Contemporary Authors®

ISSN 0010-7468

Contemporary Authors®

**A Bio-Bibliographical Guide to
Current Writers in Fiction, General Nonfiction,
Poetry, Journalism, Drama, Motion Pictures,
Television, and Other Fields**

volume 237

THOMSON

GALE

Detroit • New York • San Francisco • San Diego • New Haven, Conn. • Waterville, Maine • London • Munich

Contemporary Authors, Vol. 237

Project Editor
Julie Mellors

Editorial
Katy Balcer, Michelle Kazensky, Joshua Kondek, Lisa Kumar, Tracey Matthews, Mary Ruby, Maikue Vang

Permissions
Jacqueline Key, Lisa Kincade, Kim Smilay

Imaging and Multimedia
Lezlie Light, Kelly A. Quin

Composition and Electronic Capture
Carolyn Roney

Manufacturing
Drew Kalasky

LIBRARY OF CONGRESS CATALOG CARD NUMBER 62-52046

ISBN 0-7876-7866-X
ISSN 0010-7468

Printed in the United States of America
10 9 8 7 6 5 4 3 2 1

Contents

Indexing note: All *Contemporary Authors* entries are indexed in the *Contemporary Authors* cumulative index, which is published separately and distributed twice a year.

As always, the most recent Contemporary Authors cumulative index continues to be the user's guide to the location of an individual author's listing.

Preface

Contemporary Authors (*CA*) provides information on approximately 120,000 writers in a wide range of media, including:

- Current writers of fiction, nonfiction, poetry, and drama whose works have been issued by commercial publishers, risk publishers, or university presses (authors whose books have been published only by known vanity or author-subsidized firms are ordinarily not included)

- Prominent print and broadcast journalists, editors, photojournalists, syndicated cartoonists, graphic novelists, screenwriters, television scriptwriters, and other media people

- Notable international authors

- Literary greats of the early twentieth century whose works are popular in today's high school and college curriculums and continue to elicit critical attention

A *CA* listing entails no charge or obligation. Authors are included on the basis of the above criteria and their interest to *CA* users. Sources of potential listees include trade periodicals, publishers' catalogs, librarians, and other users of the series.

How to Get the Most out of *CA*: Use the Index

The key to locating an author's most recent entry is the *CA* cumulative index, which is published separately and distributed twice a year. It provides access to *all* entries in *CA* and *Contemporary Authors New Revision Series* (*CANR*). Always consult the latest index to find an author's most recent entry.

For the convenience of users, the *CA* cumulative index also includes references to all entries in these Thomson Gale literary series: *Authors and Artists for Young Adults, Authors in the News, Bestsellers, Black Literature Criticism, Black Literature Criticism Supplement, Black Writers, Children's Literature Review, Concise Dictionary of American Literary Biography, Concise Dictionary of British Literary Biography, Contemporary Authors Autobiography Series, Contemporary Authors Bibliographical Series, Contemporary Dramatists, Contemporary Literary Criticism, Contemporary Novelists, Contemporary Poets, Contemporary Popular Writers, Contemporary Southern Writers, Contemporary Women Poets, Dictionary of Literary Biography, Dictionary of Literary Biography Documentary Series, Dictionary of Literary Biography Yearbook, DISCovering Authors, DISCovering Authors: British, DISCovering Authors: Canadian, DISCovering Authors: Modules* (including modules for Dramatists, Most-Studied Authors, Multicultural Authors, Novelists, Poets, and Popular/Genre Authors), *DISCovering Authors 3.0, Drama Criticism, Drama for Students, Feminist Writers, Hispanic Literature Criticism, Hispanic Writers, Junior DISCovering Authors, Major Authors and Illustrators for Children and Young Adults, Major 20th-Century Writers, Native North American Literature, Novels for Students, Poetry Criticism, Poetry for Students, Short Stories for Students, Short Story Criticism, Something about the Author, Something about the Author Autobiography Series, St. James Guide to Children's Writers, St. James Guide to Crime & Mystery Writers, St. James Guide to Fantasy Writers, St. James Guide to Horror, Ghost & Gothic Writers, St. James Guide to Science Fiction Writers, St. James Guide to Young Adult Writers, Twentieth-Century Literary Criticism, 20th Century Romance and Historical Writers, World Literature Criticism,* and *Yesterday's Authors of Books for Children.*

A Sample Index Entry:

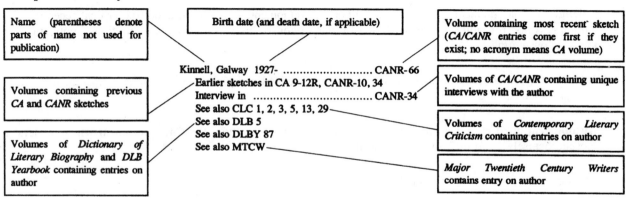

Name (parentheses denote parts of name not used for publication)

Birth date (and death date, if applicable)

Volume containing most recent sketch (*CA/CANR* entries come first if they exist; no acronym means *CA* volume)

Volumes containing previous *CA* and *CANR* sketches

Volumes of *Dictionary of Literary Biography* and *DLB Yearbook* containing entries on author

Kinnell, Galway 1927- CANR-66
Earlier sketches in CA 9-12R, CANR-10, 34
Interview in CANR-34
See also CLC 1, 2, 3, 5, 13, 29
See also DLB 5
See also DLBY 87
See also MTCW

Volumes of *CA/CANR* containing unique interviews with the author

Volumes of *Contemporary Literary Criticism* containing entries on author

Major Twentieth Century Writers contains entry on author

How Are Entries Compiled?

The editors make every effort to secure new information directly from the authors; listees' responses to our questionnaires and query letters provide most of the information featured in *CA*. For deceased writers, or those who fail to reply to requests for data, we consult other reliable biographical sources, such as those indexed in Thomson Gale's *Biography and Genealogy Master Index,* and bibliographical sources, including *National Union Catalog, LC MARC,* and *British National Bibliography.* Further details come from published interviews, feature stories, and book reviews, as well as information supplied by the authors' publishers and agents.

An asterisk (*) at the end of a sketch indicates that the listing has been compiled from secondary sources believed to be reliable but has not been personally verified for this edition by the author sketched.

What Kinds of Information Does An Entry Provide?

Sketches in *CA* contain the following biographical and bibliographical information:

- **Entry heading:** the most complete form of author's name, plus any pseudonyms or name variations used for writing

- **Personal information:** author's date and place of birth, family data, ethnicity, educational background, political and religious affiliations, and hobbies and leisure interests

- **Addresses:** author's home, office, or agent's addresses, plus e-mail and fax numbers, as available

- **Career summary:** name of employer, position, and dates held for each career post; resume of other vocational achievements; military service

- **Membership information:** professional, civic, and other association memberships and any official posts held

- **Awards and honors:** military and civic citations, major prizes and nominations, fellowships, grants, and honorary degrees

- **Writings:** a comprehensive, chronological list of titles, publishers, dates of original publication and revised editions, and production information for plays, television scripts, and screenplays

- **Adaptations:** a list of films, plays, and other media which have been adapted from the author's work

- **Work in progress:** current or planned projects, with dates of completion and/or publication, and expected publisher, when known

- **Sidelights:** a biographical portrait of the author's development; information about the critical reception of the author's works; revealing comments, often by the author, on personal interests, aspirations, motivations, and thoughts on writing

- **Interview:** a one-on-one discussion with authors conducted especially for *CA*, offering insight into authors' thoughts about their craft

- **Autobiographical essay:** an original essay written by noted authors for *CA*, a forum in which writers may present themselves, on their own terms, to their audience

- **Photographs:** portraits and personal photographs of notable authors

- **Biographical and critical sources:** a list of books and periodicals in which additional information on an author's life and/or writings appears

- **Obituary Notices** in *CA* provide date and place of birth as well as death information about authors whose full-length sketches appeared in the series before their deaths. The entries also summarize the authors' careers and writings and list other sources of biographical and death information.

Related Titles in the *CA* Series

Contemporary Authors Autobiography Series complements *CA* original and revised volumes with specially commissioned autobiographical essays by important current authors, illustrated with personal photographs they provide. Common topics include their motivations for writing, the people and experiences that shaped their careers, the rewards they derive from their work, and their impressions of the current literary scene.

Contemporary Authors Bibliographical Series surveys writings by and about important American authors since World War II. Each volume concentrates on a specific genre and features approximately ten writers; entries list works written by and about the author and contain a bibliographical essay discussing the merits and deficiencies of major critical and scholarly studies in detail.

Available in Electronic Formats

GaleNet. *CA* is available on a subscription basis through GaleNet, an online information resource that features an easy-to-use end-user interface, powerful search capabilities, and ease of access through the World-Wide Web. For more information, call 1-800-877-GALE.

Licensing. *CA* is available for licensing. The complete database is provided in a fielded format and is deliverable on such media as disk, CD-ROM, or tape. For more information, contact Thomson Gale's Business Development Group at 1-800-877-GALE, or visit us on our website at www.galegroup.com/bizdev.

Suggestions Are Welcome

The editors welcome comments and suggestions from users on any aspect of the *CA* series. If readers would like to recommend authors for inclusion in future volumes of the series, they are cordially invited to write the Editors at *Contemporary Authors*, Thomson Gale, 27500 Drake Rd., Farmington Hills, MI 48331-3535; or call at 1-248-699-4253; or fax at 1-248-699-8054.

Contemporary Authors Product Advisory Board

The editors of *Contemporary Authors* are dedicated to maintaining a high standard of excellence by publishing comprehensive, accurate, and highly readable entries on a wide array of writers. In addition to the quality of the content, the editors take pride in the graphic design of the series, which is intended to be orderly yet inviting, allowing readers to utilize the pages of *CA* easily and with efficiency. Despite the longevity of the *CA* print series, and the success of its format, we are mindful that the vitality of a literary reference product is dependent on its ability to serve its users over time. As literature, and attitudes about literature, constantly evolve, so do the reference needs of students, teachers, scholars, journalists, researchers, and book club members. To be certain that we continue to keep pace with the expectations of our customers, the editors of *CA* listen carefully to their comments regarding the value, utility, and quality of the series. Librarians, who have firsthand knowledge of the needs of library users, are a valuable resource for us. The *Contemporary Authors* Product Advisory Board, made up of school, public, and academic librarians, is a forum to promote focused feedback about *CA* on a regular basis. The six-member advisory board includes the following individuals, whom the editors wish to thank for sharing their expertise:

- **Anne M. Christensen,** Librarian II, Phoenix Public Library, Phoenix, Arizona.

- **Barbara C. Chumard,** Reference/Adult Services Librarian, Middletown Thrall Library, Middletown, New York.

- **Eva M. Davis,** Youth Department Manager, Ann Arbor District Library, Ann Arbor, Michigan.

- **Adam Janowski, Jr.,** Library Media Specialist, Naples High School Library Media Center, Naples, Florida.

- **Robert Reginald,** Head of Technical Services and Collection Development, California State University, San Bernadino, California.

- **Stephen Weiner,** Director, Maynard Public Library, Maynard, Massachusetts.

International Advisory Board

Well-represented among the 120,000 author entries published in *Contemporary Authors* are sketches on notable writers from many non-English-speaking countries. The primary criteria for inclusion of such authors has traditionally been the publication of at least one title in English, either as an original work or as a translation. However, the editors of *Contemporary Authors* came to observe that many important international writers were being overlooked due to a strict adherence to our inclusion criteria. In addition, writers who were publishing in languages other than English were not being covered in the traditional sources we used for identifying new listees. Intent on increasing our coverage of international authors, including those who write only in their native language and have not been translated into English, the editors enlisted the aid of a board of advisors, each of whom is an expert on the literature of a particular country or region. Among the countries we focused attention on are Mexico, Puerto Rico, Germany, Luxembourg, Belgium, the Netherlands, Norway, Sweden, Denmark, Finland, Taiwan, Singapore, Spain, Italy, South Africa, Israel, and Japan, as well as England, Scotland, Wales, Ireland, Australia, and New Zealand. The sixteen-member advisory board includes the following individuals, whom the editors wish to thank for sharing their expertise:

- **Lowell A. Bangerter,** Professor of German, University of Wyoming, Laramie, Wyoming.

- **Nancy E. Berg,** Associate Professor of Hebrew and Comparative Literature, Washington University, St. Louis, Missouri.

- **Frances Devlin-Glass,** Associate Professor, School of Literary and Communication Studies, Deakin University, Burwood, Victoria, Australia.

- **David William Foster,** Regent's Professor of Spanish, Interdisciplinary Humanities, and Women's Studies, Arizona State University, Tempe, Arizona.

- **Hosea Hirata,** Director of the Japanese Program, Associate Professor of Japanese, Tufts University, Medford, Massachusetts.

- **Jack Kolbert,** Professor Emeritus of French Literature, Susquehanna University, Selinsgrove, Pennsylvania.

- **Mark Libin,** Professor, University of Manitoba, Winnipeg, Manitoba, Canada.

- **C. S. Lim,** Professor, University of Malaya, Kuala Lumpur, Malaysia.

- **Eloy E. Merino,** Assistant Professor of Spanish, Northern Illinois University, DeKalb, Illinois.

- **Linda M. Rodríguez Guglielmoni,** Associate Professor, University of Puerto Rico—Mayagüez, Puerto Rico.

- **Sven Hakon Rossel,** Professor and Chair of Scandinavian Studies, University of Vienna, Vienna, Austria.

- **Steven R. Serafin,** Director, Writing Center, Hunter College of the City University of New York, New York City.

- **David Smyth,** Lecturer in Thai, School of Oriental and African Studies, University of London, England.

- **Ismail S. Talib,** Senior Lecturer, Department of English Language and Literature, National University of Singapore, Singapore.

- **Dionisio Viscarri,** Assistant Professor, Ohio State University, Columbus, Ohio.

- **Mark Williams,** Associate Professor, English Department, University of Canterbury, Christchurch, New Zealand.

CA Numbering System and Volume Update Chart

Occasionally questions arise about the *CA* numbering system and which volumes, if any, can be discarded. Despite numbers like " 29-32R," " 97-100" and "236," the entire *CA* print series consists of only 288 physical volumes with the publication of *CA* Volume 237. The following charts note changes in the numbering system and cover design, and indicate which volumes are essential for the most complete, up-to-date coverage.

CA First Revision
- 1-4R through 41-44R (11 books)
  Cover: Brown with black and gold trim.
  There will be no further First Revision volumes because revised entries are now being handled exclusively through the more efficient *New Revision Series* mentioned below.

CA Original Volumes
- 45-48 through 97-100 (14 books)
  Cover: Brown with black and gold trim.
  101 through 237 (137 books)
  Cover: Blue and black with orange bands.
  The same as previous *CA* original volumes but with a new, simplified numbering system and new cover design.

CA Permanent Series
- *CAP*-1 and *CAP*-2 (2 books)
  Cover: Brown with red and gold trim.
  There will be no further Permanent Series volumes because revised entries are now being handled exclusively through the more efficient *New Revision Series* mentioned below.

CA New Revision Series
- CANR-1 through CANR-142 (142 books)
  Cover: Blue and black with green bands.
  Includes only sketches requiring significant changes; **sketches are taken from any previously published CA, CAP, or CANR volume.**

If You Have:	You May Discard:
CA First Revision Volumes 1-4R through 41-44R and *CA Permanent Series* Volumes 1 and 2	*CA* Original Volumes 1, 2, 3, 4 Volumes 5-6 through 41-44
CA Original Volumes 45-48 through 97-100 and 101 through 237	**NONE:** These volumes will not be superseded by corresponding revised volumes. Individual entries from these and all other volumes appearing in the left column of this chart may be revised and included in the various volumes of the *New Revision Series*.
CA New Revision Series Volumes *CANR*-1 through *CANR*-142	**NONE:** The *New Revision Series* does not replace any single volume of *CA*. Instead, volumes of *CANR* include entries from many previous *CA* series volumes. All *New Revision Series* volumes must be retained for full coverage.

A Sampling of Authors and Media People
Featured in This Volume

Dominique Aury

Aury's identity as the author of the classic erotic fantasy *Histoire d'O,* was not revealed until forty years after the book's initial publication. Aury, a French author and literary editor, wrote the book under the pseudonym Pauline Réage. She was the mistress of critic and editor Jean Paulhan, and she originally wrote *Histoire d'O,* to keep the married man's interest. This influential book was translated and published in the United States as *The Story of O* where it became a popular success during the sexual liberation movement of the 1960s and 1970s. Aury's famous work continues to captivate readers and has been made into a French film and translated into more than twenty languages.

Jack Cardiff

Cardiff, who is best known as a cinematographer, has also worked as a director and actor. Born in England to parents who were vaudeville performers, Cardiff began his acting career at the early age of four. He went on to direct numerous films and won the Academy Award for best cinematography in 1947 for *Black Narcissus.* Cardiff reveals his cinematography techniques and the antics of the great twentieth-century cinema stars he worked with in his autobiography *Magic Hour: The Life of a Cameraman.* In 2001, Cardiff was honored with the Academy Award for Lifetime Achievement.

Clint Eastwood

Eastwood has earned many successes in the film industry as a popular actor, director, and producer. Early in his career, Eastwood starred in several westerns. In 1971, he directed his first feature-length film, *Play Misty for Me.* Eastwood also starred in the film, and he has done so in many of his subsequent directorial projects. Eastwood won his first Academy Awards in 1992 for Best Director and Best Picture for his film *Unforgiven.* He has since won several prestigious film awards for his work. Eastwood shares his perspective on directing films in a collection of twenty-two interviews titled *Clint Eastwood: Interviews.*

Marcella Evaristi

As a prominent Scottish feminist playwright, Evaristi has composed various autobiographical productions that are known for both their humor and insightfulness. She has also acted in many of her own stage plays. Evaristi finished her first play, *Dorothy and the Bitch,* in 1976 and has since staged twelve plays, a monologue, and a review piece. In addition to her stage successes, Evaristi has also completed several plays for television and radio broadcasts.

Mark Crispin Miller

Miller is an author and professor of media ecology whose main interests are modern propaganda, the history and tactics of advertising, American film, and media ownership. He has also provided political commentary for various documentaries, including 2004's *Hijacking Catastrophe: 9/11, Fear & the Selling of American Empire.* Many reviewers have noted that Miller writes from a left-wing perspective. His books *The Bush Dyslexicon: Observations on a National Disorder* and *Cruel and Unusual: Bush/Cheney's New World Order,* strongly criticize the George W. Bush administration.

Edmundo Paz Soldán

Paz Soldán is the author of novels and short stories, and he is a prominent contemporary Bolivian writer. He is inspired by authors like Jorge Luis Borges and Franz Kafka and is also a leading practitioner of "McOndo" literature—a form of urban realism which accepts and critiques Americanization and the "McDonalds-ization" of the Latin American world. Paz Soldán is an associate professor at Cornell University although he still spends part of the year in his native Bolivia. His first work to be translated into English was his 2001 novel, *La materia del deseo, The Matter of Desire.* The novel has autobiographical tones because it tells of a Latin-American professor caught between two worlds—his faculty position in the United States and his Bolivian home.

Audrey Thomas

After emigrating from America to Canada, Thomas found literary success with her novels, short stories, and radio plays. She has won a number of awards for her autobiographical works, including a National Magazine Award, a Commonwealth Literary Prize, and several lifetime achievement awards. Her books display an interest in feminism, experimentation, and the common theme of personal isolation and loneliness. A divorced mother of three children, Thomas is well acquainted with the problems of family life about which she often writes. An autobiographical essay by Thomas is included in this volume of *CA.*

Opal Stanley Whiteley

Whiteley was reportedly a child prodigy and the diary that she kept at the age of six was originally published in

1920 as *The Story of Opal: The Journal of an Understanding Heart*. Along with fame came skepticism, as many people argued that no child could have written such advanced prose. In her diary, Whiteley claimed to have been born in France, and that she was the abducted daughter of a French nobleman. No one has been able to prove or disprove her claims. Ultimately, Whiteley was stricken with an inherited form of schizophrenia, and she was placed in a London mental hospital, where she lived until her death. Whiteley's life continues to fascinate her followers and biographers, because the truth about Whiteley will probably never be known.

Acknowledgments

Grateful acknowledgment is made to those publishers, photographers, and artists whose work appear with these authors's essays. Following is a list of the copyright holders who have granted us permission to reproduce material in this volume of *CA*. Every effort has been made to trace copyright, but if omissions have been made, please let us know.

Photographs/Art

Sarah, Robyn: Photographs by D. R. Cowles. Courtesy of Robyn Sarah Belkin.

Sarah, Robyn: Photograph by H. Belkin. Courtesy of Robyn Sarah Belkin.

Sarah, Robyn: All photographs courtesy of Robyn Sarah Belkin. Reproduced by permission.

Thomas, Audrey: All photographs courtesy of Audrey Thomas. Reproduced by permission.

Thomas, Audrey: Photograph by Tony Bounsall. Courtesy of Audrey Thomas.

A

ADAMS, Christine A(nn) 1935-
(Christine A. Hanley, Christine A. McKenna)

PERSONAL: Born September 1, 1935, in Kittery, ME; daughter of Michael Martin (a shipyard rigger) and Bridget Mary (a registered nurse; maiden name, Scully) McKenna; married Edward S. Hanley (a business owner), June 28, 1957 (divorced 1978); married John J. Adams (a reverend), 1984 (divorced 1988); married Robert J. Butch (a licensed social worker and therapist), July 3, 1994; children: (first marriage) Edward T. Hanley, Marcia A. Hanley Firsick, Mark D. Hanley; stepchildren: Thomas J., Robert J., William J. Butch. *Ethnicity:* "Irish." *Education:* Regis College (Weston, MA), B.A., 1957; Rivier College, M.A., 1979; New Hampshire Technical Institute, counselor certification, 1985; also attended University of Lowell (now University of Massachusetts), 1982-86. *Politics:* "Independent." *Religion:* Protestant. *Hobbies and other interests:* Travel and family.

ADDRESSES: Home and office—34 Buttonwood Dr., Berwick, ME 03901. *Agent*—Frank Weimann, Literary Group, 270 Lafayette St., Ste. 1505, New York, NY 10012. *E-mail*—adamsbutch@earthlink.net.

CAREER: Writing specialist and teacher at high schools in Portsmouth, NH, 1957-58, Chelmsford, MA, 1958-86, and Lebanon, CT, 1987-97; writer, 1997—. State of Massachusetts, teacher for alcohol safety awareness program; certified addiction counselor; presenter of lectures and workshops, 1993—.

MEMBER: International Women's Writing Guild, Connecticut Authors and Publishers Association.

WRITINGS:

Claiming Your Own Life, Abbey Press (St. Meinrad, IN), 1989.

One Day at a Time Therapy, Abbey Press (St. Meinrad, IN), 1990.

(As Christine A. McKenna) *Love, Infidelity, and Sexual Addiction,* Abbey Press (St. Meinrad, IN), 1992, published under the name Christine A. Adams, iUniverse (Lincoln, NE), 2000.

Living in Love: Connecting to the Power of Love, Health Communications (Deerfield Beach, FL), 1993.

Holy Relationships, Morehouse Publishing Group (Harrisburg, PA), 1998.

Gratitude Therapy, Abbey Press (St. Meinrad, IN), 1999.

(With husband, Robert J. Butch) *Happy to Be Me: A Kid's Book about Self Esteem,* Abbey Press (St. Meinrad, IN), 2001.

ABC's of Grief: A Handbook for Survivors, edited by John D. Morgan, Baywood Publishing (Amityville, NY), 2003.

(With grandson, Harrison Edward Hanley) *Learning to Be a Good Friend: A Guidebook for Kids,* Abbey Press (St. Meinrad, IN), 2004.

Author of pamphlets for Abbey Press (St. Meinrad, IN). Contributor to periodicals, including *Marriage and Family Living, English Journal, Currents, Connecticut Parent, Computers in Education, Electronic Education, Changes,* and *Reading Improvement.* Some writings appeared under name Christine A. Hanley

Adams's books have been published in several foreign countries, including Taiwan, Indonesia, India, Thailand, the Netherlands, Sweden, Slovenia, Portugal, Brazil, Austria, Spain, Germany, England, Norway, Denmark, Belgium, France, the Philippines, South Africa, and Poland.

SIDELIGHTS: Christine A. Adams told *CA:* "My seventh-grade English teacher, Virginia Parsons, encouraged me to write and inspired me to become a teacher. She remains my mentor today. Now, I have thirty-two years of teaching experience in English literature and composition, as well as many books, magazine articles, and pamphlets to my credit. My love of learning and language was enhanced by a formal study of English at the undergraduate and graduate level. However, it did not end there! Many meaningful life experiences, combined with my passion for writing and a desire to share my knowledge of life and my gift of spirituality, enabled me to produce published works that span a period of twenty years.

"I began writing magazine articles and pamphlets in the early 1980s. In 1986 I was working in a pre-doctoral program at the University of Massachusetts in Lowell, studying technology in the learning environment. My publishing career blossomed when my education articles began appearing in the *English Journal, Electronic Education,* and *Computers in Education.*

"Then, when my life was touched by addiction, I completed an alcohol and drug addiction counselor certification program. In 1989 and 1990 I published two books about addiction. My 'carenote' pamphlets for Abbey Press, on the subjects of addiction, spirituality, and grief, were part of a line that has sold forty million pamphlets to churches and other institutions across America.

"*Living in Love: Connecting to the Power of Love* speaks to the need for love and spirituality in our lives. *Holy Relationships* outlines what it means to live in a truly holy relationship: a marriage grounded in spirituality. *ABC's of Grief: A Handbook for Survivors,* published in 2003, is a handbook for those who have lost a loved a loved one.

In 2001, my husband, Robert J. Butch, and I published *Happy to Be Me: A Kid's Book about Self Esteem,* which is now published in ten countries. In 2004, my grandson, Harrison Edward Hanley, and I collaborated on the children's book, *Learning to Be a Good Friend: A Guidebook for Kids.* This book will be published internationally as well. I look forward to writing many more children's books.

"Today I continue my pursuit of language, learning, and life by producing new manuscripts on the subjects of addiction, spirituality, and education, as well as children's books. I also travel, lecture, and present workshops. As a full-time writer, I am now entering my second life, professionally speaking, and I welcome the opportunity to refine and expand all I have learned in the first."

*   *   *

ADAMS, Norman (Edward Albert) 1927-2005

OBITUARY NOTICE— See index for *CA* sketch: Born February 9, 1927, in London, England; died March 9, 2005, in London, England. Artist, educator, illustrator, and author. Adams was renowned for his spiritual art depicting scenes from the Bible that were influenced by his own personal symbolism. He was attending the Harrow School of Art when World War II interrupted his studies. A conscientious objector, he was imprisoned for refusing to enlist and later assigned to work on a farm. With the war over, he returned to school, completing his art diploma at the Royal College of Art in 1951. Adams's interest in religious imagery was first inspired by a film he saw about the medieval painter Giotto. Scenes from the Old and New Testaments would thereafter populate his work, which mostly involved painting in oils but also other media, such as ceramics. His first important exhibit was held in 1952 at Gimpel Fils, followed by regular exhibits at the gallery Roland, Browse and Delbanco. Adams frequently painted works that related to one another in a series, such as his "Fourteen Stations of the Cross" series and his depiction of the "Seven Days of Creation." He was also an art teacher, and worked at St. Albans from 1952 until 1961, and then joined the Manchester College of Art and Design (now Manchester Polytechnic) in 1962. He left this position in 1970, but returned to teaching in 1973 as a tutor at Leeds University for three years. From 1981 until 1986 he was a professor of fine arts and department director at the University of Newcastle-upon-Tyne, and from 1986 until 1995 he was keeper of schools at the Royal

Academy of Arts. From 1986 until his 1999 retirement, he was also professor of painting at the Royal Academy. Honored in 2002 with a seventy-fifth-birthday retrospective at the Royal Academy, Adams illustrated a number of publications, including George Sullivan's children's book *Trees* (1970), John Milner's *A Decade of Painting, 1971-1981* (1981), and A. Adams's *Angels of Soho* (1988), *Island Chapters* (1991), and *Life on Limestone* (1994).

OBITUARIES AND OTHER SOURCES:

PERIODICALS

Independent (London, England), March 15, 2005, p. 36.
Times (London, England), March 18, 2005, p. 80.

*　　*　　*

ADAMSON, George (Worsley) 1913-2005

OBITUARY NOTICE— See index for *CA* sketch: Born February 7, 1913, in New York, NY; died March 5, 2005, in Exeter, England. Artist, illustrator, educator, and author. Adamson was best known as a prolific illustrator of children's books, but he was also a cartoonist and illustrated works by writers such as P. G. Wodehouse. Though born in the United States, he was raised in England beginning in 1921 after both his parents had died. Adamson initially intended to pursue a career in architecture, studying at the Wigan Mining & Technical College, but by 1930 he had decided art was more to his liking, and he enrolled at the Wigan School of Art and also attended Liverpool University. After earning a secondary teacher's art certificate at Oxford University, he embarked on a career in that field, taking jobs in Germany, France, and Portugal. When World War II began, he enlisted in the Royal Air Force, first as a navigator but then as an official war artist. With the war over, Adamson settled in Exeter, lectured for several years at Exeter College of Art, and became a freelance artist and illustrator. He contributed cartoons and artwork regularly to publications such as *Private Eye, Punch,* and *Cricket,* as well as many of England's prominent newspapers. Favoring engraving as his preferred method of illustration, Adamson was much in demand as an illustrator of children's books, his work enlivening the texts of such authors as Margaret Lovett, Norman Hunter, Richard Carpenter, Mary Cockett, and Frank Waters. In addition, he notably provided art for such well-known books as Alan Garner's *The Weirdstone of Brisingamen* (1960) and *The Moon of Gomrath* (1963). He also wrote and illustrated several of his own children's books, including *A Finding Alphabet* (1965), *Widdecombe Fair: The Famous West Country Songs in Drawings* (1966), and *Rome Done Lightly* (1972). Honored in 1981 with an illustration prize from *Punch* for his contributions to the *Short Stories of P. G. Wodehouse,* Adamson was named a fellow of the Royal Society of Painter-Printmakers in 1987.

OBITUARIES AND OTHER SOURCES:

PERIODICALS

Guardian (London, England), April 2, 2005, p. 21.
Independent (London, England), March 16, 2005, p. 33.
Times (London, England), March 18, 2005, p. 80.

*　　*　　*

ADROUNY, A. Richard 1952-

PERSONAL: Born May 7, 1952, in Aleppo, Syria; son of George A. (a biochemist and teacher) and Alice (a homemaker; maiden name, Karamanookian) Adrouny; married Karen Alyce Tamzarian (a homemaker), May 1, 1982; children: Melissa Knar, Gregory Adour. *Ethnicity:* "Armenian." *Education:* Duke University, B.S. (magna cum laude), 1973; Tulane University, M.D. and M.P.H.T.M., 1978. *Politics:* "Independent." *Religion:* Protestant. *Hobbies and other interests:* Reading, gardening, tennis.

ADDRESSES: Home—17364 Grosvenor Ct., Monte Sereno, CA 95030. *Office*—700 West Parr Ave., Ste. B, Los Gatos, CA 95032. *E-mail*—mononc@aol.com.

CAREER: Physician in private practice, specializing in medical oncology and hematology, Los Gatos, CA, 1985—. Stanford University, adjunct clinical assistant professor of medicine. Palo Alto Medical Publishing,

Inc., founder and publisher of "Care Sheets" (educational brochures for patients). Hospice of the Valley, member of board of directors, 1999-2002; American Cancer Society, volunteer.

MEMBER: American Medical Association, American Society of Clinical Oncology, American Society of Hematology, American Association for the Advancement of Science, California Medical Association, Santa Clara County Medical Association.

WRITINGS:

Understanding Colon Cancer, University Press of Mississippi (Jackson, MS), 2002.

Author of journal articles. Editorial advisor, *Gale Encyclopedia of Medicine* and *Gale Encyclopedia of Cancer,* Gale (Detroit, MI).

WORK IN PROGRESS: The Cancer-Free Zone: A Scientifically Proven Way to Reduce the Risk of Cancer; Thicker than Blood, a layperson's guide to blood clots.

SIDELIGHTS: A. Richard Adrouny told *CA:* "I am a practicing physician who is primarily motivated to write informational materials and books for patients, their families, and the general audience to help them understand complex medical subjects. I am influenced by encounters with people that I have on a daily basis in my practice. I have observed how difficult it is for people to understand complex issues related to diagnoses, treatments, and procedures. As a result, a significant sidebar to my medical career has been the writing of brochures, articles, and books on subjects that are both common and uncommon, and about which there may be a need for published articles or books.

"The process typically begins with my observation of a medical problem that may be poorly understood and appreciated. I draw on my own professional experience and the personal experiences of my patients to frame the subject matter. I then research the subject exhaustively in the scientific and medical literature to give the reader the most sound and scientifically based information possible. I am strongly oriented toward the scientific analysis of disease and try to avoid 'popular' or 'alternative' disease theories or treatments that have no scientific basis. I feel a strong ethical/moral obligation to my readers to provide accurate, scientific information that is not misleading, commercially biased, or based on emotional or empirical foundations.

"I am also motivated by the hunger that many of my patients feel for information about health and illness and the ends to which they will go to get that information. Sadly, much of that information (including material on the Internet) is misleading, inaccurate, or blatantly biased for commercial or other reasons.

"I hope in my work to provide concise, accurate, and easily understood explanations of various medical subjects."

BIOGRAPHICAL AND CRITICAL SOURCES:

PERIODICALS

Booklist, June 1, 2002, William Beatty, review of *Understanding Colon Cancer,* p. 1659.

*   *   *

ALEINIKOFF, T. Alexander
    See ALEINIKOFF, Thomas Alexander

*   *   *

ALEINIKOFF, Thomas Alexander 1952-
    (T. Alexander Aleinikoff)

PERSONAL: Born 1952. *Education:* Swarthmore College, B.A., 1974; Yale University, J.D., 1977.

ADDRESSES: Office—Georgetown University Law Center, 600 New Jersey Ave. NW, Washington, DC 20001. *E-mail*—aleinikt@law.georgetown.edu.

CAREER: Called to the Bar of the State of New York, 1978, State of Michigan, 1983; law clerk to Honorable Justice Edward Weinfeld, U.S. District Court, 1977-

78; U.S. Department of Justice, Washington, DC, attorney in Office of Legal Counsel, 1978-80, and Land and Natural Resources, 1981, general counsel for Immigration and Naturalization Service, 1994-95, executive associate commissioner for programs, 1995-97; University of Michigan, assistant professor, 1981-84, associate professor, 1984-86, professor of law, 1986-94; Georgetown University Law Center, Washington, DC, professor of law, 1997—, associate dean of research, 2003-04, dean, 2004—, executive vice president of Law Center affairs, 2004—. Former senior associate, International Migration Policy Program of Carnegie Endowment for International Peace.

AWARDS, HONORS: Alpha Sigma Nu Award, 2004, for *Semblances of Sovereignty: The Constitution, the State, and American Citizenship.*

WRITINGS:

(With David A. Martin) *Immigration: Process and Policy,* West Publishing (St. Paul, MN), 1985, 5th revised edition, also with Hiroshi Motomura, published as *Immigration and Citizenship: Process and Policy,* Thomson/West (St. Paul, MN), 2003.

(As T. Alexander Aleinikoff; editor, with John H. Garvey) *Modern Constitutional Theory: A Reader,* West Publishing (St. Paul, MN), 1989, 5th revised edition, also with Daniel A. Farber, Thomson/West (St. Paul, MN), 2004.

(As T. Alexander Aleinikoff; with Demetrios G. Papademetriou and Deborah Waller Meyers) *Reorganizing the U.S. Immigration Function: Toward a New Framework for Accountability* (Volume 7 in "International Migration Policy Program" series), Carnegie Endowment for International Peace (Washington, DC), 1998.

(As T. Alexander Aleinikoff) *Between Principles and Politics: The Direction of U.S. Citizenship Policy* (Volume 8 in "International Migration Policy Program" series), Carnegie Endowment for International Peace (Washington, DC), 1998.

(As T. Alexander Aleinikoff; editor, with Douglas Klusmeyer) *From Migrants to Citizens: Membership in a Changing World,* Carnegie Endowment for International Peace (Washington, DC), 2000.

(As T. Alexander Aleinikoff; editor, with Douglas Klusmeyer) *Citizenship Today: Global Perspectives and Practices,* Carnegie Endowment for International Peace (Washington, DC), 2001.

(As T. Alexander Aleinikoff; with Douglas Klusmeyer) *Citizenship Policies for an Age of Migration,* Carnegie Endowment for International Peace/Migration Policy Institute/Brookings Institution Press (Washington, DC), 2002.

(As T. Alexander Aleinikoff) *Semblances of Sovereignty: The Constitution, the State, and American Citizenship,* Harvard University Press (Cambridge, MA), 2002.

(As T. Alexander Aleinikoff; editor, with Vincent Chetail) *Migration and International Legal Norms,* Cambridge University Press (New York, NY), 2003.

Contributor to law journals.

SIDELIGHTS: Thomas Alexander Aleinikoff has been writing about constitutional and immigration law since the 1980s. His *Immigration: Process and Policy,* co-written with David A. Martin, has been continually revised, most recently in 2004 as *Immigration and Citizenship: Process and Policy.* In the first edition of this work the authors point out that, in studying immigration law, "major public policy issues appear repeatedly, posing deeper questions concerning national identity, membership, moral philosophy, constitutional interpretation, public law, public administration, international relations, and the limit of practical politics."

Aleinikoff and Martin address the power of the three branches of the U.S. government with regard to immigration, the federal agencies responsible, and the fact that decisions regarding immigration are under the oversight of four separate cabinet departments. They study changes in patterns of immigration, family reunification, and the definition of "child," among other factors, and conclude by studying what it means to be a citizen of the United States. Hiroshi Motomura reviewed the volume in *International Lawyer,* saying, "I can think of no other work in the field, in any format, that does such a complete yet succinct job of synthesizing the many dimensions of immigration law into a coherent whole. In this regard, the book is remarkably successful, not only in teaching immigration law, but also in defining it."

Writing as T. Alexander Aleinikoff, Aleinikoff has also produced—both alone and with others—several volumes for the Carnegie Endowment for International

Peace, including *Between Principles and Politics: The Direction of U.S. Citizenship Policy,* in which he proposes that the United States enter into agreements with other countries that would establish voting rights based on residence, eliminating the current practice of allowing dual residency. In *From Migrants to Citizens: Membership in a Changing World,* Aleinikoff and Douglas Klusmeyer study the juidical/political aspect of citizenship, or how the rights and duties of immigrants may be different from those of native-born Americans.

At the end of the nineteenth century, the U.S. Supreme Court ruled that Congress had "plenary power" to regulate immigration, Indian tribes, and newly acquired territories. The doctrine was initially used to uphold the infamous Chinese Exclusion laws that restricted land ownership and other legal perogatives; it continues to give Congress the power to control Native American tribes and territories such as Puerto Rico, as well as immigration. Peter H. Schuck wrote in *Political Science Quarterly* that the plenary power doctrine "is inconsistent with established constitutional norms and has spawned a triumphant, racist rhetoric of sovereignty. Even today, it protects some exclusionary, undemocratic policies from review on the merits." Aleinikoff notes in *Semblances of Sovereignty: The Constitution, the State, and American Citizenship* that the Warren Court, which focused on individual rights and "full and equal citizenship," failed to address these same rights as applied to permanent resident aliens, tribes, and residents of territories who do not currently enjoy full constitutional protection. He says further that the Rehnquist Court struck down policies that supported racial diversity and the sovereignty of Native tribes. Aleinikoff recommends that these peoples be included in a more egalitarian form of citizenship, a goal reflecting the agenda of those groups that seek to take the next step in the fight for human rights.

According to Peter J. Spiro in the *Michigan Law Review, Semblances of Sovereignty"* skillfully distills the doctrinal contradictions of constitutional subordination. In Aleinikoff's view, citizenship supplies both the explanation for and the answer to this subordination. Citizenship has been a powerfully equalizing force in the American constitutional tradition for those within the circle. Insofar as rights have been made contingent on citizen status, however, those outside are left without constitutional armor." As Spiro pointed out, some Puerto Ricans have renounced their

U.S. citizenship, and there is a theory that the identity of Native Americans is put at risk by citizenship. Consequently, because there is little obligation associated with citizenship, jury duty being an exception, there may be no reason not to give these groups that option, if they so choose. On the other hand, immigrants to the United States who do wish citizenship as a means of fostering ties with the larger American community are denied that status. Arguing that those who want to become U.S. citizens be allowed the right to freely apply, Aleinikoff adds that "citizenship does not guarantee a common culture for Americans. It provides the common calling of being American."

Migration and International Legal Norms is a collection of eighteen essays first presented in 2002 at a Geneva conference organized by the International Organization for Migration, the Swiss Federal Office of Refugees, the Migration Policy Institute, and the Graduate Institute of International Studies. The book's foreword notes that its purpose is to provide "a concise guide to international legal norms and standards in the field of migration." Aleinikoff's overview of the law and summary of multilateral, bilateral, and regional cooperative arrangements begins the book. Linda S. Bosniak wrote in the *American Journal of International Law* that *Migration and International Legal Norms* "might best be described as a comprehensive reference handbook on the international law of migration in its various dimensions. There is no other resource in the field that is as thorough or as authoritative."

BIOGRAPHICAL AND CRITICAL SOURCES:

BOOKS

Aleinikoff, T. Alexander, and Vincent Chetail, editors, *Migration and International Legal Norms,* Cambridge University Press (New York, NY), 2003.

Aleinkoff, Thomas Alexander, and David A. Martin, *Immigration: Process and Policy,* West Publishing (St. Paul, MN), 1985, 5th revised edition, also with Hiroshi Motomura, published as *Immigration and Citizenship: Process and Policy,* Thomson/West (St. Paul, MN), 2003.

Aleinikoff, T. Alexander, *Semblances of Sovereignty: The Constitution, the State, and American Citizenship,* Harvard University Press (Cambridge, MA), 2002.

PERIODICALS

American Journal of International Law, January, 2004, Linda S. Bosniak, review of *Migration and International Legal Norms,* p. 234.

Georgetown Immigration Law Journal, summer, 1999, Jeffrey R. O'Brien, "U.S. Duel Citizen Voting Rights: A Critical Examination of Aleinikoff's Solution," pp. 573-595.

International Affairs, July, 2001, Jean Tillie, review of *From Migrants to Citizens: Membership in a Changing World,* p. 709.

International Lawyer, winter, 1987, Hiroshi Motomura, discussion of *Immigration: Process and Policy,* pp. 261-266.

Library Journal, March 15, 2002, Steven Puro, review of *Semblances of Sovereignty: The Constitution, the State, and American Citizenship,* p. 95.

Maryland Journal of International Law and Trade, fall, 1985, review of *Immigration,* p. 248.

Michigan Law Review, February-April, 1986, Lynda S. Zengerle, review of *Immigration,* pp. 1084-1090; May, 2003, Peter J. Spiro, review of *Semblances of Sovereignty,* p. 1492.

Political Science Quarterly, fall, 2002, Peter H. Schuck, review of *Semblances of Sovereignty,* p. 536.

ONLINE

Georgetown University Law Center Online, http://www.law.georgetown.edu/ (March 23, 2005), "T. Alexander Aleinikoff."*

*   *   *

AMERT, Susan

PERSONAL: Female. *Education:* Yale University, Ph.D., 1983.

ADDRESSES: Office—Department of Foreign Languages and Literatures, 440 Smith Hall, University of Delaware, Newark, DE 19716. *E-mail*—amert@udel.edu.

CAREER: Educator and writer. Yale University, New Haven, CT, assistant professor of Russian literature, 1983-89; University of Delaware, Newark, assistant professor of Russian, 1989—.

WRITINGS:

In a Shattered Mirror: The Later Poetry of Anna Akhmatova, Stanford University Press (Stanford, CA), 1992.

SIDELIGHTS: Educator Susan Amert has studied, written about, and taught Russian language and literature since the early 1980s. Her research interests include modern Russian literature, Russian poetry, and Russian novels, and she has published articles on the novels of Fyodor Dostoevsky and Mikhail Bulgakov.

In *In a Shattered Mirror: The Later Poetry of Anna Akhmatova* Amert analyzes versed penned by famous Russian poet Anna Akhmatova, who wrote much of her more famous work before the communist revolution. Amert focuses on Akhmatova's *Poem without a Hero, The Sweetbriar Blooms, Requiem,* and *The Northern Elegies.*

Critics overall found much to praise in *In a Shattered Mirror.* Many considered Amert's work to be thorough and detailed, yet accessible to a wide audience. "Excellent use of sources, informative footnotes, extensive bibliography, and sensitive readings of texts make this book indispensable" to anyone studying Akhmatova in particular, Russian poetry in general, or even the broader topic of women's issues, according to C. A. Rydel in a review for *Choice.* Other critics observed that Amert's analysis provides an understanding not only of the poet's work but also of the poet herself. "No Akhmatovan, including scholars and knowledgeable Russian admirers, can come away from this book without a better, sounder, deeper understanding of their poet," commented *Russian Review* contributor Sidney Monas.

BIOGRAPHICAL AND CRITICAL SOURCES:

PERIODICALS

Choice, January, 1993, C. A. Rydel, review of *In a Shattered Mirror: The Later Poetry of Anna Akhmatova,* p. 802.

New York Review of Books, May 13, 1993, John Bayley, review of *In a Shattered Mirror,* p. 25.

Russian Review, January, 1994, Sidney Monas, review of *In a Shattered Mirror,* p. 132.
Times Literary Supplement, May 14, 1993, "Empress of Poets," p. 26.

ONLINE

University of Delaware Department of Foreign Languages and Literatures Web site http://www.fllt.udel.edu/ (May 5, 2005), "Susan Amert."*

*   *   *

APPLETON, Victor
 See BARRETT, Neal, Jr.

*   *   *

ARMSTRONG, Frank, III 1944(?)-

PERSONAL: Born c. 1944; married, wife's name Gabriele. *Education:* University of Virginia, Charlottesville, B.A., 1966.

ADDRESSES: Home—Coconut Grove, FL. *Office*—Investor Solutions Inc., 3250 Mary St., Ste. 207, Coconut Grove, FL 33133.

CAREER: Financial advisor and writer. Commercial pilot for Eastern Airlines; insurance agent for Connecticut General Life, beginning 1973; cofounder, Moring-Armstrong & Co. (investment advisor firm), 1984; founder and president, Investor Solutions Inc., 1992—. *Military service:* U.S. Air Force, 1966-72; served in Vietnam.

WRITINGS:

The Informed Investor: A Hype-free Guide to Constructing a Sound Financial Portfolio, AMACOM (New York, NY), 2002.

SIDELIGHTS: Author Frank Armstrong III has spent more than twenty-five years as an investment advisor. He grew up in Connecticut and Virginia, graduating from the University of Virginia in 1966 with an undergraduate degree in economics and business. After graduation, he enlisted with the U.S. Air Force and served in Vietnam, flying 400 combat missions as a pilot. After he left the Air Force in 1972, he worked as a commercial pilot with Eastern Airlines. During that same period, he also worked as an insurance agent for Connecticut General Life. Armstrong's tenure as a financial advisor began in 1984, when he cofounded Moring-Armstrong & Co., a registered investment advisor firm. Eight years later, he founded Investor Solutions Inc., a fee-based investment firm specializing in practical finance applications. Armstrong has also appeared on various television programs and has lectured nationwide on investment management.

In 2002 Armstrong published *The Informed Investor: A Hype-free Guide to Constructing a Sound Financial Portfolio.* The book serves as a practical guide to investments for people who do not have a background in finance. Armstrong explains the basics of financial economics and shows readers how to develop personal investment strategies. To build a diverse portfolio, he advises focusing on asset allocation and considering mutual funds.

Overall critics and readers responded positively to *The Informed Investor.* Many acknowledged Armstrong's efforts to make a complex topic accessible to readers who have no financial background. In a review for the *Library Journal,* Bellinda Wise wrote that "this book offers the average investor an adequate background in how to formulate a meaningful investment plan." Other critics commented on the author's positive and practical advice. *The Informed Investor* "guides readers through the basics of investing with a reassuring tone and a relatively conservative long-term strategy," observed a *Publishers Weekly* contributor.

BIOGRAPHICAL AND CRITICAL SOURCES:

PERIODICALS

Business Week, August 12, 2002, Robert Barker, review of *The Informed Investor: A Hype-free Guide to Constructing a Sound Financial Portfolio,* p. 110.
Library Journal, March 15, 2002, Bellinda Wise, review of *The Informed Investor,* p. 90.

Practical Accountant, March, 2002, "No Net Gift as Obligation Speculative," p. 14.

Publishers Weekly, February 11, 2002, review of *The Informed Investor,* p. 178.

ONLINE

800-CEO-READ, http://www.800ceoread.com/ (April 18, 2005), author profile.

American Management Association Web site, http://www.amanet.org/ (May 28, 2002), "Frank Armstrong III."

Business Week Online, http://www.businessweek.com/ (June 7, 2002), Robert Barker, "No-Hype Investment Advice: That's Author/Portfolio Manager Frank Armstrong's Sales Pitch."

Investor Solutions Inc. Web site, http://www.investorsolutions.com/ (May 28, 2002), "Frank Armstrong III."*

*   *   *

ASHCRAFT, W. Michael 1955-

PERSONAL: Born December 2, 1955, in Bossier City, LA; son of James (in business) and Lee (a seller of encyclopedias; maiden name, Wood) Ashcraft; married Carrol K. Davenport (a pastor), January 7, 1984; children: Brittany D., Kathleen L. *Ethnicity:* "White." *Education:* University of Tennessee, B.A., 1978; Southern Baptist Theological Seminary, M.Div., 1983; University of Virginia, Ph.D., 1995.

ADDRESSES: Office—Social Science Division, Truman State University, 100 East Normal, Kirksville, MO 63501-4221. *E-mail*—washcraft@truman.edu.

CAREER: Pastor of Baptist church in Madison, IN, 1984-87; James Madison University, Harrisonburg, VA, member of adjunct faculty, 1990-94; Carleton College, Northfield, MN, assistant professor, 1994-96; Truman State University, Kirksville, MO, associate professor, 1996—.

MEMBER: American Academy of Religion, Phi Kappa Phi (chapter president, 2002-03).

WRITINGS:

The Dawn of the New Cycle: Point Loma Theosophists and American Culture, University of Tennessee Press (Knoxville, TN), 2002.

Member of board of editorial consultants, *Nova Religio: Journal of Alternative and Emergent Religions.*

WORK IN PROGRESS: Editing *New Religious Movements: A Documentary Reader,* with Darack Daschke, for New York University Press (New York, NY); a history of the study of new religious movements; a biography of Judith Tyberg, American teacher of Aurobindo.

BIOGRAPHICAL AND CRITICAL SOURCES:

PERIODICALS

Church History, December, 2003, Albert R. Beck, review of *The Dawn of the New Cycle: Point Loma Theosophists and American Culture,* p. 897.

*   *   *

ASTIN, Sean (Patrick) 1971-

PERSONAL: Born Sean Patrick Duke, February 25, 1971, in Santa Monica, CA; son of Michael Tell (a rock promoter) and Patty Duke (an actor); adopted son of John Astin (an actor); married Christine Louise Harrell (an actor and producer), July 11, 1992; children: Alexandra Louise, Elizabeth Louise. *Education:* Los Angeles Valley College; University of California, Los Angeles, B.A. (honors); Stella Adler Conservatory.

ADDRESSES: Home—Los Angeles, CA. *Office*—P.O. Box 57858, Sherman Oaks, CA 91413. *Agent*—c/o Author Mail, St. Martin's Press, 175 5th Ave., New York, NY 10010.

CAREER: Actor, director, producer, and writer. Cofounder of Lava Entertainment. Member of board of directors of Patrons Association and arts council, Los Angeles Valley College.

Actor in feature films, including *The Goonies,* 1985; *White Water Summer,* 1987; *Like Father like Son,* 1987; *Staying Together,* 1989; *Memphis Belle,* 1990; *The Willies,* 1991; *Toy Soldiers,* 1991; *Encino Man,* 1992; *Where the Day Takes You,* 1992; *Rudy,* 1993; *Safe Passage,* 1994; *The Low Life,* 1995; *Courage under Fire,* 1996; *Bulworth,* 1998; *Boy Meets Girl,* 1998; *Icebreaker,* 1999; *Kimberly,* 1999; *Deterrence,* 1999; *The Sky Is Falling,* 2000; *The Last Producer,* 2000; *Lord of the Rings* (trilogy), 2001-03; *Fifty First Dates,* 2004; *Elvis Has Left the Building,* 2004; *Marilyn Hotchkiss' Ballroom Dancing and Charm School,* 2005; *Slipstream,* 2005; *Bigger than the Sky,* 2005; and *Smile,* 2005. Director and coproducer of short films *On My Honor,* 1988; and *Kangaroo Court,* 1994.

Appeared on television, including series and talk shows. Television movies include *Please Don't Hit Me, Mom,* 1981; *The Rules of Marriage,* 1982; *The B.R.A.T. Patrol,* 1986; *Harrison Bergeron,* 1995; *Party Wagon* (voice), 2004; and *Into the West* (miniseries), 2005. Director of television programs and episodes, including anthology series *Perversions of Science,* Home Box Office (HBO); and *Angel,* USA network.

MEMBER: Directors Guild of America, Screen Actors Guild, American Federation of Television and Radio Artists.

AWARDS, HONORS: Best actor award, Fort Lauderdale Film Festival, 1995, for role in *The Low Life;* Academy Award nomination, for best live-action short film, 1995, for *Kangaroo Court;* best supporting actor awards, Seattle Film Critics, and Las Vegas Film Critics Society, both 2003, both for role in *Lord of the Rings: The Return of the King.*

WRITINGS:

(With Joe Layden) *There and Back Again: An Actor's Tale* (memoir), St. Martin's Press (New York, NY), 2004.

Author of screenplay for short film *The Long and Short of It,* 2003.

WORK IN PROGRESS: Producing and directing the film *Isaac's Storm.*

SIDELIGHTS: Sean Astin, who began acting at the age of ten, reflects on his life in the entertainment business in his memoir *There and Back Again: An Actor's Tale.* Astin, who collaborated with Joe Layden to write the book, goes back to his childhood in Hollywood; raised as the son of actors John Astin and Patty Duke, Astin writes about how he would only learn much later that his biological father was actually a rock concert promoter named Michael Tell. He describes his early roles and how he established some success in the film industry, most notably playing the title role in the 1993 film *Rudy,* about a young walk-on member of the University of Notre Dame football team. By the end of the 1990s, however, Astin's career stalled when he landed the role of Samwise "Sam" Gamgee in the film version of J. R. R. Tolkien's classic "Lord of the Rings" trilogy.

Much of *There and Back Again* focuses on Astin's experience in New Zealand making the three films that comprise the trilogy, including his relationship with director Peter Jacskon and his fellow actors and the challenges they faced during filming. A maker of short films himself, Astin also describes a short movie he made while in New Zealand, using the crew and cast from the *Lord of the Rings* films. Writing in *Library Journal,* Martha Cornog noted that Astin presents a complete portrait of himself prior to landing the pivotal role of Gamgee, and "when we arrive on the set, we empathize with Astin's self-doubts while cheering him on." Cornog called the book "Highly recommended for film and general collections." A *Publishers Weekly* contributor felt that, although the author "tries to portray himself as a major star, thus exaggerating his actual status," Astin's memoir nonetheless "succeeds as a brutally frank, hard-hitting portrait of the film business."

BIOGRAPHICAL AND CRITICAL SOURCES:

BOOKS

Astin, Sean, and Joe Layden, *There and Back Again: An Actor's Tale,* St. Martin's Press (New York, NY), 2004.
Newsmakers, Issue 1, Gale (Detroit, MI), 2005.

PERIODICALS

America's Intelligence Wire, October 1, 2004, Bill O'Reilly, "Back of the Book: Interview with Sean Astin."

Entertainment Weekly, January 16, 2003, pp. 30-31; October 1, 2004, Gilbert Cruz, review of *There and Back Again,* p. 77.

Library Journal, September 1, 2004, Martha Cornog, review of *There and Back Again,* p. 151.

Publishers Weekly, September 27, 2004, review of *There and Back Again,* p. 48.

ONLINE

Internet Movie Database, http://www.imdb.com/ (March 30, 2005), "Sean Astin."

Looking Closer, http://www.lookingcloser.org/ (March 30, 2005), Jeffrey Overstreet, interview with Astin.

Sean Astin Home Page, http://www.seanastin.com (March 30, 2005).*

*　　*　　*

ATHANASIADIS, Harris

PERSONAL: Male. *Education:* McGill University, Ph.D.

ADDRESSES: Home—Hamilton, Ontario, Canada. *Agent*—c/o Author Mail, University of Toronto Press, Inc., 10 St. Mary St., Ste. 700, Toronto, Ontario M5T 1R5, Canada.

CAREER: Writer. St. Mark's Presbyterian Church, Don Mills, Ontario, Canada, minister.

WRITINGS:

The Way of the Cross: The Path to the Resurrection, St. Mark's Presbyterian Church (Don Mills, Ontario, Canada), 2001.

George Grant and the Theology of the Cross: The Christian Foundations of His Thought, University of Toronto Press (Toronto, Ontario, Canada), 2001.

Contributor to *Together in Ministry: The Theology and Practice of Ministry in the Presbyterian Church in Canada,* 2004; also contributor to periodicals, including *Presbyterian Record* and *Toronto Journal of Theology.*

SIDELIGHTS: The writings of Presbyterian minister Harris Athanasiadis include *The Way of the Cross: The Path to the Resurrection,* a collection of eighty-one brief meditations that relate to the Gospel of Mark. *Presbyterian Record* contributor Arthur Van Seters wrote that the volume "combines reflection on the biblical text with an invitation to let one's personal experience be questioned by that text."

In *George Grant and the Theology of the Cross: The Christian Foundations of His Thought* Athanasiadis studies the philosopher George Grant, who claimed that his faith (though he did not write extensively about it) inspired everything he thought and wrote. Writing in the *Presbyterian Record,* John Vissers stated that "this book is clearly written but it is not an easy read. It will, however, repay those who take the time to work through its five well-organized chapters." *Anglican Journal Online* contributor Gordon Baker also suggested that *George Grant and the Theology of the Cross* "is a great contribution to the ongoing study of George Grant's thought and will be rewarding for all those who, through an experience of the reality of the resurrection, find it necessary to struggle with the deeper significance of the Cross revealing the power and wisdom of God."

Athanasiadis told *CA:* "Writing is a wonderful vehicle for helping me think through ideas and for developing some coherence. As a writer in ideas rather than stories, my passion is to write in a way that is accessible but also compelling and persuasive. As a writer of theological and philosophical ideas, my hope is to inspire readers to openness of heart, mind and imagination. The challenge is to convey something of transcendence, of faith, of hope, of love in a way that persuades and convinces. The opportunity to write is a gift I have been privileged to taste. May it continue."

BIOGRAPHICAL AND CRITICAL SOURCES:

PERIODICALS

Books in Canada, winter, 2002, Barry Allen, review of *George Grant and the Theology of the Cross: The Christian Foundations of His Thought,* p. 23.

Canadian Literature, autumn, 2003, George Elliott Clarke, review of *George Grant and the Theology of the Cross,* p. 120.

Presbyterian Record, July, 2001, Arthur Van Seters, review of *The Way of the Cross: The Path to the Resurrection,* p. 45; September, 2001, John Vissers, review of *George Grant and the Theology of the Cross,* p. 43.

ONLINE

Anglican Journal Online, http://www.anglicanjournal. com/ (March, 2002), Gordon Baker, review of *George Grant and the Theology of the Cross.*

*   *   *

AURY, Dominique 1907-1998
(Pauline Réage)

PERSONAL: Born Anne Desclos, September 23, 1907, in France; name changed, c. 1940; died April 30, 1998 (some sources say April 26, 1998). *Education:* Lycée Fénelon (Paris, France), graduated; attended École du Louvre.

CAREER: Gallimard (publishing house), Paris, France, reader and editor, 1950-c.98; *Nouvelle Revue Française* (literary review), editor and, beginning 1953, general secretary; coeditor, beginning 1941, of *Lettres Françaises.* Worked as a translator and journalist, c. 1930s; worked for *L'Arche* magazine, c. late 1940s.

AWARDS, HONORS: Deux-Magots prize, 1955, for *Histoire d'O;* named to French Legion of Honor.

WRITINGS:

FICTION; UNDER PSEUDONYM PAULINE RÉAGE

Histoire d'O (novel), preface by Jean Paulhan, J.-J. Pauvert (Sceaux, France), 1954, new edition, 1972, translation of original edition by Jean Paulhan published as *The Story of O,* Olympia Press (Paris, France), 1954, published with illustrations by Guido Crepax as *Story of O,* Grove Press (New York, NY), 1978, translation by John Paul Hand published as *The Story of O,* Blue Moon Books (New York, NY), 1993.

The Wisdom of the Lash, with an essay by Jean Paulhan, Olympia Press (Paris, France), 1957.
Retour à Roissy: précédé de une fille amoureuse (erotic stories; sequel to *Histoire d'O*), J.-J. Pauvert (Paris, France), 1969, translated by Sabine d'Estrée published as *Return to the Château; Preceded by A Girl in Love,* Grove Press (New York, NY), 1971, published as *Retour à Roissy; Une fille amoureuse,* J.-J. Pauvert, 1975, published as *Story of O, Part II, Return to the Château; Preceded by A Girl in Love,* 1980.

OTHER

(Editor, with Jean Paulhan) *La patrie de fait tous les jours, textes français, 1939-1945,* Éditions de minuit (Paris, France), 1947.
(Compiler) *Poètes d'aujourd'hui,* preface by Jean Paulhan, Éditions de Clairefontaine (Paris, France), 1947.
Lausanne, Guilde du Livre (Lausanne, France), 1952.
Lecture pour tous (criticism), Gallimard (Paris, France), 1958, translation by Denise Folliot as *Literary Landfalls,* Chatto & Windus (London, England), 1960.
Lecture pour tous II (criticism), preface by Jean Roudaut, selected by Nicole Aboulker, Gallimard (Paris, France), 1999.
(With Nicole Grenier) *Vocation: Clandestine* (interviews), Gallimard (Paris, France), 1999.

Editor of anthology of religious poetry, Gallimard, 1943; editor, with Jean Paulhan, of anthology of writings on the French Resistance, 1947; translator of books. Contributor to *Parlez-nous d'amour,* Flammarion (Paris, France), 1986.

Histoire d'O has been translated into more than twenty languages.

ADAPTATIONS: Histoire d'O was adapted as a French film in 1974.

SIDELIGHTS: Throughout most of her life, Dominique Aury, who was born Anne Desclos, remained concealed beneath altered identities. A respected literary editor, she was also the mistress of critic and editor Jean Paulhan. In addition, she was eventually shown to be the long-unidentified author of the erotic fantasy *Histoire d'O* a book published under the pen name Pauline Réage. The true identity of Réage was kept hidden for forty years until it was finally publicly revealed by *New Yorker* writer John de St. Jorre in his 1994 article "The Unmasking of O." Aury kept her authorship a secret because she did not wish to embarrass her family and friends. In fact, when she originally wrote *Histoire d'O*—which was later translated into English as *Story of O*—it was not with the intention of having it published. Instead, it was an effort to woo the married Paulhan, because she was worried that he was losing interest in her as his mistress. Aury knew Paulhan was an admirer of the Marquis de Sade, and she thought that writing a sexual fantasy as a sort of extended love letter to Paulhan would revive their relationship. She was surprised when Paulhan encouraged her to publish the work. When the novel was released in 1954, it caused a sensation, and in the United States it became a popular success, particularly during the sexual liberation movement of the 1960s and 1970s.

Aury, whose mother abandoned her to the care of the child's grandmother, grew up living a solitary life that led her to find solace in books. She earned a teaching degree, but instead of becoming a teacher she found work as a translator. During World War II, when she abandoned her given name and adopted the name Dominique Aury, possibly because of her involvement in the French Resistance. She also worked as a literary journalist and compiled an anthology of religious poetry. Aury was trying to get the anthology published when her father introduced her to Paulhan. Paulhan had been the editor of the respected literary journal *Nouvelle Revue Française* prior to the German invasion of France and he now convinced Gallimard to publish Aury's work. Aury was enchanted by the brilliant, older married man, and the two collaborated on another journal, *Les Lettres Françaises*. Talking with De St. Jorre about these early days with Paulhan, Aury recalled that her feelings for him were not a matter of love at first sight: "It was slow, but it went very—efficiently. I didn't realize what was going on at first. . . . At first, I thought it was a caprice. But, no, it was better than that."

Although Aury could not deny her growing love for Paulhan, the fact that she became his mistress was uncomfortable for her because she felt embarrassed for Paulhan's wife and children. She especially felt guilt about his wife, who was suffering from a terminal illness. Nevertheless, she allowed Paulhan to buy a home for her, which he would regularly visit, and she remained faithful in her love to him until he died in 1968. He, on the other hand, was less-than-faithful to her, not to mention his wife, and had several other lovers besides Aury. It was this, along with her awareness that she was aging, that led her to write *Histoire d'O* as a gift to Paulhan.

Aury wrote the first sixty pages very quickly, in longhand. She surprised herself at how easily her fantasies flowed onto the paper, and was also nervous that what she had written would actually turn Paulhan away from their affair. The story had the opposite effect, however, and he urged her to write more. Aury was now working for the French publisher Gallimard, and when Paulhan presented them with the manuscript as the work of an author named Réage, it was rejected. Nevertheless, he kept trying and eventually found publisher Jean-Jacques Pauvert, who had a reputation as a risk taker. *Histoire d'O* was thus released in 1954.

Histoire d'O is the ribald tale of the eponymous woman (her name was originally Odile, after one of Aury's friends, but was shortened to O when Aury decided she did not want anyone to think she was writing about a real person so close to her), who accepts the invitation of a man named René to join him at a château in Roissy. There she allows herself to be subjected to the sadomasochistic pleasures of both the male and female guests at the home. Startlingly, O seems to enjoy the debasing treatment and even expresses bisexual yearnings. Although the book depicts graphic erotic situations that many would label pornographic, critics have been impressed by its objective descriptions and great detail, which have the effect of distancing the reader from what is happening in the story. Further, because the acts depicted in the book are well beyond the norm, both the author and reviewers have asserted that *Histoire d'O* should not be considered as rooted in reality. Therefore, as Kenneth Anderson later pointed out in the *Los Angeles Times Book Review,* this "fairy tale is not fundamentally a morality tale, in the sense of cautionary moral preachment." Anderson further explained that critics against O who complain of her passivity at such treatment are misguided: "It seems just as plausible, rather, to read O not as a person psychologically needing to be dominated, by implication caught in the grip of false consciousness or morally damaged or defunct, but instead as a person powerfully drawn to the virtues associated with hierarchy; O, although pagan, has a vocation." The reviewer continued, "O seeks virtue, but the virtue she seeks flourishes only in hierarchy, and the modern world has done its best to abolish the hierarchies spiritually necessary for her. This simple theme is taken seriously in *Story of O* and unsurprisingly is a staple theme of much of BDSM [bondage and discipline, domination and submission, sadism and masochism] fiction."

As for her own take on the novel, Aury described it to De St. Jorre as "une lettre d'amour [a love letter]. . . . Nothing else." As for "the scandalous side of *O*," the *New Yorker* writer said Aury called it "Much ado about nothing." Aury, who continued to work part time for Gallimard into her eighties, also published a sequel to her sensational novel titled *Retour à Roissy: précédé de une fille amoureuse,* but this work received much less attention. In later life, she focused mainly on her more literary, critical books, revealing herself as the writer behind Réage only four years before her death. By that time, most of the people who might have been harmed by the revelation were no longer alive.

BIOGRAPHICAL AND CRITICAL SOURCES:

BOOKS

Deforges, Régine, *O m'a dit: entretiens avec Pauline Réage,* J.-J. Pauvert (Paris, France), 1975, translation by Sabine d'Estrée as *Confessions of O: Conversations with Pauline Réage,* Viking Press (New York, NY), 1979.

PERIODICALS

Los Angeles Times Book Review, June 20, 1999, Kenneth Anderson, "The Erotics of Virtue," review of *Story of O,* p. 3.
New Yorker, August 1, 1994, John de St. Jorre, "The Unmasking of O," p. 42.
Publishers Weekly, August 1, 1994, Maureen O'Brien, "Erotic 'O' Author Outed!," p. 13.
Signs, summer, 1998, Dorothy Kaufmann, "The Story of Two Women: Dominique Aury and Edith Thomas," p. 883.

OBITUARIES

PERIODICALS

Guardian (Manchester, England), May 4, 1998, p. 13.
New York Times, May 3, 1998, section 1, p. 52.*

B

BAIRD, Nicola

PERSONAL: Female.

ADDRESSES: Office—Forest Management Foundation, 66 Warwick St., Oxford OX4 1SX, England.

CAREER: Forest Management Foundation, Oxford, England, director.

WRITINGS:

Setting Up and Running a School Library, Heinemann (Oxford, England), 1994.
A Green World? ("Viewpoints" series), Franklin Watts (New York, NY), 1997.
The Estate We're In: Who's Driving Car Culture?, Indigo (London, England), 1998.
More from Less: The More We Need, the More We Use, the More We Cause, Friends of the Earth (London, England), 2001.
The Toxic Home: Hidden Dangers around the Home, Women's Press (London, England), 2003.

Contributor to periodicals, including *New Scientist,* Manchester *Guardian,* and *New Internationalist.*

SIDELIGHTS: Nicola Baird is a freelance environmental journalist who is also director of the Forest Management Foundation, a British nonprofit organization that promotes sustainable community forest projects worldwide. She has written a number of books on environmental issues, in addition to her first book, *Setting Up and Running a School Library.* Chris Brown reviewed Baird's volume on libraryship in *School Librarian,* noting that the work's focus on managing library projects with limited resources through innovative means makdes it valuable in a range of circumstances and countries. Brown wrote that, "through a practical approach to the essentials, an enthusiastic and positive attitude is apparent throughout," and concluded that "such a wide-ranging and straightforward guide has to be an outstanding bargain for any school."

Reviewing Baird's *A Green World?* a *Books for Keeps* contributor felt that, in considering sustainable energy's place in an economic climate, the question mark of the title "is properly used." Baird followed this publication with books on car culture and consumption. She has also written for a number of publications on topics that range from chemicals and pesticides found in the human body to threats to the rainforest. *The Toxic Home: Hidden Dangers around the Home* examines cleaning products, their regulation, risks to children, products used in the garden, and how toxins can cause and exacerbate allergies and asthma. She discusses cost-effective alternatives and studies the ways in which we can minimize risk and advocate for better regulation and control of dangerous products.

BIOGRAPHICAL AND CRITICAL SOURCES:

PERIODICALS

Books for Keeps, May, 1998, review of *A Green World?,* p. 30.

School Librarian, November, 1994, Chris Brown, review of *Setting Up and Running a School Library,* p. 171.*

*   *   *

BANNISTER, Roger (Gilbert) 1929-

PERSONAL: Born March 23, 1929, in Harlow, Middlesex, England; married; wife's name, Moyra; children: four. *Education:* Oxford University, graduated; St. Mary's Hospital Medical School, graduated; attended Harvard Medical School.

ADDRESSES: Agent—c/o Author Mail, Sutton Publishing, Phoenix Mall, Thrupp, Stroud, Gloucestershire GL5 2BU, England.

CAREER: National Hospital for Nervous Diseases, London, England, director; Pembroke College, Cambridge, master. St. Mary's Hospital Medical School, Paddington, England, trustee-delegate; Sports Council of Great Britain, chairman, 1971-74; International Council for Sport and Physical Recreation, president, 1976-83.

AWARDS, HONORS: Set world track record for running the mile, 1954; Silver Pears trophy, 1954; knighted, 1975.

WRITINGS:

The Four-Minute Mile, Dodd, Mead (New York, NY), 1955, fiftieth anniversary edition published as *The First Four Minutes,* Sutton (Thrupp, Stroud, Gloucestershire, England), 2004.
(Editor) *Autonomic Failure: A Textbook of Clinical Disorders of the Autonomic Nervous System,* Oxford University Press (New York, NY), 1983, fourth revised edition, 1999.
(Editor) W. Russell Brain, *Brain's Clinical Neurology,* seventh revised edition published as *Brain and Bannister's Clinical Neurology,* Oxford University Press (New York, NY), 1992.

Also advisory editor for *Prospect: The Schweppes Book of the New Generation,* Hutchinson (London, England), 1962. Contributor to periodicals and medical journals. *Clinical Autonomic Research,* chair of editorial board, 1990—.

SIDELIGHTS: Roger Bannister has had a successful career as a neurologist, but the accomplishment that has rendered his name a household word is his record-breaking mile run, which he ran in 3:59.4 on May 6, 1954. The record lasted only seven weeks, until Australian John Landy completed the mile run in Turku, Finland, in 3:57.9. On August 7, 1954, the two runners faced each other in the British Empire Games; Landy was leading by ten yards at the halfway point, but the young doctor overcame him in the final stretch to win. The fledgling magazine *Sports Illustrated* began publishing that week and made Bannister's win its first lead story. His autobiography, *The Four-Minute Mile,* was published in a fiftieth-anniversary special edition titled *The First Four Minutes. Times Literary Supplement* contributor Michael Beloff called Bannister's memoir "the most lyrical prose description of the experience of running ever written."

Bannister came from a working-class London family. When World War II erupted, the family moved to Bath, and Bannister ran back and forth to school each day. He also ran track in high school. His academic excellence was awarded with a scholarship to attend Oxford University, where he continued to run. In 1946, while in medical school, Bannister paid a fee to run in Paddington Park, near the hospital where he worked. As *Sports Illustrated* writer Frank Deford noted, "it had helped that he was a good sort who would go over the Magdalen Bridge to the Iffley Road track at Oxford and help shovel off the snow. This was a factor in earning him a spot on the university's third team. Certainly, he was not a prepossessing physical specimen, and in fact, for a runner, he moved with an ungainly gait, rather prefiguring Monty Python's Ministry of Silly Walks." On March 22, 1947, when Bannister was being used as a pacer for the first-team Oxford runners against their Cambridge rivals, he forged ahead to win the mile by twenty yards in a time of 4:30.8. "I knew from this day," he was quoted as saying in Nelson Cordner and Roberto Quercetani's *The Milers,* "that I could develop this newfound ability."

In 1948 the nineteen-year-old Bannister ran a 4:17.2 mile at the Amateur Athletics Association championships. He declined to compete in the 1948 Olympic Games in London, instead concentrating on his studies and continuing his training. In 1951, he captured the British title in the mile, and in 1952 he competed in the Helsinki Olympic Games. He finished fourth in the 1,500 meter due to fatigue, and Bannister was criticized in the press for his unconventional training methods. At the age of twenty-five, he made his record-breaking run, with his friends Chris Chataway and Chris Brasher setting the pace.

Bannister secured the European title for the 1,500 meter, then retired from competition. He completed his medical studies and spent two decades as a researcher and neurologist. After suffering injuries in a car accident, he left private practice and concentrated on research. He maintained his ties with the athletic community, however, and served on sports councils and taught. In his professional capacity, Bannister has revised W. Russell Brain's *Brain's Clinical Neurology* and several editions of *Autonomic Failure: A Textbook of Clinical Disorders of the Autonomic Nervous System.*

Since Bannister set his track record, it has been broken by more than a thousand other athletes. Beloff noted that "today's professional athletes do not, like Bannister, run themselves into near unconsciousness; they spend every daylight hour honing their skills, training (often at altitude), resting, following a controlled diet, taking supplements (lawful or unlawful), receiving regular advice and treatment from specialists in human muscle and mind. They compete in ever more carefully crafted shoes (though there was victory before there was Nike), on ever more carefully created synthetic tracks more frequently than Bannister ever dreamed of—and for gold, not just for glory." Beloff could not help but wonder, "How fast would Bannister have run if his Chariot of Fire had been transported in a time machine to the new millennium and he had enjoyed all the advantages of his successors as world record holder?"

BIOGRAPHICAL AND CRITICAL SOURCES:

BOOKS

Bannister, Roger, *The First Four Minutes,* fiftieth anniversary edition, Sutton (Thrupp, Stroud, Gloucestershire, England), 2004.

Bascomb, Neal, *The Perfect Mile: Three Athletes, One Goal, and Less than Four Minutes to Achieve It,* Houghton Mifflin (Boston, MA), 2004.

Cordner, Nelson, and Roberto Quercetani, *The Milers,* Tafnews Press, 1985.

Dennison, Jim, *Bannister and Beyond: The Mystique of the Four-Minute Mile,* Breakaway Books, 2003.

PERIODICALS

Exceptional Parent, July, 2004, Rick Rader, "On Running Exceptionally Fast," p. 6.

Investor's Business Daily, December 19, 2003, Michael Mink, "Roger Bannister's Record Feat; Run to Glory: He Sweat the Small Stuff toward Breaking the Four-Minute Mile," p. A3.

Journal of Neurology, Neurosurgery and Psychiatry, April, 2003, Ray Chaudhuri, review of *Autonomic Failure: A Textbook of Clinical Disorders of the Autonomic Nervous System,* p. 551.

Runner's World, December, 1996, Marc Bloom, "The Single Greatest Moment" (interview), p. 50.

Sports Illustrated, December 27, 1999, Frank Deford, "Pioneer Miler Roger Bannister and Everest Conqueror Edmund Hillary Became, at Midcentury, the Last Great Heroes in an Era of Sea Change in Sport," p. 102.

Times Literary Supplement, May 14, 2004, Michael Beloff, review of *The First Four Minutes.*

ONLINE

Spokesman-Review Online (Spokane, WA), http://www.spokesmanreview.com/ (May 2, 2004), Erik Brady, "Remembering His Place in Time" (interview).*

*   *   *

BARON, Jill S. 1954-

PERSONAL: Born November 8, 1954, in Pittsburgh, PA; daughter of Lee (a merchant) and Alma (an educator; maiden name, Spann) Baron; married Dennis Ojima (a scientist), 1982; children: Claire, Kyle. *Ethnicity:* "Caucasian." *Education:* Cornell University, B.S., 1976; University of Wisconsin—Madison, M.S., 1979; Colorado State University, Ph.D., 1991.

ADDRESSES: Office—Natural Resource Ecology Laboratory, Colorado State University, Fort Collins, CO 80523.

CAREER: U.S. Geological Survey, ecologist; Colorado State University, Fort Collins, ecologist and senior research scientist at Natural Resource Laboratory;

Montana State University, distinguished lecturer at Mountain Research Center, 1997; St. Olaf College, guest speaker, 2003; member of science advisory board of Grand Canyon Monitoring and Research Center, and Glen Canyon Dam adaptive management program, 2001-03.

MEMBER: Ecological Society of America (certified senior ecologist; member of governing board).

AWARDS, HONORS: Grants from National Park Service, 1992-2003, 2002-05; Achievement Awards, Biological Resources Division, U.S. Geological Survey, 1995, 1999, 2000, 2001; Meritorious Service Award, U.S. Department of the Interior, 2002; grants from Environmental Protection Agency, 2002-05.

WRITINGS:

Biogeochemistry of a Subalpine Ecosystem, Springer-Verlag (New York, NY), 1992.
(Editor) *Rocky Mountain Futures: An Ecological Perspective,* Island Press (Washington, DC), 2002.

Contributor to periodicals, including *BioScience, Environmental Geology, Ecosystems, Paleolimnology,* and *Water Resources Research.* Associate editor, *Ecological Applications.*

WORK IN PROGRESS: Research on ecosystem dynamics and integrated assessments.

*   *   *

BARON OF WEST KIRBY
See SHEPPARD, David Stuart

*   *   *

BARONESS STRANGE
See EVANS, (Jean) Cherry (Drummond)

*   *   *

BARRETT, Neal, Jr. 1929-
(Victor Appleton, Chad Calhoun, Clay Dawson, Franklin W. Dixon, Rebecca Drury, Wesley Ellis, J. D. Hardin)

PERSONAL: Born 1929, in San Antonio, TX. *Education:* University of Oklahoma, B.A.

ADDRESSES: Agent—c/o Author Mail, Golden Gryphon Press, 3002 Perkins Rd., Urbana, IL 61802.

CAREER: Writer. Formerly worked in corporate public relations.

MEMBER: Texas Institute of Letters.

AWARDS, HONORS: Nebula award, 1990, for *Ginny Sweethips' Flying Circus;* Texas Institute of Letters Award, 2000, for *Interstate Dreams;* Theodore Sturgeon Memorial Award, for "Stairs."

WRITINGS:

NOVELS

Kelwin, Lancer Books (New York, NY), 1970.
The Gates of Time (published with *The Dwellers of the Deep,* by K. M. O'Donnell), Ace Books (New York, NY), 1970.
The Leaves of Time, Lancer Books (New York, NY), 1971.
Highwood & Annihilation Factor, Ace Books (New York, NY), 1972.
Stress Pattern, DAW Books (New York, NY), 1974.
Aldair in Albion, DAW Books (New York, NY), 1976.
Aldair: Master of Ships, DAW Books (New York, NY), 1977.
Aldair: Across the Misty Sea, DAW Books (New York, NY), 1980.
Long Days and Short Nights: A Century of Texas Ranching on the YO, 1880-1980, Y-O Press (Mountain View, TX), 1980.
(Under pseudonym J. D. Hardin) *Hard Chains, Soft Women,* Playboy Paperback (New York, NY), 1981.
Aldair: The Legion of Beasts, DAW Books (New York, NY), 1982.
Daniel Boone, Westward Trail, Miles Standish Press (Wayne, PA), 1982.
(Under pseudonym Chad Calhoun) *The River Beauty,* Banbury Books (Wayne, PA), 1982.
(Under pseudonym Victor Appleton) *Tom Swift: The Invisible Force,* Wanderer Books (New York, NY), 1983.
(Under pseudonym Wesley Ellis) *Lone Star and the Texas Gambler,* Jove Books (New York, NY), 1984.
The Karma Corps, DAW Books (New York, NY), 1984.

(Under pseudonym Rebecca Drury) *Valiant Wings,* Banbury Books (Wayne, PA), 1985.

(Under house pseudonym Franklin W. Dixon) *The Hardy Boys: The Skyfire Puzzle,* Wanderer Books (New York, NY), 1985.

Through Darkest America, Congdon & Weed (New York, NY), 1986.

The Hereafter Gang, M. V. Ziesing (Shingletown, CA), 1991.

(Under pseudonym Clay Dawson) *Long Rider: Snaketown, 1991,* Diamond Book, 1991.

Dawn's Uncertain Light, New American Library (New York, NY), 1992.

Batman in the Black Egg of Atlantis (juvenile), illustrated by Sal Amendola, Little, Brown (Boston, MA) 1992.

Pink Vodka Blues, St. Martin's Press (New York, NY), 1992.

Dead Dog Blues, St. Martin's Press (New York, NY), 1994.

Skinny Annie Blues, Kensington Books (New York, NY), 1996.

The Touch of Your Shadow, the Whisper of Your Name, Bantam (New York, NY), 1996.

Bad Eye Blues, Kensington Books (New York, NY), 1997.

Warriors' Revenge: Spider Man Super Thriller, Pocket Books (New York, NY), 1997.

Lizard's Rage: Spider Man Super Thriller, Simon & Schuster (New York, NY), 1997.

Interstate Dreams, Mojo Press, 1999.

The Prophecy Machine, Bantam Books (New York, NY), 2000.

Dungeons & Dragons (novelization of film of the same title), Wizards of the Coast, 2000.

The Day the Decorators Came, Subterranean Press (Burton, MI), 2000.

Piggs, Subterranean Press (Burton, MI), 2001.

The Treachery of Kings, Bantam Books (New York, NY), 2001.

Prince of Cristler-Coke, Golden Gryphon Press (Urbana, IL), 2004.

SHORT STORY COLLECTIONS

Slightly Off Center: Eleven Extraordinarily Exhilarating Tales, Swan Press (Austin, TX), 1992.

Perpetuity Blues and Other Stories, Golden Gryphon Press (Urbana, IL), 2000.

A Different Vintage, Subterranean Press, (Burton, MI) 2001.

Also author of novelizations of *Judge Dredd,* 1995, and *Barb Wire,* 1996. Contributor to anthologies, including *The Year's Best Science-Fiction Annual Collection,* volumes four, five, seven, ten, and eleven; *Invaders!,* 1993; *Isaac Asimov's SF-Lite,* 1993; *Omni: Best Science Fiction; The Best from Fantasy & Science Fiction; Asimov's Robots; Dark at Heart; Nebula Awards 24,* 1994; *The King Is Dead: Tales of Elvis Post-Mortem,* 1994; and *George Alec Effinger Live! From Planet Earth,* Golden Gryphon Press (Urbana, IL), 2005. Contributor of numerous short stories to magazines, including *Omni, Galaxy,* and *Isaac Asimov's Science Fiction* magazine.

ADAPTATIONS: Pink Vodka Blues was optioned by producer David Brown and purchased by Paramount Pictures, 1993.

SIDELIGHTS: Since 1960 Neal Barrett, Jr. has been writing short stories, novellas, and novels in a style uniquely his own. Barrett's work rarely falls into distinct categories or genres. Instead, fantastic elements blend with the mundane, or futuristic environments serve as homes for recognizable, fallible people. To call Barrett a science-fiction writer is to ignore his contributions to crime writing. To pin him to either category overlooks his literary novels that reflect, albeit in a quirky way, his home state of Texas. His widely anthologized short stories offer "encapsulations of the bleak implications of life in late Twentieth Century America," to quote Nick Gevers on the *Infinity Plus* Web site. Ironically, Barrett's work is so individualized, and so unpredictable, that—while well known in the writing community—he is not as famous as some of his peers who adhere to the formulaic conventions of their genres.

Barrett studied writing at the University of Oklahoma and began publishing stories in science-fiction magazines while still in his twenties. He spent many years working at various corporations in public relations before earning enough income from his fiction to devote his entire life to it. In the late 1970s he began to attract attention in the science fiction community for a series of ambitious novels, including *Stress Pattern* and the "Aldair" series, a quartet of novels featuring an earth populated by many species of sentient animals. Aldair himself is a pig, and he sets out on a quest to find out what has happened to the species that created so many thinking animals—human beings. Not until Aldair and his companions reach a distant planet do they discover the remnants of the human race, living in diminished circumstances. Nick Gevers felt that Aldair is a "remarkable protagonist" upon whom to hang a narrative. A contributor to the *St. James Guide to Science-Fiction Writers* called the "Aldair" series "one of the most entertaining and innovative of its kind."

Through Darkest America and *Dawn's Uncertain Light* offer a grim glimpse of a post-apocalyptic America in which the strong literally feed on the weak. The hero of the two novels must reconcile himself to the use of human flesh for food—or fight for the rights of those who are lobotomized as fodder for the powerful. Nick Gevers found the two novels "bleakly savage and compelling," and the *St. James Guide to Science-Fiction Writers* contributor likewise noted that the books "portray a bleak future."

Barrett has also written a series of offbeat mystery novels, each having "blues" in the title. *Pink Vodka Blues, Dead Dog Blues, Skinny Annie Blues,* and *Bad Eye Blues* all reflect their author's tongue-in-cheek affection for crime narrative, humorous characters and situations, and outrageous plot twists. "Imagine Robert Ludlum on laughing gas," a *Publishers Weekly* critic commented. In *Dead Dog Blues,* a rich Texan finds his beloved Laborador retriever dead in the backyard, wired in place so that it appears to be barking. A few days later, the man himself is murdered in a similar fashion and finding the fiendish killer falls to the task of Jack Track, a man with a past who has only recently returned to Texas. Wes Lukowsky, writing in *Booklist,* called *Dead Dog Blues* "a roller-coaster ride to hell, and the guy in the next seat is crackin' wise." A *Publishers Weekly* reviewer maintained that Barrett's humor, "plays at—but doesn't quite go over—the edge."

The same irreverence marks *Bad Eye Blues.* Mild-mannered Wiley Moss, an insect illustrator for the Smithsonian Institute, is kidnapped and dragged to the wilds of Idaho, where he is "encouraged" to paint portraits of a dozen prostitutes hired to entertain a secretive mob boss. "Those who like outdoor mysteries set in the West should read this book," suggested John Rowan in *Booklist.* A *Publishers Weekly* contributor praised Barrett as the "alpha male" of comic crime writers and characterized *Bad Eye Blues* as "a tantalizing little mystery with a double shot of big laughs."

Piggs plays itself out in a seedy strip joint in fictitious Mexican Wells, Texas. A reformed con named Jack McCooly, though capable of higher employment, works there as a waiter and dishwasher, nursing a hopeless love for one of the strippers. With dreams of a comfortable, middle-class existence with his lady love as his motivation, Jack embarks on a scheme to make some quick money, but his plans go awry with cosmic implications. In *Booklist,* Wes Lukowsky concluded that the novel "will worm its way into readers' consciousness and refuse to leave. It's very, very good." A *Publishers Weekly* correspondent also felt that Barrett's "array of dismal characters is fascinating to watch, [and] his novel fun to read."

Barrett returns to the realm of speculative fiction with works such as *The Prophecy Machine* and *Prince of Cristler-Coke.* In *The Prophecy Machine* a crafter of mechanical lizards finds himself stranded on an island and forced to repair a machine that can predict the future. The prince in the futuristic *Prince of Cristler-Coke* loses his title to rule America East as teh result of a power coup by the heirs of other dynastic corporations. Forced into "rehabilitation" in Oklahomer, the prince escapes to learn the true makeup of his "haves" and "have-nots" world.

Some critics have noted that Barrett expresses himself best in the short-story form. He has published three full collections of stories and has contributed to numerous anthologies. The tales in *Perpetuity Blues and Other Stories,* styled the "Best of Barrett" by Nick Gevers, makes America's inhabitants the poorest, most exploited, and most ruthlessly dominated people on the planet. In *Fantasy and Science Fiction,* James Sallis wrote of the collection: "Barrett's voice is not only unmistakable; you realize after a sentence or two that it's been there all along at the back of your head." The critic commended Barrett's work as "stories for adults, sent out from a rigorously individual, uncompromising vision."

Barrett's bibliography includes highly literate work such as *The Hereafter Gang* and *Interstate Dreams,* as well as pseudonymous series work and novelizations of movies. In an interview on *CrescentBlues.com,* Barrett explained: "I've written close to fifty novels in a number of different fields. This is the sort of thing a great many professional writers have to do, while they're writing great works of art. I have tried to write by a single rule: even if you're writing something when you'd rather be writing something else, write as a professional, and do the best you can. If you don't, the reader will most certainly know." He added: "I have seldom been what you'd call commercial. I'm not especially proud of the fact, but there you are. I expect I'll keep doing what I do, and writing things I love to write, and some that I don't."

BIOGRAPHICAL AND CRITICAL SOURCES:

BOOKS

St. James Guide to Science-Fiction Writers, 4th edition, St. James Press (Detroit, MI), 1996.

PERIODICALS

Analog Science Fiction and Fact, April, 2001, Tom Easton, review of *The Prophecy Machine,* p. 133.
Booklist, June 1, 1994, Wes Lukowsky, review of *Dead Dog Blues,* p. 1775; April 15, 1997, John Rowen, review of *Bad Eye Blues,* p. 1389; July, 2001, Paula Luedtke, review of *The Treachery of Kings,* p. 1991; October 15, 2001, Wes Lukowsky, review of *Piggs,* p. 384.
Fantasy and Science Fiction, December, 2000, James Sallis, review of *Perpetuity Blues and Other Stories,* p. 32.
Publishers Weekly, May 18, 1992, review of *Pink Vodka Blues,* p. 61; April 18, 1994, review of *Dead Dog Blues,* p. 49; June 17, 1996, review of *Skinny Annie Blues,* p. 50; March 31, 1997, review of *Bad Eye Blues,* p. 65; April 2, 2001, review of *A Different Vintage,* p. 45; August 27, 2001, review of *Piggs,* p. 57; August 9, 2004, review of *Prince of Cristler-Coke,* p. 235.

ONLINE

CrescentBlues.com, http://www.crescentblues.com/ (April 4, 2005), "Neal Barrett, Jr.: Genre Cocktail, Anyone?"
Infinity Plus, http://www.infinityplus.co.uk/ (April 4, 2005), Nick Gevers, "In a Genre of His Own" (interview).
Neal Barrett Home Page, http://www.nealbarrett.com (April 4, 2005).*

*   *   *

BATES, Martine
    See LEAVITT, Martine

BATHURST, Bella 1969-

PERSONAL: Born 1969, in London, England.

ADDRESSES: Home—Scotland. *Agent*—c/o Author Mail, Houghton Mifflin, Adult Editorial, 8th Floor, 222 Berkeley St., Boston, MA 02116-3764.

CAREER: Has worked as a freelance journalist and illustrator.

AWARDS, HONORS: Somerset Maugham Award, for *The Lighthouse Stevensons.*

WRITINGS:

The Lighthouse Stevensons: The Extraordinary Story of the Building of the Scottish Lighthouses by the Ancestors of Robert Louis Stevenson (nonfiction), HarperCollins (New York, NY), 1999.
Special (young adult novel), Houghton Mifflin (Boston, MA), 2002.

Contributor of articles to periodicals, including the *Washington Post,* Manchester *Guardian, Independent, Telegraph, Observer, Scotsman, Scotland on Sunday,* and London *Sunday Times.*

WORK IN PROGRESS: A book about shipwrecks.

SIDELIGHTS: Journalist and illustrator Bella Bathurst has also written both fiction and nonfiction books. In an interview on the Houghton Mifflin Web site, Bathurst commented, "It's enjoyable, writing fiction and nonfiction turn and turn about. It means I never, ever get bored."

Bathurst's first book, *The Lighthouse Stevensons: The Extraordinary Story of the Building of the Scottish Lighthouses by the Ancestors of Robert Louis Stevenson,* tells the story of a family of engineers who built were responsible for saving many lives through their work designing and contructing almost one hundred lighthouses that guarded the treacherous shores of nineteenth-century Scotland. Bathurst's story focuses primarily on four lighthouses built by the family: Skerryvore, Bell Rock, Dhu Heartach, and Muclkle Flugga.

The building of these lighthouses presented serious challenges, including the danger of transporting raw materials to wet and slippery sites, political opposition from wreckers who made their living from ship-wrecked boats, and the inadequate lighting equipment available at the time. Robert Louis Stevenson's grandfather, Robert Stevenson, became chief engineer of the newly formed Northern Lighthouse Board soon after 1786 and succeeded in creating lasting works of architecture, including the lighthouse at the infamous Bell Rock. His two sons, Alan and Tom, continued the family tradition. Although Alan died young, he left Scotland with such structures as the lighthouse at Skerryvore, which is considered a work of engineering art. The Stevenson lighthouse dynasty ended rather abruptly when Alan's son Bob became a highly regarded art historian. Tom fathered Robert Louis Stevenson, who began his career as a reluctant engineer but turned to writing novels and poetry. Nevertheless, his familiarity with Scotland's northern coast and its lighthouses served as a background for his books *Treasure Island* and *Kidnapped.*

Writing in the *Times Literary Supplement,* Karl Miller called *The Lighthouse Stevensons* "a sweetly written and suitably lucid contribution to the history of these exhilarating kindly lights and of nineteenth-century Scotland, and is full of the good stories that the sub-genre of scientific adventure requires." A *Publishers Weekly* contributor commented that "Bathurst's flamboyant and elegantly written saga is bursting with life," while Ben Downing, writing in the *New Criterion,* noted that the author "is to be commended for conveying . . . information with engaging verve and, still more, for imparting to us a keen sense of the Stevenson's accomplishments."

For her next book, Bathurst turned to fiction. *Special* focuses on adolescents as a group of girl boarding-school classmates take a two-week field trip to a Gloucestershire hostel, where they are chaperoned by two sadistic teachers. The girls come from dysfunctional families and, despite efforts by their chaperones to keep them under a watchful eye, are soon becoming involved in alcohol, drugs, and sex as they cavort with local youths from the nearby town. Although the town's temptations are great, Bathurst focuses much of the novel on the girls interactions with each other, including their jealousies and competitiveness, compounded by their general mistrust and meanness, which burst forth as they are removed from their day-to-day surroundings. The plot primarily revolves around Jules and her jealousy of the pretty, smart, and popular Caz. Nevertheless, Jules is irresistibly drawn to Caz and begins to think that she may be a lesbian, so she decides to lose her virginity with one of the town locals to prove that she is not. Other characters include Hen, an anorexic who practices self-mutilation, and Izzy, an unattractive girl who suffers from skin and respiratory allergies.

Writing in *Booklist,* Gillian Engberg noted that in *Special* Bathurst "elevates what could have been sensationalized material into a rich exploration of the subtle, often terrifying moments that define female adolescence." *New York Times Book Review* contributor William Ferguson felt that the narrative "is not strong, but the characterizations are excellent." Despite calling the author's writing "never less than fluid and pacey" and noting that the book contains "wonderful moments of insight," Geraldine Bedell noted in the *Europe Intelligence Wire* that "overall, these girls are so monotone in their mean-spiritedness that their gropings towards identity seem simply tiresome." In a review in the *Spectator,* Margaret Forster felt that the book's ending "is a little too melodramatic" and that "plenty of the themes running through it are clichéd." Nevertheless, Forster noted that the novel "explores, with great sensitivity, the discovery of personal identity, and marks a fine beginning as a novelist." *Library Journal* contributor Barbara Love concluded that *Special* is a "stunningly observed, wickedly funny, and ultimately tragic first novel."

BIOGRAPHICAL AND CRITICAL SOURCES:

PERIODICALS

Booklist, September 1, 1999, Bryce Christensen, review of *The Lighthouse Stevensons: The Extraordinary Story of the Building of the Scottish Lighthouses by the Ancestors of Robert Louis Stevenson,* p. 50; December 1, 1999, Donna Seaman, review of *The Lighthouse Stevensons,* p. 676; March 15, 2003, Gillian Engberg, review of *Special,* p. 1273.

Boston Globe, May 25, 2003, Caroline Leavitt, review of *Special,* p. D9.

Europe Intelligence Wire, October 5, 2002, Julie Myerson, review of *Special;* October 20, 2002, Geraldine Bedell, review of *Special.*

Guardian (Manchester, England), August 9, 2003, Nicola McAllister, review of *Special*, p. 20.

Kirkus Reviews, March 1, 2003, review of *Special*, p. 326.

Library Journal, March 15, 2003, Barbara Love, review of *Special*, p. 113.

New Criterion, November, 1999, Ben Downing, review of *The Lighthouse Stevensons*, p. 73.

New York Times Book Review, November 9, 2003, William Ferguson, review of *Special*, p. 28.

Publishers Weekly, August 30, 1999, review of *The Lighthouse Stevensons*, p. 64.

Quadrant, December, 1999, Oliver MacDonagh, review of *The Lighthouse Stevensons*, p. 84.

Spectator, October 12, 2002, Margaret Forster, review of *Special*, p. 67.

Times Literary Supplement, May 7, 1999, Karl Miller, review of *The Lighthouse Stevensons*, p. 26.

ONLINE

Houghton Mifflin Web site, http://www.houghtonmifflinbooks.com/ (January 28, 2005), interview with Bathurst.*

*   *   *

BEATTY, Scott 1969-

PERSONAL: Born 1969. *Education:* Iowa State University, M.A.

ADDRESSES: Home—PA. *Agent*—c/o Author Mail, CrossGen Entertainment, Inc., 4023 Tampa Rd., Ste. 2400, Oldsmar, FL 34677. *E-mail*—scott@scottbeatty.com.

CAREER: Worked as an English teacher, radio personality, and magazine editor.

WRITINGS:

COMIC BOOKS

(With Chuck Dixon) *Robin: Year One*, four volumes, DC Comics (New York, NY), 2000, published in one volume, 2002.

(With Chuck Dixon) *JLA, Terror Incognita*, DC Comics (New York, NY), 2002.

(With Chuck Dixon) *Batgirl: Year One* (collection), DC Comics (New York, NY), 2003.

WITH OTHERS; "RUSE" SERIES

Criminal Intent, CrossGen (Oldsmar, FL) 2002.

The Silent Partner, CrossGen (Oldsmar, FL), 2003.

Criminal Intent, CrossGen (Oldsmar, FL), 2003.

OTHER

Batman: The Ultimate Guide to the Dark Knight, Dorling Kindersley (New York, NY), 2001.

JLA: The Ultimate Guide to the Justice League of America, Dorling Kindersley (New York, NY), 2002.

Superman: The Ultimate Guide to the Man of Steel, Dorling Kindersley (New York, NY), 2002.

Superman, the Animated Series Guide, Dorling Kindersley (New York, NY), 2003.

Wonder Woman: The Ultimate Guide to the Amazon Princess, Dorling Kindersley (New York, NY), 2003.

Batman, the Animated Series Guide, Dorling Kindersley (New York, NY), 2003.

Batman Beyond, Dorling Kindersley (New York, NY), 2004.

Catwoman: The Visual Guide to the Feline Fatale, Dorling Kindersley (New York, NY), 2004.

(With others) *The DC Comics Encyclopedia*, Dorling Kindersley (New York, NY), 2004.

SIDELIGHTS: Scott Beatty, who has written for a long list of popular comics series, said in an interview posted at his Web site that he "grew up loving DC Comics. . . . For me, the DC bullet stood out like a beacon on the newstand."

Beatty's first work for DC was for a "Batman" comic-book series; for many of his projects, including *Robin: Year One* and *Batgirl: Year One,* he has shared writing duties with Chuck Dixon. Batgirl is the alter ego of librarian Barbara Gordon, the daughter of Gotham City's police captain. Her father rejects her idea of becoming an officer, and the FBI says she is too short to be an agent, but Barbara is determined to fight crime. Barbara's father has received help from Batman, and in an attempt to add further embarrassment, Barbara wears a Batman-like costume to the department's masquerade ball. When Barbara foils the attempt of villain Killer Moth to crash the event, the Moth dubs her "Batgirl." Emily Lloyd reviewed the collection for *School Library Journal,* calling it "a joy from start to finish, with smart, barbed dialogue, a dense plot, exuberantly drawn action, and impressive characterizations."

Beatty has written a number of guides to the most popular series' characters, including *Batman: The Ultimate Guide to the Dark Knight.* Beatty's Bat topics include Bruce Wayne, Wayne Enterprises, Batman's utility belt, the Batcave, Batmobiles, Alfred, Robin, Catwoman, the Penguin, and other characters.

Another long-time DC hero is featured in *Superman: The Ultimate Guide to the Man of Steel.* Superman has been featured by DC since 1938, and Beatty covers his entire history, with the majority of the information covering Superman post-1986. A time line lays out Superman's origins on the planet of Krypton, his childhood in Smallville, his job as a reporter for the *Daily Planet,* and his friends and his enemies. Illustrations from both the original comics and more recent works compliment the history.

Female characters are covered in *Wonder Woman: The Ultimate Guide to the Amazon Princess* and *Catwoman: The Visual Guide to the Feline Fatale.* In addition to her cat costume, transportation, and weapons, Catwoman's sometime relationship with Batman is documented, making this volume also of interest to Batman fans. Karen T. Bilton noted in *School Library Journal* that, "unlike previous books in the series, this title has overtly sexual images."

When Mark Waid left the comic-book series "Ruse," Beatty was chosen to replace him as writer. Although publisher CrossGen markets the series as a cross between *X-Files* and Sherlock Holmes, "Ruse" is actually a closer match to the televison series *The Avengers.* Instead of John Steed and Emma Peel fighting evil against a quirky cold war backdrop, "Ruse" features Simon Archard and his assistant Emma Bishop in a quasi-Victorian England setting wherein Druidism is a recognized religion and the gargoyles perched along the sides of buildings are living creatures. A *Publish-*

ers Weekly contributor, reviewing the second "Ruse" collection, *The Silent Partner,* called Simon and Emma "exceptionally clever, attractive people who make witty jibes at each other while jumping off trains and tumbling down mountains."

By the time Beatty came on board with *Ruse,* the series had won five Eisner awards. He took over completely from Waid in the third volume, *Criminal Intent.* In this go-round, Emma and Simon are separated for much of the time, and in one issue a pair of children fend off the evildoers. A *Publishers Weekly* reviewer who called *Criminal Intent* "good-natured fun" wrote that "this work deliberately exaggerates the cliches of melodramatic pop fiction right up to the edge of self-parody."

BIOGRAPHICAL AND CRITICAL SOURCES:

PERIODICALS

Booklist, January 1, 2002, Carolyn Phelan, review of *Batman: The Ultimate Guide to the Dark Knight,* p. 827; August, 2002, Carlos Orellana, review of *Superman: The Ultimate Guide to the Man of Steel,* p. 1942; May 15, 2004, Tina Coleman, review of *Catwoman: The Visual Guide to the Feline Fatale,* p. 1613.

Library Journal, September 1, 2002, Steve Raiteri, review of *Superman,* p. 152.

Publishers Weekly, May 26, 2003, review of *Ruse: The Silent Partner,* p. 51; August 11, 2003, review of *Ruse: Criminal Intent,* p. 260.

School Library Journal, September, 2002, Tim Wadham, review of *Superman,* p. 240; January, 2003, Douglas P. Davey, review of *JLA: The Ultimate Guide to the Justice League of America,* p. 146; January, 2004, Douglas P. Davey, review of *Batman, the Animated Series Guide* p. 110; April, 2004, Emily Lloyd, review of *Batgirl: Year One* p. 186; September, 2004, Karen T. Bilton, review of *Catwoman,* p. 237.

ONLINE

ComicBookResources.com, http://www.comicbook resources.com/ (August 1, 2001), Beau Yarbrough, "Scott Beatty: Profiler of the Bat" (interview).

OrcaFresh.net, http://www.orcafresh.net/ (February 26, 2005), Tim O'Shea, "Creativity Doesn't Exist in a Vacuum" (interview).

Scott Beatty Home Page, http://www.scottbeatty.com (February 26, 2005).

SilverBulletComicBooks.com, http://www.silverbullet comicbooks.com/ (February 26, 2005), Michael Deeley, "The Ultimate Guide to Scott Beatty" (interview).*

*   *   *

BECKETT, Ralph L(awrence), (Sr.) 1923-2005
(Gerald O. Doyle)

OBITUARY NOTICE— See index for *CA* sketch: Born June 6, 1923, in Salt Lake City, UT; died of cancer March 22, 2005, in Placentia, CA. Educator and author. Beckett was a former professor of speech communication at California State University, Fullerton. As a student, he attended the University of California at Los Angeles, and when World War II broke out he enlisted in the U.S. Army. After the war, he returned to school at the University of Southern California, where he earned a bachelor's degree in 1950, a master's degree in 1953, and his doctorate in 1968. His early career included such diverse jobs as professional jazz musician, produce salesman, and radio announcer and writer. By 1952, however, Beckett had entered the teaching profession, first as a teacher at South Gate High School in Los Angeles and then, beginning in 1957, as an instructor at Los Angeles Harbor College. From 1968 to 1970 he taught at the University of Missouri, then joined California State University at Fullerton, where he would remain as a professor of speech communication until taking an early retirement in 1985. Having earned his Ph.D. in speech disorders, Beckett was most fascinated by voice disorders and physiological phonetics. With Dwight Garner, he was the author of *Speech Dynamics* (1967) and *Writing the Research Paper* (1968); he was also the author of *Writing College English* (1963). More recently, however, he ventured into fiction, publishing the novel *In the Beauty of the Lilies* under the pen name Gerald O. Doyle in 2002.

OBITUARIES AND OTHER SOURCES:

PERIODICALS

Chronicle of Higher Education, April 22, 2005, p. A48.

ONLINE

California State University, Fullerton Web site, http://www.fullerton.edu/ (April 1, 2005).

*   *   *

BEECHAM, Jahnna
(Jahnna N. Malcolm, a joint pseudonym)

PERSONAL: Married Malcolm Hillgartner (a writer); children: Dash, Skye. *Hobbies and other interests:* Music, reading, traveling.

ADDRESSES: Home—Ashland, OR. *Office*—Starcatcher Press, 256 Tudor Circle, Ashland, OR 97520. *E-mail*—Malcolm@wherewelive.com.

CAREER: Actor, film producer and director, and writer. Gathering at Bigfork (playwright conference), co-founder and director with husband, Malcolm Hillgartner; Where We Live Productions (film production company), co-founder and creative director, with Hillgartner; Starcatcher Press, Ashland, OR, cofounder and publisher.

WRITINGS:

UNDER NAME JAHNNA BEECHAM

See the U.S.A. with Your Resumé: A Survival Guide to Regional Theatre, Samuel French (New York, NY), 1985.

Crazy for You, Bantam (New York, NY), 1988.

The Right Combination, Bantam (New York, NY), 1988.

The Baby-Sitters Club Guide to Baby-Sitting, Scholastic (New York, NY), 1993.

I'm Counting to One: Hope and Humor for Frazzled Parents, Sorin Books (Notre Dame, IN), 2001.

WITH MALCOLM HILLGARTNER; UNDER JOINT PSEUDONYM JAHNNA N. MALCOLM

Blubberina, Scholastic (New York, NY), 1989.

The King and Us, Scholastic (New York, NY), 1990.

The Slime That Ate Crestview, Scholastic (New York, NY), 1992.

Spirit of the West: The Story of an Appaloosa Mare, Her Precious Foal, and the Girl Whose Pride Endangers Them All, Ertl Co. (Dyersville, IA), 1996.

The Stallion of Box Canyon: The Story of a Wild Mustang and the Girl Who Wins His Trust, Ertl Co. (Dyersville, IA), 1997.

The Emerald Princess Follows a Unicorn, Scholastic (New York, NY), 1999.

Who Framed Mary Bubnik?, Starcatcher Press (Ashland, OR), 2001.

Stupid Cupids, Starcatcher Press (Ashland, OR), 2001.

Pirate's Revenge, Gateway Learning Corp. (Santa Ana, CA), 2003.

The Royal Switch, Gateway Learning Corp. (Santa Ana, CA), 2003.

The Midnight Ride, Gateway Learning Corp. (Santa Ana, CA), 2003.

Men in Green, Gateway Learning Corp. (Santa Ana, CA), 2003.

Perfect Strangers, Simon Pulse (New York, NY), 2005.

Mixed Messages, Simon Pulse (New York, NY), 2005.

Message in a Bottle, Simon Pulse (New York, NY), 2005.

The Write Stuff, Simon Pulse (New York, NY), 2005.

Author of other books for children. Author of column "A Family Journal," for *Sesame Street Parents* magazine. Author of screenplay, *The Ruby Princess Runs Away.* Author of text for interactive CD-ROM for Gateway Learning Company.

BIOGRAPHICAL AND CRITICAL SOURCES:

PERIODICALS

Publishers Weekly, June 21, 1991, review of *Makin' the Grade,* p. 64.

School Library Journal, January, 2005, Elaine Baran Black, review of *Mixed Messages,* p. 132.

ONLINE

Jewel Kingdom Web site, http://www.jewelkingdom. com/ (May 3, 2005), "Jahnna N. Malcolm."

Lovegevity Web site, http://www.lovegevity.com/ (May 3, 2005).*

BESMANN, Wendy Lowe 1954-
(Wendy Lowe)

PERSONAL: Born February 11, 1954, in Houston, TX; daughter of James (a pilot) and Evelyn (a journalist) Lowe; married Theodore Besmann (an engineer), October 24, 1982; children: Anna, David. *Ethnicity:* "Caucasian/Jewish." *Education:* San Francisco State University, B.A.; also attended Hastings College of Law. *Politics:* "Independent." *Religion:* Jewish. *Hobbies and other interests:* Meditation, philosophy and mythology, Torah studies, walking, yoga.

ADDRESSES: Home—9119 Solway Ferry Rd., Oak Ridge, TN 37830. *E-mail*—wendylb4@comcast.net.

CAREER: 13-30 Corp., Knoxville, TN, assistant editor, group editor, 1976-83; freelance writer and marketing consultant, 1983—. Also works as facilitator of focus groups. Active in local organizations, including Knoxville Jewish Alliance.

MEMBER: Insight Meditation Society, Hadassah.

AWARDS, HONORS: Milton D. Green Award, Hastings College of Law; Award of Distinction, East Tennessee Historical Society.

WRITINGS:

(Under name Wendy Lowe) *America's Wonderful Little Hotels and Inns: Western Region,* Congdon & Weed (New York, NY), fifth edition, with Barbara Crossette, 1985.

A Separate Circle: Jewish Life in Knoxville, Tennessee, University of Tennessee Press (Knoxville, TN), 2001.

Contributor to periodicals, including *Atlantic Monthly, Better Homes and Gardens, Esquire, Outside, Self, Travel and Leisure,* and *USA Today.*

WORK IN PROGRESS: A novel about "one woman's journey from madness to sanity by means of creating a personal mythology"; a nonfiction book for caregivers of mentally ill children.

SIDELIGHTS: Wendy Lowe Besmann told *CA:* "At this point in my life, my primary motivation for writing is to explain myself to myself. I want to understand the ethnic group in which I was raised, the experiences that formed me and those around me, the proud and painful journey of our country, and most especially how the human mind (including my own) operates in all its endless variety. I hope to capture the imagination and engage my reader in that same learning process.

"I have often been influenced by 'non-literary' writers (Dorothy Sayers, Mary Stewart, Ann Tyler) for their intensive research into a culture or subject and their marvelous use of language. Annie Dillard and Barbara Tuchman, for research and careful observation as well as flowing narrative, were big influences on my historical and cultural writing (particularly in the freelance travel-essay writing that began my career).

"Another major influence on my work is the situation in which my husband Ted and I have found ourselves for the past decade: raising two children with inherited mental disorders. The youngest, my son, has bipolar disorder and Asperger's syndrome (high functioning autism). Dealing with the complexity, grief, and eventual acceptance of the experience has given me a wide factual and emotional knowledge base which is the subject of my upcoming book. I hope it will be the most comprehensive and helpful work I have accomplished.

"History—with emphasis on the *story* in it—is my first passion. Next is research of all kinds. My writing method starts with research—oral and written. Next comes synthesis, my own experience mixed in; more research, writing, and rewriting. I work rather slowly but don't let it go (or be seen by others) until I'm satisfied.

"Buddhist meditation, a serious interest for the past ten years, has opened a vista of new ways to understand what I wish to communicate to myself and others. On its heels comes a fascination with how we create our personal myths—the topic of my recently completed novel. Poetry by Rumi, Mary Oliver, T. S. Eliot, and others makes me want to write language that sings. I hope I do this from time to time."

BETHE, Hans (Albrecht) 1906-2005

OBITUARY NOTICE— See index for *CA* sketch: Born July 2, 1906, in Strasbourg, Alsace-Lorraine, Germany; died of congestive heart failure March 6, 2005, in Ithaca, NY. Physicist, educator, and author. One of the giants of twentieth-century physics, Bethe was a Pulitzer Prize winner whose accomplishments included a description of how stars function and numerous contributions to the development of atomic weaponry at Los Alamos National Laboratyr during World War II. Growing up the son of scholars, he became interested in physics at a time when theories in quantum mechanics were coming to fruition. Completing his Ph.D. at the University of Munich in 1928, Bethe established himself in teaching. During the late 1920s and early 1930s, he taught at such institutions as the universities of Frankfurt, Stuttgart, Munich, and Tübingen. With the rise of the Nazis in Germany, Bethe, whose mother was Jewish, left his native land for England in 1933 to teach at the University of Manchester, the next year he was a fellow at the University of Bristol. In 1935, Bethe immigrated to the United States to accept an assistant professorship at Cornell University, where he became a full professor in just two years. He remained at Cornell for the rest of his academic career, retiring in 1975 after making the university a world-renowned center for the study of physics. Bethe came into the spotlight in the late 1930s, when he published a series of articles on the principles of nuclear physics. Published in *Reviews of Modern Physics,* these articles became known as "The Bethe Bible," and served as a guide for his colleagues in the field. Also during this time, he described the process known as the carbon cycle, a multistage process in which light is produced in some stars. It was for this accomplishment that he received the Pulitzer Prize for Physics in 1967. Because of his superlative knowledge of nuclear physics, Bethe, who had become a U.S. citizen by 1941, was courted by J. Robert Oppenheimer to join the team at Los Alamos, where scientists were hurrying to build an atomic bomb before Nazi scientists did. Persuaded to join them in 1942, Bethe headed the theoretical physics division for three years, serving also as a mentor, teacher, and even spiritual guide to his colleagues, many of whom were troubled by the implications of what they were creating. Though Bethe worked on the bomb because he felt it was necessary as a deterrent, he later became a moderating voice against nuclear weapons proliferation. In the 1950s, for example, he helped develop a means by which nuclear blasts could be detected by other nations, hoping by this development that countries limit their tests and adhere to nuclear arms treaties. From 1956 until 1964 he was on the President's Science Advisory Committee, and he opposed the proposal for developing the "Star Wars" nuclear shield in the United States during the 1980s. Because of his strong stand on such issues, Bethe was often considered to be a voice of conscience for the physics community. Among Bethe's other honors were the 1946 Presidential Medal of Merit, the 1955 Max Planck Medal, the 1959 Benjamin Franklin Medal, the 1961 Enrico Fermi Award, the 1976 National Medal of Science, the 1993 Albert Einstein Peace Prize, the 2001 Los Alamos National Laboratory Medal, and the 2001 Bruce Medal. Bethe was also the author or coauthor of numerous books, including *Elementary Nuclear Theory* (1956), *Energy Production in Stars* (1968), *Reducing the Risk of War: Geneva Can Be a Giant Step toward a More Secure Twenty-first Century* (1978), *Basic Bethe: Seminal Articles on Nuclear Physics, 1936-1937* (1986), and *Selected Works of Hans A. Bethe, with Commentary* (1997).

OBITUARIES AND OTHER SOURCES:

PERIODICALS

Chicago Tribune, March 8, 2005, section 3, p. 10.
New York Times, March 8, 2005, pp. A1, C16.
Times (London, England), March 8, 2005, p. 54.
Washington Post, March 8, 2005, p. B6.

*   *   *

BEVIS, Charles W. 1954-
(Charlie Bevis)

PERSONAL: Born 1954, in Bridgewater, MA; son of Harold (a mill foreman) and Josephine (a homemaker; maiden name, Karasiewicz) Bevis; married Kathie Crudale (a teacher); children: Scott, Kelly. *Education:* University of New Hampshire, B.A., 1975.

ADDRESSES: Home—5 Thornton Lane, Chelmsford, MA 01824.

CAREER: Worked in investment management field, Boston, MA, 1976-97; Financial Research Corp., Boston, research study editor, 1998—.

AWARDS, HONORS: McFarland-Society for American Baseball Research research award, 2003, for paper titled "Evolution of the Sunday Doubleheader and Its Role in Elevating the Popularity of Baseball."

WRITINGS:

(Under name Charlie Bevis) *Mickey Cochrane: The Life of a Baseball Hall of Fame Catcher,* McFarland and Co. (Jefferson, NC), 1998.
(Under name Charlie Bevis) *Sunday Baseball: The Major Leagues' Struggle to Play Baseball on the Lord's Day, 1876-1934,* McFarland and Co. (Jefferson, NC), 2003.

Contributor to periodicals, including *Nine: Journal of Baseball History and Culture* and *Baseball Research Journal.*

WORK IN PROGRESS: New England League: A Cultural History of One of Baseball's Oldest Minor Leagues, completion expected in 2006.

SIDELIGHTS: Charles W. Bevis told *CA:* "The cultural aspect of baseball history is what intrigues me most, not so much the game and players on the field. I was particularly taken by the lack of research and general knowledge about the struggle to play professional baseball on Sunday. Most people at the turn of the twentieth century worked six days a week, nine to ten hours a day, with Sunday the only day most could attend a ball game, yet ball games were legally prohibited that day. It was amazing to research the ways legislators thwarted initiatives for Sunday baseball (a term roughly equivalent to the political volatility of abortion today) and the ways baseball club owners tried to subvert those laws!

"Research for the book led to my paper for which I received the McFarland-Society for American Baseball Research award; it is also the focus of another paper, 'Rocky Point: A Lone Outpost of Sunday Baseball in Sabbatarian New England.' My book on the history of the New England League is also motivated by cultural elements, particularly the connection with the history of the textile and footwear industries in the region."

BIOGRAPHICAL AND CRITICAL SOURCES:

PERIODICALS

Library Journal, June 1, 1998, John M. Maxymuk, review of *Mickey Cochrane: The Life of a Baseball Hall of Fame Catcher,* p. 115.

BEVIS, Charlie
  See BEVIS, Charles W.

*   *   *

BEYERS, Charlotte K(empner) 1931-2005

OBITUARY NOTICE— See index for *CA* sketch: Born December 8, 1931, in New York, NY; died of complications from lymphoma March 10, 2005, in Palo Alto, CA. Filmmaker, journalist, and author. Beyers was well known for her documentaries on serious issues, such as AIDS and drugs. Studying journalism at Stanford University, she earned her B.A. in 1952, followed by an M.A. in 1970. After having worked as a freelance writer of science and medicine articles since 1967, in 1978 she became a correspondent to the *New York Times* and England's *Times Higher Education Supplement.* Beyers entered filmmaking for personal reasons: her second husband's brother had died from AIDS, and she decided to make an educational documentary about the disease to dispel some of the myths that surround it. Founding the company Peregrine Productions in Palo Alto, she created the 1987 film *AIDS in Your School,* which she both wrote and produced. Over a dozen other films followed, including *"A" Is for AIDS* (1989) and *Women and AIDS: The Greatest Gamble* (1993), as well as documentaries on other subjects, such as *New Crack Facts* (1990), *Night Journey to Crack* (1990), *Shadow Children* (1991), and *Working Now* (1992); she also produced such films as *Healing Circles Choices for Arthritis* (1997).

OBITUARIES AND OTHER SOURCES:

PERIODICALS

Los Angeles Times, March 17, 2005, p. B11.
New York Times, April 11, 2005, p. A21.
San Francisco Chronicle, March 19, 2005, p. B5.

*   *   *

BIRKINSHAW, Margaret 1907-2003

PERSONAL: Born August 3, 1907, in England; died January 11, 2003, in London, England; daughter of Edgar (a writer and critic) and Frieda (a concert pianist) Jepson; married Frank Birkinshaw (a physician), 1928 (separated, 1935); children: Jane, Franklin (Fay). *Education:* Attended London City College and Ealing Technical College Library School. *Hobbies and other interests:* Teaching Sunday school, theater, needlework.

CAREER: Writer, artist, and librarian. Founded an advertising agency, 1940s; worked for Hospital of St. John and St. Elizabeth, 1953-55, and British Broadcasting Corporation, London, England, 1955-63.

WRITINGS:

Via Panama, Hamish Hamilton (London, England), 1934.
Velvet and Steel, Herbert Jenkins (London, England), 1935.

Author of romance novels and serials.

SIDELIGHTS: Margaret Birkinshaw was a writer in a family of writers, and her daughter, Fay Weldon, has become a noted author. Birkinshaw's father was Edgar Jepson, a novelist and critic who could count as friends H. G. Wells and Ezra Pound, while her mother was a concert pianist. At age twenty-one, Birkinshaw married doctor Frank Birkinshaw, who had been in the company of noted soldier and author T. E. Lawrence in the Arabian desert, where Lawrence earned the name "Lawrence of Arabia."

The couple had their first child, Jane, the following year, and in 1930, they left England for New Zealand. In February, 1931, alone with her baby and pregnant with Fay, Birkinshaw survived the worst earthquake ever to be recorded in New Zealand, and she then joined her husband, who had found a position in a practice in Christchurch.

Birkinshaw published her first novel, *Via Panama,* in 1934. While praised by both the noted author George Bernard Shaw and Wells, the book caused an uproar and proved to be an embarrassment for her husband, who was then running for a seat in Parliament as a Labour candidate. The marriage was failing when she published *Velvet and Steel,* and Birkinshaw soon traveled alone to London on a cargo ship, planning to send for her children as soon as possible.

When Birkinshaw's husband threatened to take the girls to South Africa, she returned to New Zealand to collect them. In order to support her daughters, she wrote romance novels, often as many as four a year, as well as stories that were published as serials. Her manuscripts and contracts were sent and delivered by ship, but with the advent of World War II, shipping stopped, forcing Birkinshaw to find other work. Her mother joined her in 1942, and they both worked in the small ad agency Birkinshaw had set up, writing copy and working in film. In 1946, the two women and the girls returned to England.

Birkinshaw put her daughters through college, and their volatile lives kept her involved as she helped with the care of their children during difficult times. Jane, who with her three children had been abandoned by husband Guido Morris, never recovered; ill with cancer, she died in 1969, and Birkinshaw took over the care of her grandchildren. In a London *Times* obituary, a writer noted that "she managed heroically. But at heart, she was an adventurer, and the tribulations of single-parenthood by proxy for Jane in a succession of dreary towns must at times have been almost too much to bear." In 2000, Birkinshaw broke her hip, after which she moved into a residential home, then a nursing home where she died.

Although Birkinshaw never wrote her own autobiography, her daughter Fay, of whom Birkinshaw was very proud, did. Weldon, who was actually named Franklin at birth, as though she were male, reflects on her years with her parents and her early life in *Auto da Fay,* the first volume of a planned two-volume memoir. The second book will recall Weldon's life as a writer.

BIOGRAPHICAL AND CRITICAL SOURCES:

BOOKS

Weldon, Fay, *Auto da Fay: A Memoir,* Grove Press (New York, NY), 2003.

OBITUARIES

ONLINE

Times Online, http://www.timesonline.co.uk/ (January 24, 2003).*

BLACK, Ingrid
    See McCONNEL, Ian and O'HANLON, Ellis

*   *   *

BLACKSTON, Ray

PERSONAL: Male.

ADDRESSES: Home—Greenville, SC. *Agent*—c/o Author Mail, Revell Books, Baker Publishing Group, P.O. Box 6287, Grand Rapids, MI 49516-6287. *E-mail*—ray@rayblackston.com.

CAREER: Buyer and stockbroker.

WRITINGS:

"FLABBERGASTED" NOVEL SERIES

Flabbergasted, Revell (Grand Rapids, MI), 2003.
A Delirious Summer, Revell (Grand Rapids, MI), 2004.
Lost in Rooville, Revell (Grand Rapids, MI), 2005.

SIDELIGHTS: Ray Blackston is a former stockbroker and buyer who left his cubicle and cashed in his 401K in order to pursue his writing dream. Blackston's novels are popular in both the Christian and mainstream markets. The main character of his first novel, *Flabbergasted,* is substantially patterned after Blackston himself. Like the author, Jay Jarvis is a stockbroker who has recently relocated to South Carolina. He is told that he will have more luck finding women in the churches than in the bars, and he does, although some of these characters are on the quirky side. Tamara Butler noted in *Library Journal* that considering that the church environment tends to focus more on families and married couples, Blackston's debut novel "is refreshingly honest in its portrayal of young, single Christians looking for love and marriage."

Blackston, who has done missionary work in Equador, uses that experience in creating the main character of *A Delirious Summer.* Jay plays matchmaker when missionary Neil Rucker, who has been dateless for seven months, returns from Ecuador for an eight-week vacation in Greenville. There he meets the "Ladies of the Quest," a group of women who communicate via e-mail and who troll the churches of various denominations looking for eligible men. Among the singles is Beatrice Dean, age eighty-one, who is also looking for a man. When Neil becomes romantically involved with Alexis DeMoss, he, she, Beatrice, and others head south to Equador to rebuilt huts burned in a village fire. "Along with wooden huts, epiphanies arise," wrote Nancy Dorman-Hickson in *Southern Living*. A *Publishers Weekly* contributor felt that the characters "help keep the reader interested. In the end, however, it's Blackston's tongue-in-cheek humor about the lives of Christian singles that will grab the attention of readers of evangelical fiction."

BIOGRAPHICAL AND CRITICAL SOURCES:

PERIODICALS

Library Journal, June 1, 2003, Tamara Butler, review of *Flabbergasted,* p. 101; April 1, 2004, Tamara Butler, review of *A Delirious Summer,* p. 78.

Publishers Weekly, March 29, 2004, review of *A Delirious Summer,* p. 38.

Southern Living, August, 2004, Nancy Dorman-Hickson, review of *A Delirious Summer,* p. 201.

ONLINE

FaithfulReader.com, http://www.faithfulreader.com/ (November 10, 2003), interview with Blackston.

Ray Blackston Home Page, http://www.rayblackston. com (February 27, 2005).*

*   *   *

BLAKE, Andrea
  See WEALE, Anne

*   *   *

BLAKELY, Diann
  See SHOAF, Diann Blakely

BLOOM, Alan (Herbert Vawser) 1906-2005

OBITUARY NOTICE— See index for *CA* sketch: Born November 19, 1906, in Over, Cambridgeshire, England; died March 31, 2005, in Bressingham, Norfolk, England. Horticulturist and author. The founder of the famous Blooms Nurseries in Norfolk, Bloom was a renowned horticulturist who was an expert on herbaceous perennials. Inheriting a love of gardening from his father, he left school when he was only fifteen to work at a plant nursery. Soon, he joined his father's business and then started his own nursery in 1926 in Oakington, Cambridgeshire. The business prospered until World War II, during which Bloom moved his family to Canada, where he worked as a farmer. When the war was over, he returned to England and bought the two hundred acres of land that would become Blooms Nurseries. Here, Bloom specialized in herbaceous plants and bred or named some 170 new varieties of flora; he also established a new form of gardening that emphasizes planting in island bed arrangements. A recipient of the Victoria medal of honor from the Royal Horticultural Society, Bloom had other interests, too, including steam engine trains and writing. With regard to the former, he established the Bressingham Steam Museum in 1968; and as an author, he wrote the autobiographical work *Come You Here, Boy!* (1995), as well as numerous books on gardening and a work about trains titled *250 Years of Steam* (1981). For his many contributions, Bloom was named a member of the Order of the British Empire in 1997.

OBITUARIES AND OTHER SOURCES:

BOOKS

Bloom, Alan, *Come You Here, Boy!,* Ellis (Henley-on-Thames, England), 1995.

PERIODICALS

Guardian (Manchester, England), April 6, 2005, p. 25.

Independent (London, England), April 5, 2005, p. 35.

Times (London, England), April 9, 2005, p. 73.

*   *   *

BLUNT, Alison

PERSONAL: Female. *Education:* Cambridge University, B.A. (with honors); University of British Columbia, M.A., Ph.D.

ADDRESSES: Office—Department of Geography, Queen Mary, University of London, Mile End Rd., London E1 4NS, England. *E-mail*—A.M.Blunt@qmul. ac.uk.

CAREER: Educator and writer. Queen Mary College, London, London, England, reader in geography. Former chair of History and Philosophy of Geography Research Group, Royal Geographical Society/Institute of British Geographers. Member of editorial board of *Cultural Geographies* and *Transactions of the Institute of British Geographers;* member of London Women and Planning Forum steering group.

AWARDS, HONORS: Gill Memorial Award, Royal Geographical Society/Institute of British Geographers, 2002, for "research in gender geography and in particular women and imperialism"; Philip Leverhulme Prize, 2003.

WRITINGS:

Travel, Gender, and Imperialism: Mary Kingsley and West Africa, Guilford Press (New York, NY), 1994.
(Editor, with Gillian Rose; and contributor) *Writing Women and Space: Colonial and Postcolonial Geographies,* Guilford Press (New York, NY), 1994.
(With Jane Wills) *Dissident Geographies: An Introduction to Radical Ideas and Practice,* Prentice-Hall (New York, NY), 2000.
(Editor, with Cheryl McEwan; and contributor) *Postcolonial Geographies,* Continuum (New York, NY), 2002.
(Editor, with others) *Cultural Geography in Practice,* Arnold (London, England), 2003.
Domicile and Diaspora: Anglo-Indian Women and the Spatial Politics of Home, Blackwell (Malden, MA), 2005.
(With Robyn Dowling) *Home* (nonfiction), Routledge (London, England), 2006.

Contributor to books, including *A Feminist Glossary of Human Geography,* edited by L. McDowell and J. Sharp, Arnold (London, England), 1994; *Writes of Passage: Ambiguity and Contradiction in British Colonial and Post-Colonial Travel Writing,* edited by J. Duncan and D. Gregory, Routledge (London,

England), 1999; *Picturing Place: Photography and Imaginative Geography,* edited by J. Ryan and J. Schwartz, I. B. Tauris (London, England), 2003; *Key Concepts in Geography,* edited by S. Holloway, S. Rice, and G. Valentine, Sage (London, England), 2003; and *Critical Geographies,* edited by D. Sibley and others, I. B. Tauris, in press. Contributor to journals, including *International Journal of Population Geography, History Workshop Journal, Journal of Historical Geography, International Journal of Anglo-Indian Studies, Transactions of the Institute of British Geographers,* and *Gender, Place and Culture.*

SIDELIGHTS: A reader in geography at Queen Mary College, London, Alison Blunt is interested in feminism, imperialism, domesticity, travel literature, and postcolonialism as they relate to cultures in Britain, India, and elsewhere around the world. She has written, cowritten, or coedited several scholarly studies in those areas that approach geography from unique angles.

A number of Blunt's early works focus on gender and imperialism. In *Travel, Gender, and Imperialism: Mary Kingsley and West Africa* the author's "main point seems to be that, although second-class citizens at home, Englishwomen ranked above African men in the colonies because they, the women, were members of the colonizing race," commented M. D. Allen in *Belles Lettres.* Blunt focuses on the figure of Mary Kingsley, a well-known English travel writer, analyzing her writings as a way to explore issues of gender, race, and class structure in colonial Africa and England. Pointing out that Kingsley was able to indulge in activities considered the exclusive domain of British men only because she was in a land far removed from Britannia, Blunt highlights the importance of space and time with regard to gender issues. In a *Women's Studies* review, Lisa Colletta commented that Blunt "discusses how women's travel writing was influenced—and thus positioned—by notions of appropriate behavior described in conduct books for women travellers. In these books, traditional conceptions of femininity were reinforced and encouraged." Although Colletta went on to say that the author's disregard for "historical and biographical contexts" in her study is a flaw that results in a narrow perspective of her subject, she concluded that "Blunt's examination raises interesting questions about constructions of female identity within the discourse of imperialism."

Blunt tackles a similar subject in *Writing Women and Space: Colonial and Postcolonial Geographies,* which she edited with Gillian Rose. In this collection of essays, the editors cull research that "examines white women's complicity with and resistance to imperialist mappings of space, power, and difference during the colonial and postcolonial periods," reported *Geographical Review* contributor Darcy Ann Olsen. Although Olsen noted that the selected chapters only present one side of the story—that of the feminist perspective—she concluded, "Geographers will certainly be interested in reading about the use of geographical theory in feminist discourses." Karen Morin, writing in *Growth and Change,* felt that the "book as a whole provides a well written and accessible grounding in feminist poststructural theorizing in geography" and enthusiastically concluded, "I unhesitatingly invite colleagues and students across disciplines to read this fresh and imaginative collection of essays."

In addition to her works focusing on feminism, culture, and imperialism as related to geography, Blunt has written and edited works that represent more general studies. Her coedited book *Cultural Geography in Practice,* for example, is a survey that presents a solid introduction to the subject to undergraduate college students. *Dissident Geographies: An Introduction to Radical Ideas and Practice,* which she wrote with Jane Wills, covers such subjects as postcolonialism, Marxism, sexual orientation, anarchism, and gender issues as forces of resistance to existing power structures in society. Thus the authors challenge many sacred ideals, such as the necessity for capitalism to be globalized, the moral superiority of heterosexuality, and why famines are not unavoidable tragedies. Lauding *Dissident Geographies* as "an exciting book," Jeff Hopkins declared in *Canadian Geographer,* "Those geographers who are dismissive at worst or 'squeemish' at least of radical approaches to geography . . . will find a convincing and well articulated explanation of the intellectual integrity of this kind of research and how geography as a discipline and geographers as activists, colleagues, educators and researchers can help bring about positive change in society."

Blunt has also written about geographies of home and migration, focusing on the Anglo-Indian community in India, Britain, and Australia in the fifty years before and after Indian independence in 1947. Anglo-Indians are people who are of mixed European and Indian birth—a product of European imperialism—whose chosen culture is more European than Indian, even though they were born on the Asian subcontinent. This research led Blunt to complete her 2005 publication, *Domicile and Diaspora: Anglo-Indian Women and the Spatial Politics of Home.*

Blunt told *CA:* "In *Domicile and Diaspora,* I draw on interviews and focus groups with over 150 Anglo-Indians, as well as on archival research, to analyze the spatial politics of home in relation to imperialism, nationalism, decolonization and multiculturalism. The book extends feminist and postcolonial theories about home and identity in relation to critical 'mixed race' studies. Key themes include imaginative geographies of Britain as fatherland and India as motherland; the establishment of Anglo-Indian homelands; Anglo-Indian migration under the British Nationality Act of 1948 and the White Australia Policy; and the spatial politics of home for Anglo-Indians now living in India, Britain and Australia."

"My interest in critical geographies of home is also reflected in a book I have written with Robyn Dowling simply called *Home.* This book explores home as a material and an imaginative space over household, national, and transnational scales. Drawing on a wide range of historical and contemporary examples, *Home* unsettles notions of home and explores the critical intersections of home, identity and power."

BIOGRAPHICAL AND CRITICAL SOURCES:

PERIODICALS

Belles Lettres, spring, 1995, M. D. Allen, "Errant Women in 'Exotic' Lands," review of *Travel, Gender, and Imperialism: Mary Kingsley and West Africa,* p. 36.
Canadian Geographer, fall, 2001, Jeff Hopkins, review of *Dissident Geographies: An Introduction to Radical Ideas and Practice,* p. 445.
Geographical Review, April, 1995, Darcy Ann Olsen, review of *Writing Women and Space: Colonial and Postcolonial Geographies,* p. 261.
Growth and Change, winter, 1996, Karen Morin, review of *Writing Women and Space,* p. 115.
Southeastern Geographer, November, 2004, Patricia L. Price, review of *Cultural Geography in Practice,* p. 285.
Women's Studies, January, 1997, Lisa Colletta, review of *Travel, Gender, and Imperialism,* p. 125.

ONLINE

Department of Geography, Queen Mary College, London Web site, http://www.geog.qmul.ac.uk/ (April 19, 2005), "Alison Blunt."

*   *   *

BONDESON, Ulla V(iveka) 1937-

PERSONAL: Born July 10, 1937, in Malmö, Sweden; daughter of Oscar (a postmaster) and Elsa (Lindberg) Bondeson. *Education:* University of Lund, M.A., 1961, Ph.D., 1967. *Hobbies and other interests:* "Literature, culture, antiquities."

ADDRESSES: Home—Limhamnsväg 6A, 21759 Malmö, Sweden. *Office*—University of Copenhagen, Studiestraede 6, 1455 Copenhagen K, Denmark. *E-mail*—ulla.v.bondeson@jur.ku.dk.

CAREER: University of Lund, Lund, Sweden, staff member, 1960-67, lecturer, 1967-74, docent, 1974-76, associate professor, 1976-78, professor of sociology of law, 1978-79, department chair, 1989; University of Copenhagen, Copenhagen, Denmark, professor and chair of criminology, 1980—. Visiting professor at University of Minnesota, 1968, Harvard University and Yale University, 1974, University of California, 1982, University of Aix-en-Provence, 1991, and other foreign institutions.

MEMBER: International Society of Criminology (vice president), Scandinavian Council of Criminology (past president), Danish Criminalist Society (member of board of directors), American Society of Criminology, Campbell Crime and Justice Group (member of steering committee).

AWARDS, HONORS: Sellin & Glück award; Zorn Prize for U.S. research, Swedish-American Foundation.

WRITINGS:

Fången i fångsamhället: Socialisationsprocesser vid ungdomsvårdsskola, ungdomsfängelse, fängelse och internering (title means "The Prisoner in

Prison Society: Socialization Processes in Training Schools, Youth Prisons, Prisons, and Internment"), Norstedt (Stockholm, Sweden), 1974.

Kriminalvård i frihet—intention och verklighet (title means "Criminal Care at Liberty: Intention and Reality"), Liber (Stockholm, Sweden), 1977.

NADZOR (on correction in the community), Juriditjeskaja (Moscow, USSR), 1979.

Prisoners in Prison Societies, Transaction Publishers (New Brunswick, NJ), 1989.

Alternatives to Imprisonment: Intentions and Reality, Westview Press (Boulder, CO), 1994, second edition with new introduction, Transaction Publishers (New Brunswick, NJ), 2002.

Nordic Moral Climates, Transaction Publishers (New Brunswick, NJ), 2003.

Contributor to books, including *Crime Deterrence and Career Offender,* edited by Haag and Martinson, [New York, NY], 1975; and *Crime and Criminal Policy in Europe,* edited by R. Hood, Oxford University (Oxford, England), 1988. Contributor to scholarly journals in Scandinavia and elsewhere, including *Scandinavian Studies in Criminology* and *International Annals of Criminology.*

EDITOR

Rationalitet i rättssystemet (title means "Rationality in the Legal System"), Liber (Stockholm, Sweden), 1979.

(With Tamm) *Ret og retfærdighed* (title means "Law and Justice"), University of Copenhagen (Copenhagen, Denmark), 1989.

(With Peter Garde; and contributor) *Parts of Danish Law in Action,* International Academy of Comparative Law (Brisbane, New South Wales, Australia), 2002.

(And contributor) *Law and Morality,* University of Copenhagen (Copenhagen, Denmark), fifth edition, 2002.

Criminal Justice in Scandinavia, University of Copenhagen (Copenhagen, Denmark), fifth edition, 2003.

WORK IN PROGRESS: Research on criminal policy in Scandinavia and on comparative studies of moral values.

SIDELIGHTS: Ulla V. Bondeson told *CA:* "Hopefully my books on the evaluation of corrections will have an effect on developing a rational and humane criminal policy. One of my books, *Prisoners in Prison Societies,* had at least a temporary effect of reducing the number of sentences to imprisonment. Another book, *Alternatives to Imprisonment: Intentions and Reality,* led, among other things, to the abolishment of the sanction probation with institutionalization."

BIOGRAPHICAL AND CRITICAL SOURCES:

PERIODICALS

British Journal of Criminology, winter, 1996, Andrew Rutherford, review of *Alternatives to Imprisonment: Intentions and Realities,* pp. 155-156.

ONLINE

Ulla V. Bondeson Home Page, http://www.jur.ku.dk/ullavbondeson (July 19, 2004).

*   *   *

BOSNA, Valerie
(Valerie King, Sarah Montrose)

PERSONAL: Born in Annapolis, CA; married; children: one son, one daughter. *Hobbies and other interests:* Playing the piano, gardening.

ADDRESSES: Home—Phoenix, AZ. *Agent*—c/o Author Mail, Kensington Publishers, 850 Third Ave., 16th Floor, New York, NY 10023.

CAREER: Novelist, beginning 1989.

WRITINGS:

UNDER PSEUDONYM VALERIE KING; HISTORICAL ROMANCES

A Daring Wager, Zebra Books (New York, NY), 1989.
A Rogue's Masquerade, Zebra Books (New York, NY), 1989.
Reluctant Bride, Zebra Books (New York, NY), 1989.
The Fanciful Heiress, Zebra Books (New York, NY), 1990.

The Willful Widow, Zebra Books (New York, NY), 1991.
Love Match, Zebra Books (New York, NY), 1991.
Treasure, Zebra Books (New York, NY), 1992.
Cupid's Touch, Zebra Books (New York, NY), 1992.
(With Teresa Desjardins, Mona Gedney, and Emily Maxwell) *A June Wedding,* Zebra Books (New York, NY), 1992.
A Lady's Gambit, Zebra Books (New York, NY), 1992.
My Lady Vixen, Zebra Books (New York, NY), 1993.
(With Violet Hamilton, Nancy Lawrence, and Jeanne Savery) *A Mother's Love,* Zebra Books (New York, NY), 1993.
Captivated Hearts, Zebra Books (New York, NY), 1993.
The Elusive Bride,. Zebra Books (New York, NY), 1994.
Merry, Merry Mischief, Zebra Books (New York, NY), 1994.
(With Meg-Lynn Roberts and Olivia Sumner) *A Valentine Embrace: Three Tales of Regency Love,* Zebra Books (New York, NY), 1995.
Vanquished, Zebra Books (New York, NY), 1995.
Bewitching Hearts, Zebra Books (New York, NY), 1995.
(With Teresa Desjardins and Cindy Holbrook) *Bewitched by Love,* Zebra Books (New York, NY), 1996.
A Summer Courtship, Zebra Books (New York, NY), 1996.
Vignette, Zebra Books (New York, NY), 1997.
A Poet's Kiss, Zebra Books (New York, NY), 1997.
(With Nancy Lawrence and Jeanne Savery) *A Mother's Love,* edited by Violet Hamilton, Zebra Books (New York, NY), 1997
A Country Flirtation, Zebra Books (New York, NY), 1998.
(With Judith A. Lansdowne and Marcy Stewart) *My Darling Bride,* Zebra Books (New York, NY), 1998.
A Poet's Touch, Zebra Books (New York, NY), 1998.
(With Carola Dunn and Mona Gedney) *Snowflake Kittens,* Zebra Books (New York, NY), 1999.
My Lady Mischief, Zebra Books (New York, NY), 1999.
A Christmas Masquerade, Zebra Books (New York, NY), 1999.
(With Janice Bennett and Martha Kirkland) *Summer Kittens,* Zebra Books (New York, NY), 1999.

A Brighton Flirtation, Zebra Books (New York, NY), 2000.

(With Carola Dunn and Isobel Linton) *Wonderful and Wicked,* Zebra Books (New York, NY), 2000.

A London Flirtation, Zebra Books (New York, NY), 2000.

(With Jo Ann Ferguson and Jeanne Savery) *A Kiss for Mama,* Zebra Books (New York, NY), 2001.

My Lord Highwayman, Zebra Books (New York, NY), 2001.

(With Jo Ann Ferguson and Jeanne Savery) *A Kiss for Papa,* Zebra Books (New York, NY), 2002.

My Lady Valiant, Zebra Books (New York, NY), 2002.

A Rogue's Deception, Zebra Books (New York, NY), 2002.

A Rogue's Embrace, Zebra Books (New York, NY), 2002.

(With Jo Ann Ferguson and Mona Gedney) *Murder at Almack's,* Zebra Books (New York, NY), 2003.

A Daring Courtship, Zebra Books (New York, NY), 2003.

My Darling Coquette, Zebra Books (New York, NY), 2003.

A Rogue's Wager, Zebra Books (New York, NY), 2003.

A Rogue's Revenge, Zebra Books (New York, NY), 2004.

An Adventurous Lady, Zebra Books (New York, NY), 2004.

(With Jo Ann Ferguson and Cynthia Bailey Pratt) *Valentine Kittens,* Zebra Books (New York, NY), 2005.

Garden of Dreams, Zebra Books (New York, NY), 2005.

OTHER

(Under pseudonym Sarah Montrose) *The Golden Heiress,* Zebra Books (New York, NY), 1990.

Contributor to anthologies, including *Rogues and Rakes,* edited by Donna Bell, Zebra Books (New York, NY), 1996; contributor, under pseudonym Valerie King, to *A Valentine's Day Treasure,* Zebra Books, 1992; and *A Christmas to Cherish,* Zebra Books, 1992.

SIDELIGHTS: Romance writer Valerie Bosna, who writes mainly under the pseudonym Valerie King, has published over fifty romance novels and novellas since her writing career began in the late 1980s. Her specialty is the Regency romance, a specific subgenre of romance fiction in which the stories are set in the early nineteenth century. Specifically the stories are set between 1811 and 1820, when England's prince regent, the eldest son of King George III, ruled Great Britain and its empire because of his father's mental illness. The popular novel subgenre is modeled on the works of Jane Austen, the original Regency romance writer, and emphasizes manners, morality, wit, and character over gratuitous sex and passion.

"Early on," Bosna told an interviewer for the *Kensington Books Web site,* "I loved reading the novels of Georgette Heyer. I was in a bookstore one day many years ago and saw that there was a market for the kinds of books she wrote—the Regency romance—and I had a very simple thought, I can do this. So, here I am, some twenty years later, writing my novels and really enjoying the process."

Modern Regency romances tend to follow a pattern. Like the women featured in Austen's novels, the heroines of Regency romances tend to be aristocratic or from the upper middle class. Although they are bound by the conventions of the society in which they live, they often challenge those rules, much as nineteenth-century women challenged ideas about their status during the Regency period itself. Heroines are invariably forthright, spunky women, willing to challenge stereotypical ideas about the roles women should play in society. They often become involved with men of questionable character, who in their own way challenge ideas about appropriate behavior, especially that between men and women of their social class. These relationships create the conflicts that drive the novels.

In King's *A Summer Courtship,* the central conflict is between unmarried Constance Mayford, who breaks with tradition by managing her parents' estate herself in defiance of tradition. Miss Mayford has a chance encounter with a neighbor, Richard Wexham, Lord Greywell which, according to Melinda Helfer in her *RomanticTimes.com* assessment of the novel, "leaves her breathless." For his part, Helfer concluded, Lord Greywell "struggles to reconcile his feelings with the behavior he would expect from a wife."

In the case of Bosna's novels, the pivotal relationship is usually between an upper-middle-class woman and a man of the same or higher rank. In *A Brighton Flirtation,* for instance, heroine Katherine Pamberley is thrown into the company of an old acquaintance,

Captain Evan Ramsdell, while she is improving herself at the posh resort of Brighton, a favorite refuge of the regent himself. Although Ramsdell feigns a lack of romantic interest in Katherine, his stolen kisses—concealed by the bathing machines along the seashore—suggest otherwise. At the same time, however, he is distracted by his real reason for staying in Brighton: to find the assassins plotting to kill the prince regent. "Katherine," wrote Linda Hurst on the *All about Romance Web site*, "is a courageous and bright heroine who is a wonderful match for Evan, who ultimately comes to admire her courage and overlook her occasional over-exuberance—although he fights a good fight and it isn't until he nearly loses Katherine that he realizes what a treasure he has found." *Romantic Times Book Club* reviewer Teresa Roebuck called the novel an "unhurried and amusing tale of friendship unfurling . . . and hearts unaware of the nuances of love."

Because Regency novels are frequently set against the backdrop of the Napoleonic wars, King's protagonists are often involved in the war effort, sometimes as spies forced to conceal their true natures under the cover of rakish behavior. In *My Lady Valiant*, for instance, Anne Delamere kidnaps the rogue earl of Staverton, a man who first toyed with her cousin Cassie and then rejected her. Unknown to Anne, however, the earl is actually a counterintelligence agent tracking a French spy who has stolen war secrets that could jeopardize the British war effort. She agrees to assist him in his work and, in the process, finds herself falling in love with him. "Anne," explained *Booklist* contributor John Charles, ". . . knowingly flouts the conventions of her time to enjoy an adventure of her own." Praising the novel for its "Rip-roaring excitement, bloodthirsty adventurers, wild escapes and laugh-out-loud humor," Teresa Roebuck wrote in *RomanticTimes.com* that *My Lady Valiant* serves as "a treat to be savored."

BIOGRAPHICAL AND CRITICAL SOURCES:

PERIODICALS

Booklist, February 1, 2002, John Charles, review of *My Lady Valiant*, p. 928; May 15, 2002, John Charles, review of *A Rogue's Deception*, p. 1581; March 1, 2003, John Charles, review of *A Rogue's Wager*, p. 1151; May 15, 2004, John Charles, review of *A Rogue's Revenge*, p. 1603; October 15, 2004, John Charles, review of *An Adventurous Lady*, p. 394.

ONLINE

All about Romance Web site, http://www.likesbooks. com/ (February 23, 2005), Linda Hurst, review of *A Brighton Flirtation.*
Fantastic Fiction Web site, http://www.fantasticfiction. co.uk/ (February 23, 2005), "Valerie King."
Kensington Books Web site, http://www.kensington books.com/ (February 23, 2005), interview with King.
RomanticTimes.com, http://www.romantictimes.com/ (February 23, 2005), Robin Taylor, review of *A Rogue's Revenge*; Teresa Roebuck, review of *A Daring Courtship, My Darling Coquette, My Lady Valiant, My Lord Highwayman, A Rogue's Deception, A Rogue's Wager,* and *A Brighton Flirtation;* Melinda Helfer, review of *A Country Flirtation, Bewitching Hearts, My Lady Mischief, Vignette, A London Flirtation, A Summer Courtship, A Poet's Kiss,* and *A Poet's Touch;* Angela Keck, review of *A Rogue's Embrace;* Robin Taylor, review of *An Adventurous Lady;* Joan Hammond, review of *Vanquished.**

*   *   *

BOSS, Jeremy M.

PERSONAL: Male.

ADDRESSES: Office—Department of Microbiology and Immunology, Emory University, Atlanta, GA 30322-1100. *E-mail*—boss@microbio.emory.edu.

CAREER: Emory University, Atlanta, GA, faculty member, 1986-97, professor of microbiology and immunology, 1997—, director of graduate program in genetics and molecular biology.

WRITINGS:

(With Susan H. Eckert) *Academic Scientists at Work: Navigating the Biomedical Research Career,* Kluwer Academic (New York, NY), 2003, new edition, in press.

Contributor of more than fifty articles to periodicals, including *Nature, Science, Cell, Immunity, Current Opinions in Immunology, Journal of Biological Chemistry,* and *Journal of Immunology.* Deputy editor, *Journal of Immunology.*

SIDELIGHTS: Jeremy M. Boss told *CA:* "My interest in writing *Academic Scientists at Work: Navigating the Biomedical Research Career* was spawned by the great need for a resource that described the process that young scientists face as they develop their careers in academic institutions. The surprise was that there is no formal guidance for how to deal with academic processes or information or what is expected for promotion/tenure. It took me and most of my colleagues more than ten years to understand how academic institutions work.

"All of my career advice articles are written with Susan Eckert, who was the first academic administrator that I met and worked with when I took on my position as an assistant professor. Susan and I have discussed hundreds of academic topics over the last eighteen years. All of these topics have entered into our book/articles or will be in the future. I write in long sessions at the end of the day when the campus life quiets down. In the first session, the opening remarks, outline, and flow of the chapter/article is splashed on the screen. This is followed by filling in the ideas, editing, and discussions, and a final form that works for both of us. We use MS Word's 'track changes' function for our edits and discuss each change and work out a compromise. Most often, the compromise means a complete rewording of the sentence.

"My writing is influenced by the never-ending events that I witness in my profession. These events and conversations with my colleagues become fuel for ideas to write about. One of the surprises about writing is how much fun it is. I enjoy trying to place humor in the prose to keep the reader interested. Of course the goal in our writings is to educate young scientists about how the process works and how to avoid the snags and traps that can stunt a promising career."

*   *   *

BOWLBY, Alex 1924-

PERSONAL: Born 1924.

ADDRESSES: Agent—c/o Author Mail, Orion House, 5 Upper St. Martin's Ln., London WC2H 9EA, England.

CAREER: Writer and editor. *Military service:* British armed forces, served in World War II with Royal Greenjackets; later served with 21st Special Air Service regiment.

WRITINGS:

Recollections of Rifleman Bowlby, Italy 1944 (memoir), Leo Cooper (London, England), 1969.
(Editor) R. L. Crimp, *The Diary of a Desert Rat* (memoir), Leo Cooper (London, England), 1971.
Order of the Day (novella), Leo Cooper (London, England), 1974.
Roman Candle (novel), Weidenfeld and Nicolson (London, England), 1983.
Countdown to Cassino: The Battle of Mignano Gap, 1943 (history), Leo Cooper (London, England), 1995.

SIDELIGHTS: Editor and author Alex Bowlby spent much of his early career serving in the British Armed Forces, first as a member of the Royal Greenjackets during World War II and then as a member of the 21st Special Air Service regiment. He later drew on his military experiences to write a number of books, including a memoir and a novel. Bowlby also edited the memoirs of another British World War II soldier in *The Diary of a Desert Rat.*

Bowlby's first literary contribution was the 1969 memoir *Recollections of Rifleman Bowlby, Italy 1944.* In this work he documents the time he spent with the Royal Greenjackets in North Africa and Italy. Bowlby's battalion struggled in Italy when their specialized role was diminished and they were used as regular infantrymen. In that position, the battalion experienced many defeats and morale plummeted. Bowlby writes about the daily stress and struggle of that time from an intimate perspective that only a participant can provide.

In 1995, Bowlby published *Countdown to Cassino: The Battle of Mignano Gap, 1943.* The author tells the story of the overlooked but pivotal and grisly World War II battle of Mignano Gap in Italy. Through interviews with the battle's veterans, he interweaves first-person accounts of the fighting with a detailed overview of the campaign history. In fact, he explains the battle from both Allied and German perspectives, keeping an objective point of view. Critics reacted positively to Bowlby's efforts, in particular his unbiased perspective. "It is a grim story, but one in which Bowlby, unlike far too many historians of this and other campaigns, does not look for scapegoats," observed *Times Literary Supplement* contributor Michael Howard.

BIOGRAPHICAL AND CRITICAL SOURCES:

BOOKS

Bowlby, Alex, *Recollections of Rifleman Bowlby, Italy 1944,* Leo Cooper (London, England), 1969.

PERIODICALS

Times Literary Supplement, September 8, 1995, Michael Howard, review of *Countdown to Cassino: The Battle of Mignano Gap, 1943,* p. 26.

ONLINE

Orion Publishing Group Web site, http://www.orionbooks.co.uk/ (April 19, 2005), "Alex Bowlby."*

*   *   *

BOYENS, Philippa

PERSONAL: Born in Auckland, New Zealand; daughter of John (a primary school principal) and Jane Boyens; married Paul Gittins (an actor); children: Calum, Phoebe.

ADDRESSES: Agent—c/o New Line Cinema, 116 North Robertson Blvd., Los Angeles, CA 90048.

CAREER: Worked as a script reader and editor; New Zealand Writers Guild, executive director. Appeared in documentary films, including *National Geographic: Beyond the Movie—The Lord of the Rings,* 2001; *The Making of the Lord of the Rings,* 2002; *The Lord of the Rings: The Quest Fulfilled,* 2003; and *Ringers: Lord of the Fans,* 2005.

AWARDS, HONORS: Academy Award nomination for best adapted screenplay (with Fran Walsh and Peter Jackson), Academy of Arts and Sciences, 2002, for *The Lord of the Rings: The Fellowship of the Ring;* Academy Award (with Walsh and Jackson) for best adapted screenplay, 2004, for *The Lord of the Rings: The Return of the King.*

WRITINGS:

SCREENPLAYS; "LORD OF THE RINGS" TRILOGY

(With Fran Walsh and Peter Jackson; and lyricist) *The Fellowship of the Ring,* New Line Cinema, 2001.
(With Fran Walsh and Peter Jackson) *The Two Towers,* New Line Cinema, 2002.
(With Fran Walsh and Peter Jackson; and lyricist) *The Return of the King,* New Line Cinema, 2003.

WORK IN PROGRESS: King Kong, 2005; screen adaptation of the novel *The Lovely Bones* by Alice Sebold.

SIDELIGHTS: Philippa Boyens is a New Zealand-born screenwriter whose collaboration with husband-and-wife team and fellow New Zealanders Peter Jackson and Fran Walsh led to their 2004 Academy Award win for best adapted screenplay for *The Return of the King,* the third installment based on J. R. R. Tolkien's "Lord of the Rings" trilogy. The trio had been nominated, but did not win, two years earlier for the screenplay *The Fellowship of the Ring.* By the end of 2004, the film saga had garnered a total of seventeen Oscars and had grossed nearly three billion dollars worldwide. Boyens has two children and her son, Calum, had a part in the second film, *The Two Towers.*

In an interview for *21stCenturyRadio.com* Robert Hieronimus questioned Boyens regarding bringing an almost sacred work to life on the screen. "[O]ne of those things I wish [Tolkien] . . . could have seen, because I feel proud of, is the use of . . . his language that he created, and the fact that we have entire scenes in Elvish, which is great, because that's his language and it's being brought to life." Hieronimus asked Boyens if she saw a contemporary message in the trilogy with regard to industrialization—which Tolkien despised—and environmental policies. Boyens explained that the films speak to "man's impact on the environment and that connection, of course, to the Ents in film two are an extraordinary example of that. This is where nature, in effect, fights back."

Christian Century contributor Steve Vineberg reviewed the final film and reflected on all three parts of the six-plus-hour saga. "The marvel of the first film in the trilogy, *The Fellowship of the Ring,* is the way Jackson advances the narrative through a seemingly endless visual variety—a new world every fifteen minutes, as one friend expressed it to me. *The Two Towers,* racing at an almost alarming speed, is built around an extended battle sequence that rivals the fantastical wars that directors like Fritz Lang and Akira Kurosawa invented. *The Return of the King* feels like a series of valedictories, and that's largely why it's so overwhelming emotionally." Each film in the trilogy was released on DVD in an extended version, with extra footage, and all are available as a collection.

Writer and director Jackson's love of the original *King Kong* led him to remake the film, with Boyens and Walsh again cowriting. The film stars Jack Black, Naomi Watts, and Adrien Brody, with Andy Serkis, whose acting was the basis for the digital Gollum, playing the ape. Boyens has also set to work on the film version of Alice Sebold's best-selling novel *The Lovely Bones.*

BIOGRAPHICAL AND CRITICAL SOURCES:

PERIODICALS

Christian Century, January 13, 2004, Steve Vineberg, review of *The Return of the King,* p. 41.

Daily Variety, December 13, 2004, Jamie Clark, review of *The Return of the King* (extended), p. S22

Newsweek, December 6, 2004, Jeff Giles, "Kingdom Kong; Peter Jackson's *Lord of the Rings* Was One for the Ages. Now He's Remaking *King Kong,* the Movie That Changed His Young Life," p. 82.

Onfilm, December, 2003, "Six Years a Ring Bearer: An Exclusive Interview with Screenwriter Philippa Boyens," p. 15.

Village Voice, December 31, 2003, Laura Sinagra, "Where the Boys Are: Girl Talk with *Lord of the Rings* Screenwriter Philippa Boyens" (interview), p. C58.

ONLINE

21stCenturyRadio.com, http://www.21stcenturyradio. com/ (December 15, 2002), Robert Hieronimus, interview with Boyens.

Promontory Artists Association Web site, http:// promontoryartists.org/ (March 3, 2005), Jeffrey Overstreet, interview with Boyens and Fran Walsh.*

*   *   *

BOZELL, L. Brent, III 1925-

PERSONAL: Born 1925; married; children: five. *Education:* University of Dallas, B.A.

ADDRESSES: Office—Media Research Center, 325 South Patrick St., Alexandria, VA 22314; Parents Television Council, 707 Wilshire Blvd., Ste. 2075, Los Angeles, CA 90017.

CAREER: Buchanan for President campaign, financial director, 1992; Conservative Victory Committee, executive director; National Conservative Political Action Committee, president; Parents Televison Council, Los Angeles, CA, founder and chairman; Media Research Center, Alexandria, VA, founder and president; *Cybercast News Service (CNS.com),* founder.

MEMBER: Council for National Policy.

AWARDS, HONORS: Named Pew Memorial Lecturer, Grove City College, 1998.

WRITINGS:

(Editor, with Brent H. Baker) *And That's the Way It Isn't: A Reference Guide to Media Bias,* Media Research Center (Alexandria, VA), 1990.

Weapons of Mass Distortion: The Coming Meltdown of the Liberal Media, Crown Forum (New York, NY), 2004.

Author of foreword, *Pattern of Deception: The Media's Role in the Clinton Presidency,* by Tim Graham, Media Research Center (Alexandria, VA),

1996. Contributor to periodicals, including the *Washington Post, Wall Street Journal, Washington Times, New York Post, Los Angeles Times, Investors Business Daily,* and *National Review.*

SIDELIGHTS: L. Brent Bozell, III is the founder of a number of conservative and watchdog groups as well as serving as a frequent media guest and contributor to mainstream and financial newspapers. He is the son of L. Brent Bozell, Jr. and the nephew of well-known conservative writer William F. Buckley. One of Bozell's groups is the Parents Television Council (PTC), which offers guidelines for parents who want to monitor the content of children's television. Bozell's Media Research Center targets the liberal bias of the nation's media, while his Cybercast News Service is an online alternative to the established media outlets. According to Robert Kirkelbach of *Town Hall.com,* Bozell is "one of the lone purveyors of information regarding liberal media bias, compiling data and facts from news organizations nationwide."

In *Weapons of Mass Distortion: The Coming Meltdown of the Liberal Media* Bozell writes that it is apparent from the way the media covers such issues as abortion, gay rights, the environment, and gun control, that it has a liberal agenda. He comments on pundits, both left and right, and documents examples of liberal bias. A *Kirkus Reviews* critic noted that Bozell "maintains that he is talking about liberal bias in hard reporting, not commentary, yet time and again he draws on liberal commentators as exemplars of bias." These include filmmaker Michael Moore, actress Janeane Garofalo, *Boston Globe* columnist James Carroll, Jonathan Chait of the *New Republic,* and Jonathan Alter of *Newsweek.* The critic wrote that Bozell's asides, such as his reference to "the aged hippies at NPR," "tend to undercut any authorial aspirations to seriousness." A *Publishers Weekly* contributor called the volume "music to conservative ears and may even open some liberals's eyes—assuming they'll deign to read it," while *Booklist* reviewer Vanessa Bush felt that "whether readers agree with his perspective or not, those interested in the media will find this an interesting read."

Speaking to Lee Webb in an interview for the *Christian Broadcasting Network Web site,* Bozell explained why he believes that the major media are in trouble and likely to go through the "meltdown" he predicts in his book. "Since 1994, the big three broadcast networks have lost about fifty percent of their audiences. Consider that people are turning away from newspapers left and right. Consider that CNN, once the flagship of cable news, is in a complete free fall. Consider that if you want to find MSNBC on the ratings, you need a pretty good set of binoculars. . . . And ask the media, 'Why is it that everyone is leaving you?'"

BIOGRAPHICAL AND CRITICAL SOURCES:

PERIODICALS

Atlanta Journal-Constitution, September 28, 2004, Julia Malone, "Election 2004: Media Monitor Sniffs out Signs of Bias," p. A16.
Booklist, July, 2004, Vanessa Bush, review of *Weapons of Mass Distortion: The Coming Meltdown of the Liberal Media,* p. 1804.
Kirkus Reviews, May 1, 2004, review of *Weapons of Mass Distortion,* p. 427.
Library Journal, July, 2004, Judy Solberg, review of *Weapons of Mass Distortion,* p. 94.
Publishers Weekly, May 31, 2004, review of *Weapons of Mass Distortion,* p. 61.
UPI Perspectives, February 1, 2005, Pat Nason, "Analysis: Raunchy Sex on MTV?"
Washington Times, October 24, 1997, Patrick Butters, "The Right Enjoys a Liberal Dose of Joy," p. 15.

ONLINE

Christian Broadcasting Network Web, http://www.cbn.com/ (March 30, 2005), Lee Webb, interview with Bozell.
Cybercast News Service Online, http://www.cnsnews.com/ (March 30, 2005), "L. Brent Bozell."
Media Research Center Web site, http://www.mrc.org/ (March 30, 2005), "L. Brent Bozell."
MediaTransparency.org, http://www.mediatransparency.org/ (March 2, 2005), "L. Brent Bozell."
TownHall.com, http://www.townhall.com/ (March 30, 2005), Robert Zirkelbach, review of *Weapons of Mass Distortion.**

*   *   *

BRADBY, Marie

PERSONAL: Born in Alexandria, VA; married; children: one son. *Education:* Hampton University, B.A. (sociology).

ADDRESSES: Home—Louisville, KY. *Agent*—c/o Author Mail, Orchard Books/Scholastic Books, 557 Broadway, New York NY 10012. *E-mail*—mariebradby@insightbb.com.

CAREER: Author of children's books. Worked as a reporter for *Providence Journal,* Providence, RI, and *Lexington Herald,* Lexington, KY, and *Courier Journal,* Louisville, KY; staff writer for *National Geographic,* Washington, DC.

AWARDS, HONORS: American Library Association notable book citation, and International Reading Association Book Award, both 1996, both for *More than Anything Else;* Golden Kite Honor Award, for *Momma, Where Are You From?;* *Los Angeles Times* Best Book citation, 2002, for *Once upon a Farm.*

WRITINGS:

FOR CHILDREN

More than Anything Else, illustrated by Chris K. Soentpiet, Orchard Books (New York, NY), 1995.
The Longest Wait, illustrated by Peter Catalanotto, Orchard Books (New York, NY), 1998.
Momma, Where Are You From?, illustrated by Chris K. Soentpiet, Orchard Books (New York, NY), 2000.
Once upon a Farm, illustrated by Ted Rand, Orchard Books (New York, NY), 2002.
Some Friend (novel), Atheneum (New York, NY), 2004.

Contributor to *A Kentucky Christmas,* edited by George Ella Lyon.

SIDELIGHTS: Marie Bradby is the author of a number of well-received children's books, including *Momma, Where Are You From?* and *Once upon a Farm.* Bradby, a former journalist, served as a reporter for newspapers in Rhode Island and Kentucky, and has also written for *National Geographic* magazine. She began writing for children after the birth of her son, making her debut with the 1995 picture book *More than Anything Else.* In 2004 she published her first novel for middle-grade readers, *Some Friend.*

More than Anything Else concerns the childhood of African-American educator, activist, and writer Booker T. Washington. In the work, nine-year-old Booker spends his day laboring at the saltworks, though he longs for something better. With the help of his mother and a kindly stranger, he learns to read and write. *Horn Book* critic Maria B. Salvadore praised the "evocative text," and *Booklist* contributor Hazel Rochman observed, "The story will hold kids and make them want to find out more about the person and the history."

In *The Longest Wait,* a young boy named Thomas watches as his father, a mailman, ventures out in a driving blizzard. Though Thomas cannot wait to play in the snow, his mood changes after his father returns from his perilous journey and falls ill. Fortunately, Thomas's father recovers, leaving the youngster free to enjoy the winter scenery. According to Linda Perkins in *Booklist,* "the spare narrative convincingly portrays the boy's shift from excitement to anxiety to relief." Bradby's "first-person narration through Thomas's eyes is sprinkled with poetic images," noted a reviewer in *Publishers Weekly.*

A child's question to her parent evokes a flood of memories in *Momma, Where Are You From?* Bradby offers scenes from the woman's childhood, including visits from the ice man, picking beans in the field, segregated schools, cleaning clothes in a wringer washer, and the music of Duke Ellington. "As nostalgic and sentimental as an old radio show, this lyrical picture book is chock full of family reminiscences," observed a critic in *Publishers Weekly.* Reviewing *Momma, Where Are You From?* in *Booklist,* Gillian Engberg stated, "Children will be inspired by the mother's eloquent, proud answer to her daughter's essential question."

A boy recounts the pleasures of working the land in *Once upon a Farm,* "a beautiful story about a vanishing way of life," wrote Carolyn Janssen in *School Library Journal.* In simple verse, Bradby describes the family's efforts to plow the soil, harvest the crops, and enjoy the fruits of their labor. Bradby also notes how suburban sprawl has changed the rural landscape; according to a *Publishers Weekly* critic, the final spread showing "a lone bulldozer razing tall trees brings home Brady's message in a quietly dramatic style."

A coming-of-age story set in the early 1960s, *Some Friend* focuses on eleven-year-old Pearl and her complicated relationships with Lenore, a haughty troublemaker, and Artemesia, the daughter of a migrant worker. Though Pearl develops a close bond with Artemesia, she fails to step in when Artemesia is targeted for harassment by Lenore. "Bradby writes with real understanding of the conflicting feelings of a preteen who tries to keep up with the wrong kind of friend," remarked Susan Dove Lempke in *Horn Book,* and a critic in *Kirkus Reviews* called the work "a sensitive, realistic portrayal told in first person of a girl's tough lesson about the meaning of friendship."

Bradby once commented: "People often ask me if my characters are me. I tend to write in first person and in present tense, and I have given my characters bits and pieces of things that I know—all in an effort to make them seem real. But they aren't me.

"I spend a lot of time researching details to make my settings seem realistic and convincing, and to make my characters seem like someone that is very believable and that you might already know. For instance, I have taken a weaving class, hiked in the Appalachians, picked vegetables, studied stars in the night sky during a certain time of year, and [learned] how to trap muskrats in order to learn things that involve my characters. Sometimes I have to remind myself to quit researching and write the story!"

BIOGRAPHICAL AND CRITICAL SOURCES:

PERIODICALS

Booklist, July, 1995, Hazel Rochman, review of *More than Anything Else,* p. 1882; December 1, 1998, Linda Perkins, review of *The Longest Wait,* p. 669; February 15, 2000, Gillian Engberg, review of *Momma, Where Are You From?,* p. 117; February 15, 2004, Hazel Rochman, review of *Some Friend,* p. 1073.

Horn Book, September-October, 1995, Maria B. Salvadore, review of *More than Anything Else,* pp. 586-587; March-April, 2004, Susan Dove Lempke, review of *Some Friend,* pp. 178-179.

Kirkus Reviews, January 1, 2002, review of *Once upon a Farm,* p. 42; December 15, 2003, review of *Some Friend,* p. 1447.

Publishers Weekly, September 21, 1998, review of *The Longest Wait,* p. 83; April 3, 2000, review of *Momma, Where Are You From?,* p. 79; February 11, 2002, review of *Once upon a Farm,* p. 185; January 19, 2004, review of *Some Friend,* p. 77.

School Library Journal, April, 2000, Susan Hepler, review of *Momma, Where Are You From?,* p. 92; March, 2002, Carolyn Janssen, review of *Once upon a Farm,* p. 172; March, 2004, Ronni Krasnow, review of *Some Friend,* p. 203.

ONLINE

Marie Bradby Home Page, http://www.mariebradby.com (June 1, 2005).

*   *   *

BRADLEY, Celeste

PERSONAL: Married; children: two.

ADDRESSES: Home—TN. *Agent*—c/o Author Mail, St. Martin's Press, 175 5th Ave., New York, NY 10019. *E-mail*—celeste@celestebradley.com.

CAREER: Writer.

WRITINGS:

Fallen, Dorchester Publishing Company (New York, NY), 2001.
To Wed a Scandalous Spy, St. Martin's Paperbacks (New York, NY), 2005.

Contributor to *My Scandalous Bride,* St. Martin's Paperbacks (New York, NY), 2004.

LIAR'S CLUB SERIES

The Impostor, St. Martin's Paperbacks (New York, NY), 2003.
The Pretender, St. Martin's Paperbacks (New York, NY) 2003.
The Charmer, St. Martin's Paperbacks (New York, NY), 2004.
The Spy, St. Martin's Paperbacks (New York, NY), 2004.
The Rogue, St. Martin's Paperbacks (New York, NY), 2005.

SIDELIGHTS: Romance writer Celeste Bradley made her writing debut with the novel *Fallen,* the story of a notorious London bachelor and a spinster housekeeper who make a sham engagement to secure his inheritance and her independence. The pair is surprised to discover that they are strongly attracted to each other. This theme of deception and unlooked-for romance is further developed in Bradley's subsequent series of novels, the "Liars Club" books.

The first "Liar's Club" novel, *The Pretender,* focuses on Simon Montague Rain, one of a group of spies who serve the British crown during the Regency period. As part of an investigation into the murder of several fellow spies, he must infiltrate the home of the beautiful Mrs. Agatha Applequist to search for a traitor. But Agatha has her own secrets: she has arrived in London posing as a married woman so that she can travel unchaperoned to look for her missing brother James. She now wants Simon, who appears as a chimney sweep, to act as her husband at a social event. Both come to thoroughly enjoy their relationship of convenience, but it becomes problematic for Simon when it threatens his resolve to follow the Liar's Club rule of never falling in love. The often humorous adventure appealed to *Booklist* reviewer John Charles, who called the novel "a witty and delectable combination of superbly crafted characters and an intrigue-steeped plot." *Library Journal* contributor Kristin Ramsdell called the premise "a wonderful idea" and recommended the book to "readers who like their historicals laced with laughter yet on the mysterious side."

In *The Impostor* Bradley concocts a romance featuring the young widow Clara Simpson and Liar's Club member Dalton Montmorency. Under the name Sir Thorogood, she secretly pens political cartoons that anger the Crown. When Dalton poses as the cartoonist, hoping to press the real artist into revealing his identity, Clara also assumes a disguise to discover who the impostor is. When their paths cross, he thinks she is a maid and she assumes that he is a burglar, deceptions that do not dull the resulting spark of romantic interest. A *Publishers Weekly* writer called *The Impostor* a "delightful comedy of errors."

The heroine of *The Spy* is Phillipa Atwater, a young woman who is forced to assume the guise of a male tutor when her father goes missing. To her surprise, she is quickly hired by James Cunnington, whom her father bid her to watch in a cryptic message. At the same time, James is searching for Phillipa, but she does not know it. According to *Booklist* critic John Charles, *The Spy* contains "wonderfully witty writing" and is "every bit as much fun" as its predecessors.

The Charmer is the fourth installment in "The Liar's Club" series. Its central characters are spies-in-training Collis Tremayne and Rose Lacey. When their adversarial behavior threatens the school, both are tested to see if they will in fact make good spies. Rose is unsuccessful in her test mission, but she uncovers other important developments in London. Noting that allusions to pop culture are an important element in Bradley's humor, Nina C. Davis commented in *Booklist* that *The Charmer* is "sure to provide a pleasant few hours' diversion."

BIOGRAPHICAL AND CRITICAL SOURCES:

PERIODICALS

Booklist, May 1, 2003, John Charles, review of *The Pretender,* p. 1583; February 1, 2004, John Charles, review of *The Spy,* p. 954; October 1, 2004, Nina C. Davis, review of *The Charmer,* p. 315.

Library Journal, May 15, 2003, Kristin Ramsdell, review of *The Pretender,* p. 72.

Publishers Weekly, September 22, 2003, review of *The Impostor,* p. 90; May 3, 2004, review of *My Scandalous Bride,* p. 177.*

*   *   *

BRADLEY, Richard 1961-

PERSONAL: Born December 14, 1961, in Chicago, IL. *Education:* Illinois State University, B.S., 1988; University of Illinois, Chicago, M.A., 1992, Ph.D., 1997.

ADDRESSES: Office—Department of History, Central Methodist University, 411 Central Methodist Square, Fayette, MO 65248. *E-mail*—rbradley@central methodist.edu.

CAREER: Educator. Illinois State University, Normal, instructor in speech communications, 1993-94; *Sociological Quarterly,* managing editor, 1996-98; Alcorn State University, Lorman, MS, assistant professor of history, 1998-99; Central Methodist University, Fayette, MO, assistant professor of history and political science, 1999—.

MEMBER: Phi Alpha Theta, Omicron Delta Kappa.

WRITINGS:

American Political Mythology from Kennedy to Nixon (Volume 3 of "Modern American History" series), Peter Lang (New York, NY), 2000.

Contributor to encyclopedias; contributor of articles and reviews to periodicals, including *Cultural Studies.*

SIDELIGHTS: Richard Bradley's *American Political Mythology from Kennedy to Nixon* covers presidential myths at play in the presidencies of John F. Kennedy, Lyndon B. Johnson, and Richard M. Nixon. For example, with regard to Kennedy, explained Norbert Wiley in *Contemporary Sociology,* Bradley discusses three major themes, "Kennedy's martyrdom for the cause of civil rights, his mythification in the conspiratorial haze that followed, and his projection into the kingdom of Camelot." According to Wiley, "There is plenty of blarney in all three themes, but this is the nature of mythification."

The Kennedy myth is an example of what Bradley describes as "idealized generalizations about the world that motivate action." Bradley, who calls Kennedy the "good king," writes that Johnson, who was considered by many to be the "usurper to the throne," is cast as the "bad king," until that title was more recently passed on. As Andrew E. Busch noted in *Presidential Studies Quarterly,* "by the time Nixon resigned in disgrace, he had supplanted Johnson as the ultimate bad king. Bradley demonstrates the degree to which monarchical language was used by historians, journalists, politicians, and in popular culture in all three cases and contends that the radical transformation of American politics and society in that period cannot be understood without reference to the collapse of the myth of the president as good king."

Of *American Political Mythology from Kennedy to Nixon* Busch concluded, "The strength of this work lies in an interesting thesis and a number of largely forgotten points that Bradley illuminates." Wiley maintained that "one can question some of Bradley's interpretations, but he has given us a brilliant work of historical semiotics. His method could be used for other studies, such as the way September 11 mythologized George W. Bush, or the blue dress, Bill Clinton. And, it is also a welcome addition to the theory and method of semiotics."

BIOGRAPHICAL AND CRITICAL SOURCES:

PERIODICALS

Contemporary Sociology, January, 2003, Norbert Wiley, review of *American Political Mythology from Kennedy to Nixon,* p. 57.
History: Review of New Books, spring, 2001, Joe P. Dunn, review of *American Political Mythology from Kennedy to Nixon,* p. 102.
Presidential Studies Quarterly, December, 2002, Andrew E. Busch, review of *American Political Mythology from Kennedy to Nixon,* p. 815.*

* * *

BRAFF, Joshua 1967-

PERSONAL: Born 1967, in South Orange, NJ; married; wife's name Jill (a cell-phone game designer); children: Henry, Ella. *Education:* New York University, B.A.; Saint Mary's College, M.F.A. (creative writing), 1997.

ADDRESSES: Home—Berkeley, CA. *Agent*—c/o Author Mail, Algonquin Books of Chapel Hill, P.O. Box 2225, Chapel Hill, NC 27515-2225. *E-mail*—josh@joshuabraff.com.

WRITINGS:

The Unthinkable Thoughts of Jacob Green (novel), Algonquin Books of Chapel Hill (Chapel, Hill, NC), 2004.

Contributor of short fiction to literary journals, including *Alaska Quarterly* and *River Styx*.

SIDELIGHTS: Joshua Braff grew up in New Jersey, one of four children of a psychologist mother and lawyer father. The setting of his first novel, *The Unthinkable Thoughts of Jacob Green,* is also New Jersey and is about a dysfunctional Orthodox Jewish family. Braff's debut was published at about the same time his brother, actor Zach Braff, made his screenwriting and directorial debut with *Garden State,* in which Zach also acts. Both brothers have as their centerpiece suburban life and romance.

School Library Journal reviewer Susan H. Woodcock called *The Unthinkable Thoughts of Jacob Green* "a funny and thought-provoking coming-of-age journey." Jacob Green is the second child of Abram, a domineering father who is determined to mold his wife and children into the perfect Jewish family. The other children include baby Gabriel, five-year-old Dara, and older brother Asher, whom Jacob idolizes. But cursed with a learning disability, however, Jacob is not able to satisfy his father. The story opens with Abram staging a housewarming party for the neighbors at which he is trying to show that his family is exceptional. The baby is adorable, his wife, Claire, is beautiful, Dara is an outstanding swimmer, and his blond son, Jacob, reads Hebrew "so beautifully it'll make you cry."

Braff told Heidi Benson of the *San Francisco Chronicle* that "in creating Abram Green, I wanted a certain kind of guy. He's a guy that I have met a few times, in other words, friends' fathers, friends' relatives. What I did was create a hybrid of my father—who was religious and wanted the routines, but was not a maniac or a monster."

As time passes, Asher withdraws into a destructive lifestyle. He is suspended from Hebrew school when he draws a picture of a rabbi having sex with animals. Claire leaves her husband for her college professor after returning to school to pursue a doctorate. Jacob dreams of running away with Asher as the family splits in two. The "unthinkable thoughts" of the title are what help keep Jacob sane. Among his funniest are the pretend bar mitzvah thank-you notes that he creates in his mind. Not so funny is the plight of the boy who is forced by his father to write twenty such notes each evening, all of which are checked for spelling,

grammar, and syntax. Of course, Jacob is unable to write twenty perfect notes, and nearly every evening, his father throws a tantrum. Jacob also fantasizes about his live-in nanny. Even as Abram psychologically and verbally abuses Jacob, the boy continues to love him through his fear. He finally comes to realize that Asher isn't going to save him.

Alys Yablon wrote in *Jerusalem Report* that, "with a keen eye for what's going on below the surface, and a delightful means of deconstructing that reality, Jacob describes a rich fantasy life that reads like a softer version of a Woody Allen voice-over." A *Kirkus Reviews* critic concluded of *The Unthinkable Thoughts of Jacob Green* that "there's no real resolution in this primal scream ripped from adolescence: it's just painfully honest and surprisingly compassionate."

BIOGRAPHICAL AND CRITICAL SOURCES:

PERIODICALS

Booklist, July, 2004, John Green, review of *The Unthinkable Thoughts of Jacob Green,* p. 1815.

Entertainment Weekly, September 10, 2004, Scott Brown, review of *The Unthinkable Thoughts of Jacob Green,* p. 171.

Jerusalem Report, January 10, 2005, Alys Yablon, review of *The Unthinkable Thoughts of Jacob Green,* p. 41.

Kirkus Reviews, June 15, 2004, review of *The Unthinkable Thoughts of Jacob Green,* p. 548.

Library Journal, August, 2004, Kevin Greczek, review of *The Unthinkable Thoughts of Jacob Green,* p. 64.

People, August 30, 2004, "Jersey Boys: In Their Respective Film and Novel Debuts, Brothers Zach and Joshua Braff Divide and Conquer Suburbia," p. 87.

Publishers Weekly, August 2, 2004, review of *The Unthinkable Thoughts of Jacob Green,* p. 51.

San Francisco Chronicle, September 22, 2004, Heidi Benson, review of *The Unthinkable Thoughts of Jacob Green* and interview, p. E1.

School Library Journal, December, 2004, Susan H. Woodcock, review of *The Unthinkable Thoughts of Jacob Green,* p. 174.

USA Today, September 16, 2004, Jen Chaney, review of *The Unthinkable Thoughts of Jacob Green,* p. D5.

ONLINE

Joshua Braff Home Page, http://www.joshuabraff.com
(February 17, 2005).*

* * *

BRANSON, H(enry) C(lay) 1905-1981

PERSONAL: Born 1905, in Battle Creek, MI; died
1981; married; children: three daughters. *Education:*
Attended Princeton University, 1924; University of
Michigan, B.A., 1937.

CAREER: Author.

WRITINGS:

Salisbury Plain (novel), Dutton (New York, NY),
1965.

"JOHN BENT" MYSTERY SERIES

I'll Eat You Last, Simon & Schuster (New York, NY),
1941, published as *I'll Kill You Last,* Mystery
Novel of the Month (New York, NY), 1942.
The Pricking Thumb, Simon & Schuster (New York,
NY), 1942.
Case of the Giant Killer, Simon & Schuster (New
York, NY), 1944.
The Fearful Passage, Simon & Schuster (New York,
NY), 1945.
Last Year's Blood, Simon & Schuster (New York, NY),
1947.
The Leaden Bubble, Simon & Schuster (New York,
NY), 1949.
Beggar's Choice, Simon & Schuster (New York, NY),
1953.

Branson's manuscripts are maintained at Michigan
State University.

SIDELIGHTS: Crime novelist H. C. Branson derived
from his father not only his substantial American name
but also a solid Midwestern upbringing. Branson had
read the works of Sir Arthur Conan Doyle as a boy,
followed Philo Vance's cases in Paris in the pages of
Scribner's magazine and was one of the most familiar
cardholders at the Ann Arbor Public Library, where he
withdrew and consumed hundreds of mystery stories.
Following a period of physical and emotional crisis,
he decided to see if he could write detective fiction.

John Bent, Branson's series detective, is a physician
by training but does not practice in the stories. He is a
low-keyed, humane, likeable, self-assured, and wise
character; he is singularly observant and frank to the
point of being outspoken—this being perhaps his only
vice outside the pleasures of drinking and smoking, to
which he is openly devoted. In the seven novels in
which he appears, police authorities and the District
Attorney's office seem quite willing to give Bent free
run of the crime scenes and evidence, because in his
quiet, affable way, he commands respect. In his
deliberate, meticulous fashion, he evolves theories and
puzzles over them doggedly until they render up the
information and facts he wants. People and the tangles
they involve themselves in are what interested Branson, and in his fiction he gave considerable attention
to the intricacies of plotting.*

* * *

BRENDE, Eric

PERSONAL: Married, wife's name Mary (an accountant and homemaker); children: Hans, Anna,
Evan. *Education:* Degrees from Yale University, Washburn University, and Massachusetts Institute of
Technology.

ADDRESSES: Home—St. Louis, MO. *Agent*—c/o
Author Mail, HarperCollins, 10 East 53rd St., 7th
Floor, New York, NY 10022.

CAREER: Worked variously as a musician, rickshaw
driver, and soapmaker.

AWARDS, HONORS: Citation of Excellence, National
Science Foundation; graduate fellowship.

WRITINGS:

Better Off: Flipping the Switch on Technology (memoir), HarperCollins (New York, NY), 2004.

SIDELIGHTS: Eric Brende attended a graduate program at the Massachusetts Institute of Technology that studied the social effects of machines. The program got him thinking about society's overreliance on technology' after it ended, he and his wife left the Boston area and moved to a rural farming community where they could test Brende's theories about getting by without modern technology. He tells their story in *Better Off: Flipping the Switch on Technology.*

The community the Brendes joined was populated by families who lived without electricity and traveled by horse and buggy. The couple stayed for eighteen months, learning to farm and accomplish the various chores necessary to survive. They also discovered that rather than living a life of drudgery, they experienced the satisfaction of being part of a group, the members of which supported and worked with each other. As Brende told *National Catholic Reporter* contributor Rich Heffern that "in the end it saved time because you achieved so many things at once: the work, the exercise, the rich rewards of building community and friendships. The satisfactions so laborious to obtain in the technological society—bodily exercise, social ties, mental challenges—all blend together in a savory mix. It's very efficient." Brende calls this lifestyle "mini-mation" and calls the people in the community where they lived "Minimites." In order to protect their privacy, he does not identify the Minimites, and he said that they "didn't eliminate technology altogether but used it to meet ends they wanted to achieve. They take time to think deeply about alternatives, choices. They call this virtue *gelassenheit,* or self-surrender, and it flows directly from their Christian religious heritage."

In an interview with John Zmirak for *GodSpy.com,* Brende emphasized that in addition to the communal experience, "there's another whole layer of more subtle dynamics at work. When you are working with your hands, or whatever limbs, out in the field, pretty soon that work becomes self-automating. It thereby frees up the mind for conversation. Meanwhile, the labor serves as a kind of musical undercurrent that gives a certain depth to the experience." Brende said this "creates a kind of symphony of layered experiences. You're experiencing nature, hearing the birds, feeling the breeze, watching the clouds go by. Compare that to sitting virtually motionless at a video monitor watching two dimensions of reality, damaging your back and not getting any exercise for your heart, growing more socially isolated."

Mary Brende had consented to the experiment because her husband agreed to let her choose how they would live when they were through. Mary embraced what she had learned from their experience, and they moved to an older section of St. Louis, where they garden and educate their three children through a Catholic home-schooling co-op. They have no televison, computer, or other technology they feel is unnecessary. They heat with wood, and Mary uses a hand-operated washing machine. They use a half-size refrigerator and own an older car, but they walk and bike as much as possible. The Brendes live on a very modest income generated from a variety of enterprises, including his soapmaking. They live frugally and enjoy a healthier lifestyle and more leisure time. In his book, Brende makes suggestions for reducing one's dependence on technology.

Judy McAloon wrote in *School Library Journal* that "Brende's close look at technology's generally un-noticed harmful effects is a welcome relief from the usual how-to-get-ahead-in-the-rat-race attitude." *Booklist* contributor Gilbert Taylor felt that "this memorable story will warm the heart of anyone dream-ing about an alternative, closer-to-the-land lifestyle."

BIOGRAPHICAL AND CRITICAL SOURCES:

BOOKS

Brende, Eric *Better Off: Flipping the Switch on Tech-nology,* HarperCollins (New York, NY), 2004.

PERIODICALS

Booklist, July, 2004, Gilbert Taylor, review of *Better Off,* p. 1804.
Kirkus Reviews, July 1, 2004, review of *Better Off,* p. 611.
Library Journal, June 1, 2004, Wilda Williams, interview with Brende, p. 178.
National Catholic Reporter, September 17, 2004, Rich Heffern, review of *Better Off,* p. 17.
People, August 16, 2004, "Better Off" (interview), p. 53.
Publishers Weekly, May 24, 2004, review of *Better Off,* p. 52.

School Library Journal, November, 2004, Judy McAloon, review of *Better Off,* p. 178.

Science News, September 11, 2004, review of *Better Off,* p. 175.

ONLINE

GodSpy.com, http://www.godspy.com/ (November 1, 2004), John Zmirak, "The Simple Life Redux" (interview).*

*   *   *

BREWER, Gil 1922-1983
(Eric Fitzgerald, Bailey Morgan)

PERSONAL: Born 1922; died January 9, 1983.

CAREER: Author. Also worked as a warehouseman, gas station attendant, cannery worker, and book seller. *Military service:* U.S. Army; served during World War II.

WRITINGS:

"AL MUNDY" SERIES; CRIME NOVELS

13 French Street, Fawcett (New York, NY), 1951.
Satan Is a Woman, Fawcett (New York, NY), 1951.
So Rich, So Dead, Fawcett (New York, NY), 1951.
Flight to Darkness, Fawcett (New York, NY), 1952.
Hell's Our Destination, Fawcett (New York, NY), 1953.
A Killer Is Loose, Fawcett (New York, NY), 1954.
Some Must Die, Fawcett (New York, NY), 1954.
The Squeeze, Ace (New York, NY), 1955.
77 Rue Paradis, Fawcett (New York, NY), 1955.
And the Girl Screamed, Fawcett (New York, NY), 1956.
The Angry Dream, Bouregy (New York, NY), 1957, published as *The Girl from Hateville,* Zenith (Rockville Centre, NY), 1958.
The Brat, Fawcett (New York, NY), 1957.
Little Tramp, Fawcett (New York, NY), 1957.
The Bitch, Avon (New York, NY), 1958.
The Red Scarf, Bouregy (New York, NY), 1958.
The Vengeful Virgin, Fawcett (New York, NY), 1958.

Wild, Fawcett (New York, NY), 1958.
Sugar, Avon (New York, NY), 1959.
Wild to Possess, Monarch (Derby, CT), 1959.
Angel, Avon (New York, NY), 1960.
The Three-Way Split, Fawcett (New York, NY), 1960.
Backwoods Teaser, Fawcett (New York, NY), 1960.
Nude on Thin Ice, Avon (New York, NY), 1960.
Appointment in Hell, Monarch (Derby, CT), 1961.
A Taste of Sin, Berkley (New York, NY), 1961.
Memory of Passion, Lancer (New York, NY), 1963.
Play It Hard, Monarch (Derby, CT), 1964.
The Hungry One, Fawcett (New York, NY), 1966.
Sin for Me, Banner (New York, NY), 1967.
The Tease, Banner (New York, NY), 1967.
The Devil in Davos (novelization of television screenplay), Ace (New York, NY), 1969.
Mediterranean Caper (novelization of television screenplay), Ace (New York, NY), 1969.
Appointment in Cairo (novelization of television screenplay), Ace (New York, NY), 1970.

OTHER

Contributor of numerous short stories, sometimes under pseudonyms Eric Fitzgerald or Bailey Morgan, to *Zeppelin Stories, Thrilling Detective, Detective Tales, Mike Shayne Mystery Magazine,* and *Alfred Hitchcock's Mystery Magazine.*

ADAPTATIONS: Hell's Our Destination was adapted as the film *Lure of the Swamp,* 1957.

SIDELIGHTS: With the publication of his first novel, *13 French Street,* Gil Brewer began a successful career as one of the leading writers of paperback originals. Most of his more than thirty crime novels are built around a similar and classical theme: an ordinary man who becomes involved with, and is often corrupted and destroyed by, an evil or designing woman or other outside force.

Brewer's books, which easily fall into the category of noir fiction, are filled with inscrutable characters whose downfalls are instigated by their own flaws. For example, *The Red Scarf* is a tale in which the author "skillfully conveys the despair of a man with a lifelong dream after he succumbs to the temptation provided by a mob fortune," according to a *Publishers Weekly* reviewer.

Most of Brewer's books—like those by softcover contemporaries John D. MacDonald, Harry Whittington, and Day Keene—are set in the cities, small towns, and back-country areas of Florida. Brewer's style was simple and direct, with sharp dialogue and considerable passion and intensity. At times, according to some critics, he adopted an almost Hemingwayesque prose, as in his 1960s novel *The Three-Way Split.* In addition to his novels, Brewer also frequently contributed stories to the popular detective pulps of the 1950s, and also wrote for subsequent magazines.

BIOGRAPHICAL AND CRITICAL SOURCES:

PERIODICALS

Publishers Weekly, July 25, 1991, p. 40.*

*   *   *

BRUCE, Duncan A. 1932-

PERSONAL: Born 1932, in Pittsburgh, PA; wife's name, Tamara; children: two. *Education:* University of Pennsylvania, graduate of Wharton School.

ADDRESSES: Home—New York, NY. *Agent*—c/o Author Mail, Truman Talley Books/St. Martin's Press, 175 5th Ave., New York, NY 10010. *E-mail*—dbruce@ nyc.rr.com.

CAREER: Banker and writer.

AWARDS, HONORS: Recipient of arms, Lyon's Court of Scotland.

WRITINGS:

The Mark of the Scots: Their Astonishing Contributions to History, Science, Democracy, Literature, and the Arts, Carol Publishing Group (Secaucus, NJ), 1996.
The Scottish One Hundred: Portraits of History's Most Influential Scots, Carroll & Graf (New York, NY), 2000.

The Great Scot: A Novel of Robert the Bruce, Scotland's Legendary Warrior King, Truman Talley Books (New York, NY), 2004.

Editor, *Pibroch* magazine.

SIDELIGHTS: Of Scottish descent, Duncan A. Bruce has explored his ancestry in both works of nonfiction and fiction. In *The Mark of the Scots: Their Astonishing Contributions to History, Science, Democracy, Literature, and the Arts,* he documents Scottish achievement, including Scottish influence in the formation of the United States and its governance, particularly in the early presidential administrations. In *The Scottish One Hundred: Portraits of History's Most Influential Scots,* Bruce, who is among a select number of American recipients of arms from Scotland's Lyon Court, studies the lives of important Scottish figures. One notable Scot Bruce is personally tied to is Sir Edward Bruce, brother of Robert the Bruce. Bruce characterizes his most notable ancestor in his 2004 historical novel *The Great Scot: A Novel of Robert the Bruce, Scotland's Legendary Warrior King.*

Robert the Bruce was given Scottish lands after crossing the channel with William the Conqueror. Bruce's story is told through the memoirs of David Crawford, who became Robert's page after he witnessed the older man's murder of Red Comyn in 1306. David is there when Robert is crowned king of Scotland, and when he returns after seeking safety in Ireland while being hunted by England's King Edward I. Robert's defeat of Edward's army at the Battle of Loudoun Hill puts the English on the defensive. Edward II continues to wage war after the death of his father, but with Robert's 1314 victory at the Battle of Bannockburn, the English finally recognize Scotland as a separate nation in the Treaty of Northampton. Legitimized as claimant to the throne of Scotland, Robert the Bruce reigns peacefully for many years and ultimately dies in bed.

In a review of *The Great Scot,* a *Kirkus Reviews* contributor described Bruce's narration as "rather clunky," but qualified that criticism by noting that "history is everything here, so if you are a Scot or a Scotophile, you will not be the least bit disappointed."

BIOGRAPHICAL AND CRITICAL SOURCES:

PERIODICALS

Booklist, July, 2004, June Sawyers, review of *The Great Scot: A Novel of Robert the Bruce, Scotland's Legendary Warrior King,* p. 1816.

Economist, July 19, 1997, review of *The Mark of the Scots: Their Astonishing Contributions to History, Science, Democracy, Literature, and the Arts,* p. S14.

Kirkus Reviews, June 15, 2004, review of *The Great Scot,* p. 549.

ONLINE

Duncan A. Bruce Home Page, http://home.nyc.rr.com/duncanabruce (February 17, 2005).*

* * *

BRUEGGEMANN, Walter (A.) 1933-

PERSONAL: Born March 11, 1933, in Tilden, NE. *Education:* Elmhurst College, graduate; Union Theological Seminary, doctorate in divinity; St. Louis University, Ph.D.

ADDRESSES: *Office*—Columbia Theological Seminary, Decatur, GA 30031. *E-mail*—brueggemannw@ctsnet.edu.

CAREER: Biblical scholar, educator, and author. Eden Theological Seminary, faculty member, beginning 1961, professor of Old Testament, beginning 1968. Elmhurst College, academic dean, 1976; Columbia Theological Seminary, Decatur, GA, William Marcellus McPheeters Professor of Old Testament.

AWARDS, HONORS: Rockefeller Foundation fellow, 1961-63.

WRITINGS:

Peace, c. 1975, new edition, Chalice Press (St. Louis, MO), 2001.

The Bible Makes Sense, St. Mary's College Press, 1977.

God and the Rhetoric of Sexuality, Fortress Press (Philadelphia, PA), 1978.

The Prophetic Imagination, 1978, revised edition, Fortress Press (Minneapolis, MN), 2001.

Israel in Exile: A Theological Interpretation, Fortress Press (Philadelphia, PA), 1979.

Living toward a Vision: Biblical Reflections on Shalom, revised edition, Pilgrim Press (Long Island City, NY), 1982.

The Creative Word: Canon as a Model for Biblical Education, Fortress Press (Philadelphia, PA), 1982.

Kings 1, John Knox Press (Louisville, KY), 1983.

Revelation and Violence: A Study in Contextualization, Marquette University Press (Milwaukee, WI), 1986.

(With Sharon Parks and Thomas H. Groome) *To Act Justly, Love Tenderly, Walk Humbly: An Agenda for Ministers,* Paulist Press (New York, NY), 1986.

Hopeful Imagination: Prophetic Voices in Exile, Fortress Press (Philadelphia, PA), 1986.

Hope within History, John Knox Press (Louisville, KY), 1987.

Israel's Praise: Doxology against Idolatry and Ideology, Fortress Press (Philadelphia, PA), 1988.

To Pluck up, to Tear Down: A Commentary on the Book of Jeremiah, 1-25, Eerdmans (Grand Rapids, MI), 1988.

Finally Comes the Poet: Daring Speech for Proclamation, Fortress Press (Minneapolis, MN), 1989.

(Author of commentary) *First and Second Samuel,* John Knox Press (Louisville, KY), 1990.

Power, Providence, and Personality: Biblical Insight into Life and Ministry, Westminster/John Knox Press (Louisville, KY), 1990.

Abiding Astonishment: Psalms, Modernity, and the Making of History, Westminster/John Knox Press (Louisville, KY), 1991.

Interpretation and Obedience: From Faithful Reading to Faithful Living, Fortress Press (Minneapolis, MN), 1991.

To Build, to Plant: A Commentary on Jeremiah 26-52, Eerdmans (Grand Rapids, MI), 1991.

Old Testament Theology: Essays on Structure, Theme, and Text, Fortress Press (Minneapolis, MN), 1992.

Using God's Resources Wisely: Isaiah and Urban Possibility, Westminster/John Knox Press (Louisville, KY), 1993.

Biblical Perspectives on Evangelism: Living in a Three-Storied Universe, Abingdon Press (Nashville, TN), 1993.

Texts under Negotiation: The Bible and Postmodern Imagination, Fortress Press (Minneapolis, MN), 1993.

Texts for Preaching: A Lectionary Commentary, Based on the NRSV, three volumes, Westminster/John Knox Press (Louisville, KY), 1993–95.

A Social Reading of the Old Testament: Prophetic Approaches to Israel's Communal Life, edited by Patrick D. Miller, Fortress Press (Minneapolis, MN), 1994.

The Psalms and the Life of Faith, edited by Patrick D. Miller, Fortress Press (Minneapolis, MN), 1995.

The Threat of Life: Sermons on Pain, Power, and Weakness, edited by Charles L. Campbell, Fortress Press (Minneapolis, MN), 1996.

Cadences of Home: Preaching among Exiles, Westminster/John Knox Press (Louisville, KY), 1997.

Theology of the Old Testament: Testimony, Dispute, Advocacy, Fortress Press (Minneapolis, MN), 1997.

A Commentary on Jeremiah: Exile and Homecoming, Eerdmans (Grand Rapids, MI), 1998.

(Editor with George Stroup) *Many Voices, One God: Being Faithful in a Pluralistic World,* Westminster/John Knox Press (Louisville, KY), 1998.

Isaiah, Westminster/John Knox Press (Louisville, KY), 1998.

The Covenanted Self: Explorations in Law and Covenant, edited by Patrick D. Miller, Fortress Press (Minneapolis, MN), 1999.

Deep Memory, Exuberant Hope: Contested Truth in a Post-Christian World, Fortress Press (Minneapolis, MN), 2000.

First and Second Kings, Smith & Helwys (Macon, GA), 2000.

Texts That Linger, Words That Explode: Listening to Prophetic Voices, edited by Patrick D. Miller, Fortress Press (Minneapolis, MN), 2000.

Deuteronomy, Abingdon Press (Nashville, TN), 2001.

Ichabod toward Home: The Journey of God's Glory, Eerdmans (Grand Rapids, MI), 2001.

Testimony to Otherwise: The Witness of Elijah and Elisha, Chalice Press (St. Louis, MO), 2001.

(With William C. Placher and Brian K. Blount) *Struggling with Scripture,* Westminster/John Knox Press (Louisville, KY), 2001.

(Editor) *Hope for the World: Mission in a Global Context,* Westminster/John Knox Press (Louisville, KY), 2001.

Reverberations of Faith: A Theological Handbook of Old Testament Themes, Westminster/John Knox Press (Louisville, KY), 2002.

Spirituality of the Psalms, edited by Patrick D. Miller, Fortress Press (Minneapolis, MN), 2002.

Also author of *Cadences at Home: On the Art of Preaching* and *Genesis.* Contributor of hundreds of articles to periodicals.

SIDELIGHTS: Walter Brueggemann writes prolifically on biblical and theological topics. *Theological Studies* writer Dianne Bergant called him "a consummate scholar, attentive not only to critical exegesis but also to the issues that face the contemporary preacher or minister." Among his early works are *Peace,* first published in the 1970s and revised in 2001. This book examines the meanings and concepts of "shalom," the Hebrew word for peace, and views the word in relation to contemporary concerns for justice. A *Publishers Weekly* contributor noted Brueggemann's occasional "memorable or poetic turn of phrase" in the book, and called *Peace* an example of what the author "does best: squeezing the Bible to produce hardworking theology for the church."

Brueggemann's 1998 publication, *Theology of the Old Testament: Testimony, Dispute, Advocacy,* was assessed by several reviewers. The author's "hermeneutical starting point is that the Old Testament witnesses to God through speech, rather than through thought, concept, or ideas," explained Thomas Dozeman in a *Journal of Religion* review. "In fact he concludes that God only lives 'under the rhetorical enterprise of this text. Dialogue, imagination, and dialectical tension are the 'grammar of faith' in the rhetoric of the Old Testament, revealing the character of God 'in the fray.'" As a result, Dozeman continued, "testimony about God is the preferred mode of knowledge." The reviewer found that *Theology of the Old Testament* "raises many provocative questions," including one that concerns the historical criticism that "plays primarily a negative role in the book." According to Brueggemann, wrote Dozeman, historical criticism is "too objective, one dimensional, linear, monolithic, obsessed with the world behind the text, and ultimately, hegemonic in support of a privileged elite. All of these excesses are true. But the rise of historical criticism is certainly more complex, requiring a more nuanced assessment of its positive and negative impact on Old Testament theology." "Some will charge Brueggemann with conceding or asserting too much," Ben Ollenburger noted in *Interpretation,* "others with being too modest—too resolutely Christian in his interpretation, or insufficiently so." Ollenburger ultimately decided that *Theology of the Old Testament* "will provoke much discussion, not least because it engages contemporary issues—social, hermeneutical, and theological—with verve."

Obedience and law are the topics of *Interpretation and Obedience: From Faithful Reading to Faithful Living* and *The Covenanted Self: Explorations in Law and Covenant*. In the former, as well as in the volume *Abiding Astonishment: Psalms, Modernity, and the Making of History*, Brueggemann "brings the reader into conversation with a delightful array of material not limited by the boundaries of academic specialization," according to *Interpretation* reviewer Richard Nysse. The critic pointed to the opening essay in *Interpretation and Obedience*, which brings together the views of Sigmund Freud, Isak Dinesen, Robert Lifton, and others. To Nysse, Brueggemann presents "a model for working faithfully as readers and doers"; his essays "are not intended to provide a methodological road map."

The Covenanted Self begins with a discussion of the relationship between the individual and God, stressing not the legalistic meaning to this bond, but instead the "kind of delight whereby friendship ripens into love, and obligation is the chance to please and delight the other," as Brueggemann wrote. "Scholars may be disturbed by some of Brueggemann's assumptions," commented Beth Laneel Tanner in *Interpretation*, adding that the author sees in contemporary Israel's centralized structure "equivalent to the oppressive structures in the modern world."

BIOGRAPHICAL AND CRITICAL SOURCES:

BOOKS

Brueggemann, Walter, *The Covenanted Self: Explorations in Law and Covenant*, edited by Patrick D. Miller, Fortress Press (Minneapolis, MN), 1999.

God in the Fray: A Tribute to Walter Brueggemann, edited by Tod Linafelt and Timothy K. Beal, Fortress Press (Minneapolis, MN), 1998.

PERIODICALS

America, April 8, 1995, Daniel Harrington, review of *A Social Reading of the Old Testament: Prophetic Approaches to Israel's Communal Life*, p. 558; March 11, 2000, review of *Isaiah*, p. 21.

Catholic Biblical Quarterly, July, 1991, Claude Mariottini, review of *To Pluck up, to Tear Down: A Commentary on the Book of Jeremiah, 1-25*, p. 460; January, 1992, Robert Gnuse, review of

First and Second Samuel, p. 106; October, 1992, Michael Moore, review of *Abiding Astonishment: Psalms, Modernity, and the Making of History*, p. 740, Kenneth Craig, Jr., review of *Power, Providence, and Personality: Biblical Insights into Life and Ministry*, p. 741; October, 1998, Irene Nowell, review of *Theology of the Old Testament: Testimony, Dispute, Advocacy*, p. 718.

Christian Century, April 8, 1987, Donald Wells, review of *To Act Justly, Love Tenderly, Walk Humbly: An Agenda for Ministers*, p. 338; December 14, 1988, Ronald Goetz, review of *Israel's Praise: Doxology against Idolatry and Ideology*, p. 1155; October 2, 1991, Philip Blackwell, review of *Interpretation and Obedience: From Faithful Reading to Faithful Living*, p. 890; April 9, 1997, Michael Spangler, review of *The Threat of Life: Sermons on Pain, Power, and Weakness*, p. 371; June 1, 2001, Thomas Walker, review of *First and Second Kings*, p. 31.

Christianity Today, April 25, 1994, Robert Yarbrough, review of *Texts under Negotiation: The Bible and Postmodern Imagination*, p. 52.

Interpretation, January, 1990, A. Joseph Everson, review of *To Pluck up, to Tear Down*, p. 85; April, 1990, William Young, review of *Israel's Praise*, p. 200; January, 1991, Richard Boyce, review of *Finally Comes the Poet: Daring Speech for Proclamation*, p. 73; April, 1992, Murray Newman, review of *Power, Providence, and Personality*, p. 208; January, 1993, Richard Nysse, review of *Interpretation and Obedience* and *Abiding Astonishment*, p. 66; April, 1994, Elmer Martens, review of *Old Testament Theology: Essays on Structure, Theme, and Text*, p. 191; April, 1995, Thomas Dozeman, review of *Texts under Negotiation*, p. 202; January, 1998, Charles Aaron, review of *The Threat of Life*, p. 110; January, 1999, Ben Ollenburger, review of *Theology of the Old Testament*, p. 71; October, 1999, Claire Mathews McGinnis, review of *Isaiah*, p. 422; October, 2000, Beth Laneel Tanner, review of *The Covenanted Self: Explorations in Law and Covenant*, p. 432; January, 2002, Walter Harrelson, review of *First and Second Kings*, p. 84.

Journal of Church and State, summer, 1991, James Flanagan, review of *Power, Providence, and Personality*, pp. 626-627.

Journal of Religion, July, 1999, Thomas Dozeman, review of *Theology of the Old Testament*, p. 484.

Journal of the American Academy of Religion, June, 1999, Paul Hanson, review of *Theology of the Old Testament*, p. 447.

Journal of Theological Studies, April, 2000, Ronald Clements, review of *Theology of the Old Testament,* p. 178; October, 2001, R. J. Coggins, review of *Deep Memory, Exuberant Hope: Contested Truth in a Post-Christian World,* p. 1009.

Library Journal, October 1, 1986, Elise Chase, review of *Hope within History,* p. 103; April 1, 1991, Carolyn Craft, review of *Interpretation and Obedience,* p. 125; January, 1992, Craft, review of *To Build, to Plant: A Commentary on Jeremiah 26-52,* p. 139; March 1, 2002, Graham Christian, review of *Ichabod toward Home: The Journey of God's Glory,* p. 108.

Other Side, November-December, 2001, review of *Peace,* p. 12.

Publishers Weekly, May 14, 2001, review of *Peace,* p. 74.

Scottish Journal of Theology, May, 1999, Stephen Dawes, review of review of *To Pluck up, to Tear Down,* p. 107; spring, 2000, Brevard Childs, review of *Theology of the Old Testament,* p. 228.

Sojourners, November, 1999, review of *Isaiah,* p. 53; May, 2001, Jim Wallis, review of *Deep Memory, Exuberant Hope,* p. 51.

Theological Studies, September, 1989, Alan Mitchell, review of *Israel's Praise,* p. 611; June, 1991, John Endres, review of *First and Second Samuel,* p. 349; December, 1998, Richard J. Sklba, review of *Theology of the Old Testament,* p. 720; June, 2001, Dianne Bergant, review of *Deep Memory, Exuberant Hope,* p. 420.

Theology, March-April, 1997, Gillian Cooper, review of *The Psalms and the Life of Faith,* p. 135; September-October, 1998, Robert Carroll, review of *A Commentary on Jeremiah: Exile and Home-coming,* p. 371; March-April, 2000, Walter Moberly, review of *The Covented Self,* p. 127.

Theology Today, January, 1989, Terence Fretheim, review of *Israel's Praise,* p. 506; July, 1990, Donald Gowan, review of *Finally Comes the Poet,* p. 226; April, 1991, Deborah Klee Dees, review of *First and Second Samuel,* p. 108, J. Gerald Janzen, review of *Power, Providence, and Personality,* p. 114; January, 1992, Mark Hillmer, review of *Abiding Astonishment,* p. 501; July, 1994, Deborah Klee, review of *Old Testament Theology,* p. 334, Robert Kysar, review of *Texts for Preaching: A Lectionary Commentary, Based on the NRSV,* p. 338; January, 1996, Arthur Van Seters, review of *A Social Reading of the Old Testament: Prophetic Approaches to Israel's Communal Life,* p. 558; July, 1998, Erhard Gerstenberger, review of *Theology of the Old Testament,* p. 266.

Tikkun, November, 2000, review of *Deep Memory, Exuberant Hope,* p. 89.

Times Higher Education Supplement, February 18, 1994, Alan David, review of *Texts under Negotiation: The Bible and Postmodern Imagination,* p. 28.

ONLINE

Review of Biblical Literature Online, http://www.bookreviews.org/ (June 12, 2002), Dale Patrick, review of *A Commentary on Jeremiah: Exile and Homecoming.*

*   *   *

BRUNDAGE, Elizabeth

PERSONAL: Married; husband a physician; children: three. *Education:* Iowa Writers' Workshop, M.F.A.

ADDRESSES: Home—MA. *Agent*—Gretchen Koss, Viking/Penguin Group, 375 Hudson St., New York, NY 10014. *E-mail*—Elizabeth@ElizabethBrundage.com.

CAREER: Writer.

AWARDS, HONORS: James Michener Award.

WRITINGS:

The Doctor's Wife (novel), Viking (New York, NY), 2004.

Contributor to periodicals, including *Greensboro Review, Witness,* and *New Letters;* work represented in anthologies, including *I've Always Meant to Tell You: Letters to Our Mothers.*

SIDELIGHTS: Elizabeth Brundage's debut novel, *The Doctor's Wife,* is set in upstate New York, where Brundage and her husband, a physician, lived during his residency. The doctor of the story is Michael Knowles, a successful ob-gyn who agrees to help

Celina, a former girlfriend, by performing abortions in her free clinic. Annie, Michael's wife and the mother of his two children, feels neglected because Michael has little time for her, and she begins an affair with artist Simon Haas, an alcoholic womanizer she meets at St. Catherine's College, where she teaches a creative writing course. Meanwhile, Lydia, Simon's young wife, becomes an adherent of charismatic preacher Reverend Tim, who leads protests against the clinic. A *Publishers Weekly* reviewer commented that Lydia "is the enigma that fuels Brundage's examination of what happens when we are drawn to the very things that promise to destroy us."

A central protagonist in *The Doctor's Wife*, Michael begins to suffer the consequences of working at the controversial clinic when he is run off the road. The clinic is soon defaced, then bombed, and ultimately all of the workers' lives are threatened. The violence escalates with a killing and a kidnapping as Brundage's story proceeds to a conclusion, which was called "realistic yet satisfyingly dramatic" by Marianne Fitzgerald in a review of the novel for *Library Journal.*

BIOGRAPHICAL AND CRITICAL SOURCES:

PERIODICALS

Booklist, July, 2004, Ellen Loughran, review of *The Doctor's Wife,* p. 1816.
Kirkus Reviews, April 15, 2004, review of *The Doctor's Wife,* p. 344.
Library Journal, June 15, 2004, Marianne Fitzgerald, review of *The Doctor's Wife,* p. 57.
Publishers Weekly, May 31, 2004, review of *The Doctor's Wife,* p. 51.

ONLINE

Bookreporter.com, http://www.bookreporter.com/ (June 24, 2004), Carol Fitzgerald, interview with Brundage.
Bookslut.com, http://www.bookslut.com/ (July, 2004), Jessa Crispin, review of *The Doctor's Wife.*
Elizabeth Brundage Home Page, http://www.elizabeth brundage.com (February 18, 2005).*

BRYANT, Lynwood S(ilvester) 1908-2005

OBITUARY NOTICE— See index for *CA* sketch: Born December 8, 1908, in Keene, NH; died March 16, 2005, in East Sandwich, NH (one source says Center Sandwich, NH). Bryant was a professor emeritus of history at the Massachusetts Institute of Technology (MIT), where he was also a former director of MIT Press. A graduate of Harvard University, where he earned an A.B. in 1929 and an A.M. in 1938, he taught at the Roxbury Latin School in Boston, Massachusetts, for a time before joining the MIT faculty in 1937. Beginning as an instructor, he rose to full professor of history and remained at the Institute until his 1975 retirement. Though he was considered a knowledge-able generalist, Bryant had a special interest in the history of the development of automobile, diesel, and heat engines, about which he wrote in Volume Three of *A History of Industrial Power in the United States, 1780-1930: The Transmission of Power* (1991); he also contributed articles on engine history to such magazines as *Scientific American* and was an early member of the Society for the History of Technology. After retiring from MIT, Bryant remained active as a senior resident scholar at the Hagley Foundation for two years. He was also passionate about the theater, participating in a local acting troupe, the Sandwich Players.

OBITUARIES AND OTHER SOURCES:

PERIODICALS

Boston Globe, March 19, 2005.
Chronicle of Higher Education, April 29, 2005, p. A80.

ONLINE

Massachusetts Institute of Technology Web site, http:// web.mit.edu/ (March 30, 2005).

*   *   *

BULION, Leslie 1958-

PERSONAL: Born 1958, in New York, NY. *Education:* Cornell University, B.A.; University of Rhode Island Graduate School of Oceanography, M.S.; Southern Connecticut State University, M.S.W. *Hobbies and other interests:* Hiking, bicycling, cross-country skiing, scuba diving, pottery, knitting, reading, eating chocolate.

ADDRESSES: Agent—Moon Mountain Publishing, Inc., P.O. Box 188, West Rockport, ME 04865-0188. *E-mail*—leslie@lesliebulion.com.

CAREER: Children's book writer and editor.

MEMBER: Society of Children's Book Writers and Illustrators, Authors Guild, Authors League.

AWARDS, HONORS: Tassy Walden New Voices in Children's Literature Award, for Young-Adult Novel, 2001; Children's Africana Book Award, African Studies Association, 2003, for *Fatuma's New Cloth.*

WRITINGS:

Fatuma's New Cloth, illustrated by Nicole Tadgell, Moon Mountain Publishing (North Kingstown, RI), 2002.
Missing Pieces, Steck-Vaughn (Austin, TX), 2003.
One Piece at a Time, Steck-Vaughn (Austin, TX), 2004.
Tall Ships Fun, Moon Mountain Publishing (North Kingstown, RI), 2004.

Contributor to periodicals, including *Parents* and *Child.* Contributing writer to Edmin.com, 2000-02; author and editor of readers for educational publishers.

WORK IN PROGRESS: Middle-grade novel to be published in 2006 by Peachtree Publishing. Collection of insect poetry to be published by Charlesbridge Publishing, 2006.

SIDELIGHTS: Journalist and writer Leslie Bulion was inspired by her family's travels in East Africa to pen her first children's book, *Fatuma's New Cloth,* thus beginning a new branch of her career as an author. Published in 2002, the picture book follows a young girl named Fatuma as she accompanies her mother to the local market one day. Her mother promises Fatuma that, after the family shopping is done, the girl will be allowed to purchase a kanga cloth for a new dress and also stop for a treat: a cup of chai tea. While at the market many shop merchants try to impress their opinions upon young Fatuma about what constitutes the perfect chai. However, it is when Fatuma selects a brightly colored kanga cloth that the answer is

revealed. Printed within the brightly patterned cloth is the saying: "Don't be fooled by the color. The good flavor of chai comes from the sugar." In other words, there is much more to a person than just what meets the eye.

Reviewing Bulion's debut book in *School Library Journal,* Anna DeWind Walls wrote that the book's overall message is "sweet" and "the story drifts along at a dreamy pace." A *Publishers Weekly* critic commented that "Tadgell's artwork highlights the glorious colors of the area's fabrics and landscapes, and demonstrates the warmth of a closely knit community in which tradition is paramount."

BIOGRAPHICAL AND CRITICAL SOURCES:

BOOKS

Bulion, Leslie, *Fatuma's New Cloth,* Moon Mountain (North Kingstown, RI), 2002.

PERIODICALS

Publishers Weekly, May 20, 2002, review of *Fatuma's New Cloth,* p. 65.
School Library Journal, December, 2002, Anna DeWind Walls, review of *Fatuma's New Cloth,* p. 85.
Skipping Stones, March-April, 2004, review of *Fatuma's New Cloth,* p. 34.

ONLINE

Leslie Bulion Home Page, http://www.lesliebulion.com (May 3, 2005).
Moon Mountain Publishing Web site, http://www.moonmountainpub.com/ (May 3, 2005).

*   *   *

BURKE, Fred G(eorge) 1926-2005

OBITUARY NOTICE— See index for *CA* sketch: Born January 1, 1926, in Collins, NY; died of a pulmonary embolism March 11, 2005, in Newton, NJ. Educator, government official, and author. Though he also enjoyed a long and distinguished teaching career,

Burke is most often remembered for his years as the commissioner of education for the states of Rhode Island and then New Jersey. A U.S. Army Air Forces veteran, he served in the military during World War II and the Korean War before completing his education. He held a bachelor's degree from Williams College, earned in 1953, as well as an M.A. and Ph.D. from Princeton University, received in 1955 and 1958, respectively. During the late 1950s and 1960s Burke held various teaching posts. He was an associate professor of political science at Ohio Wesleyan University and he directed the school's Institute of Politics. At Syracuse University he was a professor and director of East African studies during the mid-1960s. Burke's interest in Africa led to several extended trips there; he was also a consultant to the Kenyan government in 1956, a United Nations consultant for the Economic Commission for Africa in 1968, and a training director for Peace Corps volunteers in East Africa. Returning to the United States, he served as dean of international studies and professor of social sciences and administration at the State University of New York at Buffalo from 1968 until 1970. Burke was then selected by the governor of Rhode Island to head that state's department of education. For the next four years, he strove to eliminate the gap in equality of education between rich and poor districts, and he continued to do so when he was selected in 1974 to fill the same post for the state of New Jersey. Burke's term as commissioner of education for New Jersey was tumultuous because his policies for making educators and school administrators partially accountable for the success of their students met with resistance from both groups. Burke supported what became the state's first income tax, with much of the money earmarked for schools. Although student test scores showed improvement toward the end of Burke's term, he was removed from office in 1982 when a new governor was elected. Years later, in 1990, the New Jersey Supreme Court ruled in *Abbott v. Burke* that the state must ensure that all school districts spend an equal amount on their students. Ironically, Burke was named the defendant in this suit because it was filed in 1981, while he was still in office, but he was actually pleased that the action was ruled against by the court. Leaving government bureaucracy behind, he was hired as the vice president of the University of Connecticut in 1982; ten years later, he accepted a post as senior fellow of the Phelps Stokes Fund. Burke was the author of several books on Africa, including *Africa's Quest for Order* (1964) and *Sub-Saharan Africa* (1968). He was also the author of *Public Education: Who's in Charge?* (1990).

OBITUARIES AND OTHER SOURCES:

PERIODICALS

New York Times, March 14, 2005, p. A21.
Star-Ledger (Newark, NJ), March 14, 2005, p. 11.

C

CALDER, Iain 1939-

PERSONAL: Born February 27, 1939, in Scotland; immigrated to United States, 1967; naturalized citizen; married Jane Brownlea Bell, April 17, 1965; children: Douglas William, Glen Robert Bell.

ADDRESSES: Home—Boca Raton, FL. *Agent*—c/o Author Mail, Hyperion Editorial Department, 77 West 66th St., 11th Floor, New York, NY 10023.

CAREER: Falkirk Sentinel, Falkirk, Scotland, reporter, 1955-56; *Stirling Journal,* Stirling, Scotland, reporter, 1956; *Falkirk Mail,* Falkirk, reporter, 1956-60; *Glasgow Daily Record,* Glasgow, Scotland, reporter, 1960-64; *National Enquirer,* Lantana, FL, London bureau chief, 1964-67, articles editor, 1967-73, executive editor, 1973-75, editor, 1975-91, editor-in-chief, 1991-95, editor emeritus, 1995-97, consultant, 1997—. American Media, Inc., executive vice president of publications, 1994-97. Member of board of directors, Bethesda Hospital Foundation, 1997—.

AWARDS, HONORS: Named among 500 most influential journalists in American history by Newseum (Arlington, VA).

WRITINGS:

The Untold Story: My Twenty Years Running the National Enquirer, Hyperion (New York, NY), 2004.

SIDELIGHTS: Iain Calder spent two decades as the top editor of the *National Enquirer,* America's best-known supermarket tabloid. As Calder recalls in his memoir, *The Untold Story: My Twenty Years Running the National Enquirer,* he and the paper's owner, Generoso Pope, saw an unfulfilled niche in American journalism in the early 1960s and quickly moved in to fill it with a weekly newspaper full of celebrity gossip; medical breakthroughs; advice—both paranormal and practical—on such issues as marriage, child-rearing, finding a mate, and dieting; and inspiring stories of personal courage and survival. In the *Columbia Journalism Review,* Neal Gabler wrote: "In his single-minded devotion to celebrity flotsam and jetsam, Calder seemed to be at one with his readership and onto something, too. Enquiring minds did want to know, as the old TV ads said. They wanted to be the first to know. They had a vested interest in knowing, even if what they knew really wasn't worth knowing and even if it wasn't true. In a culture where there was so much to know, knowing what others might not know was itself a form of empowerment." "Calder knew he was selling his readers resentment and hope," Gabler added. "He was also selling them the paper's own merry tawdriness."

In *The Untold Story,* Calder describes his own self-educated climb through the journalistic ranks in his native Scotland, his early years as a freelance reporter for the *National Enquirer,* and his long and productive working relationship with Pope. He also addresses the charges that the tabloid fabricated stories, categorically denying that its reporters manufactured untrue or half-true pieces, and pointing to the newspaper's record with libel lawsuits in comparison with other national and mainstream newspapers. In an interview with *NewsMax.com,* Calder said: "We tried harder—at least as hard as any newspaper—to get absolutely true stories. Our readers knew this even when celebrities would say that's not true and we're going to sue you, and six months later it would turn out that we were correct." In his book Calder details the creative techniques *National Enquirer* reporters and photographers used to obtain exclusive information, including the ground-breaking use of large teams of editors and reporters to gain blanket coverage of major stories, from the death of Elvis Presley to the O. J. Simpson murder trial. He also notes that the tabloid's publication of a cover photograph of then-Senator Gary Hart with a young woman on his lap probably changed the course of history when it wrecked Hart's bid for the U.S. presidency.

Reviewers of *The Untold Story* commended it for its breezy style and for its insider's view not only of the *National Enquirer* itself, but also of the tabloid journalism business in general. "This tell-all makes for a fun read for loyal *Enquirer* readers or anyone interested in popular culture," commented Donna Marie Smith in *Library Journal.* A *Publishers Weekly* contributor found the book "a compulsive page-turner," and added that Calder's personal tale of working his way to the top "proves just as compelling as his superstar portrayals." A critic for *Kirkus Reviews* called the work a "zippy memoir" and concluded: "If the *National Enquirer* is where reporters go to die, it must be America's most exciting retirement community."

In an interview with *Women's Wear Daily* Calder reflected on his singular career. "I'm really quite proud that I was editor of the *Enquirer,*" he said. "I've estimated that the number of publications I've sold with my name on it as editor was about 4.4 billion. I don't know if anybody else in the history of journalism could beat that record. Coming from a little mining village in Scotland, I'm quite proud of that."

BIOGRAPHICAL AND CRITICAL SOURCES:

BOOKS

Calder, Iain, *The Untold Story: My Twenty Years Running the National Enquirer,* Hyperion (New York, NY), 2004.

PERIODICALS

Booklist, May 15, 2004, Ilene Cooper, review of *The Untold Story: My Twenty Years Running the National Enquirer,* p. 1581.
Columbia Journalism Review, July-August, 2004, Neal Gabler, "Ephemera: The Rise and Rise of Celebrity Journalism," p. 48.
Editor & Publisher, May 4, 1991, Garry Boulard, "Giving People What They Want to Read," p. 46.
Kirkus Reviews, May 1, 2004, review of *The Untold Story,* p. 428.
Library Journal, June 15, 2004, Donna Marie Smith, review of *The Untold Story,* p. 79.
Publishers Weekly, May 31, 2004, Joel Hirschorn, "'Enquiring' Minds Will Want to Read This," p. 60; review of *The Untold Story,* p. 62.
Time, August 16, 2004, Andrea Sachs, "Tabloid Titan," p. G3.
Women's Wear Daily, July 2, 2004, Jeff Bercovici, "Talking the Enquirer Take on Celebrity," p. 11.

ONLINE

NewsMax, http://www.newsmax.com/ (August 19, 2004) Phil Brennan, "Editor: Bill O'Reilly Is TV's Enquirer."
Yale Journal of Ethics Online, http://www.yale.edu/yje/ (1996; May 5, 2005), Elana Zeide, "An Ethical Enquirer."*

* * *

CALHOUN, Chad
See BARRETT, Neal, Jr.

* * *

CARDIFF, Jack 1914-
(John Cardiff)

PERSONAL: Born September 18, 1914, in Yarmouth, Norfolk, England; son of John Joseph (a vaudeville performer) and Florence (a vaudeville performer) Cardiff; married Julia Lily Mickleboro, 1940 (divorced); married; wife's name, Sylvia (divorced); married; wife's name, Nicki, c. 1970; children: John, Rodney, Peter, Mason.

ADDRESSES: Agent—c/o Author Mail, Faber and Faber Ltd., 3 Queen Square, London WC1N 3AU, England.

CAREER: Cinematographer, camera operator, director, and actor. Director of films, including *This Is Colour* (short film), 1942; *Intent to Kill,* Twentieth Century-Fox, 1958; *Beyond This Place* (also known as *Web of Evidence*), 1959; *Scent of Mystery* (also known as *Holiday in Spain*), Michael Todd, 1960; *Sons and Lovers,* Twentieth Century-Fox, 1960; *The Lion,* Twentieth Century-Fox, 1962; *My Geisha,* Paramount, 1962; (director of additional sequences) *Satan Never Sleeps,* Twentieth Century-Fox, 1962; *The Long Ships,* Columbia, 1964; *Young Cassidy,* Metro-Goldwyn-Mayer (MGM), 1965; *The Liquidator,* MGM, 1966; *Dark of the Sun* (also known as *The Mercenaries*), MGM, 1968; (and producer) *The Girl on a Motorcycle* (also known as *Naked under Leather*), Claridge, 1968; *Penny Gold,* 1973; *The Mutations* (also known as *Doctor of Evil, The Freakmaker,* and *The Mutation*), Columbia, 1974; *Delius,* 1989; *Vivaldi's Four Seasons,* 1991; *The Dance of Shiva,* Epiphany Productions, 1998; *The Suicidal Dog,* BBC Films, 2000; and *One Life Later,* c. 2001. Cinematographer of films, including *The Last Days of Pompeii,* 1935; (with Hal Rosson) *As You Like It,* Twentieth Century-Fox, 1936; (with Ray Rennahan and Henry Imus) *Wings of the Morning,* Twentieth Century-Fox, 1937; *La caccia alla volpe nella campagna Romana* (short documentary film; also known as *Fox Hunting the Roman Compagna*), 1938; (as John Cardiff) *Paris on Parade* (short film), 1938; *Main Street of Paris* (short film), 1939; *World Windows,* 1939; *Peasant Island* (short film), 1940; *Green Girdle* (short film), 1941; *Plastic Surgery in Wartime* (short film), 1941; *Queen Cotton* (short film), 1941; *Western Isles* (short film), 1941; *Border Weave* (short film), 1942; *Colour in Clay* (short film), 1942; (with Claude Friese-Greene) *The Great Mr. Handel,* Midfilm, 1942; *Out of the Box* (short film), 1942; *This Is Colour* (short film), 1942; *Scottish Mazurka* (short film), 1943; (with others) *Steel* (short film), 1944; *The Western Approaches* (also known as *The Raider*), 1944; (with others) *Caesar and Cleopatra,* Eagle Lion, 1946; *Stairway to Heaven* (also known as *A Matter of Life and Death*), Universal, 1946; *Black Narcissus,* General Films Distributors, 1947; *The Red Shoes,* Eagle Lion/Rank, 1948; (with others) *Scott of the Antarctic,* Eagle Lion/Pyramid, 1949; (with others) *Under Capricorn,* Warner Bros., 1949; *The Black Rose,* Twentieth Century-Fox, 1950; *Montmartre* (short film), 1950; *The African Queen,*

United Artists (UA), 1951; *Montmartre Nocturne* (short film), 1951; *Pandora and the Flying Dutchman,* MGM, 1951; *Paris* (short film), 1951; *It Started in Paradise,* General Films Distributors, 1952; *The Magic Box,* British Lion, 1952; *The Master of Ballantrae,* Warner Bros, 1953; *The Barefoot Contessa,* UA, 1954; *Crossed Swords,* United Artists, 1954; *The Brave One,* RKO Radio Pictures, 1956; (with Aldo Tonti) *War and Peace,* Paramount, 1956; *The Big Money,* 1956, Lopert, 1962; *Legend of the Lost* (also known as *Timbuctu*), UA, 1957; *The Prince and the Showgirl,* Warner Bros., 1957; *The Vikings,* UA, 1958; (with William C. Mellor) *The Diary of Anne Frank,* Twentieth Century-Fox, 1959; *The Journey,* 1959; *Fanny,* Warner Bros., 1961; *Dark of the Sun* (also known as *The Mercenaries*), MGM, 1968; *The Girl on a Motorcycle* (also known as *Naked under Leather*), Claridge, 1968; *Scalawag,* Paramount, 1973; *Ride a Wild Pony* (also known as *Born to Run*), Buena Vista, 1976; *Behind the Iron Mask* (also known as *The Fifth Musketeer*), Columbia, 1977; *Crossed Swords* (also known as *The Prince and the Pauper*), Warner Bros., 1978; *Death on the Nile,* Paramount, 1978; *Avalanche Express,* Twentieth Century-Fox, 1979; *A Man, a Woman, and a Bank* (also known as *A Very Big Withdrawal*), Avco-Embassy, 1979; *The Awakening,* Warner Bros., 1980; *The Dogs of War,* UA, 1980; *Ghost Story,* Universal, 1981; *The Wicked Lady,* MGM/UA, 1983; *Conan the Destroyer,* Universal, 1984; *Scandalous,* Orion, 1984; *Cat's Eye* (also known as *Stephen King's Cat's Eye*), MGM/UA, 1985; *Rambo: First Blood, Part II,* TriStar, 1985; *Tai-Pan,* 1986; *Million Dollar Mystery* (also known as *Money Mania*), De Laurentiis Entertainment Group, 1987; *Call from Space,* Showscan, 1989; *The Magic Balloon,* Showscan, 1990; *Vivaldi's Four Seasons,* 1991; *The Dance of the Shiva,* 1998; *The Suicidal Dog,* 2000; and *The Tell-Tale Heart,* 2004. Also director of short documentary films for "World Window" series, including *Arabian Bazaar, Delhi, The Eternal Fire, Indian Temples, Jerusalem, Jungle, Petra, A Road in India, River Thames—Yesterday, Rome Symphony, Ruins of Palmyra and Baalbek, The Sacred Ganges, A Village in India,* and *Wanderers of the Desert,* 1937-40. Camera operator for films, including *Brewster's Millions,* 1935; *The Ghost Goes West,* 1935; *Honeymoon for Three,* 1935; *As You Like It,* Twentieth Century-Fox, 1936; *The Coronation of King George VI,* 1936; (and special effects camera operator) *The Man Who Could Work Miracles,* 1936; *Things to Come,* 1936; *Dark Journey* (also known as *The Anxious Years*), 1937; *Knight without Armour,* 1937; *The Four Feathers,* 1939; *The Life and Death of Colonel Blimp* (also known as *The Adventures of*

Colonel Blimp), 1943. Appeared in films, including *My Son, My Son,* 1918; *Billy's Rose,* 1922; *The Loves of Mary, Queen of Scots,* 1923; *Tiptoes,* 1927; *Sean O'Casey: The Spirit of Ireland,* 1965; (as himself) *A Profile of "Black Narcissus,"* Carlton International Media, 2000; (as himself) *A Profile of "The Life and Death of Colonel Blimp,"* Carlton International Media, 2000; (as himself) *A Profile of "The Red Shoes,"* Carlton Films, 2000; and *We Get to Win This Time* (video), Artisan Entertainment, 2002. Cinematographer of television miniseries, including *The Far Pavilions* (also known as *Blade of Steel*), Home Box Office (HBO), 1984; and *The Last Days of Pompeii,* ABC, 1984. Appeared as himself in television specials, including *A Matter of Michael and Emeric,* 1977; *Glorious Technicolor,* 1998; *The Hustons: Hollywood's Maverick Dynasty,* Arts and Entertainment, 1998; and *Larry and Vivien: The Oliviers in Love,* Channel 4, 2001.

AWARDS, HONORS: Academy Award for best cinematography, Academy of Motion-Picture Arts and Sciences, 1947, for *Black Narcissus;* Academy Award nominations for best cinematography, for *War and Peace* and *Fanny,* and for directing, for *Sons and Lovers;* Academy Award for Lifetime Achievement, 2001.

WRITINGS:

(With others) *The Girl on a Motorcycle* (screenplay; also known as *Naked under Leather*), Claridge, 1968.
Magic Hour: The Life of a Cameraman (autobiography), Faber & Faber (Boston, MA), 1997.

Author of another autobiography, published in 1975. Contributor to periodicals, including *American Cinematographer, Cinematographe, Screen International,* and *Time Out.*

SIDELIGHTS: Jack Cardiff is "modest, literate, gossipy, generous and one of the world's greatest cameramen," Simon Hattenstone wrote in a review of Cardiff's autobiography, *Magic Hour: The Life of a Cameraman,* in the Manchester *Guardian.* Cardiff's parents were vaudeville performers who sometimes dabbled in the new medium of film, and through them, Cardiff won his first film role in 1918, at the age of

four. But even before he reached his teens Cardiff's marketability as a child star was waning, so he moved behind the camera as an assistant.

Cardiff's big break came at age twenty-two, when Technicolor was looking to expand its color-film business into Great Britain. Cardiff interviewed to be the first British camera operator to be trained in the new technology. He was not the most scientifically competent candidate, he admits, but he was the premiere student of the use of light. Throughout his teenage years Cardiff had haunted art museums, studying the ways the great masters of painting had lit their subjects. Cardiff earned the job, he recalls in *Magic Hour,* by being able to tell the interviewers on which side of the face Rembrandt placed the key light.

Although Cardiff reveals many of the techniques of cinematography, *Magic Hour* is not merely a book for aspiring camera operators. Cardiff worked with most of the great stars of twentieth-century cinema, including Humphrey Bogart, Marilyn Monroe, Alfred Hitchcock, Ava Gardner, and Marlene Dietrich, and his "vivid evocations" of their antics on and off the set "are a treat," Lucy Maycock wrote in the London *Observer.* Overall, *Magic Hour* "is a lively, easy-going account of a remarkable career," concluded London *Sunday Times* reviewer George Perry.

BIOGRAPHICAL AND CRITICAL SOURCES:

BOOKS

Cardiff, Jack, *Magic Hour: The Life of a Cameraman,* Faber & Faber (Boston, MA), 1997.
International Dictionary of Films and Filmmakers, Volume 4: *Writers and Production Artists,* St. James Press (Detroit, MI), 1996.

PERIODICALS

Atlanta Journal-Constitution, March 29, 2001, Eleanor Ringel Gillespie, "A Few Honorary Nods to Cardiff and Lehman," p. D8.
Daily Telegraph (London, England), March 2, 2001, David Gritten, interview with Cardiff, p. 23.
Daily Variety, October 22, 2002, Adam Dawtrey, "Brits Abuzz over Biz," p. 12.

Entertainment Weekly, April 6, 2001, Ty Burr, review of *Black Narcissus,* p. 44.

Film Comment, November-December, 1985, Stephen Harvey, review of *Black Narcissus,* p. 66.

Guardian (London, England), May 10, 1996, Simon Hattenstone, review of *Magic Hour: The Life of a Cameraman,* p. 13; July 18, 1996, Caroline Sullivan, "Mood Musicians," p. 12; August 1, 1997, Tom Hutchinson, interview with Cardiff, pp. T6-T7; October 30, 1998, Gregory Street, "Wanna Make a Movie? Let the Master Show You How," p. 12.

Independent (London, England), November 21, 1997, David Benedict, interview with Cardiff, p. 26.

Los Angeles Times, April 20, 1984, Howard Rosenberg, review of *The Far Pavilions,* p. 1; April 12, 1985, Kevin Thomas, review of *Cat's Eye,* p. 4; May 22, 1985, Michael Wilmington, review of *Rambo: First Blood, Part II,* p. 1.

Maclean's, December 21, 1981, Lawrence O'Toole, review of *Ghost Story,* p. 50; February 6, 1984, Lawrence O'Toole, review of *Scandalous,* p. 54.

Mirror (London, England), March 24, 2001, Thomas Quinn, "And the Oscar Goes to . . . Jack Cardiff, 86," p. 11.

New Republic, July 1, 1985, Stanley Kauffmann, review of *Rambo: First Blood, Part II,* p. 16.

New Statesman, August 2, 1985, John Coleman, review of *Pandora and the Flying Dutchman,* p. 30.

New Yorker, March 23, 1981, Pauline Kael, review of *The Dogs of War,* pp. 138-139; June 17, 1985, Pauline Kael, review of *Rambo: First Blood, Part II,* p. 117.

New York Times, April 22, 1984, John J. O'Connor, review of *The Far Pavilions,* p. H26; March 25, 2001, Bill Desowitz, "Cinema Vermeer: A Gifted Colorist and Master of Light," p. AR17.

Observer (London, England), August 31, 1997, Lucy Maycock, review of *Magic Hour,* p. 16.

Sight and Sound, July, 2001, Geoffrey Macnab, interview with Cardiff, p. 65.

Sunday Telegraph (London, England), March 25, 2001, Chris Hastings, "Stage Fright for Briton Facing Oscar Tribute," p. 20.

Sunday Times, June 2, 1996, George Perry, review of *Magic Hour,* p. 5; February 4, 2001, Stuart Wavell, interview with Cardiff, p. NR2.

Times (London, England), August 30, 2003, Stephen Dalton, review of *Girl on a Motorcycle,* p. 6; November 24, 2003, Kate Quill, interview with Cardiff, p. 16.

Times Higher Education Supplement, June 28, 1996, Ian Christie, review of *Magic Hour,* p. 23.

ONLINE

Britmovie.com, http://www.britmovie.com/ (November 26, 2003), "Jack Cardiff."

Guild of Television Cameramen Web site, http://www. gtc.org.uk/ (November 26, 2003), Steve Hall, interview with Cardiff.

Internet Movie Database, http://www.imdb.com/ (May 25, 2004), "Jack Cardiff."*

*　　*　　*

CARDIFF, John
　　See CARDIFF, Jack

*　　*　　*

CARMEAN, Kelli 1960-

PERSONAL: Born February 8, 1960, in Athens, OH. *Education:* University of Victoria, B.A.; University of Pittsburgh, Ph.D.

ADDRESSES: Office—Department of Anthropology, Eastern Kentucky University, Richmond, KY 40475.

CAREER: Archaeologist. Eastern Kentucky University, Richmond, affiliate.

WRITINGS:

Spider Woman Walks This Land: Traditional Cultural Properties and the Navajo Nation, Altamira Press (Walnut Creek, CA), 2002.

WORK IN PROGRESS: The Village at Muddy Creek: Fort Ancient Indian Life in Central Kentucky.

*　　*　　*

CASHIN, Sheryll

PERSONAL: Born in Huntsville, AL.

ADDRESSES: Office—Georgetown University Law Center, 600 New Jersey Ave. NW, Washington, DC 20001. *E-mail*—cashins@law.georgetown.edu.

CAREER: Georgetown University, Washington, DC, professor of law; has worked as director of community empowerment board for U.S. Vice President Al Gore, and as director of community development and national economic policy for U.S. President Bill Clinton; former law clerk for Sirote & Permutt (law firm); former law clerk to Supreme Court Justice Thurgood Marshall. Television commentator on law, politics, and race relations.

WRITINGS:

The Failures of Integration: How Race and Class Are Undermining the American Dream, Public Affairs (New York, NY), 2004.

SIDELIGHTS: A former White House advisor who is currently a professor of law at Georgetown University, Sheryll Cashin has devoted much of her public career to matters of race and class. In *The Failures of Integration: How Race and Class Are Undermining the American Dream* Cashin closely examines the failed promise of segregation, analyzing the public-policy decisions that have resulted in gross racial and social inequality in America. For Cashin, such lasting segregation is the fault of both private and public choices, with public policies such as federal mortgage insurance, urban redevelopment and its public housing projects, and exclusionary zoning all playing a part in creating blacks-only enclaves throughout America and continuing exclusionary practices that are as old as America itself. Despite the fact that *Brown vs. Board of Education,* a landmark case that dismantled the country's "separate but equal" educational standard, was fifty years in the past by 2004, education in America is still segregated, Cashin contends in her book. She further argues that real socioeconomic integration begins in the schools as well as in residential neighborhoods, because segregationist policies have high costs for whites as well as blacks in America. A reviewer for *Bookwatch* summarized Cashin's thesis: "Issues of race and class are no longer theories of fairness and ethics; they are now undermining the American dream." That same reviewer praised the "hard-hitting set of realities" presented in Cashin's book.

Other reviewers found *The Failures of Integration: How Race and Class Are Undermining the American Dream* both trenchant and timely. A *Black Issues in Higher Education* critic, for instance, called Cashin's study "provocative," while Vernon Ford, writing in *Booklist,* noted that "this work supports the objectives of an American ideal that has been long lost in our current world." A contributor for *Publishers Weekly* considered *The Failures of Integration* to be a "compelling book," and further commented that Cashin "argues powerfully that such integration is crucial to build democracy and diminish racial barriers." Reviewing the same work in the *Washington Post,* Courtland Milloy concluded that "Cashin offers many solutions to these problems. But they all depend on having our consciousness raised. It's not enough for us to talk about moral values; we must walk the walk as well."

Cashin told *CA:* "*The Failures of Integration* is my first book. It was written out of passion, or anger rather. When I get in the car and drive in America I see very different neighborhoods and very different opportunities that are shaped in insidious ways by public-policy choices. I was angry mostly about the raw deal many minority poor kids receive through no fault of their own. I decided to channel five years of academic research on the subject into a book for lay audiences. In the process, I found a voice as a writer and am now committed to the writing life. I hope readers enjoy the book and will read it with an open mind."

BIOGRAPHICAL AND CRITICAL SOURCES:

PERIODICALS

Black Issues in Higher Education, May 20, 2004, review of *The Failures of Integration: How Race and Class Are Undermining the American Dream,* p. 40.

Booklist, May 15, 2004, Vernon Ford, review of *The Failures of Integration,* p. 1582.

Bookwatch, September, 2004, review of *The Failures of Integration,* p. 1.

Chicago Tribune, May 2, 2004, David J. Garrow, review of *The Failures of Integration,* p. B1.

New York Times, May 8, 2004, David L. Campbell, "If Affirmative Action Fails. . . . What Then?," p. B7.

New York Times Book Review, May 16, 2004, Samuel G. Freedman, review of *The Failures of Integration,* p. 8.

Publishers Weekly, April 12, 2004, review of *The Failures of Integration,* p. 50.

Washington Post, November 10, 2004, Courtland Milloy, "The High Price of Not Learning to Live Together," p. B1.

ONLINE

NPR Online, http://www.npr.org/ (May 4, 2004), *The Failures of Integration.*

*   *   *

CASSIDY, John 1963-

PERSONAL: Born January 31, 1963, in Leeds, England; immigrated to United States, 1984; son of John Bernard and Julie Theresa (Vaughan) Cassidy; married Patricia Mollach, August 12, 1989. *Education:* Oxford University, B.A., 1984; Columbia University, M.A., 1986; New York University, M.A., 1998.

ADDRESSES: Home—New York, NY *Office*—The New Yorker, 4 Times Sq., New York, NY 10036.

CAREER: Journalist and author. *Sunday Times,* London, England, financial correspondent, 1986-87, New York correspondent, 1987-88, Washington bureau chief, 1989-91, business editor, 1991-93; *New York Post,* New York, NY, business editor, 1993-94, deputy editor, 1994; *New Yorker,* staff writer, 1995—.

WRITINGS:

Dot.con: The Greatest Story Ever Sold (nonfiction), HarperCollins (New York, NY), 2002.

SIDELIGHTS: British journalist and writer John Cassidy has been covering economics and finance for more than fifteen years. He began his journalistic career at the London *Sunday Times,* working his way from financial correspondent to business editor over the course of five years. Cassidy then moved to the *New York Post,* where he held various editorships. In 1995, he took a writing position at the *New Yorker.* At

that publication Cassidy was nominated as a 2004 National Magazine Award finalist for his December, 2003 article, "The David Kelly Affair."

In 2002 Cassidy published his first book, *Dot.con: The Greatest Story Ever Sold.* The book serves as an overview of the Internet boom, then bust, of the 1990s. Cassidy first chronicles the technological advances leading up to the stock craze and gives profiles of well-known dot.com companies such as Netscape, Yahoo!, AmericaOnline, and Amazon. He then names key players that he believes helped inflate the technology stock bubble, including Wall Street analysts, journalists, and Federal Reserve Board chairman Alan Greenspan.

Dot.con received a mix of favorable and lukewarm reviews from critics. Many reviewers criticized Cassidy for not conducting more new reporting for the book, instead relying on information gleaned from previously published articles on the subject. "Cassidy offers little fresh reporting . . . but his narrative is well written and entertaining," wrote *Institutional Investor* contributor Steven Brull. Others lauded the author for writing a comprehensive retrospective on this important era in financial history. "This absorbing tale of an ongoing chapter in the history of the stock market is highly recommended," commented Stacey Marien in a review for the *Library Journal.*

BIOGRAPHICAL AND CRITICAL SOURCES:

PERIODICALS

American Prospect, March 11, 2002, Charles C. Mann, review of *Dot.con: The Greatest Story Ever Sold,* p. 38.

Boston Globe, February 26, 2002, Charles Stein, "The Maestro Reconsidered," p. 1.

Business Week, February 25, 2002, "How the Tech Boom Went Bust," p. 24; June 30, 2003, Hardy Green, review of *Dot.con,* p. 20.

Chicago Sun-Times, March 24, 2002, review of *Dot. con,* p. 14.

Daily Telegraph (London, England), February 2, 2002, John Lanchester, review of *Dot.con.*

Denver Post, April 7, 2002, Mark P. Couch, review of *Dot.con,* p. 1.

Economist, January 19, 2002, review of *Dot.con,* p. 85.

Guardian (Manchester, England), February 9, 2002, Robert Peston, review of *Dot.con,* p. 9; January 25, 2003, Steven Poole, review of *Dot.con,* p. 31.

Houston Chronicle, April 14, 2002, Barbara Liss, "Writer Indicts E-Business Entrepreneurs," p. 19.

Institutional Investor, March 2002, Steven Brull, "Only in America," p. 96.

Kiplinger's Personal Finance, March, 2002, Robert Frick, "*Dot-con* Dissection," p. 30.

Library Journal, March 15, 2002, Stacey Marien, review of *Dot.con,* p. 91.

Long Island Business News, March 1, 2002, review of *Dot.con,* p. 27.

Los Angeles Times, March 3, 2002, Alex Raksin, review of *Dot.con,* p. 9.

Newsweek, March 18, 2002, Adam Rogers, "Whose Bubble Is It?," p. 38.

New York Times Book Review, March 17, 2002, Hugo Lindgren, "One Is Born Every Minute," p. 14.

Publishers Weekly, January 21, 2002, review of *Dot. con,* p. 80.

San Francisco Chronicle, February 17, 2002, David Kipen, "*New Yorker* Writer Does an Autopsy of Dot.Commerce," p. 1.

Sunday Telegraph (London, England), February 3, 2002, Martin Vander Weyer, "Caught up in the Net," p. 14.

Times (London, England), February 1, 2001, Martin Waller, review of *Dot.con,* p. 27.

USA Today, March 18, 2002, Henry Pearson, "*Dot.con* Delivers Dazzling Body Blows," p. 5.

Washington Monthly, April 2002, Nicholas Thompson, review of *Dot.con,* p. 56.

ONLINE

CNET News Online, http://news.com.com/ (March 7, 2002), "Explaining the 'Dot-cons.'"

HarperCollins Web site, http://www.harpercollins.com/ (May 5, 2005), "John Cassidy."*

*   *   *

CAWSE, James N. 1945-

PERSONAL: Born November 27, 1945, in Staten Island, NY; son of Alfred J. (a judge) and Janet (a teacher; maiden name, Decker) Cawse; married Marietta Rapetti (a school counselor), July 13, 1974; children: Lauren, Jeanne. *Ethnicity:* "White." *Education:* Wesleyan University, B.A., 1967; Stanford University, Ph.D., 1973.

ADDRESSES: Office—General Electric Global Research, 1 Research Circle, Niskayuna, NY 12309. *E-mail*—cawse@berkshire.rr.com.

CAREER: Union Carbide, Charleston, WV, research chemist, 1974-79; General Electric Global Research, Niskayuna, NY, research chemist, 1980—.

MEMBER: American Chemical Society, American Society for Quality.

WRITINGS:

(Editor and contributor) *Experimental Design for Combinatorial and High Throughput Materials Development,* John Wiley and Sons (New York, NY), 2002.

Contributor to scientific journals, including *Journal of Combinatorial Chemistry, Accounts of Chemical Research, Polymer Testing,* and *Progress in Organic Coatings.*

SIDELIGHTS: James N. Cawse told *CA:* "A few years ago I was invited to join a groundbreaking effort in combinatorial chemistry at General Electric as an experimental strategist. I found that combinatorial and high throughput experimentation methods were changing the materials development world as thoroughly as they changed the drug discovery world in the last decade. Advances in chemistries, analytical techniques, preparation methods, software, and hardware have made this a tremendously exciting area to work in. Entirely new approaches were needed to deal with the explosion in experimental capability. As materials scientists, we started thinking differently, attacking research areas as entire units rather than proceeding from experiment to experiment.

"As a relatively unusual chemist with extensive training and experience in experimental design, I had the marvelous opportunity to think deeply about the key intellectual step of planning the experiments. I realized that, with the experimental horsepower now easily accessible, the experimenter really needed to map a route before careening across the landscape. In this effort I was aided by a world-class team at General Electric Global Research and, as I began to work on the book, a very strong group of contributors. It was great fun and a super education just trying to understand the mathematical, statistical, and chemical depth of their contributions!"

BIOGRAPHICAL AND CRITICAL SOURCES:

PERIODICALS

Technometrics, November, 2003, Eric R. Ziegel, review of *Experimental Design for Combinatorial and High Throughput Materials Development,* p. 365.

*   *   *

CHADWIN, Dean 1966(?)-

PERSONAL: Born c. 1966; son of Mark (an educator) and Adrienne (a real estate agent) Chadwin; married Alleen Marie Barber (an editor), May 10, 2003. *Education:* Yale University, graduated; University of Southern California, M.A.; University of Virginia, J.D.

ADDRESSES: Home—46 Kensington Oval, New Rochelle, NY 10805. *Agent*—c/o Author Mail, Verso, 180 Varick St., 10th Floor, New York, NY 10014-4606.

CAREER: Freelance sports writer.

WRITINGS:

Taking the Ice: The Mighty Ducks of Anaheim, Polestar Press (Vancouver, British Columbia, Canada), 1994, published as *Rocking the Pond: The First Season of the Mighty Ducks of Anaheim,* 1994.
Wahine Ball: The Story of Hawaii's Most Beloved Team, Mutual Publishing, 1997.
Those Damn Yankees: The Secret History of America's Greatest Sports Franchise, Verso (New York, NY), 1999.

Also contributor to periodicals, including *LA Weekly, Village Voice,* and *Honolulu Weekly.*

SIDELIGHTS: Dean Chadwin has written books focusing on professional sports franchises. His first book, *Taking the Ice: The Mighty Ducks of Anaheim,* was published in 1994 and focuses on the beginning success of the National Hockey League (NHL) expansion team by delving into the team's strategy and individual performances. Writing in the *Canadian Book Review,* Lisa Arsenault called the effort an "interesting and informative book for hockey aficionados" and noted that the author has a "nice writing style."

After publishing the story of the University of Hawaii's short-lived women's volleyball team in *Wahine Ball: The Story of Hawaii's Most Beloved Team,* Chadwin turned his focus to a long-established sports dynasty with *Those Damn Yankees: The Secret History of America's Greatest Sports Franchise.* In this book, Chadwin explores how the modern-day Yankees have built a perennial winner by outbidding other franchises for the best talent in the league, and also comments on the state of modern professional baseball. A *Publishers Weekly* contributor called the book "an engaging analysis of baseball's problems." Jim G. Burns, writing in the *Library Journal,* felt that while Chadwin criticizes the Yankees and its management too much, the book includes "cogent discussions of racism in baseball and the devolution of major league franchises into haves and have-nots." In his assessment for the *New York Times Book Review,* Allen St. John wrote, "His contention that the health of the game is threatened by the revenue gap between large-market teams and small-market teams is right on target, but his point is muddied by his anti-Yankee animus." St. John concluded that the book is "curiously refreshing."

BIOGRAPHICAL AND CRITICAL SOURCES:

PERIODICALS

Canadian Book Review, 1994, Ian A. Andrews, review of *Rocking the Pond: The First Season of the Mighty Ducks of Anaheim,* p. 138; 1994, Lisa Arsenault, review of *Taking the Ice: The Mighty Ducks of Anaheim,* p. 539.

Library Journal, June 1, 1999, Jim G. Burns, review of *Those Damn Yankees: The Secret History of America's Greatest Sports Franchise,* p. 124.

New York Times Book Review, June 20, 1999, Allen St. John, review of *Those Damn Yankees,* p. 9.

Publishers Weekly, May 3, 1999, review of *Those Damn Yankees,* p. 63.

ONLINE

BrothersJudd.com, http://www.brothersjudd.com/ (May 10, 2001), review of *Those Damn Yankees.*

Onion A.V. Club, http://www.theonionavclub.com/ (January 31, 2005), review of *Those Damn Yankees.**

*   *   *

CHAN, David Marshall 1970-

PERSONAL: Born 1970, in Los Angeles, CA. *Education:* Holds degrees from Yale University and University of California.

ADDRESSES: Home—New York, NY. *Agent*—c/o Author Mail, Publishers Group West, 1700 Fourth St., Berkeley, CA 94710.

CAREER: Writer.

AWARDS, HONORS: Columbia Fiction Prize; *Los Angeles Times* Book Prize nomination for first work of fiction, 2004, for *Goblin Fruit: Stories.*

WRITINGS:

Goblin Fruit: Stories, Publishers Group West (Berkeley, CA), 2003.

Contributor of short stories to periodicals, including *Bomb* and *Columbia.*

SIDELIGHTS: David Marshall Chan's first book of short fiction, *Goblin Fruit: Stories,* explores the vagaries of growing up Asian American in the Los Angeles metropolitan area. Warmly received by reviewers, Chan's book was nominated for the *Los Angeles Times* book prize in 2004 as a first work of fiction.

Library Journal correspondent Jim Coan explained that Chan's story collection "uses childhood and youthful innocence as a starting point to weave together tales of loss, dislocation, and imagination." In one of the stories collected, a young man describes his efforts to make it in show business after losing a brother in a horrible accident on a movie set. In another, a narrator recalls a dynamic childhood friend who has since disappeared and is believed to be dead. A *Publishers Weekly* reviewer felt that the collection "draws out the experience of growing up Asian-American in Southern California." In *Booklist,* Kaite Mediatore maintained that *Goblin Fruit* should have a wider appeal. The stories, Mediatore concluded, "have an everyman feel that will touch all readers."

BIOGRAPHICAL AND CRITICAL SOURCES:

PERIODICALS

Booklist, January 1, 2003, Kaite Mediatore, review of *Goblin Fruit: Stories,* p. 844.

Library Journal, January, 2003, Jim Coan, review of *Goblin Fruit,* p. 161.

New York Review of Books, November 6, 2003, Joyce Carol Oates, review of *Goblin Fruit.*

Publishers Weekly, November 25, 2002, review of *Goblin Fruit,* p. 41.**

*   *   *

CHIBBARO, Julie 1955-

PERSONAL: Born 1955. *Education:* Attended Hunter College of the City University of New York, 1987-91.

ADDRESSES: Home—NY. *Agent*—Jill Grinberg, Anderson Grinberg Literary Management, 244 5th Ave., 11th Floor, New York, NY 10001. *E-mail*—Julie@juliechibbaro.com.

CAREER: McKinsey & Co., New York, NY, editor, 1991-96; Channel Crossings Language and Translation, Prague, Czech Republic, teacher of English as a second language (ESL), 1996-99; GetFit.com, Redwood City, CA, editor, 1999-2000; Centre CCFA École de Langues, ELAM, Montreal, Quebec, Canada, ESL teacher, 2000-01; Rogaine, Montreal, copywriter, 2001; journalist and fiction writer, 2001—. Participant in numerous writers' conferences, workshops, and residencies in United States and Czech Republic, including Palenville Interarts Colony, 1993, Prague Summer Writer's Workshop, 1997, Squaw Valley Community of Writers, 1999 and 2001, and Vermont Studio Center, 2003.

WRITINGS:

Redemption (young-adult novel), Atheneum Books for Young Readers (New York, NY), 2004.

Contributor of short stories to periodicals, including *Optimism Monthly, Prague Review,* and *Catalyst.* Contributor of articles and reviews to periodicals, including *Prague Post, Books in Canada,* and *Montreal Gazette.*

SIDELIGHTS: Julie Chibbaro's young-adult adventure, *Redemption,* examines the possibility that English settlers arrived on North American shores almost a century before the founding of the Jamestown colony. Twelve-year-old Lily Applegate and her mother face expulsion from England in 1522 because they have harbored a religious reformer from Germany. Taking a ship bound for the New World, Lily and her mother hope to find Lily's father there, as he has been missing for some years. For both women, the perilous voyage to an unknown land brings privation and despair—Lily's mother is attacked by the very baron who demanded she leave England, and Lily suffers from the harsh conditions existing aboard the vessel. When the ship wrecks on the foreign shore, Lily and her mother must contend with the evil baron and with Native Americans, some of whom are hostile and some of whom are helpful.

Chibbaro based *Redemption* on research suggesting that a few English settlers arrived in North America prior to the main body of colonial immigration, and that these Europeans merged with Native American peoples. A *Kirkus Reviews* critic commended the novel as "a fascinating look at a little-known side of American history." Claire Rosser in *Kliatt* called *Re-*

demption "serious historical fiction," adding that readers in search of an intricate fictitious world "will be richly rewarded." *School Library Journal* contributor Anna M. Nelson wrote that Chibbaro "weaves a fast-paced and engrossing story," and in *Horn Book,* Joanna Rudge Long suggested that the author "vivifies the book with inspired descriptions." Long concluded that Chibbaro's novel is an "engrossing adventure . . . both beautifully written and thought-provoking."

Chibbaro told *CA:* "My mother wrote, though she never published. At first, I rebelled against that fact, not wanting to be like her, but when I began to see how necessary writing was to me (like breathing), I started to take it seriously.

"Great storytellers, strong feelings, serious subjects, my artist partner, and nature (human and otherwise) all influence my work. I get up every morning, write for half an hour in my journal, and go to my desk. I sit there until the afternoon, either trying to create new work, or going over what I've written until I get the shape right, making sure I've not forgotten any plot point or character detail, or any other essential issue that makes a novel valid. Afterwards, I take a walk, or a nap, and think about what needs to be covered the next day. I work from five to seven days a week.

"The most surprising thing I have learned as a writer is that writing is the only thing I can't seem to conquer. Meaning that when I think I've accurately captured an emotion or a scene, upon looking at the work the next day, I am nearly always disappointed at how short of my goal I've fallen. That kind of challenge makes me want to try again and again until I get it right. So every day I'm surprised how difficult writing is.

"I hope that the years I spend writing one book will compound into a powerful experience for the reader who takes a night or a week to read it. I hope to move my readers the way I've been moved by books, to make them think in fresh, new ways about a subject they might not have otherwise considered. I hope always to write books that are meaningful."

BIOGRAPHICAL AND CRITICAL SOURCES:

PERIODICALS

Booklist, May 15, 2004, Hazel Rochman, review of *Redemption,* p. 1628.

Bulletin of the Center for Children's Books, June, 2004, Elizabeth Bush, review of *Redemption,* p. 412.

Horn Book, July-August, 2004, Joanna Rudge Long, review of *Redemption,* p. 449.

Kirkus Reviews, May 1, 2004, review of *Redemption,* p. 439.

Kliatt, May, 2004, Claire Rosser, review of *Redemption,* p. 6.

School Library Journal, August, 2004, Anna M. Nelson, review of *Redemption,* p. 116.

ONLINE

Julie Chibbaro Home Page, http://juliechibbaro.com (February 7, 2005).

*   *   *

CIMA, Annalisa 1941-

PERSONAL: Born January 20, 1941, in Milan, Italy. *Education:* Attended school in Lausanne, Switzerland, and Geneva, Italy; degree in philosophy.

ADDRESSES: Agent—c/o Author Mail, Valdonega, via Genova 17, 37020 Arbizzano, Verona, Italy.

CAREER: Poet, painter, and critic. Founder, with Cesare Segre, of Fondazione Schlesinger, Milan, Italy, 1978. *Exhibitions:* Galleria del Cavallino, Venice, Italy, 1965; National Gallery, London, England, 1967.

WRITINGS:

6 quadri, 3 disegni, 1 serigrafia, lavori in corso, All'Insegna del Pesce d'Oro (Milan, Italy), 1968.

Eugenio Montale, via Bigli, Milano, All'Insegna del Pesce d'Oro (Milan, Italy), 1968.

Allegria di Ungaretti, All'Insegna del Pesce d'Oro (Milan, Italy), 1969.

Terzo modo (poems), All'Insegna del Pesce d'Oro (Milan, Italy), 1969, revised by Mary de Rachewiltz and translated by Sizzo de Rachewiltz as *Third Way,* New Edition (New York, NY), 1977.

La Genesi e altre poesie, All'Insegna del Pesce d'Oro (Milan, Italy), 1971.

Incontro Palazzeschi, All'Insegna del Pesce d'Oro (Milan, Italy), 1972.

Incontro Montale, All'Insegna del Pesce d'Oro (Milan, Italy), 1973.

Immobilità (poems), All'Insegna del Pesce d'Oro (Milan, Italy), 1974.

Sesamon (poems), Guanda (Parma, Italy), 1977.

Ipotesi d'amore (poems), Garzanti (Milan, Italy), 1984, translated by Jonathan Galassi as *Hypotheses on Love,* Grenfell Press (New York, NY), 1989.

Ezra Pound a Venezia da "Cici" alla salute, All'Insegna del Pesce d'Oro (Milan, Italy), 1985.

Quattro tempi, Fondazione Schlesinger (Lugano, Switzerland), 1986.

Aegri somnia/Sognidi malato, Cima (Lugano, Switzerland), 1989.

Quattro canti, Stamperia Valdonega (Verona, Italy), 1993.

Eros e il tempo, Stamperia Valdonega (Verona, Italy), 1993.

Il tempo predatore (poems), illustrated by Eugenio Montale, All'Insegna del Pesce d'Oro (Milan, Italy), 1997, new edition, 2001.

Annalisa Cima (poems; in English and Italian), translated by Frederich G. Glomblik and others, Moncalieri (Turin, Italy), 1999.

Hai ripiegato l'ultimo pagina: pensieri per Vanni Scheiwiller, preface by Maria Corti, Interline (Knavery, Italy), 2000.

A Friedrich, Edizioni Pulcinoelefante (Osnago, Italy), 2000.

Un pensiero, Edizioni Pulcinoelefante (Osnago, Italy), 2000.

Frammento da una poesiea a Friedrich, Edizioni Pulcinoelefante (Osnago, Italy), 2000.

Per Maria Corti, Edizioni Pulcinoelefante (Osnago, Italy), 2000.

To Luchino Visconti, Edizioni Pulcinoelefante (Osnago, Italy), 2000.

Il corvo bianco, Edizioni Pulcinoelefante (Osnago, Italy), 2000.

Per Maria Corti, Edizioni Pulcinoelefante (Osnago, Italy), 2000.

L'amicizia, Edizioni Pulcinoelefante (Osnago, Italy), 2000.

Canto della sopravvivenza, Edizioni Pulcinoelefante (Osnago, Italy), 2001.

Siamo, Edizioni Pulcinoelefante (Osnago, Italy), 2001.

Canti della primavera e della sopravvivenza, Stamperia Valdonega (Verona, Italy), 2001.

Gigi Guadagnucci o della metamorfosi, Edizioni di Josef Weiss (Mendrisio, Italy), 2004.

Segno del domani, con uno schizzo di Mario Botta, Edizioni di Josef Weiss (Mendrisio, Italy), 2005.

L'impossibile diviene, Edizioni di Josef Weiss (Mendrisio, Italy), 2005.

EDITOR

Con Marianne Moore, All'Insegna del Pesce d'Oro (Milan, Italy), 1968.

G. F. Malipiero a Venezia, All'Insegna del Pesce d'Oro (Milan, Italy), 1968.

(With Cesare Segre) *Eugenio Montale, profilo di un autore,* Rizzoli (Milan, Italy), 1977.

Rivoluzione die fiori, Pegaso (Lugano, Switzerland), 1986.

Eugenio Montale, *Diario postumo: prima parte* (includes verse originally published in pamphlet form as *Poesi inedite di Eugenio Montale*), Mondadori (Milan, Italy), 1991, expanded edition published as *Diario postumo: 66 poesi e altre,* 1997.

OTHER

Also author of introduction for *Logogrifi '70,* by Ezio Gribaudo, All'Insegna del Pesce d'Oro (Milan, Italy), 1970; *Di domenica,* edited by Murilo Mendes, All'Insegna del Pesce d'Oro, 1974; and *Da gilli,* edited by Jorge Guillén, All'Insegna del Pesce d'Oro (Milan, Italy), 1975. Author of preface to *Vittorio Cavicchioni,* Magma (Rome, Italy), 1973; *Di Terzat,* Grillo (Genoa, Italy), 1979; and *Egocosmo,* by Edoardo Gatti, All'Insegna del Pesce d'Oro, 1980. Contributor of poems to periodicals, including *Poetry.*

SIDELIGHTS: An Italian poet whose knowledge of philosophy and music often imbues her verses, Annalisa Cima is also a co-founder of the Schlesinger Foundation, which strives to strengthen communications and learning about cultural and scientific information between Italy and the United States. She was entrusted by the late poet Eugenio Montale to publish the poet's works after his death, and she began editing releases of Montale's works in 1969. Cima's concern for maintaining an active dialogue on the arts also has led her to publish a number of books about literature, photography, and other fields, works that often include interviews with the artists.

As a poet, Cima made an early mark on the literary scene with the critically acclaimed collection *Terzo modo,* which was translated into English as *Third Way.* This collection expresses the poet's belief in the importance of knowing oneself, and contains poems that explore the theme of being, or essence. With the follow-up poetry book *Immobilità* Cima examines the problem of the absence of love. As *Dictionary of Literary Biography* contributor Clare de Cesare Huffman noted, the poet has spent much of her life moving from town to town; thus, there is sometimes a sense of a loss of center in her verses. As Huffman wrote, "There is much 'absence' in Cima's poetry: an absent mother and an absent geographical center." Not only are these themes expressed in *Immobilità,* but Cima's poems also reveal her discomfort with abstractions and her mistrust of language, which she feels can actually be an obstacle to the search for transcendence.

These notions are further explored in *Sesamon,* in which Cima seeks to find a "resolution in thoughts that come whole and inseparable from their form, without ever falling into the trap of transient contingency," explained Huffman. With *Sesamon,* according to Huffman, Cima finally succeeds in overcoming a sense of isolation. In the volume *Ipotesi d'amore* the poet "has moved into higher poetic spheres," according to Michela Montante in *World Literature Today.* The influence of other artists, especially musicians such as Austrian composer Wolfgang Amadeus Mozart, is clearly evident here, and the poet's experience in the arts and philosophy is used to poetic advantage, wrote Montante, who declared that *Ipotesi d'amore* is clear evidence of Cima's "indisputable artistic talent."

After Montale, who had served as the Schlesinger Foundation's honorary chair, selected Cima to be the caretaker of his yet-unpublished poems, Cima was key in publishing such works as *Diario postumo: prima parte* and *Diario postumo: 66 poesi e altre.* Peter Hainsworth, reviewing the former collection in the *Times Literary Supplement,* suggested that perhaps "the general premise" of the posthumous publication of Montale's poetry is to comment on what "is left of the culture of the past" that "is now fragments and shadows."

BIOGRAPHICAL AND CRITICAL SOURCES:

BOOKS

Dictionary of Literary Biography, Volume 128: *Twentieth-Century Italian Poets,* Gale (Detroit, MI), 1993.

PERIODICALS

PN Review, January, 1998, Peter Robinson, "Montale and the Muse," pp. 27-29.
Times Literary Supplement, October 4, 1991, Peter Hainsworth, "Montale and After," review of *Diario postumo: prima parte,* p. 32; October 17, 1997, Peter Hainsworth, "The Uprightness of the Poet," review of *Diario postumo: 66 poesi e altre,* p. 23.
World Literature Today, winter, 1986, Michela Montante, review of *Ipotesi d'amore,* p. 90.

* * *

CISNEROS, Pedro (Ruben) Treto 1939-

PERSONAL: Born August 1, 1939, in Ciudad Victoria, Tamaulipas, Mexico; son of Pedro Treto Ramirez (a government employee) and María de los Angeles Cisneros Alvarado (a homemaker); married María Estela Garza Elizondo (a homemaker), September 17, 1971; children: Pedro Ruben, Pedro Pablo, Luis Arturo. *Education:* Attended Universidad Nacional Autónoma de México, 1959-64. *Religion:* Roman Catholic.

ADDRESSES: Home—Paris 2433, Col. Cumbres 2do sect, Monterey, N.L., Mexico 64310. *Office*—Nueva Orleans 4235, Frac. Lincoln, Monterey, N.L., Mexico 64310.

CAREER: XET Monterey (radio station), Monterey, Mexico, news director, 1965-67; XET (radio and television station), Monterey, sports commentator, 1968-70; Sultanes (baseball club), Monterey, general manager, 1971-78; Saltillo (baseball club), Saltillo, Mexico, general manager, 1979-81; Sultanes, president, 1982—. Mexican League of Professional Baseball, president, 1983-99. Deportes Treto Cisneros, owner.

AWARDS, HONORS: Named executive of the year, 1977; inducted into a Mexican hall of fame, 1999; named guest of honor by more than a dozen Mexican cities.

WRITINGS:

50 aniversario de los Sultanes, REDSA, 1989.
Enciclopedia del beisbol mexicano, Asociación de Equipos Profesionales de Beisbol de la Liga Mexicana (Mexico City, Mexico), 1994, 6th edition, REDSA, 2002.

The Mexican League: Comprehensive Player Statistics, 1937-2001 (bilingual in Spanish and English), McFarland and Co. (Jefferson, NC), 2002.

Contributor to magazines, including *Super Hit.*

WORK IN PROGRESS: A history of the Diablos Rojos professional baseball team; revising *Enciclopedia del beisbol mexicano.*

* * *

CLARKE, Brian

PERSONAL: Male.

ADDRESSES: Home—101 Longden Rd., Shrewsbury SY3 9EB, England.

CAREER: Journalist and broadcaster. *Times,* London, England, fishing correspondent.

AWARDS, HONORS: BP Natural World Book Prize, Wildlife Trusts, 2000, and Author's Club Best First Novel Award, 2001, both for *The Stream.*

WRITINGS:

The Pursuit of Stillwater Trout (nonfiction), A & C Black (London, England), 1975.
(With John Goddard) *The Trout and the Fly: A New Approach* (nonfiction), Doubleday (Garden City, NY), 1980.
The Stream (fiction), Swan Hill Press (Shrewsbury, England), 2000, Overlook Press (Woodstock, NY) 2004.

Author of weekly fishing column for London *Times.* Contributor of essays to *Paul McCartney, Paintings,* Little, Brown (Boston, MA), 2000.

SIDELIGHTS: Brian Clarke's first novel, *The Stream,* was also the first novel to win the United Kingdom's BP Natural World Book Prize, given to works that add to knowledge of the environment and promote its protection. The book deals with the effect, over the course of five years, of both commercial development and natural forces on a stream flowing through a rural part of England. Clarke, a devotee of fly-fishing, tells his story from the point of view of the fish, birds, mammals, and even insects that inhabit the stream and its environs, as well as from the perspective of human characters. They are all affected as the stream suffers through a drought and becomes polluted due to new industry and population growth.

The Stream is a "magnetic first novel," written in "language as spare as a prose poem," in the words of a *Kirkus Reviews* critic. A *Publishers Weekly* reviewer, on the other hand, found it "deeply flawed" and populated by stereotypical characters, but successful "as a naturalistic treatise" because of its detailed description of the stream's ecosystem. Similarly, Jim Coan wrote in *Library Journal* that the novel is "intriguing," but "conveys less dramatic impact than might be expected." On the other hand, Terry Lawson, a commentator for the *Fish and Fly* Web site, thought that Clarke "writes with real knowledge and commitment," as well as "real passion." *Booklist* contributor Donna Seaman, however, deemed *The Stream* a "powerfully evocative tale" told "in concise, vivid chapters." Godfrey Smith, writing in London's *Sunday Times,* concluded that it is a "gracefully written novel" and "a parable for our times; it's also a serendipity and a delight."

BIOGRAPHICAL AND CRITICAL SOURCES:

PERIODICALS

Booklist, July, 2004, Donna Seaman, review of *The Stream,* p. 1816.
Kirkus Reviews, April 15, 2004, review of *The Stream,* p. 345.
Library Journal, July, 2004, Jim Coan, review of *The Stream,* p. 67.
Publishers Weekly, June 28, 2004, review of *The Stream,* p. 32.
Sunday Times (London, England), April 29, 2001, Godfrey Smith, "Rhythm of Life in a Trout Stream."

ONLINE

Fish and Fly Web site, http://www.fishandfly.co.uk/ (February 25, 2005), Terry Lawson, review of *The Stream.**

CLEGG, Eileen M. 1952-

PERSONAL: Born November 6, 1952, in Monterey, CA; daughter of Dave (a chemical technician) and Iris (a language teacher; maiden name, Ridgway) Conn; married George Klineman, February, 1979 (divorced, October, 1987); married James S. Clegg (a professor and scientist), May, 1994; children: (first marriage) Justin Thomas. *Ethnicity:* "Euro-American." *Education:* University of California, Berkeley, B.A. (philosophy), 1976. *Religion:* United Church of Christ.

ADDRESSES: Home—P.O. Box 762, Bodega Bay, CA 94923. *Office*—Santa Rosa Press Democrat, 427 Mendocino Ave., Santa Rosa, CA 95402. *Agent*—Meredith Bernstein, Meredith Bernstein Literary Agency, 2112 Broadway, Ste. 503A, New York, NY 10023. *E-mail*—eileenmc@aol.com.

CAREER: Santa Rosa Press Democrat, Santa Rosa, CA, staff writer, 1979—. Writing consultant.

AWARDS, HONORS: Chairman's Award, New York Times Co., 1999, for story "One Brave Heart"; Scripps Howard National Journalism Award (with others), 1999, for series "Lessons of Alaska."

WRITINGS:

(With Susan Swartz) *Goodbye Good Girl: Letting Go of the Rules and Taking Back Your Self-Esteem,* New Harbinger Publications (Oakland, CA), 1997.
(With Betty Frain) *Becoming a Wise Parent for Your Grown Child: How to Give Love and Support without Meddling,* New Harbinger Publications (Oakland, CA), 1997.
(With Margaret McConahey, Susan Swartz, and Deborah L. S. Sweitzer) *Claiming Your Creative Self: True Stories from the Everyday Lives of Women,* New Harbinger Publications (Oakland, CA), 1998.

Contributor to periodicals.

WORK IN PROGRESS: Research on "enlightened aging" and trends toward community-building for elders.

SIDELIGHTS: Eileen M. Clegg told *CA:* "I write for the joy of exploring and sharing new perspectives, finding great stories, and putting them in the context of the latest research to inform and entertain others (and myself!). I love collaborating with others. Being 'co-creatives' is enlightening and an excellent way for extroverts to play with ideas before committing them to paper.

"*Becoming a Wise Parent for Your Grown Child: How to Give Love and Support without Meddling* was inspired by my mother's success and good humor as a 'mom of moms.' When talking about her approach with others, I began to recognize it's a rare gift for parents of adults to have the confidence and know-how to stay involved without meddling. At the same time, psychologist Betty Frain saw in her practice how vital parents are to children of any age in helping out with problems, and we wanted to explore a new model for strong multi-generational families.

"Both *Goodbye Good Girl: Letting Go of the Rules and Taking Back Your Self-Esteem* and *Claiming Your Creative Self: True Stories from the Everyday Lives of Women* were opportunities to go deep into other women's stories for nuggets of insight for making the most of today's fast-changing social context. With a little guidance, we can make up our own rules and follow the intuitive muse, instead of conforming to arcane ideas that we must conform to the expectations of the amorphous 'them'."

*   *   *

CLEMEN, Jane 1951(?)-

PERSONAL: Born c. 1951. *Education:* Holds an R.D. and L.D.

ADDRESSES: Office—Mercy Medical Center, 1111 3rd St. SW, Dyersville, IA 52040. *Agent*—c/o Author Mail, Sourcebooks, Inc., 1935 Brookdale Rd., Ste. 139, Naperville, IL 60563.

CAREER: Mercy Medical Center, Dyersville, IA, 1979—, became nutrition director. Cofounder of Fight the Fat (nutrition program).

MEMBER: American Dietetic Association.

WRITINGS:

(With others) *The Town That Lost a Ton: How One Town Lost 3,998 Pounds . . . and How You Can Too!,* Sourcebooks, Inc. (Naperville, IL), 2002.

SIDELIGHTS: Dietitian Jane Clemen and two coworkers at Mercy Medical Center in Dyersville, Illinois, collaborated with freelance writer Daniel Myerson on *The Town That Lost a Ton: How One Town Lost 3,998 Pounds . . . and How You Can Too!* to document their success with a weight-loss program they founded in 1998. She and physical therapist Bobbi Schell and director of marketing Dianne Kirkwood discovered that half of the health problems in their community were weight-related. They were hoping to begin with one hundred people, but 383 people signed up to participate in the program and actually lost nearly two tons.

Their success is attributed to the use of a buddy system to stay on course. Participants were separated into small groups of six to ten and competed with each other to see which could lose the most. The book advises that dieters should enjoy such pleasures as massage, gardening, and music to relieve stress and also includes basic good sense tips and recipes. In reviewing *The Town That Lost a Ton, Booklist* contributor Barbara Jacobs wrote that "every one of the ten chapters here is filled with great advice and sound nutrition tips."

The ten-week program expanded as more people participated from Dyersville and surrounding towns. Activities included exercise classes, dance, and power walking. Not quite half have kept the weight off, and Clemen, Schell, and Kirkwood are concentrating on that aspect of the program. They have also benefited, each having lost weight on the way to achieving their personal goals.

BIOGRAPHICAL AND CRITICAL SOURCES:

BOOKS

Clemen, Jane, and others, *The Town That Lost a Ton: How One Town Lost 3,998 Pounds . . . and How You Can Too!,* Sourcebooks (Naperville, IL), 2002.

PERIODICALS

Booklist, February 15, 2002, Barbara Jacobs, review of *The Town That Lost a Ton: How One Town Lost 3,998 Pounds . . . and How You Can Too!,* p. 979.

Publishers Weekly, February 18, 2002, review of *The Town That Lost a Ton,* p. 93.

ONLINE

USA Today Online, http://www.usatoday.com/ (February 19, 2002), Nanci Hellmich, review of *The Town That Lost a Ton.**

*   *   *

COBBLE, Dorothy Sue 1949-

PERSONAL: Born June 28, 1949, in Atlanta, GA; married, 1997; children: three. *Education:* University of California, Berkeley, B.A. (with honors), 1972; San Francisco State University, M.A., 1976; Stanford University, Ph.D., 1986.

ADDRESSES: Office—School of Management and Labor Relations, Rutgers University, 50 Labor Center Way, New Brunswick, NJ 08903. *E-mail*—cobble@rci.rutgers.edu.

CAREER: Women's History Collection, Mills College, Oakland, CA, archivist, 1976-77; San José City College and City College of San Francisco, San Francisco, CA, instructor in labor studies, 1977-80, instructor in labor studies and chairman of department at City College, 1980-86; Stanford University, Stanford, CA, instructor in history, 1979; Rutgers University School of Management and Labor Relations, New Brunswick, NJ, assistant professor of labor studies, history, and women's studies, 1986-92, founder and director of Center for Women and Work, 1992-96, associate professor of labor studies, 1992-2000, professor of labor studies and employee relations, 2000—, director of Institute for Research on Women, 2001-04. Lecturer at numerous symposia and conferences on labor issues. Member of Gender Equity Task Force, New Jersey State Employment and Training Commission, 1993-94; member of executive board, Industrial Relations Research Association, 1997-2000; member of board of trustees, National Labor College/George Meany Center, 1998-2001. Consultant to films and videos, including *The Tillie Olsen Film Project, The Women's Revolution: A Documentary,* and *Transforming America: U.S. History since 1877.*

MEMBER: American Historical Association, Organization of American Historians, American Association of University Professors.

AWARDS, HONORS: Herbert A. Gutman Book Prize, 1992, for *Dishing It Out: Waitresses and Their Unions in the Twentieth Century;* research grants from numerous foundations, including New Jersey Historical Commission, 1987-88, Henry Kaiser Family Foundation, 1989-90, National Endowment for the Humanities, 1989-90, American Historical Association, 1989-90, American Council of Learned Societies, 1989-90, Women's Bureau, U.S. Department of Labor, 1993, George Meany Center for Labor Studies, 1994, Fund for Labor Relations Studies, 1995, and Social Science Research Council, 2003-04; Woodrow Wilson fellowship, 1999-2000.

WRITINGS:

Dishing It Out: Waitresses and Their Unions in the Twentieth Century, University of Illinois Press (Urbana, IL), 1991.

(Editor) *Women and Unions: Forging a Partnership,* Cornell University Press (Ithaca, NY), 1993.

The Other Women's Movement: Workplace Justice and Social Rights in Modern America, Princeton University Press (Princeton, NJ), 2004.

The Sex of Class: Women and America's New Labor Movements, Cornell University Press (Ithaca, NY), in press.

Contributor of chapters to books, including Ronald Filippelli, editor, *Labor History in the United States,* Garland Press (New York, NY), 1990; Ava Baron, editor, *Work Engendered: Toward a New History of American Labor,* Cornell University Press (Ithaca, NY), 1991; Joanne Meyerowitz, editor, *Not June Cleaver: Women and Gender in Postwar America,* Temple University Press (Philadelphia, PA), 1994; Claire Moses and Heidi Hartmann, editors, *U.S.*

Women in Struggle: A Feminist Studies Anthology, University of Illinois Press (Urbana, IL), 1995; Cameron Macdonald and Carmen Sirianni, editors, *Working in the Service Society,* Temple University Press (Philadelphia, PA), 1996; Mary Hartman, editor, *Talking about Leadership: Conversations with Powerful Women,* Rutgers University Press (New Brunswick, NJ), 1999; Lowell Turner and others, editors, *Rekindling the Movement: Labor's Quest for Relevance in the Twenty-first Century,* Cornell University Press (Ithaca, NY), 2001; F. Colgan and Sue Ledwith, editors, *Gender, Diversity, and Trade Unions: International Perspectives,* Routledge Press (London, England), 2002; Eileen Boris and Nelson Lichtenstein, editors, *Major Problems in the History of American Workers,* 2nd edition, Houghton Mifflin (Boston, MA), 2002.

Member of editorial boards, including *Labor: Studies in Working-Class History in the Americas, International Labor and Working-Class History,* and *Feminist Studies.* Contributor of scholarly papers to numerous periodicals, including *New Labor Forum, Labor History, National Education Association Higher Education Journal, Labor Law Journal, Industrial Relations, Dissent,* and *Journal of American History.*

WORK IN PROGRESS: (With Michael Merrill) *Samuel Gompers: An Intellectual Biography; Esther Peterson and Trans-Atlantic Feminism.*

SIDELIGHTS: Dorothy Sue Cobble is an historian who focuses on the study of women's labor movements in the United States during the twentieth century. Her work covers aspects of women's studies, labor history, and the intersection between the feminist movement of the late twentieth century and the attempts by women to alter their working environments through unions. To quote Julie Greene in *Labor History,* Cobble's works have "influenced profoundly the way we understand U.S. labor history, and particularly the nature of craft unionism and its relationship to politics and the state." Eileen Boris, writing in the *Women's Review of Books,* stated that Cobble "has recovered, in the politics and thought of . . . trade unionists, a feminist legacy that in its embrace of female difference refused to conform to 'men's ways.' She provides a usable past for those of us who wish to revalue women's labors."

Cobble's *Dishing It Out: Waitresses and Their Unions in the Twentieth Century* studies the changing patterns of unionization among female restaurant workers from the beginning of the twentieth century through into the 1970s. According to Barbara M. Posadas in the *Journal of Urban History,* the book contributes "substantially to acknowledging the diversity of the white, female, paid labor force in early twentieth-century America" while also raising "tantalizing questions concerning the relationship between the working and middle classes in the early twentieth century." *Labor Studies Journal* contributor Colin J. Davis felt that the book "successfully provides the reader with a critical insight into female working-class life and action."

Women and Unions: Forging a Partnership, edited by Cobble, collects a wide variety of essays and interviews on the topics of women's issues in the workplace, the reinvigorization of the labor movement, and successes and failures in union activity among women. The book seeks to define gender-related concerns for collective bargaining, including family leave, the "glass ceiling," and the changing nature of paid employment. "*Women and Unions* is an informative, well-written, and masterfully edited collection of essays on women's workplace and union issues," wrote Francine Moccio in the *Industrial and Labor Relations Review.* "The volume's contributors address issues that are critical to women's workplace progress, and they advance the growing scholarship on women's contemporary relationship to work and unionism." In *Economic Geography,* Lee Lucas Berman concluded that Cobble "has succeeded in opening up a dialogue that crosses disciplines and professions, effectively bringing together activists of all kinds. . . . *Women and Unions* provides a wealth of information, as well as practical guidelines, about the successful implementation of certain labor strategies. As such, it is indispensable to researchers, feminist activists, and labor organizers."

In *The Other Women's Movement: Workplace Justice and Social Rights in Modern America* Cobble examines contributions to the labor movement by women and shows how women's labor unions sometimes differ with the broader, white-collar goals of the feminist movement. Janice Dunham in *Library Journal* found the work a "solid argument for the value of 'the other women's movement.'" In her review of the book, Boris observed that "Cobble's stunning reinterpretation persuasively shows that we've been looking in the wrong place for a mass movement after suffrage and before women's liberation. She names this movement 'labor feminism.'"

BIOGRAPHICAL AND CRITICAL SOURCES:

PERIODICALS

Dollars & Sense, July-August, 1994, Rose Batt, review of *Women and Unions: Forging a Partnership,* p. 34.

Economic Geography, April, 1995, Lee Lucas Berman, review of *Women and Unions,* p. 208.

Industrial and Labor Relations Review, April, 1996, Francine Moccio, review of *Women and Unions,* p. 554.

Journal of Urban History, September, 1997, Barbara M. Posadas, review of *Dishing It Out: Waitresses and Their Unions in the Twentieth Century,* p. 777.

Labor History, May, 1999, Julie Greene, "Response: Reassessing Gompers and the AFL," p. 201.

Labor Studies Journal, fall, 1993, Colin J. Davis, review of *Dishing It Out,* p. 73; fall, 1994, Peggy Kahn, review of *Women and Unions,* p. 72.

Library Journal, October 1, 2003, Janice Dunham, review of *The Other Women's Movement: Workplace Justice and Social Rights in Modern America,* p. 102.

Reviews in American History, December, 2004, Annelise Orleck, "Feminism Rewritten: Reclaiming the Activism of Working-Class Women," p. 591.

Women's Review of Books, May, 2004, Eileen Boris, "Labor Feminist Foremothers," p. 18.*

*   *   *

COCHRAN, Johnnie L., Jr. 1937-2005

OBITUARY NOTICE— See index for *CA* sketch: Born October 2, 1937, in Shreveport, LA; died of a brain tumor March 29, 2005, in Los Angeles, CA. Lawyer and author. Cochran was a high-profile attorney known for defending such well-known people as Black Panther member Elmer Pratt and football player O. J. Simpson. He earned a degree in business administration from the University of California at Los Angeles in 1959 before studying law at Loyola University, where he graduated in 1962. Hired by the city of Los Angeles's attorney's office, he worked on small cases before gaining some attention for filing an obscenity lawsuit against comedian Lenny Bruce, which Cochran lost. In 1966, he helped found and became a partner in his own firm, Cochran, Atkins, and Evans, where he specialized in brutality cases and in 1972 was on the defense team for Pratt, who had been charged with murdering a school teacher. Although Pratt was convicted, in 1997 Cochran convinced a judge to release him on grounds that important evidence had been concealed by the prosecution. Most of Cochran's fame came in the 1990s, when he became known as a defense attorney who took on cases for famous celebrities, such as the 1994 Michael Jackson trial in which the attorney successfully got the pop singer acquitted of child molestation charges. The next year, Cochran was on the team of lawyers who defended former football star O. J. Simpson, who had been charged with killing his former wife and her friend. During the trial, much of which was televised, Cochran managed to raise reasonable doubt in the jury's minds, accusing a police investigator and witness of racism and declaring that a key piece of evidence—a glove found at the scene—did not fit Simpson's hand. Simpson was found innocent in criminal court. More recently, in 2001, Cochran successfully defended rap star Sean Combs, who had been charged with illegal weapons possession. Often parodied for his flamboyant use of language and clever defense maneuvers, Cochran took the jibes in stride and noted that his success in big cases such as Simpson's allowed him to pursue less profitable cases defending people who had little money for legal fees. Founding the Cochran Firm in 1997, Cochran was not ashamed of spending lavishly on himself, and became a familiar face as a television host for Court TV and other programs. He was the author of two autobiographies: *Journey to Justice* (1996) and *A Lawyer's Life* (2002).

OBITUARIES AND OTHER SOURCES:

BOOKS

Cochran, Johnnie L., Jr., and Tim Rutten, *Journey to Justice,* Ballantine Books (New York, NY), 1996.

Cochran, Johnnie L., Jr., and Tim Rutten, *A Lawyer's Life,* Thomas Dunne Books (New York, NY), 2002.

PERIODICALS

New York Times, March 30, 2005, p. A19.

Times (London, England), March 31, 2005, p. 59.

Washington Post, March 30, 2005, pp. A1, A5.

COFFEY, Jan
    See McGOLDRICK, James A. and McGOLD-RICK, Nikoo

* * *

COLE, Stephen 1971-

PERSONAL: Born 1971, in Bedfordshire, England. *Education:* Graduate of University of East Anglia.

ADDRESSES: Home—Aylesbury, Buckinghamshire, England. *Agent*—c/o Author Mail, Bloomsbury Publishing, 38 Soho Square, London W1D 3HB, England.

CAREER: Writer. British Broadcasting Corporation, London, England, editor and writer of children's magazines, commissioning editor of science-fiction titles for BBC Worldwide, 1997, creative editor of pre-teen titles; Ladybird Books, London, former managing editor; Simon & Schuster, London, senior editor, then consulting editor, 2001; Rocket Editorial Ltd., founder, 2002.

WRITINGS:

Timeless (based on *Dr. Who* television series), BBC Books (London, England), 2003.
The Monsters Inside (based on *Dr. Who* television series), BBC Books (London, England), 2005.
To the Slaughter (based on *Dr. Who* television series), BBC Books (London, England), 2005.
Madagascar: Essential Guide (based on the animated film), Dorling Kindersley (London, England), 2005.

Author of other books for children, including film and television adaptations and spin-offs.

"WERELING" TRILOGY

Wounded, Razorbill (New York, NY), 2005.
Prey, Razorbill (New York, NY), 2005.
Resurrection, Razorbill (New York, NY), 2005.

WORK IN PROGRESS: A further teen title, due in 2006; the children's book *Astrosaurs,* for Simon & Schuster, 2006.

SIDELIGHTS: A children's book author and the founder of Rocket Editorial Ltd., Stephen Cole is the author of the popular "Wereling" trilogy, which includes the novels *Wounded, Prey,* and *Resurrection.* Cole established himself as an editor and writer in the London publishing industry by holding a series of posts at BBC Books, and after several years decided to embark on a freelance writing/editing career focusing on children's literature. In an interview on *Bloomsbury.com* Cole admitted: "I've always loved writing, and always wanted to do it for a living. I just love to write anything, from novels to articles to songs to puzzles to emails!" Many of Cole's other published works are based on films and television programs; his *The Monsters Inside,* a novel for teens based on Great Britain's popular *Dr. Who* television program, was a top sci-fi/ fantasy bestseller in 2005.

Cole's "Wereling" series opens with *Wounded,* which follows seventeen-year-old Kate Folan and sixteen-year-old Tom Anderson as they work out their feelings for each other while a dark secret keeps them apart. Kate hails from a family of werewolves, although she will not undergo the wolfen transformation unless she mates with a male werewolf. When her family finds and rescues a mortal teen who has been wounded during an accident in the woods, Kate fall for the young mortal. The news that Kate's family has "turned" Tom comes as a shock to both teens; The boy, Tom, is none too happy to discover that he is now a werewolf, while Kate is thrown into an emotional tailspin. Rather than either ignoring their growing feelings for each other or succumbing to their supernatural fate, Kate and Tom decide to search for a third option: a cure.

As the "Wereling" trilogy continues, Kate and Tom's joint quest leads them far beyond the desire to consummate their relationship. Ultimately, through the course of *Prey* and *Resurrection,* they learn of the growing power of the lupine community. When a sixteenth-century corpse unearthed in a German peat bog is rumored to be that of the first-ever werewolf, lupine powers amass even further, forcing the teens to join the struggle to end a revolution that threatens all human life on Earth.

Praising the first volume in the "Wereling" trilogy, *School Library Journal* contributor Anna M. Nelson wrote that Cole injects his story with "fast-paced action, horror, intrigue, plot twists, and a touch of romance," creating a mix that is "sure to please horror fans." In *Kliatt* Joseph DeMarco praised *Wounded* as "a solid read" that contains enough entertainment "to please even tough customers."

BIOGRAPHICAL AND CRITICAL SOURCES:

PERIODICALS

Kliatt, May, 2005, Joseph DeMarco, review of *Wounded,* p. 32.
School Library Journal, April, 2005, Anna M. Nelson, review of *Wounded,* p. 130.
Voice of Youth Advocates, April, 2005, review of *Wounded,* p. 10.

ONLINE

Bloomsbury Web site, http://www.bloomsbury.com/ (February 9, 2005), "Stephen Cole."
Wereling Web site, http://www.wereling.com/ (August 20, 2005), interview with Cole.

*   *   *

CONNELLY, Neil O., Jr.
    See CONNELLY, Neil (O'Boyle)

*   *   *

CONNELLY, Neil (O'Boyle)
    (Neil O. Connelly, Jr.)

PERSONAL: Male.

ADDRESSES: Office—Department of Languages, Mc-Neese State University, 4205 Ryan St., St. Charles, LA 70609. *Agent—* E-mail—connelly@mail.mcneese.edu.

CAREER: McNeese State University, Lake Charles, LA, associate professor.

WRITINGS:

(As Neil O. Connelly, Jr.; Reteller) Charles Dickens, *A Christmas Carol* (juvenile; "Christmas Pop-up Treasury" series), Ottenheimer Publishers (Baltimore, MD), 1993.
St. Michael's Scales (young-adult novel), Arthur A. Levine Books (New York, NY), 2002.
Buddy Cooper Finds a Way (adult novel), Simon & Schuster (New York, NY), 2004.

Contributor of short fiction to periodicals, including *Southeast Review, Review,* and *Yalobusha Review.*

SIDELIGHTS: The title of Neil Connelly's young-adult novel *St. Michael's Scales* refers to the scales held by the Catholic St. Michael, with which he weighs the worth of the souls waiting to gain entrance to heaven. Michael was also the name of fifteen-year-old Keegan Flannery's twin brother, who died during their premature birth. Keegan has carried the guilt of that death all of his life, while around him his parents' marriage dissolved, his older brother ran away, and his mother, after attempting suicide, was committed to a mental institution. Keegan feels that the scales, for him, will be empty, and so he too plans to commit suicide on his sixteenth birthday, in atonement for what he perceives to be his sins. However, he also worries that this act will exempt him from gaining a place in heaven due to St. Michael's intercession.

In the novel, Connelly portrays the guilt-obsessed culture of a 1970s Catholic school, in this case Our Lady of Perpetual Help, a crumbling building Keegan plans to burn down when he takes his own life. When the wrestling coach convinces him to fill an empty place on the wrestling team, however the scrawny Keegan agrees, feeling that the pain will be a sort of penance. After a harsh initiation, he comes to feel that he finally belongs, and begins to wrestle his inner demons as much as his opponents.

A *Publishers Weekly* critic felt that wrestling "provides a good parallel—both the weighing in ritual and the inherent struggle." Janet Hilbun wrote in *School Library Journal* that Connelly's "is a dark story, but one that is ultimately hopeful," while a *Kirkus Reviews* contributor wrote that the author "succeeds brilliantly at putting readers into the disturbed and tortured mind of its lonely protagonist." *Kliatt* reviewer Paula Rohrlick felt that "those with a Catholic background will probably best be able to relate to the religious guilt and references, but this is a story that can be appreciated by many readers."

The hero of Connelly's adult novel *Buddy Cooper Finds a Way* is the Unknown Kentucky Terror, a wrestler whose role in the ring is to lose all of his fights. Buddy is a loser in other aspects of life, as well: His wife, Alix, left him for Trevor, although she sometimes stops by for sex. Finally, Buddy gets his big chance when the head of the wrestling federation decides that he should win a match. Before it can happen, however, a fan goes on a shooting spree, hitting Buddy and two other wrestlers and killing the referee. Buddy returns to "loser" mode when he uses this tragedy to fake amnesia in order to win back Alix and his daughter. Other characters include wrestler Hardy Appleseed, who receives messages from Jesus through his hearing aid, and a group of homeless men who live in the condemned church next door. An asteroid the size of Texas that is hurtling toward Earth also figures into the plot.

Booklist critic John Green commented that the "fast-paced tragicomic plot and the eccentric cast" in *Buddy Cooper Finds a Way* "give energy to this thoughtful first novel." A *Publishers Weekly* contributor called the novel "a comic romp with a darker side," adding that it is "crafty, magical, [and] utterly enjoyable."

BIOGRAPHICAL AND CRITICAL SOURCES:

PERIODICALS

Booklist, March 15, 2002, John Green, review of *St. Michael's Scales*, p. 1251.
Entertainment Weekly, July 9, 2004, Adam B. Vary, review of *Buddy Cooper Finds a Way*, p. 94.
Horn Book, May-June, 2002, Lauren Adams, review of *St. Michael's Scales*, p. 325.
Kirkus Reviews, February 15, 2002, review of *St. Michael's Scales*, p. 252; May 1, 2004, review of *Buddy Cooper Finds a Way*, p. 409.
Kliatt, March, 2002, Paula Rohrlick, review of *St. Michael's Scales*, p. 10.
Publishers Weekly, March 25, 2002, review of *St. Michael's Scales*, p. 66; June 7, 2004, review of *Buddy Cooper Finds a Way*, p. 30.
San Francisco Chronicle, July 25, 2004, Jonathan Kiefer, review of *Buddy Cooper Finds a Way*, p. M3.
School Library Journal, June, 2002, Janet Hilbun, review of *St. Michael's Scales*, p. 134.
Times Picayune (New Orleads, LA), August 15, 2004, David Winkler-Schmit, review of *Buddy Cooper Finds a Way*, p. 6.

*　　*　　*

CONSTANTINESCU, Gheorghe M(ircea) 1932-

PERSONAL: Born January 20, 1932, in Bucharest, Romania; naturalized U.S. citizen, 1989; son of Mircea (a surgeon and obstetrician) and Elisabeta Constantinescu; married Elena Sanda, November, 1956 (marriage ended, February, 1970); married Ileana Anghelina (a clinical instructor), March 1, 1979; children: Alexandru Razvan, Adina. *Ethnicity:* "Romanian." *Education:* Faculty of Veterinary Medicine, Bucharest, Romania, D.V.M., 1955, D.M.V., 1964. *Religion:* "Orthodox Catholic." *Hobbies and other interests:* Making drawings (pen and ink, pencil, water color, and oil), sculptures, and photography.

ADDRESSES: Home—5800 Spiva Crossing Rd., Hallsville, MO 65255. *Office*—College of Veterinary Medicine, University of Missouri, 1600 East Rollins, Columbia, MO 65211-5120; fax: 573-884-6890. *E-mail*—constantinescu@missouri.edu.

CAREER: Faculty of Veterinary Medicine, Bucharest, Romania, laboratory chief, 1955; Zootechnical Research Institute, Bucharest, scientific researcher, 1958-59; Zoological Garden, Bucharest, veterinarian, 1959-62; circuit veterinarian in County Panciu, Romania, 1962-63, vice president of county agriculture council and head of breeding section, 1963-65; Faculty of Veterinary Medicine, Timisoara, Romania, associate professor of anatomy and head of department, 1965-82, associate dean, 1976-77; University of Missouri, Columbia, associate professor, 1984-92, professor of veterinary anatomy, 1992—, member of Council on International Initiatives, 2000—. Agronomic Institute, Timisoara, scientific secretary, 1974-76; Romanian College of Veterinary Pathologists, certified by Veterinary Diagnostic Laboratory, 1995. International Committee on Veterinary Gross Anatomical

Nomenclature, member, 1988—; Missouri Cattle Health Clinic and Program, member of faculty operational committee, 1997—.

MEMBER: International Society of Vertebrate Morphologists, World Association of Veterinary Anatomists, European Association of Veterinary Anatomists, Federation of American Societies for Experimental Biology, American Association of Veterinary Anatomists, American Association of Anatomists, Association of Medical Illustrators, National Computer Graphics Association, Union of Societies of Medical Sciences in Romania, Society of Veterinary Medicine in Romania, Circle of Neuropathology of the Medical Sciences Academy in Romania, Romanian Veterinary Medical Association (honorary member), Sigma Xi, Phi Zeta (Pi chapter).

AWARDS, HONORS: Doctor Honoris Causa, University of Agricultural Sciences of Banat, 1992, and University of Agronomical Sciences of Bucharest, 1995; grant from National Institutes of Health, 1998-2003; Outstanding Achievement Award, American Association of Veterinary Anatomists, 1999; honorary diploma, Faculty of Veterinary Medicine, Timisoara, Romania, 2002.

WRITINGS:

The Comparative Anatomy of Domestic Animals: Dissection Guide of Topographic Anatomy, Institutul Agronomic (Timisoara, Romania), 1967, 2nd edition, 1968.

The Anatomy and Physiology of Domestic Animals, Agro-Silvica de Stat (Bucharest, Romania), 1967, 2nd edition, Ceres (Bucharest, Romania), 1980.

The Comparative Anatomy of Domestic Animals, Agro-Silvica de Stat (Bucharest, Romania), 1969.

Textbook of Anatomy, Histology, and Embryology, Institutul Agronomic (Timisoara, Romania), 1971.

Textbook of Comparative Anatomy, Institutul Agronomic (Timisoara, Romania), volume one: *Osteology,* 1971, volume two: *Arthro-Myology,* 1973, volume three: *Neuroendocrine System,* 1973, volume four: *Splanchnology,* 1974.

The Comparative Anatomy and Physiology, Ceres (Bucharest, Romania), 1972.

(with E. Pastea, E. Muresianu, and V. Cotofan) *The Comparative and Topographic Anatomy of Domestic Animals,* Didactica si Pedagogica (Bucharest, Romania), 1978.

(With C. Radu and R. Palicica) *Dissection Guide of Topographic Anatomy,* Institutul Agronomic (Timisoara, Romania), 1979.

(With C. Radu and R. Palicica) *The Topographic Anatomy of Domestic Mammals,* Facla (Timisoara, Romania), 1982.

Clinical Dissection Guide for Large Animals, C. V. Mosby (St. Louis, MO), 1991, 2nd edition (with I. A. Constantinescu) published as *Clinical Dissection Guide for Large Animals: Horse and Large Ruminants,* 2003.

(With others) *Illustrated Veterinary Anatomical Nomenclature,* Ferdinand Enke Verlag (Stuttgart, Germany), 1992.

Guide to Regional Ruminant Anatomy Based on the Dissection of the Goat, Iowa State University Press (Ames, IA), 2001.

Clinical Anatomy for Small-Animal Practitioners, Iowa State University Press (Ames, IA), 2002.

(With Despina Tudor) *Nomina Anatomica Veterinaria: International and Romanian Terminology* (bilingual edition), Editura Vergiliu (Bucharest, Romania), 2002.

Author of scientific books published in Romanian. Contributor to books, including *Current Techniques in Small Animal Surgery,* edited by M. J. Bojrad, 3rd edition, Lea & Febiger (Media, PA), 1990. Contributor to scientific journals in the United States and abroad.

WORK IN PROGRESS: Comparative Reproductive Biology, completion expected in 2005; *Clinical Anatomy for Equine Practitioners,* 2005.

*   *   *

COOPER, Lynda Sue
See SANDOVAL, Lynda

*   *   *

CORREA, Raul 1961-

PERSONAL: Born 1961. *Education:* Columbia University, B.A., M.F.A.

ADDRESSES: Agent—c/o Author Mail, HarperCollins, 10 East 53rd St., 7th Fl., New York, NY 10022.

CAREER: Writer and educator. Taught writing to prisoners on Rikers Island, NY, and to high school students in a program at Columbia University; guest artist, Yaddo. *Military service:* U.S. Army, 1980-83; sergeant in 82nd Airborne Division.

WRITINGS:

I Don't Know but I've Been Told (novel), HarperCollins (New York, NY), 2002.

SIDELIGHTS: Raul Correa joined the U.S. Army at the age of eighteen and became a peacetime paratrooper. Correa's novel *I Don't Know but I've Been Told* is about a group of paratroopers stationed at Fort Bragg, North Carolina. The unnamed protagonist and his buddies have become soldiers in order to escape poverty and prison in a time when young men were allowed to avoid both by putting on a uniform. The story begins fifteen years later with the protagonist recalling his service during the 1980s as he recovers from a breakdown and time spent at the federal penitentiary in Fort Leavenworth, Kansas. All that keeps him going now as he wanders the streets of New York are a copy of *Huckleberry Finn*, a love letter from a pretty prostitute named Paola who he met in Panama, and his memories.

The Recon Dogs, as they were known, blow their paychecks on mescaline and marijuana, and sell plasma and stolen goods to fund their binges, including "art" they steal from motel rooms. They rely on drugs to help them jump as they undergo training in Panama and then back at Fort Bragg, where they become involved with Mr. Big, an operative who buys ordnance they steal from the base.

Reviewing Correa's novel, Ihsan Taylor wrote in the *New York Times Book Review* that "the glimpses of the languorous side of military life are frank and funny. Some of the dialogue has just the right pitch, balancing innocence and savvy." *Booklist* contributor Carrie Bissey felt that "the reward is in the pitch-perfect dialogue and in the picture Correa paints of military life." *USA Today* contributor J. Ford Huffman cited some "classic moments, such as the time Everysoldier gets back at a salesman by putting a bomb in a used-car lot." Robert J. Hughes wrote in the *Wall Street*

Journal that although *I Don't Know but I've Been Told* is based on Correa's own life, he "has given the book the full dimensions of an imaginative work, made vivid by the talents of a real writer."

BIOGRAPHICAL AND CRITICAL SOURCES:

PERIODICALS

Booklist, March 1, 2002, Carrie Bissey, review of *I Don't Know but I've Been Told*, p. 1089.
Kirkus Reviews, February 1, 2002, review of *I Don't Know but I've Been Told*, p. 121.
New York Times Book Review, Ihsan Taylor, review of *I Don't Know but I've Been Told*, p. 24.
Publishers Weekly, February 18, 2002, review of *I Don't Know but I've Been Told*, p. 71.
USA Today, May 16, 2002, J. Ford Huffman, review of *I Don't Know but I've Been Told*, p. D4.
Village Voice, May 7, 2002, Taylor Antrim, review of *I Don't Know but I've Been Told*, p. 78.
Wall Street Journal, March 15, 2002, Robert J. Hughes, review of *I Don't Know but I've Been Told*, p. W8.
Washington Post Book World, June 16, 2002, Bill Kent, review of *I Don't Know but I've Been Told*, p. 15.*

*　　*　　*

COSTAS, Bob
See COSTAS, Robert (Quinlan)

*　　*　　*

COSTAS, Robert (Quinlan) 1952-
(Bob Costas)

PERSONAL: Born March 22, 1952, in New York, NY; son of John George (an electrical engineer) and Jayne (Quinlan) Costas; married Carol Randall Krummenacher, June 24, 1983 (separated, 2001); children: Keith Michael, Taylor. *Education:* Attended Syracuse University.

ADDRESSES: Home—St. Louis, MO. *Office*—NBC Sports, 30 Rockefeller Plaza, New York, NY 10112. *Agent*—Brillstein-Grey Entertainment, 9150 Wilshire Blvd., Ste. 350, Beverly Hills, CA 90212.

CAREER: Sports journalist. Appeared in television series, including (as baseball announcer) *Game of the Week,* National Broadcasting Company (NBC), 1983-89; (as host) *NFL Live,* NBC, 1984-93; (as host) *Later with Bob Costas,* NBC, 1988-94; *The NBC Saturday Sports Showcase,* NBC, 1990; (as host) *NBA Showtime,* NBC, 1991-97; (as correspondent) *Dateline NBC,* NBC, 1992—; (as correspondent) *Now,* NBC, 1993-94; (as correspondent) *The Today Show,* NBC, 1995—; (as host, with Katie Couric) *Internight,* MSNBC, 1996; and (as host) *On the Record with Bob Costas,* Home Box Office (HBO), 2001—. Host of radio series, including *Costas Coast-to-Coast,* syndicated until 1994, Major Talk Radio Network, 1996; *The Sporting News Report;* and *Sports Flashback.* Appeared in television miniseries *Baseball,* Public Broadcasting System (PBS), 1994. Appeared in television specials, including (as moderator) *NFL '85,* NBC, 1985; (as host) *SportsWorld Looks at Sports Humor,* NBC, 1986; (as studio anchor) *1988 Winter Olympic Games,* American Broadcasting Companies (ABC), 1988; (as pregame host, with others) *1988 World Series,* NBC, 1988; (as commentator), *SportsWorld 10th Anniversary Special,* NBC, 1988; (as anchor) *1988 Summer Olympic Games,* NBC, 1988; *Friday Night Surprise!,* NBC, 1989; (as pregame host) *1989 Major League All-Star Game,* NBC, 1989; (as host) *One Year: Later),* NBC, 1989; (as host) *Two Years: Later,* NBC, 1990; *NBC All-Star Stay in School Jam,* NBC/Nickelodeon/Turner Network Television (TNT), 1991; (as host) *Play by Play: A History of Sports Television,* HBO, 1991; (as himself) *Diamonds on the Silver Screen,* syndicated, 1992; (as primetime host) *The 1992 Summer Olympics,* NBC, 1992; (as host) *An Olympic Christmas: Barcelona Memories,* NBC, 1992; (as host) *Barcelona '92: A New World Gathers,* NBC, 1992; *Five Years Later . . . with Bob Costas,* NBC, 1993; *Bob Hope: The First Ninety Years,* NBC, 1993; (as host) *Super Bowl Live,* NBC, 1993; (as host) *One Child, One Dream: The Horatio Alger Awards,* NBC, 1993; (as host) *Last Call! A Cheers' Celebration,* NBC, 1993; (as host, with others) *One on One: Classic Television Interviews,* CBS, 1993; (as himself) *TV Guide: 40th Anniversary Special,* 1993; (as host) *Forty for the Ages: Sports Illustrated's 40th Anniversary Special,* NBC, 1994; (as host) *The Horatio Alger Awards,* 1994; *Fields of Fire: Sports in the '60s,* HBO, 1995; (as host) *Great Moments of Discovery,* Discovery Channel, 1995; (as host) *The Opening Ceremonies of the 1995 Special Olympics World Games,* NBC, 1995; *The Ultimate TV Trivia Challenge,* ABC, 1995; *Baseball-a-Palooza II,* Comedy Central, 1996; *NBA at Fifty,* TNT, 1996; (as host) *Sports Illustrated Olympic Special: A Prelude to the Games,* NBC, 1996; (as pregame interviewer and commentator) *Super Bowl XXX,* NBC, 1996; (as primetime host and cohost of opening and closing ceremonies) *The 1996 Summer Olympics,* NBC, 1996; (as play-by-play commentator) *The 67th Annual Major-League Baseball All-Star Game,* NBC, 1996; *All-Star Moms,* CBS, 1997; *Long Shots: The Life and Times of the American Basketball Association,* HBO, 1997; (as play-by-play commentator) *The 48th NBA All-Star Game,* NBC, 1998; *The 69th Annual Major League Baseball All-Star Game,* NBC, 1998; *The Greek Americans,* PBS, 1998; (as commentator) *The 50th Emmy Awards,* NBC, 1998; (as host and narrator) *Yogi Berra: Deja Vu All over Again,* PBS, 1999; (as voice of himself) *When It Was a Game 3,* HBO, 2000; (as narrator) *Twice Born,* NBC, 2000; *The Sportscasters: Behind the Mike,* History Channel, 2000; *Nick News Presents Lifestory: Muhammad Ali,* Nickelodeon, 2000; (as play-by-play commentator) *The 71st Annual Major-League Baseball All-Star Game,* NBC, 2000; *The '70s: The Decade That Changed Television,* ABC, 2000; (as play-by-play commentator) *The 49th NBA All-Star Game,* NBC, 2000; (as opening ceremony host, with others, and primetime host) *2000 Olympic Games,* NBC, 2000; (as host) *Sports Illustrated's Night of Champions,* NBC, 2001; (as commentator) *The 133rd Belmont Stakes,* NBC, 2001; (as commentator) *The 127th Kentucky Derby,* NBC, 2001; (as commentator) *The 126th Preakness Stakes,* NBC, 2001; (as host) *All State Presents an All-Star Olympic Salute: Countdown to Salt Lake City,* NBC, 2002; (as host) *2002 Olympic Winter Games,* Columbia Broadcasting System (CBS), 2002; and (as himself) *100 Years of Hope and Humor,* 2003. Guest star as himself on television series, including *The Critic, Arli$$, Frasier, NewsRadio, The Larry Sanders Show, The Drew Carey Show, Space Ghost Coast to Coast, Baby Blues, Dennis Miller Live, Tracey Takes On . . . , The Brendon Leonard Show,* and *Spin City.* Appeared as himself in films, including *New York Yankees (The Movie),* Magig Video/Philo, 1987; *The Paper,* Universal, 1994; *The Scout,* Twentieth Century-Fox, 1994; *Open Season,* Legacy Releasing, 1996; *BASEketball,* Universal, 1998; *Express: Aisle to Glory,* 1998; *Race for the Record,* 1998; *Michael Jordan to the Max,* Giant Screen Sports, 2000; (as narrator) *Major-League Baseball: All-Century Team,* 2000; *Looking for Oscar,* 2000; *Pootie Tang,* Paramount, 2001; and *The Swinger,* 2001. Appeared in video *The 500 Home Run Club,* 1988. Reader of audio books, including *And the Crowd Goes Wild,* 1999; and

And the Fans Roared: The Sports Broadcasts That Kept Us on the Edge of Our Seats, Sourcebooks, 2000.

AWARDS, HONORS: Sportscaster of the Year Award, National Sportscasters and Writers Association, 1985; Best Sportscaster Award, *American Journalism Review* Reader's Poll, 1993.

WRITINGS:

Fair Ball: A Fan's Case for Baseball, Broadway Books (New York, NY), 2000.

Contributor to magazines, including *Time* and *Sporting News.*

SIDELIGHTS: Robert Costas—better known as Bob Costas—may be one of the most recognizable faces and voices in American sports journalism. Since he started announcing baseball games for nationwide broadcasts in 1983, Costas has become the voice of baseball, football, basketball, and the Olympics for many Americans. He has also interviewed scores of figures, athletic and otherwise, on his own two highly praised late-night talk shows, *Later with Bob Costas* and *On the Record with Bob Costas.* Both shows have their guests on for extended periods of time, rather than the brief segments seen on other talk shows, which allows for extended discussions of topics of interests to the guests.

Costas is also a die-hard baseball fan and a student of the business of that sport, which led him to write the book *Fair Ball: A Fan's Case for Baseball.* In *Fair Ball,* Costas lays out the problems facing professional baseball, including the lack of competitiveness of small-market teams and the meaninglessness of pennant races, and proposes solutions for them, including revenue sharing and the elimination of the wild card in the playoffs. It is a "logical, reasoned, dispassionate argument," Jay Ziemann wrote in *Nine,* and Costa's proposed restructuring of the divisions and playoff system "is straightforward and preserves the historic integrity of the leagues and team rivalries." As Paul Tuns wrote in the *National Post,* "*Fair Ball* should be required reading in the suites of Official Baseball and be the starting point for the discussion on how to ensure baseball's continued glory."

BIOGRAPHICAL AND CRITICAL SOURCES:

BOOKS

Contemporary Newsmakers 1986, Gale (Detroit, MI), 1987.
St. James Encyclopedia of Popular Culture, five volumes, St. James Press (Detroit, MI), 2000.

PERIODICALS

American Enterprise, June, 2000, interview with Costas, p. 16.
American Journalism Review, March, 1993, Penny Pagano and Jean Cobb, "The Best in the Business," pp. 32-38.
Booklist, March 15, 2000, GraceAnne A. DeCandido, review of *Fair Ball: A Fan's Case for Baseball,* p. 1290; September 1, 2000, review of *Fair Ball* (audiobook), p. 144; September 1, 2001, Mary Frances Wilkens, review of *Fair Ball* (audiobook), p. 127.
Broadcasting & Cable, April 2, 2001, Joe Schlosser, interview with Costas, p. 34; November 4, 2002, "A Powerful Franchise," p. A12.
Daily Variety, July 14, 2003, review of *On the Record with Bob Costas,* p. A9.
Denver Business Journal, March 24, 2000, Erik Spanberg, interview with Costas, p. A25.
Entertainment Weekly, January 29, 1993, Kate Meyers, "The King of Late Late Night," p. 46; July 19, 1996, pp. 30-37.
Knight Ridder/Tribune News Service, April 5, 1994, Mike Antonucci, "Bob Costas' Hour May Have Finally Arrived," p. 0405K2795; April 21, 2000, Stan Hochman, review of *Fair Ball,* p. K6210; January 12, 2001, Joe Posnanski, "Bob Costas Ponders a Quiet Life," p. K7481; February 13, 2001, Tim Kawakami, review of *On the Record,* p. K4242; May 1, 2003, Ed Sherman, "Bob Costas Expands His Field of Play," p. K3279.
Library Journal, February 1, 1998, Paul Kaplan and Morey Berger, review of *Costas on Baseball,* p. 93; April 15, 2000, Paul Kaplan, review of *Fair Ball,* p. 98.

MediaWeek, May 20, 1991, John McManus, "Bryant Bumped: Costas Tapped as Anchor of 1992 Summer Olympics," pp. 1-2.

Milwaukee Business Journal, June 23, 2000, Bruce Schoenfeld, interview with Costas, p. 12.

Multichannel News, February 19, 2001, R. Thomas Umstead, review of *On the Record with Bob Costas,* p. 22.

National Post, May 6, 2000, Paul Tuns, review of *Fair Ball,* p. 20.

Newsweek, July 22, 1996, Mark Starr, interview with Costas, p. 51.

Nine, fall, 2000, Jay Ziemann, review of *Fair Ball,* p. 112.

People, September 5, 1988, Jeff Jarvis, review of *Later with Bob Costas,* p. 15; February 1, 1993, Mark Goodman, "Bob Costas," pp. 71-74.

Publishers Weekly, May 3, 1991, March 27, 2000, review of *Fair Ball,* p. 68; June 5, 2000, review of *Fair Ball* (audiobook), p. 63.

St. Louis Business Journal, August 12, 1996, Alfred Fleishman, "Hometown Guys," p. A17.

St. Louis Journalism Review, March, 1994, Harry James Cargas, interview with Costas, pp. 10-12; July, 2000, Joe Pollack, review of *Fair Ball,* p. 10; June, 2001, Ed Bishop, interview with Costas, p. 16.

Sporting News, February 13, 1995, Steve Marantz, interview with Costas, pp. 18-20; March 5, 2001, Fritz Quindt, review of *On the Record with Bob Costas,* p. 7.

Sports Illustrated, May 12, 1986, William Taaffe, "A Fun Guy, No Kidding," pp. 62-64; April 6, 1992, Jon Scher, "Preempted: The Managerial Aspirations of Bob Costas," p. 130; July 22, 1992, Steve Wulf, "The Host with the Most," pp. 18-20; May 15, 2000, Ron Fimrite, review of *Fair Ball,* p. 8; February 5, 2001, John Walters, interview with Costas, p. 32; April 1, 2002, Richard Deitsch, interview with Costas, p. 16.

Time, August 3, 1992, David Ellis, "America's Host," p. 64; April 17, 2000, Daniel Okrent, review of *Fair Ball,* p. 84.

ONLINE

Internet Movie Database, http://www.imdb.com/ (May 27, 2004), "Bob Costas."

MSNBC Web site, http://www.msnbc.com/ (September 1, 2003), "Bob Costas."*

COTTERILL, Colin 1952-

PERSONAL: Born October 2, 1952, in London, England. *Education:* Berkshire College, teacher training diploma, 1975; Sydney University, graduate diploma, 1980; Reading University, M.A., 1984; Sydney Institute of Technology, certificate, 1999. *Hobbies and other interests:* Bicycling, listening to jazz.

ADDRESSES: Home—910 103 Condo 4, Soi Wat Pratan Porn, Suthep, Chian Mai 50200, Thailand. *Agent*—Richard Curtis, 171 East 74th St., 2nd Floor, New York, NY 10021. *E-mail*—mail@colincotterill.com.

CAREER: Teacher and curriculum developer in Israel, Australia, Japan, and Thailand, 1975-98; teacher trainer and curriculum developer for United Nations Educational, Scientific, and Cultural Organization (UNESCO), Laos, 1990-94; Prince of Songkla University, Phuket, Thailand, founder, project director, and social worker for Childwatch Phuket, 1995-97; teacher trainer in refugee camps, 1997-2000; ECPAT International, Bangkok, Thailand, training coordinator, 2000-02; Chiang Mai University, Chiang Mai, Thailand, teacher, 2002—.

WRITINGS:

Evil in the Land Without: From England to Burma, a Monster Seeks Revenge (novel), Asia Books (Bangkok, Thailand), 2003.

The Coroner's Lunch ("Siri Paiboun Mystery" series), Soho Press (New York, NY), 2004.

Thirty-three Teeth ("Siri Paiboun Mystery" series), Soho Press (New York, NY), 2005.

Other novels by Cotterill have been published in Thailand.

WORK IN PROGRESS: Additional novels in the "Siri Paiboun Mystery" series.

SIDELIGHTS: Colin Cotterill was born in London and trained as a teacher, a skill that benefited students on several continents. He produced a television series to teach language, then worked in Laos with UNESCO. Cotterill also became involved in protecting those children in Thailand who were being abused and exploited, and he worked for End Child Prostitution, Child Pornography, and Trafficking of Children for Sexual Purposes (ECPAT), an international organization that combats child prostitution and pornography, creating a program for caregivers. He continues to teach, more recently graduate students, and is spending more time writing.

During an interview with Dean James and McKenna Jordan of *Murder by the Book* online, Cotterill talked about his first books, which were published in Thailand "where the English-language readership is about eleven." Up until the time he worked for UNESCO, Cotterill wrote humor and created cartoons, but "seeing and learning about the horrors children face got me angry to start writing for effect. I wanted people to know what I knew, and I figured the best way to do that was through fiction. I wrote two novels with a theme of child protection, and I think it was quite a therapeutic activity. I think these were angry books. I was a bit calmer when I wrote a third and decided to make it a comedy (but still with a child trafficking theme).

With *The Coroner's Lunch,* Cotterill began the novel series featuring Siri Paiboun, a French-educated doctor who is appointed chief medical examiner in Vientiane, the capital of Laos, after the only doctor qualified to perform autopsies crosses the river into Thailand. The story is set following the Communist takeover of 1975, and Cotterill incorporates the history and culture of the obscure country—which he noted are almost unknown outside of Laos—in his stories. *The Coroner's Lunch* reflects the upheaval and confusion in Thailand, and in the case of Siri, who is not trained as a coroner, the novel illustrates the lack of resources he has available to efficiently perform his job, including textbooks, supplies, and staff. Cotterill related that his protagonist's character is "an amalgam of several friends in Laos. He's also a symbol of the resilience and wisdom of many of the older educated Lao People" and "represents a generation I consider to be sadly under-represented in fiction. Some of the most colorful characters I know have waved farewell to seventy and have much more to offer than a lot of these young whippersnappers that hog the limelight in novels these days."

In the series debut, an official's wife is poisoned and bodies of tortured Vietnamese soldiers are found floating in a lake, threatening to spark an "incident" between Laos and Vietnam. Siri, who is expected to sort out the deaths, turns to dreams, shamans, and spirits, as well as to medical deduction, to solve the crimes. Marilyn Stasio noted in the *New York Times Book Review* that this mystery would "be fascinating" if all it did was provide insight into this period of the country's history. "But the multiple cases spread out on Siri's examining table . . . are not cozy entertainments, but substantial crimes that take us into the thick of political intrigue," she added. A *Kirkus Reviews* contributor called *The Coroner's Lunch* "an embarrassment of riches: Holmesian sleuthing, political satire, and droll comic study of a prickly late bloomer."

Cotterill told *CA:* "I think I've always written or drawn cartoons. As an only child I had a lot of imagination to get out of my system. I always associated reading with torture. The school would force you to read a book if you were naughty. You'd just read enough to put together a synopsis and an opinion, and that opinion was always positive, or else. What finally got me hooked on reading were Marvel comics. I could get second-hand copies at the market, cheap. The earliest hero in my life was Spider Man and I can't pretend he didn't shape my personality in a number of ways.

"I loved being knocked out of my socks by my comic stories, and I loved that feeling of not knowing what was going to happen on the next page. And, despite constant criticism from 'serious writer' friends, that's how I tend to write. I don't want everything sorted out before I start to write a book. I have a few vague ideas of location, new characters, and where plots may begin, but I write as if I'm a reader. I turn the page with as much apprehension as a comic reader would. I honestly don't know the answer until I write it. So when I get to the end, I'm as drained and as satisfied as, I hope, readers will be.

"The first writing I got paid for was a funny article in a national newspaper with an illustration. I wrote the article because I wanted people to see my cartoon. I wrote several more for the same reason. I imagined the life of a cartoonist would be more fun than that of a writer. I finally got a national cartoon and gave up that awful writing stuff. No, that's not true; I continued to write for myself but swore never to open myself up to humiliation again.

"But then something happened. I started to work in child protection and a lot of reports came over my desk that were unbelievable, but true. I wanted other people to learn about the ugly things that were going on in the world. The only media I could imagine getting to a sufficiently large audience was the novel. That's when I learned just what hard work writing a novel was. I had to do it part time, evenings, weekends. I had to put down ideas as they came to me on whatever came to hand. It took me almost two years to write, then I had to face the editor. Writing is bloody hard work and it takes a little bit of your soul. I wrote two more novels based on child protection in my free time, and it helped as therapy but didn't do a lot for my bank balance.

"I enjoy every book I write for different reasons, but the book I like the most is one written in Thai. My friend translated it from handwritten notes. My mother and stepmother came to Thailand for a month following the death of my mom's second husband. It was such a peculiar time to spend a month on Phuket (where I lived at the time) with two, slightly nutty old English ladies who didn't speak a word of Thai in a little Muslim fishing village. When they left, I put together a scrapbook of cartoons, fake postcards, and fake diary inserts and sent it to them as a souvenir. I sent one photocopy to my Thai friend. She translated it, sent it to a Thai publisher, and it was sold out three months after publication. Miracle.

"I spent a lot of years doing a very stressful job. I wanted to vent my frustration by reading about something that didn't add to my stress. I wanted to see movies that weren't crammed with guts and violence. I was seeking that 'feel good' buzz that made me feel a little better about the world. The books I wrote during that period, although they had happy endings, didn't come with a 'feel good' buzz. They were there to educate and get more people angry about something everyone should be angry about.

"When I left that work, I wanted to contribute some 'feel good' to the world of literature. With my 'Lao' books, I want people to make friends with the characters, learn new things about a place few people have been, and enjoy the stories. Dr. Siri has become a close friend to me and to those very kind readers who have taken the trouble to write to me. I believe the stories make people happy; that's my aim. Again, many thanks to all the reviewers and readers who have helped make the 'Dr. Siri' series so popular.

"The idea for the project I'm working on, Books for Laos, came to me when I was in Luang Prabang, doing research for *Thirty-three Teeth*. A little girl came up to me and asked me for money for sweets. I told her sweets were bad for her, so she asked for money for a book. I was sure she'd spend the book money on sweets so (with her mother's permission) I went with her to the market. No books; on to bookshops—there were no bookshops. Then on to the printer's which had a few dusty old copies of soft-cover school texts. I bought her some sweets and sent her home. Thence began the research.

"There is a dire shortage of books at all levels in Laos. Most kids get to graduation age having never owned a book. Many schools have so few textbooks that the students have to share. A lot of new libraries around the country have an embarrassingly small number of books that aren't particularly relevant or readable (foreign language donations). So, I put together a three stage plan (findable on the contacts page of my Web site *www.colincotterill.com.*) In brief, stage one involves getting donations of multiple copies of children's picture books from publishers or bookshops, shipping them to Laos, translating them, and attaching stickers for national distribution. Stage two is the printing of locally written and illustrated books. Stage three is donations of Thai-language text books (the Lao read Thai well) for college and university libraries. This is a stop gap until the Lao Ministry of Education is able to produce large numbers of Lao language texts (a feat which, despite available money from large-donor agencies, they have been unable to accomplish). Anyone who's read my books will understand that Laos is a hard country to help. The obstacles are many and a lot of energy has to be expended on bypassing red tape. But I'm game if you are."

BIOGRAPHICAL AND CRITICAL SOURCES:

PERIODICALS

Booklist, October 1, 2004, Frank Sennett, review of *The Coroner's Lunch,* p. 313.

Kirkus Reviews, August 15, 2004, review of *The Coroner's Lunch,* p. 779.

Library Journal, December 1, 2004, Rex E. Klett, review of *The Coroner's Lunch,* p. 94.

New York Times Book Review, December 26, 2004, Marilyn Stasio, review of *The Coroner's Lunch,* p. 22.

ONLINE

Colin Cotterill Home Page, http://www.colincotterill.
com (March 9, 2005).
Murder by the Book Web site, http://www.murder
books.com/ (March 9, 2005), Dean James and
McKenna Jordan, interview with Cotterill.

* * *

CRAVER, Charles B. 1944-

PERSONAL: Born July 27, 1944, in Detroit, MI; son
of Bradford North (a research physician) and Elena (a
homemaker and writer; maiden name, Borikova)
Craver; married Kathleen Woods (a school librarian),
June 9, 1967. *Education:* Cornell University, B.S.,
1967, M.A., 1968; University of Michigan, J.D., 1971.

ADDRESSES: Home—Washington, DC. *Office*—Law
School, George Washington University, 2000 H St.
NW, B406, Washington, DC 20052. *E-mail*—ccraver@
law.gwu.edu.

CAREER: Educator, attorney, and author. George
Washington University National Law Center,
Washington, DC, professor, 1986—. Has taught at
University of Illinois, University of California at
Davis, University of Virginia, and University of
Florida. Admitted to the Bar of the State of California
and the Bar of the U.S. Supreme Court.

MEMBER: International Society of Labor Law and
Social Security, American Bar Association (member,
labor and employment law section), American Law
Institute, American Arbitration Association, National
Academy of Arbitrators, Association for Conflict
Resolution, Industrial Relations Research Association,
Society of Professionals in Dispute Resolution.

WRITINGS:

(With Harry T. Edwards and R. Theodore Clark, Jr.)
*Labor Relations Law in the Public Sector: Cases
and Materials,* Bobbs-Merrill (Indianapolis, IN),
1979, 4th edition, Michie (Charlottesville, VA),
1991.

(With Arthur B. Smith and Leroy D. Clark) *Employ-
ment Discrimination Law: Cases and Materials,*
Michie (Charlottesville, VA), 1982, published as
*Employment Discrimination Law: Selected Statutes
and Regulations,* Lexis (New York, NY), 2000.
Effective Legal Negotiation and Settlement, Michie
(Charlottesville, VA), 1986, 5th revised edition,
LexisNexis (Newark, NJ) 2005.
(With Donald P. Rothschild and Leroy S. Merrifield)
Collective Bargaining and Labor Arbitration,
Michie (Charlottesville, VA), 1988.
(With Leroy S. Merrifield and Theodore J. St. Anto-
ine) *Labor Relations Law: Cases and Materials,*
Michie (Charlottesville, VA), 1989, 11th edition,
LexisNexis (Newark, NJ), 2005.
*Can Unions Survive?: The Rejuvenation of the
American Labor Movement,* New York University
Press (New York, NY), 1993.
(With Edward J. Brunet) *Alternative Dispute Resolu-
tion: The Advocate's Perspective,* Michie
(Charlottesville, VA), 1997, 2nd revised edition,
LexisNexis (Newark, NJ), 2001.
*The Intelligent Negotiator: What to Say, What to Do,
and How to Get What You Want—Every Time,*
Prima Venture (Roseville, CA), 2002.

Contributor to numerous law journals, including *Ari-
zona Law Review, George Washington Law Review,
Judges Journal, Cornell Law Review,* and *Michigan
Law Review.*

SIDELIGHTS: Charles B. Craver cultivated an interest
in law and academia at an early age. After earning a
law degree in 1971, he clerked for Judge George
MacKinnon of the U.S. Court of Appeals for the
District of Columbia Circuit. The following year, he
took a position as an attorney with Morrison &
Foerster, specializing in labor law and general
litigation. In 1974, Craver returned to academia, working as a professor at the University of Florida College
of Law. This led to a string of other professorships, at
universities in Virginia, California, and Illinois. At
George Washington University, where he has taught
since 1986, Craver specializes in negotiation, labor
law, employment discrimination law, and public-sector
labor law. He is the author of several books on various
legal subjects and frequently contributes to law
journals.

In 1993 Craver published *Can Unions Survive?: The
Rejuvenation of the American Labor Movement.* The
book begins with an analysis of why labor unions have

diminished in popularity and power since their peak in the 1940s. Craver includes a brief history of the rise of the U.S. labor movement and the factors leading to its decline. The second half of the book is devoted to ways unions can increase their economic and political power. The book earned positive reviews overall, with critics praising Craver's accessible language and thoughtful ideas. It is "a reader-friendly . . . and provocative book that addresses the fundamental question of how the interests of rank-and-file employees should be protected," wrote Peter Feuille in a review for the *Industrial and Labor Relations Review.*

In 2002 Craver wrote and published *The Intelligent Negotiator: What to Say, What to Do, and How to Get What You Want—Every Time.* In this book he analyzes the essential elements of negotiation and gives readers guidance on how to become more effective negotiators. He also discusses common negotiating styles and provides specific language to use in certain situations. The book was well received by readers and critics, and was particularly lauded for providing straightforward and useful information. Commenting on the book in the *Journal of Business Strategy,* Bristol Lane Voss noted that *The Intelligent Negotiator* "is firmly rooted in present-day and relevant knowledge."

BIOGRAPHICAL AND CRITICAL SOURCES:

PERIODICALS

Industrial and Labor Relations Review, January, 1995, Peter Feuille, review of *Can Unions Survive?: The Rejuvenation of the American Labor Movement,* p. 353.

Journal of Business Strategy, January-February, 2003, Bristol Lane Voss, review of *The Intelligent Negotiator: What to Say, What to Do, and How to Get What You Want—Every Time,* p. 41.

ONLINE

American Law Institute Web site, http://d2d.ali-aba. org/ (April 20, 2005), "Charles Craver."

George Washington University Law School Web site, http://www.law.gwu.edu/ (April 20, 2005), "Charles Craver."

CREELEY, Robert (White) 1926-2005

OBITUARY NOTICE— See index for *CA* sketch: Born May 21, 1926, in Arlington, MA; died of complications from pneumonia March 30, 2005, in Odessa, TX. Educator and author. Creeley was an award-winning poet often associated with the Black Mountain poets and the Beat generation. Creeley lost an eye in an accident when he was two years old and his father died when he was five. Although he endured childhood poverty, insurance money from these tragedies allowed him to attend Harvard University in 1943. He left his studies toward the end of World War II to work as an ambulance driver for the American Field Service in India and Burma. Although he returned to Harvard after that, he did not receive a degree at the time; instead, he worked on a New Hampshire farm, and then left for Spain, where he was founder and publisher of Divers Press in Palma. Invited to attend the Black Mountain College by writer Charles Olson, Creeley decided to move back to America and complete his bachelor's degree from the North Carolina college in 1955. Five years later he completed a master's degree at the University of New Mexico. Because he attended Black Mountain College, he readily became associated with the Black Mountain poets, which included writers Denise Levertov and Fielding Dawson. However, he was a product of the 1960s era, too, and his free style of poetry has also been associated with Beats such as Allen Ginsberg. Creeley began publishing his poems in collections by the early 1950s, with *Le Fou* (1952) being his first title. He did not gain considerable attention until his verses appeared in the influential 1960 anthology *The New American Poetry: 1945-1960.* That same year, the poet earned his first award, the Levinson Prize, for contributions he made to *Poetry* magazine. Many more prestigious awards and grants followed, such as the Shelley Award in 1981, the Frost Medal in 1987, and the highest honor for a poet, the Bollingen Prize, which he received in 1999. As a writer, Creeley diverged from classic forms, averring that the rhythms and meters of a poem should be dictated by its content. What resulted was a very free, informal form of writing; even his use of spelling was informal, with the poet often abbreviating words such as "sd" for "said." This style was sometimes praised by critics, while others disparaged it for its lack of discipline. In addition to his experimentation with form, Creeley also favored drawing his subject matter from personal experience rather than from history or tradition. Thus, his poems, which typically are quite short, are also very personal works. Despite his publishing success he needed a steady source of income, so spent much of his time teaching university students. During the 1960s and 1970s he was a professor at the University of New Mexico, and from 1966 until 2003 he taught at the State University of New York at Buffalo, where he was David Gray Professor of Poetry and Letters from 1978 until 1989 and Samuel P. Capen Professor of Poetry and Humanities from 1989 until 2003. When he left Buffalo, he joined the faculty at Brown University. Among Creeley's numerous verse collections are such notable books as *For Love: Poems 1950-1960* (1962), *Pieces* (1968), *Hello* (1976), *Later* (1979), *The Collected Poems of Robert Creeley, 1945-1975* (1982), *Mirrors* (1983), and *Life & Death* (1993). He also published short stories, a novel titled *The Island* (1963), essay and lecture collections, and the play *Listen* (1972).

OBITUARIES AND OTHER SOURCES:

BOOKS

Creeley, Robert, *Autobiography,* Hanuman Books, 1990.

PERIODICALS

Los Angeles Times, April 1, 2005, p. B9.
New York Times, April 1, 2005, p. C13.
Times (London, England), April 1, 2005, p. 62.
Washington Post, April 1, 2005, p. B6.

*   *   *

CROOKER, Constance Emerson 1946-

PERSONAL: Born July 23, 1946, in Portland, ME; daughter of Charles W. (a Congregational minister) and Elizabeth (a tax consultant; maiden name, MacGregor; later surname, Bates) Crooker. *Ethnicity:* "Caucasian; adopted by Hispanic culture." *Education:* Reed College, B.A., 1969; Lewis and Clark College, J.D., 1977. *Politics:* "Democrat with Libertarian leanings." *Religion:* "Atheist, except when listening to Beethoven." *Hobbies and other interests:* Lindy Hop dancing, downhill skiing, playing electric guitar.

ADDRESSES: Agent—c/o Author Mail, Greenwood Publishing Group, Inc., P.O. Box 5007, Westport, CT 06881-5007. *E-mail*—ccrooker@comcast.net.

CAREER: Criminal defense lawyer in Portland, OR, 1977-2000; writer and teacher, 2000—. Tillamook Public Defender, Inc., founder and director, 1983-88; Mexican consulate, consulting attorney, 1984-2000; Hispanic Metropolitan Chamber of Commerce, member, 1990—; public speaker. Universidad Latina de América, Morelia, Michoacan, Mexico, member of adjunct faculty, 2003.

MEMBER: Oregon Defense Lawyers, Willamette Writers, Elizabeth Raintree's Writer's Consortium, Author's Lunch (chair).

WRITINGS:

Paint My Mailbox Blue: A Guide to Group Ownership and Use of Real Property, Oregon State Public Interest Research Group (Portland, OR), 1979.
The Art of Legal Interpretation: A Guide for Court Interpreters, Portland State University Continuing Education Press (Portland, OR), 1996.
Gun Control and Gun Rights, Greenwood Publishing Group (Westport, CT), 2003.

Contributor of articles and reviews to law journals and other periodicals, including *High Times, Reed, AMC Outdoors,* and *Defense Attorney.* Editor and publisher, *Spanish Language Legal Network Directory,* 1993-2000.

WORK IN PROGRESS: A text on comparative criminal law; *State of the Union,* a travel memoir; three novels, *Quiet Desperation,* a psychological mystery, *Every Secret Thing,* a murder mystery set in rural Oregon, and *Journey of the Jaguar,* an action novel set in the world of Mexican drug smugglers.

SIDELIGHTS: Constance Emerson Crooker told *CA:* "I write nonfiction in order to demystify legal areas where I am uniquely qualified to convey information not readily available to non-lawyers. My writing on the history of gun law stems from over twenty years of experience as a criminal defense lawyer, including the defense of firearms crimes. My writing on court interpretation was inspired by my many years of defending Spanish-speaking criminally accused clients and learning the importance of working with only highly qualified court interpreters.

"I retired early from the practice of criminal defense to write and teach. My three (as yet unpublished) novels all include legal themes and characters based on my colorful clients who, for myriad reasons, have found themselves on the light end of the scales of justice. The pleasure of hearing their raw colloquialisms and watching them play out their flawed humanity as they reveal themselves on the pages of my fiction is what keeps me writing."

BIOGRAPHICAL AND CRITICAL SOURCES:

PERIODICALS

School Library Journal, February, 2004, Priscilla Bennett, review of *Gun Control and Gun Rights*, p. 88.

*   *   *

CROSS, Neil 1969-

PERSONAL: Born 1969, in Bristol, England; children. *Education:* Attended college.

ADDRESSES: Home—New Zealand. *Agent*—c/o Author Mail, Charles Scribner's & Sons, 1230 Avenue of the Americas, New York, NY 10020.

CAREER: Novelist Lead singer in Atrocity Exhibition (rock band); Pan Macmillan (publisher), London, England, key accounts manager in sales department.

WRITINGS:

NOVELS

Mr. In-Between, Jonathan Cape (London, England), 1998.
Christendom, Jonathan Cape (London, England), 1999.

Holloway Falls, Scribner' (New York, NY), 2003.
Always the Sun, Scribner' (New York, NY), 2004.
Heartland, Scribner' (New York, NY), 2005.

SIDELIGHTS: During the late 1990s, while finishing college and working for a publishing company, Neil Cross made his literary debut with the dark novel *Mr. In-Between*. The plot revolves around Jon Bennett, an emotionless assassin who renews his friendship with an old school friend and begins the path to a new life when he helps that friend after the man's wife's accidental death. "I wanted to do something about a man with no redeeming qualities," Cross commented in a *PureFiction.com* interview. "Also, I'm kind of fascinated with the way assassins are portrayed in films and popular fiction as being super cool, emotionless and conscienceless." Alexander Harrison noted in the *Times Literary Supplement* that, "Although Cross shows his relish for language, he has no care for the characters he has created." Christina Patterson, writing in the London *Observer,* found Cross's prose uneven but praised the novel in general, noting that the author's "portrayal of male friendship, the rituals of working-class life and the shock of bereavement" are "superbly done."

Cross's second novel, *Christendom,* as well as his more recent *Heartland,* was inspired by one of the author's stepfathers, a Mormon as well as a white supremacist. In *Christendom,* set in a future America ruled by extreme Christian fundamentalists, a combat veteran smuggles prohibited books and films and becomes involved with an assassin. *Times Literary Supplement* contributor Stephen Goodwin judged the plot to be too similar to others of the thriller genre and the work's shock value to be overplayed at times. However, Goodwin also noted that the novel's settings are "original" and commented that "Ross handles his fast-paced, suspenseful story efficiently, and he is adept at set-piece scenes."

In *Holloway Falls* Cross tells the story of Will Holloway, a cop set up for a murder he did not commit who attempts to clear himself with the help of conspiracy theorist Jack Shepherd. Writing in the Manchester *Guardian,* David Jays commended Cross for keeping "his sentences brisk and his editorial voice bone-dry, letting us hear the fears scampering round his characters' skulls." The critic also called the story "nasty, a little deranged and very, very tense."

In *Always the Sun* Cross strays from his urban thrillers with a story about Sam, whose wife dies from a degenerative brain disorder called fatal familial insomnia. Sam and his son Jamie move to Sam's home town to start life over. When Jamie becomes the target of a school bully, Sam confronts the bully's father in a bar, is beat up, and loses the respect of his son in the process. In an effort partly to live up to his son's expectations, Sam becomes unhinged as he seeks revenge both for his son and himself. Writing in the *New Zealand Herald,* Michele Hewitson called *Always the Sun* "uneven" and noted, "You could waste a lot of good sleeping time trying to work out what sort of book this is." Shirley Dent, writing on the *Culture Wars* Web site commented that, "Apart from finding one too many plot devices veering towards the wrong side of implausibility in the last thirty or so pages, I remain convinced that this is a novel that sets out to tell a truth about society. And that truth seems to be that we are so petrified of action, that when we do act we lose all perspective and rationality."

BIOGRAPHICAL AND CRITICAL SOURCES:

PERIODICALS

Bookseller, November 7, 2003, Philip Jones, "The End of Violence: Neil Cross' Fourth Novel Explores the Powerful Emotions of Fatherhood," p. 27.
Guardian (Manchester, England), October 25, 2003, David Jays, review of *Holloway Falls,* p. 30.
Observer (London, England), April 5, 1998, Christina Patterson, review of *Mr. In-Between,* p. 16; October 25, 2003, review of *Holloway Falls,* p. 30.
Times Literary Supplement, March 27, 1998, Alexander Harrison, review of *Mr. In-Between,* p. 21; June 25, 1999, Stephen Goodwin, review of *Christendom,* p. 24.

ONLINE

Culture Wars Web site, http://www.culture wars.org.uk/ (February 1, 2005), Shirley Dent, review of *Always the Sun.*
New Zealand Herald Online, http://www.nzherald.co.nz/ (February 1, 2005), Michele Hewitson, review of *Always the Sun.*
Pulp.net, http://www.pulp.net/ (February 1, 2005), Neil Cross, "My Literary Top Ten.".
PureFiction.com, http://www.purefiction.com/ (March, 1998), interview with Cross.*

CRUSE, Harold (Wright) 1916-2005

OBITUARY NOTICE— See index for *CA* sketch: Born March 8, 1916, in Petersburg, VA; died of congestive heart failure March 25, 2005, in Ann Arbor, MI. Social critic, educator, and author. Well known as the author of *The Crisis of the Negro Intellectual* (1967), Cruse was an African-American essayist and critic of U.S. society and the media who often disparaged the value of music and theater that was derived from or emulated black culture. As a boy, he became interested in theater after an aunt introduced him to black vaudeville acts; this led to his early work in Harlem for the YMCA's theater, where he was a technical assistant. After serving in the U.S. Army during World War II, he attended the George Washington Carver School. Here, Cruse had the opportunity to hear W. E. B. Du Bois speak, and he developed a sympathy for leftist politics, joining the Communist Party and writing for its newspaper, the *Daily Worker.* Later, however, he became disenchanted with communism and left the party. During his early career, Cruse held various jobs: he worked as a film and theater critic for the *New York Labor Press,* as a teacher for the Black Arts Repertory Theatre/School, and as an office clerk for the Veterans' Administration. Meanwhile, he cofounded the Jones' Black Arts Theatre and School in New York City in 1965, where he worked as a director and stage manager; he also wrote plays but found little success as a playwright. Frustrated with the state of the arts in America, he published *The Crisis of the Negro Intellectual,* which stirred the ire of many people due to its author's criticism of jazz and the black theater. He particularly lambasted white jazz musicians, accusing them of stealing a black art form, and became infamous for criticizing George Gershwin's folk opera *Porgy and Bess.* Cruse did not limit himself to disparaging art produced by white Americans; he also criticized the writers of the Harlem Renaissance, whom he felt did not adequately address the issue of black identity. In 1968, Cruse joined the faculty at the University of Michigan, where he taught history and was named program director of the Center for Afroamerican and African Studies in 1969. In 1971 he became the center's acting director, and from 1972 until 1973 was its director. Within a few years, he became a tenured professor of history, the first African American without a college degree to become a full professor at a large university. Retiring from teaching in the mid-1980s, he continued to write, publishing *Plural but Equal: A Critical Study of Blacks and Minorities and America's Plural Society* (1987) and *The Essential Harold Cruse: A Reader* (2002).

OBITUARIES AND OTHER SOURCES:

PERIODICALS

Chicago Tribune, March 30, 2005, section 3, p. 10.
Detroit Free Press, March 28, 2005.
Los Angeles Times, April 5, 2005, p. B9.
New York Times, March 30, 2005, p. A19.
Washington Post, March 29, 2005, p. B8.

ONLINE

University of Michigan Web site, http://www.umich. edu/ (April 28, 2005).

*   *   *

CURNYN, Lynda

PERSONAL: Born in Brooklyn, NY. *Education:* Hofstra University, B.A.; New York University, M.A.

ADDRESSES: Home—New York, NY. *Agent*—Laura Dail, Laura Dail Literary Agency, 350 7th Ave., Ste. 2003, New York, NY 10001; fax: 212-947-0460. *E-mail*—lynda@lyndacurnyn.com.

CAREER: Writer. Worked for eleven years as an editor for Harlequin (publisher), New York, NY.

WRITINGS:

NOVELS

Confessions of an Ex-Girlfriend, Red Dress Ink (Don Mills, Ontario, Canada), 2002.
Engaging Men, Red Dress Ink (Don Mills, Ontario, Canada), 2003.
Bombshell, Red Dress Ink (Don Mills, Ontario, Canada), 2004.
Killer Summer, Red Dress Ink (Don Mills, Ontario, Canada), 2005.

Work represented in anthologies, including *Girls' Night In,* Red Dress Ink, 2004; and *American Girls about Town,* Downtown Press, 2004.

SIDELIGHTS: Lynda Curnyn was born in Brooklyn, raised on Long Island, and was educated and works in New York City. An English major, she became an editor with Harlequin and subsequently began writing for the romance publisher. Released by Harlequin's Red Dress imprint, her debut, *Confessions of an Ex-Girlfriend,* finds New Yorker Emma Carter alone after her boyfriend leaves for a screenwriting job in Los Angeles. Emma believes that her dating days are over, particularly because she has gained weight, but she is haunted by the world of brides due to her job as editor at a bridal magazine. Pushed to the limit when her mother, who is remarrying, enlists her to help with the wedding planning, Emma compensates for her loveless life by eating sweets and then working them off at the gym, while her two best friends, Alyssa and Jade, try to keep her upbeat. Alyssa is thinking about cheating on her long-time lover, and Jade has sworn off love in favor of casual sex. Emma is dealing with her father's alcoholism and competing with a coworker for the position of contributing editor. A *Publishers Weekly* contributor called *Confessions of an Ex-Girlfriend,* "part *Sex in the City* with more heart, and part *Bridget Jones* with less booze."

The protagonist of *Engaging Men* is Angie DiFranco, whose former boyfriends have gone on to marry other women and is now dating Kirk. Her friend, Michelle, tells her that men are like jars: Their lids have to be loosened before they will commit. Angie, an actress, is also concerned with her career; She has not been offered auditions since she accepted a part in a cable exercise show for children. *Booklist* contributor Kristine Huntley called *Engaging Men* "another fun and frothy crowd-pleaser."

In *Bombshell,* Grace Noonan, who first appeared in *Engaging Men,* is a marketing executive with a cosmetics company that has decided to change its focus from the over-thirty woman by bringing on a teenage super model. Grace, who is over thirty, dumps her boyfriend when he panics at the thought of a real commitment, which includes children, then faces her former boyfriend, the company's founder's son, when he shows up with a new woman on his arm. When Grace discovers that she may, in fact, be pregnant, she finds herself pleasantly surprised at the possibility. Reviewing the book, Huntley wrote that Curnyn's novels "keep getting better; readers will love following tough, sophisticated Grace on her quest for love and family."

BIOGRAPHICAL AND CRITICAL SOURCES:

PERIODICALS

Booklist, April 15, 2002, Kristine Huntley, review of *Confessions of an Ex-Girlfriend,* p. 1384; June 1, 2004, Kristine Huntley, review of *Bombshell,* p. 1709.

Cosmopolitan, September, 2002, Anna Holmes, "The Way 9/11 Transformed My Love Life" (interview), p. 239.
Publishers Weekly, April 1, 2002, review of *Confessions of an Ex-Girlfriend,* p. 53.

ONLINE

Lynda Curnyn Home Page, http://www.lyndacurnyn. com (March 10, 2005).
RomanticTimes.com, http://www.romantictimes.com/ (March 10, 2005), Judith Rippelmeyer, review of *Confessions of an Ex-Girlfriend.*
Steppin' out with Gena Web site, http://members.cox. net/genashowalter/ (March 10, 2005), Gena Showalter, interview with Curnyn.

D

DANNEBERG, Julie 1958-

PERSONAL: Born 1958, in Denver, CO; married; children: one daughter, one son. *Education:* University of Colorado, Boulder, B.S. *Hobbies and other interests:* Reading, gardening, biking, traveling, listening to music, sewing.

ADDRESSES: Home—Denver, CO. *Agent*—c/o Author Mail, Charlesbridge Publishing, 85 Main St., Watertown, MA 02472.

CAREER: Former special education teacher in Colorado; currently middle-school teacher in Denver, CO; writer.

AWARDS, HONORS: Best Children's Book designation, Colorado Center for the Book, 2000, for *Margaret's Magnificent Colorado Adventure;* Storyteller Award, 2000, for *First Day Jitters;* Regional Book Award, Mountains and Plains Booksellers, 2003, for *Women Artists of the West: Five Portraits in Creativity and Courage.*

WRITINGS:

Margaret's Magnificent Colorado Adventure, Westcliffe Publishers (Englewood, CO), 1999.
First Day Jitters, illustrated by Judy Love, Charlesbridge Publishing (Watertown, MA), 2000.
Amidst the Gold Dust: Women Who Forged the West, Fulcrum Resources (Golden, CO), 2001.
Women Artists of the West: Five Portraits in Creativity and Courage, Fulcrum Publishing (Golden, CO), 2002.
Women Writers of the West: Five Chroniclers of the Old West, Fulcrum Publishing (Golden, CO), 2003.
First Year Letters, illustrated by Judy Love, Charlesbridge Publishing (Watertown, MA), 2003.
Cowboy Slim, illustrated by Margot Apple, Charlesbridge Publishing (Watertown, MA), 2005.

SIDELIGHTS: Julie Danneberg spends the first hour of each day writing, whether it be personal notes in a journal, award-winning children's books, or just ideas for future projects. The busy school teacher/author draws upon her background as a third-generation resident of Colorado for inspiration, and several of her books profile notable woman who have made a mark on the American West. Danneberg is probably best known, however, for the picture books *Margaret's Magnificent Colorado Adventure, First Day Jitters,* and *First Year Letters.* These playful stories offer unconventional approaches to life-altering moments in childhood.

Margaret's Magnificent Colorado Adventure combines the history and geography of Colorado with the tale of a ten-year-old girl who keeps a journal as she travels with her parents and younger brother. Margaret faithfully records real information about the state through which she is traveling, but occasionally her temper frays when she has to deal with her annoying sibling. Danneberg's debut work, *Margaret's Magnificent Colorado Adventure* won a best children's book citation from the Colorado Center for the Book.

First Day Jitters and *First Year Letters* both feature Sarah Jane Hartwell. In *First Day Jitters* Sarah Jane faces an important milestone: It is her first day at school and she does not want to get out of bed, eat her breakfast, or face the principal and the scary students. What sets this picture book apart from so many books about children beginning school is its surprise ending, where readers discover that even adults can be afraid of new beginnings. According to Adele Greenlee in *School Library Journal,* Danneberg's joke "provides a good laugh and children may find it reassuring that they are not alone in their anxieties about new situations." Connie Fletcher, writing in *Booklist,* also found *First Day Jitters* a "wittily drawn and suspensefully told story. Fletcher concluded that Danneberg's tale is "funny and insightful."

Sarah Jane's adventures continue in *First Year Letters.* Through a classroom mailbox, Sarah Jane receives notes from the students that describe the many amusing—and distressing—incidents that mark a school year. While most of the notes Sarah Jane receives are typed, some are hand-written, and they demonstrate how students learn writing skills over the course of a year. A *Kirkus Reviews* critic called the book "both funny and touching," while in *School Library Journal* Piper L. Nyman maintained that *First Year Letters* is "easy to read," and that children "will relate to and enjoy this book." Diane Foote concluded in *Booklist* that students and teachers "will appreciate this unusual take on the ups and downs of a school year."

Danneberg has also written several books about women who lived and worked in the American West. *Women Writers of the West: Five Chroniclers of the Old West* explores the lives of Jesie Benton Fremont, Louise Clappe, Mary Hallock Foote, Helen Hunt Jackson, and Gertrude Bonnin, each of whom used her writing talents as a means of communicating individuality. The profiles in *Women Artists of the West: Five Portraits in Creativity and Courage* include Maria Martinez, Georgia O'Keefe, Laura Gilpin, Dorothea Lange, and Mary-Russell Colton. The artwork under study varies from traditional Pueblo pottery crafted by Martinez to Depression-era photographs snapped by Lange.

Amidst the Gold Dust: Women Who Forged the West offers an historical/fictitious glimpse into the life of women during the gold rush that swept Colorado and California in the nineteenth century. In *Book Report,* Tena Natale Litherland suggested that the work's characters lacked depth, but nonetheless praised Dan-

nenberg for including "interesting sidebars of historical facts." Patricia Ann Owens, reviewing the book for *School Library Journal,* liked the way the character sketches reveal "determination, perseverance, and hard work."

On her home page, Danneberg declared that she loves being a writer and enjoys the process of jotting notes as much as the efforts required to create a book that will be acceptable to editors and publishers. "Being a writer has given me the chance to learn all sorts of new things, go new places and meet new people," she said. "Also, being a writer gives me the excuse to read, read and read some more!"

BIOGRAPHICAL AND CRITICAL SOURCES:

PERIODICALS

Booklist, March 15, 2000, Connie Fletcher, review of *First Day Jitters,* p. 1386; February 1, 2003, Diane Foote, review of *First Year Letters,* p. 1000.
Book Report, September-October, 2001, Tena Natale Litherland, review of *Amidst the Gold Dust: Women Who Forged the West,* p. 74.
Kirkus Reviews, December 15, 2002, review of *First Year Letters,* p. 1848.
Kliatt, May, 2003, Carol-Ann Hoyte, review of *Women Artists of the West: Five Portraits in Creativity and Courage,* p. 41; November, 2003, Edna Boardman, review of *Women Writers of the West: Five Chroniclers of the Old West,* p. 32.
School Library Journal, May, 2000, Adele Greenlee, review of *First Day Jitters,* p. 133; June, 2001, Patricia Ann Owens, review of *Amidst the Gold Dust,* p. 167; April, 2003, Piper L. Nyman, review of *First Year Letters,* p. 118.

ONLINE

Julie Danneberg Home Page, http://www.julie danneberg.com (February 7, 2005).

*   *   *

DAVIDSON, MaryJanice (Janice Pohl)

PERSONAL: Married; children: two.

ADDRESSES: Agent—c/o Author Mail, Kensington Publishing, 850 Third Ave., New York, NY 10022. *E-mail*—maryjanice@comcast.net.

CAREER: Writer. Manager of operations for a brokerage firm.

AWARDS, HONORS: Sapphire Award for Excellence in Science-Fiction Romance, 2000, for story "Love's Prisoner."

WRITINGS:

Adventures of the Teen Furies (young-adult novel), Hard Shell Word Factory (Amherst Junction, WI), 2001.

By Any Other Name (novel), Hard Shell Word Factory (Amherst Junction, WI), 2001.

Canis Royal: Bridefight (e-book; novel), Ellora's Cave (Stow, OH), 2002.

Under Cover (short stories), Brava (New York, NY), 2003.

Beggarman, Thief (e-book; novel), Loose-ID Publications (Carson City, NV), 2004.

Undead and Unwed (novel), Berkley Sensation (New York, NY), 2004.

Undead and Unemployed (novel), Berkley Sensation (New York, NY), 2004.

The Royal Treatment (novel), Brava (New York, NY), 2004.

Undead and Unappreciated (novel), Berkley Sensation (New York, NY), 2005.

Derik's Bane (novel), Berkley Sensation (New York, NY), 2005.

Hello, Gorgeous! (novel), Brava (New York, NY), 2005.

Also author of e-books, including novels *Thief of Hearts* and *Love Lies*, for Ellora's Cave, and *Dying for Ice Cream* (young-adult), for Fiction Works, and nonfiction, including including *Escape the Slush Pile,* for Fiction Works. Contributor of short fiction to anthologies, including *Men at Work* Berkley Sensation (New York, NY), 2004; *Bite, Bad Boys with Expensive Toys; Perfect for the Beach; Cravings; How to Be a "Wicked"Woman; Naughty or Nice;* and *Secrets,* Volumes 6 and 8. Contributor, under pseudonym Janice Pohl, to *Reunions: Four Inspiring Romance Stories of Friends Reunited.*

SIDELIGHTS: MaryJanice Davidson is primarily a writer of romance novels and short stories, but she has worked in a variety of subgenres, including supernatural, science-fiction, young-adult, erotic, and inspirational romances. Her work often features copious helpings of humor and frank sexuality. The winner of a romance-writing contest sponsored by author Lori Foster, Davidson has written extensively for publication in both print and e-book form, and the success of her e-books has helped build her print career. For instance, *Undead and Unwed,* a novel about a young, single, fashion-conscious female vampire, was originally published as an e-book, and it caught the attention of an editor at Berkley. After the company published the novel in print form, it released several other books by Davidson, including two sequels to *Undead and Unwed.*

Undead and Unwed introduces readers to Betsy Taylor, a woman who joins the undead after dying in a traffic accident. Unlike most vampires, Betsy can go out in the daytime and is not bothered by religious symbols, and these qualities make her a candidate for queen of the vampires. But she also must do battle with another candidate, an evil, five-hundred-year-old vampire named Nostro. Assisting her in this effort is Eric Sinclair, a vampire who is handsome and sexy, but who nevertheless does not appeal to Betsy. Describing the novel as a "chick-lit foray into the paranormal," *Booklist* critic Diana Tixier Herald dubbed the story "sexy," "funny," and "delightful."

In *Undead and Unemployed,* Betsy has become vampire queen, but she still needs a job in the mortal world, so she goes to work in a department store selling one of her favorite things: designer shoes. Meanwhile, she has to fight off a gang of vampire-slayers and come to the aid of an enigmatic young girl. *Booklist* critic Herald praised the novel highly, calling it "wickedly clever and amusing." The series continued in 2005 with *Undead and Unappreciated.*

Vampires are not the only supernatural creatures to appear in Davidson's writings. The hero of *Derik's Bane* is attractive young werewolf Derik Gardner. His wolf pack sends him on a mission to kill Morgan le Fay, the wicked enchantress of the King Arthur legends, in order to stop what the werewolves believe is Morgan's plot to destroy the world. Morgan has been reincarnated in modern-day northern California as Dr. Sara Gunn, with whom Derik falls in love after failing to kill her. Sara, at first skeptical, eventually comes to believe she is indeed Morgan, but she claims Morgan has been falsely accused of evil intentions, and she and Derik join in fighting an Arthur-worshipping cult that is truly threatening the planet. Harriet Klausner, writing in *MBR Bookwatch,* found *Derik's Bane* "a unique well-written romantic fantasy with a Camelot twist," adding that Derik and Sara are humorous and appealing. Herald, again reviewing for *Booklist,* also noted the book's comic aspects, writing that it "will elicit delighted howls of laughter." The novel was the first in a projected "Wyndham Werewolves" series.

Hello, Gorgeous! is a venture into science fiction involving a young woman who is brought back to life after a fatal car crash through the implantation of mechanical parts. The procedure gives this "bionic woman," Caitlyn James, superpowers, so the U.S. government enlists her as a secret agent, giving her a mission to track and thwart a computer hacker. In *Booklist,* Herald predicted that readers would enjoy the novel's "over-the-top humor and raunchily funny sex scenes"

In *The Royal Treatment* Davidson envisions an alternate reality in which the state of Alaska is an independent country ruled by a monarchy. The royals like to mingle with the common people, and one day the king brings home a rootless young woman as a bride for his eldest son, the crown prince. The woman and the prince do fall in love, but they are not wholly compatible, and they must overcome their personal differences while dealing with troubles facing the kingdom. *Booklist* contributor Maria Hatton deemed the book "quirky" and "fun."

BIOGRAPHICAL AND CRITICAL SOURCES:

PERIODICALS

Booklist, March 15, 2004, Diana Tixier Herald, review of *Undead and Unwed,* p. 1274; May 1, 2004, Maria Hatton, review of *The Royal Treatment,* p. 1550; August, 2004, Diana Tixier Herald, review of *Undead and Unemployed,* p. 1908; December 1, 2004, Diana Tixier Herald, review of *Derik's Bane,* p. 641; February 1, 2005, Diana Tixier Herald, review of *Hello, Gorgeous!,* p. 948.
MBR Bookwatch, January, 2005, Harriet Klausner, reviews of *Derik's Bane* and *Men at Work;*

February, 2005, Klausner, review of *Bad Boys with Expensive Toys.*
Publishers Weekly, June 7, 2004, review of *Cravings,* p. 37; January 3, 2005, review of *Bite,* p. 42.

ONLINE

All about Romance Web site, http://www.likesbooks.com/ (March 25, 2005), Megan Frampton, review of *Under Cover.*
AllReaders.com, http://www.allreaders.com/ (March 25, 2005), L. Watson, review of *Hello, Gorgeous!*
Allscifi.com, http://www.allscifi.com/ (March 25, 2005), review of *Canis Royal: Bridefight.**

*   *   *

DAVIS, Joyce M. 1953-

PERSONAL: Born July 29, 1953, in New Orleans, LA; daughter of Albert O. (a Baptist minister) and Gloria (a teacher; maiden name, Le Conte) Davis; married Russell W. Goodman (a journalist), November 28, 1985; children: Cole Davis. *Ethnicity:* "African-American." *Education:* Attended Loyola University, 1970-73, and Center for the Formation and Perfection of Journalism, 1987-88. *Religion:* Christian.

ADDRESSES: Agent—c/o Author Mail, Palgrave Macmillan, 175 Fifth Ave, New York, NY 10010. *E-mail*—jdavis11007@msn.com.

CAREER: Times-Picayune, New Orleans, LA, assistant metropolitan editor, 1972-90; National Public Radio, Washington, DC, began as deputy foreign editor, became foreign editor, 1990-97; Knight Ridder Newspapers, Washington, DC, deputy foreign editor, 1997-2003; Radio Free Europe/Radio Liberty, Prague, Czech Republic, associate director of broadcasting, 2003—. U.S. Institute of Peace, fellow, 1983-84; Journalistes en Europe, fellow, 1987-88; Atlantic-Bruëcke, fellow, 1989. Pulitzer Prize, juror, 1999-2000. Office of the U.S. Secretary of State, cochair of Open Forum for International Women's Day, 2001; Women in International Security, member of advisory board; BMW-Herbert Quandt Transatlantic Forum, fellow; Johns Hopkins University Paul H. Nitze School of Advanced International Studies, Baltimore, MD, journalist-in-residence, 2003.

AWARDS, HONORS: Columbia-DuPont Silver Batons, 1990-91, for coverage of war in Kuwait, and 1995-96, for coverage of war in Chechnya.

WRITINGS:

Between Jihad and Salaam: Profiles in Islam, St. Martin's Press (New York, NY), 1997.
Martyrs: Innocence, Vengeance, and Despair in the Middle East, Palgrave Macmillan (New York, NY), 2003.

Contributor to periodicals.

WORK IN PROGRESS: The War within Islam: Islamic Moderates, Militants, and Terrorism.

SIDELIGHTS: Joyce M. Davis told *CA:* "My primary motivation for writing is to enlighten the American public about Islam, its leaders, and its doctrines, to help bridge the divide between Muslims and the West. I view this divide as one of the main threats to world stability in the twenty-first century. One of my earliest models in this field was Dr. John Esposito, whose work I have admired. I also have studied the works of Dr. Akbar Ahmed and other moderate Islamic thinkers.

"I write quickly and with the intention of clearly disseminating information, in the journalistic form. The most important mission of my work is to provide information and objective reporting on a most sensitive but vital topic for Americans. I have approached writing books in the same way I have done major reports for broadcast and print media—providing thorough reporting, in-depth interviews, and insights into people who are shaping world events although they are little known in the West.

"My fifteen years of reporting and supervising coverage of the Middle East led me to try to provide a deeper analysis than daily journalism allows. My work as a fellow at the United States Institute of Peace first allowed me the break from daily journalism to pursue more in-depth research and analysis. I also have been privileged to work with dedicated, talented editors who were committed to supporting my work."

BIOGRAPHICAL AND CRITICAL SOURCES:

PERIODICALS

Nation, December 15, 2003, Baruch Kimmerling, review of *Martyrs: Innocence, Vengeance, and Despair in the Middle East,* p. 23.

DAWSON, Clay
See BARRETT, Neal, Jr.

*   *   *

DAY, Brian

PERSONAL: Male. *Education:* Attended Trent University and University of Toronto.

ADDRESSES: Home—Toronto, Ontario, Canada. *Agent*—c/o Author Mail, Guernica Editions, P.O. Box 117, Station P., Toronto, Ontario, Canada M5S 2S6.

CAREER: Educator, author, and poet. Teacher in Toronto, Ontario, Canada.

AWARDS, HONORS: E. J. Pratt Medal for Poetry, 1986.

WRITINGS:

Chronicle of Celtic Folk Customs: A Day-to-Day Guide to Folk Traditions, Hamlyn (London, England), 2000.
Love Is Not Native to My Blood (poems), Guernica Editions (Buffalo, NY), 2000.
Azure (poems), Guernica Editions (Tonawanda, NY), 2004.

Also contributor to anthology *ReCreations: Religion and Spirituality in the Lives of Queer People,* Queer Press, 1999. Contributor to periodicals, including *Hart House Review, New Quarterly,* and *Arc.*

SIDELIGHTS: Brian Day is a Canadian poet and teacher whose first collection of poetry, *Love Is Not Native to My Blood,* is an ode to his own homosexuality. Using primarily tradition meters, he explores the sexuality and mythos of homosexuality in verses that are often either directly or metaphorically erotic. Calling the debut "an extraordinarily accomplished first volume," J. Reibetanz went on to note in a *University of Toronto Quarterly* review that the collection demonstrates "cultural breadth and . . .

verbal richness." Observing that Day uses "both traditional rhymed stanzas and freer forms," the critic also appreciated the poet's "considerable wit."

Day is also the author of *Chronicle of Celtic Folk Customs: A Day-to-Day Guide to Folk Traditions,* which provides information about Celtic festivals and facts about traditions of the Welsh, Irish, Scottish, Manx, Breton, and Cornish Celtic cultures. The book also includes traditional recipes.

BIOGRAPHICAL AND CRITICAL SOURCES:

PERIODICALS

Booklist, November 1, 2000, Mary Ellen Quinn, review of *Chronicle of Celtic Folk Customs: A Day-to-Day Guide to Folk Traditions,* p. 578.

Books in Canada, January-March 2002, Geoffrey Cook, review of *Love Is Not Native to My Blood,* p. 28.

Canadian Book Review Annual, 2001, review of *Love Is Not Native to My Blood,* p. 206.

University of Toronto Quarterly, winter, 2001, J. Reibetanz, review of *Love Is Not Native to My Blood,* pp. 75-76.*

*   *   *

DEVOE, Forrest, Jr.
See PHILLIPS, Max

*   *   *

DELOREAN, John Z(achary) 1925-2005

OBITUARY NOTICE— See index for *CA* sketch: Born January 6, 1925, in Detroit, MI; died of complications from a stroke March 19, 2005, in Summit, NJ. Businessperson and author. Considered a "wonder boy" innovator at General Motors, automobile executive De-Lorean created the popular Pontiac GTO but later failed to succeed with his own car company and the expensive sports car that bears his name. Born in the auto capital of the world, he endured a childhood marked by poverty after his father abandoned the family. He turned the one advantage he had, music

lessons, into a scholarship that allowed him to attend college after serving in the U.S. Army during World War II. After graduating from the Lawrence Institute of Technology in 1948, he received an M.S. in mechanical engineering from the Chrysler Institute of Engineering in 1952, while also working for Chrysler as an engineer. During the early 1950s he was an engineer and then chief of research and development for Packard Motor Co., where he developed the "ultramatic," a new form of automatic transmission. This success led to his joining General Motors (GM) in 1956 as director of advanced engineering. It was at GM that DeLorean became a famous idea man, creating a string of innovative car models that included the GTO, Firebird, and Grand Prix, and new designs of the Bonneville and Catalina models. A savvy marketer who understood what American drivers wanted, De-Lorean not only developed stylish, powerful muscle cars, but also fuel-efficient, smaller models for more conservative drivers, such as the Pinto and the Gremlin. In addition, he held dozens of patents on various instruments and improvements he invented for cars. Rising to the position of vice president and general manager at GM in 1969, and group executive for the company's North American car and truck operations in 1972, DeLorean grew tired of the bureaucratic and sluggish thinking at GM and left the company in 1973. After a year working as president of the National Alliance of Businessmen, he formed the DeLorean Motor Company in 1974 and set up a manufacturing plant in Ireland. There, after considerable problems with its design, he finally released the DeLorean DMC-12, a stainless-steel sports car with gull-winged doors, a V-6 engine, and a 25,000 dollar price tag that was out of reach for most car buyers of the mid-1970s. Because it took seven years to develop and the results were less than popular (although the car gained fame when it was used as a time machine in the movie *Back to the Future*), DeLorean only produced nine thousand cars before the factory closed in 1982. The car maker blamed lack of support from the British government, accusing Prime Minister Margaret Thatcher of sabotaging his fund raising-efforts because the government suspected his employees were sympathetic to the Irish Republican Army. Whatever the reason, DeLorean's company soon went out of business. But this was just the beginning of his troubles. In 1982, DeLorean was arrested in Los Angeles and found himself accused of dealing in cocaine as a way to raise money for his company. His defense lawyers managed to have him acquitted in 1984, by accusing the FBI of setting DeLorean up and establishing doubt concerning a police informer's statements. Nevertheless, DeLorean spent the next year in court, defending himself against dozens of law suits, including fraud. Financially ruined and with an equally befouled reputation, he struggled for many years, declaring bankruptcy in 1999 before beginning a new venture selling watches on the Internet. A small business in Texas also survived the aftermath by servicing and providing parts for the DeLorean car. At the time of his death, the automaker, who declared himself a born-again Christian, was planning a comeback. He wrote about his experiences in automotive design in the autobiography *DeLorean* (1985).

OBITUARIES AND OTHER SOURCES:

BOOKS

DeLorean, John Z., and Ted Schwarz, *DeLorean*, Zondervan (Grand Rapids, MI), 1985.

PERIODICALS

Chicago Tribune, March 21, 2005, section 4, p. 11.
New York Times, March 21, 2005, p. A16.
Times (London, England), March 22, 2005, p. 61.
Washington Post, March 21, 2005, p. B5.

*   *   *

DESURVIRE, Emmanuel 1955-

PERSONAL: Born June 7, 1955, in Boulogne, France; son of Raymond (an aircraft engineer) and Marcelle (a psychologist) Desurvire; married Cynthia Wolsfeld (an artist), November, 1995; children: Pierre-Nikolas. *Education:* University of Paris, M.S. (theoretical physics), 1981; University of Nice, Ph.D., 1983, Sc.D., 1998.

ADDRESSES: Office—Alcatel Centre de Marcoussis, 91460 Marcoussis, France. *E-mail*—emmanuel. desurvire@alcatel.fr.

CAREER: Thomson-CSF, France, staff member, 1980-3; Stanford University, Stanford, CA, postdoctoral affiliate, 1984-86; AT&T Bell Laboratories, Holmdel, NJ, member of technical staff, 1986-90;

Columbia University, New York, NY, associate professor, 1990-93; Alcatel Research, France, group leader, then joint department leader, 1996-99, predevelopment project manager at Alcatel Submarine Networks, La Villedu Bois, France, 1999-2000, director of Alcatel Technical Academy, Marcoussis, France, 2000-04. Founder and editor-in-chief, *Optical Fiber Technology* (magazine), 1991-2000. Holder of nearly three dozen patents.

MEMBER: Institute of Electrical and Electronics Engineers (fellow).

AWARDS, HONORS: Distinguished Lecturer Award, Institute of Electrical and Electronics Engineers, 1992; International Prize in Optics, 1994; Benjamin Franklin Medal in Engineering, 1998.

WRITINGS:

Erbium-Doped Fiber Amplifiers: Principles and Applications, Wiley Publishing Group (New York, NY), 1994, revised, with others, as *Erbium-Doped Fiber Amplifiers: Device and System Developments,* 2002.
Wiley Survival Guides in Global Telecommunications: Signaling Principles, Network Protocols, and Wireless Systems, Wiley Publishing Group (New York, NY), 2004.
Wiley Survival Guides in Global Telecommunications: Broadband Access, Optical Components and Networks, and Cryptography, Wiley Publishing Group (New York, NY), 2004.

Contributor to books; contributor to more than 200 technical publications, including *Scientific American, Optics & Photonic News, La Recherche,* and *Physics Today.*

WORK IN PROGRESS: Research on ultimate transmission-capacity limits in lightwave telecommunications systems, broadband access technologies, and classical and quantum information theories.

SIDELIGHTS: Emmanuel Desurvire told *CA:* "I began writing, like any scientific/engineer contributor, with involvement in book chapters. The idea of making a single-author reference book did not start until I joined academia, because my field of expertise (erbium-doped fiber amplifiers) was brand new and unpublished in any previous reference book. My motivation was driven by a concern to reconcile first-principles with engineering, and I offered to the next generation a unified and high-level account of knowledge, based upon more than 600 new technical communications in the field, on one hand, and forty years of laser history on the other. All these references were only available on paper/book support and handwritten notes at the time.

"The motivation for my second book was to update the first reference with anything fundamental that could have been missed, along with all developments that came up during the ensuing ten years. There was no attempt to improve what is now known as 'The EDFA Bible,' but I wanted to give it an inspirational/ vocational continuation with fresh revelations and thoughts. This time the writing was accomplished along with three coauthors and colleagues, internationally reputed for their own contributions to optically-amplified communication systems. We all took great pride in the team work and professional concern for carving out an objective, 'absolute' reference meant to survive troubled market times (the Internet bubble) and inspire the generation of researchers coming immediately next.

"The motivation for the third and fourth book was the phrase, 'If you want to know a field, teach it; if you want to master it, write a book.' I had always wanted to know about the rest of telecommunications; that is, the body of knowledge outside my immediate technical expertise. The intention was to establish new conceptual links (for reference purposes) between the optics and the 'coms communities', who have historical distances because of their seemingly irreconcilable, unmistakable backgrounds.

"My first book had no competition or predecessors, a unique opportunity in science and engineering! The second book offered a professional way to show that four experts can write a book without bias, in a style carefully managed, with references as complete as humanly possible—a lasting reference with added value. The third and fourth books represented a personal attempt to revisit telecom as a unified discipline, rather than a stack of disconnected layers of knowledge (as is generally known).

"Personally, I like to teach, and I like to write, the latter being a pretext and means for the former. My company recognized a need for my expanding perspectives, and further, I had no problem writing on weekend time, bringing home loads of library books, and buying my own ones when needed. Being able to move to a different field each month with lots of different books coming up every week was extremely helpful, but a bit exhausting. The Internet allowed me to solve issues which turned out not to be so 'real' (as it often happens in this case) and to discover new subject items as well. There were lots of white papers (to read diagonally), slideware (to read as if one tries to sell you something, whether existing or not), and other press articles (to read as if written by the most biased or scientifically literate professional). The Internet provided a means for a sanity check, but overall Internet information must be taken with extreme caution, for these kinds of reasons.

"My writing process includes waking up early in the morning with fresh coffee and fuzzy, not-awake thoughts. These couple of hours of writing before work are useful, if not salutary. Your mind is at its best, creative and alert, close to conception. Such an opportunity won't come at the end of the day. There is no need for an alarm clock, because you already dream of the subject and open issues you are going to address as you wake up. The dragon of the day will be defeated, no matter how scary.

"When writing, I never forget that I am 'speaking' to a real person. Readers will like it as long as the creation makes sense. Like in music, embellishments should be sparse. Seamless first-principle derivations and inventories of technical literature (with its endless queue of references and footnotes) can make a good scientific book, but one must be careful not to become utterly boring. The idea of writing is to engage the reader's interest. If thoughts like 'ha-ha!,' 'hum!,' or 'how interesting!' are absent in the author's mind, they are unlikely to appear in the reader's mind.

"I do not write biographies, essays, histories, or fiction. My endeavor is defined by expectations from technical communities. With the third book, however, I departed from this type of security. In hindsight, I could hardly have imagined that I could describe (for instance) the principle of simultaneous secret sharing in cryptography within a global telecommunications book. But the fact is that this new knowledge rightly fits into the purpose of the book.

"Why do I write about telecommunications? The subject is central to the twenty-first century, like electricity was in the early nineteenth and computers were in the second half of the twentieth. Books (meaning intense reading) make people think, and I am inspired to be the first one to jump into some cold mountain pool of knowledge and produce circles on the water surface, no matter how cold it may initially feel."

*   *   *

DEVEAU, Sarah L. 1978-

PERSONAL: Born June 15, 1978, in Halifax, Nova Scotia, Canada; daughter of Leo (a bricklayer) and Gail (an administrative assistant; maiden name, White; later surname, Bertram) Deveau; married Keith Kucharski (a manager of a circular stair company), September 11, 1999. *Ethnicity:* "Caucasian." *Education:* University of Calgary, B.A., 2001.

ADDRESSES: Agent—Carolyn Swayze, Carolyn Swayze Literary Agency, P.O. Box 39588, White Rock, British Columbia, Canada V4B 5L6. *E-mail*—sarah@ inkmarketing.ca.

CAREER: WestJet, Calgary, Alberta, Canada, writer, 2001—.

MEMBER: Canadian Authors Association.

WRITINGS:

Sink or Swim: Get Your Degree without Drowning in Debt, Dundurn Press (Toronto, Ontario, Canada), 2003.

Contributor to periodicals, including *AirLines* and *Calgary Herald.*

*   *   *

DEVINE, Bob
See DEVINE, Robert S.

DEVINE, Robert S. 1951-
(Bob Devine)

PERSONAL: Born 1951; married; children: one daughter.

ADDRESSES: Home—Corvallis, OR. *Agent*—c/o Author Mail, Anchor Books, 1745 Broadway, New York, NY 10019.

CAREER: Freelance journalist, 1982—. Former assistant editor, *Rocky Mountain* magazine.

WRITINGS:

NONFICTION

Bush versus the Environment, Anchor Books (New York, NY), 2004.

NONFICTION; UNDER NAME BOB DEVINE

Pacific Northwest, Oregon, Washington, and Alaska, National Geographic Society (Washington, DC), 1997.
Alien Invasion: America's Battle with Non-Native Animals and Plants, National Geographic Society (Washington, DC), 1998.
Guide to America's Outdoors: Pacific Northwest, photographs by Phil Schofield, National Geographic Society (Washington, DC), 2000.
Guide to America's Outdoors: Western Canada, photographs by Raymond Gehman, National Geographic Society (Washington, DC), 2002.

Contributor to periodicals, including *Atlantic Monthly, Audubon, National Geographic Traveler, Mother Jones, Sierra* and *Travel and Leisure.*

SIDELIGHTS: Robert S. Devine is a journalist who covers environmental issues, natural history, and outdoor travel for such magazines as the *Atlantic Monthly, Audubon,* and *National Geographic.* His full-length books—some published under the name Bob Devine—also make evident his deep concern about the future of America's natural environment and the potential health hazards awaiting plants and animals, including humans, if environmental degradation occurs. Devine's book *Alien Invasion: America's Battle with Non-Native Animals and Plants* details eight dangerous plant and animal pests that have proliferated in the United States after being introduced from other continents. While Devine focuses particularly on these eight invaders, he makes clear that many thousands of species of foreign plant and animal have been brought to America, for use in everything from children's aquariums to backyard gardens. A *Publishers Weekly* critic noted that Devine's book "shows how insidious" alien plants and animals can be. *Library Journal* correspondent Laura E. Lipton cited the work for its "nontechnical and readable" style.

Devine is one of many environmental journalists who have criticized the George W. Bush administration for its actions on a variety of ecological fronts. In *Bush versus the Environment* he outlines the tactics the Bush administration used to weaken federal regulations regarding the environment, from power-plant emissions to building roads through protected national forests. He cites the administration's efforts to advance its pro-business agenda without being regarded by the public at large as dangerous to the environment. "*Bush versus the Environment* is a well-researched book, a handy, perhaps even authoritative primer on the methods that Bush uses to make dangerous policies sound responsible and benign," wrote Matthew Dallek in the *Washington Post Book World*. Dallek added that Devine "offers a fresh and shrewd take on a familiar subject." *Library Journal* contributor Ilse Heidmann concluded that Devine's "lively and well-organized book offers citizens much needed insight into this part of the Bush agenda."

BIOGRAPHICAL AND CRITICAL SOURCES:

PERIODICALS

Booklist, May 1, 2004, Carol Haggas, review of *Bush versus the Environment,* p. 1528.
Kliatt, January, 2005, Nola Thiess, review of *Bush versus the Environment,* p. 32.
Library Journal, June 15, 1998, Laura E. Lipton, review of *Alien Invasion: America's Battle with Non-Native Animals and Plants,* p. 102; June 1, 2004, Ilse Heidmann, review of *Bush Versus the Environment,*

Publishers Weekly, May 18, 1998, "Spanning the Globe," p. 64; April 5, 2004, review of *Bush versus the Environment,* p. 49.
Tribune Books (Chicago, IL), January 3, 1999, Lynn Van Matres, review of *Alien Invasion,* p. 10.
Washington Post Book World, June 20, 2004, Matthew Dallek, "Taking the Measure of the Commander in Chief, from His Spiritual Life to His Approach to War," p. 10.

ONLINE

Satya Online, http://www.satyamag.com/ (October, 2004), Catherine Clyne, "Bush and the Environment" (interview with Devine).

*   *   *

DHARMAPALA, Anagarika
    See HEWAVITARNE, (Don) David

*   *   *

DIEHL, Margaret 1955-

PERSONAL: Born 1955.

ADDRESSES: Agent—c/o Author Mail, Soho Press, 853 Broadway, New York, NY 10003.

WRITINGS:

Men, Soho Press (New York, NY), 1988.
Me and You (novel), Soho Press (New York, NY), 1990.
The Boy on the Green Bicycle: A Memoir, Soho Press (New York, NY), 1999.

ADAPTATIONS: Men was adapted for a film directed by Zoe Clarke-Williams, 1997.

SIDELIGHTS: The heroine of Margaret Diehl's first novel, *Men,* lost her virginity at age fifteen, and at age twenty-one has become a woman who believes in having a wild sex life. Stella is smart and independent. She has just graduated from college, and because of the generous support of a grandmother, she can afford an upscale Manhattan apartment. As the novel begins, she is living with her former lover, whose alcoholism has cooled their status to that of friends. Stella has no qualms about her sexual appetites as she roams New York City's streets in search of conquests. While engaging in one-night stands, Stella feels almost no embarrassment or stress. As the story progresses, however, her losses are exposed: her parents deserted her as a child, and her first lover was gay. After a move to Berkeley, she meets and falls in love with Frank, a wealthy photographer, but when she reverts to her old habits, he gives her an ultimatum.

Jami McCarty wrote in a review for the *Tucson Weekly* online that, "In the style of Raymond Carver, we see what the characters do, as if watching from a window, and decide for ourselves the reasons why." In reviewing *Men,* for Chicago's *Tribune Books,* Richard Gehr wrote that the novel "can proudly take its place on the small shelf reserved for such middlebrow examples of feminist literature as Erica Jong's *Fear of Flying* and anything by Margaret Atwood."

Men are not the obsession of the protagonist of *Me and You;* alcohol is. Gwen began drinking with her father at age twelve. Her parents divorce, and, while sister Lucy goes with their mother, Gwen heads to California, where she becomes involved in an alcoholic, abusive relationship. After Lucy flies out to save her sister and bring her back to New York, Gwen joins Alcoholics Anonymous and retreats into a somewhat reclusive life, painting portraits of the dogs of wealthy women. When Lucy marries, Gwen begins an affair with Lucy's new father-in-law, Jack, a social misfit who writes science fiction.

Elizabeth Benedict pointed out in the *New York Times Book Review* that "in pursuing Jack, she is acting out the erotically charged relationship she had with her father, with the chance to rewrite the ending." Benedict concluded by saying that she admired Diehl "for taking on so boldly the subject of women drinkers in recovery and the delicate matter of fathers who, although they don't molest their daughters, inflict lasting harm with subtly seductive words and gestures." Sybil Steinberg wrote in *Publishers Weekly* that Diehl "writes convincingly about both alcohol addiction and

the joys of erotic love," while a *Kirkus Reviews* writer noted that *Me and You* "is spiked with emotionally honest, no-holds-barred sex from a woman's point-of-view."

In *The Boy on the Green Bicycle: A Memoir* Diehl describes a comfortable childhood in Montclair, New Jersey that was shattered with the loss of both a brother and a father. Diehl's older brother and idol, Jimmy, died in a bicycle accident, and her father committed suicide shortly afterward because he felt he was to blame. Diehl's mother numbed herself with alcohol and moved her three remaining children, Diehl, Charlotte, and Johnny, to New York City. Diehl writes of her surviving brother's distress and threats of suicide, her sister's cruelty, and her own painful isolation and withdrawal into a world of books and sweets.

Stacy D'Erasmo wrote in the *New York Times Book Review* that *The Boy on the Green Bicycle* "scared me, and I mean that as a compliment. Instead of simply valorizing or sentimentalizing the imagination, Diehl gives it its due as a ferocious, drug-like force. The lion who looks like a friend to the fanciful child is also, as the adult knows, a wild animal. Diehl fearlessly inhabits both points of view. The subject of her book is less her brother and her cracked family than it is the ambiguous power of her own fantasy life."

BIOGRAPHICAL AND CRITICAL SOURCES:

BOOKS

Diehl, Margaret, *The Boy on the Green Bicycle: A Memoir,* Soho Press (New York, NY), 1999.

PERIODICALS

American Journal of Psychiatry, December, 1999, Robert Michels, review of *The Boy on the Green Bicycle,* p. 2002.
Kirkus Reviews, December 15, 1989, review of *Me and You,* p. 1767.
Library Journal, May 1, 1999, Nancy R. Ives, review of *The Boy on the Green Bicycle,* p. 88.
New York Times Book Review, August 13, 1989, George Johnson, review of *Men,* p. 28; February 11, 1990, Elizabeth Benedict, review of *Me and You,* p. 28; June 13, 1999, Stacey D'Erasmo, review of *The Boy on the Green Bicycle,* p. 24.

Observer Review, February 5, 1989, Maureen Freely, review of *Men,* p. 43.

Publishers Weekly, January 19, 1990, Sybil Steinberg, review of *Me and You,* p. 96; March 29, 1999, review of *The Boy on the Green Bicycle,* p. 74.

Tribune Books (Chicago, IL), August 14, 1988, Richard Gehr, review of *Men,* p. 6.

ONLINE

Tucson Weekly Online, http://www.weeklywire.com/ (February 23, 1998), Jami Macarty, review of *Men.**

* * *

DILEO, John 1961-

PERSONAL: Born February 1, 1961, in New York, NY; son of John and Vera DiLeo; companion of Earl McCarroll. *Ethnicity:* "Italian." *Education:* Ithaca College, B.F.A. (theater arts), 1982.

ADDRESSES: Home—New York, NY; and Milford, PA. *Agent*—Diana Finch, 116 W. 23rd St., Ste. 500, New York, NY 10011. *E-mail*—jddmovies@aol.com.

CAREER: Professional stage actor, 1982-95; full-time writer, 1995—.

MEMBER: Actors' Equity Association, Screen Actors Guild.

WRITINGS:

And You Thought You Knew Classic Movies!, St. Martin's Press (New York, NY), 1999.
One Hundred Great Film Performances You Should Remember, but Probably Don't, Limelight Editions (New York, NY), 2002.

Contributor of book reviews to *Washington Post Book World* and film reviews to *Urban Refugee* (magazine).

WORK IN PROGRESS: Book about "Great Underappreciated" American films.

SIDELIGHTS: John DiLeo told *CA:* "Writing is a way for me to share my enthusiasm for my subject (American movies). Criticism is a way to express yourself through your responses to art, and I've found it to be very gratifying to organize and shape my thoughts, and then communicate them to readers. Specifically, I write about movies that are underrated or overlooked or forgotten, and I've made it my mission to bring these films the attention they deserve.

"The work of Pauline Kael had a great impact on me long before I knew I'd ever be writing film criticism, and she continues to be an inspiration. Her access to her thoughts and feelings is so uncluttered, so true, so immediate.

"After viewing a movie, I immediately begin writing down all my thoughts (in longhand), everything that I think I want to say about it. It's important to get these ideas down right away. I usually watch the movie again, this time taking extensive notes, watching key scenes multiple times. Then I put *everything* into the computer, creating the shape of the essay as I write. At this point, I have a piece that is too long and repetitive, so I begin the stripping-away process. This part always feels like sculpting to me, cutting away the extraneous bits until the final structure is revealed. When I'm close to finishing, I usually go back to the film to recheck the details of certain scenes. I know I'm done when I can read a piece and not want to change anything. An essay usually takes me five days.

"After years of living the struggling-actor life, I started writing about movies for my own amusement, or as an escape from the dissatisfactions of my acting career. I had always been a film fanatic and decided to try to use my knowledge and create something. For me, writing is very much like acting, because I'm still trying to communicate with an audience, still trying to get a laugh or entertain or make someone think. It's been an easy transition, because writing satisfies the same needs that led me to acting."

* * *

DILLON, M(artin) C(onboy) 1938-2005

OBITUARY NOTICE— See index for *CA* sketch: Born December 7, 1938, in Los Angeles, CA; died of heart failure March 10, 2005, in Verbier, Switzerland. Educator and author. Dillon was a former professor of philosophy at the State University of New York at Binghamton. He earned his B.A. from the University of Virginia in 1960, an M.A. from the University of California at Berkeley in 1964, and an M.Phil. in 1968 and Ph.D. in 1970 from Yale University. He also served in the U.S. Naval Reserve, where he achieved the rank of captain in 1960. Dillon spent the majority of his career at Binghamton, joining the faculty in 1968 and becoming a tenured professor in 1988. He also directed the undergraduate philosophy program from 1978 to 1990, was acting chair of the department in 1982, and was acting director of the law and society program from 1987 to 1988. In addition, he taught at IBM from 1986 until 1993, the same year he retired from the university. As a philosopher, Dillon was interested in existentialism and the works of Jean-Paul Sartre and Maurice Merleau-Ponty. Honored with a State University of New York Chancellor's Award for Excellence in Teaching in 1974, he wrote or edited several texts, including *Merleau-Ponty's Ontology* (1988), *Semiological Reductionism: A Critique of the Deconstructionist Movement in Postmodern Thought* (1995), and *Beyond Romance* (2001).

OBITUARIES AND OTHER SOURCES:

ONLINE

Binghamton University Department of Philosophy Web site, http://philosophy.binghamton.edu/ (May 9, 2005).
Inside Binghamton University Online, http://inside.binghamton.edu/ (March 17, 2005).

*　　*　　*

DIRR, Michael A(lbert) 1944-

PERSONAL: Born 1944. *Education:* University of Massachusetts, Amherst, Ph.D., 1972.

ADDRESSES: Home—324 Hollow Creek Lane, Watkinsville, GA 30677. *Office*—1317 Miller Plant Science Bldg., University of Georgia, Athens, GA 30602. *E-mail*—hor370@arches.uga.edu.

CAREER: Former teacher at University of Massachusetts, University of Illinois, Urbana, and Arnold Arboretum of Harvard University; University of Georgia, Athens, professor emeritus of ornamental horticulture; GIYP.com (online horticulture directory), head of trees and shrubs category of Virtual Plant Tag database.

AWARDS, HONORS: Agricultural Alumni Outstanding Teacher award, University of Georgia College of Agricultural and Environmental Sciences, 1998; L. C. Chadwick Educator Award, American Nursery and Landscape Association, 1998; D. W. Brooks Award, University of Georgia, 2000; teaching award, American Horticultural Society, 2000; Arthur Hoyt Scott Garden and Horticultural Award; educator award, American Society of Horticultural Science; silver medal, Massachusetts Horticultural Society, for excellence in horticultural writing; Slater Wight Memorial Award, Southern Nurseryman's Association; Linnaeus Award, Chicago Botanic Garden; Medal of Honor, Garden Club of America; the Michael A. Dirr Endowed Professorship at the University of Georgia was created in Dirr's honor.

WRITINGS:

Manual of Woody Landscape Plants: Their Identification, Ornamental Characteristics, Culture, Propagation, and Uses, illustrated by Bonnie L. Dirr, Stipes Pub. (Champaign, IL), 1975, 5th revised edition, 1998.
All about Evergreens, illustrated by Ron and Ronda Hildebrand, Ortho Books (San Francisco, CA), 1984.
(With Charles W. Heuser) *The Reference Manual of Woody Plant Propagation: From Seed to Tissue Culture: A Practical Working Guide to the Propagation of over 1,100 Species, Varieties, and Cultivars,* Varsity Press (Athens, GA), 1987.
(With others) *Creative Home Landscaping: How to Plan and Beautify Your Yard: With a Guide to More than 400 Landscape Plants,* Ortho Books (San Francisco, CA), 1987.
Dirr's Hardy Trees and Shrubs: An Illustrated Encyclopedia, Timber Press (Portland, OR), 1997.
Dirr's Trees and Shrubs for Warm Climates: An Illustrated Encyclopedia, Timber Press (Portland, OR), 2002.
Hydrangeas for American Gardens, illustrated by Bonnie L. Dirr, Timber Press (Portland, OR), 2004.

Also author of *Michael A. Dirr's Photo-Library of Woody Landscape Plants on CD-ROM,* PlantAmerica.

SIDELIGHTS: Horticulturist Michael A. Dirr taught for more than twenty years at the University of Georgia. Since retiring, he has continued his research work there on a part-time basis. Dirr was instrumental in establishing the University of Georgia's campus arboretum and in preparing materials for the walking tour of trees. His Georgia plant introduction program has introduced sixty-four cultivars to the nursery trade and has inspired similar programs in other states. Dirr's passion for his subject has, over the years, inspired a growing number of students to also become horticulture professionals.

Among Dirr's books is the *Manual of Woody Landscape Plants: Their Identification, Ornamental Characteristics, Culture, Propagation, and Uses,* which has been revised many times since its first publication. It has become the bible of the landscape and nursery industry and is used in many classrooms. It is also of great value to the homeowner. Carol Stocker, who reviewed the book for the *Boston Globe,* noted that because Dirr had a one-year sabbatical at the Arnold Arboretum from 1978 to 1979, "he's familiar with New England plants, and often cites individual specimens in local parks."

Dirr's Hardy Trees and Shrubs: An Illustrated Encyclopedia contains 1,650 pictures, chosen from the vast collection of plant photographs Dirr has taken over the years. This volume features plants in hardiness zones three to six, but some of the more than 500 species that are included will grow in warmer climates. The photographs included show closeups of flowers, leaves, fruit, bark, and whole specimens, sometimes in flower or with fall coloring. *Horticulture* contributor Carol Bishop Miller called the volume "a beautiful production," while *Booklist* contributor Mary Ellen Quinn felt that *Dirr's Hardy Trees and Shrubs* will become a standard garden reference.

Dirr repeated the book's format with *Dirr's Trees and Shrubs for Warm Climates: An Illustrated Encyclopedia.* This volume includes some 1,500 photographs of species and cultivars suitable for the gardens of the American South and temperate climates as far west as British Columbia. It also contains a section on cold-hardy palms. *Booklist* reviewer Alice Joyce, who called the volume "indispensable," said that there is not another garden writer who can speak "to the subject with Dirr's experience, acumen, and ability to instruct." Callie Jo Schweitzer, who reviewed

the volume for the *Quarterly Review of Biology,* praised Dirr's photographs and added that the text "is written in a welcoming manner, as if the author was standing in the garden with readers."

Hydrangeas for American Gardens consists of ten chapters that study the wide variety within the hydrangea species, not all of which are hardy in the various zones of the United States, and many of which do not resemble the familiar white, pink, or blue hydrangea (the colors of which are influence by soil conditions). Dirr includes information on care and culture, propagation, diseases, pests, and new hybridized versions. Joyce wrote that "Dirr's reigning expertise in the realm of trees and shrubs comes through once again."

In 2004 Dirr joined the team of plant experts at *GIYP. com,* the *Green Industry Yellow Pages.* The organization's Web site hosts the *Virtual Plant Tag,* an online database of information on plants. Dirr heads the trees-and-shrubs category of the database.

BIOGRAPHICAL AND CRITICAL SOURCES:

PERIODICALS

Atlanta Journal-Constitution, April 17, 2003, Martha Tate, "Garden Notes: New Mophead Will Offer Almost 'Endless' Blooms," p. HG6.
Booklist, April, 1998, Mary Ellen Quinn, review of *Dirr's Hardy Trees and Shrubs: An Illustrated Encyclopedia,* p. 1342; January 1, 2002, Alice Joyce, review of *Dirr's Trees and Shrubs for Warm Climates: An Illustrated Encyclopedia,* p. 788; June 1, 2004, Alice Joyce, review of *Hydrangeas for American Gardens,* p. 1682.
Boston Globe, June 13, 1986, Carol Stocker, review of *Manual of Woody Landscape Plants: Their Identification, Ornamental Characteristics, Culture, Propagation, and Uses,* p. 83.
Horticulture, March, 1998, Carol Bishop Miller, review of *Dirr's Hardy Trees and Shrubs,* p. 72.
Library Journal, November 15, 1997, Daniel Kalk, review of *Dirr's Hardy Trees and Shrubs,* p. 50; February 15, 2002, Deborah Anne Broocker, review of *Dirr's Trees and Shrubs for Warm Climates,* p. 134; June 1, 2004, Beth Clewis Crim, review of *Hydrangeas for American Gardens,* p. 168.

Publishers Weekly, May 31, 2004, review of *Hydrangeas for American Gardens,* p. 69.

Quarterly Review of Biology, December, 2002, Callie Jo Schweitzer, review of *Dirr's Trees and Shrubs for Warm Climates,* p. 460.

Sunset, December, 1997, Jim McCausland, review of *Dirr's Hardy Trees and Shrubs,* p. 64.

ONLINE

GIYP.com, http://www.giyp.com/ (June, 2004), "Prolific Author and Teacher, Michael Dirr Joins GIYP. com Team of Plant Experts."*

* * *

DIXON, Franklin W.
   See BARRETT, Neal, Jr.

* * *

DOYLE, Gerald O.
   See BECKETT, Ralph L(awrence), (Sr.)

* * *

DOYLE, Noreen

PERSONAL: Female. *Education:* University of Liverpool, M.A.; Texas A&M University, M.A.

ADDRESSES: Agent—Linn Prentis, 155 East 116th St., 2F/2R, New York, NY 10028. *E-mail*—Wenamun@aol.com.

CAREER: Scholar of marine archaeology and anthropology; writer.

MEMBER: International Association of Egyptologists, Egypt Exploration Society, Science Fiction and Fantasy Writers of America, Society of Children's Book Writers and Illustrators, Phi Beta Kappa, Phi Kappa Phi.

AWARDS, HONORS: Top-ten science fiction and fantasy title designation, Amazon.com, 2004, for *The First Heroes: New Tales of the Bronze Age.*

WRITINGS:

(Editor with Harry Turtledove, and contributor) *The First Heroes: New Tales of the Bronze Age,* Tor (New York, NY), 2004.

Contributor of short stories to anthologies, including Bruce Coville, editor, *Bruce Coville's UFOs,* Avon Books (New York, NY), 2000; Coville, editor, *Bruce Coville's Strange Worlds,* Avon Books, 2000; Mike Ashley, editor, *The Mammoth Book of Egyptian Whodunnits,* Carroll & Graf (New York, NY), 2002; and Harry Turtledove, editor, *Alternate Generals II,* Baen (New York, NY), 2002. Contributor of short stories to periodicals, including *Century, Realms of Fantasy,* and *Weird Tales;* contributor to *Encyclopedia of Themes in Science Fiction and Fantasy* and *Encyclopedia of Storytelling.* Editor, *The Artifact* (newsletter of Institute for Marine Archaeology).

WORK IN PROGRESS: Young adult fantasy novels; short stories.

SIDELIGHTS: Noreen Doyle's unconventional academic background—marine archaeology—has inspired her to write short stories and novellas about ancient cultures and their beliefs. One of Doyle's novellas, *Ankhtifi the Brave Is Dying,* appeared in a collection she co-edited with Harry Turtledove, titled *The First Heroes: New Tales of the Bronze Age.* All of the works in *The First Heroes* are set in the Bronze Age, but they differ widely in presentation, in setting, and in the culture they explore. Doyle's story, for instance, concerns the last days of a powerful politician of ancient Egypt who reminisces about his climb to power during the First Intermediate Period. Doyle's short stories "The Execration," "Horizon," and "Shadow of the Pyramid" are also set in ancient Egypt, revealing the author's familiarity with that civilization.

In a *Library Journal* review of *The First Heroes,* Jackie Cassada noted that the tales "bring the Bronze Age to life," while Roland Green, writing in *Booklist,* felt that Doyle and Turtledove "contribute personally to the overall quality" of the work. A *Publishers Weekly* critic concluded that, while some of the stories in the collection offer "mere historical curiosities," others "amount to beautiful and durable artifacts."

BIOGRAPHICAL AND CRITICAL SOURCES:

PERIODICALS

Booklist April 15, 2004, Roland Green, review of *The First Heroes: New Tales of the Bronze Age,* p. 1432.
Library Journal, May 15, 2004, Jackie Cassada, review of *The First Heroes,* p. 119.
Publishers Weekly, April 5, 2004, review of *The First Heroes.*

ONLINE

Noreen Doyle Home Page, http://members.aol.com/wenamun/resume.html (February 7, 2005).*

*   *   *

DRAPER, Lydia
   See GERSHGOREN NOVAK, Estelle

*   *   *

DRURY, Rebecca
   See BARRETT, Neal, Jr.

*   *   *

DUFFY, James P(atrick) 1941-

PERSONAL: Born July 13, 1941, in New York, NY; son of Michael J. and Dorothy Veronica (Somerville) Duffy; married Kathleen Mary Gallagher, September 21, 1985; children: Alexandra, Olivia. *Education:* Graduate of University of Syracuse.

ADDRESSES: Home—496 Grove Ave., Edison, NJ 08820-3647. *Agent*—c/o Author Mail, Greenwood Publishing Group, 88 Post Road West, Westport, CT 06881. *E-mail*—jp@duffy.net.

CAREER: Writer. *Military service:* U.S. Navy, 1968-72.

WRITINGS:

How to Earn a College Degree without Going to College, Stein and Day (New York, NY), 1982, revised edition, J. Wiley (New York, NY), 1994.
How to Earn an Advanced Degree without Going to Graduate School, Stein and Day (New York, NY), 1985, revised edition, J. Wiley (New York, NY), 1994.
Cutting College Costs, Barnes & Noble Books (New York, NY), 1988.
Hitler Slept Late and Other Blunders That Cost Him the War, Praeger (New York, NY), 1991.
Learn while You Sleep, Avon Books (New York, NY), 1991.
(With Lawrence R. Reich) *You Can Go Bankrupt without Going Broke: An Essential Guide to Personal Bankruptcy,* Pharos Books (New York, NY), 1992, Beard Books (Washington, DC), 2003.
(With Vincent L. Ricci) *The Assassination of John F. Kennedy: A Complete Book of Facts,* Thunder's Mouth Press (New York, NY), 1992.
(With Vincent L. Ricci) *Target Hitler: The Plots to Kill Adolf Hitler,* Praeger (Westport, CT), 1992.
(With Melvin H. Ross) *Sailboat Chartering: The Complete Guide and International Directory,* Globe Pequot Press (Old Saybrook, CT), 1993.
(With Vincent L. Ricci) *Czars: Russia's Rulers for More than One Thousand Years,* Facts on File (New York, NY), 1995.
Lincoln's Admiral: The Civil War Campaigns of David Farragut, J. Wiley (New York, NY), 1997.
College Online: How to Take College Courses without Leaving Home, J. Wiley (New York, NY), 1997.
Hitler's Secret Pirate Fleet: The Deadliest Ships of World War II, Praeger (Westport, CT), 2001.
Target America: Hitler's Plan to Attack the United States, Praeger (Westport, CT), 2004.

SIDELIGHTS: James P. Duffy's books cover a number of nonfiction subjects, ranging from earning a college degree in a nontraditional setting to military history. Included among the history titles is *Target Hitler: The Plots to Kill Adolf Hitler,* a study of the many assassination attempts against the Nazi leader. Duffy and cowriter Vincent L. Ricci devote much of their volume to describing the actions of a small group of German officers who wanted to rid Germany of its führer, particularly through the conspiracy of 1938-39 and the wartime efforts that culminated in the July 1944 bomb plot. *Historian* contributor Donald R. Tracey felt that the book presents a good general introduction, particularly for those with no knowledge of the extensive efforts undertaken to remove Hitler from power. Tracey added that the authors "have done a good job of concentrating what is known about the various attempts on Hitler's life into a brief, readable narrative."

Lincoln's Admiral: The Civil War Campaigns of David Farragut is Duffy's history of the career of the Union naval leader David G. Farragut (1801-1870), who was also America's first admiral. The motherless boy from Tennessee was not yet ten years old when he was commissioned a midshipman. His father, who served in the American Revolution, had placed his son with the family of a naval officer who took young Farragut to sea when he fought during the War of 1812. As an experienced adult officer, Farragut made the decision to fight for the Union when the country was split by civil war in 1861. His contribution to the war came through his adaptation of warfare tactics to the shallow rivers of the South. Duffy documents Farragut's capture of New Orleans in April of 1862, his action on the Mississippi River at Vicksburg and Port Hudson, and the August, 1864 Battle of Mobile Bay. Farragut was in his sixties when he achieved his greatest accomplishments. Mark A. Weitz wrote in *Historian* that "the book is an enlightening study of an important military figure of the Civil War." A *Publishers Weekly* reviewer noted that Duffy's "descriptive writing is often compelling, and includes data on wooden and ironclad warships, cannon and mines, as well as thrilling tales of ship-to-ship action." *Atlantic Monthly* contributor Phoebe-Lou Adams noted that Duffy "does not altogether overlook the people who worked those ships. After one battle, Farragut looked at the casualties laid out on the deck and quietly wept."

In *Target America: Hitler's Plan to Attack the United States* Duffy collects in one volume the available information about Axis plots, along with speculation as to what would have happened to America had Hitler defeated the USSR. Duffy projects that Hitler would have employed transatlantic bombers, for which prototypes had been built, in addition to submarines that would have curtailed East Coast shipping. *Booklist* reviewer Gilbert Taylor called the volume "engrossing coverage for readers interested in the weaponry what-ifs of World War II."

BIOGRAPHICAL AND CRITICAL SOURCES:

PERIODICALS

Atlantic Monthly, April, 1997, Phoebe-Lou Adams, review of *Lincoln's Admiral: The Civil War Campaigns of David Farragut,* p. 120.
Booklist, February 15, 1997, Roland Green, review of *Lincoln's Admiral,* p. 998; June 1, 2004, Gilbert Taylor, review of *Target America: Hitler's Plan to Attack the United States,* p. 1689.
Historian, summer, 1993, Donald R. Tracey, review of *Target Hitler: The Plots to Kill Adolf Hitler,* p. 736; winter, 2001, Mark A. Weitz, review of *Lincoln's Admiral,* p. 408.
History: Review of New Books, winter, 1998, James E. Sefton, review of *Lincoln's Admiral,* p. 96.
Publishers Weekly, February 10, 1997, review of *Lincoln's Admiral,* p. 78.

ONLINE

James P. Duffy Home Page, http://www.jp.duffy.net (March 12, 2005).*

*   *   *

DUNBAR, Polly 1980(?)-

PERSONAL: Born c. 1980, in England; daughter of Joyce Dunbar (a writer). *Education:* Graduated from Brighton University, 1999.

ADDRESSES: Home—London, England. *Agent*—Celia Catchpole, Literary Agent, 56 Gilpin Ave., London SW14 8QY, England. *E-mail*—polly@pollydunbar.com.

CAREER: Illustrator and writer.

WRITINGS:

JUVENILE LITERATURE

Help! I'm out with the In-Crowd (and Other Saturday Nightmares), Kingfisher (London, England), 1996.

Help! I've Forgotten My Brain: And Other Exam Nightmares, Kingfisher (London, England), 1996.

(And illustrator) *Dog Blue,* Candlewick Press (Cambridge, MA), 2004.

(And illustrator) *Flyaway Katie,* Candlewick Press (Cambridge, MA), 2004.

(Illustrator) Joyce Dunbar, *Shoe Baby,* Candlewick Press (Cambridge, MA), 2005.

"HOLE STORY" SERIES

Henry VIII, Scholastic (London, England), 2002.
Scrooge, Scholastic (London, England), 2002.
Cleopatra, Scholastic (London, England), 2002.

Also illustrator for *A Saucepan on His Head* (illustration anthology), Walker, and Lesley Ely's *Looking after Louis,* Frances Lincoln.

SIDELIGHTS: Juvenile book writer and illustrator Polly Dunbar demonstrated her talents early and had two books published by the time she was sixteen years old. In *Flyaway Katie,* Dunbar tells the story of Katie, who wakes up one day in a "gray" mood. As the story progresses, Katie slowly transforms her mood by intentionally brightening up her day. She puts on bright-colored clothes and lipstick and even paints her face various colors. Katie's emotional transformation is complete when she suddenly sprouts her own wings and flies into a bright-colored painting on her bedroom wall, where she soars around with the many-colored birds depicted there. Writing for *New Pages.com,* Denise Hill called *Flyaway Katie* "an absolutely delightful book." Hill went on to note that "Katie is a great role model for inspiring children to be self-empowered in controlling their emotions and to take steps to create positive changes in themselves," while a *Kirkus Reviews* contributor called the book "A joyous cure for a case of the doldrums." In a review in *Booklist,* Ilene Cooper praised Dunbar's illustrations, noting that "Children will be engaged by the artwork." The quality of Dunbar's artwork was also commented on by Wanda Meyers-Hines in *School Library Journal,* the critic noting that "The mixed-media illustrations perfectly capture Katie's transformation." Meyers-Hines went on to comment, "Told at just the right pace, this whimsical story presents a gentle reminder of the power of a child's imagination."

Dog Blue focuses on young Bertie and his wish to have a dog. Since blue is Bertie's favorite color, he would like a blue dog. Before Bertie gets a dog of his own, he satisfies his desire for one by creating his own imaginary pet. Using his imagination, he goes through all the rituals of having a pet, including playing catch—even though Bertie himself fetches the sticks he throws. Eventually, Bertie does get a dog, but the puppy is black and white. Bertie decides that, if the dog cannot be blue, he can at least name it after his favorite color. Although Bertie finally has the dog he wanted, he still uses his imagination while playing with Blue, who now watches his new owner chase sticks. Writing in *School Library Journal,* Janet M. Bair commented that Dunbar's "pencil-and-watercolor cartoon drawings are simple enough to appeal to preschoolers, but the monochromatic colors . . . are not especially eye-catching." However, a *Kirkus Reviews* contributor praised the artwork's "informal but elegant simplicity" and added that in the story "Bertie's joy comes through loud and clear." Jennifer Mattson, writing in *Booklist,* commented that "Dunbar makes clever use of page turns, unfolding the story in pithy, alliterative prose." Calling Bertie and Blue "charmers" in a review in *Horn Book,* Joanna Rudge Long also noted that "The point that make-believe can be satisfying even though a longed-for reality may turn out to be even better is gently made."

BIOGRAPHICAL AND CRITICAL SOURCES:

PERIODICALS

Booklist, June 1, 2004, Ilene Cooper, review of *Flyaway Katie,* p. 1740; July, 2004, Jennifer Mattson, review of *Dog Blue,* p. 1846.
Horn Book, September-October, 2004, Joanna Rudge Long, review of *Dog Blue,* p. 566.
Kirkus Reviews, June 15, 2004, review of *Flyaway Katie,* p. 576; July 1, 2004, review of *Dog Blue,* p. 627.
Publishers Weekly, July 5, 2004, review of *Flyaway Katie,* p. 54; August 30, 2004, review of *Dog Blue,* p. 53.
School Library Journal, September, 2004, Wanda Meyers-Hines, review of *Flyaway Katie,* and Jane M. Bair, review of *Dog Blue,* p. 158.

ONLINE

Celia Catchpole, Literary Agent, Web site http://www.celiacatchpole.co.uk/ (March 24, 2005), "Polly Dunbar."

New Pages.com, http://www.newpages.com/ (March 24, 2005), Denise Hill, review of *Flyaway Katie.*

Polly Dunbar Home Page, http://www.pollydunbar. com (March 24, 2005).*

*   *   *

DUNDES, Alan 1934-2005

OBITUARY NOTICE— See index for *CA* sketch: Born September 8, 1934, in New York, NY; died of heart failure March 30, 2005, in Berkeley, CA. Folklorist, anthropologist, educator, and author. Dundes, a professor of anthropology at the University of California at Berkeley, was a controversial analyst of modern-day folklore. Originally a student of English literature, he earned his bachelor's and master's degrees in the subject from Yale University in 1955 and 1958, respectively. Between degrees, he also served in the U.S. Navy as a lieutenant. During these studies Dundes became fascinated by the folk stories behind much of the literature he was reading, and this led to his earning a Ph.D. in folklore from Indiana University in 1962. After a year teaching English at the University of Kansas, he joined the Berkeley faculty as an assistant professor of anthropology, becoming a full professor of anthropology and folklore in 1968. Though he wrote on many subjects, ranging from the origins of biblical stories to caste systems and vampire legends, Dundes was most famous for his analysis of the cultural phenomenon of jokes. His writings analyzed their origins and explained why people found certain jokes funny. His use of humor in his classroom made his courses at Berkeley, where he is credited with establishing the master's program in folklore, extremely popular. But it was Dundes's interpretations of culture that often drew considerable fire from critics. Among his controversial explanations were the ideas that American football was actually a form of ritualized homosexuality, that Germans' interest in scatology was related to the Holocaust, and that the stories of the Bible actually originated from an oral tradition. When it came to his writings about jokes, Dundes did not shrink from discussing the most tasteless forms of humor, ranging from toilet jokes and lascivious limericks to ethnic slurs. His purpose, though, was not to stir controversy but to approach the phenomenon of humor, no matter how insensitive, from an objective, academic viewpoint. Among Dundes's many books are *Modern Folklore* (1979), *Life Is like a Chicken*

Coop Ladder: A Portrait of German Culture through Folklore (1984), *Cracking Jokes: Studies of Sick Humor Cycles and Stereotypes* (1987), *In Quest of the Hero* (1990), and *Two Tales of Crow and Sparrow: A Freudian Folkloristic Essay on Cast and Untouchability* (1997).

OBITUARIES AND OTHER SOURCES:

PERIODICALS

Chicago Tribune, April 5, 2005, Section 1, p. 15.
Los Angeles Times, April 3, 2005, p. B14.
New York Times, April 2, 2005, p. B11.
Washington Post, April 1, 2005, p. B6.

*   *   *

DUNKLE, Clare B. 1964-

PERSONAL: Born 1964, in Fort Worth, TX; married Joseph R. Dunkle (an engineer); children: two daughters. *Education:* Trinity University, B.A., 1985; Indiana University, M.L.S.

ADDRESSES: Home—PSC 2, Box 6815, APO, AE 09012. *Agent*—Merrilee Heifetz, Writers House, 21 W. 26th St., New York, NY 10010. *E-mail*—clare@ claredunkle.com.

CAREER: Writer 2001—. Coates Library, Trinity University, San Antonio, TX, librarian, 1990-99.

AWARDS, HONORS: Mythopoeic Fantasy Award, Best Books for Young Adults designation, American Library Association, Best Book selection, Bank Street College of Education, and Best Young Adult Book selection, *Locus,* all for *The Hollow Kingdom.*

WRITINGS:

By These Ten Bones (novel), Henry Holt (New York, NY), 2005.

Contributor to periodicals, including *Journal of Academic Librarianship, OCLC Micro, Library Acquisitions: Practice and Theory,* and *Journal of the Chinese Language Teachers Association.*

"HOLLOW KINGDOM" FANTASY TRILOGY

The Hollow Kingdom, Henry Holt (New York, NY), 2003.
Close Kin, Henry Holt (New York, NY), 2004.
In the Coils of the Snake, Henry Holt (New York, NY), 2005.

WORK IN PROGRESS: Rat Trap, a novel; *The Way of Water,* a novel.

SIDELIGHTS: Fantasy novelist Clare B. Dunkle began writing while living in Germany for five years while her husband, an engineer, worked for the U.S. Air Force. On her Web site, she explained that after her two teenage daughters left for boarding school in 2001, her husband suggested that she begin writing a book since she now had the time. Discussing the influences on her writing, Duncle noted that one of her earliest memories "is of my mother reading me the story of Perseus, and, as a child, I knew many of the Greek myths by heart. I also enjoyed the Norse myths, and I read collections of tales from many cultures of the world. My English professor mother taught about folk tales, nursery rhymes, and myths in her classes, and we discussed their meanings and literary devices." Dunkle has also been inspired by the texts and stories of her religion, Catholicism. "The grandeur and delicacy of these spiritual texts have had a profound effect on my writing," she noted, "and I wouldn't have it any other way."

Dunkle's *The Hollow Kingdom,* set in nineteenth-century England, is the first volume of a trilogy. In it she introduces orphaned sisters Kate and Emily Winslow, who are living with aunts at Hallow Hill, the family home to which they are heirs. The estate is located in an isolated region shrouded by the supernatural. When Marak, the local goblin king, seeks a wife, Kate is his choice. She will have none of it, however, until Emily disappears. Kate then descends into the goblin world to bargain for her sister's return. Emily is rescued, and Kate keeps her side of the bargain and agrees to marry the grotesque but kindly king. The two girls go underground into the beautiful goblin kingdom, which Emily finds enchanting but Kate does not. As time passes, Kate becomes a true queen to her people and her husband when she saves them from a wicked sorcerer who would steal their spirits.

A *Publishers Weekly* contributor called *The Hollow Kingdom* "a masterly debut," and wrote that, "paying tribute both to the elements of Victorian novels and fairy tales, first novelist Dunkle turns out a luminously polished fantasy that starts off strong and just gets better." Janice M. Del Negro noted in the *Bulletin of the Center for Children's Books* that Dunkle "creates a weirdly attractive otherworld with touches of humor that make it fully dimensional. Characterizations are solid with intriguing complications."

In *Close Kin,* the next book in the series, now eighteen-year-old Emily is the object of the affection of Seylin, who is part elf, the result of elf brides captured by the goblins long ago. When he awkwardly attempts to express his love for her, the situation goes badly, and Seylin flees the goblin kingdom to explore his elfin roots. Emily realizes she loves Seylin and goes off with the goblin Ruby to find him, even as Marak plans a strategy to add more elf blood to the goblin's gene pool. Seylin and Emily, meanwhile, discover that the few surviving elves they find no longer have their magic, their culture, or even their literacy, since they have lost everything, including their books, in the goblin-elf wars.

Reviewing *Close Kin* for *School Library Journal,* Farida S. Dowler wrote that "the narrative draws readers into a multifaceted world of strong, compelling individuals." Timnah Card commented in the *Bulletin of the Center for Children's Books* that, "as in the first book, nimble narration and sympathetic characterization involve the reader from page one."

In the Coils of the Snake is the third and final book of the trilogy. Marak now hands his reign over to Catspaw, the new goblin king, and to Miranda, the human girl who will sit beside him. Eventually, an elf opponent with real magical strength appears to face the goblins, challenging their heavy-handed tactics as well as their assumptions about their own racial superiority.

Discussing her first non-series work, Dunkle told *CA:* "I have taken on a different challenge in my fantasy/horror novel, *By These Ten Bones,* striving for as much historical accuracy as possible in the story's medieval Highland setting while still providing an exciting fantasy read. Now I am taking a break from historical fantasy altogether. My completed manuscript, *Rat Trap,* features a futuristic science-fiction dystopia full of modern slang and catchy gadgets, based loosely on the *Tale of the Pied Piper.*"

BIOGRAPHICAL AND CRITICAL SOURCES:

PERIODICALS

Booklist, November 15, 2003, Jennifer Mattson, review of *The Hollow Kingdom,* p. 608; October 1, 2004, Jennifer Mattson, review of *Close Kin,* p. 322.

Bulletin of the Center for Children's Books, February, 2004, Janice M. Del Negro, review of *The Hollow Kingdom,* p. 227; December, 2004, Timnah Card, review of *Close Kin,* p. 165.

Kirkus Reviews, October 1, 2003, review of *The Hollow Kingdom,* p. 1223; September 15, 2004, review of *Close Kin,* p. 913; April 15, 2005, review of *By These Ten Bones,* p. 472.

Publishers Weekly, November 17, 2003, review of *The Hollow Kingdom,* p. 66.

School Library Journal, December, 2003, Bruce Anne Shook, review of *The Hollow Kingdom,* p. 149; October, 2004, Farida S. Dowler, review of *Close Kin,* p. 161.

Voice of Youth Advocates, April, 2004, Stacy Dillon, review of *The Hollow Kingdom,* p. 58; December, 2004, Stacy Dillon, review of *Close Kin,* p. 402.

ONLINE

Clare B. Dunkle Home Page, http://www.claredunkle. com (March 13, 2005).

*   *   *

DUNNETT, Nigel (P.) 1962(?)-

PERSONAL: Born c. 1962, in England. *Education:* University of Bristol, B.S., 1984; Wye College, London, M.S., 1986; University of Sheffield, Ph.D., 1994.

ADDRESSES: Home—Sheffield, England. *Office*—Department of Landscape, University of Sheffield, Floor 3, Arts Tower, Western Bank, Sheffield S10 TN, England. *E-mail*—N.Dunnett@sheffield.ac.uk.

CAREER: Landscape and ecological consultant to British Forestry Commission and Game Conservancy, and to private contractors in England, Italy, and the United States, 1986-89; North Carolina State University, Raleigh, fellow in horticulture and landscape architecture, 1989-91; University of Sheffield, Sheffield, England, 1995—began as lecturer, became senior lecturer in landscape design. Creator of public meadows and roof gardens, Sheffield, England; private consultant on landscape design, urban park regeneration, and gardens. Lecturer on ecology and landscape design.

WRITINGS:

Vegetation and Climate: A Thirty-six-Year Study in Road Verges at Bibury, Gloucestershire, University of Sheffield (Sheffield, England), 1995.

(Editor with James Hitchmough) *The Dynamic Landscape: Naturalistic Planting in an Urban Context,* Spon Press (New York, NY), 2003.

(With Noël Kingsbury) *Planting Green Roofs and Living Walls,* Timber Press (Portland, OR), 2004.

Contributor to books, including *Readers Guide to the Social Sciences* and *Encyclopedia of Garden and Landscape History.* Contributor, J. Benson and M. Roe, editors, *Landscape and Sustainability,* Spon Press (New York, NY), 2000. Contributor to periodicals, including *Garden, Restoration Ecology, Functional Ecology, Garden Design Journal,* and *Journal of Ecology.*

WORK IN PROGRESS: Contributing to *The Ecology and Design of Urban Landscape Plantings,* for Spon Press, and *Aspects of Applied Biology.*

SIDELIGHTS: Nigel Dunnett is a landscape architect and college professor who works to create and restore sustainable plant life in urban areas, backyard gardens, and even on the rooftops of buildings. He has participated in projects that return vegetation to former industrial lands and even to acreage that has been chemically contaminated or over-farmed. With Noël Kingsbury, Dunnett is the coauthor of *Planting Green Roofs and Living Walls,* a work that provides step-by-step instructions for growing gardens on rooftops and in the shingles of homes or smaller structures. In the *Garden Design Journal* Dunnett wrote that rooftop gardening "can be used to create the kind of dramatic flowering meadows that are often difficult to produce at ground level." He added: "There is perhaps no better signal of environmental intent than the integration of a prominent green roof on a garden building."

In her *E* magazine review of *Planting Green Roofs and Living Walls,* Katherine Hartley observed that Dunnett and Kingsbury "illustrate the beauty and practicality of green roofs and façades." *Booklist* reviewer Alice Joyce cited the work for its "fascinating amount of data" and concluded that the material "will be welcomed by a wide audience." In *Bookwatch,* a reviewer commended the authors for introducing "an innovative horticultural field," and placed *Planting Green Roofs and Living Walls* among a group of "excellent gardening references." Edward J. Valauskas in *Library Journal* called the title a "fact-rich, well-illustrated, and accessible book."

BIOGRAPHICAL AND CRITICAL SOURCES:

PERIODICALS

Booklist, May 15, 2004, Alice Joyce, review of *Planting Green Roofs and Living Walls,* p. 1587.
Bookwatch, September, 2004, review of *Planting Green Roofs and Living Walls,* p. 2.
Garden Design Journal, October, 2004, Nigel Dunnett, "Rooftop Futures," pp. 30-34.
Library Journal, May 15, 2004, Edward J. Valauskas, review of *Planting Green Roofs and Living Walls,* p. 107.

ONLINE

University of Sheffield Landscape Department Web site, http://www.shef.ac.uk/landscape/ (February 7, 2005), "Nigel Dunnett."*

*   *   *

DURR, Bob
  See DURR, R(obert) A(llen)

DURR, R(obert) A(llen)
  (Bob Durr)

PERSONAL: Born in Brooklyn, NY. *Education:* Hofstra College, B.A. (cum laude, with honors); University of Connecticut, M.A.; Johns Hopkins University, Ph.D.

ADDRESSES: Home—Talkeetna, AK. *Agent*—c/o St. Martin's Press, 175 Fifth Ave., New York, NY 10010.

CAREER: Syracuse University, Syracuse, NY, former professor; self-employed writer, fisherman, and artist, 1968—.

MEMBER: Alaska Watercolor Society.

WRITINGS:

On the Mystical Poetry of Henry Vaughan, Harvard University Press (Cambridge, MA), 1962.
Poetic Vision and the Psychedelic Experience, Syracuse University Press (Syracuse, NY), 1970.
(As Bob Durr) *Down in Bristol Bay: High Tides, Hangovers, and Harrowing Experiences on Alaska's Last Frontier* (memoir), St. Martin's Press (New York, NY), 1999.
(As Bob Durr) *The Coldman Cometh: A Family's Adventure in the Alaska Bush* (memoir), Thomas Dunne Books (New York, NY), 2004.

SIDELIGHTS: R. A. Durr was a tenured professor who had spent several summers with his family at an isolated Alaskan lake before they made a permanent move there in 1968. They lived in temporary cabins for two years while Durr built one large enough for the family, with the help of neighbors and his eldest son. Publishing his work under the name Bob Durr, he has written two memoirs of life in Alaska: *Down in Bristol Bay: High Tides, Hangovers, and Harrowing Experiences on Alaska's Last Frontier* and *The Coldman Cometh: A Family's Adventure in the Alaska Bush.*

In *Down in Bristol Bay* he writes of his homemade boat, *Port n Storm,* from which he fishes with his son for that short period of time each year when it is possible. He writes of his drinking—a popular pastime in the isolated north—his philosophy, and of adultery. Durr, who became known as "Jungle Bob," intersperses his story with quotes from Edgar Allan Poe and William Butler Yeats. He writes that in the Native Americans he found people "whose forebears and culture glowed like a beacon in my mind, guiding me into the deep channels from so-called civilization."

A *Publishers Weekly* contributor said that "evoking the earnest soul-seeking of *Zen and the Art of Motorcycle Maintenance,* Durr spins out a metaphysics of adventure in which life is lived as a kind of 'sustained brinkmanship.'" "Brilliant, compelling, believable, and astonishingly sound, Durr's book challenges today's conventional wisdom and custom," wrote Patricia Monaghan in a *Booklist* review of *Down in Bristol Bay.*

Booklist critic Deborah Donovan wrote that Durr's second memoir, *The Coldman Cometh,* is "an adventure, a plea for an alternative lifestyle, and a survival saga by an author who still lives his story today." Durr recounts his family's story,tale, this time adding in the details of day-to-day survival and his acceptance of his need to own a chainsaw and a snowmobile. He writes of the sauna that burned down the family home, and of the subsequent task of rebuilding the house. A *Kirkus Reviews* contributor called *The Coldman Cometh* "as unadorned as the life described, aboriginal and rejoicing."

BIOGRAPHICAL AND CRITICAL SOURCES:

BOOKS

Durr, Bob, *Down in Bristol Bay: High Tides, Hangovers, and Harrowing Experiences on Alaska's Last Frontier,* St. Martin's Press (New York, NY), 1999.
Durr, Bob, *The Coldman Cometh: A Family's Adventure in the Alaska Bush,* Thomas Dunne Books (New York, NY), 2004.

PERIODICALS

Booklist, April 15, 1999, Patrician Monaghan, review of *Down in Bristol Bay,* p. 1510; June 1, 2004, Deborah Donovan, review of *The Coldman Cometh,* p. 1690.
Chicago Sun-Times, August 29, 2004, Stephen J. Lyons, review of *The Coldman Cometh,* p. 13.
Kirkus Reviews, May 1, 2004, review of *The Coldman Cometh,* p. 428.
Library Journal, April 1, 1999, Kimberly A. Bateman, review of *Down in Bristol Bay,* p. 120.
Publishers Weekly, April 19, 1999, review of *Down in Bristol Bay,* p. 46.
USA Today, August 17, 2004, review of *The Coldman Cometh,* p. B11.*

E

EASTWOOD, Clint(on, Jr.) 1930-

PERSONAL: Born May 31, 1930, in San Francisco, CA; son of Clinton and Ruth (Runner) Eastwood; married Maggie Johnson (a model), December 19, 1953 (divorced, 1982); married Dina Ruiz (a newscaster), March 31, 1996; children: (with Roxanne Tunis) Kimber L. (an actress); (first marriage) Kyle, Alison; (with Jacelyn Reeves) Kathryn Ann, Scott C.; (with Frances Fisher) Francesca Ruth; (second marriage) Morgan. *Education:* Attended Los Angeles College.

ADDRESSES: Office—Malpaso Productions, 4000 Warner Blvd., #16, Burbank, CA 91522. *Agent*—William Morris Agency, 151 South El Camino Dr., Beverly Hills, CA 90212-2704.

CAREER: Actor, director, and producer; owner of Malpaso Productions, Burbank, CA; mayor of Carmel, CA, 1986-88. Actor in films, including (uncredited; as lab technician) *Revenge of the Creature,* Universal, 1955; (uncredited; as first Saxon) *Lady Godiva* (also known as *Lady Godiva of Conventry*), Universal, 1955; (uncredited; as first pilot) *Tarantula,* Universal, 1955; (as Jonesey) *Francis in the Navy,* Universal, 1955; (uncredited; as Tom, the ranch hand) *Star in the Dust* (also known as *Law Man*), 1956; (uncredited; as Will) *Never Say Goodbye,* Universal, 1956; (uncredited; as Marine medic), *Away All Boats,* 1956; (as Lieutenant Jack Rice, roughrider) *The First Traveling Saleslady,* RKO Radio Pictures, 1956; (as Dumbo pilot) *Escapade in Japan,* Universal/RKO Radio Pictures, 1957; (as Keith Williams) *Ambush at Cimarron Pass,* Twentieth Century-Fox, 1958; (as George Moseley) *Lafayette Escadrille* (also known as *Hell Bent for Glory* and *With You in My Arms*), Warner Bros., 1958; (as the man with no name) *A Fistful of Dollars,* United Artists, 1964; (as the man with no name) *For a Few Dollars More,* United Artists, 1967; (as the man with no name) *The Good, the Bad, and the Ugly,* United Artists, 1967; (as Lieutenant Morris Pimpennel Schaffer) *Where Eagles Dare,* Metro-Goldwyn-Mayer, 1968; (as Jed Cooper) *Hang 'em High,* United Artists, 1968; (as Coogan) *Coogan's Bluff,* Universal, 1968; (as Charlie, Giovanna's husband) "Una sera come le altre," *The Witches,* Lopert, 1969; (as Pardner [Sylvester Newel]) *Paint Your Wagon,* Paramount, 1969; (as Lieutenant Kelly) *Kelly's Heroes,* Metro-Goldwyn-Mayer, 1970; (as Hogan) *Two Mules for Sister Sara,* Universal, 1970; (as Corporal John McBurney) *The Beguiled,* Universal, 1971; (as Dave Garland) *Play Misty for Me,* Universal, 1971; (as Harry Callahan [title role]) *Dirty Harry,* Warner Bros., 1971; (as title role) *Joe Kidd,* Universal, 1972; (as the stranger) *High Plains Drifter,* Universal, 1973; (as Harry Callahan) *Magnum Force,* Warner Bros., 1973; (as John "Thunderbolt" Doherty) *Thunderbolt and Lightfoot,* United Artists, 1974; (as Jonathan Hemlock) *The Eiger Sanction,* Universal, 1975; (as title role) *The Outlaw Josey Wales,* Warner Bros., 1976; (as Harry Callahan) *The Enforcer,* Warner Bros., 1976; (as Ben Shockley) *The Gauntlet,* Warner Bros., 1977; (as Philo Beddoe) *Every Which Way but Loose,* Warner Bros., 1978; (as Frank Morris) *Escape from Alcatraz,* Paramount, 1979; (in title role) *Bronco Billy,* Warner Bros., 1980; (as Philo Beddoe) *Any Which Way You Can,* Warner Bros., 1980; (as Major Mitchell Gant/Leon Sprague/Michael Lewis) *Firefox,* Warner Bros., 1982; (as Red Stovall) *Honky-tonk Man,* Warner Bros., 1982; (as Harry Callahan) *Sudden Impact,* Warner Bros., 1983; (as Wes Block) *Tightrope,* Warner Bros., 1984; (as Lieutenant Speer)

City Heat, Warner Bros., 1984; (as the preacher) *Pale Rider,* Warner Bros., 1985; (as Sergeant Thomas "Gunny" Highway) *Heartbreak Ridge,* Warner Bros., 1986; (as Harry Callahan) *The Dead Pool,* Warner Bros., 1988; (as Tommy Nowak) *Pink Cadillac,* Warner Bros., 1989; (as John Wilson) *White Hunter, Black Heart,* Warner Bros., 1990; (as Nick Pulovski) *The Rookie,* Warner Bros., 1990; (as William Munny) *Unforgiven,* Warner Bros., 1992; (as Red Garnett) *A Perfect World,* Warner Bros., 1993; (as Secret Service Agent Frank Horrigan) *In the Line of Fire,* Columbia, 1993; (as Robert Kincaid) *The Bridges of Madison County,* Warner Bros., 1995; (as Wild Bill) *Hollywood Maverick: The Life and Times of William A. Wellman,* 1995; (uncredited; as himself) *Casper,* Universal, 1995; (as Luther Whitney) *Absolute Power,* Columbia/Sony Pictures Entertainment, 1997; (as himself) *Junket Whore,* 1998; (as Steve Everett, Oakland Tribune reporter) *True Crime,* Warner Bros., 1999; (as himself) *Forever Hollywood,* 1999; (as Dr. Frank Corvin) *Space Cowboys,* Warner Bros., 1999; (as Terry McCaleb) *Blood Work,* 2002; and (as Frankie Dunn) *Million-Dollar Baby,* 2004. Director of films, including *Play Misty for Me,* Universal, 1971; *Breezy,* Universal, 1973; *High Plains Drifter,* Universal, 1973; *The Eiger Sanction,* Universal, 1975; *The Outlaw Josey Wales,* Warner Bros., 1976; *The Gauntlet,* Warner Bros., 1977; and *Bronco Billy,* Warner Bros., 1980. Director and producer of films, including *Firefox,* Warner Bros., 1982; *Honkytonk Man,* Warner Bros., 1982; *Sudden Impact,* Warner Bros., 1983; *Pale Rider,* Warner Bros., 1985; *Heartbreak Ridge,* Warner Bros., 1986; *Bird,* Warner Bros., 1988; *White Hunter, Black Heart,* Warner Bros., 1990; (executive producer) *The Rookie,* Warner Bros., 1990; *Unforgiven,* Warner Bros., 1992; *A Perfect World,* Warner Bros., 1993; *The Bridges of Madison County,* Warner Bros., 1995; *Midnight in the Garden of Good and Evil,* Warner Bros., 1997; *Absolute Power,* Columbia/Sony Pictures Entertainment, 1997; *True Crime,* Warner Bros., 1999; *Space Cowboys,* Warner Bros., 1999; *Blood Work,* 2002; *Mystic River,* Warner Bros., 2003; and *Million-Dollar Baby,* 2004. Producer of films, including *Tightrope,* Warner Bros., 1984; *The Dead Pool,* Warner Bros., 1988; (executive producer) *Thelonius Monk: Straight, No Chaser* (also known as *Straight, No Chaser*), Warner Bros., 1988; and *The Stars Fell on Henrietta,* Warner Bros., 1995. Worked on other films, including (as Western advisor [Italian prints only]), *A Fistful of Dollars,* United Artists, 1964; (uncredited; as director of suicide jumper sequence) *Dirty Harry,* Warner Bros., 1971. Composer of songs for films, including *Bronco Billy,* Warner Bros., 1980; *City Heat,* Warner

Bros., 1984; *Tightrope,* Warner Bros., 1984; *Pale Rider,* Warner Bros., 1985; *The Bridges of Madison County,* Warner Bros., 1995; "How Much I Care," *Heartbreak Ridge,* Warner Bros., 1986; "Claudia's Theme," *Unforgiven,* Warner Bros., 1992; "Big Fran's Baby," *A Perfect World,* Warner Bros., 1993; "Power Waltz" and "Kate's Theme," *Absolute Power,* Columbia/Sony Pictures Entertainment, 1997; "Why Should I Care," *True Crime,* Warner Bros., 1999; and *Space Cowboys,* Warner Bros., 1999. Appeared in television series, including (as Rowdy Yates) *Rawhide,* Columbia Broadcasting System (CBS), 1959-66; and *The Story of Hollywood,* Turner Network Television (TNT), 1988. Appeared as himself in television specials, including *Disneyland '59* (also known as *Kodak Presents Disneyland '59*), 1959; *The Man with No Name,* 1977; *Tom Synder's Celebrity Spotlight,* 1980; *All-Star Party for Clint Eastwood,* CBS, 1986; *Fame, Fortune, and Romance,* syndicated, 1986; *James Stewart: A Wonderful Life,* Public Broadcasting System (PBS), 1987; *Happy Birthday, Hollywood,* American Broadcasting Companies (ABC), 1987; *The Ultimate Stuntman: A Tribute to Dar Robinson,* 1987; *All-Star Party for Joan Collins,* CBS, 1987; *The Presidential Inaugural Gala,* CBS, 1989; (as host) *Gary Cooper: American Life, American Legend,* TNT, 1989; *The Siskel and Ebert Special,* CBS, 1990; *Sammy Davis Jr.'s 60th Anniversary Celebration,* ABC, 1990; (as host and narrator) *Here's Looking at You,* Warner Bros., ABC, 1991; *Eastwood & Co. Making "Unforgiven,"* ABC, 1992; *Clint Eastwood on Westerns,* 1992; *The Barbara Walters Special,* ABC, 1992; *Macho Men of the Movies with David Sheehan,* National Broadcasting Company (NBC), 1993; *Clint Eastwood's Favorite Films,* Cinemax, 1993; *The Twelve Most Fascinating People of 1993,* ABC, 1993; *Clint Eastwood Talking with David Frost,* PBS, 1993; *And the Winner Is,* syndicated, 1993; (as host and narrator) *Don't Pave Main Street: Carmel's Heritage,* 1994; *Hollywood Stars: A Century of Cinema,* Disney Channel, 1995; *The First 100 Years: A Celebration of American Movies,* Home Box Office (HBO), 1995; *A Personal Journey with Martin Scorsese through American Movies,* 1995; *The American Film Institute Salute to Clint Eastwood,* ABC, 1996; *Eastwood on Eastwood,* TNT, 1997; *Big Guns Talk: The Story of the Western,* TNT, 1997; *The 25th American Film Institute Life Achievement Award: A Salute to Martin Scorsese,* CBS, 1997; *American Film Institute's 100 Years . . . 100 Movies,* CBS, 1998; *The Warner Bros. Story: No Guts, No Glory: 75 Years of Stars,* TNT, 1998; *The Warner Bros. Story: No Guts, No Glory: 75 Years of Laughter,* TNT, 1998; *The Warner Bros. Story:*

No Guts, No Glory: 75 Years of Award Winners, TNT, 1998; *The Warner Bros. Story: No Guts, No Glory: 75 Years of Blockbusters,* TNT, 1998; *AFI's 100 Years . . . 100 Stars,* CBS, 1999; *James Bacon: The E! True Hollywood Story,* E! Entertainment Television, 1999; *Intimate Portrait: Marsha Mason,* Lifetime, 1999; *American Masters: Clint Eastwood: Out of the Shadows,* PBS, 2000; *The Making of "Space Cowboys,"* 2000; *James Garner: A Maverick Spirit,* Arts and Entertainment, 2000; *The Kennedy Center Honors: A Celebration of the Performing Arts,* CBS, 2000; *America: A Tribute to Heroes,* 2001; *AFI Life Achievement Award: A Tribute to Barbra Streisand,* Fox, 2001; *Kurosawa,* PBS, 2002; and *Intimate Portrait: Melody Thomas Scott,* 2002. Appeared in videos, including *Dirty Harry: The Original,* 2001; (as himself) *All on Account a Pullin' a Trigger,* 2002; (as himself) *A Decade under the Influence,* 2003; (as himself) *Leone's West,* 2004; and (as himself) *The Leone Style,* 2004. Appeared at televised awards presentations, including (as presenter) *The 42nd Annual Academy Awards,* 1970; *The 21st Annual NAACP Image Awards,* NBC, 1989; *The All-Star Pro Sports Awards,* ABC, 1990; *The Movie Awards,* CBS, 1991; *The 65th Annual Academy Awards Presentation,* ABC, 1993; *The 50th Annual Golden Globe Awards,* Turner Broadcasting System (TBS), 1993; *The 66th Annual Academy Awards Presentation,* ABC, 1994; *The 67th Annual Academy Awards,* ABC, 1995; *The 72nd Annual Academy Award Presentation,* ABC, 2000; and *The 61st Annual Golden Globe Awards,* 2004. Appeared in episodes of television series, including "Cochise, Greatest of the Apaches," *TV Reader's Digest,* ABC, 1956; "The Last Letter," *Death Valley Days,* 1956; "White Fury," *The West Point Story,* ABC, 1957; "The Charles Avery Story," *Wagon Train,* NBC, 1957; "The Lonely Watch," *Navy Log,* ABC, 1958; *Highway Patrol,* 1958; (as Red Hardigan) "Duel at Sundown," *Maverick,* ABC, 1959; "Clint Eastwood Meets Mr. Ed," *Mr. Ed,* CBS, 1962; "Clint Eastwood: The Man from Malpaso," *Crazy about the Movies,* Cinemax, 1993; and *The O'Reilly Factor,* Fox News Channel, 2001; also appeared as himself in *Wogan; The Directors,* Encore; *The Story of Hollywood,* TBS; *American Cinema,* PBS; and *Fame, Fortune, and Romance.* Director of episode "Vanessa in the Garden," *Amazing Stories,* NBC, 1985. Recorded albums, including *Eastwood after Hours—Live at Carnegie Hall,* Malpaso Records, 1997; *Music from and Inspired by the Motion Picture "Midnight in the Garden of Good and Evil,"* Malpaso Records, 1997; and *Monterey Jazz Festival: Forty Legendary Years,* Malpaso Records, 1998; performed on single "Smokin' the

Hive" with Randy Travis, 1990. Provided voice of Mitchell Gant in the video game *Firefox,* 1983. Hog's Breath Inn, Carmel, CA, owner; Pebble Beach Golf Country Club, Monterey Peninsula, CA, co-owner; former lumberjack in Oregon, steel-furnace stoker, and gas pumper; state of California, parks commissioner, 2002—. Member of National Council on the Arts, 1973. *Military service:* U.S. Army; served during 1950s.

AWARDS, HONORS: Golden Globe Award for World Film Favorite—Male, Hollywood Foreign Press Association, 1971; People's Choice Awards for Favorite Motion-Picture Actor, 1981, 1984, 1985, and 1987; named chevalier des Lettres, French government, 1985; shared Golden Apple Star of the Year Award, Hollywood Women's Press Club, 1985; People's Choice Award for All-Time Favorite, 1988; Cecil B. De Mille Award, Hollywood Foreign Press Association, 1988; Orson Welles Award for Best Directorial Achievement—English Language, 1988, and Golden Globe Award for Best Director, 1989, both for *Bird;* Hasty Pudding Man of the Year Award, Hasty Pudding Theatricals, 1991; Golden Globe Award for Best Director, Academy Awards for Best Director and Best Picture, Academy Award nomination for best actor, all Academy of Motion Picture Arts and Sciences, best picture award, Los Angeles Film Critics, and best picture award, Boston Society of Film Critics, all 1992, all for *Unforgiven;* named NATO/ShoWest Director of the Year, 1993; Irving G. Thalberg Memorial Award, Academy of Motion Picture Arts and Sciences, 1995; Life Achievement Award, American Film Institute, 1996; honorary César award (France), 1998, for career achievement; Golden Lion, Venice Film Festival, 2000, for career achievement; special tribute, Deauville Film Festival, 2000; Bronze Plaque of the City of Paris, Paris, France, 2000; Kennedy Center honor, 2000; Silver Sword Award, Maui Film Festival, 2002; Lifetime Achievement Award, Chicago Film Festival, 2002; Lifetime Achievement Award, Screen Actors Guild, 2003; Carrosse d'Or, Society of French Film Directors, Golden Coach, Cannes Film Festival, all 2003, and César Award, Fotogramas de Plata, London Critics Circle Film Award, and Sant Jordi Award, all 2004, all for *Mystic River;* recipient of and nominated for numerous other awards.

WRITINGS:

(Photographer) *Bridges of Madison County Memory Book,* Warner Books (New York, NY), 1995.

EASTWOOD   *CONTEMPORARY AUTHORS • Volume 237*

Clint Eastwood: Interviews ("Conversations with Film-makers" series), edited by Robert Kapsis and Kathie Coblantz, University Press of Mississippi (Jackson, MS), 1999.

Also wrote *Beguiled/Laser;* contributed to *A Siegel Film: An Autobiography,* by Don Siegel. Uncredited contributor to screenplay *A Fistful of Dollars,* United Artists, 1964.

SIDELIGHTS: Clint Eastwood is one of the most enduring and multi-talented men in Hollywood. He has worked on films in a variety of roles, including actor, director, producer, and composer, since 1955. As an actor, he brought to life and made legendary several rugged characters, including the "Man with No Name" in seminal "spaghetti" westerns such as *A Fistful of Dollars, For a Few Dollars More,* and *The Good, the Bad and the Ugly,* and Inspector Harry Callahan in the films *Dirty Harry, Magnum Force, The Enforcer, Sudden Impact,* and *The Dead Pool.*

Characters Eastwood played in the early part of his career often share a common persona; as described by Peter Biskind in *Premiere:* "the Man with No Name squinting in the fierce midday sun, laconic, cool, and laid-back but remorseless and vengeful at the same time, coming from nowhere, going nowhere, without a past, without a future." Although these films were box-office successes, in many cases stunningly so, they were also criticized for glorifying violence and lawlessness.

Even during his first starring role, on the long-running Western television series *Rawhide,* Eastwood showed an interest in directing. After much persuasion, he convinced the show's producers to allow him to direct advertisements for upcoming episodes. Finally, in 1971, he was given the opportunity to direct his first feature-length film, the thriller *Play Misty for Me.* Eastwood also starred in that film, playing a disc jockey who is stalked by a disturbed female fan. This set the pattern for many of his best works over the next thirty years: Eastwood both directed and starred in such successful films as *The Outlaw Josey Wales, The Bridges of Madison County,* and his highly acclaimed *Unforgiven.* That 1992 film, a revisionist Western in which Eastwood plays a gunman who has grown disgusted with violence, won Eastwood his first Academy awards, for best director and best picture.

His 2003 work, *Mystic River,* was also highly lauded and nominated for numerous awards, including Best Director and Best Picture.

A collection of interviews Eastwood gave over the years, in which he discusses his perspective on directing films, was published in 1999 as part of the "Conversations with Filmmakers" series. *Clint Eastwood: Interviews* contains twenty-two interviews, from both artistic journals and the popular press, seven of which are presented in English for the first time. The foreign interviews, which are from British, French and German publications, are particularly notable because Eastwood was respected as a director in Europe before American critics openly recognized his accomplishments. Americans "had a hard time convincing themselves I could be a director because they already had a hard time recognizing me as an actor," Eastwood commented in one interview included in the book.

Throughout his directing and producing career, Eastwood has been renowned for his ability to bring films in under budget, even in the face of uncooperative weather or other potential calamities. In some interviews, Eastwood explains why being responsible with his backers' money is so important to him. He also lays out his theory of directing, which emphasizes preparation before filming begins to save the crews and actors expensive time during the shoot. In other interviews, Eastwood talks about his love for jazz music, his political views, and his childhood. In all his interviews, Gordon Flagg noted in a review of *Clint Eastwood* for *Booklist,* "his verbal unpretentiousness corresponds well to his straightforward filmmaking."

BIOGRAPHICAL AND CRITICAL SOURCES:

BOOKS

Authors and Artists for Young Adults, Volume 18, Gale (Detroit, MI), 1996.

Eastwood, Clint, *Clint Eastwood: Interviews* ("Conversations with Filmmakers" series), edited by Robert Kapsis and Kathie Coblantz, University Press of Mississippi (Jackson, MS), 1999.

Encyclopedia of World Biography, 2nd edition, Gale (Detroit, MI), 1998.

International Directory of Films and Filmmakers, Volume 2: *Directors,* Volume 2: *Actors and Actresses,* St. James Press (Detroit, MI), 1996.

Newsmakers 1993, Issue 4, Gale (Detroit, MI), 1993.

St. James Encyclopedia of Popular Culture, St. James Press (Detroit, MI), 2000.

PERIODICALS

Back Stage West, March 6, 2003, Jenelle Riley, "In like Clint: SAG's 2003 Lifetime Achievement Award Recognizes the Actor Who Went from Being the Man with No Name to One of the Biggest Names in Hollywood," pp. 1-3.

Booklist, May 1, 1999, Gordon Flagg, review of *Clint Eastwood: Interviews,* p. 1569.

Daily Variety, May 28, 2002, Tim Ryan, "Maui to Honor Eastwood," pp. 5-6; June 25, 2002, "The 38th Chicago International Film Festival Will Honor Clint Eastwood," p. 26; February 26, 2003, Andy Klein, "Looking beyond a Tough Guise," pp. A16-A17.

Europe Intelligence Wire, May 13, 2003, "Clint Eastwood to be Honoured by French Film Directors at Cannes."

New Yorker, March 24, 2003, Lillian Ross, interview with Eastwood, p. 40.

Premiere, April, 1993, pp. 52-60.

Variety, February 28, 2000, David Rooney, "Venice Fest to Salute Eastwood," p. 31; August 28, 2000, Lisa Nesselson, September 11, 2000, "Paris Praises Clint," p. 52.

ONLINE

Internet Movie Database, http://www.imdb.com/ (May 26, 2004), "Clint Eastwood."

OTHER

Directors: Clint Eastwood (film), Media Entertainment, Inc., 2000.*

*   *   *

EBNER, Mark

PERSONAL: Male.

ADDRESSES: Home—Venice, CA. *Agent*—c/o Author Mail, Wiley Publishing, Inc., 111 River St., 5th Fl., Hoboken, NJ 07030. *E-mail*—contact@drasticmedia.com.

CAREER: Hosted *Drastic Radio with Mark Ebner,* 2000; television journalist and producer.

AWARDS, HONORS: Genesis Award, 1996, for newspaper article, "Pit Bullies."

WRITINGS:

(With Harry Knowles and Paul Cullum) *Ain't It Cool?: Hollywood's Redheaded Stepchild Speaks Out,* Warner Books (New York, NY), 2002.

(With Andrew Breitbart) *Hollywood, Interrupted: Insanity Chic in Babylon—The Case against Celebrity,* Wiley (New York, NY), 2004.

Contributor to periodicals, including *Spy, Details, Salon.com, Spin, New Times,* and *Premiere.*

SIDELIGHTS: Mark Ebner is a journalist whose first book, *Ain't It Cool?: Hollywood's Redheaded Stepchild Speaks Out,* is coauthored with Harry Knowles and Paul Cullum. The title comes from a John Travolta line in *Broken Arrow.* Knowles's memoir, the book documents how an unfortunate accident changed his life. Knowles was an overweight, twenty-something movie fan in the 1990s, when he was hit by a dolly bearing movie memorabilia and posters in an Austin, Texas, parking lot. The bedridden Knowles, who had a collection of approximately 5,000 videos, passed the time during his recovery by setting up a Web site, *Ain't It Cool News,* where he posted movie news and commentary. His spies infiltrated studios, reporting back to him on script development and other inside news, which he posted on the site, often infuriating the studios and resulting in at least one restraining order. He also wrote about movie trivia and history, and added his own tributes to his favorite celebrities.

Ain't It Cool? is, a *Publishers Weekly* contributor wrote, "valuable as a record of the Web's early entrepreneur-driven years." The Web site has survived and grown, and Knowles continues to provide scoops. In some cases, these scoops have been to the benefit of upcoming films, as when he wrote a glowing review of a *Star Wars* episode after being offered a screening. David Edelstein commented in the *New York Times Book Review* that *Ain't It Cool News* "has proven a popular place to stop in and vituperate."

With Andrew Breitbart, Ebner wrote *Hollywood, Interrupted: Insanity Chic in Babylon—The Case against Celebrity,* offering up gossip on Michael Jackson, Hugh Hefner, Eddie Murphy, and Shirley MacLaine. Some of the comments about celebrity drug use are not new, others—sometimes gleaned from such sources as celebrities' nannies—are. Rob Long wrote in the *Wall Street Journal* that readers "also take a detour through the bizarre religious faith of, say, Dyan Cannon . . . and the silly Kabbalah mutterings of Madonna. There is a lengthy stop in Scientology. In a nutshell, as it were: Kirstie Alley and Tom Cruise paid hundreds of thousands of dollars to be told that we're all beset by ancient alien spirits. And there is a huge section on the lockstep liberals who rule the town's topical debate, all of it spiced with enough sexual gossip and snarky asides to keep you turning the pages."

BIOGRAPHICAL AND CRITICAL SOURCES:

PERIODICALS

American Spectator, May, 2004, Jesse Walker, review of *Hollywood, Interrupted: Insanity Chic in Babylon—The Case against Celebrity,* p. 60.
Kirkus Reviews, January 15, 2002, review of *Ain't It Cool?: Hollywood's Redheaded Stepchild Speaks Out,* p. 87.
Los Angeles Times Book Review, April 14, 2002, Richard Schickel, review of *Ain't It Cool?,* p. R2.
New York Times Book Review, April 28, 2002, David Edelstein, review of *Ain't It Cool?,* p. 26.
Publishers Weekly, February 18, 2002, review of *Ain't It Cool?,* p. 86; February 2, 2004, review of *Hollywood, Interrupted,* p. 70.
School Library Journal, September, 2002, Jane S. Drabkin, review of *Ain't It Cool?,* p. 258.
Wall Street Journal, February 26, 2004, Rob Long, review of *Hollywood, Interrupted,* p. D8.

ONLINE

Mark Ebner Home Page, http://www.drasticmedia.com (March 31, 2005).
Modesto Bee Online, http://www.modbee.com/ (March 31, 2002), Charles Matthews, review of *Ain't It Cool?*
Time Warner Books Web site, http://www.twbookmark. com/ (March 31, 2005), "Mark Ebner."*

EDELMAN, Scott 1955-

PERSONAL: Born 1955; married, wife's name, Irene.

ADDRESSES: Office—Science Fiction Weekly, 28501 Woodview Dr., Damascus, MD 20872. *E-mail*—scott@ scottedelman.com.

CAREER: Magazine editor and author. Marvel Comics, New York, NY, writer, 1977-78; editor and writer, 1978—. Creator and editor, *Science Fiction Age,* 1991-2000; editor-in-chief, *Science Fiction Weekly,* 2000—. Former editor, *Sci-Fi Entertainment* (official magazine of Sci Fi Channel); former editor of media magazines, including *Sci-Fi Universe, Rampage, Satellite Orbit,* and *Sci-Fi Flix.* Former script writer, *Tales from the Darkside* (network television show).

AWARDS, HONORS: Four Hugo award nominations as best editor of a science-fiction magazine; Sam Moskowitz Award, 2004, for outstanding contributions to the field of science-fiction fandom.

WRITINGS:

Ovaltine Presents the Captain Midnight Action Book for Sports, Fitness, and Nutrition, Marvel Comics Group (New York, NY), 1977.
The Gift, Space and Time (New York, NY), 1990.
Suicide Art (chapbook), Necronomicon Press (New York, NY), 1992.
Texas Rattlesnake: Totally Unauthorized, Uncensored, and Raw!, Ballantine Books (New York, NY), 2000.
Warrior Queen: Totally Unauthorized Story of Joanie Laurer, Ballantine Books (New York, NY), 2000.
These Words Are Haunted (short story collection), Wildside Press (Holicong, PA), 2001.

Contributor of short stories to science-fiction and horror periodicals, and to anthologies, including Brian Stableford, editor, *Tales of the Wandering Jew,* Dedalus (Cambridge, MA), 1991; *Quick Chills II,* 1992; *Metahorror,* 1992; Ramsey Campbell and Stephen Jones, editors, *Best New Horror 4,* Carroll & Graf (New York, NY), 1993; Campbell and Jones, editors, *The Giant Book of Terror,* Magpie Books (London, England), 1994; Jones, editor, *The Mammoth Book of*

Best New Horror 8, 1997; *Horrors!: 365 Scary Stories,* 1998; Peter Crowther, editor, *Moon Shots,* DAW Books (New York, NY) 1999; Chris Reed and David Memmott, editors, *Angel Body and Other Magic for the Soul,* 2000; Jim Lowder, editor, *The Book of All Flesh,* 2001; Wil McCarthy, editor, *Once upon a Galaxy,* DAW Books, 2002; Peter Crowther, editor, *Mars Probes,* Signet Books (New York, NY), 2002; Jim Lowder, editor, *The Book of Final Flesh,* 2003; Mike Resnick, editor, *Men Writing Science Fiction as Women,* 2003; F. Brett Cox and Andy Duncan, editors, *Crossroads: Tales of the Southern Literary Fantastic,* Tor Books (New York, NY), 2004; and K. P. Burke, editor, *Quietly Now: A Tribute to Charles L. Grant,* 2004. Author of comic-book series, including "Captain Marvel," issues 49-55; "Dead of Night," issue 11; and "Omega the Unknown," issue 7, all for Marvel Comics; also contributor to DC Comics and Hanna-Barbera publications.

SIDELIGHTS: Scott Edelman is perhaps better known as a science-fiction magazine editor than he is as a writer, but over the course of three decades he has published a significant collection of horror and science-fiction short stories, as well as a novel. In his full-length work, *The Gift,* a gay couple move to a small town, only to face homophobia within their neighborhood and the unwanted attentions of a vampire in their new home. *These Words Are Haunted* collects some of editor Edelman's favorite short stories. As the title implies, horror predominates in this volume, with tales about zombies and celebrities returning from the dead. As Don D'Ammassa observed in *Science Fiction Chronicle,* Edelman's themes "are not pleasant ones," and he does not shy away from difficult psychological terrain. Nevertheless, D'Ammassa concluded that the work provides "witty, intelligent chills" for the discerning reader.

Since 2000, Edelman has served as editor of *Science Fiction Weekly,* an online magazine with nearly 175,000 registered readers. He is a frequent speaker at science fiction conventions and has been nominated for awards both as a writer and an editor.

BIOGRAPHICAL AND CRITICAL SOURCES:

PERIODICALS

Science Fiction Chronicle, October, 2001, Don D'Ammassa, review of *These Words Are Haunted,* p. 40.

ONLINE

Fantastic Fiction Web site, http://www.fantasticfiction. co.uk (February 7, 2005), "Scott Edelman."
QueerHorror.com, http://queerhorror.com (February 7, 2005), review of *The Gift.*
Scott Edelman Web site, http://www.scottedelman.com (February 7, 2005).
SFSite.com, http://www.sfsite.com (February 7, 2005), reviews of *Moon Shots* and *Once upon a Galaxy.**

*   *   *

EDELSTEIN, Alan

PERSONAL: Male. *Education:* Earned Ph.D.

ADDRESSES: Office—c/o Author Mail, Greenwood Press, 88 Post Road West, Westport, CT 06881.

CAREER: Towson University, Towson, MD, professor of sociology.

WRITINGS:

An Unacknowledged Harmony: Philo-Semitism and the Survival of European Jewry, Greenwood Press (Westport, CT), 1982.
Everybody Is Sitting on the Curb: How and Why America's Heroes Disappeared, Praeger (Westport, CT), 1996.

SIDELIGHTS: Sociologist and historian Alan Edelstein's first book dealt with an interesting phenomenon in an often-dark period of history. *An Unacknowledged Harmony: Philo-Semitism and the Survival of European Jewry* draws on European, Jewish, and Holocaust documents to tell the stories of gentiles who were drawn to favor and protect Jews from the time of the Roman Empire to the Nazi era, when philo-Semitism became a dangerous and heroic enterprise. Edelstein's next book explores heroism itself, or rather its absence. *Everybody Is Sitting on the Curb: How and Why America's Heroes Disappeared* describes the ways in which heroes as Franklin D. Roosevelt and Babe Ruth and John F. Kennedy have given way to the merely famous or to more marginal heroes that simply do not gain the national fame of previous eras.

For Edelstein, changes in social structures and cultural outlook, such as the tell-all media and the growing emphasis on political correctness and diversity, have replaced transcendent heroes with ephemeral heroes and insubstantial celebrities. While military, sports, entertainment, and politics continue to yield famous names and admired figures, there is no longer the sense of a shared national greatness embodied in such heroes. According to Edelstein, this may indicate a maturing of democracy, a refusal to accept an innately higher status for our fellow citizens. As Ray Browne pointed out in the *Journal of Popular Culture,* "this democractizing influence is not a leveling-down but a leveling-up. Instead of Kennedy being pulled down to our size, we are pushed up to his."

BIOGRAPHICAL AND CRITICAL SOURCES:

PERIODICALS

Booklist, July, 1996, review of *Everybody Is Sitting on the Curb: How and Why America's Heroes Disappeared,* p. 1798.
Journal of Popular Culture, fall, 2000, Ray Browne, review of *Everybody Is Sitting on the Curb,* p. 186.*

*   *   *

EKSTEIN, Rudolf 1912-2005

OBITUARY NOTICE— See index for *CA* sketch: Born February 9, 1912, in Vienna, Austria; died March 18, 2005, in Los Angeles, CA. Psychologist, educator, and author. Ekstein was an authority on child psychology who worked for such institutions as the Reiss-Davis Child Study Center and the Menninger Foundation. After earning his doctorate from the University of Vienna in 1937, he fled Europe with the rise to power of Adolph Hitler. Immigrating to the United States, he studied at Boston University, where he received a master's degree in 1942, and became a U.S. citizen that same year. He joined the prestigious Menninger Foundation as a training analyst in 1947, moving to

the Reiss-Davis Center in Los Angeles in 1957. Here he coordinated training and research and directed the childhood psychosis project. In 1957, Ekstein joined the Los Angeles Psychoanalytic Institute, but he left the practice of psychiatry behind in 1968 to become a professor of medical psychology at the University of California at Los Angeles. He was the author or editor of several books, such as *Children of Time and Space, of Action and Impulse* (1966) and *In Search of Love and Competence: Twenty-Five Years of Service, Training and Research at the Reiss-Davis Study Center* (1976); he also wrote or edited several sound recordings, including *Speaking of the Truth behind Fairy Tales* (1974) and *The Language of Psychotherapy* (1989).

OBITUARIES AND OTHER SOURCES:

PERIODICALS

Grand Rapids Press, March 24, 2005, p. B7.
Los Angeles Times, March 23, 2005, p. B11.

ONLINE

Menninger Clinic Web site, http://www.menninger clinic.com/ (April 29, 2005).

*   *   *

ELBOM, Gilad 1968-

PERSONAL: Born 1968, in Jerusalem, Israel. *Education:* Hebrew University; Otis College of Art and Design, M.F.A., 2003; University of North Dakota (Ph.D. candidate).

ADDRESSES: Agent—c/o Author Mail, Thunder's Mouth Press, 245 W. 17th St., 11th Fl., New York, NY 10011-5300.

CAREER: Writer. Worked as an assistant nurse in an Israeli mental institute. *Military service:* Served in the Israel Defense Forces.

WRITINGS:

Scream Queens of the Dead Sea (novel), Thunder's Mouth Press (New York, NY), 2004.

SIDELIGHTS: In his first novel, *Scream Queens of the Dead Sea,* Gilad Elbom tells the story of a young man working in an Israeli mental hospital and having an affair with a married woman named Carmel, whose husband is dying of cancer. The novel's narrator, "Gilad Elbom," not only shares the author's real name but also the fact that the author at one time worked as an assistant nurse in a mental institution in Israel. Elbom, the character, is disenfranchised and cares for little except heavy metal music and literature. He does not treat the patients he works with particularly well. The hospital is populated by an assortment of characters, from a woman who claims she is dead to a homicidal patient who says he suffers from Faith Deficit Disorder and, as a result, believes in nothing. Throughout the book, Elbom and other characters comment on the writing of the novel, from the use of punctuation to how the characters feel they are being portrayed. As the story progresses, Elbom begins to show signs of mental instability and breaks down.

Writing on *Bookslut.com,* Adam Lipkin noted that, "Linking the deteriorating state of his fictional alter-ego's mind to the political and social chaos that envelopes Israel is a nice touch." However, Lipkin added, "the wacky stuff . . . about heavy metal and movies . . . , the political commentary, the rough sex, and the look at insanity, while all well written by themselves, fail to achieve true synergy." Nevertheless, the reviewer called the debut "impressive" and "a thoroughly enjoyable read." A *Kirkus Reviews* contributor commented that in *Scream Queens of the Dead Sea,* "A potentially clever debut falls apart under the weight of the writer's fascination with his own cleverness." Misha Stone, writing in *Booklist,* noted the author's "self-indulgent" style and called the book's plot "too meandering", but added that Elbom's "acerbic wit offers more than enough compensation." A *Publishers Weekly* contributor maintained that the author's "lively present-tense narrative pulls the reader into the story" and also called the effort "a multifaceted, hilarious and excruciatingly honest novel."

BIOGRAPHICAL AND CRITICAL SOURCES:

PERIODICALS

Booklist, September 1, 2004, Misha Stone, review of *Scream Queens of the Dead Sea,* p. 60.

Kirkus Reviews, October 1, 2004, review of *Scream Queens of the Dead Sea,* p. 929.
Publishers Weekly, October 4, 2004, review of *Scream Queens of the Dead Sea,* p. 69.
Tikkun, January-February, 2005, Cynthia Hoffman, review of *Scream Queens of the Dead Sea,* p. 73.

ONLINE

Bookslut, http://www.bookslut.com/ (August, 2004), Adam Lipkin, review of *Scream Queens of the Dead Sea.**

*   *   *

ELLIS, Alice Thomas
      See HAYCRAFT, Anna (Margaret)

*   *   *

ELLIS, Wesley
      See BARRETT, Neal, Jr.

*   *   *

ESSTMAN, Barbara 1947-

PERSONAL: Born January 7, 1947, in Carroll, IA; daughter of Robert W. (a grain dealer) and Helen (a homemaker; maiden name, Culbertson) Beste; married Michael Brady Esstman, July 5, 1969 (divorced, December, 1980); children: Brian Robert, Elizabeth Brady, Mark Edward. *Education:* St. Louis University, B.A., 1969. *Hobbies and other interests:* Photography.

ADDRESSES: Home—3413 Lyrac St., Oakton, VA 22124. *Office*—The Writer's Center, 4508 Walsh St., Bethesda, MD 20815; fax: 703-620-9818.

CAREER: The Writer's Center, Bethesda, MD, writing instructor. Also worked as a writing instructor at various institutions, including George Mason University, Fairfax, VA, and American University, Washington, DC. Washington Independent Writers (board of directors).

MEMBER: PEN, George Mason University Creative Writers.

AWARDS, HONORS: *Redbook* fiction award, 1988; Virginia Commission on the Arts fellowship, 1998; National Endowment for the Arts grant, 1990; Pushcart Prize honorable mention, 1991; George Mason University Alumna of the Year Award.

WRITINGS:

The Other Anna (novel), Harcourt Brace (New York, NY), 1993.
Night Ride Home (novel), Harcourt Brace (New York, NY), 1997.
(Editor, with Virginia Hartman) *A More Perfect Union: Poems and Stories about the Modern Wedding,* St. Martin's Press (New York, NY), 1998.

ADAPTATIONS: The American Broadcasting Company (ABC) adapted *The Other Anna* for television as *Secrets; Night Ride Home* was produced by Hallmark Productions for *Hallmark Hall of Fame.*

SIDELIGHTS: Barbara Esstman's debut novel, *The Other Anna,* is set in early twentieth-century Iowa. The narrator is twelve-year-old Anna Better, who prefers the company of a housekeeper she calls the "Old One" and the woman's granddaughter, Edwina, over that of her own mother. When a family guest impregnates Edwina, she is driven from the house, but Anna's parents adopt her baby girl. Edwina is traumatized by the loss of her child and the Old One blames the family for her daughter's descent into insanity.

Esstman's second novel, *Night Ride Home,* is set in 1940s Missouri. Nora Mahler loses her son, Simon, during a horseback-riding accident when he falls from her Arabian, and her husband, Neal, kills the animal with a bullet to the head and sells off the rest of their horses. Nora is devastated by the loss of both her son and her horse and becomes withdrawn, eventually undergoing shock therapy in a mental facility under Neal's order. Nora's mother, Maggie, has her released and tries to help her daughter manage the farm, which Neal wants to sell. When Nora refuses, Neal takes their daughter, Clea, and moves with her to Chicago.

Ozzie Kline, Nora's teenage love, comes to work at the farm and brings it back to life, buying a new horse for Nora and boarding other horses. Ozzie and Nora feel their old attraction revive as they work together to restore the farm she inherited from her grandmother into a working operation.

Reviewing *Night Ride Home,* Polly Morris wrote in the *New York Times Book Review* that "Esstman tells this story skillfully through the alternating voices of her characters." *Library Journal* contributor Terrill Presky commented on Esstman's "insightful writing and find storytelling." *The Other Anna* and *Night Ride Home,* were each adapted for television with the latter having the honor of being the *Hallmark Hall of Fame*'s 200th production. The Hallmark film stars Rebecca Demornay and Keith Carradine as Nora and Neal, and Ellen Burstyn plays Maggie.

Esstman is also an editor, with Virginia Hartman, of *A More Perfect Union: Poems and Stories about the Modern Wedding.* The collection contains contributions from well-known writers, including Anne Tyler, Carson McCullers, Alice McDermott, Alice Munro, Francine Prose, and Stephen Dixon. The volume also contains poetry by Anne Sexton, Jonathan Galassi, and Sharon Olds. The contributions range from tender to lighthearted. A *Publishers Weekly* reviewer wrote that among the works of lesser-known writers, a "standout" story is "Presents," by Faye Moskowitz. The reviewer felt that "the collection as a whole nicely covers the gamut of contemporary attitudes about tying the knot."

BIOGRAPHICAL AND CRITICAL SOURCES:

PERIODICALS

Booklist, July, 1997, Jennifer Henderson, review of *Night Ride Home,* p. 1774.
Library Journal, August, 1997, Terrill Presky, review of *Night Ride Home,* p. 126.
New York Times Book Review, December 21, 1997, Polly Morrice, review of *Night Ride Home,* p. 17.
Publishers Weekly, February 15, 1993, review of *The Other Anna,* p. 188; July 28, 1997, review of *Night*

Ride Home, p. 54; April 20, 1998, review of *A More Perfect Union: Poems and Stories about the Modern Wedding,* p. 47.

Washington Post, February 7, 1999, Patricia Brennan, "Hallmark's 200th Story; Local Novelist's *Night Ride Home* Is Anniversary Choice," p. 3.

ONLINE

AuthorsDen.com, http://www.authorsden.com/ (May 7, 2005), "Barbara Esstman."

*   *   *

ETTINGER, Elzbieta 1925-2005

OBITUARY NOTICE— See index for *CA* sketch: Born September 19, 1925, in Warsaw, Poland; died of heart failure March 12, 2005, in Cambridge, MA. Educator and author. A survivor of the Holocaust, Ettinger became a writing professor at the Massachusetts Institute of Technology (MIT) and a respected novelist and biographer. After the Nazis invaded Poland, Ettinger escaped the Warsaw ghetto and fought with the resistance under the assumed identity of a Catholic Pole named Elzbieta Chodakowska. With the war over, Poland became a communist satellite of the Soviet Union, and although Ettinger believed in socialism, she criticized the new government's authoritarianism and found herself blacklisted. After earning a doctorate in American literature from the University of Warsaw, she immigrated to the United States. She worked for a time for the Radcliffe Institute (now the Bunting Institute) during the early 1970s as a senior fellow before joining the MIT faculty in 1975. Gaining a reputation as a demanding teacher, she also became known for her criticism of what she saw as the materialism and anti-intellectual culture of her adopted nation. Named Thomas Meloy Professor of Rhetoric and Literature, she remained at MIT until her retirement in 1996. Ettinger published several books over the years, including the novels *Kindergarten* (1968) and *Quicksand* (1989), both of which are set in Poland; the biography *Rosa Luxemburg: A Life* (1987); and the nonfiction *Hannah Arendt/Martin Heidegger* (1995). At the time of her death, the author was working on a biography of Arendt.

OBITUARIES AND OTHER SOURCES:

PERIODICALS

Boston Globe, March 26, 2005.
Boston Herald, April 5, 2005, p. 29.

ONLINE

Massachusetts Institute of Technology Web site, http://web.mit.edu/ (March 15, 2005).

*   *   *

EVANS, (Jean) Cherry (Drummond) 1928-2005 (Baroness Strange, Lady Strange)

OBITUARY NOTICE— See index for *CA* sketch: Born December 17, 1928, in London, England; died March 11, 2005. Politician and author. Evans was the 16th Baroness Strange, a member of the House of Lords, and a writer. Born to a life of privilege, Evans attended St. Andrews University, earning a master's degree in English and history in 1951. Although she planned to enter service in the Foreign Office, she instead married and raised a family of six children. When her father died without male heirs, she argued successfully for the title of baroness and received a seat in the House of Lords. Here she gained a reputation as a woman of charm and grace who regularly presented her colleagues with flowers from her garden. She also championed a number of causes, including aid to war widows—she was a former president of the War Widows' Association of Great Britain—and actively traveled the world on behalf of the Inter-Parliamentary Union. She resigned from the Tory Party in 1999, after which she was elected hereditary crossbench peer. In addition to her government work, Evans penned the novels *Love from Belinda* (1962) and *Lalage in Love* (1962), the biography *The Remarkable Life of Victoria Drummond, Marine Engineer* (1994), the autobiography *Creatures Great and Small* (1968), and a book of poetry titled *Love Is for Ever.*

OBITUARIES AND OTHER SOURCES:

PERIODICALS

Daily Telegraph (London, England), March 15, 2005; March 17, 2005, p. 26.
Times (London, England), March 21, 2005, p. 49.

EVARISTI, Marcella 1953-

PERSONAL: Born July 19, 1953, in Glasgow, Scotland; married Michael Body (a theater director), 1982 (separated); children: one son, one daughter. *Education:* University of Glasgow, B.A. (honors), 1974.

ADDRESSES: Home—14 Woodlands Dr., Glasgow G4 9EH, Scotland.

CAREER: University of St. Andrews, Fife, Scotland, playwright-in-residence, 1979-80; University of Sheffield, Sheffield, England, creative writing fellow, 1979-80; University of Glasgow, Glasgow, Scotland, writer-in-residence, 1984-85; University of Strathclyde, Glasgow, writer-in-residence, 1984-85. Actor in stage plays, including *Dorothy and the Bitch,* 1976; *Twelfth Night,* 1979; *Sugar and Spite,* 1981; *Mystery Bouffe,* 1982; *The Works,* 1985; *Terrestrial Extras,* 1985; *Visiting Company,* 1988; and *The Offski Variations,* 1990. Actor in radio plays, including *The Works,* 1985; and *The Hat,* 1988.

AWARDS, HONORS: Student Verse Competition prize, British Broadcasting Corporation, 1974; Arts Council bursary, 1975-76; Pye award for Best Writer New to Television, 1982, for *Eve Set the Balls of Corruption Rolling.*

WRITINGS:

STAGE PLAYS

Dorothy and the Bitch (monologue), produced in Edinburgh, Scotland, 1976.
Scotia's Darlings, produced at Edinburgh Fringe Festival, 1978.
(With Liz Lochhead) *Sugar and Spite* (revue), produced in Edinburgh, Scotland, 1978.
(With Liz Lochhead) *Mouthpieces: A Musical Satirical Revue,* produced in Edinburgh, Scotland, 1980.
Commedia (produced in Sheffield, England, 1982), Salamander Press (Edinburgh, Scotland), 1983.
Thank You for Not, in *Breach of the Peace* (review), produced in London, England, 1982.
Checking Out, produced in London, England, 1984.

The Works (produced in Edinburgh, Scotland, 1984; also see below), published in *Plays without Wires,* edited by Philip Roberts, Sheffield Academic Press, 1989.
Terrestrial Extras, produced in Glasgow, Scotland, 1985.
Trio for Strings in Three, produced in Glasgow, Scotland, 1987.
Visiting Company (monologue), produced in Glasgow, Scotland, 1988.
The Offski Variations (monologue), produced in Glasgow, Scotland, 1990.
Nightflights, produced in Dundee, Scotland, 2002.

RADIO PLAYS

Hard to Get, British Broadcasting Corporation, 1981.
Wedding Belles and Green Grasses, British Broadcasting Corporation Radio-3, 1983.
The Works (adaptation of stage play), British Broadcasting Corporation Radio-3, 1985.
The Hat, British Broadcasting Corporation Radio-3, 1988.
The Theory and Practice of Rings, British Broadcasting Corporation, 1992.
Troilus and Cressida and La-di-da-di-da, British Broadcasting Corporation, 1992.

TELEVISON PLAYS

Eve Set the Balls of Corruption Rolling, British Broadcasting Corporation, 1982.
Hard to Get (adaptation of radio play), Granada, 1983.

SIDELIGHTS: Marcella Evaristi is a Scottish feminist playwright whose autobiographical productions are marked by wit and psychological insight. In 1976 Evaristi completed her first stage play, *Dorothy and the Bitch,* which is constructed as a monologue wherein celebrated wit Dorothy Parker reflects on the nature of femininity and her own Jewish-Catholic background. Evaristi followed *Dorothy and the Bitch* with *Scotia's Darlings,* a stage production about a woman struggling to adapt to city life and a stepdaughter. "Evaristi's achievement in this early play," wrote Jan McDonald in the *Dictionary of Liter-*

ary Biography, "is to combine cutting satire with a portrayal of a protagonist who remains sympathetic even in her undeniable foolishness."

Hard to Get, another of Evaristi's notable stage plays, charts a pair of marital relationships over the course of nearly two decades. Both female characters have compromised their own aspirations and talents to survive in a male-oriented society, though both also develop the knack of rendering themselves as injured parties when interacting with males. "The men . . . are constantly frustrated by the women's propensity to cast themselves in the role of victim," said McDonald. By the play's end, though, both women have managed to realize a measure of success in pursuing their long-suppressed goals. "The personal issues are resolved," noted McDonald, "but the happy ending has been 'Hard to Get.'"

In her next staged work, *Commedia,* Evaristi presents a Scottish widow who enters into an affair with an Italian schoolteacher in Glasgow. The couple eventually travel to Italy, where they share a respite from the widow's married children. The vacation is undone when the children arrive in Italy with their spouses, and the couple's relationship dissolves after one of the children perishes in a terrorist bombing. Writing for the *New Statesman,* reviewer Benedict Nightingale summarized *Commedia* as "a play altogether pretty eloquent about people's right to resist the importunate iconography of others."

Terrestrial Extras is a production in which space invaders, assuming feminine guises, descend on Scotland—instead of their intended target, Washington, DC—and soon begin developing amusing misconceptions about life on Earth. As McDonald wrote in her profile of Evaristi, "The plight of the socially deprived, the vulnerability of women to violent male advances, and the vulgarization of a culture saturated with pap promulgated by the media are all exposed with sharp, ironic wit."

Visiting Company is another revelatory monologue on the plight of women in patriarchal society. In this play, a woman replaces her husband as guest speaker at a meeting devoted to the topic of arts funding. In the course of her speech, the heroine interjects revelatory anecdotes that expose her husband as an abusive, sexually reckless homophobe and drunk. The play ends with the heroine agreeing to sign a petition to fight policies against homosexuality. Evaristi constructs another of her monologues, *The Offski Variations,* as a series of speeches—delivered by different characters played by one actress—on what McDonald described as "the recurrent theme of parting, separation, and loss." In a *New Statesman* piece, Angela McRobbie observed that *The Offski Variations* serves as evidence of Evaristi's "true love of endless talk, sex, families and Scottish-Italian culture."

Aside from writing for the stage, Evaristi has completed plays for television and radio broadcasts. Her radio plays include *The Hat,* in which a piece of art, a collage, reflects the changes experienced by an artist's model after a younger woman has replaced her. McDonald deemed *The Hat* "sophisticated in its use of language and complex in its narrative; yet it is also moving." In another radio play, *Troilus and Cressida and La-di-da-di-da,* Evaristi provides what McDonald called "a twentieth-century feminist critique of the legend of the Trojan prince Troilus and his fickle lover." Still another radio production, *The Theory and Practice of Rings,* reveals the plight of women through representations or various marital relationships. This play ends with a husband—on the fifteenth anniversary of his marriage—announcing that he wishes to leave his wife for his pregnant lover. McDonald, who described Evaristi as "primarily a poet," contended that "her best work has been for radio."

Evaristi returned to the stage with *Nightflights,* a musical set in Italy that explores aging, love, and mortality. "Above all, it is about magic," said Ksenija Horvat in a review for *EdinburghGuide.com.* Horvat wrote that *Nightflights* signals "the return of Marcella Evaristi, the uncrowned queen of Scottish playwriting, after a decade of absence from the Scottish stage."

BIOGRAPHICAL AND CRITICAL SOURCES:

BOOKS

Contemporary Dramatists, 6th edition, St. James Press (Detroit, MI), 1999.

Contemporary Women Dramatists, St. James Press (Detroit, MI), 1994.

Dictionary of Literary Biography, Volume 233: *British and Irish Dramatists since World War II, Second Series,* Gale (Detroit, MI), 2000.

PERIODICALS

New Statesman, November 19, 1982, Benedict Nightingale, "On the Rocks," review of *Commedia,* p. 32; April 6, 1984, Paul Allen, "Gravy Train," review of *Checking Out,* p. 41; February 9, 1990, Angela McRobbie, "Freedom from the English Word: Scottish Writing in the Year of Culture," p. 33.

ONLINE

EdinburghGuide.com, http://www.edinburghguide. com/ (May, 2002), Ksenija Horvat, review of *Nightflights.**

F

FAISON, Seth 1959(?)-

PERSONAL: Born c. 1959, in Brooklyn, NY; married Siobhan Darrow (a television correspondent); children: twins. *Education:* Attended Wesleyan University.

ADDRESSES: Home—Santa Monica, CA. *Agent*—David Black Literary Agency, 156 5th Ave., New York, NY 10010. *E-mail*—sfaison@mac.com.

CAREER: Hong Kong Standard, Hong Kong, reporter, 1986-88, reporter in Beijing, 1988-91; *New York Times,* reporter in New York, NY, 1991-95, Shanghai bureau chief, 1995-2000; writer, 2000—.

AWARDS, HONORS: Pulitzer Prize, 1994, for *New York Times* articles on World Trade Center bombing.

WRITINGS:

South of the Clouds: Exploring the Hidden Realms of China, St. Martin's Press (New York, NY), 2004

SIDELIGHTS: Pulitzer prize-winning journalist Seth Faison's first book, *South of the Clouds: Exploring the Hidden Realms of China,* tells the story of his years spent wandering the back roads and alleyways of China, first as a student and then as a news reporter. From his arrival in the country in 1984 until his final departure in 2000, he experienced life in the Communist country as few Westerners have. "I wanted to capture the feeling of life in China," Faison related in an interview published on his home page, "as well as

the romance and the hardship of being an outsider in Asia. All the years I lived in China, I myself yearned to read a book about life on the ground in China, as it appears to Western eyes. That was the book I decided to try to write myself."

Faison, who shared a Pulitzer prize with other *New York Times* staff members for his reporting on the attempted 1993 World Trade Center bombing, reveals aspects of the process of his own maturing in the book as well as telling the story of China's long emergence from its Communist-era isolation. "His terse, first-hand description and analysis of protests in Tiananmen Square in 1898," wrote Victor Mallet, in the *Financial Times,* "is contemporary history at its best." "The uncovering of Chinese secrets—endless because of China's uncertainties about itself—turned out to be the answer to Faison's felt vulnerabilities," explained *Los Angeles Times* contributor Ross Terrill.

Reviewers recognized that the author's voyage through China is, in many ways, also a voyage of self-discovery. "Faison is a rarity," wrote Susan G. Baird in *Library Journal,* "a man unafraid to admit that he isn't macho and appreciates the gentler side of human interaction." "Readers will become very fond of Faison—his frank doubts about his masculinity, his willingness to wonder about his attraction to Chinese women and, yes," declared a *Publishers Weekly* contributor, "his longing for spiritual depth."

BIOGRAPHICAL AND CRITICAL SOURCES:

PERIODICALS

Booklist, October 1, 2004, George Cohen, review of *South of the Clouds: Exploring the Hidden Realms of China,* p. 296.

Financial Times, January 22, 2005, Victor Mallet, "The Chaos Years," review of *South of the Clouds,* p. 30.

Library Journal, October 1, 2004, Susan G. Baird, review of *South of the Clouds,* p. 102.

Los Angeles Times, October 12, 2004, Ross Terrill, review of *South of the Clouds.*

Publishers Weekly, September 6, 2004, review of *South of the Clouds,* p. 57.

ONLINE

Seth Faison Home Page, http://sethfaison.com (February 7, 2005).

*   *   *

FALK, John

PERSONAL: Married. *Education:* Graduated from law school.

ADDRESSES: Home—Hillsdale, NY. *Agent*—c/o Author Mail, Henry Holt & Co., 115 W. 18th St., New York, NY 10011.

CAREER: Writer, journalist, and lawyer. Spent time as a war correspondent in Bosnia; also practiced law and owned an Internet-based business.

WRITINGS:

Hello to All That: A Memoir of War, Zoloft, and Peace, Henry Holt & Co. (New York, NY), 2005.

Has written articles for several publications, including *Details, Esquire,* and *Vanity Fair.*

ADAPTATIONS: Hello to All That: A Memoir of War, Zoloft, and Peace was optioned for film; author's article about snipers titled "Shot through the Heart" and published in *Details* was adapted as the film *Shot through the Heart.*

SIDELIGHTS: Freelance writer John Falk suffered from reoccurring bouts of depression from the time he was a twelve year old but eventually found help from antidepressants. His case and recovery is known to psychologists as that of Patient X. In *Hello to All That: A Memoir of War, Zoloft, and Peace,* Falk recounts both his battle with depression and his effort, in 1993, to become a war correspondent in Sarajevo after graduating from college. He tells both stories in alternating chapters, describing how he tried to hide his depression from friends and family for years and his experiences in Sarajevo, where he befriended an anti-sniper—that is, someone who hunts down and kills snipers. In an interview with Jessa Crispin for *Bookslut.com,* Falk explained that he combined the two stories because, "they're the same guy, but they're different guys in a sense." He continued, "One guy's battling an almost unwinnable war against a chemical imbalance, if you will." The author went on to note, "On the other side is this guy whose neurological whatever is opened to life a little bit, but he's build up a lot of character flaws that keep him from living the life he wants to live and he doesn't even know it."

In a review of *Hello to All That* in *MBR Bookwatch,* Harriet Klausner wrote that Falk's memoir tells the story of surviving two wars, "a personal one that medicine cures and the other caused by human atrocities that should shame everyone." Vanessa Bush, writing in *Booklist,* noted, "This is a thoroughly engaging memoir, sometimes hilarious and sometimes horrifying." A *Publishers Weekly* contributor referred to the memoir as both "raucous" and "zany." Susan Pease called the memoir "compelling" and "ultimately uplifting" in a review in *Library Journal.* She went on to call Falk a gifted writer "whose words bring alive the human connections at stake in his struggles."

BIOGRAPHICAL AND CRITICAL SOURCES:

BOOKS

Falk, John, *Hello to All That: A Memoir of War, Zoloft, and Peace,* Henry Holt & Co. (New York, NY), 2005.

PERIODICALS

Booklist, December 15, 2004, Vanessa Bush, review of *Hello to All That,* p. 697.

Kirkus Reviews, October 1, 2004, review of *Hello to All That,* p. 947.

Library Journal, November 15, 2004, Susan Pease, review of *Hello to All That,* p. 75.

MBR Bookwatch, March, 2005, Harriet Klausner, review of *Hello to All That.*

Publishers Weekly, October 18, 2004, review of *Hello to All That,* p. 55.

ONLINE

AllReaders.com, http://www.allreaders.com/ (March 24, 2005), Harriet Klausner, review of *Hello to All That.*

BookReporter.com, http://www.bookreporter.com/ (March 24, 2005), Carole Turner, review of *Hello to All That.*

Bookslut, http://www.bookslut.com/ (March 24, 2005), Jessa Crispin, interview with Falk.

My Shelf, http://www.myshelf.com/ (March 24, 2005), review of *Hello to All That.**

* * *

FEEHAN, Christine

PERSONAL: Married; children: eleven. *Hobbies and other interests:* Martial arts.

ADDRESSES: Office—Christine Feehan Productions, P.O. Box 792, Cobb, CA 95426. *Agent*—c/o Author Mail, Penguin Group Publicity, 375 Hudson St., New York, NY 10014.

CAREER: Writer. Has taught martial arts and self-defense classes for more than twenty years.

AWARDS, HONORS: Pearl Award for Best Novella/ Short Story, for the novella *After Twilight;* Pearl Award for Best Overall Paranormal Romance, 2001, for *Dark Fire;* Career Achievement Award for Contemporary New Reality, *Romantic Times* magazine, 2003, for entire body of work.

WRITINGS:

"CARPATHIAN" ROMANCE SERIES

Dark Prince, Love Spell Books (New York, NY), 1999.

Dark Desire, Love Spell Books (New York, NY), 1999.

Dark Gold, Love Spell Books (New York, NY), 2000.

Dark Magic, Love Spell Books (New York, NY), 2000.

Dark Challenge, Love Spell Books (New York, NY), 2000.

Dark Fire, Love Spell Books (New York, NY), 2001.

Dark Guardian, Leisure Books (New York, NY), 2002.

Dark Legend, Leisure Books (New York, NY), 2002.

Dark Melody, Leisure Books (New York, NY), 2003.

Dark Symphony, Jove Books (New York, NY), 2003.

Dark Destiny, Leisure Books (New York, NY), 2004.

Dark Secret, Berkley Books (New York, NY) 2005.

ROMANCE NOVELS

The Scarletti Curse, Love Spell Books (New York, NY), 2001.

Lair of the Lion, Dorchester (New York, NY), 2002.

Shadow Game, Jove Books (New York, NY), 2003.

The Twilight before Christmas, Pocket Star Books (New York, NY), 2003.

Mind Game, Jove Books (New York, NY), 2004.

Wild Rain, Berkley Books (New York, NY), 2004.

Oceans of Fire, Jove Books (New York, NY), 2005.

Contributor to several books, including *A Very Gothic Christmas: Two Novellas,* Pocket Books (New York, NY), 2001; *Fantasy,* Jove (New York, NY), 2002; *The Only One,* Leisure Books (New York, NY), 2003; *Lover Beware,* Berkley Books (New York, NY), 2003; *Traveler* by Melanie Jackson, Love Spell Books (New York, NY), 2003; *Hot Blooded,* Jove Books, 2004; *After Twilight;* and *The Shadows of Christmas Past,* Pocket Star, 2004.

SIDELIGHTS: Christine Feehan began writing as a young girl. The first true love scene she wrote was confiscated by her teacher in math class. She went on to become a successful romance writer with the publication of *Dark Prince,* the first novel in her "Carpathian" romance series. Each book in the series focuses on immortal Carpathian vampire hunters who are also vampire-like but only kill vampires and evil people. At the center of the novels is their search for love, which is necessary if they are to be able to keep feeling emotions. In an interview with Claire E. White on *WritersWrite.com,* Feehan explained how the series evolved: "We had suffered a terrible loss in our family and I found it had robbed me of my ability to write, which was like breathing to me. I created the Carpathian world out of that darkness. I wanted them to go on no matter how bleak their existence, to hold on until the light came for them. I loved vampire stories and myths and asked myself why would someone choose to give up his soul. A life without love was the only answer I could come up with that made sense as nothing else is that important."

In the second book in the series, *Dark Desire,* Shea O'Halleran, a doctor, is called to the Carpathian mountains through her dreams of a Carpathian named Jacques. She soon learns she is the target of vampire hunters who believe she is one of the undead because of a strange blood disease she has that makes her sensitive to light and requires daily blood transfusions. When she finds Jacques, he has been buried alive, a stake plunged into his heart by an evil vampire. O'Halleran helps Jacques, and the two eventually fall in love. Writing on *AllReaders.com,* a reviewer commented that, "How Shea eventually discovers who— and what—she really is and what love is make for a deeply satisfying love story."

In *Dark Gold* heroine Alexandria Houton is a computer programmer who follows a voice that calls to her, only to find her little brother in the hands of a vampire. The vampire chains Alexandria inside a cave and begins the process of changing her into one of the undead when Aidan Savage, a Carpathian who is in San Francisco hunting vampires, comes to rescue her. Houton's fate is now sealed; she becomes an undead Carpathian. Nevertheless, she insists that she will lead a normal life, testing Savage's patience as he waits for her to accept her fate and his love. An *AllReaders.com* contributor felt the character of Savage is "such a strong personality" that other characters "seemed to pale in comparison," and went on to call the book "a great addition to the Dark series."

Dark Guardian, the eighth book in the series, pairs female cop Jaxon Montgomery with Lucian Daratrazanoff, another immortal Carpathian who hunts vampires. The two meet when Daratrazanoff rescues Montgomery after she has been shot while investigating a case at a warehouse. Montgomery has led a life of self-imposed loneliness because anyone who gets close to her is in danger of being murdered by her stepfather, Tyler Drake. Daratrazanoff, one of the oldest and most powerful Carpathian vampire hunters, has maintained his will to live by believing there is

someone out there to love and be loved by. Montgomery is determined to protect the Carpathian from her evil stepfather. The two fall in love and Daratrazanoff begins the process of turning Montgomery into a Carpathian and his mate for life. A *Publishers Weekly* contributor found it hard to believe the tough and independent female cop would so willingly submit to becoming a Carpathian, but added, "Nevertheless, Feehan's newest is a skillful blend of supernatural thrills and romance that is sure to entice readers who can stomach the occasional gory scene."

Dark Symphony tells the story of Byron Justicano, a Carpathian vampire hunter who falls for Antonietta Scarletti, a concert pianist. Scarletti is blind and has psychic powers. The Carpathian soon learns that Scarletti is the object of a murder plot associated with someone who is pilfering the Scarletti family fortune, and he is determined to save the woman he considers his life mate, even if it means his own death. Harriet Klausner, writing on *AllReaders.com,* commented that "Some amusing scenes lighten the taut intrigue; together they blend into a supreme symphony." A *Publishers Weekly* contributor noted that new readers "may be daunted by the complexity of the Carpathian world," but predicted that they will ultimately "be roped in by this unconventional and intriguing installment."

Feehan's vampire romance series has continued to garner mostly favorable reviews, a *Publishers Weekly* contributor noting that *Dark Melody* "may be her most emotionally engaging installment to date." In *Dark Destiny,* Feehan introduces her first female Carpathian vampire hunter. A *Publishers Weekly* contributor found "inconsistencies" but noted "the story has sufficient sensuality to keep readers sated." According to *Library Journal* contributor Kristin Ramsell, *Dark Secret* is characterized by "lush prose, stunning sensuality, and an emotional intensity that nearly sends the pages up in flames."

Feehan also writes other romances, including *Lair of the Lion,* which is based on the classic fairy tale "Beauty and the Beast." This gothic retelling focuses on the romance between noblewoman Isabella Vernaducci and Don Nicolai DeMarco, the latter who suffers under a family curse that causes all of the men to be perceived as "beasts." A *Publishers Weekly* contributor commented that, "Though the relationship . . . is overwrought at times . . . they're a perfectly matched pair . . . and their steamy sex scenes heat up the pages." The reviewer went on to call the author's take on the classic story "inspired."

Shadow Game focuses on a government effort to turn a group of psychics into a useful military weapon. When some of the group, known as GhostWalkers, begin to die, the psychic Lily Whitney, daughter of the doctor running the group, sets about to disband the group after her father's death and falls in love with Captain Rylan Miller, one of the GhostWalkers. Kristin Ramsdell, writing in *Library Journal,* noted that while the romance does not have "the fantasy feel of her Carpathian romances," it "is equally intense, sensual, and mesmerizing." *Mind Game* continues the story of the GhostWalkers and was called "an electrifying read, one that should satisfy her fans and cement her reputation as the reigning queen of the paranormal romance" by a *Publishers Weekly* contributor. *Wild Rain* tells the story of shape-shifters who are part human and part leopard. The story centers around the love between one of their kind and a human hiding out in the rain forest. In a review in *Publishers Weekly,* a contributor commented the author has written "a romance that feels both destined and believable."

Feehan has also written several romances with a Christmas theme. In *The Twilight before Christmas,* the author tells the story of the seven Drake sisters, who have paranormal powers and are much beloved by their local townspeople. The sisters become upset when they sense an impending danger as Christmas approaches, and soon they must deal with an evil that threatens the town. Kristin Ramsdell, writing in *Library Journal,* commented that, "Chilling, suspenseful, passionate, and rewarding, this is not your average holiday romance." Once again writing in *Library Journal,* Ramsdell called Feehan's novella "Rocky Mountain Miracle," which appeared in *The Shadows of Christmas Past,* "right on target for readers who like their holiday books laced with humor and crackling with emotional intensity."

BIOGRAPHICAL AND CRITICAL SOURCES:

PERIODICALS

Booklist, September 15, 2003, Dianna Tixier Herald, review of *Shadow Game,* p. 220; October 15, 2003, Diana Tixier Herald, review of *Dark Melody,* p. 396; July, 2004, Diana Tixier Herald, review of *Dark Destiny,* p. 1827.

Library Journal, May 15, 2003, Kristin Ramsdell, review of *The Only One,* p. 72; August, 2003, Kristin Ramsdell, review of *Shadow Game,* p. 64; November 15, 2003, Kristin Ramsdell, review of *The Twilight Before Christmas,* p. 55; November 15, 2004, Kristin Ramsdell, review of *The Shadows of Christmas Past: Two Novellas,* p. 47; January 1, 2005, Kristin Ramsdell, review of *Dark Secret,* p. 91.

MBR Bookwatch, March, 2005, Harriet Klausner, review of *Dark Secret.*

Publishers Weekly, April 8, 2002, review of *Dark Guardian,* p. 211; August 19, 2002, review of *Lair of the Lion,* p. 72; February 24, 2003, review of *Dark Symphony,* p. 58; August 11, 2003, review of *Shadow Game,* p. 263; October 20, 2003, review of *Dark Melody,* p. 42; June 28, 2004, review of *Dark Destiny,* p. 37; January 26, 2004, review of *Wild Rain,* p. 236; November 1, 2004, review of *The Shadows of Christmas Past,* p. 49; July 19, 2004, review of *Mind Game,* p. 150; August 23, 2004, review of *Hot Blooded,* p. 42.

Reviewer's Bookwatch, November, 2004, Christina Francine Whitcher, review of *Dark Challenge.*

ONLINE

AllReaders.com, http://www.allreaders.com/ (March 24, 2005), Harriet Klausner, reviews of *Wild Rain, Dark Symphony,* and *Dark Legend;* Rachelle Wadsworth, review of *Dark Prince;* Meredith Griffin, review of *Dark Magic;* Sherrie L. Jones, review of *Dark Legend;* Kayelle Allen, review of *Dark Challenge;* reviews of *Dark Gold, Dark Fire, Dark Desire,* and *Dark Guardian.*

Allscifi.com, http://www.allscifi.com/ (March 24, 2005), Harriet Klausner, reviews of *The Twilight before Christmas, Shadow Game,* and *Mind Game.*

Christine Feehan Home Page, http://www.christine feehan.com (March 24, 2005).

WritersWrite.com, http://www.writerswrite.com/ (March 24, 2005), Claire E. White, interview with Feehan.*

*   *   *

FELTRINELLI, Carlo 1962-

PERSONAL: Born 1962, in Italy; son of Giangiacomo (a publisher) and Inge (a publisher) Feltrinelli.

ADDRESSES: Home—Milan, Italy. *Office*—Giangiacomo Feltrinelli Editore, via Andegari 6, 20121 Milan, Italy.

CAREER: Giangiacomo Feltrinelli Editore, Milan, Italy, publisher.

AWARDS, HONORS: Literary Award, Salzburg Easter Festival, 2002, for *Senior Service: A Story of Riches, Revolution, and Violent Death.*

WRITINGS:

Feltrinelli: A Story of Riches, Revolution, and Violent Death, translation by Alastair McEwan, Granta Books (London, England), 2001, Harcourt (New York, NY), 2002.

SIDELIGHTS: Carlo Feltrinelli is head of the publishing house and bookstore chain founded in Milan, Italy, by his father, Giangiacomo Feltrinelli (1926-1972). The elder Feltrinelli was killed in an explosion as he attempted an act of sabotage against the Italian government. Carlo was ten years old when his father published, over the objections of the Soviet Union, *Doctor Zhivago,* by Boris Pasternak, who went on to win the Nobel Prize for literature. He gives an account of the life and death of his father in *Feltrinelli: A Story of Riches, Revolution, and Violent Death.*

Giangiacomo Feltrinelli, who was from a wealthy family, joined Italy's Communist Party in 1945 while still a teenager. While his mother distributed literature on behalf of the monarchy from her Rolls Royce, young Feltrinelli was distributing and hanging posters for the Communists. He saw publishing as a way to further his political beliefs, and founded his own publishing house in 1955. He also established the Feltrinelli Institute, which trains young leftist activists.

The biography provides a great deal of detail surrounding Feltrinelli's publishing of *Doctor Zhivago* despite strong Soviet opposition. Manchester *Guardian* reviewer Mario Fortunato felt that the transcripts of letters exchanged by Feltrinelli and Pasternak constitutes "perhaps the most successful part of the book, and certainly the most enthralling." Fortunato found

that "the greatest tribute that can be paid to Feltrinelli's work as a publisher: his active, intelligent and creative role in supporting his author."

Because of the publication of Pasternak's novel, Feltrinelli was expelled from the Italian Communist Party. With the rise of the New Left in the late 1960s, however, he assumed a leadership position. He was fascinated by Che Guevara and Fidel Castro and tried to convince the latter to publish a book of memoirs. Following his trips to Cuba, Feltrinelli tried to organize a revolutionary force, hoping to transform a conservative region of Italy into what he called "the Cuba of the Mediterranean." He supported leftist groups seeking an armed revolution by buying them guns and ammunition. Feltrinelli was also involved with the violent Red Brigades, a group that in 1978 kidnapped and murdered Italy's former prime minister, Aldo Moro. In support of such terrorist activities, Feltrinelli planted the bomb that ended his life.

Andre Schiffrin noted in the *Nation* that "in the last years of his life, Giangiacomo was in hiding; he barely saw Carlo and rarely spoke to his colleagues. He moved in the shadow world of terrorists and plotters, becoming a character in a Conrad novel rather than the millionaire publisher that he had been." Mark Falcoff, writing in *Commentary,* found that the many letters written by Feltrinelli that are reproduced in the book "reveal a man at once neurotic, self-important, self-indulgent, and at times emotionally confused."

BIOGRAPHICAL AND CRITICAL SOURCES:

PERIODICALS

Booklist, November 1, 2002, Jay Freeman, review of *Feltrinelli: A Story of Riches, Revolution, and Violent Death,* p. 472.
Commentary, February, 2003, Mark Falcoff, review of *Feltrinelli,* p. 66.
Economist, November 3, 2001, review of *Senior Service: A Story of Riches, Revolution, and Violent Death.*
Guardian (Manchester, England), January 12, 2002, Mario Fortunato, review of *Senior Service,* p. 8.
Harper's, May, 2003, Barbara Probst Solomon, review of *Feltrinelli,* p. 84.

Kirkus Reviews, September 15, 2002, review of *Feltrinelli,* p. 1364.

London Review of Books, February 7, 2002, John Foot, review of *Senior Service,* pp. 19-20.

Nation, December 2, 2002, Andre Schiffrin, review of *Feltrinelli,* p. 28.

New York Times, December 14, 2002, Alexander Stille, review of *Feltrinelli,* p. B9.

Publishers Weekly, September 16, 2002, review of *Feltrinelli,* p. 58.

Spectator, November 24, 2001, Joseph Farrell, review of *Senior Service,* p. 52.

Times Literary Supplement, December 7, 2001, Martin Clark, review of *Senior Service,* pp. 4-5.

ONLINE

SocialistWorld.net, http://www.socialistworld.net/ (June 6, 2002), Niall Mulholland, review of *Senior Service.**

* * *

FERRERAS, Francisco 1962-
   (Pipin)

PERSONAL: Born January 18, 1962, in Matanzas, Cuba; married Audrey Mestre (fourth wife, deceased, 2002).

ADDRESSES: Home—Miami, FL. *Agent*—c/o Author Mail, Regan Books, 10 E. 53rd St., 7th Fl., New York, NY 10022.

CAREER: Deep-sea diver and writer.

WRITINGS:

(With Linda Robertson) *The Dive: A Story of Love and Obsession* (memoir), Regan Books (New York, NY), 2004.

ADAPTATIONS: The Dive was adapted for film by director James Cameron.

SIDELIGHTS: Francisco "Pipin" Ferreras is a world champion free diver and author of the memoir *The Dive: A Story of Love and Obsession,* cowritten with Linda Robertson. The book recounts the love story between Ferreras and his fourth wife, Audrey Mestre, who died in 2002 while setting a new world record in the dangerous sport of free diving. During deep-sea free dives, a person goes as deep as he or she can without breathing equipment and then is pulled back to the surface. Ferreras would beat his wife's record of 170 meters (or approximately 561 feet) a year later when he dove 558 feet.

In his memoir, Ferreras tells about meeting Mestre in 1996. She was a marine biology student who had been looking for Ferreras as part of her thesis research. Before long, the two fell in love, and Mestre became the diver's fourth wife. Eventually, Mestre took up the sport herself and before long set a world record in the female diver category. But tragedy occurred on October 12, 2002, when Mestre attempted to set a new world record that would outdistance her husband's record by nearly thirty feet. Because of equipment difficulties with the cable and lift bag she was to ride to the surface, Mestre ascended too slowly, lost consciousness, and died.

Writing in the *Library Journal,* Edwin B. Burgess commented, "There may be some interest in this full account, but few readers will feel comfortable with the author's boastful self-justification in the face of this tragedy." David Pitt noted in *Booklist* that *The Dive* "is in many ways a classic love story with a couple of twists" and added that the book is "also a concise history of the sport of free diving." Pitt went on to write, "Sports memoirs are a dime a dozen, but this one stands apart." A *Publishers Weekly* contributor wrote, "With fluid writing and vivid descriptions, this compelling autobiography explores emotional depths while detailing the sport's beauty, technologies, drama and dangers."

BIOGRAPHICAL AND CRITICAL SOURCES:

BOOKS

Ferreras, Francisco, and Linda Robertson, *The Dive: A Story of Love and Obsession,* Regan Books (New York, NY), 2004.

PERIODICALS

Booklist, September 1, 2004, David Pitt, review of *The Dive,* p. 47.

Capper's, November 11, 2003, "Diver Sets New Record, Descending 558 Feet," p. 33.

Library Journal, November 15, 2004, Edwin B. Burgess, review of *The Dive,* p. 67.

Publishers Weekly, August 2, 2004, review of *The Dive,* p. 64.

Rodale's Scuba Diving, October, 1998, John Francis, "Pushing Limits, Pushing Luck," p. 17.

Skin Diver, December, 1997, Tamara Collins, "Delving into the Depths: Pipin's Dive to 500 Feet Tests the Limits of Human Potential," p. 84.

Sports Illustrated, July 17, 1995, "Sinking to New Depths," p. 8; June 16, 2003, Gary Smith, "Rapture of the Deep," p. 62; October 27, 2003, Kostya Kennedy and Mark Bechtel, "Deep Story," p. 26.

U.S. News & World Report, August 16, 2004, Thomas K. Grose, "Depths of Passion," p. 80.

ONLINE

DiveMares.com, http://www.divemares.com/ (March 24, 2005), "Cameron's Cameras Roll as Pipin Sets New Record."

OTHER

Ocean Men: Extreme Dive (film), nWave Pictures/ Sarai Inc., 2001.*

*   *   *

FINDON, Joanne 1957-

PERSONAL: Born January 28, 1957, in New Westminster, British Columbia, Canada; daughter of Harold and Alice (Blenkarn) Findon; married Steve Riddle; children: one daughter. *Education:* University of British Columbia, B.A. (medieval studies), 1982; University of Toronto, M.A., 1987, Ph.D. (medieval studies), 1994.

ADDRESSES: Home—750 Walkerfield Ave., Peterborough, Ontario K9J 4W6, Canada. *Office*— Department of English Literature, Traill College, Wallis Hall 103.2, Trent University, Peterborough, Ontario K9J 7B8, Canada. *E-mail*—jfindon@cogeco.ca.

CAREER: Educator and writer. Trent University, Peterborough, Ontario, Canada, assistant professor of English literature, 2002—.

MEMBER: Writer's Union of Canada, Canadian Society of Children's Authors, Illustrators, and Performers, Canadian Children's Book Centre.

AWARDS, HONORS: Toronto IODE Award, for *The Dream of Aengus,* 1994.

WRITINGS:

A Woman's Words: Emer and Female Speech in the Ulster Cycle, University of Toronto Press (Buffalo, NY), 1997.

Auld Lang Syne, Stoddart Kids (Buffalo, NY), 1997.

The Dream of Aengus, Stoddart Kids (Buffalo, NY), 1998.

When Night Eats the Moon, Red Deer Press (Calgary, Alberta, Canada), 1999.

Science and Technology In the Middle Ages, Crabtree (New York, NY), 2005.

Contributor of short stories to anthologies, including *The Blue Jean Collection,* Thistledown Press, 1992; and *Takes,* Thistledown Press, 1996; and *Winds through Time,* Beach Holme Publishing, 1998.

SIDELIGHTS: Canadian children's author and educator Joanne Findon is the author of the time-travel novel *When Night Eats the Moon.* In this 1999 work readers travel with main character Holly back through time to 600 B.C. and the place known as Stonehenge. Holly finds herself in Britain's Iron Age, a none-too-comfortable epoch made even less pleasant by the fact that Celtic warriors are invading the local people living near the massive stone structure that gives the place its name. Mistaken as a prophesied savior, the North American teen must now embark on a quest to help the doomed locals. "Unlike some time-travel stories, the devices here make sense, and Findon does a particularly good job explaining how the ancient history has affected Holly and her mother's relationship" commented *Booklist* critic Ilene Cooper.

Findon once commented: "I blame my two lifelong passions—writing fiction and studying the past—on American children's author Lloyd Alexander, whose books I began reading in Grade 4. His Prydain books gave me the desire to weave spells out of words and transport readers to other worlds. Alexander's inspiration for the books—the medieval Welsh tales called the Mabinogion—piqued my curiosity about early Celtic culture.

"As a result, I have spent years studying medieval history and literature, particularly Celtic literature, and have earned an M.A. and Ph.D. in medieval studies. My studies have also fed my love of writing stories inspired by times past. My first picture book, *The Dream of Aengus,* is a retelling of a haunting medieval Irish tale of love and transformation, while *Auld Lang Syne* is a nonfiction picture book about Scottish poet Robert Burns."

BIOGRAPHICAL AND CRITICAL SOURCES:

PERIODICALS

Booklist, August, 2000, Ilene Cooper, review of *When Night Eats the Moon,* p. 2138.

Canadian Review of Materials, May 26, 2000, Lorraine Douglas, review of *When Night Eats the Moon.*

Resource Links, June, 1998, review of *Auld Lang Syne,* p. 2; April, 2000, review of *When Night Eats the Moon,* p. 28.

ONLINE

Canadian Society of Children's Authors, Illustrators, and Performers Web site, http://www.canscaip.org/ (May 3, 2005), "Joanne Findon."

*   *   *

FITZGERALD, Eric
See BREWER, Gil

*   *   *

FLEMING, Fergus 1959-

PERSONAL: Born 1959. *Education:* Attended Oxford University and City University, London.

ADDRESSES: Agent—c/o Author Mail, Cassell, Orion Publishing Group, Orion House, 5 Upper St. Martin's Lane, London WC2H 9EA, England.

CAREER: Trained as an accountant and lawyer; became furniture-maker; freelance writer, 1991—.

AWARDS, HONORS: Winner of a British national poetry competition, British Broadcasting Corporation (BBC), at age ten.

WRITINGS:

NONFICTION

Barrow's Boys, Granta Books (London, England), 1998, Atlantic Monthly Press (New York, NY), 2000.

Killing Dragons: The Conquest of the Alps, Atlantic Monthly Press (New York, NY), 2000.

Ninety Degrees North: The Quest for the North Pole, Grove Press (New York, NY), 2001.

The Cuban Missile Crisis: To the Brink of World War III, Heinemann Library (Chicago, IL), 2001.

The Sword and the Cross: Two Men and an Empire of Sand, Grove Press (New York, NY), 2003.

Cassell's Tales of Endurance, Cassell (London, England), 2004.

Contributor to periodicals, including *New Statesman.*

ADAPTATIONS: Barrow's Boys was adapted as a radio play, BBC Radio 4, 1998; *Killing Dragons* was adapted as a radio play for BBC Radio 4.

SIDELIGHTS: Fergus Fleming has made a career out of chronicling the foolhardy adventures of the brave men who mapped the far reaches of the world during the nineteenth and early twentieth centuries. "There are few people writing today who can capture the lunatic spirit of adventure that possessed these often suicidal missions so well," Chris Martin declared in *Geographical.* In a *New York Times Book Review* critique of *Ninety Degrees North: The Quest for the North Pole,* Jonathan Dore noted that one of Fleming's strengths as a writer is his "admirable detachment," which makes him "always ready to be amused by pomposity." Plus, Dore continued, "He has great narrative gifts, and his brief character sketches draw readers in while pithy summaries of each expedition carry us on breathlessly from one ice hummock to the next."

Fleming's first book, *Barrow's Boys,* takes its title from John Barrow, the man who was second secretary of the British navy from 1804 until 1845. The first decade of his career was consumed with organizing the navy to defeat Napoleon and his forces, but after that threat was finally defeated in 1815, the British found themselves with far more naval officers than missions for them. It was Barrow's idea to send these idle sailors off to explore the unmapped corners of the globe, particularly the Arctic, the Antarctic, and Africa. It was a noble idea, but by most measures it proved to be a spectacular failure. These missions were usually poorly planned and frequently brought gruesome deaths for the explorers, from Captain James Tuckey, who was sent out to explore the Congo in 1816 and died of yellow fever there along with his entire party, to Sir John Franklin, who disappeared, again along with his entire party, in the Arctic in 1845. (This was after Franklin warded off starvation on an earlier Arctic expedition by eating his own boots.) Plus, Barrow's missions failed to bring the expected commercial benefits to the British Empire: There was no Northwest Passage to the Pacific Ocean to be found, and the Niger River did not in fact flow into the Congo or the Nile as Barrow had hoped. As Anthony Sattin noted in the *Sunday Times,* the stories of many of these individual missions have already been told, "but Fleming justifies the retelling . . . by setting them in the context of Barrow's personal ambition and bringing them thrillingly to life." *Washington Post Book World* reviewer Grace Lichtenstein also praised Fleming's retellings, calling *Barrow's Boys* "a rollicking narrative" and "a riveting yarn." However, as Kathleen Gorman noted in the *Journal of Popular Culture,* the book also "combines the narrative appeal of the best of the adventure books with the historical context required by scholars."

Fleming continued his history of Arctic exploration in *Ninety Degrees North.* The book begins where *Barrow's Boys* ended, in 1845, and continues through the mid-twentieth century, when the first person who is positively confirmed to have reached the North Pole, the Russian Alexander Kuznetsov, arrived there. Despite the advances in scientific knowledge and technology since the missions covered in *Barrow's*

Boys, grisly deaths during these missions were scarcely less frequent than before, and again, exceptionally negligent planning was usually to blame. Explorers were most commonly killed by scurvy—whose horrors "Fleming describes in full technicolor detail," Harry Mount noted in the *Spectator*—despite the fact that by this time it was common knowledge that lack of fruits and vegetables caused scurvy and canned produce capable of being taken on Arctic expeditions was readily available. Cold was another frequent killer, but the imperialistic British refused to accept that the native Inuit people might have something to teach them about how to survive in that weather, at least until Robert Peary came along and ordered his party to build igloos, rather than dragging along heavy and less efficient tents, and to wear furs instead of their wool uniforms. "Fleming teases out his material beautifully and at a perfect pace," Mark Cocker wrote in the Manchester *Guardian,* also stating: "Flemming is a born storyteller, and unravels this expeditionary sequence like a great saga of adventure."

Killing Dragons: The Conquest of the Alps tells the tales of the European explorers who conquered a snowy wasteland closer to home. Like Fleming's other books, it "addresses its subject with a droll, detached and sometimes pat tone of historical amusement," Elizabeth Hightower noted in the *New York Times Book Review.* The first booster of Alpine exploration, Marc-Theodore Bourrit, had to overcome the eighteenth-century certainty that the Alps were a horrible, accursed place inhabited by dragons and cretins and that the views from the highest passes were so awesome that they would drive people mad. Despite these beliefs, Bourrit succeeded in prompting enough interest in the Alps to convince some brave men to try to climb them, and by 1786 the summit of Mont Blanc (formerly Mont Maudit—Cursed Mountain) had been reached. The most popular challenge of the Alps, the Matterhorn, was finally summited in 1865 by Edward Whymper, but the achievement was overshadowed by tragedy when a broken rope cost four of the seven-person party their lives during the descent. The conquest of the Alps continued into the twentieth century, with several climbers losing their lives trying to complete the difficult the north face of the Eiger before it was successfully traversed in the 1930s. *Killing Dragons* is "energetic, wry," and "delightful," Lorraine Korman concluded in *Forbes.*

The Sword and the Cross: Two Men and an Empire of Sand also focuses on European exploration and colonialism, but unlike Fleming's earlier works it describes French rather than primarily British aspirations. The "two men" of the title are Henri Laperrine and Charles de Foucauld. Both were graduates of the prestigious St. Cyr academy who joined the Chasseurs D'Afrique and became enthusiastic participants in the French colonial project, specifically the conquest of northern Africa, although later in life they took different paths toward this goal. Laperrine rose through the French army to become the founder and commander of the "camel corps," a camel-mounted cavalry designed for desert fighting. Foucauld, on the other hand, became a monk; he lived as a semi-hermit in the Sahara desert, sometimes teaching the native Tuaregs about Christianity and French culture and sometimes providing his friend Laperrine with information and help in combatting the Tuareg resistance.

Critics again praised Fleming's writing. An *African Business* critic declared *The Sword and the Cross* to be "a vivid, haunting and sharply witty history," while *Booklist* reviewer George Cohen wrote that it "reads like the finest fiction."

BIOGRAPHICAL AND CRITICAL SOURCES:

PERIODICALS

African Business, May, 2003, review of *The Sword and the Cross: Two Men and an Empire of Sand,* p. 64.

Antioch Review, spring, 2004, Catherine Kord, review of *The Sword and the Cross,* p. 369.

Booklist, April 1, 2000, Gilbert Taylor, review of *Barrow's Boys,* p. 1427; January 1, 2001, Taylor, review of *Killing Dragons: The Conquest of the Alps,* p. 903; September 15, 2002, George Cohen, review of *Ninety Degrees North: The Quest for the North Pole,* p. 202; October 1, 2003, Cohen, review of *The Sword and the Cross,* p. 295.

Bookseller, September 6, 2002, review of *Ninety Degrees North,* p. S10; December 13, 2002, Benedicte Page, "Desert Madness," review of *The Sword and the Cross,* p. 28.

Boston Globe, February 5, 2003, Bob MacDonald, "In Cold Detail, Engaging 'Ninety'Follows Treks to North Pole," p. D5.

Forbes, March 5, 2001, Lorraine Korman, review of *Killing Dragons,* p. 116.

Geographical, November, 1998, Melanie Train, review of *Barrow's Boys,* p. 85; October, 2001, Chris Martin, "Northern Exposure," review of *Ninety Degrees North,* p. 84; December, 2004, Sarah Crowden, review of *Cassell's Tales of Endurance,* p. 101.

Guardian (London, England), November 10, 2001, Mark Cocker, "All Points North," review of *Ninety Degrees North,* p. 9.

Journal of Popular Culture, summer, 2002, Kathleen Gorman, review of *Barrow's Boys,* p. 182.

Kirkus Reviews, July 1, 2002, review of *Ninety Degrees North,* p. 931; August 15, 2003, review of *The Sword and the Cross,* p. 1056.

Kliatt, July, 2002, Michael P. Healy, review of *Killing Dragons,* p. 43.

Library Journal, February 15, 2000, Stanley Itkin, review of *Barrow's Boys,* p. 177; August, 2002, Sheila Kasperek, review of *Ninety Degrees North,* p. 125; December, 2003, Jim Doyle, review of *The Sword and the Cross,* p. 136.

Los Angeles Times, May 30, 2004, Zachary Karabell, review of *Barrow's Boys,* p. 66.

New Statesman, December 4, 1998, Roz Kaveney, review of *The Sword and the Cross,* p. R9.

New York Times Book Review, May 21, 2000, Susan Reed, "Another Fine Mess," review of *Barrow's Boys* p. 17; January 7, 2001, Elizabeth Hightower, "Thin Air and Thick Men," review of *Killing Dragons,* p. 7; November 3, 2002, Jonathan Dore, "Snow Jobs," review of *Ninety Degrees North,* p. 19.

Publishers Weekly, February 21, 2000, review of *Barrow's Boys,* p. 73; November 20, 2000, review of *Killing Dragons,* p. 54; August 26, 2002, review of *Ninety Degrees North,* p. 55; August 18, 2003, review of *The Sword and the Cross,* p. 65.

Spectator, September 29, 2001, Harry Mount, review of *Ninety Degrees North,* p. 36; March 29, 2003, Sara Wheeler, "Serving Christ and Colonialism," review of *The Sword and the Cross,* p. 50.

Sunday Times (London, England), November 1, 1998, Anthony Sattin, "Captains Courageous," review of *Barrow's Boys,* p. 8.

Time, November 11, 2002, Lev Grossman, "Blinded Me with Science: Two Gripping Tales about Daring Men Who Went to Extremes in the Pursuit of Nature's Secrets," review of *Ninety Degrees North,* p. 73; December 30, 2002, review of *Ninety Degrees North,* p. 152.

Wall Street Journal, April 18, 2000, Geoffrey Norman, "Bold, Eccentric Journeys through the Polar Ice," review of *Barrow's Boys,* p. A16.

Washington Post Book World, July 31, 2000, Grace Lichtenstein, "Going to Extremes," review of *Barrow's Boys,* p. 3.

ONLINE

Granta Online, http://www.granta.com/ (April 5, 2005), "Fergus Fleming."
Orion Books Web site, http://www.orionbooks.co.uk/ (March 14, 2005), interview with Fleming.*

*   *   *

FOLEY, Thomas W. 1931-

PERSONAL: Born December 11, 1931, in East Stroudsburg, PA; son of Robert R. and Marie J. (O'Connor) Foley; married Ruth M. Hahn (a homemaker), October 13, 1956; children: Eileen M. Stenhoff, Thomas W., John M. *Ethnicity:* "Irish." *Education:* Loyola University Chicago, B.Sc. and M.S.I.R. *Politics:* Conservative. *Religion:* Roman Catholic. *Hobbies and other interests:* Travel, birding, golf.

ADDRESSES: Home—3765 Woodsong Ct., Dunwoody, GA 30338. *E-mail*—twfoley@att.net.

CAREER: U.S. Gypsum, 1956-91, worked in labor relations in Chicago, IL, then as director of human resources in Atlanta, GA. *Military service:* U.S. Army, 1954-56.

WRITINGS:

U.S. Gypsum: A Company History, U.S. Gypsum (Chicago, IL), 1995.
Father Francis M. Craft: Missionary to the Sioux, University of Nebraska Press (Lincoln, NE), 2002.

WORK IN PROGRESS: Research on the journals of Father Francis M. Craft.

BIOGRAPHICAL AND CRITICAL SOURCES:

PERIODICALS

Catholic Historical Review, July, 2003, Harvey Markowitz, review of *Father Francis M. Craft: Missionary to the Sioux,* p. 566.

Theological Studies, December, 2003, Michael F. Steltenkamp, review of *Father Francis M. Craft,* p. 879.

*   *   *

FORATTINI, Giorgio 1931(?)-

PERSONAL: Born 1931 (some sources say 1932), in Rome, Italy.

ADDRESSES: Agent—c/o Author Mail, Arnoldo Mondadori Editore S.P.A., via Mondadori 1, 20090 Segrate, Milan, Italy.

CAREER: Oil company sales agent in Naples, Italy, and manager for a record company in Rome, Italy, 1950s; household appliances sales representative, Rome, 1967-69; advertising company art director, Rome, 1970s; *Paese Sera,* Rome, graphic designer, c. 1973-75; *La Repubblica,* Rome, satirical cartoonist, 1975-82. Worked as satirical cartoonist and graphic designer for *La Stampa,* Turin, Italy, 1982-84 and 1999-2005, and *La Repubblica* 1984-99. Contributor to *Panorama* and *L'Espresso;* created cartoons for Italian television c. 1980s; commercial artist for clients that included Alitalia and Fiat.

AWARDS, HONORS: Premio Hemingway, 2000, for journalism; civic merit award, Mayor of Trieste, Italy, 2004.

WRITINGS:

SELF-ILLUSTRATED; CARTOON COLLECTIONS

Referendum, reverendum, Feltrinelli (Milan, Italy), 1974.
Quattro anni di storia italiana, Mondadori (Milan, Italy), 1977.
Un'idea al giorno, Mondadori (Milan, Italy), 1978.
Res publica, Mondadori (Milan, Italy), 1980.
Librus, Mondadori (Milan, Italy), 1980.
Satyricon, Mondadori (Milan, Italy), 1982.
Scomodoso, Mondadori (Milan, Italy), 1983.
Pagine gialle, Mondadori (Milan, Italy), 1984.
Provocazia, Mondadori (Milan, Italy), 1986.

Nudi alla meta, Mondadori (Milan, Italy), 1986.

Il Kualunquista, Mondadori (Milan, Italy), 1988.

Giorgio e il drago, Mondadori (Milan, Italy), 1989.

Stradivarius: i songi nell'archeto, Mondadori (Milan, Italy), 1989.

Vignette Sataniche, Mondadori (Milan, Italy), 1989.

Insciaqquà, Mondadori (Milan, Italy), 1990.

Forattini classic, Mondadori (Milan, Italy), 1991.

Pizza rossa, Mondadori (Milan, Italy), 1991.

Il mascalzone, Mondadori (Milan, Italy), 1992.

Forattinopoli: storia della corruzione in Italia, Mondadori (Milan, Italy), 1993.

Bossic instinct, Mondadori (Milan, Italy), 1993.

Benito di Tacco: craxi story, 1976-1993, Mondadori (Milan, Italy), 1993.

Andreácula: andreotti story 1976-1993, Mondadori (Milan, Italy), 1993.

Karaoketto: PCUS-PCI-PDS: 1973-1994, Mondadori (Milan, Italy), 1994.

Il garante di Lady Chatterley, Mondadori (Milan, Italy), 1994.

Va' dove ti porta il rospo, Mondadori (Milan, Italy), 1995.

Giovanni Paolo secondo Forattini, 1978-1995, Mondadori (Milan, Italy), 1995.

Berluscopone, Mondadori (Milan, Italy), 1996.

Il forattone, Mondadori (Milan, Italy), 1996.

Io e il Bruco, Mondadori (Milan, Italy), 1997.

Il libro a colori del post-comunismo (political vignettes), Mondadori (Milan, Italy), 1998.

Taxgate, Mondadori (Milan, Italy), 1998.

Oscar alla regia: storia di un settennato, Mondadori (Milan, Italy), 1999.

Millennium flop, Mondadori (Milan, Italy), 1999.

Sotto il baffetto niente: ia resistibile ascesa del leader Massimo, Mondadori (Milan, Italy), 2000.

Foratt pride, Mondadori (Milan, Italy), 2000.

Glob, Mondadori (Milan, Italy), 2001.

Ciappi: un presidente di razza, Mondadori (Milan, Italy), 2001.

Kosferatu: uno spettro s'aggira per le piazze, Mondadori (Milan, Italy), 2002.

Oltre la fifa, Mondadori (Milan, Italy), 2002.

Hurk, Mondadori (Milan, Italy), 2003.

SIDELIGHTS: Giorgio Forattini has been called one of the foremost European satirical cartoonists of his generation. He completed high school, but quit his studies at a university of architectural arts in 1953 to work at an oil refinery in northern Italy and become a sales representative in the oil industry and later in other fields. Following the 1960s student revolt in his home country, satirical cartoons began to proliferate in Italian newspapers and magazines in response to the political climate. Forattini plunged headlong into the movement.

Forattini's cartoons first appeared in the daily Roman newspaper *Paese Sera.* By winning a cartoon contest run by that newspaper in the 1970s, he secured a position as a graphic designer for the publication. His first satirical political cartoons appeared in the magazine *Panorama* in 1973 and in *Paese Sera* in 1974. For the next ten years, *Panorama* published his political cartoons.

His first permanent position as a cartoonist began in 1975 when he left *Paese Sera* to join a newly founded daily called *La Repubblica* as its regular editorial cartoonist. In 1982 he moved on to Turin's daily newspaper, *La Stampa,* as a graphic designer. That paper published one of his satirical cartoons on the front page, the first time a cartoon of that kind ever appeared on the front page of a daily Italian newspaper.

In the meantime, Forattini worked in commercial advertising for Alitalia, Italy's major airline. His services were also sought by auto-maker Fiat to launch its new model, Uno, and he worked steadily during the 1980s for Italian television, contributing topical and political cartoons to that medium.

By the end of 1984, Forattini had quit *La Stampa* to return to *La Repubblica,* where his daily editorials again made the front page. During this period, he also worked for *L'Espresso* and *Panorama.* In 1999, he left *La Repubblica* to once again work for *La Stampa.* At the time, Forattini was being sued 1.6 million dollars for defamation by Prime Minister Massimo D'Alema because of a cartoon depicting D'Alema wearing a fascist-type uniform that included an armband decorated with a hammer and sickle. D'Alema was the first former communist to become prime minister of Italy, and the cartoon was published during a period of controversy over a number of Italians who had allegedly been associated with the Russian KGB.

This was not the first time D'Alema had sued Forattini. The prime minister, together with Left Democratic party leader Achille Occhetto, were awarded 60,000 dollars from a suit involving a 1991 magazine cover that pictured them as prostitutes accepting money from Soviet leader Mikhail Gorbachev. Unlike in the United States, where public figures can openly be satirized, Italy affords such individuals the same privacy protections as they do private citizens.

A contributor to *World Encyclopedia of Cartoons* noted that the Italian cartoonist's favorite subjects are the "high and mighty in all fields" and that he reviews the "principal deeds (and misdeeds) of Italian politicians." Foreign dignitaries are also fair game for Forattini, however, and he vehemently attacked U.S. President Richard Nixon and Soviet Premier Leonid Brezhnev during their terms in office. Forattini prefers to "ridicule his targets directly, at times focusing on some physical defect," never resorts to vulgarity, and uses a harsh irony to express his views of the powerful. The *World Encyclopedia of Cartoons* writer also commented that Forattini's cartoons portray a relatively upbeat and breezy style with a "pinch of optimism and confidence that raises a smile even when reality is darker than the mood of his cartoons."

By 2000, Forattini's books of cartoons and caricatures had sold more than three million copies. Many became bestsellers, and new editions have been published. *Il libro a colori del post-comunismo* contains a collection of his political vignettes originally published in the weekly journal *Panorama.*

In early 2005, Forattini was released from his contract by *La Stampa* because of his controversial cartoons, particularly one that depicted the baby Jesus in a manger, wondering whether Israeli tanks might appear to kill him again.

BIOGRAPHICAL AND CRITICAL SOURCES:

BOOKS

World Encyclopedia of Cartoons, Gale (Detroit, MI), 1980.

PERIODICALS

Boston Globe, February 6, 2000, Jeff Israely, "Cartoonist's Target Hits Back: Italy's Premier Sues over a Coverup Sketch," p. A14.
Times Literary Supplement, January 4, 1980, review of *Librus,* p. 22.

ONLINE

Giorgio Forattini Home Page, http://www.forattini.it (May 9, 2005).*

* * *

FORD, Carin T.

PERSONAL: Female.

ADDRESSES: Agent—c/o Author Mail, Enslow Publishers, Inc., Box 398, 40 Industrial Rd., Berkeley Heights, NJ 07922-0398. *E-mail*—ctfsnap@aol.com.

CAREER: Writer. Also worked as a newspaper reporter.

WRITINGS:

JUVENILE NONFICTION

Legends of American Dance and Choreography, Enslow Publishers (Berkeley Heights, NJ), 2000.
Helen Keller: Lighting the Way for the Blind and Deaf, Enslow Publishers (Berkeley Heights, NJ), 2001.
Andy Warhol: Pioneer of Pop Art, Enslow Publishers (Berkeley Heights, NJ), 2001.
Alexander Graham Bell: Inventor of the Telephone, Enslow Publishers (Berkeley Heights, NJ), 2002.
Amelia Earhart: Meet the Pilot, Enslow Publishers (Berkeley Heights, NJ), 2002.
Andy Warhol: Prince of Pop Art, Enslow Publishers (Berkeley Heights, NJ), 2002.
Andy Warhol: The Life of an Artist, Enslow Publishers (Berkeley Heights, NJ), 2002.
Thomas Edison: Inventor, Enslow Publishers (Berkeley Heights, NJ), 2002.
Helen Keller: Meet a Woman of Courage, Enslow Publishers (Berkeley Heights, NJ), 2002.
Henry Ford: The Car Man, Enslow Publishers (Berkeley Heights, NJ), 2003.
Laura Ingalls Wilder: Real-Life Pioneer of the Little House Books, Enslow Publishers (Berkeley Heights, NJ), 2003.
Thomas Jefferson: The Third President, Enslow Publishers (Berkeley Heights, NJ), 2003.

Paul Revere, Patriot, Enslow Publishers (Berkeley Heights, NJ), 2003.

Sacagawea: Meet an American Legend, Enslow Publishers (Berkeley Heights, NJ), 2003.

Walt Disney: Meet the Cartoonist, Enslow Publishers (Berkeley Heights, NJ), 2003.

The Wright Brothers: Heroes of Flight, Enslow Publishers (Berkeley Heights, NJ), 2003.

Abraham Lincoln: The Sixteenth President, Enslow Publishers (Berkeley Heights, NJ), 2003.

George Washington: The First President, Enslow Publishers (Berkeley Heights, NJ), 2003.

Dr. Seuss: Best-Loved Author, Enslow Publishers (Berkeley Heights, NJ), 2003.

Benjamin Franklin: Inventor and Patriot, Enslow Publishers (Berkeley Heights, NJ), 2003.

George Eastman: The Kodak Camera Man, Enslow Publishers (Berkeley Heights, NJ), 2003.

African-American Soldiers in the Civil War: Fighting for Freedom, Enslow Publishers (Berkeley Heights, NJ), 2004.

Levi Strauss: The Man behind Blue Jeans, Enslow Publishers (Berkeley Heights, NJ), 2004.

Lincoln, Slavery, and the Emancipation Proclamation, Enslow Publishers (Berkeley Heights, NJ), 2004.

Robert Fulton: The Steamboat Man, Enslow Publishers (Berkeley Heights, NJ), 2004.

The American Civil War: An Overview, Enslow Publishers (Berkeley Heights, NJ), 2004.

Daring Women of the Civil War, Enslow Publishers (Berkeley Heights, NJ), 2004.

Slavery and the Underground Railroad: Bound for Freedom, Enslow Publishers (Berkeley Heights, NJ), 2004.

The Battle of Gettysburg and Lincoln's Gettysburg Address, Enslow Publishers (Berkeley Heights, NJ), 2004.

Roberto Clemente: Baseball Legend, Enslow Publishers (Berkeley Heights, NJ), 2005.

Jackie Robinson: "All I Ask Is That You Respect Me as a Human Being," Enslow Publishers (Berkeley Heights, NJ), 2005.

Author of short stories have been published in national and international magazines.

SIDELIGHTS: Carin T. Ford has written numerous brief biographies and other books for young adult and middle-grade readers, from recent historical figures such as Andy Warhol and Dr. Seuss to past American presidents and notable baseball players. In *Legends of American Dance and Choreography,* Ford presents a series of brief biographies on dance legends such as Martha Graham, Fred Astaire, Bob Fosse, and Mikhail Baryshnikov. Writing in the *School Library Journal,* Carol Schene referred to the text as "concise" and "engaging," going on to state the writing "captures" each subject's "early years, key moments that led them to dance, as well as their disappointments and triumphs."

In *Helen Keller: Lighting the Way for the Blind and Deaf* Ford tells the life story of the famous blind and deaf woman, including her tutelage by Annie Sullivan, who taught Keller how to function in the world. *School Library Journal* contributor Kristen Oravec called the book "a welcome research tool and a readable narrative." Ford is also the author of several books about artist Andy Warhol, including *Andy Warhol: Pioneer of Pop Art.* In a review of the book in the *School Library Journal,* Tim Wadham commented the book retains its readers through stories of Warhol's own "idiosyncrasies" rather "than through its compelling prose."

Ford's books about America's former presidents include the brief biographies *George Washington: The First President, Thomas Jefferson: The Third President,* and *Abraham Lincoln: The Sixteenth President. School Library Journal* contributor Kristen Oravec commented the books on Jefferson and Lincoln are "good introductions" and noted the titles discuss "not only each man's accomplishments, but also his problems." Ford also writes about other notable early Americans in her books *Paul Revere, Patriot,* and *Benjamin Franklin: Inventor and Patriot.* In a review of Ford's books about Franklin and *The Wright Brothers: Heroes of Flight,* John Peters wrote in *Booklist* that "Ford adds enough context to give younger readers a sense of each figure's historical significance." Commenting in *School Library Journal* on the Franklin biography, Lucinda Snyder Whitehurst noted that while the book is too brief to fit in Franklin's many accomplishments,it would "serve its purpose for young report writers." Barbara Buckley, writing in the *School Library Journal,* called *The Wright Brothers* a "competent, accessible biography."

In *Dr. Seuss: Best-Loved Author* Ford recounts the life and work of the famous children's writer. *School Library Journal* contributor Kathleen Simonetta noted that the book "reads well, and that young researchers "will find enough information for reports." Ford profiles another author in *Laura Ingalls Wilder: Real-Life Pioneer of the Little House Books.* Ford depicts Wilder's life as a young girl living in various places such as Missouri, Kansas, and Iowa; her ultimate decision to become a writer is also discussed. Rita Soltan, writing in the *School Library Journal,* called the book "engaging for curious readers."

Ford turned to the U.S. Civil War for *Daring Women of the Civil War* and *Slavery and the Underground Railroad: Bound for Freedom.* In the former, she looks at the traditional roles of women prior to the Civil War and how that conflict caused changes in the widely held views of women, who, much like women during World War II, had to take over many of the jobs typically performed by men. Her book about the underground railroad details the rise of slavery and the true stories of both the slaves who escaped through this network of hiding places and the people who ran them. Writing in *Booklist,* Jennifer Mattson called the books "rather accessible, stand-alone discussions of individual topics" concerning the war between the states. Mattson also commented, "Well-chosen, primary-source quotations . . . bring the drama up close." *School Library Journal* contributor Kristen Oravec noted that Ford's "texts are well organized" and her "writing is straightforward."

Ford continues her focus on the Civil War with *African-American Soldiers in the Civil War: Fighting for Freedom,* in which she recounts the role of black Americans as soldiers in the conflict, from their struggle to be allowed to join the military to their heroic efforts in battle. In a review for *School Library Journal,* Laura Reed commented that "The text, illustrations, photographs, and time line all play an important role in conveying the struggles and triumphs" of African-American soldiers in the Union Army. In *The Battle of Gettysburg and Lincoln's Gettysburg Address* Ford discusses the turning point in the war between the North and the South as well as what is perhaps the most famous address ever given by a President of the United States. In terms of the battle, Ford provides detailed accounts of various encounters between the troops during battle. In focusing on Lincoln's famous speech, she points out it was not considered a great speech at the time. *School Library Journal* contributor Ann Welton called *The Battle of Gettysburg and Lincoln's Gettysburg Address* a "sound addition where books on the Civil War are in demand."

BIOGRAPHICAL AND CRITICAL SOURCES:

PERIODICALS

Booklist, June 1, 2003, John Peters, reviews of *Benjamin Franklin: Inventor and Patriot* and *The Wright Brothers: Heroes of Flight,* p. 1800; July, 2004, reviews of *Daring Women of the Civil War* and *Slavery and the Underground Railroad: Bound for Freedom,* p. 1839.

School Library Journal, July, 2000, Carol Schene, review of *Legends of American Dance and Choreography,* p. 116; May, 2001, Kristen Oravec, review of *Helen Keller: Lighting the Way for the Blind and Deaf,* p. 164; October, 2001, Tim Wadham, review of *Andy Warhol: Pioneer of Pop Art,* p. 182; April 2003, Robin L. Gibson, review of *Andy Warhol: The Life of an Artist,* p. 149; June, 2003, Kathleen Simonetta, reviews of *George Washington: The First President* and *Paul Revere, Patriot,* p. 128; September, 2003, Kristen Oravec, reviews of *Thomas Jefferson: The Third President* and *Abraham Lincoln: The Sixteenth President,* p. 197; October, 2003, Barbara Buckley, review of *The Wright Brothers,* p. 150; November, 2003, Kathleen Simonetta, review of *Dr. Seuss: Best-Loved Author,* p. 156; January, 2004, Lucinda Snyder Whitehurst, review of *Benjamin Franklin,* p. 114; May, 2004, Rita Soltan, review of *Laura Ingalls Wilder: Real-Life Pioneer of the Little House Books,* p. 166; August, 2004, Kristen Oravec, reviews of *Daring Women of the Civil War* and *Slavery and the Underground Railroad,* p. 136; October, 2004, Laura Reed, review of *African-American Soldiers in the Civil War: Fighting for Freedom,* p. 190; January, 2005, Ann Welton, review of *The Battle of Gettysburg and Lincoln's Gettysburg Address,* p. 146.

ONLINE

Carin T. Ford Home Page, http://members.aol.com/ctfsnap/ctford.htm (March 24, 2005).

Society of Children's Book Writers and Illustrators Eastern Pennsylvania Chapter Web site, http://www.scbwiepa.org/ (March 24, 2005), "Carin Ford."*

FRANK, Jerome D(avid) 1909-2005

OBITUARY NOTICE— See index for *CA* sketch: Born May 30, 1909, in New York, NY; died of complications from dementia, March 14, 2005, in Baltimore, MD. Psychiatrist, educator, activist, and author. Frank was a noted researcher, professor emeritus at Johns Hopkins University, and anti-nuclear arms activist. A graduate of Harvard University, he completed his undergraduate work in 1931, earned a Ph.D. in 1934, and finished his medical degree there in 1939. During World War II he taught at Johns Hopkins University and served with the army in the Philippines; after the war his interest in the psychological effects of battle were stirred further by his work as a research associate for the Veterans Administration. These experiences and his knowledge of the horrors of the nuclear weapons used against Japan later led to his activism against nuclear arms. He consequently helped to found the Physicians for Social Responsibility. After teaching for a year at Howard University, Frank returned to Johns Hopkins in 1949 as an associate professor of psychiatry. He became a full professor in 1959 and retired in 1974. Having worked as a clinical associate professor for the outpatient department at Johns Hopkins Hospital, he was especially interested in methods of psychotherapy treatment. His *Persuasion and Healing: A Comparative Study of Psychotherapy* (1961) has been one of the most influential texts in the field, helping to liberalize ideas about treatment, and it has been credited with spurring the development of such concepts as family and supportive psychotherapy. The third edition of the book, published in 1991, was written with his daughter, Julia Frank. The recipient of the first Oscar Pfister prize from the American Psychiatric Association, Frank was also the author of such books as *Group Methods in Therapy* (1959), *The Threats to Man: The Challenge of Ethics* (1965), and *Psychotherapy and the Human Predicament: A Psychosocial Approach* (1978).

OBITUARIES AND OTHER SOURCES:

PERIODICALS

Washington Post, March 19, 2005, p. B5.

ONLINE

JHU Gazette Online, http://www.jhu.edu/~gazette/ (April 18, 2005).

FRANKENHEIMER, John (Michael) 1930-2002
(Alan Smithee)

PERSONAL: Born February 19, 1930, in Malba (some sources cite Melba and New York), NY; died of a stroke, July 6, 2002, in Los Angeles, CA; son of Walter Martin (a stockbroker) and Helen Mary (Sheedy) Frankenheimer; married Carolyn Diane Miller, September 22, 1954 (divorced, 1961 [some sources cite 1962]); married Evans Evans (an actress), 1964 (some sources cite 1962); children: (first marriage) Lisa Jean, Kristi. *Education:* Williams College, B.A., 1951.

CAREER: Director of films, including *The Young Stranger,* Universal, 1957; *The Young Savages,* United Artists, 1961; *All Fall Down,* Metro-Goldwyn-Mayer, 1962; *Birdman of Alcatraz,* United Artists, 1962; *The Manchurian Candidate,* United Artists, 1962; *Seven Days in May,* Paramount, 1964; *The Train,* United Artists, 1965; *Grand Prix: Challenge of the Champions,* Metro-Goldwyn-Mayer, 1966; *Seconds,* Paramount, 1966; *The Fixer,* Metro-Goldwyn-Mayer, 1968; *The Extraordinary Seaman,* Metro-Goldwyn-Mayer, 1969; *The Gypsy Moths,* Metro-Goldwyn-Mayer, 1969; *I Walk the Line,* Columbia, 1970; *The Horsemen,* Columbia, 1971; *The Iceman Cometh,* American Film Institute, 1973; *Impossible Object* (also known as *Story of a Love Story*), 1973; *99 and 44/100 Percent Dead* (also known as *Call Harry Crown*), Twentieth Century-Fox, 1974; *French Connection II,* Twentieth Century-Fox, 1975; *Black Sunday,* Paramount, 1977; *Prophecy,* Paramount, 1979; *The Challenge* (also known as *Equals* and *Sword of the Ninja*), Embassy, 1982; *The Holcroft Covenant,* Universal, 1985; *52 Pickup,* Cannon, 1986; *Dead Bang,* Warner Bros., 1989; *The Fourth War,* Cannon, 1990; *Year of the Gun,* Triumph Releasing, 1991; *The Island of Dr. Moreau,* New Line Cinema, 1996; *Ronin,* United Artists, 1998; *Reindeer Games,* Dimension, 1999; and *The Hire: Ambush* (short promotional film), BMW Films, 2001. Producer of films, including (with others) *The Manchurian Candidate,* United Artists, 1962; (with others) *Seven Days in May,* Paramount, 1964; *Seconds,* 1966; (executive producer) *Grand Prix: Challenge of the Champions,* Metro-Goldwyn-Mayer, 1966; and *The Horsemen,* Columbia, 1971. Appeared in films, including (uncredited; as himself) *Grand Prix: Challenge of Champions,* Metro-Goldwyn-Mayer, 1966; (uncredited; as himself) *Lionpower from MGM,* Metro-Goldwyn-Mayer, 1967; (as the television controller) *Black Sunday,* Paramount, 1977; (as

General Sonnenberg) *The General's Daughter,* Paramount, 1999; and (as himself) *Jazz Seen: The Life and Times of William Claxton,* 2001. Appeared in videos, including (as himself) *The Manchurian Candidate Interviews,* 1988; and (as himself) *The Making of a Political Thriller,* 2001. Director of television series, including *Danger,* Columbia Broadcasting System (CBS), 1954-55; and *Playhouse 90,* CBS, 1956-61. Assistant director of television series, including *Person to Person,* CBS, 1953; *You Are There,* CBS, beginning 1953; and *The Garry Moore Show,* CBS, 1953-54. Director of television miniseries, including (and executive producer) *Andersonville,* Turner Network Television (TNT), 1996; (and producer) *George Wallace* (also known as *Wallace*), TNT, 1997; and (and executive producer) *Path to War,* 2002. Directed episodes of television series, including "The Plot against King Solomon," *You Are There,* CBS, 1954; "Portrait in Celluloid," *Climax!* (also known as *Climax Mystery Theatre*), CBS, 1955; (and producer) "The Turn of the Screw," *Ford Startime,* National Broadcasting Company (NBC), 1959; "Maniac at Large," *Tales from the Crypt* (also known as *HBO's Tales from the Crypt*), Home Box Office (HBO), 1992; also directed episodes of *DuPont Show of the Month, Mama,* and *Studio One,* all CBS; and *Sunday Showcase,* NBC. Director of television movies, including *The Browning Version,* 1959; *The Rainmaker,* HBO, 1982; (as Alan Smithee) *Riviera,* American Broadcasting Companies (ABC), 1987; *Against the Wall* (also known as *Attica! Attica!* and *Attica: Line of Fire*), HBO, 1994; (and producer) *The Burning Season* (also known as *The Life and Death of Chico Mendes*), HBO, 1994; (and executive producer) *Path to War,* HBO, 2002; also directed *The Days of Wine and Roses, For Whom the Bell Tolls,* and *Old Man.* Also directed *The Ninth Day,* 1956; and *The Blue Men* (pilot), CBS, 1959. Appeared in television specials, including *Frankenheimer,* 1971; *Reflections on Citizen Kane,* 1991; "Rod Serling: Submitted for Your Approval," *American Masters,* PBS, 1995; *Burt Lancaster,* American Movie Classics, 1997; *The Television Academy Hall of Fame,* UPN, 1999; *AFI's 100 Years, 100 Thrills: America's Most Heart-pounding Movies,* CBS, 2001; *The Inside Reel: Digital Filmmaking,* Public Broadcasting Service (PBS), 2001; *Jazz Seen: The Life and Times of William Claxton,* Bravo, 2001; and *Reel Radicals: The Sixties Revolution in Film,* 2002. Appeared in episodes of television series, including *American Cinema,* PBS, 1995; *Intimate Portrait: Janet Leigh,* Lifetime, 1996; "Angela Lansbury: A Balancing Act," *Biography,* Arts and Entertainment, 1998; "Brian Wilson: A Beach Boy's Tale," *Biography,*

Arts and Entertainment, 1999; "Rock Hudson: Acting the Part," *Biography,* Arts and Entertainment, 1999; *The Directors,* Encore, 1999; and "An Interview with John Frankenheimer," *WOAK Live,* 2000. Director of stage production *The Midnight Sun,* produced on Broadway, 1959. *Military service:* U.S. Air Force, 1951-53.

AWARDS, HONORS: Bodil Awards for best non-European film, Association of Danish Film Critics, 1965, for *Seven Days in May;* special jury award for lifetime achievement, Mystfest, 1994; Emmy awards for outstanding individual achievement in directing for a miniseries or a special, Academy of Television Arts and Sciences, 1994, for *Against the Wall,* 1995, for *The Burning Season,* and 1996, for *Andersonville;* Emmy award for outstanding directing for a miniseries or movie, 1998, for *George Wallace;* lifetime achievement award, Casting Society of America, USA, 1998; named Robert Wise Director of Distinction, Ft. Lauderdale International Film Festival, 1998; lifetime achievement award, San Diego World Film Festival, 1998; Billy Wilder Award, National Board of Review, 1999; Hollywood Discovery Award for outstanding achievement in directing, Hollywood Film Festival, 2001; inducted into Academy of Television Arts and Sciences Hall of Fame, 2002.

WRITINGS:

(With George Axelrod) *The Manchurian Candidate* (screenplay; based on the novel by Richard Condon), United Artists, 1962.
(With Gerald Pratley) *The Cinema of John Frankenheimer,* A. S. Barnes (San Diego, CA), 1969.
(With Gerald Pratley) *The Films of Frankenheimer: Forty Years in Film,* Lehigh University Press (Bethlehem, PA), 1998.

Contributor to periodicals, including *Action, Films and Filming,* and *Saturday Review.*

SIDELIGHTS: Film director John Frankenheimer only doubled as screenwriter on one of his productions, but it may well have been his best film. *The Manchurian Candidate,* a cold war-era thriller about a Korean War veteran who is brainwashed into attempting to kill the U.S. president, was adapted from a novel by Richard

Condon. It features a top-flight cast, including Frank Sinatra, Angela Lansbury, and Laurence Harvey, and was ranked number sixty-seven on the American Film Institute's list of the best one hundred American films of the twentieth century. Interest in *The Manchurian Candidate* increased when President John F. Kennedy was assassinated a year after its release and it was pulled from circulation. There are conflicting theories as to why this happened; some claimed that the film's producers did not feel it was appropriate to screen the film after Kennedy's assassination, while others cited economic considerations. When *The Manchurian Candidate* was re-released twenty-five years later, critics agreed that the passage of time had not harmed the film at all. "Not a moment of *The Manchurian Candidate* lacks edge and tension and cynical spin," Roger Ebert wrote in the *Chicago Sun-Times* upon the film's re-release. A reviewer for *TVGuide.com* even thought that this "nerve-beating masterpiece" is "more timely now than then."

In 1962, the year *The Manchurian Candidate* was first released, Frankenheimer also directed *The Birdman of Alcatraz* and *All Fall Down,* two other films which received high critical praise. "Those twelve months from Frankenheimer are better than half a century from most directors," Mark Steyn declared in his obituary of Frankenheimer for the *Spectator.* The director's career continued to soar throughout the mid-1960s, but things turned around after presidential candidate Robert Kennedy was assassinated in 1968. Frankenheimer had directed Kennedy's television commercials and was also a personal friend; on the day he was shot, Kennedy visited Frankenheimer's home and rode in his car to the hotel where he was later killed. In the wake of Kennedy's death, Frankenheimer moved to France, struggled with depression and alcoholism, and made few well-received films for many years.

Frankenheimer quit drinking in 1981, and in the 1990s he began an astonishing resurgence by directing several award-winning cable movies. He had started his career directing live televised theater for such programs as *Playhouse 90* and *Studio One;* as he reflected to *Daily Variety* interviewer Elizabeth Guider, he found a similar attitude toward high-quality television at Home Box Office (HBO) and other cable channels. Between 1994 and 1998 Frankenheimer won four Emmy awards for directing politically provocative made-for-television movies and miniseries that covered topics from the infamous Confederate prisoner of war camp at Andersonville to the life of segregationist former Alabama governor George Wallace. Frankenheimer died in 2002, bringing an abrupt end to what *Entertainment Weekly* writer Benjamin Svetkey called "one of Hollywood's greatest second acts."

BIOGRAPHICAL AND CRITICAL SOURCES:

BOOKS

Champlin, Charles, *John Frankenheimer: A Conversation with Charles Champlin,* Riverwood Press, 1995.
Encyclopedia of World Biography Supplement, Volume 22, Gale (Detroit, MI), 2002.
International Directory of Films and Filmmakers, Volume 2: *Directors,* St. James Press (Detroit, MI), 1993.

PERIODICALS

American Film, March, 1977; June, 1979.
Calgary Sun, September 24, 1998.
Chicago Sun-Times, March 11, 1988, Roger Ebert, review of *The Manchurian Candidate.*
Daily Variety, March 27, 2002, Susanne Ault, "TV Academy Picks Mix for Honors," p. 2; April 10, 2002, Army Archard, "*Seven Days in May* Was Simple," p. 6; May 17, 2002, "About an Iconoclast," p. A4, Marc Graser, "A Driving Force for a New Medium," p. A6; May 17, 2002, Elizabeth Guider, interview with Frankenheimer, pp. A1-A2, Andy Klein, "A Career Honoring Auds' Intelligence," p. A4; July 31, 2002, Army Archard, "A Special Memorial Tribute to an Extraordinary Director," p. 4; August 21, 2002, Lauren Horwitch, "ATAS Hall of Fame Taps Six," p. 3; February 4, 2003, Dave McNary, "DGA Gets an A in History," pp. 1-2.
Entertainment Weekly, February 4, 1994, Ty Burr, review of *The Manchurian Candidate,* pp. 57-58; March 7, 1997, Steve Simels, review of *The Manchurian Candidate,* p. 77; July 19, 2002, p. 19.
Newsweek, April 4, 1988, David Ansen, review of *The Manchurian Candidate,* p. 72.
People, March 7, 1988, Peter Travers, review of *The Manchurian Candidate,* p. 10; May 16, 1988, Fred Bernstein, review of *The Manchurian Candidate,* pp. 129-131.

Sight and Sound, spring, 1968.
Starlog, July, 1996.
TV Guide, August 10, 2002, pp. 36-37.
Variety, August 26, 2002, "John Frankenheimer: In His Own Words," p. S26.
Washington Post, February 13, 1988, Hal Hinson, review of *The Manchurian Candidate.*

ONLINE

Internet Movie Database, http://www.imdb.com/ (November 21, 2003), "John Frankenheimer."
Onion A.V. Club, http://www.theavclub.com/ (February 16, 2000), Scott Tobias, interview with Frankenheimer.
TVGuide.com, http://www.tvguide.com/ (December 18, 2003), review of *The Manchurian Candidate.*

OBITUARIES

BOOKS

Contemporary Theatre, Film, and Television, Volume 49, Gale (Detroit, MI), 2003.
Newsmakers, Issue 4, Gale (Detroit, MI), 2003.

PERIODICALS

Daily Variety, July 8, 2002, pp. 2-3.
Entertainment Weekly, July 19, 2002, p. 19.
Spectator, July 13, 2002, pp. 49-50.*

*   *   *

FREEMAN, David 1922-2005

OBITUARY NOTICE— See index for *CA* sketch: Born August 22, 1922, in London, England; died March 28, 2005, in London, England. Writer. A screenwriter for film and television, as well as a playwright, Freeman is best remembered as a comedic writer for British television programs, including *Benny Hill* and several popular sitcoms. He left school at the age of fourteen to become an electrician, and it was in this job that he became associated with the theater when he was hired to work for a West End production. After serving in

the Royal Navy during World War II and seeing action on the Pacific and Indian oceans, he worked as a policeman for a time before his earlier acquaintance with comedian Benny Hill led to an opportunity in television he could not pass up. Freeman helped write for Hill's landmark comedy in the 1950s and 1960s, and he also appeared in some of the show's skits; later, he worked with other comics such as Terry Scott, with whom he collaborated on the 1955 program *Great Scott—It's Maynard* and the 1980s show *Terry and June.* During the 1970s Freeman wrote for such sitcoms as *Robin's Nest* and *Bless This House,* as well as for the movie *Carry on Behind* and its television spin-off, *Carry on Laughing.* In addition to his television and film work, Freeman wrote for the stage, his most popular success being *A Bedful of Foreigners,* which debuted in 1974. Other plays by the author include *Deep and Crisp and Stolen* (1965), *Murder in a Bad Light* (1978), and *Hell's Angels: An Opera in Two Acts* (1986). He also published the books *A Hollywood Education: Tales of Movie Dreams and Easy Money* (1986) and *It's All True: A Novel of Hollywood* (2004).

OBITUARIES AND OTHER SOURCES:

PERIODICALS

Independent (London, England), April 5, 2005, p. 35.
Times (London, England), April 6, 2005, p. 54.

*   *   *

FREMES, Ruth 1930-

PERSONAL: Born January 19, 1930, in Toronto, Ontario, Canada; married Zak Sabry (a professor), May 10, 1984; children: Marji Rosenberg, Susan, Adam Shirriff, Jason Shirriff. *Education:* University of Toronto, B.A.; John F. Kennedy University, M.A. *Religion:* Jewish.

ADDRESSES: Home—Berkeley, CA. *Agent*—Andree Abecassis, Ann Elmo Agency, 756 Neilson, Berkeley, CA 94707. *E-mail*—rfremes@pacbell.net.

CAREER: Canadian Broadcasting Corp., Toronto, Ontario, radio and television host, 1960-72; Canadian Television Network, Toronto, reporter and program host, 1972-87; freelance writer. Consultant to H. J. Kaiser Foundation, U.S. Department of Agriculture, and American Dietetic Association.

AWARDS, HONORS: Award from Association of Canadian Television and Radio Artists (now Alliance of Canadian Cinema, Television, and Radio Artists), 1978, for television public-affairs programming.

WRITINGS:

NutriScore, Methuen (New York, NY), 1976.
What's Cooking: The Rate-Yourself Guide to Nutrition, five volumes, Methuen (New York, NY), 1982–87.
Down Home Healthy, U.S. Department of Agriculture (Washington, DC), 1990.
(With Nancy Carteron) *A Body out of Balance: Understanding and Treating Sjogren's Syndrome,* Putnam Publishing Group (New York, NY), 2003.

SIDELIGHTS: Ruth Fremes told *CA:* "Writing about matters of health and nutrition comes easily to me once I have knowledge that I believe others need. It is invariably helped by collaboration, usually with someone whose writing skills are inexpert but whose knowledge about a complicated subject is something the public needs.

"In the case of *A Body out of Balance: Understanding and Treading Sjogren's Syndrome,* the work sprang from the need of patients suffering with Sjogren's Syndrome to have current information and techniques for mastering their disorder. The coauthorship came about with rheumatologist Dr. Nancy Carteron, whose time was limited but whose knowledge and willingness were great.

"In the case of *NutriScore,* the work was designed to counteract the myths and claims for nutrition that were current in 1976. It was extremely successful. It became a best seller as well as a text for colleges in Canada.

"At present, I am resting, thinking, and deciding what will come next. As in the past, I feel certain that something will emerge from the process."

BIOGRAPHICAL AND CRITICAL SOURCES:

PERIODICALS

Library Journal, November 15, 2003, Lisa McCormick, review of *A Body out of Balance: Understanding and Treating Sjogren's Syndrome,* p. 90.

FUNK, David G. 1938-

PERSONAL: Born August 2, 1938, in Oak Park, IL. *Education:* Amherst College, B.A., 1960; Harvard University, Ph.D., 1965.

ADDRESSES: Agent—c/o Author Mail, Info Publications, Inc., P.O. Box 811414, Boca Raton, FL 33481-1414. *E-mail*—dgfunk@bellsouth.net.

CAREER: Wellesley College, Wellesley, MA, assistant professor of economics, 1963-66; John Hancock Life Insurance Co., Boston, MA, economist, 1966-68; Buttonwood Securities Corp. of Massachusetts, Boston, treasurer, 1968-86; Tennis Partners, Inc., Margate, FL, president, 1987—. John Magee, Inc., president, 1975-86.

WRITINGS:

Uncommon Stock Market Strategies, Info Publications (Boca Raton, FL), 2003.

SIDELIGHTS: David G. Funk told *CA:* "I wrote *Uncommon Stock Market Strategies* after witnessing the impact of the stock market meltdown on the financial hopes and dreams of many of my friends. People simply stopped reading the financial section of the newspapers and stopped opening their monthly account statements. Many swore never to buy common stocks again. Some sold their stocks, sold their houses, and quietly moved to more affordable accommodations.

"I was shocked to discover how unfamiliar these investors were with the many improved investment tools available to them, including the writing of put and call options, near simultaneous executions on the various option exchanges, and the availability of online order execution. I resolved to write a book on how to benefit from stock market volatility, based on over forty years of experience in the stock market and real estate investment industries.

"The process of writing *Uncommon Stock Market Strategies* sharpened but did not change the investment approach that I set out to write about and that had served me so well. The book utilizes the investment strategy of selling options short (writing option contracts), not buying options. The options contracts are sold (sell to open) prior to buying them (buy to close). The book targets stock market fluctuations, then stock market rates of return. Retail Wall Street does not do that, and when it does measure volatility, it uses that measure primarily as an investment indicator.

"*Uncommon Stock Market Strategies* explains an investment approach that uses common stocks, puts, and calls in an uncommon way and can benefit from price movements in either direction. It is time for stock market investors to recognize that Wall Street is a two-way street, and to structure their investment tools accordingly."

G

GAFFNEY, Elizabeth M(allory) 1966-

PERSONAL: Born December 22, 1966, in New York, NY; daughter of Richard (a painter) and Ann (a graphic designer) Gaffney; married Alexis David Boro, July 15, 1995. *Education:* Vassar College, B.A., 1988; Brooklyn College, M.F.A., 1997. *Politics:* Democrat.

ADDRESSES: Home—Brooklyn, NY. *Agent*—Darhansoff, Verrill, Feldman, 236 W. 26th St. New York, NY 10001.

CAREER: Editor and author. *Paris Review,* New York, NY, member of editorial staff, 1988-93, managing editor, 1993-95, editor-at-large, 1995-2004, advisory editor, 2004-05; writing instructor at New York University. Resident/fellow at MacDowell Colony, Peterborough, NH, 1996 and 1997; Blue Mountain Center, NY, 1999; and Yaddo, 2000, 2001, and 2004.

MEMBER: PEN, Phi Beta Kappa.

WRITINGS:

(Translator) Zoe Jenny, *The Pollen Room* (novel), Simon & Schuster (New York, NY), 1998.
(Translator) Ika Hugel-Marshall, *Invisible Woman: Growing up Black in Germany,* 2000.
(Translator) Thomas Hettche, *The Arbogast Case,* Farrar, Straus, and Giroux (New York, NY), 2003.
Metropolis (novel), Random House (New York, NY), 2005.

Contributor of short stories to literary journals, including *Mississippi Review, Brooklyn Review, North American Review, Colorado Review, Epiphany,* and *Reading Room.*

SIDELIGHTS: Elizabeth M. Gaffney has worked as a writer, editor, educator, and translator. After graduating from Vassar College in 1988, she began working on the editorial staff at the quarterly literary magazine *Paris Review.* She has held several positions there, including managing and advisory editor. Gaffney also teaches writing at New York University and has led writing seminars through professional organizations. In addition to her work on longer book projects, Gaffney is the author of many short fiction pieces, and in 2005 she published her first novel, *Metropolis.*

Gaffney first began working on novels as a translator, adapting Zoe Jenny's *The Pollen Room,* Ika Hugel-Marshall' *Invisible Woman: Growing up Black in Germany,* and Thomas Hettche's *The Arbogast Case* for English-speaking readers. In a number of reviews of this last work, critics praised Gaffney's translation skills. *New York Times Book Review* contributor Charles Wilson, for instance, called her work a "seamless translation."

Gaffney' first original work of fiction, *Metropolis,* is set in 1860s New York City. German immigrant Frank Harris fumbles through a series of jobs before getting involved with the Irish street gang the Whyos. He falls in love with pickpocket and moll Beatrice O'Gamhna, a member of the Whyos' female branch, the Why Nots. Harris finds jobs working on the construction of the

Brooklyn Bridge and the city sewer system. Together he and O'Gamhna navigate encounters with the murderer Luther Undertoe and mob bosses Johnny and Meg Dolan.

Many critics offered praise for *Metropolis,* some acknowledging Gaffney's ability to mix actual history with a compelling fictional storyline. "The novel's well-researched historical background, enlivened by descriptions of the criminal underworld and the offbeat love story, should ensure wide interest," wrote a *Publishers Weekly* contributor. Other reviewers highlighted the author's thoughtful character development. "Given its array of irresistibly colorful characters, gritty romance, and labyrinthine plot, Gaffney's tale of old New York is pure bliss," concluded Donna Seaman in *Booklist.*

Gaffney told *CA:* "My influences run from Charles Dickens, Victor Hugo, Henry James, George Sand, and Virginia Woolf to Fritz Lang and Alfred Hitchcock, to Thomas Pynchon, Philip K. Dick, Andrea Barrett, and Margaret Atwood. Almost all my ideas for writing come to me while I'm walking around New York City by myself."

BIOGRAPHICAL AND CRITICAL SOURCES:

PERIODICALS

Booklist, January 1, 2005, Donna Seaman, review of *Metropolis,* p. 814.
Denver Post, December 7, 2003, Roger K. Miller, review of *The Arbogast Case,* p. 13.
Entertainment Weekly, March 11, 2005, Gilbert Cruz, review of *Metropolis,* p. 108.
Kirkus Reviews, September 15, 2003, review of *The Arbogast Case,* p. 1145; January 15, 2005, review of *Metropolis,* p. 70.
Library Journal, January 1, 2005, Eleanor J. Bader, review of *Metropolis,* p. 95.
Newsweek, March 7, 2005, Andrew Romano, review of *Metropolis,* p. 55.
New York Times, February 28, 2005, Janet Maslin, review of *Metropolis,* p. 8.
New York Times Book Review, June 27, 1999, Jenny McPhee, review of *The Pollen Room,* p. 33; December 21, 2003, Charles Wilson, review of *The Arbogast Case,* p. 13.

Publishers Weekly, February 10, 2003, John F. Baker, "Epic New York Novel for Random," p. 56; September 29, 2003, review of *The Arbogast Case,* p. 42; December 20, 2004, review of *Metropolis,* p. 34.
Washington Post, December 16, 2003, Chris Lehmann, review of *The Arbogast Case,* p. 4.

ONLINE

Elizabeth Gaffney Home Page, http://www.elizabethgaffney.net (March 8, 2005).
New York University Web site, http://www.scps.nyu.edu/ (March 8, 2005), "Elizabeth Gaffney."

*   *   *

GARDNER, Ralph D(avid) 1923-2005

OBITUARY NOTICE— See index for *CA* sketch: Born April 16, 1923, in New York, NY; died of complications from diabetes March 30, 2005, in New York, NY. Journalist, advertising executive, and author. Gardner was best known as a biographer of Horatio Alger. He completed a journalism degree at New York University in 1942 and earned a certificate in military administration the next year from Colorado State College, just before enlisting in the U.S. Army for the duration of World War II. After the war Gardner was a foreign correspondent for the *New York Times* and was involved in founding the newspaper's international edition in Paris. He was also a bureau manager in Germany and Austria. In 1955, he left journalism to found his own advertising company, Ralph D. Gardner Advertising, in New York City. By this time, he had changed his birth surname from Goldburgh to Gardner in 1950. Gardner edited and contributed to several books in his lifetime, but he remained best known for his debut biography, *Horatio Alger; or, The American Hero Era* (1964; revised in 1971 as *Road to Success: The Bibliography of the Works of Horatio Alger*), which earned him the Prize for Literature from the Horatio Alger Society. He was also the author of *Writers Talk to Ralph D. Gardner* (1989).

OBITUARIES AND OTHER SOURCES:

PERIODICALS

New York Times, April 17, 2005, p. A31.

GELBERT, Doug 1956-

PERSONAL: Born June 26, 1956, in Wilmington, DE; son of Chester (a chemical engineer) and Lois (a homemaker) Gelbert. *Ethnicity:* "Caucasian." *Education:* University of Delaware, B.A., 1978; University of Oregon, M.B.A., 1980. *Politics:* Libertarian *Hobbies and other interests:* Golf, hiking, fishing, reading, travel.

ADDRESSES: Home—P.O. Box 467, Montchanin, DE 19710. *Office*—109 Main St., Stanton, DE 19804; fax: 302-326-0400. *E-mail*—crubay@earthlink.net.

CAREER: Cruden Bay Books, Montchanin, DE, publisher, 1993—. Dogomat, Stanton, DE, owner, 1998—. Claymont Stone School Restoration, board member.

MEMBER: Publishers Marketing Association, Chester County Canine Hiking Club (founder).

WRITINGS:

A Guide to Public Golf Courses in the Philadelphia Area, Pressbox Publications (Montchanin, DE), 1986.
Sports Hall of Fame: A Directory of over One Hundred Sports Museums in the United States, McFarland and Co. (Jefferson, NC), 1992.
Company Museums, Industry Museums, and Industrial Tours: A Guidebook of Sites in the United States that Are Open to the Public, McFarland and Co. (Jefferson, NC), 1994.
The Great Delaware Sports Book, Manatee Books (Montchanin, DE), 1995.
So Who the Heck Was Oscar Mayer, Barricade Books (New York, NY), 1996.
You Can Be a National Champion, Masters Press (Indianapolis, IN), 1997.
Civil War Sites, Memorials, and Collections, McFarland and Co. (Jefferson, NC), 1997.
The Stone School: A Vital Piece of Claymont History, Friends of the Stone School (Claymont, DE), 1997.
Revolutionary War Sites, Memorials, and Collections, McFarland and Co. (Jefferson, NC), 1998.
A Bark in the Park: New Castle County, Cruden Bay Books (Montchanin, DE), 1999.

A Bark in the Park: Delaware County, Cruden Bay Books (Montchanin, DE), 2000.
A Bark in the Park: Chester County, Cruden Bay Books (Montchanin, DE), 2000.
A Bark in the Park: Montgomery County, Cruden Bay Books (Montchanin, DE), 2000.
Teugega Country Club Centennial, Cruden Bay Books (Montchanin, DE), 2000.
Spring Lake Country Club: A Centennial Journal, Cruden Bay Books (Montchanin, DE), 2000.
The Fifty-five Best Places to Hike with Your Dog in the Philadelphia Region . . . and Fifty-five More, Cruden Bay Books (Montchanin, DE), 2001.
Starting and Running a Do-It-Yourself Dog Wash, Cruden Bay Books (Montchanin, DE), 2002.
Film and Television Locations: A State by State Guidebook to Moviemaking Sites, Excluding Los Angeles, McFarland and Co. (Jefferson, NC), 2002.
A Bark in the Park: The Fifty Best Places to Hike with Your Dog in the Baltimore Region, Cruden Bay Books (Montchanin, DE), 2002.
The Canine Hikers Bible: A Companion for the Active Dog Owner, Cruden Bay Books (Montchanin, DE), 2004.

SIDELIGHTS: Doug Gelbert told *CA:* "I have always written to discover things I want to know. Every now and then my quest for knowledge is not so esoteric, and a publisher sees it as a marketable project. My main influence has always been Lord James Balfour, one-time prime minister of England, who said, 'My ideal in life is to read a lot, write a little, play plenty of golf, and have nothing to worry about.'"

BIOGRAPHICAL AND CRITICAL SOURCES:

ONLINE

HikewithYourDog.com, http://www.hikewithyourdog.com/ (August 25, 2004), "Doug Gelbert."

*   *   *

GERSHGOREN NOVAK, Estelle 1940-
(Lydia Draper)

PERSONAL: Born January 12, 1940, in Detroit, MI; daughter of Milton (an artist) and Beatrice (a homemaker and office worker; maiden name, Rotman) Gershgoren; married Maximillian E. Novak (a professor), August 21, 1966; children: Ralph Aaron, Daniel Akiva, Rachel Aviva Novak Lederman. *Ethnicity:* "Jewish." *Education:* University of California, Los Angeles, B.A., 1961, M.A., 1962, Ph.D., 1968. *Politics:* Democrat. *Religion:* Jewish. *Hobbies and other interests:* "Tennis, on occasion."

ADDRESSES: Home—451 South El Camino Dr., Beverly Hills, CA 90212. *E-mail*—novak@humnet.ucla.edu.

CAREER: University of Southern California, Los Angeles, assistant professor, 1968-74, 1999; California State University, Northridge, lecturer, 1974-75, 1983-84, 1989-95; University of California, Los Angeles, lecturer, 1975-79, 1980-81, 1984-88, 1996-98; Loyola Marymount University, Westchester, CA, lecturer, 1999-2001.

WRITINGS:

The Shape of a Pear (poetry), Fithian Press (Santa Barbara, CA), 1996.
(Editor and contributor) *Poets of the Non-Existent City: Los Angeles in the McCarthy Era* (anthology), University of New Mexico Press (Albuquerque, NM), 2002.
The Flesh of Their Dreams (poetry), Fithian Press (Santa Barbara, CA), 2002.

Contributor to books, including *Poets of Today,* edited by Walter Lowenfels, Faber & Faber (London, England), 1964; *Reading Philip Roth,* Macmillan (New York, NY), 1988; *Literary Exile in the Twentieth Century,* Greenwood Press (Westport, CT), 1991; and *Yom HaShoah* (poetry anthology), Texas Tech University Press (Lubbock, TX), 1991. Contributor of articles and poetry in English and Yiddish to periodicals, including *Judaism, Blue Collar Review, Pemmican, Treasure House, Mosaic, Response, Poetry L.A., Colorado-North Review, Israel Today,* and *Contemporary Literature.* Some writings appear under pseudonym Lydia Draper.

WORK IN PROGRESS: The Writer as Exile: Israel Joshua Singer, a critical study of the works of Israel Joshua Singer, Yiddish novelist, 1893-1944; another collection of poetry.

SIDELIGHTS: Estelle Gershgoren Novak told *CA:* "I have been writing poetry since the age of seventeen, inspired by the very fine poet and teacher, the late Thomas McGrath. Having spent a good deal of time in the university world, I have tried to absorb as much good as I could while trying to avoid the stultifying influences that often come from institutions.

"My first love has always been poetry. My father was a fine artist and showed me how the visual world influenced all aspects of his life. Though I learned much from him about color and light, I was more attracted to the music of the word and the power that was created by the compression of great poets like William Blake or Emily Dickinson."

*   *   *

GERSHTEIN, E.
    See GERSTEIN, Emma

*   *   *

GERSHTEIN, E. G.
    See GERSTEIN, Emma

*   *   *

GERSTEIN, Emma 1903-2002
    (E. Gershtein, E. G. Gershtein)

PERSONAL: Born October 25, 1903, in Dinaburg (now Daugavpils), Russia (now Latvia); died 2002. *Education:* Graduated from Moscow University, 1925.

CAREER: Writer and literary biographer. Formerly worked in various office jobs.

WRITINGS:

(Under name E. Gershtein) *M. IU. Lermontov na Kavkaze,* [Moscow, USSR], 1942.
(Under name E. Gershtein) *Sub'ba Lermontova,* Sovetskii Pisatel (Moscow, USSR), 1964, 2nd edition, Khudozh (Moscow, USSR), 1986.

(Under name E. Gershtein) *"Geroi nashego vremeni" M. IU. Lermontova,* 1976, reprinted, CheRo (Moscow, Russia), 1997.

Anna Akhmatova o Pushkine, 1977.

(Under name E. G. Gershtein) *Novoe o Mandel'shtame: glavy iz vospominanii,* Atheneum (Paris, France), 1986.

Memuary, Inapress (St. Petersburg, Russia), 1998, translated and edited by John Crowfoot as *Moscow Memoirs: Memories of Anna Akhmatova, Osip Mandelstam, and Literary Russia under Stalin,* Overlook Press (Woodstock, NY), 2004.

(Under name E. G. Gershtein) *Pamiat' pisatelia: Stat'i i issledovaniia 30-90-kh godov,* Inapress (St. Petersburg, Russia), 2001.

SIDELIGHTS: Emma Gerstein's life spanned the twentieth century, and her friendship with several of Russia's most noted authors and her work as a literary critic make her memoirs, published four years before her death in 2002, a valuable resource for students of twentieth-century communist literature.

Gerstein—her name is sometimes transliterated as Gershtein—was born in 1903, and moved to Moscow as a child due to the demands of her father's work as a surgeon. Because surgeons were esteemed by the Bolshevik regime, the Gerstein children obtained a superior education, and Gerstein herself studied natural sciences at Moscow University. Although she originally intended to follow her father into the medical field, she eventually switched to languages and literature, graduating in 1925. After graduation, unable to establish a career in her field, she worked in a number of low-paying clerical jobs and grew increasingly depressed. This depression ultimately led to a failed suicide attempt and Gerstein was sent to a sanatorium to recover. It was there that she first met Osip and Nadezhda Mandelstam, and made her initial foray into the couple's literary circle.

Through her friendships with a number of Moscow's literary figures, Gerstein established herself as a writer, and she became a scholar of the life and work of writer Mikhail Lermontov. Her autobiographical *Moscow Memoirs: Memories of Anna Akhmatova, Osip Mandelstam, and Literary Russia under Stalin* examines mid-twentieth-century Soviet literature from the viewpoint of an insider, addressing the hardships many writers suffered under Josef Stalin's dictatorial rule.

Interestingly, Nadezhda Mandelstam, Osip Mandelstam's wife, has claimed in her memoirs that, as early as 1936, both Akhmatova and Mandelstam feared Gerstein would write about them. Nearly seventy years later, what they feared came to pass.

A *Kirkus Reviews* contributor called *Moscow Memoirs* a "searing, unsentimental portrait of Soviet intellectuals' suffering under Stalin," and added of Gerstein that "no one will come away from her detailed, pitiless record of the horrors inflicted on . . . citizens without concluding that the Soviet system was politically, economically, and morally indefensible." Anne Applebaum, writing for the *Spectator,* remarked that *Moscow Memoirs* "succeeds not because it is negative but because it humanizes its main characters, and in doing so brings to life the strange atmosphere of 1930s Moscow."

BIOGRAPHICAL AND CRITICAL SOURCES:

BOOKS

Gerstein, Emma, *Moscow Memoirs: Memories of Anna Akhmatova, Osip Mandelstam, and Literary Russia under Stalin,* translated and edited by John Crowfoot, Overlook Press (Woodstock, NY), 2004.

PERIODICALS

Choice, January, 2005, T. M. Schlak, review of *Moscow Memoirs,* p. 858.

Guardian (Manchester, England), April 17, 2004, John Crowfoot, "Witness to the Persecution"; May 15, 2004, Virginia Rounding, review of *Moscow Memoirs,* p. 14.

Kirkus Reviews, August 1, 2004, review of *Moscow Memoirs,* p. 724.

Library Journal, September 15, 2004, Maria Kochis, review of *Moscow Memoirs,* p. 57.

Russian Life, July-August, 2004, Paul E. Richardson, "Pulp Fiction," review of *Moscow Memoirs,* p. 61.

Spectator, April 24, 2004, Anne Applebaum, "Poets under Surveillance," p. 39.

Times Literary Supplement, May 14, 2004, Rachel Polonsky, "Beneath the Kremlin Crag," review of *Moscow Memoirs.*

ONLINE

Context Online, http://www.context.themoscowtimes. com/ (March 31, 2005), "Emma Gerstein."

Guardian Online, http://books.guardian.co.uk/ (Marcy 31, 2005), "Emma Gerstein."

Moscow Times Online, http://www.themoscowtimes. com/ (April 30, 2004), Oliver Ready, "Poetic License"; (March 31, 2005) "Emma Gerstein."

Overlook Press Web site, http://www.overlookpress. com/ (March 31, 2005), "Emma Gerstein."*

*   *   *

GILBERT, Lewis 1920-

PERSONAL: Born March 6, 1920, in London, England; married Hylda Henrietta Tafler; children: two sons.

ADDRESSES: Agent—c/o October Films, Spring House, 10 Spring Pl., London NW5 3BH, England.

CAREER: Director of films, including *Sailors Do Care* (documentary), G. B. Instructional, 1944; *The Ten-Year Plan* (documentary), G. B. Instructional, 1945; *Arctic Harvest* (documentary), G. B. Instructional, 1946; *Under One Roof,* 1946; *The Little Ballerina,* Universal, 1951; *The Scarlet Thread,* Butchers, 1951; *There Is Another Sun* (also known as *The Wall of Death*), 1951; *Once a Sinner,* Hoffberg, 1952; *Albert, R.N.* (also known as *Break to Freedom, Marlag "O" Prison Camp,* and *Spare Man),* Eros, 1953; *The Hundred-Hour Hunt* (also known as *Emergency!* and *Emergency Call*), Butchers, 1953; (and producer) *Johnny on the Run,* Associated British Films, 1953; *The Slasher* (also known as *Cosh Boy* and *The Tough Guy*), Lippert, 1953; *Time Gentlemen Please!* (also known as *Nothing to Lose*), Mayer-Kingsley, 1953; *The Good Die Young,* Independent Film Distributors, 1954; *The Sea Shall Not Have Them,* United Artists, 1955; *The Admirable Crichton* (also known as *Paradise Lagoon*), Columbia, 1957; *Reach for the Sky,* J. Arthur Rank, 1957; *Carve Her Name with Pride,* J. Arthur Rank, 1958; *Cast a Dark Shadow* (also known as *Angel*), Eros, 1958; *A Cry from the Street,* Eros, 1959; *Ferry to Hong Kong,* J. Arthur Rank, 1959; (and producer) *Light up the Sky!* (also known as *Skywatch!*),

British Lion, 1960; *Sink the Bismarck!,* Twentieth Century-Fox, 1960; *Loss of Innocence* (also known as *The Greengage Summer*), Columbia, 1961; *Damn the Defiant!* (also known as *H.M.S. Defiant*), Columbia, 1962; *The Seventh Dawn,* United Artists, 1964; (and producer) *Alfie,* Paramount, 1966; *You Only Live Twice,* United Artists, 1967; (and producer) *The Adventurers,* Paramount, 1970; (and producer) *Friends,* Paramount, 1971; (and producer) *Paul and Michelle,* Paramount, 1974; *Operation Daybreak* (also known as *The Price of Freedom* and *Seven Met at Daybreak*), Warner Brothers, 1976; (and producer) *Seven Nights in Japan,* Paramount, 1976; *The Spy Who Loved Me,* United Artists, 1977; *Moonraker,* United Artists, 1979; (and producer) *Educating Rita,* Columbia, 1983; (and producer, with William P. Cartlidge) *Not Quite Jerusalem* (also known as *Not Quite Paradise*), J. Arthur Rank, 1985; (and producer) *Shirley Valentine,* Paramount, 1990; (and producer) *Stepping Out,* Paramount, 1991; (and producer) *Haunted,* October Films, 1995; *Before You Go,* 2002; and (and producer) *Andre Schneider: Geben bis es Schmerzt,* Zamora Films, 2002. Also director of *The World of Gilbert* and *George;* assistant director of *Target for Today;* producer of *Spare the Rod* (television), 1959-60.

Actor in films, including (as Jem) *Dick Turpin,* Gaumont, 1933; *Divorce of Lady X,* 1937; (uncredited) *Over the Moon,* United Artists, 1940; *Alfie,* Paramount, 1966; (uncredited) *Man at St. Mark's Square, Moonraker,* United Artists, 1979; *Goodbye, Mr. Chips; The Mystery Road;* and *Room for Two.* Appeared as himself in television documentaries, including *Michael Caine: Breaking the Mold,* 1991; *Roger Moore: A Matter of Class,* Arts and Entertainment, 1995; *007: The James Bond Story,* 1999; *Best Ever Bond,* 2002; *James Bond: A BAFTA Tribute,* 2002; and *The Ultimate Film,* 2004. Appeared as himself in video documentary shorts, including *Legends,* 2000; *Ken Adam: Designing Bond,* 2000; *Inside "You Only Live Twice,"* 2000; *Inside "The Spy Who Loved Me,"* 2000; and *Inside "Moonraker,"* 2000. *Military service:* Served with Royal Air Force and U.S. Air Corps Film Unit during World War II.

AWARDS, HONORS: Named commander, Order of the British Empire; British Film Institute fellowship, 2001; Dilys Powell Award for outstanding contribution to cinema, London Film Critics' Circle, 2003.

WRITINGS:

SCREENPLAYS

Sailors Do Care (documentary), G. B. Instructional, 1944.

The Ten-Year Plan (documentary), G. B. Instructional, 1945.

Arctic Harvest (documentary), G. B. Instructional, 1946.

(With Dennis Waldock) *Marry Me!*, General Film Distributors, 1949.

The Little Ballerina, Universal, 1951.

The Hundred-Hour Hunt (also known as *Emergency!* and *Emergency Call*), Butchers, 1953.

The Slasher (also known as *Cosh Boy* and *The Tough Guy*), Lippert, 1953.

The Good Die Young, Independent Film Distributors, 1954.

The Sea Shall Not Have Them, United Artists, 1955.

The Admirable Crichton (also known as *Paradise Lagoon*, Columbia, 1957.

Reach for the Sky, J. Arthur Rank, 1957.

Carve Her Name with Pride, J. Arthur Rank, 1958.

Ferry to Hong Kong, J. Arthur Rank, 1959.

The Adventurers, Paramount, 1970.

Haunted (based on a novel by James Herbert), October Films, 1995.

ADAPTATIONS: Films based on stories by Gilbert include *Friends*, Paramount, 1971, and *Paul and Michelle*, Paramount, 1974.

SIDELIGHTS: The career of English director, producer, screenwriter, and actor Lewis Gilbert has spanned more than seven decades. As a director, his notable films include *Alfie, Shirley Valentine*, and three films featuring popular cold-war secret agent James Bond.

Gilbert was born into a show-business family: His parents performed in vaudeville and he became a child actor in silent films at the age of five. He recalled to *Variety* contributor Adam Dawtrey that, "at four years old I was looking through a curtain at people laughing. My films have never been intellectual, although I am, because they reflect my childhood touring around and watching audiences enjoy themselves." His last significant acting role, at age seventeen, was in *The*

Divorce of Lady X, where he played opposite Laurence Olivier. Gilbert's decision to leave acting was motivated by his desire to direct, and he was hired by producer Alexander Korda to fill the job of third assistant at Denham Studios. Gilbert joined the Royal Air Force after the outbreak of World War II and was transferred to the U.S. Air Corps Film Unit, where he learned alongside William Wyler as they shot training and combat films.

Gilbert's 1966 film, *Alfie*, which was produced for just one-half million dollars, is credited with propelling the career of actor Michael Caine. Gilbert saw the original play after his wife gave it rave reviews. On the recommendation of his son, Gilbert also saw *The Ipcress File*, which featured Caine, and he sensed the actor would be perfect as Alfie, the cockney chauffeur who empowers the working class as he seduces a number of beautiful women across London. Already in his thirties, Caine began his rise to stardom with this film, playing opposite Shelley Winters, Julia Foster, Shirley Anne Field, Eleanor Bron, Vivien Merchant, and Jane Asher. It was suggested to Gilbert that the film be dubbed with the voice of an American actor because the concern was that Americans would not understand Caine's accent. Gilbert resisted, the film was shown as it was originally shot, and it was a hit. The story, which includes a back-alley abortion, also helped reform the censorship code in the United States. As Gilbert noted in the Manchester *Guardian*, "the film had a big effect on my career. I was offered everything. I was flavour of the month in Hollywood."

Gilbert's first James Bond film, starring Sean Connery, was *You Only Live Twice*, and he directed Roger Moore in *The Spy Who Loved Me* and *Moonraker*. They were the only films he made for which he did not exercise artistic control, but they were attractive projects because they came with big budgets.

In *Educating Rita*, Caine plays an alcoholic English professor whose life is energized by Rita (Julie Walters), a working-class girl who joins his class as part of a remedial program. *Shirley Valentine* is an adaptation of a play by Willy Russell. Pauline Collins, in the title role, plays an Englishwoman who finds refuge in Greece after leaving her husband and children.

Shelagh Stephenson wrote the script for *Before You Go*, based on her play *The Memory of Water*. At the age of eighty-one, Gilbert directed this comedy-drama, which focuses on three sisters who have come together to attend to their dying mother. The cast includes Walters, who plays one of the daughters.

Haunted is a British ghost story adapted from a novel by James Herbert. The film stars Aidan Quinn, Kate Beckinsale, Anthony Andrews, John Gielgud, and Anna Massey. Quinn is David Ash, an American "ghost buster" who travels to London to debunk the idea of spirits that are said to be haunting a country estate. The story is typical of the traditional horror story, with a series of supernatural events culminating in a surprise ending and includes elements of romance between Quinn and the female lead, played by Beckinsale.

Gilbert has also appeared in a number of films, including documentary films that profile the James Bond films and leads. In 2003 he received the Dilys Powell Award for his lifetime contributions to the film industry.

BIOGRAPHICAL AND CRITICAL SOURCES:

PERIODICALS

Guardian (Manchester, England), May 4, 2001, Lewis Gilbert, "Friday Review: All about *Alfie*," p. 11.
Independent on Sunday (London, England), May 6, 2001, Robin Buss, "Film: Still Fancy a Bit of Rough Do You? *Alfie* Epitomised the Swinging Sixties—but How Do Its Sexual Politics Look Thirty-five Years Later?," p. 3.
Variety, February 18, 2002, Adam Dawtrey, "Lifetime Achievement: Filmmaker Gilbert Flaunts Long Legs in a Fickle Biz" (interview), p. 23.

ONLINE

Internet Movie Database, http://www.imdb.com/ (May 10, 2005), "Lewis Gilbert."*

*   *   *

GILLIATT, Mary

PERSONAL: Female.

ADDRESSES: Home—Wiltshire, England, and France. *Agent*—c/o Author Mail, Watson-Guptill Publications, 770 Broadway, New York, NY 10003.

CAREER: Interior designer and writer. Host of British television series on decorating.

WRITINGS:

English Style in Interior Decoration, photography by Michael Boys, Viking (New York, NY), 1967.
Kitchens and Dining Rooms, photography by Brian Morris and others, Viking (New York, NY), 1970.
Bathrooms, photography by Brian Morris and others, Viking (New York, NY), 1971.
A House in the Country; The Second Home, from Cottages to Castles, photography by Brian Morris, Hutchinson (London, England), 1973.
Decorating: A Realistic Guide, photography by Michael Dunne with Michael Nicholson and others, Pantheon Books (New York, NY), 1977.
(With Douglas Baker) *Lighting Your Home: A Practical Guide,* photography by Michael Dunne and others, Pantheon Books (New York, NY), 1979.
The Decorating Book, photography by Michael Dunne, Pantheon Books (New York, NY), 1981.
Making the Most of Living Rooms and Halls: A Creative Guide to Home Design, Orbis (London, England), 1983.
Making the Most of Kitchens and Dining Rooms: A Creative Guide to Home Design, Orbis (London, England), 1983.
Making the Most of Bedrooms & Bathrooms: A Creative Guide to Home Design, Orbis (London, England), 1983.
Mary Gilliatt's Mix and Match Decorating Book: An Ingenious Idea-Book with over 250,000 Combinations of Wallcoverings, Fabrics, and Floorings, Many of Which Are Available by Mail, Pantheon Books (New York, NY), 1984.
Making the Most of Children's Rooms: A Creative Guide to Home Design, Orbis (London, England), 1984.
(With Susan Zevon and Michael W. Robbins) *Decorating on the Cheap,* photography by Tom Yee, illustrations by William Ruggieri, Workman Publishing (New York, NY), 1984.
The Complete Book of Home Design, Little, Brown (Boston, MA), 1984, revised edition, 1989.
Designing Rooms for Children, Little, Brown (Boston, MA), 1985.
Setting up Home, Little, Brown (Boston, MA), 1985.
The Mary Gilliatt Book of Color, Little, Brown (Boston, MA), 1985.

English Country Style, photography by Christine Hanscomb, Little, Brown (Boston, MA), 1986.

Dream Houses, Little, Brown (Boston, MA), 1987.

The Complete Book of Home Design, Little, Brown (Boston, MA), 1989.

(With Elizabeth Wilhide) *Period Style,* Conran Octopus (London, England), 1990, Little, Brown (Boston, MA), 1991.

Mary Gilliatt's New Guide to Decorating, Little, Brown (Boston, MA), 1991.

Mary Gilliatt's Short Cuts to Great Decorating: Simple Solutions to Classic Problems, Little, Brown (Boston, MA), 1991.

The Blue and White Room, foreword by Pierre Moulin and Pierre LeVec, design by Timothy Shaner, Bantam Books (New York, NY), 1992.

Decorating with Mary Gilliatt, Little, Brown (Boston, MA), 1992.

Introduction to Decorating, Conran Octopus (London, England), 1992.

Mary Gilliatt's Interior Design Course, Watson-Guptill Publications (New York, NY), 2001.

Mary Gilliatt's Complete Room-by-Room Decorating Guide, photography by Andreas von Einsiedel, Watson-Guptill Publications (New York, NY), 2003.

Mary Gilliatt's Great Renovations and Restorations: A New Life for Older Homes, Watson-Guptill Publications (New York, NY), 2003.

Mary Gilliatt's Home Comforts with Style: A Decorating Guide for Today's Living, photography by Andreas von Einsiedel, Watson-Guptill Publications (New York, NY), 2004.

Mary Gilliatt's Dictionary of Architecture and Interior Design: Plus Essential Terms for the Home, Watson-Guptill Publications (New York, NY), 2004.

Author's articles have been published in numerous magazines.

SIDELIGHTS: Interior designer Mary Gilliatt is also a prolific writer of books on decorating and design dating back to her first publication in the late 1960s. In *Business Wire,* Beth Irons noted that Gilliatt "has incredible insight and talent, along with the ability to easily communicate a wealth of ideas about all aspects of decorating to amateurs and professional decorators alike." In her 1991 book, *Mary Gilliatt's New Guide to Decorating,* the author focuses on amateur designers and outlines a do-it-yourself approach for interior designing. She discusses stylistic approaches, decorating trends, and the basic elements of design. Much of the book focuses on specific projects, such as outlining how to install lighting and lay tile. Writing in *Interior Design,* Charles D. Gandy found that the book's "main pitfall . . . is that many topics are introduced and a smattering of information is provided . . . just enough information to be potentially dangerous." Nevertheless, Gandy went on to note that "it is an ambitious book with an incredible amount of information. If it does nothing else, it emphasizes the overwhelming complexity of our profession and the thousands of details that are essential in producing an interior of quality."

Mary Gilliatt's Interior Design Course provides a lesson in practical but creative ideas for interior design. In the first half of the book, the author discusses the basic elements of design and provides a catalog for referencing various design influences. She describes specific approaches for designing walls, windows, floors, and furnishings, as well as tips on solving specific problems—such as discolored tile grout. She also broaches choosing particular accessories and other design details. Writing in *Booklist,* Barbara Jacobs noted that the author "has mastered the art of showcasing decorating tips in an easily accessible manner." In *Mary Gilliatt's Complete Room-by-Room Decorating Guide,* the author discusses various approaches to design for each room of a house and emphasizes the options of choosing specific styles, following contemporary style elements, or taking an eclectic approach. The book also includes a history of interior design style. *Booklist* contributor Jacobs noted that the author can "turn many elegant phrases in interior home design" and wrote: "One book truly fits all."

Gilliatt focuses on updating old homes in her book *Mary Gilliatt's Great Renovations and Restorations: A New Life for Older Homes.* The book is not a how-to-guide per se, but rather a discussion of whether or not people should renovate or restore their older homes; examples include homes from the 1950s and as early as the sixteenth century. The book includes 350 photographs and a comprehensive discussion of various decorating styles common throughout Europe and the United States. Writing in *Library Journal,* Gayle A. Williamson noted the book would interest readers who "have a great interest in period decorating styles." *Booklist* contributor Jacobs called the book "Another impressive accomplishment from this doyenne of design."

In *Mary Gilliatt's Home Comforts with Style: A Decorating Guide for Today's Living* the author places an emphasis on personal comfort in decorating a home, touching on topics such as darkness in bedrooms and the need for quiet spaces. The book uses a step-by-step approach as she leads the reader through the home and includes discussions of home office space and home libraries. In addition to typical design issues such as colors and window treatments, the author discusses topics sometimes overlooked in design books, including storage, scent, and sound. Her suggestions are made in the context of the specific type of home being decorated, from apartments to detached homes. Writing in *Booklist,* Vernon Ford wrote that the book "is filled with beautiful photographs that reflect the integration of style and comfort that makes even a casual perusal delightful." In a review for *Library Journal,* Gayle Williamson commented that *Mary Gilliatt's Home Comforts with Style* contains "practical advice for every room of the home."

BIOGRAPHICAL AND CRITICAL SOURCES:

PERIODICALS

Booklist, October 15, 2001, Barbara Jacobs, review of *Mary Gilliatt's Interior Design Course,* p. 372; August, 2003, Barbara Jacobs, review of *Mary Gilliatt's Complete Room-by-Room Decorating Guide,* p. 1942; December 15, 2003, Keir Graff, brief review of *Mary Gilliatt's Complete Room-by-Room Decorating Guide,* p. 717; January 1, 2004, Barbara Jacobs, review of *Mary Gilliatt's Great Renovations and Restorations: A New Life for Older Homes,* p. 806; December 15, 2004, Vernon Ford, review of *Mary Gilliatt's Home Comforts with Style: A Decorating Guide for Today's Living,* p. 705.

Business Wire, October 7, 2004, Beth Irons, "World-Renowned Interior Designer Author Comes to Washington Metro Area for Book Signing."

HFN: The Weekly Newspaper for the Home Furnishing Network, April 1, 1996, Sarah Johnson, "Someone's in the Kitchen—And It's Mary Gilliatt," p. 30.

Interior Design, June, 1991, Charles D. Gandy, review of *Mary Gilliatt's New Guide to Decorating,* p. 122.

Library Journal, September 15, 2003, Gayle A. Williamson, review of *Mary Gilliatt's Complete Room-by-Room Decorating Guide,* p. 56; January, 2004, Gayle A. Williamson, review of *Mary Gilliatt's Great Renovations and Restorations,* p. 108; January 1, 2005, Gayle Williamson, review of *Mary Gilliatt's Home Comforts with Style,* p. 106.*

*   *   *

GLAIN, Stephen

PERSONAL: Male.

ADDRESSES: Home—Washington, DC. *Office*—Boston Globe, 135 William T. Morrissey Blvd., Boston, MA 02107. *E-mail*—glain@globe.com.

CAREER: Journalist. *Wall Street Journal,* New York, NY, journalist, 1998-2001; *Boston Globe,* Boston, MA, journalist, 2001—.

WRITINGS:

Mullahs, Merchants, and Militants: The Economic Collapse of the Arab World, St. Martin's Press (New York, NY), 2004.

Contributor to several newspapers, including *Wall Street Journal* and *Boston Globe.*

SIDELIGHTS: Journalist Stephen Glain has spent much of his career covering the economic challenges that face the Middle East for such publications as the *Wall Street Journal* and the *Boston Globe. Mullahs, Merchants, and Militants: The Economic Collapse of the Arab World,* Glain's first book, traces the history of that region's troubled economy, as well as spotlighting many Arab entrepreneurs as they struggle to make ends meet in the face of war and economic decay.

Virginia Q. Tilley, writing in the *Boston Globe,* described Glain's book as "a mosaic portrait of a region sliding toward economic crisis, through vignettes and interviews in Lebanon, Syria, Jordan, 'Palestine' (the West Bank), Iraq, and Egypt." Tilley further commented that Glain "brings a sophisticated analytical framework, as well as a discerning eye and a sense of humor" to his work. A reviewer for *Library*

Bookwatch found that Glain's analysis "surpasses the usual history and contemporary political analysis to focus on . . . the region's economic structure," while *Library Journal* contributor Nader Entessar wrote that "His approach in bringing to life the everyday struggle of ordinary people is one of the book's most distinctive aspects." A *Publishers Weekly* reviewer remarked that, "As an impressive corpus of anecdotes and a testament to Glain's exciting and wide-ranging career as a journalist, this book is a success."

BIOGRAPHICAL AND CRITICAL SOURCES:

PERIODICALS

Boston Globe, July 7, 2004, Virginia Q. Tilley, "Training a Discerning Eye on Arab Economic Collapse," p. F7.
Library Bookwatch, November, 2004, review of *Mullahs, Merchants, and Militants: The Economic Collapse of the Arab World.*
Library Journal, June 15, 2004, Nader Entessar, review of *Mullahs, Merchants, and Militants,* p. 86.
Publishers Weekly, June 14, 2004, review of *Mullahs, Merchants, and Militants,* p. 56.

ONLINE

TheGlobalist.com, http://www.theglobalist.com/ (February 23, 2005), "Stephen Glain."*

*   *   *

GLOVER, Ruth

PERSONAL: Born in Saskatchewan, Canada; married; husband's name Hal (a retired minister); children: three.

ADDRESSES: Home—The Dalles, OR. *Agent*—c/o Author Mail, Five Star, 295 Kennedy Memorial Dr., Waterville, ME 04901.

CAREER: Writer.

WRITINGS:

"WILDROSE" SERIES; ROMANCE NOVELS

The Shining Light, Beacon Hill Press (Kansas City, MO), 1994.
Bitter Thistle, Sweet Rose, Beacon Hill Press (Kansas City, MO), 1994.
A Time to Dream, Beacon Hill Press (Kansas City, MO), 1995.
Turn Northward, Love, Beacon Hill Press (Kansas City, MO), 1996.
Second-Best Bride, Beacon Hill Press (Kansas City, MO), 1997.
A Place to Call Home, Beacon Hill Press (Kansas City, MO), 1999.

"SASKATCHEWAN SAGA"; ROMANCE NOVELS

A Place Called Bliss, Fleming H. Revell (Grand Rapids, MI), 2001.
With Love from Bliss, Fleming H. Revell (Grand Rapids, MI), 2001.
Journey to Bliss, Fleming H. Revell (Grand Rapids, MI), 2001.
Seasons of Bliss, Fleming H. Revell (Grand Rapids, MI), 2002.
Bittersweet Bliss, Fleming H. Revell (Grand Rapids, MI), 2003.
Back Roads to Bliss, Fleming H. Revell (Grand Rapids, MI), 2003.

OTHER

The Letter: Based on the Novel With Love from Bliss (play), Christian Drama Publishing, 2002.

Also contributor to Christian periodicals.

SIDELIGHTS: Ruth Glover spent her childhood in the countryside of Saskatchewan, Canada. As an adult, she draws upon her intimate knowledge of the landscape to write historical romances for the "Saskatchewan Saga" and "Wildrose" series. These books have been praised by critics for their historical accuracy. In a review of Glover's debut novel, *The Shining Light,* for example, *Booklist* critic John Mort asserted that the story "has an authenticity lacking in most such efforts; Glover, who grew up on a Canadian farm, knows firsthand about gopher holes in wheat fields, clouds of mosquitoes that descend upon horses and farmers, and prairie lakes full of leeches."

The hardships experienced by immigrants and farmers in Canada play a significant role in Glover's "Wildrose" books, which begin with the story of Saskatchewan settlers in *The Shining Light.* The next book in the series, *Bitter Thistle, Sweet Rose,* features an increased dose of romance. Here, a young woman's chance meeting with a young Saskatchewan farmer blossoms into a classic love story that is "masterfully rendered," according to Mort in another *Booklist* review. In yet another installment in the series, *Second-Best Bride,* a rivalry between two sisters leads Meg to move from Toronto to the Canadian wilderness to marry the farmer that her prettier, selfish sister rejected. "Historical romances may be a dime a dozen in this genre," Melissa Hudak commented in *Library Journal,* but Gover's novel "stands out."

Glover's "Saskatchewan Saga" series is set in the town of Bliss, on the Canadian frontier. The first book, *A Place Called Bliss,* involves two women: one from a wealthy Scottish family, the other a humble servant. Both women immigrate to Canada with their husbands and both give birth during the journey, and a mistake following the births tragically links the women for decades to come.

With Love from Bliss is a story of revenge in which Kerry Ferne devises an elaborate plan to humiliate Connor Dougal, whom she blames for the death of a friend. Another romance in the series, *Seasons of Bliss,* features Tieney Caulder, who travels to the town of Bliss to be with her sweetheart, only to be devastated to learn he is already engaged to be married. Melanie C. Duncan described the latter romance in *Library Journal* as a "light historical romance for series fans."

BIOGRAPHICAL AND CRITICAL SOURCES:

PERIODICALS

Booklist, September 15, 1994, John Mort, review of *The Shining Light,* p. 112; January 15, 1995, John Mort, review of *Bitter Thistle, Sweet Rose,* p. 897.

Library Journal, February 1, 1998, Melissa Hudak, review of *Second-Best Bride,* p. 70; February 1, 2001, Melanie C. Duncan, reviews of *With Love from Bliss* and *A Place Called Bliss,* p. 77; April 1, 2002, Melanie C. Duncan, review of *Seasons of Bliss,* p. 86.

ONLINE

Romance Readers Connection Online, http://www.the romancereadersconnection.com/ (May, 2001), Wanda Augustine, review of *A Place Called Bliss.*
RomanticTimes.com, http://www.romantictimes.com/ (June 3, 2002), Bev Huston, review of *Seasons of Bliss.**

*   *   *

GOLDMAN, Joel

PERSONAL: Married; children: three. *Education:* Graduated from Kansas University.

ADDRESSES: Home—Montana. *Office*—Husch & Eppenberger LLC, 1200 Main St., Ste. 1700, Kansas City, MO 64105.

CAREER: Attorney and novelist. Trial lawyer, beginning 1977; Husch & Eppenberger (law firm), Kansas City, MO, attorney.

AWARDS, HONORS: Edgar Allan Poe Award nomination, Mystery Writers of America, 2003, for *The Last Witness.*

WRITINGS:

NOVELS

Motion to Kill, Kensington Publishing (New York, NY), 2002.
The Last Witness, Pinnacle Books (New York, NY), 2003.
Cold Truth, Pinnacle Books (New York, NY), 2004.
Deadlocked, Pinnacle Books (New York, NY), 2005.

SIDELIGHTS: Because Joel Goldman has been a trial lawyer since 1977, he has no need to conduct background research when writing legal thrillers featuring attorney Lou Mason, who works, as the author does, in Kansas City, Missouri. Goldman was inspired to write his first mystery after a conversation with one of his colleagues. As he related on his home page, "I started writing thrillers when one of my law partners complained to me about another partner. I told him we should write a murder mystery, kill the son-of-a-bitch off in the first chapter and spend the rest of the book figuring out who did it." The other lawyer never took Goldman up on the offer, so Goldman proceeded on his own. The result was 2002's *Motion to Kill,* which has been followed by several more thrillers.

Motion to Kill introduces Mason, an attorney who has just started working for a prestigious firm. While on a company retreat, he considers quitting his job in response to a request by the senior partner to alter important legal documents. The next thing he knows, the partner is found dead, and Mason is one of the main suspects. Cooperating as best he can with investigators, Mason begins his own investigation when he finds himself targeted for murder. As he delves deeper into what appears to be incriminating shenanigans at his firm, he decides to hire private investigator and friend Wilson "Blues" Bluestone to help him before he gets himself killed.

A *Publishers Weekly* reviewer remarked upon the book's "electrifying denouement," while Harriet Klausner, writing for *AllReaders.com,* wrote that *Motion to Kill* "never skips a beat." Klausner predicted that readers will be "surprised that this novel is Joel Goldman's debut" because it is of such high quality.

Suspense and thrills are again on the menu with Goldman's sequels *The Last Witness* and *Cold Truth.* In the former, Mason's friend Bluestone finds himself in big trouble after influential political insider Jack Cullan is murdered and Blues becomes the main suspect. Blues hires Mason as his attorney, but Mason soon learns that he cannot win his case because the courtroom has been rigged by politicians to favor the prosecution. He decides that the only way to save Blues is to find the true killer himself. Klausner, writing for *AllReaders.com,* praised *The Last Witness* for giving readers an "eye opening look at the American legal system."

Cold Truth involves the murder of a popular television psychologist, who is thrown from an eighth-floor window to her death. When a young woman named Jordan Hackett confesses to the killing, Jordan's parents hire Mason to defend her. Mason suspects Jordan is not telling the truth, and his careful probing leads him to the director of the youth camp where Jordan has been living. *AllReaders.com* contributor Klausner once again praised Goldman's writing, adding that "Lou is a delightful protagonist."

Mason's next case involves defending the honor of a dead man. In *Deadlocked,* after Ryan Kowalczyk is put to death by the state for killing two people fifteen years earlier, Ryan's mother and the victims' son both hire Mason to prove that it was really Whitney King, the man who fingered Ryan as the killer, who actually did the deed. "The latest Mason case is a terrific investigative thriller that makes a clear plea on the use of capital punishment; one error is one too many," according to Klausner in a *Best Reviews* online article.

Goldman told *CA:* "My work is most influenced by trying to answer the question: What happens when things go wrong? I'm more interested in characters than plot because people are more interesting, especially when they find themselves in impossible and unexpected circumstances. That's also why I enjoy writing a series; it allows me to see how the core characters evolve over time and respond to things that happen to them."

"*Deadlocked* is my favorite because it brings together many of these elements of character development and because the story raises important issues about justice and reconciliation. I also think it's the most well written of my novels and reflects my development as a writer."

BIOGRAPHICAL AND CRITICAL SOURCES:

PERIODICALS

Publishers Weekly, January 14, 2002, review of *Motion to Kill,* p. 46.

ONLINE

AllReaders.com, http://www.allreaders.com/ (February 8, 2005), Harriet Klausner, reviews of *The Last Witness, Cold Truth,* and *Motion to Kill.*

Best Reviews Web site, http://www.thebestreviews. com/ (December 18, 2004), Harriet Klausner, review of *Deadlocked.*

Joel Goldman Home Page, http://joelgoldman.com (February 17, 2005).

ReviewingTheEvidence.com, http://www.reviewingthe evidence.com/ (December, 2004), Andi Shechter, review of *Deadlocked.*

RomanticTimes.com, http://www.romantictimes.com/ (February 8, 2005), Toby Bromberg, review of *Motion to Kill.*

*   *   *

GOLLIN, James (M.) 1932-

PERSONAL: Born February 16, 1932, in St. Louis, MO; son of Joshua (a business executive) and Cecelia (Millstone) Gollin; married Jane Feder (an art critic), June 6, 1957; children: Timothy, Douglas. *Education:* Yale University, B.A., 1953, M.A., 1956.

ADDRESSES: Home—New York, NY. *Agent*—Thomas C. Wallace, T. C. Wallace Ltd., 425 Madison Ave., Ste. 1001, New York, NY 10017. *E-mail*—jgollin@ attglobal.net.

CAREER: Writer.

WRITINGS:

FICTION

The Philomel Foundation, St. Martin's Press (New York, NY), 1980.

Eliza's Galiardo, St. Martin's Press (New York, NY), 1983.

The Verona Passamezzo, Doubleday (New York, NY), 1985.

Broken Consort, St. Martin's Press (New York, NY), 1989.

OTHER

Pay Now, Die Later (nonfiction), Random House (New York, NY), 1966.

Worldly Goods (nonfiction), Random House (New York, NY), 1971.

The Star-spangled Retirement Dream (nonfiction), Scribner (New York, NY), 1981.

(With Robert W. Allardyce) *Desired Track,* American Vision Publishing, 1994.

Pied Piper: The Many Lives of Noah Greenberg, Pendragon Press (Hillsdale, NY), 2001.

Contributor to periodicals, including *American Scholar* and *Fortune.* Editor, *Early Music America,* 1995-96.

WORK IN PROGRESS: Fireworks Music, "another novel in the Antiqua Players sequence"; research on the life story of a world-famous concert musician.

BIOGRAPHICAL AND CRITICAL SOURCES:

PERIODICALS

Consumers Digest, September-October, 1981, review of *The Star-spangled Retirement Dream,* p. 25.

Library Journal, February 1, 1980, Henri C. Veit, review of *The Philomel Foundation,* p. 425; July, 1981, Harry Frumerman, review of *The Star-spangled Retirement Dream,* p. 1402.

New Yorker, July 28, 1980, review of *The Philomel Foundation,* p. 104; February 10, 1986, review of *The Verona Passamezzo,* p. 116.

New York Times Book Review, April 27, 1980, Newgate Callendar, review of *The Philomel Foundation,* p. 18; December 24, 1989, Marilyn Stasio, review of *Broken Consort,* p. 23.

Notes, June, 2002, Tom Moore, review of *Pied Piper: The Many Lives of Noah Greenberg,* p. 831.

Publishers Weekly, May 29, 1981, Genevieve Stuttaford, review of *The Star-spangled Retirement Dream,* p. 37; January 28, 1983, Barbara A. Bannon, review of *Eliza's Galiardo,* p. 72; October 20, 1989, Sybil Steinberg, review of *Broken Consort,* p. 42.

*   *   *

GONZALEZ, Francisco J.

PERSONAL: Male. *Education:* Northern Illinois University, B.A.; University of Toronto, M.A., Ph.D.

ADDRESSES: Office—Department of Philosophy and Religion, Skidmore College, 815 North Broadway, Saratoga Springs, NY 12866. *E-mail*—fgonzale@ skidmore.edu.

CAREER: Skidmore College, Saratoga Springs, NY, associate professor of philosophy.

AWARDS, HONORS: Humboldt research fellowship; National Endowment for the Humanities research fellowship.

WRITINGS:

(Editor) *The Third Way: New Directions in Platonic Studies,* Rowman & Littlefield (Lanham, MD), 1995.
Dialectic and Dialogue: Plato's Practice of Philosophical Inquiry, Northwestern University Press (Evanston, IL), 1998.

SIDELIGHTS: Francisco J. Gonzalez's *Dialectic and Dialogue: Plato's Practice of Philosophical Inquiry* was called "one of the best studies of Plato in several decades," by *Choice* reviewer M. Andic. In this work Gonzalez examines a subject that is almost never discussed in Plato scholarship: the philosopher's own conception of philosophy, including what it means to philosophize, and how we acquire the knowledge we seek. "Since Plato generally identifies philosophy with dialectic, Gonzalez's study is an investigation into the nature of dialectic," noted Laurel Dantzig in the *Review of Metaphysics.*

Gonzalez makes his points, including that Plato gives the dialectic—investigating truths and discovering fallacies through reasoned dialogue—priority over the hypothetical method, through readings of Plato's *Laches, Charmides, Cratylus, Euthydemus, Meno, Phaedo, Republic,* and *The Seventh Letter.* He also references works of contemporary scholarship in English, French, Italian, and German. Dantzig wrote that Gonzalez's readings of various dialogues "are careful and thorough, and his discussions of difficult issues, such as the Ideas and the Good, are particularly interesting and illuminating. While Gonzalez's interpretation is highly original and unorthodox, he has a good grasp on the current and not-so-current

debates in Plato scholarship." Dantzig called *Dialectic and Dialogue* "an excellent (and uncommon) combination of scholarly rigor, insight, and originality."

BIOGRAPHICAL AND CRITICAL SOURCES:

PERIODICALS

Ancient Philosophy, fall, 1997, Naomi Reshotko, review of *The Third Way: New Directions in Platonic Studies,* p. 442; spring, 2000, Peter J. Vernezze, review of *Dialectic and Dialogue: Plato's Practice of Philosophical Inquiry,* p. 199.
Choice, November, 1999, M. Andic, review of *Dialectic and Dialogue,* p. 551.
Journal of the History of Philosophy, July, 1997, J. Angelo Corlett, review of *The Third Way,* p. 458; January, 2000, Rosamond Kent Sprague, review of *Dialectic and Dialogue,* p. 113.
Review of Metaphysics, June, 2000, Laurel Dantzig, review of *Dialectic and Dialogue,* p. 930.

*   *   *

GRAFTON, C(ornelius) W(arren) 1909-1982

PERSONAL: Born 1909, in China; died 1982; children: Sue. *Education:* Earned degrees in journalism and law.

CAREER: Attorney in Louisville, KY.

AWARDS, HONORS: Mary Roberts Rinehart award, 1943.

WRITINGS:

NOVELS

The Rat Began to Gnaw the Rope (crime), Farrar & Rinehart (New York, NY), 1943.
The Rope Began to Hang the Butcher (crime), Farrar & Rinehart (New York, NY), 1944.
My Name Is Christopher Nagel, Rinehart (New York, NY), 1947.
Beyond a Reasonable Doubt (crime), Rinehart (New York, NY), 1950.

SIDELIGHTS: Attorney C. W. Grafton, the father of bestselling author Sue Grafton, only wrote a handful of novels in his lifetime, but his three mysteries, *The Rat Began to Gnaw the Rope, The Rope Began to Hang the Butcher,* and *Beyond a Reasonable Doubt* have been compared to the works of such writers as Erle Stanley Gardner, Rex Stout, and Raymond Chandler. Grafton took his first two titles from a nursery rhyme, and had he continued to write more in the series, books such as "The Water Began to Quench the Fire" and "The Stick Began to Beat the Dog" would have been next. As it is, Grafton's lawyer protagonist Gilmore Henry of Calhoun County, Kentucky, appears only in *The Rat Began to Gnaw the Rope* and *The Rope Began to Hang the Butcher.*

These books combine fast-paced plotting and a breezy style with the author's thorough knowledge of the law, as well as of the business world. His invention of crimes with their roots in events decades in the past foreshadows some of the techniques of John D. MacDonald and Ross Macdonald. More determined than some writers to root his fiction in a specific time, Grafton also conveys a strong sense of immediate pre-World War II America with war clouds conspicuous on the horizon. At times, he throws in as many topical references (prices and products; song titles; names of radio and movie stars, politicians, and sports heroes) as would someone writing a historical novel about the time.

The Rat Began to Gnaw the Rope is a complex tale about a stock manipulation scheme. Henry, a short, chubby, but likable character, is introduced as a sleuth not quite in the same mold as his predecessors. The wounds—mostly physical—he suffers during his investigations affect him more personally than the average hard-boiled hero, and he consequently comes off as a more sensitive character. In *The Rope Began to Hang the Butcher* there is more court action than in the previous Henry book; the portrait of a backwoodsy Kentucky court where the judge wanders around the room during the trial, challenging out-of-towners to tell him from advocates or spectators, is particularly unique. This time, Henry must unravel a scheme involving insurance and real estate, and he manages to do so with the all the perspicuity of the fictional Perry Mason.

Beyond a Reasonable Doubt, Grafton's return to the genre without his series character, is his best-known book. An unusual and suspenseful courtroom novel,

the story reveals early on that lawyer Jess London is guilty of the not-unjustified murder of his brother-in-law, Mitchell Sothern. The novel draws its suspense from the question of whether and how he will manage to escape punishment. Tried for the crime after recanting an earlier confession, Jess acts as his own attorney, surviving some of the narrowest escapes in courtroom fiction.

BIOGRAPHICAL AND CRITICAL SOURCES:

PERIODICALS

New York Times Book Review, February 8, 1981, review of *Beyond a Reasonable Doubt,* p. 31; September 4, 1983, review of *The Rat Began to Gnaw the Rope,* p. 19.*

* * *

GRANGER, Pip 1947-

PERSONAL: Born 1947, in Cuckfield, Sussex, England; married second husband, Ray Granger.

ADDRESSES: Home—West Country, England. *Agent*—David Higham Associates, 5-8 Lower John St., Golden Square, London W1F 9HA, England.

CAREER: Taught children with emotional and health problems in Westminster, England; literacy and special-needs teacher in Stoke Newington and Hackney, England, c. 1970s-80s.

AWARDS, HONORS: Harry Bowling Prize for fiction, 2000, for *Not All Tarts Are Apple.*

WRITINGS:

NOVELS

Not All Tarts Are Apple, Poisoned Pen Press (Scottsdale, AZ), 2002.
The Widow Ginger, Poisoned Pen Press (Scottsdale, AZ), 2003.

Trouble in Paradise, Poisoned Pen Press (Scottsdale, AZ), 2004.

No Peace for the Wicked, Bantam (New York, NY), 2005.

WORK IN PROGRESS: Another novel set in Soho, London; *Up West,* a social history of Soho, 1945-60, expected publication in 2007; a book for young adults.

SIDELIGHTS: Pip Granger began writing in the 1990s after her older brother was diagnosed with brain cancer and she had retired from teaching because of her own health problems. Her brother's illness made Granger want to write about their childhood in the Soho section of London with their father, who was at one time a part-time smuggler and knew a wide range of interesting characters. In an interview with Steve Anable for *Publishers Weekly,* Granger recalled, "I came from a criminal/bohemian background, but I didn't feel different when I was living in Soho, where such people were thick on the ground." Instead of writing a straightforward memoir, however, Granger fictionalizes her childhood experiences in *Not All Tarts Are Apple.*

Not All Tarts Are Apple takes place in London in the early 1950s and focuses on Rosie, the novel's narrator, who is being raised by an aunt and uncle since being abandoned at birth by her mother. Rosie is the favorite of the neighborhood, but when she learns that her mother, Cassandra, is an alcoholic prostitute Rosie's life becomes more complicated. She discovers that her mother had run away from a wealthy family and cruel stepfather, who has designs on the successful family engineering firm, and soon Rosie finds herself the target of a plot devised by Cassandra's stepfather. Emily Melton observed in *Booklist* that "Rosie's little-girl perspective gives the book a charm and naiveté rare in modern fiction." A *Publishers Weekly* reviewer wrote that the book is not a "conventional crime caper," adding that "anyone who appreciates fine storytelling will eagerly await further word from Rosie."

In the sequel, *The Widow Ginger,* Rosie has been legally adopted by her aunt and uncle and is happily living in Soho, where she meets all sorts of people who stop by her adoptive parents' café. When a mysterious ex-GI called the Widow Ginger is let out of prison, he looks up Rosie's uncle to collect his share of the profits from a wartime scam. The Widow Ginger's arrival causes other tensions to mount as Rosie's uncle has a falling out with his good friend, a local gangster called Maltese Joe. Before long, however, everyone bands together, united against Widow Ginger's reign of retribution and terror in the community. A *Publishers Weekly* contributor commented that "readers will warm to this unsentimental portrait of postwar London and the eccentrically lovable denizens of Rosie's Soho."

Trouble in Paradise is partly a prequel to Granger's first book about Rosie. In her interview with Anable, the author explained that part of her reason for writing a prequel was to find an older narrative voice because "I thought an adult view of the people Rosie knew would be interesting." It is the end of World II as the story begins, and though a positive outlook fills the London streets, Zelda Fluck, the novel's narrator, is dreading the return to Paradise Garden of her abusive husband, Charlie. Furthermore, Zelda's friend, local healer Zinnia Makepeace, is being harassed and vandalized, and her nephew, Tony, is hanging around with the wrong crowd. Zelda tries to get her nephew on the right path by getting him professional training for his beautiful singing voice. One day, as she sits in the café owned by Rosie's aunt and uncle, she meets Cassandra, who is pregnant with Rosie at the time, and eventually starts a new life. Sue O'Brien, writing in *Booklist,* called Granger's effort "a satisfying, compelling novel." *Chicago Tribune* contributor Dick Adler felt that the book "stands on its own shapely, sturdy legs as a marvelously evocative read," adding that Granger "has the art and imagination to bring her past back to vigorous life."

Granger told *CA:* "Both my parents were aspiring writers and I had a great uncle who wrote, so I suppose it's in the genes. I also have two nieces who are aspiring writers. I always wanted to write but didn't work up the nerve until my brother died at a young age and I felt I wanted to pay tribute by writing about a time and a place we shared (Soho, England, in the 1950s). Also, his death made me realize that I may not have time to write later, as I had always told myself. So I began writing my first novel in my late forties.

"London, and particularly Soho, influences my work obviously, also a peculiarly British comic called Frankie Howerd; I loved the way his act made you feel as if you were having a cozy gossip over the garden fence; there was an intimacy about it that made me want to write in the first person for this series of books. I also liked the intimacy of Armistead Maupin's *Tales of the City;* you felt as you read them that you were one of his gang, somehow. I loved that. Not only did I feel included, but I also felt 'safe' in a funny sort of way.

"I write in the mornings and sometimes it goes over into the afternoons, but I never start work late in the day. I write a minimum of 1,000 words a day, more if it's going well. I always begin by reading and diddling with the work I did the day before. I seem to start a novel by having a setting and throwing in more and more characters; then I seem to 'see' what they're going to do, once they're all there and interacting like mad. Sometimes, the odd character seems to do nothing at all and winds up a spare part, and then I have to go back and get rid of them. I've had to dump some characters I've grown really fond of, but I always comfort myself that they can have another book later on. Sometimes they do and sometimes they don't, but it's a comfort when they simply have to go.

"The most surprising thing I have learned as an author is that there's absolutely no glamour in it as a job, that it's a lonely old job too. And that in the actual writing process, characters can seem to take on a life of their own and do things that I wasn't expecting. My book *No Peace for the Wicked* turned into a bit of a love story and no one could have been more surprised than me, but the characters seemed to demand it. When that happens, it's terribly exciting for the writer, I find, but it must be annoying for those writers who tightly plot their books before they even begin to write. But then again, maybe it doesn't happen to them.

"Of my books, I have a bit of a soft spot for *Not All Tarts Are Apple,* because it was my first. I don't really think it's my best because my inexperience shows, I believe, although lots of readers disagree with me on that. I think *Trouble in Paradise,* was the book where I broke through to become a proper grown-up writer. At the moment I am terribly excited by my latest project, which will be called *Up West* when I've finished it. The book will be a nonfiction social history of the West End of London between 1945 and 1960. Then there's the novel I am working on as well, which as yet doesn't have a title. I'm also planning to do a book for young adults, set at the moment rock 'n' roll took off in England. Basically, I'm always most excited by a current project, whatever that may be. I

suspect it has to be that way, otherwise the writing would simply stop."

BIOGRAPHICAL AND CRITICAL SOURCES:

PERIODICALS

Booklist, September 15, 2002, Emily Melton, review of *Not All Tarts Are Apple,* p. 209; December 15, 2004, Sue O'Brien, review of *Trouble in Paradise,* p. 711.
Chicago Tribune, January 23, 2005, Dick Adler, review of *Trouble in Paradise,* p. 4.
Denver Post, November 3, 2002, Tom and Enid Schantz, review of *Not All Tarts Are Apple,* p. EE02.
Kirkus Reviews, September 1, 2003, review of *Not All Tarts Are Apple,* p. 1267; December 1, 2004, review of *Trouble in Paradise,* p. 1120.
MBR Bookwatch, January, 2005, Harriet Klausner, review of *Trouble in Paradise.*
Publishers Weekly, October 7, 2002, review of *Not All Tarts Are Apple,* p. 55; August 4, 2003, review of *The Widow Ginger,* p. 59; December 20, 2004, Steve Anable, "East End Stories" (interview), p. 40; December 20, 2004, review of *Trouble in Paradise,* p. 40.

ONLINE

AllReaders.com, http://www.allreaders.com/ (March 8, 2005), reviews of *Trouble in Paradise* and *The Widow Ginger.*
BookLoons.com, http://www.bookloons.com/ (March 8, 2005), Mary Ann Smyth, review of *Trouble in Paradise.*
David Higham Associates Web site, http://www.davidhigham.co.uk/ (March 8, 2005), "Pip Granger."
Fantastic Fiction Web site, http://www.fantasticfiction.co.uk/ (March 8, 2005), "Pip Granger."
Pip Granger Home Page, http://www.pipgranger.com (March 8, 2005).

*   *   *

GRAY, Patience (Jean Stanham) 1917-2005

OBITUARY NOTICE— See index for *CA* sketch: Born October 31, 1917, in Shackleford, Surrey, England; died March 10, 2005, in Spigolizzi, Italy. Author. Gray was best known as a food and garden writer who authored the bestselling *Honey from Weed: Fasting and Feasting in Tuscany, Catalonia, the Cyclades, and Apulia* (1986). As a young woman, she attended Queen's College, Oxford, and the University of Bonn before completing a B.Sc. at the University of London in 1939. Her interest in journalism and art history was sparked while traveling through Europe before World War II, and she gave up her original plans to study German and economics to concentrate on journalism. Hired by the British Foreign Office, she was fired when World War II started because her superiors viewed her as a risk due to her many contacts with people in Europe. Around this time, she began an affair with a married man named Thomas Gray (she took his last name, though they were never married), bearing him two children, but they were separated after he was conscripted into the military. To earn an income, she worked as a secretary and then established a research agency; she also worked as a research assistant for H.F.K. Henrion. In 1958, having won a writing competition and published the popular book *Plats du Jour* (1957) with Primrose Boyd, Gray was given a job at the London *Observer* writing the woman's page. She was also a part-time editor for the magazine *House & Garden*. Leaving the *Observer* in 1962, Gray became a textile designer. The next love of her life, sculptor Norman Mommens, was also a married man, but he divorced and the couple (they would marry, but not until 1995) moved to Italy to share their love of the rustic countryside there. They settled on a farm in Spigolizzi, where they enjoyed a Spartan life, and Gray learned a great deal about gardening and cooking. She earned extra income by designing jewelry, while Mommens focused on his art. Her love of home-grown foods and her simple lifestyle led to the book *Honey from Weed,* for which she is best remembered. She also published the books *Ring Doves and Snakes* (1989) and *Work, Adventures, Childhood, Dreams* (1999); in addition, she edited *A Catalan Cookery Book: A Collection of Impossible Recipes* (1999) by I. Davis.

OBITUARIES AND OTHER SOURCES:

PERIODICALS

Independent (London, England), March 14, 2005, p. 35.
Times (London, England), March 21, 2005, p. 50.

GRECO, Sal 1947-

PERSONAL: Born November 15, 1947, in Pittsburgh, PA; son of Sam and Ann (Hadavanic) Greco; married August 1, 1969; wife's name Terri (an administrative secretary); children: Steven, Lisa Diaz, Amy DelSignore. *Ethnicity:* "Italian." *Education:* Duquesne University, B.S.B.A., 1969. *Politics:* Republican. *Religion:* Roman Catholic.

ADDRESSES: Home and office—c/o Author Mail, Avanti Associates, 250 Pine Mountain Lane, Wexford, PA 15090.

CAREER: Worked in computer sales for companies in Pittsburgh, PA, 1969-90; CD Trader (videotape and compact disc store), Pittsburgh, owner, 1992-98; writer, 1998—. Butler Arc, member of board of directors.

WRITINGS:

Left for Dead (nonfiction), Avanti Associates (Wexford, PA), 2003.

Former newspaper columnist. Contributor to periodicals.

WORK IN PROGRESS: Abduction; a screenplay based on *Left for Dead.*

SIDELIGHTS: Sal Greco told *CA:* "I took some writing classes in the mid-eighties. I like using humor. I had a humor column in a newspaper for a year. I wrote other articles and humorous pieces for various publications. I like character-driven books and movies. I like to write dialogue.

"My writing process begins with a tablet. I draft my stories and then enter them into the computer. After that I revise and revise.

"My first book was based on the true life of a mobster turned minister. I like to write real stories about real people."

GREEN, Walon 1936-

PERSONAL: Born December 15, 1936, in Baltimore, MD; father a pilot; mother a showgirl.

ADDRESSES: Agent—ICM, 8942 Wilshire Blvd., Beverly Hills, CA 90211-1934.

CAREER: Producer, director, cinematographer, dialogue coach, consultant, and writer. Film work includes (as dialect advisor) *The Outrage,* 1964; (as dialogue coach) *Morituri,* 1965; (as director) *Spree* (also known as *Las Vegas by Night*), TransAmerica, 1967; (as director, producer, and cinematographer) *The Hellstrom Chronicle* (documentary), Cinema 5 Distributing, 1971; (as director) *The Secret Life of Plants,* Paramount, 1978; and (as executive producer) *Sniper,* TriStar, 1993. Appeared as himself in the film *The Wild Bunch: An Album in Montage,* 1996. Worked on television series, including (as producer) *National Geographic Specials,* Columbia Broadcasting System (CBS), c. 1969-70; (as producer, with others) *Hill Street Blues,* National Broadcasting Company (NBC), 1981-87; (as executive producer, with others) *Law & Order,* NBC, 1992-94; (as creative consultant) *NYPD Blue,* American Broadcasting Companies (ABC), 1993; (as executive producer, with others) *NYPD Blue,* ABC, 1994-95; (as creative consultant) *Millennium,* Fox, 1996; (as executive producer, with others) *ER,* NBC, beginning 1997; and (as executive producer) *Dragnet* (also known as *L.A. Dragnet*), ABC, 2003—. Executive producer of television movies, including *Strange New World,* 1975; and (with others) *Zero Effect,* 2002. Director of episodes of television series, including *National Geographic Specials,* CBS, 1964; and *Time-Life Specials: The March of Time,* 1965. *Military service:* Air Force Reserve.

AWARDS, HONORS: Academy Award for best documentary feature, Academy of Motion Picture Arts and Sciences, and Robert Flaterly Award for best feature-length documentary, British Academy of Film and Television Arts, both 1971, both for *The Hellstrom Chronicle.*

WRITINGS:

SCREENPLAYS

(With Roy N. Sickner and Sam Peckinpah) *The Wild Bunch,* Warner Bros., 1969.

Sorcerer (based on the French film *Wages of Fear* by Georges Arnaud), Paramount, 1977.
The Brink's Job (also known as *Big Stickup at Brink's;* based on the book by Noel Behn), MCA/Universal, 1978.
The Secret Life of Plants, Paramount, 1978.
(With David Freeman and Deric Washburn) *The Border,* Universal, 1982.
(With D. A. Metrov) *Solarbabies* (also known as *Solar Warriors*), Metro-Goldwyn-Mayer, 1986.
Crusoe (based on the book by Daniel Dafoe), Island Pictures, 1988.
(With Frank Miller) *Robocop 2,* Orion, 1990.
(With Michael S. Chernuchin and Tony Puryear) *Eraser,* Warner Bros., 1996.
The Hi-Lo Country (based on the novel by Max Evans), Gramercy, 1998.

TELEVISION SERIES; WITH OTHERS

Mysteries of the Sea, 1980.
Hill Street Blues, National Broadcasting Company, 1985–87.
Law & Order, National Broadcasting Company, 1991—.
ER, National Broadcasting Company, 1994—.
Millennium, Fox, 1997–99.
Dragnet (also known as *L.A. Dragnet*), American Broadcasting Companies, 2003—.

OTHER

(With Ronald Graham and Al Ramrus) *Strange New World* (television movie), 1975.
Robert Kennedy and His Times (television miniseries; based on the book by Arthur Schlesinger, Jr.), Columbia Broadcasting System (CBS), 1985.
(With Jeremy Thorn and Peter Lance) *Without Warning* (television movie), 1994.
(With Jake Kasdan) *Zero Effect* (television pilot), 2002.

SIDELIGHTS: Director, producer, and screenwriter Walon Green first made a name for himself in nature documentaries. He garnered three Emmy nominations for his work on *National Geographic* television specials in the late 1960s, and then in 1971 an Academy award for a film about insects, *The Hellstrom Chronicle.* In the 1980s he shifted to writing fictional films and television series, many of them in the action genre. He has written for several of the most popular television dramas of the 80s and 90s, including *Hill Street Blues* and *Law & Order,* both police shows, and *ER,* which is set in the emergency room of an inner city Chicago hospital.

Green also adapted Max Evan's novel *The Hi-Lo Country* for the screen, in something of a change of pace from his previous two films, the science-fiction thriller *Robocop 2* and *Eraser,* which stars Arnold Schwarzenegger as a U.S. marshal who must protect federal witness Vanessa Williams. *The Hi-Lo Country,* about two New Mexico cowboys recently returned from fighting in World War II who are both infatuated with the same woman, is "a compelling, very American story—the crashing to earth of the myth of the rugged individualist," Bob Ivry wrote in a review for the Bergen County, New Jersey *Record.*

BIOGRAPHICAL AND CRITICAL SOURCES:

PERIODICALS

American Film, April, 1989, Ron Shelton, review of *The Wild Bunch,* pp. 18-19.
Daily Variety, June 18, 2002, Michael Schneider, "Green Joins U's Wolf Pack," pp. 1-2.
Electronic Media, June 24, 2002, Michael Freeman and Chris Pursell, "Hollywood Notes: Green Back in *Law & Order* Fold," p. 29.
Film Comment, January-February, 1993, Nat Segaloff, interview with Green, p. 40.
Hollywood Reporter, June 18, 2002, pp. 6-7.
Independent (London, England), August 22, 1996, Adam Mars-Jones, review of *Eraser,* p. 8.
Los Angeles Times, December 30, 1998, Kenneth Turan, review of *The Hi-Lo Country,* p. 6.
Newsweek, July 1, 1996, David Ansen, review of *Eraser,* p. 62.
People, July 2, 1990, Ralph Novak, review of *Robocop 2,* p. 10; July 1, 1996, Ralph Novak, review of *Eraser,* p. 17.
Record (Bergen County, NJ), January 1, 1999, Bob Ivry, review of *The Hi-Lo Country,* p. 19.
Sight and Sound, October, 1995, Edward Buscombe, review of *The Wild Bunch,* p. 62; November, 2000, Leslie Felperin, review of *Dinosaur,* pp. 50-51.
Time, July 1, 1996, Richard Corliss, review of *Eraser,* p. 65.

Variety, May 17, 1989, review of *Three of a Kind,* p. 64; January 4, 1999, Todd McCarthy, review of *The Hi-Lo Country,* p. 97; May 15, 2000, Todd McCarthy, review of *Dinosaur,* p. 25.

ONLINE

Hollywood.com, http://www.hollywood.com/ (July 16, 2003), "Walon Green."
Internet Movie Database, http://www.imdb.com/ (July 8, 2003), "Walon Green."*

*   *   *

GREY, Johnny

PERSONAL: Male.

ADDRESSES: Home—England. *Office*—Johnny Grey Studios, Fyning Copse, Fyning Lane, Rogate, Hampshire GU31 5DH, England. *E-mail*—info@johnnygrey.co.uk.

CAREER: Johnny Grey Studios (architectural design firm), Rogate, Hampshire, England, owner.

WRITINGS:

The Art of Kitchen Design: Planning for Comfort and Style, Cassell (London, England), 1994.
Kitchen, Home Design Workbooks (New York, NY), 1997.
The Hardworking House: The Art of Living Design, Seven Dials (London, England), 2000.
Kitchen Culture: Reinventing Kitchen Design, photographs by Alex Wilson, Firefly Books (Buffalo, NY), 2004.

SIDELIGHTS: Architect Johnny Grey has focused much of his career on kitchen design. As the nephew of cooking writer Elizabeth David, he has developed a design style that emphasizes the kitchen as a social space. Grey now owns the architectural design company Johnny Grey Studios, which provides design services and project management for interior spaces including kitchens, bedrooms, and media rooms.

Grey' first book, *The Art of Kitchen Design: Planning for Comfort and Style,* outlines the history of kitchens, beginning in the seventeenth century, and then details his personal philosophy of kitchen design. The author calls special attention to the use of freestanding cupboards, pane decorations, hanging racks, and inlays. *The Art of Kitchen Design* met with favorable reviews, as many critics recognizing Grey's unique and creative approach to his subject. *Booklist* contributor Barbara Jacobs commented that the author "has produced some of the most innovative yet comfortable all-purpose rooms around."

Grey has continued to write about and design interior spaces. In 1997 he published the workbook-style volume *Kitchen,* which allows readers to develop ideas and designs for their own kitchens. Grey's more recent effort, *Kitchen Culture: Reinventing Kitchen Design,* presents the author's updated vision for kitchen design. It includes chapters on kitchen storage, ergonomics, cooking tools, lighting, floors, and work surfaces.

BIOGRAPHICAL AND CRITICAL SOURCES:

PERIODICALS

Booklist, April 1, 1995, Barbara Jacobs, review of *The Art of Kitchen Design: Planning for Comfort and Style,* p. 1371.
Library Journal, January 1997, Gayle Williamson, review of *The Art of Kitchen Design,* p. 96; September 15, 1997, Gayle Williamson, review of *Kitchen,* p. 73; January 1, 2005, Gayle Williamson, review of *Kitchen Culture: Reinventing Kitchen Design,* p. 106.
Reference & User Services Quarterly, winter, 1997, Carolyn M. Mulac, review of *Kitchen,* p. 227.

ONLINE

Firefly Books Web site, http://www.fireflybooks.com/ (March 21, 2005), "Johnny Grey."
HouseandGardenAddresses.com, http://www.houseand gardenaddresses.co.uk/ (March 21, 2005), "Johnny Grey."
Johnny Grey Studios Web site, http://www.johnnygrey. co.uk/ (March 21, 2005).*

GRUBER, Michael 1940-

PERSONAL: Born 1940, in NY; married. *Education:* Attended City College of New York; Columbia University, B.A.; University of Miami, Ph.D.

ADDRESSES: Home—Seattle, WA. *Agent*—c/o Author Mail, Morrow, 10 East 53rd Street, 7th Floor, New York, NY 10022.

CAREER: Writer. Worked as a marine biologist, and cook; policy speechwriter, c. 1970s.

WRITINGS:

Tropic of Night (novel), HarperCollins (New York, NY), 2003.
Valley of Bones (novel), William Morrow (New York, NY), 2005.
The Witch's Boy (young-adult novel), HarperTempest (New York, NY), 2005.
Jaguar (novel), Morrow (New York, NY), 2006.

Uncredited author of "Butch Karp" series by Robert K. Tanenbaum.

SIDELIGHTS: Michael Gruber worked as a ghostwriter for many of the popular "Butch Karp" legal-thriller novels before publishing his first novel under his own name. *Tropic of Night* is a critically acclaimed thriller featuring white anthropologist, Jane Doe, who nearly dies while studying shamanistic rituals in Nigeria. In the meantime, her husband, DeWitt Moore—a black writer who was also involved in the mysterious rites— essentially leaves his wife and disappears. Back in the United States, a series of bizarre murders, including Jane's sister, takes place. Doe recognizes the murders' ritualistic aspects and suspects her husband as the culprit. She teams up with Jimmy Paz, a black Cuban detective on the Miami police force who has experienced racial tensions because of his color. In an interview for *Bookreporter.com,* Gruber, a Caucasian, explained that he gained insight into his black characters "By invention, imagination and sympathy, the same way male authors can invent real female characters and female writers can invent real male ones." Noting that "the point of the book is that race is an hallucination," Gruber later added: "Not being allowed to show a fully developed brilliant black villain would really be racist."

In a review of *Tropic of Night* in the *Washington Post*, Patrick Andersen called the novel "an astonishing piece of fiction, one that expands the boundaries of the thriller genre." Anderson also commented, "The author wields his own sorcery as he lures us into the hallucinatory world of his imagination." *USA Today* contributor Marc Flores liked Gruber's characterization of Doe and his use of "multiple viewpoints such as Doe's first-person narration, her journal passages and Paz's investigation in third-person narration to skillfully advance a genre-hopping plot." A *Kirkus Reviews* contributor wrote that, "What would be overripe overplotting in lesser hands becomes wonderfully credible here, with cleverly drawn characters . . . trunkloads of ethno-botanical factoids, and interspersed sections from Jane's African logbook." Brad Hooper, writing in *Booklist*, noted that *Tropic of Night* "has movie potential written all over it, which is no criticism of its depth—simply a compliment to its strong and colorful story line."

In *Valley of Bones* Gruber brings back detective Paz to investigate the death of a foreign man who falls out of a hotel-room window and is impaled on an iron fence below. At the crime scene Paz discovers Emmylou Dideroff conversing through prayer with St. Catherine of Siena. Paz recruits psychologist Lorna Wise to help him investigate Dideroff's state of mind, and the two begin a love affair as they try to unravel the case. It is soon revealed that Dideroff is a member of the Catholic order known as the Society of Nursing Sisters of the Blood of the Christ. The evidence points to Dideroff as the murderer, but Paz thinks otherwise and sets out to track down the real killer.

Janet Maslin, writing in the *New York Times*, called *Valley of Bones* a "furiously overloaded story" and went on to suggest that the novel "is truly six different books rolled into one." Nonetheless, Maslin added, "That would amount to exasperating excess without Mr. Gruber's sharp, vivid flashes of the powerfully bizarre." A *Publishers Weekly* contributor commented that the novel "more than fulfills the promise of his dazzling *Tropic of Night*." The reviewer went on to write that "evocative prose, an erudite author, spellbinding subject matter and totally original characters add up to make this one a knockout." Frank Sennett,

writing in *Booklist*, noted that Gruber "dishes up another meaty supernatural thriller."

BIOGRAPHICAL AND CRITICAL SOURCES:

PERIODICALS

Book, March-April, 2003, review of *Tropic of Night*, p. 31.
Booklist, January 1, 2003, Brad Hooper, review of *Tropic of Night*, p. 807; December 1, 2004, Frank Sennett, review of *Valley of Bones*, p. 639.
Entertainment Weekly, January 21, 2005, Abby West, review of *Valley of Bones*, p. 93.
Kirkus Reviews, January 1, 2003, review of *Tropic of Night*, p. 12; October 1, 2004, review of *Valley of Bones*, p. 931.
Library Journal, January 1, 2005, Ken Bolton, review of *Valley of Bones*, p. 85.
MBR Bookwatch, January, 2005, Harriet Klausner, review of *Valley of Bones*.
New York Times, December 23, 2004, Janet Maslin, review of *Valley of Bones*, p. E12.
Publishers Weekly, March 11, 2002, John F. Baker, "'Scariest' Thriller for Morrow," p. 12; January 27, 2003, review of *Tropic of Night*, p. 233; November 8, 2004, review of *Valley of Bones*, p. 33; December 13, 2004, Lynn Andriani, "Hook, Line and Sinker: Michael Gruber Lures Readers in with Thrills Then Inspires Them to Contemplate Race, Faith, and the Environment," p. 39.
St. Petersburg Times, March 16, 2003, Susan Fernandez, review of *Tropic of Night*.
Sun-Sentinel (Ft. Lauderdale, FL), March 28, 2003, Oline H. Cogdill, review of *Tropic of Night*; February 2, 2005, Oline H. Cogdill, review of *Valley of Bones*.
USA Today, February 24, 2003, Marc Flores, review of *Tropic of Night*.
Washington Post, March 24, 2003, Patrick Anderson, review of *Tropic of Night*, p. C4; December 27, 2004, Patrick Anderson, review of *Valley of Bones*, p. C4.

ONLINE

Bookreporter.com, http://www.bookreporter.com/ (April, 2003), interview with Gruber.

Miami Herald Online, http://www.macon.com/mld/miamiherald/entertainment/ (January 16, 2005), Betsy Willeford, review of *Valley of Bones.*

MostlyFiction.com, http://mostlyfiction.com/ (February 17, 2005) Mary Whipple, review of *Valley of Bones.**

*   *   *

GUERRERO, Eduardo, Jr. 1916-2005
(Lalo Guerrero)

OBITUARY NOTICE— See index for *CA* sketch: Born December 24, 1916, in Tucson, AZ; died March 17, 2005, in Palm Springs, CA. Musician, composer, and author. Widely known as the "Father of Chicano Music," Guerrero composed and performed a unique blend of Mexican and American styles that gained him recognition as an award-winning musical innovator. Born into a large family in the Barrio Viejo neighborhood of Tucson that was later torn down to make way for a convention center (the subject of his song "Barrio Viejo"), Guerrero's love of music originated with his mother, who taught him to play the guitar and sing. As with many Mexican Americans, he struggled with a cultural identity that found him being rejected in Mexico by those who felt his music was too American as well as in America, for the opposite reason. Eventually, Guerrero—who went by the nickname Lalo—discovereda happy medium by blending a wide variety of styles that ranged from swing music to mambos and boleros. At times, he even ventured into children's music, recording an album reminiscent of the Chipmunks called *Las Ardillitas de Lalo Guerrero* (*Lalo's Little Squirrels*), and comedy, such as the parody songs "Mexican Mamas, Don't Let Your Babies Grow Up to Be Bus Boys" and "Pancho Lopez." By the 1970s, Guerrero was widely known for his innovative music that celebrated Chicano life, and his songs were prominently featured in the 1977 musical *Zoot Suit.* For his contributions to music, he became the first Chicano to be honored by the U.S. President with a National Medal of the Arts, which he earned in 1996; he also was presented with a Lifetime Achievement Award from the Mexican Cultural Institute and inducted into the Tejano Hall of Fame. Guerrero, who was suffering from prostate cancer at the time of his death, recorded many of his life's experiences in the biography *Lalo: My Life and Music* (2002). His life was also the planned subject of a documentary film titled *Lalo Guerrero: The Original Chicano.*

OBITUARIES AND OTHER SOURCES:

BOOKS

Guerrero, Lalo, and Sherilyn Mentes, *Lalo: My Life and Music,* University of Arizona Press (Tucson, AZ), 2002.

PERIODICALS

Chicago Tribune, March 20, 2005, section 4, p. 9.
Los Angeles Times, March 18, 2005, p. B10.
New York Times, March 19, 2005, p. B12.
Times (London, England), March 28, 2005, p.48.
Washington Post, March 26, 2005, p. B6.

*   *   *

GUERRERO, Lalo
See GUERRERO, Eduardo, Jr.

*   *   *

GULLEY, Philip 1961-

PERSONAL: Born February, 1961, in Camby, IN; married Joan Apple, June 2, 1984; children: Spencer, Sam. *Education:* Marian College, B.A.; Christian Theological Seminary, degree (with honors). *Religion:* Society of Friends (Quaker).

ADDRESSES: Home—Danville, IN. *Office*—Fairfield Friends Meeting, 7040 South County Road E., 1050, Camby, IN 46113. *E-mail*—info@philipgulleybooks.com.

CAREER: Writer and pastor. Irvington Friends Meeting, Indianapolis, IN, pastor; Fairfield Friends Meeting, Camby, IN, part-time pastor, c. 1999—.

AWARDS, HONORS: Christy Award, 2001, for *Home to Harmony.*

WRITINGS:

Front Porch Tales, Multnomah Books (Sisters, OR), 1997, published as *Front Porch Tales: Warmhearted Stories of Family, Faith, Laughter, and Love,* 2001.

Home Town Tales, Multnomah Publishers (Sisters, OR), 1998, published as *Hometown Tales: Recollections of Kindness, Peace, and Joy*, HarperSanFrancisco (San Francisco, CA), 2001.

For Everything a Season: Simple Musings on Living Well, Multnomah Publishers (Sisters, OR), 1999.

(With James Mulholland) *If Grace Is True: Why God Will Save Every Person*, HarperSanFrancisco (San Francisco, CA), 2003.

(With James Mulholland) *If God Is Love: Rediscovering Grace in an Ungracious World*, HarperSanFrancisco (San Francisco, CA), 2004.

Contributor to books, including Traci Mullins, editor, *A Grandmother's Touch: Heart-warming Stories of Love across Generations*, Vine Books (Ann Arbor, MI), 2001.

"HARMONY" SERIES

Home to Harmony, Multnomah Publishers (Sisters, OR), 2000.

Just Shy of Harmony, HarperSanFrancisco (San Francisco, CA), 2002.

Christmas in Harmony, HarperSanFrancisco (San Francisco, CA), 2002.

Signs and Wonders, HarperSanFrancisco (San Francisco, CA), 2003.

Life Goes On, HarperSanFrancisco (San Francisco, CA), 2004.

A Change of Heart, HarperSanFrancisco (San Francisco, CA), 2005.

The Scrapbook: A Christmas in Harmony Novella, HarperSanFrancisco (San Francisco, CA), 2005.

ADAPTATIONS: Home Town Tales was recorded by Multnomah Publishers (Sisters, OR), 1998.

SIDELIGHTS: Philip Gulley is a Quaker minister, and both his fiction and nonfiction writings reflect his pastoral background. Gulley offers spiritual guidance in nonfiction books such as *If God Is Love: Rediscovering Grace in an Ungracious World* and *If Grace Is True: Why God Will Save Every Person*. In his fiction he has created a world with many similarities to the one he inhabits. His novels and short stories—*Home to Harmony, Just Shy of Harmony, Signs and Wonders* and others in the "Harmony" series—are set in the imaginary town of Harmony, Indiana. By turns humorous and heartwarming, they reveal the human foibles of the congregation led by Sam Gardner, who, like his creator, serves as a pastor to the Quaker congregation in the town where he was born.

Gulley collaborated with theologian James Mulholland on *If Grace Is True* and *If God Is Love*. In the first book, the coauthors explain how they each progressed from a belief that eternal life with God requires acceptance of his saving grace to a belief that God will draw everyone into heaven, with or without their assent. "The authors did not always feel this way, and their little meditation on Christian universalism is as much autobiographical confession as theological treatise," commented a reviewer for *Publishers Weekly*. The chapters are devoted to each of the words in the phrase "why God will save every person," and the authors use anecdotal material from their own lives and ministries to illustrate their points. Their stance is theologically controversial, but the authors "stick to their guns," noted June Sawyers in *Booklist*. John Wilson, a reviewer for *Christianity Today*, found the book's premise appealing but ultimately flawed, noting that, as "in their desire to emphasize the power of God's grace, they end up trivializing human freedom." Still, Wilson praised Gulley and Mulholland for doing "what many evangelicals and orthodox Christians more generally have failed to do: they have honestly faced the church's traditional doctrines of salvation and eternal justice, even if only to reject them."

In *If God Is Love*, Gulley and Mulholland give a brief recap of the concept of universal salvation outlined in the previous book, then suggest ways of living that belief. They call upon Christians to put less emphasis on "saving" others and to strive instead to treat everyone as members of God's family. A *Publishers Weekly* writer stated that while this book may not convince everyone of the authors' theological convictions, it "details well Christ's command to love others and how to live that out."

Gulley has won a loyal audience for his "Harmony" series, beginning with *Home to Harmony*. In that book, Gulley's alter ego Sam Gardner is called to take up the pastorship of the Harmony Friends Meeting in his home town. Fresh from the seminary, the young minister has to reconcile the theology he has just studied with the humanity of his flock. As he struggles through his first year, his "journey in faith teaches through the shared medium of laughter," reported Melanie C. Duncan in *Library Journal*.

In addition to their humor, the "Harmony" books have drawn praise for their sensitive portrayal of Sam's struggles with his own doubts and difficulties. *Just Shy of Harmony,* for example, shows the young clergyman reading an article about the ten warning signs of depression, and realizing that he has seven of them. A *Publishers Weekly* reviewer called it a "refreshingly candid novel" enlivened by the author's "characteristic wry humor."

In an interview with Jana Riess for *Publishers Weekly,* Gulley commented, "I get a lot of letters from people who like the human insights of my books. My books tell them that it's okay to be broken. That being human is not a sin, and that there is grace for people. I get frustrated sometimes when I read Christian fiction. It seems unreal to me. Going to church and having the right beliefs doesn't always change your life immediately. You still struggle. And it just seems to me that somebody ought to write about that."

BIOGRAPHICAL AND CRITICAL SOURCES:

PERIODICALS

Atlanta Journal-Constitution, February 16, 2002, Don O'Briant, review of *Home to Harmony,* p. 4.

Booklist, March 1, 1997, John Mort, review of *Front Porch Tales,* p. 1111; February 15, 1999, Ray Olson, review of *For Everything a Season: Simple Musings on Living Well,* p. 1006; October 1, 2000, John Mort, review of *Home to Harmony,* p. 304; July, 2003, June Sawyers, review of *If Grace Is True: Why God Will Save Every Person,* p. 1848;

October 1, 2004, Donna Chavez, review of *If God Is Love: Rediscovering Grace in an Ungracious World,* p. 304.

Christianity Today, September, 2003, John Wilson, review of *If Grace Is True,* p. 73.

Library Journal, September 1, 2000, Melanie C. Duncan, review of *Home to Harmony,* p. 184; November 1, 2002, Shawna Saavedra Thorup, review of *Christmas in Harmony,* p. 72; April 1, 2003, Wilda Williams, review of *Signs and Wonders,* p. 84; July, 2003, Mary Prokop, review of *If Grace Is True,* p. 87; April 1, 2004, Tamara Butler, review of *Life Goes On,* p. 80; November 1, 2004, Nancy Pearl, review of *Life Goes On,* p. 135.

Publishers Weekly, August 21, 2000, Jana Riess, review of *Home to Harmony,* p. S19; February 25, 2002, review of *Just Shy of Harmony,* p. 40, Jana Riess, interview with Gulley, p. 41; September 30, 2002, review of *Christmas in Harmony,* p. 50; June 16, 2003, review of *If Grace Is True,* p. 67; March 24, 2003, review of *Signs and Wonders,* p. 59; March 1, 2004, review of *Life Goes On,* p. 50; October 25, 2004, review of *If God Is Love,* p. 44.

Tribune Books (Chicago, IL), December 23, 2002, Nancy Pate, review of *Christmas in Harmony,* p. 4.

ONLINE

AmericanProfile.com, http://www.americanprofile.com/ (February 8, 2004), Jackie Sheckler Finch, "Hometown Humorist."

BookPage.com, http://www.bookpage.com/ (April 10, 2005), Lynn Green, interview with Gulley.

Philip Gulley Home Page, http://www.philipgulley books.com (April 27, 2005).*

H

HALL, Willis 1929-2005

OBITUARY NOTICE— See index for *CA* sketch: Born April 6, 1929, in Leeds, England; died March 7, 2005, in West Yorkshire, England. Author. Hall was a popular playwright for both children's and adult theater who often collaborated with his close friend Keith Waterhouse. Hall and Waterhouse were raised in the same Yorkshire town, became friends when they were twelve, and attended the same schools. Too young to serve in the military during World War II, Hall enlisted in the British Army in 1947, spending several years in Asia, where he first put his youthful love of theater to task by creating radio plays for Chinese children. After returning to England, his play *Disciplines of War* was produced at the Edinburgh Festival in 1957. Two years later, the play had evolved into the popular *The Long and the Short and the Tall*. Hall and Waterhouse's first collaboration was *Billy Liar* (1960), which was adapted from a novel Waterhouse wrote. The two writers went on to release a wide variety of theater productions, ranging from drama and comedy to musicals and revues. Among these are *England, Our England* (1962), *All Things Bright and Beautiful* (1962), *Say Who You Are* (1965), and *Children's Day* (1969). In addition to these works, Hall was a prolific author of screenplays (including the well-received 1962 film *Whistle down the Wind*) as well as radio plays, television programs, and children's plays and musicals. In fact, much of his more recent popularity came from his musical adaptations of such children's classics as *Treasure Island* (1985) and *The Wind in the Willows* (1985). His 1989 television series *Budgie* was also popular with British audiences.

OBITUARIES AND OTHER SOURCES:

PERIODICALS

Independent (London, England), March 12, 2005, p. 44.
Times (London, England), March 14, 2005, p. 51.

*   *   *

HAMPLE, Zack 1977-

PERSONAL: Born September 14, 1977, in New York, NY; son of Stu (a writer) and Naomi (a bookseller) Hample. *Education:* Guilford College, B.A., 2000. *Religion:* "Jewish/agnostic." *Hobbies and other interests:* "Baseball, people, musical discovery, reminiscing, staying up late, throwing things, playing with kids at grown-up parties, sesame chicken, Arkanoid, singing the instrumental part, hand-eye coordination, Scrabble, dissing people in my journal, going through red lights on my bike."

ADDRESSES: Office—Argosy Book Store, 116 E. 59th St., New York, NY 10022. *E-mail*—zackSnags@aol. com.

CAREER: Guilford College, Greensboro, NC, enrollment representative, 2001; Frozen Ropes Baseball Center, New York, NY, instructor, 2002; Columbia Broadcasting Service, Inc. (CBS), New York, NY, production assistant, 2003; Argosy Book Store, New York, NY, Web master and sales associate, 2003-05; Major League Baseball Advanced Media, New York, NY, baseball writers, 2005—.

AWARDS, HONORS: $1,000 for breaking the world record on Arkanoid (a video game from 1986), Twin Galaxies, 2000.

WRITINGS:

How to Snag Major League Baseballs: More than 100 Tested Tricks That Really Work, Aladdin Paperbacks (New York, NY), 1999.

WORK IN PROGRESS: How to Watch Baseball Better, 2006; *How to Snag Major League Baseballs,* Volume II, 2007; *But I Hate Walking* (children's book), 2008.

SIDELIGHTS: Zack Hample once commented: "I've collected 2,542 baseballs at major league games. When I was younger, people used to tease me for being obsessed with something so dorky. But now that I have a book published on the subject, I'm not such a dork. Funny how that works.

"Now all I have to do is write something about my 189-pound rubber band ball."

BIOGRAPHICAL AND CRITICAL SOURCES:

PERIODICALS

Sports Illustrated, April 9, 2001, Rick Kelly, "A Ballsy Fan: If You Would Listen to Zack Hample, You'd Come Home with a Ball Every Game," p. 100.

ONLINE

Zack Hample Web site, http://www.zackhample.com (June 25, 2005).

*   *   *

HANDLER, Ruth 1916-2002
(Mrs. Elliot Handler)

PERSONAL: Born November 4, 1916, in Denver, CO; died of complications from colon surgery, April 27, 2002, in Los Angeles, CA; daughter of Jacob Joseph and Ida M. Mosko; married Elliot Handler (a furniture

designer and toy manufacturer), June 26, 1938; children: Kenneth Robert, Barbara Joyce. *Education:* Attended the University of Denver, 1935-36.

CAREER: Paramount Studios, Hollywood, CA, secretary, c. 1936-38; Mattel, Inc. (toy manufacturer), Hawthorne, CA, cofounder, 1945, executive vice president, 1945-67, president, 1967-73; co-chair of board, 1973-74; founder of Nearly Me/Ruthon, Inc. (prosthetic manufacturing firm), 1974-91. Member, White House Conference on Children and Youth business advisory council, 1970, Center Theater Group board of directors, 1971, Council of Economic Advisors advisory committee on the economic role of women, 1972, and Vista Del Mar Child Care Service board of directors; member of executive committee and chair of subcouncil on product safety, President's National Business Council for Consumer Affairs, 1971-74.

MEMBER: Los Angeles Music Center (founding member, 1965), Association of the University of Southern California.

AWARDS, HONORS: Outstanding Businesswoman, National Association of Accountants, 1961; (with husband Elliot Handler) Couple of the Year, City Hope, 1963; Woman of the Year in Business, *Los Angeles Times,* 1968; Outstanding Woman, *Ladies' Home Journal,* 1971; Advertising Woman of the Year, Western States Advertising Agencies Association, 1972; Brotherhood Award, Southern California Region of the National Conference of Christians and Jews, 1972.

WRITINGS:

(With Jacqueline Shannon) *Dream Doll: The Ruth Handler Story,* Longmeadow Press (Stanford, CT), 1994.

SIDELIGHTS: Ruth Handler is best known as the inventor of the phenomenally successful Barbie doll. Since being introduced in 1959, Barbie and her companions have been manufactured and sold in the millions, and half a century later the willowy mold-injected plastic doll is still a must-have play item for many young girls. Handler chronicles the doll's invention and success, as well as her many years of juggling motherhood and a career as a high-powered executive, in *Dream Doll: The Ruth Handler Story.*

Handler grew up in Denver, but as a young adult she moved to southern California. There she and Elliot Handler, who had been her childhood sweetheart before eventually becoming her husband, founded their first company. Elliot had long enjoyed making his own home decor, even furnishing the couple's apartment largely with pieces he designed. At Ruth's urging, he bought the necessary equipment to produce the pieces commercially, and in less than a decade the company they created was selling $2 million worth of furniture a year. Elliot soon sold his share of this business and moved on, creating a new firm, Mattel Creations, which started out producing picture frames. Then, with scraps of wood and plastic left over from the picture frame–making process, Elliot began making furniture for doll-houses. Ruth, by this time a member of the Mattel corporation, was intimately involved in the business side of the operation, even overseeing the company's sales organization. Under her leadership their doll-house line flourished, with profits of $30,000 a year. They soon branched out into other toys, making plastic ukuleles, pianos, and music boxes in the late 1940s.

Mattel's most successful toy, the Barbie doll, was conceived during an European vacation the Handlers took with their children, Barbie and Ken, in 1956. In Switzerland and Austria they saw the "Lilly" doll, which was based on a semi-pornographic European cartoon character. Handler's daughter was at this point too old to play with baby dolls, but Handler had noticed that she enjoyed playing with dolls modeling teenagers and adults. At that time the only adult dolls available in the United States were two-dimensional paper dolls, and Handler realized that she had found a niche market. Having an adult doll "gives a little girl the ability to dream about her future," Handler explained in a 1994 interview with *Lilith* contributor Susan Weidman Schneider. "A girl can interpret the adult world around her with this doll as a prop." Mattel introduced its own adult doll, Barbie, in 1959, and the company's sales quickly skyrocketed.

However, the good times at Mattel did not last forever, and within a decade the company's position began to weaken. When typical cycles of growth and loss began affecting the company, the Handlers and other members of the Mattel board tried to disguise this information in corporate financial reports. When the truth came to light, the company's stock price plummeted to $2 a share and the Handlers were indicted for fraud by the Securities and Exchange Commission. By 1974 they had been forced to leave the business they founded. At the same time Handler was struggling with breast cancer, and she mused in *Dream Doll* that perhaps the stress of her 1970 mastectomy affected her judgment during those years.

Frustrated with the prosthetic breasts that were available to her after her surgery, Handler decided to create better ones, leading her to found the company Nearly Me. This same scrappy attitude comes through in *Dream Doll,* according to some critics. *Women's Review of Books* contributor Mel McCombie wrote that Handler's "description of slights, hostility and prejudice against her gender in the workplace makes one respect her aggressive pursuit," while *New York Times Book Review* critic Amy M. Spindler noted that, despite all the setbacks in her life, Handler's tone "is unrelentingly optimistic, dotted with exclamation points and affirmative statements about herself. If Barbie could write . . . one imagines she would sound a bit like Ruth Handler."

BIOGRAPHICAL AND CRITICAL SOURCES:

BOOKS

Business Leader Profiles for Students, Volume 1, Gale (Detroit, MI), 1999.
Handler, Ruth, and Jacqueline Shannon, *Dream Doll: The Ruth Handler Story,* Longmeadow Press (Stanford, CT), 1994.
Newsmakers, Issue 3, Gale (Detroit, MI), 2003.

PERIODICALS

Chief Executive, January-February, 2003, p. 11.
Jet, p. 14.
Jewish Bulletin of Northern California, February 19, 1993, Suzan Berns, "Mattel Exec Uses Cancer Experience to Help Others," p. 19.
Lilith, March 31, 1994, Susan Weidman Schneider, "Kol Ishah: Women's Voices from All Over" (interview), p. 4.

New York Jewish Week, July 10, 1998, Susan Josephs, "Barbie's Jewish Roots," p. 30.

New York Times Book Review, February 5, 1995, Amy M. Spindler, "Bless Her Pointy Little Feet," review of *Dream Doll: The Ruth Handler Story,* p. 22.

Publishers Weekly, October 17, 1994, review of *Dream Doll,* p. 75.

Washington Post Book World, December 8, 1994, Grace Lichtenstein, "A Success beyond Ken," review of *Dream Doll,* p. 8.

Women's Review of Books, June, 1995, Mel McCombie, review of *Dream Doll,* p. 10.

ONLINE

IdeaFinder.com, http://www.ideafinder.com/ (March 23, 2005), "Inventor Ruth Handler."

Public Broadcasting Corporation Web site, http://www.pbs.org/ (March 23, 2005), *Who Made America?:* "Ruth Handler" (transcript).

OBITUARIES

PERIODICALS

Economist, May 4, 2002.
People, May 13, 2002, p. 66.
Time, May 13, 2002, p. 25.
U.S. News and World Report, December 30, 2002, p. 88.*

*   *   *

HANLEY, Christine A.
See ADAMS, Christine A(nn)

*   *   *

HARDIN, J. D.
See BARRETT, Neal, Jr.

*   *   *

HARKNESS, Peter (William) 1929-

PERSONAL: Born October 29, 1929, in Croydon, England; son of Verney Leigh (a civil servant) and Olivia Amy (a homemaker; maiden name, Austin) Harkness; married, 1955; wife's name, Margaret Rosemary (a secretary); children: Anne Olivia Harkness Chambers, Rosemary Ellice Harkness Stewart. *Ethnicity:* "Anglo Irish." *Education:* Hertford College, Oxford, B.A., 1953, M.A., 1956. *Politics:* Conservative. *Religion:* Anglican. *Hobbies and other interests:* Ecclesiology, local history, birdwatching, wild flowers, travel.

ADDRESSES: Home—7 Cloisters Rd., Letchworth Garden City SG6 3JR, England. *E-mail*—peterharkness@letchworthgc.freeserve.co.uk.

CAREER: Rose grower and breeder, 1953-89. R. Harkness and Co. Ltd., managing director, 1977-89; also managing director of Harkness New Roses Ltd. City of Glasgow, Scotland, advisor to International Rose Trials, 1986-99; Letchworth Garden City Heritage Foundation, chair, 1999-2004. Garden House Hospice, chair, 1990-96.

MEMBER: Royal National Rose Society (vice president, 1998—), Rose Growers' Association (chair, 1983-85), British Association of Rose Breeders (president, 1986-89), Worshipful Company of Gardeners (liveryman), Letchworth Garden City Rotary Club (president, 1990-91).

AWARDS, HONORS: Dean Hole Medal, Royal National Rose Society, 1996; Paul Harris fellow, Rotary, 1999.

WRITINGS:

Modern Roses, Century, 1987, published as *Modern Garden Roses,* Globe Pequot Press (Chester, CT), 1988.

The Photographic Encyclopedia of Roses, Colour Library Books (London, England), 1991.

Roses to Enjoy, Royal National Rose Society (London, England), 1993.

Roses for Today, British Association of Rose Breeders (England), 1995.

Favourite Roses, Ward Lock (London, England), 1996.

The First Seventy-five Years (local history), Osprey (Oxford, England), 1998.

All Saints . . . and Sinners (local history), Midway Clarke, 1999.

The Rose: An Illustrated History, Firefly Books (Buffalo, NY), 2003, published as *The Rose: A Colourful Inheritance,* Scriptum Cartago (London, England), 2003.

Coauthor of *Roses,* 1993. Contributor to books, including *The Royal Horticultural Society Gardeners' Encyclopedia of Plants and Flowers,* DK, 1989; *The Royal Horticultural Society A-Z Encyclopedia of Garden Plants,* DK, 1996; *Botanica's Roses,* Random House (Australia), 1998; *Welcome Rain,* 1998; and *The Royal Horticultural Society Encyclopedia of Gardening,* DK, 2002. Contributor to rose magazines. Editor, *Rose,* 1991-96.

Some of Harkness's writings have been published in German, Polish, and Dutch.

WORK IN PROGRESS: Research on roses in Hertfordshire, England.

SIDELIGHTS: Peter Harkness told *CA:* "Though writing is something I've always enjoyed as a hobby, my motivation for all save one book has been the request to write it by a commissioning editor (or in the case of the *Rose* magazine, the offer of the job as editor). The exception is *All Saints . . . and Sinners,* about my local village church, which was written out of curiosity—a desire to find out all the history of its ancient fabric and the people who have worshiped there for the past 800-plus years.

"The style of local historian Reginald Hine and his approach to subjects with a scholarly yet light touch have been an influence on my work; and the style of my brother Jack, combining wit, brevity, wisdom, and elegance, is something I'd like to have attained. Jack, who lived from 1918 to 1994, wrote rose books, two of which have classic status in rose literature.

"My writing process is to think; read all relevant sources, noting passages and their references on the word processor; write to specialists, where their input is thought useful for consultation; access material and sort it in a helpful sequence; then start writing. Undoubtedly the presence of deadlines for copy is a spur to getting the writing done."

BIOGRAPHICAL AND CRITICAL SOURCES:

PERIODICALS

Booklist, October 15, 2003, Alice Joyce, review of *The Rose: An Illustrated History,* p. 373.

Library Journal, October 1, 2003, Phillip Oliver, review of *The Rose,* p. 107.
Publishers Weekly, August 18, 2003, review of *The Rose,* p. 76.

*   *   *

HART, Jenifer (Fischer) 1914-2005

OBITUARY NOTICE— See index for *CA* sketch: Born January 29, 1914, in London, England; died March 19, 2005, in Oxford, England. Civil servant, historian, educator, and author. Hart was a former history tutor at St. Anne's College, Oxford. After graduating from Somerville College, Oxford, with a first in history in 1935, she passed the civil service exam and joined the British Home Office in 1936. Here she enjoyed one of the most successful careers of any woman to have worked for the civil service, managing to do well even when she temporarily joined the Communist Party during the 1930s. When her husband was hired to teach philosophy at New College, Oxford, Hart left government work behind and was hired at the university. She filled various positions, such as extramural studies organizer and history and politics tutor for the Society of Oxford Home Students, before joining the St. Anne's faculty as a history teacher. Here she would remain until her 1981 retirement. During this period, she also published the well-received history books *The British Police* (1951) and *Proportional Representation: Critics of the British Electoral System, 1820-1945* (1992). In 1998 Hart published her autobiography, *Ask Me No More.*

OBITUARIES AND OTHER SOURCES:

BOOKS

Hart, Jenifer, *Ask Me No More,* Peter Halban (London, England), 1998.

PERIODICALS

Independent (London, England), March 31, 2005, p. 35.
Times (London, England), March 31, 2005, p. 57.

HAYCRAFT, Anna (Margaret) 1932-2005
(Alice Thomas Ellis, Anna Margaret Lindholm, Brenda O'Casey)

OBITUARY NOTICE— See index for *CA* sketch: Born September 9, 1932, in Liverpool, England; died of lung cancer March 8, 2005, in London, England. Author. Often writing under the pen name Alice Thomas Ellis, Haycraft was associated with the Duckworth school of writers whose novels typically featured women characters in a modern British settings. Her devout, conservative Catholic beliefs were fostered when she was eighteen; abruptly quitting the Liverpool School of Art, where she had been a student, she converted to Catholicism and entered the Convent of Notre Dame de Namur in Liverpool. Unfortunately, she was compelled to leave the convent after she suffered a slipped disk. Finding work at a delicatessen, she met her future husband, Colin Haycraft. After they were married, he purchased the Duckworth publishing house, and she helped her husband by becoming the company's fiction editor. Using the Ellis pseudonym, she began writing novels for Duckworth as an outlet for self-expression, the first being *The Sin Eater* (1977). Many more novels followed, including *The Twenty-seventh Kingdom* (1982), which was shortlisted for the Booker Prize, *The Inn at the Edge of the World* (1990), which won a Writers' Guild award for best fiction, and *Fairy Tale* (1998). Her trilogy of fiction, comprised of *The Clothes in the Wardrobe* (1987), *The Skeleton in the Cupboard* (1988), and *The Fly in the Ointment* (1989), was later compiled into a single volume as *The Summer House: A Trilogy* (1994); the first book in the trilogy was later adapted as the 1992 film *Summer House*. Haycraft was also known for her columns expressing her conservative views in the *Spectator, Universe,* and the *Catholic Herald.* At one point, she was fired from the *Herald* for criticizing the archbishop of Liverpool for his ecumenism; she returned to writing for the periodical from 1998 until 2001, however. In addition to her Catholic faith, Haycraft's writing was often distinctive for its humor, which even found its way into her cookbooks, such as *Darling, You Shouldn't Have Gone to So Much Trouble* (1980), and her love of the Welsh landscape and its history, particularly noticeable in her autobiography, *A Welsh Childhood* (1990). The author also wrote nonfiction works about religion, society, and domestic life, such as *Home Life* (1986), *Loss of the Good Authority: The Cause of Delinquency* (1989, written with Tom Pitt-Aikens), and *Serpent on the Rock: A Personal View of Christian-*ity (1994). Her last book was 2000's *Valentine's Day,* which she edited.

OBITUARIES AND OTHER SOURCES:

BOOKS

Ellis, Alice Thomas, *A Welsh Childhood,* M. Joseph (London, England), 1990.

PERIODICALS

Independent (London, England), March 10, 2005, p. 35.
Los Angeles Times, March 15, 2005, p. B9.
New York Times, March 12, 2005, p. A27.
Times (London, England), March 10, 2005, p. 67.
Washington Post, March 12, 2005, p. B7.

*   *   *

HEINZ, Thomas A(rthur) 1949-

PERSONAL: Born May 1, 1949, in Evanston, IL; son of Wilbur Edward and Jeanne (Kelly) Heinz; married Ann C. Terando, February, 1999. *Education:* University of Illinois, B.Arch., 1972.

ADDRESSES: Office—Heinz and Co., 27157 St. Marys Rd., Mettawa, IL 60048.

CAREER: Architect. Central Railroad, Chicago, IL, architect engineer, 1972-77; Pensayer Co., Oak Park, IL, architect engineer, 1977-85; U.S. Post Office, Chicago, architect engineer, 1985-90; Heinz and Co., Evanston, IL, architect engineer, 1990—. Architect/engineer for Frank Lloyd Wright Room, American Wing-Metropolitan Museum of Art and thirty other Wright buildings. Former designer, John Widdicomb Furniture Co., Grand Rapids, MI.

WRITINGS:

Frank Lloyd Wright, St. Martin's Press (New York, NY), 1982.

(And photographer, with Christopher Little) *Fallingwater, A Frank Lloyd Wright Country House*, introduction by Mark Girouard, Abbeville Press (New York, NY), 1986.

Frank Lloyd Wright ("Architectural Monographs," number 18), St. Martin's Press (New York, NY), 1992.

(And photographer) *Frank Lloyd Wright. East Portfolio*, Gibbs Smith (Layton, UT), 1993.

(And photographer) *Frank Lloyd Wright. Furniture Portfolio*, Gibbs Smith (Salt Lake City, UT), 1993.

(And photographer) *Frank Lloyd Wright. Midwest Portfolio*, Gibbs Smith (Salt Lake City, UT), 1993.

(And photographer) *Frank Lloyd Wright. Stained Glass*, Gibbs Smith (Layton, UT), 1993.

(And photographer) *Frank Lloyd Wright. West Portfolio*, Gibbs Smith (Layton, UT), 1993.

Frank Lloyd Wright: Interiors and Furniture, Academy Editions (London, England), 1994.

Frank Lloyd Wright: Glass Art, Academy Editions (London, England), 1994.

(And photographer) *Frank Lloyd Wright. Chicagoland Portfolio*, Gibbs Smith (Layton, UT), 1994.

Dana House: Frank Lloyd Wright, Academy Editions (London, England), 1995.

Frank Lloyd Wright. Field Guide, Academy Editions (Chichester, West Sussex, England), Volume 1: *Upper Great Lakes: Minnesota, Wisconsin, Michigan*, 1998, Volume 2: *Metro-Chicago*, 1999, Volume 3: *West*, 1999.

(And photographer) *Frank Lloyd Wright's Stained Glass and Lightscreens*, Gibbs Smith (Salt Lake City, UT), 2000.

The Vision of Frank Lloyd Wright: Complete Guide to the Designs of an Architectural Genius, Chartwell Books (Edison, NJ), 2000.

(With Randall L. Makinson) *Greene and Greene: The Blacker House*, photographic essay by Brad Pitt, Gibbs Smith (Salt Lake City, UT), 2000.

Frank Lloyd Wright's Interiors, Grange Books (Rochester, Kent, England), 2002.

Frank Lloyd Wright's Houses, Grange Books (Rochester, Kent, England), 2002.

(With Randall L. Makinson) *Greene and Greene: Creating a Style*, Gibbs Smith (Salt Lake City, UT), 2004.

Frank Lloyd Wright Field Guide: Includes all United States and International Sites, Northwestern University Press (Evanston, IL), 2005.

Also author of articles about architecture and Frank Lloyd Wright.

SIDELIGHTS: Thomas A. Heinz is an architect and head of Heinz & Co., which makes reproductions of furniture designed by noted early twentiety-century architect Frank Lloyd Wright. Heinz's interest in Wright's work has led him to write numerous articles and books about the renowned architect's work, from Wright's buildings and furniture to his stained glass and the special window treatments that he constructed for clients. Writing in *Interior Design*, a reviewer noted that Heinz had written an "intelligent essay" for his book *Frank Lloyd Wright*, which features an eighty-page, full-color portfolio of Wright's work.

In *Frank Lloyd Wright: Glass Art* Heinz looks at the many ways Wright used glass art in his designs, from windows and doors to room dividers, skylights, sconces, and supports. In 1992's *Frank Lloyd Wright*, the author discusses how Wright constructed his art, often employing dazzling innovations in the process. In a review of both books for *Interiors*, Nayana Currimbhoy noted that they "suffer from what might be dubbed as 'Wright's Disease,' or making a little go a long way, and would probably have been better off as an article." Commenting on Heinz's *Frank Lloyd Wright: Interiors and Furniture*, Currimbhoy, however, admitted that "Heinz has produced an extensive catalogue of a vast selection of both freestanding and built-in furniture, a useful collection to the Wright library." In *Frank Lloyd Wright's Stained Glass and Lightscreens* Heinz discusses Wright's glass work and compares it to that of other noted glass makers of the early twentieth century, including Tiffany and La Farge. Writing in *Interior Design*, Stanley Abercrombie lauded the book because "it is a pleasure to see . . . [Wright's work in glass] given the full-color treatment it deserves."

Frank Lloyd Wright. Field Guide is a three-volume book focusing on Wright's work throughout the United States and includes photos, commentary, and directions to finding some of Wright's buildings. For example, volume two, *Metro-Chicago*, focuses on Chicago and the surrounding area where Wright completed the largest body of his work. *Chicago Tribune* contributor Blair Kamin felt that "Heinz does the basics well."

Heinz turned his attention to West Coast architects Charles and Henry Greene in books he wrote with Randell L. Makinson. In *Greene and Greene: Creating a Style*, the authors focus on the architectural duo's unique designs of houses, which made the Ohio-born brothers a well-known part of the California Arts and Crafts movement at the beginning of the twentieth century. The book is divided into three sections, discussing the architects' various plans, the materials they liked to work with, and interiors of the homes. Writing in *January* online, Adrian Marks observed, "One of the nicest things about *Greene & Greene: Creating a Style* is that this is a book that's meant to be read and enjoyed as much by neophytes as by architecture buffs and experts." Marks continued, "Whether you're a student of architecture, a design enthusiast or an armchair decorator, *Greene & Greene: Creating a Style* will make a valuable addition to your bookshelf or, indeed, your coffee table."

BIOGRAPHICAL AND CRITICAL SOURCES:

PERIODICALS

Chicago Sun-Times, September 21, 1997, M. W. Newman, review of *Frank Lloyd Wright. Field Guide,* Volume 1: *Upper Great Lakes: Minnesota, Wisconsin, Michigan,* p. 11; July 23, 2000, Bill Cunniff, review of *Frank Lloyd Wright's Stained Glass and Lightscreens,* p. 3.

Chicago Tribune, January 30, 1998, Blair Kamin, review of *Frank Lloyd Wright. Field Guide,* Volume 2: *Metro-Chicago,* p. 3.

Interior Design, September, 1992, review of *Frank Lloyd Wright,* p. 66; November, 1998, Stanley Abercrombie, review of *Frank Lloyd Wright. Field Guide,* Volume 2: *Metro-Chicago,* p. 78; November, 2000, Stanley Abercrombie, review of *Frank Lloyd Wright's Stained Glass and Lightscreens,* p. 146.

Interiors, September, 1994, Mayana Currimbhoy, reviews of *Frank Lloyd Wright: Interiors and Furniture, Frank Lloyd Wright: Glass Art,* and *Frank Lloyd Wright,* p. 14.

Library Journal, January 1, 2005, Gayle Williamson, review of *Greene and Greene: Creating a Style,* p. 107.

ONLINE

January Online, http://www.januarymagazine.com/ (March 8, 2005), Adrian Marks, review of *Greene and Greene: Creating a Style.*

HERBERT, Gary B. 1941-

PERSONAL: Born December 24, 1941, in Rockford, IL; son of Charles Franklin and Ruth Adele (Bogda) Herbert; married Jane Elizabeth Provancher (a teacher), August 19, 1967; children: Gregory Scott, Steven Mark. *Ethnicity:* "English." *Education:* Illinois Wesleyan University, B.A., 1965; American University, M.A., 1967; Pennsylvania State University, Ph.D., 1972. *Religion:* Protestant.

ADDRESSES: Home—2105 Hullen St., Metairie, LA 70001. *Office*—Department of Philosophy, Campus Box 138, Loyola University, New Orleans, LA 70118.

CAREER: Loyola University, New Orleans, LA, assistant professor, 1972-76, associate professor, 1976-89, professor of philosophy, 1989—.

MEMBER: American Philosophical Association (Eastern division), American Catholic Philosophical Association, American Society for Political and Legal Philosophy.

AWARDS, HONORS: Dux Academixus, Loyola University, 2001.

WRITINGS:

Thomas Hobbes: The Unity of Scientific and Political Wisdom, University of British Columbia Press (Vancouver, British Columbia, Canada), 1989.

A Philosophical History of Rights, Transaction Publishers (Piscataway, NJ), 2002.

Editor, *Human Rights Review,* 2003—.

WORK IN PROGRESS: A book on the philosophy of Immanuel Kant.

SIDELIGHTS: Gary B. Herbert told *CA:* "I spent my formative years in graduate studies at Pennsylvania State under the tutelage of Stanley Rosen and Richard Kennington. They had both been students of Leo Strauss, and it showed in their painstakingly careful analyses of texts and brilliant synoptic grasp of the philosophical history of ideas. Together, they gave my interest in classical political philosophy its direction.

"Their own teacher, Leo Strauss, authored one of the classic interpretations of the seventeenth-century political philosopher, Thomas Hobbes. There were indications in Strauss's later writings that he had changed his mind about his interpretation of Hobbes, believing that a greater emphasis on the role of Hobbes's natural philosophy was more important to Hobbes's political theory than Strauss had originally thought. Strauss promised a future work, to be written with Alexandre Kojéve, that would show how Hobbes 'opens up the way to Hegel.' No such work was ever written.

"While I do not consider my book, *Thomas Hobbes: The Unity of Scientific and Political Wisdom,* to be a fulfillment of Strauss's promise, my work and *A Philosophical History of Rights* certainly do owe a debt to the later insights of Strauss.

"My work on Hobbes, focused as it was on understanding Hobbes's political theory of natural right, led me eventually to turn to the broader philosophical history of the concept, resulting in a ten-year study of the revolutionary development of the concept of rights. That research culminated in my 2002 book.

"Since then I have followed the course of philosophical history itself, going from a study of the concept of natural right to a study of the historical and philosophical origins and development of the contemporary concept of human rights. As part of that development in my philosophical interests, I accepted an offer to become editor of *Human Rights Review.*

"In the book I am now working on, I am undertaking a reexamination of the philosophy of the eighteenth-century philosopher Immanuel Kant. The goal of the book will be to reveal an original understanding of the concept of human rights that is not so susceptible to being criticized for being an ideological tool of western bourgeois individualism and, hence, a concept that can be embraced by ethnically diverse communities and that can fulfill the promise it originally held for the international community."

HERSHKOWITZ, Allen (J.) 1955-

PERSONAL: Born April 1, 1955, in New York, NY; married Margaret Carey, September, 1982; children: three. *Education:* University of Grenoble, certificate, 1975; City College of the City University of New York, B.A. (cum laude), 1978; City University of New York, M.Phil. (political economy), 1982, Ph.D. (political economy), 1986.

ADDRESSES: Home—Westchester County, NY. *Agent*—c/o Author Mail, Island Press, 1718 Connecticut Ave. N.W., Ste. 300, Washington, DC 20009.

CAREER: City University of New York, New York, NY, instructor, 1979-82; INFORM (environmental research group), New York, NY, director of solid waste research, 1982-86; U.S. Congressional Office of Technology, Washington, DC, assessor, 1986-88; Natural Resources Defense Council, New York, NY, senior scientist, 1989—, and director of National Solid Waste Project and Paper Industry Reform Project. National Academy of Sciences, past member of National Research Council Committee on the Health Effects of Waste Incineration; Environmental Protection Agency, past member of Science Advisory Board subcommittee on sludge incineration and participant in regulatory negotiations on fugitive emissions from equipment leaks at synthetic and organic chemical manufacturing industries; New York State Department of Environmental Conservation, past chair of Commissioner's Advisory Board on Operating Requirements for Municipal Solid Waste Incinerators; Bronx Community Paper Company Project, creator. Advisor to municipalities, legislative bodies, trade groups, and environmental organizations in the United States, Europe, Japan, and Central America; leader of government fact-finding missions; delegate to United Nations Treaty Convention on the Transboundary Movements of Hazardous Wastes, 1989; testifies for national, state, and local government proceedings; consultant to investment firms. Member of board of directors of Recycled Paper Coalition and Center for Labor and Community Research. Guest speaker at educational institutions, including Harvard University, Yale University, Massachusetts Institute of Technology, Columbia University, Princeton University, University of London, and Tufts University; guest on media programs in the United States and abroad, including *Larry King Live, Crossfire,* and National Public Radio broadcasts.

MEMBER: International Society of Industrial Ecology, Pulp and Paper Technical Association of Canada, New York Academy of Sciences.

AWARDS, HONORS: Special citation, American Institute of Architects honors committee, 2002, for work on a Bronx paper mill project.

WRITINGS:

Garbage Burning: Lessons from Europe, INFORM (New York, NY), 1986.
Garbage Management in Japan, INFORM (New York, NY), 1987.
Garbage: Practices, Problems, and Remedies, INFORM (New York, NY), 1988.
Too Good to Throw Away: Recycling's Proven Record, Natural Resources Defense Council (New York, NY), 1997.
Bronx Ecology: Blueprint for a New Environmentalism, Island Press (Washington, DC), 2002.

Contributor to periodicals, including *Technology Review, New York Times, Social Research, Atlantic Monthly, Newsday, Nation, City Limits, Amicus Journal, American Book Review,* and *Environmental Impact Assessment Review.*

BIOGRAPHICAL AND CRITICAL SOURCES:

BOOKS

Harris, Lis, *Tilting at Mills: Green Dreams, Dirty Dealings, and the Corporate Squeeze,* Houghton Mifflin (Boston, MA), 2003.

PERIODICALS

New Yorker, July, 1995.
OnEarth, winter, 2003, Richard Schrader, review of *Bronx Ecology: Blueprint for a New Environmentalism,* p. 40.

*   *   *

HEWAVITARNE, (Don) David 1864-1933
(Anagārika Dharmapāla, Anagarika Dharmapala)

PERSONAL: Born September 17, 1864, in Colombo, Ceylon (now Sri Lanka); died April 29, 1933, in Sarnath, India. *Religion:* Buddhist

CAREER: Organizer of Buddhist schools and other Buddhist institutions in India, after 1884, assuming the religious name Anag_rika Dharmap_la; international speaker on behalf of Buddhism (including various visits to the United States), beginning 1888; Maha Bodhi Society, Calcutta, India, founder, 1891, founder of British chapter, c. 1926; ordained *bhikkhu* (monk), 1933.

MEMBER: Theosophical Society.

WRITINGS:

UNDER NAME ANAGĀRIKA DHARMAPĀLA

The Arya Dharma of Sakya Muni, Maha Bodhi Society (Calcutta, India), 1917.
The Life and Teachings of Buddha, 5th edition, G. A. Natesan (Madras, India), 1943.
What Did the Lord Buddha Teach?, Maha Bodhi Society (Calcutta, India), 1951.
Return to Righteousness: A Collection of Speeches, Essays, and Letters of the Anagarika Dharmapala, edited by Ananda Guruge, Anagarika Dharmapala Birth Centenary Committee, Ministry of Education and Cultural Affairs (Ceylon), 1965.
Dharmapala lipi, 1965.
"From a Tiny Seed to a Healthy Tree": The Story of Mahabodhi; Reminiscences, edited by Lakshman Jayawardane, Mahabodhi Society of Sri Lanka (Colombo, Sri Lanka), 2001.

Other writings include *Bhagavan Buddha ka `siksha,* 1949; *History of an Ancient Civilization: Ceylon under British Rule,* International Buddhist League (Los Angeles, CA), 1902; *The Psychology of Progress; or, The Thirty-seven Principles of Bodhi,* 5th edition, Maha Bodhi Society (Colombo, Ceylon), 1946; and *Anagārika Dharmapālatumaga `srestha kiyaman saha javana caritaya,* 1964. Contributor to books, including *The World's Congress of Religions,* edited by J. W. Hanson, Monarch Book Co. (Chicago, IL), 1894. Founder, *Maha Bodhi Journal,* 1892, and *British Buddhist,* c. 1926.

Some of Hewavitarne's writings have been translated into German.

BIOGRAPHICAL AND CRITICAL SOURCES:

BOOKS

Religious Leaders of America, 2nd edition, Gale (Detroit, MI), 1999.

Sangharakshita, Maha Sthavira, Flame in Darkness: The Life and Sayings of Anagarika Dharmapala, Triratna Grantha Mala (Yerawada, India), 1980.*

*   *   *

HIGHAM, Nicholas
See HIGHAM, N(icholas) J(ohn)

*   *   *

HIGHAM, N(icholas) J(ohn)
(Nicholas Higham)

PERSONAL: Male.

ADDRESSES: Office—School of History, University of Manchester, Oxford Rd., Manchester M13 9PL, England. E-mail—nick.j.higham@Manchester.ac.uk.

CAREER: University of Manchester School of History and Classics, Manchester, England, reader in history and dean of undergraduate studies in the faculty of arts.

MEMBER: Society of Antiquaries (fellow).

AWARDS, HONORS: Leslie Fox Prize, 1988.

WRITINGS:

(As Nicholas Higham; with Barri Jones) The Carvetti, Sutton (Gloucester, England), 1985, new edition, 1991.

The Northern Counties to AD 1000 ("Regional History of England" series), Longman (New York, NY), 1986.

(As Nicholas Higham) Rome, Britain, and the Anglo-Saxons, Seaby (London, England), 1992.

The Kingdom of Northumbria: AD 350-1100, Sutton (Gloucester, England), 1993.

The Origins of Cheshire, Manchester University Press (Manchester, England), 1993.

The Death of Anglo-Saxon England, Sutton (Gloucester, England), 1997.

The Norman Conquest, Sutton (Gloucester, England), 1998.

King Arthur: Myth-making and History, Routledge (New York, NY), 2002.

Contributor to books, including Blackwell's Companion to Anglo-Saxon England, Oxford University Press, 1999, and Medieval Archaeology: An Encyclopaedia, Garland (New York, NY), 2001. Contributor to periodicals, including Archaeological Journal, Northern History, Speculum, Medieval Archaeology, Welsh History Review, Britannia, and Landscapes.

"ORIGINS OF ENGLAND" TRILOGY

The English Conquest: Gildas and Britain in the Fifth Century, Manchester University Press (Manchester, England), 1994.

An English Empire: Bede and the Early Anglo-Saxon Kings, Manchester University Press (Manchester, England), 1995.

The Convert Kings: Power and Religious Affiliation in Early Anglo-Saxon England, Manchester University Press (Manchester, England), 1997.

EDITOR

The Changing Past, Manchester University (Manchester, England), 1979.

Excavations at Ordsall Hall Demesne Farm, 1978-79, Greater Manchester Archaeological Group (Manchester, England), 1980.

(With D. H. Hill) Edward the Elder, 899-924, Routledge (New York, NY), 2001.

Archaeology of the Roman Empire: A Tribute to the Life and Works of Professor Barri Jones, Archaeopress (Oxford, England), 2001.

SIDELIGHTS: An archaeologist by training, N. J. Higham is a reader of history at the University of Manchester. His 1986 book, The Northern Counties to

AD 1000, is a social and economic history of England from 685 to 1000. Filled with illustrations and maps covering the area between Hadrian's Wall and Yorkshire, the work also examines England's landscape. *Encounter* contributor Peter Levi found the book "unsmoothly written and not without jargon," but the reviewer added that Higham's effort "tells one exactly what one wants to know, and improves on those huge standard works in which one may delve in vain." *The Kingdom of Northumbria: AD 350-1100* relates the history of northern England from its years under Roman rule to the Norman Conquest. Higham combines many sources into a continuous narrative, an approach that *History Today* reviewer Catherine Hills found problematic. As Hill stated, "Because this is a synthesis it is not easy to distinguish between conventional precis of accepted wisdom, summaries of current debate which might not be universally agreed, and brief statements of new or recent research. The single authorial voice gives the same status to everything." Nevertheless, Hill called the work "well-written and lavishly illustrated."

Higham began his "Origins of England" trilogy with the 1994 book *The English Conquest: Gildas and Britain in the Fifth Century.* In this controversial work, he looks at the fall of Roman Britain and the origins of Saxon England. He examines Britsh Christian historian Gildas's *Analysis of Liber Querulus de Excidio Britanniae*—translated as *The Ruin of Britain*—which he claims "almost alone offers the opportunity to examine the 'beginnings" of England as an historical, as opposed to an archaeological, problem." Asserting that biblical and ecclesiastical sources determined the historian's ideological framework, Higham suggests that Gildas's writings were, "by implication, justifying British warfare against the Saxons." E. J. Kealy praised the work, writing in *Choice* that "Higham's challenge to accepted scholarship deserves wide reading by graduate students and scholars." *Times Literary Supplement* reviewer Patrick Sims-Williams was more skeptical, observing, "The so-called 'big bang' theory of England's origin is stimulating, ingenious and worth attention, but appears to be generated by Higham's compressed chronology rather than by Gildas's own inscrutable text."

The second volume in Higham's trilogy, *An English Empire: Bede and the Early Anglo-Saxon Kings,* concerns the political systems in southern Britain around 597 to 633 AD, as well as the Saxon empires in the age of Bede. Higham reinterprets research findings and gives an characteristically unconventional reading of Gildas. He argues that Bede tried to legitimize English dominion, and contends that stable rule existed within the small system of monarchies in England at that time. Higham also offers new insights into rural life through the relations between Britons and Anglo-Saxons. In *Choice,* J. L. Leland offered qualified praise for the volume, remarking that, "Overall, Higham's use of sources is idiosyncratic . . . but his speculations seriously challenge many received opinions." In the concluding volume of the series, *The Convert Kings: Power and Religious Affiliation in Early Anglo-Saxon England,* Higham studies the Anglo-Saxon kings' conversion to Christianity during the seventh century. The author suggests that Christianity was politically useful because its monotheism and hierarchical structure supported a growing centralized and hierarchical monarchy. As K. F. Drew noted in *Choice,* "The presentation of the theoretical foundation of Higham's argument is clear enough." Drew added, however, that "his work demonstrates the extreme weakness of the [historical] sources," many of which are drawn from the perspective of the church.

In 2002 Higham published *King Arthur: Myth-making and History,* "a sceptical survey of the debate on the historical Arthur," according to Richard Barber in the *Journal of Ecclesiastical History.* In the work, Higham analyzes the *Historia Brittonum* and the *Annales Cambriae,* two early sources of the Arthurian legend. For Higham, according to *Times Literary Supplement* reviewer Carolyne Larrington, "the essential question, mercifully, is not 'who was the real Arthur?'" Instead, Larrington noted, "the question is why and how these two histories—and no others in a period of 500 years—make use of Arthur." In the view of *Medium Aevum* contributor Stephen Knight, "Higham's scholarly and intelligent study of the early materials associated with Arthur is highly welcome."

BIOGRAPHICAL AND CRITICAL SOURCES:

PERIODICALS

Albion, fall, 2003, Patrick Wormald, review of *King Arthur: Myth-making and History,* p. 454.
Choice, January, 1995, E. J. Kealey, review of *The English Conquest: Gildas and Britain in the Fifth Century,* p. 848; March, 1996, J. L. Leland, review

of *An English Empire: Bede and the Early Anglo-Saxon Kings,* p. 1196; December, 1997, K. F. Drew, review of *The Convert Kings: Power and Religious Affiliation in Early Anglo-Saxon England,* p. 700.

Contemporary Review, February, 2003, review of *The Convert Kings,* p. 112.

Encounter, July-August, 1986, Peter Levi, review of *The Northern Counties to AD 1000,* p. 44.

English Historical Review, February, 1997, D. P. Kirby, review of *The English Conquest,* p. 155; September, 1997, Barbara Yorke, review of *An English Empire,* p. 957; February, 2003, John Blair, review of *Edward the Elder, 899-924,* p. 168.

History Today, March, 1994, Catherine Hills, "Retreading Old Ground," review of *The Kingdom of Northumbria: AD 350-1100,* p. 54; March, 1998, Barbara Mitchell, "Sparrow on the Wing," review of *The Convert Kings,* p. 56.

Journal of American Culture, September, 2003, Ray B. Browne, review of *King Arthur,* p. 417.

Journal of Church and State, spring, 1999, Donathan Taylor, review of *The Convert Kings,* p. 384.

Journal of Ecclesiastical History, October, 1998, D. P. Kirby, review of *The Convert Kings,* p. 715; January, 2004, Richard Barber, review of *King Arthur,* p. 118.

Medium Aevum, fall, 2003, Stephen Knight, review of *King Arthur,* p. 308.

Times Literary Supplement, May 26, 1995, Patrick Sim-Williams, "A British Jihad?," review of *The English Conquest,* p. 27; April 16, 1999, George Garnett, "English Heritage," review of *The Death of Anglo-Saxon England;* July 12, 2002, Carolyne Larrington, "Joshua in Camelot," review of *King Arthur.*

ONLINE

University of Manchester Web site, http://www.arts.manchester.ac.uk/ (February 15, 2005), "Dr. Nick Higham."*

*   *   *

HILL, Ernest 1961(?)-

PERSONAL: Born c. 1961, in Oak Grove, LA; son of Charley (a teacher, coach, and factory supervisor) and Katie (a teacher) Hill. *Education:* Attended Northeast Louisiana University; University of California, Berkeley, bachelor's degree (social science); Cornell University, M.A. (African studies); University of California, Los Angeles, Ph.D.

ADDRESSES: *Home*—Baton Rouge, LA. *Office*—Southern University, 2012 T. H. Harris Hall, P.O. Box 9671, Baton Rouge, LA 70813.

CAREER: Southern University, Baton Rouge, LA, writer-in-residence.

AWARDS, HONORS: Dorothy Danforth Compton doctoral fellowship.

WRITINGS:

NOVELS

Satisfied with Nothin', Pickaninny Productions (Los Angeles, CA), 1992, Simon & Schuster (New York, NY), 1996.

A Life for a Life, Simon & Schuster (New York, NY), 1998.

Cry Me a River, Dafina Books (New York, NY), 2003.

It's All about the Moon When the Sun Ain't Shining, Dafina Books (New York, NY), 2004.

SIDELIGHTS: Louisiana native Ernest Hill, a writer-in-residence at Southern University, is the author of novels that explore the African-American experience. His self-published debut, *Satisfied with Nothin',* concerns Jamie Ray Griffin, a young black man from a small Louisiana town who becomes one of the first students to integrate the local high school. His talents on the football field earn him the respect of the community and a college scholarship, but a knee injury in college ends his dreams of a professional career. Jamie's bitterness is fueled by the prejudice he faces and the injustices he witnesses, including a horrific lynching involving his cousin. "The brutal honesty of the characters' circumstances, emotions and realistic experiences make this an exceptional literary piece," remarked *Booklist* critic Lillian Lewis. *Philadelphia Tribune* contributor Kevin Omo Oni wrote that *Satisfied with Nothin'* "probes deeply into some of America's most severe societal banes—racism, complacency, and despondency."

An ultimatum leads to tragedy in *A Life for a Life,* Hill's 1998 novel. When a drug dealer kidnaps the younger brother of fifteen-year-old D'Ray Reid, D'Ray has one hour to pay the one hundred-dollar ransom. Desperate, the teen robs a convenience store, fatally wounding the clerk, a bright, young African American named Stanley Earl. While serving a life sentence for the crime, D'Ray is visited by Henry Earl, the father of the murder victim, who over time becomes a father figure to D'Ray. Henry "transcends the anger and despair he feels over his son's death," noted Mary A. McCay in the New Orleans *Times-Picayune.* He gives D'Ray "the opportunity to stand in Stanley's place, to go to college, to make something of life, as Stanley would have, and it is the opportunity for redemption." In *A Life for a Life,* Hill "has a sure hand with pacing and he renders pitch-perfect dialogue that instantly establishes character and fuels the plot with tension," noted a critic in *Publishers Weekly.* Though some critics faulted the book's sentimental ending, others praised the conclusion. As Fran Handman noted in the *New York Times Book Review,* "Despite Henry Earl's iron determination, D'Ray's redemption is far from a forgone conclusion."

Cry Me a River, published in 2003, focuses on Tyrone Stokes, a former drug addict who is released on parole after spending ten years in a Louisiana prison. He arrives home to find that his seventeen-year-old son, Marcus, is on death row for the rape and murder of a white girl. Although the execution is only eight days away, Tyrone is determined to prove his son's innocence. He begins his own investigation, assisted by an old friend, Beggar Man, and soon discovers evidence that casts doubt on Marcus's conviction. Stokes risks his own safety "to end the suffering that his son, wife, and family have endured because of his incarceration," noted *Booklist* critic Lillian Lewis; at the same time, he must "come to terms with his past . . . as well as his family's varied reactions to his presence at home and his son's situation—his mother's sadness, his sister's hostility, his estranged wife's grief, and his father-in-law's rage," Susan Larson wrote in the New Orleans *Times-Picayune.* Larson added that Hill "spins the web of family love and resentment with ease."

In 2004 Hill published his fourth novel, *It's All about the Moon When the Sun Ain't Shining.* Maurice Dupree, the story's protagonist, is preparing for his final semester at Louisiana State University and is ready to begin law school, much to the delight of his hard-working parents. Returning to his hometown during semester break, Maurice wrestles with his decision to delay marrying his longtime girlfriend, Omenita, until after he earns his law degree. Reviewing *It's All about the Moon When the Sun Ain't Shining* in *Booklist,* Vanessa Bush stated that Hill "offers a poignant portrait of a young man at a crossroads in his life," and Larson remarked in the New Orleans *Times-Picayune* that the author "writes simply yet beautifully of the tug of family ties and the pull of great dreams."

BIOGRAPHICAL AND CRITICAL SOURCES:

PERIODICALS

Afro-American Red Star, August 17, 1996, Kip Branch, "New Book *Satisfied with Nothin'* Echoes Struggles of Black Authors Richard Wright, Ralph Ellison," p. B5.

Atlanta Journal-Constitution, August 12, 1998, Don O'Briant, "Author Ernest Hill: 'Never Be Satisfied with Nothin''," p. F1; July 18, 2004, Hal Jacobs," Reading the South," review of *It's All about the Moon When the Sun Ain't Shining,* p. L5.

Booklist, August, 1996, Lillian Lewis, review of *Satisfied with Nothin',* p. 1881; June 1, 1998, Vanessa Bush, review of *A Life for a Life,* p. 1726; February 15, 2003, Lillian Lewis, review of *Cry Me a River,* p. 1043; June 1, 2004, Vanessa Bush, review of *It's All about the Moon When the Sun Ain't Shining,* p. 1700.

Chicago Independent Bulletin, September 12, 1996, Hurley Green, Sr., "Shifting Scenes: Opportunities Lost," review of *Satisfied with Nothin',* p. 4.

Kirkus Reviews, March 1, 2003, review of *Cry Me a River,* p. 334.

Library Journal, July, 1998, Shirley Gibson Coleman, review of *A Life for a Life,* p. 136.

New York Amsterdam News, December 24, 1997, Yusef Salaam, "Ernest Hill's *Satisfied with Nothin',*" p. 28.

New York Times Book Review, November 15, 1998, Fran Handman, review of *A Life for a Life,* p. 63.

Philadelphia Tribune, October 25, 1996, Kevin Omo Oni, review of *Satisfied with Nothin',* p. 11.

Publishers Weekly, July 1, 1996, review of *Satisfied with Nothin',* p. 43; June 15, 1998, review of *A Life for a Life,* p. 43.

Times-Picayune (New Orleans, LA), January 19, 1997, Mary A. McCay, "Dead End Zone," review of *Satisfied with Nothin'*, p. D7; September 6, 1998, Mary A. McCay, "'Life' Class," review of *A Life for a Life*, p. D6; May 11, 2003, Susan Larson, "Redemption Song," review of *Cry Me a River*, p. 7; July 4, 2004, Susan Larson, "Home Truths," review of *It's All about the Moon When the Sun Ain't Shining*, p. 4.*

*   *   *

HILLHOUSE, Raelynn (J.)

PERSONAL: Born in MO. *Education:* Washington University, B.A.; University of Michigan, M.A., Ph.D.; also attended Moscow State University, Moscow Finance Institute, Humboldt University (Berlin, Germany), Eberhard-Karls-Universität, and Babes-Bolyai University.

ADDRESSES: Home—HI. *Agent*—Scott Miller, Trident Media Group, 41 Madison Ave., 36th Fl., New York, NY, 10010. *E-mail*—RaelynnHillhouse@msn.com.

CAREER: Writer, educator, and health-care administrator. Also worked as a smuggler and money launderer in Eastern Europe.

MEMBER: Association for Former Intelligence Officers, International Thriller Writers, Inc.

AWARDS, HONORS: Fulbright fellowship; International Research and Exchanges Board scholarship; Foreign Languages and Area Studies fellowship; National Merit Award; Best Books designation, American Booksellers Association, 2004, for *Rift Zone*.

WRITINGS:

Rift Zone (novel), Forge (New York, NY), 2004.

Contributor to *Spirit of Aloha* and *Mystery Scene*. Contributor of articles about Eastern Europe to academic journals.

SIDELIGHTS: An expert on Central and Eastern Europe, Raelynn Hillhouse is the author of the 2004 novel *Rift Zone*, "a satisfying international thriller," according to *Booklist* critic David Wright.

Hillhouse was born in the Ozarks in Missouri, but moved to Europe at the age of twenty to pursue her education. While living in Germany, she began to run Cuban rum between East and West Berlin, smuggle jewelry and works of art from the Soviet Union to the West, and launder money from East Bloc nations. "I crossed the Iron Curtain hundreds of times and I usually had something with me I shouldn't have had," Hillhouse stated on her Web site. "I know from firsthand experience what it's like to be taken aside for questioning and have your belongings ransacked. I also know what it's like to suddenly find yourself in a situation when soldiers are pointing Kalishnikovs at you; civilian police are running toward you and everyone is yelling at you in a language you don't understand."

Rift Zone, Hillhouse's debut novel, is based on the author's own experiences. Set in 1989, the work concerns Faith Whitney, a smuggler who becomes involved in an East German plot to assassinate Soviet leader Mikhail Gorbachev. To prevent this disaster, Faith must rely on her old boyfriend Max Summers, an explosives expert, as well as on her estranged mother, a former smuggler who now operates an orphanage in Moscow.

Rift Zone received generally positive reviews. Eugen Weber, a contributor to the *Los Angeles Times Book Review*, described the novel as "evocative, gripping and convincing." In the words of *Library Journal* critic Ronnie H. Terpening, "a resourceful female protagonist, sexual undertones, explosive tension, and tradecraft galore add up to a spellbinding tale."

BIOGRAPHICAL AND CRITICAL SOURCES:

PERIODICALS

Booklist, July, 2004, David Wright, review of *Rift Zone*, p. 1798.
Kirkus Reviews, review of *Rift Zone*, p. 596.
Library Journal, Ronnie H. Terpening, review of *Rift Zone*, p. 70.

Los Angeles Times Book Review, October 17, 2004, Eugen Weber, "L. A. Confidential," review of *Rift Zone,* p. R9.

People, September 6, 2004, review of *Rift Zone,* p. 60.

St. Louis Post-Dispatch, September 8, 2004, John M. McGuire, "The Spy Who Loved It," review of *Rift Zone,* p. E1.

Tribune Books (Chicago, IL), August 22, 2004, Dick Adler, "Smugglers, Spies, Killers, and More," review of *Rift Zone,* p. 3.

ONLINE

Bookreporter.com, http://www.bookreporter.com/ (September 10, 2004), interview with Hillhouse.

Raelynn J. Hillhouse Home Page, http://www.internationalthrillers.com (March 15, 2005).

*   *   *

HOBDAY, Charles (Henry) 1917-2005

OBITUARY NOTICE— See index for *CA* sketch: Born September 9, 1917, in Eastbourne, Sussex, England; died March 2, 2005, in London, England. Author. Hobday was a leftist poet associated with the Salisbury Group and the magazine *Our Time* who later gained acclaim for his nonfiction books. Though he was of draft age, medical reasons kept him out of World War II. Instead, he completed his B.A. in 1939 and M.A. in 1941, both from Queen Mary College, London. He then worked as a teacher in London and published his poems in *Our Time.* A leftist idealist, he joined the Communist Party by 1938 and became associated with the Salisbury Group of poets who held similar beliefs, including Jack Lindsay, Edgell Rickword, *Our Time*'s editor, and Doris Lessing. Many of these poets, including Hobday, abandoned communism in protest after the Soviets invaded Hungary in 1956. Publishing poems in journals was not sufficient to earn a living, so Hobday became a subeditor for Hutchinson Publishing for two years after the war. In 1949 he joined Keesing's Publications, where he did similar work until retiring in 1982. Though Hobday would publish such poetry collections as *The Return of Cain* (1974) and *Talking of Michelangelo* (1978), it was for the non-poetic works published after his retirement that he became best known. These include the biography *Edgell Rickword: A Poet at War* (1989), the edited

collection *The Collected Poems of Edgell Rickword* (1991), and the literary study *A Golden Ring: English Poets in Florence from 1373 to the Present Day* (1998). His last books were *How Goes the Enemy?: Selected Poems 1960-2000* (2000) and *Elegy for a Sergeant* (2002), a paean to his uncle, who died fighting in World War I.

OBITUARIES AND OTHER SOURCES:

PERIODICALS

Guardian (London, England), March 16, 2005, p. 25.

Independent (London, England), March 15, 2005, p. 37.

*   *   *

HOLMES, Olivia 1958-

PERSONAL: Born September 15, 1958, in Albany, NY; daughter of J. Everitt (a science writer) and Beatrice (an historian; maiden name, Hort) Holmes; married Mario Moroni (a professor), June 10, 1989; children: Jacopo. *Ethnicity:* "White." *Education:* Yale University, B.A., 1980; University of Iowa, M.F.A., 1982; Northwestern University, Ph.D., 1994. *Politics:* Democrat.

ADDRESSES: Home—31 Gilman St., Waterville, ME 04901-5440. *Office*—Department of Italian, Yale University, P.O. Box 208311, New Haven, CT 06520-8311. *E-mail*—olivia.holmes@yale.edu.

CAREER: Yale University, New Haven, CT, assistant professor, 1996-2002, associate professor of Italian language and literature, 2002—.

MEMBER: Modern Language Association of America, Association of Italian Studies, Dante Society of America.

AWARDS, HONORS: Book Award, American Association of Italian Studies, 2000, for *Assembling the Lyric Self.*

WRITINGS:

Assembling the Lyric Self, University of Minnesota Press (Minneapolis, MN), 2000.

WORK IN PROGRESS: Dante's Two Beloved: Ethics as Erotic Choice.

*   *   *

HOOPER, Tobe 1943-

PERSONAL: Born January 25, 1943, in Austin, TX; companion of Marcia Zwilling. *Education:* Studied film at the University of Texas.

ADDRESSES: Agent—William Morris Agency, 151 El Camino Dr., Beverly Hills, CA 90212.

CAREER: Director, producer, and screenwriter. Director of films, including *Eggshells,* 1970, *The Texas Chainsaw Massacre,* 1974, *Eaten Alive,* 1976, *The Funhouse,* 1981, *Poltergeist,* 1982, *Lifeforce,* 1985, *Invaders from Mars,* 1986, *The Texas Chainsaw Massacre, Part II,* 1986, *Spontaneous Combustion,* 1989, *Leatherface: The Texas Chainsaw Massacre III,* 1990, *Tobe Hooper's Night Terrors,* 1993, *The Mangler,* 1995, *Crocodile,* 2000, and *Toolbox Murders,* 2003. Producer of films, including *The Texas Chainsaw Massacre,* 1974, and *The Texas Chainsaw Massacre, Part II,* 1986. Director of television programs, including *'Salem's Lot,* 1979, *I'm Dangerous Tonight,* 1990, *Haunted Lives . . . True Ghost Stories,* 1991, *Real Ghosts II,* 1996, *The Apartment Complex,* 1999, and episodes of *Amazing Stories, The Equalizer, Freddy's Nightmares, Tales from the Crypt, John Carpenter Presents Body Bags, Dark Skies, Perversions of Science, The Others, Night Visions,* and *Taken.* Also creator of *Down Friday Street* (film about the conservation of old homes), and Public Broadcasting Service (PBS) documentary *Peter, Paul, and Mary in Concert,* 1971; director of television commercials and of music video for Billy Idol's "Dancing with Myself," 1983. Actor in film *Sleepwalkers,* 1992, and *John Carpenter's Bodybags,* 1993; University of Texas film program, Austin, former assistant director.

WRITINGS:

SCREENPLAYS

(With Kim Hendel; and director and producer) *The Texas Chainsaw Massacre,* Bryanston, 1974.

(And director, composer, and coproducer) *The Texas Chainsaw Massacre, Part II,* Cannon, 1986.
(And director) *Spontaneous Combustion,* Taurus Entertainment, 1989.
(And creator, with Kim Hendel) *Leatherface: The Texas Chainsaw Massacre III,* New Line Cinema, 1990.
(And director) *The Mangler,* New Line Cinema, 1995.

SIDELIGHTS: Filmmaker Tobe Hooper gained dubious distinction and an immediate cult following with the 1974 release of *The Texas Chainsaw Massacre,* a notoriously horrific low-budget film about a chainsaw-wielding psychopath. The film's shocking barbarity and emphasis on sensational killing signaled a departure from mainstream Hollywood horror movies, precipitating a boom in so-called slasher films during the 1970s and 1980s. While Hooper's name is inextricably associated with the violent—and, some would argue, debased—genre he helped spawn, he has also earned critical esteem for his contributions to several television series and his work as director of the 1982 film *Poltergeist.*

The Texas Chainsaw Massacre was written by Hooper and Kim Henkel; the film's signature villain, Leatherface, was loosely modeled on Ed Gein, a Wisconsin man arrested in 1957 for the murder and dismemberment of at least fifteen individuals. It was discovered that Gein had fashioned his victim's skin and bones into clothing, furniture, and household items. Commenting on the film's ad hoc assembly and homemade special effects, Charlie Haas remarked in *New Times,* "*The Texas Chainsaw Massacre* was made in 1974, using six weeks' production time, a cast of unknown Texas-based actors, a budget of about $300,000, and part or all of eight cows, a cat, two deer, three goats, two dogs, two human skeletons, one chicken, and one armadillo."

The plot of the film is simple: a coven of cannibalistic serial killers in rural Texas terrorize a group of hapless young hippies. Stranded at a deserted house, the hippies visit a nearby farmhouse in search of gas for their van. There they encounter Leatherface, who dispatches one youth with a hammer and hangs another on a meat hook. When the murdered teens fail to return to the group, their companions set out to find them. They, too, are confronted by Leatherface, who kills the remaining two males and chases the surviving female into the farmhouse, where she discovers a menagerie of corpses and sadistic equipment. The woman manages to escape to a gas station restaurant, but is brought back to the house by the cook who, she realizes, is in cahoots with Leatherface and a demented hitchhiker whom the hippies had earlier picked up. Rather than kill the women themselves, Leatherface and the hitchhiker turn her over to their bloodthirsty grandfather who, it becomes apparent, is too feeble to kill the young woman with his hammer strikes. Again, the woman breaks free, this time flagging down a passing pickup truck and narrowly escaping Leatherface's flailing chainsaw.

Though many early reviewers of the film objected to its gratuitous violence and sickening scenes of degradation, other critics, notably sophisticates in New York and Hollywood, came to admire its aesthetic originality and emotional power. "For a low-budget horror movie," noted Hass, "it had exceptional visual style, performances, humor and special effects." But even more, Hass added, "it was absolutely terrifying." As many commentators have observed, the film's association with gruesome violence is undeserved, as the film itself contains very few scenes of actual bloodshed. Instead, like the films of Alfred Hitchcock, *The Texas Chainsaw Massacre* terrifies audiences through the mere suggestion of violence rather than in graphic displays of gore. However, citing significant differences between Hitchcock and Hooper, a *Variety* reviewer noted that Hitchcock's *Psycho* "concentrated on the causes for bloodletting, while 'Chainsaw' indulges in the effects."

Despite the mass appeal of *The Texas Chainsaw Massacre* among younger audiences, Hooper continued to work on low-budget films for the next several years. He directed *Eaten Alive,* a movie about a psychotic, Norman Bates-like motel owner who feeds a wayward prostitute and several guests to a crocodile, and *The Funhouse,* in which a group of teens spend an ill-advised night in a carnival funhouse where they are successively killed off by a hideous masked freak. Though *The Funhouse* was judged more impressive than *Eaten Alive,* both films helped solidify Hooper's reputation as an innovator in the horror genre. Between these two films, Hooper also directed the 1979 television miniseries *Salem's Lot,* an adaptation of Stephen King's best-selling horror novel.

Hooper's work on *The Funhouse* attracted the attention of filmmaker Steven Spielberg, who recruited Hooper to direct *Poltergeist,* a film produced by Spielberg. The movie, about the paranormal haunting of a suburban family whose home is built on the site of an old cemetery, was a box office hit. Commenting on the film in *Horror Film Directors, 1931-1990,* Dennis Fischer wrote, "*Poltergeist* proved an effective combining of two talents, but the end product looked more like a Spielberg movie than a Hooper movie, with the result that stories circulated that Spielberg had 'ghost'-directed the film, though Spielberg himself took an ad out in the trades to compliment Hooper on his fine direction." As Fischer added, "There is no question that producer and coscripter Spielberg had a profound effect on the overall film and that he took an active role in its complicated production, but it would also be unfair not to give Hooper any credit."

After the failure of his next two films, *Lifeforce* and *Invaders from Mars,* a remake of William Cameron Menzies's 1950 science-fiction classic, Hooper worked on a sequel to *The Texas Chainsaw Massacre.* The film was harried from the start by impossible expectations and a tight production schedule that resulted in awkward editing. The sequel reprises three key members of the original "Chainsaw" family— Leatherface, the grandfather, and the gas station cook—and introduces a new figure, Chop Top, a deranged Vietnam veteran. Instead of living in a farmhouse and preying upon hippies, as in the original, the 1980s-era sequel finds them living beneath an abandoned amusement park and brutalizing yuppies, a far less sympathetic social group.

"Unlike the first film," wrote Fischer, "*Chainsaw 2* encourages its audiences to be on the side of the maniacs by making the first victims, a pair of obnoxious yuppies in a Mercedes, so unlikable." In a *Chicago Sun-Times* review, Roger Ebert panned the sequel as crass mockery of the original. Contrasting the "raw, naked force" of the first *Chainsaw* movie with the sequel, Ebert wrote, "'Part 2' has a lot of blood and disembowelment, to be sure, but it doesn't have the terror of the original, the desire to be taken seriously. It's a geek show." As Fischer concluded, "While its sick humour is outrageous, *Chainsaw 2* in no way matches the mood of the original film to which it is supposed to be a companion piece." Hooper collaborated with Henkel on the creation of a third *Chainsaw* film, released in 1990 as *Leatherface: Texas Chainsaw Massacre III,* but declined to direct it.

During the 1990s Hooper directed three additional films: *Spontaneous Combustion, Night Terrors,* and

The Mangler all failed to impress critics or audiences. Commenting on *Spontaneous Combustion,* Fischer wrote that the film is "a mess." Critics of *The Mangler,* an adaptation of a Stephen King short story, found the film's premise—a cruel Laundromat owner runs an industrial ironing machine that preys upon humans—unbelievable and silly. Assessing the film in *Entertainment Weekly,* Glenn Kenny wrote that, "When *The Mangler* works, which is only about half the time, it's an irreverent goof." Geoffrey Cheshire, writing in *Variety,* was somewhat less charitable, concluding that *The Mangler* suffers from a "clunky narrative and lack of solid scares" that, in the end, offers "little to excite fans of 'Elm Street'-style shockers or Hooper's own 'Poltergeist.'"

While Hooper has struggled to recapture the success of his early horror films, notably *The Texas Chainsaw Massacre,* he has directed a number of less-prominent but entertaining television programs and worked on episodes for several popular television series, including *Amazing Stories, Tales from the Crypt,* and John Carpenter's Showtime series *Body Bags.*

BIOGRAPHICAL AND CRITICAL SOURCES:

BOOKS

Fischer, Dennis, *Horror Film Directors, 1931-1990,* McFarland (Jefferson, NC), 1991.

PERIODICALS

Chicago Sun-Times, August 25, 1986, Roger Ebert, review of *The Texas Chainsaw Massacre, Part II;* October 17, 2003, Roger Ebert, "'Massacre' Is Murder to Sit Through," p. 40.

Daily Herald (Arlington Heights, IL), October 17, 2003, Dann Gire, "'Massacre' Fails to Capture the Terror, Thrills of Original," p. 51.

Entertainment Weekly, December 24, 1993, Glenn Kenny, review of "Eye," pp. 66-67; August 18, 1995, Glenn Kenny, pp. 62-63; August 25-September 1, 1995, review of *Nowhere Man,* p. 98; October 17, 2003, Rebecca Ascher-Walsh, review of *Texas Chainsaw Massacre,* p. 67.

Journal Star, October 23, 2003, Brad Burke, "'Massacre' Sick and Slick but Doesn't Stick," section C, p. 3.

Knight Ridder/Tribune News Service, October 17, 2003, Glenn Lovell, section K, p. 325.

New York Times Book Review, June 4, 1982, Vincent Canby, review of *Poltergeist.*

People, August 9, 1993, David Hiltbrand, review of "Eye."

Variety, November 6, 1974, review of *The Texas Chainsaw Massacre,* p. 20; April 21, 1976, Vernee Watson, review of *Death Trap,* p. 30; March 6-12, 1995, Godfrey Cheshire, review of *The Mangler,* p. 66; September 23-29, 1996, Ray Richmond, review of *Dark Skies,* p. 51.*

*   *   *

HORNSBLOW, Doreen (?)-2001
(Sally Wentworth)

PERSONAL: Born in Watford, Hertfordshire, England; died in 2001; married Donald Alfred Hornsblow; children: one son.

CAREER: Romance novelist; Associated Newspapers Ltd., London, England, accounts clerk; Consumers' Association, Hertford, England, accounts clerk. Hertford Association of National Trust Members, founding chair, 1985, life president.

WRITINGS:

ROMANCE NOVELS UNDER PSEUDONYM SALLY WENTWORTH

Island Masquerade, Mills and Boon (London, England), 1977, Silhouette (New York, NY), 1978.

King of the Castle, Silhouette (New York, NY), 1978.

Conflict in Paradise, Silhouette (New York, NY), 1978.

Rightful Possession, Silhouette (New York, NY), 1978, published with *The Master Fiddler* by Janet Dailey and *Forest of the Night* by Jane Donnelly, Romance Treasury Association (New York, NY), 1988.

Liberated Lady, Silhouette (New York, NY), 1979.

Shattered Dreams, Mills and Boon (London, England), 1979, Silhouette (New York, NY), 1983.

The Ice Maiden, Mills and Boon (London, England), 1979, Silhouette (New York, NY), 1980.

Candle in the Wind, Mills and Boon (London, England), 1979, Silhouette (New York, NY), 1980.

Garden of Thorns, Silhouette (New York, NY), 1980.

Set the Stars on Fire, Silhouette (New York, NY), 1980.

Betrayal in Bali, Silhouette (New York, NY), 1980.

Race against Love, Mills and Boon (London, England), 1980, Silhouette (New York, NY), 1981.

Summer Love, Silhouette (New York, NY), 1981.

Say Hello to Yesterday, Silhouette (New York, NY), 1981.

King of Culla, Silhouette (New York, NY), 1981.

The Judas Kiss, Mills and Boon (London, England), 1981, Silhouette (New York, NY), 1982.

The Sea Master, Mills and Boon (London, England), 1981, Silhouette (New York, NY), 1982.

Semi-detached Marriage, New York, Silhouette, 1982.

Man for Hire, Silhouette (New York, NY), 1982.

Flying High, Mills and Boon (London, England), 1982, Silhouette (New York, NY), 1983.

Jilted, Silhouette (New York, NY), 1983.

The Lion Rock, Mills and Boon (London, England), 1983, Silhouette (New York, NY), 1984.

Backfire, Mills and Boon (London, England), 1983, Silhouette (New York, NY), 1984.

Dark Awakening, Silhouette (New York, NY), 1984.

Viking Invader, Silhouette (New York, NY), 1984.

The Wings of Love, Silhouette (New York, NY), 1985.

Fatal Deception, Silhouette (New York, NY), 1985.

The Hawk of Venice, Mills and Boon (London, England), 1985, Silhouette (New York, NY), 1986.

The Kissing Game, Silhouette (New York, NY), 1986.

Cage of Ice, Mills and Boon (London, England), 1986, Silhouette (New York, NY), 1987.

Tiger in His Lair, Mills and Boon (London, England), 1986, Silhouette (New York, NY), 1987.

Passionate Revenge, Mills and Boon (London, England), 1987, Silhouette (New York, NY), 1988.

Ultimatum, Mills and Boon (London, England), 1987, Silhouette (New York, NY), 1988.

Dishonourable Intentions, London, Mills and Boon, 1987, Silhouette (New York, NY), 1988.

Mistaken Wedding, Silhouette (New York, NY), 1988.

Satan's Island, Mills and Boon (London, England), 1988, Silhouette (New York, NY), 1989.

Driving Force, Mills and Boon (London, England), 1988, Silhouette (New York, NY), 1989.

The Devil's Shadow, Mills and Boon (London, England), 1988, Silhouette (New York, NY), 1989.

Strange Encounter, Mills and Boon (London, England), 1989, Silhouette (New York, NY), 1990.

Echoes from the Past, Mills and Boon (London, England), 1989, Silhouette (New York, NY), 1990.

Wish on the Moon, Mills and Boon (London, England), 1989, Silhouette (New York, NY), 1990.

Fire Island, Mills and Boon (London, England), 1989, Silhouette (New York, NY), 1991.

Lord of Misrule, Mills and Boon (London, England), 1990, Silhouette (New York, NY), 1991.

Taken on Trust, Mills and Boon (London, England), 1990, Silhouette (New York, NY), 1991.

Illusions of Love, Mills and Boon (London, England), 1990, Silhouette (New York, NY), 1992.

Broken Destiny, Mills and Boon (London, England), 1990, Silhouette (New York, NY), 1992.

The Devil's Kiss, Mills and Boon (London, England), 1991, Silhouette (New York, NY), 1992.

Twin Torment, Silhouette (New York, NY), 1991.

Ghost of the Past, Silhouette (New York, NY), 1991.

The Golden Greek, Mills and Boon (London, England), 1991, Silhouette (New York, NY), 1993.

Stormy Voyage, Mills and Boon (London, England), 1992, Silhouette (New York, NY), 1993.

Wayward Wife, Silhouette (New York, NY), 1992.

Yesterday's Affair, Mills and Boon (London, England), 1992, Silhouette (New York, NY), 1993.

Mirrors of the Sea, Silhouette (New York, NY), 1993.

Practise to Deceive, Silhouette (New York, NY), 1993.

Sicilian Spring, Silhouette (New York, NY), 1993.

Shadow Play, Harlequin (New York, NY), 1994.

Duel in the Sun, Harlequin (New York, NY), 1994.

To Have and to Hold, Harlequin (New York, NY), 1994.

One Night of Love, Harlequin (New York, NY), 1994.

Calum, Harlequin (New York, NY), 1995.

Francesca, Harlequin (New York, NY), 1995.

Chris, Harlequin (New York, NY), 1995.

Marriage by Arrangement, Harlequin (New York, NY), 1996.

Christmas Nights, 1996.

The Guilty Wife, Harlequin (New York, NY), 1997.

A Typical Male!, Harlequin (New York, NY), 1997.

A Very Public Affair, Mills and Boon (London, England), 1997.

(With Alison Fraser) *For the Baby's Sake,* 1997.

Runaway Fiancee, Harlequin (New York, NY), 1998.

Mission to Seduce, Mills and Boon (London, England), 1998.

(With Penny Jordan and Anne McAllister) *Christmas Presents,* Harlequin (New York, NY), 1999.

Also author of *Best of Sally Wentworth: Liberated Lady, Shattered Dreams,* 1984.

SIDELIGHTS: British author Doreen Hornsblow, who wrote under the pseudonym Sally Wentworth, was a prolific creator of contemporary romance novels. Her books are notable for their frequent integration of current women's issues, including breast cancer, abortion, and single motherhood, into their plots. For example, breast cancer is tackled in *Broken Destiny.* When Jancy is diagnosed with the disease and forced to have a mastectomy, she worries that her fiancee Duncan, who is out of the country at the time, will not continue to love her if she no longer has a perfect body. However, when Duncan receives her letter breaking off their engagement, he comes to find her and proves that he loves her regardless of how she looks. "This book is very moving, touching, and immensely encouraging to women who face the same problem," maintained a contributor to *Twentieth-Century Romance and Historical Writers.*

Abortion comes into play in *The Devil's Kiss,* one of Hornsblow's combination romance/suspense novels. When Miranda discovers that her younger sister Rosalind is pregnant and is planning to get an abortion, but will not reveal who the baby's father is, Miranda goes snooping to try to determine the baby's paternity for herself. Rosalind's expenses at the abortion clinic were paid for with a credit card belonging to one Warren Hunter, whom Miranda finds and attempts to seek revenge on. But when Warren discovers this, he explains that his credit card was stolen and he had nothing to do with Rosalind's pregnancy—which Rosalind confirms—and Warren and Miranda end up in love.

Other Hornsblow novels that mix suspense with the romance include *Christmas Nights,* about two members of a jury who are being stalked by the killer they helped convict; *The Guilty Wife,* about a lawyer's wife with a secret past; and *Runaway Fiancee,* about a woman with amnesia. *Runaway Fiancee* was praised by *RomanticTimes.com* reviewer Shannon Short, who noted its "colorful characters and emotional intensity."

Hornsblow's more traditional romances include *Marriage by Arrangement,* in which a would-be actress becomes entangled with another show-business family; she agrees to become a live-in home health aide to her instructor, only to fall in love with the teacher's son, who is a producer. *A Very Public Affair* focuses on a high-profile businessman whose personal life becomes media fodder when it is revealed, five years

after the fact, that he has a son by a woman with whom he had a one-night stand. In *Shadow Play* a woman's current relationship is endangered due to her inability to open up to her partner about past trauma in her life. Writing about *Shadow Play* for *RomanticTimes.com,* Linda Silverstein noted that "Wentworth does a splendid job portraying" her protagonist's shattered family.

BIOGRAPHICAL AND CRITICAL SOURCES:

BOOKS

Twentieth-Century Romance and Historical Writers, 3rd edition, St. James Press (Detroit, MI), 1994.

ONLINE

Fantastic Fiction Web site, http://www.fantasticfiction.co.uk/ (March 3, 2005), "Sally Wentworth."
RomanticTimes.com, http://www.romantictimes.com/ (March 3, 2005), Shannon Short, reviews of *A Duel in the Sun, A Very Public Affair, Calum, Chris, Francesca, Christmas Nights, Marriage by Arrangement, Mission to Seduce, One Night of Love, Runaway Fiancee, To Have and to Hold,* and *The Guilty Wife;* Linda Silverstein, review of *Shadow Play.*

[Sketch reviewed by husband, Don Hornsblow.]

*   *   *

HOYT, Sarah (de) A(lmeida)

PERSONAL: Born in Porto, Portugal; married; children: two sons. *Education:* M.A. (English and literature).

ADDRESSES: Home—CO. *Agent*—c/o Author Mail, Penguin/Ace Books, 375 Hudson St., New York, NY 10014. *E-mail*—sahoyt@hotmail.com.

CAREER: Writer.

WRITINGS:

SHAKESPEAREAN FANTASY NOVELS

Ill Met by Moonlight, Ace Books (New York, NY), 2001.

All Night Awake, Ace Books (New York, NY), 2002.

Any Man So Daring, Ace Books (New York, NY), 2003.

OTHER

Crawling between Heaven and Earth (stories), Dark Regions Press (Concord, CA), 2002.

Contributor to periodicals, including *Weird Tales* and *Absolute Magnitude.*

SIDELIGHTS: Sarah Hoyt's fantasy novels *Ill Met by Moonlight, All Night Awake,* and *Any Man So Daring* turn on the unusual premise that William Shakespeare not only wrote about fairies, but was personally involved with them as well. In Hoyt's debut novel, Shakespeare first appears as a struggling schoolmaster, happily married to his wife, Nan, and concerned only with being able to provide for his family. Then Nan and their daughter Susanna inexplicably vanish. Shakespeare eventually tracks them to a fairy court, where they are being held prisoner. Though he can see them, he cannot reach them. A changeling fairy named Quicksilver, who feels he has been cheated of his right to the fairy throne, enlists Shakespeare in his intrigue against the court. "This is an enjoyable story, full of great bits of historical and fairy lore," suggested Charles de Lint in a *Fantasy & Science Fiction* review. *Booklist* contributor Paula Luedtke called it "wildly imaginative and poetic," and a *Publishers Weekly* writer noted that Hoyt's depiction of Shakespeare "makes an engaging main character, and the book generally romps along."

In *All Night Awake* Shakespeare finds that he cannot continue with life as it was before he encountered the fairies. He turns to writing and learns that his chief rival in the literary world, Christopher Marlowe, was also touched by fairy enchantment. Besides being great writers, Marlowe and Shakespeare have something else in common: both were seduced by Quicksilver, who is known as Lady Silver when in feminine form.

Complications arise when Lady Silver appears in London, warning of a creature who seeks to rule both human and fairy worlds. Reviewing the book for *Chronicle,* Don D'Ammassa noted that whether imaginary or historical, Hoyt's characters are "deftly drawn and completely believable."

In the third volume of the series, *Any Man So Daring,* Marlowe has sacrificed himself to save his own soul and the life of his son. Now suspended between Heaven and Hell, he haunts Shakespeare. Meanwhile, although Shakespeare has become the most successful writer in the world, he is uneasy with his new life, and he begins to struggle with writer's block. Another fairy plot unfolds, this one threatening Will's son Hamnet. Some reviewers noted that while Hoyt's plots are engaging in themselves, the quality of her writing is also noteworthy. "Hoyt's language is so evocative and lyrical that readers are instantly involved with the characters and story," wrote Jane Halsall in *School Library Journal.* In a similar vein, Paula Luedtke noted in *Booklist:* "A great story accounts for only half the book's success; the rest depends on Hoyt's beautiful prose."

Some of Hoyt's shorter fiction is collected in *Crawling between Heaven and Earth.* Unusual plot twists and unique protagonists give the stories appeal, according to *SF Site* writer Matthew Peckham. He noted that many of the characters are "caught in that metaphorical limbo-land between heaven and earth, and so, ironically, are the stories, careening from mostly polished to occasionally jolting with overwrought phrases that refuse to sit still." Despite some flaws, Peckham believed the stories in *Crawling between Heaven and Earth* "reveal a talent for conjuring the exceptionally unusual," and he concluded: "It will certainly be interesting to see what [Hoyt produces] . . . in the years ahead."

BIOGRAPHICAL AND CRITICAL SOURCES:

PERIODICALS

Booklist, October 1, 2001, Paula Luedtke, review of *Ill Met by Moonlight,* p. 305; September 15, 2002, Joanne Wilkinson, review of *All Night Awake,* p. 212; November 1, 2003, Paula Luedtke, review of *Any Man So Daring,* p. 486.

Chronicle, November, 2002, Don D'Ammassa, review of *All Night Awake*, p. 28; December, 2002, Don D'Ammassa, review of *Crawling between Heaven and Earth*, p. 45; December, 2003, Don D'Ammassa, review of *Any Man So Daring*, p. 40.

Denver Post, October 28, 2001, Fred Cleaver, review of *Ill Met by Moonlight*, p. FF2; November 23, 2003, Fred Cleaver, review of *Any Man So Daring*, p. F14.

Fantasy & Science Fiction, September, 2001, Charles de Lint, review of *Ill Met by Moonlight*, p. 96.

Kirkus Reviews, September 15, 2001, review of *Ill Met by Moonlight*, p. 1330.

Library Journal, October 15, 2001, Jackie Cassada, review of *Ill Met by Midnight*, p. 112; October 15, 2002, Jackie Cassada, review of *All Night Awake*, p. 97; November 15, 2003, Jackie Cassada, review of *Any Man So Daring*, p. 101.

Publishers Weekly, October 1, 2001, review of *Ill Met by Moonlight*, p. 43; September 23, 2002, review of *All Night Awake*, p. 55; October 13, 2003, review of *Any Man So Daring*, p. 61.

School Library Journal, February, 2004, Nancy Menaldi-Scanlan, review of *Ill Met by Moonlight*, p. 83; April, 2004, Jane Halsall, review of *Any Man So Daring*, p. 182.

ONLINE

Best Reviews Web site, http://pnr.thebestreviews.com/ (September 15, 2002), Harriet Klausner, review of *All Night Awake*.

Bookslut.com, http://www.bookslut.com/ (February 8, 2005), Joseph J. Finn, review of *All Night Awake*.

Mythopoeic Society Web site, http://www.mythsoc.org/ (February 8, 2005), Matthew Scott Winslow, review of *Ill Met by Moonlight*.

Sarah Hoyt Home Page, http://www.sarahahoyt.com (February 8, 2005).

SFSite.com, http://www.sfsite.com/ (February 8, 2005), Matthew Peckham, review of *Crawling between Heaven and Earth.**

*   *   *

HUESTON, Marie Proeller

PERSONAL: Female.

ADDRESSES: Home—New York, NY. *Office*—Country Living Magazine Editorial, 224 West 57th St., #7, New York, NY 10019.

CAREER: Writer.

MEMBER: American Society of Journalists.

WRITINGS:

Country Living's Guide to the Best Flea Markets: How to Find (and Bargain for) Antiques and Other Treasures in the U.S. and Canada, Hearst Books (New York, NY), 2002.

Decorating with Flea Market Finds foreword by Nancy Mernit, Hearst Books (New York, NY), 2002.

Country Living: Cottage Style, Hearst Books (New York, NY), 2003.

Country Living Collection Style: Arranging and Displaying Your Treasures, Hearst Books (New York, NY), 2004.

Contributing editor, and contributor of articles, to *Country Living* magazine.

SIDELIGHTS: Marie Proeller Hueston writes about collecting and decorating trends, and has written several books published in connection with *Country Living* magazine. For example, in *Country Living: Cottage Style*, she provides decorating and design tips to turn the reader's home or apartment in a cottage-style environment. The author discusses each living area separately, including the bathrooms, bedrooms, living rooms, and kitchens and dining room, and even the garden. She also provides an assortment of decorating ideas designed to give the room's décor a cottage feel. A *Publishers Weekly* contributor noted that, "Conjuring up images of English chintz, patchwork quilts, slipcovers and easy comfortable living, the style can be applied anywhere." Writing in *Library Journal*, Gayle A. Williamson complimented the book "for its practical advice."

In *Country Living Collection Style: Arranging and Displaying Your Treasures* Hueston describes the best way for people to display their treasures and collectibles. The author discusses basic design principles for arranging objects, the best type of lighting, and even building custom shelves. *Library Journal* critic Williamson commented that "Hueston's book is recommended for all public libraries."

BIOGRAPHICAL AND CRITICAL SOURCES:

PERIODICALS

Library Journal, January, 2004, Gayle A. Williamson, review of *Country Living: Cottage Style,* p. 109; January 1, 2005, Gayle Williamson, review of *Country Living Collection Style: Arranging and Displaying Your Treasures,* p. 107.
Publishers Weekly, October 27, 2003, review of *Country Living: Cottage Style,* p. 63.*

*   *   *

HULER, Scott

PERSONAL: Married June Spence (a writer); children: Louis.

ADDRESSES: Agent—c/o Author Mail, Crown Publishers, 1745 Broadway, New York, NY 10019. *E-mail*—huler@mindspring.com.

CAREER: Writer, journalist, radio producer, and radio commentator. Nashville Public Radio, producer and reporter. Has worked as a staff writer for *Raleigh News and Observer* and *Philadelphia Daily News.*

AWARDS, HONORS: Knight-Wallace fellowship, University of Michigan, 2002-03; Public Radio News Directors Incorporated Award, 2002, 2003.

WRITINGS:

(With Gordon Bethune) *From Worst to First: Behind the Scenes of Continental's Remarkable Comeback,* Wiley (New York, NY), 1998.
A Little Bit Sideways: One Week inside a NASCAR Winston Cup Race Team, MBI Publishing Company (Osceola, WI), 1999.
On Being Brown: What It Means to Be a Cleveland Browns Fan, Gray Publishers (Cleveland, OH), 1999.
Defining the Wind: The Beaufort Scale, and How a Nineteenth-Century Admiral Turned Science into Poetry, Crown Publishers (New York, NY), 2004.

Contributor to periodicals, including *New York Times, Washington Post, Fortune,* and *Los Angeles Times.* Also contributor to radio shows, including National Public Radio's *All Things Considered, Marketplace* and *Day to Day;* and WMAL's *Voice of America News Now.*

SIDELIGHTS: Author and journalist Scott Huler is a prolific contributor to prominent newspapers such as the *New York Times, Los Angeles Times,* and *Washington Post.* While working as a copy editor for a small publisher in 1983, Huler experienced a moment of epiphany when he encountered a nondescript set of 110 words written in the nineteenth century. These words constitute the Beaufort Wind Scale, a simple descriptive table of wind speeds and descriptions attributed to English sea captain and hydrographer Admiral Sir Francis Beaufort. To Huler, however, the scale is more than a meteorological tool; to him, the succinct, even sublime descriptions rises to the stature of poetry, becoming what he dubbed "the apex of descriptive nonfiction in English."

In *Defining the Wind: The Beaufort Scale, and How a Nineteenth-Century Admiral Turned Science into Poetry* Huler describes his search to find out about the man who established the scale and whose descriptions stand as "the ultimate expression of concise, clear, and absolutely powerful writing, 110 words in six-point type." Arranged on a scale of zero to twelve, the Beaufort Scale contains descriptions of various wind effects. On the Beaufort Wind Scale, at zero, the wind is "calm; smoke rises vertically" at five, with breezes of nineteen to twenty-four miles per hour, "small trees in leaf begin to sway; crested wavelets form on inland waters." at nine, in a strong gale with winds of forty-seven to fifty-four miles per hour, "slight structural damage occurs; chimney pots and slates removed." At the highest level of twelve, in a hurricane with winds topping seventy-three miles per hour, "devastation occurs."

Beaufort himself was a hydrographer to the British Admiralty. His career spanned sixty-eight years in service to the crown. "Beaufort began his adventures at sea at age fourteen, captained a Royal Navy ship by age twenty-two, and for more than twenty years seldom seemed to step onto dry land," noted Laurence A. Marschall in *Natural History.* A shattered hip, the result of a sniper's bullet received during a fracas with

Turkish natives, ended his seagoing career in 1817, but he remained in service to the admiralty for years afterward. He knew the notorious Captain William Bligh, of the H.M.S. *Bounty,* and was the person who encouraged the captain of the H.M.S. *Beagle* to sign on a young and inexperienced naturalist named Charles Darwin. Beaufort's reputation, however, was not without blemish: he had an incestuous affair with his sister after becoming a widower in his sixties.

"What makes Huler's book exceptional . . . is his absorbing account of how he tried to empathize with Beaufort, to find out what kind of person would devise and use such as scale," Marschall noted. Huler delved deeply into historical records and archival materials to assemble his portrait of Beaufort. To experience the world as Beaufort must have, Huler sailed the seas the admiral himself had once plied. He sought personal reflections from historians, meteorologists, poets, and musicians who felt inspiration from the scale. Ironically, Huler also discovered that the 110 words of refined poetic description were probably not written by Beaufort, but by later contributors to the scale.

"Readers will be absorbed by this story of the nature of scientific inquiry and the power and value of concise, poetic observation" commented Barbara A. Genco in *School Library Journal.* Huler's book forms a "consummate example of how a writer with enough determination can mine a deep vein of curiosity and use it to produce a compelling, powerful, and, yes, interesting book," stated *Boston Globe* reviewer Anthony Doerr. Bruce Barcott, writing in the *New York Times Book Review,* called *Defining the Wind* a "sometimes arcane but ultimately enchanting stroll through maritime and science history." A *Publishers Weekly* reviewer dubbed it a "gem of a book," while *Library Journal* critic Margaret Rioux described Huler's volume as "a beautifully written portrait" of Beaufort.

BIOGRAPHICAL AND CRITICAL SOURCES:

BOOKS

Huler, Scott, *Defining the Wind: The Beaufort Scale, and How a Nineteenth-Century Admiral Turned Science into Poetry,* Crown Publishers (New York, NY), 2004.

PERIODICALS

Booklist, July, 2004, Gilbert Taylor, review of *Defining the Wind,* p. 1807.
Boston Globe, September 19, 2004, Anthony Doerr, "Of Bees and Wolves, and a Fickle Wind; Tales of Rediscovery," review of *Defining the Wind,* p. D6.
Entertainment Weekly, August 13, 2004, Wook Kim, review of *Defining the Wind,* p. 91.
Kirkus Reviews, June 15, 2004, review of *Defining the Wind,* p. 568.
Library Journal, July, 2004, Margaret Rioux, review of *Defining the Wind,* p. 114.
Natural History, November, 2004, Laurence A. Marschall, review of *Defining the Wind,* p. 51.
New York Times Book Review, October 10, 2004, Bruce Barcott, "Blowing Hot and Cold," review of *Defining the Wind,* p. 18.
Publishers Weekly, June 7, 2004, Ron Hogan, "The Beauty of the Beaufort Scale" (interview), p. 42; June 7, 2004, review of *Defining the Wind,* p. 43.
School Library Journal, December, 2004, Barbara A. Genco, review of *Defining the Wind,* p. 54.
Weatherwise, November-December, 2004, Randy Cerveny, review of *Defining the Wind,* p. 67.

*   *   *

HUNT, Everett C. 1928-

PERSONAL: Born December 28, 1928, in Stamford, CT; married Jay Kilby, 1952 (deceased); children: Gerilyn, Scott, Erik. *Education:* U.S. Merchant Marine Academy, B.S., 1951; Rensselaer Polytechnic Institute, M.S., 1958; Northeastern University, M.S., 1973; Eurotechnical University, Sc.D., 1988. *Religion:* Christian.

ADDRESSES: Home—P.O. Box 308, Warner, NH 03278.

CAREER: Engineer and author. U.S. Merchant Marine, engineer officer, 1951-52; General Electric Co., turbine design engineer and application engineer, 1954-65, turbine development project manager, 1965-66, value engineering consultant, 1966-67, engineering manager, 1967-69, quality control manager, 1969-75; Sun Shipbuilding Co., director, 1975-79; U.S. Merchant

Marine Academy, professor of engineering and department head, 1979-84; Webb Institute, professor of engineering and director of research, 1984-92; self-employed consulting engineer, 1992—. *Military service:* U.S. Navy, engineer officer, 1952-56.

MEMBER: Pan American Institute of Naval Engineers, Institute of Marine Engineering, Science, and Technology (fellow; local chair).

AWARDS, HONORS: Superior Achievement Award, U.S. Department of Transportation; Professional Achievement Award, U.S. Merchant Marine Academy.

WRITINGS:

Marine Engineering Economics and Cost Analysis, Cornell Maritime Press (Centreville, MD), 1995.
Modern Marine Engineer's Manual, 3rd edition, Cornell Maritime Press (Centreville, MD), Volume 1, 1999, Volume 2, 2002.

Author of about thirty technical articles.

*   *   *

HUNTER, Maddy

PERSONAL: Married.

ADDRESSES: Home—Madison, WI. *Agent*—c/o Author Mail, Pocket Books, 1230 Avenue of the Americas, New York, NY 10020.

CAREER: Author.

WRITINGS:

"PASSPORT TO PERIL" MYSTERY SERIES

Alpine for You, Pocket Books (New York, NY), 2003.
Top o' the Mournin', Pocket Books (New York, NY), 2003.
Pasta Imperfect, Pocket Books (New York, NY), 2004.

SIDELIGHTS: Maddy Hunter writes humorous mystery novels about amateur tour guide Emily Andrew, whose repeated efforts to lead groups of senior citizens on successful vacations of various parts of Europe always end in disaster and murder. Emily first appears in *Alpine for You,* where, finding herself without a job, she decides to accompany her grandmother on a trip to Switzerland. The vacation is a bomb from the start, with Emily having an unpleasant time with the senior citizens in the group tour. Things go from bad to worse when their guide is murdered. Emily suddenly finds herself with a new job as substitute tour guide, and finds a new love interest in attractive inspector Etienne Miceli in a debut mystery that *Murder Express* reviewer Lelia Taylor called "delightfully fresh, with a great deal of humor."

In *Top o' the Mournin'* Emily returns, this time with another group of seniors traveling through Ireland. Murder is in the cards again, when two staff members at a castle are killed. Fortunately for Emily, Etienne is on the case, too, though a wrench is thrown into the works by Emily's ex-husband, Jack. *RomanticTimes.com* reviewer Samantha J. Gust found Hunter's story "funny and full of suspense."

Never a good advertisement for the joys of travel, Hunter's series continues to fin humor in all the things that can go wrong on a vacation, including lost luggage and cantankerous traveling companions Italy is the destination for Emily's third adventure, *Pasta Imperfect.* Emily, who has now found a job working at a bank, is also in charge of the Windsor City Bank Senior Travel Club. The seniors hook up with a romance publisher's tour, and when one of the aspiring authors on the trip is killed, it is handsome Etienne who is once more on the case.

BIOGRAPHICAL AND CRITICAL SOURCES:

ONLINE

AllReaders.com, http://www.allreaders.com/ (February 8, 2005), Harriet Klausner, review of *Pasta Imperfect.*
Murder Express, http://www.murderexpress.net/ (November, 2002), Lelia Taylor, review of *Alpine for You.*

Mystery Reader, http://www.themysteryreader.com/ (February 8, 2005), Jennifer Monahan Winberry, review of *Pasta Imperfect.*

RomanticTimes.com, http://www.romantictimes.com/ (February 8, 2005), Samantha J. Gust, review of *Alpine for You.**

I-J

IOANID, Radu

PERSONAL: Born in Bucharest, Romania.

ADDRESSES: Office—U.S. Holocaust Memorial Museum, 100 Raoul Wallenberg Pl. SW, Washington, DC 20024-2126.

CAREER: Museum director and writer. U.S. Holocaust Memorial Museum, Washington, DC, associate director of international programs.

WRITINGS:

Urbanizarea n Romania: Implicatii Social-Economice, Editura Stiintifica si Enciclopedica (Bucharest, Romania), 1978.
The Word of the Archangel: Fascist Ideology in Romania, translated by Peter Heinegg, East European Monographs (Boulder, CO), 1990.
The Holocaust in Romania: The Destruction of Jews and Gypsies under the Antonescu Regime, 1940-1944, Ivan R. Dee (Chicago, IL), 2000.
(Author of introduction and notes) Mihail Sebastian, *Journal, 1935-1944,* translated by Patrick Camiller, Ivan R. Dee (Chicago, IL), 2000.
The Ransom of the Jews: The Story of the Extraordinary Secret Bargain between Romania and Israel, Ivan R. Dee (Chicago, IL), 2005.

SIDELIGHTS: Radu Ioanid has written or edited several books about his native land of Romania. In *The Holocaust in Romania: The Destruction of Jews and Gypsies under the Antonescu Regime, 1940-1944* Ioanid explores anti-Semitism in Romania during World War II and describes the role of Romanian leaders, including Ion Antonescu, in passing legislation that led to the deportation of Jews as well as their resettlement in Romanian ghettos. Ioanid gathered much of the material from the United States Holocaust Memorial Museum where he works and from the National Archives, both located in Washington, D.C. He also uses testimonies from survivors and material from Jerusalem's Yad Vashem. Writing in *Booklist,* George Cohen called the book the "definitive account of the Holocaust in Romania."

The Ransom of the Jews: The Story of the Extraordinary Secret Bargain between Romania and Israel recounts a little-known episode in Romanian history in which Romanian leaders Gheorghe Gheorghiu-Dej and then Nicolae Ceausescu demanded money from Israel to allow Romanian Jews to immigrate there during the 1950s and 1960s. Ioanid draws much of the story from secret Romanian documents and interviews to detail this uneasy relationship between the two countries. Writing in the *Library Journal,* Maria C. Bagshaw called the author's work "carefully documented" and "essential for academic collections." A *Publishers Weekly* contributor commented that "Ioanid does a service in reporting on this sordid tale of exploitation and the trade in human beings."

Ioanid also wrote the introduction and notes for *Journal, 1935-1944,* written by Romanian writer Mihail Sebastian and focusing on the problems encountered by the Romanian Jewish population during World War II. Writing in the *New Criterion,* Anne Applebaum called the book "a small reminder of how thin is the veneer of Western civilization, how close to the surface are brutality and hatred."

BIOGRAPHICAL AND CRITICAL SOURCES:

PERIODICALS

Booklist, November 1, 1999, George Cohen, review of *The Holocaust in Romania: The Destruction of Jews and Gypsies under the Antonescu Regime, 1940-1944,* p. 506.
Library Journal, January 1, 2005, Maria C. Bagshaw, review of *The Ransom of the Jews: The Story of the Extraordinary Secret Bargain between Romania and Israel,* p. 128.
New Criterion, March, 2001, Anne Applebaum, review of *Journal, 1935-1944,* p. 66.
Publishers Weekly, November 15, 2004, review of *The Ransom of the Jews,* p. 52.*

*   *   *

JACOBSTEIN, J(oseph) Myron 1920-2005

OBITUARY NOTICE— See index for *CA* sketch: Born January 27, 1920, in Detroit, MI; died March 25, 2005, in Danville, CA. Librarian, lawyer, educator, and author. Jacobstein was a former law professor and librarian at Stanford University. While he was attending Columbia University, the United States entered World War II and he enlisted in the U.S. Air Forces. Stationed in New Mexico, he spent the duration stateside. After the war, Jacobstein completed a B.A. at Wayne State University in 1946, followed by his master's degree in library science at Columbia University and a law degree in 1952 from the Chicago-Kent College of Law. The next year, he was admitted to the State Bar of Illinois. While working on his law degree, he was employed as a librarian at the University of Chicago Library. Combining his two interests, he then became assistant law librarian for the University of Illinois in the mid-1950s. From 1955 until 1959 he did similar work for Columbia University, after which Jacobstein joined the University of Colorado, where he was a professor of law and law librarian for four years. Finally, in 1963, he joined the Stanford faculty as a law professor and librarian. He remained

there until his 1987 retirement. In addition to his academic work, Jacobstein was on the executive board of the American Association of Law Libraries from 1973 to 1975 and was the organization's president from 1978 until 1979. For this work, he was honored with the Distinguished Service Award from the American Association of Law Libraries in 1987. Jacobstein was also the author or editor of several books on law and legal research, including *Fundamentals of Legal Research* (1973; seventh edition, 1998), *Legal Research Illustrated: An Abridgment of Fundamentals of Legal Research* (second edition, 1981; sixth edition, 1994), and *The Rejected: Sketches of the Twenty-six Men Nominated for the Supreme Court but Not Confirmed by the Senate* (1993).

OBITUARIES AND OTHER SOURCES:

PERIODICALS

American Libraries, May, 2005, p. 57.
San Francisco Chronicle, April 2, 2005, p. B5.

ONLINE

Stanford Report Online, http://news-service.stanford.edu/ (April 13, 2005).

*   *   *

JOHANSEN, Ruthann Knechel 1942-

PERSONAL: Born 1942; married, husband's name Bob; children: Erik, Sonia. *Education:* Manchester College, B.S.; Columbia University Teachers College, M.A.; Drew University, Ph.D.

ADDRESSES: Home—51385 Hunting Ridge Trail, Granger, IN 46530. *Office*—104 O'Shaughnessy, University of Notre Dame, Notre Dame, IN 46556. *E-mail*—johansen.9@nd.edu.

CAREER: Rutgers University, New Brunswick, NJ, visiting lecturer in English, 1981-84; Stockton State College, Pomona, NJ, assistant professor of American literature, 1985-86; Bethany Theological Seminary,

Oak Brook, IL, member of adjunct faculty, 1992; University of Notre Dame, Notre Dame, IN, assistant professor, 1990-94, associate professor, 1995-99, professional specialist and associate director, College of Arts and Letters core course, 1999. Visiting scholar, Harvard Divinity School, 1992-93; participant in MacArthur Foundation summer seminar on peace studies, 1988, and Ford Foundation summer seminar on cultural diversity, 1991.

AWARDS, HONORS: Outstanding Young Women of America award, 1973; Evelyn Ortner Prize, Drew University, 1981; research grant, Stockton State College, 1985; Elizabeth Agee prize, 1992, for *The Narrative Secret of Flannerty O'Connor: The Trickster as Interpreter;* Kroc Institute fellow, 1993; grant from Lilly Foundation, 1998; Kaneb Teaching Award for Excellence in Undergraduate Teaching, University of Notre Dame, 1999.

WRITINGS:

Coming Together: Male and Female in a Renamed Garden, Brethren Press (Elgin, IL), 1977.
The Narrative Secret of Flannery O'Connor: The Trickster as Interpreter, University of Alabama Press (Tuscaloosa, AL), 1994.
Listening in the Silence, Seeing in the Dark: Reconstructing Life after Brain Injury, University of California Press (Berkeley, CA), 2002.

Contributor of articles to periodicals, including *Flannery O'Connor Bulletin, Fellowship,* and *Brethren Life and Thought.*

WORK IN PROGRESS: Research on narrativity and selfhood.

SIDELIGHTS: Ruthann Knechel Johansen is a professor whose book *The Narrative Secret of Flannery O'Connor: The Trickster as Interpreter* analyzes the artistic vision of novelist Flannery O'Connor. In Johansen's view, O'Connor's religious faith and her artistic viewpoint were inextricably linked. The author contends that they were also both closer to the viewpoint held by medieval scholars than by modern readers. In making her point, Johansen . . . relates O'Connor's writing to the narrative tradition of storytelling, which draws the listener into mythic realms. "Johansen's text is difficult and oftentimes reads as if it were written for O'Connor scholars," noted D. Coshnear in *Choice.* "However, she painstakingly defines her terms and her complex critical framework." Sarah Gordon, a contributor to *Southern Humanities Review,* noted: "Johansen's clear intent . . . is to explain how the strangeness and indeed the harshness of O'Connor's fiction may be understood in light of the author's firm Christianity and to suggest the presence of the numinous in her stories of the Southern backwoods." Gordon found that "Johansen is at her best in discussing biblical sources and linguistic conventions."

Johansen's personal life is the subject of *Listening in the Silence, Seeing in the Dark: Reconstructing Life after Brain Injury.* When the author's son Erik was fifteen years old, he was in an automobile accident that caused him to suffer severe brain injury and coma. Uncertain as to whether he would live or die, Johansen and her husband struggled to communicate with their child and with the medical team around him. When he did begin to regain consciousness, Erik had no memory of himself or of how to perform the basic activities of daily living. Johansen reflects on the variety of forces that combined to help bring her son back from his coma. She recounts the initial trauma, the early stages of recovery and rehabilitation, and finally, the long process of readjusting to life in a permanently altered state. *Listening in the Silence, Seeing in the Dark* is "a deeply moving story of a struggle to selfhood," according to Jodith Janes in *Library Journal.* The book speaks honestly of the monumental difficulties involved in Erik's recovery, including strain on family bonds, which led to his eventually being placed in a rehabilitation home. Such decisions are never easy, and the author's "candor is rare enough to distinguish this book from similar accounts of families dealing with stricken children," stated William Beatty in *Booklist.* *Listening in the Silence, Seeing in the Dark* goes beyond personal memoir, in Beatty's opinion; through the story of her own family, Johansen "pursues questions of justice, compassion, and responsibility."

BIOGRAPHICAL AND CRITICAL SOURCES:

BOOKS

Johansen, Ruthann Knechel, *Listening in the Silence, Seeing in the Dark: Reconstructing Life after Brain Injury,* University of California Press (Berkeley, CA), 2000.

PERIODICALS

American Literature, December, 1994, review of *The Narrative Secret of Flannery O'Connor: The Trickster as Interpreter,* pp. 881-882.

Booklist, March 15, 2002, William Beatty, review of *Listening in the Silence, Seeing in the Dark: Reconstructing Life after Brain Injury,* p. 1192.

Choice, January, 1995, review of *The Narrative Secret of Flannery O'Connor,* p. 781.

Contemporary Sociology, July, 2003, Michele S. Smith, review of *Listening in the Silence, Seeing in the Dark,* p. 520.

Library Journal, March 15, 2002, Jodith Janes, review of *Listening in the Silence, Seeing in the Dark,* p. 102.

Mississippi Quarterly, winter, 1995, David J. Knauer, review of *The Narrative Secret of Flannery O'Connor,* p. 127.

Southern Humanities Review, winter, 1997, review of *The Narrative Secret of Flannery O'Connor,* p. 77.

Southern Literary Journal, spring, 1996, Anne Rowe, review of *The Narrative Secret of Flannery O'Connor,* p. 121.*

* * *

JONG-FAST, Molly 1978-

PERSONAL: Born 1978; daughter of Erica Jong (a novelist) and Jonathan Fast (a novelist and screenwriter); married; children: one son. *Education:* Attended New York University, Barnard College, and Wesleyan University; Bennington College, M.F.A.

ADDRESSES: Home—New York, NY. *Agent*—c/o Author Mail, Villard, 1745 Broadway, New York, NY 10019.

CAREER: Writer.

WRITINGS:

Normal Girl (novel), Villard Books (New York, NY) 2000.

The Sex Doctors in the Basement: True Stories from a Semi-Celebrity Childhood (memoir), Villard Books (New York, NY), 2005.

Has published essays and articles in the *New York Times, W, Cosmopolitan, Mademoiselle, Marie Claire,* London *Times, Elle, Modern Bride,* and *Forward.*

ADAPTATIONS: Normal Girl was adapted as a screenplay by Bret Easton Ellis.

SIDELIGHTS: Molly Jong-Fast comes from a family of famous novelists: her mother is literary superstar Erica Jong (*Fear of Flying*); her father is Jonathan Fast (*The Beast*); and her grandfather is Howard Fast (*Spartacus*). She told *Philadelphia Inquirer* reporter Jennifer Weiner that she has been writing since she was four years old and stated, "I always thought that books were the most important thing in the world." Jong-Fast published the semi-autobiographical novel *Normal Girl* when she was age twenty-one, and has more recently completed a collection of biographical essays, *The Sex Doctors in the Basement: True Stories from a Semi-Celebrity Childhood.* Both books present the more outrageous, horrific, and sometimes humorous aspects of growing up a privileged child in New York City. The fact that Jong-Fast has become a writer has been considered newsworthy. Reviews have credited her with a deft use of humorous observation, while profiles have been riveted on the connections between her writing and her personal life.

One of Jong-Fast's reasons for writing *Normal Girl* was that she wanted to present an unglamorized account of substance abuse. Bulimic as a teenager and an alcoholic by age sixteen, the author also used cocaine, LSD, sleeping pills, and diet pills. At age nineteen she was sent to the Hazelden rehabilitation clinic. In interviews she speaks of struggling to grow up and create a sense of self-worth. Finding her identity as a writer has also been difficult, but she is proud of not shying away from writing because of the fear of being measured against her mother's success. Jong-Fast has not read any of the books written by her mother, who she called "the self-styled queen of erotica" in the South Africa *Sunday Times Online.* Interviewer Philip Delves Broughton perceived that, in contrast to Jong, the author "has donned the wimple of moral conservatism." While she remains close to her mother, Jong-Fast has reversed roles in an ironic way. As *Los Angeles Times* writer Louise Roug pointed out, the daughter was mortified by people identifying her with children portrayed in her mother's fiction; Jong now faces the same kind of comparisons to the often absent, socialite mother in *Normal Girl.*

The central character in *Normal Girl* is nineteen-year-old Miranda Woke, a rich Manhattan drug abuser with rich, drug-abusing friends. Miranda fears that she contributed to the death of her boyfriend by overdose, an event she cannot remember. She returns to partying, but due to the intervention of a former boyfriend is soon sent to a rehabilitation clinic. Her divorced socialite mother and architect father are too busy to have much influence. Throughout, Jong-Fast comments on the social ills rampant in New York City, and she makes fun of the self-obsession, cult of celebrity, and devotion to "The Next Big Thing-ism."

Critics were most impressed with *Normal Girl*'s satirical edge. Writing for the *New Statesman,* Tim Teeman called the author "a precise observer" and remarked that her "observations on Miranda's drug and alcohol dependency are sharper, cleverer, and more self-aware than the stuff about her new, clean life." A *Publishers Weekly* writer observed that "while it is witty at times, this tale of meltdown and resurrection is ultimately too much like its protagonist: sexy but superficial." With its "interesting and eventually sympathetic heroine," *Booklist* reviewer Kristine Huntley called the book a "promising first novel."

In *The Sex Doctors in the Basement: True Stories from a Semi-Celebrity Childhood,* Jong-Fast offers gossipy chapters from real life. The pitfalls of attending the posh Manhattan Day School, meeting her mother's boyfriends, watching her grandfather marry a woman half his age, and meeting with the psychiatrists her mother hopes will help Molly lose weight are among the book's acid anecdotes. While a *Publishers Weekly* reviewer called the work "a memoir that's long on jokes but short on substance," a *Kirkus Reviews* critic praised the collection's "neurotic, very funny essays."

BIOGRAPHICAL AND CRITICAL SOURCES:

PERIODICALS

Booklist, May 1, 2000, Kristine Huntley, review of *Normal Girl,* p. 1652.

Entertainment Weekly, July 31, 1998, Alexandra Jacobs Flamm, "Between the Lines," p. 66; June 30, 2000, Clarissa Cruz, "Family Fare: Does Having a Famous Last Name Lead to Literary Fame? It Sure Doesn't Hurt," review of *Normal Girl,* p. 124.

Kirkus Reviews, January 1, 2005, review of *The Sex Doctors in the Basement: True Stories from a Semi-Celebrity Childhood,* p. 35.

Los Angeles Times, September 10, 2001, Louise Roug, "She's Her Mother's Daughter, but Her Life's Plot Is All Her Own," p. E2.

New Statesman, May 29, 2000, Tim Teeman, "Talk Show," review of *Normal Girl* p. 56.

New York Times, June 18, 2000, Alex Witchel, "Counterintelligence," section 9, p. 2.

Philadelphia Inquirer, June 5, 2000, Jennifer Weiner, "Novelist Molly Jong-Fast Has Been Writing since She Was Four."

Publishers Weekly, July 20, 1998, Judy Quinn, "About a 'Girl'" p. 112; May 8, 2000, review of *Normal Girl,* p. 204; December 20, 2004, review of *The Sex Doctors in the Basement,* p. 43.

ONLINE

Beatrice Web site, http://www.beatrice.com/interviews/ (April 23, 2005), Ron Hogan, interview with Jong-Fast.

Bookreporter.com, http://www.bookreporter.com/ (June 23, 2000), interview with Jong-Fast.

Sunday Times Online (South Africa), http://www.suntimes.co.za/ (April 4, 1999) Philip Delves Broughton, "Desperately Flying from Erica" (interview).*

K

KANARIS, Jim 1964-

PERSONAL: Born December 18, 1964, in Montreal, Quebec, Canada. *Education:* Concordia University, B.A. (theology/philosophy), 1993; McGill University, M.A. (religious studies), 1995, Ph.D. (religious studies), 2000. *Religion:* Protestant.

ADDRESSES: *Office*—McGill University, 3520 University St., Montreal, Quebec H3A 2A7, Canada. *E-mail*—jim.kanaris@mcgill.ca.

CAREER: McGill University, Montreal, Quebec, Canada, professor of religion, 2000—.

WRITINGS:

Bernard Lonergan's Philosophy of Religion: From Philosophy of God to Philosophy of Religious Studies, State University of New York Press (Albany, NY), 2002.
(Editor, with Mark Doorley, and contributor) *In Deference to the Other: Lonergan and Contemporary Continental Thought,* State University of New York Press (Albany, NY), 2003.

Contributor to books, including *Explorations in Contemporary Continental Philosophy of Religion,* edited by D-P. Baker and P. Maxwell, Rodopi (New York, NY), 2003. Contributor of articles and reviews to periodicals, including *Studies in Religion/Sciences Religieuses, ARC,* and *Method: Journal of Lonergan Studies.*

BIOGRAPHICAL AND CRITICAL SOURCES:

PERIODICALS

Theological Studies, December, 2003, Robert M. Doran, review of *Bernard Lonergan's Philosophy of Religion: From Philosophy of God to Philosophy of Religious Studies,* p. 896.

ONLINE

Jim Kanaris Home Page, http://pages.infinit.net/jkanaris (September 24, 2004).

*   *   *

KARPIN, Michael

PERSONAL: Male.

ADDRESSES: *Agent*—c/o Author Mail, Holt/Metropolitan, 115 W. 18th St., New York, NY 10011.

CAREER: Former editor-in-chief of Israeli television news program *Mabat;* editor and anchor of *Second Look* television program. Director of documentary films, including *The Road to Rabin Square,* 1997, and *A Bomb in the Basement: Israel's Nuclear Option,* 2001.

WRITINGS:

Gilgulim ba-sheleg, Domino (Jerusalem, Israel), 1983.

Resimot mi-Kikar Pushkin, Yedi'ot aharonot (Tel-Aviv, Israel), 1993.

(With Ina Friedman) *Murder in the Name of God: The Plot to Kill Yitzhak Rabin,* Metropolitan Books (New York, NY), 1998.

SIDELIGHTS: Michael Karpin is an Israeli journalist who collaborated with Ina Friedman to write *Murder in the Name of God: The Plot to Kill Yitzhak Rabin,* an account of the 1995 assassination of the Israeli prime minister. The authors describe the crime, analyze the political-religious conflicts that motivated the killer, and suggest that the man who pulled the trigger may have been sanctioned to do so by the religious right. Describing the political climate in Israel, Karpin and Friedman portray a country sharply divided between Orthodox Zionists and Zionists who are non-religious and democratic. Rabin's participation in the 1993 Oslo peace agreement, which turned some land over to the Palestinians, marked him as a traitor by those who believed that modern Israel must encompass the entire biblical extent of Israel. According to Karpin and Friedman, right-wing groups tolerated actions of extremists, and their rabbis cited biblical support for killings in the name of religion. *Murder in the Name of God* dismisses the notion that Rabin was responsible for his own death, or that the blame rested with Rabin's right-hand man, Shimon Peres. The authors criticize left-wing factions for their failure to condemn radical rabbis, and the security force that was to have protected Rabin is also subjected to negative comment. Rabin was shot by a twenty-five-year-old law student, an Orthodox Jew named Yigal Amir. While it is generally reported that he acted alone in shooting Rabin, the authors suggest that Amir was only one member of a conservative faction that sanctioned killing for religious reasons.

Murder in the Name of God is "not only a chilling profile of the murderer but also an expose of the right-wing zealotry that created him," according to a reviewer for *Publishers Weekly.* The authors achieve "significant success" in their attempt to "describe the social, religious, and political background against which the murder took place," stated David B. Green in a *Mediterranean* review. The book was also highly recommended by Guilain Denoeux in *Middle East Policy,* both for the way it "skillfully pieces together information about key participants" and for its success in offering "a unique look into the world of Jewish religious messianism and ultranationalist extremism in

both Israel and the United States." Karpin further explored Rabin's assassination in a controversial documentary, *The Road to Rabin Square.* It shows the climate of hatred that built up in the years preceding Rabin's assassination, including footage of demonstrators carrying posters with bulls-eyes over Rabin's face. Karpin interviewed the assassin and his family, as well.

Karpin is also the director of the film *A Bomb in the Basement: Israel's Nuclear Option,* which investigates the development and probable extent of Israel's nuclear-weapons program. According to Karpin, Shimon Peres forged ties with the French in the 1950s on the strength of their shared fear of North African nationalist movements. This led to French cooperation in helping Israel to obtain what was needed to start a nuclear-weapons program. Extreme secrecy about nuclear capabilities has long been a hallmark of the Israeli government, but censors allowed Karpin's film to be released despite its candor. Karpin was quoted in the *Boston Globe* as saying that perhaps this was due to his timing; terrorist attacks on the World Trade Center in New York City had happened only days before. "It could be that after September 11 they decided that perhaps the time has come to reveal a little bit more about the Israeli nuclear project," he said. "But this is only my speculation."

BIOGRAPHICAL AND CRITICAL SOURCES:

PERIODICALS

Booklist, September 1, 1998, Mary Carroll, review of *Murder in the Name of God: The Plot to Kill Yitzhak Rabin,* p. 3.

Boston Globe, November 11, 2001, Dan Ephron, review of *A Bomb in the Basement.*

Guardian (Manchester, England), April 17, 1999, Colin Shindler, review of *Murder in the Name of God,* p. 9.

Issues of the American Council for Judaism, spring, 1999, Allan C. Brownfeld, review of *Murder in the Name of God.*

Library Journal, September 15, 1998, Sanford R. Silverburg, review of *Murder in the Name of God,* p. 98.

Mediterranean, January 10, 1999, David B. Green, "A Political Act."

Middle East Policy, June, 1999, Guilain Denoeux, review of *Murder in the Name of God,* p. 203.

New Statesman, March 5, 1996, Tim Franks, review of *Murder in the Name of God,* p. 54.

New York Jewish Week, May 16, 1997, Larry Derfner, review of *A Bomb in the Basement,* p. 49.

Publishers Weekly, October 26, 1998, review of *Murder in the Name of God,* p. 49.

San Francisco Chronicle, November 22, 1998, review of *Murder in the Name of God,* p. 3.

Washington Monthly, December, 1998, Joshua A. Brook, review of *Murder in the Name of God,* p. 40.*

*　　　*　　　*

KAUFMAN, Pamela

PERSONAL: married; husband's name Charlie (a writer); children: two sons. *Education:* Earned Ph.D.

ADDRESSES: Agent—c/o Author Mail, Three Rivers Press, 1745 Broadway, New York, NY 10019.

CAREER: Novelist. Formerly worked as an actress; former educator.

WRITINGS:

HISTORICAL FICTION

Shield of Three Lions, Crown (New York, NY), 1983, reprinted, Three Rivers Press (New York, NY), 2002.

Banners of Gold (sequel to *Shield of Three Lions*), Crown (New York, NY, 1986, reprinted, Three Rivers Press (New York, NY), 2002.

The Book of Eleanor, Crown (New York, NY), 2002.

SIDELIGHTS: Pamela Kaufman's debut novel, *Shield of Three Lions,* is a work of historical fiction in which Lady Alix of Wanthwaite, an adolescent, loses her family and her lands along the Scottish border in an attack. Because she feels the only hope of regaining her inheritance is by pleading her case to King Richard the Lionhearted, she cuts her hair, dresses as a boy, and travels to Richard's encampment to be taken on as a page. Calling herself Alexander, she is befriended by Enoch, a Scottish knight who becomes her protector.

Along the way, Alix/Alexander meets such figures as Robin Hood and the archbishop of Canterbury, as well as prostitutes, rogues, entertainers, and other colorful characters. Against the background of the Third Crusade, the beautiful young boy attracts the homosexual advances of Richard, while Alix, who suspects that Richard knows her true gender, mistakes his intentions as heterosexual. Richard eventually learns the truth, and Alix flees to her home to find that her castle, as well as her hand, has been given to Enoch.

Christine B. Vogel wrote in the *Washington Post Book World* that in *Shield of Three Lions* "Kaufman has captured all the pageantry, chivalry, and stench-filled realities of medieval life with a fineness of detail that bespeaks prodigious and painstaking research. Add to that her sensitivity, humor and highly creative writer's touch and you have a truly original and extraordinarily memorable story." *Los Angeles Times Book Review* contributor Elizabeth Wheeler felt that "Kaufman takes her history seriously. She skillfully re-creates an era of mystery and brutality, presenting an exceptional picture of the time without violating or expanding the conventions of the historical romance." A *Publishers Weekly* reviewer called *Shield of Three Lions* a "rollicking, bawdy, glorious work," and noted Kaufman's clear portrayal of Alix, whose "deepening perceptions of love, sex, human nature and honor are right on the mark and hilarious to boot."

In *Banners of Gold* Richard's mother, Eleanor of Aquitaine, has Lady Alix—who is now married to Enoch—abducted and brought from Scotland to France because Richard has announced that the young woman is the one with whom he wants to have children. Although Richard is married at the time, and childless, he consumates his desire for Alix, placing her life in danger. When Richard dies, Alix escapes to a nunnery to avoid the fate planned for her by Eleanor and Prince John, Richard's evil brother. A *Kirkus Reviews* contributor noted that Kaufman "drives her tale at a satisfying gallop" and called the book "Sound historical entertainment."

The Book of Eleanor is a fictional memoir penned as though by one of the most significant women in medieval history, Eleanor of Aquitaine, wife and mother of kings. Eleanor's history unfolds in the cell where she has been imprisoned by her second husband, the ruthless Henry II of England, after organizing a rebellion against him led by their sons. Eleanor had married Louis VII of France for political reasons while she was still in her teens and her sexually repressed husband was so jealous that he took her with him on the Crusades, where she experienced a freedom unknown to women of her time. She eventually convinced the pope to annul their marriage and then married Henry. In Kaufman's novel, Eleanor finds love with Baron Rancon, although the actual history of this affair is unknown. A *Publishers Weekly* contributor wrote that Kaufman's "presentation of one of history's larger-than-life heroines as an early feminist will engage and entertain readers with an interest in the life stories of powerful women."

Kaufman told *CA:* "My writing process is like making ovals across a page for penmanship; I redo everything. Since I write about women in the Middle Ages and since almost nothing is known about them, I write out the story, then rewrite and rewrite again until it sounds comfortable. I work all day every day. Obviously I do a lot of research, but try not to let it show. I like a humorous tone, especially high comedy. I've been an actress on Broadway and that shows: I'm aware of the laugh and waiting for it. I taught for many years as a professor and that shows as well: I teach myself first, then others.

"I like to laugh and laugh most while I'm writing, so I suppose *Shield of Three Lions* made me laugh most. I'm quite fond of my latest book, *The Prince of Poison;* it has a wonderful villain and a major theme: Magna Carta. And of course, it has humor."

BIOGRAPHICAL AND CRITICAL SOURCES:

PERIODICALS

Kirkus Reviews, September 1, 1986, review of *Banners of Gold,* p. 1314; December 15, 2001, review of *The Book of Eleanor,* p. 1705.
Library Journal, September 1, 1983, Andrea Lee Shuey, review of *Shield of Three Lions,* p. 1721; April 1, 2002, Wendy Bethel, review of *The Book of Eleanor,* p. 140.
Los Angeles Times Book Review, November 20, 1983, Elizabeth Wheeler, review of *Shield of Three Lions,* p. 14.

Publishers Weekly, July 29, 1983, review of *Shield of Three Lions,* p. 61; September 12, 1986, review of *Banners of Gold,* p. 79; January 7, 2002, review of *The Book of Eleanor,* p. 45.
Washington Post Book World, September 18, 1983, Christine B. Vogel, review of *Shield of Three Lions,* p. 8; November 30, 1986, Jeanne McManus, review of *Banners of Gold,* p. 8.
West Coast Review of Books, Volume 12, issue 4, review of *Banners of Gold,* p. 35.

ONLINE

RomanticTimes.com, http://www.romantictimes.com/ (May 11, 2005), Kathe Robin, review of *The Book of Eleanor.**

* * *

KEMP, Simon 1952-

PERSONAL: Born February 6, 1952, in Liverpool, England; married Cora Beryl Baillie; children: one daughter. *Education:* University of Auckland, B.A., 1973, M.S. (with first class honors), 1975, D.Phil., 1980.

ADDRESSES: Office—Department of Psychology, University of Canterbury, Christchurch, New Zealand; fax: 64-3-364-2181.

CAREER: Department of Social Welfare, Wellington, New Zealand, assistant research officer, 1975-76; Technical University, Munich, West Germany (now Germany), research scientist at Institute of Electroacoustics, 1980-81; University of Canterbury, Christchurch, New Zealand, lecturer, 1981-86, senior lecturer, 1986-95, associate professor of psychology, 1996—. Christian Albrecht University, fellow at Institute of Psychology, 1988-89.

MEMBER: International Association for Research in Economic Psychology (member of governing board), American Psychological Association (foreign affiliate), Cheiron.

AWARDS, HONORS: Alexander von Humboldt Foundation fellowship for Germany, 1987; grants from Medical Research Council, Deafness Research Foundation, Oticon Foundation (New Zealand), Marsden Fund, Foundation for Research, Science and Technology, New Zealand Department of Inland Revenue, and New Zealand Department of Labour.

WRITINGS:

Medieval Psychology, Greenwood Press (Westport, CT), 1990.

Cognitive Psychology in the Middle Ages, Greenwood Press (Westport, CT), 1996.

(Editor, with P. E. Earl, and contributor) *The Elgar Companion to Consumer Research and Economic Psychology,* Edward Elgar Publishing (Northampton, MA), 1999.

Public Goods and Private Wants: A Psychological Approach to Government Spending, Edward Elgar Publishing (Northampton, MA), 2002.

Contributor to books, including *Human Suggestibility: Advances in Theory, Research, and Application,* edited by J. F. Schumaker, Routledge, Chapman & Hall (New York, NY), 1991. Contributor to periodicals, including *Psychological Research, Audiology, Acustica, Perceptual and Motor Skills, Perception and Psychophysics, Journal of Speech and Hearing Research, Psychological Medicine,* and *Journal of the Acoustical Society of America.* Coeditor, *Journal of Economic Psychology;* member of editorial board, *New Zealand Journal of Psychology.*

SIDELIGHTS: Simon Kemp told *CA:* "I have published in a variety of areas. I started my career doing auditory psychophysics. Over the last ten years or so, my research has concentrated mainly on long-term memory, psychology in the Middle Ages, and economic psychology. Although these areas are somewhat disparate, the thread of cognitive psychology runs through them. Thus, I have been particularly interested in cognitive theories (for example, that of the inner senses) put forth by medieval scholars. Similarly, much of my work in economic psychology has been concerned with people's memory for prices and with the utilities that people assign to goods and services that the government provides. A recent article attempted to explain the way people misremember past dates and the past prices of goods using a common theory."

*   *   *

KENNAN, George F(rost) 1904-2005

OBITUARY NOTICE— See index for *CA* sketch: Born February 16, 1904, in Milwaukee, WI; died March 17, 2005, in Princeton, NJ. Historian, diplomat, ambassador, educator, and author. A key figure in the cold war between the United States and the former Soviet Union, Kennan was considered the architect of the so-called "containment" policy that many believed was responsible for ending the threat of nuclear war with the Soviets. He was also a brilliant writer, winning two Pulitzer prizes and several National Book awards. Interested in Russian history from an early age—he was related to another George Kennan, a scholar of czarist Russia—Kennan earned a B.A. from Princeton University in 1925 and then joined the U.S. State Department, where he was trained at the Foreign Service School and learned fluent Russian. When the U.S. government officially recognized the USSR, Kennan was sent to Moscow as part of U.S. ambassador William C. Bullitt's team. Here, Kennan became intimately aware of Soviet leader Josef Stalin's harsh style of government, while also becoming familiar with the inherent strengths and weaknesses of Soviet diplomacy. He left Moscow in 1935 to serve as consul in Vienna, followed by a post as second secretary in Prague. A year in Czechoslovakia was followed, in 1939, with the unenviable assignment of working in Berlin as World War II was heating up. When the United States entered the war in 1941, Kennan and the fellow diplomats were imprisoned by the German government, spending several months in confinement before a prisoner exchange found Kennan in Lisbon, Portugal. After spending a year in London as a counselor, he returned to Moscow, this time as a minister-counselor. It was while serving in this post that Kennan wrote the famous correspondence that would become known as "the Long Telegram." In it, he explained to the U.S. State Department the history and outlook of Soviet policy and how he predicted it would affect American foreign policy. A startling revelation to many was Kennan's assertion that the Soviets would not honor a treaty if they felt it was to their disadvantage; on the other hand, he felt that they would back down from conflict in the face of powerful political and military opposition. Later, in 1947, Kennan elaborated upon his view of Soviet politics in an article published in *Foreign Affairs*. These two pieces of writing have since been considered the foundation of America's containment policy against the Soviets, in which the United States vigilantly worked to prevent the USSR from expanding its influence into other countries in Europe and Asia. Kennan, however, would later hold that the U.S. government interpreted his ideas too militaristically and generally, erroneously emphasizing military force over political deterrence, and resisting Soviet influence in every case, instead of focusing on important hot spots such as Eastern Europe. After World War II, Kennan continued to work for the U.S. State Department in important positions. He served as director of policy planning in 1947 and as counselor from 1949 to 1950. In 1952 he was named U.S. ambassador to the Soviet Union, and from 1961 until 1963 he was the ambassador to Yugoslavia. Kennan's later years were spent in academia. He joined Princeton University's Institute for Advanced Study in 1956, teaching there, with the exception of his time in Yugoslavia, until his retirement as professor emeritus in 1974. A moderate political thinker, Kennan argued against nuclear proliferation and felt that the United States was becoming too militaristic and that the federal government too often ignored the opinions of the intellectual community. One example of his attempt to be the voice of reason came a few months before the United States invaded Iraq as a reaction to the September 11, 2001, terrorist attacks. Kennan deemed this a bad move, predicting that it would likely result in America becoming entangled in that country for years. Honored many times for his work in diplomacy, Kennan received such prestigious honors as the Albert Einstein Peace Prize and the Presidential Medal of Freedom. An active and acclaimed author, he also earned the Pulitzer and National Book Award for *Russia Leaves the War* (1956), is the first volume of his two-volume *Soviet-American Relations, 1917-1920*, a second Pulitzer and National Book Award, as well as an Overseas Press Club award, for his *Memoirs, 1925-1950*, and many other prizes. Among his other publications are *American Diplomacy, 1900-1950* (1951), *The Decline of Bismarck's European Order: Franco-Russian Relations, 1875-1890* (1979), *The Fateful Alliance: France, Russia, and the Coming of the First World War* (1984), *Sketches from a Life* (1989), and *At a Century's Ending: Reflections, 1982-1995* (1996).

OBITUARIES AND OTHER SOURCES:

PERIODICALS

Chicago Tribune, March 18, 2005, section 1, p. 11.
Los Angeles Times, March 18, 2005, pp. A1, A4-A5.
New York Times, March 19, 2005, p. B11.
Times (London, England), March 19, 2005, p. 80.
Washington Post, March 18, 2005, pp. A1, A11.

*   *   *

KERIK, Bernard B. 1955-

PERSONAL: Born September 4, 1955; son of Donald and Patricia Kerik; married; second wife's name, Halah; children: Lisa; (second marriage) Celine, Angeline. *Education:* Empire State College, State University of New York, B.S.

ADDRESSES: Agent—c/o Author Mail, HarperCollins, 10 East 53rd St. 7th Floor, New York, NY 10019.

CAREER: Law enforcement officer. King Faisal Specialist Hospital, Riyadh, Saudi Arabia, chief of investigations for security office, 1982-84; Passaic County Jail, Passaic, NJ, warden, 1986, also served as Training Officer and Commander of the Special Weapons and Operations Units; New York Police Department (NYPD), New York, NY, served a variety of positions in uniformed and plains-clothes duty, 1986-94; New York City Department of Corrections, New York, NY, executive assistant to the commissioner and director of Investigations Units, then first deputy commissioner, c. 1994-97, commissioner, 1998-2001; City of New York, NY, police commissioner, 2000-01; interim minister of the interior, Iraq, 2003; senior vice president at Giuliani Partners, until 2004; chief executive officer of Giuliani-Kerik, LLC, until 2004. Served on New York City Gambling Control Commission, beginning 1997; former chair of annual fundraiser, Michael Buczek Foundation. *Military service:* U.S. Army; military policeman.

AWARDS, HONORS: Medal of Valor, New York Police Department.

WRITINGS:

The Lost Son: A Life in Pursuit of Justice, ReganBooks (New York, NY), 2001.

(With others) *New York City Police Department Equal Employment Opportunity Policy,* Police Department of the City of New York (New York, NY), 2001.

(Author of foreword) *In the Line of Duty: A Tribute to New York's Finest and Bravest,* ReganBooks (New York, NY), 2001.

ADAPTATIONS: The Lost Son was adapted as a film by Miramax.

SIDELIGHTS: Bernard B. Kerik is a former law enforcement officer who rose through the ranks to become New York City's police commissioner. Following the terrorists attacks the city on September 11, 2001, he gained an even higher profile and completed his autobiography, *The Lost Son: A Life in Pursuit of Justice.* In the book, Kerik paints much of his life as a quest to come to terms with his abandonment by his mother. During research for this book, he discovered that his mother had become a prostitute and was probably murdered. He grew up with his father and credits the process of earning a black belt in the martial arts with turning his life around. Kerik went on to serve in the U.S. military and then began a career in corrections that led him to the New York Police Department (NYPD). He recounts some of his exploits in the department in his autobiography, such as an undercover assignment to buy drugs in Harlem that resulted in a bust of Columbian drug lords and the seizure of millions of dollars of cocaine. In addition to his rise in law enforcement, Kerik writes about his relationship with former New York mayor Rudi Giuliani.

After the book's publication, Kerik served as interim minister of the interior in Iraq, where he trained members of the postwar the Iraqi police department. He was also nominated by President George W. Bush to replace Tom Ridge as Homeland Security secretary, but Kerik declined the nomination following allegations that he had abused his authority for personal advantage. Sam Somer wrote on the *California Law Enforcement Command College* Web site that he "liked this inspirational book and would highly recommend it for others to read." Writing in the *New Yorker,* Rebecca

Mead noted that Kerik's book is a "testament to the rough-edged authenticity that endeared him" to the president. However, the reviewer also reflected on Kerik's downfall and commented, "The next edition of the book presents an opportunity for him to address various inconsistencies that have now come to light."

BIOGRAPHICAL AND CRITICAL SOURCES:

BOOKS

Kerik, Bernard B., *The Lost Son: A Life in Pursuit of Justice,* ReganBooks (New York, NY), 2001.

PERIODICALS

Atlanta Journal-Constitution, December 4, 2004, Julia Malone and Eunice Moscoso, "Nominee Started as Beat Cop for Homeland Security, Bush Looks Back to 9/11," p. A6.

New Yorker, January 10, 2005, Rebecca Mead, "Busted," p. 27.

New York Times, November 9, 2001, Christopher Drew, "Family Secret Is Revealed in Autobiography," p. D1.

Publishers Weekly, November 26, 2001, Daisy Maryles, "A Top Cop's Tale," p. 15.

Successful Meetings, March, 2002, Michelle Gillan Fisher, "Walking a New Beat: New York City's Former Top Cop Is Now Patrolling the Speaker's Circuit," p. 156.

Washington Post, December 9, 2004, Richard Cohen, "The Commish of Homeland Insecurity," p. A33.

ONLINE

AllReaders.com, http://www.allreaders.com/ (February 25, 2005), review of *The Lost Son: A Life in Pursuit of Justice.*

California Law Enforcement Command College Web site, http://www.commandcollee.com/ (March 16, 2005), Sam Somers, review of *The Lost Son.*

Empire State College Web site, http://www.esc.edu/ (March 16, 2005), "Bernard B. Kerik Nominated Homeland Security Secretary."

OTHER

In Memoriam: New York, 9/11/01 (film), Home Box Office, 2002.*

KING, John O(zias) 1923-2001

PERSONAL: Born July 18, 1923, in Madison, WI; died of congestive heart failure, May 9, 2001; son of Paul Clark and Margaret (Ozias) King; married; wife's name, Jan. *Education:* University of Houston, M.A.; Vanderbilt University, Ph.D., 1966.

CAREER: Historian, educator, and writer. University of Houston, Houston, member of faculty, beginning 1961, served as department chairman, professor of U.S. history, 1975-96, then professor emeritus. *Military service:* U.S. Army, 1942-45; Bronze Star, Combat Infantry Badge.

WRITINGS:

The Early History of the Houston Oil Company of Texas, 1901-1906, Texas Gulf Coast Historical Association (Houston, TX), 1959.

Joseph Stephen Cullinan: A Study of Leadership in the Texas Petroleum Industry, 1897-1937, Vanderbilt University Press (Nashville, TN), 1970.

(With George T. Thomas) *The Woodlands: A New Community Development, 1964-1983,* Texas A&M University Press (College Station, TX), 1987.

SIDELIGHTS: John O. King was an education and an historian who chronicled the Texas petroleum boom and also wrote about the development of an innovative town near Houston, Texas. King's book *Joseph Stephen Cullinan: A Study of Leadership in the Texas Petroleum Industry, 1897-1937* tells the story of a Pennsylvania oilman who arrived in Texas in 1897 and eventually founded the Texas Oil Company, the forerunner of Texaco.

King also cowrote *The Woodlands: A New Community Development, 1964-1983,* with George T. Thomas. This book focuses on the efforts of George Mitchell, founder of the Mitchell Energy and Development Corporation, to create a "new town" financed partially through the Housing and Urban Development's New Communities program. This program was an attempt to provide government funding to carry on an idea developed in the 1960s: the creation of new towns that would solve the urban problems associated with big inner cities. These communities were to provide better access to residential, commercial, and recreational facilities, while being environmentally friendly and attractive with a low-density population. Writing in the *Business History Review,* Marc A. Weiss noted that the book "tells in considerable detail the story of the trials, tribulations, and triumphs of this . . . experiment in community building." The reviewer also wrote that "the content is important; this is one of a few books to document with facts and figures the history of a modern large-scale community development project from the viewpoint of a single real estate firm."

BIOGRAPHICAL AND CRITICAL SOURCES:

PERIODICALS

American Historical Review, April, 1972.

Business History Review, winter, 1988, Marc A. Weiss, review of *The Woodlands: A New Community Development, 1964-1983,* p. 717.

Choice, April, 1971, review of *Joseph Stephen Cullinan: A Study of Leadership in the Texas Petroleum Industry, 1897-1937.*

Journal of American History, June, 1971, G. T. White, review of *Joseph Stephen Cullinan: A Study of Leadership in the Texas Petroleum Industry, 1897-1937.*

Library Journal, T. M. Bogie, February 15, 1971, review of *Joseph Stephen Cullinan: A Study of Leadership in the Texas Petroleum Industry, 1897-1937.*

OBITUARIES

ONLINE

Cullinan & Cullinane Family Genealogy Project, http://freepages.genealogy.rootsweb.com/~ccfgpw/ (February 12, 2003).*

*   *   *

KING, Valerie
    See BOSNA, Valerie

*   *   *

KINGDON, Jonathan

PERSONAL: Male. *Education:* University of Southern California, Los Angeles, Ph.D.

ADDRESSES: Office—Department of Zoology, Oxford University, Tinbergen Building, South Parks Road, Oxford OX1 3PS, England. *E-mail*—jonathan. kingdon@bioanth.ox.ac.uk.

CAREER: Oxford University Department of Zoology, Oxford, England, senior research associate at Institute of Biological Anthropology.

AWARDS, HONORS: Natural World Book Prize, British Petroleum/Wildlife Trusts, 1990, for *Island Africa: The Evolution of Africa's Rare Animals and Plants;* Cherry Kearton Medal and Award, 1998.

WRITINGS:

East African Mammals: An Atlas of Evolution in Africa, Academic Press (London, England), 1971, University of Chicago Press (Chicago, IL), 1984.
Mammalia Africana: An Exhibition of Drawings from "East African Mammals: An Atlas of Evolution in Africa," Academic Press (London, England), 1981.
African Mammal Drawings: The Wellcome Volume, Pangolin Prints (Islip, NY), 1983.
Kilimanjaro: Animals in a Landscape, British Broadcasting Corporation (London, England), 1983.
Island Africa: The Evolution of Africa's Rare Animals and Plants, Princeton University Press (Princeton, NJ), 1989.
(With others) *A Primate Radiation: Evolutionary Biology of the African Guenons,* Cambridge University Press (New York, NY), 1989.
Arabian Mammals: A Natural History, Academic Press (London, England), 1990.
Self-made Man: Human Evolution from Eden to Extinction, Wiley (New York, NY), 1993, published as *Self-made Man and His Undoing,* Simon & Schuster (London, England), 1993.
The Kingdon Field Guide to African Mammals, Princeton University Press (Princeton, NJ), 1997.
Lowly Origin: Where, When, and Why Our Ancestors First Stood Up, Princeton University Press (Princeton, NJ), 2003.
The Kingdon Pocket Guide to African Mammals, Princeton University Press (Princeton, NJ), 2005.

SIDELIGHTS: Evolutionary biologist, writer, and artist Jonathan Kingdon was born and raised in East Africa, and educated both there and in Great Britain.

He has traveled extensively, teaching and conducting research across Europe, Asia, Africa, Australia, and North America. Kingdon serves as a senior research associate at Oxford University's Institute of Biological Anthropology and is considered one of the foremost authorities in the world on African mammals. In addition to working as a scientist and writer, he is also an accomplished artist: Wedgwood commissioned him to produce a piece of art as part of their "Earthlife" collection in 1986, and his drawings have also served as illustrations for several of his books.

In *Island Africa: The Evolution of Africa's Rare Animals and Plants,* Kingdon offers an in-depth look at the flora and fauna of Africa from a range of perspectives. His main focus is to investigate why certain plants and animals are found in certain regions of the plateau continent, but he also succeeds in explaining the evolutionary events that led to the diversity of Africa's ecosystem, providing reasons why certain species are rare or extinct. For the lay reader, Kingdon provides a wealth of hand-drawn illustrations that bring the subject to life. A contributor to the *Economist* observed that "this is a book that marries the old tradition of the explorer-naturalist with that of a modern scientist." *Island Africa* was awarded the Natural World Book Prize from British Petroleum and the Wildlife Trusts in 1990.

Self-made Man: Human Evolution from Eden to Extinction chronicles more than the phases of man's evolution. Kingdon proposes that humankind has always has a fascination with tools—both making and mastering them—and it is man's ability to advance his technology that has enabled humankind to evolve. In discounting the influence of natural selection according to the theories of Charles Darwin, he explores the dispersal of humans across the various continents through the centuries, and looks at the common genetic traits of the five traditional races of mankind, stressing how technology developed within each group based on the region where they eventually settled. From there he explains a number of ideas, including the theory that Africans have darker skin tones because they are descendents of sea-faring people whose prolonged exposure to the sun via their advanced technology—boats—forced their skin to mutate as a form of self-preservation.

Marek Kohn, in a review for *New Statesman and Society,* took issue with Kingman's hypothesis in *Self-made Man,* writing that, "because his tone is pleasantly unstrident, it's . . . easy to overlook the hardness of his theoretical position. He's an out-of-Africa man, no quarter given." Kohn added that, granted, "artifacts (including fire) enabled humans to occupy various habitats, where they diversified and—to some extent— adapted. But the vision of technology as the prime mover of human evolution is a glaring instance of the great anthropological predilection for discovering ourselves in ancient ruins." A contributor to *Publishers Weekly* called the book a "provocative and lively saga of human origins."

Lowly Origin: Where, When, and Why Our Ancestors First Stood Up examines that phase of evolution that separates man from the animals: his conversion to walking erect. Kingdon discusses the conditions imposed by ecology, geography, and physiology that led humans to take their first upright steps. William H. Kimbel, in *American Scientist,* called the book "an original and engaging account of human evolution as the evolution of 'just one more African mammal,'" but added: "unfortunately, Kingdon populates the terrain with stand-ins for the real hominids, whose histories await a more discerning and persuasive rendering than that on offer here." Nonetheless, the reviewer called the book "the best popular account of that subject I have read." *Natural History* contributor Ian Tattersall remarked that Kingdon's work "is a landmark for its thoroughness in integrating the story of human evolution . . . with that of the evolving landscapes and habitats of the African continent."

BIOGRAPHICAL AND CRITICAL SOURCES:

PERIODICALS

American Scientist, May-June, 2004, William H. Kimbel, "Becoming Bipeds," review of *Lowly Origin: Where, When, and Why Our Ancestors First Stood Up,* pp. 274-276.

Bioscience, September, 2004, Bernard Wood, "Exploring Human Origins," review of *Lowly Origin,* pp. 866-888.

Economist, March 30, 1991, review of *Island Africa: The Evolution of Africa's Rare Animals and Plants,* p. 86; March 27, 1993, review of *Self-made Man: Human Evolution from Eden to Extinction,* p. 97.

Natural History, November, 2003, Ian Tattersall, "Stand and Deliver," pp. 60-63.

New Statesman and Society, March 26, 1993, Marek Kohn, review of *Self-made Man,* p. 39.

Publishers Weekly, July 26, 1993, review of *Self-made Man,* p. 52.

Science, May 19, 1989, Colin P. Groves," Corcopithecus and Company," review of *A Primate Radiation: Evolutionary Biology of the African Guenons,* pp. 860-861.

Science News, September 13, 2003, review of *Lowly Origin,* p. 175.

Washington Post Book World, July 20, 2003, Mark Parascandola, "More Fallout from the Darwin Thesis: From Barnacles to Standing up Straight," p. T8.

ONLINE

Akademika Web site, http://www.akademika.no/ (February 9, 2005), "Jonathan Kingdon."

Cafe Scientific Web site, http://www.cafescientific.com.au/ (February 9, 2005), "Jonathan Kingdon."

Princeton University Press Web site, http://www.pupress.princeton.edu/ (February 9, 2005), "Jonathan Kingdon."*

*   *   *

KIRSTEN, Wulf 1934-

PERSONAL: Born June 21, 1934, in Klipphausen, Germany. *Education:* University of Leipzig, graduated 1964, certified as a teacher.

ADDRESSES: Agent—c/o Author Mail, Ammann Verlag, Postfach 163, 8032 Zurich, Switzerland.

CAREER: Worked variously as a baker, construction worker, clerk, and teacher; Aufbau (publisher), Berlin, West Germany (now Germany), editor, 1965-87; freelance writer, 1987—.

AWARDS, HONORS: Louis Fürnberg prize, 1972; City of Weimar literature and art prize, 1983; Johannes R. Becher prize, 1985; Peter Huchel prize, 1987; Heinrich Mann prize, 1989; German Association of Protestant Bookshops book prize, 1990; Literature of the Arts prize, 1991; Elisabeth Langgässer prize, 1993;

Fedor Malchow prize for poetry, 1994; Weimar prize, 1994; Erwin Strittmatter prize, 1995; Henning Kaufmann Foundation prize, 1997; Horst Bienek prize, 1999; Marie Luise Kaschnitz prize, 2000; Schillerring, German Schiller Association, 2002; honorary doctorate, Friedrich Schiller University, 2003; Eichendorff prize, Wangener Society for Literature and the Arts, 2004; Konrad Adenauer award, 2005.

WRITINGS:

Die Schlacht bei Kesselsdorf: ein Bericht; Kleewunsch: ein Kleinstadtbild, Aufbau (Berlin, West Germany), 1984.

Winterfreuden: zwei Prosatexte, Ulrich Keicher (Warmbronn, West Germany), 1987.

Wulf Kirsten: Texte, Dokumente, Materialien, Elster (Moos, West Germany), 1987.

Eintragung ins Grundbuch: Thüringen im Gedicht, Hain (Rudolstadt, Germany), 1996.

Texten: Reden und Aufstätze, Ammann (Zürich, Switzerland), 1998.

Die Prinzessinnen im Krautgarten (autobiography; title means "The Princesses in the Herb Garden"), Ammann (Zürich, Switzerland), 2000.

POETRY

Wulf Kirsten, Neues Leben (Berlin, West Germany), 1968.

Satzanfang, Aufbau (Berlin, West Germany), 1970.

Der Landgänger, Sassafras (Düsseldorf, West Germany), 1976.

Ziegelbrennersprache, J. G. Bläschke (Darmstadt, West Germany), 1977.

Der Bleibaum, Aufbau (Berlin, West Germany, 1977.

Die Erde bei Meissen, Reclam (Leipzig, West Germany), 1986.

Veilchenzeit, Ulrich Keicher (Warmbronn, West Germany), 1989.

Stimmenschotter: Gedichte 1987-1992, Ammann (Zürich, Switzerland), 1993.

Wettersturz: Gedichte, 1993-1998 (title means "Weather Fall: Poems 1993-1998"), Ammann (Zürich, Switzerland), 1998.

Also author of *Poesiealbum 4,* 1968

EDITOR

Die Akte Detlev von Liliencron, Aufbau (Berlin, West Germany), 1968.

(With Herbert Greiner-Mai) *Ein Fischer sass im Kahne: die schönsten dt. Balladen d. 19. Jahrhunderts,* Aufbau (Berlin, West Germany), 1974, reprinted, 1998.

(With Ulrich Berkes) *Vor meinen Augen, hinter sieben Bergen: Gedichte vom Reisen* (poetry), Aufbau (Berlin, West Germany), 1977.

With Wilhelm Müller, *Rom, Römer und Römerinnen* (travel), Rütten & Leoning (Berlin, West Germany), 1978.

With Franz Carl Weiskopf, *Unter fremden Himmeln: ein Abriss der deutschen Literatur im Exil 1933-1947: mit einem Anhang von Textproben aus Werken exilierter Schriftsteller,* Aufbau (Berlin, West Germany), 1981.

(With Konrad Paul) *Deutschsprachige Erzählungen, 1900-1945* (fiction), three volumes, Aufbau (Berlin, West Germany), 1981.

(With Konrad Paul) *Liebesgeschichten: von Arthur Schnitzler bis Hermann Broch,* Reclam (Stuttgart, West Germany), 1986.

Franz Hodjak, *Sehnsucht nach Feigenschnaps,* Aufbau (Berlin, West Germany), 1988.

(With Ursula Heukenkkamp and Heinz Kahlau) *Die Eigene Stimme: Lyrik der DDR* (poetry), Aufbau (Berlin, West Germany), 1988.

Rudolf Hartig *Apostel einer besseren Menschlichkeit: der Expressionist Rudolf Hartig (1893-1962),* Isele (Eggingen, Germany), 1997.

Wilhelms Haus, *Erzählungen,* Wartburg (Weimer, Germany), 2000.

(With Holm Kirsten) *Stimmen aus Buchenwald: ein Lesebuch* (essays), Wallstein (Göttingen, Germany), 2002.

Other works include (editor, with Wolfgang Trampe) *Don Juan über Sund* (poetry); *Heumond: frühe Erzählungen; Es waren zwei Königskinder: eine Auswahl deutscher Volkslieder* (folk songs), 1989; and *Veränderte Landschaft,* [Leipzig, West Germany], 1979. Author's work also represented in anthologies.

SIDELIGHTS: Wulf Kirsten, a German poet and writer, is the son of a stonecutter, and before becoming a full-time writer, he himself worked at a number of different jobs. An editor with the publishing house

Aufbau in West Berlin for more than two decades, Kirsten was actually qualified to teach, although he did so for a very short time. He describes his wartime childhood in the 2000 autobiography *Die Prinzessinnen im Krautgarten,* the title of which which translates as "The Princesses in the Herb Garden."

The title of Kirsten's memoir reflects the author's interest in nature, which had served as the primary theme of his poetry since the 1960s. Kirsten's poems are a realistic mirror of his surroundings; as Jeffrey Adams wrote in a review of the collection *Wettersturz: Gedichte 1993-1998* for *World Literature Today,* Kirsten's landscape poetry is comparable to that of fellow Germans Johannes Bobrowski and Peter Huchel. These poets "avoided fusing nature imagery with transcendent values," as Adams wrote, "preferring to decipher the signs of history and society embedded in the natural world. Nevertheless, the intertextual presence of Romantic precursors in Kirsten's poems sets up a useful contrast between their vision of nature as a set of hieroglyphs revealing nature's transcendent mystery and Kirsten's reinvention of nature poetry as the esthetic transcription of a localized, regional landscape that records the history of its inhabitants."

Kirsten interprets nature using language that paints a picture of rural life in days past, and he writes of those who work in the earth, in contrast to the contemporary tendency to dismiss the lives of simple farmers. He also refers to the effects of militarization and industrialization on German culture. The poems of *Wettersturz* contain no capitalization or division into stanzas. Instead, according to Adams, they "run on in an uninterrupted stream from beginning to end, creating a monolithic presence on the page. . . . Kirsten's confidence in his sturdy words is unshaken by the inevitable existential losses and failings of the human condition, which he registers in melancholy but unsentimental tones."

BIOGRAPHICAL AND CRITICAL SOURCES:

BOOKS

Kirsten, Wulf, *Die Prinzessinnen im Krautgarten,* Ammann (Zürich, Switzerland), 2000.
Wallace, Ian, editor, *Neue Ansichten: The Reception of Romanticism in the Literature of the GDR,* pp. 191-211.

PERIODICALS

German Life and Letters, January, 1987, Axel Goodbody, "Reading Nature's Secret: A Romantic Motif in Wulf Kirsten's Nature Poetry," pp. 158-174.
World Literature Today, spring, 2000, Jeffrey Adams, review of *Wettersturz: Gedichte, 1993-1998,* p. 406.*

*   *   *

KITCHIN, C(lifford) H(enry) B(enn) 1895-1967

PERSONAL: Born October 17, 1895, in Harrogate, Yorkshire, England; died April 2, 1967. *Education:* Attended Clifton College, Bristol, Exeter College, Oxford, and Lincoln Inn, London.

CAREER: Lawyer and novelist. *Military service:* British Army, 1916-18.

WRITINGS:

NOVELS

Streamers Waving, Hogarth Press (Oxford, England), 1925.
Mr. Balcony, Hogarth Press (Oxford, England), 1927, with a new introduction by Francis King, 1989.
The Sensitive One, Hogarth Press (Oxford, England), 1931.
Olive E., Constable (London, England), 1937.
Birthday Party, Constable (London, England), 1938.
The Auction Sale, Secker and Warburg (London, England), 1949, with an introduction by Lord David Cecil, Chatto and Windus (London, England), 1971.
The Secret River, Secker and Warburg (London, England), 1956.
Ten Politt Place, Secker and Warburg (London, England), 1957.
The Book of Life, Davies (London, England), 1960, Appleton-Century-Crofts (New York, NY), 1961.
A Short Walk in Williams Park, Chatto and Windus (London, England), 1971.

"MALCOLM WARREN" SERIES

Death of My Aunt, Hogarth (Oxford, England), 1929, Harcourt (New York, NY), 1930.

Crime at Christmas, Hogarth (Oxford, England), 1934, Harcourt (New York, NY), 1935.

Death of His Uncle, Constable (London, England), 1939, Harper (New York, NY), 1984.

The Cornish Fox, Secker and Warburg (London, England), 1949.

OTHER

Curtains (poetry), Blackwell (Oxford, England), 1919.

(Editor, with Vera M. Britain and Alan Porter) *Oxford Poetry, 1920,* Blackwell (Oxford, England), 1920.

Winged Victory (poetry), Blackwell (Oxford, England), 1921.

Jumping Joan and Other Stories, Secker and Warburg (London, England), 1954.

Contributor to anthologies, including *The Second Ghost Book,* Barrie (London, England), 1952.

SIDELIGHTS: C. H. B. Kitchin never received popular acclaim for his detective novels or for his more literary efforts. Although he began his career writing poetry, he turned to novels in the mid-1920s with *Streamers Waving* and *Mr. Balcony.* William Reynolds, writing in the *Dictionary of Literary Biography,* found that these novels "combine brilliant wit with serious underlying intentions." In *Mr. Balcony,* for example, Kitchin's story revolves around a man who travels to Africa on a yacht with several guests. During the voyage, he murders one of his guests, marries and impregnates another, and ends up becoming involved with natives who castrate him. Reynolds noted that the novel "conceals terror beneath a meticulously described surface."

Kitchin is best remembered for the detective novels he introduced in 1929 with his first and most famous work in this genre, *Death of My Aunt.* The entire story takes place over four days and focuses on a young stock broker named Malcolm Warren. Invited by his wealthy aunt, Catherine Cartwright, to her home in the English countryside for a consultation on her finances, Malcolm becomes a prime suspect when his aunt sud-denly dies. Kitchin wrote three more mysteries featuring Malcolm. However, according to a contributor in the *St. James Guide to Crime & Mystery Writers,* the author "mistakenly chose to stress characterization at the expense of puzzle and plot," thus limiting his audience. Nevertheless, his detective stories did have admirers, especially *Death of My Aunt.* As Reynolds noted, "Those who praise the novel do so because its characters are clearly drawn and believable, particularly in the way Cartwright's wealth influences her relatives' dealing with her and with one another."

Kitchin admitted that he had only a tangential interest in the detective novel, and he wrote his last such book in 1949. His other mainstream novels, such as *The Sensitive One* and *Olive E.,* provide a bleak worldview. His most highly praised non-detective novels were *The Auction Sale* and *The Book of Life,* with critics differing on which book was his best work. *The Auction Sale* focuses on Miss Elton, who once worked as a private secretary in a wealthy country household. As the book begins in 1938, Miss Elton is attending an auction of the estate of her former employer. She tries to avoid listening to the conversations around her that mention the upcoming war; instead she focuses on her memories of her happy life living among the gentry. The novel depicts a changing society, the values of genteel life, and the gentry's traditional values as they are subsumed in a more democratic society. According to a reviewer for *NewImprovedHead.com,* Kitchin deftly develops this theme but has a much broader scope in mind. The reviewer commented, "Much like the magician who has a beautiful assistant do something that distracts attention from the dirty work of subterfuge being performed elsewhere on the stage, Kitchin carefully makes every detail of his novel relevant to an analysis of the value of genteel life while at the same time developing his main theme without our really noticing it." The reviewer went on to comment that "Kitchin's assessment of the value of gentility is ultimately irrelevant, since he was in fact not writing about a specific ideal, but about the effects of ideals in general." Calling the book "interesting and engaging," the reviewer also noted, "Kitchin's analysis of his theme . . . is intelligent and humane."

BIOGRAPHICAL AND CRITICAL SOURCES:

BOOKS

Dictionary of Literary Biography, Volume 77: *British Mystery Writers, 1920-1939,* Gale (Detroit, MI), 1989.

St. James Guide to Crime & Mystery Writers, 4th edition, St. James Press (Detroit, MI), 1996.

PERIODICALS

Books, February, 19, 1935, review of *Crime at Christmas,* p. 16.

Boston Transcript, January 23, 1935, review of *Crime at Christmas,* p. 2.

Canadian Forum, March, 1935, review of *Crime at Christmas.*

Chicago Daily Tribune, January 26, 1935, review of *Crime at Christmas,* p. 10.

New York Times, March 9, 1930, E. C. Beckwith, review of *Death of My Aunt,* p. 23; January 27, 1935, review of *Crime at Christmas,* p. 13.

New York World, February 9, 1930, review of *Death of My Aunt,* p. 11.

Outlook, February 12, 1930, review of *Death of My Aunt.*

Saturday Review, November 9, 1929, review of *Death of My Aunt.*

Saturday Review of Literature, March 15, 1930, review of *Death of My Aunt;* January 26, 1935, review of *Crime at Christmas.*

Springfield Republican, May 25, 1930, review of *Death of My Aunt,* p. 7; February 24, 1935, review of *Crime at Christmas,* p. 7.

Times (London, England), October 24, 1929, review of *Death of My Aunt,* p. 849.

Times Literary Supplement, October 18, 1934, review of *Crime at Christmas,* p. 712.

ONLINE

NewImprovedHead.com, http://www.newimproved head.com/ (February 1, 2005), review of *The Auction Sale.**

*   *   *

KLISE, Kate

PERSONAL: Born in Peoria, IL. *Education:* Graduated from Marquette University.

ADDRESSES: Home—Norwood, MO. *Home and office*—P.O. Box 744, Mountain Grove, MO 65711.

CAREER: Writer and journalist. Former correspondent for *People* magazine.

AWARDS, HONORS: Young Adults' Choice Award, Children's Book Council, 1999, for *Regarding the Fountain,* and 2000, for *Letters from Camp;* Juvenile Fiction Award, Friends of American Writers, 2002, for *Trial by Journal.*

WRITINGS:

FOR CHILDREN

Regarding the Fountain: A Tale, in Letters, of Liars and Leaks, illustrated by M. Sarah Klise, Avon (New York, NY), 1998.

Letters from Camp, illustrated by M. Sarah Klise, Avon (New York, NY), 1999.

Trial by Journal, illustrated by M. Sarah Klise, HarperCollins (New York, NY), 2001.

Regarding the Sink: Where, Oh Where, Did Waters Go?, illustrated by M. Sarah Klise, Harcourt (Orlando, FL), 2004.

Shall I Knit You a Hat?: A Christmas Yarn, illustrated by M. Sarah Klise, Henry Holt (New York, NY), 2004.

Deliver Us from Normal, Scholastic (New York, NY), 2005.

Regarding the Trees: A Splintered Saga Rooted in Secrets, illustrated by M. Sarah Klise, Harcourt (Orlando, FL), 2005.

SIDELIGHTS: Kate Klise writes children's books, many of which are designed and illustrated by her sister, M. Sarah Klise. Called a "comic epistolary novel" by a critic in the *New York Times Book Review,* the duo's first collaboration was *Regarding the Fountain: A Tale, in Letters, of Liars and Leaks.* The sisters' story is told through a series of drawings, letters, newspaper clippings, memos, and school announcements, a story-telling device Klise uses in many of the duo's illustrated novels. The story focuses on the need to replace a leaking drinking fountain at the Dry Creek Middle School. When the school's principal decides to get the new fountain from Flowing Waters Fountains, he expects to receive a traditional fountain. To his surprise, and to the delight of the children, owner Florence Waters turns out to be an artist who creates fountains that are individually sculpted pieces of art. Her ideas for the school fountain include an ice-skating rink, chocolate milk dispenser, natural whirlpool, and exotic birds. The story includes a subplot about the disappearance of the town's water supply, featuring villains Dee Eel, president of Dry Creek Water Company, and Sally Mander, head of the Dry Creek Swimming Pool. Clues to the mystery surrounding the missing water are uncovered by a fifth-grade class working on a history project about the town. A *Publishers Weekly* contributor called the book a "good-natured story with an irrepressible main character." Writing in *Kirkus Reviews,* a critic dubbed *Regarding the Fountain* "a tale overflowing with imagination and fun," while Rita Soltan wrote in *School Library Journal* that Klise "cleverly establishes character traits and motive" and called the book "fresh, funny, and a delight to read."

Letters from Camp focuses on Camp Happy Harmony, where brothers and sisters who cannot get along are sent to learn to love and respect each other. The camp's owners, however, are a group of singers turned con artists who are bent on killing each other and who use the children to do the work of the camp, including cleaning septic lines, building fences, and painting, all the while making them wear strange uniforms and sing bizarre songs. The children are kept in line through drugged food served in the Wysteria Cafeteria. The campers learn to cooperate, and brothers and sisters eventually learn to care for each other, as they solve the mysteries of Camp Happy Harmony. A *Publishers Weekly* contributor found the book a "bit less satisfying" than *Regarding the Fountain,* but also noted that "the humor is obvious but kid-friendly, the mystery simple yet fun to solve." Writing in *Booklist,* Debbie Carton commented that the story is "all in all, an entirely satisfying camp adventure that even those who have never been to camp will relish."

In *Regarding the Sink: Where, Oh Where, Did Waters Go?* Florence Waters once again takes center stage as the sixth-grade kids of Geyser Creek Middle School want her to replace a dilapidated cafeteria sink. The only problem is that Florence has vanished while on a trip to China, but the children are determined to find her. Meanwhile, to further complicate the children's lives, beans have become the staple of school lunches as part of slimy Senator Sue Ergass's moneymaking scam, which includes feeding cows nothing but beans so they produce more methane gas. A *Kirkus Reviews* contributor called the book "an amusing sequel," while in *Horn Book,* Susan P. Bloom commented, "To their credit, the Klises provide a satisfying denouement to this utter mayhem." In a review for *School Library Journal,* Jean Gaffney called *Regarding the Sink* "a clever, unconventional reading experience."

Shall I Knit You a Hat?: A Christmas Yarn tells of a Mother Rabbit who knits a hat for her son to protect him from an oncoming blizzard. Little Rabbit loves his hat and never takes it off, but he is concerned for his other animal friends and suggests that he and his mother make hats for all of them as Christmas gifts. "The Klises consistently sound notes of tenderness and humor," noted a *Publishers Weekly* contributor of the book. J. D. Biersdorfer, writing in the *New York Times Book Review,* called *Shall I Knit You a Hat?* "a nice change of pace" and noted that "the Klise sisters team up to show that the giving is just as important as the gift."

Klise's other books include *Trial by Journal,* the story of the first juvenile juror in one state's history who records her experience for a research paper assignment. In *Regarding the Trees: A Splintered Saga Rooted in Secrets,* a middle-school principal's plans to have the school trees trimmed before his administrative evaluation encounters problems caused by a town gender war, dueling chefs, and student tree protests. In *Deliver Us from Normal* Klise tells the story of twelve-year-old Charlie, who lives in Normal, Illinois, but whose poor family is far from normal. Charlie is picked on in school and embarrassed about his family and their unusual lifestyle. When the family decides to leave Normal and live on a junky houseboat, Charlie is at first distressed that his life will never ever be normal, but he eventually learns that not being normal has its benefits. In a review for *Flamingnet.com,* Caroline Devilbiss called *Deliver Us from Normal* "an enlightening tale of self discovery and adolescence, of the importance of family and confidence."

BIOGRAPHICAL AND CRITICAL SOURCES:

PERIODICALS

Booklist, August, 1998, Susan Dove Lempke, review of *Regarding the Fountain: A Tale, in Letters, of Liars and Leaks,* p. 2006; July, 1999, Debbie Carton, review of *Letters from Camp,* p. 1946; September 1, 2004, Francisca Goldsmith, review of *Regarding the Sink: Where, Oh Where, Did Waters Go?,* p. 124.
Horn Book, May-June, 1998, Nancy Vasilakis, review of *Regarding the Fountain,* p. 345; September-October, 2004, Susan P. Bloom, review of *Regarding the Sink: Where, Oh Where, Did Waters Go?,* p. 588.

Kirkus Reviews, December 15, 1997, review of *Regarding the Fountain,* pp. 1835-1836; July 15, 2004, review of *Regarding the Sink,* p. 688.

New York Times Book Review, September 20, 1998, review of *Regarding the Fountain,* p. 32; December 19, 2004, J. D. Biersdorfer, review of *Shall I Knit You a Hat?: A Christmas Yarn,* p. 26.

Publishers Weekly, January 12, 1998, review of *Regarding the Fountain,* p. 60; June 28, 1999, review of *Letters from Camp,* p. 79; September 27, 2004, review of *Shall I Knit You a Hat?,* p. 61.

School Library Journal, June, 1998, Rita Soltan, review of *Regarding the Fountain,* p. 147; October, 2004, Jean Gaffney, review of *Regarding the Sink,* p. 170.

ONLINE

Flamingnet.com, http://flamingnet.com/ (February 17, 2005), Caroline Devilbiss, review of *Deliver Us from Normal.*

Kate and Sarah Klise Home Page, http://www.kateandsarahklise.com (February 1, 2005).

*   *   *

KNOBLOCK, Glenn A. 1962-

PERSONAL: Born February 17, 1962, in Parma Heights, OH; son of William (an engineer) and Ceceilia (in customer service; maiden name, Delaney) Knoblock; married Teresa Hensing (a care giver), September, 1981; children: John Andrew, Anna Elizabeth. *Ethnicity:* "Caucasian." *Education:* Bowling Green State University, B.A., 1984. *Politics:* Democrat.

ADDRESSES: Home—P.O. Box 2, 26 Elm St., Wolfboro Falls, NH 03896. *E-mail*—glennknob1@juno.com.

CAREER: Writer, historian, and lecturer. Mayor's Blue Ribbon Cemetery Committee, Portsmouth, NH, ex-officio member.

WRITINGS:

A History of First Parish Burial Ground in Rollinsford, New Hampshire from 1730, privately printed, 1996.

Historic Burial Grounds of the New Hampshire Seacoast, Arcadia (Mount Pleasant, SC), 1999.

New Hampshire Covered Bridges, Arcadia (Mount Pleasant, SC), 2002.

Strong and Brave Fellows: New Hampshire's Black Soldiers and Sailors of the American Revolution, McFarland and Co. (Jefferson, NC), 2003.

Black Submariners in the U.S. Navy, 1940-1975, McFarland and Co. (Jefferson, NC), 2004.

Brewing in New Hampshire, Arcadia (Mount Pleasant, SC), 2004.

"With Great Sacrifice and Bravery": The Career of Polish Ace Wackaw Lalkowski, Merriam Press (Bennington, VT), 2004.

WORK IN PROGRESS: Black Coast Guardsmen of World War II.

SIDELIGHTS: Glenn A. Knoblock told *CA:* "Since my earliest teenage years I've considered myself a historian, so it was just a matter of time before I put my research on various historical matters into print. One of my prime motivators for the books I write is to preserve many aspects of history that might otherwise be lost. In a number of my books, my intent was not to rewrite history that has already been written, but to present and preserve the achievements of the everyday man and woman that are often overlooked, or lost altogether. This is particularly true of my works in the area of African-American military history.

"While I have received a good amount of acclaim for my work, none of it would be possible without the support and encouragement of my wife, Terry."

*   *   *

KONIECZNY, Vladimir 1946-

PERSONAL: Born 1946, in Germany; immigrated to Canada, 1951. *Education:* Earned B.A. and M.A. degrees. *Hobbies and other interests:* Playing flute and alto saxophone.

ADDRESSES: Agent—c/o Author Mail, Napoleon Publishing/RendezVous Press, 178 Willowdale Ave., Ste. 201, Toronto, Ontario M2N 4Y8, Canada.

CAREER: Writer and educator. Vancouver School Board, Vancouver, British Columbia, Canada, former English and music instructor; Simon Fraser University, Vancouver, former director of publications and foundations for advancement office and part-time instructor in writing and publishing program; freelance writer specializing in corporate communications.

WRITINGS:

Struggling for Perfection: The Story of Glenn Gould (biography; for juveniles), Napoleon Publishing (Toronto, Ontario, Canada), 2004.

SIDELIGHTS: An amateur musician, a writing instructor, and a corporate communications specialist, Vladimir Konieczny is an avid fan of Canadian pianist Glenn Gould. In his biography for young readers, *Struggling for Perfection: The Story of Glenn Gould,* Konieczny profiles a musician famous for his tremendous skill at the keyboard as well as his eccentricities. Gould was a child prodigy who went on to have an important concert and recording career. However, his public performances were limited by his dislike of performing with an orchestra, which he saw as competition, and by his desire to perform perfectly. Because of this second preoccupation, Gould made many recordings. He is also known for his habit of humming while playing and for refusing to shake hands because of the possibility of injury.

Konieczny's book, designed for upper-elementary school readers, offers short chapters under headings such as "American Debuts" and "The Last Concert." He also includes a time line, glossary, and a variety of photographs and drawings. Critics described the biography as interesting and readable. The book is "refreshing," according to *Booklist* reviewer Jennifer Mattson, who particularly enjoyed the wealth of visual material. Writing for *School Library Journal,* Robyn Walker commented that *Struggling for Perfection* "stands above others of the genre."

BIOGRAPHICAL AND CRITICAL SOURCES:

PERIODICALS

Booklist, July, 2004, Jennifer Mattson, review of *Struggling for Perfection: The Story of Glenn Gould,* p. 1840.

Resource Links, June, 2004, Rosemary Anderson, review of *Struggling for Perfection,* p. 30.
School Library Journal, September, 2004, Robyn Walker, review of *Struggling for Perfection,* p. 228.*

*   *   *

KOSSOFF, David 1919-2005

OBITUARY NOTICE— See index for *CA* sketch: Born November 24, 1919, in London, England; died March 23, 2005, in Hatfield, Hertfordshire, England. Actor, broadcaster, and author. Kossoff was a character actor well known for playing wise, elderly Jews or Russian scientists, but later in life he became an active anti-drug campaigner after his son Paul died of an overdose. Abandoning formal education while still in elementary school, he enrolled in art school with plans of working in interior design. By the late 1930s, though, he was working as an aircraft draftsman for the DeHaviland Aircraft Co., where he remained for the duration of World War II. His acting career began in 1942 when Kossoff made his debut in a Unity Theatre production of *The Spanish Village.* He continued to act and direct at the Unity for three more years before finding a job with the BBC Radio's repertory company during World War II. He left the BBC in 1951 and returned to the stage, acting at such venues as the Arts Theater, Embassy Theatre, and Mermaid, often cast as Jewish characters in such plays as *The Tenth Man* and the comedy *Come Blow Your Horn at the Prince of Wales.* Another specialty was Russian characters, which he performed in plays such as *The Iron Petticoat,* as well as in films such as *The Good Beginning* and *The Ring of Spies.* Many of his films were B-movies, though he had notable appearances in the Peter Sellers movies *The Mouse That Roared* (1959) and its sequel, *Mouse on the Moon* (1963). One of his greatest successes came on the radio where, beginning in 1961, he regularly read Bible stories and often interpreted tales such as Jonah and the Whale. He focused mainly on the Old Testament, but also told stories from the New Testament, though with less success. This work resulted in his first book, *Bible Stories Retold* (1968). Other similar books include the children's book *Bible Stories* (1973) and *You Have a Minute, Lord? A Sort of Prayer Book* (1977). Kossoff also wrote a play, *On Such a Night* (1969) in which he acted, too. But his life changed dramatically after one of his sons, Paul, got involved in drugs as a rock musician and later died. As a result, Kossoff decided to dedicate his life to fighting drugs, creating the show *The Late Great Paul,* which he performed as a touring program, free of charge. Though this took up much of his time, Kossoff also occasionally appeared as an actor, his last film role being in the 1994 movie *Staggered.* His last book, *The Old & the New,* was published in 2002. Elected a fellow of the Royal Society of Arts in 1969, Kossoff was also honored with a British Academy of Film and Television Arts award in 1956.

OBITUARIES AND OTHER SOURCES:

PERIODICALS

Daily Telegraph (London, England), March 24, 2005, p. 1.
Herald (Glasgow, Scotland), March 25, 2005, p. 20.
Independent (London, England), March 25, 2005, p. 35.
Times (London, England), March 24, 2005, p. 66.

*   *   *

KOZAK, Warren 1951-

PERSONAL: Born 1951, in WI.

ADDRESSES: Agent—c/o Author Mail, HarperCollins 10 E. 53rd St., 7th Floor, New York, NY 10022.

CAREER: Journalist and writer for network news anchors.

AWARDS, HONORS: Benton fellowship, University of Chicago, 1993.

WRITINGS:

The Rabbi of 84th Street: The Extraordinary Life of Haskel Besser, HarperCollins (New York, NY), 2004.

Also contributor to numerous media outlets, including *PBS, NPR, Wall Street Journal,* and *Washington Post.*

SIDELIGHTS: On the day World War II broke out, young Haskel Besser and his family fled Poland for Palestine, fearing the rising tide of anti-Semitism that was engulfing their homeland. Eventually they moved to the United States, where Besser grew up to be one of New York's most beloved Hasidic rabbis, as well as a commercial real-estate developer, like his father. In 1988, network news journalist Warren Kozak met Besser, and the two developed a warm friendship that inpired Kozak to become Besser's biographer.

The Rabbi of 84th Street: The Extraordinary Life of Haskel Besser recounts Besser's relatively happy childhood growing up in a home that was a meeting place for European intellectuals as well as a place devoted to piety. The rise of Nazism shattered this world, and Kozak's "loving, simply written portrait," in the words of *Library Journal* reviewer Herbert E. Shapiro, chronicles the journey that ultimately took Besser to a small synagogue in Manhattan's upper west side, where the octogenarian has continued to start his day teaching a class on the Talmud at 6:30 a.m. In addition to the rabbi's spiritual influence, Kozak also provides insights into the man's intellectual strengths, such as his library filled with 1,000 books and his encyclopedic knowledge of classical music. In short, according to a *Publishers Weekly* contributor, "Kozak's inspiring and poignant biography of this legendary man is a wonderful concoction of fascinating details and enlightening stories."

BIOGRAPHICAL AND CRITICAL SOURCES:

PERIODICALS

Booklist, July, 2004, George Cohen, review of *The Rabbi of 84th Street: The Extraordinary Life of Haskel Besser,* p. 1802.
Library Journal, July, 2004, Herbert E. Shapiro, review of *The Rabbi of 84th Street,* p. 90.
Publishers Weekly, May 10, 2004, review of *The Rabbi of 84th Street,* p. 53.

ONLINE

HarperCollins Web site, http://www.harpercollins.com/ (February 23, 2005), "Waren Kozak."*

KRANCHER, Jan A. 1939-

PERSONAL: Born September 1, 1939, in Malang, Java, Indonesia; naturalized U.S. citizen; son of Ludwig Adolf and Henriette Jeane (Klaare) Krancher; married Irene Joyce Hauber (a homemaker), March 1, 1965; children: Glenn Clifford, Sheldon Anthony, Corinne Henriette Krancher-Bruno. *Ethnicity:* "Dutch-Indonesian." *Education:* State College of Tropical and Subtropical Agriculture, Deventer, Netherlands, diploma, 1960; University of Hawaii at Manoa, B.S., 1967; California State University, Fresno, M.S., 1976; Donsbach University, Ph.D., 1985. *Politics:* Republican. *Religion:* Church of Jesus Christ of Latter-day Saints (Mormons).

ADDRESSES: Home—831 West Princeton, Visalia, CA 93277-4778. *E-mail*—drjanphd@aol.com.

CAREER: Worked as agriculturist and plant breeder in Salinas Valley, CA, for eight years; manager of plant breeding station in San Joaquin Valley, CA; County Environmental Health, Fresno, CA, registered environmental health specialist, 1973-82; Bechtel Engineering, manager of health services in Saudi Arabia, 1982-85; Tulare County Health and Human Services Agency, registered environmental health specialist, 1985-2003; retired. Environmental health and industrial hygiene specialist for companies in Saudi Arabia, including Al-Jubail Petrochemical Co., 1982-85; Everclean Services, Inc., senior food safety auditor, 2000-03. Nutritionist, 1961—. *Military service:* U.S. Army, interpreter and translator, 1962-65; served in Germany; became sergeant.

MEMBER: National Environmental Health Association.

AWARDS, HONORS: Scroll of appreciation, Lord Mayor of Augsburg, Germany; named contributing author of the year, *Journal of Environmental Health,* 1993.

WRITINGS:

(Editor and translator) *The Defining Years of the Dutch East Indies, 1942-1949: Survivors' Accounts of Japanese Invasion and Enslavement of Europeans and the Revolution That Created Free Indonesia,* McFarland and Co. (Jefferson, NC), 1996.
(Translator from Dutch) *Toean Petoro from Mamasa,* Xlibris (Philadelphia, PA), 2002.

Contributor of articles in Dutch and English to periodicals, including *Journal of Environmental Health.*

WORK IN PROGRESS: Captions and subtitles for *The Indies POW Camp Experience,* a collection of original drawings by a Dutch prisoner of war.

BIOGRAPHICAL AND CRITICAL SOURCES:

ONLINE

Krancher Consult Environmental Health Professional, http://www.krancher.org/ (December 28, 2004).

L

LADY STRANGE
See EVANS, (Jean) Cherry (Drummond)

* * *

LAMANTIA, Philip 1927-2005

OBITUARY NOTICE— See index for *CA* sketch: Born October 23, 1927, in San Francisco, CA; died of heart failure March 7, 2005, in San Francisco, CA. Author. Lamantia was a respected surrealist and mystic poet associated with the Beat generation. Though he had a promising start as a young poet, drugs and depression, as well as an unwillingness to promote his work, relegated Lamantia to relative obscurity among the Beats. He started writing verses in high school, and found early success at age sixteen when one of his poems appeared in the magazine *View;* not long afterwards, another piece by the poet was accepted and printed in the journal *VVV.* Strongly influenced at a young age by surrealist painters such as Joan Miro and Salvador Dali, whose works he had a chance to see at the San Francisco Museum of Art, Lamantia was more interested in pursuing the literary life than staying in school. He dropped out of high school to work as an assistant editor for *View* in New York City, where he met such literary figures as Andre Breton. Returning to California in 1947, he attended the University of California at Berkeley for two years, but dropped out again before completing his degree. It was at this time that Beat poets such as Allen Ginsburg were making their debut, and Lamantia befriended Ginsburg and other Beat writers, including Jack Kerouac. He worked on his poetry and participated in the famous 1955 live reading at the Sixth Gallery in San Francisco that many consider the official launch of the Beat movement. Having by this time published the collections *Erotic Poems* (1946), *Ekstasis* (1959), and *Destroyed Works: Hypodermic Light, Mantic Notebook, till Poems, Spansule* (1962), Lamantia established himself as a surrealist who was also preoccupied with religion and mysticism. A recluse, he shied away from publicity and often disappeared from the literary limelight altogether. At one point, he lived with the Cora Indians and experimented with peyote in an effort to get in touch with his spirituality. Drugs, unfortunately, were a long-lasting bane for the poet, and this, compounded by fits of depression, severely limited his output. Eventually, however, he managed to get off drugs, finding steady work in 1978 as a lecturer at the San Francisco Art Institute. Among his other collections are *Selected Poems: 1943-1966* (1967), *Becoming Visible* (1981), and *Bed of Sphinxes* (1997).

OBITUARIES AND OTHER SOURCES:

PERIODICALS

Chicago Tribune, March 20, 2005, section 4, p. 9.
Los Angeles Times, March 18, 2005, p. B11.
New York Times, March 21, 2005, p. A16.

* * *

LANG, Kenneth R(obert) 1941-

PERSONAL: Born November 16, 1941; son of Robert Raymond and Clara (Barnes) Lang; married Marcella Greco; children: Marina, Julia, David. *Education:* University of Colorado, B.S.; Stanford University, Ph.D.

ADDRESSES: Office—Department of Physics and Astronomy, Robinson Hall, Tufts University, Medford, MA 02155. *E-mail*—klang@emerald.tufts.edu.

CAREER: Tufts University, Medford, MA, professor of physics and astronomy, 1974—National Aeronautics and Space Administration, Washington, DC, senior scientist, 1990-92.

MEMBER: International Astronomy Union, Royal Astronomy Society, American Astronomy Society.

AWARDS, HONORS: Fulbright fellow in Italy; Danforth fellowship; California Institute of Technology, fellow, 1972-73.

WRITINGS:

Astrophysical Formulae: A Compendium for the Physicist and Astrophysicist, Springer-Verlag (New York, NY), 1974.
(Editor, with Owen Gingerich) *A Source Book in Astronomy and Astrophysics, 1900-1975,* Harvard University Press (Cambridge, MA), 1979.
Wanderers in Space: Exploration and Discovery in the Solar System, Cambridge University Press (New York, NY), 1991.
Astrophysical Data: Planets and Stars, Springer-Verlag (New York, NY), 1992.
Sun, Earth, and Sky, Springer-Verlag (New York, NY), 1995.
The Sun from Space, Springer (New York, NY), 2000.
The Cambridge Encyclopedia of the Sun, Cambridge University Press (New York, NY), 2001.
The Cambridge Guide to the Solar System, Cambridge University Press (New York, NY), 2003.

SIDELIGHTS: A prominent astronomer and educator, Kenneth R. Lang is the author of a number of encyclopedic works on the solar system and the greater universe, as well as of several highly specialized treatments of scientific formulae for experts in the field. *Astrophysical Data: Planets and Stars,* for instance, compiles rare tables containing data about globular clusters and emission nebulae, as well as tables on the physical characteristics of known planets and the magnitudes and distances of stars. *Astronomy* contributor Dave Bruning was disappointed by some major errors in these star charts, but concluded that the hard-to-find tables "alone are worth the price of this book," although he cautioned buyers to locate a corrected edition.

More appealing to the amateur astronomer is Lang's *The Sun from Space,* which "presents a lucid and coherent view of the perspectives opened up over the past decade by three spacecraft," in the words of *Science* contributor J. R. Jokipii. After a short introduction discussing the scientific nature of the sun, Lang focuses on the three unmanned spacecraft which were sent to examine phenomena such as sunspots and solar wind in the 1990s. These explorations have dramatically enhanced man's understanding of the star that dominates Earth, and Jokipii concluded, "I can recommend *The Sun from Space* to anyone interested in a coherent and accurate account of the recent advances in our understanding of the Sun and the many ways in which it affects our lives."

Lang expanded his studies of this heavenly body in *The Cambridge Encyclopedia of the Sun.* "Well conceived and brilliantly executed," according to Craig DeForest in *Astronomy,* "Lang's work has a flair and beauty that make it an excellent coffee-table book or gift book. But the attention to detail and clear explanations also make it a well-rounded coursebook for professors teaching solar physics." Lang covers the magnetic atmosphere of the sun, the mysterious solar interior, the influence of solar wind, and numerous other phenomena while drawing on a minimum of equations and an extensive index which allows scientists and laypeople alike to explore a range of topics. He also discusses the various instruments scientists use to gather data on the familiar stellar body.

In *The Cambridge Guide to the Solar System* Lang provides a similar treatment for the planets orbiting the Sun. A "cross between an encyclopedia and an introductory textbook," in the words of *Library Journal* reviewer Barbarly Korper McConnell, the book discusses both historical and scientific information concerning the Sun, the planets that orbit it, and the moons that orbit those planets, as well as the comets and asteroids that travel throughout the solar system. For a *Booklist* contributor, "The photographs are stunning, the numerous charts and graphs are exemplary, and the narrative is bulging with all the important information about the solar system that is available to date."

BIOGRAPHICAL AND CRITICAL SOURCES:

PERIODICALS

Astronomy, February, 1993, Dave Brunning, review of *Astrophysical Data: Planets and Stars,* p. 95; March, 2002, Craig DeForest, review of *The Cambridge Encyclopedia of the Sun,* p. 89.

Booklist, December 15, 2001, review of *The Cambridge Encyclopedia of the Sun,* p. 748; May 15, 2004, review of *The Cambridge Guide to the Solar System,* p. 1652.

Library Journal, April 1, 2004, Barbara Korper McConnell, review of *The Cambridge Guide to the Solar System,* p. 86.

Publishers Weekly, June 25, 2001, review of *The Cambridge Encyclopedia of the Sun,* p. 60.

Science, April 27, 2001, J. R. Jokipii, review of *The Sun from Space,* p. 645.*

* * *

LEAVITT, Martine 1953-
(Martine Bates)

PERSONAL: Born July 19, 1953, in Taber, Alberta, Canada; daughter of James (in the military) and Mary Webster; married first husband, c. 1975 (divorced); married Greg Leavitt, 1995; children: (first marriage) Sterling, Sarah, Rachel, Russell, Candace, Derek; (second marriage) Dallas. *Education:* University of Calgary, graduated (first class honors), 1996; Vermont College, M.F.A., 2003.

ADDRESSES: Home—908 Emerson Rd., High River, Alberta T1V 1B1, Canada. *E-mail*—wmleavitt@aol.com

CAREER: Copy editor for SMART Technologies, Inc.; freelance writer.

MEMBER: Canadian Society of Children's Authors, Illustrators, and Performers, Writer's Union of Canada.

AWARDS, HONORS: American Association of Mormon Letters Award, for *Dragon's Tapestry, Prism Moon,* and *Taker's Key;* Our Choice Award, Canadian Children's Book Centre, for *Prism Moon* and *Taker's Key;* finalist, American Association of Mormon Letters Award, and Best Books for Young Adults designation, American Library Association, 2002, both for *The Dollmage;* Mr. Christie Award for Young Adult Literature, Benjamin Franklin Award, and Top Fifty International Best Books for Young Adults designation, all 2004, all for *Tom Finder;* named laureate, Governor General's award (Canada), 2004, for *Heck Superhero.*

WRITINGS:

NOVELS

The Dollmage, Red Deer Press (Calgary, Alberta, Canada), 2001.
Tom Finder, Red Deer Press (Calgary, Alberta, Canada), 2003.
Heck, Superhero, Front Street Books (Asheville, NC), 2004.

FANTASY TRILOGY; UNDER NAME MARTINE BATES

The Dragon's Tapestry, Red Deer College Press (Red Deer, Alberta, Canada), 1992.
The Prism Moon, Red Deer Press (Calgary, Alberta, Canada), 1993.
The Taker's Key, Red Deer Press (Calgary, Alberta, Canada), 1998.

WORK IN PROGRESS: Lord Death, a fantasy, for Front Street Books.

SIDELIGHTS: Canadian young-adult novelist Martine Leavitt wrote her first three books, an award-winning fantasy trilogy featuring Marwen the Oldwife's apprentice, under the name Martine Bates. The trilogy follows Marwen's adventures as she progresses to her magical destiny as a wizard who falls in love with a prince.

Leavitt's *The Dollmage* revolves around the title character, a wise woman of Seekvalley who protects the people of her village with her magic and her secrete ability to make story dolls. When Dollmage realizes that her power is weakening, she sets out to choose a successor. She knows her successor will be born on a certain date, but on that date twin girls are born in Seekvalley. Dollmage chooses Reenoa as her successor, but Annakey also has magical powers. When catastrophe is about to strike the village, Annakey must convince Dollmage that she can help despite the fact that no one believes she has the powers to so. Writing in *Resource Links,* Ingrid Johnston called the book a "compelling fantasy" and went on to comment that the author "creates a world of magic that is easy to believe in with characters that we come to care about." *School Library Journal* contributor Patricia A. Dollisch noted that Leavitt has created "a tightly plotted story of pride, jealousy, magic, passion, and regret," and called *The Dollmage* a "book that is extraordinary for its characterizations and plot."

In *Tom Finder* Leavitt tells the story of fifteen-year-old Tom, who is living on the streets and knows nothing about himself except his first name. As he tries to figure out who he is, a First Nations medicine man tells the teen he is a "Finder" and that he can help Tom discover his true identity but only after Tom helps find the medicine man's missing son, Daniel. During his quest to find Daniel, Tom has the feeling that Mozart's *The Magic Flute* has played a crucial role in his life, and questions are answered at a performance of the noted opera.

Erin Lukens Darr wrote in *Kliatt* that *Tom Finder* "provides an eye-opening view of the hardships of those less fortunate whom we often ignore" due to Leavitt's "depth and insight." *Resource Links* contributor Donna K. Johnson Alden also praised the book as "an excellent young adult novel, rich in character development, a compelling plot, a realistic male protagonist who easily engages a reader's sympathies—and valuable for its social message of homelessness in a modern Canadian city."

Heck, Superhero is about a thirteen year old who has artistic talents, especially as a cartoonist. Life has been hard for Heck's mother and they now live day-by-day on little money. Heck turns to drawing cartoon superheroes as a way to cope with his harsh reality. When his mother, who slips in and out of depression, disappears from his life, Heck finds himself on the streets with no home and no money. For the first time in his life, his superheroes cannot help him cope. As he searches for his mother, he encounters a mentally unstable teenager who ends up jumping to his death. This situation leads Heck to realize that he must ask for help if he is ever to find his mother and get his life together.

Betty Carter, writing in *Horn Book* noted that "Heck . . . emerges as a true hero, a complex boy armed with optimism, wit, heart, and commitment." *Booklist* contributor Shelle Rosenfeld felt that some parts of *Heck, Superhero,* such as the teen's encounter with drugs, are "more appropriate for mature readers" and that the ending seems "rushed." Nevertheless, the critic added that "Heck is a well-drawn, sympathetic protagonist who learns that compassion is a superpower, and that asking for help can be the most heroic act of all."

BIOGRAPHICAL AND CRITICAL SOURCES:

PERIODICALS

Booklist, October 1, 2004, Shelle Rosenfeld, review of *Heck, Superhero,* p. 323.
Horn Book, January-February, 2005, Betty Carter, review of *Heck, Superhero,* p. 96.
Kirkus Reviews, September 1, 2004, review of *Heck, Superhero,* p. 869.
Kliatt, November, 2003, Erin Lukens Darr, review of *Tom Finder,* p. 16.
Resource Links, June, 2002, Ingrid Johnston, review of *The Dollmage,* p. 26; October, 2003, Donna K. Johnson Alden, review of *Tom Finder,* p. 36.
School Library Journal, August, 2002, Patricia A. Dollisch, review of *The Dollmage,* p. 192; October, 2004, Maria B. Salvadore, review of *Heck, Superhero,* p. 171.

ONLINE

Canadian Society of Children's Authors, Illustrators, and Performers Web site, http://www.canscaip.org/ (February 11, 2005), "Martine Leavitt."
Front Street Books Web site, http://www.frontstreet books.com/ (February 11, 2005), "Martine Leavitt."
Martine Leavitt Home Page, http://www.martineleavitt. com (February 11, 2005).

*   *   *

LEHR, Dick 1944(?)-

PERSONAL: Born c. 1944. *Education:* Harvard College, B.A., 1976; University of Connecticut School of Law, J.D., 1984.

ADDRESSES: Home—MA. *Office*—c/o Boston Globe, 135 William T. Morrissey Blvd., Boston, MA 02125.

CAREER: Journalist for *Old Lyme Gazette,* Lyme, CT, 1977-79, and *Hartford Courant,* Hartford, CT, 1979-83; *Boston Globe,* Boston, MA, general assignment, legal affairs, Spotlight Team reporter, and feature writer, 1985—.

AWARDS, HONORS: Associated Press (AP) Sports Editors award for best news story, 1989; AP Sevellan Brown Award, 1989, 1990, 1996, 1997; Scripps Howard Public Service Award, 1991; John S. Knight journalism fellowship, at Stanford University, 1991-92; Loeb Award, 1992; Hancock Award, 1992; Pulitzer Prize for nomination for investigative reporting, 1997; AP Managing Editors Public Service Award, 1998; Edgar Allan Poe Award for Best Fact Crime, Mystery Writers of America, 2001, for *Black Mass: The Irish Mob, the FBI, and a Devil's Deal.*

WRITINGS:

(With Gerard O'Neill) *The Underboss: The Rise and Fall of a Mafia Family,* St. Martin's Press (New York, NY), 1989.

(With Gerard O'Neill) *Black Mass: The Irish Mob, the FBI, and a Devil's Deal,* Public Affairs (New York, NY), 2000.

(With Mitchell Zuckoff) *Judgment Ridge: The True Story behind the Dartmouth Murders,* HarperCollins (New York, NY), 2003.

SIDELIGHTS: Writer and reporter Dick Lehr has served on the staff of several New England newspapers since graduating from the University of Connecticut School of Law, including the *Hartford Courant* and the *Boston Globe.* Over the course of his career, he has won several awards for journalism, including a John S. Knight journalism fellowship, the Scripps Howard Public Service Award, and the Associated Press's Managing Editors Public Service Award. In 1997, he was a finalist for the Pulitzer Prize in investigative reporting. He has also coauthored a number of true crime books, combining his writing talents with his legal knowledge and a reporter's skill for digging up the facts and examining the motivations behind a given event.

Lehr's first book, *The Underboss: The Rise and Fall of a Mafia Family,* which he cowrote with Gerard O'Neill, examines the structure of the Mafia in Boston by focusing on the Angiulo family. Lehr and O'Neill then turn their attention to the Irish mob, partnering once again to write *Black Mass: The Irish Mob, the FBI, and a Devil's Deal.* Based on a news story they originally broke, the book traces the lives of South Boston FBI agent John J. Connolly, Jr., and James "Whitey" Bulger, also from South Boston and a hardened criminal, and examines how the two mens' lives ultimately intersected. It started with Connolly using Bulger as an informant, but led to his encouraging Bulger and Bulger's friend and co-informant Stephen Flemmi to provide information that would enable agents to bring down key players in the Italian mob—thereby eliminating Bulger's competition. Not only did Connolly proceed to disregard standard procedure for dealing with informants, but he involved his supervisor and other coworkers as well, ultimately leading to a conspiracy that included more that a dozen local FBI agents. While the FBI was able to decrease Italian mob activity in Boston, their methods allowed Bulger and Flemmi to increase their own businesses to fill part of the gap.

Washington Post Book World contributor Peter H. Stone remarked that "through diligent investigative reporting, *Black Mass* succeeds admirably in showing just how fragile FBI integrity can be when the good guys lose sight of truth, the rules, and the law." Alan M. Dershowitz wrote in the *New York Times Book Review* that the book "should prompt a re-evaluation of the uses and misuses of informers by law enforcement officials throughout the country." William Bratton, reviewing for the *Boston Globe,* commented: "The book is a great read—it reels you in and holds you. O'Neill and Lehr have the remarkable ability to put you in the room and on the street where the action takes place. The dialogue is vital, gutsy, down and dirty." *Black Mass* was awarded the Mystery Writers of America's Edgar Allan Poe Award for Best Crime Fact book in 2001.

For *Judgment Ridge: The True Story behind the Dartmouth Murders* Lehr collaborated with Mitchell Zuckoff and traveled to small-town America in order to report the gruesome murders of two Dartmouth College professors who were stabbed to death in their homes by a pair of teenage boys. The murders occurred in early 2001, when Robert Tulloch and Jim

Parker, residents of nearby Chelsea, Vermont, decided they wanted to move to Australia and that the way to earn the money for their trip was by stealing it. Later police uncovered the true motivation for the brutal murders as, not robbery, but curiosity: Robert wanted to know what it would be like to kill someone. *Booklist* critic Vanessa Bush called the book "a chilling and revealing look at a crime that fueled concerns about adolescents and violence." A contributor to *Publishers Weekly* found the work "meandering yet irresistibly absorbing," noting that Lehr and Zuckoff "appear to have been reluctant to omit any mundane detail or passing commentary, [thus] bogging down their energetic narrative." Douglas McCollam, reviewing for the *Washington Post Book World,* commented that the authors "convincingly explore those particular strands of teenage DNA that sometimes mutate into murder: the extreme self-possession, the feelings of invulnerability and the desire to defy authority. *Judgment Ridge* is a scary and depressing examination of what can happen when that mutation goes unchecked."

BIOGRAPHICAL AND CRITICAL SOURCES:

PERIODICALS

Atlantic Monthly, August, 2000, Phoebe-Lou Adams, review of *Black Mass: The Irish Mob, the FBI, and a Devil's Deal,* p. 98.

Book, September, 2000, Rob Stout, review of *Black Mass,* p. 82.

Booklist, June 1, 2000, Mary Carroll, review of *Black Mass,* p. 1814; November 15, 2001, Ted Hipple, review of *Black Mass,* p. 591; September 15, 2003, Vanessa Bush, review of *Judgment Ridge: The True Stories behind the Dartmouth Murders,* p. 188.

Boston Globe, June 7, 2000, David Nyhan, "Read All about It: The Vicious Record of Whitey Bulger and His Protectors," p. A19; August 13, 2000, William Bratton, review of *Black Mass,* p. D1.

Denver Post, November 16, 2003, Robin Vidimos, "Double Murder Probe Comes down to Why," p. F13.

Kirkus Reviews, July 15, 2003, review of *Judgment Ridge,* p. 953.

Library Journal, June 1, 2000, Charlie Cowling, review of *Black Mass,* p. 162; August, 2003, Deirdre Bray Root, review of *Judgment Ridge,* p. 106.

New York Times Book Review, July 16, 2000, Alan M. Dershowitz, "Stoolies," review of *Black Mass,* p. 16; November 2, 2003, Andrea Higbie, review of *Judgment Ridge,* p. 28.

Publishers Weekly, May 22, 2000, review of *Black Mass,* p. 86; July 21, 2003, review of *Judgment Ridge,* pp. 186-187.

Reason, January, 2004, Jesse Walker, "The Blurry Blue Line" review of *Black Mass,* p. 14.

St. Louis Post-Dispatch, June 4, 2000, Harry Levins, "Boston Scandal Inspires Both Novel and True Story," p. F10.

Telegram and Gazette (Worcester, MA), June 20, 2000, Lee Hammel,"Authors Doubt FBI Aimed Leaks at Mob," p. A2; October 10, 2003, Pamela H. Sacks, "Duo Didn't Rush to 'Judgment': 'Dartmouth Murders' Authors Patiently Pursued Teens' Motives in Zantop Slayings," p. C1.

Tribune Books (Chicago, IL), December 24, 2000, David Wise, review of *Black Mass,* p. 1.

Washington Post Book World, July 16, 2000, Peter H. Stone, "Crime Tsars" review of *Black Mass,* p. X9; September 14, 2003, Douglas McCollam, "The Death Penalty on Trial, a Down-Home Defense and Teens Who Kill," p. T6.

ONLINE

BookBrowse.com, http//www.bookbrowse.com/ (February 9, 2005), "Dick Lehr."

HarperCollins Web site, http://www.harpercollins.com/ (February 9, 2005), "Dick Lehr."*

*   *   *

LEICK, Gwendolyn 1951-

PERSONAL: Surname is pronounced "Like"; born February 25, 1951, in Öberaichwald, Austria; daughter of Reginald (a physician) and Herta (a social worker; maiden name, Schescherul) Leick; married Charlemagne Kanon, July 31, 2001; children: George Sebastian, Joseph Ibrahim. *Ethnicity:* "Austrian." *Education:* Karl Franzens University, Dr.Phil., 1977; London School of Oriental and African Studies, London, postdoctoral study, 1977-79. *Religion:* Roman Catholic.

ADDRESSES: Home—97-99 Sclater St., London E1 6HR, England. *Office*—Chelsea College of Art and

Design, University of the Arts, John Islip St., London SW1 P4RG, England. *E-mail*—gwendolynl@onetel. net.uk.

CAREER: Property owner and manager in southern Austria, 1972-77; Theater of Mistakes, public relations manager, 1979-84; University of Reading, Reading, England, part-time lecturer in ancient Near Eastern archaeology and literature, 1982-89; University of Glamorgan, Pontypridd, Glamorgan, Wales, senior lecturer in anthropology, 1991-96; Chelsea College of Art and Design, University of the Arts, London, England, senior lecturer in history and theory of design, 1995—. Part-time lecturer at City University, London, 1980-83, National University of Wales, Cardiff, 1991-94, and American International University, London, 1995—.

MEMBER: Royal Anthropological Institute (fellow), Institute for Learning and Teaching in Higher Education.

WRITINGS:

Dictionary of Ancient Near Eastern Architecture, Routledge (New York, NY), 1988.
Dictionary of Ancient Near Eastern Mythology, Routledge (New York, NY), 1991, 2nd edition, 1999.
Sex and Eroticism in Mesopotamian Literature, Routledge (New York, NY), 1994.
Who's Who in the Ancient Near East, Routledge (New York, NY), 1999.
Mesopotamia: The Invention of the City, Penguin Books (New York, NY), 2002.
Historical Dictionary of Mesopotamia, Scarecrow Press (Lanham, MD), 2003.
The Babylonians: An Introduction, Routledge (New York, NY), 2003.

Contributor to books, including *Encyclopedia of World Mythology,* edited by A. Cotterell, Dempsey Parr, 1999. Contributor of articles and reviews to periodicals, including *Folklore.*

Some of Leick's writings have been published in Spanish and Italian.

WORK IN PROGRESS: General editor of *The Babylonian World,* publication by Routledge (New York, NY) expected in 2006; research on urbanization processes in antiquity and present-day Africa.

SIDELIGHTS: Gwendolyn Leick told *CA:* "I studied Assyriology because I thought it was a difficult, arcane, and somewhat esoteric subject which would not lead to a normal career. I discovered that, while I was not particularly gifted to do epigraphic work—transcribing and translating cuneiform tablets—I could communicate and transmit the results of Assyriological scholarship to a wider audience, to make the field more accessible. That's why I began to write encyclopedic dictionaries as the most user-friendly, concise, and straightforward way to access information on matters concerning the ancient Near East.

"I am generally interested in processes of intellectual transmission across languages, cultures, periods, and customs. I have taught all sorts of subjects without being a specialist, but as a curious explorer. This mentality of being able to sit on the fence was probably fostered by the fact that I am an immigrant to the United Kingdom, having left my native Austria at the age of twenty-five, lured by the British Museum and the cosmopolitan life in London. I wanted to become a writer in English because it is for me the most accommodating, rich, and ecumenical of modern languages which allows so many people, regardless of their original language, to find a worldwide audience."

BIOGRAPHICAL AND CRITICAL SOURCES:

PERIODICALS

Antiquity, September, 1995, Timothy Taylor, review of *Sex and Eroticism in Mesopotamian Literature,* p. 632.
Booklist, December 15, 2003, Mary Ellen Quinn, review of *Historical Dictionary of Mesopotamia,* p. 765.
Journal of Near Eastern Studies, October, 2003, Robert D. Biggs, review of *Who's Who in the Ancient Near East,* p. 290.

*   *   *

LEIGH, Tera 1964-

PERSONAL: Born 1964. *Education:* Western State University, Fullerton, CA, J.D., 1993; studied makeup at Joe Blasco, Hollywood, CA.

ADDRESSES: Office—6965 El Camino Real #105-431, Carlsbad, CA 92009. *E-mail*—tera@teraleigh.com.

CAREER: Artist and attorney. Has worked as an esthetician and as a secretary. Admitted to the Bar of the State of California, 1993. Law Office of Curtis L. Gemmil, Whittier, CA, personal injury investigator, 1986-89, supervisor of Investigative and Research Department, 1990-92, attorney, 1993-95; attorney in private practice, Whittier, 1995—; artist's consultant on law, 2001-04; freelance legal consultant, 2004—. Founder and chief executive officer of ToleNet (online decorative painting company; president of Memory Box Project (nonprofit organization), 2001—. Spokesperson for Robert Simmons Sapphire Brush line, 2002-05; has also been a guest artist for Paintideas.com, Rustoleum, 2004, and Hewlett-Packard.com scrapbook Web site, 2004-05. Appeared as a guest on numerous television and radio shows, including *Aleen's,* The Nashville Network (TNN), *Creative Living with Sheryl Borden,* Public Broadcasting System (PBS); *Scrapbooking,* DIY Network; and *It's Christopher Lowell Show,* Discovery Network.

MEMBER: Housing Industry Association, Society of Creative Designers, Society of Decorative Painters.

AWARDS, HONORS: Best Artist Award, Joe Blasco Makeup Academy, 1983; American Jurisprudence Award, Trusts, 1991; Crafts/Craftrends Award of Excellence (with others), 2001, (solo recipient), 2003; Top Ten Craft/Hobby Book designation, American Library Association, 2002, for *Complete Book of Decorative Painting,* and 2003, for *How to Be Creative If You Never Thought You Could;* More than Words award, Harlequin Enterprises, 2004; Special Recognition Award, Housing Industry Association, 2003; Designers with Heart Award, Society of Craft Designers, 2004.

WRITINGS:

The Complete Book of Decorative Painting, North Light Books (Cincinnati, OH), 2001.
How to Be Creative If You Never Thought You Could, North Light Books (Cincinnati, OH), 2003.
Faux Mosaics, North Light Books (Cincinnati, OH), 2004.

Also contributor to *Crafters' Internet Handbook: Research, Connect, and Sell Your Crafts Online,* Muska & Lipman Publishing, 2002; and *Everything Crafts: Easy Projects,* Adams Media (Cincinnati, OH), 2005. Has contributed columns and articles to numerous decorative arts magazines, including *Artist's Magazine Sketchbook, Craft & Needlework Age, Country Marketplace, Create & Decorate, Decorative Artists Workbook, Paintworks, Priscilla's Club* Online magazine, *Quick & Easy Painting,* and *Tole World.* Member of editorial board, *PaintWorks* and *Quick & Easy Painting.*

SIDELIGHTS: Tera Leigh was a practicing lawyer who committed herself to becoming an artist in 1999. In an interview on the *Another Girl at Play* Web site, Leigh said, "My first creative goals were to create a product line and write a reference book to make it easier for people to learn how to paint." Her first book, *The Complete Book of Decorative Painting,* focuses on folk-art painting and discusses such aspects of the craft as faux finishes, brush-stroke techniques, and realistic interpretations. She also details how to do surface preparation, master floating techniques, and complete the job with finishing. Much of her instruction is presented in a question-and-answer format, such as "I can't draw a straight line. How can I paint?" Leigh also tells readers they can get the most out of classes and seminars, and she lists the major decorative arts conventions throughout the world. In an interview on the *Kota Press* Web site, Leigh noted that she wanted to "write a good reference book on painting that would fill a gap I thought existed between other books currently available." Writing in *Booklist,* Barbara Jacobs commented on the "depth and breadth of the detail" in the book and called it a "bible for novices and experienced painters."

In *How to Be Creative If You Never Thought You Could,* Leigh presents readers with fifteen projects, guiding them through each step with the focus on becoming creative in the crafts. She discusses working with a variety of media and techniques, including metal, paper, mosaics, collage, and painting. She also discusses the need for confidence while producing crafts and guides the reader in generating ideas. Daniel Lombardo, writing in *Library Journal,* commented, "The result is a good choice for most craft collections." *Booklist* contributor Whitney Scott noted that the book "goes beyond abstractions and sensitivity-training exercises" and "will be a key starting point for beginners." Keir Graff, also writing in *Booklist,* included *How to Be Creative If You Never Thought You Could* among his top-ten craft and hobby books in 2003, and wrote, "Crafts novices who doubt their creative ability will welcome Leigh's advice."

Leigh guides the reader through twenty step-by-step projects in *Faux Mosaics.* She demonstrates how to paint on grout, create beautiful tiles with various papers, and glaze the tiles. Among the projects are decorating a necklace, a jewelry box, and coasters. Many of the projects can be completed in just a few hours, and the reader learns how to apply mosaic designs to almost any surface. A reviewer writing for *Expressions* liked the accompanying photography and called Leigh's instructions "super clear." Stephanie Zvirin, writing in *Booklist,* also praised "Leigh's precise, easy-to-follow instructions."

BIOGRAPHICAL AND CRITICAL SOURCES:

PERIODICALS

Booklist, January 1, 2002, Barbara Jacobs, review of *The Complete Book of Decorative Painting,* p. 792; March 1, 2003, Whitney Scott, review of *How to Be Creative If You Never Thought You Could,* p. 1135; December 15, 2003, Keir Graff, review of *How to Be Creative If You Never Thought You Could,* p. 717; July, 2004, Stephanie Zvirin, review of *Faux Mosaics,* p. 1809.
Expression, November-December, 2004, review of *Faux Mosaics,* p. 98.
Library Journal, March 15, 2003, Daniel Lombardo, review of *How to Be Creative If You Never Thought You Could,* p. 82.

ONLINE

Another.GirlatPlay.com, http://another.girlatplay.com/ (February 11, 2005), interview with Leigh.
Kota Press Web site, http://www.kotapress.com/ (February 11,2005), interview with Leigh.
Tera Leigh Home Page, http://teraleigh.com (February 11, 2005).

*   *   *

LEITH, Denise J. 1954-

PERSONAL: Born April 4, 1954, in Sydney, New South Wales, Australia. *Education:* Macquarie University, Ph.D.

ADDRESSES: Agent—c/o Author Mail, Random House Australia, 20 Alfred St., Milsons Point, New South Wales 2061, Australia. *E-mail*—deniseleith@ iprimus.com.au.

CAREER: Writer and academic specializing in international relations.

WRITINGS:

The Politics of Power: Freeport in Suharto's Indonesia, University of Hawaii Press (Honolulu, HI), 2002.
Bearing Witness: The Lives of War Correspondents and Photojournalists, Random House Australia (Milsons Point, New South Wales, Australia), 2004.

SIDELIGHTS: Dense J. Leith told *CA:* "I was not so much 'interested' in writing but, rather, I felt compelled to write about contemporary international political issues—particularly with regard to human rights and war. I believe writing and the opportunity to be published is an extraordinary privilege and responsibility.

"My work is most influenced by the myriad individuals who are committed to writing or speaking with honesty and integrity about critical political and social issues. I cannot abide lies and deceptions and journalists who uncritically report these as 'news.'

"The most I can hope for with my work is to encourage people to continually examine their own place and responsibility within the world."

*   *   *

LEVINE, Eliot 1967-

PERSONAL: Born January 5, 1967, in MA; son of Earle M. and Barbara A. (Parlow) Levine; married Madge C. Evers; children: Jesse. *Education:* Massachusetts Institute of Technology, B.S., 1989; University of Maryland, M.S., 1995, Ph.D., 1998.

ADDRESSES: Agent—c/o Author Mail, Teachers College Press, 1234 Amsterdam Ave., New York, NY 10027.

CAREER: Teacher and research consultant.

WRITINGS:

One Kid at a Time: Big Lessons from a Small School, Teachers College Press (New York, NY), 2001.

BIOGRAPHICAL AND CRITICAL SOURCES:

PERIODICALS

Education Next, summer, 2003, Robin J. Lake, review of *One Kid at a Time: Big Lessons from a Small School,* p. 83.
Library Journal, February 1, 2002, Terry Christner, review of *One Kid at a Time,* p. 112.

*   *   *

LINDHOLM, Anna Margaret
    See HAYCRAFT, Anna (Margaret)

*   *   *

LINOWITZ, Sol M(yron) 1913-2005

OBITUARY NOTICE— See index for *CA* sketch: Born December 7, 1913, in Trenton, NJ; died March 18, 2005, in Washington, DC. Businessperson, diplomat, lawyer, and author. Linowitz was a former executive for Xerox who also served in the Johnson and Carter administrations as a diplomat, most notably negotiating the turn-over of the Panama Canal to the Panamanians. Completing his undergraduate work at Hamilton College in 1935, he then studied law at Cornell University, where he earned his J.D. with highest honors in 1938. Admitted to the Bar of New York State that same year, he joined the Sutherland & Sutherland law firm in Rochester. When America entered World War II, he applied his legal skills to the Office of Price Administration as an assistant general counsel and later enlisted in the navy as a legal officer. With the war over, he returned to practicing law as a partner in the Sutherland, Linowitz & Williams firm, which later became Harris, Beach, Keating, Wilcox & Linowitz. During this time, his legal assistance for Haloid

Company, the first producer of commercial copiers, turned into a full-time job after the company became Xerox Corporation. Named general counsel and chair of the board of directors in 1958, he worked there for the next eight years while Xerox became a leading business machines company. Linowitz entered the world of politics in 1966, when he accepted President Lyndon Johnson's invitation to be U.S. ambassador to the Organization of American States and U.S. representative to the Inter-American Committee on the Alliance for Progress. He held this post for three years before returning to law as a senior partner with Coudert Brothers. While still working for Coudert, President Jimmy Carter approached Linowitz with another offer: serving as co-negotiator for the Panama Canal treaties from 1977 to 1978. The canal was originally built by the United States, with the first ships navigating it by 1914. However, the nation of Panama, which won independence in 1903, had long disliked the fact that so much of its territory was controlled by a foreign power. Though many politicians saw the canal as a matter of national security for the United States, President Carter felt that an equitable agreement could be reached, and Linowitz was key in having a treaty signed that eventually, in 1999, turned over all authority over the canal to Panama. Long afterwards, Linowitz would consider this his greatest achievement. He continued his involvement with Latin America as co-chair of the Inter-American Dialogue from 1981 until 1992 and was also involved in talks between Israel and the Palestinians as special Middle East negotiator for Carter from 1979 until 1981. During the Carter administration, he also was chair of the Presidential Committee to End World Hunger. After retiring from law as senior counsel for Coudert Bros. in 1994, he published *The Betrayed Profession: Lawyering at the End of the Twentieth Century* (1994), which was highly critical of the way the legal profession had evolved into a business concerned only with making money. Honored with the Presidential Medal of Freedom in 1998, Linowitz was also the author of several other books, including *This Troubled Urban World* (1974), *World Hunger: A Challenge to American Policy* (1980), and *The Making of a Public Man: A Memoir* (1985).

OBITUARIES AND OTHER SOURCES:

BOOKS

Linowitz, Sol M., *The Making of a Public Man: A Memoir,* Little, Brown (Boston, MA), 1985.

PERIODICALS

Chicago Tribune, March 19, section 2, p. 11.
Los Angeles Times, March 19, 2005, p. B16.
New York Times, March 19, 2005, p. B12.
Times (London, England), April 8, 2005, p. 70.
Washington Post, March 19, 2005, p. B6.

*   *   *

LINSLEY, Leslie

PERSONAL: Married Jon Aron (a photographer and illustrator).

ADDRESSES: Home—Nantucket, RI. *Office*—Zero India St., Nantucket Island, MA 02554. *E-mail*—info@leslielinsley.com.

CAREER: Writer and designer. *Craftclick.com,* chief editorial consultant; former craft-pages editor, *Family Circle* magazine. Owner and operater of Leslie Linsley Nantucket (studio and crafts store), Nantucket, RI. Commercial spokesperson. Frequent guest on television shows such as *Good Morning America, Oprah,* and *Today.* Lecturer and guest speaker at women's groups throughout the country.

WRITINGS:

Decoupage: A New Look at an Old Craft, photography by husband, Jon Aron, Nelson (London, England), 1975.
Decoupage Designs: Seventy-five Projects You Can Do with Color Prints, line drawings by Jon Aron, Doubleday (Garden City, NY), 1975.
You Can Decoupage the Plain and Uglies around Your House, illustrated by Jon Aron, C. R. Gibson Co. (Norwalk, CT), 1975.
The Art of Creative Acrylic (Hyplar) Crafts, photography by Jon Aron, M. Grumbacher (New York, NY), 1976.
The Decoupage Workshop, photography by Jon Aron, Doubleday (Garden City, NY), 1976.
Scrimshaw: A Traditional Folk Art, a Contemporary Craft, photography by Jon Aron, Hawthorn Books (New York, NY), 1976.

Decoupage for Young Crafters, photography by Jon Aron, Dutton (New York, NY), 1977.
Decoupage on Glass, Wood, Metal, Rocks, Shells, Wax, Soap, Plastic, Canvas, Ceramic, photographs by Jon Aron, Chilton Book Co. (Radnor, PA), 1977.
Wildcrafts, photography by Jon Aron, Doubleday (Garden City, NY), 1977.
Fabulous Furniture Decorations, photography by Jon Aron, Crowell (New York, NY), 1978.
Army/Navy Surplus: A Unique Source of Decorating Ideas, photography by Jon Aron, Dell (New York, NY), 1979.
Custom Made, photographs by Jon Aron, Harper & Row (New York, NY) 1979.
New Ideas for Old Furniture, photographs by Jon Aron, Crowell (New York, NY) 1980.
(With Jon Aron) *Photocraft,* Dell (New York, NY), 1980.
The Great Bazaar, photographs by Jon Aron, Delacorte Press (New York, NY), 1981.
Making It Personal with Monograms, Initials, and Names, photographs by Jon Aron, R. Marek Publishers (New York, NY), 1981.
Air Crafts: Playthings to Make and Fly, photographs by Jon Aron, Lodestar Books (New York, NY), 1982.
Leslie Linsley's Christmas Ornaments and Stockings, photographs by Jon Aron, St. Martin's Press (New York, NY), 1982.
Million-Dollar Projects from the Five-and-Ten-Cent Store, photographs by Jon Aron, St. Martin's Press (New York, NY), 1982.
America's Favorite Quilts, illustrations by Michael Strahm and Jeffrey Tarr, photographs by O. E. Nelson, Delacorte Press (New York, NY), 1983.
Quick and Easy Knit and Crochet, St. Martin's Press (New York, NY), 1983.
Afghans to Knit and Crochet, photographs by Jon Aron, illustrated by Greg Worth, St. Martin's Press (New York, NY), 1984.
Leslie Linsley's Night before Christmas Craft Book, design and photographs by Jon Aron, St. Martin's Press (New York, NY), 1984.
Carry-along Crochet, Sedgewood Press (New York, NY), 1985.
Country Decorating with Fabric Crafts, photographs by Jon Aron, St. Martin's Press (New York, NY), 1985.
First Steps in Quilting, Doubleday (Garden City, NY), 1986.
First Steps in Stenciling, illustrations by Peter Peluso, Jr., photographs by Jon Aron, Doubleday (New York, NY), 1986.

The Weekend Quilt, St. Martin's Press (New York, NY), 1986.

Calico Country Crafts, St. Martin's Press (New York, NY), 1987.

First Steps in Counted Cross Stitch, photographs by Jon Aron, Doubleday (New York, NY), 1987.

Country Patchwork and Quilting, illustrations by Peter Peluso, Jr., and Robby Smith, photographs by Jon Aron, Sedgewood Press (New York, NY), 1988.

(With the National Needlework Association) *Quilts across America: The Making of the Great American Quilt Banner,* St. Martin's Press (New York, NY), 1988.

A Rainbow of Afghans, photographs by Jon Aron, Sedgewood Press (New York, NY), 1989.

Country Weekend Patchwork Quilts: Twenty-six Quilts to Make with Time-saving Shortcuts and Techniques, illustrations by Robby Smith and Peter Peluso, Jr., photographs by Jon Aron, Sedgewood Press (New York, NY), 1990.

The Illustrated Afghan, photographs by Jon Aron, Sedgewood Press (New York, NY), 1990.

Nantucket Style, photographs by Jon Aron, Rizzoli International Publications (New York, NY), 1990.

A Quilter's Country Christmas: More than Fifty Projects to Make Your Home, Gifts, and Decorations Extra Special for the Holidays, St. Martin's Press (New York, NY), 1990.

Hooked Rugs: An American Folk Art, photographs by Jon Aron, C. Potter (New York, NY), 1992.

Key West Houses, photographs by Jon Aron, Rizzoli International Publications (New York, NY), 1992.

Leslie Linsley's Weekend Decorating: 1,001 Quick Home Decorating Ideas, Tips, and How-Tos, Warner Books (New York, NY), 1993.

More Weekend Quilts: Nineteen Classic Quilts to Make with Shortcuts and Quick Techniques, St. Martin's Press (New York, NY), 1993.

Pretty Patchwork, photographs by Jon Aron, Meredith Press (New York, NY), 1993.

Small Patchwork and Quilting, illustrations by Robby Savonen, photographs by Jon Aron, Meredith Press (New York, NY), 1993.

Leslie Linsley's Country Christmas Crafts: More than Fifty Quick-and-Easy Projects to Make for Holiday Gifts, Decorations, Stockings, and Tree Ornaments, photographs by Jon Aron, St. Martin's Griffin (New York, NY), 1995.

Leslie Linsley's Fifteen-Minute Decorating Ideas, illustrations by Jon Aron, St. Martin's Griffin (New York, NY), 1996.

Leslie Linsley's Quick Christmas Decorating Ideas, illustrations by Jon Aron, St. Martin's Griffin (New York, NY), 1996.

Totally Cool Grandparenting: A Practical Handbook of Time-tested Tips, Activities, and Memorable Moments to Share—for the Modern Grandparent, St. Martin's Griffin (New York, NY), 1997.

First Home: A Decorating Guide and Sourcebook for the First Time Around, illustrations by Jon Aron, Quill (New York, NY), 1998.

Crafts for Dummies, IDG Books Worldwide, Inc. (Indianapolis, IN), 1999.

Leslie Linsley's High-Style, Low-Cost Decorating Ideas, St. Martin's Griffin (New York, NY), 1999.

Leslie Linsley's Decoupage: Design, Create, Display, photographs by Jon Aron, Bulfinch Press (New York, NY), 2004.

A Nantucket Christmas, photographs by Jeffrey Allen, Bulfinch Press (New York, NY), 2004.

Contributor to periodicals, including *Boston Herald.* Author of weekly column, *"Home Style,"* for *Nantucket Inquirer.*

SIDELIGHTS: Author, crafts expert, and style specialist Leslie Linsley is the prolific author of more than sixty books on handcrafts, home decorating, and related subjects. She is a frequent guest on television shows such as *Good Morning America, Oprah,* and *Today,* and is a frequent lecturer and guest speaker at women's groups throughout the country. Due to her broad area of expertise, Linsley has served as a commercial spokesperson for a variety of popular home and craft products.

One of Linsley's specialties is decoupage, the art of applying decorative paper cutouts to furniture, storage boxes, plates, and other accessories. Her own decoupage projects sold at high-end retailers such as Tiffany & Co. and Bergdorf-Goodman when interest in the art form was at its height during the 1970s, and these sales helped Linsley fund her college education, noted a writer in *Good Housekeeping.* In *Leslie Linsley's Decoupage: Design, Create, Display* Linsley offers "many inspiring ideas" and "easy-to-follow instructions" for using decoupage to decorate and embellish a room or object's style, commented Gayle Williamson in *Library Journal.* Linsley guides readers through the process of locating pieces that lend themselves to decoupage decoration, determining which design to use, and creating the decoupage applique itself. She covers use of materials such as flowers, wallpaper, fabric, and paper. Thorough information on the materials needed for decoupage arms the reader with the techniques and know-how to successfully begin practicing the art. Linsley also includes instructions for making her specialty item: decoupaged glass plates.

Leslie Linsley's High-Style, Low-Cost Decorating Ideas provides a detailed selection of budget-minded decorating tips and techniques. Linsley suggests starting with designs found at popular commercial outlets such as Pier 1 or Crate & Barrel. She gives advice on effects created by innovative painting; luxurious-looking but economical sewing projects; and small touches such as cashmere rugs that enhance a room's appeal. Linsley outlines "almost infinite possibilities for dollar-stretching decorating," commented Barbara Jacobs in *Booklist*.

Linsley addresses one of America's favorite traditional handcrafts in *America's Favorite Quilts,* and includes detailed designs and pattern pieces for well-known quilt styles such as Broken Star, Tree of Life, Log Cabin, Little Red Schoolhouse, and Turkey Tracks. Linsley provides guidance and instructions that are "clear and perfectly geared for beginners," according to a reviewer in *People*.

For crafters and decorators short on time, Linsley offers suggestions on what can be accomplished with a quarter of an hour in *Leslie Linsley's Fifteen-Minute Decorating Ideas*. The author offers quick decorating ideas applicable to every room in the house. She covers seasonal decorating, professional shortcuts, outdoor decorating, new products and materials, and holiday decorating. New trends in decorating are condensed to allow readers to apply the latest style techniques in the shortest amount of time. Linsley also provides tips on lifestyle issues such as time management and control of clutter. "Decorating creativity (and common sense) abounds" in Linsley's book, commented Jacobs in a *Booklist* review.

First Home: A Decorating Guide and Sourcebook for the First Time Around focuses on the decorating needs of first-time homeowners who wish to infuse their new dwellings with a stylish flair. Linsley gives readers what Jacobs called a "very logical sequence of

how-to-think decorating," and carefully explains the many options available to first-time home decorators as well as the advantages and disadvantages of different decorating styles and choices. She includes a number of resources for the best places to find additional information on all aspects of decorating, including online resources. Linsley endorses creating a master plan for home decorating, but she also encourages readers to veer from it if the circumstances, and decorating opportunities, are right. Practical and budget-conscious tips are interspersed with style-minded suggestions. She also provides instructions for the motivated do-it-yourselfer desiring to take on painting, carpeting, and wallpapering tasks. Her suggestions encourage first-timers to find their own style while creating comfortable and practical decor.

Leslie Linsley's Quick Christmas Decorating Ideas contains a series of Yuletide-themed decorating ideas. The author covers topics such as ornaments, table decorations and centerpieces, gift wrapping, lighting, wreaths, door decorations, and more. She includes tips on creating appealing Christmas card and floral displays as well as decorations for the ubiquitous Christmas tree. Many of her suggestions revolve around holiday entertaining and decorating for Christmas get-togethers. All of Linsley's suggestions are "eminently workable," Jacobs noted.

Linsley is also the author of *Crafts for Dummies,* part of IDG Books' enormously popular series of subject guidebooks for absolute beginners. Here Linsley focuses largely on the fundamentals of crafting, with detailed information on basic tools, materials, and techniques. The book includes suggestions on crafting with paint, fabric, paper, needlework, and other materials and dispenses simple yet practical advice for making quilts, pillows, decorative frames, and other handcrafts.

BIOGRAPHICAL AND CRITICAL SOURCES:

PERIODICALS

Booklist, February 15, 1996, Barbara Jacobs, review of *Leslie Linsley's Fifteen-Minute Decorating Ideas,* p. 981; October 15, 1996, review of *Leslie Linsley's Quick Christmas Decorating Ideas,* p. 382; March 1, 1998, Barbara Jacobs, review of

First Home: A Decorating Guide and Sourcebook for the First Time Around, p. 1085; July, 1999, Barbara Jacobs, review of Leslie Linsley's High-Style, Low-Cost Decorating Ideas, p. 1916.

Crafts 'n' Things, November, 1990, review of A Quilter's Country Christmas, p. 16.

Creative Crafts, April, 1982, review of Making It Personal with Monograms, Initials, and Names, p. 12.

Good Housekeeping, May, 2004, "Discover Decoupage: To Give Your Furniture a Pretty Face-Lift, Says Author and Expert Leslie Linsley, All You Need Are Scissors, Glue, and an Amazing Glaze," p. 170; December, 2004, Caroline Hwang, "Trimmed with Tradition: In Her New Book, A Nantucket Christmas, Leslie Linsley Shows How the Simplest Decorations Can Be the Most Stylish," p. 110.

Horn Book, August, 1982, Karen Jameyson, review of Air Crafts: Playthings to Make and Fly, p. 423.

Houston Chronicle, October 2, 1999, Madeleine McDermott Hamm, review of Leslie Linsley's High-Style, Low-Cost Decorating Ideas, p. 1.

Library Journal, June 1, 1980, Constance Ashmore Fairchild, review of Photocraft, p. 1297; June 1, 1980, Constance Ashmore Fairchild, review of New Ideas for Old Furniture, p. 1297; March 1, 1981, Constance Ashmore Fairchild, review of The Great Bazaar, p. 549; January 1, 1982, review of Making It Personal with Monograms, Initials, and Names, p. 88; November 1, 1982, review of Leslie Linsley's Christmas Ornaments and Stockings, p. 2088; May 1, 1983, Janice Zlendich, review of Quick and Easy Knit and Crochet, p. 900; May 1, 1986, Janice Zlendich, review of First Steps in Quilting, p. 115; November 1, 1986, Mary Hemmings, review of The Weekend Quilt, p. 89; September 1, 1990, Barbara Bartos, review of Nantucket Style, p. 218; June 1, 1995, review of Leslie Linsley's Weekend Decorating, p. 70; May 15, 1996, Gayle A. Williamson, review of Leslie Linsley's Fifteen-Minute Decorating Ideas, p. 60; May 15, 1998, Gayle A. Williamson, review of First Home: A Decorating Guide and Sourcebook for the First Time Around, p. 84; May 15, 1999, Gayle A. Williamson, review of Leslie Linsley's High-Style, Low-Cost Decorating Ideas, p. 94; September 15, 2004, Gayle A. Williamson, review of Leslie Linsley's Decoupage: Design, Create, Display, p. 56.

People, April 9, 1984, review of America's Favorite Quilts, p. 22.

Publishers Weekly, March 21, 1980, review of New Ideas for Old Furniture, p. 65; October 16, 1981, Genevieve Stuttaford, review of Making It Personal with Monograms, Initials, and Names, p. 73; August 20, 1982, review of Leslie Linsley's Christmas Ornaments and Stockings, p. 67; April 22, 1983, review of Quick and Easy Knit and Crochet, p. 97; November 18, 1983, review of America's Favorite Quilts, p. 64; May 16, 1986, Sybil Steinberg, review of The Weekend Quilt, p. 68; June 8, 1990, Genevieve Stuttaford, review of Nantucket Style, p. 41; April 6, 1998, review of First Home, p. 75; June 7, 1999, review of Leslie Linsley's High-Style, Low-Cost Decorating Ideas, p. 79.

School Library Journal, December, 1982, review of Million-Dollar Projects from the Five-and-Ten-Cent Store, p. 90; February, 1983, Patricia Homer, review of Air Crafts: Playthings to Make and Fly, p. 70.

ONLINE

Leslie Linsley Home Page, http://www.lesleylinsley.com (April 21, 2005).*

*   *   *

LINZ, Cathie

PERSONAL: Married.

ADDRESSES: Home—Chicago, IL. *Agent*—c/o Author Mail, Silhouette Books, P.O. Box 5190, Buffalo, NY 14240-5190. *E-mail*—cathielinz@aol.com.

CAREER: Writer, novelist, and librarian. Worked in a university law library.

MEMBER: Romance Writers of America.

AWARDS, HONORS: National Service Award, Romance Writers of America; Storyteller of the Year Award, *Romantic Times.*

WRITINGS:

ROMANCE NOVELS

Remembrance of Love, Dell (New York, NY), 1982.
Wildfire, Dell (New York, NY), 1983.

A Summer's Embrace, Dell (New York, NY), 1983.
A Charming Strategy, Dell (New York, NY), 1984.
A Private Account, Dell (New York, NY), 1984.
Winner Takes All, Dell (New York, NY), 1984.
Pride and Joy, Dell (New York, NY), 1985.
A Glimpse of Paradise, Dell (New York, NY), 1985.
Tender Guardian, Dell (New York, NY), 1985.
Lover and Deceiver, Dell (New York, NY), 1986.
Continental Lover, Dell (New York, NY), 1986.
A Handful of Trouble, Dell (New York, NY), 1987.
Change of Heart, Silhouette Books (New York, NY), 1988.
A Friend in Need, Silhouette Books (New York, NY), 1988.
As Good as Gold, Silhouette Books (New York, NY), 1989.
Smiles, Silhouette Books (New York, NY), 1990.
Handyman, Silhouette Books (New York, NY), 1991.
Smooth Sailing, Silhouette Books (New York, NY), 1991.
Flirting with Trouble, Silhouette Books (New York, NY), 1992.
Male Ordered Bride, Silhouette Books (New York, NY), 1993.
Escapades, Silhouette Books (New York, NY), 1993.
Midnight Ice, Silhouette Books (New York, NY), 1994.
One of a Kind Marriage, Silhouette Books (New York, NY), 1994.
Bridal Blues, Silhouette Books (New York, NY), 1994.
Baby Wanted, Silhouette Books (New York, NY), 1995.
A Wife in Time, Silhouette Books (New York, NY), 1995.
Husband Needed, Silhouette Books (New York, NY), 1997.
The Rancher Gets Hitched, Harlequin (Toronto, Ontario, Canada), 1999.
The Cowboy Finds a Bride, Harlequin, (Toronto, Ontario, Canada) 1999.
The Lawman Gets Lucky, Harlequin (Toronto, Ontario, Canada), 2000.
Between the Covers, Harlequin (Toronto, Ontario, Canada), 2001.
A Prince at Last, Silhouette Books (New York, NY), 2002.

"THREE WEDDINGS AND A GIFT" TRILOGY

Michael's Baby, Silhouette Books (New York, NY), 1996.

Seducing Hunter, Silhouette Books (New York, NY), 1996.
Abbie and the Cowboy, Silhouette Books (New York, NY), 1996.

"MARRIAGE MAKERS" TRILOGY

Too Sexy for Marriage, Harlequin (Toronto, Ontario, Canada), 1998.
Too Stubborn to Marry, Harlequin (Toronto, Ontario, Canada), 1998.
Too Smart for Marriage, Harlequin (Toronto, Ontario, Canada), 1998.

"MEN OF HONOR" SERIES

Daddy in Dress Blues, Silhouette Books (New York, NY), 2000.
Stranded with the Sergeant, Silhouette Books (New York, NY), 2001.
The Marine and the Princess, Silhouette Books (New York, NY), 2001.
Married to a Marine, Silhouette Books (New York, NY), 2002.
Sleeping Beauty and the Marine, Silhouette Books (New York, NY), 2003.
Her Millionaire Marine, Silhouette Books (New York, NY), 2004.
Cinderella's Sweet-talking Marine, Silhouette Books (New York, NY), 2004.
The Marine Meets His Match, Silhouette Books (New York, NY), 2004.

Contributor to *Dangerous Men and Adventurous Women: Romance Writers on the Appeal of the Romance,* edited by Jayne Anne Krentz, University of Pennsylvania Press (Philadelphia, PA), 1992.

Author's works have been translated into twenty languages.

SIDELIGHTS: Romance novelist Cathie Linz has written nearly fifty romances, mostly for Silhouette Books. She has been writing and publishing for more than two decades. Linz's novels are often characterized as "sweet," although her characters are sexually aware and drawn to each other. "Some describe these books as sweet because there are no consummated love scenes without marriage in them, but actually my books are very sensual in the build-up, in the building of sexual tension," Linz remarked in an interview for *RomanceEverAfter.com.*

Many of Linz's more recent novels have involved military themes, combining the hard-edged life of a U.S. marine with the more gentle pursuits of romance. As she stated in her *RomanceEverAfter.com* interview, Linz got the idea to use a military man as her hero after a marine spoke at her Chicago-area writers' group. One novel features Curt Blackwell, a marine who learns that the leg wound he suffered in Bosnia has curtailed his active service and restricted him to a desk job. On the plus side, however, he finds out he is the father of a three-year-old girl named Blue and locates her. In a short amount of time, Blackwell has to become what the book's title implies, a *Daddy in Dress Blues.* Intent on making his time with his daughter as rewarding as possible, he asks a preschool teacher, Jessie Moore, to give a crash course in parenting. Blackwell fails to realize, however, that the hauntingly familiar Jessie is the same woman who gladly surrendered her virginity to him twelve years before and who was devastated by his rejection. Jessie struggles to come to terms with her past while she helps the man she once loved cope with his present situation. Suzie Housley, writing for *Myshelf.com,* commented that Linz's "wonderful writing style is unique and her writing, a pure joy to read."

In *Between the Covers* Linz "displays a wonderful talent for combining beautifully created characters, scintillating dialogue, and sassy humor into an absolutely delicious story," remarked Leena Hyat on *TheBestReviews.com.* Shane Huntington, a handsome police officer, faces a problem when he is told by his family's lawyer that he must marry before his thirtieth birthday or risk losing his inheritance. A confirmed bachelor, Shane chafes under the marriage mandate which he sees as just another attempt by his family to control him—they were, after all, scandalized when he decided to join the police force rather than become a doctor. He asks librarian Paige Turner to help him find the perfect wife. Paige has recently started over in Chicago, leaving behind a failed relationship and seeking solace as a quiet librarian. Although she had vowed never again to fall for a handsome man with a wild scheme, she is unable to deny her attraction to Shane. Against her better judgment, the cautious Paige agrees to help. As their plan unfolds, Paige and Shane realize

that she may be offering more than reference help and that his perfect wife may be closer than he thought. Hyat called the book "a hilarious, sexy, and full-of-fun romp that is not to be missed" by romance readers.

Linz returns to a military theme with *Married to a Marine.* Kelly Hart has nursed a crush on Justice Wilder since she was a teenager. Back then, he was her older sister's boyfriend, and Kelly was beneath his notice. His marriage to her sister lasted only two years. Now a physical therapist, Kelly has been called upon to help Justice recover from an injury he suffered while saving a child from a burning car. Hardheaded Justice does not want help, even after Kelly travels to his island hideaway in a soaking downpour to meet with him. Justice agrees to let her stay, but Kelly's long-term crush and Justice's newfound interest move them ever closer to falling for each other. *TheBestReviews.com* critic Cynthia Meidinger called *Married to a Marine* "a great read" with "a strong, fast-paced plot," while *Booklist* reviewer John Charles named it "a sweetly sexy, gently humorous romance."

In *Sleeping Beauty and the Marine* journalist Cassandra Jones is indignant when military hero Sam Wilder ignores her at a press conference in favor of one of her blonde competitors. Assigned to do a magazine profile on the marine, she undergoes a makeover that turns her into a physically stunning "whiplash blonde." No matter how hard the two try to keep things businesslike between them, they find themselves strongly attracted and getting closer all the time. Linz "expertly maneuvers the simmering sexual chemistry between her hero and heroine into a sweetly satisfying romance" novel, Charles commented in another *Booklist* review.

Marine Striker Kozlowski, the hero of *Her Millionaire Marine,* is not happy to have to go back to Texas to run his grandfather's oil company, King Oil, but he has been ordered to do so by his superiors. When assertive but beautiful attorney Kate Bradley offers to help, Striker declines. Kate is just as relieved to not have to deal with the handsome marine, whom she views as little more than a grandstander addicted to danger. As they come together more and more often for business, they soon realize that they might not be the opposites they thought they were. Linz "adds just the right dash of humor and bit of sizzle into this subtly sensual contemporary romance," Charles commented in *Booklist.*

In *The Marine Meets His Match* Captain Rad Kozlowski needs a decoy to put the overzealous daughter of a general off his romantic trail. He asks bookseller Serena Anderson, who has disapproved of the marine ever since he spoke during a fifth-grade career day, to pose as his fiancée. Kozlowski, the owner of the building that houses Serena's bookstore, sweetens the deal by offering to cut her rent in half for a year. Unable to resist, Serena agrees, thinking that a few months of play-acting would be worth the effort. When Kozlowski's family hears of the engagement, Rad and Serena find themselves moving closer to a real engagement. "Funny, upbeat, and heartwarming," was *Library Journal* contributor Kristin Ramsdell's assessment of the book. Writing again for *Booklist,* Charles observed that in *The Marine Meets His Match* Linz "excels at crafting a satisfying sensual yet sweetly humorous form of chemistry between her love interests."

BIOGRAPHICAL AND CRITICAL SOURCES:

PERIODICALS

Booklist, September 15, 2002, John Charles, review of *Married to a Marine,* p. 214; February 1, 2003, John Charles, review of *Sleeping Beauty and the Marine,* p. 976; May 1, 2004, John Charles, review of *Her Millionaire Marine,* p. 1550; July, 2004, John Charles, review of *Cinderella's Sweet-talking Marine,* p. 1827; September 1, 2004, John Charles, review of *The Marine Meets His Match,* p. 72.

Library Journal, August, 2004, Kristin Ramsdell, review of *The Marine Meets His Match,* p. 55.

ONLINE

Cathie Linz Home Page, http://www.cathielinz.com (April 12, 2005).

MyShelf.com, http://www.myshelf.com/ (April 12, 2005), Suzie Housley, review of *Daddy in Dress Blues.*

RomanceEverAfter.com, http://www.romanceeverafter.com/ (April 12, 2005), interview with Linz.

TheBestReviews.com, http://www.thebestreviews.com/ (July 4, 2001), Leena Hyat, review of *Between the Covers;* (August 29, 2002) Cynthia Meidinger, review of *Married to a Marine;* (March 19, 2003) Kathy Boswell, review of *Sleeping Beauty and the*

Marine; (May 14, 2004) Kathy Boswell, review of *Her Millionaire Marine;* (July 23, 2004) Kathy Boswell, review of *Cinderella's Sweet-talking Marine;* (April 12, 2005) "Cathie Linz."*

*   *   *

LITWAK, Eugene 1925-

PERSONAL: Born June 23, 1925, in Detroit, MI. *Education:* Wayne State University, B.A., 1948; Columbia University, Ph.D., 1948.

ADDRESSES: Office—Department of Sociomedical Sciences, Columbia University, 600 West 168 St., 7th Floor, New York, NY 10032. *E-mail*—el12@columbia.edu.

CAREER: Educator and sociologist. Cornell University Housing Research Center, Ithaca, NY, research associate, 1951-53; Johann-Wolfgang Goethe University, Frankfurt, Germany, instructor and research associate, 1953; University of Chicago, Chicago, IL, assistant director of Family Study Center and instructor in sociology, 1953-56; Columbia University, New York, NY, instructor, then assistant professor, 1956-59, professor, 1972-85, professor of sociology and public health and head of Division of Sociomedical Sciences at the School of Public Health, 1985-96; University of Michigan School of Social Work, Ann Arbor, 1959-71, associate professor, then professor. Visiting professor at University of Tel Aviv, 1970 and 1971, and at Andrus School of Gerontology, University of Southern California, 1992.

MEMBER: American Sociological Association (president of family section, 1969-70; member of William J. Goode book award committee, family section, 1988-89), Sociological Research Association, Eastern Sociological Society (member of executive committee, 1985-87).

AWARDS, HONORS: Center for Advanced Study in the Behavioral Sciences fellow, 1966-67; National Institute of Mental Health special fellow, 1966-67; Ford Foundation visiting scholar, Hungarian Academy of Science, 1967; Australian National University, School of Social Sciences fellow, 1984.

WRITINGS:

Relationship between School-Community Coordinating Procedures and Reading Achievement, Center for Advanced Study in the Behavioral Sciences (Stanford, CA), 1966.

(With Henry J. Meyr) *School, Family, and Neighborhood: The Theory and Practice of School-Community Relations,* Columbia University (New York, NY), 1974.

Helping the Elderly: The Complementary Roles of Informal Networks and Formal Systems, Guilford Press (New York, NY), 1985.

Contributor, with D. Jessop and H. Moulton, to *Family Caregiving across the Life Spans,* edited by E. Kahana, D. Biegel, and M. Wykle, Sage Publications, 1994. Contributor of articles to academic journals, including *Community Mental Health Journal, Journal of Health and Social Behavior, Contemporary Jewry, Marriage and Family Review,* and *American Sociological Review. Research on Aging,* associate editor; *Marriage and Family Living,* associate editor, 1962-68; *Social Problems,* associate editor, 1964-66; *Sociometry,* consulting editor; *Journal of Health and Social Behavior,* associate editor, 1987-89. Member of editorial board, *Journal of Gerontology,* 1989-83, and *Trans-Action.*

SIDELIGHTS: Eugene Litwak is a sociologist who has studied primary groups and formal organizations, including the ways in which such groups are linked to each other and how variations in formal organizational structure relate to optimal delivery of services. For example, in his 1985 book, *Helping the Elderly: The Complementary Roles of Informal Networks and Formal Systems* Litwak focuses on how informal primary groups—such as children, close friends, spouses, and neighborhoods—and large secondary and formal organizations—such as nursing homes and other service providers—can work together to provide care for the elderly who cannot take care of themselves. Litwak points out that informal primary groups deal better with uncertainty and idiosyncratic needs while formal organizations are best at providing routine services, such as bathing, feeding, and medical services. In a review for *Contemporary Sociology,* Sarah H. Matthews commented, "Contrary to popular wisdom . . . primary groups and formal organiza-

tions can exist side by side, complementing one another and avoiding conflict and friction."

BIOGRAPHICAL AND CRITICAL SOURCES:

PERIODICALS

American Journal of Sociology, March, 1976, review of *School, Family, and Neighborhood: The Theory and Practice of School-Community Relations,* p. 1230; July, 1986, Sharon M. Keigher, review of *Helping the Elderly: The Complementary Roles of Informal Networks and Formal Systems.*

Annals of the American Academy of Political and Social Sciences, March, 1976, review of *School, Family, and Neighborhood,* p. 157.

Choice, November, 1974, review of *School, Family, and Neighborhood,* p. 1362; January, 1986, J. S. McCrary, review of *Helping the Elderly: The Complementary Roles of Informal Networks and Formal Systems.*

Contemporary Sociology, September, 1986, Sarah H. Matthews, review of *Helping the Elderly.*

Journal of Marriage and Family, May, 1975, review of *School, Family, and Neighborhood,* p. 459.

Library Journal, December 1, 1973, review of *School, Family, and Neighborhood,* p. 3555.

Social Worker, January, 1987, review of *Helping the Elderly: The Complementary Roles of Informal Networks and Formal Systems,* p. 86.

ONLINE

Columbia University Department of Sociology Web site, http://www.sociology.columbia.edu/ (February 1, 2005), "Eugene Litwak."*

*   *   *

LORD ROLL OF IPSDEN
See ROLL, Eric

*   *   *

LOWE, Wendy
See BESMANN, Wendy Lowe

LYONS, Richard K. 1961-

PERSONAL: Born February 10, 1961, in Palo Alto, CA; son of J. Richard (a commercial pilot) and Ida P. Lyons; married; wife's name Jennifer N. (a securities analyst); children: Jake C., Nicole A. *Ethnicity:* "Caucasian." *Education:* University of California, Berkeley, B.S. (with highest honors), 1982; Massachusetts Institute of Technology, Ph.D., 1987. *Politics:* Democrat.

ADDRESSES: Home—460 Michigan Ave., Berkeley, CA 94707. *Office*—Haas School of Business, University of California, Berkeley, CA 94720-1900; fax: 510-643-1420. *E-mail*—lyons@haas.berkeley.edu.

CAREER: Stanford Research Institute (now SRI International), Menlo Park, CA, research analyst in financial industries fivision, 1983-84; Columbia University, New York, NY, began as assistant professor, became associate professor of business and international affairs, 1987-93; University of California, Berkeley, professor of business, 1993—, Schwabacher fellow, 1994, member of executive committee, Institute of Business and Economic Research, 1994-96, chair of Finance Group at Haas School of Business, 2001-02. Organization for Economic Cooperation and Development, research assistant in Paris, France, 1985; Foundation for Advanced Information and Research, Tokyo, Japan, visiting scholar, 1989; National Bureau of Economic Research, research associate; guest speaker at educational institutions, including Stanford University and University of Grenoble. Matthews Asian Funds, chair of board of directors; iShares Inc., member of board of directors; Barclays Global Investors Funds, Inc., member of board of directors; consultant to International Monetary Fund, World Bank, Federal Reserve Bank, and European Commission. Holder of copyrights for musical works; former general building contractor, State of California.

MEMBER: Council on Foreign Relations, Phi Beta Kappa, Beta Gamma Sigma.

AWARDS, HONORS: International affairs fellow, Council on Foreign Relations, 1993; grants from National Science Foundation, 1994-97, 1997-2000, 2000-03.

WRITINGS:

The Microstructure Approach to Exchange Rates, MIT Press (Cambridge, MA), 2001.

Contributor to books, including *European Integration: Trade and Industry,* edited by A. Winters and A. Venables, Cambridge University Press (New York, NY), 1991; *Political Economy, Growth, and Business Cycles,* edited by Z. Hercowitz and L. Leiderman, MIT Press (Cambridge, MA), 1992; *International Financial Contagion,* edited by S. Claessens and K. Forbes, Kluwer (Boston, MA), 2001; *New Developments in Exchange Rate Economics,* edited by L. Sarno and M. Taylor, Edward Elgar Publishing (Northampton, MA), 2002; and *Central Banking, Monetary Theory, and Practice: Essays in Honor of Charles Goodhart,* edited by P. Mizen, Edward Elgar Publishing (Northampton, MA), 2003.

Contributor to scholarly journals, including *Journal of Financial Economics, American Economic Review, Journal of Monetary Economics, Journal of Development Economics, World Bank Economic Review,* and *European Economic Review.* Associate editor, *Journal of Financial Markets, Emerging Markets Review, California Management Review, Finance Research Letters,* and *Journal of International Finance Markets, Institutions, and Money.*

BIOGRAPHICAL AND CRITICAL SOURCES:

ONLINE

University of California, Berkeley Web site, http://faculty.haas.berkeley.edu/ (October 25, 2004), "Richard K. Lyons."

M

MacDONOGH, Katharine

PERSONAL: Female. *Education:* Somerville College, Oxford, graduated 1975.

ADDRESSES: *Agent*—c/o Author Mail, St. Martin's Press, 175 5th Ave., New York, NY 10010.

CAREER: Worked as a translator and editor in Paris, France.

MEMBER: International Napoleonic Society (fellow).

WRITINGS:

Reigning Cats and Dogs: A History of Pets at Court since the Renaissance, St. Martin's Press (New York, NY), 1999.

Other works include *Napoleon against the World* and *The Flight of the Eagle.*

SIDELIGHTS: Katharine MacDonogh's *Reigning Cats and Dogs: A History of Pets at Court since the Renaissance* is filled with facts and anecdotes about the pets kept by royals and aristocrats in the United Kingdom, France, Russia, and Asia. She notes that dogs were banned from the palaces of Ming emperors, who loved their cats, but that canines were favored by artists, like Van Dyck, because they were easier to control for a sitting.

MacDonogh writes of dogs who changed history and suggests that Henry VIII might have been denied a divorce if his representative's greyhound had not knocked over the stool on which the ailing Pope Clement VII's gouty foot was resting. She writes of the affection of lonely queens for their little dogs and the devotion of kings who could trust no one but their canine companions. She also notes that as a child, King George V was forced to eat on the floor with the dogs because his table manners were so poor, and that he removed his clothes, claiming that if the dogs did not have to dress for dinner, neither did he. Other dogs were used to taste their masters' food to ensure that it was safe to eat. Cats caught mice, especially in monasteries, where there tended to be great numbers, and some dogs and cats were merely pets.

Manchester *Guardian* reviewer Anne Solway wrote that "probably your average royal pet could not believe its luck. Throughout most of the era covered, animals were treated with hideous cruelty, for which the British were especially notorious: at Elizabeth I's coronation, a bonfire was topped by a Pope-shaped wicker figure filled with live cats." Solway also felt that royal pets played "the role of the tension-relieving Fool, who can get away with things no one else dares to do without setting an Awful Precedent." A *Publishers Weekly* critic called *Reigning Cats and Dogs* "a work to be browsed for pleasure or consulted for reference." *Booklist* contributor Margaret Flanagan concluded her review by saying, "Chock-full of irresistibly eccentric tidbits, this unique history will appeal to both court watchers and pet lovers."

BIOGRAPHICAL AND CRITICAL SOURCES:

PERIODICALS

Booklist, November 15, 1999, Margaret Flanagan, review of *Reigning Cats and Dogs: A History of Pets at Court since the Renaissance,* p. 597.

Guardian (Manchester, England), September 18, 1999, Anne Solway, review of *Reigning Cats and Dogs,* p. 8.

New York Times Book Review, February 27, 2000, Alida Becker, "All the King's Pets," review of *Reigning Cats and Dogs,* p. 35.

Publishers Weekly, October 18, 1999, review of *Reigning Cats and Dogs,* p. 65.

Times Literary Supplement, October 22, 1999, E. S. Turner, "Corgi and Bess," review of *Reigning Cats and Dogs,* p. 13.*

*   *   *

MacPHERSON, Myra

PERSONAL: Married Jack Gordon.

ADDRESSES: Home—FL and Washington, DC. *Agent*—c/o Author Mail, Indiana University Press, 601 North Morton St., Bloomington, IN 47404.

CAREER: Journalist. Former political reporter for *Washington Post.* Member of board of directors, St. Francis Center Community, Washington, DC.

WRITINGS:

The Power Lovers: An Intimate Look at Politics and Marriage, Putnam (New York, NY), 1975.

Long Time Passing: Vietnam and the Haunted Generation, Doubleday (Garden City, NY), 1984, updated edition, Indiana University Press (Bloomington, IN), 2001.

She Came to Live out Loud: An Inspiring Family Journey through Illness, Loss, and Grief, Scribner (New York, NY), 1999.

Contributor to magazines and the Internet.

SIDELIGHTS: Myra MacPherson, former political reporter for the *Washington Post,* has written books on a variety of political themes. Her first, *The Power Lovers: An Intimate Look at Politics and Marriage,* looks candidly at the personal lives of political couples throughout U.S. history. Through her research and interviews, MacPherson discovers that while partners in political marriages handle the stress of long work hours and the public eye differently, commonalities surface. The author contends that politicians, being often egocentric, make difficult partners, while their spouses are often lonely and left at home to raise children. Covering such topics as divorces, campaigning spouses versus the stay-at-home types, and campaign-trail groupies, the author details several relationships that succeed despite their political confines. Citing Lyndon and Lady Bird Johnson and former Michigan Congresswoman Martha Griffiths and her husband, Hicks, she adds that these couples are the exception.

Some critics believed that MacPherson was off target in her analyses of the primarily male politician's mind. Jane O'Reilly, for example, wrote in the *New York Times Book Review,* "The trouble with the book is that the author, in defiance of her own research, believes that unhappy political marriages could be happy if politics changed. But some men do not wish to be home taking walks in the woods." Writing in the *Washington Post Book World,* a reviewer observed, "Most politicians come out of this . . . reporter's irresistible expose looking power-mad, shallow, and narcissistic and their long-suffering wives loyally dishonest."

MacPherson's *Long Time Passing: Vietnam and the Haunted Generation* focuses on the complex war and its effect on those Americans who came of age during the 1960s and 1970s. She interviewed more than five hundred people for the book, including veterans and their parents, deserters, psychologists, and historians, whose voices she uses to vividly portray the experiences of those most affected during and after the war. She also devotes a section to people who avoided the war in Vietnam, punctuating how America's poor fought this war. Writing in the *Washington Post Book World,* Jack Beatty commented that the author "does justice to an extraordinary range of experience and emotion. Rage, shame, battle lust, a dark rainbow of guilt and regret and grief—these are just a few of the feelings that Myra MacPherson elicits from the veterans with the kind of skillful emphatic questioning a master psychologist might envy. There have been many books on the Vietnam War, but few have captured its second life as memory better than *Long Time Passing.*" An updated version of the book was published in 2001, after which MacPherson went on a speaking tour to universities to discuss Vietnam.

In *She Came to Live out Loud: An Inspiring Family Journey through Illness, Loss, and Grief* MacPherson details the illness of Anna Johannessen, a middle-aged woman from Maryland who was diagnosed with breast cancer in 1989 at age thirty-seven. MacPherson takes a political angle in her story, using the woman's eventual death to explain how Americans deal with sickness and death. A *Publishers Weekly* contributor commented that "MacPherson occasionally gushes in her praise of Anna and her family, but she succeeds in bringing readers into the dying woman's intimate world and in conveying everyone's grief." Bette-Lee Fox, writing in the *Library Journal,* asserted that "this thoughtful and moving portrait conveys death and grieving as positive, life-affirming processes." *New York Times Book Review* contributor Sara Ivry concluded that *She Came to Live out Loud* is "a rich description of an optimistic, charismatic woman who stubbornly refused to allow illness to run her life."

BIOGRAPHICAL AND CRITICAL SOURCES:

PERIODICALS

Booklist, December 15, 1998, Danise Hoover, review of *She Came to Live out Loud: An Inspiring Family Journey through Illness, Loss, and Grief,* p. 708.

Chicago Tribune, April 16, 2002, Mike Conklin, "Vietnam Packing 'Em in on Campus," p. 1.

Library Journal, January, 1999, Bette-Lee Fox, review of *She Came to Live out Loud,* p. 131.

Los Angeles Times Book Review, June 10, 1984, Elizabeth Janeway, review of *Long Time Passing: Vietnam and the Haunted Generation,* pp. 1, 7.

Nation, June 23, 1984, p. 763.

National Review, December 19, 1975, Anne Crutcher, review of *The Power Lovers: An Intimate Look at Politics and Marriage,* pp. 1489-1490.

New York Times, June 24, 1984, Donald Knox, review of *Long Time Passing,* p. 9.

New York Times Book Review, November 30, 1975, Jane O'Reilly, review of *The Power Lovers,* pp. 8, 17; May 9, 1999, Sara Ivry, review of *She Came to Live out Loud,* p. 27.

Publishers Weekly, January 4, 1999, review of *She Came to Live out Loud,* p. 81.

Washingtonian, May, 1999, p. 50.

Washington Post Book World, August 31, 1975, review of *The Power Lovers,* p. 1; June 3,1984, Jack Beatty, review of *Long Time Passing,* pp. 1, 14.

OTHER

Mothers and Daughters (sound recording), 1997, National Public Radio (Washington, DC).*

*   *   *

MAGNUSSON, A. L.
   See MAGNUSSON, Lynne (Augusta)

*   *   *

MAGNUSSON, Lynne (Augusta) 1953-
   (A. L. Magnusson)

PERSONAL: Born 1953.

ADDRESSES: Agent—c/o Author Mail, Cambridge University Press, Edinburgh Bldg., Shaftesbury Rd., Cambridge CB2 2RU, England.

CAREER: University of Waterloo, Waterloo, Ontario, Canada, associate professor of English; Queen's University, Kingston, Ontario, professor of English and literature.

WRITINGS:

(Editor and author of introduction, with C. Edward McGee, as A. L. Magnusson) *The Elizabethan Theatre XI,* P. D. Meany (Port Credit, Ontario, Canada), 1990.

Shakespeare and Social Dialogue: Dramatic Language and Elizabethan Letters, Cambridge University Press (New York, NY), 1999.

(With others) *Reading Shakespeare's Dramatic Language: A Guide,* Arden (London, England), 2000.

(Editor and author of introduction, with C. Edward McGee) *The Elizabethan Theatre XV: Papers Given at the Fifteenth and Sixteenth International Conferences on Elizabethan Theatre Held at the University of Waterloo, Waterloo, Ontario,* P. D. Meany (Toronto, Ontario, Canada), 2002.

(With others) *Shakespeare and the Language of Translation,* Arden (London, England), 2004.

SIDELIGHTS: Lynne Magnusson is a Shakespeare scholar who has edited volumes of conference papers and written books, including *Shakespeare and Social Dialogue: Dramatic Language and Elizabethan Letters.* In the first section of this 1999 release, Magnusson uses politeness theory to study the relationships among the characters of *Henry VIII,* as well as in the sonnets. In the second section, she examines social relations through references to letter writing as found in various Renaissance manuals. According to *Studies in English Literature, 1500-1900* contributor Meredith Anne Skura, "Magnusson . . . calls attention to a neglected dimension of dialogue, in this case its socially determined structure. She argues that dialogue on stage as well as off functions not just semantically, to express meaning, but also socially, to establish and maintain relationships between characters. Because critics often neglect this dimension, Magnusson cautions, they need to be careful about finding psychological or stylistic significance in lines that may be predetermined by social convention rather than created on the spot by the character speaking—or by the playwright."

"Although *Shakespeare and Social Dialogue* is not a long book," noted H. R. Woudhuysen in the *Times Literary Supplement,* "it is a dense one that opens up a relatively new subject." As Wayne A. Rebhorn described in the *Journal of English and Germanic Philology,* "Magnusson has written a splendid book that offers both a compelling method of close reading and a number of careful, discriminating analyses of Renaissance English texts. Like the New Historicists, Magnusson is interested in the ways that literary works articulate the social and political world around them, and she demonstrates in admirable detail how linguistic texture reveals—indeed constructs—social, cultural, and ideological practices."

In her introduction to the book, noted William Dodd in *Shakespeare Quarterly,* "Magnusson expresses surprise at 'how few stylistic studies of Shakespeare's work since the emergence of the new historicism have taken up the challenge to relate linguistic texture to social, cultural, and ideological practices and . . . how few historicist studies have found ways to reengage linguistic detail or texture in any sustained way that accords with their theoretical principles and political enterprise.'" Dodd continued: "*Shakespeare and Social Dialogue* thus aims to begin filling this gaping gulf. But it does much more than that. Though unassumingly written and cautiously argued, it has important implications not only for the analysis of Shakespearean and dramatic dialogue in general but also for the current debate over the nature of character in literature and drama."

BIOGRAPHICAL AND CRITICAL SOURCES:

PERIODICALS

Criticism, summer, 2000, Gary Schneider, review of *Shakespeare and Social Dialogue: Dramatic Language and Elizabethan Letters,* p. 384.

Journal of English and Germanic Philology, April, 2001, Wayne A. Rebhorn, review of *Shakespeare and Social Dialogue,* p. 270.

Renaissance Quarterly, autumn, 2001, review of *Reading Shakespeare's Dramatic Language: A Guide,* p. 999.

Shakespeare in Southern Africa (annual), 2001, Ronald Hall, review of *Reading Shakespeare's Dramatic Language,* p. 107.

Shakespeare Quarterly, spring, 2001, William Dodd, review of *Shakespeare and Social Dialogue,* p. 154.

Shakespeare Studies (annual), 2001, William H. Sherman, review of *Shakespeare and Social Dialogue,* p. 232.

Studies in English Literature, 1500-1900, spring, 2000, Meredith Anne Skura, review of *Shakespeare and Social Dialogue,* p. 355.

Times Literary Supplement, June 18, 1999, H. R. Woudhuysen, review of *Shakespeare and Social Dialogue,* p. 31.*

*   *   *

MAIER, Philipp 1971-

PERSONAL: Born November 6, 1971, in Reutlingen, Germany. *Education:* University of Saarbrücken, B.A., 1994; University of Góttingen, M.A., 1997; Dutch Network of Economics, diploma, 2000; University of Groningen, Ph.D., 2001.

ADDRESSES: Home—F. Bolstraat 15, 1072 LA Amsterdam, Netherlands. *E-mail*—p.maier@dnb.nl.

CAREER: Regional Office for Statistics, Stuttgart, Germany, intern, 1995; European Central Bank, researcher, 2001; Netherlands Central Bank, Amsterdam, economist in Monetary and Economic Policy Department, 2001-03, senior economist, 2003—.

AWARDS, HONORS: Wicksell Prize, best paper by a young economist, European Public Choice Conference, 2000.

WRITINGS:

Political Pressure, Rhetoric, and Monetary Policy: Lessons for the European Central Bank, Edward Elgar Publishing (Northampton, MA), 2002.

Contributor to books, including *History of the Bundesbank: Lessons for the ECB,* edited by J. de Haan, Routledge (London, England), 2000. Contributor to periodicals, including *European Journal of Political Economy, International Organization, Public Choice, Journal of Comparative Economics, Journal of Policy Modeling, Journal of Macroeconomics,* and *Kredit und Kapital.*

BIOGRAPHICAL AND CRITICAL SOURCES:

ONLINE

Philipp Maier Home Page, http://www.philipp-maier.de (October 26, 2004).

*   *   *

MALCOLM, Jahnna N.
See BEECHAM, Jahnna

*   *   *

MALET, (Baldwyn) Hugh (Grenville) 1928-2005

OBITUARY NOTICE— See index for *CA* sketch: Born February 13, 1928, in Salisbury, England; died March 13, 2005, in Taunton, England. Educator, historian, and author. Malet is best remembered as the author of books about his travels on the English and Irish canals,

including *Voyage in a Bowler Hat* (1960; second edition, 1985). Graduating from King's College, Cambridge, in 1951, he joined the Sudan Political Service as a district commissioner. He left this post in 1955 after Sudan won independence from Britain, and worked in industrial relations for Shell Petroleum in Egypt. Returning home in 1959, Malet was a freelance writer and broadcaster for two years, during which time he bought a sixteen-foot boat he named the *Mary Ann.* Knowing little about where he was going, he resolved to travel the canals and other waterways of Britain, recording his adventures of personal discovery in what became *Voyage in a Bowler Hat.* His travels left a lifelong impression on him, and he would later work to help preserve the canal system, which was so important to Britain's history. Malet worked as an editor for the *National Christian News* from 1961 to 1962, and then served as director of studies and lecturer in philosophy for Brasted Place Theological Training College for eleven years. Toward the end of this period, he published another book about canal voyages with *In the Wake of the Gods: On the Waterways of Ireland* (1972); he also published two biographies on the duke of Bridgewater: *The Canal Duke* (1961) and *Bridgewater: The Canal Duke, 1736-1803* (1977; third edition, 1990). In 1973, Malet was hired as a lecturer in local history and fine arts at Salford University, and he would continue to teach there until he retired in 1985. His later books were *O. W. Malet and the Conservation of Taunton Castle* (1988), *The Bridgewater Canal: A Pictorial History* (1990), and *The Blue Anchor Pilgrimage* (1994).

OBITUARIES AND OTHER SOURCES:

PERIODICALS

Independent (London, England), May 7, 2005, p. 61.

*   *   *

MARTENS, Kurt 1870-1945

PERSONAL: Born January 21, 1870, in Leipzig, Germany; committed suicide February 16, 1945, in Dresden, Germany; son of Heinrich Oscar and Henriette (Erckel) Martens; married Mary Fischer, 1899; children: Hertha Helena. *Education:* Attended University in Heidelberg; studied law in Berlin. *Religion:* Roman Catholic.

CAREER: Novelist and author of short fiction. Lawyer, 1895-96.

WRITINGS:

Sinkende Schwimmer: Novellistische Skizzen aus dem Strudel der Zeit, Hochsprung (Berlin, Germany), 1892.

Wie ein Strahl verglimmt (three-act play), Wild (Leipzig, Germany), 1895.

Die gehetzten Seelen: Novellen, Fontane (Berlin, Germany), 1897.

Roman aus der Décadence, Fontane (Berlin, Germany), 1898.

Aus dem Tagebuch einer Baronesse von Treuth und andere Novellen, Fontane (Berlin, Germany), 1899.

Die Vollendung (novel), Fleischel (Berlin, Germany), 1902.

Kaspar D Hauser (four-act play), Fleischel (Berlin, Germany), 1903.

Katastrophen: Novellen, Fleischel (Berlin, Germany), 1904.

Kreislauf der Liebe: eine Geschichte von besseren Menschen, Fleischel (Berlin, Germany), 1906.

Der Freudenmeister (four-act play), Fleischel (Berlin, Germany), 1907.

Drei Novellen von adeliger Lust, Fleischel (Berlin, Germany), 1909.

Literatur in Deutschland: Studien und Eindrücke, Fleischel (Berlin, Germany), 1910.

Die alten Ideale, Volume 1: *Deutschland marschiert: ein Roman von 1813,* Fleischel (Berlin, Germany), 1913, Volume 2: *Pia: der Roman ihrer zwei Welten,* Fleischel (Berlin, Germany), 1913, Volume 3: *Hier und drüben: Roman,* Grethlein (Leipzig, Germany), 1915.

Geschmack und Bildung: Kleine Essays, Fleischel (Berlin, Germany), 1914.

Verse, Bachmair (Munich, Germany), 1914.

Jan Friedrich: der Roman eines Stätsmannes, Grethlein (Leipzig, Germany), 1916.

Die großen und die kleinen Leiden: Novellen, Grethlein (Leipzig, Germany), 1917.

Der Alp von Zerled (novel), Grethlein (Leipzig, Germany), 1920.

Schura: Novelle, Hillger (Berlin, Germany), 1920.

Schonungslose Lebenschronik 1870-1900, Rikola (Vienna, Austria), 1921.

Die Pulververschwörung 1603-1606, Deutscher Verlag (Leipzig, Germany), 1922.

Zwischen Sumpf und Firmament: Novellen, Paetel (Munich, Germany), 1922.

(Editor) *Die deutsche Literatur unserer Zeit: in Charakteristiken und Proben,* Rösl (Munich, Germany), 1922, enlarged edition, Franke (Berlin, Germany), 1933.

Abenteuer der Seele: Novelletten, Reclam (Leipzig, Germany), 1923.

Des Geliebten doppelte Gestalt (novel), Scherl (Berlin, Germany), 1923.

Schonungslose Lebenschronik: Zweiter Teil 1901-1923, Rikola (Vienna, Austria), 1924.

Blausäure: Ein Schuß im Wiener Wald: Kriminal-Novellen, Sieben Staebe (Berlin, Germany), 1929.

Gabriele Bach: Roman einer Deutschen in Paris, Neff (Berlin, Germany), 1935.

Die Tänzerin und der Blinde, Limpert (Berlin, Germany), 1935.

Feldherr in fremdem Dienst: Schicksale des Grafen Matthias von der Schulenburg: Historische Erzählung, Möhring (Leipzig, Germany), 1936.

Die junge Cosima (novel), Janke (Leipzig, Germany), 1937.

Forsthaus Ellermoor (novel), Seyfert (Dresden, Germany), 1937.

Verzicht und Vollendung (novel), Steuben (Berlin, Germany), 1941.

(Translator and adapter, with Hertha Martens) Sudraka, *Vasantasena,* Drehbühne (Berlin, Germany), 1943.

Contributor to periodical *Das literarische Echo.*

SIDELIGHTS: While German writer Kurt Martens wrote numerous novels and novella-length works during his career, he remains best known for his literary friendship with novelist Thomas Mann. In the early part of Martens's career, he and Mann shared thoughts about writing and shared admiration for each other; Mann even dedicated his well-known novella *Tonio Kröger* to Martens as a token of their camaraderie. Gradually, however, as Mann's star rose and Martens's fell, the friendship faded. After Dresden was bombed during World War II, two of Martens's manuscripts, along with his household, perished in flames, and he committed suicide in the ruins of his home shortly after.

Martens was born on January 21, 1870 in the city of Leipzig. His parents, Heinrich Oscar and Henriette Erckel Martens, were wealthy; as George C. Schoolfield put it in the *Dictionary of Literary Biography,* Martens came from "a patrician and conservative home." He was educated thoroughly at boarding school, though he later described his schooldays in harrowing terms. Schoolfield explained: "The burden of Martens's first volume [of his autobiography, *Schonungslose Leben-schronik* or "Unsparing chronicle of life," 1921] . . . was the harmful effect his upbringing in boarding schools had had upon him. Some of the teachers had been excellent . . . but the headmaster was unaware of what went on outside the classroom, and Martens had early been introduced to homosexual practices. These involvements, however much Martens claims to regret them, are recounted with a great deal more ardor than are his later heterosexual adventures and the vague and hasty story of his engagement and marriage." Regardless of his difficulties in boarding school, Martens pursued his education diligently, eventually attending the University at Heidelberg, and then studying law in Berlin.

In 1895, Martens moved to Dresden to begin a legal career, but a year later he decided to focus wholly on his writing. In 1896, he began to compose his first and best novel, *Roman aus der Décadence,* a semi-autobiographical story about Just, a young trainee in the Leipzig court system.

In Martens's story, Just seems to be uncertain of his position in the world; though he is courting the genteel Alice, he still sleeps with a beggar he calls Amaryllis. While Just wrestles with his own societal position, he gradually loses his friend, the jurist Erich Luttwitz, when Erich becomes increasingly decadent. Finally, Just watches passively as Erich throws a "death festival" in a rented mansion. There, Erich provides his guests with lavish music and theater, until the guests become crazed with art and begin to revel orgiastically in the audience. Erich sweeps away to marry a wealthy widow, leaving Just to consider his own position in this society. Alice, his genteel love interest, marries another man; another likely wife, Esther, is already secretly married. The novel ends while Just is deciding whether to become a revolutionary—but the reader never knows what Just has decided.

Roman aus der Décadence, evoked some interest from critics, but, as Schoolfield remarked, "Martens lacks that 'elevation' of which Thomas Mann would speak; as Just's narrative voice is dryly unimpassioned, so Martens is incapable of making almost any of his characters or milieu seem alive." Nevertheless, the novel solidified Martens's career as a writer. One year after its publication, Martens moved to Munich, married Mary Fischer (with whom he had one daughter, Hertha Helena), and became a novelist.

After his first success, the remainder of the author's career proved to be anticlimactic. Though as a young editor Mann had accepted a story of Martens's for his magazine, *Simplicissimus,* Mann became increasingly critical of Martens's work. When his autobiography, *Schonungslose Lebenschronik,* was published in 1921, Mann reviewed it shortly though with some kindness. As Schoolfield suggested, Mann "must have been flattered by Martens's tributes to his exceptional talent, yet pained by the crass revelations Martens made about himself in an often wooden and pedantic style."

Throughout the 1920s and 1930s, Martens continued to write about the same subject that had initially interested him: the conflict between wealth and birth. Increasingly, however, he wrote in the mode of entertainment rather than the mode of social critique. *Der Alp von Zerled,* for example, tells the tale of a talented young lawyer, Roderich, who becomes obsessed with the aristocratic daughter of the house of Zerled—but also becomes obsessed with the girl's governess. Ultimately, the poor lawyer is slain by the nobility whom he both emulates and despises.

In *Verzicht und Vollendung,* Martens's last published novel, he fantasizes that ill-fated King Louis XVII escapes the French revolution to live in a sort of muted moral glory over his would-be assassins. Martens often used an historical frame in order to comment on the struggles between the wealthy middle class and the aristocracy. While in his writing he seems, ultimately, to support a social hierarchy based on birthright, throughout his career he wavered between the importance of accumulating wealth and significance of the accident of birth.

BIOGRAPHICAL AND CRITICAL SOURCES:

BOOKS

Dictionary of Literary Biography, Volume 66: *German Fiction Writers, 1885-1913,* Gale (Detroit, MI), 1988, pp. 391-395.*

MARTIN, Shannon E. (Rossi) 1952-

PERSONAL: Born April 3, 1952, in OH; daughter of Robert J. (an artist) and Mary K. (an educator; maiden name, Rust) Rossi; married Edwin A. Martin, Jr. (a photographer); children: Zachary Rosenbarger, Jacob Rosenbarger. *Education:* Indiana University—Bloomington, B.A., M.A., 1987; University of North Carolina at Chapel Hill, Ph.D., 1993.

ADDRESSES: Office—Department of Communication and Journalism, 5724 Dunn Hall, University of Maine at Orono, Orono, ME 04469-5724; fax: 207-581-1286. *E-mail*—shannon.martin@umit.maine.edu.

CAREER: Annenberg Washington Program, Washington, DC, fellow, 1994; Rutgers University, member of faculty, 1993-2001; University of Maine at Orono, teacher of communication and journalism and director of Maine Center for Student Journalism. *Star-Ledger,* Newark, NJ, research librarian, 1999-2000.

AWARDS, HONORS: Senior Fulbright scholar in Bosnia-Herzegovina, 2002-03.

WRITINGS:

Bits, Bytes, and Big Brother: Federal Information Control in a Technological Age, Praeger Publishers (Westport, CT), 1995.
(With Kathleen Hansen) *Newspapers of Record in a Digital Age,* Praeger Publishers (Westport, CT), 1998.
(Editor, with David Copeland) *The Function of Newspapers in Society: A Global Perspective,* Greenwood Press (Westport, CT), 2003.

Contributor to books, including *Perspectives on Media and the Persian Gulf War,* edited by Robert Denton, Praeger Publishers (Westport, CT), 1993; and *Law, Information, and Information Technology,* edited by Eli Lederman and Ron Shapira, Kluwer Law International, 2001. Contributor to periodicals, including *Information and Communication Technology Law, Communications and the Law, Communication Law and Policy, Newspaper Research Journal, New Jersey Journal of Communication, Journalism and Mass Communication Quarterly,* and *Information Management Journal.*

WORK IN PROGRESS: Research on federal and state public-information access and control-policy issues, computer-assisted reporting, online and digital news services development and policy issues, and information law and policy issues.

BIOGRAPHICAL AND CRITICAL SOURCES:

ONLINE

University of Maine Web Site, http://www.umit.maine.edu/ (December 5, 2004), "Shannon E. Martin."

*   *   *

MAVERICK, Liz

PERSONAL: Female. *Education:* Holds several degrees, including an M.B.A. and C.P.A. *Hobbies and other interests:* Travel.

ADDRESSES: Home—San Francisco, CA. *Agent*—c/o Author Mail, Love Spell, 200 Madison Ave., Ste. 200, New York, NY 10016. *E-mail*—lizmaverick@yahoo.com.

CAREER: Former accountant and Web site developer; works variously as freelance travel writer and novelist.

WRITINGS:

What a Girl Wants, New American Library (New York, NY), 2004.
The Shadow Runners, Love Spell (New York, NY), 2004.
Adventures of an Ice Princess, New American Library (New York, NY), 2004.

Contributor of travel articles to numerous periodicals.

WORK IN PROGRESS: Card Sharks.

SIDELIGHTS: Novelist Liz Maverick started her career as a tax accountant, later working as a Web site developer, believing that she needed to work in something she considered an industry. She started writing her first novel on her laptop computer while riding the train to work and discovered that she was meant to be an author. She writes both contemporary women's fiction and futuristic romance novels, as well as freelancing as a travel writer, which enables her to indulge her passion for seeking out new places. Her writing has taken her to France, Antarctica, and Indonesia, among other locales.

Maverick's first novel, *What a Girl Wants,* follows the adventures of Haley Jane Smith, a single woman working in the Silicon Valley dot-com world and trying to find both the perfect job and the perfect boyfriend. When the man working one cubicle over dies, Haley decides the only saving grace is Grant Hutchinson, the police detective assigned to investigate the case. Kristine Huntley, in a review for *Booklist,* called the book a "charming debut novel." However, a contributor for *Kirkus Reviews* remarked that "mean-spirited characters and elaborately snotty prose don't do much for this lifeless first outing." But Harriet Klausner commented in *AllReaders.com* that "readers wanting an offbeat amusing contemporary will enjoy this maverick of a tale."

In *Adventures of an Ice Princess* Maverick sends her heroines—three young women from Northern California—to work at the South Pole as part of a scientific community. Each woman leaves behind her own personal troubles, including a long-term boyfriend, an eliminated job, and a newly sold business. *Booklist* critic Aleksandra Kostovski noted the improbability of the situation, but remarked that "in Maverick's hands it's not so unthinkable." She concluded that the book is "an outlandishly funny adventure."

Maverick explores the future in *The Shadow Runners,* a romance set in a 2176 Australia that relies heavily on the nation's history. When Jenny Red's father is arrested, Jenny and the rest of her family find themselves in the royal palace's servants' quarters, and then the Newgate penal colony. Jenny meets Shadow Runner D'ekker Han Valoreen, the prince's half brother, who convinces her to assist him in his quest to improve the situation at Newgate. The pair inevitably fall in love, despite the differences in their circumstance.

BIOGRAPHICAL AND CRITICAL SOURCES:

PERIODICALS

Booklist, February 1, 2004, Kristine Huntley, review of *What a Girl Wants,* p. 954; October 1, 2004,

Aleksandra Kostovski, review of *Adventures of an Ice Princess,* p. 316.
Kirkus Reviews, December 1, 2003, review of *What a Girl Wants,* p. 1375.

ONLINE

AllReaders.com, http://www.allreaders.com/ (February 23, 2005), Harriet Klausner, review of *What a Girl Wants.*
AllScifi.com, http://www.allscifi.com/ (February 23, 2005), "Liz Maverick."
Liz Maverick Home Page, http://www.lizmaverick.com (February 23, 2005).
New American Library, http://nalauthors.com/ (February 23, 2005), "Liz Maverick."*

*   *   *

MAZIS, Glen A. 1951-

PERSONAL: Born April 4, 1951, in Woodbury, NJ; son of Bernard (an engineer) and Charlotte (a secretary; maiden name, Fischman) Mazis; married Bonnie Winters, August, 1981 (divorced, July, 1986). *Ethnicity:* "Jewish." *Education:* State University of New York at Binghamton, B.A., 1972; Yale University, M.A., 1974, Ph.D., 1977. *Politics:* Democrat. *Religion:* Zen Buddhist. *Hobbies and other interests:* Running marathons, tennis, kayaking, hiking, gardening.

ADDRESSES: Home—264 West Front St., Marietta, PA 17547. *Office*—School of Humanities, Pennsylvania State University Harrisburg, Route 230, Middletown, PA 17051. *E-mail*—glenmazis@aol.com.

CAREER: Northern Kentucky University, Highland Heights, associate professor of philosophy, 1980-86; Wesleyan University, Canton, NY, visiting associate professor of philosophy, 1986-89; St. Lawrence University, Canton, visiting associate professor of philosophy, 1989-91; Pennsylvania State University Harrisburg, Middletown, professor of philosophy and humanities, 1991—. Soka University, professor, 2000-02; also taught at Louisiana State University and University of Illinois at Urbana/Champaign.

MEMBER: American Philosophical Association, Society for Phenomenological and Existential Philosophy, Merleau-Ponty Circle.

AWARDS, HONORS: Danforth fellow, 1972; Lion Award, Soka University, 2002.

WRITINGS:

Emotion and Embodiment: Fragile Ontology, Peter Lang Publishing (New York, NY), 1993.
The Trickster, Magician, and Grieving Man: Reconnecting Men with Earth, Bear (Santa Fe, NM), 1994.
Earthbodies: Rediscovering Our Planetary Senses, State University of New York Press (Albany, NY), 2002.

Contributor of articles and poetry to academic journals and literary magazines, including *Many Mountains Moving, Sou'wester, Willow Review, Ellipsis,* and *Spoon River Poetry Review.*

WORK IN PROGRESS: The Other Time of Encounter, a poetry collection; *The Fullness of the Body Is the Emptiness of Reality; Utopia U,* a "satiric academic novel"; *Humans/Animals/Machines: The Promise and Dangers of Blurred Boundaries.*

SIDELIGHTS: Glen A. Mazis told *CA:* "My primary motivation to write is to be a witness to the particular features of this planet and the life of embodiment that seem to go unnoticed in the Western intellectual tradition. The power of emotion, the depths of the senses, the insight of creative imagination have been pushed aside for far too long in the West and now in the world of globalization. For me, the hours spent writing are magical hours: they pass in a rhythm that is enveloping and embracing. Merleau-Ponty has been my guiding spirit as a philosopher, as well as Nietzsche and so many other thinkers on the edge. As a poet, there are so many teachers from Auden, Dylan Thomas, Yeats, to so many people writing now, like Piercy, Twitchell, Nye, Kinell, Collins, et cetera. As I get older, writing is more about the joys of rewriting, cutting, shaping, paring. It is an exciting time!"

BIOGRAPHICAL AND CRITICAL SOURCES:

PERIODICALS

Booklist, April 1, 1994, Pat Monaghan, review of *The Trickster, Magician, and Grieving Man: Reconnecting Men with Earth,* p. 1411.

McCONNEL, Ian
(Ingrid Black, a joint pseudonym)

PERSONAL: Married Ellis O'Hanlon (a journalist); children: three.

ADDRESSES: Home—Belfast, Northern Ireland. *Agent*—c/o Author Mail, St. Martin's Press, 175 Fifth Ave., New York, NY 10019.

CAREER: Writer.

WRITINGS:

WITH WIFE, ELLIS O'HANLON; UNDER JOINT PSEUDONYM INGRID BLACK

The Dead, Headline (London, England), 1993, Thomas Dunne Books (New York, NY), 2004.
The Dark Eye, Headline (London, England), 2004.

ADAPTATIONS: Production rights to *The Dead* were sold to the British Broadcasting Corporation.

SIDELIGHTS: Ian McConnel and his wife, Ellis O'Hanlon, have collaborated on mystery novels published under the joint pseudonym Ingrid Black. Their first effort, *The Dead,* introduces the character of Saxon, a former agent with the Federal Bureau of Investigation. A woman who is never identified by any other name, Saxon has given up her work in law enforcement to write true-crime stories. Having traveled to Dublin to research a story about Ed Fagan, a Bible-obsessed serial killer, she remains in the city even when her book project fails to pan out. Meanwhile, Nick Elliott, a newspaper reporter, does succeed in publishing a book on Fagan, who is also known as the "Night Hunter" and who remains at large. After Elliott's book comes out, he is contacted by someone who threatens to kill five prostitutes within the next week. Saxon goes into action to try to stop the murders, aided by her lover, Detective Chief Superintendent Grace Fitzgerald of the Dublin police force. This debut novel was praised by Jenny McLarin in *Booklist* as "a refreshing change of pace: Its serial killer offers a new twist on psychotic behavior, and its heroine is not just another cop." Saxon's "combination of sarcasm and smarts will have readers clamoring for more," predicted McLarin. A *Kirkus Reviews* writer advised that "Forensic analysis and intellectual speculation overshadow action, but sublimely prickly Saxon is a solid foundation for debut mystery-monger Black to build a series on." The authors' evocation of "gritty, moody Dublin" was noted with approval by a reviewer for *Publishers Weekly,* who concluded: "A string of plausible suspects keeps the reader guessing and the suspense at fever pitch."

BIOGRAPHICAL AND CRITICAL SOURCES:

PERIODICALS

Booklist, May 1, 2004, Jenny McLarin, review of *The Dead,* p. 1501.
Kirkus Reviews, April 15, 2004, review of *The Dead,* p. 362.
Publishers Weekly, May 3, 2004, review of *The Dead,* p. 174.

ONLINE

Mystery Women, http://www.mysterywomen.co.uk/ (December 13, 2004), Lizzie Hayes, review of *The Dead.**

*   *   *

McGOLDRICK, James A.
    (Jan Coffey, a joint pseudonym, May McGoldrick, a joint pseudonym)

PERSONAL: Married; wife's name, Nikoo (a mechanical engineer); children: two sons. *Education:* Ph.D. in sixteenth-century British literature.

ADDRESSES: Home—Litchfield County, CT. *Agent*—c/o Author Mail, Signet Publicity, 375 Hudson St., New York, NY 10014. *E-mail*—mcgoldmay@aol.com.

CAREER: Writer. Has worked as a professor of English literature.

MEMBER: Romance Writers of America.

WRITINGS:

(With wife, Nikoo McGoldrick) *Marriage of Minds: Collaborative Fiction Writing,* Heinemann (New York, NY), 2000.

WITH WIFE, NIKOO MCGOLDRICK, UNDER JOINT PSEUDONYM MAY MCGOLDRICK

The Thistle and the Rose, Penguin USA (New York, NY), 1995.
Angel of Skye, Penguin USA (New York, NY), 1996.
Heart of Gold (originally published as *Cloth of Gold*), Penguin USA (New York, NY), 1996.
The Beauty of the Mist, Penguin USA (New York, NY), 1997.
The Intended, Penguin Putnam (New York, NY), 1998.
Flame (originally published as *The Jeweled Cup*), Penguin Putnam (New York, NY), 1998.
The Dreamer (book one of "Highland Treasure" trilogy), Onyx (New York, NY), 2000.
The Enchantress (book two of "Highland Treasure" trilogy), Onyx (New York, NY), 2000.
The Firebrand (book three of "Highland Treasure" trilogy), Onyx (New York, NY), 2000.
The Promise, Signet (New York, NY), 2001.
The Rebel, Signet (New York, NY), 2002.
Tess and the Highlander, HarperCollins Young Adult (New York, NY), 2002.
Borrowed Dreams (book one in "Scottish" trilogy; originally published as *Lord of Scandal*), Signet (New York, NY), 2003.
Captured Dreams (book two in "Scottish" trilogy), Signet (New York, NY), 2003.
Dreams of Destiny (book three in "Scottish" trilogy), Signet (New York, NY), 2004.

WITH WIFE, NIKOO MCGOLDRICK; UNDER JOINT PSEUDONYM JAN COFFEY

Trust Me Once, Mira Books (New York, NY), 2001.
Twice Burned, Mira Books (New York, NY), 2002.
Triple Threat, Mira Books (New York, NY), 2003.
Fourth Victim, Mira Books Books (New York, NY), 2004.
Five in a Row, Mira Books (New York, NY), 2005.
Tropical Kiss, HarperCollins Young Adult (New York, NY), 2005.

SIDELIGHTS: Husband and wife writing team James A. and Nikoo McGoldrick have written numerous novels under their joint pseudonyms May McGoldrick and Jan Coffey. Each had their own careers before they began to write together: James was a professor of English literature and Nikoo was a mechanical engineer. However, they also loved writing. Nikoo had started to write stories when she was twelve years old in an attempt to cope with the death of her best friend in a car accident. Unfortunately, her parents were not supportive, and so she turned her attention to math and science, attending engineering school to secure a solid career path. James began writing stories as a child of seven, using his friends as an audience for his action-packed creations. After college, he came close to selling a screenplay to actor/director Robert Redford, but when that failed he turned to the more reliable career of academics.

Neither McGoldrick gave up writing entirely, and they spent more than a decade attempting to get their individual work accepted by a publisher. Not until they joined forces and began writing in tandem, though, did they finally succeed. When their younger son underwent heart surgery, the event forced the couple to reassess their priorities and the direction of their lives. They started out writing a short story together, and when that placed in a national contest, they turned their eyes toward full-length fiction. A love of history made historical romances a natural choice. Within five days of submitting their first effort, they had an agent, and three months later a multi-book contract with a major New York publisher. May McGoldrick, their first joint pseudonym, was the result of an editor's suggestion that they write under a feminine name; May was James's grandmother. They created their second pseudonym, Jan Coffey, to use with more-suspenseful novels.

In an interview for *RomanceReview.com,* James and Nikoo described the benefits of working as a team. "The biggest pleasure that we've found in the actual act of writing is the feeling of complementing each other. While we don't really have specialty areas, Nikoo could be characterized as the screenwriter type (she loves writing dialogue), and Jim is more the poetic type. He loves imagery and language, descriptive passages." Of course, teamwork has its drawbacks as well, as they noted. "Having two heads doesn't necessarily mean that you have twice the brain . . . or you could write twice as fast. Feeding times are difficult . . . bathroom times are hell." The McGoldricks further explained their interest in historicals in an interview on their own Web site, stating that "history in general offers the writer so many opportunities to create stories. We know (or learn) the names and the events, but the human dimension is not generally recorded. This means that there are huge gaps left in the records, just dying for storytellers to flesh out."

The McGoldricks write both stand-alone novels and series. As May McGoldrick, they are responsible for both the "Highland Treasure" trilogy, consisting of *The Dreamer, The Enchantress,* and *The Firebrand,* and the "Scottish" trilogy, made up of *Borrowed Dreams, Captured Dreams,* and *Dreams of Destiny.* The "Highland Treasure" books follow the adventures of the three Percy sisters as they attempt to unite the clues they possess in order to locate their family's treasure, while at the same time falling for three very different Highland warriors. *AllReaders.com* critic Marilyn Malone called the first volume "an enjoyable read," while a contributor to *Publishers Weekly* stated that *The Enchantress* "is tender and the narrative is enhanced by strong secondary characters."

The "Scottish" trilogy allowed the McGoldricks to delve more deeply into Scotland's history and culture, focusing on strong female characters struggling to survive in the latter part of the eighteenth century. Harriet Klausner, in a review of *Borrowed Dreams* for *AllReaders.com,* remarked that "this engaging Georgian romance works on several layers besides the obvious romance"; regarding *Dreams of Destiny,* Klausner commented that Georgian enthusiasts "will take immense delight." The reviewer added that "the story line is action-packed, but at its best when the lead couple banter and try to trump one another." *Booklist* critic Shelley Mosley called the last installment of the "Scottish" series, *Dreams of Destiny,* "an entertaining book filled with murder, suspense, and humor, and a satisfying conclusion," noting that the book can also be read on its own.

Scotland is not the only setting for the McGoldricks' historical novels. In *The Promise* heroine Rebecca Neville flees England when she believes that she has killed her employer. She boards a ship bound for America, and when the woman assisting her dies during the voyage, Rebecca raises the woman's child as if he were her own. Ten years later, when the boy's father discovers his whereabouts, Rebecca is forced to return to England. John Charles remarked in *Booklist* that the authors' "gift for characterization extends from the . . . courageous heroine and wounded hero . . . to a fascinating cast of secondary characters." *The Rebel* serves as a sequel of sorts, with the hero's best friend moving into the role of a protagonist when he finds himself apprehending an Irish rebel who turns out to be a woman. Charles called this volume a "vivid, compelling historical."

The McGoldricks have won numerous awards for their novels from various chapters of the Romance Writers Association and *Romantic Times*. In addition to their fiction, they have written a nonfiction work on how their writing partnership works: *Marriage of Minds: Collaborative Fiction Writing*.

BIOGRAPHICAL AND CRITICAL SOURCES:

PERIODICALS

Booklist, September 15, 1998, Pat Engelmann, review of *Flame,* p. 210; August, 2001, John Charles, review of *The Promise,* p. 2100; July, 2002, John Charles, review of *The Rebel,* p. 830; June 1, 2004, Shelley Mosley, review of *Dreams of Destiny,* p. 1711.

Library Journal, July, 2000, Robert Moore, review of *Marriage of Minds: Collaborative Fiction Writing,* p. 110.

New York Times, February 8, 1998, Diane Nottle, "And They All Lived Happily Ever After," review of *Heart of Gold,* p. 14.

Publishers Weekly, July 31, 2000, review of *The Enchantress,* p. 77; June 10, 2002, review of *The Rebel,* p. 46.

ONLINE

All about Romance Web site, http://www.likesbooks. com/ (February 23, 2005), "May McGoldrick."

AllReaders.com, http://www.allreaders.com/ (February 23, 2005), Marilyn Malone, review of *The Dreamer;* Rebecca Herman, reviews of *Flame, Tess and the Highlander,* and *The Firebrand;* Harriet Klausner, reviews of *Dreams of Destiny, Borrowed Dreams, Twice Burned, Triple Threat, Fourth Victim, The Rebel,* and *The Promise.*

Fantastic Fiction Web site, http://www.fantasticfiction. co.uk/ (February 23, 2005), "May McGoldrick."

HarperChildrens Web site, http://www.harperchildrens. com/ (February 23, 2005), "May McGoldrick."

May McGoldrick Home Page, http://www. maymcgoldrick.com (February 23, 2005).

MyUnicorn.com, http://www.myunicorn.com/ (February 23, 2005), "May McGoldrick."

New American Library Web site, http://nalauthors.com/ (February 23, 2005), "May McGoldrick."

RomanceReview.com, http://www.aromancereview. com/ (February 23, 2005), interview with McGoldrick.*

*   *   *

McGOLDRICK, May
    See McGOLDRICK, James A. and McGOLD-RICK, Nikoo

*   *   *

McGOLDRICK, Nikoo
    (Jan Coffey, a joint pseudonym, May McGoldrick, a joint pseudonym)

PERSONAL: Married James A. McGoldrick (a writer); children: two sons.

ADDRESSES: Home—Litchfield County, CT. *Agent*—c/o Author Mail, Signet Publicity, 375 Hudson St., New York, NY 10014. *E-mail*—mcgoldmay@aol.com.

CAREER: Writer. Has worked as a mechanical engineer.

MEMBER: Romance Writers of America.

WRITINGS:

(With husband, James A. McGoldrick) *Marriage of Minds: Collaborative Fiction Writing,* Heinemann (New York, NY), 2000.

WITH HUSBAND, JAMES A. MCGOLDRICK, UNDER JOINT PSEUDONYM MAY MCGOLDRICK

The Thistle and the Rose, Penguin USA (New York, NY), 1995.

Angel of Skye, Penguin USA (New York, NY), 1996.

Heart of Gold (originally published as *Cloth of Gold*), Penguin USA (New York, NY), 1996.

The Beauty of the Mist, Penguin USA (New York, NY), 1997.

The Intended, Penguin Putnam (New York, NY), 1998.

Flame (originally published as *The Jeweled Cup*), Penguin Putnam (New York, NY), 1998.

The Dreamer (book one of "Highland Treasure" trilogy), Onyx (New York, NY), 2000.

The Enchantress (book two of "Highland Treasure" trilogy), Onyx (New York, NY), 2000.

The Firebrand (book three of "Highland Treasure" trilogy), Onyx (New York, NY), 2000.

The Promise, Signet (New York, NY), 2001.

The Rebel, Signet (New York, NY), 2002.

Tess and the Highlander, HarperCollins Young Adult (New York, NY), 2002.

Borrowed Dreams (book one of "Scottish" series; originally published as *Lord of Scandal*), Signet (New York, NY), 2003.

Captured Dreams (book two of "Scottish" series), Signet (New York, NY), 2003.

Dreams of Destiny (book three of "Scottish" series), Signet (New York, NY), 2004.

WITH HUSBAND, JAMES A. MCGOLDRICK, UNDER JOINT PSEUDONYM JAN COFFEY

Trust Me Once, Mira Books (New York, NY), 2001.

Twice Burned, Mira Books (New York, NY), 2002.

Triple Threat, Mira Books (New York, NY), 2003.

Fourth Victim, Mira Books (New York, NY), 2004.

Five in a Row, Mira Books (New York, NY), 2005.

Tropical Kiss, HarperCollins Young Adult (New York, NY), 2005.

SIDELIGHTS: For sidelights, see *CA* entry on James A. McGoldrick.

BIOGRAPHICAL AND CRITICAL SOURCES:

PERIODICALS

Booklist, September 15, 1998, Pat Engelmann, review of *Flame,* p. 210; August, 2001, John Charles, review of *The Promise,* p. 2100; July, 2002, John Charles, review of *The Rebel,* p. 830; June 1, 2004, Shelley Mosley, review of *Dreams of Destiny,* p. 1711.

Library Journal, July, 2000, Robert Moore, review of *Marriage of Minds: Collaborative Fiction Writing,* p. 110.

New York Times, February 8, 1998, Diane Nottle, "And They All Lived Happily Ever After," review of *Heart of Gold,* p. 14.

Publishers Weekly, July 31, 2000, review of *The Enchantress,* p. 77; June 10, 2002, review of *The Rebel,* p. 46.

ONLINE

All About Romance, http://www.likesbooks.com/ (February 23, 2005), "May McGoldrick."

AllReaders.com, http://www.allreaders.com/ (February 23, 2005), Marilyn Malone, review of *The Dreamer;* Rebecca Herman, reviews of *Flame, Tess and the Highlander,* and *The Firebrand;* Harriet Klausner, reviews of *Dreams of Destiny, Borrowed Dreams, Twice Burned, Triple Threat, Fourth Victim, The Rebel,* and *The Promise.*

Fantastic Fiction Web site, http://www.fantasticfiction.co.uk/ (February 23, 2005), "May McGoldrick."

HarperChildrens Web site, http://www.harperchildrens.com/ (February 23, 2005), "May McGoldrick."

May McGoldrick Home Page, http://www.maymcgoldrick.com (February 23, 2005).

MyUnicorn.com, http://www.myunicorn.com/ (February 23, 2005), "May McGoldrick."

New American Library Web site, http://nalauthors.com/ (February 23, 2005), "May McGoldrick."

RomanceReview.com, http://www.aromancereview.com/ (February 23, 2005), interview with McGoldrick."*

*   *   *

McKENNA, Christine A.
See ADAMS, Christine A(nn)

*   *   *

McLEOD, Kembrew 1970-

PERSONAL: Born 1970. *Education:* James Madison University, B.S., 1993; University of Virginia, M.A., 1995; University of Massachusetts—Amherst, Ph.D., 2000.

ADDRESSES: Office—Department of Communication Studies, 105 Becker Communication Studies Bldg., University of Iowa, Iowa City, IA 52242-1498. *E-mail*—kembrew@kembrew.com.

CAREER: University of Massachusetts, Amherst, oral-skills program consultant, 1998-99, visiting professor, 1999; University of Iowa, Iowa City, assistant professor of communications, 2000—. Producer of documentary films *Money for Nothing: Behind the Business of Pop Music,* 2002, and *Copyright Criminals,* 2005.

MEMBER: International Association for the Study of Popular Music, International Communication Association, National Communication Association.

AWARDS, HONORS: Rosa Luxemburg Award for Social Consciousness, New England Film and Video Festival, 2002, for *Money for Nothing.*

WRITINGS:

Owning Culture: Authorship, Ownership, and Property Law, Peter Lang (New York, NY), 2001.
Freedom of Expression: Overzealous Copyright Bozos and Other Enemies of Creativity, Doubleday (New York, NY), 2005.

Contributor to books, including *Pop Music and the Press,* edited by S. Jones, Temple University Press (Philadelphia, PA), 2002; *Critical Cultural Policy: A Reader,* edited by J. Lewis and T. Miller, Blackwell (Malden, MA), 2002; and *Recyclables: Critical Approaches to Cultural Recycling,* edited by T. Kendall. Contributor of articles and music criticism to periodicals, including *Popular Music & Society, Electronic Book Review, Journal of Popular Music Studies, Popular Music, Journal of Communication, New York Times, Village Voice,* and *Rolling Stone.*

WORK IN PROGRESS: Ill Communication: An Unintentional Beastie Boys Guide to Popular Culture; Do You Wanna Dance? Punk and Disco in 1977.

SIDELIGHTS: Communications professor Kembrew McLeod is known for his studies examining the ways in which artists establish ownership over their works. A music critic as well as a scholar, his works *Owning Culture: Authorship, Ownership, and Property Law* and *Freedom of Expression: Overzealous Copyright Bozos and Other Enemies of Creativity* trace the complications involved in establishing the rights of creative people to the product of their labor and their imaginations. "Who'da thunk that I would become a university professor after I failed my senior year of high school?" McLeod wrote in a biographical essay published on his home page. "Thanks to some inspiring teachers along the way, I decided to give the profession a try because it appeared to allow me the most freedom of any career option." "To use a Grateful Dead-invoking cliche (yecchhh)," he concluded, "it's been a long strange trip, one that includes dancing, deconstruction and—in one instance—a fellow grad student catching on fire. After five years in Iowa City chasing the children of the corn through the field of dreams, I still solomnly swear to put the 'ass' back in assistant professor."

McLeod's chosen topic in *Owning Culture* is the effect of the rapidly changing information distribution industry during the 1990s. "McLeod explores such diverse and disparate subjects as the trademarking of corporate logos," wrote William S. Walker in a *Journal of Popular Culture* review of the book, "the patenting of indigenous knowledge, and the restrictions placed on free expression by copyright protections." In fact, the author views copyright as less a legal device intended to protect an individual artist than as a way for companies to control property. "All intellectual property law, then, according to McLeod," Walker concluded, "forms a web of legal and extralegal restrictions that ultimately serve to reinforce the hegemony of American corporations."

Freedom of Expression takes McLeod's chosen subject a step further. "The notion of intellectual property," declared a *Publishers Weekly* contributor, "now extends well beyond digital music sampling to biology (gene patenting) and 'scents and gestures'—and laws governing it, the author says, are being wielded like a bludgeon." "McLeod ponders the conflict between traditions that have encouraged openness versus the modern slide toward monopoly protectionism," stated Vernon Ford in *Booklist.* "When privatization usurps the cultural commons," wrote a *Kirkus Reviews* contributor, "the free flow of ideas is impeded, and scientific research inhibited."

BIOGRAPHICAL AND CRITICAL SOURCES:

PERIODICALS

Booklist, December 15, 2004, Vernon Ford, review of *Freedom of Expression: Overzealous Copyright Bozos and Other Enemies of Creativity,* p. 694.
Journal of Popular Culture, February, 2004, William S. Walker, review of *Owning Culture: Authorship, Ownership, and Property Law,* p. 536.
Kirkus Reviews, November 15, 2004, review of *Freedom of Expression,* p. 108.
Publishers Weekly, December 20, 2004, review of *Freedom of Expression,* p. 45.

ONLINE

Kembrew McLeod Home Page, http://kembrew.com (April 4, 2005).
University of Iowa Department of Communication Studies Web site, http://www.uiowa/edi/~commstud/ (April 4, 2005), "Kembrew McLeod."*

*   *   *

McWILLIAMS, Wilson Carey 1933-2005

OBITUARY NOTICE— See index for *CA* sketch: Born September 2, 1933, in Santa Monica, CA; died of a heart attack March 29, 2005, in Flemington, NJ. Political scientist, educator, and author. McWilliams was cofounder of the Institute for the Study of Civic Values at Rutgers University, where he was also a professor of political science. After earning his B.A. from the University of California at Berkeley in 1955, he served in the U.S. Army as a lieutenant for two years. Returning to civilian and student life at Berkeley, he finished his M.A. in 1960 and Ph.D. in 1966. McWilliams's academic career began at Oberlin College, where he was an instructor in the 1960s while studying for his graduate degrees. A three-year period at Brooklyn College of the City University of New York was followed in 1970 by his joining the faculty at Rutgers. Here he taught political science from 1970 until his death. As a scholar, his main concern was the study of morality in politics, which led to the founding of the Institute for the Study of Civic Values in 1973; he was still serving as the institute's president when he died. McWilliams fervently believed in the democratic process and the value of America's system of elections, often offering his analysis of presidential elections in books cowritten with Gerald M. Pomper, such as *The Election of 1980: Reports and Interpretations* (1981). In addition to this work and his teaching, McWilliams wrote and edited several other books, including *The Idea of Fraternity in America* (1973), which won a National Historical Society prize, *The Politics of Disappointment: American Elections, 1976-1994* (1995), and *Beyond the Politics of Disappointment? American Elections, 1980-1998* (2000).

OBITUARIES AND OTHER SOURCES:

PERIODICALS

New York Times, April 11, 2005, p. A21; April 15, 2005, p. A2.

ONLINE

Commonweal Online, http://www.commonweal magazine.org/ (April 22, 2005).
Daily Targum Online, http://www.dailytargum.com/ (March 31, 2005).

*   *   *

MEADE, Holly

PERSONAL: Female

ADDRESSES: Agent—c/o Author Mail, Marshall Cavendish, 99 White Plains Rd., Tarrytown, NY 10591.

CAREER: Children's book writer and illustrator.

AWARDS, HONORS: Caldecott honor book selection, American Library Association, for *Hush! A Thai Lullaby.*

WRITINGS:

SELF-ILLUSTRATED CHILDREN'S BOOKS

John Willy and Freddy McGee, Marshall Cavendish (New York, NY), 1998.

A Place to Sleep, Marshall Cavendish (New York, NY), 2001.

Inside, Inside, Inside, Marshall Cavendish (New York, NY), 2005.

ILLUSTRATOR

Nancy Van Laan, *This Is the Hat: A Story in Rhyme,* Joy Street Books (Boston, MA), 1992.

Phillis Gershator, *Rata-Pata-Scata-Fata: A Caribbean Story,* Joy Street Books (Boston, MA), 1993.

Libba Moore Gray, *Small Green Snake,* Orchard Books (New York, NY), 1994.

Nancy Van Laan, *Sleep, Sleep, Sleep: A Lullaby for Little Ones around the World,* Little, Brown (Boston, MA), 1995.

Betty G. Birney, *Pie's in the Oven,* Houghton (Boston, MA), 1996.

Minfong Ho, *Hush!: A Thai Lullaby,* Orchard Books (New York, NY), 1996.

Diane Karter Appelbaum, *Cocoa Ice,* Orchard Books (New York, NY), 1997.

Laurie M. Carlson, *Boss of the Plains: The Hat That Won the West,* DK Ink/DK Publishing (New York, NY), 1998.

Judith Heide Gilliland, *Steamboat: The Story of Captain Blanche Leathers,* DK Publishing (New York, NY), 2000.

Melinda Long, *When Papa Snores,* Simon & Schuster Books for Young Readers (New York, NY), 2000.

(And reteller) Brothers Grimm, *The Rabbit's Bride,* Marshall Cavendish (New York, NY), 2001.

Ann-Jeanette Campbell, *Queenie Farmer Had Fifteen Daughters,* Silver Whistle/Harcourt (San Diego, CA), 2002.

Reeve Lindbergh, *On Morning Wings,* Candlewick Press (Cambridge, MA), 2002.

Cari Best, *Goose's Story,* Melanie Kroupa Books/Farrar, Straus (New York, NY), 2002.

Florence Parry Heide and Sylvia Van Clief, *That's What Friends Are For,* Candlewick Press (Cambridge, MA), 2003.

Phyllis Root, *Quack!,* Candlewick Press (Cambridge, MA), 2004.

C. M. Millen, *Blue Bowl Down,* Candlewick Press (Cambridge, MA), 2004.

Mingfong Ho, *Peek!: A Thai Hide-and-Seek Story,* Candlewick Press (Cambridge, MA), 2004.

OTHER

Hop!, illustrated by Petra Mathers, Candlewick Press (Cambridge, MA), 2004.

SIDELIGHTS: Holly Meade is a renowned children's book illustrator who has gone on to pen her own children's stories. Her first illustrated work, *This Is the Hat: A Story in Rhyme,* was written by Nancy Van Laan and tells the story of a man who loses his hat while walking during a storm. The hat is then occupied, in turn, by various creatures, including a crow. A *Publishers Weekly* contributor commented that, "In Meade's illustrative debut, torn paper collages in happy blues, greens and magentas perfectly partner the text." Jim Jaske, writing in *Booklist,* noted that Meade's illustrations "add a friendly air to the story."

In *Rata-Pata-Scata-Fata: A Caribbean Story,* Meade's illustrations help tell Phillis Gershator's story of a daydreaming youth named Junjun who believes himself capable of making magic wishes come true. *Booklist* contributor Julie Corsaro observed that Meade's collages "rhythmically echo" the story. Writing in *Horn Book,* Ellen Fader felt that Meade's illustrations "evoke the essence of a Caribbean landscape [and] invite readers into young Junjun's tropical world."

Small Green Snake by Libba Moore Gray tells the story of a defiant young garter snake who ignores his mother's warning and roams away from home, only to be captured and held in a glass jar. When the snake escapes after the jar is broken, his adventure inspires his siblings to also venture forth. A *Publishers Weekly* contributor commended Meade's "bold, graphic artwork." In her second book with Nancy Van Laan, *Sleep, Sleep, Sleep: A Lullaby for Little Ones around the World,* Meade illustrates the story of both human and animal mothers soothing their offspring to sleep. Leone McDermott wrote in *Booklist* that Meade's collages possess "a tender quality."

Meade's collaboration with writer Minfong Ho on *Hush!: A Thai Lullaby,* was described by *Booklist* contributor Janice del Negro as "visually arresting," because "the comforting earth tones suit the quiet nature of the story." Writing in the *School Library Journal,* John Philbrook noted that Meade's collages generate a "somnolent atmosphere." Meade also illustrated author Betty G. Birney's *Pie's in the Oven,* a story about a young boy waiting to eat his grandmother's pie. *Booklist* contributor Ilene Cooper noted that Meade's collages "look like thick oil paintings" and are "deftly rendered, full of life, and demanding a second look."

Cocoa Ice, by Diana Karter Appelbaum, tells the story of an unusual tie between a Caribbean girl and an American girl living in New England: their business-men fathers trade cocoa for ice. Writing in the *School Library Journal,* Luann Toth commented that, "Meade's vibrant cut-paper and gouache illustrations capture the action, industry, and natural beauty of each locale." In *Boss of the Plains: The Hat That Won the West,* Meade's illustrations help tell author Laurie M. Carlson's story of John Baterson Stetson, who created the famous brand of western Stetson hats. *New York Times Book Review* contributor Anne Scott MacLeod noted that Carlson and Meade "clearly explain felting and hat making." MacLeod went on to praise Meade's illustrations as "exuberant."

After several years of focusing on her career as an illustrator, Meade wrote her first children' book, *John Willy and Freddy McGee.* The story focuses on two curious guinea pigs who forsake the safety of their cage and wander off to freedom. They soon hop onto a billiards table and scurry through the tunnels circulating beneath the tabletop. Their fun is disrupted, however, when an inquisitive cat begins flicking billiard balls into the pockets. As the balls roll through the tunnels, the guinea pigs must dodge the balls and get past the cat to make it back safely to their cage. Writing in *Booklist,* John Peters noted that Meade's text "has a roll and bounce to it that effectively capture the pace and excitement" of the guinea pigs' escapade. *School Library Journal* contributor Joy Fleishhacker deemed Meade's book "a fine tale" and noted that her "colorful, cut-paper collages work in harmony with the text, adding details and extending the action of the story."

Meade returned to her role as illustrator for Judith Heide Gilliland's *Steamboat: The Story of Captain Blanche Leathers,* which tells the true story Blanche Douglas, the first woman steamboat captain on the Mississippi River. A *Publishers Weekly* contributor praised Meade's work, pointing out that the book contains "two climactic collages in midnight blue and black tones [that] detail Blanche's triumphant test run on a moonless night." As the illustrator for Melinda Long's *When Papa Snores,* Meade was praised by *Booklist* contributor Kathy Broderick for her illustrations that "capture the energy of the story and the personalities of the characters." A *Horn Book* contributor noted that "Meade's lively line keeps the simple story moving and gives expressive charm not only to the little girl but also to the overactive household objects."

Meade has applied her artistic and authorial talents to the classic Brothers Grimm fairytale *The Rabbit's Bride.* The story focuses on a young girl who is supposed to chase a white rabbit from a cabbage patch but ends up being charmed by the rabbit. After becoming betrothed to the animal, she finds that the rabbit is not as nice as he seems. Tina Hudak, writing in the *Library Journal,* felt that Meade made a wrong decision in deciding to change the story's ending into a happier one because "the entire story loses the folktale flavor and raison d'etre." Hudak added, "The artwork, done in vibrant watercolors, effectively illustrates the rabbit's changing personality from harmless to demonic, but the effect may be too scary for young readers." *Booklist* contributor Ilene Cooper called the book "an interesting version of a little-told tale."

In *A Place to Sleep,* which Meade wrote and illustrated, the author uses a riddle format to get readers to think about where various animals sleep. The text also gives young readers facts about how animals sleeping, such as the fact that elephants sleep standing up and fish sleep with their eyes open. A *Kirkus Reviews* contributor commented that the "alliterative text is rich in wordplay," while a *Publishers Weekly* contributor called the book's design "innovative" and commended Meade for writing "a soothing bedtime read for young animal lovers." Writing in the *School Library Journal,* Cathie Reed commented that,, "With its oversized format, stunning art, and lyrical text, this is a great choice for story hours as well as bedtime reading."

While Meade's own stories have met with favorable reviews, she has continued to illustrate other authors' books. Among these titles is *On Morning Wings* by Reeve Lindbergh, which was adapted from Psalm 139. Carolyn Phelan, writing in *Booklist,* noted that "the simplicity, clarity, and grace of both the words and the illustrations make this a lovely and potentially moving picture book." Meade has also illustrated the 2003 republication of the 1968 book about friendship titled *That's What Friends Are For,* by Florence Parry Heide and Sylvia Van Clief. *School Library Journal* contributor Lauralyn Persson called the illustrations "fresh and lively." In a review in the *Chicago Tribune,* Mary Harris Russell dubbed Meade's illustrations for C. M. Millen's *Blue Bowl Down* "luminous and comforting."

BIOGRAPHICAL AND CRITICAL SOURCES:

PERIODICALS

Booklist, November 15, 1992, Jim Laske, review of *This Is the Hat: A Story in Rhyme,* p. 611; April

15, 1994, Julie Corsaro, review of *Rata-Pata-Scata-Fata: A Caribbean Story*, p. 1541; September 15, 1994, Hazel Rochman, review of *Small Green Snake*, p. 132; December 15, 1995, Leone McDermott, review of *Sleep, Sleep, Sleep: A Lullaby for Little Ones around the World*, p. 715; April 15, 1996, Janice del Negro, review of *Hush!: A Thai Lullaby*, p. 1443; July, 1996, Ilene Cooper, review of *Pie's in the Oven*, p. 1828; November 1, 1997, Lauren Peterson, review of *Cocoa Ice*, p. 466; September 1, 1998, John Peters, review of *John Willy and Freddy McGee*, p. 127; February 1, 2000, Kathy Broderick, review of *When Papa Snores*, p. 1056; May 15, 2001, Ilene Cooper, review of *The Rabbit's Bride*, p. 1754; September 1, 2001, Lauren Peterson, review of *A Place to Sleep*, p. 117; March 1, 2002, Denise Wilms, review of *Queenie Farmer Had Fifteen Daughters*, p. 1148; March 1, 2002, Ilene Cooper, review of *Steamboat: The Story of Captain Blanche Leathers*, p. 1147; September 15, 2002, Carolyn Phelan, review of *On Morning Wings*, p. 233; January 1, 2003, review of *On Morning Wings*, p. 798.

Chicago Tribune, June 6, 2004, Mary Harris Russell, review of *Blue Bowl Down*, p. 2.

Horn Book, September-October, 1994, Ellen Fader, review of *Rata-Pata-Scata-Fata*, p. 574; March-April, 1995, Ellen Fader, review of *Small Green Snake*, p. 183; November-December, 1995, Hanna B. Zeiger, review of *Sleep, Sleep, Sleep*, p. 739; May-June, 1998, Martha V. Parravano, review of *Boss of the Plains: The Hat That Won the West*, p. 356; March, 2000, review of *Steamboat*, p. 211; September, 2000, review of *When Papa Snores*, p. 552; May 1, 2002, Hazel Rochman, review of *Goose's Story*, p. 1520.

Kirkus Reviews, August 1, 2001, review of *A Place to Sleep*, p. 1129; April 1, 2002, review of *Queenie Farmer Had Fifteen Daughters*, p. 488; April 15, 2002, review of *Goose's Story*, p. 562; June 15, 2002, review of *On Morning Wings*, p. 884; April 15, 2003, review of *That's What Friends Are For*, p. 608.

New York Times Book Review, May 17, 1998, Anne Scott MacLeod, review of *Boss of the Plains*, p. 23.

Publishers Weekly, October 26, 1992, review of *This Is the Hat*, p. 69; April 4, 1994, review of *Rata-Pata-Scata-Fata*, p. 79; September 5, 1994, review of *Small Green Snake*, p. 108; March 25, 1996, review of *Hush!*, p. 82; May 4, 1998, review of *Boss of the Plains*, p. 213; August, 17, 1998, review of *John Willy and Freddy McGee*, p. 71; April 3, 2000, review of *Steamboat*, p. 80; February 12, 2001, review of *The Rabbit's Bride*, p. 211; October 1, 2001, review of *A Place to Sleep*, p. 60; April 1, 2002, review of *Queenie Farmer Had Fifteen Daughters*, p. 82; May 5, 2003, review of *That's What Friends Are For*, p. 223.

School Library Journal, October, 1992, Alexandra Marris, review of *This Is the Hat*, p. 98; September, 1994, Jody McCoy, review of *Small Green Snake*, p. 184; January, 1996, Ruth K. MacDonald, review of *Sleep, Sleep, Sleep*, p. 97; March, 1996, John Philbrook, review of *Hush!*, pp. 175-176; September, 1996, Kathy Piehl, review of *Pie's in the Oven*, p. 170; January, 1998, Luann Toth, review of *Cocoa Ice*, p. 80; September, 1998, Joy Fleishhacker, review of *John Willy and Freddy McGee*, p. 177; March, 2000, Susan Hepler, review of *Steamboat*, p. 224; May, 2001, Tina Hudak, review of *The Rabbit's Bride*, p. 142; September, 2001, Cathie Reed, review of *A Place to Sleep*, p. 199; August, 2002, Jeanne Clancy Watkins, review of *Goose's Story*, p. 148; August, 2002, Jeanne Clancy Watkins, review of *Queenie Farmer Had Fifteen Daughters*, p. 148; December, 2002, Marian Drabkin, review of *On Morning Wings*, p. 126; May, 2003, Lauralyn Persson, review of *That's What Friends Are For*, p. 120.

ONLINE

Houghton Mifflin Education Place Online, htt://www.eduplace.com/ (February 16, 2005), "Holly Meade."*

*   *   *

MEADOWS, Graham (W.) 1934-

PERSONAL: Born August 31, 1934, in Bristol, England. *Ethnicity:* "Caucasian." *Education:* University of Bristol, B.V.Sc., 1958.

ADDRESSES: Home and office—Graham Meadows, Ltd., 1559 State Highway 16, Woodhill, RD2, Helensville 1250, New Zealand. *Agent*—Ray Richards, Richards Literary Agency, 49c Aberdeen Rd., Castor Bay, Auckland, New Zealand. *E-mail*—graham@gmpl.co.nz.

CAREER: Writer and photographer. Veterinarian, in Evesham, England, 1958-67; Matamata Veterinary Club, Matamata, New Zealand, veterinarian, 1967-71; Auckland Zoo, Auckland, New Zealand, curator and veterinarian, 1975-80; Animal Concepts Ltd., managing director, 1975—World Wildlife Fund, regional coordinator, 1980-82; Graham Meadows Ltd., Helensville, New Zealand, founder and managing director, 2003—. Host of television programs for New Zealand television.

WRITINGS:

JUVENILE NONFICTION; SELF-ILLUSTRATED

Animal Sanctuaries, Shortland Publications (Auckland, New Zealand), 1988.

Zoos Past and Present, Shortland Publications (Auckland, New Zealand), 1988.

The Underwater Zoo, Shortland Publications (Auckland, New Zealand), 1988.

Extinction Is Forever, Shortland Publications (Auckland, New Zealand), 1989.

Photography, Shortland Publications (Auckland, New Zealand), 1989.

Discovering the Past, Shortland Publications (Auckland, New Zealand), 1989.

Animals Talk Too, Shortland Publications (Auckland, New Zealand), 1989.

Who Looks after Me?, Shortland Publications (Auckland, New Zealand), 1989.

Pets Need People, Shortland Publications (Auckland, New Zealand), 1990.

Animal Friends, Shortland Publications (Auckland, New Zealand), 1990.

Cass Becomes a Star, Shortland Publications (Auckland, New Zealand), 1990.

Dogs, Dogs, Dogs, Shortland Publications (Auckland, New Zealand), 1991.

Fascinating Facts about Animals, Shortland Publications (Auckland, New Zealand), 1991.

Rabbits, Shortland Publications (Auckland, New Zealand), 1991.

All about Donkeys, Shortland Publications (Auckland, New Zealand), 1992.

Cats, Cats, Cats, Shortland Publications (Auckland, New Zealand), 1992.

Nests, Shortland Publications (Auckland, New Zealand), 1993.

In the Park, Shortland Publications (Auckland, New Zealand), 1993.

Look Out!, Shortland Publications (Auckland, New Zealand), 1993.

Toes, Wendy Pye Ltd. (Auckland, New Zealand), 1994.

Cats, Lands End Publishing (Auckland, New Zealand), 1995.

A Visit to the Vet, Lands End Publishing (Auckland, New Zealand), 1995.

Happy Face, Sad Face, Lands End Publishing (Auckland, New Zealand), 1995.

Hot Potato, Cold Potato, Lands End Publishing (Auckland, New Zealand), 1995.

Big and Little, Lands End Publishing (Auckland, New Zealand), 1995.

Watching the Whales, Lands End Publishing (Auckland, New Zealand), 1995.

The Bird Barn, Lands End Publishing (Auckland, New Zealand), 1996.

Duck Magic, Shortland Publications (Auckland, New Zealand), 1996.

Lady and the Champ, Celebration Press (Lebanon, IL), 1996.

After the Rain, Shortland Publications (Auckland, New Zealand), 1997.

Hands, Hands, Hands, Shortland Publications (Auckland, New Zealand), 1997.

Beaks, Shortland Publications (Auckland, New Zealand), 1997.

Animals Are Not like Us: Horses, Ashton Scholastic (Sydney, New South Wales, Australia), 1998.

Animals Are Not like Us: Pigs, Ashton Scholastic (Sydney, New South Wales, Australia), 1998.

Animals Are Not like Us: Dogs, Ashton Scholastic (Sydney, New South Wales, Australia), 1998.

Animals Are Not like Us: Cats, Ashton Scholastic (Sydney, New South Wales, Australia), 1998.

Keeping Clean, Getting Dirty, Macmillan Education (Sydney, New South Wales, Australia), 1999.

Whales Have Tails, Macmillan Education (Sydney, New South Wales, Australia), 1999.

Some Animals Have Horns, Macmillan Education (Sydney, New South Wales, Australia), 1999.

Eating, Macmillan Education (Sydney, New South Wales, Australia), 1999.

This Is My Garden, Macmillan Education (Sydney, New South Wales, Australia), 1999.

A Bean Bonanza, Barrie Publishing (Melbourne, Australia), 1999.

The Glass Bottle, Barrie Publishing (Melbourne, Australia), 1999.

The Pine Tree, Barrie Publishing (Melbourne, Australia), 1999.

Champions in the Making, Barrie Publishing (Melbourne, Australia), 1999.

Behind the Scenes at the Zoo, Barrie Publishing (Melbourne, Australia), 1999.

Making a Motorway, Barrie Publishing (Melbourne, Australia), 1999.

A Vet's Day, Barrie Publishing (Melbourne, Australia), 1999.

Taking Off, Barrie Publishing (Melbourne, Australia), 1999.

Pets and Other Animals, Bridgehill Publishing (Alexandra, New Zealand), 1999.

"DOMINIE WORLD OF ANIMALS" SERIES; JUVENILE NONFICTION; AND ILLUSTRATOR

(With Claire Vial) *Lions,* Dominie Press (Lebanon, IL), 1999.

(With Claire Vial) *Elephants,* Dominie Press (Lebanon, IL), 1999.

(With Claire Vial) *Zebras,* Dominie Press (Lebanon, IL), 1999.

(With Claire Vial) *Giraffes,* Dominie Press (Lebanon, IL), 1999.

(With Claire Vial) *Baboons,* Dominie Press (Lebanon, IL), 1999.

(With Claire Vial) *Hippos,* Dominie Press (Lebanon, IL), 1999.

(With Claire Vial) *Rhinos,* Dominie Press (Lebanon, IL), 1999.

(With Claire Vial) *Leopards,* Dominie Press (Lebanon, IL), 1999.

(With Claire Vial) *Kangaroos,* Dominie Press (Lebanon, IL), 1999.

(With Claire Vial) *Koalas,* Dominie Press (Lebanon, IL), 1999.

(With Claire Vial) *Foxes,* Dominie Press (Lebanon, IL), 2000.

(With Claire Vial) *Gorillas,* Dominie Press (Lebanon, IL), 2000.

(With Claire Vial) *Otters,* Dominie Press (Lebanon, IL), 2000.

(With Claire Vial) *Wolves,* Dominie Press (Lebanon, IL), 2000.

(With Claire Vial) *Polar Bears,* Dominie Press (Lebanon, IL), 2000.

(With Claire Vial) *Brown Bears,* Dominie Press (Lebanon, IL), 2000.

(With Claire Vial) *Orang-utans,* Dominie Press (Lebanon, IL), 2000.

(With Claire Vial) *Tigers,* Dominie Press (Lebanon, IL), 2000.

(With Claire Vial) *Cheetahs,* Dominie Press (Lebanon, IL), 2000.

(With Claire Vial) *Pandas,* Dominie Press (Lebanon, IL), 2000.

"DOMINIE WORLD OF AMPHIBIANS AND REPTILES" SERIES; JUVENILE NONFICTION; AND ILLUSTRATOR

(With Claire Vial) *About Amphibians,* Dominie Press (Lebanon, IL), 2001.

(With Claire Vial) *Introducing Frogs and Toads,* Dominie Press (Lebanon, IL), 2001.

(With Claire Vial) *Newts and Salamanders,* Dominie Press (Lebanon, IL), 2001.

(With Claire Vial) *Fascinating Frogs,* Dominie Press (Lebanon, IL), 2001.

(With Claire Vial) *About Reptiles,* Dominie Press (Lebanon, IL), 2001.

(With Claire Vial) *Introducing Lizards,* Dominie Press (Lebanon, IL), 2001.

(With Claire Vial) *Introducing Snakes,* Dominie Press (Lebanon, IL), 2001.

(With Claire Vial) *Tortoises and Turtles,* Dominie Press (Lebanon, IL), 2001.

(With Claire Vial) *Constricting Snakes,* Dominie Press (Lebanon, IL), 2001.

(With Claire Vial) *Chameleons,* Dominie Press (Lebanon, IL), 2001.

"DOMINIE WORLD OF INVERTEBRATES" SERIES; JUVENILE NONFICTION; AND ILLUSTRATOR

(With Claire Vial) *Introducing Invertebrates,* Dominie Press (Lebanon, IL), 2002.

(With Claire Vial) *Introducing Arthropods,* Dominie Press (Lebanon, IL), 2002.

(With Claire Vial) *Ants,* Dominie Press (Lebanon, IL), 2002.

(With Claire Vial) *Beetles,* Dominie Press (Lebanon, IL), 2002.

(With Claire Vial) *Butterflies and Moths,* Dominie Press (Lebanon, IL), 2002.

(With Claire Vial) *Flies,* Dominie Press (Lebanon, IL), 2002.

(With Claire Vial) *Grasshoppers and Crickets,* Dominie Press (Lebanon, IL), 2002.

(With Claire Vial) *Snails and Slugs,* Dominie Press (Lebanon, IL), 2002.

(With Claire Vial) *Spiders and Scorpions,* Dominie Press (Lebanon, IL), 2002.

(With Claire Vial) *Wasps and Bees,* Dominie Press (Lebanon, IL), 2002.

"DOMINIE WORLD OF BIRDS" SERIES; JUVENILE NONFICTION; AND ILLUSTRATOR

(With Claire Vial) *What Is a Bird?,* Dominie Press (Lebanon, IL), 2004.

(With Claire Vial) *Perching Birds,* Dominie Press (Lebanon, IL), 2004.

(With Claire Vial) *Non-Perching Birds,* Dominie Press (Lebanon, IL), 2004.

(With Claire Vial) *Where Birds Are Found,* Dominie Press (Lebanon, IL), 2004.

(With Claire Vial) *Bird Feathers and Flight,* Dominie Press (Lebanon, IL), 2004.

(With Claire Vial) *What Birds Eat,* Dominie Press (Lebanon, IL), 2004.

(With Claire Vial) *Bird Migration,* Dominie Press (Lebanon, IL), 2004.

(With Claire Vial) *How Birds Keep in Touch,* Dominie Press (Lebanon, IL), 2004.

(With Claire Vial) *Bird Families and Life Cycles,* Dominie Press (Lebanon, IL), 2004.

(With Claire Vial) *Birds and People,* Dominie Press (Lebanon, IL), 2004.

ADULT NONFICTION; AND ILLUSTRATOR

Graham Meadows on Pets, Wilson and Horton (Auckland, New Zealand), 1979.

Graham Meadows' Guide to Pet Care, Pan Books (Auckland, New Zealand), 1988.

(With Howard Loxton) *The Noble Cat,* David Bateman Ltd. (Auckland, New Zealand), 1990.

An Illustrated Guide to Dogs, Reed Publishing (Auckland, New Zealand), 1992.

An Illustrated Guide to Cats, Reed Publishing (Auckland, New Zealand), 1993.

A New Zealand Guide to Cattle Breeds, Reed Publishing (Auckland, New Zealand), 1996.

Sheep Breeds of New Zealand, Reed Publishing (Auckland, New Zealand), 1997.

(With Elsa Flint) *Before You Call the Vet: Horses, Ponies, and Donkeys,* Reed Publishing (Auckland, New Zealand), 1998.

(With Elsa Flint) *The Dog Owner's Handbook,* Struik Publishing, 2001.

(With Elsa Flint) *The Cat Owner's Handbook,* Struik Publishing, 2001.

(With Elsa Flint) *The Chunky Cat Book,* New Holland Publishing, 2003.

OTHER

A Seal on the Motorway (adult novel), Hodder and Stoughton (Auckland, New Zealand), 1982.

The Adventures of Granny Gatman (juvenile fiction), Dominie Press (Lebanon, IL), 1999.

Columnist for a New Zealand newspaper. Author of television series.

SIDELIGHTS: Graham Meadows practiced for nine years as a veterinarian in England before immigrating to New Zealand. There he practiced for an additional four years before taking on the position of curator and veterinarian at the Auckland Zoo. In addition to his career as an animal doctor, Meadows is also a prolific author who has written over one hundred books, most of which seek to educate children about animals. Among his many titles are *An Illustrated Guide to Dogs: Their Selection and Care, Cats, Dogs, Newts and Salamanders,* and *Introducing Frogs and Toads.* Skilled in the use of a camera, Meadow has illustrated many of his books with his own photographs.

Meadows once commented: "My writing stems from my passion, which is to interest my readers, especially children, and provide them with information that not only answers their questions but also gets them thinking. Coming from a veterinary background, my main focus has been in animals, natural history and conservation, but plenty of other subjects interest me and are incorporated into my books.

"I write mainly for children because they are the future. I try to stimulate their interest in a particular subject, and get them to think about issues, in particular the need to respect all forms of life, and have concern for conservation, recycling, and the future of our environment.

"My inspiration for subjects almost always stems from sights that I have seen or photographs that I have taken. The image of a duck preening beside a lake prompted me to write a children's nonfiction book titled *Keeping Clean, Getting Dirty.*

"My writing has certainly changed, and improved, over the last twenty years. In the early days I wrote the subject matter first and then looked for the photograph to match it. Now I usually select the photograph that best shows the subject matter, and then write the text to describe it."

BIOGRAPHICAL AND CRITICAL SOURCES:

ONLINE

Graham Meadows Photo Library Online, http://www.gmphotolibrary.com/ (February 9, 2005).

New Zealand Book Council Web site, http://www.bookcouncil.org.nz/ (February 9, 2005), "Graham Meadows.".

Reed Publishing Web site, http://www.reed.co.nz/ (February 9, 2005), "Graham Meadows."

*   *   *

MENEGHELLO, Luigi 1927(?)-

PERSONAL: Born 1927 (some sources say 1922), in Malo, Vicenza, Italy; naturalized British citizen; son of Gaetano (an artisan) and Giuseppina (a teacher) Meneghello; married; wife's name Katia. *Education:* University of Udine, degree in philosophy.

ADDRESSES: Home—England. *Agent*—c/o Giangiacomo Feltrinelli Editore, via Andegart 6, 20121 Milan, Italy.

CAREER: University of Reading, Reading, England, emeritus professor of Italian literature, 1947-80, then emeritus.

WRITINGS:

Libera nos a malo (title means "Free Us from Evil") Feltrinelli (Milan, Italy), 1963.

I piccoli maestri Feltrinelli (Milan, Italy), 1964, translation published as *The Outlaws,* Harcourt (New York, NY), 1967.

Pomo pero: Paralipomeni d'un libro di famiglia, Rizzoli (Milan, Italy), 1974.

Fiori italiani (title means "Italian Flowers"), Rizzoli (Milan, Italy), 1976.

Il Tremaio: Note sull'interazione tra lingua e dialetto nelle scritture letterarie, P. Lubrica (Bergamo, Italy), 1986.

Jura: Ricerche sulla natura delle forme scritte, Garzanti (Milan, Italy), 1987.

Bau-sète, Rizzoli (Milan, Italy), 1988.

Leda e la schioppa, P. Lubrica (Bergamo, Italy), 1988.

Che fate, quel giovane?, Moretti & Vitali (Bergamo, Italy), 1990.

Maredè, maredè, Rizzoli (Milan, Italy), 1991.

Colin-maillard, Le Promeneur (Paris, France), 1991.

Rivarotta, Moretti & Vitali (Bergamo, Italy), 1992.

Il dispatrio, Rizzoli (Milan, Italy), 1993.

Opere, Rizzoli (Milan, Italy), 1993.

Mambor: Opere anni '60, Galleria Cinguetti (Verona, Italy), 1993.

Promemoria: Lo sterminio degli d'europa, 1939-1946, in un Resoconto di "Ugo Varnai"(1953) del libro "The Final Solution" de Gerald Reitlinger," Mulino (Bologna, Italy), 1994.

Il turbo e il chiaro, Società Dante Alighieri, Comitato Veneziano (Venice, Italy), 1995.

La materia di Reading e altri reperti, Rizzoli (Milan, Italy), 1997.

Le carte: materiali manoscritti inediti, 1963-1989, trascritti e ripuliti nei tardi anni Novanta, Rizzoli (Milan, Italy), Volume I: *Ani Sessanta,* 1999, Volume II: *Anni Settanta,* 2000, Volume III: *Anni Ottanta,* 2001.

Trapianti: Dall'inglese al vicentino, Rizzoli (Milan, Italy), 2002.

SIDELIGHTS: Luigi Meneghello is an Italian novelist whose books, which are frequently autobiographical, combine sardonic humor with a search for truth. Meneghello's life is an interesting subject for autobiography, as he was a member of the Italian Resistance in World War II and eventually became an expatriate in England. Language is one of his fascinations, and he has written of his experiences adapting to English, and of the variations between standard Italian and the regional dialect of his native region of Veneto.

Born in the small village of Malo, Meneghello grew up in a home that encouraged free thought—an attitude that was unusual for that time and place. At a young age he rebelled against both the teachings of the Catholic Church and the government's fascist ideology, which was taught in the local schools. In high school and as a young adult, he became involved in the underground resistance movement battling Italy's Fascist government and its alliance with Nazi Germany. During the final months of World War II, Italy suffered tremendously because of the war, being "invaded and reinvaded, occupied and reoccupied acre by acre," explained Harvey Sachs in *Antioch Review.* "The disasters of international and civil war were complicated and augmented by political strife, physical deprivation, and moral degradation. Italy suffered greater devastation during the last twenty months of the war than in all her previous, turbulent history." Eventually, Meneghello decided in 1947 to leave the country and go to England to study at the University of Reading. He planned to remain there for less than a year, but after several months, he asked to stay on and eventually became a British citizen. At the University of Reading, he worked to create an Italian-based curriculum.

In 1963, Meneghelli published his first book, *Libera nos a malo.* It recounts tales from his youth in Malo, expressing his affection for that time and place, and humorously recounting the villagers' imperiousness to the control Italy's totalitarian government was trying to impose upon all Italians. One of the aims of fascist dictator Benito Mussolini was to standardize the numerous regional dialects into a single standardized language. While use of dialects was even made illegal, most of the peasant population spoke standard Italian only as a second language, and found it inadequate for much expressive thought. Though the book is humorous in tone, it also takes a serious look at the attempt to take away the culture of a people. Reviewing *Libera nos a malo* for the *Times Literary Supplement,* Filippo Donini praised the author's approach: "By dealing lightly with a serious matter Meneghello has rendered his criticism much more effective. The reader who would have skipped even half a page of sermonizing will delight in the innumerable anecdotes, jokes and sallies."

Many of Meneghelli's subsequent books have dealt with similar subject matter. *Fiori italiani* tells of a boy's education during the rise of Italian fascism and

of that system's eventual collapse. Reviewing the book for the *Times Literary Supplement,* Donini stated that at times it "reads more like an essay than a novel or an autobiography, an essay on Fascist education and on the Italian character in general, a subject on which Meneghello has some interesting, not always very flattering things to say. He says them, however, with such grace and humour that their sting is almost neutralized." Another book in this vein is *Bau-sète,* which focuses mainly on Meneghello's life during the interval between the final days of the war and his departure for England. "As always he has some excellent comic pages, with affectionately ironic portrayals of his friends and his younger self, the more so as he moves erratically forwards," noted Peter Hainsworth in the *Times Literary Supplement.*

In *Il dispatrio* Meneghello turns his attention from Italy to England. He presents his life in Britain as a comfortable ensconcement in academia: a string of many meetings with top thinkers, formal dinners, and numerous visits to library and museums. He discusses few of the harsh realities he and many Italians experienced as immigrants to Great Britain. *World Literature Today* contributor Luigi Monga advised that *Il dispatrio* "makes for good reading" and is "A funny, perceptive, and captivating autobiography."

Reflecting in the *Times Literary Supplement* on Meneghello's significance as a writer, Peter Hainsworth wrote: "All his books, singly and together, are modest attempts at large-scale sabotage. Some of the targets are cliches or orthodoxies of thought and language, a favourite one being the high rhetoric which has played such a damaging role in Italian culture and history. But the most serious enemy is time, with its power simply to carry everything away—lives, languages, things, cultures—and the memory of them."

BIOGRAPHICAL AND CRITICAL SOURCES:

BOOKS

Meneghello, Luigi, *Libera nos a malo,* Feltrinelli (Milan, Italy), 1963.

Meneghello, Luigi, *I piccoli maestri,* Feltrinelli (Milan, Italy), 1964, translation published as *The Outlaws,* Harcourt (New York, NY), 1967.

Meneghello, Luigi, *Pomo pero: Paralipomeni d'un libro di famiglia,* Rizzoli (Milan, Italy), 1974.

Meneghello, Luigi, *Fiori italiani,* Rizzoli (Milan, Italy), 1976.

Meneghello, Luigi, *Jura: Ricerche sulla natura delle forme scritte,* Garzanti (Milan, Italy), 1987.

Meneghello, Luigi, *Bau-sète,* Rizzoli (Milan, Italy), 1988.

Meneghello, Luigi, *Il dispatrio,* Rizzoli (Milan, Italy), 1993.

PERIODICALS

Antioch Review, spring, 1994, Harvey Sachs, "Resisting," p. 231.

Italianist: Journal of the Department of Italian Studies, University of Reading, Volume 9, 1989, pp. 7-51.

South Carolina Review, May, 1993, pp. 265-282.

Studi Novecenteschi, December, 1990, John A. Scott, "Luigi Meneghello; or, The Dialectics of Dialect," pp. 357-377.

Times Literary Supplement, July 2, 1976, Filippo Domini, review of *Libera nos a malo,* p. 832; October 14, 1977, Filippo Donini, review of *Fiori italiani,* p. 1187; January 1, 1988, Peter Hainsworth, review of *Jura: Ricerche sulla natura delle forme scritte,* p. 22; April 21, 1989, Peter Hainsworth, review of *Bau-sète,* p. 418; January 1, 1988, p. 22.

World Literature Today, autumn, 1988, Gaetano A. Iannace, review of *Jura,* p. 644; summer, 1994, Luigi Mongo, review of *Il dispatrio,* p. 547; spring, 1997, Franco Marenco, "The Rise and Fall of Irony," p. 303.*

*   *   *

MICKLETHWAIT, (Richard) John 1962-

PERSONAL: Born August 11, 1962; son of Richard Miles and Jane Evelyn (Codrington) Micklethwait; married Fevronia Read, 1992; children: Richard Thomas, Guy William, Edward Hugh. *Education:* Magdalen College, Oxford, graduated.

ADDRESSES: Home—London, England. *Office*—c/o Economist, 25 St. James' St., London SW1A 1HG, England.

CAREER: Journalist. Economist, London, England, finance writer, 1987-89, media correspondent, 1989-90, Los Angeles correspondent, 1990-93, business editor, 1993-97, New York bureau chief, 1997-99, U.S. editor, 2000—.

WRITINGS:

(With Adrian Wooldridge) *The Witch Doctors: Making Sense of the Management Gurus,* Times Books (New York, NY), 1996.

(With Adrian Wooldridge) *A Future Perfect: The Challenge and Hidden Promise of Globalization,* Crown Business (New York, NY), 2000.

Globalisation: The Economist, Economist (London, England), 2002.

(With Adrian Wooldridge) *The Company: A Short History of a Revolutionary Idea,* Modern Library (New York, NY), 2003.

(With Adrian Wooldridge) *The Right Nation: Conservative Power in America,* Penguin (New York, NY), 2004.

Contributor to periodicals, including *New York Times, Spectator, Los Angeles Times, Wall Street Journal,* and Manchester *Guardian.*

SIDELIGHTS: Speaker and journalist John Micklethwait has worked for the *Economist* magazine since 1987, when he joined the staff as a writer. He rose steadily, eventually gaining the position of New York bureau chief before becoming editor of the London-based magazine's U.S. edition. Micklethwait appears regularly on television and radio.

The Witch Doctors: Making Sense of the Management Gurus, which Micklethwait coauthored with fellow *Economist* journalist Adrian Wooldridge, addresses the proliferation of experts who promise to teach their readers or students the secrets of successful management skills. The book examines the most popular management theorists, analyzing their advice and finding that, while some of it is useless, there is still a multi-million dollar business that hinges on management, and therefore some of the lessons must be worth learning. Andrew Stuttaford, in the *National Review,* called *The Witch Doctors* "a succinct guide. If something can be said in a couple of pages, that's all the authors use . . . this is a management book that the reader will actually be able to finish." Robert D. Gulbro, contributing to *Business Horizons,* remarked that "this book is must reading for business managers who desire guidance in helping them avoid the pitfalls of hiring just any consultant. It should also be read by students of management, because it helps clarify the study of management theories."

Micklethwait again teams with Wooldridge for *A Future Perfect: The Challenge and Hidden Promise of Globalization,* a volume that makes a case for the potential benefits of a truly global economy. Over the course of the book, they not only revisit traditional reasons to proliferate a global economy, but address standard critiques and shortcomings and illustrate how they might be overcome. A reviewer for *Publishers Weekly* opined that the book praises globalization to the exclusion of sufficient time to "address the extent of its destabilizing economic effects or the havoc it has wreaked on many countries," but overall remarked that the book constitutes "an estimable effort." However, Jagdish Bhagwati, in a *Foreign Affairs* review, commented that the authors "write gloriously. As journalists, they have learned the art of making a point vividly by buttressing it with an apt anecdote, a striking interview, or a telling quote. Yet the book's substance is what really makes it stand out." He added that "given such an overwhelming agenda, they cannot hope to paint on this immense canvas without incurring minor blemishes of detail and errors of judgment. But judged in its entirety . . . the book is a spectacular success." *Economist* contributor Hamish McRae took issue with the book's structure, stating that, "as befits the Internet age, the reader is whisked on a series of lightning swoops about the globe. . . . It is fun in its way, but a bit bewildering." Overall, however, McRae praised Micklethwait and Wooldridge, noting that "they welcome the benefits but they are also commendably sensitive to the threats globalization might pose. They make the really big point that it supports individual liberties: the freedom of people to make their own choices, rather than having them determined by national governments."

The Company: A Short History of a Revolutionary Idea traces the concept of forming a company from near its inception through the present day. The idea was to create an entity that could be treated in some respect as a human being, allowing governments access to major projects and investments without having the money on hand. In certain instances, companies became almost synonymous with the nations they represented, such as the British East India Company. In modern business dealings, companies such as IBM and Procter and Gamble are involved in aspects of life and culture that extend far beyond the products they sell. A contributor to *Kirkus Reviews* called *The Company* "an entertaining and even charming excursion in business history, largely unburdened by formulas and numbers but full of debate-stirring data all the same." Michael Arndt, reviewing for *Business Week,* wrote that "if *The Company* has a shortcoming, it is that it is too short." He concluded that "the ground they do cover is worth exploring."

The Right Nation: Conservative Power in America examines the nature of conservatism in the United States, analyzing how it has become more popular through the decades and looking at the nation's steady right-ward trend. A reviewer for *Publishers Weekly* observed that "this epochal political transformation is rarely analyzed with the degree of dispassionate clarity that Micklethwait and Wooldridge bring to their penetrating analysis." Alexandra Starr, in a review for *Business Week,* noted that "what makes the volume all the more impressive is that Micklethwait and Wooldridge are addressing audiences on both sides of the Atlantic. In trying to explain to Europeans why Americans have skewed so far to the Right, they identify one of the more intriguing aspects of U.S. politics: Voters often craft their political identities based on their values, not their economic interests." Michael Kazin, writing for *Mother Jones,* called the volume "a vividly detailed study of why conservatives rule American politics," and "an immensely valuable book."

BIOGRAPHICAL AND CRITICAL SOURCES:

PERIODICALS

American Prospect, July, 2004, James P. Pinkerton, "God and Man in the GOP," review of *The Right Nation: Conservative Power in America,* pp. 34-36.

Booklist, October 15, 1996, David Rouse, review of *The Witch Doctors: Making Sense of the Management Gurus,* p. 388; November 1, 1998, David Rouse, review of *The Witch Doctors,* p. 474; May 15, 2000, review of *A Future Perfect: The Challenge and Hidden Promise of Globalization,*

p. 1707; February 15, 2003, Mary Whaley, review of *The Company: A Short History of a Revolutionary Idea,* p. 1024; June 1, 2004, Bryce Christensen, review of *The Right Nation,* p. 1676.

Business Horizons, September-October, 1997, Robert D. Gulbro, review of *The Witch Doctors,* pp. 73-74.

Business Week, March 24, 2003, Michael Arndt, "An Ode to 'The Money-Spinner,'" review of *The Company,* p. 22; June 7, 2004, Alexandra Starr, "America's Right Turn," p. 26.

Christian Century, December 14, 2004, Kenneth J. Heineman, review of *The Right Nation,* pp. 43-47.

Contemporary Review, April, 2004, review of *The Company,* p. 253.

Economist, November 16, 1996, Hamish McRae, review of *The Witch Doctors,* pp. S12-S13; July 15, 2000, Hamish McRae, "Economic Globalization: Good for Liberty," p. 4.

Entertainment Weekly, March 14, 2003, Aynda Wheaton, review of *The Company,* p. 70.

Forbes, August 7, 2000, Caspar W. Weinberger, review of *A Future Perfect,* p. 49.

Foreign Affairs, July-August, 2000, Jagdish Bhagwati, "Globalization in Your Face: A New Book Humanizes Global Capitalism," p. 134; September-October, 2004, Nicholas van de Walle and others, review of *The Right Nation,* p. 164.

Government Finance Review, August, 2000, Nick Greifer, review of *A Future Perfect,* p. 57.

Harvard Business Review, March-April, 1997, Eileen Shapiro, review of *The Witch Doctors,* pp. 142-146.

Insight on the News, June 26, 2000, Rex Roberts, "Going Global," p. 26.

Institutional Investor International Edition, May, 2000, Deepak Gopinath, "Back to the Future," p. 104.

Kirkus Reviews, January 1, 2003, review of *The Company,* p. 43.

Library Journal, March 1, 2003, Dale Farris, review of *The Company,* pp. 100-101; June 1, 2004, William D. Pederson, review of *The Right Nation,* p. 158.

Management Today, July, 2000, Howard Davies, "Mish-Mash of Half Truths," review of *A Future Perfect,* p. 41.

Mother Jones, July-August, 2004, Michael Kazin,"All the Right Moves," pp. 81-82.

National Review, April 7, 1997, Andrew Stuttaford, review of *The Witch Doctors,* pp. 50-51.

Naval War College Review, winter, 2002, Lawrence E. Modisett, "Is This the End of the Nation-State?," pp. 133-140.

New Statesman, September 27, 2004, Robert Reich, "The Right-Wing Revolution: Ordinary Americans Are Fighting the Wrong Class War," pp. 70-72.

Newsweek International, April 10, 2000, Michael Elliott, "Globalization Is Good for You," p. 4.

Publishers Weekly, October 21, 1996, review of *The Witch Doctors,* p. 67; April 24, 2000, review of *A Future Perfect,* p. 72; February 3, 2003, review of *The Company,* pp. 65-66; May 10, 2004, review of *The Right Nation,* pp. 50-51.

Reason, November, 2000, Brink Lindsey, "Trade Winds," review of *A Future Perfect,* p. 70; November, 2004, Brian Doherty, "Right-wingers Redux: Are We a Conservative Nation? Does It Matter?," pp. 62-66.

School Library Journal, June, 2003, review of *A Future Perfect,* p. SS55.

Training, September, 2000, Theodore Kinni, review of *A Future Perfect,* p. 143.

Washington Monthly, January-February, 1997, Tim Carvell, review of *The Witch Doctors,* pp. 48-50; June, 2004, Michael Lind, "Frontier Myth: The Spirit of the American Pioneer Did Not Inspire Modern-Day Conservatism," pp. 52-53.

ONLINE

Economist Online, http://www.economist.com/ (February 9, 2005), "John Micklethwait."

Foreign Affairs Online, http://www.foreignaffairs.org/ (February 9, 2005), "John Micklethwait."

London Speaker Bureau Web site, http://www.londonspeakerbureau.co.uk/ (February 9, 2005), "John Micklethwait."

Orion Books Web site, http://www.orionbooks.co.uk/ (February, 9, 2005), "John Micklethwait."

Town Hall.com, http://www.townhall.com/bookclub/ (February 9, 2004), "John Micklethwait."*

*   *   *

MILLER, Mark Crispin 1949(?)-

PERSONAL: Born c. 1949. *Education:* Northwestern University, B.A., 1971; Johns Hopkins University, M.A., 1973, Ph.D., 1977.

ADDRESSES: Office—New York University, The Steinhardt School of Education, Cutlure &

Communication, East Bldg., 239 Greene St., 7th Floor, New York, NY 10003. *Agent*—c/o Author Mail, W. W. Norton & Company, Inc., 500 Fifth Ave., New York, NY 10110.

CAREER: Educator and writer. New York University, New York, NY, professor of media ecology. Also involved with directing the Project on Media Ownership (PrOMO).

Has appeared in a one-man show in New York, in the short film *Exceed,* 2001, and in the documentaries *Orwell Rolls in His Grave,* 2003, and *Hijacking Catastrophe: 9/11, Fear & the Selling of American Empire,* 2004.

WRITINGS:

Boxed In: The Culture of TV, Northwestern University Press (Evanston, IL), 1988.
(Editor and contributor) *Seeing through Movies,* Pantheon Books (New York, NY), 1990.
The Bush Dyslexicon: Observations on a National Disorder, Norton (New York, NY), 2001.
Cruel and Unusual: Bush/Cheney's New World Order, Norton (New York, NY), 2004.
Spectacle: Operation Desert Storm and the Triumph of Illusion, 2005.

Contributor to *Conglomerates and the Media,* New Press, 1997, and to various publications and Web sites, including *BuzzFlash.* Author of introduction to *Propaganda* by Edward Bernays, Ig Publishing (New York, NY), 2005.

WORK IN PROGRESS: Mad Scientists: Paranoid Delusion and the Craft of Propaganda.

SIDELIGHTS: Mark Crispin Miller is an expert in media and culture and a political commentator whose wide-ranging interests include modern propaganda, the history and tactics of advertising, American film, and media ownership. In his first book, *Boxed In: The Culture of TV,* Crispin critiques the pernicious effects of television on American life and culture. One of the major problems Crispin observes is that television has become a tool of marketers who seek to make people passive consumers without the ability to individually

discriminate between what they really need and want and what the television commercials tell them is necessary to make them happy. Miller argues that advertisers have become quite adept at manipulating the viewer, especially those who are aware of and mock ads. Miller believes that to overcome this psychological defense against advertisements, many ads, as well as television shows, have incorporated irony to flatter the viewers as "being in the know" yet at the same time belittling them by saying they are either part of the joke or the brunt of it.

Miller's book also serves as a broader cultural critique of television's pervasive hold on society, which the author demonstrates through looks at such wide-ranging television programming as game shows and political new coverage.

Writing a review of *Boxed In* for the *Nation,* Jackson Lears commented that Miller has "produced the most probing critique of contemporary television that I have ever seen" and called the author "the funniest as well as the most perceptive media critic at work today." *Atlantic Monthly* contributor Sven Birkerts called Miller a "lucid and witty" thinker and added that the "essays are the most provocative writing on the subject since Marshall McLuhan first made it a subject."

In *Seeing through Movies,* Miller gathers together six essays by various writers looking at the significance and impact of mass culture films on society. In his essay, Miller focuses on the merger between advertising and cinema, from blatant product displays in the films to the insistence on feel-good, happy endings. Miller also wrote the book's introduction, which *Video Age International* contributor Fred Hift called "provocative" and noted that it "superbly summarizes the Hollywood trends . . . stressing the dominance of 'marketing' over quality." Michael Cornfield, writing in *Washington Monthly,* felt that when the critics "concentrate on what they find in batches of films, instead of what they think the films mean, their work shines with insight." Cornfield also noted that in his essay, "Miller excels at detailing the pernicious effects advertising divisions have had on entertainment divisions."

Miller analyzes the political arena in his next book, *The Bush Dyslexicon: Observations on a National Disorder.* On the surface, the book, published in 2001 after George W. Bush's election to his first term as U.S. president, is a compendium of the president's malapropisms, grammatical gaffes, and less-than-informed comments, which the author suggests might be partially due to dyslexia. The author's deeper purpose is to contend that Bush and his colleagues mastered the political use of television to sell their ideas and decisions to the public via a sophisticated propaganda machine. Throughout the book Miller uses the candidate's campaign quotes, television interviews, and debates to show how Bush maintained a strict adherence to talking points. Nevertheless, Miller argues that a careful viewer could discover Bush's real thoughts through translating his various malapropisms and body language. Miller also accuses the general public of being too willing to pay attention only to the buzzwords and themes without thinking substantively about the issues.

Many reviewers have noted that Miller writes from an extreme left-wing political bias. Jill Ortner, writing in the *Library Journal,* noted that "Miller makes no effort to be unbiased and is sometimes openly contemptuous, but the analysis is thoughtful and the quotes are accurate and well documented." *Nation* contributor Elayne Tobin felt that "crucial parts of the book read like sour grapes and detracts from the moments of sharp observation that Miller offers elsewhere." A *Publishers Weekly* contributor noted, "While Miller is sometimes vague in his arguments, he has produced a sharp-edged polemic questioning the wisdom of how we elect our leaders."

Miller continues his attack on Bush and his administration with *Cruel and Unusual: Bush/Cheney's New World Order.* In this view of the Bush administration, Miller argues that Bush and vice president Dick Cheney are actually outside the mainstream of American political traditions and are creating a nation that the Founding Fathers would have found appalling in its contempt for the democratic process, overemphasis on religion, and reckless militarism. In an interview on *BuzzFlash.com,* Miller noted, "I wrote *Cruel and Unusual* to make the case that Bush & Co. is fundamentally un-American—an order wholly alien to the spirit of our founding documents." In the book, Miller chastises both the Bush administration for manipulating the American people and the media for allowing those in charge to do it. A *Publishers Weekly* contributor wrote, "While such arguments are familiar, as is the indignant tone, Miller's thoroughness and clarity

in tracking down the sources of the policies he decries, and the ways in which they are disseminated, set the book apart." Writing in *Booklist,* Alan Moores thought the "sometimes dyspeptic tone will probably not convert anyone on the other side of the aisle," but added that the book "is a critical contribution to America's internal, life-or-death debate over foreign and domestic policy." Michael A. Genovese noted in the *Library Journal* that *Cruel and Unusual* "may be too polemical for mainstream tastes" but concluded: "Lively, entertaining, and hard-hitting, this book is a searing indictment of the Bush administration."

BIOGRAPHICAL AND CRITICAL SOURCES:

PERIODICALS

American Film, November, 1990, Andy Klein, review of *Seeing through Movies,* p. 40.

Atlantic Monthly, September, 1988, Sven Birkerts, review of *Boxed In: The Culture of TV,* p. 94.

Booklist, July, 2004, Alan Moores, review of *Cruel and Unusual: Bush/Cheney's New World Order,* p. 1812.

Entertainment Weekly, June 8, 2001, Mike Flaherty, review of *The Bush Dyslexicon: Observations on a National Disorder,* p. 71.

Kirkus Reviews, May 1, 2004, review of *The Bush Dyslexicon,* p. 432.

Library Journal, June 1, 2001, Jill Ortner, review of *The Bush Dyslexicon,* p. 192; July, 2004, Michael A. Genovese, review of *Cruel and Unusual,* p. 104.

Los Angeles Times, August 22, 2001, Mary McNamara, review of *The Bush Dyslexicon,* p. E1.

Nation, January 9, 1989, Jackson Lears, review of *Boxed In,* p. 59; August 5, 2002, Elayne Tobin, review of *The Bush Dyslexicon,* p. 40.

Progressive, September, 2001, Frank Fuller, review of *The Bush Dyslexicon,* p. 44.

Publishers Weekly, May 11, 1990, Penny Kaganoff, review of *Seeing through Movies,* p. 255; September 29, 1997, review of *Conglomerates and the Media,* p. 77; May 7, 2001, review of *The Bush Dyslexicon,* p. 233; May 31, 2004, review of *Cruel and Unusual,* p. 60.

Video Age International, February, 1991, Fred Hift, review of *Seeing through Movies,* p. 11.

Washington Monthly, July-August, 1990, Michael Cornfield, review of *Seeing through Movies,* p. 552.

Washington Post, July 29, 2001, Trevor Butterworth, review of *The Bush Dyslexicon,* p. T4.

ONLINE

BuzzFlash.org, http://www.buzzflash.com/ (July 23, 2004), interview with Crispin.

International Movie Database, http://www.imdb.com/ (February 23, 2005), listing of films author has appeared in.

New York University Web site, http://www.education. nyu.edu/ (February 23, 2005), "Mark Crispin Miller."

OffOffOff.com, http://www.offoffoff.com/ (February 23, 2005), Joshua Tanzer, "Never Can Say Good Buy."

Public Broadcasting Service Web site, http://www.pbs. org/ (March 23, 2005), interview with Miller.

Stay Free! Web site, http://www.stayfreemagazine.org/ (February 23, 2005), Carrie McLaren, "Mad Crispin Miller on Conspiracies, Media, and Mad Scientists."*

*   *   *

MINER, Robert C. 1970-

PERSONAL: Born 1970. *Education:* Rice University, B.A., 1993; University of Notre Dame, M.A., 1995, Ph.D., 1999.

ADDRESSES: Home—TX. *Office*—Baylor University, Tidwell 306, Waco, TX 76797. *E-mail*—Robert_ Miner@baylor.edu.

CAREER: Author and educator. St. Edmund's College, Cambridge, Cambridge, England, visiting scholar, 1996; University of Notre Dame, Notre Dame, IN, lecturer in philosophy, 1997; Xavier University, Cincinnati, OH, visiting assistant professor of philosophy, 1998-99; Boston College, Boston, MA, assistant professor of philosophy, 1999-2002; Baylor University, Waco, TX, assistant professor of philosophy in honors college, 2002-04, associate professor, 2004—.

WRITINGS:

Vico, Genealogist of Modernity, University of Notre Dame Press (Notre Dame, IN), 2002.

Truth in the Making: Knowledge as Construction in Theology and Philosophy, Routledge (New York, NY), 2003.

Contributor of numerous scholarly articles and book reviews to publications, including *International Philosophical Quarterly* and *Epistemologia.*

SIDELIGHTS: Author and educator Robert C. Miner serves as an associate professor of philosophy in the honors college at Baylor University, in Waco, Texas. His research interests include seventeenth-and eighteenth-century philosophy, twelfth and thirteenth century theology, ancient protreptic, and the works of philosopher Giambattista Vico (1668-1744). Miner's writings include a biography of Vico, *Vico, Genealogist of Modernity,* and a volume on theology and philosophy titled *Truth in the Making: Knowledge as Construction in Theology and Philosophy.*

Vico is remembered primarily for reviving the Italian humanist tradition and his belief that imagination could be considered a form of knowledge, as well as for his attacks on the theories of Descartes and Enlightenment views of history. Miner presents Vico as an Orthodox Catholic thinker—as opposed to having traditional, more Marxist views—and examines the philosopher's belief that the subject should be the starting point for any analysis of doctrine. Thora Ilin Bayer, in the *Review of Metaphysics,* commented that "Miner wishes to establish that Vico is not a secular skeptic or cynic but a believer in traditional Christian doctrine." She added that "in terms of Vico scholarship two aspects of Miner's work make it especially interesting: his thesis that Vico's philosophy is normative and his grounding of Vico's new science in Vico's Universal Law." *Library Journal* reviewer David Gordon wrote that Miner's work "offers original insight and understanding into a seminal, if occasionally neglected, figure."

Truth in the Making offers readers a map of the way knowledge and creative power relate through an examination of the history of philosophical enquiry. Miner traces philosophy back to early ideals of creativity in relation to religious thought, going on to explore how knowledge in different disciplines interacts, from mathematics to philosophy to theology.

BIOGRAPHICAL AND CRITICAL SOURCES:

PERIODICALS

Library Journal, April 1, 2002, David Gordon, review of *Vico, Genealogist of Modernity,* p. 111.
Review of Metaphysics, March, 2004, Thora Ilin Bayer, review of *Vico,* p. 638.

ONLINE

Baylor University Web site, http://www.baylor.edu/ (November 12, 2004), "Robert C. Miner."
Notre Dame Press Web site, http://ndpress.undpress. nd.edu/ (November 12, 2004), "Robert C. Miner."

*   *   *

MITCHINSON, Wendy 1947-

PERSONAL: Born December 12, 1947, in Hamilton, Ontario, Canada; daughter of Cameron and Frances (Davis) Mitchinson; married Res Lingwood (a sculptor), May 22, 1971. *Education:* York University, B.A., 1970, M.A., 1971, Ph.D., 1977.

ADDRESSES: Office—Department of History, University of Waterloo, Waterloo, Ontario N2L 3G1, Canada. *E-mail*—wlmitchi@watarts.uwaterloo.ca.

CAREER: Mount Saint Vincent University, Halifax, Nova Scotia, Canada, began as lecturer, became assistant professor of history, 1975-77; University of Windsor, Windsor, Ontario, Canada, assistant professor, 1977-81, associate professor of history, 1981-85; University of Waterloo, Waterloo, Ontario, associate professor, 1985-91, professor of history, 1991—. University of Western Ontario, J. M. S. Carless Lecturer, 1985, 1997; McMaster University, visiting professor at Hannah Institute for the History of Medicine, 1988-89; University of New South Wales, guest lecturer, 1991; University of Manitoba, James A. Jackson Memorial Lecturer, 1993; University of Saskatchewan, Bilson Memorial Lecturer, 1995; Universidad de Oriente, Santiago de Cuba, Canadian Studies Lecturer, 1997; Laurentian University, Angus Gilbert Memorial Lecturer, 1998. Rockefeller Study Center, Bellagio, Italy, scholar-in-residence, 1994; Fundación Valparaíso, Almeríia, Spain, scholar-in-residence, 1997.

MEMBER: Canadian Historical Association, Canadian Association of University Teachers, Canadian Society for the History of Medicine.

AWARDS, HONORS: Woman of Distinction Award, Young Women's Christian Association (Toronto, Ontario, Canada), 1991, for *Canadian Women: A History;* Thérèsè Casgrain fellowship, 1993-94.

WRITINGS:

(Editor, with Ramsay Cook) *The Proper Sphere: Woman's Place in Canadian Society,* Oxford University Press (Toronto, Ontario, Canada), 1976.
(Editor, with Janice Dickin McGinnis, and contributor) *Essays in Canadian Medical History,* McClelland & Stewart (Toronto, Ontario, Canada), 1988.
(With Alison Prentice and others) *Canadian Women: A History,* Harcourt Brace Jovanovich (Toronto, Ontario, Canada), 1988, 2nd edition, 1996.
The Nature of Their Bodies: Women and Their Doctors in Victorian Canada, University of Toronto Press (Toronto, Ontario, Canada), 1991.
(Coeditor) *Canadian Women: A Reader,* Harcourt Brace Jovanovich (Toronto, Ontario, Canada), 1996.
(Editor, with Franca Iacovetta, and contributor) *On the Case: Explorations in Social History,* University of Toronto Press (Toronto, Ontario, Canada), 1998.
Giving Birth in Canada, 1900-1950, University of Toronto Press (Toronto, Ontario, Canada), 2002.

Contributor to books, including *The Benevolent State: The Growth of Welfare in Canada,* edited by Allan Moscovitch and Jim Albert, Garamond Press (Toronto, Ontario, Canada), 1987; *The History of Marriage and the Family in Western Society,* edited by R. Phillips, CPSI (Toronto, Ontario, Canada), 1995; *Great Dames,* edited by Janice Dickin McGinnis and E. Cameron, University of Toronto Press (Toronto, Ontario, Canada), 1997; *The Politics of Women's Health: Exploring Agency and Autonomy,* edited by Susan Sherwin and others, Temple University Press (Philadelphia, PA), 1998; and *Intersections: Women on Law, Medicine, and Technology,* edited by Kerry

Petersen, Dartmouth Publishing (Aldershot, England), 1997. Contributor to periodicals, including *Histoire Sociale, International Journal of Women's Studies, Journal of Canadian Studies, Atlantis, Environments,* and *Health and Canadian Society. Canadian Historical Review,* member of editorial board, 1998-2001, coeditor, 2001-04; member of editorial board, *Canadian Bulletin of Medical History,* 1983-87, *Canadian Journal of Women and the Law/La revue canadienne de la femme et le droit,* 1985-88, *Ontario History,* 1986-90, and *Scientia Canadensis,* 1987-90.

WORK IN PROGRESS: Research on the medical treatment of women in Canada, 1900-1950.

*   *   *

MITROKHIN, Vasili (Nikitich) 1922-2004

PERSONAL: Born in 1922; defected to England, 1992; died January 23, 2004, in England.

CAREER: Soviet Foreign Intelligence Service, senior officer, 1948-84; defected to Great Britain, 1992.

WRITINGS:

I segreti del KGB in Italia, P. Manni (Lecce, Italy), 1999.

Sword and the Shield: The Mitrokhin Archive and the Secret History of the KGB, Basic Books (New York, NY), 1999, published as *The Mitrokhin Archive: The KGB in Europe and the West,* Allen Lane (London, England), 1999.

(Editor) *KGB Lexicon: The Soviet Intelligence Officer's Handbook,* Frank Cass (Portland, OR), 2002.

SIDELIGHTS: Vasili Mitrokhin began working as a Soviet intelligence agent when he was a young man, but early in his career, he learned of his government's persecution of dissidents and became disenchanted with Soviet ideology. With a position that gave him access to huge numbers of classified documents, Mitrokhin began a silent form of dissidence, memorizing and copying information, which he frequently smuggled out of the office in his shoe. For years he

kept up his activities, hiding his papers around his home—under the floor, in a butter churn, and in other unlikely places.

Mitrokhin's chance to break for freedom came after the fall of the Iron Curtain. Mitrokhin tried to turn himself in to the United States's Central Intelligence Agency, but he was turned down. He instead surrendered himself to British authorities, who gave him asylum and provided him and his family with new identities. Mitrokhin was able to provide British intelligence with some of the most complete and extensive information on Soviet activities ever revealed in the West. His notes included the identities of thousands of spies, locations of hidden arms caches, facts about Soviet agents in England, various plots to disrupt international and internal politics, a plan to break the legs of ballet dancer Rudolf Nureyev after he defected to the West, and documents from as early as 1971 identifying Cardinal Archbishop Karol Wojtyla—who later became Pope John Paul II—as a dangerous threat to the Soviet bloc.

Sword and the Shield: The Mitrokhin Archive and the Secret History of the KGB is derived from the documents smuggled out of the Soviet bloc by Mitrokhin. According to a writer for the *Harvard International Review, Sword and the Shield* is more important for what it tells us about the inner workings of Soviet intelligence than for any specific bit of intelligence smuggled out by Mitrokhin, and provides "a detailed, compelling, and at times startling account of what the KGB and its predecessors knew and did over their 75-year history." According to the reviewer, the book is divided into two phases: the first details the period from 1917 to 1945, when the Soviet Union's spying capabilities were the best in the world, while the second focuses on the period following World War II, when real achievements became rare. *Sword and the Shield* is "never an easy read," noted Donald P. Steury in *History: Review of New Books,* but it "nonetheless demonstrates convincingly the role of the KGB in corrupting the Soviet state."

BIOGRAPHICAL AND CRITICAL SOURCES:

BOOKS

Sword and the Shield: The Mitrokhin Archive and the Secret History of the KGB, Basic Books (New York, NY), 1999, published as *The Mitrokhin Archive: The KGB in Europe and the West,* Allen Lane (London, England), 1999.

PERIODICALS

Alberta Report, October 11, 1999, Jeff M. Sellers, review of *Sword and the Shield: The Mitrokhin Archive and the Secret History of the KGB,* p. 10.

Bulletin of the Atomic Scientists, May, 2000, Melvin A. Goodman, review of *Sword and the Shield,* p. 64.

Harvard International Review, spring, 2000, review of *Sword and the Shield,* pp. 84-85.

History: Review of New Books, winter, 2000, Donald P. Steury, review of *Sword and the Shield,* p. 77.

Insight on the News, October 18, 1999, Jamie Dettmer, review of *Sword and the Shield,* p. 6; March 25, 2002, Hans S. Nichols, review of *Sword and the Shield,* p. 6.

Los Angeles Times, October 24, 1999, Timothy Naftali, review of *Sword and the Shield,* p. 7.

Maclean's, September 27, 1999, review of *Sword and the Shield,* p. 53.

New Republic, October 25, 1999, Harvey Klehr, review of *Sword and the Shield,* p. 41.

New Statesman, October 4, 1999, Richard Gott, review of *The Mitrokhin Archive: The KGB in Europe and the West,* p. 53.

New York Times, October 31, 1999, Joseph E. Persico, review of *Sword and the Shield.*

Popular Mechanics, April, 2000, Jim Wilson, "Red Terror," p. 74.

Time, September 27, 1999, review of *Sword and the Shield,* p. 58.

OBITUARIES

PERIODICALS

America's Intelligence Wire, January 29, 2004.*

*   *   *

MOLE, Gary D(avid) 1964-

PERSONAL: Born September 20, 1964, in Birmingham, England; son of Edward John and Margaret Rose (Loach) Mole; married Nicole Hochner (a university lecturer), March 16, 1997; children: Rakefet Shulamit, Pin'has Moshe. *Ethnicity:* "Jewish." *Education:* Fitzwilliam College, Cambridge, B.A., 1987, M.A., 1990, Ph.D., 1992. *Politics:* "Left-wing." *Religion:* Jewish.

ADDRESSES: Home—9/8 Rehov Nahal Hever, Madi'in 71700, Israel. *Office*—Department of French, Bar-Ilan University, Ramat-Gan 52900, Israel. *E-mail*—molega@mail.biu.ac.il.

CAREER: Cambridge University, Pembroke College, Cambridge, England, lecturer and fellow, 1990-95; Bar-Ilan University, Ramat-Gan, Israel, senior lecturer in French and department head, 1995—.

MEMBER: Society of French Studies, Group for War and Cultural Studies, Modern Language Association of America.

AWARDS, HONORS: Milgat award, Government of Israel, 1996-99.

WRITINGS:

(Translator) Emmanuel Lévinas, *Beyond the Verse: Talmudic Readings and Lectures,* Athlone Press (London, England), 1994.

Lévinas, Blanchot, Jabès: Figures of Estrangement, University Press of Florida (Gainesville, FL), 1997.

Beyond the Limit-Experience: French Poetry of the Deportation, 1940-1945, Peter Lang Publishing (New York, NY), 2002.

Author of scholarly articles.

WORK IN PROGRESS: Discourses of Jewish Identity in France, 1945-1980, completion expected in 2005.

SIDELIGHTS: Gary D. Mole told *CA:* "As a professional academic I have no choice but to continue to research and to publish articles and books. But beyond this necessity, I write because I believe that outside the classroom—with undergraduates and graduates—I have knowledge I wish to share with fellow academics and other interested readers.

"No subject I have ever written on has been dictated to me. I research only those areas that I believe important, whether it be modern French poetry or the novel, the influence of Jewish thought on contemporary French philosophy, the poetry of the deportation and the Shoah (Holocaust), or indeed medieval French poets, on whom I have also written.

"At the end of the day, I write to be read, in the hope that someone out there can learn something from the hours I spend in libraries and books. It is this—the teacher-student relationship—that guides my writing."

*   *   *

MONTELEONE, Elizabeth E.

PERSONAL: Married Thomas F. Monteleone (a writer and editor).

ADDRESSES: Home—Grantham, NH. *Agent*—c/o Author Mail, Warner Books, 1271 Avenue of the Americas, New York, NY 10020.

CAREER: Writer and editor.

AWARDS, HONORS: Bram Stoker Award, Horror Writers Association, 2003, for *Borderlands 5: An Anthology of Imaginative Fiction.*

WRITINGS:

EDITOR

(With Craig Slaight and Jennifer Esty) *The Smith and Kraus Play Index for Young Actors Grades 6-12: A Guide to 500 Plays,* Smith & Kraus (Lyme, NH), 2000.
(Editor, with husband, Thomas F. Monteleone) *Borderlands 5: An Anthology of Imaginative Fiction,* Borderlands Press (Fork, MD), 2003.
(Editor, with Thomas F. Monteleone) *From the Borderlands,* Warner Books (New York, NY), 2004.

Also contributor of short fiction to books, including anthology *Shivers II,* Cemetery Dance Publications.

SIDELIGHTS: Elizabeth E. Monteleone is a writer and editor who has collaborated with her husband, Thomas F. Monteleone, on a contribution to the "Borderlands" anthology series of dark fantasy fiction. Their co-edited *Borderlands 5: An Anthology of Imaginative Fiction* contains twenty-five selections. According to a *Publishers Weekly* contributor, the anthology includes "a healthy quotient of offbeat efforts." The reviewer noted that most of the stories "are triumphs of mood or narrative trickery over storytelling" and added that "the wealth of relatively new writers featured is encouraging."

Another co-editing project, *From the Borderlands* also contains twenty-five stories by well-known writers of horror like Stephen King as well as by new authors. Writing on *MyShelf.com,* a reviewer noted, "These stories are not pure horror, yet all are strange in some respect and have aspects of horror in them. All are unforgettable." The reviewer went on to comment, "If you've never read one of the Borderlands series, this book will quickly make you a fan."

Monteleone also collaborated with Craig Slaight and Jennifer Esty to produce *The Smith and Kraus Play Index for Young Actors Grades 6-12.* The book includes an index of more than 500 plays appropriate for school children from the elementary grades through high school. In addition to providing information on the plays' authors, styles, and cast requirements, the coauthors include detailed plot summaries and information on how to acquire scripts. Writing in the *School Library Journal,* Cris Riedel noted the that the index contains "an eclectic mix" of plays and also wrote, "there is much to recommend this title."

BIOGRAPHICAL AND CRITICAL SOURCES:

PERIODICALS

Booklist, March 1, 2004, Ray Olson, review of *Borderlands 5: An Anthology of Imaginative Fiction,* p. 1145.
Publishers Weekly, January 19, 2004, review of *Borderlands 5,* p. 57.
School Library Journal, November, 2000, Cris Riedel, review of *The Smith and Kraus Play Index for Young Actors Grades 6-12,* p. 96.

ONLINE

MyShelf.com, http://www.myshelf.com/ (February 23, 2005), review of *From the Borderlands.**

*   *   *

MONTROSE, Sarah
   See BOSNA, Valerie

*   *   *

MOORE, Kathryn

PERSONAL: Female.

ADDRESSES: Agent—c/o Author Mail, Stackpole Books, 5067 Ritter Rd., Mechanicsburg, PA 17055.

CAREER: Colonial Williamsburg, Williamsburg, VA, historical interpreter; teacher of American history in Lee's Summit, MO.

WRITINGS:

(Editor, with D. M. Giangreco) *Dear Harry: Truman's Mailroom, 1945-1953: The Truman Administration through Correspondence with "Everyday Americans,"* Stackpole Books (Mechanicsburg, PA), 1999.
(With D. M. Giangreco) *Eyewitness D-Day: Firsthand Accounts from the Landing at Normandy to the Liberation of Paris* (includes audio CD), edited and with a foreword by Norman Polmar, Barnes & Noble Books (New York, NY), 2004.

Author of the self-published *Manhole Covers of Fort Wayne, IN,* 1988. Contributor to periodicals, including *American Heritage, Kansas City Star, Milwaukee Journal Sentinel,* and *Washington Times.*

WORK IN PROGRESS: First Lady of Monticello, a biography of Martha Jefferson, the wife of Thomas Jefferson.

SIDELIGHTS: Kathryn Moore is editor, with D. M. Giangreco, of *Dear Harry: Truman's Mailroom, 1945-1953: The Truman Administration through Correspondence with "Everyday Americans."* The coeditors drew on letters and other communications, primarily from the Harry S Truman Library in Independence, Missouri, that reflect the feelings of citizens over Truman's two presidential terms, from 1945 to 1953. His eight years were spent addressing many crises, and he bore the brunt of a great deal of criticism for his actions, which included integrating the civil service and armed forces and recognition of Israel as a nation-state. Most of the letters respond to the particular incidents that serve as the subjects of the book's ten chapters. Chapters most often deal with more than one subject, although several cover a single subject, such as Truman's relieving General Douglas MacArthur of his command, the atomic bomb, and the Korean War.

Infantry reviewer Albert N. Garland recommended the book, saying that "it gives flavor to the times. It brings back memories of the many problems we faced after World War II, and how many were solved. But there were others that are still around; for example, Truman believed in some form of national health service. Each president faces and will face his own set of problems and his own crises. Truman's actions, reactions, and decisions present a good guide to follow." *New York Times Book Review* contributor Stanley Weintraub noted that while most of the letters to Truman were critical, some supported his actions, for example when he ordered that a Native American soldier who had died in Korea be buried in Arlington National Cemetery, after authorities at another cemetery with a whites-only policy refused to do so. "The country was with him," noted Weintraub. "His mail reflected the turbulent, dynamic postwar nation he inherited as accidental President and tried to steer toward the future."

Moore and Giangreco—the editor of the U.S. Army's *Military Review*—also collaborated in writing *Eyewitness D-Day: Firsthand Accounts from the Landing at Normandy to the Liberation of Paris,* which comes with a CD on which is recorded a number of interviews. While some are with former German soldiers, most are interviews with soldiers, sailors, airmen, and medical personnel who served with the Allied forces that assembled on the southern shores of England on May 30, 1944. The operation began on June 5, but inclement weather caused a temporary delay. D-Day began on June 6, 1944, commanded by General Dwight D. Eisenhower, who made the decision to go ahead in spite of worsening conditions rather than postpone the launch for weeks until the tides would favor a later landing. In spite of the casualties suffered, D-Day initiated the liberation of German-occupied France and eventually the Nazi grip on Europe. The volume is enhanced by many black-and-white photographs and a foldout map that identifies the ships that were damaged and destroyed. It also includes the history of related incidents, including the plot to kill German dictator Adolf Hitler.

BIOGRAPHICAL AND CRITICAL SOURCES:

PERIODICALS

Infantry, May-August, 2000, Albert N. Garland, review of *Dear Harry: Truman's Mailroom, 1945-1953: The Truman Administration through Correspondence with "Everyday Americans,"* p. 51.
Library Journal, April 1, 2005, David Lee Poremba, review of *Eyewitness D-Day: Firsthand Accounts from the Landing at Normandy to the Liberation of Paris,* p. 108.
New York Times Book Review, October 24, 1999, Stanley Weintraub, review of *Dear Harry,* p. 47.*

*   *   *

MORGAN, Bailey
   See BREWER, Gil

*   *   *

MORGAN, Nicola 1961-

PERSONAL: Born November 11, 1961, in England. *Education:* Earned M.A.

ADDRESSES: Agent—c/o Author Mail, Walker Books, 87 Vauxhall Walk, London SE11 5HJ, England. *E-mail*—author@nicolamorgan.co.uk.

CAREER: Writer. Former teacher of English; founder, Magic Readers, 1994—; founder, Child Literacy Centre.

AWARDS, HONORS: Fleshmarket named an American Library Association Best Book for Young Adults.

WRITINGS:

Louis and the Night Sky, Oxford University Press (New York, NY), 1990.
Once in a Blue Moon, Oxford University Press (New York, NY), 1992.
Bouncy Gets Wet, Egmont (London, England), 1999.
Come down, Silky!, Egmont (London, England), 1999.
The Lost Key, Egmont (London, England), 1999.
At Home with Dad, Egmont (London, England), 1999.
Sam at the Museum, Egmont (London, England), 1999.
The Tree House, Egmont (London, England), 1999.
Sam's Birthday, Egmont (London, England), 1999.
Sam's Jungle, Egmont (London, England), 1999.
Sam's New School, Egmont (London, England), 1999.
Tiger Tales, Egmont (London, England), 1999.
Silky and Bouncy, Egmont (London, England), 1999.
Silky Is Lost, Egmont (London, England), 1999.
People Who Made History in Ancient Greece, Hodder Wayland (London, England), 2000.
Mondays Are Red, Hodder (London, England), 2002, Delacorte (New York, NY), 2003.
Fleshmarket, Hodder (London, England), 2003, Delacorte (New York, NY), 2004.
Sleepwalking, Hodder (London, England), 2004.
Chicken Friend, Candlewick Press (Cambridge, MA), 2005.
The Leaving Home Survival Guide, Walker Books (London, England), 2005.
Blame My Brain, Walker Books (London, England), 2005.

Also author of "I Can Learn" series, 18 volumes, Egmont (London, England), "Learning Rewards" series, seven volumes, Egmont, and "Thomas the Tank Engine" series, twelve volumes, Egmont.

SIDELIGHTS: Nicola Morgan was a teacher for sixteen years, first as an English instructor and then as a specially qualified expert in reading problems. Drawing on her expertise in this field, she has written many books for young children who are just learning to read, many of these aimed at the home-schooling market. More recently, Morgan has fulfilled a life-long ambition to write novels, and has produced the young-adult novels *Mondays Are Red, Fleshmarket,* and *Sleepwalking.*

Mondays Are Red tells of Luke, a fourteen year old who wakes up from a coma to discover that he is suffering from synesthesia, a condition in which the senses blur together and one seems to taste sounds, feel colors, and hear feelings. In this confused, hallucinatory condition, Luke struggles against a haunting presence named Dreeg, who is bent on encouraging him to do evil. A critic for *Kirkus Reviews* praised Morgan's "magnificent imagery" when describing the unusual medical condition. Hillias J. Martin, in *School Library Journal,* praised Morgan's "hallucinogenic imagery" as "well conceived and sophisticated."

Morgan sets *Fleshmarket* in nineteenth-century Edinburgh, Scotland. Robbie Anderson is a fourteen year old whose mother has just died after surgery. He and his little sister, Essie, are quickly abandoned by their distraught father and left to make their own ways in the world. Essie becomes a beggar, while Robbie works as a delivery boy. As life becomes more difficult for him, Robbie develops a growing hatred for Dr. Robert Knox, the surgeon who operated on his late mother. In addition to becoming convinced that Knox could have saved his mother, Robbie also discovers that the doctor is buying corpses to dissect, and some of these corpses are of murder victims. "Morgan's story is fast paced and absorbing," Anna M. Nelson wrote in *School Library Journal.* Betty Carter, reviewing the novel for *Horn Book,* wrote that "the fully realized setting and the character development of a young man facing interenal demons . . . make this novel memorable."

Sleepwalking is a science-fiction tale set in England, 150 years in the future. In this future world, most people are Citizens, content to have the state provide all their needs. Citizens' personalities are regulated by government-prescribed drugs, and implanted computer chips limit their ability to use language to analyze or question the authorities. But there are also Outsiders, those who live in the countryside where the government has little control. The Outsiders are content to live quietly until a plague hits their community, pushing them to launch a revolt against the government that is led by four teenagers attempting to infiltrate government headquarters. A critic for the Manchester *Guardian* called *Sleepwalking* "an intriguing read, as well as a thrilling one." "Morgan is a verbal sculptress," noted the reviewer for the London *Sunday Herald,* "creating images of vivid physicality so that the world of the Outsiders and Citizens is entirely credibly drawn.

BIOGRAPHICAL AND CRITICAL SOURCES:

PERIODICALS

Booklist, March 1, 2005, Chris Sherman, review of *Chicken Friend,* p. 1198.

Bookseller, February 18, 2005, review of *The Leaving Home Survival Guide,* p. 40.

Bulletin of the Center for Children's Books, October, 2004, Elizabeth Bush, review of *Fleshmarket,* p. 92.

Europe Intelligence Wire, October 8, 2002, Lindsey Fraser, review of *Mondays Are Red.*

Guardian (Manchester, England)October 19, 2004, review of *Sleepwalking.*

Horn Book, September-October, 2004, Betty Carter, review of *Fleshmarket,* p. 594; May-June, 2005, Joanna Rudge Long, review of *Chicken Friend,* p. 332.

Independent, October 15, 2004, review of *Sleepwalking.*

Journal of Adolescent and Adult Literacy, March, 2005, Juliet R. Heyden, review of *Fleshmarket,* p. 523.

Kirkus Reviews, October 1, 2003, review of *Mondays Are Red,* p. 1228; July 15, 2004, review of *Fleshmarket,* p. 691; February 15, 2005, review of *Chicken Friend,* p. 234.

Observer (London, England), October 24, 2004, review of *Sleepwalking.*

Publishers Weekly, November 17, 2003, review of *Mondays Are Red,* p. 66.

School Library Journal, November, 2003, Hillias J. Martin, review of *Mondays Are Red,* p. 143; September, 2004, Anna M. Nelson, review of *Fleshmarket,* p. 213; April, 2005, Steven Engelfried, review of *Chicken Friend,* p. 138.

Scotsman, October 16, 2004, review of *Sleepwalking.*

Sunday Herald, October 31, 2004, review of *Sleepwalking.*

ONLINE

Child Literacy Centre Web site, http://www.child literacy.com/ (May 31, 2005), "About Nicola Morgan."

Nicola Morgan's Web site, http://www.nicolamorgan. co.uk (May 31, 2005).

MORTIMER, Richard

PERSONAL: Male.

ADDRESSES: Office—Westminster Abbey Library, East Cloister, London SW1P 3PA, England.

CAREER: Westminster Abbey, London, England, keeper of muniments.

WRITINGS:

(Editor) *Leiston Abbey Cartulary and Butley Priory Charters,* Boydell Press (Ipswich, Suffolk, England), 1979.

(Editor, with Christopher Harper-Bill) *Stoke by Clare Catulary: BL Cotton Appx. XXI,* three volumes, Boydell Press (Ipswich, Suffolk), 1982–84.

(Editor, with James C. Holt) *Acta of Henry II and Richard I,* Paradigm Print (Gateshead, England), 1986.

Angevin England: 1154-1258, Blackwell (Cambridge, MA), 1994.

(Editor, with Anthony Harvey) *The Funeral Effigies of Westminster Abbey,* Boydell Press (Rochester, NY), 1994.

(Editor) *Charters of St. Bartholomew's Priory, Sudbury,* Boydell Press (Woodbridge, Suffolk, England), 1996.

(Editor, with Lindy Grant) *Westminster Abbey: The Cosmati Pavements,* Ashgate Publishing (Burlington, VT), 2002.

(Editor, with Tim Tatton-Brown) *Westminster Abbey: The Lady Chapel of Henry VII,* Boydell Press (Rochester, NY), 2003.

(Editor, with C. S. Knighton) *Westminster Abbey Reformed: 1540-1640,* Ashgate Publishing (Burlington, VT), 2003.

SIDELIGHTS: An historian with a strong interest in medieval and early modern art and architecture, Richard Mortimer is also an expert on Westminster Abbey, where he is the keeper of the muniments. In *The Funeral Effigies of Westminster Abbey,* edited with Anthony Harvey, the authors examine the medieval portrait effigies of medieval kings and queens that were carried at their funeral processions as well as the tradition of creating beautifully dressed wax figures

that began with Charles II. He also discusses the creator of the statues of national heroes, such as Admiral Horatio Nelson, that were designed to satisfy the curiosity of a public willing to pay to see their image. "It is obviously essential reading for those interested in the personages whose effigies survive, and for historians of costume," concluded Jennifer Loach in the *English Historical Review.*

In *Westminster Abbey: The Cosmati Pavements,* co-edited with Lindy Grant, Mortimer and his fellow essayists examine the history of the glass, marble, and stone pavement laid down in the Great Sanctuary during the thirteenth century. The Roman look of the Pavement in a building otherwise northern French and English in its inspiration has long fascinated art historians, and the essays examine the work in the context of similar pavements in England, as well as providing descriptions of how it was constructed and conserved. In addition, essayists look at the interplay between biblical and cosmological symbolism in the inscriptions that reveals a sophisticated interest in numerology and calendrical analysis. "The essays are accompanied by numerous drawings and photographs which make this volume essential for any understanding of this unique mediaeval survival," according to a *Contemporary Review* contributor.

More recently, Mortimer has co-edited *Westminster Abbey: The Lady Chapel of Henry VII.* The last great example of medieval architecture, the chapel is the culmination of three hundred years of gothic style. The burial place of fifteen kings and their consorts, the chapel provides a vivid representation of the transition from medieval to Renaissance tombs in England, as well as numerous examples of gothic sculpture. The book also provides a short history of the cult of the Virgin in the twelfth century and an explanation of the restoration the chapel underwent in the 1990s.

In addition to his work on the famed and magnificent Westminster Abbey, Mortimer has also edited *Charters of St. Bartholomew's Priory, Sudbury.* A contrast to the Abbey in many ways, St. Bartholomew's was a small, backwater priory usually housing a prior and two monks; at one point, the monks actually considered trading in their lands and priory house for a few shops in London. Fortunately for the collection, they decided not to, and the 130 surviving charters provide a look at the economic and social structure of a medieval religious house and its surrounding borough.

While much of Mortimer's work focuses on the specialized details and manuscripts that focus on specific cultural objects, he has also produced a general study suitable for use as a textbook. *Angevin England: 1154-1258* covers the politics, sociology, and economics of this important period in England's development. "This is, generally speaking, rather a well-written and thoughtful work, with a range of interesting and scholarly material," noted *English Historical Review* contributor H. Ridgeway. "The pace is brisk, but all chapters avoid superficiality and display a good eye for the essential points."

BIOGRAPHICAL AND CRITICAL SOURCES:

PERIODICALS

Contemporary Review, August, 2003, review of *Westminster Abbey: The Cosmati Pavements,* p. 125.

English Historical Review, April, 1997, H. Ridgeway, review of *Angevin England: 1154-1258,* p. 436; April, 1997, Jennifer Loach, review of *The Funeral Effigies of Westminster Abbey,* p. 465; June, 1998, Nicholas Vincent, review of *Charters of St. Bartholomew's Priory, Sudbury,* p. 716.

Journal of Ecclesiastical History, January, 1998, Gervase Rosser, review of *Charters of St. Bartholomew's Priory, Sudbury,* p. 163; October, 2003, Julian Gardner, review of *Westminster Abbey: The Cosmati Pavements,* p. 752.

*   *   *

MOSES, Sheila P. 1961-

PERSONAL: Born 1961, in Rich Square, NC.

ADDRESSES: Home—Atlanta, GA. *Agent*—c/o Author Mail, Margaret K. McElderry Books, 1230 Avenue of the Americas, New York, NY 10020.

CAREER: Writer and theatrical producer.

AWARDS, HONORS: Coretta Scott King Author Honor book, 2005, for *The Legend of Buddy Bush.*

WRITINGS:

(With Dick Gregory) *Callus on My Soul: A Memoir,* Longstreet Press (Atlanta, GA), 2000.

The Legend of Buddy Bush, Margaret K. McElderry Books (New York, NY), 2004.

I, Dred Scott: A Fictional Slave Narrative Based on the Life and Legal Precedent of Dred Scott, Margaret K. McElderry Books (New York, NY), 2005.

The Obituary, Margaret K. McElderry Books (New York, NY), 2005.

SIDELIGHTS: Sheila P. Moses writes across genres, working as a poet, playwright, novelist, and biographer. The ninth of ten children, she was born and raised in Rich Square, North Carolina, a setting she mined for her novel *The Legend of Buddy Bush,* in which twelve-year-old Pattie Mae shares Moses's childhood home. Moses depicts the issues of racism and segregation in North Carolina in 1947, following Pattie Mae and her family through their daily lives in a time before the civil rights movement, when Pattie Mae's uncle, the title character, escapes a near-lynching by the Ku Klux Klan. A contributor to *NimbleSpirit.com* commented that Moses "creates an appealing voice for her main character . . . a girl on the cusp of a young womanhood that is upon her, perhaps, too soon and under too stressful circumstances." In *Kirkus Reviews,* a contributor noted that the first-person narrative is not always appropriate to Moses's multi-layered tale, but called *The Legend of Buddy Bush* "an important story."

I, Dred Scott: A Fictional Slave Narrative Based on the Life and Legal Precedent of Dred Scott is Moses's take on the infamous U.S. Supreme Court case. Inspired by the simple plaque outside the Old Courthouse in St. Louis, where Scott was tried in 1850, Moses decided to delve deeper into the history of the events surrounding the trial as well as Scott's background. The result is a book written as if from Scott's point of view, though Moses discovered more about Scott's owners than about Scott himself. In order to write as authentically as possible, she researched other slave narratives and studied interviews with former slaves. Claire Rosser, in a review for *Kliatt,* called Moses's effort "an accessible vehicle to tell about this important legal case."

BIOGRAPHICAL AND CRITICAL SOURCES:

PERIODICALS

Ebony, January, 2005, review of *The Legend of Buddy Bush,* p. 27.

Kirkus Reviews, November 15, 2003, review of *The Legend of Buddy Bush,* p. 1361.

Kliatt, January, 2005, Claire Rosser, review of *I, Dred Scott: A Fictional Slave Narrative Based on the Life and Legal Precedent of Dred Scott,* p. 10.

USA Today, February 4, 2005, Bob Minzesheimer, review of *I, Dred Scott.*

Washington Post, February 6, 2005, review of *I, Dred Scott,* p. D8.

ONLINE

DallasBlack.com, http://new.dallasblack.com/ (February 23, 2005), "Sheila P. Moses."

NimbleSpirit.com, http://www.nimblespirit.com/ (February 23, 2005), "Sheila P. Moses."

Simon and Schuster Web site, http://www.simonsays.com/ (February 23, 2005), "Sheila P. Moses."

Washington Post Online, http://www.washingtonpost.com/ (February 23, 2005), "Sheila P. Moses."*

* * *

MOUNTAIN, Fiona 1974(?)-

PERSONAL: Born c. 1974, in England; married Tim Mountain (a music composer); children: Daniel, James, Gabriel.

ADDRESSES: Home—Oxfordshire, England. *Agent*—c/o Emily Furniss, Orion Publishing Group, Orion House, 5 Upper Saint Martin's Ln., London WC2H 9EA, England. *E-mail*—info@fionamountain.com.

CAREER: BBC Radio One, London, England, former press officer; currently runs her own public relations firm in Oxfordshire, England.

WRITINGS:

Isabella (historical romance novel), Orion Publishing Group (London, England), 1999.

Pale as the Dead ("Natasha Blake" mystery novel), Orion Publishing Group (London, England), 2002, St. Martin's/Minotaur (New York, NY), 2004.

Bloodline ("Natasha Blake" mystery novel), Orion Publishing Group, (London, England), 2004.

SIDELIGHTS: Fiona Mountain grew up in Sheffield, England, then moved to London at the age of eighteen and began working for the British Broadcasting Corporation as a press and public relations consultant. After nearly a decade, she moved to the Cotswolds, where she lives with her husband, Tim Mountain, and their three sons, and runs a public relations firm. In addition to her PR work, she is the author of several novels, including the "Natasha Blake" detective series.

Mountain's first novel, *Isabella,* is an historical love story based on the true events behind the mutiny on the HMS *Bounty.* Shortlisted for the Romantic Novel of the Year Award, the story follows Fletcher Christian's cousin, Isabella Curwen, a rich young heiress with whom Christian was apparently in love.

In her subsequent novels, Mountain has incorporated the detective skills required for her to research the historical background of Christian and his cousin into the story itself, turning her attention to writing mysteries. *Pale as the Dead* is set in modern times but deals with the study of genealogy, delving into a family's past. Natasha Blake is not your everyday detective; she is a genealogist. When a young girl goes missing, Natasha's investigation leads her into a mystery surrounding the girl's obsession with Lizzie Siddal, the famous wife of pre-Raphaelite poet Dante Gabriel Rossetti.

In a profile for *Shots* online, Mountain explained her reason for concentrating on the science of genealogy: "It . . . seemed the right time to write this kind of book. Not only is genealogy now the most popular hobby in the UK, but there are more web sites devoted to it than any other subject, except pornography." She went on to remark that "it is a real thrill to find, staring up at you from the indexes, or some obscure manuscript or old book, a name, a person you've been searching for. By piecing together strands of evidence of a person's existence they are suddenly made real. And . . . you want to go on breathing the life back into them."

GraceAnne A. DeCandido, in a review of *Pale as the Dead* for *Booklist,* commented that "Mountain captures the silken creepiness of much of the . . . story without quite revealing its gorgeous artistic legacy." A reviewer for *Publishers Weekly* remarked that the novel's ending is "anticlimactic," but added that "the premise of a genealogist sleuth holds plenty of potential." Harriet Klausner, in a review for *AllReaders.com,* called the book an "exhilarating opening debut of a fascinating 'detective,'" and went on to state that "this is a unique tale starring a delightful individual who makes a fine sleuth whether it is the past or the present."

Bloodline continues the adventures of the geneologist. In this volume, Natasha finds herself embroiled in a mystery that links an old man's murder to a pair of World War II soldiers, one British and one German, and a secret that has been hidden for decades.

BIOGRAPHICAL AND CRITICAL SOURCES:

PERIODICALS

Booklist, June 1, 2004, GraceAnne A. DeCandido, review of *Pale as the Dead,* p. 1708.

Denver Post, August 1, 2004, Tom and Enid Schantz, "Caesar Embroils Detective in Conflict," review of *Pale as the Dead,* p. F12.

Kirkus Reviews, June 1, 2004, review of *Pale as the Dead,* p. 521.

Publishers Weekly, June 21, 2004, review of *Pale as the Dead,* p. 46.

ONLINE

AllReaders.com, http://www.allreaders.com/ (February 23, 2005), Harriet Klausner, review of *Pale as the Dead.*

Fantastic Fiction Web site, http://www.fantasticfiction.co.uk/ (February 23, 2005), "Fiona Mountain."

Fiona Mountain Home Page, http://www.fionamountain.com (February 23, 2005).

Orion Books Web site, http://www.orionbooks.com/ (February 23, 2005), "Fiona Mountain."

Shots Online, http://www.shotsmag.co.uk/ (February 23, 2005), "Fiona Mountain."*

*   *   *

MRS. ELLIOT HANDLER
See HANDLER, Ruth

MURPHY, David E. 1921-

PERSONAL: Born June 23, 1921, in Utica, NY; son of Howard Leo and Anne K. (Brown) Murphy; married Marian Escovy, February 29, 1944 (died February, 1978); married Star Hellmann (a Central Intelligence Agency employee), January 6, 1979; children: Steven J., Vincent B., Gerald H., Barbara A. *Ethnicity:* "Irish." *Education:* Attended Cortland College (now State University of New York), 1942, and University of California, Berkeley, 1943-44, 1946. *Politics:* "Independent." *Hobbies and other interests:* Boating, swimming.

ADDRESSES: Agent—c/o Author Mail, Yale University Press, P.O. Box 209040, New Haven, CT 06520-9040.

CAREER: Central Intelligence Agency (CIA), Washington, DC, career officer, beginning 1947, served in Korea and Japan, chief of combined OSO/OPC Soviet Operations Base, Munich, Germany, 1951-52, deputy chief for Soviet operations, Washington, DC, 1953-59, chief of Berlin Operations Base, 1959-61, representative on Berlin Task Force, deputy chief (became chief) of East European Division of Clandestine Services, 1961-63, chief of Soviet Russian Division, 1963-68, special assistant to ambassador to France, 1968-74, national intelligence officer, 1974-75; Science Applications International, intelligence specialist, beginning 1979; retired, late 1980s. *Military service:* Served in Germany and France during World War II.

AWARDS, HONORS: Notable Book of the Year, *New York Times,* 1997, for *Battleground Berlin: CIA vs. KGB in the Cold War.*

WRITINGS:

(With Sergei A. Kondrashev and George Bailey) *Battleground Berlin: CIA vs. KGB in the Cold War,* Yale University Press (New Haven, CT), 1997.

What Stalin Knew: The Enigma of Barbarrosa, Yale University Press (New Haven, CT), 2005.

Contributor to professional journals.

SIDELIGHTS: David E. Murphy was a career officer with the Central Intelligence Agency (CIA) during one of the most volatile periods in twentieth-century American history, from the end of World War II in 1945 until the construction of the Berlin Wall in 1961. With Sergei A. Kondrashev and George Bailey, he documents these years in *Battleground Berlin: CIA vs. KGB in the Cold War.* Murphy told *CA* that "the reason for writing this particular book was the need I felt to make available to historians an insider's account of intelligence operations which did so much to shape the policies and actions of all governments involved in this key Cold War city." Murphy and Kondrashev, a retired KGB (Soviet secret police) general, drew on documents from their respective agencies, their work augmented that of Bailey, a former director of Radio Liberty and a German affairs expert.

Joseph E. Persico wrote in the *New York Times Book Review* that the book "is hardly a romp for the general reader. Microscopic descriptions of cogs within cogs in the spy bureaucracies, a flood of acronyms and a rain of polysyllabic Russian names create, at times, pages that only a Sovietologist could love. Yet the book does present a remarkably balanced view of the Berlin spy wars."

Kondrashev, who rose to become the deputy head of the KGB, had under his supervision the spy George Blake, who from his position within British intelligence delivered American and British agents to Moscow. Kondrashev was successful in retrieving eighty-seven photocopies of documents, as well as portions of approximately 250 files from the closely guarded KGB (now SVR) archives, although he was unable to secure documentation about Soviet officers who were sent abroad as foreign nationals, nor was he able to provide documents from the program responsible for spreading propaganda to influence Western opinion.

Murphy goes into detail about such subjects as the 400-yard Berlin tunnel the Americans dug into East Berlin so that they could tap Soviet-sector phone lines. In fact, the KGB knew of the tunnel's existence from the beginning, having been informed by Blake, and they leaked only inconsequential information and even invented false information to deceive the Americans. Murphy notes in an appendix the real value of the tunnel.

The Berlin Wall was erected to stem the flow of refugees from East to West Germany. Murphy, who briefed President John F. Kennedy when the wall was erected, said in a *CNN.com* online chat that "the administration was perfectly prepared to stand by and allow the East Germans to take whatever measures they thought necessary, to regulate the outflow of refugees. What did come as a surprise to them was the reaction of the West Berliners. The cable, which was sent to President Kennedy by [West Berlin Mayor] Willy Brandt, emphasized that the West Berlin population was indeed shocked at the fact that the West took no action to counter the closure of the sector borders. They interpreted this as perhaps the first step of the West's abandonment of West Berlin." As a result of the Berlin Wall and Stasi (East German security), communications between the CIA and its informants and contacts in East Germany were severely curtailed.

Understandably, both sides of all issues are not presented in *Battleground Berlin*, nor are there always equally balanced profiles of various spies. However, as Oleg Gordievsky wrote in the *Times Literary Supplement*, Murphy's book "is the first serious attempt by Russian and American writers, working together, to write the objective history of the intelligence war between East and West."

In *What Stalin Knew: The Enigma of Barbarrosa* Murphy studies the intelligence war between Soviet dictator Joseph Stalin and German dictator Adolf Hitler from 1939 to 1941. He shows that Stalin believed, based partly on letters from Hitler to that effect, that Germany would never invade the Soviet Union. On June 22, 1941, however, Hitler did just that. In spite of warnings from his own generals, Stalin was unprepared, a failing that ultimately cost the lives of million of people.

BIOGRAPHICAL AND CRITICAL SOURCES:

PERIODICALS

Booklist, October 1, 1997, Roland Green, review of *Battleground Berlin: CIA vs. KGB in the Cold War,* p. 292.

History: Review of New Books, spring, 1998, Julius W. Friend, review of *Battleground Berlin,* p. 161.

Journal of American History, December, 1999, Manfred Berg, review of *Battleground Berlin,* p. 1383.

Library Journal, September 15, 1997, Daniel K. Blewett, review of *Battleground Berlin,* p. 91.

Los Angeles Times Book Review, October 12, 1997, Markus Wolf and Tennent H. Bagley, review of *Battleground Berlin.*

New York Review of Books, October 23, 1997, Thomas Powers, review of *Battleground Berlin,* pp. 60-64.

New York Times, October 1, 1997, Richard Bernstein, review of *Battleground Berlin.*

New York Times Book Review, September 28, 1997, Joseph E. Persico, review of *Battleground Berlin,* p. 15.

Publishers Weekly, July 21, 1997, review of *Battleground Berlin,* p. 189.

Times Literary Supplement, November 14, 1997, Oleg Gordievsky, review of *Battleground Berlin,* p. 11.

ONLINE

CNN Online, http://www.cnn.com/ (May 17, 2005), "Cold War Chat: David E. Murphy—Former CIA Berlin Chief."*

*   *   *

MURRAY, Charles Shaar 1950(?)-

PERSONAL: Born c. 1950.

ADDRESSES: Agent—c/o Author Mail, St. Martin's Press, 175 5th Ave., New York, NY 10010.

CAREER: Writer. Former editor of *New Musical Express,* England.

WRITINGS:

(With Roy Carr) *David Bowie: An Illustrated Record* (biography), Avon (New York, NY), 1981.

Crosstown Traffic: Jimi Hendrix and the Post-war Rock 'n' Roll Revolution (biography), St. Martin's Press (New York, NY), 1989, published as *Crosstown Traffic: Jimi Hendrix and Post-war Pop,* Faber and Faber (London, England), 1989.

Shots from the Hip (articles), Penguin (New York, NY), 1991.

Blues on CD: The Essential Guide, Kyle Cathie (London, England), 1994.

Boogie Man: The Adventures of John Lee Hooker in the American Twentieth Century (biography), St. Martin's Press (New York, NY), 2000.

Contributor to anthology *This Old Guitar: Making Music and Memories from Country to Jazz, Blues to Rock,* Voyageur Press (Stillwater, MN), 2003. Contributor to periodicals, including Manchester *Guardian.*

SIDELIGHTS: Charles Shaar Murray has followed the music scene for several decades and is the author of several autobiographies of prominent artists in the business. His first, cowritten with Roy Carr, is *David Bowie: An Illustrated Record.* A study of Bowie's career, the book includes a discography and reproduces a collection of concert programs, press releases, and articles about the rock star. *Crosstown Traffic: Jimi Hendrix and the Post-war Rock 'n' Roll Revolution* (published in England as *Crosstown Traffic: Jimi Hendrix and Post-war Pop,*) was written several years later as a tribute to Hendrix, who died in 1970 at the age of twenty-seven of an overdose of sleeping pills. In the book, Murray notes that Hendrix was heavily influenced by the legendary blues singer and guitarist Robert Johnson and by B. B. King, Buddy Guy, Albert King, and Muddy Waters.

Born in Seattle, Hendrix was of mixed race—black, white, and Cherokee—and he played his black-inspired music to audiences that were primarily white. He began his career playing for Little Richard and with various rock bands before being transported to London by his agent, Chas Chandler, former bass player with the band the Animals. It was in London that the flamboyant guitarist became a pop icon, impressing audiences and other musicians, including Eric Clapton. His famous rendition of "The Star-Spangled Banner," at the conclusion of the Woodstock Festival, is replayed to this day. Hendrix's career lasted just four years.

Publishers Weekly contributor Genevieve Stuttaford said that Murray "augments solid musical scholarship with astute social and historical commentary, and meets the challenge admirably." Jeremy Harding wrote in the *London Review of Books,* "In a sparkling homage, far more readable than most books about pop music, Murray argues that the extravagant left-hander who introduced a new vocabulary to rock guitar-playing was the unsung progenitor of a jazz we will never know."

A selection of Murray's articles from two decades are collected in *Shots from the Hip.* Murray also wrote *Blues on CD: The Essential Guide,* which documents recordings from the 1920s to the 1990s, including those by artists Bessie Smith and Ma Rainey to contemporary blues masters like Kinsey Report and Saffire/Uppity Blues Women. *Library Journal* contributor Rick Anderson noted that "Murray's fresh and friendly writing and profound mastery of the subject matter make this guide worth acquiring."

Murray returned to biography with *Boogie Man: The Adventures of John Lee Hooker in the American Twentieth Century,* drawing in part on interviews with friends, family, and Hooker himself. Born in the Mississippi Delta, Hooker first played blues guitar as a child in the 1920s. Murray traces the musician's career from Memphis to Detroit and finally to San Francisco, chronicling Hooker's worldwide status in the 1960s rock culture. Because Hooker could not read music, each time he performed a song it sounded unique. Hooker influenced musicians like Clapton, Bonnie Raitt, Van Morrison, and ZZ Top. He had been playing more than forty years when he had his first hit album, *The Healer,* which also featured Raitt and Carlos Santana, although his seminal album, *Canned Heat,* had been recorded two decades earlier in the 1960s.

"As Murray sees it, nobody else but Hooker could have come up with the particular style and sound that have made him the legendary bluesman that he is," wrote Paula Friedman in the *Los Angeles Times.* "It is a view that might seem a mere truism, yet Murray makes the case compellingly clear." Friedman concluded that "Murray provides an intelligent analysis of the various strains of popular music with which Hooker's blues became entwined. Folk, pop, rhythm and blues and rock 'n' roll all came under the sway of Hooker's emotionally intense, rich, broody voice."

Murray contributed to the anthology *This Old Guitar: Making Music and Memories from Country to Jazz, Blues to Rock,* a history and tribute to acoustic and electric guitars of various makes. The volume includes historical photographs, memoirs, and stories as well as quotes from famous guitarists, including Clapton, Waters, King, Hendrix, Pete Townsend, and T-Bone Walker.

BIOGRAPHICAL AND CRITICAL SOURCES:

PERIODICALS

Booklist, October 15, 2000, Mike Tribby, review of *Boogie Man: The Adventures of John Lee Hooker in the American Twentieth Century,* p. 406.
Library Journal, October 1, 1981, Lauren Fleishman, review of *David Bowie: An Illustrated Record,* p. 1929; September 15, 1994, Rick Anderson, review of *Blues on CD: The Essential Guide,* p. 73; October 1, 2000, David Szatmary, review of *Boogie Man,* p. 102.
London Review of Books, May 24, 1990, Jeremy Harding, "Got to Keep Moving," review of *Crosstown Traffic: Jimi Hendrix and Post-war Pop,* p. 19.
Los Angeles Times, October 26, 2000, Paula Friedman, "A Blues Career of Enduring Eloquence," review of *Boogie Man,* p. E1.
New York Times Book Review, January 20, 1991, Robert Waddell, review of *Crosstown Traffic: Jimi Hendrix and the Post-war Rock 'n' Roll Revolution;* March 18, 2001, Michael E. Ross, review of *Boogie Man,* p. 17.
Publishers Weekly, June 22, 1990, Genevieve Stuttaford, review of *Crosstown Traffic: Jimi Hendrix and the Post-war Rock 'n' Roll Revolution,* p. 40.
Rolling Stone, November 9, 2000, David Thigpen, review of *Boogie Man,* p. 42.
Sunday Times (London, England), October 24, 1999, Robert Sandall, review of *Boogie Man,* p. 42.
Village Voice Literary Supplement, March, 1992, Richard Gehr, "Vicious and His Circle: Taking Aim at the Sex Pistols," review of *Shots from the Hip,* p. 27.*

*   *   *

MURRAY, William 1926-2005

OBITUARY NOTICE— See index for *CA* sketch: Born April 8, 1926, in New York, NY; died of a heart attack March 9, 2005, in New York, NY. Journalist and author. Murray was a former staff writer for the *New Yorker* who turned his passion for horse racing into popular mystery novels and nonfiction books. After spending several childhood years with his mother and her family in Italy after his parents divorced, he was brought back to America, where he attended Phillips Exeter Academy, Harvard University, and the Manhattan Conservatory. After serving in the U.S. Army Air Forces during World War II, Murray lived in Rome for a time, where he studied voice for five years in the hope of becoming an opera singer. Unfortunately, he felt his voice just was not good enough to perform in major opera productions, and so he took up a second interest: journalism. Having worked in Rome as a part-time writer for *Time* magazine, he returned to New York City and got a job as a reader of fiction submissions to the *New Yorker* in 1956. By 1961 he was a full-time staff writer, and he later moved back to Italy and wrote a regular column on the country for the magazine. Besides opera and Italy, Murray, who left the *New Yorker* in the mid-1980s and moved to Del Mar Heights near San Diego's Del Mar racetrack, had a passion for horse racing. He became an expert on the subject, and used this knowledge to write a series of mystery novels and several nonfiction titles, the latter including the well-received *The Wrong Horse: An Odyssey through the American Racing Scene* (1992). Among his many mystery novels, which have been noted for their exciting depictions of the sport, are *The Sweet Ride* (1967), which was adapted as a movie, *The Mouth of the Wolf* (1977), *Tip on a Dead Crab* (1985), and *I'm Getting Killed Right Here* (1991). Another novel, *Malibu* (1980), was turned into a television miniseries. Murray also published books about Italy, such as *Italy: The Fatal Gift* (1982), which was an American Library Association notable book, and *The Last Italian: Portrait of a People.* In addition, his autobiographical *Janet, My Mother, and Me: A Memoir of Growing up with Janet Flanner and Natalia Danesi Murray* (2000) relates his memories of his mother's affair with Flanner after his parents divorced. Two more titles were scheduled for publication after Murray's death, including the mystery novel *Dead Heat* and the nonfiction *Fortissimo: Backstage at the Opera with Sacred Monsters and Young Singers.* Although he never became a famous opera star, Murray continued to indulge his interest in singing later in life as a performer with the Gilbert and Sullivan Opera Company in San Diego.

OBITUARIES AND OTHER SOURCES:

PERIODICALS

Chicago Tribune, March 11, 2005, section 1, p. 9.
Los Angeles Times, March 11, 2005, p. B10.
New York Times, March 12, 2005, p. A27.
Washington Post, March 12, 2005, p. B6.

N-O

NAYLOR, R. T(homas) 1945-

PERSONAL: Born 1945. *Education:* Cambridge University, Ph.D.

ADDRESSES: Office—Department of Economics, McGill University, Leacock Bldg., Rm. 443, 855 Sherbrooke St. W., Montreal, Quebec H3A 2T7, Canada. *E-mail*—thomas.naylor@mcgill.ca.

CAREER: McGill University, Montreal, Quebec, Canada, professor of economics. University of Toronto Centre for Peace and Conflict Studies, senior fellow; York University Nathanson Centre for the Study of Organized Crime and Corruption, research associate.

WRITINGS:

The History of Canadian Business, 1867-1914, J. Lorimer (Toronto, Ontario, Canada), 1975, revised edition, Black Rose Books (New York, NY), 1997.
Dominion of Debt: Centre, Periphery and the International Economic Order, Black Rose Books (Montreal, Quebec, Canada), 1985.
Canada in the European Age, 1453-1919, New Star Books (Vancouver, British Columbia, Canada), 1987.
Hot Money and the Politics of Debt, Linden Press (New York, NY), 1987, 2nd edition, Black Rose Books (New York, NY), 1994.
Bankers, Bagmen, and Bandits: Business and Politics in the Age of Greed, Black Rose Books (New York, NY), 1990.

Patriots and Profiteers: On Economic Warfare, Embargo Busting, and State-Sponsored Crime, McClellan & Stewart (Toronto, Ontario, Canada), 1999, published as *Economic Warfare: Sanctions, Embargo Busting, and Their Human Cost,* Northeastern University Press (Boston, MA), 2001.
Wages of Crime: Black Markets, Illegal Finance, and the Underworld Economy, Cornell University Press (Ithaca, NY), 2002, revised edition, 2004.

Crime, Law, and Social Change, senior editor and contributor.

SIDELIGHTS: Canadian-based economist R. Thomas Naylor has written a number of volumes on economic history and theory. His first, *The History of Canadian Business, 1867-1914,* is based on much original research and traces Canada's economic history from its colonial roots. Naylor covers financial institutions and the investment of capital, the development of Canadian railroads, patents and technology, and the country's expansion and development. In commenting on the book for *Business History Review,* Richard W. Pollay called it "an impressive work."

Naylor covers a broader time period in *Canada in the European Age, 1453-1919,* a study of the economic history of Canada in relation to concurrent European economic expansion. The book covers a time when Britain and France vied for the rich resources of Canada and when the United States was beginning to form a stronger relationship with its northern neighbor. Bryan D. Palmer wrote in *American Historical Review* that Naylor's "sweeping accounts . . . conform to no contemporary intellectual trend." Palmer went on to note, "Refreshingly sardonic and elegantly sarcastic, he writes with wit and unusual antagonism to the powerful."

Jane M. Wilson reviewed the second edition of *Hot Money and the Politics of Debt* in the *Canadian Book Review Annual,* noting that Naylor's "sardonic and fascinating exposé of financial black markets culminates in the international debt crisis of the mid-1980s that threatened the entire banking system." Naylor follows billions of dollars as they pass through the hands of drug traffickers, arms dealers, banks, governments and their intelligence agencies, tax evaders, the International Monetary Fund, and the Vatican. A *Journal of Economic Literature* contributor noted that Naylor makes the case that international debt and the "hot money" of his title "are two sides of the coin of peekaboo finance."

In *Patriots and Profiteers: On Economic Warfare, Embargo Busting, and State-Sponsored Crime* Naylor studies the profiteering taking place as far back as Elizabethan times. In *Quill & Quire,* Andrew Allentuck noted that the author "sees trade sanctions as gifts to gangsters who make money trading in goods that are otherwise unavailable," and added that "Naylor's research is authoritative and his conclusions startling." The book describes bribes made by firms in the U.S. military-industrial complex as well as black markets, both of which have profited from shortages after those with wealth and power took control of limited resources and economic opportunities not available to the lower and middle classes. Naylor comments that criminals sometimes become national heroes and that nations and empires have even been created from the profits of crime.

Naylor continues his study of global corruption in *Wages of Crime: Black Markets, Illegal Finance, and the Underworld Economy,* which focuses on wealthy, industrialized countries. In the wake of the post-September 11, 2001 terrorist attacks, Naylor contends, new, more restrictive laws that encroach on individual rights will not be effective in curtailing international crime. He theorizes that the publicized numbers summarizing the amount and movement of worldwide illegal capital are fabricated and that no one knows the actual details of the world's black-market economy. According to Naylor, such numbers are exaggerated to justify the expansion of the prison-industrial complex

and law enforcement agencies that are inefficient and ineffective. In the book's introduction he writes: "Never in history has there been a black market tamed from the supply side. From Prohibition to prostitution, from gambling to recreational drugs, the story is the same. Supply-side controls act to encourage production and increase profits." *Barron's* contributor Neil Lipschutz wrote, "This wide-ranging, well-researched recent history of various illegal activities contains many anecdotes, on topics ranging from drug-running and gun-running to the underworld of gold."

BIOGRAPHICAL AND CRITICAL SOURCES:

BOOKS

Naylor, R. T., *Wages of Crime: Black Markets, Illegal Finance, and the Underworld Economy,* Cornell University Press (Ithaca, NY), 2002.

PERIODICALS

American Historical Review, June, 1989, Bryan D. Palmer, review of *Canada in the European Age, 1453-1919,* pp. 901-902.
Barron's, May 6, 2002, Neil Lipschutz, review of *Wages of Crime: Black Markets, Illegal Finance, and the Underworld Economy,* p. 46.
Books in Canada, August, 1988, J. L. Granatstein, "The Sun Also Sets," review of *Canada in the European Age, 1453-1919,* p. 23.
Business History Review, autumn, 1976, Richard W. Pollay, review of *The History of Canadian Business, 1867-1914,* p. 409.
Canadian Book Review Annual, 1994, Jane W. Wilson, review of *Hot Money and the Politics of Debt,* p. 304.
Canadian Historical Review, March, 1986, Peter Wylie, review of *Dominion of Debt: Centre, Periphery and the International Economic Order,* p. 105; September, 1989, Donald G. Paterson, review of *Canada in the European Age, 1453-1919,* pp. 437-438.
Choice, February, 1977, review of *The History of Canadian Business, 1867-1914,* p. 1638; September, 1988, R. W. Winks, review of *Canada in the European Age, 1453-1919,* p. 208; December, 1994, A. R. Sanderson, review of *Hot Money and the Politics of Debt,* p. 649.

Ethics & International Affairs, October, 2002, Joy Gordon, "United States Economic Statecraft for Survival, 1933-1991: Of Sanctions and Strategic Embargoes," review of *Economic Warfare: Sanctions, Embargo Busting, and Their Human Cost,* p. 177.

Journal of Criminal Law and Criminology, winter-spring, 2003, Bard R. Ferrall, review of *Wages of Crime,* p. 821.

Journal of Economic Literature, March, 1995, review of *Hot Money and the Politics of Debt,* p. 323; December, 1997, review of *The History of Canadian Business, 1867-1914,* p. 2170.

Library Journal, April 1, 2002, Tim Delaney, review of *Wages of Crime,* p. 125.

Quill & Quire, April, 1987, H. S. Bhabra, "Shedding More Heat than Light on Money Scandals," review of *Hot Money and the Politics of Debt,* p. 31; June, 1999, Andrew Allentuck, review of *Patriots and Profiteers: On Economic Warfare, Embargo Busting, and State-Sponsored Crime,* p. 59.

Saturday Night, September, 1976, Robert Collison, "Canada Has Always Been a Client State," review of *The History of Canadian Business, 1867-1914,* p. 60.

ONLINE

Counterpunch.org, http://www.counterpunch.org/ (June 21, 2003), Standard Schaefer, "The Wages of Terror" (interview).*

*   *   *

NORTH, Andrew
    See NORTON, Andre

*   *   *

NORTON, Alice Mary
    See NORTON, Andre

*   *   *

NORTON, Andre 1912-2005
    (Andrew North, Alice Mary Norton, Allen Weston)

OBITUARY NOTICE— See index for *CA* sketch: Born February 17, 1912, in Cleveland, OH; died of conges-

tive heart failure March 17, 2005, in Murfreesboro, TN. Author. Norton was an award-winning author of fantasy and science fiction for adults and children. During the early 1930s, she studied at what is now Case Western University with the intention of becoming a teacher. However, the Great Depression forced her to leave the university and work at the Cleveland Public Library as a children's librarian through the 1930s and 1940s. During this time, she also briefly ran her own book store and worked for the Library of Congress. Next, she worked as a reader for Gnome Press, where she was exposed to a great deal of science fiction from 1950 until she left the publisher in 1958. Norton, who had been writing since high school and published her first novel, the children's fantasy *Rogue Reynard,* in 1947, started publishing science fiction after joining Gnome. Her first sci-fi novel was 1952's *Star Man's Son, 2250 A.D.* She had changed her birth name from Alice Mary Norton to Andre Norton in 1934 because male genre authors were more widely accepted and published than women, and she eventually adopted Andre as her legal name. Becoming a full-time writer by the end of the 1950s, Norton published well over one hundred titles during her lifetime. This included books in the mystery, spy, gothic, historical, and adventure genres, but she found the most success with fantasy and science fiction, much of it geared toward children and young adults. Her "Witch World" series, which included over two dozen books published over three decades, was one of her most popular writing endeavors, and she also published other series titles, such as the "Solar Queen" and "Time Traders" books. The first woman to receive the Gandalf Grand Master of Fantasy Award and the first to win the Grand Master Award from the Science Fiction and Fantasy Writers of America, Norton remained a dominant figure in these genres for over fifty years, winning numerous other prizes. She also tried to assist fellow genre authors by opening the High Hallack Genre Writers' Research Library in Murfreesboro, Tennessee, in 1999. She was compelled to close it in 2004, however, due to her ill health. Norton's last novel was *Three Hands of Scorpio,* which was scheduled to be published posthumously.

OBITUARIES AND OTHER SOURCES:

PERIODICALS

Los Angeles Times, March 19, 2005, p. B17.
New York Times, March 18, 2005, p. A23.
Washington Post, March 19, 2005, p. B7.

O'HANLON, Ellis
(Ingrid Black, a joint pseudonym)

PERSONAL: Married Ian McConnel (a journalist); children: three.

ADDRESSES: Home—Belfast, Northern Ireland. *Agent*—c/o Author Mail, St. Martin's Press, 175 5th Ave., New York, NY 10019.

CAREER: Writer.

WRITINGS:

WITH HUSBAND, IAN MCCONNEL, UNDER PSEUDONYM INGRID BLACK

The Dead, Headline (London, England), 1993, Thomas Dunne Books (New York, NY), 2004.
The Dark Eye, Headline (London, England), 2004.

ADAPTATIONS: Production rights to *The Dead* were sold to the British Broadcasting Corp. (BBC).

SIDELIGHTS: For Sidelights, see sketch on Ian McConnel, elsewhere in this volume.

BIOGRAPHICAL AND CRITICAL SOURCES:

PERIODICALS

Booklist, May 1, 2004, Jenny McLarin, review of *The Dead,* p. 1501.
Kirkus Reviews, April 15, 2004, review of *The Dead,* p. 362.
Observer (London, England), February 29, 2004, Henry McDonald, "Chick-Lit Flourishes in Singletons' Dublin."
Publishers Weekly, May 3, 2004, review of *The Dead,* p. 174.

ONLINE

AllReaders.com, http://www.allreaders.com/ (January 20, 2005), Harriet Klausner, review of *The Dead.*

Mystery Women Web site, http://www.mysterywomen. co.uk/ (December 13, 2004), Lizzie Hayes, review of *The Dark Eye* and *The Dead.**

*   *   *

O'CASEY, Brenda
See HAYCRAFT, Anna (Margaret)

*   *   *

ODOM, Mel 1950-

PERSONAL: Born 1950; married; wife's name Sherry; children: five. *Education:* Virginia Commonwealth University, B.A.; attended graduate school in England.

ADDRESSES: Home—Moore, OK. *Agent*—Simon Pulse, 1230 Avenue of the Americas, New York, NY 10020. *E-mail*—DenimByte@aol.com.

CAREER: Former illustrator for such publications as *Blueboy, Playboy,* and *Omni;* CBS records, sleeve illustrator; illustrated cover art for numerous books.

AWARDS, HONORS: Illustrator of the Year, *Playboy,* 1980; Gold Medal in the editorial class, Society of Illustrators, 1982, Silver Medal in the Book Class, 1987.

WRITINGS:

Dreamer: Drawings, introduction by Edmund White, Penguin (New York, NY), 1984.
(With Warren Norwood) *Stranded,* Lynx Omeiga Books (New York, NY), 1989.
Freelancers, TSR (Lake Geneva, WI), 1995.
I Have No Mouth, and I Must Scream: The Official Guide, preface by Harlan Ellison, Prima Publishers (Rocklin, CA), 1995.
Angel Devoid: Face of the Enemy, Prima Publishers (Rocklin, CA), 1996.
F.R.E.E. Fall, TSR (Lake Geneva, WI), 1996.
Leisure Suit Larry: Love for Sail, Prima Publishers (Rocklin, CA), 1996.

Oddworld Abe's Oddysee: Unlock the Official Secrets, GW Press (Auburn, CA), 1997.

Redneck Rampage—in Your Face!: Unlock the Secrets, GW Press (Auburn, CA), 1997.

Shadow Warrior: The Unauthorized Game Secrets, Prima Publishers (Rocklin, CA), 1997.

Zork Grand Inquisitor: Unauthorized Game Secrets, Prima Publishers (Rocklin, CA), 1997.

(With Michael Brown) *A, D, and D Descent to Undermountain: Unlock the Secrets,* GW Press (Auburn, CA), 1997.

(With Ted Chapman) *Blood: The Official Strategy Guide,* Prima Publishers (Rocklin, CA), 1997.

Duke Nukem Sixty-four, GW Press (Auburn, CA), 1997.

Duke Nukem PSX: Unlock the Secrets, GW Press (Auburn, CA), 1997.

Ecstatica II: The Official Strategy Guide, Prima Publishers (Rocklin, CA), 1997.

The Lost Library of Cormanthyr, TSR (Lake Geneva, WI), 1997.

Nightmare Creatures: The Official Strategy Guide, Prima Publishers (Rocklin, CA), 1997.

Black Dahlia: Prima's Official Strategy Guide, Prima Publishers (Rocklin, CA), 1998.

Glover: Prima's Official Strategy Guide, Prima Publishers (Rocklin, CA), 1998.

Nightmare Creatures Sixty-four: Prima's Official Strategy Guide, Prima Publishers (Rocklin, CA), 1998.

Spacestation Silicon Valley: Prima's Official Strategy Guide, Prima Publishers (Rocklin, CA), 1998.

Rayman Two, the Great Escape: Prima's Official Strategy Guide, Prima Publishers (Rocklin, CA), 1999.

Rising Tide, TSR (Renton, WA), 1999.

Under the Fallen Stars, TSR (Renton, WA), 1999.

Xena, Warrior Princess, Prima Publishers (Rocklin, CA), 1999.

Young Hercules (based on the teleplay by Andrew Dettman and Daniel Truly), Pocket Books (New York, NY), 1999.

(With Blaine Dee Pardoe) *My Blood Betrayed,* New American Library (New York, NY), 1999.

Croc Two: Prima's Official Strategy Guide, Prima Publishers (Rocklin, CA), 1999.

Draconus: Cult of the Wyrm, Prima Publishers (Roseville, CA), 1999.

Hybrid Heaven: Prima's Official Strategy Guide, Prima Publishers (Rocklin, CA), 1999.

(With Donato Tica and Jeff Barton) *Jet Force Gemini,* Prima Publishers (Rocklin, CA), 1999.

Legacy, Pocket Books (New York, NY), 1999.

Legacy of Kain: Soul Reaver, Prima Publishers (Roseville, CA), 1999.

Silent Scope: Prima's Official Guide, Prima Publishers (Roseville, CA), 2000.

Snowday, Pocket Books (New York, NY), 2000.

Realms of the Deep, Wizards of the Coast (Renton, WA), 2000.

Die Hard Trilogy Two: Viva Las Vegas, Prima Publishers (Roseville, CA), 2000.

Mummy Dearest!, Pocket Books (New York, NY), 2000.

Redemption, Pocket Books (New York, NY), 2000.

Rugrats in Paris: The Movie, Prima Publishers (Roseville, CA), 2000.

The Sea Devil's Eye, Wizards of the Coast (Renton, WA), 2000.

(With Michael A. Sommers) *Gene Marshall: Girl Star,* Hyperion (New York, NY), 2000.

Bruja, Pocket Books (New York, NY), 2001.

Pirate Pandemonium, Pocket Books (New York, NY), 2001.

Revenant, Pocket Books (New York, NY), 2001.

The Rover, Tor (New York, NY), 2001.

The Sea of Mist, HarperEntertainment (New York, NY), 2001.

The Black Road, Pocket Books (New York, NY), 2002.

The Jewel of Turmish, Wizards of the Coast (Renton, WA), 2002.

Hunters of the Dark Sea, Tor (New York, NY), 2003.

The Destruction of the Books, Tor (New York, NY), 2004.

A Conspiracy Revealed, Simon Pulse (New York, NY), 2005.

Lord of the Libraries, Tor (New York, NY), 2005.

The Mystery Unravels, Simon Pulse (New York, NY), 2005.

Contributor to periodicals, including *Today's Christian Woman.*

NOVELIZATIONS

Sabrina Goes to Rome (based on the teleplay by Daniel Berendsen), Pocket Books (New York, NY), 1998.

Vertical Limit (based on the screenplay by Robert King and Terry Hayes), Pocket Books (New York, NY), 2000.

Tomb Raider (based on the screenplay by Patrick Massett, John Zinman, and Simon West), Pocket Books (New York, NY), 2001.

Tom Clancy's Net Force: High Wire (based on characters created by Tom Clancy and Steve Pieczenik), Berkley Jam Books (New York, NY), 2001.

Crossings (based on *Buffy the Vampire Slayer*), Simon Pulse (New York, NY), 2002.

Image (based on *Angel*), Simon Pulse (New York, NY), 2002.

Shades (based on *Roswell*), Simon Pulse (New York, NY), 2002.

Tiger Tale (based on *Sabrina the Teenage Witch*), Simon and Schuster (New York, NY), 2002.

Cursed (based on *Buffy the Vampire Slayer*), Simon Pulse (New York, NY), 2003.

"LEFT BEHIND" SERIES

Apocalypse Dawn, Tyndale House (Wheaton, IL), 2003.

Apocalypse Burning, Tyndale House (Wheaton, IL), 2004.

Apocalypse Crucible, Tyndale House (Wheaton, IL), 2004.

SIDELIGHTS: Mel Odom studied fashion illustration at Virginia Commonwealth University and went on to do graduate work in England. He then spent nine months creating a portfolio prior to moving to New York City in 1975, where he attempted to garner attention in the art market. Some of his earliest successes were erotic works he sold to *Blueboy,* a gay magazine, and to *Playboy.* In addition to erotic subjects, he began to sell to mainstream clients. His art frequently graced book covers, as well as record sleeves and the science-fiction magazine *Omni.* Odom did book covers for such series as "Kay," "Hazel," "Nancy Collins," and and a number of books by Ruth Rendell. One of the more identifiable aspects of his cover styles was the use of a face as the entire design, with the eyes standing out in particular. In addition to his artistic endeavors, Odom is the author of numerous books, including fantasy, science-fiction, horror, and young-adult novels, many of them linked in some manner to computer games, television, or film.

Among Odom's novels are several fantasies for young readers involving librarian Edgewick Lamplighter. *The Rover* tracks the adventures of Lamplighter as he fol-

lows a messenger who is sent to deliver a package to the Yonderling Docks and is shanghaied by pirates. *School Library Journal* reviewer Linda G. Sinclair remarked that "readers will enjoy the wealth of creatures in this tale of magic, mystery, and self-discovery." Sally Estes, in a review for *Booklist,* called the book "a surefire page-turner," adding that "the characterizations are simply delicious."

With *The Destruction of the Books,* Odom returns to the world of Edgewick Lamplighter. One hundred years have passed since the events of *The Rover,* and Wick is now a grandmagicster in charge of a secret collection of books. Sally Estes, in a review for *Booklist,* remarked that, "as before, plenty of humor tempers the wild action." A contributor to *Kirkus Reviews* opined that "Odom's bouncy, funny, cliff-hanger adventure is perfect for the Potter crowd, with enough puns, wry asides, and satirical send-ups to amuse Tolkien fans." A reviewer for *Publishers Weekly* stated that "the narrative moves along at a snappy pace, with much good humor, zest, and color." Harriet Klausner, in a review for *AllSci-Fi.com,* called *The Destruction of the Books* "an engaging epic fantasy that reaches out to a wide range of readers with its amusing often ironic humor."

Odom also has written several volumes of the popular "Left Behind" series, including *Apocalypse Burning* and *Apocalypse Crucible.* These books are based on biblical teachings having to do with the end of the world and the second coming of Jesus Christ. In an essay for *Today's Christian Woman,* Odom stated that "no one can completely understand everything that will happen in the Last Days, but I believe that overcoming the evil that will be loosed on the world will come from what God has already taught so many people." Odom addresses these themes from various angles, having also written several novelizations based on the television series *Buffy the Vampire Slayer* and *Angel,* both of which deal with fighting evil.

BIOGRAPHICAL AND CRITICAL SOURCES:

PERIODICALS

Advocate, November 21, 2000, Matthew Link, review of *Gene Marshall: Girl Star,* p. 66.

Booklist, July, 2001, Sally Estes, review of *The Rover,* p. 1992; January 1, 2002, review of *The Rover,* p. 764; April 15, 2002, Ray Olson, review of *The*

Rover, p. 1387; August, 2003, Michael Gannon, review of *Hunters of the Dark Sea,* p. 1957; July, 2004, Sally Estes, review of *The Destruction of the Books,* p. 1829.

Kirkus Reviews, May 15, 2004, review of *The Destruction of the Books,* p. 478.

Kliatt January, 2005, Claire Rosser, review of *Hunter's League,* p. 16.

Library Journal, august, 2001, Jackie Cassada, review of *The Rover,* p. 171; June 15, 2004, Jackie Cassada, review of *The Destruction of the Books,* p. 62.

Publishers Weekly, January 25, 1999, review of *Rising Tide,* p. 93; September 25, 2000, review of *Gene Marshall,* p. 49; April 2, 2001, Karen Raugust, "Star of Page and Screen," review of *Gene Marshall,* p.24; June 18, 2001, review of *The Rover,* p. 63; June 28, 2004, review of *The Destruction of the Books,* p. 36.

School Library Journal, January, 2002, Linda G. Sinclair, review of *The Rover,* p. 171.

Today's Christian Woman, November-December, 2003, Mel Odom, "An Author Speaks: Mel Odom Shares Why Family Means Everything to Him," p. 20; March-April, 2004, review of *Apocalypse Cruicible,* p. 8; May-June, 2004, "An Author Speaks: Mel Odom Reveals his Heart in the Writing of Apocalypse Crucible," p. 18

ONLINE

AllSciFi.com, http://www.allscifi.com/ (April 16, 2005), "Mel Odom."

Olaf Krusche Web site, http://www.o-love.net/ (April 16, 2005), "Mel Odom."*

*   *   *

OPPEDISANO, Jeannette M. 1943-

PERSONAL: Born 1943. *Education:* State University of New York at Albany, B.A. (English education), 1972, M.S. 1975; Rensselaer Polytechnic Institute, Ph.D., 1992.

ADDRESSES: Office—School of Business, Southern Connecticut State University, 501 Crescent St., New Haven, CT 06515. *E-mail*—oppedisano_j@southernct. edu.

CAREER: Educator. Southern Connecticut State University School of Business, New Haven, chair and professor of management; Skidmore College, Saratoga Springs, NY, director of Camp Start-Up. Co-designer of faculty development program for *CASE Journal;* president of Whistling Wynds (life-strategy/management consultant).

WRITINGS:

Historical Encyclopedia of American Women Entrepreneurs: 1776 to the Present, Greenwood Press (Westport, CT), 2000.

Contributor to periodicals, including *NWSA Journal.*

SIDELIGHTS: Jeannette M. Oppedisano is the author of *Historical Encyclopedia of American Women Entrepreneurs: 1776 to the Present.* A gathering of 120 mini-profiles, the work highlights Oppedisano's academic interest in women's multidisciplinary entrepreneurship and philanthropy, as well as her ongoing research in innovation and change management.

Including businesswomen from Clara Barton to Jane Addams, Lydia Pinkham, and Oprah Winfrey, Oppedisano's collection of biographies consists of women from various ethnic, religious, racial, and geographic backgrounds. Fields of endeavor from making pottery to repairing automotive transmissions are also spotlighted in this survey. The author demonstrates how women have taken the same sort of risks as their male counterparts for over two centuries and have gone on to have an impact not only locally, but also nationally and internationally. In a *Booklist* review, a contributor felt that in her goal of showing "women's contributions to the nation's economy" and of providing "role models to young women," Oppedisano "has succeeded admirably." The same reviewer concluded that the book is an "outstanding addition to the field of women's studies."

BIOGRAPHICAL AND CRITICAL SOURCES:

PERIODICALS

Booklist, February 15, 2001, review of *Historical Encyclopedia of American Women Entrepreneurs: 1776 to the Present,* p. 1180.

ONLINE

BookNews.com, http://www.booknews.com/ (July 7, 2004), review of *Historical Encyclopedia of American Women Entrepreneurs.*

CaseWeb.org, http://www.caseweb.org/ (July 6, 2004), "CASE Association."

Greenwood Publishing Group Web site, http://info.greenwood.com/ (July 6, 2004).

International Association for Business and Society Newsletter Online, (July 6, 2004), "Jeannette Oppedisano."

Southern Connecticut State University School of Business Web site, http://schoolofbusiness.southernct.edu/ (July 6, 2004), "Jeannette Oppedisano."*

* * *

ORR, Elaine Neil 1954-

PERSONAL: Born 1954, in Nigeria; married; husband's name, Andy; children: Joel. *Education:* Campbellsville University, B.A. (art); University of Louisville, M.A. (English); Emory University, Ph.D. (literature and theology).

ADDRESSES: Home—Raleigh, NC. *Office*—North Carolina State University, 201 Tompkins Hall, Box 8105, Raleigh, NC 27695. *E-mail*—elaine@unity.ncsu.edu.

CAREER: Educator and writer. North Carolina State University, Raleigh, professor of English. Previously instructor in English at Spalding University, Louisville, KY.

AWARDS, HONORS: Southeast Booksellers Association Book Award nominee for creative nonfiction, 2004, for *Gods of Noonday;* grants and fellowships from National Endowment for the Humanities, North Carolina Arts Council, Virginia Center for the Creative Arts, and North Carolina Humanities Council.

WRITINGS:

Tillie Olsen and a Feminist Spiritual Vision, University of Mississippi Press (Jackson, MI), 1987.

Subject to Negotiation: Reading Feminist Criticism and American Women's Fictions, University of Virginia Press (Charlottesville, VA), 1997.

Gods of Noonday: A White Girl's African Life, University of Virginia Press (Charlottesville, VA), 2003.

Contributor of articles and poems to journals and magazines, including *Southern Cultures, Missouri Review, Kalliope, Louisville Review, Black Mountain Review, Modern Language Quarterly, South Atlantic Review,* and *Journal of Narrative Technique.*

SIDELIGHTS: In *Subject to Negotiation: Reading Feminist Criticism and American Women's Fictions,* Elaine Neil Orr examines works of women writers, including *Song of Solomon* by Toni Morrison, *Woman on the Edge of Time* by Marge Piercy, *The House of Mirth* by Edith Wharton, *Their Eyes Were Watching God* by Zora Neale Hurston, and *The Optimist's Daughter* by Eudora Welty. Writing in the *Mississippi Quarterly,* Barbara Ladd observed that "the idea that feminist criticism is or can be a negotiation rather than an oppositional or subversive criticism is at the center" of Orr's book. Ladd, however, felt that Orr's reading and examination of works by Morrison and Piercy are more successful than her similar treatment of works by the other authors. Further, Ladd noted that Orr's "surprising moments [of] clarity" in the study are "almost always unsustained."

Born in Nigeria to missionary parents, Orr was brought up in Africa until she was a teenager and then was sent to the United States for her education. In her forties, Orr became seriously ill from kidney failure and needed dialysis and a transplant. She harkened back to her Nigerian past and a Yoruba saying that in order to journey forward, you need to journey back. This she does in *Gods of Noonday: A White Girl's African Life,* "a beautifully composed and poignant" memoir, as Cori Yonge described the book in the *Mobile Register Online.* Orr recounts her life as the daughter of Baptist medical missionaries in Nigeria. Throughout her youth she thought of herself as part African and part American. Yonge went on to note that "at a time when other children her age were slouching on the sofa watching June and Ward Cleaver in black and white, Orr was plunging into the clear, cold water of the Ethiope River and swimming against its swift currents." For Yonge, Orr's is a "courageous attempt to recapture and to understand her African life while dealing with the uncertainty of illness." Similarly, Kathleen Driskell called Orr's book a "shimmering memoir" in the Louisville, *Courier-Journal.* Driskell further commented that a book such as Orr's, describing a privileged youth in comparison to the childhoods of Nigerians, "could easily drift into a polemic about colonialism." Instead, Driskell pointed out, "Orr's memoir is more thoughtful than radical." The same critic concluded that Orr "balances the constellation of all with admirable talent in this very readable book."

Speaking with Yolanda Rodriquez in an interview for the *Atlanta Journal-Constitution,* Orr explained the title of her book: "It's in response to [Joseph Conrad's novel] *Heart of Darkness,* that conveys the idea of Africa as a place full of evil that has been abandoned by the gods," Orr noted to Rodriguez. "My experience of Nigeria is a place where God dwells and a place full of light. It's 'gods' because the Yoruba believe in one God, but they believe in many faces of God."

BIOGRAPHICAL AND CRITICAL SOURCES:

BOOKS

Gods of Noonday: A White Girl's African Life, University of Virginia Press (Charlottesville, VA), 2003.

PERIODICALS

Atlanta-Journal Constitution, January 21, 2004, Yolanda Rodriguez, interview with Orr, p. F3.

Courier-Journal (Louisville, KY), November 9, 2003, Kathleen Driskell, review of *Gods of Noonday: A White Girl's African Life.*

Mississippi Quarterly, fall, 1998, Barbara Ladd, review of *Subject to Negotiation: Reading Feminist Criticism and American Women's Fictions,* p. 738.

Tennessean, February 8, 2004, Michael E. Jackson, review of *Gods of Noonday.*

ONLINE

MaximsNews.com, http://www.maximsnews.com/ (July 6, 2004), "Elaine Orr."

Mobile Register Online, http://www.al.com/ (July 6, 2004), Cori Yonge, review of *Gods of Noonday.*

Novello Festival of Reading Web site, http://www.novellofestival.net/ (July 6, 2004), "Elaine Neil Orr."

Official Elaine Neil Orr Web site, http://www.elaineneilorr.com (July 6, 2004).

SouthernScribe.com, http://www.southernscribe.com/ (July 6, 2004), Pam Kingsbury, review of *Gods of Noonday.**

P

PATTERSON, Ted 1944-

PERSONAL: Born July 6, 1944, in Mansfield, OH; son of Theodore R. and Helen (Stuhldreher) Patterson; married Diana E. Gillett, June 26, 1971; children: Michael T., Clare E. *Ethnicity:* "Caucasian." *Education:* University of Dayton, B.A., 1966; Miami University (Oxford, OH), M.A., 1968. *Politics:* Republican.

ADDRESSES: Home—522 Anneslie Rd., Baltimore, MD 21212.

CAREER: WCBM-Radio, Baltimore, MD, newscaster, sportscaster, and host of sports talk shows. Entertainment and Sports Network (ESPN; cable television network), reporter from Baltimore for *NFL Game Day.*

WRITINGS:

Day by Day in Orioles History, Leisure Press (New York, NY), 1984, foreword by Boog Powell, Sports Publishing (Champaign, IL), 1999.
The Baltimore Orioles: Forty Years of Magic from Thirty-third Street to Camden Yards, Taylor Publishing (Dallas, TX), 1994, revised edition, 2000.
Football in Baltimore: History and Memorabilia, photographs by Edwin H. Remsberg, foreword by Raymond Berry, Johns Hopkins University Press (Baltimore, MD), 2000.
The Golden Voices of Baseball (with compact discs), Sports Publishing (Champaign, IL), 2002.
The Golden Voices of Football, Sports Publishing (Champaign, IL), 2004.

SIDELIGHTS: Ted Patterson told *CA: "The Golden Voices of Baseball* was actually researched from 1966 through 1969, with taped interviews of pioneer and prominent sports broadcasters. The tapes were used for two companion compact discs in the book, each lasting seventy-four minutes. The book is heavily illustrated with never-before-seen photographs."

*   *   *

PAZ SOLDÁN, (José) Edmundo 1967-

PERSONAL: Born 1967, in Cochabamba, Bolivia; married, 1998; children: one son. *Education:* University of Alabama, Huntsville, B.A., 1991; University of California Berkeley, M.A., 1993, Ph.D., 1997.

ADDRESSES: Home—103 2nd St., Ithaca, NY 14850. *Office*—312 Morrill Hall, Cornell University, Ithaca, NY 14850. *E-mail*—jep29@cornell.edu.

CAREER: Writer and educator. Cornell University, Ithaca, NY, visiting assistant professor, 1997-2004, associate professor, 2004—.

MEMBER: Modern Language Association, Latin-American Studies Association, Latin-American Studies Program.

AWARDS, HONORS: Erich Guttentag prize, 1992, for *Días del papel;* Juan Rulfo Short-Story Award, 1997, for "Dochera"; Premio Nacional de Literatura (Bolivia), 2003, for *El delirio de Turing;* Romulo Gállegos award finalist.

WRITINGS:

Las máscaras de la nada (title means "Masks of Nothingness"), Editorial Los Amigos de Libro (La Paz, Bolivia), 1990.

Días de papel (title means "Days of Paper"), Editorial Los Amigos de Libro (La Paz, Bolivia), 1991.

Desapariciones, Ediciones Centro Simón I. Patiño (Bolivia), 1994.

Alrededor de la torre, Editorial Nuevo Milenio (La Paz, Bolivia), 1997.

Dochera y otros cuentos (short stories), Editorial Nuevo Milenio (La Paz, Bolivia), 1998.

Rio fugitivo (title means "Fugitive River"), Alfaguara (La Paz, Bolivia), 1998.

Simulacros, Santillano (La Paz, Bolivia), 1999.

Amores imperfectos (title means "Imperfect Loves"), Alfaguara (La Paz, Bolivia), 2000.

(Co-author) *Latin American Literature and Mass Media,* Garland (New York, NY), 2000.

(Editor, with Alberto Fuguet) *Se habla español: Voces latinas en USA,* Alfaguara (Miami, FL), 2000.

Sueños digitales (title means "Digital Dreams"), Alfaguara (La Paz, Bolivia), 2000.

(With Alejandro Grimson) *Migrantes bolivianos en la Argentina y los Estados Unidos,* Programa de las Naciones Unidas para el Desarrollo (La Paz, Bolivia), 2000.

La materia del deseo, Alfaguara (Miami, FL), 2001, translated by Lisa Carter as *The Matter of Desire,* Houghton Mifflin (Boston, MA), 2003.

Alcides Arguedas y la narrativa de la nación enferma, Plural Editores (La Paz, Bolivia), 2003.

El delirio de Turing, Alfaguara (La Paz, Bolivia), 2003, translated by Lisa Carter as *Turing's Delirium,* Houghton (Boston, MA), 2006.

SIDELIGHTS: Edmundo Paz Soldán "is perhaps Bolivia's most notable contemporary author," according to a reviewer for *Publishers Weekly.* One of the leading practitioners of so-called "McOndo" literature, Paz Soldán rejects the "levitating grandmothers, clouds of butterflies, or velvet curtains of prose that mark the work of Latin American writers from Gabriel García Márquez to Isabel Allende," as Robin Dougherty noted in the *Boston Globe.* Instead he affects a gritty urban reality in his novels and short stories, an acceptance and critique of globalization and the Americanization of the Latin American world. The term "McOndo" refers to this cultural imperialism, taking its name

from a title of an anthology by a "bad boy of Chilean letters," as Ed Morales termed writer Alberto Fuguet in *Library Journal.* McOndo "satirizes the McDonalds-ization of Gabriel García Márquez's fictitious town, Macondo," Morales further noted. Paz Soldán breaks free of such literary progenitors and stereotypes, taking inspiration instead from writers like Jorge Luis Borges and Franz Kafka.

Educated in the United States, Paz Soldán is an associate professor at Cornell University, but he spends part of the year in his native Bolivia. The winner of numerous literary prizes in his own country, his first work to be translated into English was his 2001 novel, *La materia del deseo, The Matter of Desire.* The story of a Latin-American professor caught between two worlds—his faculty position in the United States and his Bolivian home—the novel has autobiographical elements. Like his fictional protagonist Pedro Zabalaga, Paz Soldán also earned his doctorate at the University of California at Berkeley; also like his protagonist, he teaches at a New York university and misses his home in Bolivia. In the novel, Zabalaga escapes an affair with Ashley, a graduate student, to return to his native Rio Fugitivo, a fictional Bolivian town that Paz Soldán has featured in many of his stories and novels. Back in Bolivia, Zabalaga becomes involved in trying to uncover the secret of his revolutionary father's disappearance. The threads Zabalaga follows in this search lead to startling revelations; meanwhile, this part of the story alternates with the story of the affair between Pedro and Ashley.

Reviewers generally responded favorably to *The Matter of Desire,* but a critic for *Publishers Weekly* found the novel's dual storylines uneven. While Pedro's affair "is a standard tale of star-crossed lovers," according to the contributor, "less familiar, and more engaging, is the throbbing world of Rio Fugitivo, flooded with American culture but still haunted by years of oppression." Allison Block, reviewing *The Matter of Desire* in *Booklist,* called it a "taut, gritty tale of two different Americas." According to Block, the novel is a blend of "history, existentialism, and romantic and political passion" that adds up to an "edgy, urban vision that sizzles from the start." A contributor to *Americas* wrote that the author "paints a vivid picture of political and moral corruption in Bolivia," and Jack Shreve, reviewing the same novel in *Library Journal,* felt that Paz Soldán is "especially insightful about the inexorable suffusion southwards of American pop culture and values."

Cultural globalism infuses much of Paz Soldán's work. In the title story of his award-winning 1998 collection, *Dochera y otros cuentos,* he uses the metaphor of a crossword puzzle to indicate the modern condition. For *World Literature* critic Naomi Lindstrom, the "diabolical 'Dochera' is the one true standout in the collection, but throughout, the fiction is amusing, stylish, and full of surprises." In *Sueños digitales* ("Digital Dreams"), Paz Soldán "paints a portrait of young people living in a sophisticated, urban Latin American society," according to Morales. In the book, a magazine editor attempts to discern reality in his life from the virtual reality of the digitally enhanced photographs he works with. Reviewing the Spanish-language version of that book, *Library Journal* critic Lourdes Vazquez praised Paz Soldán for creating a "fast-paced, easy-to-read novel."

El delirio de Turing (translated as *Turing's Delirium*) won the 2003 Premio Nacional de Literatura in Bolivia. According to Carmen Ospina in *School Library Journal,* this novel is characteristically "steeped in references to information-age U.S. culture and postmodern world of Rio Fugitivo." In the novel, Turing is a hacker and cryptographer living in Rio Fugitivo, Bolivia, who is battling the forces of multinationals. Ospina described the tale as a "novel about betrayal, fraud, and hidden truths."

Paz Soldán told *CA:* "I remember reading Emilio Salgari's novels when I was ten years old and getting lost in his world. I started writing in order to tell stories and hope to get readers lost in my fictional world. My main literary influences are Latin-American writers such as Borges and Vargas Llosa, but I am also influenced by the popular culture around me, movies and music and the internet. I usually write in the morning; when I am writing the first draft of a novel I focus on the main storyline, and afterwards I start adding layers, giving texture to the descriptions, depth and shades to the characters, and tying all the subplots into the main one.

"The most surprising thing is to see how books travel from one place to another, allowing me to find readers in unexpected places. And also, realizing that once the book is published you surrender control over its meaning. Readers do whatever they want with your books, which is wonderful. My favorite book is the last one I wrote, maybe because in a way I'm still living in that world."

BIOGRAPHICAL AND CRITICAL SOURCES:

PERIODICALS

Americas, September-October, 2002, review of *La materia del deseo,* p. 61.
Booklist, April 1, 2004, Allison Block, review of *The Matter of Desire,* p. 1349.
Boston Globe, April 18, 2004, Robin Dougherty, "Between the Lines with Edmundo Paz Soldán," p. E9.
Kirkus Reviews, March 1, 2004, review of *The Matter of Desire,* p. 199.
Library Journal, June 1, 2001, Ed Morales, "The New America's Virtual Truth," p. 21, and Lourdes Vazquez, review of *Sueños digitales,* p. 26; April 1, 2004, Jack Shreve, review of *The Matter of Desire,* p. 124.
M2 Best Books, November 7, 2003, "Latin American Author New Identity Inspires New Book."
Publishers Weekly, May 10, 2004, review of *The Matter of Desire,* p. 38.
School Library Journal, June, 2003, Carmen Ospina, "Paz Soldán Wins Bolivia's Fifth National Literature Prize," p. 12.
World Literature Today, spring, 1999, Naomi Lindstrom, review of *Dochera y otros cuentos,* p. 303; summer-autumn, 2001, Luis Larios, review of *Se habla español: Voces latinas en USA,* p. 223.

*   *   *

PERRICONE, Nicholas V. 1948(?)-

PERSONAL: Born c. 1948, in Branford, CT; son of Vincent (a stonemason) and Mary (a homemaker) Perricone; married (divorced, 1986); married, 1995; second wife's name, Madeleine (a homemaker); children: (first marriage) Nicholas, Jeffrey; (second marriage) Caitlin. *Education:* Michigan State University Medical School, M.D.

ADDRESSES: Office—N. V. Perricone, M.D., Ltd., 377 Research Parkway, Meriden, CT 06450; fax: 203-379-0817. *E-mail*—publicrelations@nvperriconemd.com.

CAREER: Dermatologist and author. Worked in private practice, Meriden, CT, beginning 1986; Yale University Medical School, New Haven, CT, assistant clinical professor of dermatology, ending 2002; Veterans' Hospital, CT, chief of dermatology; founder of N. V. Perricone, M.D., Cosmeceuticals, 1999, and of a Madison Avenue boutique, New York, NY, c. 2004. Michigan State University's College of Human Medicine, adjunct professor of medicine, c. 2002—; International Symposium on Aging Skin, chair. Also worked for CT Muscular Dystrophy Association; as a salesperson for McKesson Chemical Co., mid-1970s; and as a fragrance salesperson. Holds dozens of U.S. and international patents for the treatment of skin and systemic disease. Producer of television ocumentaries for Public Broadcast Service. *Military service:* U.S. Army Reserves, ending 1971.

MEMBER: New York Academy of Sciences (fellow), American College of Nutrition (fellow), American Academy of Dermatology (fellow), Society of Investigative Dermatology (fellow).

AWARDS, HONORS: Norman E. Clark, Sr., Lecture Award, 2000, American College for Advancement in Medicine; Eli Whitney Award, Connecticut Intellectual Property Law Association, 2002, for contributions to science, invention, and technology.

WRITINGS:

The Wrinkle Cure: Unlock the Power of Cosmeceuticals for Supple, Youthful Skin, Rodale (Emmaus, PA), 2000.

The Perricone Prescription: A Physician's Twenty-eight-Day Program for Total Body and Face Rejuvenation Daybook, HarperResource (New York, NY), 2002.

The Acne Prescription: The Perricone Program for Clear and Healthy Skin at Every Age, HarperResource (New York, NY), 2003.

The Perricone Promise: Look Younger, Live Longer in Three Easy Steps, Warner Books (New York, NY), 2004.

Contributor to *The Basic Principles and Practice of Anti-Aging Medicine and Age Management for the Aesthetic Physician and Surgeon,* 2003; contributor to journals, including *Skin and Aging; Archives of Gerontology and Geriatrics,* member of editorial board.

ADAPTATIONS: The Wrinkle Cure: Unlock the Power of Cosmeceuticals for Supple, Youthful Skin was adapted for audio, Simon and Schuster Audio, 2001.

SIDELIGHTS: Nicholas V. Perricone is a board-certified clinical and research dermatologist and the founder of N. V. Perricone, M.D., Cosmeceuticals. After completing his internship in pediatrics at Yale University Medical School, Perricone did his residency at Henry Ford Hospital in Michigan. There, he first theorized that wrinkles, which are often accompanied by inflammation, could be treated with antioxidants that reduce this cellular inflammation. He began his practice in 1986 in Meriden, Connecticut, and attempted to demonstrate his theories to companies that included Johnson & Johnson. When they expressed no interest, he decided to write his first book, *The Wrinkle Cure: Unlock the Power of Cosmeceuticals for Supple, Youthful Skin.* Perricone proposes that by eating a diet rich in antioxidants and omega-3 fatty acids (he emphasizes the value of eating salmon), as well as by applying topical antioxidants like vitamin C and alpha lipoic acid, skin can be kept healthy and the effects of aging and other damage can be reversed.

Perricone's claims have been met with skepticism by several medical professionals. Dr. Jeffrey Dover, a clinical associate professor of dermatology at the Yale University School of Medicine, told *People* reviewer Galina Espinoza that "to suggest that altering your diet will slow down the aging process is not believable to most dermatologists." "Yet," said Espinoza, "Dover admits that 'some of [Perricone's] products make sense; his diet is really good. And the guy is a brilliant marketer.'"

Perricone's line of cosmeceuticals, which were originally introduced in upscale department stores like Nordstrom, was a more-than-$50 million annual business by 2003, and the celebrities who swore by his products included actresses Julia Roberts and Kim Cattrall. Along with his line of skincare products, Perricone also promotes a diet that includes fruits and vegetables, adequate water, good fats like olive oil and nuts, and lean protein. Perricone became an adjunct professor at Michigan State University's College of Human Medicine c. 2002 and has since become a major donor to the university, beginning with his $5 million pledge to establish the Perricone Division of Dermatology there.

Sally Beatty noted in the *Wall Street Journal* that, "Many dermatologists claim an inherent conflict of interest exists between doctors administering care and selling their own products. . . . Others go a step further, saying Dr. Perricone hasn't proved some of his more sensational claims." Perricone has stated that since his products are sold through stores and he sees only a limited number of patients, the conflict argument does not apply to him. "And he defends the more sensational language in *The Wrinkle Cure*," noted Beatty, "by saying it is a lot more responsible than the often exaggerated claims made by cosmetics companies in magazine advertising. 'The cosmetic industry has an awful one hundred-year history of making incredible promises and then basically putting oil and water and emulsions in a jar,' says Dr. Perricone."

Perricone's books all promote the same healthy lifestyle. *The Perricone Prescription: A Physician's Twenty-eight-Day Program for Total Body and Face Rejuvenation Daybook* was a best-seller. He continues to promote a diet devoid of starchy foods and writes that some foods, for example cereals, bananas, and breads, all of which have a high glycemic index, cause a spike in blood sugar that prompts an insulin response by the body, thereby storing, rather than burning fat, and leading to inflammation. He offers a month's worth of menus, plus a three-day plan to kick-start results. Perricone recommends an exercise program and spends approximately one third of the book discussing antioxidants, vitamin supplements, and creams.

As a *Publishers Weekly* reviewer pointed out, *The Acne Prescription: The Perricone Program for Clear and Healthy Skin at Every Age* repeats the advice found in Perricone's other books, but the contributor felt that the book may interest new readers. The work targets readers of all ages, and particularly adolescents and young adults with acne. In addition to his twenty-eight-day diet program, he offers information on yoga exercises and dietary supplements that may help improve skin. The reviewer felt that although Perricone's theories are not embraced by some in the dermatological field, "one can hardly argue against a regimen that dictates a healthy diet, regular exercise, and good hygiene."

BIOGRAPHICAL AND CRITICAL SOURCES:

PERIODICALS

Flare (Toronto, Ontario, Canada), November, 2002, review of *The Perricone Prescription: A Physi-*

cian's Twenty-eight-Day Program for Total Body and Face Rejuvenation Daybook, p. 88.
Knight-Ridder Tribune News Service, May 24, 2004, Soo Youn, "Celebrity Dermatologist to Open Flagship Boutique in NYC," p. 1.
Library Journal, June 1, 2003, Susan B. Hagloch, review of *The Perricone Prescription,* p. 85.
Nutrition Action Health Letter, July-August, 2003, "A New Wrinkle," p. 6.
People, September 9, 2002, Galina Espinoza, "Very Berry Smooth: Dr. Nicholas Perricone Says the Secret to Young Skin Lies in Salmon and Blueberries," p. 101.
Publishers Weekly, March 6, 2000, review of *The Wrinkle Cure: Unlock the Power of Cosmeceuticals for Supple, Youthful Skin,* p. 101; July 8, 2002, review of *The Perricone Prescription,* p. 47; August 18, 2003, review of *The Acne Prescription: The Perricone Program for Clear and Healthy Skin at Every Age,* p. 76.
Time, October 21, 2002, Andrea Sachs, "Skin Deep: A Dermatologist Says He Can Reverse Wrinkles. Others Are Unconvinced" (interview), p. A11.
Wall Street Journal, November 14, 2003, Sally Beatty, "New Wrinkle," p. A1.
Washington Post, December 17, 2002, Stefanie Weiss, review of *The Perricone Prescription,* p. F1.

ONLINE

Nicholas V. Perricone Home Page, http://www.nv perriconemd.com (July 14, 2004).*

*   *   *

PEVAR, Stephen L. 1946-

PERSONAL: Born November 29, 1946, in Brooklyn, NY; son of Nathan (in sales) and Mildred (a homemaker; maiden name, Friedman) Pevar; married Laurel Hoskins (a graphic designer), October 3, 1992; children: Lianna, Elena. *Education:* Princeton University, A.B. (cum laude), 1968; University of Virginia, J.D. (with honors), 1971. *Politics:* Democrat. *Religion:* Jewish.

ADDRESSES: Office—American Civil Liberties Union, 32 Grand St., Hartford, CT 06106. *E-mail*—rightsofindians@aol.com.

CAREER: American Civil Liberties Union, Hartford, CT, senior staff counsel, 1976—.

WRITINGS:

The Rights of Indians and Tribes: The Basic ACLU Guide to Indian and Tribal Rights, 2nd edition, Southern Illinois University Press (Carbondale, IL), 1992, 3rd edition published as *The Rights of Indians and Tribes: The Authoritative ACLU Guide to Indian and Tribal Rights,* 2002.
The Rights of American Indians and Their Tribes (young adult), Puffin Books (New York, NY), 1997.

SIDELIGHTS: Stephen L. Pevar told *CA:* "I am motivated by a desire to use the law as a tool for social change, to increase social justice. My work with the American Civil Liberties Union helps me protect civil liberties and to help bring the law to where it ought to be.

"Living on the Rosebud Sioux Indian Reservation opened my eyes to injustices suffered by Indians and by poor people in general. As with my work for the American Civil Liberties Union, I was motivated by a desire to help people and make a difference. I hope my book does both."

BIOGRAPHICAL AND CRITICAL SOURCES:

PERIODICALS

Booklist, January 1, 1998, Stephanie Zvirin, review of *The Rights of American Indians and Their Tribes,* p. 788; January 1, 2000, Dona Helmer, review of *The Rights of Indians and Tribes: The Basic ACLU Guide to Indian and Tribal Rights,* p. 960.

* * *

PHILLIPS, Douglas A. 1949-

PERSONAL: Born October 7, 1949, in Volga, SD; son of Alan M. and Carolyn (a homemaker; maiden name Hook) Phillips; married Marlene Francis (a nurse) October 3, 1970; children: Christopher, Angela. *Education:* Northern State University, B.D., 1971, M.S., 1975; University of Alaska, Anchorage, Administration certification. *Politics:* Democrat. *Religion:* Christian.

ADDRESSES: Agent—c/o Author Mail, Chelsea House Publishers, 1974 Sproul Rd., Ste. 400, Broomall, PA 19008. *E-mail*—Douglas_phillips@cox.net.

CAREER: Gettysburg Public Schools, Gettysburg, PA, teacher, 1973-75, 1975-78; Division of Elementary and Secondary Education, Pierre, SD, director of social studies, 1978-81; Anchorage School District, director of social studies, 1981-99; Center for Civic Education, Calabasas, CA, senior consultant, 1996-2005; author, 2002—.

MEMBER: National Council for Geographic Education (president), Council for the Social Studies (South Dakota and Arkansas chapters).

AWARDS, HONORS: Named South Dakota Outstanding Young Educator, 1977; Distinguished Teaching Achievement Award, National Council for Geographic Education, 1985; named Mr. Social Studies of Alaska, Alaska Council for the Social Studies, 1988; Outstanding Service Award, National Council for the Social Studies, 1991; Outstanding Achievement in American History award, National Society of the Daughters of the American Revolution, 1991; Keizai Koho fellowship to Japan, 1991; Howard Cutler Award, Alaska Council for Economic Education, 1997; South Dakota Friend of Law-related Education Award, 1997; Friend of Children Award, Alaska State Council PTA, 1999.

WRITINGS:

The Pacific Rim Region: Emerging Giant, Enslow Publishers (Hillside, NJ), 1988.
Alaska, Japan, and the Pacific Rim: A Teacher's Resource Guide, Alaska Center for International Business, 1988.
India, Chelsea House Publishers (Philadelphia, PA), 2003.
Japan, Chelsea House Publishers (Philadelphia, PA), 2003.
Bosnia and Herzegovina, Chelsea House Publishers (Philadelphia, PA), 2004.
Nigeria, Chelsea House Publishers (Philadelphia, PA), 2004.
Indonesia, Chelsea House Publishers (Philadelphia, PA), 2005.

WORK IN PROGRESS: Vietnam, East Asia, and *Southeast Asia,* all for Chelsea House.

SIDELIGHTS: Douglas A. Phillips commented: "As a child I always felt that my purpose in life was to bring the world a little big closer together. Obviously this was a far-fetched dream and one that I had little notion of how to address and perhaps I never will achieve the 'purpose.'

"I was born into a solid and loving mid-American family with roots going back to the Revolutionary War and beyond. Dad was employed by Northwestern Bell Telephone Company and was an inventor all his life. Electronic and building mysteries were never left unsolved. From the home-made electric snow blower (made long before snow blowers), to our first television, to a home-made travel trailer, my father could make anything. He also like to travel as he'd grown up in a military reserve family and had gotten around the country quite a bit. My mother was the home stabilizer and nurturer that would be the envy of any child. She supported my father's camping adventures as we explored most of the United States. By my eighteenth year, I had seen America first as we'd traveled by trailer to forty-six states and all of the southern Canadian provinces. What was left? The world!

"As an eight-year-old Cub Scout, I started my preparation for traveling the world. I was a stamp collector. Each stamp told a story of other places with interesting people, languages, places, and cultures. By the time I was a young married adult the internal quest of bringing the world a little closer together played out. I was a middle-school teacher in South Dakota who taught civics, economics, and geography. Here I tried to share my passion with talented young folks who possessed boundless energy as they identified and got local governments to pass public policies on issues of importance to them. Bike trails were established, stop lights added, and other issues resolved in Brookings, South Dakota as students took action as young citizens. I love students and teaching.

"But there were other paths ahead in curriculum development and teacher training. Seeing first-hand the influence a teacher has, I wanted to try and have a broader impact. Teacher training is an activity I love, and I have worked with thousands of teachers in over 3,500 training sessions. Most of these were in the United States or Canada until the mid-1990s, when I was able to serve as a senior consultant for the Center for Civic Education in Calabasas, California. This organization has provided me with the opportunity of training in civic education around the world, an activity I continue today. The furthest corners of the world suddenly have had their doors opened to me. Bosnia and Herzegovinia, Kazakhstan, India, Madagascar, Nigeria, Tunisia, Macedonia, Malaysia, Russia, Argentina, Latvia, Hungary, Croatia, Serbia & Montenegro, and even Palestine have been venues where I have been blessed to have conducted training for educators in civic education. I was able to facilitate the work of incredible educators from Bosnia and Herzegovinia in an ongoing curriculum development effort that resulted in the first unified civics curriculum for the country after the war. All of these efforts have shown me the wonderful character of dedicated educators no matter how low their pay is. Stories about these teaching heroes are locked into my memory.

"In addition to working overseas, I have an enduring interest in seeing the world and meeting its people. So far the journey has included over eighty countries and my curiosity remains intact; I continue to revisit many dear places and people as well as explore new venues.

"Have I achieved the purpose revealed in my childhood? I don't believe so, but I've come to appreciate that the goal may really consist of maintaining the course and belief that a person can work to bring the world a little bit closer together. The task has gotten more difficult for Americans after the invasion of Iraq and the tragedy of 9/11, but I believe we must maintain the course of trying to bring the world a little closer together. Writing is another vehicle that allows us to be invited into someone's mind and heart. It can form a bridge from the writer to others that can be utilized to bring the world a little closer together rather than dividing it."

BIOGRAPHICAL AND CRITICAL SOURCES:

PERIODICALS

School Library Journal, November, 2003, Dian S. Marton, review of *India,* p. 165.

*   *   *

PHILLIPS, Max
(Forrest DeVoe, Jr.)

PERSONAL: Married.

ADDRESSES: Home—New York, NY. *Agent*—Dunow, Carlson & Lerner, c/o A+ Hosting Inc., 10620 Southern Highlands Pkwy, Ste. 110-491, Las Vegas, NV 89141.

CAREER: Cofounder of Hard Case Crime (imprint), New York, NY.

AWARDS, HONORS: Academy of American Poets Prize; National Endowment for the Arts fellowship.

WRITINGS:

Snakebite Sonnet, Little, Brown (Boston, MA), 1996.
The Artist's Wife, Holt (New York, NY), 2001.
Fade to Blonde, Hard Case Crime (New York, NY), 2004.
(As Forrest DeVoe, Jr.) *Into the Volcano: A Mallory and Morse Novel of Espionage*, HarperCollins (New York, NY), 2004.

Contributor of short fiction and poetry to periodicals, including *Atlantic Monthly* and *Story*.

SIDELIGHTS: New York-based writer Max Phillips is the author of several mystery novels. He is also the cofounder, with Charles Ardai, of the Hard Case Crime imprint, which aims to publish or reprint hard-boiled crime fiction by such noted authors as David Dodge, Ed McBain, Erle Stanley Gardner, Lawrence Block, and Stephen King.

Phillips's own writing covers a range of styles, from literary to genre. His first novel, *Snakebite Sonnet*, takes place over two decades, beginning in 1970, and recounts the adventures of ten-year-old Nick as he assists a beautiful college sophomore when she is bitten by a snake. The incident prompts Nick to fancy himself in love with this older woman, and his feelings continue as he goes on with his life and grows up. Megan Harlan, in a review for *Entertainment Weekly,* called Phillips's writing "a gorgeous mesh of erotic exactitude, heaps of wit, and generous, weary wisdom." A contributor for *Publishers Weekly* suggested that Phillips "flirts with excess," but concluded that he "demonstrates a poet's ear for lyric precision and a comic's for surefire punch lines." Joanne Wilkinson, writing for *Booklist,* dubbed the book "an uncommonly well crafted first novel."

In *The Artist's Wife,* Phillips tells the fictionalized memoir of the colorful Alma Mahler, wife of Austrian composer Gustav Mahler. The book follows Alma, the daughter of a landscape painter and a lieder singer, through her relationships with men, including architect Walter Gropius and author Franz Werfel, as well as her experiences as a minor composer in her own right. Alma had a reputation as something of a wild woman, and the novel depicts her joyful exuberance. A contributor for *Publishers Weekly* remarked that Phillips's "well-informed presentation of the historical milieu is overpowered by the self-centered sensuality of his protagonist." Elise Harris, in a review for the *Nation,* commented that the author's "overreliance on Alma's diaries has done him a disservice as a novelist, because he cannot get away from her own idea of herself." She went on to conclude, however, that the book presents "an amusing facsimile of the woman and her peculiar gifts." Brad Hooper, in a review for *Booklist,* found the depiction of Alma to be "vivid and viable."

Fade to Blonde represents a change in style for Phillips. This hard-boiled thriller, published by Phillips's Hard Case Crime imprint, tells the story of former boxer Ray Corson, who has tried his hand at writing screenplays and, failing at that, turned to detective work. Corson is hired by Rebecca LaFontaine to protect her from Lance Halliday, a Hollywood porn producer whom she has recently spurned. In a review for *Publishers Weekly,* a contributor remarked that Phillips "deftly balances his lovestruck hero's terse yet tender introspection with hard-hitting physical action," concluding that "they do write 'em like they used to."

BIOGRAPHICAL AND CRITICAL SOURCES:

PERIODICALS

Booklist, June 1, 1996, Joanne Wilkinson, review of *Snakebite Sonnet,* p. 1677; April 1, 2001, Brad Hooper, review of *The Artist's Wife,* p. 1452.
Daily News (New York, NY), June 1, 2004, Ethan Sacks, "New York City Pair Writes New Chapter for Pulp Novels."
Entertainment Weekly, July 12, 1996, Megan Harlan, review of *Snakebite Sonnet,* p. 52.
Nation, December 3, 2001, Elise Harris, "The Insatiable Fiction of Desire," review of *The Artist's Wife,* p. 25.

Newsweek, June 3, 1996, Jeff Giles and David Gates, "First Time for Everyone," review of *Snakebite Sonnet,* p. 74.

New York Times, July 8, 2001, Sarah Boxer, review of *The Artist's Wife,* p. 7.

Publishers Weekly, Aprill 22, 1996, review of *Snakebite Sonnet,* p. 58; June 4, 2001, review of *The Artist's Wife,* p. 55; August 2, 2004, review of *Fade to Blonde,* p. 57.

ONLINE

Hard Case Crime Web site, http://www.hardcasecrime. com/ (April 16, 2005), "Max Phillips."

MostlyFiction.com, http://mostlyfiction.com/ (April 16, 2005), "Max Phillips."

*   *   *

PILLER, Charles 1955-

PERSONAL: Born January 9, 1955, in Chicago, IL; son of Jack (a teacher) and Alice (a medical technologist; maiden name, Shakow) Piller; married Surry Bunnell (a registered nurse), August 26, 1984; children: Nathan. *Education:* Lone Mountain College, B.A., 1977. *Religion:* Jewish.

ADDRESSES: Agent—c/o Author Mail, Basic Books, 387 Park Ave. South, Twelfth Floor, New York, NY 10016. *E-mail*—charles.piller@latimes.com.

CAREER: Journalist and author. Carquinez Coalition, Contra Costa County, CA, executive director, 1980-81; Institute of Industrial Relations, University of California, Berkeley, senior writer, 1981-82; University of California Medical Center, San Francisco, writer and editor for *Synapse* (news weekly), 1982—; *Los Angeles Times,* Los Angeles, CA, staff writer. U.S. Senate, consultant to Subcommittee on Oversight of Government Management, 1987—; *MacWorld,* associate editor; affiliated with Bay Area Committee on Occupational Safety and Health.

MEMBER: National Writers Union, Northern California Science Writers Association, Media Alliance.

WRITINGS:

Labor Educator's Health and Safety Manual, University of California Press (Berkeley, CA), 1982.

(With Keith R. Yamamoto) *Gene Wars: Military Control over the New Genetic Technologies,* Beech Tree Books (New York, NY), 1988.

The Fail-Safe Society: Community Defiance and the End of American Technological Optimism, Basic-Books (New York, NY), 1991.

Contributor to periodicals, including *Los Angeles Times, Philadelphia Inquirer, San Francisco Chronicle, Baltimore Sun, Cleveland Plain Dealer, San Jose Mercury News, Oakland Tribune,* Toronto *Globe and Mail, Nation, Medical Self Care, Redbook, PC World, San Francisco Focus,* and *Chicago Tribune.*

SIDELIGHTS: Charles Piller, a journalist who has written extensively about technology and computer science, is also the author of a number of books. Among these is *Gene Wars: Military Control over the New Genetic Technologies,* which Piller wrote with molecular biologist Keith R. Yamamoto. Piller and Yamamoto present possible scenarios in which biological and chemical weapons could be employed by the military, then provide a look at historical instances where such means were used. They note that the U.S. Army began to investigate the use of biological warfare (BW) at Fort Detrick, Maryland, during World War II; diseases that were studied included plague, yellow fever, typhus, and botulism. This work was advanced with data that had been accumulated by the Japanese, who had used thousands of prisoners as guinea pigs during the war. During the 1950s and 1960s, U.S. Army scientists conducted animal experiments and secret open-air testing in its Utah proving grounds. The authors draw on documents, which, by law, must be unclassified, but which are very vague in their descriptions and difficult to obtain. They "provide a devastating analysis of the military's use of deception and secrecy to avoid governmental control," noted Clifton E. Wilson in *Library Journal.*

In 1925 the United States and one hundred other nations signed the Geneva Protocol, which prohibited the use of poison gas and bacteriological weapons. Also signed was the 1972 Biological Warfare Convention, which prohibits the development, production, or stockpiling of microbial or other biological toxins or agents. The authors write that the United States and other countries continue their research, defending their right do to so because, they say, they must be able to defend themselves from such attacks. The authors feel that research must be limited and that all information regarding defense against such threats should be made public. "Biologists do not yet have the strong link to weapons research that physicists and engineers have," noted Warren E. Leary in the *New York Times Book Review,* "and it is early enough to prevent such an attachment from forming."

The authors concede that responsible governments must defend themselves and develop the means to do so. However, according to Leary, the authors argue that the Pentagon, "with hundreds of millions of dollars to award in biological research contracts and a history of secrecy . . . cannot be trusted to protect the public's interest. Biologists must assume some of this responsibility by deciding against working on war projects." In addition, a *Kirkus Reviews* contributor wrote that Piller and Yamamoto show that the Pentagon "is actively meddling in certain aspects of biological research."

Gene Wars also addresses how the DNA of a plant or animal can be manipulated, which brings into question the possibility of altering food crops or developing deadlier viruses. Daniel Kevles, writing in the *Los Angeles Times Book Review,* concluded by saying that "the value of *Gene Wars* lies in the chilling report it provides of the U.S. BW program and in the alarm it raises against permitting the arms race to expand into a new and insidious arena."

The Fail-Safe Society: Community Defiance and the End of American Technological Optimism was called a "thoughtful middle alternative to sometimes reactionary activism and technocracy" by a *Publishers Weekly* writer. The book is Piller's study of the growing number of Americans who oppose scientific projects and experiments close to where they live. While Americans supported such scientific pursuits in the 1950s, the ensuing environmental disasters and threats, beginning with Love Canal, led to the founding of the syndrome known as "Not in My Backyard," NIMBY. Piller studies a number of cases, including one involving the Department of Energy's Rocky Flats nuclear weapons plant near Denver, Colorado. The plant employed a large number of residents, but in the mid-

1980s the site was found to be contaminated and the area groundwater to contain plutonium, and it was closed in 1989. Another NIMBY three-year battle was fought and lost in Monterey County, California, when a local group protested the testing of a genetically engineered bacteria as a form of frost control for crops.

Because of NIMBY activism, the building of waste dumps, factories, and research laboratories has more recently slowed to a crawl. Piller defines the two types of NIMBY protestors: those who are focused on a single project in their community, and outside environmentalists who come in to support local protestors. Piller's solution entails raising environmental standards and involving the communities themselves. "Piller may not have all the answers," wrote Peter Aldhous in *Nature,* "but his book is a thought-provoking starting point for an important and necessary debate."

BIOGRAPHICAL AND CRITICAL SOURCES:

PERIODICALS

Booklist, March 15, 1988, review of *Gene Wars: Military Control over the New Genetic Technologies,* p. 1208.

Choice, September, 1988, E. Lewis, review of *Gene Wars,* p. 211.

Kirkus Reviews, February 15, 1988, review of *Gene Wars,* p. 266; July 15, 1991, review of *The Fail-Safe Society: Community Defiance and the End of American Technological Optimism,* p. 914.

Library Journal, July, 1988, Clifton E. Wilson, review of *Gene Wars,* p. 84; September 15, 1991, Christopher R. Jocius, review of *The Fail-Safe Society,* p. 108.

Los Angeles Times Book Review, May 8, 1988, Daniel Kevles, review of *Gene Wars,* p. 2.

Nature, January 9, 1992, Peter Aldhous, review of *The Fail-Safe Society,* p. 124.

New York Times Book Review, March 27, 1988, Warren E. Leary, review of *Gene Wars,* p. 44.

Publishers Weekly, February 12, 1988, review of *Gene Wars,* p. 78; July 5, 1991, review of *The Fail-Safe Society,* p. 54.

Technology Review, July, 1992, Phil Brown, review of *The Fail-Safe Society,* pp. 68-70.*

PINTI, Pietro 1927-

PERSONAL: Born 1927, in Tuscany, Italy; married.

ADDRESSES: Agent—c/o Author Mail, Arcade Publishing, 141 5th Ave., Floor 8, New York, NY 10010.

CAREER: Has worked as a farmer and a cook.

WRITINGS:

(With Jenny Bawtree) *Pietro's Book: The Story of a Tuscan Peasant,* Arcade Publishing (New York, NY), 2004.

SIDELIGHTS: As a tourist destination and a setting for memoirs and movies, Tuscany has earned a reputation for old-world charm and simple pleasures. There is, of course, another side, and in *Pietro's Book: The Story of a Tuscan Peasant* Pietro Pinti reveals the grinding poverty, oppression, and ignorance that have also shaped the history of the region. Born into a family of twelve children in 1927, Pinti grew up in the shadow of fascism and social upheaval, and the impact of World War II is a central part of his story. But he also provides an insight into the traditional rhythms of northern Italian life, such as the *padrone* who actually owned the peasants' land and passed out benefits based on the peasant's success or failure in farming that land. He takes the reader through a typical peasant's year, from making chestnut wood ladders in January to pressing olive oil in December. In addition, as *Geographical* contributor Christian Amodeo noted, the book is "crammed with comical, predictable and reassuring anecdotes and rhymes—gems of peasant humour that poke fun at people in authority or fellow peasants' hilarious reactions to modern technology." At the same time, there is an undertone of sadness in the book, which after all is a tribute to a vanished world and a lost way of life. For *Booklist* reviewer GraceAnn A. DeCandido, "This small, cherishable book is as close to living history as one gets."

BIOGRAPHICAL AND CRITICAL SOURCES:

BOOKS

Pinti, Pietro, and Jenny Bawtree, *Pietro's Book: The Story of a Tuscan Peasant,* Arcade Publishing (New York, NY), 2004.

PERIODICALS

Booklist, May 15, 2004, GraceAnn A. DeCandido, review of *Pietro's Book,* p. 1595.
Geographical, September, 2003, Christian Amodeo, review of *Pietro's Book,* p. 55.
Library Journal, July, 2004, Joseph L. Carlson, review of *Pietro's Book,* p. 92.*

*   *   *

PIPIN
See FERRERAS, Francisco

*   *   *

PLOTKIN, Fred 1956(?)-

PERSONAL: Born c. 1956; son of Edward (a trombonist) and Bernice (a public information office worker) Plotkin. *Education:* University of Wisconsin, B.A. (Italian Renaissance history); graduated from University of Bologna (opera production); Columbia University M.A. (journalism).

ADDRESSES: Agent—c/o Author Mail, Little Brown and Co., 148 Yorkville Ave., Toronto, Ontario M5R 1C2, Canada.

CAREER: Author, lecturer, and food critic. New York Metropolitan Opera, New York, NY, performance manager and program guide editor. Has worked at La Scala (opera house), Milan, Italy, and as a tour guide at Lincoln Center, New York, NY.

AWARDS, HONORS: Fulbright scholar.

WRITINGS:

The Authentic Pasta Book, Simon and Schuster (New York, NY), 1985.
(With Dana Cernea) *Eating Healthy for a Healthy Baby: A Month-by-Month Guide to Nutrition during Pregnancy,* Crown Trade Paperbacks (New York, NY), 1994.

Opera 101: A Complete Guide to Learning and Loving Opera, Hyperion (New York, NY), 1994.

Italy for the Gourmet Traveler, Little, Brown (Boston, MA), 1996.

Italy Today the Beautiful Cookbook: Contemporary Recipes Reflecting Simple, Fresh Italian Cooking, food photography by Peter Johnson, Collins Publishers (New York, NY), 1997.

Recipes from Paradise: Life and Food on the Italian Riviera, Little, Brown (Boston, MA), 1997.

La Terra Fortunata: The Splendid Food and Wine of Friuli-Venezia Giulia, Broadway Books (New York, NY), 2001.

Classical Music 101: A Complete Guide to Learning and Loving Classical Music, Hyperion (New York, NY), 2002.

Contributor to publications, including *Opera News, New York Times, Gourmet,* and *Los Angeles Times.*

SIDELIGHTS: A connoisseur of fine food and Italian cooking, Fred Plotkin began his writing career with *The Authentic Pasta Book.* Although some of the recipes in this book are easy for beginners, most of them are for intermediate to experienced cooks. Along with general information on sauces and pastas, Plotkin provides detailed directions for making, cooking, serving, and eating pasta. Plotkin describes recipes and cooking styles specific to each region of Italy. *Booklist* reviewer John Brosnahan described the book as a "wonderful collection," and a *Library Journal* reviewer praised the recipes as "quick . . . [yet] unusual and delicious."

Plotkin has written and coauthored a number of other books on Italian gourmet cooking. *Recipes from Paradise: Life and Food on the Italian Riviera* includes a generous selection of recipes from the Italian Riviera, a region also known as Liguria. Plotkin "does an admirable . . . job of collecting authentic versions" of these recipes, noted a *Publishers Weekly* reviewer. Included in the book are recipes for pesto, focaccia, and a variety of fish. "Serious research makes this book a fascinating read" both for the recipes and for the information on Liguria itself, the *Publishers Weekly* reviewer commented.

Italy for the Gourmet Traveler offers in-depth information on the best places to dine in some 300 cities and villages throughout Italy. "Practical advice, such as

making reservations, goes hand-in-hand with colorful descriptions" of Italian restaurants and eateries, remarked *Booklist* reviewer Alice Joyce. Plotkin includes cultural details of the areas in which the restaurants can be found. The book also contains a glossary of Italian food terms, city profiles, restaurant reviews, indexed recipes, and local anecdotes. David Naudo, writing in *Library Journal,* called the book "an entertaining, comprehensive guide."

In *La Terra Fortunata: The Splendid Food and Wine of Friuli-Venezia Giulia* Plotkin "does what he does best—focuses on a lesser-known part of Italy and brings it to life," observed a reviewer in *Publishers Weekly.* A multicultural region bordering on Austria and the former Yugoslavia, Friuli-Venezia Giulia has multiple ethnic influences infusing its foods. Plotkin discusses these influences in the course of presenting 150 recipes and also includes a detailed history of the region, plus information about local vineyards. A *Publishers Weekly* reviewer called the book "an outstanding volume."

In *Opera 101: A Complete Guide to Learning and Loving Opera* Plotkin, who is a former performance manager for the New York Metropolitan Opera, provides a helpful guide readers new to the topic. The book "provides an excellent 400-year history [of opera] that could have been published as a booklet on its own," commented Brad Hooper in *Booklist.* Plotkin explains the basic parts of an opera performance, including how to understand the plots and staging, how to learn the story that is being sung, and how to appreciate each singer's voice and technique. He also discusses opera etiquette, with detailed advice on how tickets are purchased and when to applaud. Ken Ringle of the *Washington Post Book World,* while applauding Plotkin's knowledge about and love of opera, remarked that the book is not as accessible to beginners as it should be, but agreed that Plotkin's analyses of operas "are valuable for their scholarship and insight." He also noted that Plotkin's lists of outstanding recordings of operas are "valuable guides through the bewildering forest of artists and conductors past and present."

Plotkin turns his attention to another source of cultured music in *Classical Music 101: A Complete Guide to Learning and Loving Classical Music.* The book "is an amazingly complete volume, considering the scope of its content," remarked *Strings* reviewer Meg

Eldridge. Coverage includes topics such as the type and history of musical instruments found in a symphony orchestra; tone quality, or timbre; and the "voices" of the orchestra. Plotkin explains topics such as the process of musical composition, the ins and outs of conducting and orchestra, the role of singers in classical music, and how to appreciate a live performance. A discography and resource guide rounds out the book's contents. Eldridge concluded that Plotkin "addresses what it means to really listen to and appreciate music."

BIOGRAPHICAL AND CRITICAL SOURCES:

PERIODICALS

American Record Guide, September-October, 2002, Donald R. Vroon, review of *Classical Music 101: A Complete Guide to Learning and Loving Classical Music,* p. 252.

Booklist, August, 1985, John Brosnahan, review of *The Authentic Pasta Book,* pp. 1614-1615; November 15, 1994, Brad Hooper, review of *Opera 101: A Complete Guide to Learning and Loving Opera,* p. 569; November 15, 1994, p. 595; July, 1996, Alice Joyce, review of *Italy for the Gourmet Traveler,* p. 1792.

Library Journal, August, 1985, review of *The Authentic Pasta Book,* p. 95; May 15, 1996, David Nudo, review of *Italy for the Gourmet Traveler,* p. 77; May 15, 1997, Judith C. Sutton, review of *Italy Today the Beautiful Cookbook: Contemporary Recipes Reflecting Simple, Fresh Italian Cooking,* p. 96; April 15, 2001, Judith Sutton, review of *La Terra Fortunata: The Splendid Food and Wine of Friuli-Venezia Giulia,* p. 126.

Music Educators Journal, May, 2003, review of *Classical Music 101,* p. 51.

New York Times, August 30, 2002, Glen Collins, "Off with the Cellphone (Even If It Plays Beethoven)," biography of Fred Plotkin, p. B2.

Opera News, April, 2003, Alan Wagner, review of *Classical Music 101,* p. 79.

Publishers Weekly, June 21, 1985, review of *The Authentic Pasta Book,* p. 94; November 7, 1994, review of *Opera 101,* p. 71; August 4, 1997, review of *Recipes from Paradise: Life and Food on the Italian Riviera,* pp. 70-71; March 19, 2001, review of *La Terra Fortunata,* p. 95.

Strings, October, 2002, Meg Eldridge, review of *Classical Music 101,* p. 90.

Washington Post Book World, January 22, 1995, Ken Ringle, review of *Opera 101,* p. 2.

ONLINE

Smithsonian Study Tours Web site, http://www. smithsonianstudytours.org/ (July 27, 2004), "Fred Plotkin."*

*   *   *

POETHEN, Johannes 1928-2001

PERSONAL: Born September 13, 1928, in Wickrath, Nordrhein-Westfalen, Germany; died May 9, 2001, in Stuttgart, Germany. *Education:* Studied German literature at University of Tübingen.

CAREER: Freelance writer and poet, beginning 1947; Süddeutschen Rundfunks (South Germany Broadcasting), head of literature department; produced essays for radio. *Military service:* Served in German military.

MEMBER: PEN; German Writers' Union.

AWARDS, HONORS: Hugo Jacobi poetry prize, 1959; Forderpreis der Städt Köln, 1962; Forderpreis zum Immerman Preis der Städt Düsseldorf, 1967; Stuttgart literature prize, 1990.

WRITINGS:

Lorbeer über gestirntem Haupt; sechs Gesänge, E. Diederich (Düsseldorf, Germany), 1952.

Risse des himmels. Gedichte (poems), Bechtle (Esslingen, Germany), 1956.

Stille im trockenken Dorn. Neue Gedichte (poems), Bechtle (Esslingen, Germany), 1958.

Ankunft und Echo: Gedichte und Prosagedichte (poems), Fischer (Frankfurt, Germany), 1961.

Gedichte (poems), Moderner Buch-Club (Darmstadt, Germany), 1963.

Wohnstatt zwischen den Atemzügen. Gedichte, (poems), Claassen (Hamburg, Germany), 1966.

Kranichtanz. Mit 7 Fotografiken, Collispress (Stuttgart, German), 1967.

(Editor) Wolfgang Weyrauch, *Lyrik aus dieser Zeit, 1967-68* (poems), Bechtle (Munich, Germany), 1967.

Aus der unendlichen Kälte; vierzehn Gedichte, sieben Sprüche, drei Fragmente (collection; includes poems), J. G. Bläschke (Darmstadt, Germany), 1969.

(With Helmut A. P. Grieshaber) *Im Namen der Trauer,* Claassen (Düsseldorf, Germany), 1969.

Gedichte: 1946-1971 (poems), Claassen (Hamburg, Germany), 1973.

Rattenfest im Jammertal: Gedichte 1972-1975 (poems), Claassen (Düsseldorf, Germany), 1976.

Der Atem Griechenlands (travel essays; originally written for radio), Claassen (Düsseldorf, Germany), 1977.

Ach Erde du alte: Gedichte 1976-1980 (poems), Klett-Cotta (Stuttgart, Germany), 1981.

(With Rudel Horst) *Stuttgart* (pictorial), G. Rüber (Schwieberdingen, Germany), 1983.

Schwarz das All: vier Zyklen Gedichte (poems), U. Keicher (Scheer, Germany), 1984.

Auch diese Wörter: Neue Gedichte (poems), Drumlin Verlag (Weingarten, Germany), 1985.

Eines Morgens über dem Golf: Vierzehn Gedichte (poems), U. Keicher (Warmbronn, Germany), 1986.

Urland Hellas: Reisen in Griechenland (essays; originally written for radio), Drumlin Verlag (Weingarten, Germany), 1987.

Wer hält mir die Himmelsleiter: Gedichte 1981-1987 (poems), G. Braun (Karlsruhe, Germany), 1988.

Ich bin nur in Wörtern: Johannes Poethen zum sechzigsten Geburtstag (collection), U. Keicher (Warmbronn, Germany), 1988.

Stuttgarter Lesebuch: 25 Autoren stellen sich vor (literary criticism), G. Braun (Karlsruhe, Germany), 1989.

Auf der Suche nach Apollon: sieben griechische Götter in ihrer Landschaft: Essays, Heliopolis (Tübingen, Germany), 1992.

Die Möwen der Hagia Sophia: vierzehn Gedichte (poems), U. Keicher (Warmbronn, Germany), 1992.

Zwischen dem All und dem Nichts: Gedichte, 1988-1993 (poems), Edition Isele (Eggingen, Germany), 1995.

Von Kos bis Korfu: sieben Inseln: Mythen, Geschichte, Gegenwart (essays), Edition Isele (Eggingen, Germany), 1998.

Nach all den Hexametern: letzte Gedichte 1995-2000 (poems), edited by Usch Pfaffinger and Ruth Theil, Ithaka (Stuttgart, Germany), 2001.

Contributor to periodicals.

SIDELIGHTS: German writer Johannes Poethen spent his career playing with words and images and creating his own version of modern poetry. He was fascinated with Greece and Greek mythology and by the contrast between the sun-drenched south and the colder, darker north.

Poethen was born in Wickrath, Nordrhein-Westfalen, Germany, and grew up and went to school in Cologne until 1943. He spent the next few years living in various places, including Austria and Bavaria, as he continued his studies. After completing his military service, he resumed his education, completing studies in German literature at the University of Tübingen. He then became a freelance writer and a contributor to various German newspapers.

Poethen wrote his first poem, "Sonette," at the age of seventeen, clearly influenced by the work of Hölderlin and Reiner Maria Rilke. The poem was published in 1947 in the *Neuen Runschau* in Stockholm, Sweden, and again in 1949 in *Zeitschrift.* Poethen found his poetic path in 1952 when his poetry collection titled *Lorbeer über gestirntem Haupt; sechs Gesänge* was published. This early work exemplified the basic themes, motives, and central motifs that would characterize the body of Poethen's poetry.

Poethen tended to create poetic circles in his work and to focus on two particular German landscapes: the technological, angst-ridden north and the devout south. These contrasting locales form the images of Metopia (an unreal place) and Utopia (a perfect nonexistent place). For Poethen, poetry was a word game, to which ideological and sociological categories did not apply; it was an autonomous world with its own laws. He worked toward the fusion of intuition and rationality, of enthusiasm and calculation, a concept he explores in the poem "Labor der Träume."

Poethen's poetry is full of double meanings, and his words can mean many different things. Jürgen P. Wallman wrote in *Universitas* that, for Poethen, poetry was a form of meditation, in that one can read for the strictest, most realistic meaning of the words but also then explore the multitude of possible meanings such words could have. In his poetic language, Poethen took jargon and casual speech and used them to create daring combinations of words and images. His 1987 collection *Rattenfest im Jammertal: Gedichte 1972-1975* defined him as a radical poet; he continued to employ that style in subsequent works.

Poethen's final poems are rich in literary allusions, taken from traditional poetry and from church music. However, he took these images and modified them considerably from the originals, making them his own. His most mature poems use a language that is simpler and more direct and an artistic calculation that is more precise than that of his works from the 1970s. There is also an autobiographical element in his poetry volumes *Schwarz das All: vier Zyklen Gedichte* and *Auch diese Wörter: Neue Gedichte.*

Mythology occupied a central place in Poethen's writing. According to Wallman, the poet believed the psychological theory that mythology illustrates reality and that it is therefore the poet's task to be a writer of myths. For Poethen, myths bear a strong relationship to landscape, particularly the Greek landscape, and he embraced the possibility that myth and reality can fuse momentarily in the dazzling clarity of this landscape.

Poethen combined his interest in Greek mythology with an enthusiasm for travel that played an important role in his life; he spent a great deal of time in Mediterranean countries, particularly in Greece. He wrote a number of radio essays on Greece from the 1950s through the 1980s that were later collected and published as *Der Atem Griechenlands* and *Urland Hellas: Reisen in Griechenland.* Other works by Poethen that deal with Greek mythology and travel are *Auf der Suche nach Apollon: sieben griechische Götter in ihrer Landschaft: Essays,* and *Von Kos bis Korfu: sieben Inseln: Mythen, Geschichte, Gegenwart.* He also produced travel works that focus on his homeland. *Stuttgart* is a pictorial description of the German city. In addition, Poethen wrote books of German literary criticism, including *Stuttgarter Lesebuch: 25 Autoren stellen sich vor.*

Poethen was the head of the literature department at South Germany Broadcasting in Stuttgart. During his lifetime, he received recognition for his work and was awarded several literary prizes during the 1950s and 1960s.

BIOGRAPHICAL AND CRITICAL SOURCES:

BOOKS

Garland, Mary, *The Oxford Companion to German Literature,* 3rd edition, Oxford University Press (New York, NY), 1997.

PERIODICALS

Neue Deutsche Hefte, Volume 35, issue 3, 1988, Jürgen P. Wallman, review of *Ich bin nur in Wörtern: Johannes Poethen zum sechzigsten Geburtstag,* p. 650.
Universitas, Volume 26, issue 7, 1971, Jürgen P. Wallman, "Der Lyriker Johannes Poethen und sein Werk in der deutschen Lyrik der Gegenwart," p. 749.*

*   *   *

POHL, Janice
    See DAVIDSON, MaryJanice

*   *   *

POOLE, Robert M. 1950(?)-

PERSONAL: Born c. 1950, in NC. *Education:* University of North Carolina, B.A., 1971.

ADDRESSES: Agent—c/o Author Mail, Penguin Group, 345 Hudson St., New York, NY 10014.

CAREER: Winston-Salem Journal, Winston-Salem, NC, former reporter; Media General News Service, Washington, DC, former correspondent; *Boston Herald,* Boston, MA, former Washington correspondent; *National Geographic,* writer and executive editor, 1980-2001.

AWARDS, HONORS: Washington Journalism Center, fellow, 1974.

WRITINGS:

Explorers House: National Geographic and the World It Made, Penguin Press (New York, NY), 2004.

SIDELIGHTS: A former executive editor at the *National Geographic,* Robert M. Poole has produced a history of the well-known magazine and its rise from an academic journal with limited appeal to its more-recent iconic status. *Explorers House: National Geographic and the World It Made* begins with the vision of Gardner Green Hubbard, founder of the National Geographic Society, to bring geographic discoveries to a wider audience. The real tale begins with Hubbard's son-in-law, famed inventor Alexander Graham Bell, who gained control of the Society in 1898 when the magazine had a circulation of only one thousand. In addition to a wealth of journalistic ideas, such as stories on waltzing mice and the impact of yellow fever, Bell pushed for pictorial content, a decision that would bear fruit in the magazine's reputation for containing magnificent history of photography.

While *National Geographic* did well under Bell, it really took off under the editorship of his son-in-law, Gilbert Grosvenor, and the Grosvenor family has been closely linked with the magazine ever since. As *Library Journal* reviewer Donna Marie Smith noted, "Poole's book reads like an intriguing family saga while remaining a well-researched text." Indeed, commented a reviewer for the *Economist,* "Poole presents a plausible case for nepotism," revealing the impact that the public-spirited family had on bringing interesting stories and far-flung places to the attention of the American populace without obsessing about the bottom line. "Poole is not, however, blinkered by his association with the publication and writes candidly about bigoted editors, vapid articles, and dumb business decisions," as noted to *Booklist* reviewer Gilbert Taylor. The result, in the words of a *Kirkus Reviews* contributor, is a "gratifyingly evenhanded chronicle of the society's personalities and initiatives."

BIOGRAPHICAL AND CRITICAL SOURCES:

PERIODICALS

Booklist, October 1, 2004, Gilbert Taylor, review of *Explorers House: National Geographic and the World It Made,* p. 295.

Economist, October 16, 2004, review of *Explorers House,* p. 82.
Kirkus Reviews, September 1, 2004, review of *Explorers House,* p. 852.
Library Journal, February 1, 2005, Donna Marie Smith, review of *Explorers House,* p. 94.
Publishers Weekly, September 13, 2004, review of *Explorers House,* p. 68.

ONLINE

OntheMedia.org, http://www.onthemedia.org/ (December 17, 2004), Brooke Gladstone, interview with Poole.*

* * *

**PROCTOR, Michael
(Mike Proctor)**

PERSONAL: Born in NM. *Education:* California State University, Long Beach, B.A., 1970; earned secondary school and community college teaching credentials; completed additional training in law enforcement.

ADDRESSES: Agent—Grayson Literary Agency, 1342 18th St., San Pedro, CA 90732. *E-mail*—duckworks@cox.net.

CAREER: Substitute teacher for public schools in El Segundo and Anaheim, CA, 1970-72; City of Westminster, CA, police officer, 1972-96, retiring as detective, 2004; Duck Works Criminal Consulting, writer, lecturer, and consultant on stalking and threat management, 1996—. National Center for Victims of Crime, registered stalking expert; testified in numerous court cases; guest on media programs, including *20/20, America's Most Wanted, Unsolved Mysteries,* and broadcasts of the Cable News Network and Court TV; guest on radio talk shows.

MEMBER: Association of Threat Assessment Professionals.

AWARDS, HONORS: Police photographers award, *Law and Order,* 1978; Public Safety Merit Awards, Westminster Chamber of Commerce, 1989, 1995; award from Association of Reserve Officers, 1999; Defender of Justice Award, California State Assembly, 2003; Lifetime Achievement Award, City of Westminster, 2003.

WRITINGS:

(As Mike Proctor) *How to Stop a Stalker,* Prometheus Books (Amherst, NY), 2003.

Contributor to periodicals, including *Law and Order* and *Journal of California Law Enforcement.*

WORK IN PROGRESS: A "true-crime" novel, under a pseudonym.

SIDELIGHTS: Michael Proctor told *CA:* "My life revolves around helping and educating people, professionals as well as the public, on matters that can make their lives safer and more productive. That was the primary reason for writing *How to Stop a Stalker.*

"In regard to my other ongoing works, they are inspired by and based on the dark, depraved world I love to work in. Writing allows me to give the reader a brief glimpse into this strange, interesting, and at time sick environment that I encounter every day.

"My writing process is simple. I merely transcribe what I see, absorb, and feel. Oftentimes, life is truly stranger than fiction. What I see and experience is then scribbled upon the page with my own dash of sarcasm, in the hopes of assisting the reader to better digest the material that is being presented."

BIOGRAPHICAL AND CRITICAL SOURCES:

ONLINE

Detective Mike Proctor Home Page, http://www. detectivemikeproctor.com (December 5, 2004).

*   *   *

PROCTOR, Mike
    See PROCTOR, Michael

R

RANK, Mark Robert 1955-

PERSONAL: Born May 18, 1955, in Milwaukee, WI; son of Robert Arthur and Hallie Jean (Hughes) Rank; married Anne Elizabeth Deutch, September 15, 1984; children: Elizabeth and Katherine. *Education:* University of Wisconsin, Madison, B.A. (with honors), 1978, M.S., 1980, Ph.D., 1984.

ADDRESSES: Home—St. Louis, MO. *Office*—Washington University, Campus Box 1196, One Brookings Dr., St. Louis, MO 63130. *E-mail*—markr@ wustl.edu.

CAREER: Professor and author. University of North Carolina, Chapel Hill, professional fellow, 1984-85; Washington University, St. Louis, MO, assistant professor, 1985-89, professor of social welfare, 1989—.

MEMBER: American Sociological Association, National Council on Family Relations.

AWARDS, HONORS: Feldman Award, Groves Conference on Marriage and the Family, 1991; Founders Day Distinguished Faculty Award, Washington University, 1995; Faculty Award to Improve Learning, William T. Kemper Foundation, 1998; Outstanding Research Award, Society of Social Work and Research, 2001; Distinguished Faculty Award, George Warren Brown School of Social Work, Washington University, 2005; Access to Equal Justice Award, School of Law, Washington University, 2005.

WRITINGS:

Demographic Characteristics of Wisconsin's Welfare Recipients, University of Wisconsin (Madison, WI), 1984.
Living on the Edge: The Realities of Welfare in America, Columbia University Press (New York, NY), 1994.
(Editor, with Edward L. Kain) *Diversity and Change in Families: Patterns, Prospects, and Policies,* Prentice Hall (Englewood Cliffs, NJ), 1995.
One Nation, Underprivileged: Why American Poverty Affects Us All, Oxford University Press (New York, NY), 2004.

Contributor to academic journals, including *Social Work, Demography, Social Forces, Journal of Marriage and the Family, American Sociological Review, Journal of Gerontology, Review of Economics and Statistics, Journal of Policy Analysis and Management, Psychological Science, Journal of Law and Social Policy,* and *Social Science Quarterly.*

SIDELIGHTS: Educator and author Mark Robert Rank has long had an interest in poverty issues. He earned his doctorate at the University of Wisconsin in the field of sociology, and began teaching shortly thereafter at Washington University in St. Louis. In 1989, he joined the university's school of social work, and became Herbert S. Hadley Professor of Social Welfare. His research and teaching specialties focus on social welfare, economic inequality, and social policy. In addition to writing books addressing these topics, Rank regularly contributes to academic and trade journals concerned with these issues. He has also provided his expertise to members of the U.S. Congress.

In 1994, Rank wrote his first book on the subject of American poverty. *Living on the Edge: The Realities of Welfare in America.* is based on ten years of interviews and sociological research involving welfare recipients in the state of Wisconsin. His focus is to show readers why people turn to the welfare system, what it is like to survive on welfare, and what the country can do to improve the system. The result is a combination of statistical data and personal stories from individuals and families living on welfare.

Overall, *Living on the Edge* was well received by readers and reviewers. Many critics acknowledged Rank's efforts to reach beyond an academic audience by providing narrative and personal accounts of life within the welfare system. "Rank strives manfully, and to some extent successfully, to reach both scholar and general reader," wrote *Booklist* contributor Roland Gilbert. Others praised Rank for trying to refute stereotypes about welfare recipients, while acknowledging the fact that his research only focuses on a specific segment of the welfare population. "Rank's effort to attack popular stereotypes is undermined by his failure to deal head on with the issue of the so-called urban underclass," observed Fred Block in a review for *Political Science Quarterly.*

In 2004, Rank wrote his next book on the subject of poverty, *One Nation, Underprivileged: Why American Poverty Affects Us All.* With this work he analyses the state of poverty in the United States, using definitions, statistics, and an overview of poverty's structural causes. He also argues that reducing poverty is in the country's self-interest because a majority of Americans will experience poverty or near-poverty at some point in their lives. Rank then outlines policies that could reduce poverty but have yet been untried.

Critics again recognized the merits of Rank's efforts in *One Nation, Underprivileged.* John Iceland, in a review for *Social Forces* called Rank's work "an admirable and thoughtful book that is likely to stimulate lively discussions on poverty at a time when renewed attention on this issue is needed." Other reviewers acknowledged Rank's attempts to expose the truth behind why the U.S. continues to have a problem with poverty. "The author debunks the traditional belief that the poor are largely responsible for their own condition," wrote *Booklist* contributor Allen Weakland.

Rank told *CA:* "Throughout my writings, I have attempted to change the way that we have traditionally understood the issues of poverty, inequality, and social welfare. My work consistently challenges my readers to look beyond the stereotypes, to the deeper meanings and realities underlying these critical social and economic issues."

BIOGRAPHICAL AND CRITICAL SOURCES:

PERIODICALS

America, November 22, 2004, Cecilio Morales, "The Face of the Poor Is Ours," p. 16.
Booklist, April 15, 1994, Roland Gilbert, review of *Living on the Edge: The Realities of Welfare in America,* p. 1491; May 15, 2004, Allen Weakland, review of *One Nation, Underprivileged: Why American Poverty Affects Us All,* p. 1584.
Canadian Review of Sociology and Anthropology, February, 1996, Julia S. O'Connor, review of *Living on the Edge,* p. 119.
Choice, December 2004, K. J. Bauman, review of *One Nation, Underprivileged: Why American Poverty Affects Us All,* p. 743.
Michigan Law Review, May 1996, Lisa A. Crooms, review of *Living on the Edge,* p. 1953.
New Leader, June 6, 1994, Earl Shorris, review of *Living on the Edge,* p. 23.
Political Science Quarterly, winter, 1994, Fred Block, review of *Living on the Edge,* p. 933.
Progressive, January 1995, Ruth Conniff, review of *Living on the Edge,* p. 47.
Public Administration Review, May-June, 1996, Edward T. Jennings, Jr., review of *Living on the Edge,* p. 305.
Social Forces, September 2004, John Iceland, review of *One Nation, Underprivileged,* p. 439.

ONLINE

Washington University in St. Louis Web site, http://gwbweb.wustl.edu/ (February 10, 2005), "Mark Rank."

*　　*　　*

RATHENAU, Walther 1867-1922

PERSONAL: Born September 29, 1867, in Berlin, Germany; assassinated June 24, 1922, in Berlin, Germany; son of Emil (an entrepreneur) and Mathilde Rathenau. *Education:* Doctorate in physics, 1889. *Politics:* Democrat (German). *Religion:* Jewish.

CAREER: Industrialist, business executive, statesman, and author. Allgemeine Elektrizitatsgesellschaft (electric company), Berlin, Germany, member of research and management, beginning c. 1899, president, 1915-21; Government of Germany, War Raw Materials Department, director, 1914-15, member of German socialization committee, 1920, minister of reconstruction, 1921, appointed foreign secretary of Germany, 1922.

WRITINGS:

Walther Rathenau-Gesamtausgabe, G. Muller (Munich, Germany), 1900.

Impressionen, S. Hirzel (Leipzig, Germany), 1902.

Reflexionen, S. Hirzel (Leipzig, Germany), 1912.

Zur Kritik der Zeit, S. Fischer (Berlin, Germany), 1912.

Probleme der Friedenswirtschaft, S. Fischer (Berlin, Germany), 1917.

Deutschlands rohstoffversorgung, S. Fischer (Berlin, Germany), 1917.

Eine streitschrift vom glauben (letter), S. Fischer (Berlin, Germany), 1917.

Vom aktienwesen, eine geschaftliche Betrachtung, S. Fischer (Berlin, Germany), 1918.

Die neue Wirtschaft, S. Fischer (Berlin, Germany), 1918.

Rathenau-Brevier. Hrsg. von Erich Schairer (letters), E. Diederichs (Jena, Germany), 1918.

Von kommenden Dingen, S. Fischer (Berlin, Germany), 1918, translation by Eden and Cedar Paul published as *In Days to Come,* Allen and Unwin (London, England), 1921.

Gesammelte Schriften (collected works), S. Fischer (Berlin, Germany), 1918.

An Deutschlands Jugend, S. Fischer (Berlin, Germany), 1918.

Zeitliches, S. Fischer (Berlin, Germany), 1918.

Autonome Wirtschaft, E. Diederichs (Jena, Germany), 1919.

Der Kaiser, S. Fischer (Berlin, Germany), 1919.

Nach der Flut, S. Fischer (Berlin, Germany), 1919.

Kritik der dreifachen Revolution; Apologie, S. Fischer (Berlin, Germany), 1919.

Der neue Stät, S. Fischer (Berlin, Germany), 1919, translation published as *The New Society,* Harcourt, Brace, and Howe (New York, NY), 1921.

Die neue Gesellschaft, S. Fischer (Berlin, Germany), 1919.

Was wird werden?, S. Fischer (Berlin, Germany), 1920.

Der Kaiser; eine Betrachtung von Walther Rathenau, S. Fischer (Berlin, Germany), 1921.

Zur Mechanik des Geistes, S. Fischer (Berlin, Germany), 1922.

Cannes und Genua; vier Reden zum Reparationsproblem, mit einem Anhang, S. Fischer (Berlin, Germany), 1922.

Kunstphilosophie und Asthetik, zusammengestellt und eingeleitet von Wolfgang Schumann, G.D.W. Callwey (Munich, Germany), 1923.

Gesammelte reden, S. Fischer (Berlin, Germany), 1924.

Gesammelte Schriften (collected works), S. Fischer (Berlin, Germany), 1925–29.

Briefe (letters), 4 volumes, C. Reissner (Dresden, Germany), 1926–30.

Ausgewählte reden, von Walther Rathenau, edited with introductions and notes by James Taft Hatfield, Knopf (New York, NY), 1928.

Nachgelassene Schriften, S. Fischer (Berlin, Germany), 1928.

Briefe an eine Liebende (letters), C. Reissner (Dresden, Germany), 1931.

Blanche Trocard: Shauspiel in zwei Akten (play), Koetschau-Verlag (Berlin, Germany), 1947.

Walther Rathenau in Briefe und Bild (letters and photographs), A. Leber (Frankfurt, Germany), 1967.

Tagebuch, 1907-1922 (diary), Droste Verlag (Düsseldorf, Germany), 1967.

Hauptwerke und Gesprache, G. Müller (Munich, Germany), 1977.

Schriften (collected writings), Berlin-Verlag (Berlin, Germany), 1981.

SIDELIGHTS: Walther Rathenau was a German statesman and industrialist who came to prominence in the early twentieth century. The son of the famous German-Jewish entrepreneur Emil Rathenau, who had founded and directed Allgemeine Elektrizitatsgesellschaft, Germany's electric supplier, for many years, Walther studied electrochemistry, earning a doctorate in physics. After his father's death in 1915, Rathenau took over control of AEG. The indefatigable young man was involved in a wide variety of business enterprises. He also delved deeply into politics, philosophy, and economics, publishing many articles on these topics.

Believing that some economic planning was necessary to a healthy economy, Rathenau he organized the German War Raw Materials Department at the beginning of World War I. Despite these activities, he pressed for an early settlement of hostilities. At war's end Rathenau joined the German government, serving on the socialization committee and as a technician at the Spa Conference on Disarmament. Accepting the new Weimar Republic, the republican regime that was created after Germany's defeat and which lasted until 1933, Rathenau was named to the Ministry of Reconstruction in 1921, a post through which he hoped to rebuild the German economy. He is known for coauthoring and signing in 1922 the controversial Treaty of Rapallo, an arms and weapons agreement between Germany and Soviet Russia. German racists, however, believed Rathenau to be part of an alleged Jewish conspiracy to take over the world. On June 24, 1922, two young nationalist fanatics murdered him.

Throughout his lifetime Rathenau was a patron of the arts and an author, publishing, among other works, five didactic volumes on philosophical and contemporary issues. Since his death, a steady stream of his publications have continued to appear. These include collected works, correspondence, and even the play *Blanche Trocard: Shauspiel in zwei Akten*. In 1974 a number of people interested in protecting Rathenau's intellectual legacy founded the Walther Rathenau Society.

BIOGRAPHICAL AND CRITICAL SOURCES:

BOOKS

Felix, David, *Walther Rathenau and the Weimar Republic: The Politics of Reparations*, Johns Hopkins Press (Baltimore, MD), 1971.

Joll, James, *Three Intellectuals in Politics*, Pantheon (New York, NY), 1961.

Kessler, Harry, *Walther Rathenau: His Life and Work*, translated by W. D. Robson-Scott and Lawrence Hyde, Harcourt (New York, NY), 1930, reprinted, AMS Press (New York, NY), 1975.

Loewenberg, Peter, *Walther Rathenau and Henry Kissinger: The Jew as a Modern Statesman in Two Political Cultures*, Leo Baeck Institute (New York, NY), 1980.

PERIODICALS

Judaism, summer, 1995, Carole Fink, "The Murder of Walther Rathenau," p. 259.

ONLINE

Walther Rathenau Society Web site, http://www.walther-rathenau.de/ (July 22, 2004).*

*   *   *

RAUBER, Paul

PERSONAL: Male.

ADDRESSES: Office—Sierra Club National Headquarters, 85 Second St., 2nd Fl., San Francisco, CA 94105.

CAREER: Journalist and author. *Sierra* magazine, senior editor; columnist for *East Bay Express*.

WRITINGS:

(With Carl Pope) *Strategic Ignorance: Why the Bush Administration Is Recklessly Destroying a Century of Environmental Progress*, Sierra Club Books (San Francisco, CA), 2004.

Contributor to periodicals, including *Sierra* and *East Bay Express*. Scriptwriter for film *Counting Sheep*.

SIDELIGHTS: Journalist and author Paul Rauber frequently writes on topics such as the environment, national politics, travel, and food. He worked for many years as a columnist for the California alternative weekly newspaper *East Bay Express*, then became a senior editor at *Sierra*, the national magazine of the Sierra Club. He has also worked with Green TV, writing the script for the film *Counting Sheep*, which tells the story of the Sierra Nevada, bighorn sheep.

In 2004, Rauber cowrote the book *Strategic Ignorance: Why the Bush Administration Is Recklessly Destroying a Century of Environmental Progress* with Carl Pope, the Sierra Club's executive director. In it the authors claim that the administration of President George W. Bush is responsible for deliberately neglecting environmental concerns in the United States. Rauber and Pope cite numerous examples to support their claim, as well as present ten solutions to heal the environmental damage they argue has been caused by the Bush administration.

Critics had much to praise about *Strategic Ignorance.* Some recognized the book's well-founded arguments as one major asset. "One might suspect that a Sierra Club book would be biased, but its arguments are well supported and logically presented, with few editorial asides or coaching," wrote Nancy Moeckel in a review for the *Library Journal.* Other critics noted the authors' ability not only to examine the big picture, but also to find and present the little things that factor into this environmental problem. "The real energy of the book comes from its accumulation of small facts to paint the picture," observed a *Publishers Weekly* contributor.

BIOGRAPHICAL AND CRITICAL SOURCES:

PERIODICALS

Booklist, May 1, 2004, Carol Haggas, review of *Strategic Ignorance: Why the Bush Administration Is Recklessly Destroying a Century of Environmental Progress,* p. 1528.

E, September-October, 2004, Katherine Hartley, "The Wrecking Crew," p. 62.

Library Journal, June 15, 2004, Nancy Moeckel, review of *Strategic Ignorance,* p. 93.

Publishers Weekly, March 29, 2004, review of *Strategic Ignorance,* p. 49; April 26, 2004, Judith Rosen, "Bushed," p. 29.

Sierra, September-October, 1993, Paul Rauber, "Coyotes and Town Dogs," p. 132; November-December, 1993, Paul Rauber, "Always Getting Ready," p. 104; May-June, 1994, Paul Rauber, "Not in Our Backyard," p. 82; September-October, 1994, Paul Rauber, "The Geography of Childhood," p. 78; November-December, 1994, Paul Rauber, "Fields of Greens," p. 100; September-October, 1995, Paul Rauber, "Losing Ground," p. 90.

ONLINE

GreenTV.org, http://greentv.org/ (February 10, 2005), "Paul Rauber."*

READING, Richard P(atrick) 1962-

PERSONAL: Born March 12, 1962, in Evanston, IL; son of Ronald R. and Mary (Nolan) Reading; married Lauren McCain (an environmentalist), August 3, 2001. *Education:* Trinity College (Hartford, CT), B.S. (biology), 1984; Yale University, M.S. (environmental studies), 1986, M.S. and M.Phil. (wildlife ecology), 1991, Ph.D. (wildlife ecology), 1993.

ADDRESSES: Home—1452 Hudson St., Denver, CO 80220. *Office*—Denver Zoological Foundation, 2900 E. 23rd Ave., City Park, Denver, CO 80205. *E-mail*—rreading@denverzoo.org; rreading@du.edu.

CAREER: Trinity College Department of Biology, Hartford, CT, independent researcher, 1985; New York Zoological Society, menagerie keeper, 1986-88; Northern Rockies Conservation Cooperative, research associate, 1988—; Bureau of Land Management, wildlife management biologist, 1991-94; Nature Conservation International, Berlin, Germany, research associate, beginning 1994; Denver Zoological Foundation, Denver, CO, director of conservation biology, 1996—. University of Denver, associate research professor, 1997—, affiliated faculty of animal sciences and biology, 1998-2002; University of Montana, affiliated faculty in School of Forestry, 2001—; Denver Museum of Nature and Science, research associate, 2002—. Consultant to Victoria, Australia, Department of Conservation and Natural Resources, 1991-94, UNDP/Global Environmental Fund and Mongolia Ministry for Nature and the Environment, 1994-95, and German Technical Advisory Group, 1995-97. Member, Lynx-Wolverine advisory team to Colorado Division of Wildlife, 1998-2001; scientific advisor, Southern Plains Lands Trust, Pritchett, CO, 1999—; member of board of directors, Argali Wildlife Research Center, Ulaanbaatar, Mongolia, 1999—, Southern Plains Land Trust, 2001-03, Predator Conservation Alliance, 2001—, Mongolian Conservation Coalition, 2001—, and Denver-Ulaanbaatar sister cities committee, 2003—; member, AZA Special Task Force on Science and Technology, 2000-03; scientific advisor, Center for Native Ecosystems, 2000—; member of board of trustees, Colorado-Mongolian Project Cultural and Education Exchanges, 2000-04; member, reintroduction and Caprinae groups of IUCN Species Survival Commission.

MEMBER: Society for Conservation Biology, Wildlife Society, American Association for the Advancement of

Science, American Institute of Biological Sciences, Natural Areas Association, Cenozoic Society, Large Herbivore Initiative.

AWARDS, HONORS: Yale University fellowship, 1988-93; Certificate of Appreciation, Ministry of Natural Resources and Environment (Victoria, Australia), 1997; Certificate of Appreciation, Colorado Division of Wildlife, 2001; E-chievement Award, E-Town Radio and Whole Food, 2003; Certificate of Appreciation, Southern Plains Land Trust (Pritchett, CO), 2003; grants from Chicago Zoological Society, Earthwatch, Edna Sussman Fund, National Fish & Wildlife Foundation, Trust for Mutual Understanding, U.S. Bureau of Land Management, and other organizations.

WRITINGS:

Black-footed Ferret Annotated Bibliography, 1986-1990, U.S. Department of the Interior, Bureau of Land Management, Montana State Office, 1990.

(Editor with TIm W. Clark and Alice L. Clarke) *Endangered Species Recovery: Finding the Lessons, Improving the Process,* Island Press (Washington, DC), 1994.

Latin-Mongolian-Russian-English-German Dictionary of the Vertebrate Species of Mongolia, Sukhbaatar Publishing House (Ulaanbaatar, Mongolia), 1995.

(With Brian Miller and Steve Forrest) *Prairie Night: Black-footed Ferrets and the Recovery of Endangered Species,* Smithsonian Institution Press (Washington, DC), 1996.

Protected Areas Rangers Training Manual, Mongolian Ministry for Nature and the Environment (Ulaanbaatar, Mongolia), 1996.

(Editor with Brian Miller) *Endangered Animals: A Reference Guide to Conflicting Issues,* Greenwood Press (Westport, CT), 2000.

Ecology and Conservation of Wild Bactrain Camels, Camelus bactrianus ferus, Mongolian Conservation Coalition & Admon Printing (Ulaanbaatar, Mongolia), 2002.

Contributor to periodicals, including *Journal of Phycology, Bulletin of Marine Science, Anthrozoös, Conservation Biology, Northern Rockies Conservation Cooperative News, Species, Zoo Review, Zoogoer, Reintroduction News, Endangered Species, Grasslands Gazette, CMS Bulletin,* and *Biological Conservation.* Contributor to books.

Author's works have been translated into Mongolian.

SIDELIGHTS: Richard P. Reading is currently the director of conservation biology at the Denver Zoological Foundation, in addition to his numerous other posts. As part of his work as a wildlife biologist, Reading has spend many years involved in the conservation issues surrounding the species and ecosystem in Mongolia. He is currently a major participant in the Mongolia Carnivore Project, a scientific research project studying the biology and conservation of meat-eating animals living in the grassland and semi-desert steppes of that region. The project studies the ecology, behavior, and community-level interactions among steppe carnivores with a goal of developing sufficient conservation measures to ensure the long-term survival of these creatures and preserve their native habitat.

Reading is the author or coeditor of several books, among them *Endangered Animals: A Reference Guide to Conflicting Issues.* Edited by Reading and colleague Brian Miller, the book seeks to raise awareness of the issues surrounding endangered species and the importance and impact of these pressing issues. The book presents specific case studies that provide an in-depth explanation of the species involved, including their history, threats, current status, and physical description. Erica B. Lilly, reviewing the book for the *Reference & User Services Quarterly,* commented that Reading "does an excellent job of updating similar early works that also describe endangered species," and added that the book's "strength is in the scholarly, yet fully accessible treatment of each species." Paul Haschak, writing in *Library Journal,* cited the book's comprehensive bibliography, and concluded of *Endangered Animals* that, "Although the number of animals is limited, this guide is recommended for academic libraries requiring more detailed, scholarly information" on specific species.

BIOGRAPHICAL AND CRITICAL SOURCES:

PERIODICALS

Booklist, January 1, 2001, review of *Endangered Animals: A Reference Guide to Conflicting Issues,* p. 1010.

Library Journal, February 15, 2001, Paul Haschak, review of *Endangered Animals*, p. 156.

Reference & User Services Quarterly, spring, 2001, Erica B. Lilly, review of *Endangered Animals*, p. 287.

ONLINE

Mongolia Carnivore Project Web site, http://www.wildcru.org/ (May 3, 2005).*

*   *   *

RÉAGE, Pauline
    See AURY, Dominique

*   *   *

RESNICOW, Herbert 1921-1997

PERSONAL: Born May 28, 1921, in New York, NY; died of congestive heart failure April 4, 1997, in Roslyn, NY; son of Isadore (a grocer) and Fannie Gold (a homemaker) Resnicow; married Melly Engelberg (a teacher), July 14, 1946; children: Norman, Eva, David, Ruth. *Education:* Attended Brooklyn College, 1937-38, and Cooper Union Institute of Technology, 1938-41; Brooklyn Polytechnic Institute, B.S. (civil engineering), 1947. *Politics:* Democrat. *Religion:* Jewish.

CAREER: Civil engineer and mystery writer. Architect, engineer, project manager, and builder of buildings in New York, NY, 1946-86; full-time writer, 1986-97. Also served as president or vice president of Narco Construction Corporation, HRB Holding Corporation, West View Hill Corporation, Harbinger Development Corporation, and Modular Technics Corporation. Temple Sholom, member of board of governors, 1953-54. *Military service:* U.S. Army Corps of Engineers, served overseas during World War II.

AWARDS, HONORS: Edgar Allan Poe Award nomination, Mystery Writers of America, 1984, for *The Gold Solution*.

WRITINGS:

MYSTERY NOVELS; "GOLD" SERIES

The Gold Solution, St. Martin's Press (New York, NY), 1983.
The Gold Deadline: A Whodunit, St. Martin's Press (New York, NY), 1984.
The Gold Frame: A Whodunit, St. Martin's Press (New York, NY), 1984.
The Gold Curse: A Whodunit, St. Martin's Press (New York, NY), 1986.
The Gold Gamble, St. Martin's Press (New York, NY), 1988.

MYSTERY NOVELS; "CROSSWORD" SERIES

Murder across and Down, Ballantine (New York, NY), 1985.
The Seventh Crossword, Ballantine (New York, NY), 1985.
The Crossword Code, Ballantine (New York, NY), 1986.
The Crossword Legacy, Ballantine (New York, NY), 1987.
The Crossword Hunt, Ballantine (New York, NY), 1987.
The Crossword Trap, Ballantine (New York, NY), 1988.

MYSTERY NOVELS; "BAER" SERIES

The Dead Room, Dodd Mead (New York, NY), 1987.
The Hot Place, St. Martin's Press (New York, NY), 1991.

OTHER MYSTERY NOVELS

(With Fran Tarkenton) *Murder at the Super Bowl*, Morrow, 1986.
(With Pelé) *The World Cup Murder*, Wynwood Press (New York, NY), 1988.
(With Tom Seaver) *Beanball*, Morrow (New York, NY), 1989.
(With Ed Koch) *Murder at City Hall*, Kensington Books (New York, NY), 1995.

Contributor to periodicals, including *Armchair Detective, MRA Journal,* and *Mystery and Detective Monthly.*

SIDELIGHTS: Mystery author Herbert Resnicow began writing fiction while working as an architect and engineer in the New York City area. He wrote his first novel, *The Gold Solution,* during a lonely period in the summer of 1982 when a building project prevented him from accompanying his wife on vacation. The novel, featuring brilliant but abrasive engineering consultant Alexander Magnus Gold, was nominated for an Edgar Allan Poe Award from the Mystery Writers of America and inspired further "Gold" novels. In 1986, then in his mid-sixties, Resnicow finally abandoned his demanding construction career to write fiction full-time, having already authored two additional "Gold" novels in his spare time.

Each of Resnicow's "Gold" novels centers upon the unnatural demise of a Manhattan cultural figure: a famous architect in *The Gold Solution;* a ballet dancer in *The Gold Deadline;* the director of an art museum in *The Gold Frame;* an opera star in *The Gold Curse;* and a Broadway actress in *The Gold Gamble.* In each case Gold, the engineer-turned-private eye, is assisted by Norma, his talkative and unusually tall wife.

The first installment of the "Gold" series was well received by critics. *Washington Post Book World* reviewer Jean M. White described *The Gold Solution* as "an engaging, light-hearted tale," concluding that "Resnicow writes brightly with bouncy humor." While the next installment, *The Gold Deadline,* was generally deemed an unworthy successor, the third and fourth novels in the series received better reviews. Commenting on *The Gold Frame* in *Armchair Detective,* Robert A. W. Lowndes wrote, "This is one of the finest puzzle-murder mysteries of recent times." In a review of *The Gold Curse,* a Toronto *Globe and Mail* critic observed that "the plot is well-crafted . . . and Resnicow makes good use of the inside world of opera." The final installment, *The Gold Gamble,* also received positive reviews. According to *Armchair Detective* critic Allen J. Hubin, *The Gold Gamble* is "a pleasantly amusing story of the cerebral (i.e., lots of talk about alibis and timing) variety."

In addition to his "Gold" books, Resnicow has authored a series of "Crossword" novels and two books based on the character Ed Baer. The "Crossword"

novels feature actual crossword puzzles in the story, each of which conceals a clue to the mystery and is integral to the narrative. The protagonist of Resnicow's "Baer" novels, *The Dead Room* and *The Hot Place,* is a widowed venture capitalist who, with his philosopher son Warren, solves the murder of an acoustical engineer in the first book and a country club executive in the second.

New York Times Book Review critic Newgate Callendar described *The Dead Room* as "a pleasant piece of work," while Hubin, again writing in *Armchair Detective,* concluded that it is "nicely entertaining." Commenting on *The Hot Place, Armchair Detective* reviewer Maria Brolley characterized the book as "a fun-to-read mystery," while a *Publishers Weekly* critic praised the novel as a "lively tale" with a "delightful" protagonist. However, a *Kirkus Reviews* critic found fault in the novel's "over-elaborate plot" and "repetitive, talky" narrative.

Resnicow has also collaborated with three professional sports stars—football quarterback Fran Tarkenton, Brazilian soccer great Pelé, and baseball pitcher Tom Seaver—and a New York political figure to produce murder mysteries relevant to his coauthors' respective backgrounds. For example, *Murder at the Super Bowl,* a book written with Tarkenton, centers on the murder of a championship football coach, while *Murder at City Hall,* written with former New York City mayor Ed Koch, involves Koch's role in solving a fictional murder that occurs at city hall while he is in office. Though reviewers dismissed *Murder at City Hall* as a crass exercise in self-promotion for Koch, critics found more to recommend in *Murder at the Super Bowl.* According to Callendar, again writing in the *New York Times Book Review,* Resnicow does "a thoroughly professional job" in translating Tarkenton's insider knowledge into a football thriller. As Callendar added, "thanks to Fran Tarkenton, there is a good deal of background information about football and football players that most readers will find of unusual interest." Commenting on the book in *Globe and Mail,* Margaret Cannon wrote, "It's not earth-shaking, but it's good clean fun—just like football used to be."

Resnicow once told *CA:* "My books are all classic whodunits, puzzle mysteries in which all clues are presented clearly at least twice. The murders are 'locked room' (i.e., impossible) crime problems in which howdunit and whydunit must be solved to find whodunit. Readers and reviewers claim that the lead characters in my books bear a suspicious resemblance to myself (I suffered a heart attack before I was forty-nine like Alexander Magnus Gold) physically and in personality. I hotly deny this and would like to point out that Alexander Magnus Gold is a quarter inch taller, and my wife, Melly, is only five inches taller, not seven."

BIOGRAPHICAL AND CRITICAL SOURCES:

PERIODICALS

Armchair Detective, summer, 1986, Charles Shibuk, review of *The Gold Frame,* p. 332; winter, 1987, Robert A. W. Lowndes, review of *The Gold Frame,* p. 91; spring, 1988, Allen J. Hubin, review of *The Dead Room,* p. 148; summer, 1990, Allen J. Hubin, review of *The Gold Gamble,* pp. 276-277; summer, 1991, Maria Brolley, review of *The Hot Place,* p. 346.

Booklist, September 15, 1988, review of *The Gold Gamble,* p. 123; September 15, 1995, Emily Melton, review of *Murder at City Hall,* p. 143.

Globe and Mail (Toronto, Ontario, Canada), August 30, 1986, review of *The Gold Curse;* November 22, 1986, Margaret Cannon, review of *Murder at the Super Bowl.*

Kirkus Reviews, November 1, 1984, review of *The Gold Frame,* p. 1024; May 1, 1987, review of *The Dead Room,* p. 680; August 15, 1988, review of *The Gold Gamble,* p. 1196; December 1, 1990, review of *The Hot Place,* p. 1643.

New York Times Book Review, November 27, 1983, review of *The Gold Solution;* November 16, 1986, Newgate Callendar, review of *Murder at the Super Bowl,* p. 38; August 2, 1987, Newgate Callendar, review of *The Dead Room,* p. 29; October 30, 1988, Marilyn Stasio, review of *The Gold Gamble,* p. 28.

Publishers Weekly, October 26, 1984, review of *The Gold Frame,* p. 98; May 8, 1987, review of *The Dead Room,* p. 64; August 19, 1988, review of *The Gold Gamble,* p. 61; November 16, 1990, review of *The Hot Place,* p. 48; July 24, 1995, review of *Murder at City Hall,* p. 49.

Washington Post Book World, November 20, 1983, Jean M. White, review of *The Gold Solution,* pp. 10-11.

West Coast Review of Books, Volume 13, number 2, 1987, review of *The Dead Room,* p. 27.

OBITUARIES

PERIODICALS

New York Times, April 12, 1997, p. 28.*

*   *   *

RIOTTA, Gianni 1954-

PERSONAL: Born 1954, in Palermo, Italy; married; children: two. *Education:* University of Palermo (philosophy), 1975; Columbia University, M.S. (journalism), 1984.

ADDRESSES: Home—New York, NY, and Turin, Italy. *Agent*—c/o Author Mail, Farrar, Straus and Giroux, 19 Union Square W., New York, NY 10001.

CAREER: Novelist and journalist. RAI (Italian public radio), New York, NY, host of *Un Certo Discorso,* 1983, host of *Milano-Italia* (talk show) for RAI 3, 1993-94; *La Stampa,* special correspondent in Rome, Italy, 1986-88, coeditor in Turin, Italy, 1998—; *Corriere della Sera* (Italian daily), correspondent and columnist, including in New York, NY, 2002. Founded monthly magazine *Global* and online European magazine *Golem.*

AWARDS, HONORS: Fulbright fellow; Florio prize, 2002, for *Prince of the Clouds.*

WRITINGS:

(With Michele Melillo) *Le interviste del manifestoa,* preface by Rossana Rossanda, Cooperativa "Manifesto 80" (Rome, Italy), 1983.

Ultima dea, Feltrinelli (Milan, Italy), 1994.

Ombra: un capriccio Veneziano, Rizzoli (Milan, Italy), 1995.

Principe delle nuvole (novel), Rizzoli (Milan, Italy), 1997, translation by Stephen Sartarelli published as *Prince of the Clouds,* illustrated by Matteo Pericolil, Farrar, Straus, and Giroux (New York, NY), 2000.

N.Y. undici Settembre: diario di duna guerra, Einaudi (Turin, Italy), 2001.
Alborada, Rizzoli (Milan, Italy), 2002.

Contributor to periodicals *Washington Post, Le Monde, Foreign Policy, La Vanguardia,* and others.

SIDELIGHTS: Italian journalist and author Gianni Riotta has had a distinguished career in the Italian press and is considered an expert on America due to his longtime position as a U.S. correspondent for several Italian newspapers and other publications. His family is based in New York, but he often travels between the United States and Italy, where he has been coeditor of *La Stampa* since 1998. Riotta is also an accomplished novelist who has also written short stories and a collection of essays on the aftermath of the September 11, 2001, terrorist attacks in New York City and Washington, D.C.

Although his novels are well known in Italy and other parts of Europe, Riotta remained largely unknown in the United States until the publication of *Prince of the Clouds,* his first novel to be published in English. According to Riotta, he first developed his idea for the novel about a soldier who believes the rules of war can be applied to life while covering a small coup in a small island in the Caribbean, where he and fellow reporters ended up in an ambush.

In *Prince of the Clouds* Riotta examines love, life, and war as he tells the story of Carlo Terzo, a colonel in the Italian army during World War II. Although he did not see battle during the war, Terzo sets out to write a "Manual for Strategic Living" based on his premise that the rules of war and principles of military history apply equally to day-to-day life. As Terzo works on his book following the war, he becomes more and more enmeshed in the nonmilitary life, marrying a countess from Russia who ends up dying from cancer and becoming entangled in the forbidden and doomed romance of two students he is tutoring. Terzo also becomes involved in a communist rally that turns violent and in which he finally takes a position of command and uses his knowledge of warfare to help resolve the situation. Although he has faced personal crisis and tragedy, Terzo remains committed to his work; and, as pointed out by *World Literature Today* contributor Rufus S. Crane, it has "rescued him and made him a survivor, thereby establishing its worth."

Writing in the *Seattle Times,* Alix Wilber noted that, "Though *Prince of the Clouds* is firmly rooted in reality, a shimmer of magic envelops it. There is something reminiscent of *The Arabian Nights* in the way Riotta weaves gripping details of great historical battles into the fabric of his modern-day story." Michael Pye, writing in the *New York Times Book Review,* noted that the book has some "didactic pretensions and some deeply irritating devices at the end," but added that the book "also has life and substance." A *Publishers Weekly* contributor commented that "this lofty but poignant and seductive novel ambitiously distills tragic romance, political conflict and military history into one man's struggle to draw wisdom from the mistakes and triumphs of the past."

BIOGRAPHICAL AND CRITICAL SOURCES:

PERIODICALS

New York Times Book Review, May 21, 2000, Michael Pye, review of *Prince of the Clouds,* p. 21.
Publishers Weekly, May 1, 2000, review of *Prince of the Clouds,* p. 50.
World Literature Today, winter, 2001, Rufus S. Crane, review of *Prince of the Clouds,* p. 160.

ONLINE

Camden Conference 2004 Web site, http://camden conference.org/ (July 14, 2004), "Gianni Riotta."
Encyclopedia Multimediale delle Scienze Filosofiche Online, http://www.emsf.rai.it/ (July 14, 2004), "Gianni Riotta."
Seattle Times Online, http://seatletimes.nwsource.com/ (June 6, 2000), Alix Wilber, review of *Prince of the Clouds.**

*   *   *

ROBERTS, John Stuart 1939(?)-

PERSONAL: Born c. 1939.

ADDRESSES: Agent—c/o Author Mail, Metro Publishing Ltd., 19 Gerrard St., London W1V 7LA, England.

CAREER: Formerly head of television department at British Broadcasting Corp. (BBC) Wales.

WRITINGS:

Siegfried Sassoon, Richard Cohen (London, England), 1998.

Editor, *Everyman* and *Heart of the Matter.*

SIDELIGHTS: John Stuart Roberts chronicles the life of a celebrated British poet from World War I in the biography *Siegfried Sassoon.* Sassoon came from a privileged background, the child of a Jewish businessman and an artistic English mother. Although the family had wealth, it did not ensure a happy childhood for Sassoon. His parents's marriage did not last long, and Sassoon's mother was left to raise three boys on her own. She was extremely protective of them and strove to keep them at home as much as possible. According to Elizabeth Lowry in the *Times Literary Supplement,* "Roberts's account of Sassoon's sheltered boyhood and youth, written in commendably clear prose punctuated by moments of quiet humour, makes poignant reading."

Sassoon began writing poetry at a very young age. When he entered combat in World War I and came face to face with the horrors of war, he was forever changed. His powerful poetry describes the grim realities of that conflict, looking beyond nationalities and ideologies to show that war desecrates humanity on all sides. Sassoon was nearly killed in the trenches, but survived, to be haunted by the war for the rest of his life. He became restless, eventually lost his focus as a poet, and took up a frenetic social life. Reporting on this period, Roberts "descends, through no fault of his own, into a bathetic saga of weekend parties, long lunches, vapid dinners, silly soirees, random jaunts around the country, literary in-fighting (it seems that Sassoon had survived the war chiefly in order to bicker with the Sitwells) and humiliating homosexual entanglements," reported Lowry. Eventually, the poet seemed to find some peace in his conversion to Roman Catholicism. Lowry concluded, "This is an immensely readable biography which is made even more moving by having a truly tragic subject." Discussing his book in an interview with Michele Fry for the *Counter-Attack* Web site, the author stated that he

hoped to "elucidate"Sassoon's life rather than to bring out every sensational detail of the writer's socializing. Roberts commented: "Of course you can be sensational and sell a million copies, but that, to my mind, is not what biography is about."

BIOGRAPHICAL AND CRITICAL SOURCES:

PERIODICALS

Guardian (Manchester, England), July 3, 1999, Stephen MacDonald, review of *Siegfried Sassoon,* p. 9.
Spectator, June 26, 1999, Nicholas Harman, review of *Siegfried Sassoon,* p. 33.
Times Literary Supplement, August 20, 1999, Elizabeth Lowry, review of *Siegried Sassoon,* pp. 4-5.

ONLINE

Counter-Attack Web site, http://www.sassoonery.demon.co.uk/ (April 10, 2005), Michele Fry, interview with John Stuart Roberts.*

*   *   *

ROLL, Eric 1907-2005
(Lord Roll of Ipsden)

OBITUARY NOTICE— See index for *CA* sketch: Born December 1, 1907, in Nova Sulita, Austria-Hungary (now Ukraine); died March 30, 2005. Economist, civil servant, banker, and author. Roll was a former economics professor and government undersecretary who played a key roll in the post-war Marshall Plan and advocated that Britain join the European Economic Union. Born in a town on the foothills of the Carpathian mountains, he immigrated to England, where he earned a bachelor's degree from the University of Birmingham in 1928 and a Ph.D. there two years later. Not long afterward he joined the University of Hull faculty as a professor of economics and commerce. He remained there until 1946, though during World War II he also part of a British Food Mission responsible for distributing food from America to Europe. Entering government service in 1946 as an assistant secretary for the Ministry of Food, he was involved in the landmark Marshall Plan that helped save post-war Europe from starvation and economic collapse. A series of other government posts followed, including undersecretary for economic planning in the treasury department in 1948; head of the United Kingdom's delegation to NATO meetings in Paris in 1952; under-secretary of the Ministry of Agriculture, Fisheries, and Food from 1953 to 1957; deputy leader for negotiations for the European Economic Community from 1961 to 1963; economics minister and head of his country's treasury delegation to Washington, D.C., from 1963 to 1964; and undersecretary of state to Britain's newly formed Department of Economic Affairs from 1964 to 1966. In this last position, Roll attempted to move Britain out of its economic inertia, away from the "Old Labor" mindset, and into a more international frame of mind. He felt that the country should join with the rest of Europe to form a stronger economic unit with a shared currency. Retiring from the civil service in 1966, Roll applied his economics knowledge to banking, serving as director of the Bank of England from 1968 to 1977 and as deputy chair, chair, and eventually president of S. G. Warburg & Co. from 1967 to 1995. For his service to his country, Roll—who was also chancellor of the University of Southampton from 1974 to 1984—was made a companion of the Order of the Bath in 1956, a knight commander of St. Michael and St. George in 1962, and a life peer in 1977. He was the author of several books on economics and the history of economics, including *A History of Economic Thought* (1938; fifth edition, 1992), *The Uses and Abuses of Economics, and Other Essays* (1978), and *Where Are We Going? The Next Twenty Years* (2000).

OBITUARIES AND OTHER SOURCES:

PERIODICALS

Guardian (Manchester, England), April 2, 2005, p. 21.
Times (London, England), April 1, 2005, p. 63.

ONLINE

New Economist Online, http://neweconomist.blogs. com/ (April 3, 2005).
Telegraph Online, http://www.telegraph.co.uk/ (April 1, 2005).

ROMAN, Lawrence 1921-

PERSONAL: Born May 30, 1921, in Jersey City, NJ; son of Irving (a grocer) and Bessie Dora (Roud) Roman; married Evelyn Mildred Zirkin, April 29, 1946; children: Steven, Catherine. *Education:* University of California, Los Angeles, B.A., 1943.

ADDRESSES: Home—4097 Sapphire Dr., Encino, CA 91436.

CAREER: Playwright and screen writer.

MEMBER: Writers Guild, Dramatists Guild, Producers Guild.

AWARDS, HONORS: Peabody Award, for *The Ernest Green Story.*

WRITINGS:

PLAYS

Under the Yum-Yum Tree (produced on Broadway, 1960; also see below), Dramatists Play Service (New York, NY), 1961.
P.S. I Love You, produced on Broadway, 1965.
Buying Out, produced in Buffalo, NY, 1970.
Crystal, Crystal Chandelier, produced in Stockbridge, MA, 1972.
Alone Together, (produced on Broadway, 1984), Doubleday (Garden City, NY), 1983.

Also author of *If! If! If!,* 1979; *Grapes and Raisins* (also known as *Moving Mountains); To Tell the Truth; Coulda, Woulda, Shoulda,* first produced in Berlin, Germany; *A Hearty Welcome,* produced in Bonn, Germany; and *Make Me a Match,* produced in Hamburg, Germany and Canada.

SCREENPLAYS, EXCEPT AS INDICATED

Vice Squad, United Artists, 1953.
(With John K. Butler) *Drums across the River,* Universal, 1954.
(With others) *Naked Alibi,* Universal, 1954.

One Desire, Universal, 1955.

(With others) *The Man from Bitter Ridge,* Universal, 1955.

A Kiss before Dying, United Artists, 1956.

(With others) *The Sharkfighters,* United Artists, 1956.

Slaughter on Tenth Avenue, Universal, 1957.

(With John W. Cunningham) *Day of the Bad Man,* Universal, 1958.

Under the Yum-Yum Tree (adaptation of his play), Columbia Pictures, 1963.

The Swinger, Paramount Pictures, 1966.

Paper Lion (adaptation of the book by George Plimpton), United Artists, 1968.

(With others) *Soleil Rouge,* National General Pictures, 1971.

A Warm December, National General Pictures, 1973.

(And producer) *McQ,* Warner Brothers, 1974.

The Ernest Green Story (teleplay), Disney Channel, 1991.

Also author of screenplays *The Mayflower Number, Abracadabra, Skeletons, Lovers Three, Three Wishes for Jamie,* and *Final Verdict.* Author of teleplays, including *Omar Bradley: A Soldier's Story,* 1981; *Anatomy of an Illness* (based on the book by Norman Cousins), 1982; and *Badge of the Assassin* (based on the book by Robert Tanenbaum).

SIDELIGHTS: Lawrence Roman has had a long and prestigious career in theater and films. His plays have been produced in the United States and Europe, and he adapted his Broadway hit *Under the Yum-Yum Tree* into a film starring Jack Lemmon. John Wayne starred in Roman's original screenplay *McQ,* and Sidney Poitier had the lead in 1973's *A Warm December.* Roman also adapted George Plimpton's *Paper Lion* for the screen.

Roman wrote the script for the television movie adaptation of *Anatomy of an Illness,* the autobiography of *Saturday Review* editor Norman Cousins. In the film, Cousins (played by Ed Asner) suffers from a crippling illness that does not respond to treatment, and he embarks on his own holistic regime that includes high doses of vitamin C and a diet of fresh vegetables prepared by his wife (Millie Perkins). His doctor (Eli Wallach) goes along with his wishes, believing that it cannot hurt, and the story ends with Cousins returning to work, healthy and happy.

Alone Together, Roman's 1980s Broadway production, starred Janis Paige and Kevin McCarthy as parents whose adult sons have returned to the nest just as they are about to enjoy life after thirty years of raising children. Among Roman's more recent efforts is his screenplay *The Ernest Green Story,* which aired on the Disney Channel. It is set in Little Rock, Arkansas, during the turbulent period following the *Brown v. Board of Education* Supreme Court decision, when nine black high school students transferred to that city's all-white Central High School. Ernest Green (Morris Chestnut), the first black student to graduate from Central, is the focus of the film, which also stars Ruby Dee, Ossie Davis, and Avery Brooks. Rod Granger wrote in *Multichannel News* that *The Ernest Green Story* "is a compelling look at the atmosphere of hate surrounding those students and the bravery they evidenced to right a historical wrong."

BIOGRAPHICAL AND CRITICAL SOURCES:

PERIODICALS

Chicago Sun-Times, September 12, 1985, Lynn Voedisch, review of *Alone Together,* p. 70.

Multichannel News, December 21, 1992, Rod Granger, review of *The Ernest Green Story,* p. 9.

New York Times, May 15, 1984, John J. O'Connor, review of *Anatomy of an Illness;* October 22, 1984, Frank Rich, review of *Alone Together.*

*   *   *

ROSEN, Marvin 1933-

PERSONAL: Born March 5, 1933, in New York, NY; son of Samuel (a clothing manufacturer) and Sophie (a homemaker) Rosen; married Joyce Barron (a nurse and marketer) May 19, 1988; children: Jacqueline, Betsy, Michael, Jennifer. *Education:* University of Massachusetts, B.A., 1956; University of Pennsylvania, M.A., 1958; University of Pennsylvania, Ph. D., 1961. *Religion:* Jewish. *Hobbies and other interests:* Writing, gardening, hiking.

ADDRESSES: Home—462 Meetinghouse Ln, Media, PA 19063. *E-mail*—docmarv_2000@yahoo.com.

CAREER: Psychologist. Albert Einstein Hospital, psychologist, 1961-62; University of Pennsylvania, Philadelphia, instructor in psychology, 1962-63; Elwyn Institute, Elwyn, PA, clinical psychologist, 1963-2002; Interboro School District, administrator and vice president, 2003—. *Military service:* U.S. Army Reserve, 1957-63.

MEMBER: American Psychological Association.

AWARDS, HONORS: Research award, American Association of Mental Retardation.

WRITINGS:

(Editor with Gerald R. Clark and Marvin S. Kivitz) *The History of Mental Retardation: Collected Papers,* University Park Press (Baltimore, MD), 1976.

(With Gerald R. Clark and Marvin S. Kivitz) *Habilitation of the Handicapped: New Dimensions in Programs for the Developmentally Disabled,* University Park Press (Baltimore, MD), 1977.

Notes and Blots from a Psychologist's Dest, Nelson-Hall (Chicago, IL), 1978.

(With Edwin D. Arsht) *Psychological Approaches To Family Practice: A Primary-Care Manual,* University Park Press (Baltimore, MD), 1979.

(Editor with Marie Skodak Crissey) *Institutions for the Mentally Retarded: A Changing Role in Changing Times,* PRO-ED (Austin, TX), 1986.

Treating Children in Out-of-Home Placements, Haworth Press (New York, NY), 1998.

(With Walter Rosen and Beth Allen) *Welcome to Junior's: Remembering Brooklyn with Recipes and Memories from Its Favorite Restaurant,* Morrow (New York, NY), 1999.

(Consulting editor) Michele Alpern, *The Effects of Job Loss on the Family,* Chelsea House (Philadelphia, PA), 2002.

(Consulting editor) Heather Lehr Wagner, *Dealing with Terminal Illness in the Family,* Chelsea House (Phildelphia, PA), 2002.

(Consulting editor) Heather Lehr Wagner, *The Blending of Foster and Adopted Children into the Family,* Chelsea House (Philadelphia, PA), 2002.

(Consulting editor) Michele Alpern, *Teen Pregnancy,* Chelsea House (Philadelphia, PA), 2002.

Dealing with the Effects of Rape and Incest, Chelsea House (Philadelphia, PA), 2002.

Understanding Post-Traumatic Stress Disorder, Chelsea House (Philadelphia, PA), 2003.

The Effects of Stress and Anxiety on the Family, Chelsea House (Philadelphia, PA), 2003.

(Consulting editor) Sara L. Latta, *Dealing with the Loss of a Loved One,* Chelsea House (Philadelphia, PA), 2003.

(Consulting editor) Michele Alpern, *Overcoming Feelings of Hatred,* Chelsea House (Philadelphia, PA), 2003.

(Consulting editor) Michele Alpern, *Let's Talk: Sharing Our Thoughts and Feelings during Times of Crisis,* Chelsea House (Philadelphia, PA), 2003.

The ABC's of Love, 1st Books (Bloomington, IN), 2004.

Demystifying Dreams, i-Universe (Lincoln, NB), 2004.

Meditation and Hypnosis, Chelsea House (Philadelphia, PA), 2005.

Sleep and Dreaming, Chelsea House (Philadelphia, PA), 2005.

Contributor to periodicals, including *Journal of the American Academy of Child and Adolescent Psychiatry.*

WORK IN PROGRESS: Sleep and Dreaming and *Hypnosis and Meditation,* both for Chelsea House Publishers.

SIDELIGHTS: Marvin Rosen is a licensed clinical psychologist who has authored several works that focus on the psychological effects of a changing society. Educated at Cornell University and the University of Pennsylvania, Rosen interned at the V.A. Hospital at Perry Point, Maryland. He worked as a child psychologist at the Albert Einstein Hospital in Philadelphia and then began a thirty-eight-year career at Elwyn, Inc. in Elwyn, Pennsylvania. In addition to maintaining a private practice in psychology, Rosen was principal investigator during a lengthy follow-up study of persons who left the institution for independent living, started a pre-school language program for at-risk three and four year olds, directed a head trauma program, and helped develop a program for emotionally disturbed youngsters in out-of-home placements. While at Elwyn, Rosen authored or edited several textbooks.

Retiring in January of 2002, Rosen quickly decided that the retiree lifestyle was not for him. He returned to work part-time as a school psychologist at Interboro

School District in Delaware County, Pennsylvania. In addition to serving as consulting editor for several books by other authors, he has also penned books such as *Dealing with the Effects of Rape and Incest* and *Understanding Post-Traumatic Stress Disorder,* both of which are geared toward a young-adult readership.

Rosen lives with his wife Joyce in Media, Pennsylvania, fifteen miles south of Philadelphia, where he is the proud father of four married children and several grandchildren.

BIOGRAPHICAL AND CRITICAL SOURCES:

PERIODICALS

School Library Journal, October, 2002, Libby K. White, review of *Dealing with the Effects of Rape and Incest,* p. 193.

*   *   *

ROSTENBERG, Leona 1908-2005

OBITUARY NOTICE— See index for *CA* sketch: Born December 28, 1908, in New York, NY; died of heart problems March 17, 2005, in New York, NY. Bookseller and author. A rare book dealer, Rostenberg is best remembered for being the co-discoverer of the risqué stories published pseudonymously by Louisa May Alcott. After graduating from New York University in 1930, she completed her Ph.D. work at Columbia University, but her dissertation was rejected. Because of this, Rostenberg could not teach at the university level, and she therefore worked for book dealer Herbert Reichner for ten years. Close friend Madeleine Stern encouraged her to open her own used book store, and she finally did so in 1944. Stern and Rostenberg became partners the next year, opening Leona Rostenberg & Madeleine Stern Rare Books. The friends traveled around Europe, finding unique books and bringing them back to their store for sale. They also spent a great deal of time researching authors in the library. It was during one of their research trips that Rostenberg discovered a letter from a publisher to Louisa May Alcott requesting more of her racy stories, which she had been publishing under

the pen name A. M. Barnard. Further digging revealed that Alcott wrote stories involving violence, drugs, and other unsavory practices in order to help support her family. In 1943, Rostenberg broke the news about these unknown stories by the beloved author of the genteel *Little Women* in the journal *Papers of the Bibliographical Society of America.* Her partner, Stern, also used this information in her 1950 biography of Alcott and a 1975 collection of edited stories. Rostenberg, on the other hand, continued publishing academic books, such as *English Publishers in the Graphic Arts, 1599-1700: A Study of the Print-Sellers and Publishers of Engravings, Art and Architectural Manuals, Maps, and Copy-Books* (1963) and *An Antiquarian's Credo* (1976). These works eventually convinced Columbia University to at last award her a Ph.D. in 1973. With Stern, she also published several works about old and rare books, as well as two autobiographical works about herself and Stern: *Old Books, Rare Friends: Two Literary Sleuths and Their Shared Passion* (1997) and *Bookends: Two Women, One Enduring Friendship* (2001).

OBITUARIES AND OTHER SOURCES:

PERIODICALS

Los Angeles Times, March 31, 2005, p. B11.
New York Times, March 24, 2005, p. C22.
Washington Post, April 2, 2005, p. B6.

*   *   *

ROTH, John D. 1960-

PERSONAL: Born 1960, in Holmes County, OH; married Ruth Miller; children: Sarah, Leah, Hannah, Mary. *Education:* University of Chicago, Ph.D., 1989. *Religion:* Mennonite.

ADDRESSES: Office—Department of History, Goshen College, 1700 South Main St., Goshen, IN 46526.

CAREER: Goshen College, Goshen, IN, professor of history, 1988—, and director of Mennonite Historical Library.

WRITINGS:

(Editor) *Engaging Anabaptism: Conversations with a Radical Tradition,* Herald Press (Scottdale, PA), 2001.
Choosing against War: A Christian View, Good Books (Intercourse, PA), 2002.

Editor, *Mennonite Quarterly Review.*

WORK IN PROGRESS: A history of European Mennonites in the seventeenth and eighteenth centuries.

BIOGRAPHICAL AND CRITICAL SOURCES:

PERIODICALS

Booklist, August, 2002, Steven Schroeder, review of *Choosing against War: A Christian View,* pp. 1894-1895.

ONLINE

Goshen College Web site, http://www.goshen.edu/ (August 19, 2002), "Advocating Pacifism Post-9/11: Roth Book Explains Christian Peace Movement."*

* * *

ROTHOLZ, James M. 1951-

PERSONAL: Born September 25, 1951, in Colorado Springs, CO; son of Max B. (a bank president) and Mary Louise (Kirkpatrick) Rotholz; married Louise Penniman (a certified public accountant), 1979; children: Abigail Michal, Jesse. *Ethnicity:* "Scots-Irish/German Jew." *Education:* Attended University of Texas, 1969-71; Gordon College, B.A., 1977; Washington State University, M.A. (cultural anthropology), 1992, Ph.D. (cultural anthropology), 1995. *Politics:* "Independent." *Religion:* Protestant. *Hobbies and other interests:* Walking, camping, travel, culture study.

ADDRESSES: Agent—c/o Author Mail, Haworth Press, Inc., 21 East Broad St., Hazleton, PA 18201. *E-mail*—jmrotholz@aol.com.

CAREER: Consortium of North American Christian Colleges, post-earthquake reconstruction volunteer in Guatemala, 1976; World Concern, relief and development worker in Somalia, 1981-82; United Mission to Nepal, water systems coordinator, 1984-85; Food for the Hungry International, country director for Ethiopia, 1989-91; Washington State University, assistant professor of anthropology, 1996; writer, 1996—.

WRITINGS:

Chronic Fatigue Syndrome, Christianity, and Culture: Between God and an Illness, Haworth Press (Hazleton, PA), 2002.

Contributor to books, including *Stricken: Voices from the Hidden Epidemic of Chronic Fatigue Syndrome,* edited by Peggy Munson, Haworth Press (Hazleton, PA), 2000. Contributor to periodicals, including *CFIDS Chronicle, Practicing Anthropology,* and *Trumpeter: Journal of Ecosophy.*

WORK IN PROGRESS: *Walking the Spirit: Embracing Life as a Spiritual Journey.*

SIDELIGHTS: James M. Rotholz told *CA:* "I have wondered many times exactly what motivates me to write, in that writing is such a vexing affair for me. Simply put, my language skills are ill suited to the task of providing adequate form to the wide array of inspiring thoughts that run swirling through my head. Certainly a complete inventory of motivational impulses runs deeper than I can peer with the conscious mind. Yet lurking somewhere in the thick of things lies an inescapable compulsion to communicate to others some truth regarding life, and to do it in such a way as to offer a fresh and, hopefully, illuminating perspective. To reach for such a lofty goal, I attempt to combine a personal and experiential approach along with a cultural and religious perspective. Those are the perspectives that have shaped my world view and continue to give rise to whatever uniqueness my writing may represent.

"I first seriously took up writing in response to a chronic illness. I needed to wrestle with the life-changing issues involved, and to form some kind of coherent framework around which to build my then-shattered life. It worked . . . to a degree. But the framework remains unfinished, and the writing goes on. Life, unlike words on a page, never completely succumbs to neatly arranged units, and I, as every other sentient being, must continually renegotiate who, what, and where I am in the greater scheme of things. That fact, and the permanent tensions that exists between lived experience and the formal theories that attempt to explain it, means that the final word on any topic will never be written. Yet the unexplained challenges of life are precisely what motivate me to continue writing. It is an ongoing quest to probe, understand, and inspire. The more I do of it, the more forcefully I realize just how inadequate I am to the task. It's not that my literary inadequacies are so overwhelming a problem, but that the inestimable riches of life are far too extensive and too sublime to allow me to do more than shine a dim light on a vast and wondrous landscape that beckons human exploration.

"I have never read that much. It's an unfortunate habit I retain from my youth, reinforced by poor health and a dimming wit. Yet, most likely for that very reason I have drawn tremendous inspiration from those notable works I have encountered; namely, the Russian masters Tolstoy and Dostoevsky, the incomparable Europeans Blake, Pascal, and Kierkegaard, and the American literary giants Whitman, Thoreau, and Twain. More contemporary authors who have greatly influenced and inspired me are Malcolm Muggeridge, Henri Nouwen, Edward O. Wilson, and Annie Dillard. Each has been remarkably successful in doing what I can only feebly aspire to—capturing in words something of the brilliance of life that perpetually flashes all about."

BIOGRAPHICAL AND CRITICAL SOURCES:

PERIODICALS

Townsend Letter for Doctors and Patients, July, 2003, Jule Klotter, review of *Chronic Fatigue Syndrome, Christianity, and Culture: Between God and an Illness,* p. 26.

*   *   *

ROUGHAN, Howard

PERSONAL: Married; wife's name, Christine; children: Trevor. *Education:* Dartmouth College, graduated, 1988.

ADDRESSES: Home—Weston, CT. *Agent*—c/o Author Mail, Warner Books, 1271 Avenue of the Americas, New York, NY 10020.

CAREER: Writer. Former advertising executive, New York, NY.

WRITINGS:

NOVELS

The Up and Comer, Warner Books (New York, NY), 2001.
The Promise of a Lie, Warner Books (New York, NY), 2004.
(With James Patterson) *Honeymoon,* Little, Brown and Co. (New York, NY), 2005.

ADAPTATIONS: The Up and Comer was adapted for audio, read by Frank Whaley, Time Warner, 2001, and as an electronic book.

SIDELIGHTS: Howard Roughan's debut novel, *The Up and Comer,* features Philip Randall, an attorney who is destined for partnership in a prestigious Manhattan firm and whose wife, Tracy, comes from a wealthy Greenwich, Connecticut family. Philip spends most of his time defending criminals and some of his time sleeping with Jessica, his mistress. Philip's "perfect" life is strained, however, when old prep school chum Tyler Mills comes to town and, after spying on Philip, decides to blackmail his former friend over the affair. However, Philip will do anything to ward off threat to his lifestyle.

Harriet Klausner wrote in an *AllReaders.com* review that *The Up and Comer* "is a forceful thriller that succeeds because the key characters come across as human" and "Roughan is clearly an up and coming author worth following." *Publishers Weekly* contributor Jeff Zaleski also praised Roughan's characterizations, writing that "auxiliary characters, particularly Philip's robust boss, Jack Devine, and Jack's kind, innocuous wife, Sally, are well-drawn and convincing, adding the depth and humanity necessary to counteract Philip's almost robotic duplicity." *Booklist* critic Mary Frances Wilkens considered the story "fast moving and involving; mercifully, Philip emerges as at least partially sympathetic in the end."

The protagonist of *The Promise of a Lie* is psychologist David Remler, author of a book that explains why people commit unexpected crimes. David's book was propelled up the best-seller lists when he gave expert testimony in the case of a rabbi accused of murder that resulted in the rabbi's conviction. David's new patient, Samantha Kent, tells him she is so afraid of her Wall Street businessman husband that she has thoughts of killing him. After their second session, she calls David and tells him she has done just that. David rushes to their apartment, where he finds the body, but no Samantha. The police discover a knife missing from the victim's kitchen in David's apartment, a match to one found at the murder scene. David has no alibi, and since he failed to notify the police before going to the apartment, he becomes the main suspect. He is shocked when he discovers that the woman claiming to be Samantha is actually an imposter. David, who is being framed by the woman impersonating the real Samantha Kent, then goes on trial.

Library Journal critic Ronnie H. Terpening felt that the courtroom scenes in *The Promise of a Lie* are responsible for developing the story into "an engrossing read that's hard to put down." A *Publishers Weekly* contributor called Roughan's novel "smoothly written, briskly paced and nicely constructed, with surprises that are genuinely startling," while *Booklist* critic David Pitt dubbed it "compulsively readable. . . . A smart, thoroughly engaging thriller."

BIOGRAPHICAL AND CRITICAL SOURCES:

PERIODICALS

Booklist, May 1, 2001, Mary Frances Wilkens, review of *The Up and Comer,* p. 1640; March 1, 2004, David Pitt, review of *The Promise of a Lie,* p. 1143.
Entertainment Weekly, June 8, 2001, Thom Geier, review of *The Up and Comer,* p. 71.
Library Journal, March 1, 2004, Ronnie H. Terpening, review of *The Promise of a Lie,* p. 109.
Publishers Weekly, April 30, 2001, Jeff Zaleski, review of *The Up and Comer,* p. 50; February 9, 2004, review of *The Promise of a Lie,* p. 57.

ONLINE

AllReaders.com, http://www.allreaders.com/ (July 8, 2004), Harriet Klausner, reviews of *The Up and Comer* and *The Promise of a Lie.**

RUSSERT, Tim(othy) 1950-

PERSONAL: Born May 7, 1950, in Buffalo, NY; son of Tim (a sanitation foreman and truck driver) Russert; married Maureen Orth (a writer); children: Luke. *Education:* Graduate of John Carroll University and Cleveland-Marshall College of Law.

ADDRESSES: Office—NBC News, 30 Rockefeller Plaza, New York, NY 10112. *E-mail*—mtp@msnbc.com.

CAREER: Journalist and attorney. U.S. Senate, Washington, DC, special counsel, 1977-82; Office of the Governor, Albany, NY, counsel, 1983-84; National Broadcasting Corporation (NBC), began in 1984, managing editor and moderator of *Meet the Press,* 1991—, political analyst for *NBC Nightly News* and *Today,* anchor of *The Tim Russert Show* (CNBC), contributing anchor for MSNBC, and senior vice president and Washington bureau chief of NBC News. Trustee of Freedom Forum's Newseum; member of board of directors, Greater Washington Boys and Girls Club and America's Promise-Alliance for Youth; lecturer.

AWARDS, HONORS: Fatherhood awards include Father of the Year, National Father's Day Committee, 1995, Dream Dad, *Parents,* 1998, and Father of the Year, National Fatherhood initiative, 2001; Joan S. Barone Award, Radio and Television Correspondents, and Walter Cronkite Award, Annenberg Center, 2000, for interviews with presidential nominees George W. Bush and Al Gore; Edward R. Murrow Award (shared), 2001, for overall excellence in television; named the best and most influential journalist in Washington, DC, *Washingtonian,* 2001; John Peter Zenger Award; American Legion Journalism Award; Congressional Medal of Honor Society Journalism Award; Allen H. Neuharth Award for excellence in journalism; David Brinkley Award for excellence in communication; recipient of dozens of honorary doctorates.

WRITINGS:

(With Bill Novak) *Big Russ and Me: Father and Son; Lessons of Life* (memoir), Miramax/Hyperion (New York, NY), 2004.

SIDELIGHTS: Tim Russert is a television journalist whose role as host of the popular Sunday morning talk show *Meet the Press* has made him one of the country's most influential political commentators. *Esquire* contributors Tom Carson and Barry Sonnenfeld wrote that Russert has come to play the role that was previously occupied by news giants Ted Koppel, Sam Donaldson, and Dan Rather: "A decade into his tenure there," they said, "Russert is widely regarded as the capital's toughest inquisitor, the journalist who asks the hard questions and doesn't let anyone off the hook. Yet one reason Russert never makes the powers that be squirm, except individually, is that he's refereeing a game whose rules he's eager to endorse, playing a time-honored role in Washington media culture." Earlier in his career, in 1985, Russert arranged for an unprecedented live broadcast of Pope John Paul II for the *Today* show. In 1986 and 1987 he led news teams that broadcast from South America, Australia, and China.

Russert was born into an Irish-Catholic working-class family in South Buffalo, New York. He was educated by Jesuits and nuns, served as an altar boy, and was greatly influenced by the adults in his life, most notably by his father, who, as he notes in his memoir *Big Russ and Me: Father and Son; Lessons of Life,* continues to be a guiding light. A *Kirkus Reviews* contributor wrote that "Russert, the kid from blue-collar South Buffalo who now grills the prominent and powerful, writes in a style as unadorned as the snow in the land of the Bills."

Time critic John F. Dickerson noted that "some grown men have trouble embracing their fathers in public. Russert hugs his for twenty-one chapters in *Big Russ and Me . . .* , a memoir that is part tribute to his dad and part guidebook for the author's college-age son, Luke." A high-school dropout, Big Russ served in World War II and returned home to work for the sanitation department during the day and drive a newspaper truck at night. Young Russ also worked for the sanitation department during the summer and was the first in his family to graduate from college. He later went on to earn a law degree, and he worked on the staffs of politicians Daniel Patrick Moynihan and Mario Cuomo.

America writer Terry Golway noted that *Big Russ and Me* is the "sort of literary work that some of us have been longing for—a book in which nuns and priests

actually inspire the young people in their charge. It is also a portrait of a chapter in American life that now seems as distant as the Jazz Age." Russert writes that religion was a vital part of his home life and schooling. Crosses hung above beds, grace was said at meals, and during May, the Virgin Mary's month, his mother would honor her each day with a candle and fresh flowers from the garden. Golway said, "I suspect that not many memoirs from powerful Washington figures recall with such love and affection these rituals of a Catholic childhood, circa 1960. That's what makes this book so genuinely sweet and likeable—there's not a dishonest page in it."

Appraising Russert's influence within the sphere of mainstream journalism, *New Yorker* writer Nicholas Lemann commented: "Russert probably holds the distinction of being the journalist whose work Washington talks about most obsessively. . . . Russert performs a journalistic function on *Meet the Press* in the sense that he peppers officials with questions, but even if you don't live in Washington it's obvious that he's a bigger deal than most of his guests. His role is that of a luminous fixed star in political space, around whom other bodies must orient themselves."

BIOGRAPHICAL AND CRITICAL SOURCES:

BOOKS

Russert, Tim, and Bill Novak, *Big Russ and Me: Father and Son; Lessons of Life* (memoir), Miramax/Hyperion (New York, NY), 2004.

PERIODICALS

America, June 7-14, 2004, Terry Golway, review of *Big Russ and Me: Father and Son; Lessons of Life,* p. 22.
Booklist, March 1, 2004, Vanessa Bush, review of *Big Russ and Me,* p. 1099.
Esquire, January, 2004, Tom Carson and Barry Sonnenfeld, "The Daunting Guy: There Was Koppel and, before Him, Donaldson and Rather. Now It's Russert Who Is Reputed to Have the Power to Sway Elections and Afflict the Comfortable," p. 48.
Kirkus Reviews, March 15, 2004, review of *Big Russ and Me,* p. 263.

Library Journal, July, 2004, Katherine E. Merrill, review of *Big Russ and Me,* p. 94.

New Yorker, May 24, 2004, Nicholas Lemann, review of *Big Russ and Me,* p. 82.

People, May 17, 2004, Eric Felten, review of *Big Russ and Me,* p. 49.

Publishers Weekly, April 5, 2004, Jerome Joseph Gentes, "From *Meet the Press* to Meet the Parent" (interview), p. 54; May 24, 2004, Daisy Maryles, review of *Big Russ and Me,* p. 24.

Sports Illustrated, May 24, 2004, Richard Deitsch, interview with Russert, p. 24.

Time, May 24, 2004, John F. Dickerson, review of *Big Russ and Me,* p. 83.

ONLINE

Meet the Press Online, http://msnbc.msn.com/ (July 8, 2004), "Tim Russert."*

S

SADIE, Stanley (John) 1930-2005

OBITUARY NOTICE— See index for *CA* sketch: Born October 30, 1930, in Wembley, Middlesex, England; died of amyotrophic lateral sclerosis March 21, 2005, in Cossington, England. Editor, music critic, and author. Sadie is best remembered as the editor responsible for *The New Grove Dictionary of Music and Musicians,* a volume considered the bible in its field. A Cambridge University alumnus, he earned his B.A. and Mus.B. in 1953, followed by a master's degree in 1957 and a Ph.D. in 1958. During his early career, Sadie was a music critic for the London *Times,* and was also a lecturer at the Trinity College of Music from 1957 to 1965. Leaving teaching behind, he became an editor for the *Musical Times* in 1967 and remained there through 1987. Sadie made his distinctive mark on music history after accepting the job of editor for the sixth edition of Grove's dictionary of music. Tracing its roots back to the nineteenth century, when the reference book was first compiled by Sir George Grove, the dictionary still focused on western music of the eighteenth and nineteenth centuries at the time Sadie took over. Sadie, however, had more ambitious plans. Heading a team of dozens of researchers and writers, he compiled and contributed to an expanded, twenty-volume resource that contains entries on music and musicians from all over the world, and includes modern musical forms such as pop and jazz. The changes were so extensive that the dictionary was re-christened *The New Grove Dictionary of Music and Musicians* (1980). Sadie continued work on this project for many years, issuing a second edition in 2001 that encompasses twenty-nine volumes. He also edited such guides as *The History of Opera* (1990), the four-volume *The New Grove Dictionary of Opera* (1992), and *The Billboard Illustrated Encyclopedia of Classical Music* (2000). In addition to his editorial work Sadie, whose favorite period was the eighteenth century, was the author of works about composers, such as *Handel* (1962), *Mozart* (1966), *Beethoven* (1967), and *Handel Concertos* (1972). Named a commander of the Order of the British Empire in 1982, his interest in music history also led to his role in preserving Handel's home in London. At the time of his death, Sadie had just completed a book about the early life of Mozart.

OBITUARIES AND OTHER SOURCES:

PERIODICALS

Los Angeles Times, March 27, 2005, p. B12.
New York Times, March 23, 2005, p. A20.
Times (London, England), March 23, 2005, p. 61.
Washington Post, March 24, 2005, p. B6.

*   *   *

SANDOVAL, Lynda 1965(?)-
(Lynda Sue Cooper)

PERSONAL: Born c. 1965; married (a police officer), 1994. *Education:* Earned B.S., 1994. *Hobbies and other interests:* Quilting, hiking, gardening, making jewelry.

ADDRESSES: Home—P.O. Box 62080, Littleton, CO 80162-0901; and P.O. Box 1915, Wheat Ridge, CO 80034. *E-mail*—lynda@lyndasandoval.com.

CAREER: Writer. Wheat Ridge Police Department, Wheat Ridge, CO, police officer, 1991-98; currently works part time as an emergency medical dispatcher, Littleton, CO, police and fire departments.

AWARDS, HONORS: Rising Star, Golden Quill, and Beacon awards, all from regional chapters of Romance Writers of America, all 2002.

WRITINGS:

ROMANCE NOVELS

Unguarded Hearts, Kensington Publishing (New York, NY), 1999.
Unsettling, HarperCollins Rayo (New York, NY), 2004.
One Perfect Man, Silhouette Books (New York, NY), 2004.
And Then There Were Three, Silhouette Books (New York, NY), 2004.
Borderline Personalities, HarperCollins Rayo (New York, NY), 2004.

"THREE AMIGAS" SERIES; ROMANCE NOVELS

Look of Love, Kensington Publishing (New York, NY), 1999.
Dreaming of You, Encanto (New York, NY), 2000.
One and Only, Kensington Publishing (New York, NY), 2001.
Thief of Hearts, Encanto (New York, NY), 2001.

Dreaming of You was translated into Spanish.

OTHER

(As Lynda Sue Cooper) *True Blue: An Insider's Guide to Street Cops for Writers,* Gryphon Books for Writers (Memphis, TN), 1999.
Who's Your Daddy? (young adult), Simon Pulse (New York, NY), 2004.

Author of numerous articles; contributor to *Border-Line Personalities: A New Generation of Latinas Dish on Sex, Sass, and Cultural Shifting,* edited by Robyn Moreno and Michelle Herrera Mulligan.

WORK IN PROGRESS: Romance novels tentatively titled *Chicks Ahoy, Hooked!, Hidden Truths,* and *The Premonition Mission.*

SIDELIGHTS: Lynda Sandoval is a romance writer who worked as a police officer for several years before turning to writing full time in 1998. In an interview with Robin Vidimos for the *Denver Post,* she related, "I actually think being a police officer parallels being a writer because there are long stretches of not much happening punctuated by exciting events." One of Sandoval's earliest books, in fact, was not a romance novel but a guide for writers called *True Blue: An Insider's Guide to Street Cops for Writers.*

For the most part, Sandoval focuses on romance novels, which are often set within the Hispanic-American community, such as the four books in her "Three Amigas" series. In the first book in the series, *Look of Love,* scientist Esme Jaramillo is invited to appear on television's *Barry Stillman Show* to talk about her work in gene cloning. The shy Esme, however, is shocked to learn that the show's makeup artist, Gavino Mendez, has altered her looks because she is actually on an episode devoted to beauty make-overs for ugly bookworms. Esme tromps off stage and goes into semi-seclusion. Gavino, who developed a rapport with Esme while doing her makeup, feels guilty and goes to Colorado to find Esme and apologize. Esme shows reluctance at first to let Gavino into her life after he finds her, but she eventually rents him an apartment over her garage, leading to a love affair. Writing on *AllReaders.com,* a reviewer noted that *Look of Love* "is a classic Cinderella story, but written so beautifully and with such wonderful characters that you don't even care."

Also in the series, *One and Only* tells the story of Danny and Pilar Valenzuela, childhood sweethearts who married early. Danny is a cop who works long hours to support his family, but Pilar is unhappy with the constant demands of her husband's job. When he comes home from work one day, he finds his bags packed; Pilar wants him to leave. The ensuing story shows how both Danny and Pilar look at their life and their marriage and what needs to be changed to make it work. Writing on *EscapetoRomance.com,* Deborah Barber observed, "This isn't a book with great depth . . . but I believe that if you are looking for a book of conflict and compassion, this is a great little read."

Thief of Hearts, the fourth book in the "Three Amigas" series, features a ladies man named Isaias Pacias who rescues elementary schoolteacher Graciela Inez Obregon from a car accident. Graciela, who used to be a "party girl," decides to hunt down Isaias a year after the accident to thank him personally for rescuing her. Meanwhile, Pacias thinks that she is dead and the accident has changed his life, leading him to study to be an emergency medical technician. Pacias now learns through a newspaper article that Graciela is searching for her "Samaritan Soulmate." Eventually, the two get together and a romance evolves. "Both characters evolve in ways that are solid and believable," according to Vidimos. In a review on the *All about Romance* Web site, Heidi L. Haglin praised Sandoval for creating realistic secondary characters, going on to call *Thief of Hearts* "an excellent book, and a touching love story about refreshingly real characters."

In *Unsettling* Sandoval once again turns to her experience as a cop to write about Lucy Olivera, a Denver drug officer who is tough on the streets but afraid of personal commitments, largely because her family believes that its women are all cursed with failed first marriages. Marrying a fellow cop named Ruben, Lucy flees from their wedding reception and goes on a road trip with three friends to find a medicine woman who can lift the curse she believes will ruin her marriage. During the trip, each of the four friends face and come to terms with their own inner demons. Writing in the *Washington Post,* Pamela Regis commented, "In classic road-trip fashion, each confronts her fears in a sometimes panic-stricken, often hilarious trek." *BookLoons.com* reviewer Rashmi Srinivas felt that the tone of the book "is overwhelmingly Latino, with all the corresponding spiciness. Overall, this is one of those tales that leaves readers feeling satisfied, happy, and richer."

Sandoval turns from romance to the young-adult audience with *Who's Your Daddy?,* a story about three sixteen-year-old friends who are social outcasts at their school. They are also without boyfriends, largely because of their fathers' occupations, which include being a cop and a famous jazz musician. The three girls get together and search for love by conducting a Celtic ritual called the "Dumb Supper." Eventually, they each meet a boy who is a potential date for their junior prom. Sandoval tells the stories from the perspective of each of the girls through alternating viewpoint chapters. The storyline is also revealed in the form of the instant messages and e-mails the girls send to each other. "Overall this is a charming, warm story, if not especially innovative," according to a *Publishers Weekly* contributor. Lynn Evarts, writing in *School Library Journal,* commented that "The lessons get a bit heavy-handed . . . but teenagers will respond to the unfairness of parental punishments and the unpredictability of love." More enthusiastic, *Kliatt* contributor Stephanie Squicciarini dubbed *Who's Your Daddy?* a "laugh-out-loud novel" and said "Sandoval is an author to watch."

BIOGRAPHICAL AND CRITICAL SOURCES:

PERIODICALS

Denver Post, August 11, 2002, Robin Vidimos, "Romance Genre a Springboard for Ex-Cop," p. EE02.
Kliatt, September, 2004, Janis Flint-Ferguson, review of *Who's Your Daddy?,* p. 26; January, 2005, Stephanie Squicciarini, review of *Who's Your Daddy?,* p. 17.
Publishers Weekly, September 16, 2003, John F. Baker, "Rayo Preempts Latina Cop's Book," p. 14; May 31, 2004, review of *Unsettling,* p. 52; December 20, 2004, review of *Who's Your Daddy?,* p. 60.
School Library Journal, January, 2005, Lynn Evarts, review of *Who's Your Daddy?,* p. 126.
Washington Post, July 11, 2004, Pamela Regis, review of *Unsettling,* p. T13.

ONLINE

All about Romance Web site, http://www.likesbooks.com/ (March 8, 2005), Heidi L. Haglin, review of *Thief of Hearts.*
AllReaders.com, http://www.allreaders.com/ (March 8, 2005), reviews of *Look of Love* and *Unsettling.*
BookLoons.com, http://www.bookloons.com/ (March, 2005), Rashmi Srinivas, review of *Unsettling.*
eReader.com, http://www.ereader.com/ (March 8, 2005), "Lynda Sandoval."
EscapetoRomance.com, http://www.escapetoromance.com/ (March 8, 2005), Deborah Barber, review of *One and Only.*
Romance Reader Web site, http://www.theromancereader.com/ (March 8, 2005), Cathy Sova, interview with Sandoval.*

SARAH, Robyn 1949-

PERSONAL: Born October 6, 1949, in New York, NY; daughter of Leon Lipson and Toby (Palker) Belkin; married Fred Louder (a graphic designer and printer), 1970 (divorced); married D. R. Cowles (a photographer), 1991; children: (first marriage) two. *Education:* McGill University, B.A., 1970, M.A., 1974; Conservatoire de Musique du Quebec, Concours Diploma in clarinet, 1972.

ADDRESSES: Home—Montreal, Quebec, Canada.

CAREER: Villeneuve Publications, Montreal, Quebec, co-founder, 1976, publisher, 1976-87. Member of English faculty at Champlain Regional College, 1975-2000.

WRITINGS:

POETRY

Shadowplay, Fiddlehead Poetry Books (Fredericton, New Brunswick, Canada), 1978.

The Space between Sleep and Waking, Villeneuve Publications (Montreal, Quebec, Canada), 1981.

Three Sestinas, Villeneuve Publications (Montreal, Quebec, Canda), 1984.

Anyone Skating on That Middle Ground, Vehicle Press (Montreal, Quebec, Canada), 1984.

Becoming Light, Cormorant Books (Dunvegan, Ontario, Canada), 1987.

The Touchstone: Poems New and Selected, Anansi (Concord, Ontario, Canada), 1992.

Questions about the Stars, Brick Books (London, Ontario, Canada), 1998.

A Day's Grace, Porcupine's Quill (Erin, Ontario, Canada), 2003.

SHORT STORIES

A Nice Gazebo, Véhicule Press (Montreal, Quebec, Canda), 1992.

Promise of Shelter, Porcupine's Quill (Erin, Ontario, Canada), 1997.

Robyn Sarah

OTHER

Contributor to anthologies, including, *Canadian Poetry Now: Twenty Poets of the '80s,* edited by Ken Norris, Anansi, 1984; *The New Canadian Poets, 1970-1985,* edited by Dennis Lee, McClelland & Stewart, 1985; *Best Canadian Stories '86,* edited by Helwig and Martin, Oberon, 1986; *More Stories by Canadian Women,* edited by Sullivan, Oxford University Press, 1987; *Fifteen Canadian Poets X 2,* edited by Geddes, Oxford University Press, 1988; *Poetry by Canadian Women,* edited by Sullivan, Oxford University Press, 1989; *The Journey Prize Anthology 6,* McClelland & Stewart, 1993; *Fifteen Canadian Poets X 3,* edited by Gary Geddes, Oxford University Press, 2001; *Poetry: An Introduction,* edited by Michael Meyer, Bedford/St. Martin's, 2001; *The Bedford Introduction to Literature: Reading, Thinking, Writing,* edited by Michael Meyer, Bedford/St. Martin's, 2002; *Contemporary Jewish Writing in Canada,* edited by Michael Greenstein, University of Nebraska Press, 2004; and *The Norton Anthology of Poetry,* edited by Margaret Ferguson, Mary Jo Salter, and Jon Stallworthy, W. W. Norton, 2005. Contributor to periodicals, including *Books in Canada, Canadian Forum, Malahat Review, Threepenny Review, Poetry, New England Review, Hudson Review, North American Review,* and *New Quarterly.* Columnist for Gazette Books, 2000-01.

SIDELIGHTS: Although writer Robyn Sarah was born in New York, her parents were Canadian, and shortly after she was born, the family returned to Canada. Sarah—her name is a pseudonym—has lived in Montreal since 1953, and she began publishing her poetry in periodicals while finishing her studies at McGill

University. According to *Literary Montreal Online,* Sarah is "considered one of Canada's finest poets." She was the co-founder of a small press, Villeneuve Publications, based in Montreal, which published some of her own titles, as well as books by August Kleinzahler and A. F. Moritz, among others. She has written articles on education and literacy for Canadian newspapers, as well as book reviews and a regular column, "Poetic License" for Gazette Books from 2000 through 2001.

In an online interview with Stephen Brockwell for *Poetics.ca,* Sarah discussed the changes her poetry has made over the years. "I am almost entirely a creature of impulse," the poet explained of her varied output, "and my artistic choices are most often intuitive, unconscious, or stumbled-on, always very much 'of the moment.'" In discussing her themes with Brockwell, Sarah commented, "The passage of time has been my primary theme, as a poet, ever since *The Space between Sleep and Waking.*" In a review of *A Day's Grace* for the *Association of English-language Publishers of Quebec Web site,* Bert Almon commented that "Sarah's poems heft some weighty emotions. . . . Such poems, disconsolate or joyful, are indeed little machines that move the heart."

Sarah once told *CA:* "I think the music of words, the sound and rhythm of them, is above all what informs my writing, whether it is poetry or fiction. My poems most often germinate from a combination of words—a phrase, maybe a line or two—with a sound that pleases me. I call these 'tinder words.' The rest of the poem evolves from them, sometimes at once, sometimes months or years later."

AUTOBIOGRAPHICAL ESSAY: Robyn Sarah contributed the following autobiographical essay to *CA:*

A WRITER IN THE MAKING

How does one tell the story of one's life? Where does one begin? "I was born" would seem the obvious point of departure, but is it the real beginning? I was born in New York City on October 6, 1949. But that blunt fact conceals more than it reveals about who I am.

A few years ago, I came across a quote from the writings of Hannah Arendt which struck me forcefully and has continued to resonate as I contemplate my life. It was this: *"The history of any given personality is far older than the individual as a product of nature, begins long before the individual's life, and can foster or destroy the elements of nature in his heritage. Whoever wants aid and protection from History, in which our insignificant birth is almost lost, must be able to know and understand it."*

I have come to understand that historical forces are, to a much greater degree than I could ever have guessed as a young woman, responsible for who I am. History, "in which our insignificant birth is almost lost", engineered the coming-together of forbears whose genetic material I would inherit; forces of history directed the passage of those individuals through geography; histories determined the cultural environment of the communities that received me (one more post-war Baby Boom baby) in my allotted place and time. The language I speak, the language whose literature provided my inspiration as a writer, the attitudes, beliefs, habits and assumptions—even some of the quirks of character that I call my own—are all to a greater or lesser degree accidents of history. As my New York City birth was an accident of history, during what was only a brief sojourn there for my Canadian parents.

My mother was several months pregnant with me when my father was accepted into graduate school at Columbia University. Before I turned three they were back in Canada, but I brought with me the advantage of dual citizenship. This may well have been at the back of my parents' minds in choosing an American university. Both of them children of immigrants, first in their families to attend university at all, they were keenly aware of their own life advantages. Children of the Depression, young Jews whose high-school years were marked by watching the world go to war with Hitler, they might have had the thought that if one New World citizenship was good for a Jew, two would be even better.

Another of my life advantages—namely, that my mother tongue is English, the world's dominant language—I owe not only to my grandparents' having emigrated (in the wake of the First World War) from eastern Europe to Canada in the 1920s, but to a particular phase in Quebec history. In bicultural Montreal where my mother's parents settled, there were two main linguistic communities and two school boards: a French Catholic one that did not admit Jewish students, and an English Protestant one that welcomed them. So my mother was educated and socialized in English and assimilated, as a first new-generation Canadian, to Quebec's smaller but then-dominant Anglo community. But times and agendas change. Since the late 1970s, Quebec's protectionist language laws have obliged new immigrants (except those who were themselves educated in English) to send their children to French schools, thereby ensuring that the new generation assimilates to the province's French-language community (a majority in Quebec, a minority in Canada). In Montreal in the 1980s, even as a longstanding Quebec resident, I had to produce documentation to prove I had been educated in English in order for my own children to be permitted to attend English schools.

I have few and hazy memories of my earliest childhood, the not quite three years when, with my young parents, I lived in New York City. We were domiciled at first on an island in the East River called North Brother, in apartment housing reserved for married WWII veterans who were pursuing higher education in the city. My father took a ferry to get to school, and one of my earliest memories is of watching tugboats on the river, which we could see from our windows. I remember the roof of our later apartment building at the corner of 119th and Amsterdam, where I used to play while my mother hung the washing; I remember being carried down stone steps from the street into the subway, where it seemed suddenly to be nighttime, and some while later emerging up similar stairs to the surprise of sunshine and day again. Strange to say, after we returned to Canada I was not to visit New York again until well into my fourth decade, but whenever I go there, I see things that look hauntingly familiar. I have tried to find where we lived—the building near campus was called Laureate Hall—but it apparently no longer exists. And North Brother Island, which became a rehab center for drug addicts after we left, eluded me for years; no New Yorker I asked could tell me which island it was. A recent Internet search explained why: apparently the island was abandoned in the mid-1950s and allowed to revert to wilderness. I have learned that the building complex we lived in once formed part of a hospital for contagious diseases, that the island also housed a tuberculosis sanatorium (vacant when we lived there), and that for thirty years it was the enforced home of Typhoid Mary, who died there.

My parents met in Montreal on the *McGill Daily,* early in 1946. My mother, two years ahead of my father in

The author's parents, Toby and Leon, at Toby's McGill University graduation dance, 1947. They had just broken off their engagement.

her undergraduate program, was night editor of the university paper while he, in her words, was "just a lowly cub reporter." A latecomer to university, he was fresh out of the Royal Canadian Air Force; a monthly allowance from the Department of Veterans' Affairs allowed him to study full time. His parents, like my mother's, had come to Canada in the 1920s—his from the Ukraine (he was born in Kiev) and hers from Galicia (Poland). His had settled in Ottawa, where his mother had relatives and his father set up shop as a tailor.

Does everyone romanticize their parents' courtship? I always thought my parents' story so romantic. They were, from all I have gathered, deeply in love; they were thwarted in their wish to marry when my mother graduated. Her parents were strongly opposed, had hoped for better for their only daughter than a tailor's son, and believed in any case that they were too young, that they would not be able to manage financially on his Veterans' Allowance and should wait at least until he finished school. In deference, my mother broke off the engagement, but the unhappy pair soon got secretly re-engaged. My father applied for a transfer to the University of British Columbia to finish his B.A., and the two of them hatched a new plan. He would hitch-hike to Vancouver in July, scout out work, put things in order for his school year, and find them a place to live. My mother meanwhile would take shorthand courses, work, and save money toward a train ticket to join him in the fall. She would tell her parents she wanted to take a trip to get over him. They would marry as soon as she arrived: essentially, it was elope-ment in installments. To conceal the fact that they were still in contact, she rented a post office box where she could receive his letters in secret.

And wonderful letters he wrote her, almost daily for a period of nearly five months, all the way across Canada and then from Vancouver as he established himself. He wrote about his rides, about Canada's spectacular changing scenery as he traveled west, about people he met, about his dreams and high hopes for their shared future. His letters were filled with post-war optimism, with the excitement of the road and of embarking on a new life, as they were filled, too, with love and longing and impatience to have her with him. En route across the country, he would stop in towns and cities, check in at the local Y to shower, shave, do laundry, catch up on sleep, and write to my mother. And the whole while, he was also scribbling away at short stories (whose plots he described in his letters), for my father had literary ambitions, and was hoping to write some stories he could sell while wait-ing to resume his studies. On arrival in Vancouver, he found lodging in the Veterans' residence area of UBC, took on a job as carpenter's assistant, and immediately checked his first two books out of the university library: *The Contemporary Short Story* and *Breaking into Print.*

By the time my mother joined him in late November, their secret was out: shortly before her departure, they agreed to break the news to their families. My mother's parents, days before they were to see their only child off on a solo journey to the far end of the continent, were so relieved to know someone was wait-ing for her in Vancouver that, tardily, they gave the marriage their blessing. After a four-day train ride, my mother was reunited with her impatient fiancé, and on

November 24, 1947, the two were married at Hillel House on the campus of UBC. As UBC's first-ever campus wedding, it was covered by the local press as well as by the university paper, the *Ubyssey.*

If I linger on the subject of this courtship and of my father's letters, it is because those letters, now in my possession, are most of what I know of my father. The cruel ending to my parents' idyll came not even six years later, when he was killed in a car crash while homeward bound to Ottawa after a short trip to Toronto. He was thirty, working for the Canadian government, and close to completing his Ph.D. in international law at Columbia. My mother was twenty-seven. I was a few months short of my fourth birthday, and my brother, born in Ottawa, was not yet three months old.

*

The impact of my father's death on all of our lives is something I can hardly measure. My parents had just bought a home in Ottawa, a semi-detached cottage, jointly with my father's brother and his wife who had already moved into their half. When my Ottawa grandmother, devastated by the death of her firstborn, said she did not feel she could take on daytime care of two small children at her age, my mother, with some bitterness, sold her half of the new house and moved back to Montreal. Her parents gave up their apartment, and together they found and rented, on Côte Ste. Catherine Road, an upper duplex large enough to share. There they set up house and my mother went out to work. My Montreal grandmother, "Granny," became primary caregiver to my brother and me, and we lived as one family until shortly after my mother remarried, four years later.

Those childhood years when my grandparents lived with us—the "Silverman years" we called them, after the landlord couple who lived in the lower duplex—are where my remembered childhood begins, and they remain extraordinarily vivid in memory to this day. I would not have thought this to be the case for my brother, who was three and a half years younger than I. But in 1990, at my grandmother's funeral, when I asked him if he could remember those years at all, he said, "Those years are the only part of my childhood that I do remember."

In my fifties at this writing, I'm amazed that my grandmother, fifty-three at the time of my father's

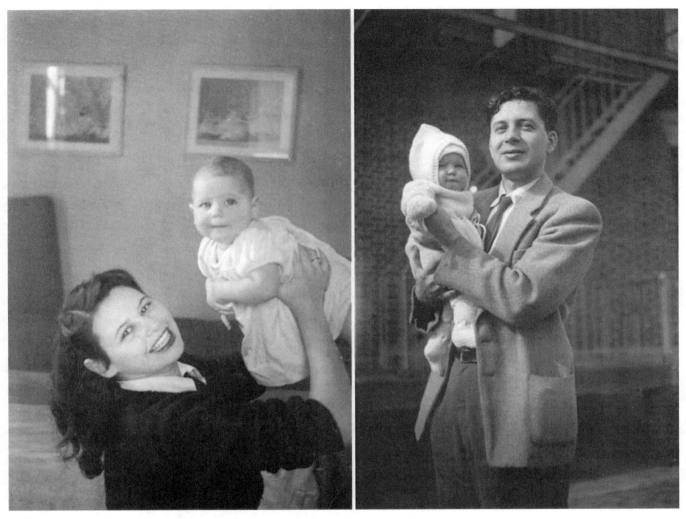

Robyn as a baby, with her mother (left) and father (right), North Brother Island, New York, 1950

death, found the stamina to take on the job. Not only was she past the half-century mark: she was frail. A survivor of tuberculosis (TB) in the 1930s, she had undergone several operations to collapse portions of both lungs, and the slightest exertion left her short of breath; the single flight of stairs to our upper was taxing, she had to take the steps a few at a time. But take on the job she did, with vigor and finesse, as though it were the most natural thing in the world. In the last year of her life she once remarked to me, "Do you know, all those years at Silverman's, I took only one vacation? Once only, I went away for two weeks; to the country, to a friend. Not a weekend, not a day off, in nearly five years! And it was I who did everything. When your mother came home from work, she wanted you children to be finished with your supper, bathed, already in pajamas—everything done, so she could relax with her dinner and then play with

you, read to you before bed. So I made two suppers, I cleaned up twice, first for you and your brother, then for your mother and my husband." It startled me to hear she had taken a two-week vacation: I could not remember her ever being away. And it startled me more, all those decades later, to realize that she might have longed for a day off, might have had other wants, other relationships. Her life had seemed to exist, with her blessing, entirely for our service.

Just as cataclysms of history send their shock waves through the life of a generation, so cataclysms of personal history send shock waves through individual lives. I was born in the wake of two world wars, waves that had quieted, yet still brushed my life in ways I would not understand until much older. Our three-generation household, our little ark, carried that baggage as well as the baggage of personal cataclysm.

(Left) The author, age four, with her brother and grandmother, Montreal, 1953. (Right) The author's grandmother in 1958

My father's death, a childhood given for me and my brother, was the central trauma of my life though I did not know it as such then; its aftershocks would hit me later, in waves, through all succeeding phases of my life, sometimes recognized for what they were, sometimes not. But more immediate for me in those years were past traumas in the lives of my mother and grandmother.

For my mother, to be suddenly widowed so early in her marriage must have echoed the central trauma of her own early childhood: namely, having her mother suddenly taken from her life, not to return for a full eight years. That is the length of time my grandmother spent incarcerated in the Mount Sinai Sanatorium in the Laurentians. For my grandmother, the trauma was to be stricken with TB at age thirty-one: losing the best years of life, as she used to put it, to a deadly

(and stigmatized) disease. But the worst of it was the forced separation from her only child, five years old at the time she got sick. There was, for my grandmother, a bittersweet irony to the burden of childcare that my father's death thrust upon her later years. The childhood years she missed out on with her own child were in a sense given back to her in me, the granddaughter who came to live with her at almost the same age as the daughter she had to leave. And my infant brother was given to her keeping as if in lieu of the son she had been denied.

My grandfather was a shy and laconic man who worked long hours (at that time, a six-day week) as a cutter in a clothing factory. When home, he disappeared behind the Yiddish newspapers. He was not a strong presence in my life. But my grandmother ran a tight ship and was in many ways the perfect parent to my brother and me: more patient than any young mother could have been, supremely gentle and tender, watchful and responsive, cajoling our compliance rather than commanding it. Not only did she never raise her voice or lift a hand to us, she made it clear that she valued and enjoyed our company. The three of us were a little society. Through the myriad small daily rituals and ministrations, she talked to us, told us stories, asked us questions, encouraged us to express ourselves. She shared whatever she saw, whatever she loved: she would call us to the window to see the sunset, or the moon rising, or Jack Frost patterns on the glass; would show us how every snowflake was six-sided and each one was different; would point out to us the beauties of the deep red Indian rug on the floor in her room, in whose intricate design she said she could find something new every day.

My knowledge of the world expanded its borders as I took in the stories of my Granny's life—above all stories of her blissful early childhood in what she called the Old Country, where she was the middle child with two older brothers and two younger sisters, loving parents, and a grandfather she adored. But stories about her adult life in Canada often came to an abrupt end with the words, "Then I got sick." As if a giant's foot had come down upon her life. I heard about the terrible sickness called TB, and about The San, the big hospital in the mountains where she had to live, "like being in jail," for eight years. Health, I heard over and over again, was the only thing worth wishing for in life, "because without our health, it's no good to have anything else."

Every childhood is full of mystery, and every childhood has a dark underside, sensed in spite of all efforts to make nice. The dark underside of my childhood was threefold. There was the TB, whose impact was still palpable in that household. There was the death of my father, whose name was almost never spoken; a silence about my father. And there was the Nazi Holocaust, which had not yet been given that name and was never mentioned around me, but which had claimed the lives of one of my grandmother's sisters and at least one brother. This was a second silence, the silence about the war and my grandmother's family. Perhaps I should not say it was a silence. The language of our little home was primarily English, but between themselves, the grown-ups often spoke in Yiddish, a language I did not learn. No effort was made to teach it to me, and I believe I

must have sensed that whatever it was they were talking about in that language, it was something I did not want to know.

In 1953, when we moved in to Silverman's, my grandmother still had hopes that one brother might be alive. There were sometimes phone calls from strangers, people who had the same last name and had somehow tracked her down. I remember the tense excitement when she was called to the phone, then how in the course of a brief conversation in Yiddish her face would fall, her voice would change. "Another Hirschhorn," she would say, putting the telephone down, "not related. Well. That's that."

Though I could not have understood it at the time, it must have been the war, not just time and distance, that gave my grandmother's stories of her early childhood their glow and intensity, the feeling of a paradise lost and unrecoverable. I knew from an early age that I was named Sarah after her sister, Sarah Leah (affectionately called Salah) who was now dead. But my grandmother never spoke of the adult Sarah who died; she spoke of the childhood Sarah, the younger sister who was fair-haired in a family all dark-haired, whose long hair she used to braid. It was not until I was seventeen, standing in Yad VaShem, the Holocaust Memorial Museum in Jerusalem, that it first dawned on me, with a shock, that Sarah must have died in the Holocaust.

My grandmother's youngest sister, Ruzha, was alive. She had gone to Palestine in 1936, with her Zionist husband who had come back to Poland to visit his parents and find himself a bride. Every few weeks, a crackly airmail envelope arrived from Ruzha in the reborn state of Israel—a letter in Polish, sometimes containing snapshots of her children, my second cousins, the youngest of whom, a boy, was my own age. The letters were always an occasion. My grandmother would show me the pictures, tell me all about the family, and talk glowingly of Israel, "our own country," which to me sounded as unimaginably far away and unattainable as that other place, "the Old Country." My grandparents were Labour Zionists, had met as *landsleit* in a Montreal Labour Zionist organization, and had hoped in the twenties to go to Palestine themselves, but were thwarted by the TB.

*

Meanwhile, in Montreal, Canada, somewhere between these two mythical (to me) countries, I began my schooling and socialization as a Jewish Canadian in an English Protestant school in a French Catholic province of an English-speaking country. I was a minority within a minority within a minority, and my evolving consciousness was a minority consciousness—confused and ambivalent. It was heightened by having a working mother and no father. Even though most of the children in my class were, like me, Jews of the second generation to be born in Canada, I was different and felt it. Maybe I wasn't as different as Renata, who arrived mid-year in our third-grade class speaking only German, and had to sit at a special desk at the front, under the teacher's watchful eye, but I was different enough.

In the 1950s the Protestant schools of Montreal provided an education that was, vestigially, still heavily British Empire. Day began with reciting the Lord's Prayer, followed by saluting the flag and singing the anthem. In kindergarten we were still saluting the Union Jack and singing "God Save the Queen." Later it was the Red Ensign and "O Canada," but morning exercises always finished with "God Save the Queen," and Queen Elizabeth II's coronation picture graced our classroom walls in grade school. Some of our textbooks—our spellers, grammar books, and later, in high school, our Latin books—were published in England.

When I came home from school, my grandmother always asked me, "What did you learn today?" I remember, in kindergarten, singing a song for her—it was "Away in a Manger," about the Little Lord Jesus with no crib for a bed. I was chagrined to see her face darken in dismay; Granny who always loved to hear me sing! What was the matter? "This isn't ours," was all she would say.

Out on the street, as I began learning to read, I sounded out strange words: what was an "Arrêt Stop"? What was an "École School"? Those were French words, I was told. So I inferred yet another world in proximity to which I did not belong. In third grade we began studying French. But when I proudly tried out my first simple sentence on the one little French girl on our block, she did not understand me, and when I asked her to say in French what I thought I had said, I scarcely recognized the words she spoke. Our English-speaking teachers taught us the language in an accent that was incomprehensible to our French fellow citizens.

Robyn as a child, 1957

My mother worked full time as press officer for the Canadian Jewish Congress, also serving as editor for its monthly bulletin. But she went out of her way to maximize the little time she had with her children; she wanted me to have every opportunity she had missed during her own childhood. She read to me nightly, taught me to read phonetically before I could be taught at school by new methods she did not trust, signed me up at the local children's library. When she saw that I would come home from school and pick out songs by ear on my toy piano, she bought an apartment-sized upright piano on the installment plan, and after a couple of false starts with unsuitable teachers, I began lessons with a high school friend of hers who had studied at the Quebec Conservatory. My mother, like my grandmother, told me stories of her childhood, but most of them centered around her happy times at summer camp, a Labour Zionist camp she attended from the age of five as a charity camper. Those were her only good childhood memories. When I was older, I heard the sadder stories: about various foster families she lived with, about the frightening once-a-year visits to her mother in The San, and the stigma she felt about not having a real home or parents to look after her. Camp was the one place where she felt like everybody else, because there, nobody else had their parents either. She longed for family life, for siblings and normalcy, but learned to play the happy-go-lucky, because she did not like people to feel sorry for her.

It was my mother who put the writing bee in my bonnet. She came home from work one day toward the end of my first-grade year with a strange gift: a bright orange scribbler, unsuitable for crayoning because the pages were lined. She explained it was a book for writing stories in. I wrote my first story that night, and on her prompting, brought it to school next day. The teacher read it to the class and encouraged others to write their own stories. Practically from that time, a writer was what I wanted to be when I grew up, though that ambition was to jockey with other enthusiasms. I did not then know it had also been one of my father's dreams.

To her credit, my mother made sure my brother and I stayed in contact with our father's family. Twice a year, over Christmas holidays and in the summer, we were taken by train to Ottawa (if not by her, then by our Granny, until we were old enough to travel by ourselves) for a visit to the other grandparents, who occupied the lower flat of a triplex they owned on Arlington Avenue near Bank Street.

We loved these visits and everything that went with them: the train trip, the grandeur of the old CPR train stations, the old-world atmosphere of our Ottawa grandparents' home: full of crystal and knick-knacks, a Russian-alphabet perpetual calendar on the telephone stand, the phone always ringing, and relatives we didn't remember from year to year (there were so many!) dropping in at all hours to see the children, or gathering around our *Bobeh*'s generous table. Our father's mother was one of nine children, several of whom ended up in Ottawa with families of their own. Our grandfather had his tailor shop in the front room, and we loved to play there, going through his buckets of brass military buttons, battle ribbons, and crests; marvelling at how, in an idle hour, he could make a stuffed animal or a pinwheel cushion out of scraps of fabric; fascinated by his strong horseshoe magnet which, held under a cardboard tray, would drag straight

pins into clusters and move them magically about; watching him roll a giant cigarette on his wooden guillotine cigarette machine which then chopped it into five to add to his round tobacco tin. This *Zayda* could not have been more different from the one in Montreal: he would get down on his hands and knees and play horsie with us, hide and jump out at us from behind the stuffed chairs, tickle us until we howled. He used to take us on long walks, through Paterson Creek Park to Ottawa's Museum of Natural History, where we were awestruck by the dioramas and where he—an avid fisherman—would spend what seemed to us an inordinate amount of time gazing raptly at the rows of glazed specimen fish mounted on a panel over the stairs.

Another highlight of our Ottawa visits was being taken by our uncle to the CKOY radio station where, in those years, he was the voice of the six o'clock news. Most exciting was to watch the teletype machine in its cubicle, the latest news tapped out as if by an invisible typist, on a continuous roll of paper cascading onto the floor. This uncle was the only one who ever spoke to us about our father, saying his name out loud, reminiscing about the wonderful brother he had been. Inarticulately, how we loved him for that! For, in Ottawa as in Montreal, there was otherwise a silence about our father, his name spoken in hushed tones, by grownups whispering in Yiddish over our heads. I remember creeping into our grandparents' bedroom all by myself, sometimes, to steal a look at his picture on the bureau. I had my own picture of him in a little wallet my mother had given me, but this was a big framed picture and different. But I did not want my grandmother to catch me looking at it.

At the end of my first-grade year, my mother remarried. At first her parents stayed on in the house and she continued to work, but tensions built, and it was decided the cohabitation should end. My grandparents took an apartment of their own, a block away, and for the next year or so my brother and I came home from school to their house, and waited for my mother to collect us on her way home from work. I was grieved to have my grandmother move out, even though I still saw her nearly every day. My relationship with my stepfather was distant. He was divorced—a rarity in those days—and had left a five-year-old son; he carried a burden of guilt that interfered with his ease in assuming the role of father to my brother and me.

But soon there was a new baby sister at home, and my mother stopped working. Hard on the heels of these

The author at Conservatoire, after a chamber music recital, 1970

school, though I distinguished myself academically and was encouraged in my writing by a couple of fine teachers. I missed close friends from my old school and neighborhood, and did not easily make new ones. The trade-off was an expanding family: in short order, a second baby sister, then a baby brother. It made for a lively household. There was always plenty of noise and activity, providing diversion and a smokescreen for my general unhappiness.

A melancholy, introverted child, I preferred my friendships one-to-one, was uncomfortable in groups. I was a bookworm, devouring eight to ten books weekly. I still wanted to be a writer—of children's books, I thought then—and I still scribbled, periodically beginning novels in a burst of enthusiasm, but tiring of them after a chapter or two. At this time I also began writing poetry—for the most part, absolutely undistinguished and cliché-ridden rhyming verse—which nonetheless won admiration from grownups. I continued playing piano, changing teachers at eleven when my mother's friend stopped giving lessons. My new teacher was an unusual man: a consummate musician and eclectic thinker, a profound influence on me. Among other things he introduced me to tenets of Eastern philosophy, Zen and Taoist, which he incorporated into his teaching; and he gave me unusual things to read, such as Chinese poetry of the Tang Dynasty in English translation, which I began at once to imitate.

High school began a happier chapter in my life. By sheer luck, Montreal West High School had a superb music program; its concert bands regularly took top prizes in city and inter-city competitions. Since my piano teacher did not think it a bad idea for me to take up a second instrument, I enrolled in this program, choosing clarinet as my instrument. The school band was soon the center of my life. I loved the music, the camaraderie, and the teacher, who quickly became confidant and mentor. Like my piano teacher, he took a paternal interest in my intellectual development and introduced me to some of his favorite writers, notably A. E. Housman, whose stamp is heavy on poems I wrote at that age. One of them ("To the Memory of My Father") I included on the dedication page of my 2003 poetry collection, *A Day's Grace,* published in the fiftieth anniversary year of my father's death.

My progress on clarinet was such that within a year I was playing in the senior as well as the junior band, and successfully auditioned for the full-scholarship

huge changes, my parents bought a bungalow in a raw new housing development, and we moved to suburban Côte St. Luc. Visits to my grandmother were now only once a week. I did not greatly like my new program of Quebec's Conservatoire de Musique et d'Art Dramatique. There, after school and on weekends, I embarked on a full musical education, all of it free: private lessons on clarinet, mandatory classes in theory, solfege and musical dictation, plus classes in ensemble playing, both orchestra and chamber music. My teacher was then first-chair clarinetist in the Montreal Symphony Orchestra. At age fifteen, I entered the Orchestre du Conservatoire as one of its youngest members, assuming the chair of first clarinetist myself. I still remember the sink-or-swim feeling of my first rehearsal (at which the orchestra sight-read Beethoven's Fourth) as I nervously counted bars toward my solo entries.

Playing in an orchestra thrilled me, and I now believed this was the career I wanted. But at the same time I became more serious about the piano, embarking on some of the more challenging repertory. Musical collectivities (band, orchestra, chamber groups) fostered new friendships and, for the first time, a social setting in which I felt I belonged. At Conservatoire, it was an extremely diverse one: students ranged in age from about thirteen to thirty, came from both language groups, and represented many nationalities (as did the teachers.) Instruction was primarily in French, as were all communications from *la Direction*. Standards were high (a passing grade was 80%) and we were expected to conduct ourselves with the seriousness of professionals.

*

At this juncture my stepfather, whose restlessness had driven him through several career changes, entered the Canadian Civil Service and was appointed to a post in Ottawa. To say that I was upset at the idea of moving—of being torn from my new life at Conservatoire, from my high school class in our graduating year, from my friends and beloved music teachers—would be to understate the case. My grandparents came to the rescue, offering to take me in so I could remain in Montreal to finish high school. Since it was understood I would then apply to McGill, it amounted to leaving home at fifteen, though I felt it was home that was leaving me. My mother fretted that I was too young for this separation. I felt a great wrench at the thought of leaving her, leaving the comfortable pandemonium of our household and especially my little sisters and baby brother, but there was never any doubt how I would decide.

I think it must have been while packing for the move to Ottawa that my mother unearthed my father's 1947 letters and gave them to me to read. She had told me the story of her unusual elopement, but the letters were a revelation. To read them was to hear my father's inner voice. I spent a weekend immersed in them, amazed at the ways in which I was similar to him. Most surprising to me was his dream of becoming a published writer. Though it appeared to have taken a back seat to music, writing was still a vital interest for me; I harbored a quiet certainty that whatever else I might become or do in my life, I would always write. I was not to see my father's letters again for twenty-five years. Then, unexpectedly, on a rare visit to my brother, they passed into my keeping. Unbeknownst to me, my brother had had them in his possession since late adolescence, and he thought it was my turn. Among the letters were some papers I did not remember having seen before, including drafts of stories my father had written for Earle Birney's writing course at UBC, with Birney's comments on them.

From April of 1965 until I graduated from high school a year and a half later, I lived once again with my grandparents. And again, in retrospect, their selflessness amazes me. To share their small apartment with a teenager (I slept on a folding cot in their living room) was already a sacrifice of privacy; to share it with one who practiced two hours of clarinet and at least one hour of piano daily (they borrowed a piano for me) was saintly. Though initially nervous about the arrangement, I felt immediately at home under their roof, and became much closer to my grandmother as we again shared talk and daily routines. Much as I missed the brouhaha of family life, it was sweet to be center of attention in that simple, peaceful, rather Spartan household where I could focus with great concentration on my music and studies. It was during this period that I discovered a writer who was to become a major influence: Katherine Mansfield. Her short story, "Miss Brill," in our school English anthology, electrified me, and the school librarian directed me to her *Collected Stories* and a biography. My grandmother read the biography too. Just I was fascinated to learn that Mansfield had started out as a classical musician, so my grandmother could relate to her struggles with TB and repeated separations from her husband in search of treatment.

In the fall of 1966 I entered McGill University as a full-scholarship student in the music faculty, and moved into Royal Victoria College, the women's residence. A miserable summer in Ottawa had confirmed me in my love for Montreal, which I claimed as my city. Once I had adjusted to the traffic noise, it was intoxicating to live downtown and to have a room of my own, even if the washroom facilities were shared with thirty-nine other women. For my first year only, the old pre-Sixties codes of RVC were still in force: skirts and nylons in the Dining Room, strict curfews, boys allowed only in the ground-floor Common Rooms, an elaborate sign-out and sign-in Leaves system. I found this cloistered life more quaint than irritating (others were less enchanted, and a fair amount of cheating went on), but the Victorian regulations were tossed out in my second year.

Rather to my surprise, I loved residence life. But within a year I knew it had been a mistake for me to enroll in the bachelor of music program. Hearing my dorm-mates discussing their courses in psychology, anthropology, art history, and philosophy, I felt envious: my program was too specialized, too narrow. I was still attending Conservatoire (using transfer credits, in order to stay with certain teachers). Could I manage a double program at the university level, as I had done through high school? I effected a switch to Arts and began my second year as a B.A. student, majoring in philosophy, while continuing my musical studies at Conservatoire.

The summer between—the summer of 1967—was a landmark in my life. At my technique exam that spring, the Conservatoire's Directeur-Général extended an unexpected invitation. He was assembling a choir to represent French Canada at Israel's Zimriya, a triennial international choral festival to be held in July. Knowing I was Jewish, he asked if I would like to join the choir and come along to see Israel. My parents consented, some funds were found toward my fare, and I worked for six weeks in the Civil Service's student summer employment program to earn the rest. What a summer that was, the summer of '67, a summer that brought together all the diverse threads of my identity. This was the summer that Montreal hosted the World's Fair, Expo '67; it was Canada's Centennial Year. On the fairground, Canada's brand-new Maple Leaf flag flew side by side with Quebec's Fleur-de-Lys. Quebec nationalism was stirring, but for the moment a shared pride in our country's bicultural heritage prevailed.

Robyn with future husband Fred Louder in the McGill Ghetto, 1970, in front of the building he was living in when they met. At the time of this photo, it had been vacated for demolition.

Even as I read up on Jewish history and the story of Israel in preparation for our trip, the fate of that young nation hung in the balance as it went to preemptive war against a coalition of Arab neighbour-states pledged to its annihilation. Briefly it looked as if our trip would be called off, but Israel prevailed in a miraculous six-day campaign applauded by the Western world. In that heady atmosphere, a mere ten days after the reunification of Jerusalem, our choral group landed at Lodd Airport and began a three-week singing tour. I experienced Israel not only through my own eyes as a young diaspora Jew, but vicariously through the eyes of the French-language fellow Canadians with whom I was living and travelling: their wholehearted enthusiasm was deeply warming to me. During this visit I also had the opportunity, albeit briefly, to meet my grandmother's surviving sister and her three children. The trip powerfully affected me, and I wanted very much to find a way to go back and to stay longer, but on returning to Canada the whole episode gradually faded and became dreamlike. I was not to see Israel again until 1998.

Summer of '68 was the summer I refused to go home to Ottawa. I was eighteen. Having decided to move out of residence into an apartment of my own in the fall, I found a summer job as a typist, and (to maximize my savings) took a small, cheap furnished room—the cheaper for being shared with an old high school friend—in the area just off-campus known as the McGill Ghetto, an enclave of decaying Victorian mansions long since converted to rooming-houses. This was a blissful summer. Despite my nine-to-five workday, I managed to write three short stories and a sheaf of new poems—the first serious writing I had done since high school—and I and my roommate made the city's downtown our playground in the evenings. When fall came and school resumed, we moved to a small apartment, the first of several I was to occupy in the same neighborhood over the next few years.

The McGill Ghetto was home not only to students from out of town, but also to a growing number of Americans living in Canada to dodge the draft, as well as to a motley collection of elderly ne'er-do-wells, artist-bohemians, counterculture types, and foreign political refugees. Far more than my classes at McGill, it was this diverse and fascinating milieu that nurtured me. For the first time, I found myself among aspiring writers, painters, and musicians who were self-directed. Dropping out was cool, being in school was not. Many of my peers quit university to travel or simply to "do their thing," whatever it happened to be—living hand to mouth on odd jobs, unemployment insurance, or whatever other sources of income they could find. On campus, it was a time of political foment. The Vietnam War did not have the same immediacy to us in Canada, but there were enough Americans at and around McGill to make the anti-war movement felt. Marxist-Leninists, Maoists, radical feminists, and anarchists were all in evidence on campus. Quebec nationalism was in ascendancy and the radical FLQ (Front de Libération du Québec) whose first isolated terrorist acts had shocked Montreal even before I started high school, was becoming more of a presence. (This group would, in October of 1970, stun the country with the kidnapping of British High Commissioner James Cross and the kidnapping-murder of provincial Justice Minister Pierre Laporte,

prompting Prime Minister Trudeau to suspend civil liberties with passage of the War Measures Act.)

I took little interest in the political activity that swirled around me in those years; something in me mistrusted politicos of all stripes. But I was deeply drawn to the artists and bohemians. In July of 1970 I married Fred Louder, an American who had spent his high school years on the U.S. naval base at Argentia, Newfoundland, and had come to study classics at McGill though his real passion was writing poetry. His twin brother was a self-taught classical guitarist. Among our friends and close neighbours were Philadelphia-born pianist (later harpsichordist, harpsichord builder, and organist) Robert Sigmund, whom we helped to build his first harpsichord in a basement apartment on Prince Arthur Street; Dutch-born poet Peter Van Toorn; Polish-born painter Leopold Plotek; and Dublin-born theater director (later, radio producer and writer) Philip Coulter. As urban development encroached on the McGill Ghetto in the early 1970s, we all moved several blocks uptown to the Plateau Mont Royal neighborhood known as Mile End, an area—once Jewish, by then largely Greek and Chinese—that was beginning to be discovered by students and counterculture types willing to pool resources to share its large, wonderfully affordable flats.

*

How and when did I become a writer? On one level, I felt myself to be one from earliest childhood. It was an inner sureness I had, whether or not I was actively writing. Recognition for my writing came both at home and at school: poems and essays printed in school publications, read or recited at assemblies; occasional prizes in youth writing contests. Before I entered university, my mother sent a manuscript of my high school poetry to Canadian poet-lawyer F. R. Scott, whom she'd known in her own McGill years, and he wrote back encouragingly, with the suggestion that I immerse myself in the moderns. (My stepdad, in a gesture that touched me deeply, went out quietly and bought most of the poetry section of Classics Bookstore, the basis of my permanent poetry library.) But the inner sureness was something else. It had more to do with the fact that, given an idle moment, there was never anything I wanted to do so much as scribble; and it had to do with recognizing myself when I read biographies of writers. So it was a small shock to me, in those McGill Ghetto years, to find myself among other scribblers my age who not only thought of themselves privately as writers, but took themselves seriously enough to go public with it. They did not hesitate to show their work to writer-professors on campus; they gave poetry readings; some, like Van Toorn, had already begun to publish in magazines. What was I waiting for?

Around this time I was beginning to admit to qualms about a career in music. I had come to find rehearsal and performance schedules a straitjacket, and the company of professional-track musicians lacking in stimulation, compared to the eclectic amateurs I had been meeting. I made a private vow to commit myself more seriously to my writing, but in the meantime I was still enrolled in two school programs that had nothing to do with it and that took up vast amounts of my time and energy.

Unhappy in these inner divisions, I somehow managed to complete my B.A. with first-class honors in philosophy, and accepted a teaching assistantship in the expectation that I would work toward an M.A. in philosophy. But my heart wasn't in it. Nor was it, any more, in my formal musical studies. Seduced by scholarship money, I continued to go through the motions of both, but this was a period of deep confusion and anxiety for me, exacerbated by the fact that my husband and most of our friends had dropped out of university and were working here and there in theater and other creative ventures. In the end I was to maneuver a transfer to English, persuading the department to let me exercise its rarely invoked creative option of handing in a fiction or poetry manuscript in lieu of an M.A. thesis. And I was to graduate from Conservatoire, but not with the standing I'd hoped for.

In 1972 I applied and was hired to teach music and humanities at Champlain Regional College, a brand-new community college on Montreal's South Shore. It was not a full-time post, a good thing, because I was still finishing McGill and because I found teaching, initially at least, enormously stressful. Particularly shocking to me was the decline in literacy, as evidenced by the writing of my students, in the years since I had graduated from high school. But even part time, the pay was better than any I'd seen before, and it left my summers free. For my M.A. I prepared a manuscript of poems, many of which I had actually written during my years in the philosophy department. I found the courage to show some of these to poet-

professor Louis Dudek, whose good opinion was deeply validating, and in spring of 1973 I took the big step of shipping out my first poems to magazines. Braced to paper my wall with rejection slips, I got lucky with one of my first tries: Prism International accepted two poems, publishing them under my adopted pseudonym of Robyn Sarah.

Why a *nom de plume*? It was not so much that I wanted anonymity as that I felt ambivalent about my surnames. My mother had felt it best for me to assume my stepfather's name when she remarried, so that all her children would have the same last name. On marrying I took my husband's name. But I did not want publish my poetry under a name shared with a poet-husband. I would have liked to revert to my father's name, which was no longer my legal name and which I had not used since the age of six, but to do so now might hurt my stepdad's feelings. Yet I felt that publishing under my stepfather's name would be an affront to my father's memory. It was a happy thought that I could drop all three names and simply use my two given ones.

Many years later, visiting the newly opened Holocaust memorial museum in Montreal, I learned that one of the early laws enacted against the Jews in Nazi Germany was the requirement that every citizen of Jewish extraction assume an added name: Israel for a man, Sarah for a woman. I felt this added a dimension to my pseudonym. Just as it stood in memory of the Sarah for whom I was named—my grandmother's sister, last heard from in Lvov in 1941—so it could also stand in memory of all the other Sarahs.

In June of 1974, Fred and I packed up the contents of our flat, storing most of our belongings with friends, and took off for Vancouver Island on the West Coast. I left my job, giving up two years' accumulated seniority without a second thought. The idea was to live cheaply on savings and unemployment insurance till our money ran out: maybe buy an old truck we could live in and travel around, maybe rent a fisherman's cabin, maybe grow our own food. . . . After that it was open-ended; maybe we would stay on. My immediate plan was to write a book; Fred had, on principle, no plan. Planlessness, like going out west, was part of the ethos of the times; you were supposed to "go with the flow," you were supposed to "be here now." Psychedelic drug culture and Eastern religions had permeated the thinking of our generation. We ourselves were not hippies—we were both too cautious by nature, and too intellectual—but these ideas were the air we breathed, and they were seductive. For me, there was the need to break with academia and years of rigorous musical discipline. There may also have been a wish to retrace my parents' footsteps westward, and there was certainly a desire to spend time by the sea, something I had never done.

We weren't good candidates for the plunge we'd taken. Quickly we found that we fit nowhere: the locals dismissed us as hippies based on our dress and transient status, but the hippies didn't know what to make of us either. (You went out west with a knapsack, not with a trunk full of books and an antiquated manual typewriter. You spent your evenings smoking grass and banging on bongoes, not re-reading *War and Peace.*) After a few misadventures with derelict vehicles, and some time spent in East Sooke with friends who were squatting in an abandoned farmhouse (where we witnessed the home birth of their child), we rented a small, equipped beach cabin with a view across the Strait of Juan de Fuca. There we settled into a daily routine of reading and writing. It should have been a dream, but I was culture-shocked, and more homesick for Montreal and our friends than I could have anticipated.

I was working on an autobiographical novel at the time, a lyrical memoir of early childhood, begun in Montreal just prior to our departure. I was also writing poems and stories and shipping them out to magazines—collecting rejection slips to be sure, but also some acceptances. For petty cash, both of us freelanced for the local weekly, the *Sooke Mirror.* Once a week we drove in to Victoria to plunder the library. Through that long, rainy winter I immersed myself in Katherine Mansfield and D. H. Lawrence, reading not only their fiction but journals and letters, finding it instructive (if sobering) to realize that by the time they were our age, Mansfield and her husband Middleton Murry were seasoned book reviewers and had edited two literary journals. In the end, our western sojourn did not last even a full year. But it was during those ten months on Vancouver Island, a period sliced exactly in half by my twenty-fifth birthday, that I would say my writer's life began.

The novel I had thought I was embarked on came to naught. Having completed the first section, I was forced to conclude that I had written a fifty-page prose

The author in Sooke, Vancouver Island, 1975

poem, richly musical, but completely lacking in narrative drive. It was painful to shelve it, but I pulled myself together, now determined to expand my McGill manuscript into a publishable poetry collection. I also undertook regular book reviewing for the *Daily Colonist* in Victoria, under the byline R. S. Louder. But the fulcrum event of this period was probably our meeting an amateur letterpress printer (a transplanted Californian, owner of the local health food store) who had begun to produce limited editions on an 1890s-model Chandler & Price platen press. He offered to give us a demonstration lesson in typesetting and printing, and it was in his rustic print shop (next to the goat shed, behind the organic vegetable garden) that we met August Kleinzahler, another itinerant poet, whose first chapbook we were destined to publish in Montreal two years later.

We returned to Montreal at the end of April, 1975, a little torn to leave the Island just as we were beginning to find our footing, but low on cash and weary of the west-coast mentality. We hungered for talk that was about books and ideas, rather than boats, building, gardens, and fish. (Edward Ward-Harris, British-born books editor of the *Daily Colonist,* put it succinctly when he told us, "The only culture we have out here

Robyn in her study in Mile End, Montreal

is yogurt." Disappointed that we were leaving, though he understood why, he continued to send me books to review in Montreal.) We now had a plan: we wanted to find jobs and save up to buy a letterpress of our own. We would publish limited-edition chapbooks and support ourselves with commercial printing. It wasn't very realistic, but who is realistic at age twenty-five? We would also start a literary magazine, something we could do even before we had the press. And why stop there? I also wanted to get a book of my own published and have a baby—preferably in that order, but whichever happened first. It all seemed quite possible, even if for the moment we were flat broke and had nowhere to live.

And it all did, eventually, materialize—all except the income from the press, which was never adequate and was to keep me, more or less unhappily, in the teaching harness for many years to come. On arrival in Montreal, I reapplied to Champlain—this time to teach

English—and squeaked in for September with a partial course load. After rooming with friends for a few months, we found a cheap third-floor walkup on Ville-neuve (the street that was to give its name to our imprint), and in that modest five-room flat we started *Versus,* the first of two literary magazines we were to co-edit, and acquired the printing press we could afford: a tabletop, hand-cranked platen similar to the one that once served Leonard and Virginia Woolf for their Hogarth Press. Fred taught himself typography and presswork out of books; I learned typesetting only. Kleinzahler, with whom we'd kept in touch and who contributed poems to *Versus,* showed up in Montreal with a manuscript of poems which we decided to make our debut publication; and my own manuscript of poems got finished and duly shipped off to a small press, which accepted it for publication in the coming year. In June of 1977, two years after our return to Montreal, we launched Villeneuve's first chapbook, Kleinzahler's *The Sausage Master of Minsk,* just days before our first child, a son, was born. And January

1978 saw the publication (if to no fanfare) of my own first poetry collection, *Shadowplay.*

*

Divisions of energy have characterized my life. Through high school I was obliged to balance music with academics; in university, I opted for a double program of music and philosophy. For whatever reason—a subconscious fear of commitment, reluctance to put all eggs in one basket, maybe just a restless need for variety—my focus was always split: artistically, between writing and music; as a musician, between piano and clarinet; as a writer, between poetry and fiction. Villeneuve Publications, a separate if related interest that operated on a moonlight basis as we found time for it, became yet another diversion. But financial necessity meant that a chunk of my time had also to go into a whole new vocation, teaching,

about which I was profoundly ambivalent, enjoying the classroom, but resenting the work taken home nightly, the pressure of preparation and the drudgery of marking. To this brew, I was about to add the classic woman's dilemma and greatest division of them all: that of balancing family and career. Again, the ethos of the times was my guide: feminism said that I had the right to both, that it could be done, that the institution of marriage had to remake itself to allow for both. But family and *two* careers? Pregnant for the first time, I wrote in my journal, "I can be a teacher/ writer/editor and I'm sure I could be a mother/writer/ editor, but don't see how I can possibly be a teacher/ mother/writer/editor."

The next two decades of my life can be summed up as a quest for solutions to that "how," a great juggling act, the strain of which would eventually end the marriage. By 1979 we had a second child, a daughter, born at home. I stayed on extended unpaid maternity

The author with her grandmother, 1989, a few months before the elderly woman died

leave from Champlain for as long as we could afford it—eighteen months—but still found little time to write, between the demands of house and children, and our slow push to keep Villeneuve operational (we followed Kleinzahler's book with chapbooks by A. F. Moritz, Brian Bartlett, and Jack Hannan.) Thirteen new poems of my own were my total output between 1976 and 1981. Yet these poems, many of which record the struggle of a would-be writer-turned-mother, are the beginnings of my mature work; they are where I found my voice. In 1981 we gathered them into a chapbook, *The Space between Sleep and Waking,* and printed it under our own imprint in an edition of 300 copies. For such a tiny publication, it garnered a surprising amount of attention: the poems struck a timely chord, especially with women. The opening poem, "Maintenance," which begins, "Sometimes the best I can do/ is homemade soup, or a patch on the knee/ of the baby's overalls./ Things you couldn't call poems . . . " was to be anthologized seven times in the next eight years.

All frustrations aside, the children brought me enormous joy and I resigned myself to a vastly slowed-down pace as a writer in the interest of being with them as much as possible. But I resented more and more that I had to continue teaching for us to make ends meet. I did not teach a full load (the college accommodated my requests for partial leaves, while teachers scrambling for seniority were glad to pick up the sections I dropped) yet Parkinson's Law prevailed: even when there was less of it, the work I brought home seemed to take just as much time. By the time I had published enough to be eligible for the Canada Council's arts grants program, our expenses had gone up just enough so that the extra money (when I was lucky in the competition) only allowed me to continue my pattern of partial leaves; it was never enough for me to stop teaching altogether, even for a semester.

In similar fashion, printing technology undermined the progress of our little shop. The advent of computer graphics and desktop publishing made equal mockery of our hopes for a commercially viable letterpress shop and of our labor-of-love literary productions. The commercial work brought in less and less money for more and more expenditure of time; Villeneuve Publications slowed to a trickle. Neither of us was practical or worldly enough to re-vision our enterprise and forge a workable game plan. The press faltered along on a mixture of denial and good intentions until

the summer of 1987, when a flash flood inundated our basement print shop and brought an end to any remaining illusions. The marriage ended not long after.

What did all of this mean to me as a writer? It meant frustration and fragmentation, writing in little bursts as time permitted (and if inspiration favored me at those moments); it meant, for many years, writing mostly poetry because I could hope to finish a poem in such stolen pockets of time, but found it much harder to sustain the energy of a short story through endless interruptions and shelvings; a novel was unthinkable. It meant that, even if I was lucky enough to get a few poems or the odd story written, it might be weeks or months before I could snatch the time to type up clean copy, write a cover letter, and submit the work for publication. My free summers were not free at all, because the children were home from school and I could not afford child care. For years, the ongoing and largely thankless job of being my own agent was what tended to go by the boards: a little writing I could manage, a little typesetting for Villeneuve now and then, but there was no time to nurture a career. It added up to tortoise-style progress as a writer; often I felt like a fraud.

But little successes sustained me: a magazine acceptance here, an invitation to read there, a request to reprint a poem or broadcast a story. Heartening response to *The Space between Sleep and Waking* came from one writer for whom I had deepest regard, Adele Wiseman. Respected poet-editors Gary Geddes and Dennis Lee anthologized my poems; Québecois poet Michel Beaulieu approached me to translate *The Space between Sleep and Waking* into French (a project aborted by his untimely death of a heart attack in 1985, at the age of forty-three.) Taken together, there was just enough encouragement to keep me going through two more small-press poetry collections: *Anyone Skating on That Middle Ground* (1984) and *Becoming Light* (1987). It was not until 1992, when my New and Selected Poems, *The Touchstone,* was being readied for publication, that it occurred to me I finally had enough stories to consider bringing out a slim volume of those as well. My fiction debut, *A Nice Gazebo,* saw publication that same year, its earliest story ("Première Arabesque") having been written on Vancouver Island in the fall of 1974, eighteen years earlier.

The trajectory of a life often makes more sense in retrospect. What felt piecemeal, irrational, and chaotic at the time was actually surprisingly directional: amid

"By the sea of Galilee. I spent a month in Israel with my husband in the spring of '98. Our housesitter was our friend Yann Martel, who began writing Life of Pi *in our house that month."*

digression and necessary compromise, I now discern slow but steady progress along a chosen path. I was not prolific, and I did not achieve major recognition at an early age, but looking back, I feel that nothing was wasted. My years as a musician honed my ear and shaped my formal aesthetic as a writer. My studies in philosophy lent thoughtful substance to my poetry and fiction. Teaching forced me to conquer shyness and evolve a public persona as speaker and reader; it also gave me, for many years, a sense of legitimacy in the world, something that painfully eludes an obscure artist. Hand typesetting and letterpress publishing taught me to appreciate the integrity of a book and made me a stringent self-editor. Finally, having children put me in touch with universal, elemental emotions and pulled me into the mainstream of human life.

Today, in my sixth decade, I am remarried, sharing my life with a visual artist, a photographer whose work has opened whole new vistas to me; I have left teach-ing for full-time writing, have published a second collection of short stories and two more books of poetry, have added two genres (personal essay and journalism) to my writer's repertory—and can only wait to see what sense the future will make of my now.

BIOGRAPHICAL AND CRITICAL SOURCES:

PERIODICALS

ARC, Volume 36, 1996, Kathleen O'Donnell, "Interweaving Voices: An Interview with Robyn Sarah," pp. 23-32; Volume 42, 1999, Kenneth Sherman, review of *Questions about the Stars,* pp. 68-74.

Books in Canada, Volume 16, issue 9, 1987, Marc Côte, review of *Becoming Light,* p. 31; Volume 27, 1998, review of *Promise of Shelter,* p. 7; Volume 28, issue 2, 1999, Eric Ormsby, review of *Questions about the Stars,* pp. 11-12; Volume 30, issue 4, 2001, "Talking Poetry in Letters: Robyn Sarah and John Unrau on Free Verse vs. Chopped Prose," pp. 34-35.

Canadian Jewish News, August 6, 1998; February 26, 2004, review of *A Day's Grace.*

Canadian Literature, Volume 122-123, 1989, Robert J. Merrett, review of *Becoming Light,* pp. 223-226; Volume 134, 1992, D. G. Jones, "Maintenance Music: The Poetry of Robyn Sarah," pp. 191-198.

Canadian Materials, Volume 14, issue 2, 1986, review of *Anyone Skating on That Middle Ground,* p. 89.

Canadian Woman Studies, Volume 6, issue 4, Margaret Avison, review of *Anyone Skating on That Middle Ground;* Volume 13, issue 3, 1993, Deborah Jurdjevic, review of *The Touchstone: Poems New and Selected,* pp. 108-109.

Globe & Mail (Toronto, Ontario, Canada), March 30, 1985; June 18, 1988; May 29, 1992, review of *A Nice Gazebo;* January 24, 2004, review of *A Day's Grace.*

Hudson Review, Volume 57, issue 2, 2004, review of *A Day's Grace,* pp. 325-334.

Matrix, Volume 51, 1998, pp. 10-11.

Paragraph, Volume 19, issue 2, 1997, Debra Martens, "In Concert with Robyn Sarah," pp. 15-18.

Poetry Canada Review, Volume 7, issue 2, 1985-86, review of *Anyone Skating on That Middle Ground,* pp. 38-39.

Quill & Quire, Volume 58, issue 11, Rhea Tregebov, review of *The Touchstone: Poems New and Selected,* p. 28; Volume 64, issue 8, Ruth Panofsky, review of *Questions about the Stars,* p. 31.

OTHER

Association of English-language Publishers of Quebec Web site, http://www.aelaq.org/ (March 5, 2005), Bert Almon, review of *A Day's Grace.*

Poetics.ca, http://www.poetics.ca/ (March, 2003), Stephen Brockwell, interview with Sarah.

University of Toronto Library's Canadian Poetry Index Online, http://www.library.utoronto.ca/canpoetry/ (March 15, 2005), "Robyn Sarah."

*   *   *

SCALIA, Laura J. 1959-

PERSONAL: Born 1959. *Education:* New York University, B.A.; Yale University, M.A., M.Phil., Ph.D.

ADDRESSES: Office—University of Houston, Department of Political Science, 4800 Calhoun Rd., Houston, TX 77204.

CAREER: Educator and author. University of Houston, Houston, TX, currently assistant professor of political science.

WRITINGS:

America's Jeffersonian Experiment: Remaking State Constitutions, 1820-1850, Northern Illinois University Press (DeKalb, IL), 1999.

Contributor to *Political Research Quarterly.*

SIDELIGHTS: Laura J. Scalia, an educator and author in the field of political science, focuses primarily on political thought and American government, particularly democratic theory and American ideas of freedom and self-government during the nineteenth century. Her first book, *America's Jeffersonian Experiment: Remaking State Constitutions, 1820-1850,* compares seven state constitutions and ten constitutional conventions during the first half of the nineteenth century in the context of the studies by revisionist scholars J. G. A. Pocock, Gordon Wood, and Bernard Bailyn. Scalia investigates the notions of sovereignty and inalienable rights as they pertained to individual states, using the opposing beliefs of Thomas Jefferson and James Madison as a framework. Michael O'Brien wrote in a review for the *Times Literary Supplement* that Scalia "believes that scholars have underestimated the diversity of American political thought by concentrating too much on Washington, while scanting the States, which were by instinct more Jeffersonian and less Madisonian, more experimental and less cautious."

Scalia concentrates on the debates occurring during the constitutional conventions in an effort to examine the political thought of a generation slightly removed from the original founding fathers. The main question at hand is whether it is wise to allow the flexibility of frequent revision to state constitutions—a system Jefferson favored—or whether it is preferable to restrict such alterations—as Madison recommended. John Dinan commented in the *Journal of American History* that "this is certainly an important question and one that has attracted a good deal of recent attention from constitutional scholars, as well as constitution makers in emerging democracies," but he noted that "Scalia's principal conclusion . . . is likely to be carefully scrutinized. Some scholars are likely to reach different conclusions." However, in a review for *Publius*, Peter J. Galie stated that "the monograph fulfills its claim of enriching our 'understanding of the nature and purpose of constitutions' and contributes to the growing body of literature that is directing our attention to the historical significance and continuing importance of the state constitutions."

BIOGRAPHICAL AND CRITICAL SOURCES:

PERIODICALS

Journal of American History, March, 2001, John Dinan, review of *America's Jeffersonian Experiment: Remaking State Constitutions, 1820-1850,* p. 1480.
Political Research Quarterly, December, 1996, Laura J. Scalia, "The Many Faces of Locke in America's Early Nineteenth-Century Democratic Philosophy," p. 807.
Publius, fall, 1999, Peter J. Galie, review of *America's Jeffersonian Experiment,* p. 115.
Times Literary Supplement, October 15, 1999, Michael O'Brien, review of *America's Jeffersonian Experiment,* p. 37.*

*   *   *

SCHMITZ, Neil

PERSONAL: Male. *Hobbies and other interests:* Native American literature and family history genre.

ADDRESSES: Office—State University of New York at Buffalo, Department of English, 306 Clemens Hall, Box 604610, Buffalo, NY 14260-4610. *E-mail*—nschmitz@buffalo.edu.

CAREER: Educator and author. State University of New York at Buffalo, professor of English.

AWARDS, HONORS: Chancellor's Award for excellence in teaching, State University of New York at Buffalo, 1980; John Simon Guggenheim Memorial Foundation fellow, 1984.

WRITINGS:

Of Huck and Alice: Humorous Writing in American Literature, University of Minnesota Press (Minneapolis, MN), 1983.
White Robe's Dilemma: Tribal History in American Literature, University of Massachusetts (Amherst, MA), 2001.

Contributor of articles to literary journals, including *Partisan Review, Magazine of Wisconsin History, American Literary History,* and *Arizona Quarterly,* and essays to *Columbia Literary History of the United States,* Columbia University Press, 1988; *The Best of "American Literature," Essays on Humor,* Duke University Press, 1992; and *The Cambridge Companion to Mark Twain,* Cambridge University Press, 1995.

SIDELIGHTS: A longtime professor of English at the State University of New York at Buffalo, Neil Schmitz has written extensively about American literature, his subjects spanning a study of humorous writing, U.S. Civil War studies, and Native American literature.

In his first book, *Of Huck and Alice: Humorous Writing in American Literature,* Schmitz delves into the style of American humor and how it serves the purpose of his basic premise, which is that humor "transforms the effect of error, the result of wrong, and reformulated pains as pleasure." The author discusses how the meaning of the term "humor" has changed over time and he looks at several early examples of humor in the writings of satirist James Russel Lowell and the yarns of George Washington Harris. Schmitz's primary focus, however, is on the writings of novelist Mark Twain, poet Gertrude Stein, and George Herriman, creator of the "Krazy Kat" cartoons. For example, in his analysis of Twain, he delves into how Twain turned everyday American speech that was often vulgar in nature into "Huckspeech," thus influencing American humor and writing for generations. In his book, Schmitz also comments on such diverse American humorists as Osea Biglow, Harpo Marx, Lenny Bruce, and many others.

Writing in the *Journal of American Studies,* John S. Whitley commented that he wished "that Schmitz had developed his argument in detail with reference to at least one writer of more recent times." Whitley went on to call *Of Huck and Alice* "an original and brilliant contribution, not merely to the attempts to define American humour, but to an understanding of American culture." *American Literature* contributor Hamlin Hill found part of the book "self-defeating" because of the author's "quirky" analysis and "self-conscious and precious" language. Still, Hill called the book "a personal tour-de-force" and added that "there are frequent insights which are provocative and even brilliant."

In *White Robe's Dilemma: Tribal History in American Literature* Schmitz turns his attention to Native-American tribal history and the influence of Indian representation in American literature and history. For the most part he focuses on the Mesquakie tribe of Iowa. White Robe was a tribal leader who refused to make an alliance with the French and instead went to war, which led to his death. For Schmitz, White Robe's refusal to ally his tribe with a more powerful "nation" illustrates the tribe's effort to oppose Western influence on their culture. In his discussion, Schmitz highlights the differences between Western historical accounts of the Mesquakie and their own history. Schmitz's analysis of Western writing's impact on Native Americans also considers many other sources of American literature about and by Indians, including chapters on Standing Bear and Black Elk.

As noted by John E. Dockall in *Library Journal*, in *White Robe's Dilemma* "Schmitz ranges far afield in his assessment of the impact of published literature as a whole on Native Americans, their views of self, and the influence of these views in a variety of social arenas." Raymond J. DeMallie, writing in the *Journal of American History*, said that the book "is ultimately about how history is written and who has the rights to it." DeMallie went on to note that, in a sense, Schmitz is a "victim of his own argument" because "he has written American Indians out of the modern world, as though they were able to escape the influences of modern life while at the same time living in it." Nevertheless, the reviewer went on to note that "Schmitz nonetheless forces the reader into considering a different dimension of historical understanding. This volume raises important issues in new ways for anyone writing—or reading—American Indian history."

BIOGRAPHICAL AND CRITICAL SOURCES:

BOOKS

Schmitz, Neil, *Of Huck and Alice: Humorous Writing in American Literature*, University of Minnesota Press (Minneapolis, MN), 1983.

PERIODICALS

American Literature, May, 1984, Hamlin Hill, review of *Of Huck and Alice*, pp. 275-276.
Choice, July-August, 1983, review of *Of Huck and Alice*, p. 1599.
Journal of American History, December, 2002, Raymond J. DeMallie, review of *White Robe's Dilemma: Tribal History in American Literature*, p. 1084.
Journal of American Studies, August, 1985, John S. Whitley, review of *Of Huck and Alice*, pp. 271-272.
Library Journal, September 1, 2001, John E. Dockall, review of *White Robe's Dilemma*, p. 192.
Modern Philology, November, 1985, Milton Rickels, review of *Of Huck and Alice*, p. 215.

ONLINE

State University of New York at Buffalo Web site, http://www.english.buffalo.edu/ (July 24, 2004), "Neil Schmitz."*

*   *   *

SCHNABEL, Timothy B. 1963-

PERSONAL: Born March 2, 1963, in Elkhart, IN; son of John (a professor) and Pat Schnabel. *Ethnicity:* "Caucasian." *Education:* West Virginia University, B.S., 1985. *Politics:* Democrat. *Religion:* Lutheran.

ADDRESSES: Agent—c/o Author Mail, Shanem Publishing, 8491 Sunset Blvd., Ste. 1700, West Hollywood, CA 90069. *E-mail*—tbs2000@aol.com.

CAREER: Writer.

MEMBER: Publishers Marketing Association.

WRITINGS:

The Gift-Giving Handbook for the Inept Man: Thousands of Gift-Giving Ideas to Make His Life Easier and Her Life Better, Shanem Publishing (West Hollywood, CA), 2003.

SIDELIGHTS: Timothy B. Schnabel told *CA:* "My first work, along with the books I am currently putting on paper, are based on topics close to my heart. I prefer writing projects that will entertain, but I also enjoy projects that will help people learn and grow."

BIOGRAPHICAL AND CRITICAL SOURCES:

PERIODICALS

Library Journal, November 15, 2003, Douglas C. Lord, review of *The Gift-Giving Handbook for the Inept Man: Thousands of Gift-Giving Ideas to Make His Life Easier and Her Life Better,* p. 86.

*   *   *

SCIOLINO, Elaine

PERSONAL: Female. *Education:* New York University, master's degree, 1971.

ADDRESSES: Office—New York Times, 229 West 43rd St., New York, NY 10036.

CAREER: Newsweek, New York, NY, member of staff, 1972-84, including foreign correspondent in Paris, 1978-80, Rome bureau chief 1980-82, and roving international correspondent based in New York, 1983-84; *New York Times,* New York, NY, general assignment reporter, 1984-85, U.N. bureau chief, 1985-87, diplomatic correspondent, 1987-91, intelligence beat, 1991-92, chief diplomatic correspondent, 1991-96, senior writer in Washington bureau, 1996—.

AWARDS, HONORS: Page One Award, 1978; National Headliners Award for outstanding coverage of a major news event by a magazine (shared), 1981; Edward R. Murrow Press fellow, Council on Foreign Relations, 1982-83; citation for magazine reporting abroad, Overseas Press Club, 1983; senior fellow and specialist, United States Institute of Peace, 1998-99. Honorary doctorates from Syracuse University, Canisius College, and Dowling College.

WRITINGS:

Outlaw State: Saddam Hussein's Quest for Power and the Gulf Crisis, Wiley (New York, NY), 1991.
Persian Mirrors: The Elusive Face of Iran, Free Press (New York, NY), 2000.

SIDELIGHTS: Elaine Sciolino, a senior writer with the *New York Times,* was the first woman to become the Edward R. Murrow Press fellow at the Council on Foreign Relations and the first woman to hold the post of chief diplomatic correspondent for the *New York Times.* In her role as the *New York Times* roving international correspondent, she covered the Iranian revolution, the Iran hostage crisis, the Iran-Iraq War, the invasion of Grenada, and the U.S. Marine position in Lebanon.

Sciolino's first two books draw on her vast Middle East experiences. In *Outlaw State: Saddam Hussein's Quest for Power and the Gulf Crisis* she provides a historical overview of Iraq, charts Iraqi dictator Saddam Hussein's rise to power, and discusses the international interactions during the period of Iraq's invasion of Kuwait. Marvin Zonis, writing in the *New York Times Book Review,* noted that while the book "covers much of the ground of other instant books on the crisis in the Persian Gulf, [it] makes more tangible the notion that much of the 'Arab world' . . . has become a tangled web of deceit, political illegitimacy and intellectual decay." Zonis, who called Sciolino an "industrious and resourceful reporter," defined three crucial issues that evolve as Sciolino recounts the abuses the Iraqis and citizens of the Arab world were subjected to: First is Hussein's despicable character and the exposé of Kuwait's emir Sheik Jaber al-Ahmed Al-Sabah, for what Zonis called an "appalling lack of sophistication in dealing with Mr. Hussein . . . his abysmal lack of leadership after the invasion . . . and, throughout, his utter disdain for his own people and for his allies, including the United States." Second is the Arab world's intellectual bankruptcy; third is the devastation caused in Iraq during the invasion by the United States. Sciolino writes, "Even the economic infrastructure of the country, so painstakingly built up over the previous two decades . . . was dismantled. The allies justified hitting these targets for what they called important military value." Zonis noted, however, that just what that military value was "has never been explained by the United States." Zonis concluded his review by commenting, "Since this book was completed, much of the victory of the United States in the gulf war has turned sour. . . . But, as Elaine Sciolino makes all too uncomfortably clear, little else could have been expected. This, after all, is the Middle East."

By the time she wrote *Persian Mirrors: The Elusive Face of Iran,* Sciolino had spent more than twenty years covering Iran as a reporter—during a revolution, a war, and seizure of an embassy—and was one of only two female journalist to accompany the Ayatollah Khomeini on his midnight flight from exile in Paris to his triumphant return to Iran in 1979. According to a reviewer for the *Chicago Sun-Times,* "Sciolino reveals a country at war with itself, battling to sustain an Islamic state even as it invents new and creative ways around its own religious restrictions . . . a culture in which [the counterposed forces of] Islam and democracy struggle to coexist." While Reuel Marc Gerecht of the *Wall Street Journal* was more skeptical than Sciolino regarding the intent of Islamic clerical reformers, he concluded, "She has done a good job of showing the contradictory forces that have animated the Iranian soul since the Islamic revolution."

BIOGRAPHICAL AND CRITICAL SOURCES:

BOOKS

Outlaw State: Saddam Hussein's Quest for Power and the Gulf Crisis, Wiley (New York, NY), 1991.

PERIODICALS

Booklist, October 1, 2000, Vanessa Bush, review of *Persian Mirrors: The Elusive Face of Iran,* p. 319.
Business Week, November 6, 2000, review of *Persian Mirrors,* p. 20.
Chicago Sun-Times, October 22, 2000, review of *Persian Mirrors,* p. 15.
Economist, January 20, 2001, review of *Persian Mirrors,* p. 5.
Foreign Affairs, winter, 1991, William B. Quandt, review of *Outlaw State: Saddam Hussein's Quest for Power and the Gulf Crisis,* p. 203.
Library Journal, January, 2001, Eric Bryant and others, review of *Persian Mirrors,* p. 56; January, 2003, Nancy Pearl, review of *Persian Mirrors,* p. 192.
New York Review of Books, January 30, 1992, Theodore Draper, "The True History of the Gulf War," pp. 38-45.
New York Times, September 27, 2000, Ira Lapidus, review of *Persian Mirrors,* p. E8.
New York Times Book Review, June 23, 1991, Marvin Zonis, review of *Outlaw State,* p. 8; October 22, 2000, Diane Johnson, review of *Persian Mirrors,* p. 12.
Wall Street Journal, October 10, 2000, Reuel Marc Gerecht, review of *Persian Mirrors,* p. A24.

ONLINE

Public Broadcasting Service Web site, http://www.pbs.org/ (July 28, 2004), *Frontline:* "Gunning for Saddam."*

* * *

SEMPA, Francis P. 1959-

PERSONAL: Born August 13, 1959, in Scranton, PA; son of Frank F. and Minerva (Pidick) Sempa; married Mary E. Hergert (a homemaker), September 10, 1988; children: Eileen, Francis, Mary Grace, John, Abigail. *Ethnicity:* "Polish/Russian." *Education:* University of Scranton, B.S. (political science), 1981; Pennsylvania State University, J.D., 1984. *Politics:* Republican. *Religion:* Roman Catholic. *Hobbies and other interests:* Tennis.

ADDRESSES: Home—201 Amity Ave., Old Forge, PA 18518. *Office*—U.S. Attorney's Office, Federal Building, North Washington Ave., Scranton, PA 18503. *E-mail*—msempa@yahoo.com.

CAREER: Pennsylvania Superior Court, Lock Haven, law clerk, 1985-86; Lackawanna County District Attorney's Office, Scranton, PA, assistant district attorney, 1986-89; Pennsylvania Office of the Attorney General, Wilkes Barre, deputy attorney general, 1989-2002; U.S. Attorney's Office, Scranton, assistant U.S. attorney, 2002—. Wilkes University, adjunct professor of political science.

MEMBER: Center for the Study of the Presidency.

WRITINGS:

Geopolitics: From the Cold War to the Twenty-first Century, Transaction Publishers (New Brunswick, NJ), 2002.

Author of introduction, *The Problem of Asia: Its Effect upon International Politics,* by Alfred Thayer Mahan, Transaction Publishers (New Brunswick, NJ), 2003. Contributor of articles and reviews to periodicals, including *Strategic Review, National Review, National Interest, American Diplomacy, Human Rights Review,* and *Presidential Studies Quarterly.*

WORK IN PROGRESS: Introduction to *The Interest of America in International Conditions* by Alfred Thayer Mahan, for Transaction Publishers (New Brunswick, NJ).

SIDELIGHTS: Francis P. Sempa told *CA:* "Since 1986, I have written articles and book reviews on historical and foreign-policy topics for several publications. In my writing, I have been greatly influenced by the works of James Burnham, Halford Mackinder, Nicholas Spykman, and Alfred Thayer Mahan, as well as by more-contemporary writers on foreign policy and geopolitics.

"I write on historical and foreign-policy topics because I love to read, study, and think about history, especially the history of international relations. I have chosen to write about Burnham, Makinder, Spykman, and Mahan because their ideas and concepts are still relevant to current international relations theory, and much of their writings and ideas is unknown, except to specialists in the field."

*   *   *

SHADID, Anthony 1969(?)-

PERSONAL: Born c. 1969, in Oklahoma City, OK; married (separated); children: Laila. *Education:* Attended University of Oklahoma; University of Wisconsin, degree in journalism and political science, 1990; attended American University in Cairo, 1991-92, and Columbia University, 1992-94.

ADDRESSES: Office—Washington Post, 1150 15th St. NW, Washington, DC 20071.

CAREER: Journalist. Associated Press, news editor of Los Angeles, CA, bureau, international desk editor, New York, NY, 1993-94, Middle East correspondent, Cairo, Egypt, 1995-99; *Boston Globe,* Boston, MA, foreign correspondent, 1999-2002; *Washington Post,* Washington, DC, Islamic affairs correspondent, 2002—. Joe Alex Morris, Jr., Memorial lecturer, Nieman Foundation for Journalism, Harvard University, 2004.

AWARDS, HONORS: Bob Considine Award, Overseas Press Club, 1997; George Polk Award, 2003, for foreign reporting; American Society of Newspaper Editors' Award, for deadline news reporting by an individual; Michael Kelly Award, 2004; Pulitzer Prize for international reporting, 2004.

WRITINGS:

Legacy of the Prophet: Despots, Democrats, and the New Politics of Islam, Westview Press (Boulder, CO), 2001.

SIDELIGHTS: In 2002 Anthony Shadid was shot while covering the Israeli-Palestinian conflict near the headquarters of Palestinian leader Yassar Arafat in the West Bank city of Ramallah while reporting for the *Boston Globe.* He went on to win a Pulitzer prize in 2004 for his work as a foreign correspondent for the *Washington Post* for his reportage of the war with Iraq and its aftermath. The Pulitzer board cited his "extraordinary ability to capture, at personal peril, the voices and emotions of Iraqis as their country was invaded, their leader toppled and their way of life upended."

Shadid, the grandson of Lebanese immigrants, studied Arabic at the American University in Cairo and became a fluent speaker of the language. His language skills, coupled with his understanding of the culture and politics of the Middle East, have enabled him to write with knowledge and detail about the region and its people. His *Legacy of the Prophet: Despots, Democrats, and the New Politics of Islam* is based on a four-part series produced for the Associated Press in 1996. Shadid, who was then based in Cairo, Egypt, spent nearly a year interviewing students, activists, religious sheikhs, and politicians. In the book, he points out that the Muslim religion is divided into many different sects, as is the Christian religion, and that these sects are susceptible to change and adaptation. He argues that many Westerners, especially those who identify terrorism with Islam, do not understand the religion. "While criticizing the brutality of Islamic regimes such as Sudan's or the violence of zealots, he shows that for many Muslims the politicization of their faith is mainly about protecting the 'disinherited,'" noted Kiran Nihalani in *New Internationalist.* As Shadid points out, most people in the Middle East derive their sense of identity from being Muslims first. Their nationality or pan-Arab identity comes second.

Shadid begins the book by introducing the reader to the identity issue faced by the um'ma (global Muslim community), then reviews the literature that explains the evolution of political Islam. He notes the political goal of religious violence and that militant Islam is an expression of injustice. In the third chapter, he looks at the terrorist attacks of September 11, 2001, through the eyes of the perpetrators. He differentiates between Islamic internationalists, who have adopted jihad, or holy war, as the sixth pillar of Islam, and Islamic nationalists, who seek partnership through democracy.

Rolin Mainuddin wrote in *Perspectives on Political Science* that Shadid emphasizes that "on the one hand, globalization—and the concomitant Western hegemony—threatens the political, economic, and cultural identity of the um'ma. . . . Viewed as a revisionist force, on the other hand, political Islam is resented and misunderstood in the West. The um'ma is not uniform in its political organization: it includes both authoritarian and democratic regimes. Faith is no longer enough for mobilizing the destitutes; success is predicated on implementing social services that address everyday needs of the people." Mainuddin concluded by calling *Legacy of the Prophet* "a timely contribution."

On the eve of the U.S. invasion of Iraq, Shadid phoned Phil Bennett, the *Washington Post*'s assistant managing editor, asking that he be permitted to stay, even as other correspondents were pulling out. His request granted, Shadid stayed in the country and continued covering the region that had come to dominate the headlines. Shadid was writing a story about the Shiite uprising when he received word that he had won the Pulitzer Prize, journalism's highest honor. Sherry Ricchiardi noted in *American Journalism Review* that "Shadid's 'voice of the people' trademark resonates with supporters. They view his interviews with Iraqis in remote villages, marketplaces and Baghdad slums as filling a gap in American coverage." Ricchiardi said that it is through the eyes of these interviewees "that readers see how U.S. policies are playing out."

BIOGRAPHICAL AND CRITICAL SOURCES:

PERIODICALS

American Journalism Review, June-July, 2004, Sherry Ricchiardi, "Voice of the People" (profile of Anthony Shadid), p. 44.

First Things, December, 2001, Daniel Pipes, review of *Legacy of the Prophet: Despots, Democrats, and the New Politics of Islam,* p. 61.
Military Review, March-April, 2002, Simon J. Hulme, review of *Legacy of the Prophet,* p. 109.
New Internationalist, November, 2001, Kiran Nihalani, review of *Legacy of the Prophet,* p. 33.
Perspectives on Political Science, winter, 2002, Rolin Mainuddin, review of *Legacy of the Prophet,* p. 57.
Washington Report on Middle East Affairs, April 30, 2001, Adila Masood, "Shadid Introduces *Legacy of the Prophet* at CCAS (Center for Contemporary Arab Studies, Georgetown University)," p. 86.

ONLINE

Editor & Publisher Online, http://www.mediainfo.com/ (April 5, 2004), Mark Fitzgerald, "Pulitzer Winner Shadid: 'Embedded in the Soul' of Iraq."*

*   *   *

**SHEPPARD, David Stuart 1929-2005
(Baron of West Kirby)**

OBITUARY NOTICE— See index for *CA* sketch: Born March 6, 1929, in Reigate, Surrey, England; died of cancer March 5, 2005, in West Kirby, Merseyside, England. Bishop, cricket player, and author. A former bishop of Woolwich who was known for his efforts to alleviate racial tensions between blacks and whites in England, Sheppard was also an accomplished cricket player who captained the England team in 1954. Graduating in 1953 from Trinity Hall, Cambridge, he earned a master's degree at Ridley Hall in 1955. Ordained a minister in the Church of England that year, his first two years with the church were spent as a curate in Islington. As warden of the Mayflower Family Centre in Canning Town from 1957 to 1969, Sheppard worked closely with poverty-stricken families of many races. Concerned about strained racial relationships between blacks and the government and Anglican church, he strove to address such problems as poor housing and unemployment while chair of the central religious advisory committee, the Liverpool Manpower Services Commission, and the General Synod's Board for Social Responsibility. He also was a key player in writing the 1985 report "Faith in the City: A Call for Action by Church and Nation," which helped quell negative public opinion about blacks after the riots of that year. In addition to his church work, Sheppard, who was named bishop of Woolwich in 1969 and bishop of Liverpool in 1975, was a gifted cricket player. He played for Sussex from 1947 to 1962, and for England from 1950 to 1963, serving as captain of the Sussex team in 1953 and of the England team in 1954. He was also an author of several books, including *Parson's Pitch* (1964; later published as *Built as a City: God and the Urban World Today,* 1974), *Bias to the Poor* (1983), *The Other Britain* (1984), and three books with Archbishop Derek Worlock: *Better Together: Christian Partnership in a Hurt City* (1988), *With Christ in the Wilderness,* and *With Hope in Our Hearts* (1994). Named a life peer in 1998, Sheppard's autobiography, *Steps along Hope Street: My Life in Cricket, the Church, and the Inner City,* was published in 2002.

OBITUARIES AND OTHER SOURCES:

BOOKS

Sheppard, David Stuart, *Steps along Hope Street: My Life in Cricket, the Church, and the Inner City,* Hodder & Stoughton (London, England), 2002.

PERIODICALS

Daily Post (Liverpool, England), March 7, 2005, p. 6.
Independent (London, England), March 7, 2005, p. 34.
Times (London, England), March 7, 2005, p. 49.

*   *   *

SHERWONIT, Bill 1950-

PERSONAL: Surname is pronounced "Sure-*wan*-it"; born January 4, 1950, in Bridgeport, CT; son of Edward and Victoria (a secretary; maiden name, Schmollinger) Sherwonit; married Dulcy Boehle (a special-education teacher and speech therapist); children: Tiaré Neill. *Education:* Bates College, B.S. (cum laude), 1971; University of Arizona, M.S., 1974; attended Pierce College, 1978-80. *Hobbies and other interests:* Reading, music, hiking, bird feeding and watching, recreational basketball, wilderness exploration, natural history studies, environmental/ conservation activism.

ADDRESSES: Home—7601 Soldotna Dr., Anchorage, AK 99507. *E-mail*—akgriz@hotmail.com.

CAREER: Worked as an exploration geologist in Alaska, c. 1974-80; *Simi Valley Enterprise,* Simi Valley, CA, sports writer and editor, 1980-82; *Anchorage Times,* Anchorage, AK, sports writer, 1985-87, outdoors writer and editor, 1987-92; freelance nature writer and photographer, Anchorage, 1992—. University of Alaska, Anchorage, adjunct instructor in creative writing, 1993—; presenter of writing workshops; public speaker, including appearances at Kachemak Bay Writers Conference, Alaska Nature Writing Institute, Sitka Symposium, Alaska Public Lands Information Center, and Eagle River Nature Center; guest on media programs. Chugach State Park citizens advisory board, member, 2000-03, chair of trails committee, 2002-03.

MEMBER: Outdoor Writers Association of America, Association for the Study of Literature and the Environment.

AWARDS, HONORS: First place award, Associated Press Sports Editors, 1985; Sierra Cup, Sierra Club (Alaska chapter), 1989, for work at *Anchorage Times;* Mountain Literature Award finalist, 2001, for *Denali: A Literary Anthology;* award from Wildlife Federation of Alaska; multiple awards from Outdoor Writers Association of America, Alaska Press Club, and Society of Professional Journalists.

WRITINGS:

To the Top of Denali: Climbing Adventures on North America's Highest Peak, Alaska Northwest Books (Portland, OR), 1990, revised edition, 2000.
Iditarod: The Great Race to Nome, Alaska Northwest Books (Portland, OR), 1991.
Alaska's Accessible Wilderness: A Traveler's Guide to Alaska's State Parks, Alaska Northwest Books (Portland, OR), 1996.
Alaska Ascents: World Class Mountaineers Tell Their Stories, Alaska Northwest Books (Portland, OR), 1996.

Alaska's Bears, Alaska Northwest Books (Portland, OR), 1998.

Denali: A Literary Anthology, Mountaineers Books (Seattle, WA), 2000.

Denali: The Complete Guide, Alaska Northwest Books (Portland, OR), 2002.

Wood-Tikchik: Alaska's Largest State Park, Aperture Foundation (New York, NY), 2003.

(Editor, with Andromeda Romano-Lax and Ellen Bielawski) *Travelers' Tales: Alaska,* Travelers' Tales (San Francisco, CA), 2003.

Work represented in anthologies, including *The Last New Land: Stories of Alaska Past and Present,* edited by Wayne Mergler, Alaska Northwest Books (Portland, OR), 1996; *Danger! True Stories of Trouble and Survival,* edited by James O'Reilly, Sean O'Reilly, and Larry Habegger, Travelers' Tales (San Francisco, CA), 1999; *Earth beneath, Sky Beyond: Nature and Our Planet,* edited by Whitney Scott, Outrider Press (Crete, IL), 2000; *Arctic Refuge: A Circle of Testimony,* edited by Carolyn Servid and Hank Lentfer, Milkweed Editions (Minneapolis, MN), 2001; and *Take Two—They're Small: Writings about Food,* edited by Whitney Scott, Outrider Press (Crete, IL), 2002. Contributor to periodicals, including *Alaska, Audubon, Backpacker, Christian Science Monitor, Climbing, National Wildlife, National Parks, Orion, Outside, Paddler, Sea Kayaker, Sierra, Wilderness,* and *Writing Nature.*

WORK IN PROGRESS: Two works of literary nonfiction: *Living with Wildness: An Alaskan Odyssey* (tentative title) and a book about the Arctic wilderness.

SIDELIGHTS: Bill Sherwonit told *CA:* "I entered the 'writing life' in my late twenties, after getting an advanced degree in geology and working several years in that field. While a geologist, I found myself surrounded by people who were passionate about their work in a way I was not. Over time, I realized I did not want to spend my life working as a geologist; I decided to seek a career and lifestyle that I could be passionate about. As the late mythologist Joseph Campbell (well known for his advice to 'follow your bliss') might put it, I went in search of my bliss. I didn't know what that might be, so I took a leap of faith into the unknown. That leap led me into journalism. Taking classes at a junior college in California, I became excited at the possibilities. I joined the student newspaper as a sports writer (later to become sports editor), and that in turn led to my first job as a journalist: reporting on sports at the *Simi Valley Enterprise.*

"Though I'd decided not to build a career in geology, the profession had blessed me with a gift: it introduced me to Alaska. I fell in love with the state—especially its wild landscapes—my first summer there, in 1974. Though I later moved to California, I knew I would return to Alaska some day. I did, in 1982, reincarnated as a sports writer. I worked at the *Anchorage Times* from 1982 through 1992 (when the newspaper went out of business, after losing a newspaper war to the *Anchorage Daily News*), first as sports writer, then as the paper's outdoors writer and eventually editor.

"Almost immediately after I'd learned that the *Times* was folding in 1992, two thoughts streaked through my mind: I will continue to live in Alaska; and I will continue to write. It would be no easy task in a state with few newspapers or magazines. That led to another leap of faith, into the world of freelancing. Since 1992 I have survived—and in many ways, thrived—as a freelance writer. I now follow the bliss of nature writing in the place where I feel most at home, Alaska. It's an ideal combination.

"Through nature writing, I explore my relationship with the world. Through many different sorts of audiences (from the general audiences that read the local newspaper to those who read magazines such as *Orion*), I get to share my perspectives, opinions, and revelations—and perhaps get people to consider different ways of being in the world. Through writing I gain a sense of purpose. It's what I love to do. The writers who inspire me the most are those who write about nature and our species' complicated relationships with more-than-human nature, in one fashion or another (though some would hardly consider themselves nature writers). These include Alaska's own Richard Nelson and Sherry Simpson, as well as Loren Eiseley, Edward Abbey, Barry Lopez, Terry Tempest Williams, David James Duncan, Scott Russell Sanders, David Quammen, and Kathleen Dean Moore, among others. Others important to my writing craft and life include people with whom I've worked in local writing groups, particularly Andromeda Romano-Lax and Ellen Bielawski.

"Though I began writing as a journalist, I find myself ever more attracted to creative nonfiction, particularly the personal essay form (and longer, book-length narratives). This is the direction of growth for me as a writer. It's where my learning curve—and passion—is leading me."

BIOGRAPHICAL AND CRITICAL SOURCES:

ONLINE

Bill Sherwonit Home Page, http://www.billsherwonit. alaskawriters.com (November 1, 2004).

* * *

SHOAF, Diann Blakely 1957-
(Diann Blakely)

PERSONAL: Born 1957, in Anniston, AL. *Education:* Sewanee University of the South, B.A. (art history); Vanderbilt University, M.A., 1980; attended New York University, 1981; Vermont College, M.F.A., 1989.

ADDRESSES: Home—Nashville, TN. *Agent*—c/o Author Mail, Story Line Press, Three Oaks Farm, P.O. Box 1240, Ashland, OR 97520-0055.

CAREER: Author and teacher. Harpeth Hall School, Nashville, TN, teacher, beginning 1987, and former writer-in-residence; also teacher at Belmont University, Nashville, TN, and Watkins Institute, Nashville; temporary adjunct professor, Vermont College.

AWARDS, HONORS: Walter E. Dankin poetry fellow, Sewanee Writers' Conference, 1993; Robert Frost fellow, Bread Loaf Writers' Conference, 1994; Pushcart Prize, 1994 and 1995; Di Castagnoa Award, Poetry Society of America, 2001, for *Cities of Flesh and the Dead;* Harold Stirling Vanderbilt fellow, Vanderbilt University.

WRITINGS:

Hurricane Walk (poems), BOA Editions (Brockport, NY), 1992.
(As Diann Blakely) *Farewell, My Lovelies* (poems), Story Line Press (Ashland, OR), 2000.

Author of *Cities of Flesh and the Dead* and *Rain at Our Door: Duets with Robert Johnson.* Coeditor of *Each Fugitive Moment,* a collection of essays on the life and work of Lynda Hull. Works from Shoaf's books have appeared in *New England Review, Paris Review, Southern Review, Yale Review, Parnassus, Oxford American,* and *Pushcart Prize* anthologies XIX and XX, among others. Contributor to *Bookshelf.* Assistant poetry editor, *Antioch Review,* 1997—.

SIDELIGHTS: Born in the small town of Anniston, Alabama, Diann Blakely Shoaf moved with her parents at a young age to the city of Birmingham but spent school holidays and summers in Anniston with her maternal grandparents in their large home. In their back yard, Shoaf's grandparents housed a black couple who worked for them, the wife as Shoaf's nanny. According to a *Poetry Net* Web site essayist, "The intricately schizoid relationship, at once intimate and taboo-ridden, loving and exploitative, between such blacks and such whites was probably no more mind-boggling to [Shoaf] than to other children; nonetheless, the South and its racial divide, which became cruelly and explosively obvious in Birmingham during the early '60s, recurs as one of the central urgencies of her work."

Published as part of the "New Poets Series," Shoaf's *Hurricane Walk* was described as an impressive first collection by several reviewers, and Pat Monoghan indicated in *Booklist* that, "mincing no words," Shoaf thrusts the reader into the emotional center of each poem. The collection captures characters in the throws of every-day life—painting gripping portraits of mundane and ordinary activities. Joyce Peseroff noted in *Ploughshares* that "Shoaf writes about the self's desire to escape—from consciousness, from flesh—into art and nature, into otherness; finally, into death," and called the collection "rich in wit, humor, and irony." A reviewer for *Publishers Weekly* commented that Shoaf expresses an "eerie" and "horrific vision" in the "uneven" collection. The reviewer noted that, early in the collection, Shoaf's unique voice is evident in the speakers as they probe their ordinary, everyday, boring lives; the reviewer called Shoaf's poems "feminist yet focused on an ever-present lover." The reviewer felt that by the final third of the book, as speakers becomes more at ease with their lovers' presence, Shoaf's voice becomes less evident; to compensate, according to the critic, she writes through the voices of mythical or historic figures, "and the results are unimpressive." Frank Allen, reviewing the collection for *Library Journal,* called the forty poems "well polished" and "combining a purifying sensibility with compassion for loss."

Denise Duhamel, commenting in *Ploughshares* on *Farewell, My Lovelies,* said that Shoaf's second collection is "decidedly female poetry—tough, stylized, and heart-smart. . . . Her voice is an in-your-face voice, an almost performance-poetry voice, yet her poems are full of craft and gorgeousness." Writing in the *Women's Review of Books,* Lisa M. Steinman noted that the poems in this collection—published under the name Diann Blakely—contain "distinctly narrative elements . . . [that] often yield to the lyrical, as stories become icons of the soul." Many scenes contain distinct memories from the poet's own childhood and her personal reflections about race and class.

BIOGRAPHICAL AND CRITICAL SOURCES:

PERIODICALS

Booklist, September 1, 1992, review of *Hurricane Walk,* p. 27.
Library Journal, August 1992, review of *Hurricane Walk,* p. 106.
Ploughshares, winter 1992, Joyce Peseroff, review of *Hurricane Walk,* p. 238; fall 2000, Denise Duhamel, review of *Farewell, My Lovelies,* p. 227.
Publishers Weekly, August 24, 1992, review of *Hurricane Walk,* p. 73; January 10, 2000, review of *Farewell, My Lovelies,* p. 247.
Women's Review of Books, September 200, Lisa M. Steinman, review of *Farewell, My Lovelies,* p. 15.

ONLINE

Poetry Net, http://members.aol.com/poetrynet/ (August 13, 2004), "Diann Blakely."*

*　　*　　*

SHORT, Bobby
See SHORT, Robert Waltrip

SHORT, Robert Waltrip 1924-2005
(Bobby Short)

OBITUARY NOTICE— See index for *CA* sketch: Born September 15, 1924, in Danville, IL; died of leukemia March 21, 2005, in New York, NY. Musician and author. A fixture at the Café Carlyle in New York since 1968, Short was a popular pianist and vocalist known for his renditions of jazz and other popular standards. Performing from the age of nine, when his father died, Short was playing professionally and making appearances at the Apollo by the time he was just thirteen. He decided to return to his home town in 1938 and finish his high school education, before resuming his career as a full-time performer. During his travels, he became friends with such well-known singers and musicians as Nat King Cole, Art Tatum, and Lena Horne. Despite his extensive experience, Short still felt like an amateur for many years. In 1954 he met composer Phil Moore, who later became his manager. Moore helped Short polish his style and find his musical niche, and by the 1960s the pianist felt he was at last a worthy entertainer. Not long after participating in a Greenwich Village revue of Cole Porter songs in 1965, he was hired by the Carlyle hotel, where he became a permanent act. Short's fashionable clothing and classy performances made the Café Carlyle a cultural icon of New York City that was admired by the likes of film director Woody Allen, who often made reference to the café in his movies. In addition to his performing career, however, Short was also an accomplished jazz scholar who tried to share his knowledge of African-American music with others. He was the author of two autobiographical books: *Black and White Baby* (1971) and *Bobby Short: The Life and Times of a Saloon Singer* (1995).

OBITUARIES AND OTHER SOURCES:

BOOKS

Black and White Baby, Dodd, Mead (New York, NY), 1971.
Short, Bobby, and Robert Mackintosh, *Bobby Short: The Life and Times of a Saloon Singer,* C. Potter (New York, NY), 1995.

PERIODICALS

Chicago Tribune, March 22, 2005, section 1, p. 5.
Los Angeles Times, March 22, 2005, p. B8.

New York Times, March 22, 2005, p. C17.
Times (London, England), March 23, 2005, p. 62.

*   *   *

SIDEL, John T. 1966-

PERSONAL: Born June 4, 1966, in New York, NY; son of Stephen and Nancy (Jarmon) Sidel; married Eva-Lotta Elisabeth Hedman (an academic and writer), June 25, 1999; children: Matilda Hedman. *Education:* Yale University, B.A. (summa cum laude) and M.A., both 1988; Cornell University, Ph.D., 1995.

ADDRESSES: Office—Department of Government, London School of Economics and Political Science, University of London, Houghton St., London WC2A 2AE, England. *E-mail*—jtsidel@yahoo.com.

CAREER: University of London, London, England, reader in politics at London School of Oriental and African Studies, 1994-2004, professor of politics at London School of Economics and Political Science, 2004—.

MEMBER: Association for Asian Studies (member of Southeast Asia Council).

AWARDS, HONORS: British Academy grant.

WRITINGS:

Capital, Coercion, and Crime: Bossism in the Philippines, Stanford University Press (Stanford, CA), 1999.
(With Eva-Lotta E. Hedman) *Philippine Politics and Society in the Twentieth Century: Colonial Legacies, Post-Colonial Trajectories,* Routledge (New York, NY), 2000.

WORK IN PROGRESS: Riots, Regions, Jihad: Religious Violence in Indonesia; Liberalism, Communism, Islam, on "nationalist" struggles in Southeast Asia.

BIOGRAPHICAL AND CRITICAL SOURCES:

PERIODICALS

Pacific Affairs, fall, 2003, Paul D. Hutchcroft, review of *Capital, Coercion, and Crime: Bossism in the Philippines,* p. 505.

SIGERSON, Davitt

PERSONAL: Married; children: two daughters. *Education:* Studied history at Oxford University.

ADDRESSES: Home—New York, NY. *Agent*—c/o Author Mail, Random House, Inc., 1745 Broadway, New York, NY 10019.

CAREER: Songwriter, record producer, and music journalist. Former president of Polydor Records; president and chief executive officer of EMI Records, beginning 1994; chair of Island Records U.S., 1998—. Composer of sound recordings *David Sigerson,* ZE Records, 1980, and *Falling in Love Again,* Island Records, 1984.

WRITINGS:

Faithful (novel), Nan A. Talese/Doubleday (New York NY), 2004.

WORK IN PROGRESS: A second novel.

SIDELIGHTS: Music company executive Davitt Sigerson's first novel, *Faithful,* appeared after he had already enjoyed a successful career as a songwriter and record producer. Sigerson, as quoted in *Publishers Weekly,* said that his novel focuses on "marital sex and parenthood, ecstatically and painfully entwined." Many critics have agreed that *Faithful,* in the words of a *Publishers Weekly* reviewer, is a "racy debut." Allison Block, writing in *Booklist,* called the novel an "unapologetically erotic novel."

In *Faithful* Nick Clifford, a London trader and man-about-town, marries Trish, a sexy flight attendant. Trish soon falls into an extramarital affair with her first love, the wealthy and generous Joe Somerville. Although Trish finds that she is carrying husband Nick's baby, but she chooses to stay with Joe, all the while carrying on a clandestine liaison with Nick. Discouraged by the situation, Nick eventually moves to New York to work.

Critics were not especially kind to Sigerson's first fictional effort. A *Publishers Weekly* reviewer, for one, noted that the book "manages to prove that even stormy sex can be ho-hum." A *Kirkus Reviews* critic similarly called the book "dumb, thin, meretricious, absurd," while *Library Journal* contributor Kellie Gillespie dubbed the story "both intriguing and disappointing." In the *New York Times Book Review,* Emily Nussbaum wrote that *Faithful*'s "sophistication is paper-thin" but that it "might be just what the beach bag ordered."

BIOGRAPHICAL AND CRITICAL SOURCES:

PERIODICALS

Booklist, March 1, 2004, Allison Block, "Lust in the Afternoon," p. 1138.
Entertainment Weekly, November 29, 2002, Matthew Flamm, "Between the Lines: The Inside Scoop on the Book World," p. 109.
Kirkus Reviews, January 1, 2004, review of *Faithful,* p. 14.
Library Journal, February 1, 2004, Kellie Gillespie, review of *Faithful,* p. 125.
New York Times Book Review, May 23, 2004, Emily Nussbaum, "Some Like It Hot," p. 10.
Publishers Weekly, January 26, 2004, review of *Faithful,* p. 118; February 23, 2004, review of *Faithful,* p. 50.*

*   *   *

SILVEY, Anita 1947-

PERSONAL: Born September 3, 1947, in Bridgeport, CT; married. *Education:* Indiana University, B.S., 1969; University of Wisconsin, M.A., 1970.

ADDRESSES: Home—101 Whitewood Rd., Westwood, MA 02090. *E-mail*—readermail@anitasilvey.com.

CAREER: Little, Brown and Co., Boston, MA, editorial assistant in children's book department, 1970-71; *Horn Book* magazine, Boston, assistant editor, 1971-75, editor-in-chief, 1985-95; *New Boston Review,* Boston, founder and managing editor, 1975-76; Houghton Mifflin Company, Boston, managing advertising and promotion for children's division, 1976-1984, vice president and publishers of children's

books, 1995-2001. Instructor at Simmons College Graduate School of Library Science, Boston, and St. Michaels College, Burlington, VT. Former president, Children's Book Council; former board member, International Board on Books for Young People, United States section.

MEMBER: International Reading Association, American Library Association, Associations of American Publishers, New England Round Table (chair, 1978-79).

AWARDS, HONORS: Book Women Award, Women's National Book Association, 1987, as one of Seventy Women Who Have Made a Difference; award from City of Fort Wayne, IN, 1994, as one of the city's thirty eight famous sons and daughters; honorary M.F.A., Vermont College, 2000.

WRITINGS:

EDITOR

Children's Books and Their Creators, Houghton Mifflin (Boston, MA), 1995, updated edition published as *The Essential Guide to Children's Books and Their Creators,* 2002.
Help Wanted, Little, Brown (Boston, MA), 1997.
(Author of introduction) *Keat's Neighborhood: An Ezra Jack Keats Treasury,* Viking (New York, NY), 2002.
One Hundred Best Books for Children, Houghton Mifflin (Boston, MA), 2004.

OTHER

Editor, Vermont Folklife Center children's book series, 2003—; member of editorial board, *Cricket* magazine.

SIDELIGHTS: Anita Silvey has worked for many years in children's book publishing and is the editor of several books focusing on children's literature. In an interview with Teri Lesesne for *Teacher Librarian,* Silvey related that, in her opinion, a great book for children "maintains high standards of literary and artistic merit, speaks to both children and adults on different levels, and stands the test time."

In *Children's Books and Their Creators* Silvey gathers more than eight hundred entries focusing authors, various genres, and historical issues in children's publishing. In addition, seventy-five authors and illustrators write about their work. In her 2002 update, *The Essential Guide to Children's Books and Their Creators,* Silvey includes one hundred new articles that add new authors and their works, while keeping only 375 of the articles from the previous work. Writing in *Library Journal,* Kelli Perkins commented that, "Like its acclaimed predecessor, this guide offers brief but meaty articles." *School Library Journal* contributor Suzanne Crowder wrote that *The Essential Guide to Children's Books and Their Creators* "holds a wealth of information about children's literature in an easily accessible, alphabetized format," and she concluded that Silvey's effort is a "solid, handy resource."

In *Help Wanted: Short Stories about Young People Working* Silvey selects a diverse collection of twelve short stories that focus on young adults and their first jobs or work-like experiences. Among the authors included are Borden Deal, Ray Bradbury, Gary Soto, Michael Dorris, and Judith Ortiz Cofer. A *Publishers Weekly* contributor praised the selections for "their uncommon themes, settings, and situations." The reviewer went on to note, "Defining work in broad terms, this enticing collection offers a little something for everyone." Writing in *Booklist,* Stephanie Zvirin noted that "the collection is generally strong and varied."

Silvey provides a preferred children's reading list in *One Hundred Best Books for Children.* In her interview with Lesesne, Silvey explained how she narrowed down the list, focusing on books over the past millennium that target children up to age twelve and allowed only one book per author or illustrator onto the list. She also consulted lists drawn up by others citing the best books of the twentieth century. She explained that she "then interviewed 1,000 to 2,000 people about their favorite books as children, the ones they remembered the most vividly. Then I reread 1,000 books in six months. In the final stages, I simply agonized over the final list." In the book, Silvey provides a plot synopsis and appropriate age range of the reader for each book. She also includes some stories about how the books were created, told from an insider's perspective, and an extensive "Beyond the Hundred Best" list of books that focus on special interests.

Silvey's "long experience as a book reviewer and editor makes her list pretty much spot-on," wrote Ilene Cooper in a *Booklist* review of *One Hundred Best Books for Children.* In *Commentary* Joseph Bottum attested, "There is little that is opinionated or annoying in her selections; neither is there much surprising or exciting." Roger Sutton, writing in *Horn Book,* commented, "The choices . . . are wise, although some of the most contemporary ones . . . are more arguable than definitive." *Library Journal* contributor Marianne Orme concluded, "Teachers, librarians, and home-schoolers will particularly enjoy the way Silvey spices her annotations with entertaining anecdotes."

BIOGRAPHICAL AND CRITICAL SOURCES:

PERIODICALS

Booklist, November 1, 1997, Stephanie Zvirin, review of *Help Wanted: Short Stories about Young People Working,* p. 461; March 15, 1999, review of *Help Wanted,* p. 1300; November 1, 2001, Gillian Engberg, review of *Help Wanted,* p. 478; July, 2004, Ilene Cooper, review of *One Hundred Best Books for Children,* p. 1802.

Commentary, April, 2004, Joseph Bottum, review of *One Hundred Best Books for Children,* p.68.

Horn Book, November-December, 1997, Roger Sutton, review of *Help Wanted,* p. 682; January-February, 2003, Roger Sutton, review of *The Essential Guide to Children's Books and Their Creators,* p. 106; July-August, 2004, Roger Sutton, review of *One Hundred Best Books for Children,* p. 473.

Library Journal, October 1, 2002, Kelli Perkins, review of *The Essential Guide to Children's Books and Their Creators,* p. 81; April 1, 2004, Marianne Orme, review of *One Hundred Best Books for Children,* p. 94.

Publishers Weekly, October 9, 1995, Diane Roback, "Top-Level Shifts in Children's Publishing," p. 14; June 17, 1996, Amy Meeker, interview with Silvey, p. 26; August 4, 1997, review of *Help Wanted,* p. 76; October 21, 2002, review of *The Essential Guide to Children's Books and Their Creators,* p. 77.

School Library Journal, July, 2001, "Silvey Departs Houghton," p. 16; March, 2003, Suzanne Crowder, review of *The Essential Guide to Children's Books and Their Creators,* p. 263.

Teacher Librarian, October, 2004, Teri Lesesne, "Keeping Books Alive" (interview), p. 47.

ONLINE

Anita Silvey Home Page, http://www.anitasilvey.com (February 25, 2005).

Horn Book Web site, http://www.hbook.com/ (February 25, 2005), "Anita Silvey."

* * *

SINGER, Margaret
See SINGER, Margaret Thaler

* * *

SINGER, Margaret Thaler 1921-2003
(Margaret Singer)

PERSONAL: Born July 29, 1921, in Denver, CO; died of complications from pneumonia November 23, 2003, in Berkeley, CA; married Jerome R. Singer (a physics professor), 1955; children: Sam, Martha. *Education:* Denver University, B.A., M.A., Ph.D., 1943.

CAREER: University of Colorado School of Medicine, psychiatry department, 1944-52; Walter Reed Army Institute of Research, Washington, DC, psychologist, 1953-57; University of California, Berkeley, adjunct professor of psychology, 1958-91, professor emeritus, 1991-2003. Researched schizophrenia at National Institute of Mental Health, U.S. Air Force, and Massachusetts Institute of Technology; taught at University of Rochester and Albert Einstein College of Medicine. Board member, Kaiser Foundation Research Institute Review Board, and American Family Foundation.

MEMBER: American Psychosomatic Society (president, 1972-73).

AWARDS, HONORS: Hofheimer Prize for Research, 1966, and Stanley R. Dean Award for Research, 1976, both from American College of Psychiatrists; two-time nominee, Nobel Prize; received awards from American Psychiatric Association, American Association for Marriage and Family Therapy Association, and Mental Health Association of the United States.

WRITINGS:

(With Janja Lalich) *Cults in Our Midst: The Hidden Menace in Our Everyday Lives,* foreword by

Robert Jay Lifton, Jossey-Bass Publishers (San Francisco, CA), 1995, revised edition, 2003.
(With Janja Lalich) *"Crazy" Therapies: What Are They?, Do They Work?,* illustrated by Jim Coughenour, Jossey-Bass Publishers (San Francisco, CA), 1996.

Contributor to numerous professional journals and popular periodicals.

SIDELIGHTS: A trained clinical psychologist, Margaret Thaler Singer became one of the world's foremost experts on cults and brainwashing, authoring more than one hundred articles and interviewing about 4,000 former cult members. As Ivan Oransky stated in the *Lancet,* "Singer was, for almost fifty years, a champion of people who had been kidnapped, brainwashed, or worse by cults and other groups." She also authored two books on the subject with Janja Lalich, a former cult member. *Cults in Our Midst: The Hidden Menace in Our Everyday Lives* is considered "a landmark in the field," according to *Los Angeles Times* contributor Dennis McLellan, while *"Crazy" Therapies: What Are They?, Do They Work?* "deals with the negative and harmful impacts of New Age psychiatric therapies," as McLellan explained.

Singer's work in brainwashing began in 1953 when she went to work at Walter Reed Institute of Research in Washington, D.C., interviewing soldiers who had been prisoners of war in Korea and had undergone psychological and physical manipulation that left many with an aversion to their own country. Singer studied the techniques employed by the North Koreans in this brainwashing and indoctrination. When she and her physics professor husband moved to California, Singer found herself coincidentally placed in what was fast becoming the capital of cultism. Increasingly she was consulted by parents whose children suddenly disappeared, swallowed up by some religious cult or another. Working as adjunct psychology professor at the University of California at Berkeley, Singer began investigating the world of religious cults and their use of brainwashing techniques. Although her research into schizophrenia and its affects on speech patterns is the work for which her professional peers knew her best, Singer became known to the general public for her role as an expert witness in high-profile trials such as that of Patty Hearst as well as various legal cases such as those involving the Unification Church of Rev. Sun Myung Moon. She was also a regular media consultant on incidents such as the mass suicides at the People's Temple in Guyana in 1978, the Branch Davidians in Waco, Texas, in 1993, and the Heaven's Gate cult deaths. She also interviewed Charles Manson, whose cult followers had murdered Sharon Tate and others in 1969.

Singer drew on such experiences in *Cults in Our Midst*, a "well-researched, enlightening introduction to a serious subject," as Mary Carroll noted in a *Booklist* review. From her copious research and interviews of former cult members, Singer explored the nature of cults and how they operate. Her book also explains these groups' threat to society as a whole and details methods by which reluctant members can escape such cults. A *Publishers Weekly* reviewer described *Cults in Our Midst* as "an instructive report on the cult phenomena." In 2003, shortly before her death, Singer updated *Cults in Our Midst*, extending her analysis to show the connection between terrorism and cults.

In *"Crazy" Therapies*, again written with Lalich, Singer took on the host of treatments advocated by New Age therapists, from aroma therapy to chakra and aura readings, searches into past lives, alien-abduction therapy, and rebirthing, among many others. In an article for *Harvard Mental Health Letter*, coauthors Singer and Lalich wrote: "These practitioners purport to bring about such results as inner-child healing, clear frequencies, programming release, finding one's missing self, rebalancing the body's energies, personal empowerment, planetary healing, and alignment of fluid intelligence systems. . . . These methods are not just ineffective, misleading, and therefore a waste of time. Often they are actively abusive and damaging. Clients become accustomed to magical thinking that makes them look for instant solutions to daily problems."

Singer's work earned her numerous enemies among cults, whose members were known to leave dead rats on her doorstep, threatening letters in her mailbox, and hack into her computer. Undeterred, Singer continued her work right up to the time of her death, her most recent projects involving con artists and the frauds they perpetrate on senior citizens such as herself.

BIOGRAPHICAL AND CRITICAL SOURCES:

PERIODICALS

Booklist, April 15, 1995, Mary Carroll, review of *Cults in Our Midst: The Hidden Menace in Our Everyday Lives,* p. 1456.

Harvard Mental Health Letter, December, 1997, Margaret Singer and Janja Lalich, *"Crazy" Therapies: What Are They?, Do They Work?,* p. 5.

NCAHF Newsletter, November-December, 1992, "Cultologists Sue Social Science Associations," p. 2.

Publishers Weekly, March 6, 1995, review of *Cults in Our Midst,* p. 49.

OBITUARIES

PERIODICALS

Family Process, March, 2004, p. 5.
Guardian (Manchester, England), December 2, 2003, p. 29.
Lancet, January 31, 2004, p. 403.
Los Angeles Times, November 28, 2003, p. B16.
New York Times, December 7, 2003, p. A56.
San Francisco Chronicle, November 25, 2003, p. A19.*

*   *   *

SKAGGS, (Barbara) Gayle 1952-

PERSONAL: Born July 29, 1952, in Warrensburg, MO; daughter of James C. (an auto mechanic) and Dorothy N. (an elementary teacher; maiden name, Norman) Saunders; married Robert L. Skaggs (a graphic artist), June 1, 1974; children: Elizabeth Anne Skaggs Stabler, Sarah Christine Skaggs Taylor. *Education:* Central Missouri State University, B.S.E. *Religion:* Southern Baptist. *Hobbies and other interests:* Christian missionary activities (including work in Mexico), a television ministry.

ADDRESSES: Home—1820 West McCarty, Jefferson City, MO 65109. *Office*—Cole County R-5 Schools, P.O. Box 78, Eugene, MO 65032.

CAREER: Art teacher at schools in Chilhowee, MO, 1974-75; librarian at schools in Ridgeway, MO, 1977-78; elementary art teacher in Lathrop, MO, 1978-80, and Hannibal, MO, 1981-82; high school librarian in Jefferson City, MO, 1985-94; elementary librarian in Bourbon, MO, 1995-96, and Conway, MO, 1996-98;

high school librarian in Pleasant Hope, MO, 1998-99; Cole County R-5 Schools, Eugene, MO, elementary librarian, 1999—. Workshop presenter.

MEMBER: Missouri State Teachers Association.

WRITINGS:

(And illustrator) *Bulletin Boards and Displays,* McFarland and Co. (Jefferson, NC), 1993.

(And illustrator) *Off the Wall!,* McFarland and Co. (Jefferson, NC), 1995.

(And illustrator) *On Display: Twenty-five Themes to Promote Reading,* McFarland and Co. (Jefferson, NC), 1999.

Reading Is First: Great Ideas for Teachers and Librarians, illustrated by husband Robert L. Skaggs, McFarland and Co. (Jefferson, NC), 2003.

WORK IN PROGRESS: "A book for teachers and librarians that presents a step-by-step approach to promoting reading for a school year based on a U.S.A. theme; *First Century,* a hands-on vacation bible School."

SIDELIGHTS: Gayle Skaggs told *CA:* "I am a wife and mother before anything else. My husband Bob and I have been married since 1974 and are blessed to have two wonderful daughters and two beautiful granddaughters. I love being a grandmother!

"Next to my family, I am very much involved in my church. I am a born-again believer in Jesus Christ, and it is a privilege to share my faith with others. I try to go on mission trips each year where I work in vacation bible schools, construction projects, et cetera, to tell others about the Lord. This year I painted a large painting of Christ that was hung on the wall of one of the men's cell blocks at the Santa Adelida Prison in Matamoros, Mexico. Our team also worked with the inmates to paint Bible verses and symbols on the walls surrounding their baseball field. It was an awesome experience!

"My current project is to begin a library in a school in the 'Squatter's camp' in Matamoros, Mexico. 700 children attend this school and they have no books to read. Being able to read is powerful and it could open up a better life for these children.

"My mother is a retired elementary teacher. As a teenager, I helped her create items to decorate her classroom. She encouraged me to be creative and express myself artistically. We had very little money for supplies, so I had to learn to make things with found materials or to look at everyday items in a new way. Even though I am not a great artist, I have found that you don't have to be a fantastic artist to create effective displays. My motivation is to encourage others to create eye-catching, colorful displays to excite children about reading. My books are designed to simplify the process for the busy educator.

"It is exciting to be able to combine my art abilities and the look of the library. I look at the library as if it were a store and the children are my customers. Some customers need a little more persuasion to buy than others, so that is my challenge.

"When I first became a librarian at a large high school, one of my responsibilities was to promote the library and reading in displays and bulletin boards. I looked for ideas in the books we had in the library, and I was not impressed. Everything looked old, dated, and tired. I decided to create my own bulletin board book to help other librarians and teachers to create great displays at little or no cost. I drew all the pictures for the books myself so that the reader could see how simple the process could be. One of my goals was to get the reader to start thinking more three-dimensionally instead of just using the traditional, flat display. I really used a lot of carpet tubes for many of the suggested ideas!

"After the first book was published, I was asked to conduct workshops for our school district, and eventually I led several workshops for the Missouri Association of School Librarians at their annual meeting. The next two books were done in a similar style.

"*Reading Is First: Great Ideas for Teachers and Librarians* was written to address the current elementary reading programs, such as 'Accelerated Reader' and 'Reading Counts.' Many librarians and teachers have the responsibility of coming up with a theme each year to promote the program. The book contains themes complete with promotion ideas to tie reading to every other part of the school. This book is special to me because my husband created all the illustrations.

"When I make up my mind to write a book, and that is a big commitment of time and energy, I like to do that by using all of my free time after school and on weekends to accomplish the task. Everything I want to include just seems to flow out quickly! Sometimes I wonder if any of my ideas will be useful and then I think about my own school and how well they have worked there. Our school can't be all that different from other elementary schools. It is such a treat to hear one of my students say 'WOW' when they enter my library or participate in a reading promotion.

"*Reading is First* is special because I worked with my husband to complete it. It was a joy to work with him. . . . This book has many great ideas for the librarian or teacher who has to promote a reading program."

BIOGRAPHICAL AND CRITICAL SOURCES:

PERIODICALS

Booklist, October 1, 1995, Stephanie Zvirin, review of *Off the Wall!*, p. 330; July, 1999, Ilene Cooper, review of *On Display: Twenty-five Themes to Promote Reading*, p. 1960.
Reference and User Services Quarterly, fall, 1999, Michael A. Perry, review of *On Display*, p. 110.
School Library Journal, November, 2003, Edith Ching, review of *Reading Is First: Great Ideas for Teachers and Librarians*, p. 175.

*   *   *

SMITH, Mary Burnett 1931-

PERSONAL: Born 1931; married. *Education:* Temple University, M.A. (education).

ADDRESSES: Home—PA. *Agent*—c/o Author Mail, William Morrow & Company, 10 East 53rd St., 7th Floor, New York, NY 10022.

CAREER: School teacher in Philadelphia, PA, until 1992.

AWARDS, HONORS: Fiction Short Story Award, *Ebony* magazine.

WRITINGS:

Miss Ophelia (novel), Morrow (New York, NY), 1997.
Ring around the Moon (novel), Morrow (New York, NY), 1998.

SIDELIGHTS: Mary Burnett Smith's first novel about a young black girl growing up in post-World War II Virginia, was a debut well received by critics. Narrated by the now-grown-up Isabelle—once known as Belly—it recounts the events of the summer of 1948, when she went away to care for sick relatives. In a strange town, Belly is lonely, and her aunt is mean, but the girl finds sympathy and kindness from her new piano teacher, Miss Ophelia. In this setting, Belly learns many new lessons about people and adulthood, including discrimination within races, abortion, religious hypocrisy, and adultery.

Critics praised Smith for a well-told tale, and especially for her fine crafting of Belly's character. A *Kirkus Reviews* critic, for one, called *Miss Ophelia* a "gently affecting tale" and credited Smith with having "richly realized the ritual courtesies and dynamic village unity of an isolated community." A *Publishers Weekly* reviewer called the book "exceptional" and noted, "The plot isn't terribly original, but Smith . . . handles it with notable delicacy, capturing the complex way in which Belly half-comprehends the lives of the adults around her." Beth E. Anderson, writing for *Library Journal*, deemed Belly to be "so genuinely rendered that the reader must struggle to remember that this is a work of fiction."

Smith's second novel, *Ring around the Moon*, resembles her first in several ways. Also set in the 1940s, it is narrated by a young African-American girl who watches her parents struggle to keep their marriage intact. On a sweltering July night, nine-year-old Amy Beale is present as her mother gives her father—a gambler, drinker, womanizer, and wife beater—one more chance to save the marriage over the course of a "trial year." Amy chronicles the final year of this disastrous relationship and recounts its effects on herself and her two brothers. She also reminisces on her struggles with self-image, her desperate need for friendship, and the cruel jokes and taunts she suffered from other children because of her light complexion and reddish hair. A *Publishers Weekly* reviewer commented on the book's "fine dialogue and vivid characters," while Joanne Wilkinson noted in *Booklist* that the author's "impressionistic writing style is perfectly matched to her material."

BIOGRAPHICAL AND CRITICAL SOURCES:

PERIODICALS

Booklist, September 1, 1997, Lillian Lewis, review of *Miss Ophelia,* p. 61; October 1, 1998, Joanne Wilkinson, review of *Ring around the Moon,* p. 309.

Kirkus Reviews, July 1, 1997, review of *Miss Ophelia,* pp. 979-980.

Library Journal, August 1997, Beth E. Anderson, review of *Miss Ophelia,* p. 136.

Publishers Weekly, July 21, 1997, review of *Miss Ophelia,* p. 182; September 7, 1998, review of *Ring around the Moon,* p. 83.*

*   *   *

SMITH, Nicola

PERSONAL: Married Geoff Hansen (a photographer); children: one daughter. *Education:* Columbia University, M.F.A.

ADDRESSES: Home—White River Junction, VT. *Agent*—c/o Author Mail, Lyons Press, P.O. Box 480, Guilford, CT 06437. *E-mail*—nsmith@harvest-book. com.

CAREER: Freelance writer.

WRITINGS:

Harvest: A Year in the Life of an Organic Farm, photographs by Geoff Hansen, Lyon's Press (Guilford, CT), 2004.

SIDELIGHTS: In her first book, *Harvest: A Year in the Life of an Organic Farm,* freelance writer Nicola Smith and her husband, freelance photographer Geoff Hansen, chronicle the lives of their neighbors, Jennifer Megeysi and Kyle Jones. Megeysi and Jones, both of whom have graduate degrees in wildlife conservation, own and operate a twenty-acre organic farm in Vermont called Fat Rooster Farm. Running Fat Rooster Farm is hard work, and in her "well-written profile" Smith" presents a realistic look at the pleasures and enormous difficulties of farming for a living," Ilse Heidmann wrote in *Library Journal.* Among the difficulties are the long hours spent not only caring for the livestock and crops but also on the business aspects of running a farm, such as manning booths at farmers' markets and hauling produce to commercial customers such as restaurants. Then, after these tasks have been completed, the couple must report to the part-time jobs that they have been forced to take, since they cannot support themselves on the farm income alone. This stress takes a toll on Jones and Megeysi's relationship, and Smith provides a "close-up view of the private, painful, and real negotiations necessary to keep the farm running," noted *Booklist* reviewer Gillian Engberg. A *Publishers Weekly* reviewer also praised Smith's attention to the human side of small farms, commenting that "Megeysi may be one of the most vividly drawn farm women since *Letters of a Woman Homesteader.*"

BIOGRAPHICAL AND CRITICAL SOURCES:

PERIODICALS

Booklist, October 1, 2004, Gillian Engberg, review of *Harvest: A Year in the Life of an Organic Farm,* p. 290.

Library Journal, November 1, 2004, Ilse Heidmann, review of *Harvest,* p. 112.

Publishers Weekly, September 20, 2004, review of *Harvest,* p. 54.

ONLINE

Geoff Hansen Home Page, http://www.geoffhansen. com/ (February 15, 2005).

Globe Pequot Press, http://www.globepequot.com/ (February 15, 2005), "*Harvest.*"

Harvest, http://www.harvest-book.com/ (February 15, 2005).*

*   *   *

SMITHEE, Alan
See FRANKENHEIMER, John (Michael)

SONGER, C. J.

PERSONAL: Born in NY; married (husband a former police detective); children: two. *Education:* University of Minnesota, B.F.A. (theatre); Florida State University at Tallahassee, M.F.A. (theatre).

ADDRESSES: Home—P.O. Box 393, Simi Valley, CA 93062. *E-mail*—redsfox@aol.com.

CAREER: Novelist and columnist. Worked for the Glendale, CA, police department.

MEMBER: California Rifle and Pistol Association.

WRITINGS:

"MEG GILLIS" CRIME NOVEL SERIES

Bait, Scribner (New York, NY), 1998.
Hook, Scribner (New York, NY), 1999.
Line, Scribner (New York, NY), 2003.

OTHER

Contributor to periodicals, including *Women & Guns.* Author of column "View from the Home Front" for *Firing Line* (magazine of the California Rifle and Pistol Association).

Author's works have been translated into German.

WORK IN PROGRESS: A fourth "Meg Gillis" crime novel.

SIDELIGHTS: Mystery novelist C. J. Songer is well acquainted with the day-to-day details of a life of crime and law enforcement. For many years, she worked for the Glendale, California, police department, and her husband is a former Glendale police officer and robbery/homicide detective. "Cops have been a constant in my life for the past eighteen years— sometimes more, sometimes less, but always there," Songer said in an interview with Cathy Sova on *TheMysteryReader.com.* Songer is also an ardent supporter of weapons and self-defense training. She has trained at a number of prominent shooting schools throughout the country, including Gunsite, and has participated in invitation-only shooting competitions and tactical matches emphasizing street survival skills. "I'm not particularly gung-ho about guns, myself, because I think good defense is as much or more the grit of the person as it is the weapon, and so I really take pains not to train to be 'weapon-reliant,'" Songer remarked in a *BooksnBytes.com* interview with Jon Jordan. Still, she advocates at least a basic level of firearms knowledge for defense of self and others, stating, "How the heck can you understand what the issues are or what you can do about them until you understand how guns work and how other people think about them?"

Songer also holds degrees in theatre from the University of Minnesota and Florida State University at Tallahassee. She admits to a love of science fiction, but "decided to write mysteries because of the combustible conflict of coming from a liberal arts/liberal family background," and her work at the Glendale police department, she commented to Sova.

Songer has successfully conbined her training into a successful run of mystery novels featuring character Meg Gillis. *Bait* introduces Gillis, an ex-police officer and cop widow whose police-officer husband was killed in an unsolved shooting. She is co-owner of a business selling home-security systems. When Meg's business partner, Mike Johnson, who is also an ex-cop, fails to show up at work one Saturday morning, she gives it little thought beyond annoyance, thinking that one of his many romantic trysts must have delayed him again. However, when a mysterious phone call meant for Mike reports a kidnapping, her police senses go on alert. Investigating, Meg finds clues to a possible murder, one in which she has inadvertently become the prime suspect. While she is grilled by the police, she is asked uncomfortable questions about Mike's business practices that involve possible drug sales and blackmailing of customers. Detective sergeant Joe Reilly presses the investigation, but Meg is not sure if Reilly is out to solve the crime, implicate her completely, or cover up some wrongdoing of his own. When Meg's stolen car is recovered, it is covered in blood and she realizes she is the victim of a carefully orchestrated frame-up.

"The author's strength in this debut novel lies in her own past experience on the police force, and the nuances of police investigation tactics," commented reviewer Martha Moore on *TheMysteryReader.com.* "Songer clearly has a good feel for police work and strong dialogue among her cop and ex-cop characters." A *Publishers Weekly* reviewer called *Bait* a "convoluted, often enticing tale," while Rex E. Klett remarked in *Library Journal* that the book displays "forceful, gutsy prose, winning characters, and a caustic look at police procedure."

In *Hook* Meg helps out her business partner, Mike, by serving legal papers on suspected wife abuser Rudolfo de la Peña. When she meets Rudolfo, however, Meg has trouble believing that the sophisticated gentleman is really an abusive brute. When Rudolfo is found dead, Meg suspects a set-up, a theory that is reinforced by the looming presence of a couple of unsavory thugs. She sets out to find answers, and her often-frustrating investigation finally leads to motives in the volatile politics and brutal military dictatorships of Pena's native Argentina. A *Publishers Weekly* critic commented that *Hook* "falters" in areas such as dialogue, pacing, and character action. "In the end," the *Publishers Weekly* reviewer stated, "*Hook* will snare readers, but not firmly."

"I've always written," Songer said in the interview with Sova, "so to me writing is a natural expression, an art form, my effort at giving a gift. A way to translate, perhaps, between different cultures and feelings. That sounds high-falutin', and truthfully, I don't know that anyone else perceives my books that way, or will care very deeply, but still I have this obligation, the need to express [and] to give back a little, to honor the people and the influences as best I can."

BIOGRAPHICAL AND CRITICAL SOURCES:

PERIODICALS

Booklist, July, 1998, David Pitt, review of *Bait,* p. 1866.
Library Journal, July, 1998, Rex E. Klett, review of *Bait,* p. 141.
Publishers Weekly, June 15, 1998, review of *Bait,* p. 45; November 15, 1999, review of *Hook,* p. 58.

ONLINE

BooksnBytes.com, http://www.booksnbytes.com/ (July 20, 2004), Jon Jordan, interview with Songer.

C. J. Songer Home Page, http://hometown.aol.com/ redsfox/ (July 20, 2004).
CrescentBlues.com, http://www.crescentblues.com/ (July 27, 2004), Donna Andrews, interview with Songer.
TheMysteryReader.com, http://www.themysteryreader. com/ (July 20, 2004), Cathy Sova, interview with Songer; (July 20, 2004) Martha Moore, review of *Bait.* *

*   *   *

SPARROW, Elizabeth 1928-

PERSONAL: Born 1928.

ADDRESSES: Agent—c/o Author Mail, Boydell & Brewer, 668 Mount Hope Avenue, Rochester, NY 14620-2731.

CAREER: Independent scholar and writer.

WRITINGS:

Secret Service: British Agents in France, 1792-1815, Boydell Press (Rochester, NY), 1999.

Contributor to periodicals, including *Historical Journal.*

SIDELIGHTS: An acknowledged authority on the beginnings of the British secret service, Elizabeth Sparrow is the author of *Secret Service: British Agents in France, 1792-1815.* In the book, Sparrow follows the origins of the British secret service, especially in relation to the Alien Office, a British government department that was created to deal with immigrant issues. In reality, the agency was overseeing the British government's spying efforts in Europe. Sparrow had discovered many unknown documents of the agency in the late 1980s and spent a decade studying them and other documents from archives in France and Switzerland in order to write her book. Focusing primarily on the British efforts to spy on arch-enemy France, Sparrow begins by delving into efforts underway to influence who would rule France following the French Revolution, including working with such factions as the modern monarchists. Eventually Napoleon Bonaparte took control of France, ending such intrigue, and the second part of Sparrow's book looks at the British spying efforts following Bonaparte's ascent to power, including, as pointed out by Dave Hollins in a review on *Napoleonseries.org,* Britain's "channeling of money and operations in France to divert Napoleon's attention." According to Sparrow, it was not long before such covert actions raised the stakes to increasing internal dissent to bring about Napoleon's downfall. British spies were so successful in some of their infiltration efforts that they often controlled much of the Paris police. Nevertheless, not everything went smoothly, such as when British agents were captured in 1804 as part of a plot to assassinate Napoleon.

Through the course of *Secret Service* Sparrow delves into the roles of many individuals, including William Windham, who was believed to be a minor government minister and dilettante but who in reality was in charge of British spying efforts. She also discusses William Wickham, an agent stationed in Switzerland who tried to bring about the collapse of revolutionary France. Sparrow also delves into the mysterious identity of the Scarlet Pimpernel, the shadowy figure on whom Baroness Orczy modeled the hero of her novel of the same name. In fact, Sparrow indicates, Orczy's fictional hero was based on three agents: Xandrin; low-level aristocrat Louis Bayard; and Richard Cadman Etches, who Sparrow believes is the primary source for the fictional Scarlet Pimpernel.

Several reviewers noted that Sparrow's intense research and detailed discussion of the facts tends to "get in the way of a good story," as John Crossland wrote in the London *Sunday Times.* However, Crossland went on to note that "if you have the stamina to stay with this marathon of plotting, there are rewards and some surprises." *English Historical Review* contributor Clive Emsley remarked that in *Secret Service* "Sparrow exposes an astonishing tale." M. R. D. Foot, writing in the *Spectator,* commented that "the whole history of the world war against revolutionary and Napoleonic France now has to be rewritten."

BIOGRAPHICAL AND CRITICAL SOURCES:

PERIODICALS

English Historical Review, June, 2000, Clive Emsley, review of *Secret Service: British Agents in France, 1792-1815,* p. 746.

Spectator, June 17, 2000, M. R. D. Foot, review of *Secret Service,* pp. 48-49.
Sunday Times (London, England), February 20, 2000, John Crossland, review of *Secret Service,* p. 41.

ONLINE

Jane Austin Centre in Bath Web site, http://www.janeausten.co.uk/ (July 14, 2004), review of *Secret Service.*
Napoleonic-Literature.com, http://www.napoleonic-literature.com/ (July 14, 2004), review of *Secret Service.*
Napoleonseries.org, http://www.napoleonseries.org/ (February, 2000), Dave Hollins, review of *Secret Service.**

*   *   *

SPENDER, (John) Humphrey 1910-2005

OBITUARY NOTICE— See index for *CA* sketch: Born April 19, 1910, in London, England; died of heart failure March 20, 2005, in Ulting, Essex, England. Photographer, textile designer, and author. Spender belonged to a breed of documentary photographers that included Walter Evans, who recorded black-and-white images of ordinary life during the Depression Era. After studying at the University of Freiburg, he attended courses at the British Architectural Association and qualified as an architect in 1933. Instead of going into this field, however, Spender returned to his boyhood love of photography and opened up his own studio in London. In 1937, he was hired to be the official photographer for England's Mass Observation project, an initiative similar to the photography program administered by the U.S. Works Progress Administration at the time. From 1937 until 1938, Spender recorded images of working-class Brits, taking the pictures for which he would later become known after his work was rediscovered in the 1970s. Spender also gained recognition for his contributions to the magazine *Picture Post* and for a series of photographs that included his brother, poet Stephen Spender, and novelist Christopher Isherwood. During World War II, Spender worked for the British War Office, notably saving the lives of a group of war prisoners when he informed the Royal Air Force that they had incorrectly identified a prisoner camp as a military target. By the 1950s, despite his previous success, Spender put away his camera to focus on other artistic pursuits, including painting and wallpaper and textile design. He also taught at the Royal College of Art. His photographs have been collected in such books as *Mass Observation: The First Year's Work* (1938), *Britain Revisited* (1968), and *Humphrey Spender's Humanist Landscapes: Photo-Documents, 1932-1942* (1997).

OBITUARIES AND OTHER SOURCES:

PERIODICALS

Independent (London, England), March 14, 2005, p. 34.
Los Angeles Times, March 26, 2005, p. B17.
New York Times, March 20, 2005, p. A27.
Times (London, England), March 15, 2005, p. 58.

* * *

STEINHAUER, Olen

PERSONAL: Married. *Education:* Emerson College, graduate study in creative writing.

ADDRESSES: Home—Budapest, Hungary. *Agent*—c/o Author Mail, St. Martin's Press, Inc., 175 5th Ave., New York, NY 10010.

CAREER: Has worked as a librarian, teacher, manual laborer, film producer, and author. Co-producer, with Krista Steinhauer, of film documentary *Central Square,* 1999.

AWARDS, HONORS: Fulbright fellowship; production grant, Massachusetts Institute of Technology, for film *Central Square;* Ellis Peters Historical Dagger Award nomination, Crime Writers' Association, Anthony Award for Best Historical Novel, Bouchercon, and Macavity Award for Best Novel, and Edgar Allan Poe Award, both from Mystery Writers of America, all 2004, all for *The Bridge of Sighs.*

WRITINGS:

The Bridge of Sighs, St. Martin's Minotaur (New York, NY), 2003.
The Confession, St. Martin's Minotaur (New York, NY), 2004.

Also contributor of poems and stories to literary journals; creator of online journal.

Steinhauer's books have been translated into Swedish, French, and Japanese.

ADAPTATIONS: Blackstone Audiobooks recorded audiocassette versions of *The Bridge of Sighs,* 2003, and *The Confession,* 2004.

WORK IN PROGRESS: Essay "The Errant Compass," about living in voluntary exile; several film scripts; three novels; autobiographical vignettes; an online newsletter.

SIDELIGHTS: Olen Steinhauer, an American known for penning crime novels set in Eastern Europe during the cold war, traces his interest in that part of the world to stints as an exchange student in Croatia and as a Fulbright scholar in Romania. With two successful novels to his credit Steinhauer found an important niche for himself in the field of crime writing. On his Web site, Steinhauer wrote that he finds such writing "satisfying" in its "mixture of European setting and criminal element." He chooses unnamed countries for his settings, he said, because his focus is on "the psychological reality . . . , not in the absolute reality of all the details."

Steinhauer's first book, drawn from his Ph.D. thesis, is *The Bridge of Sighs.* Set in 1948, the year of the Berlin Airlift, the story follows Emil Brod, a young homicide inspector for the People's Militia, as he tries to solve two murders in a small Eastern European country. Brod's police colleagues treat him with disdain, thinking that he is a spy, and he is not even given a gun. He undergoes many other obstacles as he moves from location to location to solve the murder of a well-known songwriter, Janos Crowder, who has been found beaten to death in his apartment. The fact that the murdered man was politically well connected makes the rookie inspector's job all the more difficult.

Critical response to *The Bridge of Sighs* was positive, and the novel received several awards. In the *Houston Chronicle,* P. G. Koch wrote that "what [Steinhauer] does best . . . is reimagine the palpable dangers of that perilously tilted postwar landscape." Edna Boardman, writing in *Kliatt,* called the novel a "richly drawn detective mystery." Ronnie H. Terpening wrote in *Library Journal* that the book is an "intelligent, finely polished debut, loaded with atmospheric detail."

Steinhauer continues his series with a second novel, *The Confession.* This story, set in another unnamed Eastern European country in 1956, follows an older homicide inspector, Ferenc Kolyeszar, as he investigates a murder and the apparent suicide of a prominent Communist Party member's wife. Kolyeszar has to deal not only with the intricacies of a totalitarian system, but also with his own crumbling marriage and his grisly memories of World War II. David Wright, in a review for *Booklist,* wrote that although the premise of a detective troubled by personal "demons is hardly new . . . seldom is it presented with such depth and personal intensity."

Other critics were equally impressed with *The Confession.* Terpening, in *Library Journal,* called the novel "a gripping and fully realized portrayal of a man whose strengths, flaws, struggle, and ultimate fall are emblematic of the fate of Eastern Europe itself." Another reviewer for *Publishers Weekly* commented on the "deaths and deceptions snowballing grotesquely" and said that "the novel makes readers wonder just what Steinhauer will do for the next book in his series."

Steinhauer's other writing projects include a novel about another intriguing character caught in the vicissitudes of an unstable Eastern Europe. Along with two other planned novels, he was working on a lengthy essay about life in voluntary exile, several film scripts, and his own online newsletter.

BIOGRAPHICAL AND CRITICAL SOURCES:

PERIODICALS

Booklist, January 1, 2004, David Wright, review of *The Confession,* p. 835.
Entertainment Weekly, March 12, 2004, Michelle King, review of *The Confession,* p. 120.
Houston Chronicle, May 4, 2003, P. G. Koch, "Shades of Gray: Nominal Hero Seen in Terrifying Light," p. 19.
Kliatt, November, 2003, Edna Boardman, review of *The Bridge of Sighs,* p. 44.

Library Journal, December, 2002, Ronnie H. Terpening, review of *The Bridge of Sighs,* p. 184; January, 2004, Ronnie H. Terpening, review of *The Confession,* p. 166, Scott R. DeMarco, review of *The Bridge of Sighs,* p. 183.
Publishers Weekly, January 20, 2003, review of *The Bridge of Sighs,* p. 59; December 1, 2003, review of *The Confession,* p. 38.

ONLINE

Olen Steinhauer Home Page, http://www.olen steinhauer.com (July 25, 2005).*

*   *   *

STUDLAR, Gaylyn

PERSONAL: Female. *Education:* Texas Tech University, B.A. (music); University of Southern California, M.A. (music), Ph.D. (communication), 1984.

ADDRESSES: Office—University of Michigan, Program in Film and Video Studies, 2512 Frieze, 105 South State St., Ann Arbor, MI 48109. *E-mail*—gstudlar@umich.edu.

CAREER: Film scholar, author, and educator. Emory University, Atlanta, GA, associate professor; University of Michigan, Ann Arbor, professor of women's studies and director of program in film and video studies, 1995—, Rudolph Arnheim Collegiate Professor of Film Studies, 2000—. American Museum of the Moving Image, New York, NY, guest curator.

WRITINGS:

In the Realm of Pleasure: Von Sternberg, Dietrich, and the Masochistic Aesthetic, University of Illinois (Urbana, IL), 1988.
This Mad Masquerade: Stardom and Masculinity in the Jazz Age, Columbia University Press (New York, NY), 1996.

EDITOR

(With David Desser) *Reflections in a Male Eye: John Huston and the American Experience,* Smithsonian Institution Press (Washington, DC), 1993.

(With Matthew Bernstein) *Visions of the East: Orientalism in Film,* Rutgers University Press (New Brunswick, NJ), 1997.

(With Kevin S. Sandler) *Titanic: Anatomy of a Blockbuster,* Rutgers University Press (New Brunswick, NJ), 1999.

(With Matthew Bernstein) *John Ford Made Westerns: Filming the Legend in the Sound Era,* Indiana University Press (Bloomington, IN), 2001.

Contributor of critical essays to scholarly periodicals and books, including *Mob Culture,* edited by Esther Sonnet and Lee Grievson, Cambridge University Press (Cambridge, England), 2003, and *Interdisciplinary Literary Studies: A Journal of Criticism and Theory.*

WORK IN PROGRESS: From Girls to Women: Female Transformation in Classical Hollywood and *Harem Envy: Hollywood Orientalism and American Sexuality, 1919-1929.*

SIDELIGHTS: Theorist Gaylyn Studlar has written and edited several works of film criticism focusing on issues of gender and ethnicity. Her publications evince a highly theoretical approach to film and are based on the author's understanding of different schools of psychoanalysis, semiotics, colonialism, and feminist theory. Studlar specializes in American film, particularly from the 1910s and 1930s, but she has also edited critical collections that deal more broadly with twentieth-century film history in the United States and abroad.

In the Realm of Pleasure: Von Sternberg, Dietrich, and the Masochistic Aesthetic examines the subject of masochism in six 1930s-era films—including *Morocco* (1930) and *The Devil Is a Woman* (1935)—all directed by Josef von Sternberg and starring Marlene Dietrich. Influenced by the work of French theorist Giles Deleuze, Studlar contends that the films exhibit a type of masochistic pleasure different from that identified by earlier film theorists, notably Laura Mulvey and her view of women as passive objects of a voyeuristic male gaze. As reviewer Nancy Warring explained in the *Women's Review of Books,* "Studlar argues instead that cinematic pleasure belongs to everyone who has ever been an infant. . . . [Her] account of visual pleasure is a far cry from the male-sadistic, controlling pleasure commonly associated with spectatorship in modern film theory." *Choice* reviewer J. E. Gates found Studlar's work to signal "an important redirec-

tion in feminist film study that could lead the way to further questioning of the Freudian bias existing in current theories of gender difference." Likewise, *Film Quarterly* contributor Vivian Sobchack observed that, "despite it's flaws," *In the Realm of Pleasure* "is an important and extremely valuable [book] and should be read—no less for its rigorous and provocative argument than for its model applications of Peircean semiotics and rhetorical tropes to the von Sternberg/Dietrich films."

In *This Mad Masquerade: Stardom and Masculinity in the Jazz Age* Studlar examines the films of four male stars from the silent era—Douglas Fairbanks, John Barrymore, Rudolph Valentino, and Lon Chaney—and places their respective embodiment of masculinity in the American social context of the time. In particular, Studlar suggests that the masculine identities acted out by each of the actors reflect a transformation of gender roles and underlying social expectations during the 1920s.

As *Film Quarterly* critic Shari Roberts wrote, "Studlar's central argument is that Fairbanks works hegemonically to enforce normative masculinity, while the other three stars progressively function to transgress and, with Chaney, to negate this norm." Summarizing the significance of Chaney in Studlar's analysis, Roberts wrote, "Chaney's grotesque performances constitute an anti-modern, masochistic, self-reflexive, and subversive revelation of the Other, which is the masquerade that is masculinity." Though finding fault in Studlar's theoretical reticence and conspicuous neglect of race, class, and sexual orientation as integral issues, Roberts commended the book's "exemplary" self-contained chapters, noting that the work "certainly serves as a useful contribution to the continually growing wealth of scholarly studies on stars, spectatorship, and social constructions." *Choice* reviewer J. I. Deutsch called *This Mad Masquerade* a "well-documented and incisive analysis of how the roles and performances of these four stars represented changing notions of masculinity."

Studlar has also served as an editor of several critical collections. *Reflections in a Male Eye: John Huston and the American Experience,* coedited with David Desser, is a collection of twelve essays on the films of American director John Huston. The volume provides positive and negative takes on the director's work, as well as an interview with Huston and two short stories by the filmmaker. Though best known for his films of the 1940s and 1950s—notably *The Maltese Falcon* (1941), *Treasure of the Sierra Madre* (1948), and *The African Queen* (1951)—Huston worked up until his death in 1987. *Reflections in a Male Eye* focuses on academic debates concerning the significance and lasting value of Huston's oeuvre. According to *Sight and Sound* contributor Peter Matthews, "Studlar's and Desser's anthology is the more welcome in that it attempts—partially and with mixed success—to wrestle free from the deadening grip of structural determinism. Nearly all the contributors treat Huston not merely as the reflex of this or that ideological formation or institutional setting, but as an artist with specific traits whose films can be distinguished, argued over, liked or disliked." However, commenting on the critical perspective suggested by the book's title, Matthews argued that Huston is "too complicated an animal to be pinned down by the terms of a 'masculinity' debate."

Visions of the East: Orientalism in Film, which Studlar edited with Matthew Bernstein, is a collection of essays that examine the presentation of North African, Middle Eastern, and Asian cultures in Western films. Studlar contributed an essay on "fan magazine orientalism," according to *Library Journal* reviewer Robert W. Metlon, who noted that "the audience for this book is clearly academic." While acknowledging several outstanding selections, *Film Quarterly* commentator Gina Marchetti found shortcomings in the volume's lack of focus and inadequate elaboration of Edward Said's postcolonial theory, notably his influential concept of Orientalism, which ostensibly frames the collection's theoretical perspective. "Rather than having a clear sense of the issues and theoretical approaches to Orientalism to be covered by the anthology," wrote Marchetti, "the editors seem to have taken a haphazard approach, too much on some topics and films, not enough on others, and absolutely noting at all on certain key issues."

Studlar has also coedited critical collections on director James Cameron's *Titanic* and on the work of noted filmmaker John Ford. *Titanic: Anatomy of a Blockbuster,* edited by Studlar and Kevin S. Sandler, contains fourteen critical essays on the 1997 box-office phenomenon *Titanic,* directed by Cameron and starring Leonardo DiCaprio and Kate Winslet. As *Artforum International* critic Vernon Shetley observed, "the extraordinary popularity and monumental banality [of *Titanic*] cries out for the sophisticated skepticism that the best practitioners of cultural criticism bring to mass-media texts." However, Shetley remarked,

"revelations" of this order "are in short supply" in Studlar and Sandler's collection. Dismissing the volume as an *academic instant book* that seeks to seize upon a "'hot' topic," Shetley found the majority of the collection's selections jargon-ridden and superficial.

In *John Ford Made Westerns: Filming the Legend in the Sound Era,* edited by Studlar and Matthew Bernstein, the volume's academic contributors selected consider Ford's Westerns in light of ideological issues involving gender, class, and race. Among the book's nine essays is one by Studlar, "Sacred Duties, Poetic Passions," in which she addresses the issue of femininity in Ford's Westerns. While noting that some readers might object to the book's ideological emphasis, reviewer David Boyd praised the collection in the online journal *SensesofCinema.com.* According to Boyd, "the overall standard of this volume is very high indeed: every one of the essays has something to say, and says it clearly and persuasively."

BIOGRAPHICAL AND CRITICAL SOURCES:

PERIODICALS

Artforum International, October, 1999, Vernon Shetley, review of *Titanic: Anatomy of a Blockbuster,* p. 32.

Choice, March, 1989, J. E. Gates, review of *In the Realm of Pleasure: Von Sternberg, Dietrich, and the Masochistic Aesthetic,* p. 1176; January, 1997, J. I. Deutsch, review of *This Mad Masquerade: Stardom and Masculinity in the Jazz Age,* p. 804.

Film Quarterly, spring, 1990, Vivian Sobchack, review of *In the Realm of Pleasure,* pp. 43-46; summer, 1994, Doug K. Holm, review of *Reflections in a Male Eye: John Huston and the American Experience,* p. 52; spring, 1998, Shari Roberts, review of *This Mad Masquerade,* p. 62; fall, 1998, Gina Marchetti, review of *Visions of the East: Orientalism in Film,* p. 93.

Library Journal, March 15, 1993, Richard W. Grefrath, review of *Reflections in a Male Eye,* p. 80; February 1, 1997, Robert W. Melton, review of *Visions of the East,* p. 81.

Sight and Sound, August, 1993, Peter Matthews, review of *Reflections in a Male Eye,* p. 36.

Women's Review of Books, December, 1988, Nancy Waring, review of *In the Realm of Pleasure,* p. 15.

ONLINE

SensesofCinema.com, http://www.sensesofcinema.com/ (December, 2001), David Boyd, review of *Titanic.**

T

TANGE, Kenzo 1913-2005

OBITUARY NOTICE— See index for *CA* sketch: Born September 4, 1913, in Osaka, Japan; died of heart failure March 22, 2005, in Tokyo, Japan. Architect, educator, and author. Tange, often recognized for his design for the Peace Memorial Park that honors those who died in Hiroshima, was a prize-winning architect whose work combined the best of modern and traditional, East and West designs. He earned his architecture degree at the University of Tokyo in 1938, and then worked for the firm Kunio Maekawa before returning to the university as a graduate student in 1942. He earned a Ph.D. in 1945 and completed his doctoral thesis in 1959. Tange, who was influenced by Swiss architect Le Corbusier through his work with that designer's disciple, Maekawa, thereafter combined an active career as both a working architect and a teacher. He began teaching architecture at the University of Tokyo in 1946, and in 1961 he became a partner in the firm Kenzo Tange & Urtec, which later became Kenzo Tange Associates. Tange made a name for himself early in his career, when his bid to rebuild the central core of the nuclear-bomb-devastated Hiroshima was accepted in 1951. The result was the Peace Memorial Park, which artfully includes a park, hotel, library, museum, and offices. This and later structures designed by Tange are notable for their eclectic and effective combination of old and new, Eastern and Western architecture. He also helped encourage the acceptance of the Metabolist school, which sought ways to accommodate Japan's rapidly growing population through such solutions as floating structures and buildings with replaceable components. Tange designed important buildings worldwide, including the Tokyo City Hall, the Nanyang Technological Institute, the World Square in Australia, King Faisal's Palace in Saudi Arabia, the Bulgarian Embassy and Chancellery, the Japanese Embassy in Mexico City, St. Mary's Cathedral, the Olympic Gyms in Tokyo, and additions to the Minneapolis Art Museum. He was recognized for his accomplishments in 1987, when he was awarded the prestigious Pritzker Prize. Retiring from teaching in 1974, Tange continued to lecture at universities and publish books. Among his writings are *Japan in the Future* (1966), *Man and Architecture* (1970), *Architecture and City* (1970), and *Kenzo Tange* (1987).

OBITUARIES AND OTHER SOURCES:

PERIODICALS

Chicago Tribune, March 23, 2005, section 3, p. 9.
Los Angeles Times, March 24, 2005, p. B10.
New York Times, March 23, 2005, p. A20.
Times (London, England), March 25, 2005, p. 67.
Washington Post, March 24, 2005, p. B6.

*   *   *

TAYLOR, Theodore W(alter) 1913-2005

OBITUARY NOTICE— See index for *CA* sketch: Born December 22, 1913, in Berkeley, CA; died March 12, 2005, in Falls Church, VA. Government official and author. Taylor was a longtime employee of the U.S. Department of the Interior where he specialized in Native American affairs, later publishing four books on the subject. Graduating in 1935 from the University of Arizona, he went to Syracuse University to earn an M.A. in public administration in 1938. Later, in 1960, he completed his Ph.D. at Harvard University in this subject. During the late 1930s he was a manager for the Rural Electrification Administration in Washington, D.C.; he then joined the Department of Agriculture as an administrative assistant, soon rising to the job of director of the Federal Extension Service. When the United States entered World War II, Taylor worked in personnel for the U.S. Navy's Bureau of Ships. When the war was over, he joined the Department of the Interior, initially working as a budget officer for the Office of Territories and Island Possessions. His interest in Native-American affairs was sparked in 1950, when he became chief of the Branch of Management Planning for the Bureau of Indian Affairs. Before leaving the Department of the Interior in 1959, he spent three years as mobilization officer for defense electrical power. Taylor next joined the Smithsonian Institution, where he was an assistant to the secretary from 1959 to 1965. He returned to the Bureau of Indian Affairs as deputy commissioner in 1966, remaining there until 1974, with the exception of a year spent at the Brookings Institution. Taylor was assistant to the bureau's commissioner from 1971 to 1974. In his later years he continued to work as a freelance consultant and writer, publishing the books *The States and Their Indian Citizens* (1972), *American Indian Policy* (1983), and *The Bureau of Indian Affairs* (1984). He also edited *Federal Public Policy: Personal Accounts by Ten Senior Civil Service Executives* (1984).

OBITUARIES AND OTHER SOURCES:

PERIODICALS

Washington Post, March 15, 2005, p. B7.

*   *   *

TAYLOR, Timothy (F.) 1960-

PERSONAL: Born July 10, 1960.

ADDRESSES: Office—Department of Archaeological Sciences, University of Bradford, Bradford, West Yorkshire BD7 1DP, England. *E-mail*—T.F.Taylor@Bradford.ac.uk.

CAREER: University of Bradford, Bradford, England, reader in archaeology. Guest on television programs, including *Sex BC,* 2002, and *National Geographic.*

WRITINGS:

The Prehistory of Sex: Four Million Years of Human Sexual Culture, Bantam Books (New York, NY), 1996.
The Buried Soul: How Humans Invented Death, Beacon Press (Boston, MA), 2004.

Contributor to *Encyclopedia of Prehistory 4: Europe,* edited by Peter N. Peregrine and Melvin Ember, Kluwer Academic (New York, NY), 2001. Contributor to periodicals, including *Nature, British Archaeology,* and *Scientific American.*

WORK IN PROGRESS: Research on the later prehistoric societies of southeastern Europe; conducting the excavation of a Bronze Age burial site in Yorkshire, England.

SIDELIGHTS: Timothy Taylor has explored ancient cultural practices related to sex and death in his books *The Prehistory of Sex: Four Million Years of Human Sexual Culture* and *The Buried Soul: How Humans Invented Death.* In the former, Taylor attempts to survey changing sexual attitudes and customs beginning in the australopithecine period and continuing into the European Middle Ages, and beyond. Such breadth takes in a tremendous amount of subject matter, and as *Antiquity* reviewer Marcia-Anne Dobres pointed out, the author risks giving a superficial account because of the scope of his book. Dobres found, however, that Taylor's "attempt is valiant and for the most part successful," and commented that the author "is to be commended for keeping his vision focused far out on the horizon and never losing sight of his main point: that from its very origins, human sexual culture has never been focused simplistically on procreation and (genetic) reproductive success. Rather, it has everywhere and always involved pleasure, pain, preference, prejudice and politics." Dobres did not agree with all of Taylor's conclusions but nevertheless rated *The Prehistory of Sex* as a valuable resource.

In his book Taylor suggests that even ancient cultures may have known enough about medicinal plants to use them as aphrodisiacs or contraceptives. Drawing on evidence from burial sites and other archeological digs, he states that ancient cultures may have practiced cross-dressing and other practices that certainly have no link to reproduction. Ancient statues, long thought to be representations of Earth Mother goddesses, may have simply been the prehistoric equivalent of modern pornography. *The Prehistory of Sex* does contain much speculation, but as Laurence A. Marschall pointed out in *Sciences*, "The hard evidence may support a wide range of wild and entertaining ideas, but one thing is clear: the tapestry of human sexual culture has always been a rich and varied one. The images that we see on these pages . . . indicate that, whatever your predilection, someone in the past had it too." Megan Harlan, reviewing the book in *Entertainment Weekly*, commented that while the author's "energetic arguments don't always coalesce, they do breathe imaginative sensual life into long-discarded shards and bones."

In *The Buried Soul* Taylor looks at ancient practices and superstitions surrounding death. He covers nearly two million years of history in a survey that is "vast, ambitious, and contentious," according to Katherine Ashenburg in *American Scholar*. The author believes that cannibalism was one of the earliest ways of disposing of the dead: it served a spiritual need to keep the dead among the living, and also fulfilled the practical function of removing the body. The earliest burials took place some 120,000 years ago, marking a shift in human understanding of mortality and morality that made cannibalism taboo. *The Buried Soul* is a frequently "grisly" book, according to *American Scholar* reviewer Ashenburg, and the author "boldly" incorporates his own experiences and perceptions of death into his analysis. Ashenburg concluded, "Taylor's childhood and his professional research forged a deep conviction that modern people still scapegoat the vulnerable, torture the innocent, and live harnessed to profound superstitions." Bob Chapman, writing in the *Journal of the Royal Anthropological Institute*, also noted the unique perspective offered by Taylor in *The Buried Soul*, stating: "The choice of examples and themes makes this an eclectic and individual book."

BIOGRAPHICAL AND CRITICAL SOURCES:

PERIODICALS

American Scholar, autumn, 2004, Katherine Ashenburg, review of *The Buried Soul: How Humans Invented Death*, p. 165.

Antiquity, December, 1997, Marcia-Anne Dobres, review of *The Prehistory of Sex: Four Million Years of Human Sexual Culture*, p. 1095; March, 2003, Philip Rahtz, review of *The Buried Soul*, p. 202.
Booklist, September 1, 1996, Donna Seaman, review of *The Prehistory of Sex*, p. 43; June 1, 2004, Donna Chavez, review of *The Buried Soul*, p. 1680.
Entertainment Weekly, October 4, 1996, Megan Harlan, review of *The Prehistory of Sex*, p. 56.
Journal of the Royal Anthropological Institute, September, 2004, Bob Chapman, review of *The Buried Soul*, p. 737.
Maclean's, September 6, 2004, review of *The Buried Soul*, p. 95.
New Scientist, September 28, 2002, Kate Douglas, interview with Taylor, p. 46.
New Statesman, October 18, 1996, Christopher Badcock, review of *The Prehistory of Sex*, p. 42.
Publishers Weekly, June 24, 1996, review of *The Prehistory of Sex*, p. 40.
Sciences, November-December, 1996, Laurence A. Marschall, review of *The Prehistory of Sex*, p. 40.

ONLINE

University of Bradford Web site, http://www.brad.ac.uk/ (March 2, 2005), "Tim Taylor."

*   *   *

TEDLOW, Richard S. 1947(?)-

PERSONAL: Born c. 1947. *Education:* Yale, B.A., 1969; Columbia M.A., 1971, Ph.D., 1976 (history).

ADDRESSES: Office—Harvard Business School, Entrepreneurial Management Unit, Cambridge, MA 02163. *E-mail*—rtedlow@hbs.edu.

CAREER: Business instructor, writer, and consultant. Harvard Business School, Cambridge, MA, professor, 1979—, currently Class of 1949 Professor of Business Administration.

AWARDS, HONORS: Giants of Enterprise: Seven Business Innovators and the Empires They Built selected as one of the top ten business books of 2001 by *Business Week*.

WRITINGS:

Keeping the Corporate Image: Public Relations and Business, 1900-1950, J.A.I. Press (Greenwich, CT), 1979.

(With A. D. Chandler, Jr.) *The Coming of Managerial Capitalism: A Casebook on the History of American Economic Institutions* (with teaching guide), Irwin (Homewood, IL), 1985.

(With R. John, Jr.) *Managing Big Business: Essays from the Business History Review,* Harvard Business School Press (Cambridge, MA), 1986.

New and Improved: The Story of Mass Marketing in America, Basic Books (New York, NY), 1990, second edition, Harvard Business School Press (Cambridge, MA), 1996.

The Rise of the American Business Corporation, Harwood Academic Press (Chur, Switzerland), 1991.

(Editor, with G. Jones, and contributor) *The Rise and Fall of Mass Marketing,* Routledge (London, England), 1993.

(Editor, with A. D. Chandler, Jr. and T. K. McCraw) *Management Past and Present: A Casebook on American Business History,* Southwestern Publishing Company (Cincinnati, OH), 1996.

Giants of Enterprise: Seven Business Innovators and the Empires They Built, HarperBusiness (New York, NY), 2001.

The Watson Dynasty: The Fiery Reign and Troubled Legacy of IBM's Founding Father and Son, HarperBusiness (New York, NY), 2003.

Contributor to encyclopedias and dictionaries, including *Dictionary of American Biography, The Reader's Encyclopedia of American History, The Encyclopedia of the United States in the Twentieth Century, Oxford Encyclopedia of American History, Oxford Companion to United States History,* and *Encyclopedia of American Economic History,* and to books, including *Trade Associations in Business History,* edited by Hiroaki Yamazaki and Matao Miyamoto, University of Tokyo Press, 1988; *Fundamentals of Pure and Applied Economics,* Harwood, 1991; and *The Global Market: Developing a Strategy to Manage across Borders,* edited by John A. Quelch and Rohit Deshpandé, Jossey-Bass, 2004. Contributor to periodicals, including *American Quarterly, Business History Review, Business and Economic History, Zeitschrift für Unternehmensgeschichte, World Link, New York Times, Harvard Business Review,* and *Journal of Macromarketing.*

Tedlow's works have been translated into French and Japanese.

WORK IN PROGRESS: The American: The Life and Times of Andy Grove.

SIDELIGHTS: Richard S. Tedlow is a professor at Harvard Business School and the author of numerous books dealing with aspects of business from entrepreneurial history to managerial style and mass marketing. In 1985's *The Coming of Managerial Capitalism: A Casebook on the History of American Economic Institutions* Tedlow and collaborator A. D. Chandler, Jr., examine the transformation of managerial capitalism by such firms as Standard Oil and Du Pont, as well as by more modern diversified corporations such as General Electric.

In *New and Improved: The Story of Mass Marketing in America* Tedlow draws his examples from the rivalries between Coca-Cola and Pepsi Cola, and General Motors and Ford. Brand names and their marketing is at the heart of this "exhaustive, lively casebook," as *Publishers Weekly* critic Genevieve Stuttaford described it. Reviewing the same title in *Business History Review,* Daniel Pope concluded that "those who read and contemplate the story Tedlow presents so well will gain a broader and deeper understanding of American business and society." Likewise, T. A. B. Corley, writing in *Business History,* praised the manner in which Tedlow "has made a skillful use of the plentiful archives, and thereby has given an example for other scholars to follow." With *The Rise of the American Business Corporation* Tedlow provides a short course on the subject to "introduce this material to non-specialists lacking the time to read more substantial accounts," according to Christopher Scmitz in *Business History.* Tony Freyer, writing in the *Business History Review,* described the book as an exploration of "the growth of the business corporation as an organization entity within the course of American history, from its colonial beginnings to the present." Freyer further commented that, "using case studies and anecdotes, [Tedlow] portrays well the causes and consequences of . . . the managerial revolution."

Tedlow serves up seven stories of business titans in his *Giants of Enterprise: Seven Business Innovators and the Empires They Built.* These men include Andrew Carnegie of Carnegie Steel, George Eastman of Eastman Kodak, Henry Ford of Ford Motor Company, Thomas J. Watson, Sr. of Internatioal Business Machines (IBM), Charles Revson of Revlon, Sam Walton of Wal-Mart, and Robert Noyce of Intel. In his book, Tedlow "narrates the often-twisted roads to riches of some of America's greatest entrepreneurs" as Jill Lerner noted in the *Boston Business Journal.* The author presents mini-biographies that hone in on the style and tactics of men whose careers span a century-and-a-half of American history. According to Lerner, "In Tedlow's unvarnished accounts of the seven entrepreneurs, it becomes clear these men were indeed giants, though not gods." It also becomes clear that each had a succinct message which they were able to put across efficiently, as in Noyce's "Intel Inside" or Walton's "Always the low price. Always."

Further praise for Tedlow's *Giants of Enterprise* came from a *Business Week* reviewer, who called the book an "engrossing gallery of executive portraits," and added that Tedlow "performs a great service by bringing their stories together in one volume." The same critic went on to note that Tedlow "deftly explores [the executives'] backgrounds and the psychological impulses that drove them" in this book informed by "passionate and fluid writing." Writing in *Training,* Jane Bozarth felt that Tedlow "has intimate knowledge of his subjects and is able to draw incisive parallels and contrasts among them." Bozarth continued that Tedlow's "talent at getting to the essence of their stories makes this an excellent overview of the history of American enterprise."

Tedlow continues his case-history approach to the study of managerial styles in *The Watson Dynasty: The Fiery Reign and Troubled Legacy of IBM's Founding Father and Son.* Expanding on the mini-biography of Thomas J. Watson Sr. from *Giants of Enterprise,* Tedlow devotes an entire volume to Watson, father and son, who helped shaped the destiny and workings of IBM, or "Big Blue" as the corporation is popularly known. Tedlow demonstrates how "shaky" were the beginnings of both father and son, as *Library Journal* contributor Carol J. Elsen pointed out, and "offers insight into how the complex and often volatile personalities of father and son created the corporate ethos of IBM."

BIOGRAPHICAL AND CRITICAL SOURCES:

PERIODICALS

Booklist, November 1, 2001, Eileèn Hardy, review of *Giants of Enterprise: Seven Business Innovators and the Empires They Built,* p. 452.

Boston Business Journal, December 7, 2001, Jill Lerner, review of *Giants of Enterprise,* p. 21.
Business History, October, 1991, T. A. B. Corley, review of *New and Improved: The Story of Mass Marketing in America,* p. 121; January, 1993, Christopher Scmitz, review of *The Rise of the American Business Corporation,* p. 97; April, 1994, Sue Bowden, review of *The Rise and Fall of Mass Marketing,* p. 133.
Business History Review, summer, 1985, review of *The Coming of Managerial Capitalism: A Casebook on the History of American Economic Institutions,* p. 312; winter, 1990, Daniel Pope, review of *New and Improved,* p. 780; spring, 1993, Tony Freyer, review of *The Rise of the American Business Corporation,* p. 153;
Business Week, December 10, 2001, p. 21; December 17, 2001, "Remembering the Titans," p. 18.
Computerworld, December 10, 2001, Kathleen Melymuka, "Learning Some Lessons from Titans of Industry," p. 44.
Library Journal, September 1, 2001, Steven J. Mayover, review of *Giants of Enterprise,* p. 200; November 1, 2003, Carol J. Elsen, review of *The Watson Dynasty: The Fiery Reign and Troubled Legacy of IBM's Founding Father and Son,* p. 95.
Publishers Weekly, February 23, 1990, Genevieve Stuttaford, review of *New and Improved,* p. 210;
Training, April, 2002, Jane Bozarth, review of *Giants of Enterprise,* p. 56.

ONLINE

Harvard Business School Web site, http://dor.hbs.edu/ (July 26, 2004), "Richard S. Tedlow."*

*   *   *

THAYER, Cynthia

PERSONAL: Born in New York, NY; married; husband's name, Bill. *Education:* Degree in English and theater.

ADDRESSES: Home—Gouldsboro, ME. *Agent*—c/o Author Mail, St. Martin's Press, 175 Fifth Avenue, New York, NY 10010.

CAREER: Farmer and writer. Darthia Farm, Gouldsboro, ME, owner and operator. Former teacher, basketmaker, and weaver. Maine St. Andrew's Pipes and Drums, bagpiper.

WRITINGS:

(With Nathan D. Hamilton) *The Moosehead Lake Region,* Arcadia (Dover, NH), 1995.
Strong for Potatoes (novel), St. Martin's Press (New York, NY), 1999.
A Certain Slant of Light (fiction), St. Martin's Press (New York, NY), 2000.

ADAPTATIONS: An abridged audio version of *Strong for Potatoes* was released by Audio Literature.

SIDELIGHTS: Considering herself a "late bloomer," Cynthia Thayer began writing at the age of forty-eight partly because arthritis was restricting her weaving abilities. As a writer noted on the *Folkcal Archives* Web site, while Thayer maintains she "cannot write well about herself . . . she does write about what she knows, from the blueberry fields of Washington County to the tunes played on a Celtic chanter, and it is this familiarity that makes her characters and her stories ring true."

Thayer's first novel, *Strong for Potatoes,* is the story of Blue Willoughby, who lost an eye and suffered a leg injury after being struck by a golf cart while shooting a film as a child. As time passes, Blue receives little support from her dysfunctional parents. She becomes pregnant by her prom date and turns to her full-blooded Passamaquoddy Indian grandfather and his neighbors on the tribe's Maine reservation for support. Blue's grandfather teaches her the healing value of nature and Native American ways and she learns to weave beautiful baskets that are "strong for potatoes." With her grandfather's support, Blue is able to face motherhood and her awakening lesbian sexuality.

A reviewer for *Publishers Weekly* called the novel a "well-crafted, if somewhat maudlin, debut." Janet A. Ingraham Dwyer, reviewing the book in *Library Journal,* referred to two "unforgettable" passages about death that "center" the novel. Dwyer called one

"shocking and audacious" and the other "unusually tranquil." "Thayer's first novel is written with skill and patience, like one of Blue's handcrafted ash baskets," declared Jennifer Henderson in *Booklist.*

Thayer's critically acclaimed second novel, *A Certain Slant of Light,* is also set in the unglamorous and tough landscape of rural Maine. The narrator, Peter, was a bagpiper until his wife and two children died in a house fire. Ridden with guilt, Peter moves to the coast of Maine, his only companions being an old Passamaquoddy woman and a dog—until the arrival during a severe winter storm of a pregnant woman on the run from an abusive husband. Peter cannot turn her away. In *World and I,* Joan Silber commented that at the very beginning of the story, Thayer sets the tone with her description of place: "A bare, spare, and orderly atmosphere has been evoked. . . . Place is not only geography but a system of values, and sober self-reliance is at home here." A *Publishers Weekly* critic commented that "Thayer's tale is deeply poetic and quasi-Freudian. . . . Her characters are plainspoken and lucid as well as complex."

BIOGRAPHICAL AND CRITICAL SOURCES:

PERIODICALS

Booklist, January 1, 1998, Jennifer Harrison, review of *Strong for Potatoes,* p. 779; August, 2000, Kristin Kloberdanz, review of *A Certain Slant of Light,* p. 2117.
Dover Community News, November 9, 2001, review of *A Certain Slant of Light.*
Library Journal, January, 1998, Janet A. Ingraham Dwyer, review of *Strong for Potatoes,* p. 146; July, 2000, Reba Leiding, review of *A Certain Slant of Light,* p. 2117.
Publishers Weekly, November 17, 1997, review of *Strong for Potatoes,* p. 54; June 26, 2000, review of *A Certain Slant of Light,* p. 2117.
San Francisco Chronicle, April 10, 1998, Karen Sorlie Russo, review of *Strong for Potatoes,* p. D13.
World and I, December, 2000, Joan Silber, review of *A Certain Slant of Light,* p. 242.

ONLINE

Folkcal Archives Web site, http://lists.svaha.com/ pipermail/folkcal/ (February 10, 2003), *Sound Portrait of the Artist:* "Cynthia Thayer."
Maine Writers, http://www.waterboro.lib.me.us/ maineaut/ (June 15, 1999), "Cynthia Thayer."*

THOMAS, Audrey (Callahan) 1935-

PERSONAL: Born November 17, 1935, in Binghamton, NY; immigrated to Canada; daughter of Donald Earle (a teacher) and Frances (Corbett) Callahan; married Ian Thomas (a sculptor and art teacher), December 6, 1958 (divorced, 1978); children: Sarah, Victoria, Claire. *Education:* Smith College, B.A., 1957; University of British Columbia, M.A., 1963.

ADDRESSES: Home—R.R. 2, Box 11, C-50, Galiano Island, British Columbia V0N 1P0, Canada.

CAREER: Writer and educator. Visiting assistant professor of creative writing, Concordia University, 1978; visiting professor of creative writing, University of Victoria, 1978-79; writer-in-residence, Simon Fraser University, 1981-82, University of Ottawa, 1987, University of Toronto, 1993, University of Victoria, University of British Columbia, and David Thompson University Centre; Scottish-Canadian Exchange Fellow in Edinburgh, 1985-86; visiting professor, Concordia University, 1989-90, Dartmouth College, 1994, 1996.

MEMBER: PEN, Writers Union of Canada, Writers Guild of Canada.

AWARDS, HONORS: Atlantic Monthly magazine First award, 1965; CBC Literary Competition, second prize for fiction, 1980, second prize for memoirs, 1981; second prize for fiction, National Magazine Awards, 1980; second prize, *Chatelaine* Fiction Competition, 1981; British Columbia Book Prize: Ethel Wilson Fiction Prize, 1985, for *Intertidal Life,* 1990, for *Wild Blue Yonder,* and 1995, for *Coming down from Wa;* Marian Engel Award, 1987; Canada-Australia Literary Prize, 1989-90; Governor General's Literary Award nomination, and Commonwealth Literary Prize, both 1996, both for *Coming down from Wa;* W. O. Mitchell Book Prize, 2001; Terasen Lifetime Achievement Award, 2003; Matt Cohen Award, for lifetime of distinguished work, 2004.

WRITINGS:

NOVELS

Mrs. Blood, Bobbs-Merrill (Indianapolis, IN), 1970.
Munchmeyer and Prospero on the Island, Bobbs-Merrill (Indianapolis, IN), 1972.

Audrey G. Thomas

Songs My Mother Taught Me, Bobbs-Merrill (Indianapolis, IN), 1973.
Blown Figures, Talonbooks (Vancouver, British Columbia, Canada), 1974, Knopf (New York, NY), 1975.
Latakia, Talonbooks (Vancouver, British Columbia, Canada), 1979.
Intertidal Life, Stoddart Press (Toronto, Ontario, Canada), 1984.
Graven Images, Viking (Toronto, Ontario, Canada), 1993.
Coming down from Wa, Viking (Toronto, Ontario, Canada), 1995.
Isobel Gunn (novel), Viking (Toronto, Ontario, Canada), 1999.
Tattycoram, Goose Lane Editions (Fredericton, New Brunswick, Canada), 2005.

SHORT-STORY COLLECTIONS

Ten Green Bottles, Bobbs-Merrill (Indianapolis, IN), 1967.

Ladies & Escorts, Oberon (Ottawa, Ontario, Canada), 1977.

Two in the Bush, and Other Stories, McClelland & Stewart (Toronto, Ontario, Canada), 1979.

Real Mothers, Talonbooks (Vancouver, British Columbia, Canada), 1981.

Goodbye Harold, Good Luck, Viking/Penguin (Toronto, Ontario, Canada), 1986.

Wild Blue Yonder, Penguin (Toronto, Ontario, Canada), 1990.

The Path of Totality, Penguin (Toronto, Ontario, Canada), 2001.

Contributor of short fiction to anthologies, including *Personal Fictions: Stories by Munro, Wiebe, Thomas, and Blaise,* edited by Michael Ondaatje, Oxford University Press (New York, NY), 1977, to periodicals, including *Atlantic Monthly, Maclean's, Saturday Night, Toronto Life, Capilano Review, Fiddlehead, Canadian Literature,* and *Interface.*

RADIO PLAYS

(With Linda Sorenson and Keith Pepper) *Once Your Submarine Cable Is Gone, What Have You Got?,* Canadian Broadcasting Corp. (CBC-Radio), 1973.

Mrs. Blood, CBC-Radio, 1975.

Untouchables, CBC-Radio, 1981.

The Milky Way, CBC-Radio, November 26, 1983.

The Axe of God, in *Disasters! Act of God or Acts of Man?,* CBC-Radio, 1985.

The Woman in Black Velvet, CBC-Radio, 1985.

In the Groove, CBC-Radio, 1985.

On the Immediate Level of Events Occurring in Meadows, in *Sextet,* CBC-Radio, 1986.

Also author of fourteen other radio plays.

ADAPTATIONS: Isobel Gunn was adapted as an audiobook.

WORK IN PROGRESS: Two novels, one set in the 1830s in London and the Gold Coast of Africa; the other, a contemporary novel.

SIDELIGHTS: An American-born Canadian author of novels, short stories, and radio plays, Audrey Thomas has won a number of literary prizes, yet, as Urjo Kareda observed in *Saturday Night,* "somehow she has never achieved her rightful place in the hierarchy of Canada's best writers. Her writing tends to be racier, ruder, more raw than that of her contemporaries in the Ontario-centered, female-dominated literary establishment." Thomas's work, as a number of critics have noted, is autobiographical in nature, and it displays an interest in feminism and a love of experimentation, both with language and literary devices.

Employing these techniques in different ways to shed light on her common theme of personal isolation and loneliness, the author has said that her stories are about "the terrible gap between men and women," quoted Margaret Atwood in her *Second Words: Selected Critical Prose.* "Language," Thomas told Liam Lacey in a *Globe and Mail* interview, "is where men and women get into trouble, I think, . . . they think they mean the same things by the same words when they really don't." The author also sometimes expands the theme of adult relationships to involve children, who are often the casualties of broken marriages. *Saturday Night* contributor Eleanor Wachtel maintains that as a writer who reveals these "politics of the family, . . . Audrey Thomas [is] one of [our] most astute commentators."

A divorced mother of three children, Thomas is well acquainted with the problems of family life about which she writes. Having resided in such places as Ghana, England, Scotland, and Greece, she also "likes to tell her stories of Americans or Canadians set down in an alien culture so that their problems will appear more starkly," wrote *Open Letter* critic George Bowering. The author's first novel, *Mrs. Blood,* is about one such character who suffers a miscarriage while living in Africa. It is a stream-of-consciousness novel in which the protagonist, Isobel Cleary, while lying in the hospital, contemplates the problems of her marriage and her painful affair with another man. Critics like Joan Caldwell, a *Canadian Literature* reviewer, were particularly impressed by the writing skills demonstrated in this first effort. "*Mrs. Blood* is accomplished writing," praised Caldwell; "it does not bear the marks of a first novel and it must surely not be Audrey Thomas's last."

Thomas has written two sequels to *Mrs. Blood, Songs My Mother Taught Me* and *Blown Figures.* The first of these takes Isobel back to her childhood, an unhappy time in her life during which she is caught between her parents—an "inadequate man and [a] compulsive angry woman," as *Saturday Night* contributor Anne Montagnes described them. Longing for love, Isobel does not find happiness until she gets a job at an asylum, where, as Constance Rooke related in the *Dictionary of Literary Biography*, "she learns something of compassion and something of the madness which has been concealed in her family. Finally, she chooses to be vulnerable." The subject of madness is also a part of *Blown Figures*, which takes up the story of Isobel with her return to Africa to find the body of her miscarried baby. "She is now clearly schizophrenic and addresses many of her remarks to a Miss Miller—an imaginary confidante," explained Rooke. "Blatantly experimental, *Blown Figures* has numerous nearly blank pages which serve to isolate the fragments (cartoons, one-liners, and so forth) which appear here. The novel depends heavily on Africa as a metaphor for the unconscious." Atwood, in a *New York Times Book Review* article, praised the book, noting that, "In hands less skillful than Miss Thomas's, such devices could spell tedious experimentation for its own sake, self-indulgence, or chaos. But she is enormously skillful, and instead of being a defeating pile of confusions 'Blown Figures' is amazingly easy to read."

The novels *Munchmeyer and Prospero on the Island, Latakia,* and *Intertidal Life* concern male-female relationships and also have in common protagonists who are women writers. These characters, reported Wayne Grady in *Books in Canada,* are "trying to come to terms in their books with the fact that they have been rejected by men who have loved them." Of these books, critics have generally found *Intertidal Life,* the story of a woman named Alice whose husband leaves her after fourteen years of marriage, to be the most significant effort. Grady called *Intertidal Life* "undoubtedly Thomas's best novel to date." Although Kareda felt that this novel "doesn't rank with Audrey Thomas's finest writing," he asserted that "its desire to reach us, to tell so much, to keep questioning, are the strengths of an exceptional, expressive will."

According to Alberto Manguel in the *Village Voice, Intertidal Life* seems to resolve an issue that was raised in Thomas's earlier work. The novel "appears as the culmination of the search for a character that was never quite defined before. Perhaps in the much-neglected *Blown Figures* or in *Songs My Mother Taught Me,* there are sketchier versions of Alice

circling the primary question: Who am I? In *Intertidal Life* the question is answered." Rooke explained further that, in being separated from her husband, Alice is able to assert her independence while overcoming her feelings of isolation by becoming "inextricably involved with others and most particularly with [her] female friends and children."

Graven Images features Charlotte Corbett, a character much like Thomas: an American-born writer, divorced and living in British Columbia. Charlotte is on a search for her ancestors, traveling to England to trace her heritage and discover who founded the clan in the eleventh century. Accompanied by her friend Lydia, a woman who was taken to Canada as a child to avoid the Nazi bombing during World War II and is on a parallel quest to locate her own family, the two women arrive in England just as a hurricane hits the island. Writing in *Books in Canada,* Elisabeth Harvor explained that "Thomas is not often a very introspective writer. She instead reserves her love for the surface of life and for the thousands of details that make up the surface. . . . This preference for the surface has a tendency to make *Graven Images* seem somewhat trivial." In contrast, Nancy Wigston in *Quill & Quire* noted that "Charlotte's voice is one of absolute candour; her insights into the multiple phases of women's lives pile up like the gifts she is constantly buying for friends and family. Cluttered and subtle like Charlotte herself, this book is like one of those gifts: special and resonant with meaning."

Coming down from Wa introduces a male protagonist while once again exploring the issues of heritage and nationality. In this novel, declared Lynne Van Luven in *Books in Canada,* "Thomas charts new terrain for herself and tackles a powerful subject, human cupidity, in a broader political context than ever before." The story tells of a young Canadian, William Kwame MacKenzie, and his struggle to understand his own past and that of both his parents. He travels from British Columbia to Ghana in West Africa in an attempt to resolve his doubts about his history. "One could make the case that the novel's disguised theme is Canada's loss of innocence vis a vis foreign aid to the Third World," theorized *Quill & Quire* contributor Jerry Horton; "what seemed possible and even noble in the 1960s has proven enormously complicated from both pragmatic and ethical points of view." The author, Van Luven stated, "has dared to expand her own repertoire in writing such a novel, and she is to be highly praised for that."

While *Coming down from Wa* gave readers Thomas's first male protagonist, *Isobel Gunn* stands as a different kind of first for Thomas: it is her first work of historical fiction. While living in Scotland in the 1980s, Thomas heard the story of a woman from the Orkney Isles of Scotland named Isobel Gunn. Immigrating to western Canada, Gunn became the only white woman to work at Hudson's Bay Company, a fort at the bottom of the Bay, in the early 1800s. She had disguised herself as a man in order to get the position, but her gender was revealed when she gave birth to a son during her work shift. When Thomas later visited the Orkney Isles, she heard the story again. "I just kept hearing about her and I thought: I really want to do something with this," Thomas explained to Linda Richards of *January Online.* After spending four years doing research and finding that very little factual information actually existed about Gunn's life, Thomas began to write her novel. "It was enough of a frame on which to embroider her well-told tale," Thomas told Richards. Critics agreed; a critic for *Herizons* noted that while the truth of Gunn's story will never be known, "The well-balanced *Isobel Gunn* is both a credible historic reading of events and a darn good read." Susan McClelland, writing for *Macleans,* considered the work a "captivating and tragic new novel," and commented, "it is the courageous Isobel who lingers in the reader's imagination."

Writing in the *Reference Guide to Short Fiction,* Lorraine M. York claimed that "What sets Thomas apart from almost any other writer in Canada is her rich melange of self-conscious fabulation, feminism, and autobiography." These themes that Thomas explores in her novels are also echoed in her short-story writing, which, along with the work she has done for radio, has amounted to a large oeuvre since the 1970s. But, lamented Atwood, despite this concerted effort and "its ambition, range and quality, she has not yet received the kind of recognition such a body of work merits, perhaps because she is that cultural hybrid, an early-transplanted American. Of course her work has flaws; everyone's does. She can be sentimental, repetitious, and sometimes merely gossipy. But page for page, she is one of [Canada's] best writers."

AUTOBIOGRAPHICAL ESSAY: Audrey Thomas contributed the following autobiographical essay to *CA:*

Several years ago my mother wrote me a letter and enclosed a clipping. The former secretary of one of the first ladies, Lady Bird Johnson perhaps, had just written a book which was auctioned to a New York publisher for some incredible amount of money: thousands and thousands of dollars. Wasn't it about time, wrote my mother, that I admitted I was not a success as a writer, gave up this foolish dream, and went back to what I studied in college, was it medieval history? Perhaps I could get a job teaching. What I studied in college was Anglo-Saxon and Middle English, but my mother is old, very old, so it didn't bother me that she had got it mixed up. What did bother me was my own reaction, after all these years, to her not-so-subtle ways of putting me down. I laughed but I also felt again the self-doubt that has plagued me all my life about my writing: that I had somehow, as usual, ended up chained to a large hungry dog (my writing) and would give anything if someone would come along and release me, unchain me, shoot the damn dog, or at least find the dog another home. Maybe the old lady was right—give it up.

Easier said than done, of course, so I put the letter away and kept on with the only thing I know how to do. It would appear that I have no choice, although it wasn't my first choice or even my second. But therein lies a tale.

I come from a small city in western New York State, at the junction of the Chenango and Susquehanna Rivers. My mother's family had been in that general area since 1790, first in northern Pennsylvania (they named the town of New Milford) and then across the line in Conklin, New York. They had been in Massachusetts for over a hundred years before they "went west" so they were a very old family indeed. They made their money in lumber, and one branch of the family was in the acid factory business up and down the east branch of the Delaware until the 1930s. My grandfather came in on the very end of this—my mother talks about going to live near Shinhopple where they were not allowed to play with the company children. She remembers seeing men with huge arms, stripped to the waist and covered in sweat, feeding the furnaces which were the first step in the "destructive distillation" process which led, eventually, to acetate of lime. Some of those villages still remain: Acidalia, Burntwood, Methol, Corbett, New York, and I have been to see them. However, by the time I was born my grandfather lived in Binghamton and was head of the mechanical engineering department at IBM. THINK, said a brass plaque on his enormous desk. He

Father, Donald Earle Callahan

was my hero when I was a child. I remember my grandmother, his wife, only vaguely. She wasn't a well woman and she died a day or two after a heart attack at my kindergarten Christmas party. My grandfather lived another thirty years after her death; the last time I saw him he called me by her name—"Is that you, Grace?" (Still in his own house then and not senile, he quickly corrected himself and made a nice attempt to admire his great-granddaughter Sarah. We were on our way from England to British Columbia, where we were to settle, but I had taken the baby on a side trip to show her off to my mother and father, my sister, my grandfather. It seemed terribly important to do this even though it meant I would travel by train from Boston to Vancouver by myself, with the baby, as my husband went on ahead once our ship docked at Montreal.)

My father's family had also been in the area for a long time and also came there from Massachusetts. He was a member of the Sons of the American Revolution,

somebody having fought in the Revolution but I can't remember who, some connection with General Joseph Warren and the Battle of Bunker Hill. His father died before I was born but had run a very successful hardware and sporting goods store, Callahan and Douglas, for years before he sold it to his partner. He was a keen fisherman and so was my father. One of my favorite breakfasts as a child was brook trout freshly caught, rolled in cornmeal, and fried in a cast-iron frying pan. I love living out here by the ocean, feasting on salmon and cod, oysters, clams and crab, but there are days when I yearn for the clear lakes and brooks of my childhood and the silvery treasures, laid so carefully on ferns, in my father's creel. My father talked a lot about that sporting-goods store—I think he missed it and would have liked that sort of a life for himself, discussing lures and rods and guns. He loved to "jaw," as my mother called it. Instead, he taught general science and history at a high school across the river. And although he had two degrees I never saw him read a serious book the whole time I lived at home. He read *Life* and *U.S. News and World Report* and the *National Geographic,* a lifetime wedding gift from my grandfather Corbett. (My mother read the *Ladies' Home Journal,* the *Woman's Home Companion,* and *McCall's.*)

I think my father, a short, rather nervous man, was ill-suited to be a high school teacher, and one of the ways he showed this seemed very peculiar when I was young. My grandfather Corbett had a summer camp in the Adirondack Mountains, and we went there every summer until I was seventeen years old and he was forced to sell it. We left home the day after school was out (returning at least twice to make sure the gas stove had been turned off and the notes had been left out for the milkman and the mailman) and we didn't come back until Labor Day. Our first stop was the Esso station to fill up with gas. "Yep," my father would say to the owner, whom he knew, "Me and the missus and the kids are headin' up to camp for the summer." And as we progressed—a stop at Utica for lunch, a stop at the General Store in Pisco, if it was still open by the time we got there, a stop at Red's Baits to get worms and other crawly things that lived in soil-filled trays in an old shed—his diction and accent became more and more "country boy." It drove my mother nuts, but then just about everything my father did or didn't do drove her nuts. (It was years before I real-

Mother, Frances Waldron (Corbett) Callahan

ized that husbands and wives actually shared one bedroom.)

*

Both my mother and father thought of "success" in terms of money, nice cars, nice *things.* They argued about money all the time, terrible arguments and nearly every night. Neither could manage money and although a teacher's pay was very low in those days compared with the salaries in any other profession (teachers were like nurses and ministers; they were expected to have a vocation) I don't think we needed to be as hard-up as we were. My father was always asking his unmarried sister, Ethel (who was a maths professor at an upstate college), to bail us out; my mother would ask her father. Sometimes my parents hid when bill collectors came to the door. Sometimes the telephone was cut off. After my grandmother Callahan, who had been crippled for years, was moved up to Syracuse with my

uncle and his family (they all lived next door but my mother didn't speak to them), we moved into the family home, a dreary house with faded brown wallpaper and a general air of decay. Except for a few months near the end of his life, when they wanted to be closer to my sister and her family in Massachusetts, they lived there until my father died. (They rented, they didn't own; my aunt owned the house, another thorn in my mother's side.) There were attempts to fix the place up from time to time, but I remember it as shabby and depressing. It had a nice backyard, however, with an apple tree, a cherry tree (pie cherries), and a small vegetable and flower garden. My father tended all this and was very proud of his tomatoes and his roses. His other great interest, besides fishing, was the Masons, and at one point he was master of his lodge. He used to pace up and down in his room upstairs at the back of the house practicing his degrees: "Hail, Brother from the South!" etc. All of this was very secret stuff, of course, but we couldn't help overhearing from time to time. He loved the Masons (successful men belonged to the Masons) and always took us to the annual father-daughter banquet and talent night where we knew he wished we could twirl batons or play the piano. (I wrote poetry but it never occurred to me that poetry might come under the classification of entertainment. My poems were not humorous.) He also liked parades and took us to the Shriners parade every year. I think there was a streak of showman in him. He told me that when he was a child he had wanted to join the circus and that later he had wanted to be a minister. There was something wistful about him although I had nothing but contempt for the way he measured success and the way he engaged in these dreadful quarrels with my mother. I see now that he tried to escape, in his own way, tried to make some kind of a life for himself outside the home, and I wish I had known him better.

The last time I saw my father was the winter of 1963, when he and my mother had rented a small house in Holbrook, Massachusetts. My sister had phoned me to say that he was terribly ill and that, although he didn't know it, he was dying. "When are you going to come and see him?" she said. "At the funeral?" I left my husband and the youngest child and flew with our eldest, then four-and-a-half, to the United States Kennedy had been shot just a few weeks before and the country was still in a state of stunned disbelief. There was a lot of snow and Sarah had fun playing with her cousins although she ended up with tonsillitis and the trip back to British Columbia was a nightmare.

The night before we left I sat up with my father and watched *Goodbye, Mr. Chips,* of all things. The rest of the family insisted he didn't know that he was dying, but I was sure he did. I wanted to talk to him about it and about his life, but I didn't know how to begin. I was a graduate student at the time, taking a leisurely M.A. because the children were so young, and earning babysitting money by teaching freshman English. He was very proud of all this and talked a bit about his days at Cornell. I asked him if he remembered when he was getting his M.A. and we all went up to Ithaca with him, how he used to bring home stuff from the experimental farm: three-legged turkeys and blue eggs, things like that. I wanted to *cheer him up.* I should have taken his hand, but we had been trained by our mother to be such a non-touching family I was afraid to do so. We sat side by side while the tears rolled down my cheeks. "I always cry in sentimental films," I told him.

He died in June and had a Masonic funeral. My mother sold the house (*her* father had died in July) and moved to Massachusetts. She gave away a lot of my childhood toys and books, threw away my box of school certificates and awards, and cleared out a lifetime of old magazines from the spare room. I couldn't help her because we'd gone to Africa to work for two years. When we stopped in to see her on our way, she told me I had killed my father because he was so afraid for us "going out there." She'd worked herself into such a fury about that and other things by the time we left that she began running after the taxi that was taking us to the station, running down the street in her nightdress, barefoot, yelling. My husband held my hand tight: "Don't look back," he said, "just don't look back. It will all be all right."

When you have parents who behave like children, parents who refuse to take charge of their own lives, then how can you ever be a child yourself? *They* are having the tantrums, the crying spells, the fights. You learn very early on to keep your mouth shut if you know what's good for you. But you can't help seeing and hearing; you hear because even with the pillow over your head the voices come up the hot air registers; you see the broken dishes, the smashed picture frames, and the endless letters, written on secretarial pads, shoved under your bedroom door during the night. You feel trapped and helpless and at the same time furious—that they won't behave, that they can't be relied upon to act like other parents, that they have

staked everything on you and your sister: "We stayed together for your sake; we sacrificed everything for you."

If you can't open your mouth to question any of this and if you don't keep a journal because there is nowhere safe to hide it, you memorize, you can't help but memorize. You can't get rid of all this and so it remains inside you, imprinted. My ex-husband still says "you have an incredible memory!" and I do, I do. He says it, now, with admiration, but I see myself like Marley's ghost, clanking along through life, weighed down by all this memory.

In *A Prayer for Owen Meaney,* John Irving says "Your memory is a monster; you forget, it doesn't; you think you have a memory; it has you." Only I don't forget; so am I a monster, too?

*

My first choice for "what I want to do with my life" was "visual artist." Why, I don't know, as I have no talent in this direction at all. My mother had gone to Pratt Art Institute for a while (she said recently that she had wanted to be an interior decorator) and her old drawing board was used in the kitchen as a pastry board. She also sharpened pencils with a paring knife; nobody else's mother did this. I never saw her draw anything and still don't know whether she herself had any talent for design. A few years ago I bought her a drawing pad and some crayons and suggested that she might like to do some sketching. Last year she gave them back to me, unused. "You might as well give these to the grandchildren." Her father could draw. I have hanging in my guest cottage a large pencil drawing he did when he was at Stevens Institute. It's a very carefully rendered drawing of a column, a geometrical figure, and a round bean pot. It looks very "modern" and yet he drew it in 1887. It has a photographic quality as well; this was a young man who understood angles and volumes and lines. Did *he* suggest that I should take up drawing? I know only that he bought me a complete set of oil colours, in a wooden box, when I was in junior high school, and I did some *copies* of paintings that weren't bad and some charcoal drawings of log cabins in the snow. And once I answered one of those Famous Artists ads which appeared regularly in the magazines my mother read: CAN YOU DRAW THIS PICTURE? Since I was good at copying I sat down and drew the picture (I think it was the head of a girl) and not long afterwards a salesman came to the door. I didn't sign up for the course he was offering; perhaps it cost too much money or perhaps I knew in my heart that I wasn't any good at this. I did, later on, take visual art for a year when I was at college, but I think it was more because I loved being around an art room than because I had any illusions about myself as an artist. I do remember one painting, however (done in poster paints I think), that would have been a psychiatrist's delight. The painting showed a group of girls in yellow slickers and yellow rain hats on one side of a street; on the other stands a solitary girl in a red velvet party dress. My professor saw it; I'm surprised, now, that he didn't ask me about it. I gave the girl black hair but she was obviously me.

I still like being around visual artists. I married one, lived with another, and my eldest daughter is both an artist and an art therapist at a veterans' hospital. All three of my daughters, in fact, have a strong sense of colour and design and were encouraged, when young, to explore paint and clay and printmaking. I think they were very lucky to have a father who would "play" with them in this way. Of course there were books around, lots of books, but they had the added pleasure of "making a mess" and nobody minded. A friend said to me one day that she didn't know anybody else who wrote about landscape the way I do. I think that's an exaggeration, but I do think that I have "the painter's eye" if not the rest of the equipment. When I write I actually see the place I'm writing about, see where the sun is (if there is a sun), see where the shadows fall. However, working with black marks on white paper isn't nearly so satisfying as squeezing out a colour, mixing it with another, laying it on. My vegetable garden is my canvas now, I suppose; I can get very excited seeing my purple burgundy beans climbing the fence with the orange and gold nasturtiums, the ruffled purple lettuce next to the dusty green broccoli.

There was a war on when I was young, but it was all happening "over there." The quarrels of my parents were much more frightening to me than the possibility of an enemy attack. I remember the posters, which seemed to be everywhere. "Shhh. The Enemy May Be Listening" or "Loose Lips SINK SHIPS"—and I remember air-raid drills at school where we went down into the basement and put our heads between our knees. My father tried to enlist but he was over forty

"With my sister (I'm on the left). The hand-tinted picture was taken for my grandfather, who kept it on his desk in a frame that said 'The pin-up girls of L.B. Corbett,'" about 1942

and had flat feet so they turned him down. He was welfare commissioner for part of the war, however, and he enjoyed that very much. How he got the job and what qualifications he had, God knows; it probably had something to do with the Masons and the fact he was a Democrat. (My mother was a Republican; she liked to think she cancelled out his vote.) Now he had a big desk and even a secretary, Betty, who took dictation. We had a cocker spaniel named Skippy and my father would stand at the door saying, "Where are we going, Skippy? City Hall? City Hall? City Hall?" until the dog was nearly frantic. My father loved being a big shot, even if he was only a minor big shot (and out on his ear as soon as the Republicans came back in.) Later, he worked briefly as an inspector for the OPA and traveled the state checking up on businesses and staying in hotels; he loved that, too (and of course it got him away from home).

I remember my mother kneading a bag of margarine (called "oleo" then) with a small colour capsule inside. Margarine didn't come coloured then, you had to do it yourself. (I don't think it came coloured in Canada until fairly recently.) She was working this and working this but it never lost its streaky appearance and my father hated it—"none of that ersatz stuff for me!"

I was good at singing and loved all the war songs: "Don't Sit Under the Apple Tree," "Comin' in on a

Wing and a Prayer," "From the Halls of Montezuma (to the shores of Tripoli)." We listened to Kate Smith every Sunday and prayed for our boys in church. At my grandfather's summer place, things went on much as usual. He had a housekeeper who knew how to get extra treats from butchers and grocers so we ate very well. On the outhouse he tacked up a sign you usually saw at the gas station: IS THIS TRIP NECESSARY?, and bought toilet paper printed with the faces of Hitler, Mussolini, and Hirohito. "Wipe out the Axis" it said. But not a single member of our family was "over there." Some cousins were in the ROTC but I don't think they ever went overseas. The war wasn't real to me; it was something happening somewhere else. I don't think I had any idea, then, what was happening to the Jews; it certainly wasn't talked about at school. Children today are so much more aware of what's going on in the world—they are bombarded with images of suffering, starvation, and death. I suppose they still believe, here in North America, that wars always happen someplace else, but teachers talk about things that never came up in my youth: prejudice, racism, the possibility of war itself being wrong. I do not think we should take away the innocence of children or make them feel guilty if they are white and middle class. But to make them aware of a wider world than their own safe neighborhood is not a bad thing.

We were at my grandfather's the day the war ended in the Pacific; this was the only time I ever saw him take a drink. My father, who had been a bugler boy in the First World War, although he got influenza and never went overseas, took down the bugle which hung on the front porch and played TAPS.

And that was that. The only other thing I remember is seeing the front page of a newspaper with a picture of the mushroom cloud and a reference to President Truman. Because I was fascinated by words from a very early age, I could never take his name seriously. It was like having a president named Mr. Goodfellow. But what he'd done was real all right and now he was a hero.

(A few years ago in Ottawa I saw a traveling exhibition of paintings done by survivors of the atom bomb; I believe most of them had been children at the time. I stood in the corridor and wept.)

*

From the time I was nine until I was about thirteen I wrote poetry. Some of it won prizes in the annual contests sponsored by *Scholastic* magazine. I wish I still had some of these poems so that I could include an example here. All I remember is the opening lines of one: Beyond the gates of sunset lies / the shining realm of Paradise, where little boys with golden curls / stoop down to sing with little girls. I wish I could forget THAT! The others were of the same ilk: princes and princesses, knights and lepers—dreadful stuff. I'm surprised I didn't become a writer of greeting card verse. I think I wrote this stuff to *please,* and to try and elevate my soul from the drab reality of the house at 13 Chestnut Street. It was like covering a cake of shit with sickly, sugary icing and hoping no one would notice what was really inside.

I never admitted to anyone what my life at home was like, and my sister and I never talked about it; we still don't. People must have known, though, at least about my parents' improvidence. The milkman knew, the electricity company, the telephone company, the insurance agent, the department stores where expensive dresses for my sister and me were put on layaway every year, the dancing-school teacher, the dentist (who would wait until I was in the chair, with the drill turned on, before he said, "Would you ask your mother to call me about her bill?"), the bank managers. And all of these people had families; some of them had children at our school. I wrote those poems because it seemed to me that these were the sort of poems teachers (and judges of contests) expected from nice little girls. Perhaps, if I wrote enough of them, they would think I *was* a nice little girl, just like all the others. It took me a long long time to get over the feeling that I had to please people with my writing, that I shouldn't write about anything dark if I wanted to be liked and/or accepted. And I have never got over the fear of being in debt; I pretty well have to know, down to the last dollar, what I have in the bank. I'm amazed at people who don't balance their chequebooks—how can they stand it? I still see the awkward bill collectors turning their hats in their hands, looking sideways at my mother and father: "Well, perhaps if you put a little something on the account?"

When I sold my first published story (to the *Atlantic Monthly*), we were living out in West Africa. They wrote and asked for a brief biography and where to send the cheque. (Five hundred U.S. dollars! A fortune!) I wrote them a (very) brief history of my life and at the end I put, "to speak of something as sordid as money, please don't send the cheque here, but deposit it in my bank account in Canada." Shortly after that I received a letter from Edward Weeks. He said I should get one thing straight right at the beginning of my career; there was nothing sordid about money except the lack of it.

My children used to say, "You must have really liked school, you're so smart." But I didn't. I hated it most of the time and wished I didn't have to go. I was shy and awkward and always on the outside of things. And I wasn't really all that bright; learning did not come easy to me, only reading. I spent half my time looking out the window and the other half trying not to be called upon. Junior high was even worse, except that I took journalism instead of English (this was an option if your English grades were high) and finally had a group I belonged to. (I think we all had the same homeroom.) I learned about column inches and layout and design, went round to local businesses and shops drumming up advertisers, wrote feature articles, book reviews, sports columns. I think that was in grades seven and eight but it might have been for three years, I can't remember. The editor of the *West Junior Leader* was the daughter of the editor of the Binghamton *Sun*. Naturally I thought *I* was a far better writer, and the two of us were rivals. As my mother would say, I felt she got the job through "pull."

I also played in the junior high school orchestra and sang in the glee club, for music was my second choice after art. One winter—I think I was in the third grade—I came down with a cold that turned into severe bronchitis and I was forced to stay home from school for weeks and weeks. I didn't really mind because the old radio, a small, wooden table-top model with its wonderful glowing tubes in the back, was brought up to my room. I slept, I listened to soap operas ("The Romance of Helen Trent," "Ma Perkins," "Young Dr. Malone," "Our Gal Sunday"), I cut out pictures from ladies' magazines and stuck them on white paper, designing "rooms." I must have been quite sick because once I saw a sign on the front door: Please Don't Ring Bell—Sick Child. Even today, if I get a cold it easily slides into bronchitis and I have a permanent cough, rather like a smoker's cough. I suppose that all started that winter.

One day my grandfather came to see how I was and he brought me a small violin in a case lined with purple plush. I thought that violin was absolutely beautiful. I would take it out and run my fingers up and down the rich, honey-coloured wood, smell the block of resin used to lubricate the bow, pluck notes on the strings. I still don't know why he decided to buy me this present but I wanted to get better fast so that I could take lessons. We did have my grandmother Callahan's piano downstairs in the living room, and my sister had begun piano lessons but there wasn't much interest in music in the family except for listening to the Lucky Strike Hit Parade once a week. My sister and I both sang in the junior choir at the First Presbyterian Church, and I continued to sing in choirs and glee clubs right up to the time I graduated from university. (I still slip into a church from time to time on a Sunday morning, in order to sing a few of those lovely old hymns.) My father knew some Gay Nineties songs and taught me "A Bicycle Built for Two," "Bill Bailey," and "The Band Played On" ("Casey would waltz with the strawberry blonde"), a song I particularly liked because my hair, when I was very small, was red-gold. And up in the attic there was a gramophone with two horns, one for everyday, functional, adult brassy colour, and one for special occasions—a morning-glory horn. This had been left behind when my uncle and his family moved up to Syracuse. There were wax records too, stored in padded cardboard cylinders. Every so often my father would get out this gramophone and play a few songs or recitations. Strangely enough the only one I can remember was about Jealousy, the Green-eyed Monster. The voices were scratchy and faint, like the voices of the Munchkins in *The Wizard of Oz,* but I was fascinated. Who knows where that gramophone ended up; how I should love to have it today!

My mother had an old beau named Harvey Fairbanks; his wife was a peripatetic music teacher and often visited our school. Harvey Fairbanks gave violin lessons at the big music store near our church and it was arranged that I would take a half-hour lesson once a week at some bargain price (I seem to remember it was fifty cents) "for old times' sake." Later on I would visit that store many times, as a teenager, to select a record and go into one of the soundproof booths to listen. We didn't have a record player although my sister finally got one as a present the year *South Pacific* appeared. Mostly I listened to music on the radio or in one of those booths at Weeks and Dickinsons.

The music studios, very cramped and tiny, were on the second floor. Harvey Fairbanks taught me some simple tunes and told me I had to practise, practise, practise in order to strengthen my fingers. But it was hard to practise at home in the living room with my father trying to read the evening paper, my mother working on the evening quarrel, and our dog howling whenever I hit a high note. And I was lazy about it as well; playing the violin was hard work! However, by the time I reached junior high I knew enough to win a place in the second violin section of the school orchestra. We didn't do much except supply a kind of underpadding for the first violins. There were two boys in this section who could *really* play, had real talent, but of course they were looked down upon by the other boys—and a lot of the girls. It just wasn't "manly" to play the violin. I remember one song, "Dark Eyes," where all the second violins did was go *uh-uh uh-uh uh-uh* throughout the entire piece. *La la la:la la* went the melody and paused: *uh-uh,* we replied, *La la la:la la* (*uh-uh* and so on). At some point, perhaps when I entered junior high, my grandfather gave me *his* violin, which was very old and came with a battered wooden case. I had never heard my grandfather play the violin but he must have, perhaps in his youth. I hated that case, so shabby and beat-up; I was beginning to fall for my mother's belief in appearance and "nice things." I must have made quite a fuss because eventually I was given, for Christmas, a new violin case from Weeks and Dickinsons, but I was already losing interest in pursuing the violin in any serious fashion. By the time I was in senior high I had ceased playing altogether, and the violin went up to the attic. I still think music is the highest art form and envy those of my friends who stuck to their music lessons and derive great pleasure from playing. (This is usually the piano or the recorder.) I recently went to a drumming workshop here on the island where I live, twenty-four of us and a wonderful assortment of African drums. By the end of the afternoon our hands were buzzing, but we were actually producing music. It was wonderful, and now all those yearnings have begun again.

*

My grandfather had a record player up at his camp; it was the latest thing, with a device which allowed several records to be stacked, one on top of the other, a new one dropping in place when the old one had finished. One record was Fritz Kreisler (violin music!), one was North American Bird Songs (a set), one was Bob Hope, Bing Crosby, and Jerry Colonna. My grandfather was very fond of Bob Hope and Bing

Crosby and during the winters he took us to the latest "Road" movie, although my mother thought they were too risqué (her word). Afterwards we went to the Ritz Tearoom where the hostess, a tall blonde in a black dress, took us to our seats. My grandfather was a flirt, even in his seventies, and if we called him "Grandpa" when the blonde with the peek-a-boo bob was around, he'd say, "Now that did I tell you girls?" We were supposed to call him "Uncle Larry."

He was very sarcastic towards both my mother and father, particularly my father, who smoked and who therefore represented a fire hazard when we were up in the woods. He usually walked up from his house on Walnut Street to eat Christmas dinner with us but would make cutting remarks about all the fancy gifts under the tree. I was always a little frightened of him but he was, in fact, a good grandfather. (I know now what a stern, cold father he was and how his children suffered because of this.) I think it was those summers at his camp that kept me sane. My parents didn't dare to quarrel so much—at least not inside or where he could hear them—and my sister and I were allowed a lot of freedom. The cottage, a big log house with a screened porch in front and a workshop and garage underneath, was on a rise above the lake. The nights were very cool—we wore drop-seat pajamas with feet in them called "Dr. Dentons"—but by midday it was high summer and we were down on the sand in our bathing suits, running in and out of the water or taking out the rowboat which was ours exclusively, "The PinUp Girl."

It took a long time for the lake to drop off so we were quite safe, even when small, and once we learned to row a boat we were trusted on the water by ourselves. My grandfather had a series of housekeepers with unusual names (Mrs. Thing, Bertha Pullum, Johnnie Coffee) and that also allowed my mother some freedom as she didn't have to cook or plan meals. She often went fishing with my father over at T-Lake mountain, and I liked to think they were actually happy together at those times. They could be like the children they were, with no real responsibilities (as my grandfather was paying for everything). My mother sometimes complained about the fact that we lived off my grandfather every summer because my father wasn't a "good provider" and she often resented the housekeepers, particularly the very attractive Mrs. Coffee, but in her heart I felt she liked having someone else in charge of all the domestic and financial arrangements.

"My grandfather's summer camp in the Adirondack Mountains"

There was a huge stone fireplace in the main room, with a buffalo rug on the floor in front of it. My grandfather got up about 5 A.M. and lit the fire (and the fire in the woodstove in the kitchen; even after we got electricity and an electric stove, breakfast was usually cooked on the woodstove), and after a while we raced in with our clothes and dressed in the warmth from the fireplace. Now I cook on a woodstove in the winters and enjoy coming downstairs in my nightgown and lighting the fire. Even as I write this, the wood is snapping and crackling and giving off a kind of purr. There is no other sound like it.

We ate very well. Fresh-squeezed oranges (a job for my sister and myself, using a metal contraption that looked something like an earth-mover's shovel), pancakes, bacon, and maple syrup for breakfast; fried chicken and corn on the cob for dinner, or fish and coleslaw and baked potatoes; sandwiches and soup for supper. And there were always blueberry pies or a dish of boiling blueberries and sugar, with dumplings plopped in called "blueberry grunt." Wild blueberries grew in profusion all along the sandy road which led out to the main road. It didn't take long to pick a bucket or two as well as a posy of black-eyed Susans, Queen Anne's lace, and clover.

The waters of the lake were so clear you could see to the bottom even when you were quite a ways off shore. Clear and cool. We ran across the burning sand in mid-afternoon, our feet about to burst into flame, or that's the way it felt, and ran out into that lovely cool water. Out here in British Columbia the ocean is cold;

it turns your bones to glass and you hesitate, will I, won't I, on all but the hottest day. Not the same thing at all.

My grandfather sold the place in 1953. The camp burned down shortly afterwards and, as he had sold it "lock, stock and barrel" as my mother said, a great chunk of my childhood went up with the house: the big old radio next to my grandfather's chair, the slippery black sofa stuffed with horsehair, the cotton Navajo blankets and lumberjack shirts that hung on pegs by the back door, the stereopticon with its views of foreign castles and cathedrals, the jars of arrowheads, the old books for rainy days, the Ouija board on which we tried to foretell our futures, the beds we slept in, everything.

I've been back once. The people who bought from my grandfather are there still. He has a business in Amsterdam, New York, and there's a float plane moored at the entrance to the creek. They said my grandfather had installed a sawdust-burning furnace shortly before he sold the place and something went awry. They've built a nice house on the property and they were certainly welcoming but I couldn't wait to leave. Everything had shrunk from the mythic to the ordinary; I doubt I'll ever visit there again.

*

When I entered senior high school I became very depressed. My teachers did not inspire me, not even my Latin teacher, and I felt very alone and awkward. Both my parents had gone to this high school and my sister seemed to be doing fine. She was very active in the drama society and had joined a "second-string" sorority after neither of us had been pledged to either of the "top" sororities, Delta Kappa or Tau Epsilon. Sororities were a big thing in those days and your whole social life revolved around them. There were meetings every Friday night and after the meetings the boys (who had their own fraternities) came over, milled about, and joined up with the girls for Saturday movie dates. I was very ashamed that we hadn't been asked to join, especially as my mother was so upset about it, as was my father. My mother wept and my father muttered and of course they fought about who was to blame. There was also the implication that it was our fault as well and that we had let them down. I think now it probably *was* our fault, if fault is the right word. Neither of us knew much about socializing and we had become very self-centered. One could argue that our upbringing had caused this, but I don't think we should be let off that easily. We were older now; we could see through a lot of the pettiness and envy of our mother, the weak-willed behaviour of our father, and yet we continued to view life through their eyes—as victims as "acted upon." It took me a long time to get over this, and the feeling still creeps in occasionally through various cracks and crevices. And I long ago forgave my parents; it seems to be harder to forgive myself!

One day, in study hall, I talked to a girl I knew slightly. She said she hated high school too and was going away to boarding school in just a few weeks. Her father worked in one of the big banks; I'd seen him when we were dragged in by our parents as ocular proof that they needed yet another loan, so I imagine he made a fairly good salary. I went home and told my mother I hated school and wanted to go to boarding school. She asked me if I was crazy—where would they get the money for something like that when our father couldn't keep us out of debt as it was. I said the girl had mentioned scholarships; maybe I could get a scholarship or something.

I don't know why my mother agreed to write. Did she sense how desperate I was or was she so used to asking for money, for favours, that she saw nothing out of the ordinary about writing such a letter? I still don't know what she said, but a few weeks later they drove me to New Hampshire and deposited me at St. Mary's-in-the-Mountains; I was the recipient of a Bishop's scholarship, me, a Presbyterian! There had been an early snowfall but the leaves were still on the sugar maples. I felt as though I were in Paradise, truly, as they drove away and left me there surrounded by all that beauty. This turned out to be one of the happiest years of my life.

I am not going to give a blow by blow description of the rest of my life up to now but St. Mary's was such a turning point for me that I must try and set down why this was so. This was a small school, maybe not more than seventy girls, Anglican, and with great emphasis on strong minds in strong bodies. Classes were small, teachers were dedicated, and the girls themselves were a mix—tall, short, pretty, plain, shy, outgoing. We wore a uniform, grey skirt and navy blazer for class, navy ski pants and pale blue parka

when we skiied on nearby Cannon Mountain. Of course there were party dresses for various social functions and some of these girls came from very wealthy families, but most of the time we could simply forget about what we wore. That was a great plus for me, right from the start. Secondly, classes were small and we were given not only the set texts but as much extra work as we wanted. It was *okay,* in fact it was great, to want to learn more. My English teacher, seeing that I had finished all the books for the year by Christmas, gave me Tolstoy, Dostoevsky, Chekhov, Thomas Mann, Ibsen, even, I seem to recall, Gertrude Stein. He told me I wrote very well and had I ever tried my hand at writing stories? The history teacher gave a special class in Far Eastern history; until then I had known little or nothing about China or Japan. I began to realize how truly ignorant I was, but this didn't depress me at St. Mary's. I suppose what I discovered was the joy of learning and that joy led to other joys. Soon I was quite a cheerful person, dreaded going home for Christmas, couldn't wait to get back.

I was in the choir and we sang not only at school but on Sundays, in red robes and white surplices, in the choir of the Anglican church in Littleton. We sang our responses in Latin; we sang a sevenfold A-men. The music teacher had just come from England (she was quite young and I don't think she was English although she affected an English accent) and was full of the works of Ralph Vaughan Williams. On Sunday afternoons there was Music Appreciation and I heard whole operas for the first time, heard Strindberg, Dvorak, Erik Satie.

And then there were the sports. I had never been terribly good at sports (my eyesight has been bad since I was seven) but I'd played grass hockey and volleyball back home as well as softball. I was also a good runner. Now I learned lacrosse and how to ski. I was never good at either of these things but I was out there trying and nobody made fun, quite the opposite. I loved coming in from outdoors on a winter afternoon, my whole body glowing and alive.

When the school decided to put on *Macbeth,* I tried out for one of the witches. I closed my eyes and tried to imagine the blasted heath, the thin scratchy voices of the witches, who weren't evil themselves but knew evil when they saw it. After I spoke there was a sudden burst of applause. I had discovered another aspect of my personality: I could "do" voices. (This has proved very useful when I do public readings of my own work.)

There were just two flies in the ointment, as my mother would say: the minister who taught us religious studies and was also the priest at the local church, and the headmistress herself. I did not get along with either of them. Rightly or wrongly I felt that the headmistress picked on me, that she didn't like scholarship girls and was the only member of staff who looked down on me. The minister didn't like me because, like the Queen of Sheba, I asked him "hard questions." I was becoming known among the other girls for my rather sarcastic "wit" and I expect I gave the minister a hard time just to show off. Anyway, whatever the cause, I didn't get my scholarship renewed. Mother wrote to another place, in Massachusetts, and I went there for my final year of school. It was all right but it wasn't the same as that lovely little school tucked up in the mountains of New Hampshire. After that year I knew, somehow, that I would survive, that I was never trapped unless I chose to be trapped, that my "background" was simply that and I should start getting on with my life and let my parents cope with theirs as best they could. Not a bad lesson to learn when you are sixteen.

*

There is a family story that my mother trots out from time to time. She says that when I was about three and my grandmother Corbett was still alive but frail, lying on the big sofa up at the woods and requesting that "somebody take that child down to the beach," I shouted back up at the house, "Well I don't care! Someday I'm going to Europe!" It's probably apocryphal although I did know at a very early age—because of the stereopticon and some old photograph albums—that there was such a place and that it was far away. Nobody in the Callahan family had been to Europe since they came over from Ireland before the Revolution but my aunt, my mother's sister, had been to Europe in her youth and my grandfather's parents, accompanied by their youngest daughter Mabel, had done the grand tour. That was when Mabel danced with the Prince of Wales. ("Before he met Mrs. Simpson, of course," says my mother.) And when I was in grade school there was a series of rather sugary books about children from other lands ("Little Anne of England," "Little Jan of Holland," "Little Marie of France"; I'm making these up because I can't really remember the titles, but you get the idea.) There was also the ubiquitous *National Geographic* with the pictures of sturdy, happy people from other parts of

the world. Every so often the magazine would come with a map which my father unfolded carefully and I borrowed from him later.

I didn't know any people in Binghamton who had been to Europe, although certain fathers and sons had been overseas during the war, not only in Europe but also in the Pacific, the Far East. Girls at St. Mary's and the school I went to later had been to Europe, usually with their families, but I imagined going on my own, perhaps living in Paris or London for a while, writing books which would be instantly acclaimed. The more I read, the more I wanted to travel.

I won a scholarship to Smith College, which had (probably still has) a junior year abroad, but I knew I could never afford that and it still wasn't exactly what I had in mind. Then, near the middle of my second year, I became friends with a girl who intended to head off to St. Andrew's in Scotland for her junior year. A friend of her older sister had done this and loved it. Why didn't I come along? She had a copy of the catalogue, which was nothing like the glossy catalogues put out by American colleges: just a thick book listing rules and regulations and all the courses offered. Scotland was cheap and if we went as nonmatriculating students we need pay only twenty-five pounds (about seventy-five U.S. dollars) in tuition. I went home at spring break and told my parents I wanted to go to Europe for my junior year. How would I get the money? I'd go back to The Hill, I said.

In 1884 or shortly before, the first inebriate asylum was opened on a hill to the east of our city centre: two hundred and fifty-two acres of land high above the Susquehanna and Chinango rivers. The cornerstone was laid by the Grand Master of the Free and Accepted Masons, and part of his speech is recorded in *A History of Broome County* (with illustrations), 1885:

> As I looked last night at the flaming comet in our sky, and saw it inclined and plumed like a pen [there had been a comet in the sky the night before] fit and ready for the Almighty's own hand, I could not but feel that if He should seize it and inscribe with its diamond point upon the sky the chief event of this *annus mirabilis* it would be the foundation of a policy and a usage that we now celebrate—of an institution, the first of its kind in the world, which proclaims that mercy is better than justice; nay, that mercy is an exacter justice.

Whether there weren't enough inebriates who were willing to come forward or what, I don't know, but the experiment failed. Within a few years, the place had become the Binghamton Asylum for the Chronic Insane, called by the locals "The Hill." I had heard of The Hill, not just in the ordinary way—that everybody in town had heard of it and knew where it was—but because my mother's sister had spent some time there after her second suicide attempt. However, it wasn't the sort of place you went for a field trip with Brownies or Scouts and I had never even been near it until I started to look for a summer job that would pay real money, at the end of my freshman year. I had seen an ad for someone to demonstrate hair brushes at a local department store and, as I had an abundance of nice-coloured hair, I went downtown for an interview. But I had got up late and the job was taken by the time I arrived. What to do? I went over to the New York State Employment Commission and told the woman behind the desk I had to have a job. Could I type? No. Could I instruct children in riding? No. Could I drive a car? No. She said she didn't see how she could help me since I had no skills. "Isn't there *anything?*" I said. "I really need the money."

She hesitated, then handed me an index card. "There's an opening for two orderlies at The Hill. You could start tomorrow."

"You mean—work at the insane asylum?" She nodded. "It just says someone in good health and prepared to work hard."

I could see by her face she knew I wasn't going to take it. College girl, too good for that sort of thing.

"I'll take it," I said.

My sister, who was away somewhere that summer, had a friend whose father was a doctor. My parents said I had to call him up to make sure it was safe to work there. My father, who hated mention of illness of any kind, kept muttering and shaking his head, but I knew it was my mother who would decide. And the doctor said it would be perfectly all right to work there—they'd never put me on the Violent Ward. In fact, his daughter was looking for a job as well; he'd mention to her that The Hill had two openings for female orderlies. When she came home she called and said she was coming too.

The next day we borrowed her brother's convertible and drove up for our interview. Naturally we were hired on the spot—they were very short-staffed—and half an hour later we had caps and a series of keys which were fastened to a lanyard tied around our waists. She was to go to one ward, I to another. We looked at one another: "We thought we'd be together," I said. The director shook his head. No, we were to act as "reliefs"; we'd be moved around from ward to ward wherever we were needed. He took Joan up to her ward while I waited in his office, then he came down and got me. I was on the fourth floor of the main building, Ward 88. He knocked on the heavy metal door and after a few minutes a nurse unlocked the door and we stepped in. Even today I don't know why I didn't turn and run. The noise! The smell!

"Welcome to the Shit Ward," she said, taking my arm and leading me down the long corridor. "Come and I'll introduce you to our ladies."

Joan quit the next day; I stayed all that summer and went back the next. If anything made me a writer (if writers are made, not born) I think it was The Hill. For although my family life was pretty terrible emotionally, I had, in fact, led a sheltered existence. I wasn't even allowed to go to funerals when I was young. Ward 88 was crammed full of mad old ladies, incontinent, abusive, hideous to look at (most of them), terrifying. I had not known there were people like this in the world, *women* like this. Skin and bones, most of them, with huge bedsores painted with gentian violet. This was still the era of straitjackets and "baths" (with canvas covers and a hole for the patient's head so she stuck up like a pie bird in a pie).

I worked on other wards besides Ward 88—the shock ward (insulin shock, which is terribly dangerous and makes you fat, as well as electroconvulsive therapy, where I often had the job of holding down a patient's legs), an ambulatory ward, the operating room. In fact, during my second summer I worked almost exclusively in the O.R., witnessed lobotomies and amputations as well as the birth of two babies, born to women who had no idea what was happening. I worked 7:00 to 3:30; I worked 3:30 to 11:00; I worked midnight to 8:00. I made friends with the nurses and some of the other orderlies. The world of The Hill became much more real than the world outside, down in the town. When I wasn't working there, I was asleep. And at the end of the second summer, with a little help from the

"The wonderful ship that took me to Europe for the first time"

Daughters of the American Revolution (another of my mother's letters) and all my savings, I flew to Boston to join my friend and we set sail for England. Boston-Halifax-St. John's-Liverpool. It took us twelve days to cross the Atlantic and by the time we stepped ashore, I felt ready for anything that life could offer; I felt free. (It wasn't until several years later that I began to have nightmares about The Hill.)

*

About fifteen years ago I made a sentimental pilgrimage to St. Andrew's and to No. 10 Hope Street which in my student days was a co-ed boarding house. Now it was a bed-and-breakfast run by a dour Scots woman who was very reluctant to let me in the door when I said I had lived there as a student. She obviously didn't like students very much even though she lived in a town which depended on the university for a lot of its revenue. (It is also the home of the Royal and Ancient Golf Course; no doubt many of her clients were well-behaved golfers, not rowdy undergraduates.)

I went up to the top floor where we had a room directly opposite the stairs. The room was unoccupied so she let me have a look in although she stayed right behind me, looking from time to time at her watch. I had had no brothers and so had never shared a house with boys before; it took me a while to get used to a boy coming out of the (bitterly cold) bathroom in his dressing gown, to the way people popped in and out of rooms, sometimes without knocking. We all had various interests outside the house but we were also the Hope Street Gang and would go en bloc to the movies, where we sat in the shilling seats and smoked and made rude comments if we didn't like the film, or went to the Cross Keys for beer and crisps and noisy discussions about Life. On Tuesdays we gathered in one room and listened to the *Goon Show.* We made fun of the food we got, the inevitability of it—Mondays, bangers and mash and turnips; Tuesdays, floating mince and mash and tinned peas; Wednesdays, rissoles; Thursdays, stewing steak with gravy; Fridays, plaice and chips. I can't remember Saturdays and Sundays, probably a "joint" of some kind on Sunday. Porridge (always) for breakfast. Pot after pot of tea.

The academic work was hard and nobody stood over you to read that book by Wednesday or get that essay in. At that time only about five percent of young people went on to university so it was still a privilege, not a right. Most of the students were on grants and had very little spare cash. But they knew how to have fun (there were lots of parties and dances and walks along the sea) as well as how to make best use of their study time. After the first quarter, when I nearly failed Moral Philosophy because I hadn't read the books the professor had "suggested" we read, I smartened up and learned how to study myself. I think that basic grounding in self-discipline, setting aside a certain portion of the day for intellectual work, has been of great benefit to me as a self-employed writer. When I am working on a story or a novel, particularly when I am working on the first few drafts and have no deadlines, no editors, no *anyone* breathing down my neck, I have to set myself a schedule and try to stick to it. Now I find it hard to work for anyone else!

At the end of the academic year my roommate and I went walking in the Highlands and on Skye, staying in youth hostels, hitchhiking occasionally when we got tired. I have always been drawn to hills and mountains and the sometimes bleak beauty of the Highlands really spoke to me. The weather held and we came back feeling very fit after our year of books and bangers and beer. During the long Easter break, we had gone to Spain and now we decided to go to Scandinavia (her grandfather was Danish), Holland, and Italy. It was safe to hitchhike in those days; we never had any trouble even though she was very blonde and I was a redhead. We were followed a lot in Italy (*che belizza! che belizza!*) but no one really accosted us. Times have changed; a woman would be a fool to hitchhike in most parts of Europe any more. (And perhaps our innocence protected us; I don't know.)

One of the many songs we learned at parties was "Come Landlord Fill the Flowing Bowl" (before it doth run over). The refrain is:

> For tonight we'll merry, merry be
> For tonight we'll merry, merry be
> For tonight we'll merry, merry be
> Tomorrow we'll be sober

The first novel I attempted to write, about that year at St. Andrew's, was called *Tomorrow We'll Be Sober.* I think I wanted it to be a cross between *Zuleika Dobson* and *Our Hearts Were Young and Gay.* I abandoned it fairly early on and God knows where it is now; I'd love to have it. I was so in love with the whole student world of St. Andrew's that I even toyed with the idea of staying on. I would have to learn Greek in order to matriculate and I would have to find some more money; the last didn't worry me so much even though I was on a student visa and forbidden to work. There

were always odd jobs about and after The Hill I knew I could do anything, however unpleasant, if I needed to. But I was a scholarship student at Smith and I felt a certain duty to return and finish my degree. Maybe obligation is a better word. So, in late August I sailed for home (via the port of Montreal) on the *Franconia.* There were quite a lot of college kids on that ship; they seemed terribly *immature* to me, especially the giggly girls. After all, I hadn't just spent the summer cruising around Europe with my pals; I'd been a student. I'd had an affair. I'd actually lived there. I wasn't a *tourist.* What a snob I must have seemed to the others! What a phoney.

But one thing was real—I knew I was going back just as soon as possible. I'd been bitten. The New World would never again hold the attraction of the Old. Or so I thought—leaning on the rail as we sailed up the St. Lawrence on that warm afternoon in August 1956.

By November 1957, having graduated from Smith and worked in a bookstore and then the advertising department of a department store ("Crisp as an autumn breeze these pleated skirts are just the thing for the smart schoolgirl"), I had saved enough money for a passage back across the water. In the late summer I had also become engaged (wasn't that what all our mothers wanted?) to a man I had known at St. Andrew's. I already knew, by the time I sailed, that this wasn't going to work out but I decided I wanted to go anyway. I shared a room in a house in Ladbroke Grove near the Holland Park Tube Station with a friend from our house at Smith, and I answered ad after ad trying to find work in London. The Aliens Act had come in and I had to prove that I was better qualified to do the job than a British person. I couldn't type or do shorthand and I had no real "qualifications" other than a B.A. so I soon became very discouraged. I tried the BBC, the film studios (I almost got a job with Columbia Pictures, doing publicity, but there was no particular reason why they should hire an American so the home office said no). I think my lowest day came when I answered an ad for a temporary nanny, went all the way to Highgate, only to discover that my future employer would be an American woman who only wanted a girl with "a good English accent." (She apologized for not having made that clear in the ad.) December was cold and bleak and foggy. Sometimes, when you crossed the street, you could only see the orange globes at the sides of the zebra crossings. It was like living in a bag of damp, dirty white wool, and the ambulances went all night, taking the elderly to hospital with pneumonia. For the first time I understood what a pea-soup fog really was. Just before Christmas, when all I had left was a few pounds and my return passage, a young man I'd met on the ship suggested I try Birmingham, where his father was a teacher. Apparently they were always short of teachers in Birmingham. I said I didn't have a teaching certificate. He said that didn't matter; I could teach with a degree.

I really didn't want to leave London. Why would a would-be writer go to *Birmingham?* Who, of note, had ever come from Birmingham? I liked London; I liked the parks and the museums and galleries. I even got to see some good plays (parts of them) by hanging around theatres waiting for doctors to be called out on emergencies! I was never afraid in London, even in those Dickensonian fogs. I went to free lectures and struck up conversations in coffeehouses (espresso bars were just becoming the rage) and pubs. This sometimes led to free coffee or lager or even a meal. But I knew I couldn't stay if I had no work at all, and my visitor's visa would run out in a few months.

*

Just before Christmas I took the train to Birmingham, talked to my friend's father who set up an interview with the Education Authority, and I was hired on the spot, to begin the first week of January. They sent me back to London with a letter for the home office saying it wasn't a question of someone else doing the job better, there was no one to do the job. (They were 500 teachers short in Birmingham at that time.) The night before I was (reluctantly) to leave London, the man I loved called me up. We hadn't seen each other for a while because all we did was fight. He wanted to know how I was doing and would I like to meet again and talk. I remember holding the black receiver in my hand (the telephone was in the downstairs hall) and thinking, "I can't go to Birmingham; I love this man; surely we can work something out.") "I've got a job in Birmingham," I said, "teaching primary school. I leave tomorrow." "Best of luck," he said, and I never saw him again.

Someday soon I intend to write an entire book about my time in Birmingham at Bishop Ryder's Church of England Infant and Junior School, a fancy name for what was really a very old school in the slums. I had Class 3, ages six and seven, and I think there were about forty-eight of them, all but a few (the boy whose father was a fireman, the little girl whose father made coffins) very noisy, cheeky, and dirty. I had a high, slant-top desk at the top of the room and took attendance in a huge register, dipping a pen in an inkwell. "John Fulford?" "Here, Miss." "June Binnell?" "Yes, Miss." At break I sold biscuits from three separate tins at three separate prices. Janine Dodgers were the most expensive, a penny ha'penny. There were also Lincoln biscuits and something else I can't remember. The children all crowded round shouting out their orders and I was always short at the end of the week. Every schoolchild in England got a free pint of milk at break but a lot of my children didn't like it—they preferred tea—until I suggested to the headmistress that perhaps they could have chocolate milk. Trucks were lorries, elevators were lifts, cookies were biscuits, your "front passage" was what you peed out of, not the entrance way in your house. When it was my turn to supervise school dinners, I and another teacher walked the school down a few blocks to the Salvation Army Hall where good, nourishing food was ladled out by two deaf mutes. (Eventually the hall was burnt down by some of the older boys at the school.)

The other teachers were mostly much older than I was, very good at their jobs, and knew how to keep order as well as teach; they overlooked the bedlam coming from my classroom and gave me lots of good advice. I'm not sure what those children learned (except a lot of songs; they loved to sing), but I learned a lot.

I lived with two other young teachers miles away in a house owned by the Education Authority and used to teach home economics to secondary school students. My housemates were *real* teachers, had been to teacher training college, and both had steady boyfriends whom I suppose they eventually married. There was a good fish-and-chips shop at the end of the road where I got off the bus, so I would often bring home big newspaper-wrapped bundles of fish-and-chips or roe-and-chips, and we'd sit around the kitchen table eating all this lovely, greasy food and drinking endless cups of tea. We paid almost no rent, but we had to make sure the place was spotless on Monday mornings.

I discovered Birmingham was full of culture: the Birmingham Rep, the City of Birmingham Orchestra, the wonderful art gallery, the Cathedral, the excellent

"My oldest child, Sarah, at her christening with Ian's mother at my back, his grandmother holding Sarah, and me in the very '50s 'bandeau pul veil.' We were about to sail for Canada," Sussex, England, 1959.

library. And I hadn't been there long when I met a young man in his final year at the Birmingham College of Arts and Crafts on Margaret Street, the first college to be built outside London during the arts and crafts movement. He had a book in his pocket. It turned out he always had a book in his pocket. I think, in many ways, he was better read than I was. He introduced me to the happy-go-lucky world of the Art College (just to go in the door of that place made me feel good) and soon he was doing the art lesson, on Friday afternoons, for my little monsters.

We "courted" in pubs and coffee bars and curry houses. We spent Saturdays wandering around the Bull Ring listening to the hawkers, watching the Strong Man get loose from his heavy chains (he was married to a girl at the Art College), eating cockles off the end of a pin. He invited me to come out to Solihull, where he lived, to meet his parents. He said he wanted to

emigrate, to see the world; I said I had wanted to settle in England but I too wanted to see the world. I don't know whether we "fell" in love so much as realized, gradually, how very much we had in common, that we loved one another, yes, but would also be good companions in the adventure of our lives. We decided to get married. (His parents had quite liked me up to then but they didn't like Americans much and they never expected their son to marry one. They never got over it.)

In 1959, with our infant daughter, Sarah, we sailed to Montreal on the old *Empress of France,* in the cheapest cabin on D-deck, right next to the engine room (the baby seemed to find the thud-thud soothing) and then came to British Columbia where we have lived—more or less—ever since. I had never seen the Pacific Ocean until then and I am now a complete convert to the Pacific Northwest. Although Ian and I are no longer together, we live very similar lives on separate islands in the same archipelago between the mainland and Vancouver Island. We have vegetable gardens and he has geese and ducks and chickens (I had chickens until recently) and we live in wood houses on land that we own and love. We have three daughters all very much "West Coasters" and all just a ferry-ride away. It seems impossible that thirty-four years have gone by since I held the baby up to the train window as we sped across Canada ("these are the lakes these are the hills these are the prairies these are the prairies these are the prairies—this is your country now, Baby"). I wrote to someone the other day, "If Time flies, he goes by Concorde." There are two little grandsons in Victoria. Is that possible?

*

I have not said much about our time in West Africa, where Ian was offered a job at the (then) Kwame Nkrumah University of Science and Technology in Kumasi, Ghana. We sent a telegram "yes" and then said to one another, "Where's Ghana?" It had been the Gold Coast when we were in school. My family said, "You're taking your children to *Africa?" His* mother said, "Lucky you, fancy having servants." (We were there when Nkrumah was overthrown and overnight, almost, his name was painted out from everything; it was like something out of *Alice in Wonderland.*) I was pregnant with our third child when we arrived and lost the baby when I was nearly seven months along and I nearly bled to death, a horrible experience in every way. I was ill for a long time, both in body and spirit, and lived on the edge of a breakdown for several years. But about six months after I got out of hospital I wrote a story, a very stylized story, trying to come to terms with what had happened. (Nobody wanted to talk about it. After all, it wasn't as though I had *known* her, was it? I must "buck up" and not mope.) I would have had more sympathy with a broken leg.

I sent the story off to the *Atlantic Monthly*—I had several encouraging letters from them in the past few years—and two months later they wrote and said they'd taken it as an Atlantic "First." I sat staring at the letter with the tears rolling down my face. I would give anything to have had the baby rather than the letter! However, it was from that moment on that I decided to write about reality, about what it was like to be a woman in the second half of the twentieth century, decided that I had to be *true,* not "nice," if I was to be an artist (and was to save my soul).

Edward Weeks saw the story and wrote me a letter from Atlantic Monthly Press. Robert Amussen at Bobbs-Merrill saw the story and wrote me a letter from Bobbs-Merrill in New York. Both wanted to know if I was working on a novel. I wrote back, to both, that I could only imagine writing short stories as I had two young children and my life was very fragmented. Atlantic Monthly Press said they'd be delighted to see a book of stories when I finished. They heaped praise on me, comparisons to "the early James Joyce" and Katherine Mansfield. Bob Amussen said, "We'll sign for a book of stories right now if you will do a novel later on." I was in such despair and confusion at that time I couldn't imagine a "later on" but Ian, who I think now must have been terribly worried about my sanity, said "sign it, sign it." I think maybe he held my hand as I signed it, I don't remember.

The *Atlantic Monthly* story came out in June 1965, almost thirty years ago. I have been writing stories, novels, and radio plays (radio is a great passion of mine; I don't own a TV) ever since. Looking back on this time I would say that writing has never brought me happiness, that it has got in the way of my human relationships, that if I knew how to do something else I would. "It's so *isolating!*" I said to one of my daughters last year. "I want colleagues; I want office parties." She just laughed. Most people envy me because I am my own boss and can take a day off,

without asking permission, if I want to. But I have no dental plan, no company pension to look forward to, and I pay all my medical plan myself. (How fortunate I am to live in Canada with its national health care plan!) I teach from time to time at universities but I don't really like university life; I think, on the whole, it's death to artists. I'm glad, most of the time, that I didn't opt for *that* life, but I get a little wistful when I discover somebody is getting $91,000 a year teaching Canadian literature and I'm on the reading list! But money (or the lack of it) isn't my real problem. I've never had much and I can't imagine I ever will. Money doesn't bring automatic happiness, although it's useful when the old fridge packs in or the dentist hands you a bill you'll have trouble paying. I *did* think writing well, as best as I knew how, and trying to be a good mother and good wife would bring happiness—and for a while, a long while, it did. But writing by itself? Forget it. And I am more and more cynical about the publishing world. Publishers are looking for profits—can we blame them? And people like me, who have a small but loyal following, are barely tolerated any more. I never get an advance over $10,000 (Canadian), and for my last book, which took seven *years,* that was paid out in three installments, the last $3,333 on the week of publication. How is one to keep on writing with "encouragement" like that? I can't get an agent because I've written too many books, have too big a backlist of critically acclaimed but financially unsuccessful titles. Agents want to discover people or snap up people who've become "hot." I'm not even lukewarm. Believe me, I've tried and been turned down again and again. Without an agent to negotiate for me (I used to have an agent but she retired, then I had another but he moved to Dublin), I haven't a chance of pulling together enough money to give me some peace of mind. There are days—more and more frequent—when I hate the writing, when the appetite of the large dog seems insatiable, when I have the feeling he will eventually eat me up. I still feel I should be doing something useful. The world is in a "terrible state of chassis" and there must be something I could do to help, something more useful than chronicling what it's like to be a woman in the second half of the twentieth century. I don't think that what I have to say about it is very important. Eliot again: "The great poet, in writing himself, writes his time." What about the not-so-great, the really-rather-ordinary-but-she-has-a-way-with-words? Some days I want to say to young writers—don't do it, run from it as fast as you can. It's not worth it, none of it. Find something else to do, less isolating, more fun, with colleagues and office parties. Artists can't really share—or only

"I'm pregnant with Claire, Vickie on left, Sarah on right," Stanley Park, Vancouver, 1967

with people who would pass them by on the street. Give the large dog back while it's still a puppy or you'll end up discovering you don't own it, it owns you.

Audrey Thomas contributed the following update to *CA* in 2005:

Several years ago my middle daughter, Victoria, said, "I guess writers don't retire, do they?" (This was around the time her father retired from his permanent part-time position as a teacher of painting and sculpture.) "No," I replied, "or hardly ever—not even when they should." I told her how a friend and I had fantasized about a Last Novel Award, where a writer, for a nice sum of money, agreed never to write, or at least never to publish, again. This was really to be aimed at writers whose work we disliked intensely,

but of course it remained a fantasy. Where would we get the funding? What writer would ever agree? Now that I am about to turn seventy I think I might agree never to publish again if someone would give me a golden handshake. I doubt I could stop writing, but the publishing side gets more and more problematic. I can foresee a time when I may have to stop publishing because no one will want my work.

Penguin Canada, my publisher for the last twenty years, turned down my last manuscript, or the fiction editor did, and my agent got one of those letters that usually go out to peddlers of first manuscripts, you know the sort; they end with the editor saying another publishing house would no doubt better serve the writer, "but I send her every good wish for the future." I did call her up and ask if anyone had read it besides herself and she said no. Of course that is the prerogative of a senior editor; s/he doesn't really have to show it to anyone else; but you would have thought that after twenty years she might have passed it along to one or two others. However, the book has just come out with Goose Lane, a small and highly respected press in New Brunswick. They've done a lovely job and it's getting good reviews so we'll see what happens. The editor at Goose Lane told me that the rumour in the industry is that I am a loose cannon, that I seem to write about whatever I please and publishers therefore have trouble promoting me. I think that's a fair assessment—I do write about whatever ever captures my interest and what pleases me lately is historical fiction. My last novel before this one was historical, the current novel is historical with a twist, but the novel before that was set in West Africa and very much a contemporary novel.

Isobel Gunn was based on a real woman from the Orkney Islands off the northern tip of Scotland. In the early nineteenth century she disguised herself as a man and signed on with the Hudson Bay Company. I did an enormous amount of research, both in Orkney itself (walking the land, searching through the archives at the Kirkwall library and the Hudson Bay archives in Winnipeg). Although I have two degrees I'm not really an academic and wasn't sure how all this research would transform itself into a novel, but once I got caught up in the life of Isobel Gunn herself, once I could imagine her in Orkney making her great decision and then working as "John Fubbister" at Albany Fort at the bottom of the Bay, the words just rolled out. (Because I grew up in the United States, I knew very little about the Hudson Bay Company; now I feel I could probably give a lecture or two on this "Company of Adventurers" as they call themselves. Imagine a business empire founded on a fashion in beaver hats.)

"John Fubbister worked willingly and well," as it says in the old log books, and was discovered to be a woman only about twenty minutes before her baby was born. (That will do it every time.)

The reviews were good—my reviews are generally good—but no one wanted it in the States or England. I am hoping someday to see the material made into a mini-series or even an opera. Isobel is a strong character and there are other fascinating players in the drama, including the known father of her child, John Scarth (who may or may not have raped her). No white women were allowed at the Bay at that time, although

the "factories" (forts where the beaver skins were collected and shipped back to England) depended upon native women to sew the hundreds of pairs of moccasins the men needed, to act as interpreters and, in many cases, to serve as "country wives" for the men.

Realizing that I could do this kind of research without going mad, I turned my hand to another novel that depended on historical research.

For years, whenever I visited London I stayed at a place for overseas graduates in Mecklenburgh Square, Bloomsbury. When I came out of the square and onto Guildford Street, which I did nearly every morning, to get to the Russell Square tube station or the buses along Southampton Row, I passed a large, gated playground with a curious sign: CORAM FIELDS PLAYGROUND FOR CHILDREN. NO ADULTS ADMITTED UNLESS IN THE COMPANY OF A CHILD. The Brits are fond of signs; they put them everywhere and some can be quirky. I still remember the old Blackwell's in Oxford with its sign as you headed down the stairs to the paperback cellar: MIND YOUR EGGHEAD. This sign was quirky. Surely it was usually the other way around—no children admitted unless in the company of an adult? Finally I asked someone, who told me that the playground was on the grounds where the old Foundling Hospital had stood for over two hundred fifty years. "Coram" referred to the retired sea-captain who had founded the hospital. I thought I had come across the name Coram before but couldn't place it.

My informant said that if I were really interested, there was a small museum located in the shortcut between Mecklenburgh Square and Brunswick Square. I went right away to the museum, met the curator, and was shown around. I won't go into elaborate detail here, but I discovered that a lot of famous people had been associated with "The Foundling" (as Londoners used to call it) including Hogarth, who designed the boys' and girls' uniforms (I saw replicas in the museum; they looked itchy) and the composer Handel who was associated with the chapel, donated a keyboard and a fair copy of the *Messiah* when he died. Benefit performances of the *Messiah* were put on for years and raised hundreds of pounds for the hospital.

The most moving exhibits were found in two glass-lidded cases, keepsakes and mementos left by the mothers when they gave their babies over to the

Sarah's wedding, August 1997: Leonard McCabe, Sarah McCabe, Claire Thomas, Victoria Thomas

hospital: a mother-of-pearl fish; half a metal heart, a letter pointing out that it was a "good baby" and did not cry overmuch, a tiny cap.

The curator mentioned that Charles Dickens had been associated with the hospital when he lived just around the corner in Doughty Street and that he even rented a pew in the chapel. The choir was famous and many fashionable men and women came to the chapel on Sundays. Dickens even used the name Coram in one of his books.

"Of course," I said, "*Little Dorrit.* Tattycoram."

I went away thinking that there was a novel in all this, but wasn't sure where or how to begin. I was working on something else but I stored all this knowledge away until the beginning of 2001 when I received a grant to work on this novel (in my proposal I said I wanted to write the "life" of a fictional character from one of Dickens's novels, a girl named Tattycoram). I wrote to

the Coram Foundation to find out where the archives might be located and whether they were on microfilm. The reply said they were at the London Metropolitan Archives, were quite extensive, and very little was on microfilm. If I wanted to see them I would have to come to London. For £50 they could, however, send me a copy of the index. I agreed, and was very glad I did, as the index is over a thousand pages long.

During the winter I re-read *Little Dorrit,* read all of Dickens's published letters and several biographies, both old and new. I also marked items in the index that I thought would be of particular interest to me. Then, on September 9, 2001, I flew to London, arriving on September 10.

I got up very early the next day, even though I was tired, as I knew I could afford only a month there (I call London the one-meal-a-day city) and felt I mustn't waste a minute. I was at the Metropolitan Archives when the doors opened and I worked there all day until my eyes felt like fuzzy tennis balls, reading letters faded to sepia, household accounts, anything and everything related to the Foundling Hospital in the nineteenth century. It must have been around 4:30 P.M. when I set off back to Mecklenburgh Square. I hadn't yet discovered that by taking numerous shortcuts I could walk to the archives, so I got on the tube at Farringdon, then changed at King's Cross for the Piccadilly line. I was trying to stay awake when an announcement came over the loudspeaker: "Due to the incidents in America today, there will be no planes flying from Heathrow." (The Piccadilly line is the line that goes out to Heathrow.) I came out of my daze at this announcement and immediately thought, "Bush has been assassinated." This was not such a bizarre thought for a former American; presidents do get assassinated in the U.S. And when the British say "incident," they mean "death." If you hear this over the loudspeaker, "Due to the incident at Oxford Circus this train will not be stopping at that station," you can be pretty sure that someone has fallen, jumped, or been pushed onto the rails. But "incidents"? They must have got Cheney as well. I am no fan of the Bush administration, but in my view assassination is never the way to go. I like to see connivers in high office impeached or publicly humiliated, so I did feel a twinge of something—maybe annoyance, maybe sympathy—and wondered who had done the deed. (That awful term, "claiming responsibility.") It wasn't until I came up to the surface that I found out what really happened.

It was a strange time to be in London, for there were rumours that London might be next. [Editor's Note: This piece was written before the bombings that occurred in London on July 7, 2005, and the subsequent attempts on July 23.] I found I had switched from the Underground to buses; I wanted to be above ground if anything happened. By day I was immersed in the past; in late afternoon I emerged into the anxious present. I kept thinking of those lines from Yeats's "Second Coming," relating the line about conviction to those who should be leading and what they lacked, and his words about passion and intensity to the creators of anarchy and chaos. It was Thursday afternoon, or possibly Friday, when I heard a plane flying overhead. The skies had been so silent for the last few days that the sound cut through my consciousness like a chainsaw. I said to myself, don't look up, keep walking, you knew flights were going to be resumed today; it was today, wasn't it?; yet I couldn't help myself, I stopped and looked up at the sky. All

around me people had stopped and were doing the same thing. Sheepish, we smiled at one another when the plane passed out of sight.

The novel I was working on in September of 2001 was *Tattycoram,* which has just come out. I am already at work on another, on two more, one historical, set on the "Gold Coast" of Africa in the mid-nineteenth century and the other more or less contemporary. I hear my daughter's voice: "Mom, writers don't retire, do they?"

My mother, with whom I began my essay in 1993, is now dead. She lived to be 98, and although she was in a care home, she was bedridden for only the last ten days of her life. I went to see her (I was actually heading east on a book tour when my sister called), sat by her side and held her icy hand. She didn't want to talk—she kept her eyes closed the whole time I was there—so I pressed her hand once and was pleased when she pressed back. I tried pressing twice and she did the same. Every so often we played this little hand-pressing game as I sat with her through the long afternoon. My sister had been reading a book about giving the dying person permission to leave and I knew I was supposed to say, "You can let go, Mother, it's all right, just let go." I didn't do this. Maybe I was afraid she would suddenly sit up in bed and yell at me to mind my own business.

The doctor said she might hang on for days and my sister said I should probably go back up to Canada and do the rest of my readings, so I was back on my island when she actually died. I had stopped in Montpelier on the way down and bought some scented stocks at a florist. (My father, who was the gardener in the family, used to grow old-fashioned flowers like stocks.) The nurse brought a vase, but I took some of them and laid them on Mother's pillow. "Do you remember the stocks in Daddy's garden? Remember how sweetly they smelled?"

She didn't open her eyes but whispered, "lovely, lovely." Those were the last words she ever spoke to me.

Do I miss her? I don't miss her bitterness, her self-absorption and self-pity, her inability to accept people as they are, her wild accusations. I do miss her use of language. My mother was born in 1897 and used old-fashioned colourful words like gumption, high-falutin, shenanigans, smithereens, lollygag. I feel that the English language, for all that new words are being introduced every day, has lost a lot of its vigour, at least in everyday speech. When I listen to teenagers—or even to those older than that—it would seem that every other "fuckin'" word is, "like, fuck."

So I miss my mother in that way and I'm glad she lived long enough for me to cease being afraid of her. I actually cared about her by the end. I think she was a manic-depressive, what we now call by the much less-interesting term, bipolar.

In the spring of 1995 I was teaching at Dartmouth (had talked myself into a job there for a winter-spring term once before, as my mother grew near death, and now I was back even though she had died in the autumn). My sister and her husband and I drove up to the Adirondacks to scatter Mother's ashes—she was the first person in our family to be cremated. The ashes were beside me on the back seat, in a box inside a Stop and Shop paper bag. Every so often my brother-in-law would call out to me, "How's Mother doing back there?" and I would say, "Just fine, thanks." We had decided the best place for the ashes would be in the trout stream near where we spent all our childhood summers. When she and Daddy went fishing, she was probably the happiest she ever allowed herself to be.

We stayed overnight at the Irondaquoit Inn, on Piseco Lake, now a bed-and-breakfast but a private club for men when we were growing up. When we awoke the next morning it had turned cold and was snowing—in mid-May. We sat in the car and read the poems we had chosen, or rather, I read the poem I had chosen, as my sister, for some obscure reason, decided not to read hers. My brother-in-law read a short passage from the Bible, then we stepped out of the car and walked over to the stream. With numb fingers I opened the box and we took turns flinging handfuls of Mother's ashes into the rushing water. A wind had sprung up and some of the ashes, along with snowflakes, blew back into our faces. There seemed to be grit between my teeth for a week afterwards.

The same year that Mother died I sold some papers to the National Library of Canada and assumed a mortgage on a small house, a cottage really, in

Victoria, on Vancouver Island. My middle daughter lives here and my grandsons officially live here, but William is now twenty and has just finished his second year of university and Nicholas, eighteen, graduates from high school on June 16. They are fast moving out into their own worlds.

I like the little house, said to be the smallest house in Victoria, although I am sure I've seen at least two that are smaller. For the past five years I have come from my small island to this bigger island (*much* bigger island) during "the rainy season" or the part of it that extends from January through May. It's hard to call it "winter" when the climate here is so mild compared to the rest of Canada. The sea is just a block away and I can see water and the distant Olympic mountains from my back stoop. I take courses in choral singing, which I have always loved—how wonderful to do something as part of a group—and a playwriting workshop, as I'd like to try my hand at a stage play. Victoria's core is small and I can walk to just about anywhere I want to go; otherwise, I hop on a bus. When I'm on Galiano I rent the house out and except for my very first tenants this has been a pleasurable experience. The hardest part of the whole enterprise is carting things over in boxes in January and then packing it all up again in the spring. One day I suppose I'll have to get rid of one place or the other (maybe both?) and decide where I would really like to spend the rest of my days. The west coast of Canada has become a very desirable place to live and real estate prices keep going up. This means that taxes keep going up as well. Right now I have the best of both possible worlds.

Since I wrote my first essay, one of my daughters has married, two have divorced and one has happily remarried. At the moment all seem healthy and happy and very very busy. My youngest, Claire, and her husband Jason, went to China in February (along with Vickie, the next up, for support) and picked up their adopted baby daughter, Amy Shu. "Shu" was part of her name at the orphanage and it means "pretty girl." She is certainly that, and her new parents decided it should be a permanent part of her name. She comes from a part of China that speaks Mandarin and I often think of that old Far Side cartoon as I watch her watching us speak. You remember the one about what you say to your dog ("Now Rex, I want you to be a good dog Rex while I'm out, and Rex, no barking" etc. etc. etc.) and what the dog hears ("blah blah blah Rex, blah blah Rex, blah blah blah blah Rex"). What babies

Claire Thomas ("my youngest!"), with husband, Jason Chan, picking up their adopted daughter, Amy Shu, in China, 2005

of Amy's age mostly hear (she is now seventeen months old) is blah blah blah plus their name, but blah blah blah in Mandarin must sound very different from blah blah blah in English. To add to her confusion, Jason's parents, who are Chinese, speak Cantonese! She is very sociable, which I find rather surprising, and has already accumulated an impressive amount of "stuff," brought to her from adoring relations and friends. Sarah, my oldest daughter, and her husband have no children, but they are so impressed by the whole procedure that they are now going the same route. Perhaps we shall have another small grandchild by this time next year.

I remember an interview with Martin Amis that was broadcast on the CBC many years ago. The interviewer asked him what he thought was the biggest hurdle facing women artists. He said, "The pram in the hall." (It sounds more like Virginia Woolf than Amis, doesn't it?) It is certainly true that it's hard—make that impossible—to write with small children running around. I solved this by writing only during "the school day,"

beginning at 9 A.M. and packing up around 2:30 P.M., before they arrived home. I worked on the kitchen table for years, so I quite literally had to pack up. It's only in the last few years that I've had a small writing studio built in the garden both on Galiano and in town. No more kitchen table, except occasionally in December when I simply want to be close to my big wood stove and its companionable warmth. I still tend to write during the school day and shall probably do so until I drop; I still write in longhand on lined yellow sheets. I send the final draft to Carole Robertson, in Montreal, who has been my typist since 1989. I told her once that it was such a relief, putting that envelope in the mail, I called it "sending the children to camp." Now we share a little joke between us: I e-mail her (yes, I do have an ancient computer) that the manuscript is on the way; I say "the babies are off." When she receives the parcel she e-mails "the babies have arrived."

Writing by hand is a little like drawing, I think, and perhaps that is one reason why I like it so much. Also,

I like to travel but I don't like to worry about expensive gear that might get damaged, lost or stolen. I buy Pilot Hi-Tech fine-point pens by the box. I would love to use a fountain pen, but the ink would seep through on this porous paper. (By the way, on the ground floor of the Dickens Museum on Doughty Street, there is a library and reference room. School groups can come in, learn more about Dickens and try their hand at writing with a quill pen. I, too, had a go at writing my name this way. What came out was shaky letters with very uneven strokes and lots of blots. How on earth did he do it—all those huge novels written with a quill pen.)

I'm not sure I have much more to say. Not one of my novels or books of stories has ever become a best-seller. Maybe my old mother was right all along and I should have given all this up years ago. My financial situation is always slightly precarious, but I do have a small government pension now and I augment this with occasional readings, workshops and articles. I also have very generous friends. I've won a few awards with healthy chunks of cash attached and once a year I get a cheque from Canadian PLR.

Many of the people I know who opted for the career plus salary are now retired and actively involved in good causes that require a lot of meetings, usually in the daytime. I am a member of the Writers' Union of Canada (was chair in 2002) and write letters to Members of Parliament about causes I believe in—I do the same for P.E.N. Canadian Centre and Amnesty—but I rarely attend meetings. I think the world is in a terrible state and often feel guilty about not being more actively involved, especially as regards aid to African women and children. How history will condemn us if we turn our backs on Africa!

It has been forty years since my first published story appeared in the *Atlantic Monthly.* How is that possible?? I once wrote to a friend that if time flies, he goes by Concorde, yet now even the Concorde flies no more and soon no one will get the allusion. Would I have kept at it, the writing, if I had known how difficult it is to make a living? Probably. I finish a book in a state of mental, physical, and financial exhaustion. I vow "Never again!" Then I read something or hear something or see something and I get that little tingle of excitement and curiosity and I'm off. The Cheshire Cat told Alice that we are all mad or we wouldn't be her. Is the creative impulse a kind of madness? I'm beginning to think it is. Our heads are full of voices and visions; we see sights that aren't the same as what we see out the kitchen window. We laugh or cry as we make little black marks on white paper. We need to persuade others that the worlds we see are real. Is this not a form of madness? We can call it by a fancier name, but I suspect we writers, painters, composers, we ARTISTS, are walking a fine line, most of the time, between sanity and something else. (And strangely enough, by walking that line, we stay sane.)

BIOGRAPHICAL AND CRITICAL SOURCES:

BOOKS

Atwood, Margaret, *Second Words: Selected Critical Prose,* House of Anansi (Toronto, Ontario, Canada), 1982.
Authors in the News, Volume 2, Gale (Detroit, MI), 1976.
Contemporary Literary Criticism, Gale (Detroit, MI), Volume 7, 1977, Volume 13, 1980, Volume 37, 1986.
Dictionary of Literary Biography, Volume 60: *Canadian Writers since 1960, Second Series,* Gale (Detroit, MI), 1987.
Reference Guide to Short Fiction, St. James Press (Detroit, MI), 1994.

PERIODICALS

Books in Canada, December, 1979; February, 1982; May, 1985; March, 1993, review of *Graven Images,* p. 46; October, 1995, review of *Coming down from Wa,* pp. 35-37.
Canadian Book Review Annual, 1995, review of *Coming down from Wa,* p. 187; 1999, review of *Isobel Gunn,* p. 187; 2002, review of *The Path of Totality,* p. 202.
Canadian Forum, May-June, 1974; June-July, 1980; July-August, 1993, Gwendolyn Guth, review of *Graven Images,* pp. 39-40; November, 1999, Thomas Wharton, review of *Isobel Gunn,* pp. 39-43.
Canadian Literature, autumn, 1971; summer, 1975; winter, 1992, pp. 139-40; summer, 1994, review of *Graven Images,* p. 8; winter, 2000, review of *Isobel Gunn,* p. 186; winter, 2002, Elizabeth Hodgson, "Crossing the Bay," pp. 181-183; winter, 2003, review of *The Path of Totality,* p. 147.

Essays on Canadian Writing, fall, 1992, pp. 43-50.

Fiddlehead, January, 1983.

Globe and Mail (Toronto, Ontario, Canada), April 16, 1977; April 18, 1987; September 22, 1990; November 3, 1990.

Herizons, summer, 2000, review of *Isobel Gunn,* p. 32.

Los Angeles Times Book Review, February 10, 1985.

Macleans, December 20, 1999, Susan McClelland, "New World Tragedy," p. 110; April 23, 2001, "Heroine Worship," p. 66; May 16, 2005, "When Writers Become Characters," p. 62.

Mosaic, fall, 1993, pp. 69-86.

New York Times Book Review, February 1, 1976.

Open Letter, summer, 1976.

Paragraph, fall, 1993, review of *Graven Images,* p. 39.

Prairie Fire, winter, 2000, interview with Thomas, pp. 44-50.

Quill & Quire, March, 1993, review of *Graven Images,* p. 46; September, 1995, review of *Coming down from Wa,* p. 68; November, 1999, review of *Isobel Gunn,* p. 34; September, 2001, review of *The Path of Totality,* p. 48.

Resource Links, June, 1997, review of *Coming down from Wa,* pp. 232-233.

Room of One's Own, Volume 10, numbers 3-4, 1986.

Saturday Night, July, 1972; May, 1974; April, 1982; January, 1985.

University of Toronto Quarterly, summer, 2000, Ed Kleiman, "Audrey Thomas Looks back on the Cauldron of History," p. 660.

Village Voice, August 6, 1985.

Wascana Review, fall, 1976.

ONLINE

Canadian Writers Union Web site, http://www.writersunion.ca/ (August 7, 2005), "Audrey Thomas."

January Online, http://epe.lac-bac.gc.ca/ (January 1-8, 2001), Linda Richards, interview with Thomas.

Library and Archives of Canada Web site, http://www.collectionscanada.ca/ (August 7, 2005).

Terasen Lifetime Achievement Award Web site, http://www.bcbookworld.com/ (August 7, 2005), "Audrey Thomas."

*   *   *

TISSEYRE, Michelle 1947-

PERSONAL: Born 1947; daughter of Pierre (a publisher) and Michelle (a television host) Tisseyre.

ADDRESSES: Agent—c/o Key Porter Books, 6 Adelaide St., 10th Fl., Toronto, Ontario, Canada M5C 1H6.

CAREER: Journalist and literary translator.

WRITINGS:

La passion de Jeanne (novel), Robert Laffront (Paris, France), 1997, translated by Tisseyre as *Divided Passions,* Key Porter Books (Toronto, Ontario, Canada), 1999.

TRANSLATOR

Robert Sutherland, *Le mystère de l'île au roc noir* (title means "The Mystery of Black Rock Island"), Éditions Pierre Tisseyre (St. Laurent, Quebec, Canada), 1999.

Emily Carr, *Klee Wyck,* Éditions Pierre Tisseyre (St. Laurent, Quebec, Canada), 2000.

Robert Sutherland, *Meurtres au lac des Huards* (title means "Murder at Lake of the Huards"), Éditions Pierre Tisseyre (St. Laurent, Quebec, Canada), 2000.

Robert Sutherland, *Si deux meurent* (title means "If Two Die"), Éditions Pierre Tisseyre (St. Laurent, Quebec, Canada), 2001.

SIDELIGHTS: Michelle Tisseyre, a Canadian journalist and literary translator, also found success as a novelist when her debut work *La passion de Jeanne* remained on the bestseller lists in Quebec for more than four months. In 1999 Tisseyre, the daughter of Quebec publisher Pierre Tisseyre and popular television host Michelle Tisseyre, translated her own work into English as *Divided Passions.*

Described as "an engaging blend of romance and political intrigue" by a *Resource Links* contributor, *Divided Passions* is based on the life of the author's maternal grandparents. The book concerns Jeanne Langlois, the only daughter of a prominent French-Canadian politician and his controlling, pious wife. To placate her mother, at age sixteen Jeanne entered a Carmelite convent in Manitoba, but found the strict conditions overwhelming and left the order, only to rush into a thankless marriage with a young lawyer of

Irish descent. "While the language difference could suggest, as does the title, [an] account of a family struggling to breach the linguistic divide, this conflict is really of no consequence here," noted Jane Koustas in the *University of Toronto Quarterly*. "The story is instead a romanticized 'slice of life' glimpse at upper-crust Montreal society." Amid the tumult of World War I and the Great Depression, Jeanne struggles to raise a child after her marriage disintegrated, and learns to chart her own course in a rapidly changing world. "Confronted with a failed marriage to an abusive, alcoholic husband, who seemingly has never stopped loving her, Jeanne finally finds happiness in the arms of another man, at considerable expense to her reputation and, no doubt, to that of Tisseyre's mother's entire family," Koustas added.

Quill & Quire reviewer Mary Soderstrom stated that in *Divided Passions* Tisseyre produces "a popular novel filled with as much romance as social observation," and added that the author "skillfully weaves in political argument with historical fact," as in her description of the conscription debates during World War I. A critic in *Books in Canada* remarked that the author "writes with flair and confidence, tells a good story, and uses her knowledge of Quebec politics to good advantage," while Soderstrom observed that *Divided Passions* "is skillfully translated by the author herself, a feat that is as remarkable as her book is engaging."

"The main interest for English readers lies, perhaps, not in the novel's literary worth but in its popularity," Koustas wrote of *Divided Passions*. "Tisseyre's novel hits a nostalgic chord. This is a privileged glimpse into what sells in Quebec."

BIOGRAPHICAL AND CRITICAL SOURCES:

PERIODICALS

Booklist, May 15, 1998, review of *La passion de Jeanne,* p. 1610.
Books in Canada, October, 1999, review of *Divided Passions,* p. 36.
Quill & Quire, April, 1999, Mary Soderstrom, review of *Divided Passions,* p. 27.
Resource Links, October, 2000, review of *Divided Passions,* p. 49.
University of Toronto Quarterly, winter, 2000-01, Jane Koustas, review of *Divided Passions.**

*   *   *

TROTTER, Sharland 1943(?)-1997

PERSONAL: Born c. 1943, in Robstown, TX; died of cancer November 25, 1997, in Brookline, MA; married Robert Kuttner (a journalist), 1971; children: Gabriel, Jessica. *Education:* Attended Goucher College; Harvard University, Ed.D., 1987.

CAREER: Clinical psychologist and writer. Psychologist in private practice, Boston, MA; research fellow at Radcliffe College, Cambridge, MA; staff member at Fresh Pond Day Treatment Center, Cambridge, and Westwood Lodge (psychiatric hospital), Westwood, MA. Former editor-in-chief of American Psychological Association's *Monitor on Psychology*.

Worked as an editor in publishing houses in New York, NY; a member of "Nader's Raiders" in Washington, DC, c. 1971; and a staff member at the Massachusetts Advocacy Center, Boston, MA, c. 1979.

WRITINGS:

(With Franklin D. Chu) *The Madness Establishment: Ralph Nader's Study Group Report on the National Institute of Mental Health,* Grossman Publishers (New York, NY), 1974.
(Editor, with Evelyn B. Thoman) *Social Responsiveness of Infants: A Round Table,* The Company (New Brunswick, NJ), 1978.
(With Robert Kuttner) *Family Re-Union: Reconnecting Parents and Children in Adulthood,* Free Press (New York, NY), 2002.

SIDELIGHTS: Sharland Trotter was a clinical psychologist who cowrote the book *Family Re-Union: Reconnecting Parents and Children in Adulthood* with her journalist husband, Robert Kuttner. The book focuses on relationships between adults and their parents and how they can form stronger bonds of friendship. The authors look at the relationship between parents and children beginning with the time children first leave home, usually to go to college, and on through the years until the time of the parents' impending death. In fact, the authors came up with the idea for the book when their own son was heading off to college. The book is made more poignant by the fact that Trotter discovered she had cancer when she and her husband began working on the book. As a result, the book includes a look at how Trotter and her family deal with her illness, which eventually led to her death in 1997 prior to the book's publication. The authors also include real-life examples from various families and from literature, as well as examples from their own lives to discuss their theme and to offer suggestions on forming essentially a new parent-child relationship as the child becomes an adult. In a review in *Adolescence,* Roslyn Heights commented that the book "offers hope that, no matter what our personal circumstances, it is never too late to create loving, respectful family ties." Pam Matthews, writing in the *Library Journal,* felt that "Trotter's last days tend to eclipse the titular theme." A *Publishers Weekly* contributor called the book "a thoughtful rumination on the nature and intricacies of adult child and parent relationships."

BIOGRAPHICAL AND CRITICAL SOURCES:

PERIODICALS

Adolescence, summer, 2004, Roslyn Heights, review of *Family Re-Union: Reconnecting Parents and Children in Adulthood,* p. 400.
Library Journal, March 15, 2002, Pam Matthews, review of *Family Re-Union,* p. 97.
Publishers Weekly, April 15, 2002, "What Life Has in Store," review of *Family Re-Union,* p. 57.

ONLINE

Simon & Schuster Web site, http://www.simonsays.com/ (June 7, 2002), "Sharland Trotter."

OBITUARIES AND OTHER SOURCES

PERIODICALS

Boston Globe, November 27, 1997, p. B39.*

U-V

UTGOFF, Victor A.

PERSONAL: Male. *Education:* Massachusetts Institute of Technology, B.S. (aeronautics and astronautics), 1960; Purdue University, Ph.D. (electrical engineering), 1970.

ADDRESSES: Office—Institute for Defense Analyses, 4850 Mark Center Dr., Alexandria, VA 22311.

CAREER: During early career, worked for various research and aerospace companies; National Security Council staff, senior member, 1977-81; Institute for Defense Analyses, Alexandria, VA, currently deputy director of strategy, forces, and resources division.

AWARDS, HONORS: Andrew J. Goodpaster Award, Institute for Defense Analyses, 1999, for excellence in research.

WRITINGS:

(With Barry M. Blechman) *Fiscal and Economic Implications of Strategic Defenses,* Westview Press (Boulder, CO), 1986.
The Challenge of Chemical Weapons: An American Perspective, foreword by W. Y. Smith, St. Martin's Press (New York, NY), 1991.
(With others) *The American Military in the Twentieth Century,* St. Martin's Press (New York, NY), 1993.
(Editor and contributor) *The Coming Crisis: Nuclear Proliferation, U.S. Interests, and World Order,* MIT Press (Cambridge, MA), 2000.

Also author of papers related to nuclear, biological, and chemical weapons.

SIDELIGHTS: Victor A. Utgoff, a prominent official at the Institute for Defense Analyses, has written extensively about military matters, especially about the threat of nuclear, biological, and chemical weapons. He first collaborated with Barry M. Blechman on *Fiscal and Economic Implications of Strategic Defenses,* then wrote *The Challenge of Chemical Weapons: An American Perspective.* He also contributed to *The American Military in the Twentieth Century,* a book that asks important questions about the implications of a downsized U.S. military force. Donald M. Snow, writing in *Armed Forces and Society,* called the information in this book "valuable" but suggested that it is meant primarily for force planners in the Pentagon and the U.S. Capitol. "For the more general reader looking for a discussion of broader principles and strategic alternatives," the critic added, the many details in the book could be "overwhelming."

Utgoff has also edited *The Coming Crisis: Nuclear Proliferation, U.S. Interests, and World Order,* a timely series of essays by recognized scholars on an important global issue. The book raises many questions about what the United States should do with its nuclear arsenal if deterrence should fail. In the first half of the book, the authors discuss the reasons nation-states decide to acquire or develop nuclear weapons. Essays in the second half address the possibility of nuclear crises between the United States and a regional nuclear power, and the consequences of such confrontations.

Several critics found *The Coming Crisis* a useful contribution to the growing literature on nuclear proliferation. In the *Marine Corps Gazette,* John M. Manson wrote that, while some of the essays "are tedious and can overcomplicate relatively straightforward issues," the book "is a good read for the serious scholar of international security affairs." Jon Greene commented in the *Naval War College Review* that the main premise of the book is that "sooner or later the proliferation of nuclear weapons is going to lead to a confrontation between the United States and a nuclear-armed state. . . . All students of national security policy owe it to themselves to consider the policy implications."

BIOGRAPHICAL AND CRITICAL SOURCES:

PERIODICALS

Armed Forces and Society, winter, 1995, Donald M. Snow, review of *The American Military in the Twentieth Century,* p. 308.

Marine Corps Gazette, July, 2001, John Manson, review of *The Coming Crisis: Nuclear Proliferation, U.S. Interests, and World Order,* p. 77.

Naval War College Review, summer, 2001, Jon Greene, review of *The Coming Crisis,* p. 169.

ONLINE

Johns Hopkins University Applied Physics Laboratory Web site, http://www.jhuapl.edu/ (July 26, 2004), "Victor Utgoff."*

*   *   *

VANBURKLEO, Sandra F.

PERSONAL: Female. *Education:* Hamline University (St. Paul, MN), B.A. (history); University of Minnesota, M.A., Ph.D.

ADDRESSES: Office—Department of History, Wayne State University, 3133 Faculty/Administration Bldg., Detroit, MI 48202.

CAREER: Wayne State University, Detroit, MI, professor of history.

WRITINGS:

"Belonging to the World": Women's Rights and American Constitutional Culture, Oxford University Press (New York, NY), 2001.

(Editor, with Kermit Hall and Robert Kaczorowski) *Constitutionalism and American Culture: Writing the New Constitutional History,* University Press of Kansas (Lawrence, KS), 2002.

Also contributor to books, including *The Research Process in Political Science,* edited by W. P. Shively, Peacock, 1984; *By and for the People: Constitutional Rights in American History,* edited by Kermit Hall, Harlan Davidson, 1991; *Political Trials,* second edition, edited by Michal Belknap, Greenwood/Praeger, 1994; and *Seriatim: The Supreme Court before John Marshall,* New York University Press, 1998. Contributor to journals, including *Michigan Historical Review, Magazine of History, Constitution,* and *Journal of the Early Republic.* Also contributor of entries to encyclopedias and dictionaries, including *Oxford Companion to the Supreme Court,* edited by Kermit Hall, Oxford University Press, 1992; *Biographical Dictionary of U.S. Supreme Court Justices,* edited by Melvin Urofsky, Garland Press, 1994; *American National Biography,* edited by John Garraty, Oxford University Press, 1997-98; and *Oxford Companion to American Law,* Oxford University Press, 2002.

SIDELIGHTS: Sandra F. VanBurkleo has produced a study of the evolution of women's rights in America and was coeditor of another book of essays on American constitutional history in its cultural context. According to Judith A. Baer in the *Journal of Women's History,* VanBurkleo's full-length work, *"Belonging to the World": Women's Rights and American Constitutional Culture,* "confirms the tension between gender equality and male dominance throughout U.S. history." *"Belonging to the World"* chronicles the development of what VanBurkleo likes to call "speech communities": that is, groups that gradually allowed women in different historical periods to find a public voice. Regarding the pre-colonial period she discusses the ways in which Ann Hutchinson and Ann Hibbens, for example, were punished for their refusal to keep silent. During the American Revolution and the New Republic, VanBurkleo contends, many women achieved increased economic power but did not achieve political emancipation. The "speech communities" that developed among early women's rights activists in the mid-and late-nineteenth century, she maintains, presaged the later emergence of political and economic rights in their insistence that women should be able to speak freely in public.

The gradual emergence of the suffrage movement, according to VanBurkleo, was accompanied by an entrenched ideology that women were morally superior to men and thus should have a greater voice in government. The alliance of other activist groups such as the Women's Christian Temperance Union with the suffragists added other "speech communities" to the mix and thus strengthened women's power in eventually getting the vote. VanBurkleo also reports on a number of court cases that were pivotal in achieving women's rights, and she also brings the debate up to the present day in her discussion of women's economic status, sexual harassment issues, and the problem of violence against women.

In her review, Baer said that VanBurkleo's book, along with Nancy Cott's *Public Vows: A History of Marriage and the Nation,* "could have been significantly better if [the authors] had brought more insights of contemporary feminist theory to bear on the analysis," but the critic concluded that *"Belonging to the World"* is a valuable contribution to women's history. Dorothy McBride Stetson commented in *Political Science Quarterly* that VanBurkleo exhibits "an almost breathless urgency to temper generalizations about American law with attention to variations among states, regions, classes, and races." VanBurkleo, McBride concluded, has provided "a tool for arranging the movement in periods and an explanation for the diversity of feminist activism." *Reviews in American History* contributor Allison M. Parker called the book a "comprehensive view of women's public and political attempts to gain their rights," with a "synthesis of American women's history that also provides readers with a useful new perspective regarding the importance of public speech for equality and citizenship."

VanBurkleo also coedited and contributed to *Constitutionalism and American Culture: Writing the New Constitutional History,* a festschrift in memory of historian Paul Murphy, who pioneered the study of constitutional history in its political and social context. According to Stuart Banner, writing in the *Journal of American History,* the twelve essays in the collection

are "an eclectic bunch" that cover subjects such as the framers of the Constitution and their own concepts of history, efforts to achieve equal constitutional protection for women, the Warren court's idea of equality, and the history of constitutional thought on race and civil society. VanBurkleo's essay covers the nineteenth-century women's movement as it relates to the idea of freedom of speech. Banner concluded that "one could not ask for a better sampler of this particular genre of constitutional history."

BIOGRAPHICAL AND CRITICAL SOURCES:

PERIODICALS

Journal of American History, September, 2003, Stuart Banner, review of *Constitutionalism and American Culture: Writing the New Constitutional History,* p. 628.
Journal of Women's History, summer, 2002, Judith A. Baer, "Public and Private Rule: The Wife and the Citizen," p. 182.
Law and Social Inquiry, fall, 2002, review of *Constitutionalism and American Culture,* p. 1007.
Political Science Quarterly, fall, 2002, Dorothy McBride Stetson, review of *"Belonging to the World": Women's Rights and American Constitutional Culture,* p. 538.
Reviews in American History, March, 2003, Alison M. Parker, "Women's Rights and 'Speech Communities' in American Legal History," p. 66.

ONLINE

Wayne State University Web site, http://www.cla.wayne.edu/ (July 26, 2005), "Sandra F. VanBurkleo."*

* * *

Van SICKLE, Emily 1910-2005

OBITUARY NOTICE— See index for *CA* sketch: Born October 23, 1910, in Vicksburg, MS; died of dementia, March 10, 2005, in Rockville, MD. Secretary and author. Van Sickle is best remembered for her memoir describing her years in a Japanese internment camp in the Philippines during World War II. Earning a bachelor's degree from Goucher College in 1931, she moved with her family to the Philippines in 1935 and two years later married an international businessman. When Japan invaded the Philippines, the couple was imprisoned, along with thousands of other Americans living on the island. Van Sickle endured nearly intolerable conditions from 1942 until the camp was liberated in 1945. The only bright point of those years was the kindness of local priests who interceded on the couple's behalf to try and gain some leniency from the Japanese military. The Japanese were about to execute a plan to kill all the prisoners when Allied forces rescued them. After the war Van Sickle's husband suffered ill health as a result of the poor camp conditions and died within a few years. During the late 1960s and early 1970s, she found work as a business administrator and part-time secretary for American University. She also worked for the Postal Rate Commission for two years, and continued working in various jobs until the mid-1980s. Her memoir *The Iron Gates of Santo Tomas: The Firsthand Account of an American Couple Interned by the Japanese in Manila, 1942-1945* was published in 1992 and was still in print at the time of her death.

OBITUARIES AND OTHER SOURCES:

PERIODICALS

Washington Post, March 26, 2005, p. B5.

*   *   *

VICKERY, Margaret Birney 1963-

PERSONAL: Born 1963; married Peter Vickery (an attorney); children: two. *Education:* Oberlin University, received degree, 1985; Stanford University, Ph.D., 1993.

ADDRESSES: Home—190 University Dr., Amherst, MA 01002-3818.

CAREER: Architectural historian and author. Worked for Victorian Society, London, England; lecturer on Victorian architecture and the arts and crafts movement.

WRITINGS:

Buildings for Bluestockings: The Architecture and Social History of Women's Colleges in Late Victorian England, University of Delaware Press (Newark, DE) 1999.

SIDELIGHTS: Margaret Birney Vickery is an architectural historian and author whose debut book, *Building for Bluestockings: The Architecture and Social History of Women's Colleges in Late Victorian England,* examines the trends in building design for university dormitories that were intended for the use of women. College housing for men followed a standard structure throughout England, with stacked staircases that led to each room. However, when women first began to gain admittance to degree programs and the universities undertook providing housing for these new students, a more domestic, house-like architecture was employed. Vickery focuses her study on six colleges that were among the first to admit women: Girton and Newnham at Cambridge University, Lady Margaret Hall and Somerville at Oxford, and Westfield and Royal Holloway, London. These dormitories were designed with private rooms off of hallways instead of stairs, and they tended to be smaller than their counterparts built for men. J. Mordaunt Crook commented in a review for the *Times Literary Supplement* that "the author's scrutiny of elevations and plans reinforces the view that there was indeed a women's collegiate style, understated . . . communal and—the word continues to recur—domestic."

Vickery focuses on the way traditional expectations of women's roles in society came into play in the architectural decisions, even as the women in question were making strides toward greater equality in society. Crook went on to note that "if women had to leave home for the purposes of higher education, then at least they should live like ladies." In her review for *Journal of Women's History,* Valerie S. Rake found fault with Vickery's decision to narrow the scope of her study to gender, stating that "she does not . . . explore the class, race, or sexual implications of these projects." Instead, Vickery concentrates on more conventional influences, making a point to acknowledge that factors such as under-funding and compromise also affected the final outcome of the architectural designs. William Whyte, in a review for the *English Historical Review,* stated that Vickery "forces historians to re-examine their understanding of these colleges, and to reassess the role of building in expressing ideas and identity. No one interested in nineteenth-century architecture or education can afford to ignore this book."

BIOGRAPHICAL AND CRITICAL SOURCES:

PERIODICALS

English Historical Review, September, 2000, William Whyte, review of *Buildings for Bluestockings: The Architecture and Social History of Women's Colleges in Late Victorian England,* p. 1011.
Journal of Women's History, summer, 2001, Valerie S. Rake, review of *Buildings for Bluestockings,* p. 221.
Oberlin Alumni, winter, 2000, review of *Buildings for Bluestockings.*
Times Literary Supplement, August 16, 2000, J. Mordaunt Crook, "Staging Posts for Heroic Women."

ONLINE

Peter Vickery's Home Page, http://www.progressive lawyer.com/ (July 26, 2005).*

*   *   *

VOSKO, Leah F.

PERSONAL: Female. *Education:* Ph.D., 1998.

ADDRESSES: Office—York University, Atkinson College, Third Floor, School of Social Science, 90 Pond Rd., Toronto, Ontario M3J 1P3, Canada. *E-mail*—lvosko@yorku.ca.

CAREER: Educator and author. McMaster University, Hamilton, Ontario, Canada, former assistant professor of labor studies and political science; York University, Toronto, Ontario, Canada research chair in feminist political economy; University of Toronto, Institute for Work and Health, Toronto, adjunct scientist. Principal investigator for the Community University Research

Alliance of Contingent Work and Gender and Work database. Virtual scholar-in-residence for Law Commission of Canada, 2003-04.

WRITINGS:

Temporary Work: The Gendered Rise of a Precarious Employment Relationship, University of Toronto Press (Toronto, Ontario, Canada), 2000.
(Editor, with others) *Studies in Political Economy: Developments in Feminism,* Women's Press (Toronto, Ontario, Canada), 2002.
(Editor, with Wallace Clement) *Changing Canada: Political Economy as Transformation,* McGill-Queen's University Press (Montreal, Quebec, Canada) 2003.
(With Cynthia Cranford, Judy Fudge, and Eric Tucker) *Self-employed Workers Organize: Law, Policy, and Unions,* McGill-Queen's University Press (Montreal, Quebec, Canada), 2004.
(Editor, with Jim Stanford) *Challenging the Market: The Struggle to Regulate Work and Income* McGill-Queen's University Press (Montreal, Quebec, Canada), 2004.

SIDELIGHTS: Educator and author Leah F. Vosko is an associate professor at York University who also serves as principal investigator for the Community University Research Alliance of Contingent Work, based at York University and involving a team drawn from six community groups as well as McMaster University, the University of Quebec at Montreal, George Brown College, and the University of Toronto.

Vosko explores the growth of the temporary employment industry in Canada in her book *Temporary Work: The Gendered Rise of the Precarious Employment Relationship.* Here she traces the industry's history and development, as well as how corporate use of temporary workers has evolved from hiring a few people to fill in for ill or vacationing employees to staffing entire departments with agency workers on a long-term basis. Vosko points out that much of this shift occurred simultaneously with the post-World War II influx of female, immigrant, and non-white individuals into the work force, and that such workers are treated more as commodities to be bought and sold than as standard employees.

In a review for *Resources for Feminist Research* Tania Das Gupta stated that "what is particularly valuable in this study is the intertwining of a feminist analysis of this process as the protagonists in this story over-whelmingly emerge as women." She went on to note, however, that while men are becoming much more common within the temporary employment field, "Vosko argues that despite the . . . trend, the varieties of jobs available for temporary workers are clearly gendered in terms of the division of labour, i.e., who gets to do what kind of job, the kinds of salary and working conditions each has, and the overall feminized character of all temporary work relationships which is based on the old image of the 'Kelly Girl.'" Chris Schenk, writing for *Capital and Class,* called Vosko's book "the most insightful analysis to date on the rise and evolution of temporary work in Canada," and went on to remark that "activists concerned with the plight of contingent workers and researchers needing to ground their examination of labour market trends will benefit from this study."

BIOGRAPHICAL AND CRITICAL SOURCES:

PERIODICALS

Canadian Journal of Sociology, January-February 2001, Dr. Jackie Krasas Rogers, review of *Temporary Work: The Gendered Rise of a Precarious Employment Relationship.*

Capital and Class, autumn, 2001, Chris Schenk, review of *Temporary Work: The Gendered Rise of a Precarious Employment Relationship,* p. 51.

Labour/Le Travail, spring, 2002, Ester Reiter, review of *Temporary Work,* p. 277.

Resources for Feminist Research, spring-summer, 2001, Tania Das Gupta, review of *Temporary Work,* p. 205.

W

WAIWAIOLE, Lono

PERSONAL: Born in San Francisco, CA.

ADDRESSES: Home—Hilo, HI. *Agent*—c/o Author Mail, St. Martin's Press, 175 5th Ave., New York, NY 10010. *E-mail*—mail@lonowaiwaiole.com.

CAREER: Teacher of social studies and English in secondary schools in Portland, OR, 1989-2003; high-school teacher of English in HI, 2003—. Worked variously as a newspaper editor, associate editor of a magazine, director of publications and sports information at a liberal-arts college, and as a professional poker player.

WRITINGS:

Wiley's Lament (mystery novel), St. Martin's Minotaur (New York, NY), 2003.
Wiley's Shuffle (mystery novel; sequel to *Wiley's Lament*), St. Martin's Minotaur (New York, NY), 2004.

SIDELIGHTS: Lono Waiwaiole's mysteries *Wiley's Lament* and *Wiley's Shuffle* are dark, violent novels featuring a gritty protagonist known only as Wiley. Living a marginal life in Portland, Oregon, Wiley makes ends meet by playing poker; when necessary, he supplements his income by robbing drug dealers. Wiley's life becomes even more bleak when his daughter Lizzie, who works for an escort service, is found brutally murdered in a motel room. Wiley sets out to hunt down her killer. He suspects a man named Leon, a wealthy kingpin in Portland's sex industry and a former lover of Lizzie's. Wiley finally locates Leon but is ultimately convinced of his innocence, and the two join forces to find the real killer, a rogue agent of the Drug Enforcement Agency. Reviewing *Wiley's Lament* for Chicago's *Tribune Books,* Dick Adler warned that the novel is "extremely violent," but added that the author "makes it all worthwhile" and is capable of "writing that tears at the heart."

The events of *Wiley's Lament* resonate in the sequel, *Wiley's Shuffle.* This novel finds Wiley losing badly while playing poker at Leon's casino. When he gets a call from his friend Miriam, a prostitute who is in trouble with her boss, Wiley hurries to help her. His innate goodness, hidden deep inside his disreputable exterior, makes Wiley "the quintessential noir anti-hero," according to a *Kirkus Reviews* writer. *Wiley's Shuffle,* added the critic, pits the title character against a pimp named Dookie, "a true monster, maybe the most unregenerate, over-the-top baddie in recent crime fiction." Wiley's struggle to protect Miriam leads him to Las Vegas, Nevada, through Los Angeles, California, and finally all the way up the West Coast back to Portland. According to Frank Sennett in *Booklist,* Waiwaiole brings the story to life with "crackling dialogue and explosively entertaining characters."

BIOGRAPHICAL AND CRITICAL SOURCES:

PERIODICALS

Booklist, June 1, 2004, Frank Sennett, review of *Wiley's Shuffle,* p. 1709.

Kirkus Reviews, December 15, 2002, review of *Wiley's Lament,* p. 1812; April 15, 2004, review of *Wiley's Shuffle,* p. 367.

Library Journal, February 1, 2003, Rex Klett, review of *Wiley's Lament,* p. 121.

Publishers Weekly, February 10, 2003, review of *Wiley's Lament,* p. 166; May 31, 2004, review of *Wiley's Shuffle,* p. 55.

Tribune Books (Chicago, IL), March 30, 2003, Dick Adler, review of *Wiley's Lament,* p. 2.

ONLINE

Harriet Klausner's Review Archive, http://harriet klausner.wwwi.com/ (March 2, 2005), Harriet Klausner, review of *Wiley's Shuffle.*

Lono Waiwaiole Home Page, http://lonowaiwaiole. com (March 14, 2005).*

* * *

WASSIL-GRIMM, Claudette 1948(?)-

PERSONAL: Born c. 1948. *Education:* William Patterson College, B.A., 1970, M.Ed., 1972; University of Arizona, M.F.A., 1983.

ADDRESSES: Home—Parkersburg, WV. *Agent*—c/o Author Mail, The Overlook Press, 141 Wooster Street, New York, NY 10012.

CAREER: Editor and writer. Has appeared on numerous radio and television shows. Worked in education before turning to writing full time.

WRITINGS:

(With Virginia M. Fontana and the staff of Hunter House) *Charting Your Way Thru' PMS: A Woman's Appointment Book and Planning Guide,* Borgo press (San Bernardino, CA), 1985.

How to Avoid Parents' Mistakes When You Raise Your Children, illustrations by Jonathan Grimm, Pocket Books (New York, NY), 1990.

Where's Daddy? How Divorced, Single, and Widowed Mothers Can Provide What's Missing When Dad's Missing, Overlook Press (Woodstock, NY), 1994.

Diagnosis for Disaster: The Devastating Truth about False Memory Syndrome and Its Impact on Accusers and Families, Overlook Press (Woodstock, NY), 1995.

The Twelve-Step Journal, Overlook Press (Woodstock, NY), 1996.

Served as editor for several books, including *The House of Marriage,* William Summers, M.D., Erdmann Publishing; *Grandparenting in the 90s* and *Love and Power/Parent and Child,* both by Glenn Austin, both Erdmann Publishing; and for *Getting High in Natural Ways; An Info Book for Teens; Helping Your Child Succeed After Divorce;* and *Menopause without Medicine,* all published by Hunter House, Inc.

SIDELIGHTS: Claudette Wassil-Grimm has written several books in the fields of family health and psychology and is a certified instructor of conflict resolution techniques. For her books, she draws largely from extensive interviews with people who have survived and overcome the problems she writes about, such as parents who grew up in dysfunctional families and went on to become successful parents or women who were sexually abused but have reunited with their families. In *Where's Daddy? How Divorced, Single, and Widowed Mothers Can Provide What's Missing When Dad's Missing,* Wassil-Grimm discusses such issues as why fathers disappear from their children's lives and provides potential approaches to compensate for the father's absence by, for example, making sure there is some type of male presence in the child's life. A *Publishers Weekly* contributor noted, "The author covers. . . issues. . . in a constructive yet realistic spirit, aiding single mothers without bad-mouthing fathers." In a review in the *Journal of Marital and Family Therapy,* Sandra A. Jensen and Alan J. Hawkins noted that, although the book targets single mothers, it "can also be a great resource for therapists and the general public." They went on to write, "The book's format, with its engaging narratives and chapter-end summaries, makes it easy and enjoyable to read."

Diagnosis for Disaster: The Devastating Truth about False Memory Syndrome and Its Impact on Accusers and Families examines several views about the supposed "recovery" of suppressed memories in child sexual abuse cases. For the book, the author interviews several people who later retracted their claims about child sexual abuse and discusses such issues as the dramatic increase in such claims and the possible causes for such reports, including the encouragement of overzealous therapists. Writing in *Booklist,* Kathryn Carpenter noted, "Wassil-Grimm's . . . book is a tough read because of both the complexity of the issues and their emotional charge." A *Publishers Weekly* contributor called the book "a clearly written handbook that is also a cogent critique of the excesses of the sexual abuse 'recovery movement'."

BIOGRAPHICAL AND CRITICAL SOURCES:

PERIODICALS

Booklist, January 15, 1995, Kathryn Carpenter, review of *Diagnosis for Disaster: The Devastating Truth about False Memory Syndrome and Its Impact on Accusers and Families,* p. 884.

Choice, September, 1995, review of *Diagnosis for Disaster.*

Journal of Marital and Family Therapy, January, 1997, Sandra A. Jensen and Alan J. Hawkins, review of *Where's Daddy? How Divorced, Single, and Widowed Mothers Can Provide What's Missing When Dad's Missing,* p. 99.

Kirkus Reviews, December 15, 1994, review of *Diagnosis for Disaster.*

Publishers Weekly, December 19, 1994, review of *Diagnosis for Disaster,* p. 40; June 20, 1994, review of *Where's Daddy?,* p. 89.*

*   *   *

WEALE, Anne
(Andrea Blake)

PERSONAL: Married Malcolm Blakeney; children: one son. *Hobbies and other interests:* Walking, reading, sketching, gardening, sewing, and visiting art galleries and museums.

ADDRESSES: Agent—c/o Author Mail, eHarlequin. com, P.O. Box 5190, Buffalo, NY 14240-5190. *E-mail*—anne@anneweale.com.

CAREER: Writer and journalist. Former staff reporter for *Eastern Evening News,* Norwich, England, *Western Daily Press,* Bristol, England, and *Yorkshire Evening Press,* York, England.

WRITINGS:

ROMANCE NOVELS

Winter Is Past, Mills & Boon (London, England), 1955, Harlequin (New York, NY), 1961.

The Lonely Shore, Mills & Boon (London, England), 1956, Harlequin (New York, NY), 1966.

The House of Seven Fountains, Mills & Boon (London, England), 1957, Harlequin (New York, NY), 1960.

Never to Love, Mills & Boon (London, England), 1958, Harlequin (New York, NY), 1962.

Sweet to Remember, Mills & Boon (London, England), 1958, Harlequin (New York, NY), 1964.

Castle in Corsica, Mills & Boon (London, England), 1959, Harlequin (New York, NY), 1960.

Hope for Tomorrow, Mills & Boon (London, England), 1959, Harlequin (New York, NY), 1965.

A Call for Nurse Templar, Mills & Boon (London, England), 1960, published as *Nurse Templar,* Harlequin (New York, NY), 1961.

Until We Met, Mills & Boon (London, England), 1961, Harlequin (New York, NY), 1964.

The Doctor's Daughters, Mills & Boon (London, England), 1962, Harlequin (New York, NY), 1963.

The House on Flamingo Cay, Mills & Boon (London, England), 1962, Harlequin (New York, NY), 1963.

If This Is Love, Mills & Boon (London, England), 1963, Harlequin (New York, NY), 1964.

The Silver Dolphin, Harlequin (New York, NY), 1963.

All I Ask,, Harlequin (New York, NY), 1964.

Islands of Summer, Mills & Boon (London, England), 1964, Harlequin (New York, NY), 1965.

Three Weeks in Eden, Mills & Boon (London, England), 1964.

Doctor in Malaya, Harlequin (New York, NY), 1965.

Girl about Town, Mills & Boon (London, England), 1965.

The Feast of Sara, Mills & Boon (London, England), 1965, Harlequin (New York, NY), 1966.

Christina Comes to Town, Harlequin (New York, NY), 1966.

Terrace in the Sun, Harlequin (New York, NY), 1966.

The Sea Waif, Harlequin (New York, NY), 1967.

South from Sounion, Harlequin (New York, NY), 1968.

The Man in Command, Harlequin (New York, NY), 1969.

Sullivan's Reef, Harlequin (New York, NY), 1970.

That Man Simon, Harlequin (New York, NY), 1971.

A Treasure for Life, Harlequin (New York, NY), 1972.

The Fields of Heaven, Harlequin (New York, NY), 1974.

Lord of the Sierras, Harlequin (New York, NY), 1975.

The Sun in Splendour, Mills & Boon (London, England), 1975.

Now or Never, Harlequin (New York, NY), 1978.

The River Room, Mills & Boon (London, England), 1978.

Separate Bedrooms, Mills & Boon (London, England), 1979.

Stowaway, Mills & Boon (London, England), 1979, Harlequin (New York, NY), 1983.

The Girl from the Sea, Mills & Boon (London, England), 1979.

The First Officer, Mills & Boon (London, England), 1980.

The Last Night at Paradise, Mills & Boon (London, England), 1980.

Touch of the Devil, Mills & Boon (London, England), 1980, Harlequin (New York, NY), 1982.

Blue Days at Sea, Mills & Boon (London, England), 1981.

Passage to Paxos, Mills & Boon (London, England), 1981.

Rain of Diamonds, Mills & Boon (London, England), 1981.

Bed of Roses, Mills & Boon (London, England), 1981, Harlequin (New York, NY), 1982.

Antigua Kiss, Worldwide (Toronto, Ontario, Canada), 1982.

Portrait of Bethany, Harlequin (New York, NY), 1982.

Wedding of the Year, Mills & Boon (London, England), 1982.

Frangipani, Harlequin (New York, NY), 1982.

All That Heaven Allows, Harlequin (New York, NY), 1983.

Ecstasy, Mills & Boon (London, England), 1983 Harlequin (New York, NY), 1984.

Flora, Worldwide (Toronto, Ontario, Canada), 1983.

Yesterday's Island, Harlequin (New York, NY), 1983.

Summer's Awakening, Mills & Boon (London, England), 1984.

Girl in a Golden Bed, Mills & Boon (London, England), 1986.

All My Worldly Goods, St. Martin's Press (New York, NY), 1987.

Lost Lagoon, Century (London, England), 1987.

Night Train, Mills & Boon (London, England), 1987.

Neptune's Daughter, Mills & Boon (London, England), 1987.

Catalan Christmas, Mills & Boon (London, England), 1988.

Do You Remember Babylon?, Mills & Boon (London, England), 1989, Harlequin (New York, NY), 1990.

Time and Chance, Century (London, England), 1989, St. Martin's Press (New York, NY), 1990.

The Fountain of Delight, St. Martin's Press (New York, NY), 1990.

Thai Silk, Mills & Boon (London, England), 1990.

Sea Fever, Mills & Boon (London, England), 1990.

Pink Champagne, Mills & Boon (London, England), 1991.

Footprints in the Sand, Mills & Boon (London, England), 1992.

The Singing Tree, Mills & Boon (London, England), 1992.

The Man from Madrid, Harlequin (New York, NY), 2004.

Also author of *Turkish Delights,* 1993, *Tequila Sunrise,* 1994, *Seascape,* 1995, *Never Go Back,* 1995, *Sophie's Secret,* 1996, *A Night to Remember,* 1996, *A Marriage Has Been Arranged,* 1997, *The Youngest Sister,* 1997, *The Impatient Virgin,* 1998, *The Bartered Bride,* 1998, *Sleepless Nights,* 1999, *Desert Honeymoon,* 1999, *Worthy of Marriage,* 2000, *A Spanish Honeymoon,* 2002, and *Sea Change,* 2002.

ROMANCE NOVELS; UNDER PSEUDONYM ANDREA BLAKE

September in Paris, Harlequin (New York, NY), 1963.

Now and Always, Harlequin (New York, NY), 1964.

Whisper of Doubt, Harlequin (New York, NY), 1965.

Night of the Hurricane, Harlequin (New York, NY), 1965.

OTHER

Columnist, *"Bookworm on the Net,"* for *Bookseller* (magazine).

SIDELIGHTS: Anne Weale is a prolific romance novelist who has written dozens of romances and has used her extensive world travels as background for her stories. She has written tales set in England, New England, Fiji, Thailand, Europe, and other locations, and is noted for her detailed descriptions of place. Her novel *Yesterday's Island,* for example, is set on Nantucket, an island off the coast of Massachusetts that once served as a major port for whaling ships. In addition to the romantic story told in *Yesterday's Island,* readers of the novel can also learn a great deal about whaling and the history and customs of the historic port.

Weale told *CA:* "I was first published in my twenties. In the early years of my career I observed the restrictions imposed by magazine editors who paid high fees for serialization rights. Later, when I was established, I wrote three ground-breaking novels, *Blue Days at Sea* (1981), which had the first black hero and heroine in a Mills & Boon romance, followed by *Antigua Kiss* (1982), and *Ecstasy* (1983), which helped to pave the way for more realistic love scenes than had been permitted earlier. My recent romances have been inspired by the village in Spain which is my winter home. I spend the summer months on an island off the coast of France. I'm still an enthusiastic traveler in my mid-seventies, and my most recent journey was to the High Atlas Mountains in North Africa."

BIOGRAPHICAL AND CRITICAL SOURCES:

BOOKS

Twentieth-Century Romance and Historical Writers, 3rd edition, St. James Press (Detroit, MI), 1994.

PERIODICALS

Publishers Weekly, October 5, 1990, Sybil Steinberg, review of *The Fountain of Delight,* p. 90.

ONLINE

eHarlequin.com, http://www.eharlequin.com/ (March 2, 2005), interview with Weale.
RomanticTimes.com, http://www.romantictimes.com/ (March 14, 2005), Kimberley Harvey, review of *The Man from Madrid* and *A Spanish Honeymoon;* Shannon Short, reviews of *Worthy of Marriage, Desert Honeymoon, A Marriage Has Been Arranged,* and *The Bartered Bride.*

*　*　*

WENTWORTH, Sally
　See HORNSBLOW, Doreen

WESTON, Allen
　See NORTON, Andre

*　*　*

WHITE, Sheldon H(arold) 1928-2005

OBITUARY NOTICE— See index for *CA* sketch: Born November 30, 1928, in New York, NY; died of heart failure March 17, 2005, in Boston, MA. Psychologist, educator, and author. White was an authority on developmental psychology whose research into how children learn greatly influenced the federal government's Head Start program and children's educational shows for public television. A Harvard University graduate who completed his B.A. in 1951, he went on to earn an M.A. from Boston University in 1952 and a Ph.D. from Iowa State University in 1957. White then taught psychology at the University of Chicago through the early 1960s along with one year teaching at Harvard. In 1965 he returned to Harvard as an associate professor, eventually becoming Roy E. Larsen Professor of Educational Psychology in 1968. He retired from the Harvard faculty in 2001. During the 1960s, White conducted research that would later profoundly influence the Head Start program for early education; in fact, he chaired the Department of Health and Human Services committee that evaluated the program from 1991 to 1993. From 1968 until 1970, he worked with the Children's Television Workshop as it developed the landmark educational series for children *Sesame Street.* In addition, White served as a consultant to the RAND Corporation, the Huron Institute, and the Educational Testing Service. He was the author or coauthor of several books, including *To End a Silence—Or Begin One* (1976) and *Childhood: Pathways of Discovery* (1979).

OBITUARIES AND OTHER SOURCES:

PERIODICALS

Chicago Tribune, March 21, 2005, section 4, p. 9.
Los Angeles Times, March 21, 2005, p. B7.
New York Times, March 26, 2005, p. B6.

*　*　*

WHITELEY, Opal
　See WHITELEY, Opal Stanley

WHITELEY, Opal Stanley 1897-1992
(Opal Whiteley)

PERSONAL: Born 1897; died 1992, in London, England.

CAREER: Writer.

AWARDS, HONORS: American Book Award, Before Columbus Foundation, 1988, for *The Singing Creek where the Willows Grow: The Rediscovered Diary of Opal Whiteley.*

WRITINGS:

The Fairyland around Us, self-published (Los Angeles, CA), 1918.

(As Opal Whiteley) *The Story of Opal: The Journal of an Understanding Heart,* Atlantic Monthly Press (Boston, MA), 1920.

(As Opal Whiteley) *The Flower of Stars,* self-published (Washington, DC), 1923.

Elizabeth Lawrence, *Opal Whiteley: The Unsolved Mystery* (contains *The Story of Opal: The Journal of an Understanding Heart*) Putnam (London, England), 1962.

Benjamin Hoff, editor, *The Singing Creek where the Willows Grow: The Rediscovered Diary of Opal Whiteley,* Ticknor & Fields (New York, NY), 1986, revised edition published as *The Singing Creek Where the Willows Grow: The Mystical Nature Diary of Opal Whiteley,* Penguin Books (New York, NY), 1995.

ADAPTATIONS: The Story of Opal: The Journal of an Understanding Heart was adapted by Robert Lindsey Nassif as *Opal: A New Musical Adventure,* Samuel French, 1993; and by Jane Boulton as *Opal,* Macmillan, 1976, revised as *Opal: The Journal of an Understanding Heart,* Tioga Publishing, 1984, revised as *Only Opal: The Diary of a Young Girl,* illustrated by Barbara Cooney, Philomel Books, 1995.

SIDELIGHTS: The life of Opal Stanley Whiteley, which spanned the years from 1897 to 1992, continues to fascinate her followers and biographers. This is in part because the absolute truth about Whiteley will probably never be known.

Whiteley was reportedly a child prodigy with an unquenchable thirst for learning. She spent much of her time in the woods communing with nature, and as a very young girl gave the barnyard and wild creatures elaborate names and sought refuge in a tree she called Michael Raphael. Whiteley entered school at age three and skipped two grades. At age six, she began keeping a diary, which she hid in a hollow log. A jealous sister ripped it to pieces, but when she was in her twenties *Atlantic Monthly* editor Ellery Sedgwick told Whiteley to bring the pieces to his mother's home, where they were reassembled. The diary was written phonetically in a childish scrawl, all in capital letters and with no punctuation. The book, which was published in a limited edition in 1920, brought Whiteley some measure of fame: it resulted in her being called a genius on the one hand, and a fraud on the other.

Whiteley was supposedly born in Oregon and raised in a logging camp, along with the five other children of Edward and Elizabeth Whiteley. However, in her diary, *The Story of Opal: The Journal of an Understanding Heart,* Whiteley claims to have been born in France, where her actual parents had taught her to read and write, thus accounting for the French phrases that appear in her diary. She claimed that she had been adopted by the Whiteleys and was actually the daughter of French naturalist and nobleman Henri Duc d'Orleans. Following publication of the diary, the duke's family accepted their new American relative, but later disowned her, claiming her to be a fraud.

Following the original publication of the diary, skeptics charged that no child of six could have written such advanced prose. Whiteley's case was further damaged by magazine reports that claimed that she had admitted that her diary was a hoax. Whiteley's family, shamed and angered, disowned her. In 1920 her grandmother was quoted in a newspaper as saying that Whiteley "was always a queer girl." She talked about the whippings the girl received from her and from Whiteley's mother. The diary was out of print a year after its publication, and Whiteley left the United States for India, and then England, where she lived in poverty. Her mental health was fragile, a result of an inherited form of schizophrenia, and she was discovered, starving, in 1948 and placed in a London mental hospital, where she lived until her death.

In the *Washington Post Book World,* Bruce Brown maintained that Whiteley was, in fact, the French princess she claimed to be. "Both her biological mother and father—who may never have married—were killed in separate, nearly simultaneous incidents in 1901," wrote Brown. Françoise, supposedly Whiteley's real name, "remembers traveling with her nanny to see her grandfather ('Grandpére,' Robert, duke of Chartres), but somehow on the way the little girl was either lost or abducted, and launched on a crazy journey that carried her to the far side of another continent, and into another culture, language and identity." Brown noted other circumstantial evidence to make Whiteley's case, including the fact that the child wrote about all of the rivers that were in the vicinity of the home of the Duc d'Orleans.

In 1986 another Whiteley defender appeared. Benjamin Hoff, author of *The Tao of Pooh,* published Whiteley's diary, along with his commentary, as *The Singing Creek where the Willows Grow: The Rediscovered Diary of Opal Whiteley.* In a *Chicago Tribune,* article, Paul Galloway noted that Hoff "has used his skills to make a persuasive case that Opal Whiteley's diary is the real thing, written by an uncommonly bright little girl who was enraptured by the world around her and was able to communicate that rapture in a rare, beautiful and unusual way." Hoff spent three years investigating Whiteley's story. While he concluded that she was the daughter of the Oregon couple and that her alternate view of her past was a fantasy, he also believed that the diary was indeed her own work. Hoff includes in his book a sixty-six page introduction that contains a biography of Whiteley and a history of his research, as well as a thirty-nine-page conclusion.

Whiteley's life has been memorialized by a number of writers. Jane Boulton, who traveled to London to meet Whiteley, adapted the diary into verse in 1976. Boulton later collaborated with Caldecott medalist Barbara Cooney, who illustrated a version designed especially for children. Another writer, Robert Lindsey Nassif, created a musical based on Whiteley's life and diary. Nassif saw Whiteley in London on nearly a dozen occasions. She repeatedly told Nassif that she was pleased to hear about Hoff's book, but was not happy that he called her Opal Whiteley in the title. During their interviews, she continued to refer to herself as Francoise d'Orleans.

BIOGRAPHICAL AND CRITICAL SOURCES:

BOOKS

Beck, Kathrine, *Opal: A Life of Enchantment, Mystery, and Madness,* Viking (New York, NY), 2003.

Hoff, Benjamin, *The Singing Creek where the Willows Grow: The Rediscovered Diary of Opal Whiteley* (includes *The Story of Opal: The Journal of an Understanding Heart*), Ticknor & Fields (New York, NY), 1986, revised edition published as *The Singing Creek Where the Willows Grow: The Mystical Nature Diary of Opal Whiteley,* Penguin Books (New York, NY), 1995.

Lawrence, Elizabeth, *Opal Whiteley: The Unsolved Mystery* (contains *The Story of Opal: The Journal of an Understanding Heart,* Putnam (London, England), 1962.

Whiteley, Opal, *The Story of Opal: The Journal of an Understanding Heart,* Atlantic Monthly Press (Boston, MA), 1920.

PERIODICALS

Chicago Tribune, December 26, 1986, Paul Galloway, "Mystery of a Little Girl's Diary," p. 1.

Horn Book, May-June, 1994, Mary M. Burns, review of *Only Opal: The Diary of a Young Girl,* p. 338.

New York Times Book Review, November 21, 1976, Betty Jean Lifton, review of *Opal.*

Publishers Weekly, July 12, 1976, review of *Opal;* September 13, 1976, Robert Dahlin, review of *Opal,* p. 85; July 25, 1986, review of *The Singing Creek where the Willows Grow,* p. 177; January 17, 1994, M. P. Dunleavey, review of *Only Opal,* p. 35.

Washington Post Book World, June 16, 1985, Bruce Brown, review of *The Story of Opal,* p. 10.

ONLINE

Opal Whiteley Memorial Page, http://www.efn.org/ (August 12, 2004).*

*   *   *

WILEY, Roland John

PERSONAL: Born in CA. *Education:* Stanford University, B.A. (music; with honors in choral conducting); Harvard University, Ph.D., 1974.

ADDRESSES: Office—c/o Department of Music, University of Michigan, Ann Arbor, MI 48109. *E-mail*—rjwiley@umich.edu.

CAREER: Educator, author, and consultant. University of Michigan, Ann Arbor, professor of music, 1974—; Royal Opera House, Covent Garden, London, England, production consultant, 1983—.

AWARDS, HONORS: De la Torre Bueno Prize, Dance Perspectives Foundation, 1998, for *The Life and Ballets of Lev Ivanov: Choreographer of "The Nutcracker" and "Swan Lake";* National Endowment for the Humanities fellowship; Guggenheim fellowship; Mellon fellowship.

WRITINGS:

Tchaikovsky's Swan Lake: The First Production in Moscow and St. Petersburg, Wiley (Cambridge, MA), 1974.

(Compiler and author of commentary) *A Production Plan for Nutcracker,* Wiley (Cambridge, MA), 1984.

Tchaikovsky's Ballets: Swan Lake, Sleeping Beauty, Nutcracker, Oxford University Press (New York, NY), 1985.

(Editor, with Malcolm Hamrick Brown) *Slavonic and Western Music: Essays for Gerald Abraham,* UMI Research Press (Ann Arbor, MI), 1985.

A Century of Russian Ballet: Documents and Accounts, 1810-1910, Oxford University Press (New York, NY), 1990.

The Life and Ballets of Lev Ivanov: Choreographer of The Nutcracker and Swan Lake, Oxford University Press (New York, NY), 1997.

(Author of introduction) Charles-Louis Didelot, *Three King's Theatre Ballets, 1796-1801: Originally Published in London 1796-1801,* Stainer & Bell (London, England), 1994.

Author of numerous academic articles.

SIDELIGHTS: A professor of music at the University of Michigan at Ann Arbor, Roland John Wiley specializes in the music of the nineteenth century, with a particular focus on Russian music and ballet. He also serves as production consultant to the Royal Opera House, in Covent Garden, London, on revivals of *The Nutcracker* and *Swan Lake.*

The Life and Ballets of Lev Ivanov: Choreographer of The Nutcracker and Swan Lake, sheds light on the life of a little-recognized Russian choreographer. Ivanov

served as assistant to fellow choreographer Marius Petipa, yet was never mentioned in either Petipa's letters or Tchaikovsky's. Using Ivanov's memoirs and various documentary materials, Wiley reconstructs the choreographer's life and reviews his works, devoting a chapter each to *The Nutcracker* and *Swan Lake.* James Munson, in *Contemporary Review,* commented that, "at last, after all these years, we have the first biography and proper evaluation of the man who created so much that delights the civilised eye." Those "delights" consist of an hour and a half of surviving choreography, consisting of the second scene of *Swan Lake* and the famous meeting between Odette, the swan queen, and Prince Siegfried. *Wall Street Journal* reviewer Joan Acocella remarked that "everyone who knows anything about ballet knows this scene, and it was made by Ivanov." Regarding Wiley, she went on to say that "he has done a Herculean job of research, pored over every newspaper, read every ballet memoir, examined every box of documents. But Mr. Wiley is not just a chronicler. He knows the context. . . . He is a sophisticated guide."

BIOGRAPHICAL AND CRITICAL SOURCES:

PERIODICALS

Contemporary Review, December, 1997, James Munson, review of *The Life and Ballets of Lev Ivanov: Choreographer of The Nutcracker and Swan Lake,* p. 326.

New Criterion, September 18, 1999, Laura Jacobs, "Tchaikovsky at the Millennium."

New York Review of Books, February 13, 1986, Robert Craft, review of *The Life and Ballets of Lev Ivanov.*

New York Times, October 14, 1998, "A Dance Book Award," p. E8.

Wall Street Journal, November 18, 1997, Joan Acocella, "In the Shadow of Greatness," p. 1.*

*   *   *

WILLIAMS, Barnaby (?)-2001(?)

PERSONAL: Died c. 2001.

CAREER: Novelist and author of short fiction.

WRITINGS:

The Comeback, P. Davies (London, England), 1974.

The Racers (short stories), New English Library (London, England), 1981.

Stealth Bomber, Sphere (London, England), 1990.

Knight of the Divine Wind, Macdonald (London, England), 1991.

Revolution: A Novel of Russia, Simon & Schuster (London, England), 1994.

Anno Domini: The Crucifixion of the True Faith, Simon & Schuster (New York, NY), 1995.

Killing Place, Mainstream (Edinburgh, Scotland), 1995.

Crusaders, Simon & Schuster (London, England), 1996.

Death before Dishonour, Simon & Schuster (London, England), 1997.

Soldiers of God, Severn House (Sutton, Surrey, England), 2000.

SIDELIGHTS: Since the 1970s, author Barnaby Williams has written thrillers and short stories based on historical or quasi-historical events. Some of his works foreshadow events that have occurred since the novels were published. *The Comeback,* his first novel, was published in 1974, and tells the story of a former Royal Air Force pilot who is caught up in the revolutionary politics of a tumultuous African state. In order to combat the revolutionary underground, the protagonist needs the assistance of strike aircraft of the sort he used to fly. In *Stealth Bomber,* Williams tracks the efforts of a renegade Islamic-oriented group that tries to bring two superpowers closer and closer to a nuclear holocaust.

Death before Dishonour is a multi-generational novel that tells the story of the fictional de Clare family and the machinations of members of different branches of this widespread and ancient lineage. The de Clares begin as important members of the British aristocracy during the Norman Conquest and remain so into the twentieth century. The First World War, however, has brought the family down, killing off most of the male members of its branches. Protagonist Fish de Clare ends up the only male survivor of his family after the accidental death of his uncle and the suicide of his elder brother. Fish survives World War I only to die in the evacuation of Dunkirk that begins World War II. Thus, the family title goes to his son, Gawaine; Fish's

widow, Vi, is left with the unenviable job of protecting their son from the meddling of cousin Godfrey—who by spying for the Soviets, "plays Lucifer to Fish's Gabriel in the black-and-white moral universe Williams paints," according to a *Publishers Weekly* reviewer. Barbara Love, writing for *Library Journal,* declared *Death before Dishonour* "an old-fashioned, cracking good yarn."

BIOGRAPHICAL AND CRITICAL SOURCES:

PERIODICALS

Books, June, 1990, review of *Stealth Bomber,* p. 22.

Books & Bookmen, April, 1974, Trevor Allen, review of *The Comeback,* p. 110.

Library Journal, October 1, 1999, Barbara Love, review of *Death before Dishonour,* p. 136.

Publishers Weekly, September 27, 1999, review of *Death before Dishonour,* p. 70.*

*   *   *

WINDAWI, Thura al- 1983(?)-

PERSONAL: Female. Born c. 1983. *Education:* Attended University of Baghdad and University of Pennsylvania.

ADDRESSES: Agent—c/o Author Mail, Viking/Penguin Group, 375 Hudson St., New York, NY 10014.

WRITINGS:

Thura's Diary: My Life in Wartime Iraq (young adult), translation by Robin Bray, Viking (New York, NY), 2004.

SIDELIGHTS: Thura al-Windawi is the daughter of a British-educated father and a middle-class Iraqi woman who has written *Thura's Diary: My Life in Wartime Iraq,* a memoir of the time leading up to and including the U.S. invasion that began in March 2003. A British journalist who saw al-Windawi's diary helped get it translated and published. The book contains the thoughts and observations of a young woman whose life changed after her country came under attack. Al-Windawi writes of family moments, including baking bread with her mother and listening to her sister's protestations over the wearing of a head scarf. Most of the details involve the U.S war on Iraqi dictator Saddam Hussein's government and that conflict's aftermath, including how a childhood friend died trying to help others in his Baghdad neighborhood.

Al-Windawi expresses mixed feelings toward both Hussein and the country's U.S. liberators. As Elizabeth Bush pointed out in the *Bulletin of the Center for Children's Books,* "Readers are not required to sort out a political position on the Iraqi conflict." Alison Follos wrote in *School Library Journal,* that al-Windawi's "focus is on explicitly and calmly exposing the ravages of war on the vulnerable members of society."

Al-Windawi studied pharmacology in Baghdad, and when her story reached the admissions department of the University of Pennsylvania, she was offered a four-year scholarship to continue her studies there. She told Rebecca Bellville of *Citypaper.net* that "the message that I want from my diary is that I want peace. After I came here, people are different and everyone has a good heart inside their hearts, and I want to take this message back to Iraq."

BIOGRAPHICAL AND CRITICAL SOURCES:

BOOKS

Al-Windawi, Thura, *Thura's Diary: My Life in Wartime Iraq* (young adult), translation by Robin Bray, Viking (New York, NY), 2004.

PERIODICALS

Booklist, May 15, 2004, John Green, review of *Thura's Diary,* p. 1613.
Bulletin of the Center for Children's Books, July-August, 2004, Elizabeth Bush, review of *Thura's Diary,* p. 452.
Horn Book, July-August, 2004, Christine M. Heppermann, review of *Thura's Diary,* p. 464.
School Library Journal, July, 2004, Alison Follos, review of *Thura's Diary,* p. 114.

ONLINE

Citypaper.net, http://citypaper.net/ (April 8, 2004), Rebecca Bellville, interview with al-Windawi.*

*   *   *

WINGROVE, Elizabeth Rose 1960-

PERSONAL: Born 1960. *Education:* Brandeis University, Ph.D.

ADDRESSES: Office—University of Michigan, Office of Political Science, 7648 Haven Hall, Ann Arbor, MI 48109; fax: 734-764-3522. *E-mail*—ewingrove@ umich.edu.

CAREER: Author and educator. University of Michigan, Ann Arbor, associate professor of political science and women's studies.

MEMBER: American Political Science Association.

AWARDS, HONORS: Foundations of Political Thought Best Paper award, American Political Science Association, 1997, for "Republican Romance."

WRITINGS:

Rousseau's Republican Romance, Princeton University Press (Princeton, NJ), 2000.

Contributor to volumes including *Citizenship after Liberalism,* edited by Karen Slawner and Mark Denham, Peter Lang Publishing Group (New York, NY), 1998. Contributor to periodicals including *Signs: Journal of Women in Culture and Society, Women and Politics,* and *Political Theory.*

SIDELIGHTS: Political scholar Elizabeth Rose Wingrove expands on the connection between sex and politics in *Rousseau's Republican Romance,* an exploration of the sexual politics of republicanism in French enlightenment philosopher Jean-Jacques Rousseau's works. The book also seeks to find a means of analytically linking together Rousseau's literary works on sex and sexuality with his political writings and treatises. "Wingrove's confident, complex, and provocative book takes up the central Rousseaun questions of power and will," commented Eve Grace in *American Political Science Review*.

In *Rousseau's Republican Romance*, "Wingrove convincingly argues that for Rousseau, consent always involves willing the circumstances of one's own domination, and is thus always a form of submission," explained Rebecca Kukla in *Hypatia*. This concept of "consensual nonconsensuality" allows individuals to constrain their behavior according to society's overall wishes and "is the precondition for our participation in social norms" and other forms of overarching social control, Kukla noted. "The problem of how to harmonize obedience and liberty is generally understood to be resolved by him through the doctrine of submission to the general will, by which each citizen sovereignly commands the law that in turn subjects him or her," Grace observed. Wingrove argues that "this interplay of power and will . . . is the stuff of romance, and romance the stuff of democratic self rule," in which the ideals of man and citizen "are simultaneously formed through induction into a heterosexual and political order," Grace noted. Wingrove, then, "reveals a Rousseau who introduces eros into the essential heart of republican citizenry, and relations of authority and coercion into the essential heart of romantic love," Kukla commented.

"Wingrove's book is an important and impressive contribution to Rousseau scholarship," Kukla noted, "and those of us who write directly on Rousseau will find her book helpful, interesting, and worth citing often." Although the book generates new understanding of Rousseau's works, Kukla found that it is was weakened because Wingrove does not apply this new understanding to a larger political or philosophical world and generalize her conclusions outside the sphere of Rousseau's writings. However, the critic wrote that *Rousseau's Republican Romance* constitutes "an important contribution to the theoretical history of gender," and concluded that "as a work of hermeneutic scholarship . . . is a success." Reviewing the book on *PoliticalStudies.org*, Ethan Putterman called Wingrove's w1ork "an original and engaging analytical bridge between Rousseau's literary and political writings."

BIOGRAPHICAL AND CRITICAL SOURCES:

PERIODICALS

American Political Science Review, December, 2000, Eve Grace, "Rousseau, Nature, and the Problem of the Good Life," review of *Rousseau's Republican Romance,* p. 922.
Hypatia, spring, 2002, Rebecca Kukla, review of *Rousseau's Republican Romance,* p. 174.

ONLINE

American Political Science Association Web site, http://www.apsanet.org/ (July 26, 2004), "Foundations of Political Thought Award Winners."
PoliticalStudies.org, http://www.politicalstudies.org/ (August 20, 2004), Ethan Putterman, review of *Rousseau's Republican Romance.*
Princeton University Press Web site, http://www.pupress.princeton.edu/ (July 26, 2005), "Rousseau's Republican Romance."
University of Michigan Web site, http://www.umich.edu/ (July 26, 2005), "Elizabeth Wingrove."*

*   *   *

WOHL, Ellen E.

PERSONAL: Born 1962. *Education:* Arizona State University, B.S. (geology), 1984; University of Arizona, Ph.D. (geosciences), 1988.

ADDRESSES: Office—College of Natural Resources, Colorado State University, Fort Collins, CO 80523-1401. *E-mail*—ellenw@cnr.colostate.edu.

CAREER: Colorado State University, Fort Collins, assistant professor, 1989-96, associate professor, 1996-2000, professor of geology, 2000—.

MEMBER: Geological Society of America (fellow; second vice chair, Quaternary Geology and Geomorphology Division), American Geophysical Union, Geological Society of America.

AWARDS, HONORS: Fulbright fellowship to Israel, 1991; Gladys W. Cole Memorial Award, Geological Society of America, 1995; Japan Society for the Promotion of Science fellowship, 1996; G. K. Gilbert Award for Excellence in Geomorphological Research, Association of American Geographers' Geomorphology Specialty Group, 2000; Water Center Award for Outstanding contributions to Interdisciplinary Water Education, Colorado State University, 2001.

WRITINGS:

Rain Forest into Desert: Adventures in Australia's Tropical North, University Press of Colorado (Niwot, CO), 1994.
(Editor, with Keith J. Tinkler) *Rivers over Rock: Fluvial Processes in Bedrock Channels,* American Geophysical Union (Washington, DC), 1998.
(Editor) *Inland Flood Hazards: Human, Riparian, and Aquatic Communities,* Cambridge University Press (Cambridge, England), 2000.
Mountain Rivers, American Geophysical Union (Washington, DC), 2000.
Virtual Rivers: Lessons from the Mountain Rivers of the Colorado Front Range, Yale University Press (New Haven, CT), 2001.
Disconnected Rivers: Linking Rivers to Landscapes, Yale University Press (New Haven, CT), 2004.

Contributor to journals, including *Geomorphology, Journal of Geology, Ecological Applications, Water Resources Bulletin,* and *Geological Society of America Bulletin.* Associate editor, *Geomorphology, Geological Society of America Bulletin,* and *Water Research.*

SIDELIGHTS: Ellen E. Wohl's books and articles on geography, geology, and water issues are useful to government officials, civil engineers, and students in fields such as hydrology, hydraulics, geography, and geology. She published a book on Australia's rain forest and edited another on fluvial processes in bedrock before editing her better-known *Inland Flood Hazards: Human, Riparian, and Aquatic Communities.* This book studies three major river basins: the Colorado in the United States and Mexico, the Tone in Japan, and the Ganges and Brahmaputra in Bangladesh. A general reference on flood hazards, the book covers such subjects as physical control of flooding, biological flood processes, and the effects of human actions on flooding. Hadrian F. Cook wrote in the *Geographical Journal* that *Inland Flood Hazards* is "well presented, well written and thoroughly referenced," and *Quarterly Review of Biology* contributor Brett Roper commented that "the breadth of this book makes it an ideal inclusion in many different libraries."

Wohl produced a monograph on mountain rivers before publishing her next book, *Virtual Rivers: Lessons from the Mountain Rivers of the Colorado Front Range,* which is accessibly written for both lay readers and professionals. In it she outlines in graphic detail, using illustrations and nontechnical language, how human actions have profoundly altered the form and function of river basins. Rivers become "virtual" when humans divert their courses, dam them, or otherwise change their natural flow. She concentrates on rivers in a particular area of Colorado, beginning with the effects of the Gold Rush in 1859 and ending in the 1990s.

William Wyckoff pointed out in the *Geographical Review* that Wohl is asking readers to "give western rivers the respect they deserve" by questioning how ecosystems have been damaged in the past by unwise human manipulation. In the *Quarterly Review of Biology,* Steven P. Canton noted that the author tends to sermonize and that she "may have tried to put too much information in a relatively short volume." Still, he adde, her book is "fascinating," and its message "should lead to many lively discussions."

Wohl has continued to pursue her interest in human interactions with river systems in *Disconnected Rivers: Linking Rivers to Landscapes.* In this volume, she discusses topics such as pollution by humans, commercial impacts on rivers, bureaucratic bungling, and attempts at rehabilitation of river systems.

BIOGRAPHICAL AND CRITICAL SOURCES:

PERIODICALS

Environment, June, 2002, Robert Harriss, review of *Virtual Rivers: Lessons from the Mountain Rivers of the Colorado Front Range,* p. 39.
Geographical Journal, March, 2003, Hadrian F. Cook, review of *Inland Flood Hazards: Human, Riparian, and Aquatic Communities,* p. 95.

Geographical Review, October, 2002, William Wyckoff, review of *Virtual Rivers,* p. 14.

Quarterly Review of Biology, September, 2001, Brett Roper, review of *Inland Flood Hazards,* p. 371; September, 2002, Steven P. Canton, review of *Virtual Rivers,* p. 353.

ONLINE

Colorado State University Web site, http://www.cnr.colostate.edu/ (July 26, 2004), "Ellen Wohl."

*   *   *

WOOD, Peter (W.) 1953-

PERSONAL: Born 1953. *Education:* Graduate of Haverford College and Rutgers University; University of Rochester, Ph.D. (anthropology), 1987.

ADDRESSES: Office—Boston University, 143 Bay State Rd., Boston, MA 02215. *E-mail*—pwood@bu.edu.

CAREER: Educator and author. Boston University, Boston, MA, associate professor of anthropology.

WRITINGS:

Diversity: The Invention of a Concept, Encounter Books (San Francisco, CA), 2003.

A Bee in the Mouth: Anger in America Now, Encounter Books (San Francisco, CA), 2004.

Contributor to *Partisan Review, Society, National Review Online, American Conservative, Claremont Review of Books,* and *American Spectator.*

SIDELIGHTS: Anthropologist Peter Wood is the author of *Diversity: The Invention of a Concept.* In this "erudite, elegant" book, to quote Matt Feeney in the *Weekly Standard,* Wood offers a wide-ranging examination of the diversity movement. He traces the origins of this modern movement to two key events: President Lyndon B. Johnson's 1965 executive order allowing the use of affirmative action in federal

contracts, and the 1978 Supreme Court decision *Regents of the University of California v. Bakke,* in which the Court opened the door for race to be used as a factor in college admissions. Spurred by events such as these, a race-based concept of diversity gained prominence in virtually all walks of American life, from college campuses to the corporate world. Wood argues that the diversity movement, rather than transforming American society for the better, has "achieved a substantial record of increased social discord and cultural decline," in the words of Carol Iannone in *National Review.*

Reviewers praised *Diversity* for its exhaustive treatment of a concept that has become ingrained—and divisive—in contemporary American life. Remarking on the author's "brilliant biography of the concept of diversity," Feeney noted that "chapters on the Bakke fiasco, diversity myths on college campuses, and the business world's craven and faddish diversity fixation are so dolefully illuminating it actually hurts." Writing in the *Los Angeles Times,* Jim Sleeper called the book "a wonderful surprise." While noting that the work "has its slippery patches," Sleeper maintained that "any liberal who claims to value intellectual as well as racial diversity and wants to engage the other side's best arguments without shouting should try Wood." *Washington Post* contributor Edward Countryman criticized Wood's "vague and undocumented assigning of blame" but added that *Diversity* "is worth reading" because its anthropologist author's "sense of how things fit together overcomes his polemic." "Diversity has finally found its poet and philosopher, in the form of a clever antagonist named Peter Wood," commented Stanley Kurtz in *National Review Online.* Wood's "extraordinary" book, continued Kurtz, "spills the beans about diversity—about its flimsiness and mendacity . . . but also about its complex cultural accomplishments and appeal, however unfortunate or insidious these may be."

BIOGRAPHICAL AND CRITICAL SOURCES:

BOOKS

Wood, Peter, *Diversity: The Invention of a Concept,* Encounter Books (San Francisco, CA), 2003.

PERIODICALS

Booklist, December 1, 2002, Ray Olson, review of *Diversity: The Invention of a Concept,* p. 634.

Commentary, June, 2003, Chester E. Finn, Jr., review of *Diversity,* p. 71.

Library Journal, February 1, 2003, Mark Bay, review of *Diversity,* p. 107.

Los Angeles Times, August 10, 2003, Jim Sleeper, "Courting Diversity: Two Warnings Ignored," p. R5.

National Review, June 2, 2003, Carol Iannone, review of *Diversity.*

Wall Street Journal, February 26, 2003, Adam Wolfson, "What Makes a Difference," p. D10.

Washington Post, April 6, 2003, Edward Countryman, "Mosaic Law," p. T8.

Weekly Standard, January 27, 2003, Matt Feeney, review of *Diversity,* p. 43.

ONLINE

Boston University Web site, http://www.bu.edu/ (July 26, 2004), "Peter W. Wood."

National Review Online, (March 19, 2003), Stanley Kurtz, "Diversity, like You've Never Seen It."

*   *   *

WORRALL, Simon

PERSONAL: Born in England. *Education:* Bristol University.

ADDRESSES: Home—East Hampton, NY. *Agent*—c/o Author Mail, Penguin Group USA, 375 Hudson St., New York, NY 10014.

CAREER: Journalist. Began career in England working with Royal Shakespeare Company and Royal Court theatre as a dramaturge.

WRITINGS:

The Poet and the Murderer: A True Story of Literary Crime and the Art of Forgery, Dutton (New York, NY), 2002.

Contributor to periodicals, including *Sunday Review, New Yorker, Paris Review, Times Weekend Review, London Review, Die Ziet, Esquire, Harper's, National Geographic, Independent, New Republic,* and *New Yorker.*

SIDELIGHTS: In *The Poet and the Murderer: A True Story of Literary Crime and the Art of Forgery* journalist Simon Worrall tells the true story of forger-turned-murderer Mark Hofmann. As told by Worrall, Hofmann was raised in a devout Mormon family and went to England at the age of nineteen as a missionary for the church. However, it is soon revealed that Hofmann harbors deep hostilities toward the Church of Jesus Christ of Latter-day Saints. In an effort to mock and embarrass the Morman church, Hofmann, who deals in rare books, begins to forge documents concerning the church's founding and beliefs. Embarrassed by these documents, which they believe are real, church leaders ultimately buy them all from Hofmann. Buoyed by his success with Mormon leaders, Hofmann develops an increasing hubris that results in his continued forgery of documents, not only those supposedly originating from early Mormon leaders but also documents by such notable Americans as George Washington, Paul Revere, and Abraham Lincoln. He eventually produces a newly discovered poem by Emily Dickinson that sold for approximately 21,000 dollars at auction. Supremely confident of his abilities to forge documents and make money, Hofmann spent lavishly and went deeply into debt. When he was pursued by creditors, he hatched a plan that involved bombings and murder and ultimately killed two people in the historic document field. He was captured when a bomb explodes in his own car and police discovered his criminal activities while investigating the bombing. The explosion could have been an accident, a suicide attempt, or an attempt by Hofmann to set himself up as a potential victim and divert growing suspicion away from his forgery activities. In the end, his illegal activities are completely exposed, and he is sentenced to prison.

Lloyd Rose, reviewing *The Poet and the Murderer* in the *Washington Post,* commented, "The book is weighed down periodically by Worrall's efforts to invest his entertaining detective story with deeper meaning," and is "handicapped by an overemphatic prose style." Nevertheless, the reviewer added, "if Worrall is a lead-footed stylist, he's a keen, hardworking investigator, and the story he tells is fascinating." Writing in the *Emily Dickinson Journal,* Ellen Louise Hart commented that *The Poet and the Murderer* "is riddled with error" concerning Dickinson and her works, and argued that Worrall is misguided in his efforts to compare Dickinson to Hofmann by "claiming they both lived secret double lives." The reviewer added: "In trying to appeal to a range of audiences Worrall's narrative becomes an awkward mesh of investigative journalism and selective details from other studies and biographies, presented through fictionalizing and simplification." "Yet," Hart also noted, "this slippery book remains worthy of our attention for two reasons: it contributes new information to the Hofmann case, and the event of the forgery has a place in Dickinson Studies."

Other reviewers consistently praised the book. A *Publishers Weekly* contributor called *The Poet and the Murderer* a "compelling debut," while Jamie Spencer, writing in the *St. Louis Post-Dispatch,* commented: "Worrall is not just a good story-spinner and not just a crackerjack researcher. Best of all, he makes incisive judgments." In a review for the *Library Journal,* Clay Stalls wrote that "Worrall's book stands as an entertaining addition to the corpus of work on Mark Hofmann." *Booklist* contributor Connie Fletcher viewed *The Poet and the Murderer* as "a compelling case study of forgery" and called it "[a] true-crime standout."

BIOGRAPHICAL AND CRITICAL SOURCES:

PERIODICALS

Artforum, fall, 2002, Paul Maliszewski, review of *The Poet and the Murderer: A True Story of Literary Crime and the Art of Forgery,* p. 46.

Book, May-June, 2002, Eric Wargo, review of *The Poet and the Murderer,* p. 78.

Booklist, April 1, 2002, Connie Fletcher, review of *The Poet and the Murderer,* p. 1287.

Emily Dickinson Journal, Volume 11, issue 2, 2002, Ellen Louise Hart, review of *The Poet and the Murderer,* p. 114.

Guardian (Manchester, England), August 10, 2002, Blake Morrison, review of *The Poet and the Murderer,* p. 10.

Harper's, May, 2002, Guy Davenport, review of *The Poet and the Murderer,* p. 71.

Kirkus Reviews, February 15, 2002, review of *The Poet and the Murderer,* p. 245.

Library Quarterly, April, 2003, Clay Stalls, review of *The Poet and the Murderer,* p. 235.

Publishers Weekly, February 25, 2002, review of *The Poet and the Murderer,* p. 49.

St. Louis Post-Dispatch, May 19, 2002, Jamie Spencer, review of *The Poet and the Murderer,* p. F10.

Spectator, Nicholas Harman, review of *The Poet and the Murderer,* p. 47.

Village Voice, May 9, 2000, Cynthia Cotts, "The Silence of the Lamb," p. 34.

Washington Post, June 9, 2002, Lloyd Rose, review of *The Poet and the Murderer,* p. T06.

ONLINE

Penguin Group USA Web site, http://www.penguin putnam.com/ (March 30, 2005), "Simon Worrall."*

* * *

WRIGHT, Robin M. 1950-

PERSONAL: Born 1950. *Education:* Stanford University, Ph.D., 1981.

ADDRESSES: Agent—c/o Author Mail, Duke University Press, P.O. Box 90660, Durham, NC 27708-0660.

CAREER: Universidade Estadual de Campinas, Brazil, director of Center for Research in Indigenous Ethnology and associate professor of anthropology.

WRITINGS:

(Editor, with Ismaelillo) *Native Peoples in Struggle,* E.R.I.N. Publications (Bombay, NY), 1982.

(Translator) *Hydroelectric Dams on Brazil's Xingu River and Indigenous Peoples,* edited by Leinad Auer de O. Santos and Lucia M. M. de Andrade, Cultural Survival (Cambridge, MA), 1990.

Cosmos, Self, and History in Baniwa Religion: For Those Unborn, University of Texas Press (Austin, TX), 1998.

(Translator and editor, with others) *Waferinaipe ianheke = A sabedoria dos nossos antepassados: histórias dos hohodene e dos walipere-dakenai do Rio Aiari,* narrated by José Marcellino Cornelio, ACIRA/FOIRN (Rio Aiari, Amazonas, Brazil), 1999.

(Editor) *Transformando os deuses: os múltiplos sentidos da conservão entre os povos indígenas no Brasil* (title means "Transforming the Gods: Multiple Senses of Conversion among Indigenous Peoples in Brazil"), FAPESP (São Paulo, Brazil), 1999.

(Editor, with Neil L. Whitehead) *In Darkness and Secrecy: The Anthropology of Assault Sorcery and Witchcraft in Amazonia,* Duke University Press (Durham, NC), 2004.

Contributor to scholarly collections of essays and journals, including *Annual Review of Anthropology.*

SIDELIGHTS: An anthropology professor at Brazil's Universidade Estadual de Campinas, Robin M. Wright has edited and written several works on that country's indigenous peoples. The Baniwa Indians of the northwest Amazon are the subject of his 1998 title *Cosmos, Self, and History in Baniwa Religion: For Those Unborn.* For more than a century, these native people have prophesied the end of the current world civilization and the subsequent re-creation of the original paradise. Such prophecies are passed on by tribal shamans and have their roots deep in the tribe's myths of origin and creation. In his book, Wright looks at the Baniwa religion, and notes how such beliefs have also led to widespread conversion to evangelical Christianity. Wright divides his work into four parts that trace aspects of Baniwa religion from its shaman-istic roots to the arrival of the first Christian missionaries.

Reviewing *Cosmos, Self, and History in Baniwa Religion,* Thomas Griffiths noted in *Cultural Survival Quarterly* that "Wright brings together more than two decades of his ethnographic and archival research on the relationships between Baniwa religion, history, and social action." Griffiths further praised Wright's book for the "fabulous ethnographic detail it provides on Baniwa cosmology, ritual and ethnohistory." *Journal of Latin American Studies* contributor Peter Riviere found *Cosmos, Self, and History in Baniwa Religion* a "good and serious book."

BIOGRAPHICAL AND CRITICAL SOURCES:

PERIODICALS

Cultural Survival Quarterly, December 31, 1999, Thomas Griffiths, review of *Cosmos, Self, and History in Baniwa Religion: For Those Unborn,* p. 75.
Journal of Latin American Studies, February, 2000, Peter Riviere, review of *Cosmos, Self, and History in Baniwa Religion,* p. 268.

ONLINE

Duke University Press Web site, http://www.dukeu press.edu/ (February 2, 2005), "Robin Wright."
UNICAMP Departmento de Antopologia Web site, http://www.unicamp.br/ (February 12, 2005), "Robin M. Wright."*

* * *

WRIGHT, Stephen 1946-

PERSONAL: Born 1946. *Education:* Attended Ohio State University and University of Iowa.

ADDRESSES: Office—New School University, Cre-ative Writing Program, 66 West 12th St., Room 507, New York, NY 10011.

CAREER: Novelist. New School University, New York, NY, faculty member. Taught at Princeton University, Brown University, and Goucher College. *Military service:* U.S. Army, 1969-70, intelligence of-ficer in Vietnam.

AWARDS, HONORS: Maxwell Perkins Prize, 1983, for *Meditations in Green;* Guggenheim fellowship, 1989; Whiting Writers Award, 1990; Lannan Literary Award, 1994, for *Going Native.*

WRITINGS:

NOVELS

Meditations in Green, Charles Scribner's Sons (New York, NY), 1983.
M31: A Family Romance, Harmony Books (New York, NY), 1988.
Going Native, Farrar, Straus & Giroux (New York, NY), 1994.

Contributor to periodicals, including *Esquire, Ontario Review,* and *Antioch Review.* Also contributor to *Avant-Pop: Fiction for a Daydream Nation,* edited by Larry McCaffery, Black Ice Books (Boulder, CO), 1993.

SIDELIGHTS: Stephen Wright stepped onto the literary scene in 1983 with the publication of his debut novel, *Meditations in Green,* a work inspired by his harrowing experiences as a soldier during the Vietnam War. Frequently compared to *Catch-22,* Joseph Heller's classic antiwar satire, *Meditations in Green* was greeted by critics as the work of a promising new author. Wright grew up in Cleveland, Ohio, and attended Ohio State University during the 1960s. However, when his grades slipped, he became eligible for the draft and was sent to Vietnam as an intelligence officer. After returning from service, Wright resumed his studies at Ohio State, majoring in English, but eventually left to attend the Iowa Writer's Workshop, where he studied under John Cheever, John Irving, and Vance Bourjaily. Wright's first novel was the result of that two-year program.

Meditations in Green revolves around the experiences of Specialist Four James Griffin, a U.S. intelligence advisor in Vietnam who escapes the horror, tedium, and madness of the war through drug use. The novel's title alludes to the green of the jungle's dense foliage, including its many hallucinogenic plants, and the narrative structure alternates between Griffin's first-person reflections as a heroin-addicted veteran and vivid third-person accounts of combat and mayhem in Southeast Asia.

Though several reviewers regarded the book's shifting narrative presentation as a distraction, most praised *Meditations in Green* as one of the best fictional accounts of the Vietnam War to date. *New York Times Book Review* contributor Walter Kendrick described the work as a "brilliant, scarifying first novel," while *Washington Post Book World* critic William Boyd noted, "its portrayal of the U.S. military machine and mind at their most brutally callous and complacent is a terrifying indictment." Though praising Wright's "eyewitness testimony," Boyd wondered about the literary merit of war novels in general, suggesting that their documentary imperative inevitably overwhelms their artistic pretensions. As Kendrick observed, "[Wright's] novel is lurid, extravagant, rhapsodic and horrific by turns—sometimes all at once. Its structure is needlessly complicated, and its superheated prose often gets wearisome. Yet for all its self-conscious excesses, it has overwhelming impact—the impact of an experience so devastating that words can hardly contain it."

M31: A Family Romance is set in the American Midwest and involves an eccentric family at the center

of a UFO cult. Living in an abandoned church whose centerpiece is a mock spacecraft, husband and wife Dash and Dot preside over a clan of damaged children—including an autistic daughter whom they believe is a conduit for alien transmissions—while proselytizing salvation in galaxy M31. Among their new-age followers is Gwen, an alien abductee who narrates much of the novel.

Praising *M31* in the *New York Times Book Review,* Francine Prose attributed the novel's success to Wright's "beautifully written, sharply detailed" prose and "metaphoric imagination," which she found especially effective in satirizing contemporary American mass culture. *People* reviewer Jess Cagle, on the other hand, viewed Wright's prose as occasionally "self-indulgent," but noted that "more often it is haunting." *New York Times* critic Michiko Kakutani found much to appreciate in Wright's "electrically wired prose" and the novelist's depiction of Middle America's dark underside. "Wright has an instinct for reinventing some of the essential American myths," wrote Kakutani, "and his ease in combining the mundane and the extravagant, the domestic and the bizarre, lend this novel dense luminosity." Describing the book as a "funny, disturbing novel," Prose remarked, "*M31* is not just a galley of grotesques but a visionary novel—a vision of American life turned incestuous and lethal."

Going Native, Wright's third novel, is a loosely linked series of stories that trace the cross-country trajectory of Wylie Jones, a married suburban father who unexpectedly abandons his banal existence by driving away in a stolen car. Wylie's journey is described obliquely through the perspectives of those with whom he comes into contact, including a crack-house couple, a solitary truck driver, a science-fiction-writing motel owner, representatives of the porn industry, Las Vegas lesbians, and Hollywood eco-tourists. *New York Times* reviewer Kakutani hailed *Going Native* as "an uncompromising 1990's version of 'On the Road' that gives us an alarming picture of a country pitched on the edge of an emotional and social abyss." While praising Wright's "absolutely brilliant maximalist prose," a *Publishers Weekly* reviewer described *Going Native* as "the darkest of novels," remarking that the book's narrative structure is both "compelling and alienating." *People* reviewer Joseph Olshan noted that *Going Native* reveals "Wright's raw, poetic sensibility," adding that the novel has "the impact of an X-acto knife slitting open the belly of American life."

Over the years Wright's work has drawn comparison to that of Thomas Pynchon, a writer whom Wright has said he admires. Commenting on Wright's "grammatically complex, ironic, sarcastic" style in the *Review of Contemporary Fiction,* Steven Moore compared Wright's fiction to "an issue of the *National Enquirer* as cowritten by [James] Joyce and Pynchon." According to Moore, *Going Native* is a "brilliant" novel that "should promote Wright to the ranks of America's finest novelists."

BIOGRAPHICAL AND CRITICAL SOURCES:

PERIODICALS

Christian Science Monitor, November 4, 1983, John A. Glusman, review of *Meditations in Green,* p. B10.

Contemporary Literature, summer, 1998, interview with Wright, pp. 156-179.

New Leader, November 28, 1983, Tom Graves, review of *Meditations in Green,* pp. 14-15.

New York Times, June 29, 1988, Michiko Kakutani, review of *M31: A Family Romance,* p. C25; January 7, 1994, Michiko Kakutani, "On the Road across the Alarming '90s Landscape," p. C31.

New York Times Book Review, November 6, 1983, Walter Kendrick, review of *Meditations in Green,* pp. 7, 24; July 17, 1988, Francine Prose, review of *M31,* p. 11.

People, October 24, 1988, Jess Cagle, review of *M31,* p. 40; May 2, 1994, Joseph Olshan, review of *Going Native,* p. 39.

Publishers Weekly, January 24, 1994, Michael Coffey, "Stephen Wright," pp. 35-36; October 25, 1998, review of *Going Native,* p. 43.

Review of Contemporary Fiction, summer, 1994, Steven Moore, review of *Going Native,* p. 202.

Wall Street Journal, October 13, 1983, Tom Carhart, review of *Meditations in Green,* p. 26.

Washington Post Book World, October 30, 1983, William Boyd, review of *Meditations in Green,* pp. 3, 11.

ONLINE

ALTX.com, http://www.altx.com/ (August, 2004), David Kushner, interview with Wright.*

Y-Z

YASHAR, Deborah J. 1963-

PERSONAL: Born 1963. *Education:* University of California, Berkeley, Ph.D.

ADDRESSES: Office—Princeton University, Woodrow Wilson School of Public and International Affairs, 219 Bendheim Hall, Princeton, NJ 08544. *E-mail*—dyashar@princeton.edu.

CAREER: Educator and author. Woodrow Wilson School of Public and International Affairs, Princeton University, Princeton, NJ, associate professor of politics and international affairs.

AWARDS, HONORS: Fellowships from Fulbright, Joint Committee on Latin-American Studies of the American Council of Learned Societies/Social Science Research Council, U.S. Institute of Peace, Helen Kellogg Institute for International Studies at University of Notre Dame, and Princeton's Class of 1934 University Preceptorship.

WRITINGS:

Demanding Democracy: Reform and Reaction in Costa Rica and Guatemala, 1870s-1950s, Stanford University Press (Stanford, CA), 1997.
Contesting Citizenship in Latin America: The Rise of Indigenous Movements and the Postliberal Challenge, Cambridge University Press (New York, NY), 2005.

Also contributor to books; contributor to periodicals, including *World Politics* and *Comparative Politics.*

WORK IN PROGRESS: Civil Wars and Peace Accords: Prospects for Democracy.

SIDELIGHTS: An associate professor of politics and international affairs at Princeton University, Deborah J. Yashar focuses her research on the comparative study of democracies. In 1997's title *Demanding Democracy: Reform and Reaction in Costa Rica and Guatemala, 1870s-1950s* Yashar takes an historical look at democracy and authoritarianism in these two Central American countries. Fabrice Edouard Lehoucq, writing in the *Journal of Latin-American Studies,* noted that Yashar's thesis is that "the political divergence of Costa Rica and Guatemala after the 1940s is a product of the way elites responded to subaltern classes in the 1940s and 1950s." Lehoucq further commented that Yashar explains how Costa Rican "dominant classes divided in the face of popular demands for participation, [while] in Guatemala, by contrast, they remained sealed. The result was the institutionalisation of Costa Rican democracy and the continuation of authoritarianism in Guatemala."

Mitchell A. Seligson, reviewing *Demanding Democracy* in the *American Political Science Review,* commented that Yashar's "richly detailed and nuanced case studies of Guatemala and Costa Rica should give pause to those who have been disparaging the utility of area studies research in political science." Seligson also praised *Demanding Democracy* as "well-written and carefully researched," noting that it "rests its scholarship on a wealth of secondary and archival sources, coupled with transcriptions of the author's illuminating interviews with key political figures who participated in many of the events described." Lowell Gudmundson, writing in the *Canadian Journal of History,* felt that Yashar's book "will be widely read by both social scientists and historians and each group of readers will find much to admire in its pages." Further praise came from *Comparative Political Studies* contributor Gretchen Casper, who observed the "richness of Yashar's research and the significance of her findings." Kirk S. Bowman, writing in the *Hispanic American Historical Review,* approved of the "innovative and provocative theory" found in Yashar's "accessible and important work."

BIOGRAPHICAL AND CRITICAL SOURCES:

PERIODICALS

American Political Science Review, September, 1998, Mitchell A. Seligson, review of *Demanding Democracy: Reform and Reaction in Costa Rica and Guatemala, 1870s-1950s,* p. 740.

Canadian Journal of History, August, 1998, Lowell Gudmundson, review of *Demanding Democracy,* p. 335.

Comparative Political Studies, February, 1998, Gretchen Casper, review of *Demanding Democracy,* p. 125.

Hispanic American Historical Review, August, 1999, Kirk S. Bowman, review of *Demanding Democracy,* p. 582.

Journal of Latin American Studies, October, 1998, Fabrice Edouard Lehoucq, review of *Demanding Democracy,* p. 663.

ONLINE

Princeton University Web site, (July 26, 2004), "Deborah J. Yashar."*

*   *   *

YOUNG, Virginia G(arton) 1919-2005

OBITUARY NOTICE— See index for *CA* sketch: Born January 16, 1919, in Mountain View, MO; died March 16, 2005 (one source says March 15), in Columbia, MO. Consultant and author. Young was an influential library consultant and authority on library trusteeship who wrote and lectured widely on the subject. She graduated from Southwest Missouri State College (now University) in 1939, and completed her library science degree the next year at the University of Missouri. Though she was qualified to work as a librarian, Young spent her next years as a wife and mother. Later in life, however, she became active on library committees and organizations from the local to the national level. In 1955, she became a member of the Missouri State Library Commission, where she remained active for many years. She served in other posts along the way, including on the advisory committee to the U.S. Commissioner of Education's library services branch during the early 1960s. From 1963 until 1965 she was at the U.S. Department of Defense as a member of the Defense Advisory Committee on Women in the Services. Young was best known for her library organization work. She served several terms as president and trustee of the Missouri State Library Commission, was a president of the Daniel Boone Regional Library and the American Library Trustees Association, a cofounder and president of the University of Missouri's Friends of the Libraries, and onetime delegate to the International Federation of Library Associates. Her expertise on the role of the library trustee led her to write the book *The Trustee of a Small Public Library* (1962; revised edition, 1978), and edit the influential text *The Library Trustee: A Practical Guidebook* (1964; fifth edition, 1995). For her valuable service to the library community, Young was made an honorary life member of the American Library Association. In 2002, she was also honored when the boardroom of the Columbia Public Library was named after her.

OBITUARIES AND OTHER SOURCES:

PERIODICALS

Library News Notes (Columbia, MO), March 18, 2005.

ONLINE

American Library Association Web site, http://www.ala.org/ (April 1, 2005).

Columbia Daily Tribune Online, http://www.show menews.com/ (March 18, 2005).

YUNKER, James A.

PERSONAL: Male. *Education:* Fordham University, B.A. (magna cum laude), 1965; University of California, Berkeley, M.A. (economics), 1966; Northwestern University, Ph.D. (economics), 1971.

ADDRESSES: Office—Western Illinois University, College of Business and Technology, Stipes Hall 442, Macomb, IL 61455. *E-mail*—JA-Yunker@wiu.edu.

CAREER: Author, economist, and educator. Western Illinois University, Macomb, assistant professor, 1968-74, associate professor, 1974-78, professor of economics, 1978—.

WRITINGS:

Socialism in the Free Market, Nellen Publishing Company (New York, NY), 1979.
Integrating Acquisitions: Making Corporate Marriages Work, Praeger (New York, NY), 1983.
Socialism Revised and Modernized: The Case for Pragmatic Market Socialism, Praeger (New York, NY), 1992.
World Union on the Horizon: The Case for Supranational Federation, University Press of America (Lanham, MD), 1993.
Capitalism versus Pragmatic Market Socialism: A General Equilibrium Evaluation, Kluwer Academic Publishers (Boston, MA), 1993.
Economic Justice: The Market Socialist Vision, Rowman & Littlefield Publishers (Lanham, MD), 1997.
Toward Genuine Global Governance: Critical Reactions to "Our Global Neighborhood," Praeger (Westport, CT), 1999.
Common Progress: The Case for a World Economic Equalization Program, Praeger (Westport, CT), 2000.
On the Political Economy of Market Socialism: Essays and Analyses, Ashgate (Burlington, VT), 2001.
Capital Management Effort: Theory and Applications, Ashgate (Burlington, VT), 2004.

Contributor to scholarly journals and publications, including *Eastern Economic Journal, Review of Quantitative Finance and Accounting, Public Finance Review, Journal of Economic Education, Journal of* *Post-Keynesian Economics, Journal of Comparative Economics, Journal of Developing Areas, Review of Business and Economic Research, Annals of Public and Cooperative Economy, Library Acquisitions: Practice and Theory, Nebraska Journal of Economics and Business,* and *Comparative Economic Studies.*

SIDELIGHTS: A prolific author and economist, James A. Yunker is the author of numerous books and dozens of magazine and journal articles on economic topics and related subjects. Yunker's work focuses on market socialism, world government, and capital wealth. In a statement posted on the *Western Illinois University* Web site, Yunker commented that "one of the nice things about economics is that its concepts and methods can be sensibly applied to a tremendous range of interesting problems and issues."

Socialism Revised and Modernized: The Case for Pragmatic Market Socialism collects twenty-five papers published by Yunker in a variety of publications since 1973. Yunker offers a radical—at least to capitalists—idea for switching the current American economic system into one based on pragmatic market socialism, a system "designed to ameliorate great inequality in the distribution of unearned property returns while preserving the efficiency of the contemporary capitalist system," according to Gladys Parker Foster in the *Journal of Economic Issues.*

In modern developed nations, particularly the United States, "the question is how to reconcile the rising output potential provided by technological progress with the efficient reductions in input use, especially labor use, that currently create substantial unemployment in market economies," stated Holland Hunter in *Comparative Economic Studies.* Technology continues to fulfill its promise by reducing the need for human labor, but workers whose jobs and incomes are displaced by technology struggle to retain reasonable employment, livable wages, and appreciable economic purchasing power.

Yunker suggests a major shift to the tenets of pragmatic market socialism. In the current system, business corporations reap all the benefits of the capitalist system, retaining huge wealth and generating tremendous profits that enrich only the corporation and its shareholders. Under pragmatic market socialism, all large, established corporations would be owned by the public rather than by stockholders. Foster explained that "the proposal envisions publicly owned business enterprises as operating independently, autonomously, and for profit as they do now, with all profit paid to a national government agency (the BPO). The BPO would distribute all but five percent retained for expenses and for incentives to the public in the form of a social dividend that is proportional to personally earned labor income or pension income." Yunker argues that private entrepreneurship should be excluded from the plan, allowing risk-taking entrepreneurs and small-business owners to retain ownership of their companies and company assets.

Socialism Revisited and Modernized "provides a lucid, cohesive, and in its own terms plausible explication of the argument that a 'pragmatic market socialist' economy would be morally superior to contemporary actually existing capitalist societies," commented John E. Elliott in the *Review of Social Economy.* "Yunker's presentation is spirited but moderate, and his critique of 'capitalist apologetics' is irreverent but fair-minded." Holland called the book "an intriguing and potentially very important book" that "seeks to answer a basic economic question."

Economic Justice: The Market Socialist Vision also focuses on Yunker's theories of pragmatic market socialism. The book argues "persuasively against all of our objections and fears" regarding an untried and unfamiliar market system, remarked Doug Brown in *Journal of Economic Issues.* Yunker revisits his argument for public ownership of *Fortune* 500 companies that do not have entrepreneurial owners. Current stockholders would be compensated when their companies reverted to public ownership; boards of directors would still exist; and private individuals who are not entrepreneurs would be excluded from capital markets. Brown noted that the book also "covers a lot of twentieth-century socialist history and some economic theory and engages the student in the debate about whether or not socialism is dead in either theory or practice." Although Brown remarked that Yunker does not adequately cover how such a system could come into existence, he still called the book "very readable."

BIOGRAPHICAL AND CRITICAL SOURCES:

PERIODICALS

Comparative Economic Studies, spring, 1993, Holland Hunter, review of *Socialism Revised and Modernized: The Case for Pragmatic Market Socialism,* p. 121.

Journal of Economic Issues, December, 1988, Doug Brown, review of *Economic Justice: The Market Socialist Vision,* p. 1189; September, 1993, Gladys Parker Foster, review of *Socialism Revised and Modernized,* p. 964.

Review of Social Economy, summer, 1993, John E. Elliott, review of *Socialism Revised and Modernized,* p. 241.

ONLINE

Western Illinois University Web site, http://www.wiu.edu/ (July 27, 2005), "James A. Yunker."*

*   *   *

ZAKRZEWSKI, Sigmund F. 1919-2005

OBITUARY NOTICE— See index for *CA* sketch: Born September 15, 1919, in Buenos Aires, Argentina; died March 4, 2005, in Amherst, NY. Researcher, environmental scientist, educator, and author. Zakrzewski was best known as an authority on environmental toxicology. Though born in Argentina, he was raised in Poland, and when Poland was invaded by the Germans, he enlisted in the. Captured in 1939, he spent the duration of World War II as a prisoner of war. Afterward, he studied chemistry and biochemistry at the University of Hamburg, where he earned a master's degree in 1952 and a Ph.D. in 1954. During the early 1950s, Zakrzewski worked as a research associate in pharmacology at Case Western University and Yale University, where he was also a postdoctoral fellow from 1954 to 1956. He then joined the Roswell Park Cancer Institute in Buffalo, New York, where he did cancer research for the next three decades, specializing in chemotherapy advances. His interest in the environment was spurred after he took a course at the Massachusetts Institute of Technology in 1980 offered by the Environmental Protection Agency. Becoming aware of the negative effects a poisoned environment could have not only on people's health but also on civilization as a whole, Zakrzewski made educating people about these hazards his goal for the rest of his life. Retiring from the cancer institute in 1987, he taught classes in environmental toxicology at the State University of New York at Buffalo. He also published several books on the subject, including *Principles of Environmental Toxicology* (1991; third edition, 2002),

Climate, Weather Patterns, and Human Behavior (1996), *A Life in the Twentieth Century* (1999; second edition, 2002), and *Environmental Toxicology* (2002).

OBITUARIES AND OTHER SOURCES:

PERIODICALS

Buffalo News (Buffalo, NY), March 8, 2005, p. D6.

* * *

ZUCKERT, Michael P. 1942-

PERSONAL: Born 1942; married. *Education:* Cornell University, B.A., 1964; University of Chicago, M.A., 1967, Ph.D., 1974.

ADDRESSES: Office—University of Notre Dame, 450 Decio Faculty Hall, Notre Dame, IN 46556. *E-mail*—Michael.Zuckert.1@nd.edu.

CAREER: Author, consultant, and educator. University of Notre Dame, Notre Dame, IN, professor of political science. Previously professor of political science at Carlton College; served as consultant to Public Broadcasting Service and U.S. Department of Education.

WRITINGS:

The Garden Died: An Interpretation of Locke's First Treatise, University of Chicago Press (Chicago, IL), 1974.

Natural Rights and the New Republicanism, Princeton University Press (Princeton, NJ), 1994.

The Natural Rights Republic: Studies in the Foundation of the American Political Tradition, University of Notre Dame Press (Notre Dame, IN), 1996.

Launching Liberalism: On Lockean Political Philosophy, University Press of Kansas (Lawrence, KS), 2002.

(Editor, with Thomas S. Engeman) *Protestantism and the American Founding,* University of Notre Dame Press (Notre Dame, IN), 2004.

Editor, with wife, of journal *Interpretation.*

SIDELIGHTS: Michael P. Zuckert is an author and scholar of political science with a particular interest in the political philosophy of John Locke and other foundational philosophies of the United States. In his book *The Natural Rights Republic: Studies in the Foundation of the American Political Tradition* he provides a close analysis of the Declaration of Independence and the beliefs that it illustrates, with close attention to the political thought of Thomas Jefferson and the role of "natural rights." Zuckert emphasizes the role of liberalism in the founding document over classic republican and communitarian views. *American Political Science Review* contributor Robert Webking remarked that Zuckert "maintains and, indeed, further clarifies the basic importance of natural rights for Americans while suggesting that three alternative explanations of America may contribute something to the way Americans see themselves and political life." Christopher Wolfe, in a review for *First Things,* remarked that "Zuckert is very persuasive in making his case for the natural rights republic. His critiques of alternative views are particularly powerful. Zuckert confronts his opponents head-on, portraying them fairly, but then going . . . for the jugular." Wolf did question, however, "whether one can move from careful textual analysis of the Declaration and other major public documents to such a conclusive characterization of the nature of the American regime."

With *Launching Liberalism: On Lockean Political Philosophy* Zuckert offers a fresh look at seventeenth-century English philosopher Locke's writings and political philosophies in a collection of essays and lectures written over a twenty-five-year period. Reviewers noted that the structure of the book makes it less cohesive than it might have been if written as a single entity rather than a compilation. Barry Shain, in a review for *Modern Age,* wrote that "although the title suggests that the essays' focus is on liberalism, or at least on Locke's political philosophy, neither is the case. . . . [Locke] serves mainly as a portable backdrop for the particular concern of each essay." However, Thomas G. West, in a review for the *Claremont Institute Web site,* remarked that "the book's considerable merits confirm . . . that Zuckert . . . is one of the foremost Locke scholars of his generation." West particularly praised Zuckert's analysis of Locke's *First Treatise* and the chapter on Locke's analysis of language usage. He did take issue, however, with Zuckert's assertion that Locke believed that self-ownership led to the concept of human beings bearing rights or moral responsibility toward each other. West wrote, "it is hard to see how each self's ownership of itself could ever generate a moral obligation, given Locke's strict definition of moral law. As Zuckert himself correctly points out, the only source of moral obligation that Locke recognizes is a law whose punishment is imposed by a lawgiver." However, these different potential interpretations of Locke's political beliefs are what keep the material interesting. *Perspectives on Political Science* reviewer Richard Boyd stated that "Zuckert's Locke emerges as altogether original in his ability to assimilate, and to be assimilated by, other accepted traditions of his day and after. It is precisely this aspect of Locke that makes him so puzzling and controversial."

BIOGRAPHICAL AND CRITICAL SOURCES:

PERIODICALS

American Political Science Review, December, 1995, Edward J. Erier, review of *Natural Rights and the New Republicanism,* p. 1018; June 1998, Robert Webking, review of *The Natural Rights Republic: Studies in the Foundation of the American Political Tradition,* p. 453.

English Historical Review, April, 1997, Mark Goldie, review of *Natural Rights and the New Republicanism,* p. 476.

Ethics, January, 1999, review of *The Natural Rights Republic,* p. 493.

First Things, May, 1998, Christopher Wolfe, review of *The Natural Rights Republic,* p. 52; January, 2003, Joshua Mitchell, "In the Beginning Was the Word," p. 62.

Journal of Modern History, March, 1997, John Dunn, review of *Natural Rights and the New Republicanism,* p. 122.

Modern Age, fall, 2003, Barry Shain, "Locke and Liberal Origins," p. 366.

Perspectives on Political Science, summer, 1998, Eduardo A. Velasquez, review of *The Natural Rights Republic,* p. 162; spring, 2003, Richard Boyd, review of *Launching Liberalism: On Lockean Political Philosophy,* p. 119.

Review of Metaphysics, June, 1998, Roger Paden, review of *The Natural Rights Republic,* p. 968.

ONLINE

Claremont Institute Web site, http://www.claremont.org/ (July 26, 2005), Thomas G. West, "Nature and Happiness in Locke."

University of Notre Dame Web site, http://www.nd.edu/ (July 26, 2005), "Michael P. Zuckert."*